GREAT IDEAS IN RETAILING

In conjunction with other professors, the text authors have prepared a companion book entitled *Great Ideas in Retailing* to enhance your learning experience. *Great Ideas* is keyed to *Retail Management: A Strategic Approach* and contains these features:

- **Chapter-based exercises (1 per chapter)** – suitable for class discussion.
- **Short cases** – 25 cases that are generally 2-4 pages in length. These are appropriate for shorter assignments or for in-class discussion.
- **Long cases** – five cases ranging in length from 5-9 pages. These cases are suitable as major class assignments.
- **A team assignment** – a seven-part project. Students develop and implement a detailed plan for establishing a retail store.

To purchase this supplement, visit www.mypearsonstore.com.

Once there, you have the option to purchase this supplement stand-alone using ISBN 0-13-608799-X.

MATH FOR MERCHANDISING: A RETAILER'S HANDBOOK

Math for Merchandising: A Retailer's Handbook is an easy-to-use reference tool that illustrates how daily merchandising operations, products, and strategies are developed, planned, measured, and evaluated. The handbook shows how theory is put into practice and gives merchants a means to develop, substantiate, and manage business initiatives with sound decisions.

To purchase this supplement, visit www.mypearsonstore.com.

Once there, you have the option to purchase this supplement stand-alone using ISBN 0-13-609503-8.

RETAIL MANAGEMENT

RETAIL MANAGEMENT
A Strategic Approach

eleventh edition

Barry Berman
Hofstra University

Joel R. Evans
Hofstra Univeristy

Prentice Hall

Boston   Columbus   Indianapolis   New York
San Francisco   Upper Saddle River   Amsterdam   Cape Town   Dubai   London
Madrid   Milan   Munich   Paris   Montreal   Toronto   Delhi   Mexico City   Sao Paulo
Sydney   Hong Kong   Seoul   Singapore   Taipei   Tokyo

Library of Congress Cataloging-in-Publication Data

Berman, Barry.

    Retail management: a strategic approach/Barry Berman, Joel R. Evans.—11th ed.

      p. cm.

    Includes index.

    ISBN-13: 978-0-13-608758-8

    ISBN-10: 0-13-608758-2

    1. Retail trade—Management.   I. Evans, Joel R.   II. Title

HF5429.B45 2010

658.8'7—dc22

2009013911

Editorial Director: Sally Yagan
Editor in Chief: Eric Svendsen
Acquisitions Editor: James Heine
Product Development Manager: Ashley Santora
Editorial Project Manager: Kierra Kashickey
Director of Marketing: Patrice Lumumba Jones
Senior Marketing Manager: Anne Fahlgren
Senior Managing Editor: Judy Leale
Project Manager: Ann Pulido
Senior Operations Supervisor: Arnold Vila
Senior Art Director: Janet Slowik
Art Director: Michael Fruhbeis
Text and Cover Designer: Michael Fruhbeis
Manager, Visual Research: Beth Brenzel
Manager, Rights and Permissions: Zina Arabia
Image Permission Coordinator: Ang'john Ferreri
Manager, Cover Visual Research & Permissions: Karen Sanatar
Lead Media Project Manager: Lisa Rinaldi
Editorial Media Project Manager: Denise Vaughn
Full-Service Project Management: Elm Street Publishing Services
Composition: Integra Software Services Pvt. Ltd.
Printer/Binder: Quebecor World Color/Versailles
Cover Printer: Lehigh-Phoenix Color/Hagerstown
Text Font: Times

Credits and acknowledgments borrowed from other sources and reproduced, with permission, in this textbook appear on appropriate page within text.

Microsoft® and Windows® are registered trademarks of the Microsoft Corporation in the U.S.A. and other countries. Screen shots and icons reprinted with permission from the Microsoft Corporation. This book is not sponsored or endorsed by or affiliated with the Microsoft Corporation.

10 9 8 7 6 5 4 3 2 1

Prentice Hall
is an imprint of

www.pearsonhighered.com

ISBN 10:   0-13-608758-2
ISBN 13: 978-0-13-608758-8

Brief Contents

Contents

Preface

Welcome to *Retail Management: A Strategic Approach.* Our major goal is to present you with the most current, comprehensive, reader-friendly book on retail management that is possible. We want you to get thoroughly immersed in the subject matter, see how retail strategies are formed, look at the activities of a wide range of actual retailers (large and small, goods and services, domestic and global), and explore the possibility of a full-time career in retail management. Read through this preface and see what's available to you.

The concept of a strategic approach to retailing is the cornerstone of this book. With a strategic approach, the fundamental principle is that the retailer has to plan for and adapt to a complex, changing environment. Both opportunities and constraints must be considered. A retail strategy is the overall plan or framework of action that guides a retailer. Ideally, it will be at least one year in duration and outline the mission, goals, consumer market, overall and specific activities, and control mechanisms of the retailer. Without a pre-defined and well-integrated strategy, the firm may flounder and be unable to cope with the environment that surrounds it. Through our text, we want you to become a good retail planner and decision maker and be able to adapt to change.

Since the first edition of *Retail Management: A Strategic Approach,* we have sought to be as contemporary and forward-looking as possible. We are proactive rather than reactive in our preparation of each edition. That is why we take this adage of Wal-Mart's founder, the late Sam Walton, so seriously: "Commit to your business. Believe in it more than anybody else."

What's New to This Edition

1. All data and examples are as current as possible and reflect the current economic situation. We believe it is essential that our book take into account the economic environment that has adversely affected so many businesses and consumers.
2. The opening vignettes are all updated and highlight the titans of retailing.
3. The applied boxes in each chapter are all new or substantially updated. Here are the topics:
   a. *Technology in Retailing*
   b. *Retailing Around the World*
   c. *Ethics in Retailing*
   d. *Careers in Retailing*
4. There are 30 shorter cases, as well as 8 comprehensive cases—all new or substantially revised. Every case is based on real companies and real situations.
5. Substantive changes have been made in each chapter. For example, in **Chapter 1: An Introduction to Retailing,** to properly capture the importance of the economic situation facing retailers today, we introduce a new chapter appendix: "Understanding the Recent Economic Downturn in the United States and Around the Globe." The appendix covers the events leading to the economic downturn, the global nature of the downturn, the effect of the downturn on retailing, and strategic retailing options in weak economic times.
6. **Our Web site, www.pearsonhighered.com/berman, has been fully updated and enhanced.** It includes an updated Computer-assisted Strategic Retail Management Planning template, linked to the content presented in Chapter 3: Strategic Planning in Retailing along with additional resources and career information to enhance your learning experience.

The Berman and Evans Pre-Quiz

To highlight the interesting and useful information presented in *Retail Management: A Strategic Approach,* here's a brief pre-quiz. (Wow! Who ever heard of STARTING a book with a quiz?) It's a fun trivia quiz, based on one piece of information that we write about in each chapter. When you finish reading our book, you'll know the answers to all of these questions and a whole lot more. Text page references are provided for the trivia pre-quiz. Please: No peeking until after you complete the quiz. See how many questions you can answer:

1. **Chapter 1:** About how many people are employed by traditional retailers (including food and beverage service firms) in the United States? (see page 7)
2. **Chapter 2:** In 1985, women bought 70 percent of men's products. Due to the increased shopping done by men, what percentage of men's products are bought by women today? (see page 33)
3. **Chapter 3:** Who is Leslie Wexner, and what is his contribution to retailing? (see page 57)
4. **Chapter 4:** Suppose you want to open your own store and you decide to become a franchisee for Jazzercise. What franchise fee will you have to pay? What percentage of your sales must you pay as an ongoing cost of doing business? (see page 119)
5. **Chapter 5:** What is scrambled merchandising? [Hint: It does not involve eggs or an omelet.] Why do so many retailers engage in it? (see page 126)
6. **Chapter 6:** How many hours per week does the typical U.S. Web user spend on the Web? [Compare this with how many hours per week that YOU spend on the Web.] (see page 162)
7. **Chapter 7:** Name 3 of the top 10 reasons shoppers leave an apparel store without buying anything. (see pages 199–200)
8. **Chapter 8:** What is the Universal Product Code? Why is it important for retailers? (see page 225)
9. **Chapter 9:** What is a parasite store? [No, it is not a bug.] (see page 258)
10. **Chapter 10:** Where is the world's largest shopping center (megamall)? (see page 284)
11. **Chapter 11:** Andrea Jung and Mary Sammons are female chief executives of what two firms? (see page 323)
12. **Chapter 12:** What do Mervyns, Linens 'n Things, Sharper Image, Steve & Barry's, and Goody's Family Clothing all have in common? (see page 344)
13. **Chapter 13:** How many credit and debit cards are in use in the United States? (see page 365)
14. **Chapter 14:** In terms of dollar sales, what percentage of U.S. retail revenues are contributed by private brands such as Sears' Kenmore and Craftsman products? (see page 400)
15. **Chapter 15:** TJX (the parent of T.J. Maxx and Marshall's) attributes a large part of its merchandising success to its reliance on opportunistic buying. What is this? (see page 417)
16. **Chapter 16:** What are the LIFO and FIFO methods of accounting in inventory management? (see page 441)
17. **Chapter 17:** When manufacturers or wholesalers seek to control the retail prices of their goods and services, it is called vertical price fixing. Is this practice legal in the United States? (see pages 468–469)
18. **Chapter 18:** Inside most supermarkets, a straight traffic flow places displays and aisles in a rectangular pattern. What U.S. football term is also used to denote this type of traffic flow? [This one is really easy for you sports fans.] (see page 516)
19. **Chapter 19:** Among these retail store types, which one spends the highest percentage of its sales on advertising: apparel and accessories stores, department stores, drugstores, eating places, furniture stores, grocery stores, hotels and motels, movie theaters, or shoe stores? (see page 533)
20. **Chapter 20:** In retail management, what is gap analysis? [Hint: It does not require a dental procedure at your local dentist.] (see page 578)
21. **Appendix: Careers in Retailing (bonus question):** True or false? According to Careers-in-Marketing.com: "Retail is one of the fastest growing, most dynamic parts of the world economy. Careers in retail are people-oriented, fast-paced, and exciting." (see page 597)

What Is Covered in Retail Management

Retail Management: A Strategic Approach has eight parts.

Part One introduces the field of retailing, the basics of strategic planning, the importance of building and maintaining customer and supplier relations, and the decisions to be made in owning or managing a retail business.

In **Part Two,** retail institutions are examined in terms of ownership types, as well as store-based, nonstore-based, electronic, and nontraditional strategy mixes. The wheel of retailing, scrambled merchandising, the retail life cycle, and the Web are covered.

Part Three focuses on target marketing and information-gathering methods, including discussions of why and how consumers shop and the retailing information system and data warehouse.

Part Four presents a four-step approach to location planning: trading-area analysis, choosing the most desirable type of location, selecting a general locale, and deciding on a specific site.

Part Five discusses the elements involved in managing a retail business: the retail organization structure, human resource management, and operations management (both financial and operational).

Part Six deals with merchandise management—developing and implementing merchandise plans, the financial aspects of merchandising, and pricing.

In **Part Seven**, the ways to communicate with customers are analyzed, with special attention paid to retail image, atmosphere, and promotion.

Part Eight deals with integrating and controlling a retail strategy.

At the end of the text, **Appendix: Careers in Retailing** highlights career opportunities in retailing. There is also a comprehensive **Glossary.**

To give you the best possible learning experience, these features are included in every chapter:

- ▶ An opening vignette that highlights the best-known retailers around: Amazon.com, Best Buy, Costco, Dunkin' Donuts, eBay, The Gap, Inc., Home Depot, Ikea, Limited Brands, Macy's, Mary Kay, McDonald's, Mrs. Fields, Nordstrom, Pearle Vision, Staples, Starbucks, Stew Leonard's, Target, and Wal-Mart.
- ▶ Chapter objectives.
- ▶ Chapter overview.
- ▶ Reader-friendly coverage of all the important topics pertaining to that chapter.
- ▶ A colorful design with numerous photos and figures that illustrate important points.
- ▶ Margin notes with links to key Web sites.
- ▶ Four real-world boxes on "Technology in Retailing," "Retailing Around the World," "Ethics in Retailing," and "Careers in Retailing."
- ▶ A chapter summary tied directly to the chapter goals.
- ▶ A list of key terms and their page references.
- ▶ Questions for discussion.
- ▶ A Web-based exercise to stimulate thought.
- ▶ Chapter endnotes (conveniently located at the back of the book).

To provide extra coverage for five special topics, we also include these chapter-ending appendixes: Chapter 1—"Understanding the Recent Economic Downturn in the United States and Around the Globe," Chapter 2—"Planning for the Unique Aspects of Service Retailing," Chapter 3—"The Special Dimensions of Strategic Planning in a Global Retailing Environment," Chapter 4—"The Dynamics of Franchising," and Chapter 6—"Multi-Channel Retailing."

At the end of each of the eight parts in *Retail Management,* there are a variety of short and long cases. They deal with such firms as Abercrombie's Ruehl No. 925, Bed Bath & Beyond, BJ's, Borders, Costco, IMAX, Netflix, Publix Super Markets, 7-Eleven, Shutterfly, Sony, Trader Joe's, and Von Maur. In all, there are 30 short cases and 8 long cases.

The E-volution of *Retail Management: A Strategic Approach*

As Bob Dylan once said, "The times, they are a changing." What does this mean? The "E" word—electronic—now permeates our lives. From a consumer perspective, gone are the old electric typewriters, replaced by PCs, BlackBerrys and other PDAs, and cell phones. Snail mail is giving way to E-mail and MySpace and Facebook. Looking for a new music CD? Well, we can go to the store—or order it from Amazon.com (**www.amazon.com**) or download some tracks from iTunes to create our own CDs/DVDs.

Are you doing research? Then hop on the Internet express to gain access to millions of facts at your fingertips. The Web is an anytime (24/7/365), anywhere medium that is transforming—and will continue to transform—our behavior.

From a retailer perspective, we see four formats—all covered in *Retail Management*—competing in the new millennium (cited in descending order of importance):

▶ **Combined "bricks-and-mortar" and "clicks-and-mortar" retailers.** These are store-based retailers that also offer Web shopping, thus providing customers the ultimate in choice and convenience. Virtually all of the world's largest retailers, as well as many medium and small firms, fall into this category. This is clearly the fastest-growing format in retailing, exemplified by such different firms as Barnes & Noble (**www.barnesandnoble.com**), Costco (**www.costco.com**), and Target (**www.target.com**).

▶ **Clicks-and-mortar retailers.** These are the new breed of Web-only retailers that have emerged in recent years, led by Amazon.com (**www.amazon.com**). Rather than utilize their own physical store facilities, these companies promote a "virtual" shopping experience: wide selections, low prices, and convenience. Among the firms in this category are Priceline (**www.priceline.com**)—the discount airfare, hotel, and more retailer—and toy retailer eToys (**www.etoys.com**).

▶ **Direct marketers with clicks-and-mortar retailing operations.** These are firms that have relied on traditional nonstore media such as print catalogs, direct selling in homes, and TV infomercials to generate business. Almost all of them have added Web sites to enhance their businesses. Leaders include Lands' End (**www.landsend.com**) and QVC (**www.qvc.com**). These direct marketers will see a dramatic increase in the proportion of sales coming from the Web.

▶ **Bricks-and-mortar retailers.** These are companies that rely on their physical facilities to make sales. They do not sell online, but use the Web for providing information, customer service, and image building. Auto dealers typically offer product information and customer service online, but conduct their sales transactions at retail stores. Firms in this category represent the smallest grouping of retailers. Many will need to rethink their approach as online competition intensifies.

We have access to more information sources than ever before, from global trade associations to government agencies. The information in *Retail Management,* Eleventh Edition, is more current than ever because we are using the original sources themselves and not waiting for data to be published months or a year after being compiled. We are also able to include a greater range of real-world examples because of the information at company Web sites.

Will this help you, the reader? You bet. Our philosophy has always been to make *Retail Management* as reader-friendly, up-to-date, and useful as possible. In addition, we want you to benefit from our experiences, in this case, our E-xperiences.

E-xciting E-features

To reflect these E-xciting times, *Retail Management: A Strategic Approach,* Eleventh Edition, incorporates a host of E-features throughout the book—and at our wide-ranging, interactive Web site (**www.pearsonhighered.com/berman**).

The Eleventh Edition has a very strong integration of the book with this Web site:

▶ A special section of our Web site is devoted to each chapter.
▶ In each chapter, there are multiple references to Web links regarding particular topics (such as free online sources of secondary data).
▶ Every chapter has a number of margin notes that refer to company Web sites.
▶ Every chapter concludes with a short Web exercise.
▶ At our Web site, for each chapter, there are chapter objectives, a chapter overview, a listing of key terms, interactive study guide questions, hot links to relevant Web sites, and more.
▶ Our Web site contains extra math questions for Chapters 9, 12, 16, and 17.
▶ Our Web site includes in-depth exercises that apply key course concepts through free company downloads and demonstrations. There are several for each part of the book.
▶ The Web site even includes hints for solving cases, a listing of key online secondary data sources, and descriptions of retail job opportunities and career ladders.
▶ With regard to in-text content, each chapter includes important practical applications of the Web within the context of that chapter.

But, that's not all! *Retail Management,* Eleventh Edition, is packed with other E-features:

▶ The interactive online study guide provides correct answers and text page references for more than 50 questions per chapter—about 1,100 in all!
▶ Our Web site (**www.pearsonhighered.com/berman**) also includes:
 ■ More than 1,000 hot links.
 ■ A full glossary.
 ■ A lot of career material, including a directory of hundreds of retailers and their online addresses. We have hot links directly to the career sections of leading retailers.
 ■ A list of popular search engines.
 ■ A list of free online secondary data sources.
 ■ Hints on how to solve a case study.
 ■ Interactive computer exercises tied into the text—16 in all.
 ■ An interactive strategic planning template that places the retail planning process into a series of steps that are integrated with Figure 3-1 in the book.
 ■ A list of major trade associations—with hot links to their Web sites.
 ■ Information from the Federal Trade Commission (useful for consumers and potential franchisees) and the Small Business Administration (useful for entrepreneurs).
 ■ Links to free downloads and demos that encourage you to visit specific Web sites to gather useful information and try out innovative software.
▶ The endpapers of *Retail Management* show the Web addresses for more than 200 retailers around the globe.
▶ A number of "Technology in Retailing" boxes cover E-applications.
▶ Many cases have E-components.
▶ At the Web site (**www.pearsonhighered.com/berman**):
 ■ The section entitled "Retail Careers" has four basic categories.
 ● *General Information.* We discuss the career preparation process in terms of these steps: assessing yourself, acquiring job leads, writing a résumé and cover letter, and doing well with the personal interview and post-interview activities.
 ● *Internships.* In planning a career, a well-balanced approach during college is often the key to long-run success. What does this mean? A person should take his or her college education seriously, participate in co-curricular and extracurricular activities, and begin to acquire meaningful work experience.
 ● *Job Hunting Guide.* The job-hunting process consists of several steps, which are discussed in detail: collecting information, applying for a job, job-search methods, evaluating a job offer, and becoming familiar with job-hunt-related search engines.

- *Types of Retail Jobs.* We provide in-depth information on these retail jobs: buyers and merchandise managers, customer service representatives, restaurant and food service managers, retail managers, retail sales workers, and travel agents. We also cite numerous other positions in retailing, present several flow charts demonstrating career path growth, and offer links to retailers' career sites.
- Web site addresses are provided for more than 700 U.S. retailers, about 180 retailers outside the United States, and more than 50 professional and trade associations.

Careers! Careers! Careers!

We recognize that many of you may be contemplating a career in retailing/retail management. We have a great deal of material that should help you decide whether such a career is for you, learn more about the broad range of careers in retailing, and obtain contact information about potential employers. Here are the major career-oriented features of *Retail Management: A Strategic Approach* and our Web site:

- ► Our strategic approach to the field of retail management enables you to learn about the key concepts that should be grasped by anyone who wants to pursue a professional career in retailing/retail management.
- ► Each chapter has a "Careers in Retailing" box that traces the career path of real people in such areas as store management, operations, merchandising, information technology, human resource management, online retailing, loss prevention, finance, logistics, and advertising. The information in these boxes is from the National Retail Federation, the leading association in retailing.
- ► Chapter 11 covers retail organizations and human resource management.
- ► The appendix presents an overview of career opportunities, complete with salary ranges for a variety of jobs in retailing.
- ► The endpapers cite the Web addresses of more than 200 leading retailers around the globe.

Great Ideas in Retailing

In conjunction with a number of your professors, we have prepared a companion book titled *Great Ideas in Retailing* to further enhance your learning experience. *Great Ideas* is keyed to *Retail Management: A Strategic Approach* and contains these features:

- ► Chapter-based exercises (one per chapter)—suitable for class discussion.
- ► Short cases—25 cases that are generally two to four pages in length. These are suitable for shorter assignments or for in-class discussion.
- ► Long cases—five cases ranging in length from five to nine pages. All of these cases are suitable as major class assignments.
- ► A team assignment broken down into seven parts. It entails developing and implementing a detailed plan for establishing a retail store.

Concluding Remarks

We consider ourselves to be as reader-friendly as possible. Please feel free to send us feedback regarding any aspect of *Retail Management* or its package. We promise to reply to any correspondence.

Sincerely,

Professor Barry Berman (E-mail at **mktbxb@hofstra.edu**),
Zarb School of Business, Hofstra University, Hempstead, NY 11549

Professor Joel R. Evans (E-mail at **mktjre@hofstra.edu**),
Zarb School of Business, Hofstra University, Hempstead, NY, 11549

About the Authors

Barry Berman

Joel R. Evans

Barry Berman (Ph.D. in Business with majors in Marketing and Behavioral Science) is the Walter H. "Bud" Miller Distinguished Professor of Business and Professor of Marketing and International Business in the Zarb School of Business at Hofstra University. He is also the director of Hofstra's Executive MBA program. **Joel R. Evans** (Ph.D. in Business with majors in Marketing and Public Policy) is the RMI Distinguished Professor of Business and Professor of Marketing and International Business in the Zarb School of Business at Hofstra University. He is also the coordinator for Hofstra's Master of Science programs in Marketing and Marketing Research. The Zarb School of Business at Hofstra University is fully accredited by AACSB International.

While at Hofstra, each has been honored as a faculty inductee in Beta Gamma Sigma honor society, has received multiple Dean's Awards for service, and has been selected as the Teacher of the Year by the Hofstra MBA Association. For several years, Drs. Berman and Evans were co-directors of Hofstra's Retail Management Institute and Business Research Institute. Both regularly teach undergraduate and graduate courses to a wide range of students.

Barry Berman and Joel R. Evans have worked together for 30 years in co-authoring several best-selling texts, including *Retail Management: A Strategic Approach*, Eleventh Edition. They have also consulted for a variety of clients, from "mom-and-pop" retailers to *Fortune* 500 companies. They are co-founders of the American Marketing Association's Special Interest Group in Retailing and Retail Management. They have co-chaired the Academy of Marketing Science/American Collegiate Retailing Association's triennial conference several times and edited the conference proceedings. They have been featured speakers at the annual meeting of the National Retail Federation, the world's largest retailing trade association. Each has a chapter on retailing in Dartnell's *Marketing Manager's Handbook*.

Barry and Joel are both active Web practitioners (and surfers), and they have written and developed all of the content for the comprehensive, interactive Web site that accompanies *Retail Management* (**www.pearsonhighered.com/berman**). They may be reached through the Web site or by writing to **mktbxb@hofstra.edu** (Barry Berman) and **mktjre@hofstra.edu** (Joel R. Evans).

Acknowledgments

Many people have assisted us in the preparation of this book, and to them we extend our warmest appreciation.

We thank the following reviewers, who have reacted to this or earlier editions of the text. Each has provided us with perceptive comments that have helped us to crystallize our thoughts and to make *Retail Management* the best book possible:

M. Wayne Alexander, Morehead State University
Larry Audler, University of New Orleans
Ramon Avila, Ball State University
Betty V. Balevic, Skidmore College
Stephen Batory, Bloomsburg University
Leta Beard, University of Washington
Joseph J. Belonax, Western Michigan University
Ronald Bernard, Diablo Valley College
Charles D. Bodkin, University of North Carolina at Charlotte
Charlane Bomrad, Onondaga Community College
John J. Buckley, Orange County Community College
David J. Burns, Youngstown State University
David A. Campbell, Southern Illinois University
John W. Carpenter, Lake Land College
Joseph A. Davidson, Cuyahoga Community College
Peter T. Doukas, Westchester Community College
Blake Escudier, San Jose State University
Jack D. Eure, Jr., Southwest Texas State University
Phyllis Fein, Westchester Community College
Letty Fisher, Westchester Community College
Myron Gable, Shippensburg University
Linda L. Golden, University of Texas at Austin
James Gray, Florida Atlantic University
Barbara Gross, California State University–Northridge
J. Duncan Herrington, Radford University
Mary Higby, University of Detroit, Mercy
Terence L. Holmes, Murray State University
Charles A. Ingene, University of Mississippi
Marilyn Jones, Bond University
Marvin A. Jolson, University of Maryland
David C. Jones, Otterbein College
Carol Kaufman-Scarborough, Rutgers University
Ruth Keyes, SUNY College of Technology
Maryon King, Southern Illinois University
Stephen Kirk, East Carolina University
John Lanasa, Duquesne University
Dana Lanham, University of North Carolina at Charlotte
J. Ford Laumer Jr., Auburn University
Marilyn Lavin, University of Wisconsin–Whitewater
Dennis G. Lee, Southwest Georgia Technical College
Richard C. Leventhal, Metropolitan State College
Michael Little, Virginia Commonwealth University
John Lloyd, Monroe Community College
Ann Lucht, Milwaukee Area Technical College
Robert Lupton, Central Washington University
Vincent Magnini, Longwood University
James O. McCann, Henry Ford Community College
Sanjay S. Mehta, Sam Houston State University

Frank McDaniels, Delaware County Community College
Ronald Michman, Shippensburg University
Jihye Park, Iowa State University
Howard C. Paul, Mercyhurst College
Roy B. Payne, Purdue University
Susan Peters, California State Polytechnic University, Pomona
Dawn I. Pysarchik, Michigan State University
Julian Redfearn, Kilgore College
Curtis Reierson, Baylor University
Barry Rudin, Loras College
Julie Toner Schrader, North Dakota State University
Steven J. Shaw, University of South Carolina
Ruth K. Shelton, James Madison University
Gladys S. Sherdell, Bellarmine College
Jill F. Slomski, Gannon University
Randy Stuart, Kennesaw State University
John E. Swan, University of Alabama, Birmingham
Ruth Taylor, Texas State University–San Marcos
Lisa Taylor Weaver, Las Positas College
Moira Tolan, Mount Saint Mary College
Anthony Urbanisk, Northern State University
Anu Venkateswaran, Wilberforce University
Lillian Werner, University of Minnesota
Kaylene C. Williams, California State University, Stanislaus
Mathew C. Williams, Clover Park Technical College
Terrell G. Williams, Western Washington State University
Yingjiao Xu, Ohio University
Ugur Yucelt, Pennsylvania State University, Harrisburg

Special recognition is due to the National Retail Federation, TNS Retail Forward, and Retail Image Consulting for their cooperation and assistance in providing career materials, case studies, and photos for this edition. We also appreciate the efforts of our Prentice Hall colleagues who have worked diligently on this edition. As always, thank you to Diane Schoenberg for the editorial assistance. And thanks to Matthew Wettan, Kunal Swani, and Stacey Evans.

Barry Berman
Joel R. Evans
Hofstra University

RETAIL MANAGEMENT

PART 1 An Overview of Strategic Retail Management

Welcome to *Retail Management: A Strategic Approach*, 11e. We hope you find this book to be informative, timely, and reader-friendly. Please visit our Web site (**www.pearsonhighered.com/berman**) for interactive, useful, up-to-date features that complement the text—including chapter hot links, a study guide, and much more!

In Part One, we explore the field of retailing, establishing and maintaining relationships, and the basic principles of strategic planning and the decisions made in owning or managing a retail business.

Chapter 1 describes retailing, shows why it should be studied, and examines its special characteristics. We note the value of strategic planning, including a detailed review of Target Corporation (a titan of retailing). The retailing concept is presented, along with the total retail experience, customer service, and relationship retailing. The focus and format of the text are detailed.

Chapter 2 looks at the complexities of retailers' relationships—with both customers and other channel members. We examine value and the value chain, customer relationships and channel relationships, the differences in relationship building between goods and service retailers, the impact of technology on retailing relationships, and the interplay between ethical performance and relationships in retailing. The chapter ends with an appendix on planning for the unique aspects of service retailing.

Chapter 3 shows the usefulness of strategic planning for all kinds of retailers. We focus on the planning process: situation analysis, objectives, identifying consumers, overall strategy, specific activities, control, and feedback. We also look at the controllable and uncontrollable parts of a retail strategy. Strategic planning is shown as a series of interrelated steps that are continuously reviewed. A detailed computerized strategic planning template, available at our Web site, is described. At the end of the chapter, there is an appendix on the strategic implications of global retailing.

Source: Monkey Business Images/Dreamstine LLC-Royalty Free.

1

An Introduction to Retailing

Chapter Objectives

1. To define retailing, consider it from various perspectives, demonstrate its impact, and note its special characteristics

2. To introduce the concept of strategic planning and apply it

3. To show why the retailing concept is the foundation of a successful business, with an emphasis on the total retail experience, customer service, and relationship retailing

4. To indicate the focus and format of the text

A perfect example of a dream come true is the story of Sam Walton, the founder of Wal-Mart (**www.walmart.com**). From a single store, Wal-Mart has grown to become the largest company in the world in terms of revenues. And today it dwarfs every other retailer. Wal-Mart consistently ranks among America's top 50 most admired corporations according to *Fortune* magazine.

As a store owner in Bentonville, Arkansas, Sam Walton had a simple strategy: to take his retail stores to rural areas of the United States and then sell goods at the lowest prices around. Sam was convinced that a large discount format would work in rural communities. Wal-Mart's strategy is based on everyday low prices (which reduces its advertising costs), having the lowest prices on 1,500 key items, and on a low cost distribution system.

Walton's first discount store opened in 1962 and used such slogans as "We sell for less" and "Satisfaction guaranteed," two of the retailer's current hallmarks. By the end of 1969, Wal-Mart had expanded to 31 locations. Within a year, Wal-Mart became a public corporation and rapidly grew on the basis of additional discount stores and global expansion. In 2008, Wal-Mart began pricing hundreds of generic prescriptions at $10 for a 90-day supply.

Wal-Mart has become a true textbook example of how a retailer can maintain growth without losing sight of its original core values of low overhead, the use of innovative distribution systems, and customer orientation—whereby employees swear to serve the customer. "So help me, Sam."[1]

Source: Reprinted by permission of Susan Berry, Retail Image Consulting, Inc.

OVERVIEW

Retailing encompasses the business activities involved in selling goods and services to consumers for their personal, family, or household use. It includes every sale to the *final* consumer—ranging from cars to apparel to meals at restaurants to movie tickets. Retailing is the last stage in the distribution process.

Retailing today is at a complex crossroads. On the one hand, retail sales are at their highest point in history. Wal-Mart is the leading company in the world in terms of sales—ahead of ExxonMobil, Toyota, and other manufacturing giants. New technologies are improving retail productivity. There are lots of opportunities to start a new retail business—or work for an existing one—and to become a franchisee. Global retailing possibilities abound. On the other hand, retailers face numerous challenges. The weak economy in recent years has had a major impact on many retailers, their suppliers, and consumers around the world. Many consumers are bored with shopping or do not have much time for it. Some locales have too many stores, and retailers often spur one another into frequent price cutting (and low profit margins). Customer service expectations are high at a time when more retailers offer self-service and automated systems. Some retailers remain unsure what to do with the Web; they are still grappling with the emphasis to place on image enhancement, customer information and feedback, and sales transactions.

These are the key issues that retailers must resolve:

"How can we best serve our customers while earning a fair profit?"

"How can we stand out in a highly competitive environment where consumers have so many choices?"

"How can we grow our business while retaining a core of loyal customers?"

Our point of view: Retail decision makers can best address these questions by fully understanding and applying the basic principles of retailing in a well-structured, systematic, and focused retail strategy. That is the philosophy behind *Retail Management: A Strategic Approach.*

Visit Blue Nile's Web site (**www.bluenile.com**) and see what drives one of the world's "hot" retailers.

Can retailers flourish in today's tough marketplace? You bet! Just look at your favorite restaurant, gift shop, and food store. Look at the growth of Costco, Dunkin' Donuts, and Blue Nile (the online jewelry retailer). What do they have in common? A desire to please the customer and a strong market niche. To prosper in the long term, they all need a strategic plan and a willingness to adapt, both central thrusts of this book. See Figure 1-1.

In Chapter 1, we look at the framework of retailing, the value of developing and applying a sound retail strategy, and the focus and format of the text. A special appendix at the end of this chapter looks at the impact of the recent economic downturn on retailers in the United States and around the world.

The Framework of Retailing

To appreciate retailing's role and the range of retailing activities, let's view it from three perspectives:

▶ Suppose we manage a manufacturing firm that makes vacuum cleaners. How should we sell these items? We could distribute via big chains such as Best Buy or small neighborhood appliance stores, have our own sales force visit people in their homes (as Aerus—formerly Electrolux—does), or set up our own stores (if we have the ability and resources to do so). We could sponsor TV infomercials or magazine ads, complete with a toll-free phone number.

▶ Suppose we have an idea for a new way to teach first graders how to use computer software for spelling and vocabulary. How should we implement this idea?

FIGURE 1-1

Boom Times for Dunkin' Donuts

Dunkin' Donuts is the largest coffee-and-baked-goods chain in the world. It sells high-quality coffee, bagels, donuts, and other baked goods. And it now features smoothies and other new menu items to stay ahead of competitors.

Source: Reprinted by permission of Susan Berry, Retail Image Consulting, Inc.

We could lease a store in a strip shopping center and run ads in a local paper, rent space in a local YMCA and rely on teacher referrals, or do mailings to parents and visit children in their homes. In each case, the service is offered "live." But there is another option: We could use an animated Web site to teach children online.

▶ Suppose that we, as consumers, want to buy apparel. What choices do we have? We could go to a department store or an apparel store. We could shop with a full-service retailer or a discounter. We could go to a shopping center or order from a catalog. We could look to retailers that carry a wide range of clothing (from outerwear to jeans to suits) or look to firms that specialize in one clothing category (such as leather coats). We could surf around the Web and visit retailers around the globe.

Service businesses such as Jiffy Lube (www.jiffylube.com) are engaged in retailing.

There is a tendency to think of retailing as primarily involving the sale of tangible (physical) goods. However, retailing also includes the sale of services. And this is a big part of retailing! A service may be the shopper's primary purchase (such as a haircut) or it may be part of the shopper's purchase of a good (such as furniture delivery). Retailing does not have to involve a store. Mail and phone orders, direct selling to consumers in their homes and offices, Web transactions, and vending machine sales all fall within the scope of retailing. Retailing does not even have to include a "retailer." Manufacturers, importers, nonprofit firms, and wholesalers act as retailers when they sell to final consumers.

Let's now examine various reasons for studying retailing and its special characteristics.

Reasons for Studying Retailing

Learn more about the exciting array of retailing career opportunities (www.allretailjobs.com).

Retailing is an important field to study because of its impact on the economy, its functions in distribution, and its relationship with firms selling goods and services to retailers for their resale or use. These factors are discussed next. A fourth factor for students of retailing is the broad range of career opportunities, as highlighted with a "Careers in Retailing" box in each chapter, Appendix A at the end of this book, and our Web site (**www.pearsonhighered.com/berman**). See Figure 1-2.

FIGURE 1-2

A Good Source for
Careers in Retailing
Information

Source: Reprinted by permission of
the National Retail Federation.

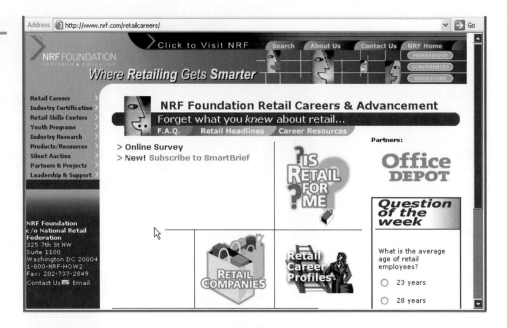

THE IMPACT OF RETAILING ON THE ECONOMY

Retailing is a major part of U.S. and world commerce. Retail sales and employment are vital economic contributors, and retail trends often mirror trends in a nation's overall economy.

According to the Department of Commerce, annual U.S. retail store sales are nearly $5 trillion—representing one-third of the total economy. Telephone and mail-order sales by nonstore retailers, vending machines, direct selling, and the Web generate hundreds of billions of dollars in additional yearly revenues. And personal consumption expenditures on financial, medical, legal, educational, and other services account for another several hundred billion dollars in annual retail revenues. Outside the United States, retail sales are several trillions of dollars per year.

CAREERS
IN RETAILING

The Vast Career Opportunities in Retailing

Current career material from the National Retail Federation (NRF) is presented in each chapter of *Retail Management.* Included are an overview of retailing careers, illustrative retail career profiles (Chapters 2 through 7), and specific kinds of retailing jobs (Chapters 8 through 20). At the NRF's Web site (**www.nrf.com/retailcareers**), a lot of additional information may also be found.

Retailing has been and continues to be an industry with enormous prospects for growth. It offers perhaps the greatest variety of opportunities for ambitious and hard-working people. Some of the major retail career areas are distribution, logistics, and supply chain management; entrepreneurship; finance; human resources; information technology (IT) and E-commerce; loss prevention; marketing and advertising; merchandise planning and buying; retail industry support; sales and sales-related operations; store management; and store operations.

Career paths in the dynamic, expanding retail industry are exciting, varied, and lucrative. At the store level alone,

a general manager of a department store oversees an average sales volume of $25 million to $30 million and employs an average of 150 people. Average department store manager salaries start at $80,000 and exceed $100,000. Most retailing companies encourage employees at all levels of the company, even management and corporate employees, to have solid, store-level (i.e., sales associate) experience. Some even require it. And, most of the skills you are using to succeed as a sales associate are needed as you move up the ladder—skills such as problem solving and decision making, teamwork, dedication to courtesy and customer service, "people skills" (the ability to interact effectively with different personalities), a good work ethic and reliability, enthusiasm and initiative, cross-cultural awareness, and communication skills (listening, speaking, and writing).

Source: Reprinted by permission of the National Retail Federation.

Durable goods stores—including motor vehicles and parts dealers; furniture, home furnishings, electronics, and appliance stores; and building materials and hardware stores—make up one-third of U.S. retail store sales. Nondurable goods and services stores—including general merchandise stores; food and beverage stores; health- and personal-care stores; gasoline stations; clothing and accessories stores; sporting goods, hobby, book, and music stores; eating and drinking places; and miscellaneous retailers— together account for two-thirds of U.S. retail store sales.

The world's 100 largest retailers generate more than $2.8 trillion in annual revenues. They represent 19 nations. Thirty-six of the 100 are based in the United States, 11 in Great Britain, 9 in France, 9 in Germany, and 6 in Japan.[2] Table 1-1 shows the 10 largest U.S. retailers. In 2007, they produced more than $930 billion in sales. As of 2008, they operated about 36,000 stores and had 4.3 million employees. Visit our Web site for links to a lot of current information on retailing (**www.pearsonhighered.com/berman**).

> The *Occupational Outlook Handbook* (www.bls.gov/oco) is a great source of information on employment trends.

Retailing is a major source of jobs. In the United States alone, 25 million people— about one-sixth of the total labor force—work for traditional retailers (including food and beverage service firms, such as restaurants). Yet this figure understates the true number of people who work in retailing because it does not include the several million persons employed by service firms, seasonal employees, proprietors, and unreported workers in family businesses or partnerships.

From a cost perspective, retailing is a significant field of study. In the United States, on average, 32 cents of every dollar spent in department stores, 47 cents spent in furniture and home furnishings stores, and 28 cents spent in grocery stores go to the retailers to cover operating costs, activities performed, and profits. Costs include rent, displays, wages, ads, and maintenance. Only a small part of each dollar is profit. In 2007, the 10 largest U.S. retailers' after-tax profits averaged 3.4 percent of sales.[3] Figure 1-3 shows costs and profits for Walgreens, a drugstore chain.

RETAIL FUNCTIONS IN DISTRIBUTION

Retailing is the last stage in a **channel of distribution**—all of the businesses and people involved in the physical movement and transfer of ownership of goods and services from

TABLE 1-1   The 10 Largest Retailers in the United States

Rank	Company	Web Address	Major Retail Emphasis	2007 Sales (millions)	2007 After-Tax Earnings	2008 Number of Stores	2008 Number of Employees
1	Wal-Mart	**www.walmart.com**	Full-line discount stores, supercenters, membership clubs	$378,799	$12,731	7,200+	2,000,000+
2	Home Depot	**www.homedepot.com**	Home centers, design centers	84,740	4,395	2,200+	350,000+
3	CVS Caremark	**www.cvscaremark.com**	Drugstores	76,330	2,637	6,300+	190,000+
4	Kroger	**www.kroger.com**	Supermarkets, convenience stores, jewelry stores	70,235	1,181	4,300+	320,000+
5	Costco	**www.costco.com**	Membership clubs	64,400	1,083	540+	140,000+
6	Target	**www.target.com**	Full-line discount stores, supercenters	63,367	2,849	1,680+	365,000+
7	Walgreens	**www.walgreens.com**	Drugstores	53,762	2,041	5,900+	160,000+
8	Sears Holdings	**www.sears.com**	Department stores, specialty stores	50,703	826	3,800+	350,000+
9	Lowe's	**www.lowes.com**	Home centers	48,283	2,809	1,500+	215,000+
10	Safeway	**www.safeway.com**	Supermarkets	42,286	888	1,900+	200,000+

Sources: 2008 *Fortune* 500; and company annual reports.

FIGURE 1-3

The High Costs and Low
Profits of Retailing—
Where the Typical $100
Spent with Walgreens in
2008 Went

Source: Computed by the authors
from *Walgreens 2008 Annual
Report*.

Manufacturer's costs and profits

Retailer's
operating,
personnel,
advertising, and
other costs

Retailer's
income
taxes

Retailer's
after-tax
profits

$71.84 $22.36 $2.15 $3.65

producer to consumer. A typical distribution channel is shown in Figure 1-4. Retailers often act as the contact between manufacturers, wholesalers, and the consumer. Many manufacturers would like to make one basic type of item and sell their entire inventory to as few buyers as possible, but consumers usually want to choose from a variety of goods and services and purchase a limited quantity. Retailers collect an assortment from various sources, buy in large quantity, and sell in small amounts. This is the **sorting process**. See Figure 1-5.

Another job for retailers is communicating both with customers and with manufacturers and wholesalers. Shoppers learn about the availability and characteristics of goods and services, store hours, sales, and so on from retailer ads, salespeople, and displays. Manufacturers and wholesalers are informed by their retailers with regard to sales forecasts, delivery delays, customer complaints, defective items, inventory turnover, and more. Many goods and services have been modified due to retailer feedback.

For small suppliers, retailers can provide assistance by transporting, storing, marking, advertising, and pre-paying for products. Small retailers may need the same type of help from their suppliers. The tasks performed by retailers affect the percentage of each sales dollar they need to cover costs and profits.

Retailers also complete transactions with customers. This means having convenient locations, filling orders promptly and accurately, and processing credit purchases. Some retailers also provide customer services such as gift wrapping, delivery, and installation. To make themselves even more appealing, many firms now engage in **multi-channel retailing**, whereby a retailer sells to consumers through multiple retail formats (points of contact). Most large retailers operate both physical stores and Web sites to make shopping easier and to accommodate consumer desires. Some firms even sell to customers through retail stores, mail order, a Web site, and a toll-free phone number. See Figure 1-6.

Sherwin-Williams (www.
sherwin-williams.com) is
not only a manufacturer
but also a retailer.

For these reasons, products are usually sold through retailers not owned by manufacturers (wholesalers). This lets the manufacturers reach more customers, reduce costs, improve cash flow, increase sales more rapidly, and focus on their area of expertise. Select manufacturers such as Sherwin-Williams and Polo Ralph Lauren do operate retail

FIGURE 1-4

A Typical Channel of
Distribution

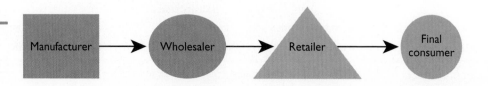

Manufacturer → Wholesaler → Retailer → Final consumer

FIGURE 1-5

The Retailer's Role in the
Sorting Process

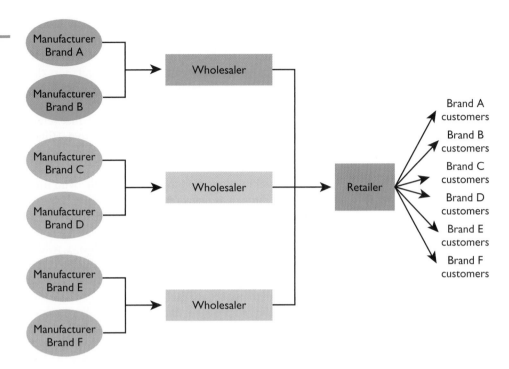

facilities (besides selling at traditional retailers). In running their stores, these firms complete the full range of retailing functions and compete with conventional retailers.

THE RELATIONSHIPS AMONG RETAILERS AND THEIR SUPPLIERS

Relationships among retailers and suppliers can be complex. Because retailers are part of a distribution channel, manufacturers and wholesalers must be concerned about the caliber of displays, customer service, store hours, and retailers' reliability as business partners. Retailers are also major customers of goods and services for resale, store fixtures, computers, management consulting, and insurance.

These are some issues over which retailers and their suppliers have different priorities: control over the distribution channel, profit allocation, the number of competing retailers handling suppliers' products, product displays, promotion support, payment terms, and operating flexibility. Due to the growth of large chains, retailers have more power than ever.

FIGURE 1-6

Brooks Brothers and Multi-Channel Retailing
Brooks Brothers clothing can be purchased at its stores in shopping centers, in downtown business districts, through its Web site (**www.brooksbrothers.com**), and at its outlet stores. This makes it quite convenient for customers.

Source: Reprinted by permission of Susan Berry, Retail Image Consulting, Inc.

Unless suppliers know retailer needs, they cannot have good rapport with them; as long as retailers have a choice of suppliers, they will pick those offering more.

Channel relations tend to be smoothest with **exclusive distribution**, whereby suppliers make agreements with one or a few retailers that designate the latter as the only ones in specified geographic areas to carry certain brands or products. This stimulates both parties to work together to maintain an image, assign shelf space, allot profits and costs, and advertise. It also usually requires that retailers limit their brand selection in the specified product lines; they might have to decline to handle other suppliers' brands. From the manufacturers' perspective, exclusive distribution may limit their long-run total sales.

Channel relations tend to be most volatile with **intensive distribution**, whereby suppliers sell through as many retailers as possible. This often maximizes suppliers' sales and lets retailers offer many brands and product versions. Competition among retailers selling the same items is high; retailers may use tactics not beneficial to individual suppliers, because they are more concerned about their own results. Retailers may assign little shelf space to specific brands, set very high prices on them, and not advertise them.

With **selective distribution**, suppliers sell through a moderate number of retailers. This combines aspects of exclusive and intensive distribution. Suppliers have higher sales than in exclusive distribution, and retailers carry some competing brands. It encourages suppliers to provide some marketing support and retailers to give adequate shelf space. See Figure 1-7.

The Special Characteristics of Retailing

Three factors that most differentiate retailing from other types of business are noted in Figure 1-8 and discussed here. Each factor imposes unique requirements on retail firms.

The average amount of a sales transaction for retailers is much less than for manufacturers. The average sales transaction per shopping trip is well under $100 for department stores, specialty stores, and supermarkets. This low amount creates a need to tightly control the costs associated with each transaction (such as credit verification, sales personnel, and bagging); to maximize the number of customers drawn to the retailer, which may place more emphasis on ads and special promotions; and to increase impulse sales by more aggressive selling. However, cost control can be tough. For instance, inventory management is often expensive due to the many small transactions to a large number of

FIGURE 1-7

Comparing Exclusive, Intensive, and Selective Distribution

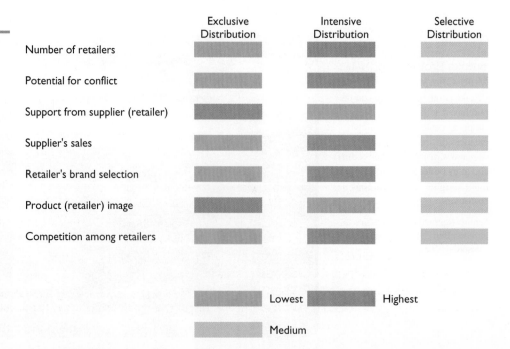

FIGURE 1-8

Special Characteristics
Affecting Retailers

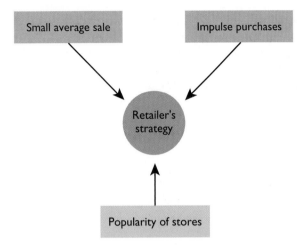

customers. A typical supermarket has several thousand customer transactions *per week,* which makes it harder to find the proper in-stock level and product selection. Thus, retailers are expanding their use of computerized inventory systems.

Final consumers make many unplanned or impulse purchases. Surveys show that a large percentage of consumers do not look at ads before shopping, do not prepare shopping lists (or do deviate from the lists) once in stores, and make fully unplanned purchases. This behavior indicates the value of in-store displays, attractive store layouts, and well-organized stores, catalogs, and Web sites. Candy, cosmetics, snack foods, magazines, and other items are sold as impulse goods when placed in visible, high-traffic areas in a store, catalog, or Web site. Because so many purchases are unplanned, the retailer's ability to forecast, budget, order merchandise, and have sufficient personnel on the selling floor is more difficult.

Macy's (**www.macys.com**) has a Web site to accompany its traditional stores and catalogs.

Retail customers usually visit a store, even though mail, phone, and Web sales have increased. Despite the inroads made by nonstore retailers, most retail transactions are still conducted in stores—and will continue to be in the future. Many people like to shop in person; want to touch, smell, and/or try on products; like to browse for unplanned purchases; feel more comfortable taking a purchase home with them than waiting for a delivery; and desire privacy while at home. This store-based shopping orientation has implications for retailers; they must work to attract shoppers to stores and consider such

RETAILING AROUND THE WORLD

Selling Luxury Cars in China

Although China is usually referred to as a developing country, its super-luxury segment (especially in Beijing, Shanghai, and Shenzhen) is extremely important to auto makers and retailers. According to a research report by CapGemini (**www.capgemini.com**) and Merrill Lynch (**www.ml.com**), 38 percent of Asia's ultra-high-net-worth people (those with more than $30 million in assets) are Chinese.

In China, taxes can double the cost of a Rolls-Royce (**www.rolls-roycemotorcars.com**), raising the total price of the car to $800,000. In contrast, in the United States, taxes add 15 percent of the cost to a car. Until five years ago, Rolls-Royce had no retail facilities in China and its overall brand awareness was low. The company began

to build relationships with China's super rich by hosting cocktail parties at its dealerships.

In 2007, 170 Rolls-Royce cars were sold in China and Hong-Kong, making it the second-largest market for English luxury autos. In response to the rapid increase in demand, Rolls-Royce has opened larger showrooms in Beijing and Shanghai and is developing plans to open in Shenzhen and Hangzhou. To underscore the importance of the Chinese market, Daimler had the world debut for its LK-Class SUV at the Beijing auto show.

Source: Bruce Einhorn, "Rolls-Royce Targets China's Really-Rich," **www.businessweek.com/globalbiz** (May 7, 2008).

factors as store location, transportation, store hours, proximity of competitors, product selection, parking, and ads.

The Importance of Developing and Applying a Retail Strategy

A **retail strategy** is the overall plan guiding a retail firm. It influences the firm's business activities and its response to market forces, such as competition and the economy. Any retailer, regardless of size or type, should utilize these six steps in strategic planning:

1. Define the type of business in terms of the goods or service category and the company's specific orientation (such as full service or "no frills").
2. Set long-run and short-run objectives for sales and profit, market share, image, and so on.
3. Determine the customer market to target on the basis of its characteristics (such as gender and income level) and needs (such as product and brand preferences).
4. Devise an overall, long-run plan that gives general direction to the firm and its employees.
5. Implement an integrated strategy that combines such factors as store location, product assortment, pricing, and advertising and displays to achieve objectives.
6. Regularly evaluate performance and correct weaknesses or problems when observed.

To illustrate these points, the background and strategy of Target Corporation—one of the world's foremost retailers—are presented. Then the retailing concept is explained and applied.

Target Corporation: The Winning Approach of an Upscale Discounter![4]
COMPANY BACKGROUND

See the mass/class approach of Target Corporation (**www.target.com**).

Target Corporation describes itself as "an upscale discounter that provides quality merchandise at attractive prices in clean, spacious, and guest-friendly stores. The first Target store opened in Roseville, Minnesota, in 1962. In addition, the company operates an online business called Target.com. Just like our Bullseye logo, our history comes full circle. Our department-store roots evolved into discount-store savvy. Our first-in-the-industry innovations led to retail revolutions. And our community-minded founder fostered a national philanthropic mindset."

Hoover's recent profile of Target reports that:

> Target and its larger grocery-carrying incarnation, SuperTarget, have carved out a niche by offering more upscale, fashion-forward merchandise than rivals Wal-Mart and Kmart. After years of struggling to turn around its Marshall Field's and Mervyn's department store divisions, the discounter sold them both in 2004. Target also owns apparel supplier Associated Merchandising Corp. and issues Target Visa and its proprietary Target Card.

Today, Target Corporation has nearly 1,700 stores in 48 states with more than 360,000 employees. About 240 stores are SuperTarget outlets, which are larger and carry more merchandise than typical Target stores. And the Target.com Web site is quite popular. The firm is the sixth largest U.S. retailer (in terms of revenues).

THE TARGET CORPORATION'S STRATEGY: KEYS TO SUCCESS

Throughout its existence, Target has adhered to a consistent, far-sighted, customer-oriented strategy—one that has paved the way for its long-term achievements.

GROWTH-ORIENTED OBJECTIVES. "Our mission is to make Target the preferred shopping destination for our guests by delivering outstanding value, continuous innovation, and an exceptional guest experience by consistently fulfilling our Expect More. Pay Less. brand promise. To support our mission, we are guided by our commitments to great value, the community, diversity, and the environment."

FIGURE 1-9

"Expect More. Pay Less" at Target

This very successful chain projects a strong image through a combination of low prices and plentiful, quality merchandise.

Source: Reprinted by permission of Susan Berry, Retail Image Consulting, Inc.

APPEAL TO A PRIME MARKET. The firm is strong with middle-income, well-educated adults. The median age of customers is 42, the median annual household income is about $60,000, one-third have children at home, and one-half have completed college.

DISTINCTIVE COMPANY IMAGE. Target has done a superb job of positioning itself. It is a discount department store chain with everyday low prices. It has linoleum floors, shopping carts, and a simple layout. See Figure 1-9. But Target is also perceived as an upscale discounter: "Expect more of everything. More great design, more choices, and more designer-created items that you won't find anywhere else. And pay less. It's as simple as that. We team up with world-class designers—people like Michael Graves, Liz Lange, and Sonia Kashuk—to create exclusive products to decorate and delight."

FOCUS. The chain never loses sight of its discount store niche: "In this increasingly competitive retail landscape, we strive to remain relevant to our guests by surprising and delighting them with a constant flow of affordable new merchandise, an evolving store design that meets their changing shopping needs, and a convenient array of goods and services that includes food, pharmacy, and Starbucks."

STRONG CUSTOMER SERVICE FOR ITS RETAIL CATEGORY. The firm prides itself on offering excellent customer service for a discount store: "We are committed to consistently delighting our guests. We strive to exceed their expectations, adding this and trying that to provide the perfect blend of style, substance, and oh-so-satisfying shopping."

MULTIPLE POINTS OF CONTACT. Target reaches its customers through extensive advertising, stores in 48 states, a toll-free telephone service center (open 7 days a week, 17 hours per day), and a Web site.

EMPLOYEE RELATIONS. Target calls its employees "team members" and says: "We consider our team member relations to be good. We offer a broad range of company-paid benefits to our team members, including a pension plan, 401(k) plan, medical and dental plans, a retiree medical plan, short-term and long-term disability insurance, paid vacations, tuition reimbursement, various team member assistance programs, life insurance, and merchandise discounts. Eligibility for, and the level of, these benefits varies depending on team members' full-time or part-time status and/or length of service."

INNOVATION. Target often introduces clever, unique innovations. In 2008, it began offering gift cards with built-in digital cameras: "The retailer's gift cards are packing a 1.2-megapixel chip, which isn't all that awesome camera-wise—but you can also buy diapers, laundry detergent, clothes, and so forth with it. Name one other camera that allows you to do *that*. The card is available in increments of $50 to $1,000, and comes with 8MB of memory, which should hold about 50 images."

COMMITMENT TO TECHNOLOGY. Target is devoted to new technologies: "We continue to invest in technology and infrastructure, including implementation of enhanced guest-service systems and construction of new perishable-food and general merchandise distribution centers and our second Target.com fulfillment center."

COMMUNITY INVOLVEMENT. Target believes in giving back: "Since 1946, Target has given 5 percent of its income to communities." In recent years, that has meant "over $3 million each and every week."

CONSTANTLY MONITORING PERFORMANCE. "We strive for continuous improvement in everything we do. We are committed to efficient expense management with focused attention on both delivering results today and preparing for our future."

TARGET ADAPTS TO A DIFFICULT ECONOMY

Due to the difficult economic conditions in recent years, even outstanding retailers such as Target have been affected. In 2007, Target's sales growth and profit growth slowed considerably from 2006. Then, in 2008, Target's sales grew very little; same-store sales actually declined, and the companywide growth was a result of adding new stores. During 2008, company profitability actually declined, largely because of higher credit card expenses.

Overall, Target's new chief executive officer (CEO) says that:

> As we look ahead, we will remain focused on the fundamentals of our business while continuing to pursue innovative solutions and establish new best practices throughout the company. Specifically, we are diligently working to drive top-line growth and thoughtfully manage our expenses. By prioritizing our investments and focusing our resources on areas that increase speed and efficiency, and reduce work and cost, while preserving our brand and overall shopping experience for our guests, we will rise above the current economic challenges.

More specifically, Target has been taking these actions:

▶ Running ads that show people spending more time at home.
▶ Opening fewer new stores.
▶ Placing more emphasis on the "Pay Less" part of its slogan.
▶ Matching Wal-Mart prices whenever possible.
▶ Adding more designers with special collections for Target.
▶ Carrying more food items in traditional Target stores.
▶ Tightening credit terms for customers.

The Retailing Concept

As we just described, Target Corporation has a sincere long-term desire to please customers. In doing so, it uses a customer-centered, chainwide approach to strategy development and implementation; it is value-driven; and it has clear goals. Together, these four principles form the **retailing concept** (depicted in Figure 1-10), which should be understood and applied by all retailers:

1. *Customer orientation.* The retailer determines the attributes and needs of its customers and endeavors to satisfy these needs to the fullest.
2. *Coordinated effort.* The retailer integrates all plans and activities to maximize efficiency.
3. *Value driven.* The retailer offers good value to customers, whether it be upscale or discount. This means having prices appropriate for the level of products and customer service.
4. *Goal orientation.* The retailer sets goals and then uses its strategy to attain them.

FIGURE 1-10

Applying the Retailing
Concept

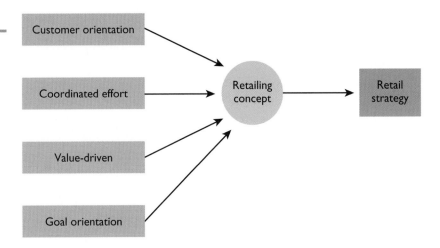

Unfortunately, this concept is not grasped by every retailer. Some are indifferent to customer needs, plan haphazardly, have prices that do not reflect the value offered, and have unclear goals. Some are not receptive to change, or they blindly follow strategies enacted by competitors. Some do not get feedback from customers; they rely on supplier reports or their own past sales trends.

The retailing concept is straightforward. It means communicating with shoppers and viewing their desires as critical to the firm's success, having a consistent strategy (such as offering designer brands, plentiful sales personnel, attractive displays, and above-average prices in an upscale store); offering prices perceived as "fair" (a good value for the money) by customers; and working to achieve meaningful, specific, and reachable goals. However, the retailing concept is only a strategic guide. It does not deal with a firm's internal capabilities or competitive advantages but offers a broad planning framework.

Let's look at three issues that relate to a retailer's performance in terms of the retailing concept: the total retail experience, customer service, and relationship retailing.

THE TOTAL RETAIL EXPERIENCE

One consumer may shop at a discount retailer, another at a neighborhood store, and a third at a full-service firm; nonetheless, these diverse customers all have something crucial in common: They each encounter a total retail experience (including everything from parking to checkout counter) in making a purchase. According to *Chain Store Age*,

> The way to stand out in a crowded marketplace is to operate in a distinctive way that invites notice, and people notice things that reduce clutter and enhance value. At the moment, many companies are choosing remodels over ground-up stores to increase shopping basket size. For effectiveness and efficiency, new designs are bringing the same voice and touchpoints to all of a retailer's formats. Opportunities for competitive differentiation are everywhere—new brands and formats, services, presentations, interactivity. Even small touches can encourage shoppers to buy often and stay loyal. Companies must continuously capitalize on innovation and make strategic adjustments in the store. Innovation can't wait until business picks up. Retail moves so quickly and competitively, the only constant is the ongoing push for the ideas that will lead to better performance.[5]

The **total retail experience** includes all the elements in a retail offering that encourage or inhibit consumers during their contact with a retailer. Many elements, such as the number of salespeople, displays, prices, the brands carried, and inventory on hand, are controllable by a retailer; others, such as the adequacy of on-street parking, the speed of a consumer's Internet connection, and sales taxes, are not. If some part of the total retail experience is unsatisfactory, consumers may not make a purchase—they may even decide not to patronize a retailer again: "Think about scenarios that play out every day. Where is

**ETHICS
IN RETAILING**

McDonald's Introduces a More Well-Rounded Menu

McDonald's (**www.mcdonalds.com**) now offers sliced apples, called Apple Dippers, as an alternative to French fries, in its Happy Meals. To increase the acceptability of healthy foods, McDonald's has launched a series of campaigns, such as *Shrek the Third*–branded carrot sticks, milk, and fruit bags. McDonald's has also added a line of premium salads and fruit parfaits geared to adults. Some of McDonald's meals (such as warm chicken salad and Berrynice yogurt) have qualified for the American Heart Foundation's "Tick" endorsement (**www.americanheart.org**).

McDonald's hopes that the healthy menu additions will reduce criticism that the franchisor and its restaurants offer only fat- and salt-laden foods to an unsuspecting public, including small children. Since 2005, a number of state laws have been passed that make the use of trans-fat oils illegal, require calorie counts on menus, and even outlaw new fast-food franchises.

What remains to be seen is the extent to which these healthier alternatives or legislation will result in positive changes in consumer behavior. Although a large percentage of consumers say they want healthy foods, few McDonald's customers actually buy its salads. The healthy items are also more costly for McDonald's to purchase, as well as to store.

Sources: "Does McDonald's Deserve Its Tick?" *B&T Magazine* (February 17, 2007), p. 6; Melanie Warner, "The Nutrition-Conscious Take a Bite Out of Fast Food," **www.businessweek.com/lifestyle/content** (September 17, 2007); and Jennifer R. Scott, "McDonald's Introduces 'Go Active' Meal," **http://weightloss.about.com/cs/eatsmart/a/aa041804a.htm** (July 30, 2008).

the 'fast' in the fast food industry, when drive-up or walk-in service can now take up to ten or fifteen minutes? Why are there so many automated telephone cues that offer recorded messages warning that due to high call volume, wait times may be many minutes long? How about local businesses, such as dry cleaners and specialty stores, whose staff do not care enough to remember names of frequent patrons?"[6]

In planning its strategy, a retailer must be sure that all strategic elements are in place. For the shopper segment to which it appeals, the total retail experience must be aimed at fulfilling that segment's expectations. A discounter should have ample stock on hand when it runs sales but not plush carpeting; a full-service store should have superior personnel but not have them perceived as haughty by customers. Various retailers have not learned this lesson, which is why some theme restaurants are in trouble. The novelty has worn off, and many people believe the food is only fair while prices are high.

A big challenge for retailers is generating customer "excitement" because many people are bored with shopping or have little time for it. Here is what one retailer, highlighted in Figure 1-11, does:

Build-A-Bear Workshop (www.buildabear.com) even offers a great online shopping experience.

Build-A-Bear Workshop is the only global company that offers an interactive make-your-own stuffed animal retail-entertainment experience. The company currently operates more than 400 Build-A-Bear Workshop stores worldwide. In December 2007, Build-A-Bear Workshop extended its in-store interactive experience online with the launch of its virtual world at **www.buildabearville.com**. We offer an extensive and coordinated selection of merchandise, including over 30 different styles of animals to be stuffed and a wide variety of clothing, shoes, and accessories for the stuffed animals. Our concept appeals to a broad range of age groups and demographics, including children, teens, parents, and grandparents. Our stores, which are primarily located in malls, are destination locations and draw guests from a large geographic reach.[7]

CUSTOMER SERVICE

Customer service refers to the identifiable, but sometimes intangible, activities undertaken by a retailer in conjunction with the basic goods and services it sells. It has a strong impact on the total retail experience. Among the factors comprising a customer service strategy are store hours, parking, shopper friendliness of the store layout, credit acceptance, salespeople, amenities such as gift wrapping, rest rooms, employee politeness, delivery policies, the time

FIGURE 1-11

The Build-A-Bear
Experience: Never Boring
High shopper interactivity
and customized products—in a
child-friendly store environment—
make Build-A-Bear Workshop a
fun place to shop.

Source: Reprinted by permission
of Susan Berry, Retail Image
Consulting, Inc.

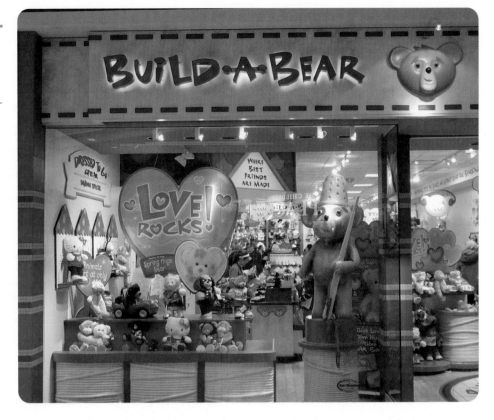

At Lands' End (**www.
landsend.com**), customer
service means "Guaranteed.
Period."

shoppers spend in checkout lines, and customer follow-up. This list is not all inclusive, and it differs in terms of the retail strategy undertaken. Customer service is discussed further in Chapter 2.

Satisfaction with customer service is affected by expectations (based on the type of retailer) and past experience, and people's assessment of customer service depends on their perceptions—not necessarily reality. Different people may evaluate the same service quite differently. The same person may even rate a firm's customer service differently over time due to its intangibility, although the service stays constant:

> Costco shoppers don't expect anyone to help them to their car with bundles of commodities. Teens at Abercrombie & Fitch would be pretty turned off if a tuxedo-clad piano player serenaded them while they shopped. And Wal-Mart customers would protest loudly if the company traded its shopping carts for oversized nylon tote bags. On the other hand, helping shoppers to their cars when they have an oversized purchase is part of the service package at P.C. Richard & Sons, piano music sets the mood at Nordstrom, and nylon totes jammed full of value-priced apparel are in sync with the Old Navy image. Service varies widely from one retailer to the next, and from one shopping channel to the next. The challenge for retailers is to ask shoppers what they expect in the way of service, listen to what they say, and then make every attempt to satisfy them.[8]

Interestingly, despite a desire to provide excellent customer service, a number of outstanding retailers now wonder if "the customer is always right." Are there limits? Ponder this scenario: "Chronic returnaholics can be very crafty. Some buy expensive items with credit cards to earn rewards or airline points and then return the items during certain periods of the billing cycle when the points will not be removed from their account. Some buy large quantities of items, try to sell them on the Internet or in private shops, and then return them for a refund if they don't sell. Some interior designers will buy items for a specific event such as an open house and then return the items for a refund."[9]

FIGURE 1-12

A Customer Respect Checklist

Source: Adapted by the authors from Leonard L. Berry, "Retailers with a Future," *Marketing Management* (Spring 1996), p. 43. Reprinted by permission of the American Marketing Association.

✓ Do we trust our customers?

✓ Do we stand behind what we sell? Are we easy to deal with if a customer has a problem? Are frontline workers empowered to respond properly to a problem? Do we guarantee what we sell?

✓ Is keeping commitments to customers—from being in stock on advertised goods to being on time for appointments—important in our company?

✓ Do we value customer time? Are our facilities and service systems convenient and efficient for customers to use? Do we teach employees that serving customers supersedes all other priorities, such as paperwork or stocking shelves?

✓ Do we communicate with customers respectfully? Are signs informative and helpful? Is advertising above reproach in truthfulness and taste? Are contact personnel professional? Do we answer and return calls promptly—with a smile in our voice? Is our voice mail caller-friendly?

✓ Do we treat all customers with respect, regardless of their appearance, age, race, gender, status, or size of purchase or account? Have we taken any special precautions to minimize discriminatory treatment of certain customers?

✓ Do we thank customers for their business? Do we say "thank you" at times other than after a purchase?

✓ Do we respect employees? Do employees, who are expected to respect customers, get respectful treatment themselves?

RELATIONSHIP RETAILING

As with the retailers profiled in this book, we want to engage in relationship retailing. So please visit our Web site (**www.pearsonhighered. com/berman**).

The best retailers know it is in their interest to engage in **relationship retailing**, whereby they seek to establish and maintain long-term bonds with customers, rather than act as if each sales transaction is a completely new encounter. This means concentrating on the total retail experience, monitoring satisfaction with customer service, and staying in touch with customers. Figure 1-12 shows a customer respect checklist that retailers could use to assess their relationship efforts.

To be effective in relationship retailing, a firm should keep two points in mind:

1. Because it is harder to lure new customers than to make existing ones happy, a "win–win" approach is critical. For a retailer to "win" in the long run (attract shoppers, make sales, earn profits), the customer must also "win" in the long run (receive good value, be treated with respect, feel welcome by the firm). Otherwise, that retailer loses (shoppers patronize competitors) and customers lose (by spending time and money to learn about other retailers).
2. Due to the advances in computer technology, it is now much easier to develop a customer data base with information on people's attributes and past shopping behavior. Ongoing customer contact can be better, more frequent, and more focused. This topic is covered further in Chapter 2.

The Focus and Format of the Text

There are various approaches to the study of retailing: an institutional approach, which describes the types of retailers and their development; a functional approach, which concentrates on the activities that retailers perform (such as buying, pricing, and personnel practices); and a strategic approach, which centers on defining the retail business, setting objectives, appealing to an appropriate customer market, developing an overall plan, implementing an integrated strategy, and regularly reviewing operations.

We will study retailing from each perspective but center on a *strategic approach*. Our basic premise is that the retailer has to plan for and adapt to a complex, changing environment.

TECHNOLOGY IN RETAILING

Load Testing Web Sites

According to a recent report by Jupiter Research (**www.jupiterresearch.com**), 33 percent of dissatisfied online shoppers attribute their dissatisfaction to a Web site's being too slow. An additional 28 percent state that error messages are a cause of dissatisfaction. Three-quarters of online shoppers state that when a site freezes or has a confusing ordering process, they will never shop from that site again. Twenty-seven percent note that they will tell their friends and family members about these negative experiences.

To guard against such issues, retailers need to regularly "stress test" and "load test" their Web under full capacity and transaction conditions. Through such testing, retailers simulate what will actually occur when Web site traffic

peaks (such as in an important holiday season, when demand for a product offering is unexpectedly high, or when there is a major promotion). Stress testing and load testing are also important when a retailer significantly revises its Web site design. Load testing can be done with in-house developed applications, through licensed software, and through use of outsourced service operators.

Without proper load testing, a firm may lose significant sales and profits. In eBay's early days, it lost $3 million in revenues due to a single 22-hour outage on its Web site.

Source: Ken Magill, "Carrying the Load," *2008 Multichannel Merchant Buyer's Guide*, pp. 54–55.

Both opportunities and threats must be considered. By engaging in strategic retail management, the retailer is encouraged to study competitors, suppliers, economic factors, consumer changes, marketplace trends, legal restrictions, and other elements. A firm prospers if its competitive strengths match the opportunities in the environment, weaknesses are eliminated or minimized, and plans look to the future (as well as the past). Look at the appendix to Chapter 1, which examines the impact of a weak economic situation on retailers and consumers alike.

Retail Management: A Strategic Approach is divided into eight parts. The balance of Part One looks at building relationships and strategic planning in retailing. Part Two characterizes retailing institutions on the basis of their ownership; store-based strategy mix; and Web, nonstore-based, and other nontraditional retailing format. Part Three deals with consumer behavior and information gathering in retailing. Parts Four through Seven discuss the specific elements of a retailing strategy: planning the store location; managing a retail business; planning, handling, and pricing merchandise; and communicating with the customer. Part Eight shows how a retailing strategy may be integrated, analyzed, and improved. These topics have special end-of-chapter appendixes: the impact of the economy (Chapter 1), service retailing (Chapter 2), global retailing (Chapter 3), franchising (Chapter 4), and multi-channel retailing (Chapter 6). There are also three end-of-text appendixes: retailing careers, an overview of the comprehensive Web site accompanying *Retail Management*, and a glossary. And our Web site includes "How to Solve a Case Study" (**www.pearsonhighered.com/berman**), which will aid you in your case analyses.

To underscore retailing's exciting nature, four real-world boxes appear in each chapter: "Careers in Retailing," "Ethics in Retailing," "Retailing Around the World," and "Technology in Retailing."

Chapter **Summary**

In this and every chapter, the summary is related to the objectives stated at the beginning of the chapter.

1. *To define retailing, consider it from various perspectives, demonstrate its impact, and note its special characteristics.* Retailing comprises the business activities involved in selling goods and services to consumers for personal,

family, or household use. It is the last stage in the distribution process. Today, retailing is at a complex crossroads, with many challenges ahead.

Retailing may be viewed from multiple perspectives. It includes tangible and intangible items, does not have to involve a store, and can be done by manufacturers and others—as well as retailers.

Annual U.S. store sales are approaching $5 trillion, with other forms of retailing accounting for hundreds of billions of dollars more. The world's 100 largest retailers generate $2.8 trillion in yearly revenues. About 25 million people in the United States work for retailers (including food and beverage service firms), which understates the number of those actually employed in a retailing capacity. Retail firms receive up to 40 cents or more of every sales dollar as compensation for operating costs, the functions performed, and the profits earned.

Retailing encompasses all of the businesses and people involved in physically moving and transferring ownership of goods and services from producer to consumer. In a distribution channel, retailers perform valuable functions as the contact for manufacturers, wholesalers, and final consumers. They collect assortments from various suppliers and offer them to customers. They communicate with both customers and other channel members. They may ship, store, mark, advertise, and pre-pay for items. They complete transactions with customers and often provide customer services. They may offer multiple formats (multi-channel retailing) to facilitate shopping.

Retailers and their suppliers have complex relationships because retailers serve in two capacities. They are part of a distribution channel aimed at the final consumer, and they are major customers for suppliers. Channel relations are smoothest with exclusive distribution; they are most volatile with intensive distribution. Selective distribution is a way to balance sales goals and channel cooperation.

Retailing has several special characteristics. The average sales transaction is small. Final consumers make many unplanned purchases. Most customers visit a store location.

2. *To introduce the concept of strategic planning and apply it.* A retail strategy is the overall plan guiding the firm. It has six basic steps: defining the business, setting objectives, defining the customer market, developing an overall plan, enacting an integrated strategy, and evaluating performance and making modifications. Target Stores' strategy has been particularly well designed and enacted, even though it has been affected by the tough economy in recent years.

3. *To show why the retailing concept is the foundation of a successful business, with an emphasis on the total retail experience, customer service, and relationship retailing.* The retailing concept should be understood and used by all retailers. It requires a firm to have a customer orientation, use a coordinated effort, and be value driven and goal oriented. Despite its straightforward nature, many firms do not adhere to one or more elements of the retailing concept.

The total retail experience consists of all elements in a retail offering that encourage or inhibit consumers during their contact with a retailer. Some elements are controllable by the retailer; others are not. Customer service includes identifiable, but sometimes intangible, activities undertaken by a retailer in association with the basic goods and services sold. It has an effect on the total retail experience. In relationship retailing, a firm seeks long-term bonds with customers rather than acting as if each sales transaction is a totally new encounter with them.

4. *To indicate the focus and format of the text.* Retailing may be studied by using an institutional approach, a functional approach, and a strategic approach. Although all three approaches are covered in this book, our focus is on the strategic approach. The underlying principle is that a retail firm needs to plan for and adapt to a complex, changing environment.

Key Terms

retailing (p. 4)
channel of distribution (p. 7)
sorting process (p. 8)
multi-channel retailing (p. 8)

exclusive distribution (p. 10)
intensive distribution (p. 10)
selective distribution (p. 10)
retail strategy (p. 12)

retailing concept (p. 14)
total retail experience (p. 15)
customer service (p. 16)
relationship retailing (p. 18)

Questions for Discussion

1. What is your favorite apparel retailer? Discuss the criteria you use in making your selection. What can a competing firm do to lure you away from your favorite firm?

2. What kinds of information do retailers communicate to customers? To suppliers?

3. What are the pros and cons of a firm such as Polo Ralph Lauren having its own retail facilities and E-commerce Web site (**www.ralphlauren.com**), as well as selling through traditional retailers?

4. Why would one retailer seek to be part of an exclusive distribution channel while another seeks to be part of an intensive distribution channel?

5. Describe how the special characteristics of retailing offer unique opportunities and problems for local hardware stores.

6. What is the purpose of developing a formal retail strategy? How could a strategic plan be used by a restaurant chain?

7. On the basis of the chapter description of Target Corporation, present five suggestions that a new retailer should consider.

8. Explain the retailing concept. Apply it to your school's bookstore.

9. Define the term "total retail experience." Then describe a recent retail situation in which your expectations were surpassed, and state why.

10. Do you believe that customer service in retailing is improving or declining? Why?

11. How could a small Web-only retailer engage in relationship retailing?

12. What checklist item(s) in Figure 1-12 do you think would be most difficult for Home Depot, as the world's largest home improvement retailer, to address? Why?

Web **Exercise**

Visit About.com: Retail Industry (http://retailindustry. about.com). Describe the site and give several examples of what a prospective retailer could learn from it.

Note: Stop by our Web site (www.pearsonhighered. com/berman) to experience a number of highly interactive,

appealing Web exercises based on actual company demonstrations, and sample materials related to retailing.

Appendix Understanding the Recent Economic Downturn in the United States and Around the Globe

During 2008 and 2009, the economies of the United States and many other countries around the globe declined or were stagnant. In some instances, the effects were devastating. Millions of people lost their jobs, had trouble paying their mortgages (and may have lost their homes), and became pessimistic about the future. Financial institutions had to write off bad debt, and several leading banks and brokerage houses were forced to merge and sometimes went out of business. As a result, this period was tumultuous for retailers. Long-time firms such as Circuit City, Mervyn's, Linens 'n Things, Fortunoff, and Sharper Image—and newer star retailers such as Steve & Barry's—had to shut down. Numerous other retailers suffered losses and had to run frequent sales to generate business.

In this appendix, we present a brief overview of the events leading to the economic downturn, the impact of the downturn on economies around the world, and the effect of the economic downturn on retailing. We also discuss some of the strategic options that retailers are pursuing and should pursue to sustain their business amid a weak economy.

The Events Leading to the 2008–2009 Economic Downturn

Several interrelated factors led to the 2008–2009 economic downturn. These included risky mortgage loans by banks and other financial institutions that were at the heart of the asset base behind mortgage-backed securities, declines in the auto and housing industries (due in part to the decline in consumer confidence and to the reduced availability of credit for auto leases and loans), and high oil prices (which reduced the desirability of gas-guzzling cars and SUVs).

In the period just before the economic downturn, low interest rates and the availability of easy credit enabled banks and other lending institutions to lower down payment and income guideline requirements for home mortgages. Prior to this time, consumers wishing to purchase a home typically made down payments equal to 10 to 20 percent of the home's purchase price; the balance would be financed through a mortgage. Then, in the mid-2000s, as a result of the reduced credit guidelines, many home buyers were able to finance up to 100 percent of the purchase price. Some of these borrowers took out adjustable-interest mortgages that had low initial "teaser rates" that would reset to higher rates in future years. New homeowners often favored adjustable-rate mortgages, where the interest rate fluctuated.

Further aggravating the risky environment created by lending institutions was the fact that some of these loans were made to speculators who purchased homes that were under construction and then sought to "flip"—resell—them at a profit upon their completion. A number of people who received mortgages during this time would have been ineligible for these loans based on the previous guidelines set by the financial institutions.

According to one estimate, subprime loans—those made to buyers with a weak credit rating—accounted for 25 percent of the mortgage market in 2005 and 2006 (up from about 8 percent in the mid-1990s). As of December 2008, U.S. consumers owed about $848 billion on subprime mortgages. Another category of loan, called "Alt A" loans, made to borrowers with unreliable incomes or other factors, made up another 15 percent of the mortgage market.[1] Banks and other financial institutions that underwrote these chancy mortgages hoped that steadily increasing home values would provide them with security against future defaults.

These mortgages were then bundled by financial institutions into mortgage-backed securities that resembled bonds but were backed by mortgages. To compensate for loan portfolios where the homeowners had weak underlying credit scores, a $1,000 bond could be backed by $1,200 or so in mortgages. The mortgage-backed securities were commonly purchased by hedge funds and other investors, who then used these securities as collateral to borrow additional money. As part of the borrowing agreement, lenders could force the investors to pre-pay part of their debt when the underlying asset value in their portfolio dropped below a given level (due to such factors as late or nonpayment issues or declines in the market price of the underlying real-estate).

A large number of mortgage borrowers (new homeowners) were forced to stop making monthly payments when they lost their jobs or when they realized that, due to declines in housing prices, their mortgage loans were now greater than the value of their homes (or that they could not sell or profitably rent real-estate they had hoped to flip). By the end of September 2008, the national subprime delinquency rate jumped to 33.9 percent, a 60 percent increase over the prior 12-month period. At that time, 11.2 percent of all subprime loans ($93 billion) were in foreclosure. The high foreclosure rate, requirements by banks that investors pay down debt or put up more collateral, and the uncertainty in assessing the true value of mortgage-backed securities caused global credit markets to freeze up.[2]

Although some major financial institutions that had invested heavily in these securities received government bailouts as an alternative to their going bankrupt, others ultimately closed. Under the Emergency Economic Stabilization Act of 2008, the U.S. Treasury was authorized to purchase up to $700 billion in assets of financial institutions, especially mortgage-backed securities. This legislation sought to restore liquidity to banking institutions and to open credit markets that had all but shut down.

The U.S. government also provided up to $100 billion in assistance to Fannie Mae (which makes loans to mortgage bankers, brokers, and other primary mortgage market makers) and Freddie Mac (which purchases loans from lending institutions). Aside from rising delinquencies and foreclosures, both Fannie Mae and Freddie Mac were affected by higher funding costs and the lack of investor demand for their long-term debt. The American International Group (AIG), which guaranteed mortgage-backed securities, also received a $150 billion government commitment for loans. Among the casualties of the subprime mortgage crisis were Bear Stearns, which ultimately was folded into J.P. Morgan Chase; Lehman Brothers, which closed down; and Washington Mutual, which became the largest bank failure in history.

High mortgage foreclosure rates, forced sales by speculators, and the low availability of mortgages after the subprime mortgage crisis all contributed to declining home values (particularly in Florida, Nevada, California, and Texas, where home construction had previously boomed). As of early 2009, the median home value in the Unites States had dropped to $180,000—the lowest level since March 2004.

In addition to the subprime credit crisis, the economic downturn was spurred by high oil prices, which reached a peak price of $147 a barrel in July 2008 (before dropping down to below $40 in late 2008 and early 2009). Not only did the high price of oil lead to higher heating and driving costs, it also drastically reduced the demand for fuel-guzzling cars and SUVs. These vehicles were among the best-selling and most-profitable ones made by General Motors, Ford, and Chrysler. Car sales for all brands of cars—both foreign and domestic—were also negatively affected by both low consumer confidence and the reluctance of finance companies to lease or finance car purchases to all but the most creditworthy households. In December 2008, General Motors and Chrysler accepted $17.4 billion in government-backed loans. The bailout required both firms to radically restructure by mid-2009 and to develop comprehensive plans to become profitable again. To the U.S. government, the overriding concern was that without a bailout, the economic effects of the two firms entering into bankruptcy would extend far beyond the auto industry and worsen an already poor overall economy—in the United States and globally.

As a result of the combined effect of lower home values, lower stock prices, and lost jobs, the Federal Reserve reported that U.S. households lost nearly $7.1 trillion in net worth during 2008.[3] In addition, the December 2008 holiday season was the worst one for retailers in decades.

The Impact of the Downturn on Economies Around the World

The effects of the 2008–2009 downturn were also felt throughout the world. One global credit insurer, Euler Hermes, estimated that about 35,000 western European retail businesses would become insolvent in 2009, up 17 percent from 2008. Retailing was the second-worst-hit sector in Europe—after the manufacturing sector.[4]

A research study involving 2,700 consumers in Germany, France, Great Britain, Italy, and Spain by the firm Boston Consulting found that 56 percent of the adults who were surveyed planned to cut discretionary spending in 2009 by an average of 12 percent.[5] Among the key European retail bankruptcies were Woolworths, a chain selling toys and housewares; MFI, a furniture retailer; and The Pier, a housewares chain.

According to another forecast, European nations were expected to have an extremely low economic growth rate of 0.2 percent in 2009, with a slow recovery to 1.6 percent growth in 2010. As Business Monitor International noted: "Virtually every economic indicator in Europe looked weak. Whether you were looking at consumer confidence, factory orders, or unemployment, the outlook was not bright. Compounding the danger was the deterioration of financial markets, which would continue to restrict credit growth and hurt both investment and private consumption."[6]

The slowdown in the U.S. and European markets also affected Asia. In the second half of 2008, the rate of economic growth in China slowed to the lowest figure in five years. This occurred despite the reduction of domestic interest rates three times between September and November 2008 and the halt of the appreciation of the yuan relative to the U.S. dollar by the Chinese government.

The Effect of the Economic Downturn on Retailing

The 2008–2009 economic downturn had a major impact on all types of retailers, including those selling to a more upscale clientele. According to Lew Frankfort, the chairman and chief executive officer of Coach, "No social or economic class has been immune from this crisis. The customer is fragile. She's worried about her future."[7]

To further illustrate the effect of this economic downturn on a broad range of retailers, for several months, comparable year-to-year same-store sales fell for many retail companies, as reported by *Women's Wear Daily* and other sources. Even such illustrious retail chains as Neiman Marcus, Saks, and Nordstrom faced sales declines. A report from MasterCard Inc.'s Spending Pulse unit noted that U.S. luxury sales during the crucial November 1 to December 24, 2008, holiday season dropped significantly—including 35 percent for jewelry, 14 percent for footwear, and 14 percent for men's apparel sales.[8]

As already noted, the overall 2008 holiday season was the worst in years. Total 2008 U.S. retail sales (excluding automobiles) fell from the 2007 period by 5.5 percent in November 2008 and by 8 percent in December (through Christmas eve). Because some retailers earn as much as 40 percent of their annual profits during the holiday season (for toy merchants, it can be 50 percent of profits), several bankruptcies were necessary in early 2009 for financially weak firms.

The 2008–2009 retail bankruptcies were undertaken under a tougher set of rules than in the previous economic downturn. Prior to 2005, U.S. firms had an unlimited amount of time to file a restructuring plan after filing for bankruptcy. Since 2005, these filings have had to be submitted within 18 months. Under earlier laws, retailers had two years or more (via extensions) to determine which store locations to keep. Today, retailers under bankruptcy protection must make store-closing decisions within 210 days. Retailers in bankruptcy also now need to pay suppliers and utilities during the retailers' bankruptcy period. Under the older laws, suppliers and utilities had to wait until a company emerged from bankruptcy before being paid. Lastly, due to concerns from lenders who were burnt with mortgage-backed securities, troubled retailers have found it much more difficult to get financing. As a result of these factors, many retailers that entered bankruptcy were unable to restructure and, thus, forced to close.

Among the bankruptcies that were quickly followed by company closings were Steve & Barry's, Mervyn's, Sharper Image, and Tweeter. Although all of these companies were adversely affected by the overall economy, the specific causes of their declines were somewhat different.

Steve & Barry's featured inexpensive licensed celebrity and athlete collections, such as Bitten by Sarah Jessica Parker, Dear by Amanda Bynes, Eleven by Venus Williams, and Starbury by Stephon Marbury. Two funds, Bay Harbour Management and York Capital Management, bought the retailer out of bankruptcy in September 2008 for $168 million. They later decided to shut it down. According to bankruptcy documents, the chain was not able to get adequate financing during the rough economic environment. And some of Steve & Barry's stores had sales of less than $100 per square foot, barely enough to cover operating and staffing costs.[9]

Mervyn's, a California-based department store chain, was acquired from Target by Cerberus Capital Management, Sun Capital Partners, and Lubert-Adler in July 2004 for $1.65 billion. To raise funds, the new owners closed down and resold 90 of Mervyn's underperforming stores, as well as two of its four distribution centers. Additional capital was raised by selling below-market leases on many of its retail properties to outside companies. These properties were then re-leased by Mervyn's at prevailing market rents. Saddled with substantial costs, low sales due to the weak economy, and the expansion of J.C. Penney and Kohl's into western markets, the chain floundered.[10]

Sharper Image, a 184-store chain that specialized in distinctive electronics and gadgets, ultimately succumbed to liquidation due to overreliance on a single product: an air purifier called the Ionic Breeze. Although air purifiers accounted for 28 percent of Sharper Image's sales in 2005, they dropped to 9.4 percent of total sales in 2007.[11] In 2003, *Consumer Reports* published a report stating that Sharper Image's Ionic Breeze cleaners did not clean the air. In a follow-up 2005 report, *Consumer Reports* suggested that the product might be dangerous due to the small amount of ozone it generated. Lawsuits from Ionic Breeze owners and Sharper Image investors followed.

Tweeter, a 94-store electronics chain, faced a dour retail situation due to its reliance on selling and installing high-end audio systems. It faced declining sales as consumers shifted attention to home entertainment systems. In addition, many of Tweeter's high-end brands became more widely available, and Tweeter faced additional competition from firms specializing in system installation. Lastly, Tweeter's gross profits from flat-panel HD

TV sales plummeted as the retail prices of these televisions dropped and the economy weakened.[12]

Some analysts believed that retailers that were number two or three in market share in their respective markets were particularly vulnerable to bankruptcy or liquidation. This was especially the case for retailers that used heavy debt to fund their expansion during the recent period when interest rates were low and credit availability was high. Retailers owned by private equity firms that were acquired during the pre-2008 boom years—due to their strong cash flow and property assets—were also financially stressed.

Due to shoppers' concern about the viability of retailers in bankruptcy, the sales of gift cards were affected. It was widely publicized by the media that gift card recipients would be treated as unsecured creditors when a retailer entered into bankruptcy protection. Consumers Union estimated that unused Sharper Image gift cards totaled $20 million.[13]

Strategic Options for Retailers in Weak Economic Times

Among major retailers, Wal-Mart, Costco, BJ's, and other value-based companies far outperformed the industry. As Wal-Mart's outgoing chief executive officer H. Lee Scott noted: "This is the kind of environment that Sam Walton built this company for." The president of the Retail Metrics research firm added that Wal-Mart was "a primary destination for a lot of people who may not have gone there before, but who elected to go there for the price and the value."[14]

BJ's and Costco did particularly well with food items, as more consumers saved money by eating at home versus at casual or traditional restaurants. Supermarkets such as Supervalu built up their prepared foods and convenience foods sections as an alternative to more costly eating out. Supervalu's chief executive officer stated that "Supervalu, like many retailers, delivered more meal solutions in a value-priced way, so that people could pick things that were ready to go or only need limited preparation, and bring them home."[15] And McDonald's did well as many people switched to inexpensive fast-food restaurants as their dining-out options.

The rent-to-own store was another retail format that outperformed the industry—largely as a result of the scarce credit available to some furniture and appliance shoppers. For example, in the third quarter of 2008 alone, Aaron Rents—the second-largest U.S. rent-to-own retailer with about 1,600 stores—added 26,000 new customers. This 18 percent jump was the largest increase for that quarter in five years. At the same time, Aaron Rents' same-store sales rose 5.7 percent.[16]

Off-price apparel chains such as Marshalls, Burlington Coat Factory, and Syms also drew new shoppers because of the many customers who became more value driven. In addition, these off-price chains gained significant opportunistic buying opportunities due to overstocked channel members, as well as the unsold merchandise of bankrupt or liquidating retailers.

Let's look at several strategic options that are available to retailers to increase their performance during troubled economic times:

▶ *Increase the firm's cash position.* When retail sales drop and credit for retailers is more restrictive, retailers typically work hard to increase their cash holdings. Specific strategies include marking down merchandise (not just for holidays and special events) to stimulate inventory turnover, canceling orders (where possible), seeking to delay payments to suppliers, placing fewer orders to reduce inventory levels, putting off expansion plans, cutting back on remodeling, and pressing suppliers for additional markdown allowances. As Tim Belk, the chief executive of Belk Department Stores, stated: "Like many retailers, we continued to experience the effects of a severe economic slowdown. However, we maintained a strong balance sheet and positive cash flow, which placed us in a good position to weather the downturn. This was the result of the diligent efforts of our managers and associates across the country to manage inventory, expenses, and capital investments."[17]

▶ *Rethink existing store formats.* At Wal-Mart, smaller-format stores will play a larger role in the future in order to increase sales per square foot and lower rent and utility costs. Wal-Mart's average supercenter is now 140,000 to 170,000 square feet, versus 195,000 square feet a few years ago. To make the new strategy work, Wal-Mart needs to reduce product assortments and maximize supply chain efficiencies so stockouts are kept down despite lower in-store inventory levels.

▶ *Keep stores open longer hours.* In December 2008, Toys "R" Us kept its Times Square, New York, flagship store open continuously for 134 hours. Wal-Mart, H&M, and Macy's also added "extreme hours" at select locations. To lure shoppers, Toys "R" Us' Times Square store offered a 15 percent discount for purchases made between midnight and 5 A.M.

▶ *Begin the holiday season early.* One estimate is that stores typically place orders up to four to seven months in advance. Thus, due to the combined effects of a recession, poor credit availability, and an atmosphere of consumer caution, stores may then have 15 to 20 percent or more excess holiday inventory. As a result, many retailers promote major holidays well ahead of time and conduct special sales events even before a holiday season begins. For example, many retailers now reduce prices on Christmas items before Thanksgiving.

▶ *Re-introduce layaway plans.* The concept of layaways started during the Great Depression as a way of enabling customers to purchase items without using a credit card. Through a layaway plan, a customer pays the product's total cost in installments (plus a small fee) before being allowed to take it home. In a traditional layaway program, a customer has 30 days to pay for an item after leaving an initial payment. Although layaway programs deny instant gratification to the purchaser, the customer has no danger of overextending his or her credit. Until the 2008–2009 economic downturn, Kmart was the only major U.S. retailer with a layaway program. Now, Sears, T.J. Maxx, Marshalls, and Burlington Coat Factory—along with many regional chains and local stores—offer layaway programs. Recently, Kmart extended the payment times for its layaway plan to up to eight weeks.

2

Building and Sustaining Relationships in Retailing

Chapter Objectives

1. To explain what "value" really means and highlight its pivotal role in retailers' building and sustaining relationships

2. To describe how both customer relationships and channel relationships may be nurtured in today's highly competitive marketplace

3. To examine the differences in relationship building between goods and service retailers

4. To discuss the impact of technology on relationships in retailing

5. To consider the interplay between retailers' ethical performance and relationships in retailing

Stew Leonard's (**www.stewleonards.com**) is a four-store supermarket chain with units in Connecticut and New York. Each square foot of selling space has been estimated by one source to account for as much as $3,750 in sales. It is listed in the *Guinness Book of Records* for having the greatest sales per area of any single food store in the United States! In addition, its stores have a higher profit margin than the average supermarket. Every year, the company attracts thousands of business leaders who attend "Stew Leonard's University" to learn about its successful practices.

Stew Leonard's bases its store strategy on "retailtainment" and on building and maintaining customer relationships. One of Stew Leonard's tactics is to be known as the "Disneyland of Dairy Stores" by being as exciting as possible for shoppers of all ages. Stew Leonard's processes milk in full view of customers while the "Farm Fresh Five," a band of milk-carton robots, sing. The parking lot even has a petting zoo. Day-in, day-out, Stew Leonard's offers free samples from its in-house bakeries and dairies. There are also special activities on major holidays. For example, local music groups and dancers perform on St. Patrick's Day and at Halloween the chain features hayrides and pumpkin-carving contests.

Stew Leonard's prides itself on its customer service. The retailer's shopper relationships are built on the concept that the "Customer Is Always Right." Carved into 6-foot-high, 6,000-pound boulders at the entrance to the firm's Norwalk and Danbury, Connecticut, stores are two rules: "Rule 1: The customer is always right. Rule 2: If the customer is wrong, reread Rule 1."[1]

Source: Reprinted by permission of Susan Berry, Retail Image Consulting, Inc.

OVERVIEW

To prosper, a retailer must properly apply the concepts of "value" and "relationship" so (1) customers strongly believe the firm offers a good value for the money and (2) both customers and channel members want to do business with that retailer. Some firms grasp this well. Others still have some work to do. Consider GameStop's forward-thinking view:

GameStop
(**www.gamestop.com**)
is—first and foremost—a
customer-driven retailer.

> GameStop is the world's largest video game retailer. With over 4,400 stores located throughout the United States and 15 countries, we are the retail destination for gamers around the world. Our GameStop, EB Games, and Electronics Boutique retail locations set us apart in the industry. Everything that we offer our customers—from our expansive selection of new products to our knowledgeable associates to our value-added pre-owned products—is geared to deliver customer satisfaction. We complement our store network with GameStop.com and EBgames.com, and publish *Game Informer,* one of the industry's largest circulation video game magazines. Together, we hold a passion for gaming, a commitment to our industry, and a disciplined business perspective to continuously drive value with shareholders, customers, vendors, and employees.[2]

As retailers look to the future, this is the looming bottom line on value: "Consumers will demand more for less from the shopping experience. Time and budget constrained consumers will spend less time shopping, make fewer trips, visit fewer stores, and shop more purposefully. Different strokes will satisfy different folks. Consumers will shop different formats for different needs. Specifically, they will split the commodity shopping trip from the value-added shopping trip. Consumers are becoming more skeptical about price. Under the barrage of sales, price has lost its meaning; gimmicks have lost their appeal. To regain consumer confidence, pricing by retailers and manufacturers alike will become clearer, more sensible, and more sophisticated."[3] See Figure 2-1.

This chapter looks at value and the value chain, relationship retailing with regard to customers and channel partners, the differences in relationship building between goods and service retailers, technology and relationships, and ethics and relationships. There is also a chapter appendix on service retailing.

Value and the Value Chain

In many channels of distribution, there are several parties: manufacturer, wholesaler, retailer, and customer. These parties are most apt to be satisfied with their interactions when they have similar beliefs about the value provided and received, and they agree on the payment for that level of value.

From the perspective of the manufacturer, wholesaler, and retailer, **value** is embodied by a series of activities and processes—a value chain—that *provides* a certain value for the consumer. It is the totality of the tangible and intangible product and customer service attributes offered to shoppers. The level of value relates to each firm's desire for a fair profit and its niche (such as discount versus upscale). Where firms may differ is in rewarding the value each provides and in allocating the activities undertaken.

From the customer's perspective, **value** is the *perception* the shopper has of a value chain. It is the customer's view of all the benefits from a purchase (formed by the total retail experience). Value is based on the perceived benefits received versus the price paid. It varies by type of shopper. Price-oriented shoppers want low prices, service-oriented shoppers will pay more for superior customer service, and status-oriented shoppers will pay a lot to patronize prestigious stores.

FIGURE 2-1

The Walking Company:
Providing Extra Value for
Customers

As The Walking Company
(**www.thewalkingcompany.com**)
says, "We search the world over,
so you can walk the world in
comfort. Whether you purchase a
fashion comfort sandal to wear
while dining out, comfortable
dress shoes to commute to the
city, an ultimate comfort clog to
use while on your feet all day at
work, or a new pair of
performance shoes to reach your
personal fitness goals, our highly
trained sales staff can help you
with all of your comfort shoe
needs. Customer service is our
number one priority, and your
satisfaction is guaranteed." The
firm has stores around the
country and a shopper-friendly
Web site.

Source: Reprinted by permission of
Susan Berry, Retail Image
Consulting, Inc.

Why is "value" such a meaningful concept for every retailer in any kind of setting?

▶ Customers must always believe they get their money's worth, whether the retailer sells $20,000 Patek Phillipe watches or $40 Casio watches.
▶ A strong retail effort is required so that customers perceive the level of value provided in the manner the firm intends.
▶ Value is desired by all customers; however, it means different things to different customers.
▶ Consumer comparison shopping for prices is easy through ads and the World Wide Web. Thus, prices have moved closer together for different types of retailers.
▶ Retail differentiation is essential so a firm is not perceived as a "me too" retailer.
▶ A specific value/price level must be set. A retailer can offer $100 worth of benefits for a $100 item or $125 worth of benefits (through better ambience and customer service) for the same item with a $125 price. Either approach can work if properly enacted and marketed.

Peapod (**www.peapod.com**)
offers a unique value chain
with its home delivery
service.

A retail **value chain** represents the total bundle of benefits offered to consumers through a channel of distribution. It comprises store location and parking, retailer ambience, the level of customer service, the products/brands carried, product quality, the retailer's in-stock position, shipping, prices, the retailer's image, and other elements. As a rule, consumers are concerned with the results of a value chain, not the process. Food shoppers who buy online via Peapod care only that they receive the brands ordered when desired, not about the steps needed for home delivery at the neighborhood level.

Some elements of a retail value chain are visible to shoppers, such as display windows, store hours, sales personnel, and point-of-sale equipment. Other elements are not visible, such as store location planning, credit processing, company warehouses, and many merchandising decisions. In the latter case, various cues are surrogates for value: upscale store ambience and plentiful sales personnel for high-end retailers; shopping carts and self-service for discounters.

There are three aspects of a value-oriented retail strategy: expected, augmented, and potential. An *expected retail strategy* represents the minimum value chain elements a given customer segment (e.g., young women) expects from a type of retailer (e.g., a mid-priced apparel retailer). In most cases, the following are expected value chain elements: store cleanliness, convenient hours, well-informed employees, timely service, popular products in stock, parking, and return privileges. If applied poorly, expected elements cause customer dissatisfaction and relate to why shoppers avoid certain retailers.

Compare T.J. Maxx (**www.tjmaxx.com**) and Lord & Taylor (**www. lordandtaylor.com**).

An *augmented retail strategy* includes the extra elements in a value chain that differentiate one retailer from another. As an example, how is Sears different from Saks? The following are often augmented elements: exclusive brands, superior salespeople, loyalty programs, delivery, personal shoppers and other special services, and valet parking. Augmented features complement expected value chain elements, and they are the key to continued customer patronage with a particular retailer.

Today Barnes & Noble (**www.bn.com**) relies on both its stores and its Web site for revenues.

A *potential retail strategy* comprises value chain elements not yet perfected by a competing firm in the retailer's category. For example, what customer services could a new upscale apparel chain offer that no other chain offers? In many situations, the following are potential value chain elements: 24/7 store hours (an augmented strategy for supermarkets), unlimited customer return privileges, full-scale product customization, instant fulfillment of rain checks through in-store orders accompanied by free delivery, and in-mall trams to make it easier for shoppers to move through enormous regional shopping centers. The first firms to capitalize on potential features gain a head start over their adversaries. Barnes & Noble and Borders accomplished this by opening the first book superstores, and Amazon.com became a major player by opening the first online bookstore. Yet, even as

---

CAREERS IN RETAILING   Katie: Co-owner of an Online Retail Store

During college, Katie held several internships, one in interior design and another at a law office. After earning a bachelor's degree in English with a minor in art history, Katie decided to earn a professional designation in merchandise marketing from a fashion institute to pursue her goal of opening her own retail store.

Katie's first retail experience was as an assistant manager for a regional specialty store chain, where she applied customer service and sales skills—the heart of the retail business. She also learned day-to-day tasks such as working a cash register, doing markdowns, folding (believe it or not, there's a trick to it based on merchandising—many retailers have their own specifications), and so forth. Katie progressively gained more responsibilities, such as managing employees, developing schedules, and doing the payroll. These responsibilities more fully prepared her for her next position.

Katie was recruited to be a sales manager for an international specialty store chain; and it was a perfect fit for her career aspirations of launching her own boutique. The store was located on Rodeo Drive, which offered networking opportunities with the clientele she intended to target as an entrepreneur. It was also a nice pay raise!

Katie feels she was born to be an entrepreneur. She met her business partner at the fashion institute, where they were grouped together in an entrepreneurship class. At first, as a class project, they brainstormed opening a store. Through research, opening a store evolved to developing an online boutique, and continued work on this project led to "What if we really did this? We can do this."

Today, Katie works out of her online boutique's office and warehouse. She comments that there is always something to be done and things change so frequently. So there is no real routine.

Source: Reprinted by permission of the National Retail Federation.

pioneers, firms must excel at meeting customers' basic expectations and offering differentiated features from competitors if they are to grow.

There are five potential pitfalls to avoid in planning a value-oriented retail strategy:

▶ *Planning value with just a price perspective.* Value is tied to two factors: benefits and prices. Most discounters now accept credit cards because shoppers want to purchase with them.
▶ *Providing value-enhancing services that customers do not want or will not pay extra for.* Ikea knows most of its customers want to save money by assembling furniture themselves.
▶ *Competing in the wrong value/price segment.* Neighborhood retailers generally have a tough time competing in the low-price part of the market. They are better off providing augmented benefits and charging somewhat more than large chains.
▶ *Believing augmented elements alone create value.* Many retailers think that if they offer a benefit not available from competitors that they will automatically prosper. Yet, they must never lose sight of the importance of expected benefits. A movie theater with limited parking will have problems even if it features first-run movies.
▶ *Paying lip service to customer service.* Most firms say, and even believe, customers are always right. Yet, they may act contrary to this philosophy—by having a high turnover of salespeople, charging for returned goods that have been opened, and not giving rain checks if items are out of stock.

To sidestep these pitfalls, a retailer could use the checklist in Figure 2-2, which poses a number of questions that must be addressed. The checklist can be answered by an owner/corporate president, a team of executives, or an independent consultant. It should be reviewed at least once a year or more often if a major development, such as the emergence of a strong competitor, occurs.

FIGURE 2-2

A Value-Oriented Retailing Checklist

Answer yes or no to each question.

✓ Is value defined from a consumer perspective?

✓ Does the retailer have a clear value/price point?

✓ Is the retailer's value position competitively defensible?

✓ Are channel partners capable of delivering value-enhancing services?

✓ Does the retailer distinguish between expected and augmented value chain elements?

✓ Has the retailer identified meaningful potential value chain elements?

✓ Is the retailer's value-oriented approach aimed at a distinct market segment?

✓ Is the retailer's value-oriented approach consistent?

✓ Is the retailer's value-oriented approach effectively communicated to the target market?

✓ Can the target market clearly identify the retailer's positioning strategy?

✓ Does the retailer's positioning strategy consider trade-offs in sales versus profits?

✓ Does the retailer set customer satisfaction goals?

✓ Does the retailer periodically measure customer satisfaction levels?

✓ Is the retailer careful to avoid the pitfalls in value-oriented retailing?

✓ Is the retailer always looking out for new opportunities that will create customer value?

Retailer Relationships

In Chapter 1, we introduced the concept of *relationship retailing,* whereby retailers seek to form and maintain long-term bonds with customers, rather than act as if each sales transaction is a new encounter with them. For relationship retailing to work, enduring value-driven relationships are needed with other channel members, as well as with customers. Both jobs are challenging. See Figure 2-3. Visit our Web site for links related to relationship retailing issues (**www.pearsonhighered.com/berman**).

Customer Relationships

Loyal customers are the backbone of a business. Thus, it is important that they be cultivated. Here's why: "A Walker Information study revealed that while 79 percent of customers said they were satisfied, only 41 percent of them were categorized as loyal. The reason given for not buying again or switching was customer service. Do you know what your customers value today? It might be different than it was in January. Can they leave your property and say 'that experience was really good value'?"[4]

In relationship retailing, there are four factors to keep in mind: the customer base, customer service, customer satisfaction, and loyalty programs and defection rates. Let's explore these next.

THE CUSTOMER BASE

Retailers must regularly analyze their customer base in terms of population and lifestyle trends, attitudes toward and reasons for shopping, the level of loyalty, and the mix of new versus loyal customers.

The U.S. population is aging. One-fourth of households have only one person, one-sixth of people move annually, most people live in urban and suburban areas, the number of working women is high, middle-class income has been rising very slowly, and African American, Hispanic American, and Asian American segments are expanding. Thus, gender roles are changing, shoppers demand more, consumers are more diverse, there is less interest in shopping, and time-saving goods and services are desired.

FIGURE 2-3

J.C. Penney: An Emphasis on Solid Retail Relationships

J.C. Penney wants its customers to be fully satisfied with the shopping experience—and to return over and over. It also seeks to have strong relationships with the many suppliers from which it buys merchandise.

Source: Reprinted by permission of Susan Berry, Retail Image Consulting, Inc.

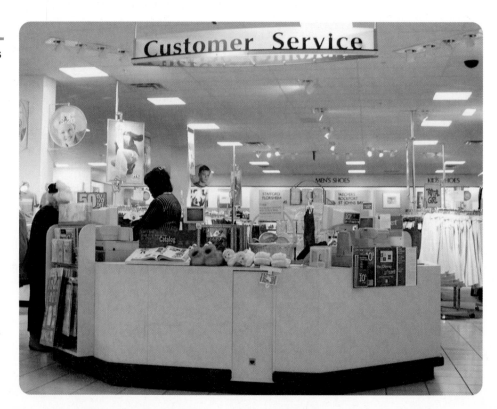

Consider the following about U.S. consumers:

▶ In an average month, shoppers visit 14 different stores. Due to time constraints and pre-shopping on the Internet, consumers now spend an average of less than 75 minutes when visiting a shopping mall.

▶ About 56 percent of households shop at supermarkets at least once per week, 20 percent at drugstores, 7 percent at membership clubs such as Costco, 6 percent at home improvement or hardware stores, and 3 percent at traditional department stores.

▶ In 1985, women bought 70 percent of men's products; today, they buy less than 25 percent due to the increased shopping done by men. Women do more product research before shopping and are less apt to be influenced by ads than are men.

▶ Consumers' most important reasons to shop at a given *food store* are high-quality fresh foods, good value, and healthy food alternatives. Consumers give *department stores* high marks for the brands and styles carried, but lower marks for prices. Consumers at *supercenters* and *discount department stores* tend to be households in the family life stages, often in the down- and middle-income brackets. These retailers are popular for many different product categories.[5]

It is more worth nurturing relationships with some shoppers than with others; they are the retailer's **core customers**—its best customers. And they should be singled out:

> Most businesses have a mix of good, better, and best customers. Unfortunately, there are bad customers as well, and they can be a waste of time and money. Good customers might be good because they spend lots of money. They might be good because they come back often. Bad customers are the ones who are never satisfied and almost always cost more to serve than they spend. The trick is to identify the best customers and see what characteristics differentiate these profitable customers from all the rest. Then focus your strategies on the segments most apt to produce the new best customers.[6]

A retailer's desired mix of new versus loyal customers depends on that firm's stage in its life cycle, goals, and resources, as well as competitors' actions. A mature firm is more apt to rely on core customers and supplement its revenues with new shoppers. A new firm faces the dual tasks of attracting shoppers and building a loyal following; it cannot do the latter without the former. If goals are growth-oriented, the customer base must be expanded by adding stores, increasing advertising, and so on; the challenge is to do this in a way that does not deflect attention from core customers. Although it is more costly to attract new customers than to serve existing ones, core customers are not cost-free. If competitors try to take away a firm's existing customers with price cuts and special promotions, a retailer may feel it must pursue competitors' customers in the same way. Again, it must be careful not to alienate core customers.

CUSTOMER SERVICE

As described in Chapter 1, *customer service* refers to the identifiable, but sometimes intangible, activities undertaken by a retailer in conjunction with the goods and services it sells. It has an impact on the total retail experience. Consistent with a value chain philosophy, retailers must apply two elements of customer service: **Expected customer service** is the service level that customers want to receive from any retailer, such as basic employee courtesy. **Augmented customer service** includes the activities that enhance the shopping experience and give retailers a competitive advantage. AutoZone does a good job with both expected and augmented customer services:

AutoZone (**www.autozone. com**) has a unique style of customer service.

> AutoZone offers thousands of parts and accessories. But the best product we offer is our customer service—and you get that free of charge. Our stores have friendly, knowledgeable people who are glad to help you. "AutoZoners always put customers first!" That's the first line of AutoZone's pledge and it's the most important thing we do. We go the extra mile to make sure you get the help you

need. We have created our shopping experience with the customer in mind. We're constantly changing our stores to bring you the newest and most exciting products. And you always know when you enter our stores you'll find a great selection of quality merchandise at low prices.[7]

The attributes of personnel who interact with customers (such as politeness and knowledge), as well as the number and variety of customer services offered, have a strong effect on the relationship created. Although planning a superior customer service strategy can be complex, a well-executed strategy can pay off in a big way. Just a decade ago, independent pharmacies were perceived by many experts as an "endangered species." But today, they have found a strong marketplace niche based on personal service, as praised recently by *Consumer Reports*:

> In each of our drugstore surveys, begun in 1998, readers have ranked independents above the other types of store, probably because of their focus on prescription drugs, which account for 92 percent of everything they sell. Readers gave pharmacists at independent stores high marks for being accessible, approachable, easy to talk to (when sought out), and knowledgeable about prescription and nonprescription products. Independents also stock medical supplies (wheelchairs, walkers, canes, and braces) that might be missing from other types of stores and will customize medicines for patients with special needs. Waits are uncommon, and many independents offer home delivery. On independents' Web sites, you can usually order refills, shop for medical equipment, track purchases, and do a little research.[8]

Nordstrom (**www. nordstrom.com**) really believes in empowering its employees to better serve customers.

Some retailers realize that customer service is better when they utilize **employee empowerment**, whereby workers have the discretion to do what they believe is necessary—within reason—to satisfy the customer, even if this means bending the rules. One well-known practitioner of employee empowerment is Nordstrom: "Our people and the passion they have for service make all the difference. We trust one another's integrity and ability. Our only rule: use good judgment in all situations. Be empowered. Want to go above and beyond for a customer? Make a suggestion? Try something new? We want you to take the initiative and we'll support your efforts to deliver exceptional service. Have an idea? Want to talk? If it's important to you, we're listening. And if you've got a great idea, we want to hear about it."[9]

To apply customer service effectively, a firm must first develop an overall service strategy and then plan individual services. Figure 2-4 shows one way a retailer may view the customer services it offers.

FIGURE 2-4

Classifying Customer Service

Source: Adapted by the authors from Albert D. Bates, "Rethinking the Service Offer," *Retailing Issues Letter* (December 1986), p. 3. Reprinted by permission.

	Cost of Offering the Customer Service	
	High	**Low**
Value of the Customer Service to the Shopper — **High**	**Patronage Builders** — High-cost activities that are the primary factors behind customer loyalties. Examples: transaction speed, credit, gift registry	**Patronage Solidifiers** — The "low-cost little things" that increase loyalty. Examples: courtesy (referring to the customer by name and saying thank you), suggestion selling
Low	**Disappointers** — Expensive activities that do no real good. Examples: weekday deliveries for two-earner families, home economists	**Basics** — Low-cost activities that are "naturally expected." They don't build patronage, but their absence could reduce patronage. Examples: free parking, in-store directories

DEVELOPING A CUSTOMER SERVICE STRATEGY.   A retailer must make the following vital decisions.

What customer services are expected and what customer services are augmented for a particular retailer? Examples of expected customer services are credit for a furniture retailer, new-car preparation for an auto dealer, and a liberal return policy for a gift shop. Those retailers could not stay in business without them. Because augmented customer services are extra elements, a firm could serve its target market without such services; yet, using them enhances its competitive standing. Examples are delivery for a supermarket, an extra warranty for an auto dealer, and gift wrapping for a toy store. Each firm needs to learn which customer services are expected and which are augmented for its situation. Expected customer services for one retailer, such as delivery, may be augmented for another. See Figure 2-5.

What level of customer service is proper to complement a firm's image? An upscale retailer would offer more customer services than a discounter because people expect the upscale firm to have a wider range of customer services as part of its basic strategy. Performance would also be different. Customers of an upscale retailer may expect elaborate gift wrapping, valet parking, a restaurant, and a ladies' room attendant, whereas discount shoppers may expect cardboard gift boxes, self-service parking, a lunch counter, and an unattended ladies' room. Customer service categories are the same; performance is not.

Should there be a choice of customer services? Some firms let customers select from various levels of customer service; others provide only one level. A retailer may honor several credit cards or only its own. Trade-ins may be allowed on some items or all. Warranties may have optional extensions or fixed lengths. A firm may offer one-, three-, and six-month payment plans or insist on immediate payment.

Should customer services be free? Two factors cause retailers to charge for some customer services: (1) Delivery, gift wrapping, and some other customer services are labor intensive. (2) People are more apt to be home for a delivery or service call if a fee is imposed. Without a fee, a retailer may have to attempt a delivery twice. In settling on a free or fee-based strategy, a firm must determine which customer services are expected (these are often free) and which are augmented (these may be offered for a fee), monitor competitors and profit margins, and study the target market. In setting fees, a retailer must also decide if its goal is to break even or to make a profit on certain customer services.

How can a retailer measure the benefits of providing customer services against their costs? The purpose of customer services is to enhance the shopping experience in a manner

Staples (**www.staples.com**) offers free delivery on orders of $50 or more.

FIGURE 2-5

H-E-B: Going Above and Beyond

H-E-B (**www.heb.com**) operates customer-friendly stores in Texas and Mexico: The chain's "commitment to excellence has made it one of the nation's largest independently owned food retailers. Yet H-E-B's success has not changed its commitment to giving the customer exceptional service, low prices, and friendly shopping."

Source: Reprinted by permission of TNS Retail Forward.

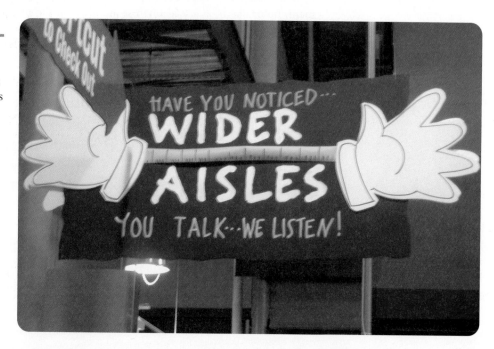

that attracts and retains shoppers—while maximizing sales and profits. Thus, augmented customer services should not be offered unless they raise total sales and profits. A retailer should plan augmented customer services based on its experience, competitors' actions, and customer comments; when the costs of providing these customer services increase, higher prices should be passed on to the consumer.

How can customer services be terminated? Once a customer service strategy is set, shoppers are likely to react negatively to any customer service reduction. Nonetheless, some costly augmented customer services may have to be dropped. In that case, the best approach is to be forthright by explaining why the customer services are being terminated and how customers will benefit via lower prices. Sometimes a firm may use a middle ground, charging for previously free customer services (such as clothing alterations) to allow those who want the services to still receive them.

PLANNING INDIVIDUAL CUSTOMER SERVICES. Once a broad customer service plan is outlined, individual customer services are planned. A department store may offer credit, layaway, gift wrapping, a bridal registry, free parking, a restaurant, a beauty salon, carpet installation, dressing rooms, clothing alterations, pay phones, rest rooms and sitting areas, the use of baby strollers, delivery, and fur storage. The range of typical customer services is shown in Table 2-1 and described next. Most retailers let customers make credit purchases; and many firms accept personal checks with proper identification. Consumers' use of credit rises as the purchase amount goes up. Retailer-sponsored credit cards have three key advantages: (1) The retailer saves the fee it would pay for outside card sales. (2) People are encouraged to shop with a given retailer because its card is usually not accepted elsewhere. (3) Contact can be maintained with customers and information learned about them. There are also disadvantages to retailer cards: Startup costs are high, the firm must worry about unpaid bills and slow cash flow, credit checks and follow-up tasks must be performed, and customers without the firm's card may be discouraged from shopping. Bank and other commercial credit cards enable small and medium retailers to offer credit, generate added business for all types of retailers, appeal to mobile shoppers, provide advertising support from the sponsor, reduce bad debts, eliminate startup costs for the retailer, and provide data. Yet, these cards charge a transaction fee and do not yield loyalty to the retailer.

All bank cards and most retailer cards involve a **revolving credit account**, whereby a customer charges items and is billed monthly on the basis of the outstanding cumulative balance. An **option credit account** is a form of revolving account; no interest is assessed if a person pays a bill in full when it is due. When a person makes a partial payment, he or she is assessed interest monthly on the unpaid balance. Some credit card firms (such as American Express) and some retailers offer an **open credit account**, whereby a consumer must pay the bill in full when it is due. Partial, revolving payments

TABLE 2-1 Typical Customer Services

Credit	Miscellaneous	
Delivery	• Bridal registry	• Rest rooms
Alterations and installations	• Interior designers	• Restaurant
Packaging (gift wrapping)	• Personal shoppers	• Babysitting
Complaints and returns handling	• Ticket outlets	• Fitting rooms
Gift certificates	• Parking	• Beauty salon
Trade-ins	• Water fountains	• Fur storage
Trial purchases	• Pay phones	• Shopping bags
Special sales for regular customers	• Baby strollers	• Information
Extended store hours		
Mail and phone orders		

are not permitted. A person with an open account also has a credit limit (although it may be more flexible).

For a retailer that offers delivery, there are three decisions: the transportation method, equipment ownership versus rental, and timing. The shipping method can be car, van, truck, rail, mail, and so forth. The costs and appropriateness of the methods depend on the products. Large retailers often find it economical to own their delivery vehicles. This also lets them advertise the company name, have control over schedules, and use their employees for deliveries. Small retailers serving limited trading areas may use personal vehicles. Many small, medium, and even large retailers use shippers such as UPS if consumers live away from a delivery area and shipments are not otherwise efficient. Finally, the retailer must decide how quickly to process orders and how often to deliver to different locales.

For some retailers, alterations and installations are expected customer services—although more retailers now charge fees. However, many discounters have stopped offering alterations of clothing and installations of heavy appliances on both a free and a fee basis. They feel the services are too ancillary to their business and not worth the effort. Other retailers offer only basic alterations: shortening pants, taking in the waist, and lengthening jacket sleeves. They do not adjust jacket shoulders or width. Some appliance retailers may hook up washing machines but not do plumbing work.

Within a store, packaging (gift wrapping)—as well as complaints and returns handling—can be centrally located or decentralized. Centralized packaging counters and complaints and returns areas have key advantages: They may be situated in otherwise dead spaces, the main selling areas are not cluttered, specialized personnel can be used, and a common policy is enacted. The advantages of decentralized facilities are that shoppers are not inconvenienced, people are kept in the selling area (where a salesperson may resolve a problem or offer different merchandise), and extra personnel are not required. In either case, clear guidelines as to the handling of complaints and returns are needed.

Gift certificates encourage shopping with a given retailer. Many firms require certificates to be spent and not redeemed for cash. Trade-ins also induce new and regular shoppers to shop. People may feel they are getting a bargain. Trial purchases let shoppers test products before purchases are final to reduce risks.

Retailers increasingly offer special customer services to regular customers. Sales events (not open to the general public) and extended hours are provided. Mail and phone orders are handled for convenience.

London's Topshop: Pulling Out All the Stops

The United States has plenty of stores aimed at fashion-loving young women—but there is nothing in America that directly compares with Topshop's megastore (**www.topshop.co.uk**) located on Oxford Street in London. The flagship store generates annual sales per square foot of $2,000 (versus $400 per square foot for Gap stores). What makes this Topshop store so appealing is that it has been able to strike a balance between discount retailing (the store's more costly items rarely sell for over $200) and its luxury brand status and cutting-edge fashions.

Topshop offers its shoppers a "world of make-believe." The London megastore includes a hair salon (offering blowouts for $42), a manicure station, a candy shop, and even a concierge who can arrange to get rock concert tickets for customers. Many of the stores have personal shoppers, who help customers select outfits. The chain also has Topshop Express units, which arrange to have purchases delivered to the shopper's home or office within three hours. These amenities are unusual for a mass-market retailer that attracts young shoppers.

To keep the excitement going and the merchandise fresh, the flagship store gets three deliveries each day. This encourages shoppers to return on a weekly basis to examine the store's new fashion merchandise.

Sources: Elizabeth Esfahani, "High Class, Low Price," **www.money.cnn.com/magazines/business2** (February 16, 2007); and Jennifer Reingold, "The British (Retail) Invasion," **www.money.cnn.com/2008/07/01** (July 3, 2008).

Other useful customer services include a bridal registry, interior designers, personal shoppers, ticket outlets, free (or low-cost) and plentiful parking, water fountains, pay phones, baby strollers, rest rooms, a restaurant, babysitting, fitting rooms, a beauty salon, fur storage, shopping bags, and information counters. A retailer's willingness to offer some or all of these services indicates to customers a concern for them. Therefore, firms need to consider the impact of excessive self-service.

CUSTOMER SATISFACTION

Customer satisfaction occurs when the value and customer service provided through a retailing experience meet or exceed consumer expectations. If the expectations of value and customer service are not met, the consumer will be dissatisfied: "Retail satisfaction consists of three categories: *shopping systems satisfaction,* which includes availability and types of outlets; *buying systems satisfaction,* which includes selection and actual purchasing of products; and *consumer satisfaction,* which is derived from the use of the product. Dissatisfaction with any of the three aspects could lead to customer disloyalty, decrease in sales, and erosion of the market share."[10]

Only "very satisfied" customers are likely to remain loyal in the long run. How well are retailers doing in customer satisfaction? Many have much work to do. The American Customer Satisfaction Index (**www.theacsi.org**) annually questions thousands of people to link customer expectations, perceived quality, and perceived value to satisfaction. Overall, retailers consistently score only about 75 on a scale of 100. Gasoline stations usually rate lowest in the retailing category (with scores around 70). To improve matters, retailers should engage in the process shown in Figure 2-6.

Most consumers do not complain when dissatisfied. They just shop elsewhere. Why don't shoppers complain more? (1) Because most people feel complaining produces little or no positive results, they do not bother to complain. (2) Complaining is not easy. Consumers have to find the party to whom they should complain, access to that party may be restricted, and written forms may have to be completed.

Try out some of StatPac's surveys (**www.statpac.com/online-surveys/examples.htm**) for measuring customer satisfaction.

To obtain more feedback, retailers must make it easier for shoppers to complain, make sure shoppers believe their concerns are addressed, and sponsor ongoing customer satisfaction surveys. As suggested by software firm StatPac, retailers should ask such questions as these and then take corrective actions:

1. "Overall, how satisfied or dissatisfied are you with the store?"
2. "How satisfied or dissatisfied are you with the *price* of the items you purchased?"
3. "How satisfied or dissatisfied are you with the *quality* of the merchandise?"
4. "Please tell us something we could do to improve our store."[11]

LOYALTY PROGRAMS

Consumer loyalty (frequent shopper) programs reward a retailer's best customers, those with whom it wants long-lasting relationships. According to *Profit* magazine, about

FIGURE 2-6

Turning Around Weak Customer Service

Source: Figure and its discussion developed by the authors from information in Jeff Mowatt, "Keeping Customers When Things Go Wrong," *Canadian Manager* (Summer 2001), pp. 23, 28.

Focus on Customer Concerns	Empower Frontline Employees	Show That You Are Listening	Express Sincere Understanding	Apologize and Rectify the Situation
"Employees must view customer complaints as *concerns*. This will shift a negative situation into one that is positive, helpful, and productive."	"You can often prevent customers from becoming upset if you empower frontline employees to make reasonable on-the-spot decisions."	"When a customer voices dissatisfaction, listen without interrupting. Then prove that you've heard him or her. That means repeating and paraphrasing."	"Upset customers need to know that you care—not just about their problem—but about their frustration. So, empathize. Use phrases like, 'I'd feel the same way if I were you.'"	"Say, 'I'm sorry.' Even when you suspect the customer is wrong, it's better to give him or her the benefit of the doubt. On top of an exchange or refund, give a token of appreciation for the inconvenience."

90 percent of all U.S. households participate in at least one loyalty program.[12] And here's what consumers want:

> Shoppers will change their buying behavior in response to a reward if they judge the value of that reward to be higher than its cost to make a future purchase or to give out an E-mail address, for example. An important step in designing rewards is to make sure customers perceive them as being valuable. Our team grouped reward types into five categories and identified the groups of shoppers most likely to view them as valuable:

> ► *Economic rewards* include things such as price reductions and purchase vouchers. People most concerned about their budgets will perceive these types of rewards as valuable.
> ► *Hedonistic rewards* include things such as points that can be exchanged for spa services or participation in games or sweepstakes. These rewards have more emotional value and will attract people who shop for pleasure.
> ► *Social-relational rewards* include things such as mailings about special events or the right to use special waiting areas at airports. Consumers who want to be identified with a privileged group will value these kinds of rewards.
> ► *Informational rewards* include things such as personalized beauty advice or information about new goods or services. They will attract consumers who like to stick with one brand or store.
> ► *Functional rewards* include things such as access to priority checkout counters or home delivery. Consumers who want to reduce the time they spend shopping will value these most.[13]

Great Britain's Tesco (www. tesco.com/clubcard) has a strong loyalty program (Tesco Clubcard) for its supermarket customers.

What do good customer loyalty programs have in common? Their rewards are useful and appealing, and they are attainable in a reasonable time. The programs honor shopping behavior (the greater the purchases, the greater the benefits). A data base tracks behavior. There are features that are unique to particular retailers and not redeemable elsewhere. Rewards stimulate both short- and long-run purchases. Customer communications are personalized. Frequent shoppers feel "special." Participation rules are publicized and rarely change.

When a retailer studies customer defections (by tracking data bases or surveying consumers), it can learn how many customers it is losing and why they no longer patronize the firm. Customer defections may be viewed in absolute terms (people who no longer buy from the firm at all) and in relative terms (people who shop less often). Each retailer must define its acceptable defection rate. Furthermore, not all shoppers are "good" customers. A retailer may feel it is okay if shoppers who always look for sales, return items without receipts, and expect fee-based services to be free decide to defect. Unfortunately, too few retailers review defection data or survey defecting customers because of the complexity of doing so and an unwillingness to hear "bad news."

Channel Relationships

Within a value chain, the members of a distribution channel (manufacturers, wholesalers, and retailers) jointly represent a **value delivery system**, which comprises all the parties that develop, produce, deliver, and sell and service particular goods and services. These are the ramifications for retailers:

► Each channel member is dependent on the others. When consumers shop with a certain retailer, they often do so because of both the retailer and the products it carries.
► All activities in a value delivery system must be enumerated and responsibility assigned for them.

▶ Small retailers may have to use suppliers outside the normal distribution channel to get the products they want and gain adequate supplier support. Although large retailers may be able to buy directly from manufacturers, smaller retailers may have to buy through wholesalers handling such accounts.

▶ A value delivery system is as good as its weakest link. No matter how well a retailer performs its activities, it will still have unhappy shoppers if suppliers deliver late or do not honor warranties.

▶ The nature of a given value delivery system must be related to target market expectations.

▶ Channel member costs and functions are influenced by each party's role. Long-term cooperation and two-way information flows foster efficiency.

▶ Value delivery systems are complex due to the vast product assortment of super-stores, the many forms of retailing, and the use of multiple distribution channels by some manufacturers.

▶ Nonstore retailing (such as mail order, phone, and Web transactions) requires a different delivery system than store retailing.

▶ Due to conflicting goals about profit margins, shelf space, and so on, some channel members are adversarial—to the detriment of the value delivery system and channel relationships.

When they forge strong positive channel relationships, members of a value delivery system better serve each other and the final consumer. Here's how:

> At Wal-Mart and Sam's Club, we're 100 percent committed to giving our customers unbeatable value, reliable quality, and friendly service. Working closely with our suppliers to drive out unnecessary costs allows us to pass the savings on to our shoppers. We realize it takes a lot of time and effort to become a Wal-Mart or Sam's Club supplier, therefore, we may not be the proper fit for every business. If you run a small business and you don't have the capacity to distribute products on a national level, you might qualify for our Local Purchases program. To initiate the partnership process, just ask the store manager or food merchandiser at any Wal-Mart store for a Local Purchases program questionnaire. This questionnaire includes step-by-step instructions and requirements for becoming one of our local suppliers.[14]

Ace (**www.acehardware. com**) prides itself on strong relationships with its suppliers.

> Since the Ace Hardware cooperative structure allows our buyers to negotiate with combined buying power of over 4,800 locations, our store owners have a significant advantage over nonaffiliated stores. Our regional and state-of-the-art distribution centers and computerized ordering give you efficient access to more than 70,000 items in every major hardware category. Your Ace Hardware store will also be equipped with a proprietary computerized management system, which will provide accurate sales transaction processing, detailed sales and expense information, and extensive inventory management and ordering features to help you run a "tight ship."[15]

One relationship-oriented practice that some manufacturers and retailers use, especially supermarket chains, is *category management*, whereby channel members collaborate to manage products by category rather than by individual item. Successful category management is based on these actions: (1) Retailers listen better to customers and stock what they want. (2) Profitability is improved because inventory matches demand more closely. (3) By being better focused, shoppers find each department to be more desirable. (4) Retail buyers have more responsibility and accountability for category results. (5) Retailers and suppliers share data and are more computerized. (6) Retailers and suppliers plan together. Category management is discussed further in Chapter 14.

Figure 2-7 shows various factors that contribute to effective channel relationships.

FIGURE 2-7

Elements Contributing to
Effective Channel
Relationships

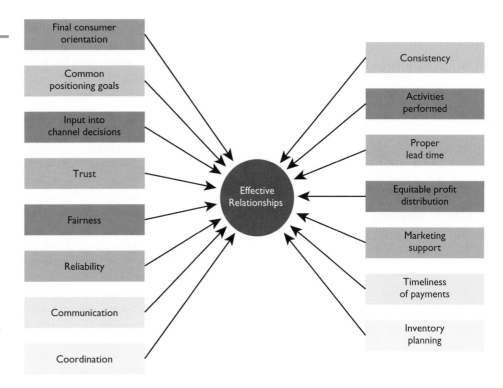

The Differences in Relationship Building Between Goods and Service Retailers

The consumer interest in services makes it crucial to understand the differences in relationship building between retailers that market services and those that market goods. This applies to store-based and nonstore-based firms, those offering only goods *or* services, and those offering goods *and* services.

Goods retailing focuses on the sale of tangible (physical) products. **Service retailing** involves transactions in which consumers do not purchase or acquire ownership of tangible products. Some retailers engage in either goods retailing (such as hardware stores) or service retailing (such as travel agencies); others offer a combination of the two (such as video stores that rent, as well as sell, movies). The latter format is the fastest growing. Consider how many pharmacies offer film developing, how many department stores have beauty salons, how many hotels have gift shops, and so on.

Service retailing encompasses such diverse businesses as personal services, hotels and motels, auto repair and rental, and recreational services. In addition, although several services have not been commonly considered a part of retailing (such as medical, dental, legal, and educational services), they should be when they entail final consumer sales. There are three kinds of service retailing:

▶ **Rented-goods services**, whereby consumers lease and use goods for specified periods of time. Tangible goods are leased for a fixed time, but ownership is not obtained and the goods must be returned when the rental period is up. Examples are Hertz car rentals, carpet cleaner rentals at a supermarket, and video rentals at a 7-Eleven.

▶ **Owned-goods services**, whereby goods owned by consumers are repaired, improved, or maintained. In this grouping, the retailer providing the service never owns the good involved. Illustrations include watch repair, lawn care, and an annual air-conditioner tune-up.

▶ **Nongoods services**, whereby intangible personal services are offered to consumers who then experience the services rather than possess them. The seller offers personal expertise for a specified time in return for a fee; tangible goods are not involved. Some examples are stockbrokers, travel agents, real-estate brokers, and personal trainers.

Please note: The terms *customer service* and *service retailing* are not interchangeable. Customer service refers to the activities undertaken *in conjunction with* the retailer's main business; they are part of the total retail experience. Service retailing refers to situations in which services *are sold to* consumers.

Cheap Tickets (**www. cheaptickets.com**) makes itself more tangible through its descriptive name.

There are four unique aspects of service retailing that influence relationship building and customer retention: (1) The intangibility of many services makes a consumer's choice of competitive offerings tougher than with goods. (2) The service provider and his or her services are sometimes inseparable (thereby localizing marketing efforts). (3) The perishability of many services prevents storage and increases risks. (4) The aspect of human nature involved in many services makes them more variable.

The intangible (and possibly abstract) nature of services makes it harder for a firm to develop a clear consumer-oriented strategy, particularly because many retailers (such as opticians, repairpeople, and landscapers) start service businesses on the basis of their product expertise. The inseparability of the service provider and his or her services means the owner-operator is often indispensable and good customer relations are pivotal. Perishability presents a risk that in many cases cannot be overcome. Thus, revenues from an unrented hotel room are forever lost. Variability means service quality may differ for each shopping experience, store, or service provider. See Figure 2-8.

FIGURE 2-8

Characteristics of Service Retailing That Differentiate It from Goods Retailing and Their Strategic Implications

Source: Adapted by the authors from Valarie A. Zeithaml, A. Parasuraman, and Leonard L. Berry, "Problems and Strategies in Service Marketing," *Journal of Marketing*, Vol. 49 (Spring 1985), p. 35. Reprinted by permission of the American Marketing Association.

Characteristics of Service Retailing | Selected Strategic Implications

Intangibility
- No patent protection is possible for services.
- It is difficult to display and communicate services and service benefits.
- Service prices are difficult to set.
- Quality judgment by customers may be subjective. Two dimensions of quality judgment are process quality (judged by the customer during the service) and output quality (judged by the customer after the service is performed).
- Some services involve performances/experiences.

Inseparability
- The consumer may be involved in the production of services.
- Centralized mass production of services is difficult.
- If a popular employee leaves a firm, customers may switch to the new company where that person now works.

Perishability
- Services cannot be inventoried.
- The effects of seasonality can be severe.
- Planning employee schedules can be complex.

Variability
- Standardization and quality control are hard to achieve.
- Services may be delivered by employees who are beyond the immediate influence of management (at the customer's home, on the road, etc.).
- Customers may perceive variability in the service quality from one occasion to the next occasion, even if such variability does not actually occur.

FIGURE 2-9

Selected Factors Affecting Consumer Perceptions of Service Retailing

Sources: Adapted by the authors from Leonard L. Berry, Kathleen Seiders, and Dhruv Grewal, "Understanding Service Convenience," *Journal of Marketing*, Vol. 66 (July 2002), pp. 1–17; and Hung-Chang Chiu, "A Study on the Cognitive and Affective Components of Service Quality," *Total Quality Management*, Vol. 13 (March 2002), pp. 265–274.

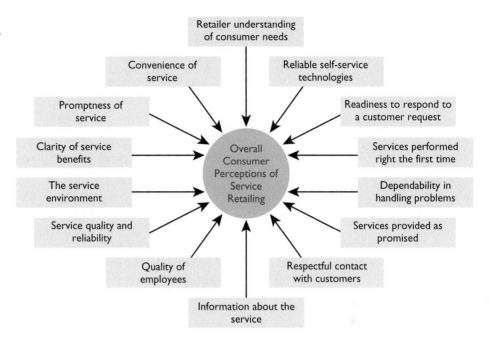

Service retailing is much more dependent on personal interactions and word-of-mouth communication than goods retailing:

> Relationship marketing benefits the customer, as well as the firm. For services that are personally important, variable in quality, and/or complex, many customers will desire to be "relationship customers." Medical, banking, insurance, and hairstyling services illustrate some or all of the significant factors—importance, variability, and complexity—that would cause many customers to desire continuity with the same provider, a proactive service attitude, and customized service delivery. The intangible nature of services makes them difficult for customers to evaluate prior to purchase. The heterogeneity of labor-intensive services encourages customer loyalty when excellent service is experienced. Not only does the auto repair firm want to find customers who will be loyal, but customers want to find an auto repair firm that evokes their loyalty. Knowledge of the customer combined with social rapport built over a series of service encounters facilitate the tailoring of service to customer specifications. Relationship marketing does not apply to every service situation. However, for those services distinguished by the characteristics discussed here, it is potent.[16]

Figure 2-9 highlights several factors that consumers may consider in forming their perceptions about the caliber of the service retailing experience offered by a particular firm. The appendix at the end of this chapter presents an additional discussion on the unique aspects of operating a service retailing business.

Technology and Relationships in Retailing

Technology is beneficial to retailing relationships if it facilitates a better communication flow between retailers and their customers, as well as between retailers and their suppliers, and there are faster, more dependable transactions.

These two points are key in studying technology and its impact on relationships in retailing:

1. In each firm, the roles of technology and "humans" must be clear and consistent with the goals and style of that business. Although technology can facilitate customer service, it may become overloaded and break down. It is also viewed as impersonal by some consumers. New technology must be set up efficiently with minimal disruptions to suppliers, employees, and customers.

2. Shoppers expect certain operations to be in place, so they can rapidly complete credit transactions, get feedback on product availability, and so on. Firms have to deploy some advances (such as a computerized checkout system) simply to be competitive. By enacting other advances, they can be distinctive. For instance, consider the paint store with computerized paint-matching equipment for customers who want to touch up old paint jobs.

Throughout this book, we devote a lot of attention to technological advances via "Technology in Retailing" boxes and in-chapter discussions. Here, we look at technology's effects in terms of electronic banking and customer–supplier interactions.

Electronic Banking

Electronic banking involves both the use of automatic teller machines (ATMs) and the instant processing of retail purchases. It allows centralized record keeping and lets customers complete transactions 24 hours a day, 7 days a week at bank and nonbank locations—including home or office. Besides its use in typical financial transactions (such as check cashing, deposits, withdrawals, and transfers), electronic banking is now used in retailing. Many retailers accept some form of electronic debit payment plan (discussed further in Chapter 13), whereby the purchase price is immediately deducted from a consumer's bank account by computer and transferred to the retailer's account.

Worldwide, there are more than 1.1 billion ATMs—360,000 in the United States alone—and people make billions of ATM transactions yearly.[17] ATMs are located in banks, shopping centers, department stores, supermarkets, convenience stores, hotels, and airports; on college campuses; and at other sites. With sharing systems, such as the Cirrus and Plus networks, consumers can make transactions at ATMs outside their local banking areas and around the world.

A highly touted new version of electronic payment is called the *smart card* by industry observers. The smart card contains an electronic strip that stores and modifies customer information as transactions take place. Its acceptance is important for retailers and shoppers alike:

> In the United States, when a consumer presents a payment to a merchant, the merchant typically makes a request for authorization before accepting the payment. Personal information, such as an account number, address, or telephone number, is often enough to initiate a payment. A serious weakness of this system is that criminals who obtain personal information can impersonate an honest consumer and commit payments fraud. A key to improving security—and reducing payments fraud—might be payment smart cards. These cards have an embedded computer chip that encrypts messages to aid authorization. If properly configured, payment smart cards could provide direct benefits to consumers, merchants, banks, and others. These groups would be less vulnerable to the effects of fraud and the cost of fraud prevention would fall. Smart cards could also provide indirect benefits to society by allowing a more efficient payments system. Smart cards have already been adopted in other countries, allowing a more secure payments process and a more efficient payments system.[18]

Customer and Supplier Interactions

Technology is changing the nature of retailer–customer and retailer–supplier interactions. If applied well, benefits accrue to all parties. If not, there are negative ramifications. Here are several illustrations.

Retailers widely use point-of-sale scanning equipment. Why? By electronically scanning products (rather than having cashiers "ring up" each product), retailers can quickly complete transactions, amass sales data, give feedback to suppliers, place and receive orders faster, reduce costs, and adjust inventory. There is a downside to scanning: the error rate. This can upset consumers, especially if they perceive scanning to be inaccurate. Yet, according to research on scanning, scanner errors in reading prices occur very infrequently; although consumers believe that most errors result in overcharges, overcharges and undercharges are equally likely. One way to assure consumers is to display more information at the point of purchase.

An increasingly popular point-of-sale system involves self-scanning (which is discussed further in Chapter 13). Here's how a basic system works:

> With a customer-operated point-of-sale (POS) station—also called a "self-scanning checkout"—customers pay for and bag their own merchandise without interacting with a human cashier, although a support person is typically nearby and available. The station includes a touch-screen display, barcode scanner, weighing scale, credit card reader and cash reader, and deposit unit. After the customer scans the item's barcode, the item is placed in the bag, which is hanging on a scale. If the weight of the additional item does not jive with the item just scanned, the customer is asked to rescan it, otherwise an alarm will notify the attendant.[19]

Other technological innovations are also influencing retail interactions. Here are three examples:

Neiman Marcus pioneered the electronic gift card (**www.neimanmarcus.com**).

▶ Many retailers think they have the answer to the problem of finding the perfect gift—the electronic gift card: "Even the most creative shoppers can run out of gift ideas. And even the most gracious recipients sometimes hate the gifts they receive. Thus, the popularity of the gift card." Annual gift card sales in the United States exceed $90 billion, and about three-quarters of shoppers buy them during the peak holiday shopping period. However, about 10 percent of gift cards are not redeemed by their recipients.[20]

▶ Interactive electronic kiosks (discussed further in Chapter 6) are gaining in use. For example, the Embassy Direct Registration Kiosk offers self-service check-in capabilities to Embassy Suites hotel guests. "The easy-to-use automated kiosk is designed for your convenience when checking in, checking out, and printing your boarding pass. With a simple swipe of a credit card, you'll receive: suite check-in, ability to select your suite, disbursement of your room key, printing of registration information, check-out, printing of folio, airline check-in, personalized messaging, and coupons for hotel services."[21] Figure 2-10 shows a McDonald's interactive kiosk.

▶ More retailers are using Web portals to exchange information with suppliers: "Since our introduction as an Internet-based communications network exclusively serving retail chain drugstores, ChainDrugStore.net (**www.chaindrugstore.net**) has evolved into the industry's essential link between pharmacy and more than 200 manufacturing and managed care organizations. As the link between manufacturers, managed care organizations, and pharmacies, more than 60,000 stores and 48,000 pharmacies rely on us to access crucial information. By providing pharmacies with the right information at the right time, ChainDrugStore.net ensures that every pharmacy operator has access to the relevant product information and market analytics needed to manage a profitable business."[22]

Ethical Performance and Relationships in Retailing

Ethical challenges fall into three interconnected categories: *Ethics* relates to the retailer's moral principles and values. *Social responsibility* involves acts benefiting society. *Consumerism* entails protecting consumer rights. "Good" behavior depends not only on the retailer but also on the expectations of the community in which it does business.

Throughout this book, in "Ethics in Retailing" boxes and chapter discussions, we look at many ethical issues. Here we study the broader effects of ethics, social responsibility, and consumerism. Visit our Web site for links on retailers' ethical challenges (**www.pearsonhighered.com/berman**).

FIGURE 2-10

Interactive Marketing at McDonald's

Through this kiosk, parents can place a food order for their children and themselves, and the completed order will be delivered to the McDonald's play area.

Source: Reprinted by permission of Susan Berry, Retail Image Consulting, Inc.

Ethics

In dealing with their constituencies (customers, the general public, employees, suppliers, competitors, and others), retailers have a moral obligation to act ethically. Furthermore, due to the media attention paid to firms' behavior and the high expectations people have today, a failure to be ethical may lead to adverse publicity, lawsuits, the loss of customers, and a lack of self-respect among employees.

When a retailer has a sense of **ethics**, it acts in a trustworthy, fair, honest, and respectful manner with each of its constituencies. Executives must articulate to employees and channel partners which kinds of behavior are acceptable and which are not. The best way to avoid unethical acts is for firms to have written ethics codes, to distribute them to employees and channel partners, to monitor behavior, and to punish poor behavior—and for top managers to be highly ethical in their own conduct. See Figure 2-11.

 **TECHNOLOGY IN RETAILING** Contactless Cards Come to Retailing

Unlike traditional credit cards with magnetic stripes, contactless cards can be swiped from any direction and do not require a signature for transactions of $25 or less. In addition, transactions can move along faster since there is no small change to be counted or exchanged. MasterCard's PayPass (**www.paypass.com**), American Express' ExpressPay (**www.americanexpress.com/expresspay**), and Visa's PayWave (**www.visa.com/paywave**) systems all operate in a similar manner. Unlike card-based credit transactions, the contactless cards contain microprocessor chips that can store large quantities of data, such as adding consumer purchases to a retailer's loyalty program.

Contactless cards are a natural for fast-food restaurants, drive-through windows, and gasoline stations. Although McDonald's (**www.mcdonalds.com**) and AMC Theatres (**www.amctheatres.com**) are among the retailers that offer contactless payment terminals at their locations, overall consumer and retailer acceptance of this technology has been slow. And consumers typically have little use for a technology that's not widely accepted by merchants. At the same time, merchants have little interest in using a payment form without a large customer base. One credit-card company executive calls this a "chicken-and-the-egg" type problem.

To increase acceptance of contactless technology, credit-card firms need to develop and promote a common message about the benefits of this new technology for both merchants and consumers. Currently, MasterCard, American Express, and Visa use different appeals.

Sources: "Contactless Needs a Unified Message," *Cash & Payments* (December 2007), p. 40; and Linda Punch, "Spreading North? Contactless in Canada," *Cards & Payments Marketplace 2008*, p. 28.

FIGURE 2-11

Eddie Bauer: Strong Ethical Sensibilities

Source: Reprinted by permission of Eddie Bauer, Inc.

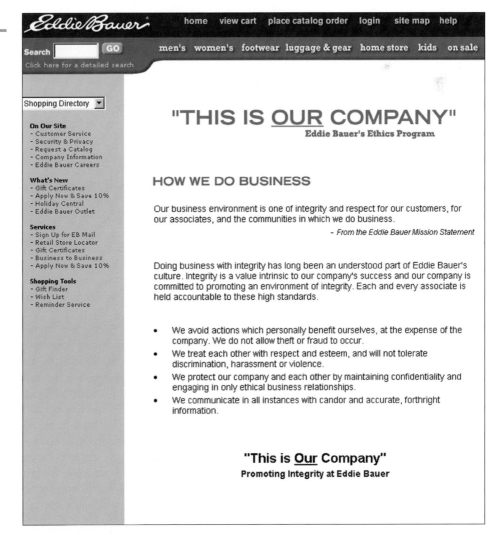

Society often may deem certain behavior to be unethical even if laws do not forbid it. Most observers would agree that practices such as these are unethical (and sometimes illegal, too):

▶ Raising prices on scarce products after a natural disaster such as a hurricane.
▶ Not having adequate merchandise on hand when a sale is advertised.
▶ Charging high prices in low-income areas because consumers there do not have the transportation mobility to shop out of their neighborhoods.
▶ Selling alcohol and tobacco products to children.
▶ Having a salesperson pose as a market researcher when engaged in telemarketing.
▶ Defaming competitors.
▶ Selling refurbished merchandise as new.
▶ Pressuring employees to push high-profit items, even if these items are not the best products.
▶ Selling information from a customer data base to other parties.

The Direct Marketing Association makes its complete ethics code available at its Web site (**www.dmaresponsibility. org/Guidelines**).

Many trade associations promote ethics codes to member firms. For example, here are some provisions of the Direct Marketing Association's ethics code:

Article 1: All offers should be clear, honest, and complete.

Article 5: Disparagement of any person or group on grounds addressed by federal or state laws that prohibit discrimination is unacceptable.

Article 8: All contacts should disclose the name of the sponsor and each purpose of the contact; no one should make offers or solicitations in the guise of one purpose when the intent is a different one.

Article 24: No sweepstakes promotion should represent that a recipient or entrant has won a prize or that any entry stands a greater chance of winning a prize than any other entry when this is not the case.

Article 32: Firms should be sensitive to the issue of consumer privacy.

Article 46: A firm should not knowingly call or send a voice solicitation message to a consumer who has an unlisted or unpublished phone number except where the number was provided by the consumer to that marketer for that purpose.[23]

Social Responsibility

A retailer exhibiting **social responsibility** acts in the best interests of society—as well as itself. The challenge is to balance corporate citizenship with a fair level of profits for stockholders, management, and employees. Some forms of social responsibility are virtually cost-free, such as having employees participate in community events or disposing of waste products in a more careful way. Some are more costly, such as making donations to charitable groups or giving away goods and services to a school. Still others mean going above and beyond the letter of the law, such as having free loaner wheelchairs for persons with disabilities besides legally mandated wheelchair accessibility to retail premises.

Most retailers know socially responsible acts do not go unnoticed. Although the acts may not stimulate greater patronage for firms with weak strategies, they can be a customer inducement for those otherwise viewed as "me too" entities. It may also be possible to profit from good deeds. If a retailer donates excess inventory to a charity that cares for the ill, it can take a tax deduction equal to the cost of the goods plus one-half the difference between the cost and the retail price. To do this, a retailer must be a corporation and the charity must use the goods and not sell or trade them.

The Ronald McDonald House program (**www. rmhc.org**) is one of the most respected community outreach efforts in retailing.

This is what some retailers are doing. McDonald's founded Ronald McDonald House so families can stay at a low-cost facility instead of a costly hotel when their seriously ill children get medical treatment away from home. Target is among the many retailers that no longer sells cigarettes. Wal-Mart's environmental goals "are simple and straightforward: to be supplied 100 percent by renewable energy, to create zero waste, and to sell products that sustain our natural resources and the environment."[24] J.C. Penney requires

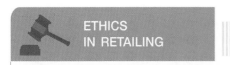

Are Retailer Loyalty Programs in Sync with Their Customers?

Even though a large proportion of retailers have loyalty programs, many firms neglect to concentrate on the natural loyalty that is generated by treating their customers well. According to some analysts, a loyalty program that offers free merchandise at the expense of old-fashioned excellent service may backfire. Retailers also need to rethink the notion that their regular customers are loyal, when they may shop there only because the store locations are convenient.

Fred Reichheld, an expert on loyalty programs, believes that there are four basic behaviors of loyal customers: They come back for more, they increase their purchases, they bring their friends, and they invest their precious time for free. Thus, retailers need to distinguish between artificial and genuine loyalty.

There several ethical issues to keep in mind with regard to loyalty programs. For example, some institutions—such as airlines and hotels—have awarded so many free miles or points that it is extremely difficult to use the earned credits during the times requested or on a direct flight. This is especially true for popular destinations during peak periods. Most airlines have also increased their mileage requirements or discontinue members' total mileage credits if an account is inactive for a given time period.

Sources: Joan S. Adams, "The Do's and Don'ts of Loyalty Programs," *Supply House Times* (May 2008), pp. 24, 26; and Steve McKee, "The Problem with Loyalty Programs," **www.businessweek.com/smallbiz/content** (August 14, 2008).

all suppliers to sign a code of conduct that underage labor is not used. Hannaford Bros.' pledge sums up the role of a socially involved retailer:

> Our business depends on the people who shop at our stores and the people who work for us. When we help our communities, the places where our customers and associates and their families live and work become better, healthier, and more prosperous. Each year, Hannaford donates about $4 million in charitable donations and sponsorships within the communities we serve. With the help of customers and associates, Hannaford also raises hundreds of thousands of dollars through in-store fundraising programs. These funds go to community health programs and programs dedicated to families and children. Every year, Hannaford gives millions of pounds of groceries to hunger-relief programs, through regional food banks and donations to soup kitchens and food pantries.[25]

Consumerism

Consumerism involves the activities of government, business, and other organizations to protect people from practices infringing upon their rights as consumers. These actions recognize that consumers have basic rights that should be safeguarded. As President Kennedy said nearly 50 years ago, consumers have the *right to safety* (protection against unsafe conditions and hazardous goods and services), the *right to be informed* (protection against fraudulent, deceptive, and incomplete information, advertising, and labeling), the *right to choose* (access to a variety of goods, services, and retailers), and the *right to be heard* (consumer feedback, both positive and negative, to the firm and to government agencies).

Retailers and their channel partners need to avoid business practices violating these rights and to do all they can to understand and protect them. These are some reasons:

Learn more about ADA (www.ada.gov).

▶ Some retail practices are covered by legislation. One major law is the **Americans with Disabilities Act (ADA)**, which mandates that persons with disabilities be given appropriate access to retailing facilities. As Title III of the Act states: "Public accommodations [retail stores] must comply with basic nondiscrimination requirements that prohibit exclusion, segregation, and unequal treatment. They also must comply with specific requirements related to architectural standards for new and altered buildings; reasonable modifications to policies, practices, and procedures; effective communication with people with hearing, vision, or speech disabilities; and other access requirements. Additionally, public accommodations must remove barriers in

FIGURE 2-12

Understanding the
Americans with Disabilities
Act

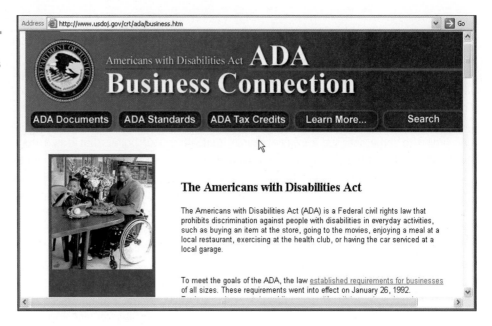

existing buildings where it is easy to do so without much difficulty or expense, given
the public accommodation's resources." ADA affects entrances, vertical transportation, width of aisles, and store displays.[26] See Figure 2-12.

▶ People are more apt to patronize firms perceived as customer-oriented and not to
shop with ones seen as "greedy."

▶ Consumers are more knowledgeable, price-conscious, and selective than in the past.

▶ Large retailers may be viewed as indifferent to consumers. They may not provide
enough personal attention for shoppers or may have inadequate control over employees.

▶ For some shoppers, the increasing use of self-service causes frustration.

▶ Innovative technology is unsettling to many consumers, who must learn new shopping behavior (such as how to use electronic video kiosks).

▶ Retailers are in direct customer contact, so they are often blamed for and asked to
resolve problems caused by manufacturers (such as defective products).

One troublesome issue for consumers involves how retailers handle *customer privacy*.
A consumer-oriented approach, comprising these elements, can reduce negative shopper
feelings: (1) Notice—"A company should provide consumers with a clear and conspicuous
notice regarding its information practices." (2) Consumer choice—"A company should provide consumers with an opportunity to decide whether it may disclose personal information
about them to unaffiliated third parties." (3) Access and correction—"Companies should
provide consumers with an opportunity to access and correct personal information that they
have collected about the consumers." (4) Security—"Companies should adopt reasonable
security measures to protect the privacy of personal information." (5) Enforcement—"The
firm should have in place a system by which it can enforce its privacy policy."[27]

To avoid customer relations problems, many retailers have devised programs to protect consumer rights without waiting for government or consumer pressure to do so. Here
are examples.

For almost 100 years, J.C. Penney has adhered to the general principles of the
"Penney Idea":

> To serve the public, as nearly as we can, to its complete satisfaction; to expect
> for the service we render a fair remuneration and not all the profit the traffic
> will bear; to do all in our power to pack the customer dollar with value, quality,
> and satisfaction; to continue training ourselves and our associates so the service
> we give will be more intelligently performed; to improve constantly the human
> factor in our business; to reward men and women in our firm by participation in
> what the business produces; and to test our every policy, method, and act—
> "Does it square with what is right and just?"[28]

About 40 years ago, the Giant Food supermarket chain devised a consumer bill of rights (based on President Kennedy's), which it still follows today: (1) Right to safety—Giant's product safety standards, such as age-labeling toys, go beyond those required by the government. (2) Right to be informed—Giant has a detailed labeling system. (3) Right to choose—Consumers who want to purchase possibly harmful or hazardous products (such as foods with additives) can do so. (4) Right to be heard—A continuing dialog with reputable consumer groups is in place. (5) Right to redress—There is a money-back guarantee policy on products. (6) Right to service—Customers should receive good in-store service.[29]

A number of retailers have enacted their own programs to test merchandise for such attributes as value, quality, misrepresentation of contents, safety, and durability. Sears, Wal-Mart, A&P, Macy's, and Target are just a few of those doing testing. See Figure 2-13. Among the other consumerism activities undertaken by many retailers are setting clear procedures for handling customer complaints, sponsoring consumer education programs, and training personnel to interact properly with customers.

Consumer-oriented activities are not limited to large chains; small firms can also be involved. A local toy store can separate toys by age group. A grocery store can set up displays featuring environmentally safe detergents. A neighborhood restaurant can cook foods in low-fat vegetable oil. A sporting goods store can give a money-back guarantee on exercise equipment, so people can try it at home.

FIGURE 2-13

Voluntary Product Testing at Target Stores

Source: Reprinted by permission of Target Stores.

Target's Responsibility

At Target, toys are an important part of our business. We want the toys you buy to meet Target's and the U.S. Government's high standards of quality, value, and safety. Therefore, we abide by all U.S. Consumer Product Safety Regulations. Target also utilizes an independent testing agency. They test samples of all toys we sell to help ensure your child's safe play.

All toys sold at Target are tested to be certain they are free from these dangers:

Sharp edges

Toys of brittle plastic or glass can be broken to expose cutting edges. Poorly made metal or wood toys may have sharp edges.

Small parts

Tiny toys and toys with removable parts can be swallowed or lodged in child's windpipe, ears, or nose.

Loud noises

Noise-making guns and other toys can produce sounds at noise levels that can damage hearing.

Sharp points

Broken toys can expose dangerous points. Stuffed toys can have barbed eyes or wired limbs that can cut.

Propelled objects

Projectiles and similar flying toys can injure eyes in particular. Arrows or darts should have protective soft tips.

Electrical shock

Electrically operated toys that are improperly constructed can shock or cause burns. Electric toys must meet mandatory safety requirements.

Wrong toys for the wrong age

Toys that may be safe for older children can be dangerous when played with by little ones.

Chapter **Summary**

1. *To explain what "value" really means and highlight its pivotal role in retailers' building and sustaining relationships.* Sellers undertake a series of activities and processes to provide a given level of value for the consumer. Consumers then perceive the value offered by sellers, based on the perceived benefits received versus the prices paid. Perceived value varies by type of shopper.

A retail value chain represents the total bundle of benefits offered by a channel of distribution. It comprises store location, ambience, customer service, the products/brands carried, product quality, the in-stock position, shipping, prices, the retailer's image, and so forth. Some elements of a retail value chain are visible to shoppers. Others are not. An expected retail strategy represents the minimum value chain elements a given customer segment expects from a given retailer type. An augmented retail strategy includes the extra elements that differentiate retailers. A potential retail strategy includes value chain elements not yet perfected in the retailer's industry category.

2. *To describe how both customer relationships and channel relationships may be nurtured in today's highly competitive marketplace.* For relationship retailing to work, enduring relationships are needed with other channel members, as well as with customers. More retailers now realize loyal customers are the backbone of their business.

To engage in relationship retailing with consumers, these factors should be considered: the customer base, customer service, customer satisfaction, and loyalty programs and defection rates. In terms of the customer base, all customers are not equal. Some shoppers are more worth nurturing than others; they are a retailer's core customers.

Customer service has two components: expected services and augmented services. The attributes of personnel who interact with customers, as well as the number and variety of customer services offered, have a big impact on the relationship created. Some firms have improved customer service by empowering personnel, giving them the authority to bend some rules. In devising a strategy, a retailer must make broad decisions and then enact specific tactics as to credit, delivery, and so forth.

Customer satisfaction occurs when the value and customer service provided in a retail experience meet or exceed expectations. Otherwise, the consumer will be dissatisfied.

Loyalty programs reward the best customers, those with whom a retailer wants to develop long-lasting relationships. To succeed, they must complement a sound value-driven retail strategy. By studying defections, a firm can learn how many customers it is losing and why they no longer patronize it.

Members of a distribution channel jointly represent a value delivery system. Each one depends on the others; and every activity must be enumerated and responsibility assigned. Small retailers may have to use suppliers outside the normal channel to get the items they want and gain supplier support. A delivery system is as good as its weakest link. A relationship-oriented technique that some manufacturers and retailers are trying, especially supermarket chains, is category management.

3. *To examine the differences in relationship building between goods and service retailers.* Goods retailing focuses on selling tangible products. Service retailing involves transactions where consumers do not purchase or acquire ownership of tangible products.

There are three kinds of service retailing: rented-goods services, where consumers lease goods for a given time; owned-goods services, where goods owned by consumers are repaired, improved, or maintained; and nongoods services, where consumers experience personal services rather than possess them. Customer service refers to activities that are part of the total retail experience. With service retailing, services are sold to the consumer.

The unique features of service retailing that influence relationship building and retention are the intangible nature of many services, the inseparability of some service providers and their services, the perishability of many services, and the variability of many services.

4. *To discuss the impact of technology on relationships in retailing.* Technology is advantageous when it leads to an improved information flow between retailers and suppliers, and between retailers and customers, and to faster, smoother transactions.

Electronic banking involves both the use of ATMs and the instant processing of retail purchases. It allows centralized records and lets customers complete transactions 24 hours a day, 7 days a week at various sites. Technology is also changing the nature of supplier–retailer–customer interactions via point-of-sale equipment, self-scanning, electronic gift cards, interactive kiosks, and other innovations.

5. *To consider the interplay between retailers' ethical performance and relationships in retailing.* Retailer challenges fall into three related categories: Ethics relates to a firm's moral principles and values. Social responsibility has to do with benefiting society. Consumerism entails the protection of consumer rights. "Good" behavior is based not only on the firm's practices but also on the expectations of the community in which it does business.

Ethical retailers act in a trustworthy, fair, honest, and respectful way. Firms are more apt to avoid unethical behavior if they have written ethics codes, communicate them to employees, monitor and punish poor behavior, and have ethical executives. Retailers perform in a socially responsible manner when they act in the best interests of society through recycling and conservation programs and other efforts. Consumerism activities involve government, business, and independent organizations. Four consumer rights are basic: to safety, to be informed, to choose, and to be heard.

Key Terms

value (p. 28)
value chain (p. 29)
core customers (p. 33)
expected customer service (p. 33)
augmented customer service (p. 33)
employee empowerment (p. 34)
revolving credit account (p. 36)
option credit account (p. 36)

open credit account (p. 36)
customer satisfaction (p. 38)
consumer loyalty (frequent shopper) programs (p. 38)
value delivery system (p. 39)
goods retailing (p. 41)
service retailing (p. 41)
rented-goods services (p. 41)

owned-goods services (p. 41)
nongoods services (p. 42)
electronic banking (p. 44)
ethics (p. 46)
social responsibility (p. 48)
consumerism (p. 49)
Americans with Disabilities Act (ADA) (p. 49)

Questions for Discussion

1. When a consumer dines at an upscale restaurant, what factors determine whether the consumer feels that he or she got a fair value? How does the perception of value differ when that same consumer shops at a fast-food restaurant?

2. What are the expected and augmented value chain elements for each of these retailers?
   a. Best Buy.
   b. Ikea.
   c. Local hair salon.

3. Why should a retailer devote special attention to its core customers? How should it do so?

4. What is the connection between customer service and employee empowerment? Is employee empowerment always a good idea? Why or why not?

5. How would you measure the level of customer satisfaction with your favorite electronics store?

6. Devise a consumer loyalty program for Radio Shack.

7. What are the unique aspects of service retailing? Give an example of each.

8. What are the pros and cons of ATMs? As a retailer, would you want an ATM in your store? Why or why not?

9. Will the time come when most consumer purchases are made with self-scanners? Explain your answer.

10. Describe three unethical, but legal, acts on the part of retailers that you have recently encountered. How have you reacted in each case?

11. Differentiate between social responsibility and consumerism from the perspective of a retailer.

12. How would you deal with consumer concerns about privacy in their relationships with retailers?

Web **Exercise**

Visit the U.S. Web site of H&M (www.hm.com/us), the worldwide apparel chain. Click on "Customer Service" at the top of the home page. Comment on the information you find there. Does H&M have customer-oriented policies? Explain your answer.

Note: Stop by our Web site (www.pearsonhighered.com/ berman) to experience a number of highly interactive, appealing Web exercises based on actual company demonstrations and sample materials related to retailing.

Appendix Planning for the Unique Aspects of Service Retailing

We present this appendix because service retailing in the United States and around the world is growing steadily and represents a large portion of overall retailing. In the United States, consumers spend 60 percent of their after-tax income on such services as travel, recreation, personal care, education, medical care, and housing. About 80 percent of the labor force works in services. Consumers spend billions of dollars each year to rent such products as power tools and party goods (coffee urns, silverware, wine glasses, etc.). People annually spend $150 billion to maintain their cars. There are 85,000 beauty and barber shops, 40,000 laundry and cleaning outlets, 50,000 hotels and motels, and 25,000 sports and recreation clubs. During the past 35 years, the prices of services have risen more than the prices of many goods. Due to technological advances, automation has substantially reduced manufacturing labor costs, but many services remain labor-intensive due to their personal nature.[1]

Here, we look at the abilities required to be a successful service retailer, how to improve the performance of service retailers, and the strategy of a Baldrige Award winner.

Abilities Required to Be a Successful Service Retailer

The personal abilities required to succeed in service retailing are usually quite distinct from those in goods retailing:

▶ With service retailing, the major value provided to the customer is some type of retailer service, not the ownership of a physical product produced by a manufacturer.
▶ Specific skills are often required, and these skills may not be transferable from one type of service to another. TV repairpeople, beauticians, and accountants cannot easily change businesses or transfer skills. The owners of appliance stores, cosmetics stores, and toy stores (all goods retailers) would have an easier time than service retailers in changing and transferring their skills to another area.
▶ More service operators must possess licenses or certification to run their businesses. Barbers, real-estate brokers, dentists, attorneys, plumbers, and others must pass exams in their fields.
▶ Owners of service businesses must enjoy their jobs and have the aptitude for them. Because of the close personal contact with customers, these elements are essential and difficult to feign.

Many service retailers can operate on lower overall investments and succeed on less yearly revenues than goods retailers. A firm with four outdoor tennis courts can operate with one worker who functions as clerk/cashier and maintenance person. A tax-preparation firm can succeed with one accountant. A watch repair business needs one repairperson. In each case, the owner may be the only skilled worker. Operating costs can be held down accordingly. On the other hand, a goods retailer needs a solid product assortment and inventory on hand, which may be costly and require storage facilities.

The time commitment of a service retailer differs by type of business opportunity. Some businesses, such as a self-service laundromat or a movie theater, require a low time commitment. Other businesses, such as house painting or a travel agency, require a large time commitment because personal service is the key to profitability. More service firms are in the high rather than the low time-investment category.

Improving the Performance of Service Retailers

Service tangibility can be increased by stressing service provider reliability, promoting a continuous theme (the Hertz #1 Club Gold), describing specific results (a car tune-up's improving gas consumption by one mile per gallon), and offering warranties (hotels giving automatic refunds to unhappy guests). Airlines have Web sites where customers can select flights and make their reservations interactively. These sites are a tangible representation of the airlines and their logos.

Demand and supply can be better matched by offering similar services to market segments with different demand patterns (Manhattan tourists versus residents), new services with demand patterns that are countercyclical from existing services (cross-country skiing during the winter at Denver golf resorts), new services that complement existing ones (beauty salons adding tanning booths), special deals during nonpeak times (midweek movie theater prices), and new services not subject to existing capacity constraints (a 10-table restaurant starting a home catering service).

Standardizing services reduces their variability, makes it easier to set prices, and improves efficiency. Services can be standardized by clearly defining each task, determining the minimum and maximum times needed to complete each task, selecting the best order for tasks to be done, and noting the optimum time and quality of the entire service. Standardization has been successfully applied to such firms as quick-auto-service providers (oil change and tune-up firms), legal services (for house closings and similar proceedings), and emergency medical care centers. If services are standardized, there is often a trade-off (e.g., more consistent quality and convenience in exchange for less of a personal touch).

Besides standardizing services, retailers may be able to make services more efficient by automating them and substituting machinery for labor. Thus, real-estate attorneys often use computerized word-processing templates for common paragraphs in house closings. This means more consistency in the way documents look, time savings, and neater documents with fewer errors. Among the service firms that automate at least part of their operations are banks, car washes, bowling alleys, airlines, phone services, real-estate brokers, and hotels.

The location of a service retailer must be carefully considered. Sometimes, as with TV repairs, house painting, and lawn care, the service is "delivered" to the customer. The firm's location becomes a client's home, and the actual retail office is rather insignificant. Many clients might never even see a service firm's office; they make contact by phone or personal visits, and customer convenience is optimized. The firm incurs travel expenses, but it also has low (or no) rent and does not have to maintain store facilities, set up displays, and so on. Other service retailers are visited on "specific-intent" shopping trips. Although a customer may be concerned about the convenience of a service location, he or she usually does not select a skilled practitioner such as a doctor or a lawyer based on the location. It is common for doctors and attorneys to have offices in their homes or near hospitals or court buildings. A small store can often be used because little or no room is needed for displaying merchandise. A travel agency may have six salespeople and book millions of dollars in trips, but fit into a 500-square-foot store.

To improve their pricing decisions, service retailers can apply these principles to "capture and communicate value through their pricing":[2] Satisfaction-based pricing recognizes and reduces customer perceptions of uncertainty that service intangibility magnifies. It involves service guarantees, benefit-driven pricing, and flat-rate pricing. Relationship pricing encourages long-term relationships with valuable customers. It entails long-term contracts and price bundling. Efficiency pricing shares cost savings with customers that arise from the firm's efficiently executing service tasks. It is related to the concept of cost leadership.

Negotiated pricing occurs when a retailer works out pricing arrangements with individual customers because a unique or complex service is involved and a one-time price must be agreed on. Unlike traditional pricing (whereby each consumer pays the same price for a standard service), each consumer may pay a different price under negotiated pricing (depending on the nature of the unique service). A moving company charges different fees, depending on the distance of the move, who packs the breakable furniture, the use of stairs versus an elevator, access to highways, and the weight of furniture.

Contingency pricing is an arrangement whereby the retailer does not get paid until after the service is performed and payment is contingent on the service's being satisfactory. A real-estate broker earns a fee only when a house purchaser (who is ready, willing, and able to buy) is presented to the house seller. Several brokers may show a house to prospective buyers, but only the broker who actually sells the house earns a commission. This technique presents risks to a retailer because considerable time and effort may be spent without payment. A broker may show a house 25 times, not sell it, and, therefore, not be paid.

One customer type is often beyond the reach of some service firms: the do-it-yourselfer. And the number of do-it-yourselfers in the United States is growing, as service costs

FIGURE A2-1

Lessons in Service Retailing from the Best Firms

Source: Figure developed by the authors based on information in Robert C. Ford, Cherrill P. Heaton, and Stephen W. Brown, "Delivering Excellent Service: Lessons from the Best Firms," *California Management Review,* Vol. 44 (Fall 2001), pp. 39–56.

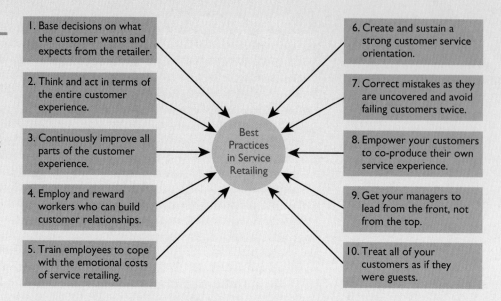

1. Base decisions on what the customer wants and expects from the retailer.
2. Think and act in terms of the entire customer experience.
3. Continuously improve all parts of the customer experience.
4. Employ and reward workers who can build customer relationships.
5. Train employees to cope with the emotional costs of service retailing.

Best Practices in Service Retailing

6. Create and sustain a strong customer service orientation.
7. Correct mistakes as they are uncovered and avoid failing customers twice.
8. Empower your customers to co-produce their own service experience.
9. Get your managers to lead from the front, not from the top.
10. Treat all of your customers as if they were guests.

increase. The do-it-yourselfer does a car tune-up, paints the house, mows the lawn, makes all vacation plans, and/or sets up a darkroom for developing film. Goods-oriented discount retailers do well by selling supplies to these people, but service retailers suffer because the labor is done by the customer.

Figure A2-1 highlights 10 lessons that service retailers can learn from the best in the business, such as Walt Disney Company, Marriott International, Ritz-Carlton, and Southwest Airlines.

The Strategy of Pal's Sudden Service: A Baldrige Award Winner[3]

The Baldrige Award is given by the president of the United States to businesses—manufacturing and service, small and large—and to education and healthcare organizations that apply and are judged to be outstanding in seven areas: leadership; strategic planning; customer and market focus; measurement, analysis, and knowledge management, human resource focus; process management; and business results. One of the few retailers (and the only restaurant) to win this award is Pal's Sudden Service, a privately owned, quick-service restaurant chain with 21 locations (as of 2009), all within 60 miles of Kingsport, Tennessee. The firm distinguishes itself by offering competitively priced food of consistently high quality, delivered rapidly, cheerfully, and without error.

For every organizational and operational activity, Pal's has a process. Its Business Excellence Process is the key integrating element and ensures that customer needs are met in each transaction. Carried out under the leadership of Pal's top executives and its owner-operators, the Business Excellence Process spans all facets of operations from strategic planning (done annually) to online quality control.

Pal's goal is to provide the "quickest, friendliest, most accurate service available." Achieving this is a challenge in an industry with annual employee turnover rates of more than 200 percent. The company's success in reducing turnover among frontline production and service personnel, most of whom are between the ages of 16 and 32, is a key advantage. Owner-operators and assistant managers have primary responsibility for training based on a four-step model: show it, do it, evaluate it, and perform it again. Employees must demonstrate 100 percent competence before they can work at a specific job task.

Pal's order handout speed has improved more than 30 percent since 1995, decreasing to 20 seconds, almost four times faster than its top competitor. Order errors are rare, averaging less than 1 for every 2,000 transactions. The firm aims to reduce its error rate to 1 in 5,000 transactions. In addition, Pal's has consistently received the highest health inspection scores in its market.

Hop over to Pal's Sudden Service (www.palsweb.com). See why it's a big winner!

3

Strategic Planning in Retailing

Chapter Objectives

1. To show the value of strategic planning for all types of retailers

2. To explain the steps in strategic planning for retailers: situation analysis, objectives, identification of consumers, overall strategy, specific activities, control, and feedback

3. To examine the individual controllable and uncontrollable elements of a retail strategy, and to present strategic planning as a series of integrated steps

4. To demonstrate how a strategic plan can be prepared

While working at his father's general clothing store, Leslie Wexner urged his father to concentrate on sportswear due to its higher sales rates. His father insisted that a clothing store needed a wide variety of merchandise, including formal and business clothes. He angrily told Leslie, "You'll never be a merchant." So, at age 26, Leslie Wexner founded The Limited—now Limited Brands (**www.limitedbrands.com**). He started in 1963 with one small store after getting a $5,000 loan from an aunt. Today, Limited Brands has annual sales of $10 billion.

Clearly, Wexner's specialty store strategy has worked. Limited Brands currently does business through more than 2,900 specialty stores nationwide, as well as through the Web and catalog sales. Over the years, Wexner built a large retailing and marketing conglomerate, which currently includes Victoria's Secret and La Senza (which both sell lingerie and sleepwear), Bath & Body Works, C. O. Bigelow (beauty and personal care), The White Barn Candle Company (personal-care and beauty items, and home fragrances), and Henri Bendel (specialty stores). Major retail brands that have been spun off during the past several years include Lane Bryant, Abercrombie & Fitch, Lerner New York, The Limited Too, The Limited, and Express.

Wexner has certainly been an ace merchant. He was one of the first retailing executives to understand the importance of developing a network of foreign suppliers that could manufacture goods at low cost and at blazing speed. This enabled his stores to rapidly respond to hot fashion trends without the risks associated with large inventories. Wexner also had the insight to reposition Victoria's Secret, which was a rather sleazy six-store chain based in San Francisco at the time Wexner bought it. Now, it is the leader in intimate apparel.[1]

Source: Reprinted by permission of TNS Retail Forward.

OVERVIEW

In this chapter, we cover strategic retail planning—the foundation of our book—in detail. As noted in Chapter 1, a **retail strategy** is the overall plan or framework of action that guides a retailer. Ideally, it will be at least one year long and outline the retailer's mission, goals, consumer market, overall and specific activities, and control mechanisms. Without a defined and well-integrated strategy, a firm may be unable to cope with the marketplace. This is the advice offered by the U.S. Small Business Administration:

> Too many people think strategic planning is something meant only for big businesses, but it is equally applicable to small businesses. Strategic planning is matching the strengths of your business to available opportunities. You need to collect and analyze information about the business environment. You need to have a clear understanding of your business—its strengths and weaknesses—and develop a clear mission and objectives. This often involves more work than expected. If you are to survive and prosper, you should take the time to identify the niches in which you are most apt to succeed and identify the resources that are necessary.[2]

My Strategic Plan (**www.mystrategicplan.com**) has a lot of useful planning tools for retailers at its Web site. Click on "Resources."

The process of strategic retail planning has several attractive features: It provides a thorough analysis of the requirements for doing business for different types of retailers. It outlines retailer goals. A firm determines how to differentiate itself from competitors and develop an offering that appeals to a group of customers. The legal, economic, and competitive environment is studied. A firm's total efforts are coordinated. Crises are anticipated and often avoided.

Strategic planning can be done by the owner of a firm, professional management, or a combination of the two. Even among family businesses, the majority of high-growth companies have strategic plans.

The steps in planning and enacting a retail strategy are interdependent; a firm often starts with a general plan that gets more specific as options and payoffs become clearer. In this chapter, we cover each step in developing a retail strategy, as shown in Figure 3-1. Given the importance of global retailing, a chapter appendix explores the special dimensions of strategic planning in a global retailing environment. Visit our Web site (**www.pearsonhighered.com/berman**) for several links on strategic planning.

Situation Analysis

Situation analysis is a candid evaluation of the opportunities and threats facing a prospective or existing retailer. It seeks to answer two general questions: What is the firm's current status? In which direction should it be heading? Situation analysis means being guided by an organizational mission, evaluating ownership and management options, and outlining the goods/service category to be sold.

A good strategy anticipates and adapts to both the opportunities and threats in the changing business environment. **Opportunities** are marketplace openings that exist because other retailers have not yet capitalized on them. Ikea does well because it is the pioneer firm in offering a huge selection of furniture at discount prices. **Threats** are environmental and marketplace factors that can adversely affect retailers if they do not react to them (and, sometimes, even if they do). Single-screen movie theaters have virtually disappeared because they have been unable to fend off the inroads made by multi-screen theaters.

FIGURE 3-1

Elements of a Retail
Strategy

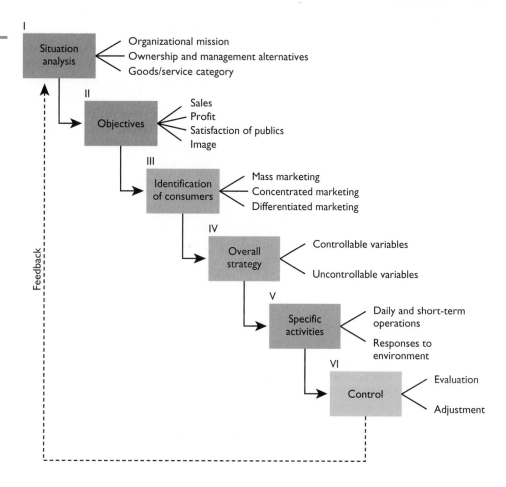

A firm needs to spot trends early enough to satisfy customers and stay ahead of competitors, yet not so early that shoppers are not ready for changes or that false trends are perceived. Merchandising shifts—such as stocking fad items—are more quickly enacted than changes in a firm's location, price, or promotion strategy. A new retailer can adapt to trends easier than existing ones with established images, ongoing leases, and space limitations. Well-prepared small firms can compete with large retailers.

During situation analysis, especially for a new retailer or one thinking about making a major strategic change, an honest, in-depth self-assessment is vital. It is all right for a person or company to be ambitious and aggressive, but overestimating one's abilities and prospects may be harmful—if the results are entry into the wrong retail business, inadequate resources, or misjudgment of competitors.

Organizational Mission

An **organizational mission** is a retailer's commitment to a type of business and to a distinctive role in the marketplace. It is reflected in the firm's attitude toward consumers, employees, suppliers, competitors, government, and others. A clear mission lets a firm gain a customer following and distinguish itself from competitors. See Figure 3-2.

One major decision is whether to base a business around the goods and services sold or around consumer needs. A person opening a hardware business must decide if, in addition to hardware products, a line of bathroom vanities should be stocked. A traditionalist might not carry vanities because they seem unconnected to the proposed business. But if the store is to be a do-it-yourself home improvement center, vanities are a logical part of the mix. That store would carry any relevant items the consumer wants.

FIGURE 3-2

The Focused
Organizational Mission of
Frisch's Restaurants

The company operates and licenses family restaurants under the trade name Frisch's Big Boy. These facilities are located in Ohio and Kentucky. Additionally, the firm operates two hotels with restaurants in metropolitan Cincinnati, where it is headquartered. Trademarks that the company has the right to use include "Frisch's," "Big Boy," "Quality Hotel," and "Golden Corral."

Source: Reprinted by permission of Frisch's Restaurants.

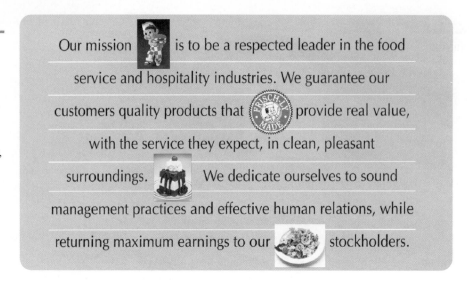

Our mission is to be a respected leader in the food service and hospitality industries. We guarantee our customers quality products that provide real value, with the service they expect, in clean, pleasant surroundings. We dedicate ourselves to sound management practices and effective human relations, while returning maximum earnings to our stockholders.

A second major decision is whether a retailer wants a place in the market as a leader or a follower. It could seek to offer a unique strategy, such as Taco Bell becoming the first national quick-serve Mexican food chain. Or it could emulate the practices of competitors but do a better job in executing them, such as a local fast-food Mexican restaurant offering five-minute guaranteed service and a cleanliness pledge.

See how Tiffany's Web site (www.tiffany.com) is consistent with its upscale mission.

A third decision involves market scope. Large chains often seek a broad customer base (due to their resources and recognition). It is often best for small retailers and startups to focus on a narrower customer base, so they can compete with bigger firms that tend not to adapt strategies, as well to local markets.

Although the development of an organizational mission is the first step in the planning process, the mission should be continually reviewed and adjusted to reflect

---

CAREERS IN RETAILING

Rex: Store Manager

While at college, Rex was a stock and sales associate for a national department store chain. After graduating, Rex was promoted to merchandise manager. His responsibilities included buying and merchandising products for the home department. Rex was then promoted and transferred to another store as senior department manager for the chain. His next promotions were to senior department manager, operations manager, and assistant store manager.

At that point, Rex was promoted to district business planning manager for the men's division for 15 stores. This promotion was only offered to a select number of highly rated management associates. The district position gave Rex experience working in a variety of store sizes and markets. Buying, building floor plans, and districtwide marketing promotions were involved. As a district planning manager, Rex worked more with corporate staff members and helped in building plans for the region. All of these skills and experiences helped build Rex's knowledge in various store-level

activities that he now uses as a store manager. Rex was transferred to another state to achieve his goal of promotion to store manager.

As a store manager for his national department store chain, Rex earns $75,000 to $100,000 annually. He also receives health and dental insurance, a 401(k) and retirement plan, stock options, and bonuses from his employer. Rex reviews daily reports on sales, inventory, gross profit, and sales forecasting. Weekly, he sends in the forecast for the monthly profit plan. This involves estimating sales, markdowns, salary costs, and various other costs. It is Rex's responsibility to communicate with corporate staff about merchandise needs and trends that the store is experiencing. There are many reports that Rex goes through to evaluate where the store is, where it has been, and where it needs to go to maximize sales and profits.

Source: Reprinted by permission of the National Retail Federation.

changing company goals and a dynamic retail environment. Here are examples of well-conceived retail organizational missions:[3]

> McDonald's holds a leading share in the globally branded quick-service restaurant segment of the informal eating-out market in virtually every country in which we do business. Our customers are the reason for our existence. We demonstrate our appreciation by providing them with high quality food and superior service, in a clean, welcoming environment, at a great value.

> PetSmart is the largest specialty retailer of services and solutions for the lifetime needs of pets. The company operates pet stores, a growing number of in-store cat and dog boarding facilities and Doggie Day Camps, and is a leading online provider of pet supplies and pet care information. PetSmart provides a broad range of competitively priced pet food and pet supplies; and it offers complete pet training, pet grooming, and pet adoption services.

> At Zumiez, we do what others have only dreamed: providing our customers with cutting-edge clothing styles, music, and hard goods for skate, snow, surf, and active young lifestyles. Everything we do revolves around our customer— they are the hearts of our company.

Ownership and Management Alternatives

An essential aspect of situation analysis is assessing ownership and management alternatives, including whether to form a sole proprietorship, partnership, or corporation—and whether to start a new business, buy an existing business, or become a franchisee.[4] Management options include owner-manager versus professional manager and centralized versus decentralized structures. Consider that "There is no single best form of ownership for a business. That's partly because the limitations of a particular form of ownership can often be compensated for. For instance, a sole proprietor can often buy insurance coverage to reduce liability exposure. Even after you have established your business as a particular entity, you may need to re-evaluate your choice of entity as the business evolves. An experienced attorney and tax advisor can help you decide which form of ownership is best for your business."[5]

A **sole proprietorship** is an unincorporated retail firm owned by one person. All benefits, profits, risks, and costs accrue to that individual. It is simple to form, fully controlled by the owner, operationally flexible, easy to dissolve, and subject to single taxation by the government. It makes the owner personally liable for legal claims from suppliers, creditors, and others; it can also lead to limited capital and expertise.

A **partnership** is an unincorporated retail firm owned by two or more persons, each with a financial interest. Partners share benefits, profits, risks, and costs. Responsibility and expertise are divided among multiple principals, there is a greater capability for raising funds than with a proprietorship, the format is simpler to form than a corporation, and it is subject to single taxation by the government. Depending on the type of partnership, it, too, can make owners personally liable for legal claims, can be dissolved due to a partner's death or a disagreement, binds all partners to actions made by any individual partner acting on behalf of the firm, and usually has less ability to raise capital than a corporation.

A **corporation** is a retail firm that is formally incorporated under state law. It is a legal entity apart from individual officers (or stockholders). Funds can be raised through the sale of stock, legal claims against individuals are not usually allowed, ownership transfer is relatively easy, the firm is assured of long-term existence (if a founder leaves, retires, or dies), the use of professional managers is encouraged, and unambiguous operating authority is outlined. Depending on the type of corporation, it is subject to double taxation (company earnings and stockholder dividends), faces more government rules, can require a complex process when established, may be viewed as impersonal, and may separate ownership from management. A closed corporation is run by a limited number of persons who control ownership; stock is not available to the public. In an open corporation, stock is widely traded and available to the public.

FIGURE 3-3

A Checklist to Consider When Starting a New Retail Business

Source: Adapted by the authors from *Small Business Management Training Instructor's Guide*, No. 109 (Washington, DC: U.S. Small Business Administration, n.d.).

Name of Business _____

A. Self-Assessment and Business Choice
✓ Evaluate your strengths and weaknesses.
✓ Commitment paragraph: Why should you be in business for yourself? Why open a new business rather than acquire an existing one or become a member of a franchise chain?
✓ Describe the type of retail business that fits your strengths and desires. What will make it unique? What will the business offer customers? How will you capitalize on the weaknesses of competitors?

B. Overall Retail Plan
✓ State your philosophy of business.
✓ Choose an ownership form (sole proprietorship, partnership, or corporation).
✓ State your long- and short-run goals.
✓ Analyze your customers from their point of view.
✓ Research your market size and store location.
✓ Quantify the total retail sales of your goods/service category in your trading area.
✓ Analyze your competition.
✓ Quantify your potential market share.
✓ Develop your retail strategy: store location and operations, merchandising, pricing, and store image and promotion.

C. Financial Plan
✓ What level of funds will you need to get started and to get through the first year? Where will they come from?
✓ Determine the first-year profit, return on investment, and salary that you need/want.
✓ Project monthly cash flow and profit-and-loss statements for the first two years.
✓ What sales will be needed to break even during the first year? What will you do if these sales are not reached?

D. Organizational Details Plan
✓ Describe your personnel plan (hats to wear), organizational plan, and policies.
✓ List the jobs you like and want to do and those you dislike, cannot do, or do not want to do.
✓ Outline your accounting and inventory systems.
✓ Note your insurance plans.
✓ Specify how day-to-day operations would be conducted for each aspect of your strategy.
✓ Review the risks you face and how you plan to cope with them.

Sole proprietorships account for 75 percent of all U.S. retail firms that file tax returns, partnerships for 5 percent, and corporations for 20 percent. In terms of sales volume, sole proprietorships account for just 5 percent of total U.S. retail store sales, partnerships for 8 percent, and corporations for 87 percent.[6]

Starting a new business—being entrepreneurial—offers a retailer flexibility in location, operating style, product lines, customer markets, and other factors, and a strategy is fully tailored to the owner's desires and strengths. There may be high construction costs, a time lag until the business is opened and then until profits are earned, beginning with an unknown name, and having to form supplier relationships and amass an inventory of goods. Figure 3-3 presents a checklist to consider when starting a business.

Buying an existing business allows a retailer to acquire an established company name, a customer following, a good location, trained personnel, and facilities; to operate immediately; to generate ongoing sales and profits; and to possibly get good lease terms or financing (at favorable interest rates) from the seller. Fixtures may be older, there is less flexibility in enacting a strategy tailored to the new owner's desires and strengths, and the growth potential of the business may be limited. Figure 3-4 shows a checklist to consider when purchasing an existing retail business.

By being a franchisee, a retailer can combine independent ownership with franchisor support: strategic planning assistance; a known company name and loyal customer following; cooperative advertising and buying; and a regional, national, or global (rather than local) image. However, a franchisee contract may specify rigid operating standards, limit the product lines sold, and restrict supplier choice; the franchisor company is usually paid

FIGURE 3-4

A Checklist for Purchasing an Existing Retail Business

NAME OF BUSINESS _____

✓ Why is the seller placing the business up for sale?

✓ How much are you paying for goodwill (the cost of the business above its tangible asset value)?

✓ Have sales, inventory levels, and profit figures been confirmed by your accountant?

✓ Will the seller introduce you to his or her customers and stay on during the transition period?

✓ Will the seller sign a statement that he or she will not open a directly competing business in the same trading area for a reasonable time period?

✓ If sales are seasonal, are you purchasing the business at the right time of the year?

✓ In the purchase of the business, are you assuming existing debts of the seller?

✓ Who receives proceeds from transactions made prior to the sale of the business but not yet paid by customers?

✓ What is the length of the lease if property is rented?

✓ If property is to be purchased along with the business, has it been inspected by a professional engineer?

✓ How modern are the storefront and store fixtures?

✓ Is inventory fresh? Does it contain a full merchandise assortment?

✓ Are the advertising policy, customer service policy, and pricing policy of the past owner similar to yours? Can you continue old policies?

✓ If the business is to be part of a chain, is the new unit compatible with existing units?

✓ How much trading-area overlap is there with existing stores?

✓ Has a lawyer examined the proposed contract?

✓ What effect will owning this business have on your lifestyle and on your family relationships?

continuously (royalties); advertising fees may be required; and there is a possibility of termination by the franchisor if the agreement is not followed satisfactorily.

Strategically, the management format also has a dramatic impact. With an owner-manager, planning tends to be less formal and more intuitive, and many tasks are reserved for that person (such as employee supervision and cash management). With professional management, planning tends to be more formal and systematic. Yet, professional managers are more constrained in their authority than an owner-manager. In a centralized structure, planning clout lies with top management or ownership; managers in individual departments have major input into decisions with a decentralized structure.

A comprehensive discussion of independent retailers, chains, franchises, leased departments, vertical marketing systems, and consumer cooperatives is included in Chapter 4.

Goods/Service Category

Entrepreneur magazine (www.entrepreneur.com) addresses many of the issues facing new and growing firms as they plan their strategies.

Before a prospective retail firm can fully design a strategic plan, it selects a **goods/service category**—the line of business—in which to operate. Figure 3-5 shows the diversity of goods/service categories. Chapter 5 examines the attributes of food-based and general merchandise store retailers. Chapter 6 focuses on Web, nonstore, and other forms of nontraditional retailing.

It is advisable to specify both a general goods/service category and a niche within that category. Jaguar dealers are luxury auto retailers catering to upscale customers. Wendy's is an eating and drinking chain known for its quality fast food with a menu that emphasizes hamburgers. Motel 6 is a chain whose forte is inexpensive rooms with few frills.

A potential retail business owner should select a type of business that will allow him or her to match personal abilities, financial resources, and time availability with the requirements of that kind of business. Visit our Web site (www.pearsonhighered.com/berman) for links to many retail trade associations, which represent various goods/service categories.

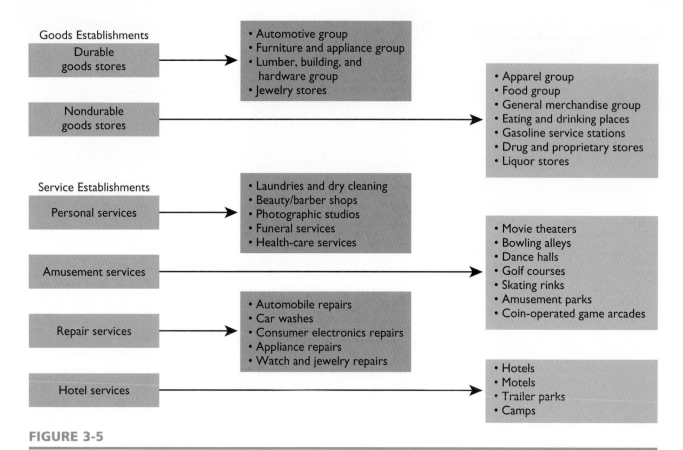

FIGURE 3-5

Selected Kinds of Retail Goods and Service Establishments

Personal Abilities

Personal abilities depend on an individual's aptitude—the preference for a type of business and the potential to do well; education—formal learning about retail practices and policies; and experience—practical learning about retail practices and policies.

An individual who wants to run a business, likes to use initiative, and has the ability to react quickly to competitive developments will be suited to a different type of situation than a person who depends on others for advice and does not like to make decisions. The first individual could be an independent operator, in a dynamic business such as apparel; the second might seek partners or a franchise and a stable business, such as a stationery store. Some people enjoy customer interaction; they would dislike the impersonality of a self-service operation. Others enjoy the impersonality of mail-order or Web retailing.

In certain fields, education and experience requirements are specified by law. Stockbrokers, real-estate brokers, beauticians, pharmacists, and opticians must all satisfy educational or experience standards to show competency. For example, real-estate brokers are licensed after a review of their knowledge of real-estate practices and their ethical character. The designation "broker" does not depend on the ability to sell or have a customer-oriented demeanor.

Some skills can be learned; others are inborn. Accordingly, potential retail owners have to assess their skills and match them with the demands of a given business. This involves careful reflection about oneself. Partnerships may be best when two or more parties possess complementary skills. A person with selling experience may join with someone who has the operating skills to start a business. Each partner has valued skills, but he or she may be unable to operate a retail entity without the expertise of the other.

TABLE 3-1 Some Typical Financial Investments for a New Retail Venture

Use of Funds	Source of Funds
Land and building (lease or purchase)	Personal savings, bank loan, commercial finance company
Inventory	Personal savings, manufacturer credit, commercial finance company, sales revenues
Fixtures (display cases, storage facilities, signs, lighting, carpeting, etc.)	Personal savings, manufacturer credit, bank loan, commercial finance company
Equipment (cash register, marking machine, office equipment, computers, etc.)	Personal savings, manufacturer credit, bank loan, commercial finance company
Personnel (salespeople, cashiers, stockpeople, etc.)	Personal savings, bank loan, sales revenues
Promotion	Personal savings, sales revenues
Personal drawing account	Personal savings, life insurance loan
Miscellaneous (equipment repair, credit sales [bad debts], professional services, repayment of loans)	Personal savings, manufacturer and wholesaler credit, bank credit plan, bank loan, commercial finance company

Note: Collateral for a bank loan may be a building, fixtures, land, inventory, or a personal residence.

Financial Resources

Many retail enterprises, especially new, independent ones, fail because the owners do not adequately project the financial resources needed to open and operate the firm. Table 3-1 outlines some of the typical investments for a new retail venture.

Novice retailers tend to underestimate the value of a personal drawing account, which is used for the living expenses of the owner and his or her family in the early, unprofitable stage of a business. Because few new ventures are immediately profitable, the budget must include such expenditures. In addition, the costs of renovating an existing facility often are miscalculated. Underfunded firms usually invest in only essential renovations. This practice reduces the initial investment, but it may give the retailer a poor image. Merchandise assortment, as well as the types of goods and services sold, also affects the financial outlay. Finally, the use of a partnership, corporation, or franchise agreement will affect the investment.

Table 3-2 illustrates the financial requirements for a hypothetical used-car dealer. The initial personal savings investment of $300,000 would force many potential owners to rethink the choice of product category and the format of the firm: (1) The plans for a 32-car inventory reflect this owner's desire for a balanced product line. If the firm concentrates on subcompact, compact, and intermediate cars, it can reduce inventory size and lower the investment. (2) The initial investment can be reduced by seeking a location whose facilities do not have to be modified. (3) Fewer financial resources are needed if a partnership or corporation is set up with other individuals, so that costs—and profits—are shared.

American Express (**http://home.americanexpress.com/home/open.shtml**) offers financial support and advice for small firms.

The U.S. Small Business Administration (**www.sba.gov/services/financialassistance**) assists businesses by guaranteeing thousands of loans each year. Such private companies as Wells Fargo and American Express also have financing programs specifically aimed at small businesses.

Time Demands

Time demands on retail owners (or managers) differ significantly by goods or service category. They are influenced both by consumer shopping patterns and by the ability of the owner or manager to automate operations or delegate activities to others.

Many retailers must have regular weekend and evening hours to serve time-pressed shoppers. Gift shops, toy stores, and others have extreme seasonal shifts in their hours. Mail-order firms and those selling through the Web, which can process orders during any part of the day, have more flexible hours.

Some businesses require less owner involvement, including gas stations with no repair services, coin-operated laundries, and movie theaters. The emphasis on automation, self-service, standardization, and financial controls lets the owner reduce the time investment.

TABLE 3-2 Financial Requirements for a Used-Car Dealer

Total investments (first year)	
Lease (10 years, $60,000 per year)	$ 60,000
Beginning inventory (32 cars, average cost of $12,500)	400,000
Replacement inventory (32 cars, average cost of $12,500)[a]	400,000
Fixtures and equipment (painting, paneling, carpeting, lighting, signs, heating and air-conditioning system, electronic cash register, service bay)	60,000
Replacement parts	75,000
Personnel (one mechanic)	45,000
Promotion (brochures and newspaper advertising)	35,000
Drawing account (to cover owner's personal expenses for one year; all selling and operating functions except mechanical ones performed by the owner)	40,000
Accountant	15,000
Miscellaneous (loan payments, etc.)	100,000
Profit (projected)	40,000
	$1,270,000
Source of funds	
Personal savings	$ 300,000
Bank loan	426,000
Sales revenues (based on expected sales of 32 cars, average price of $17,000)	544,000
	$1,270,000

[a]Assumes that 32 cars are sold during the year. As each type of car is sold, a replacement is bought by the dealer and placed in inventory. At the end of the year, inventory on hand remains at 32 units.

Other businesses, such as hair salons, restaurants, and jewelry stores, require more active owner involvement.

Intensive owner participation can be the result of several factors:

▶ The owner may be the key service provider, with patrons attracted by his or her skills (the major competitive advantage). Delegating work to others will lessen consumer loyalty.
▶ Personal services are not easy to automate.
▶ Due to limited funds, the owner and his or her family must often undertake all operating functions for a small retail firm. Spouses and children work in 40 percent of family-owned businesses.
▶ In a business that operates on a cash basis, the owner must be around to avoid being cheated.

Off-hours activities are often essential. At a restaurant, some foods must be prepared in advance of the posted dining hours. An owner of a small computer store cleans, stocks shelves, and does the books during the hours the firm is closed. A prospective retail owner also has to examine his or her time preferences regarding stability versus seasonality, ideal working hours, and personal involvement.

Objectives

Kroger (**www.kroger.com**) is one of the leading food-based retailers in the United States.

After situation analysis, a retailer sets **objectives**, the long-run and short-run performance targets it hopes to attain. This helps mold a strategy and translates the organizational mission into action. A firm can pursue goals related to one or more of these areas: sales, profit, satisfaction of publics, and image. Some retailers strive to achieve all the goals fully; others attend to a few and want to achieve them really well. Think about this array of goals for the Kroger Company:

Our business model is straight-forward: increase annual earnings per share through strong and sustainable identical sales growth, slightly improved operating margins, and fewer shares outstanding. Investments in our customers' shopping experience help us drive strong and sustainable identical sales growth. These investments can take several forms—including improved customer service, better product quality and selection, and lower prices. We fund these investments through operating cost reductions and productivity enhancements in several areas of our business. A cornerstone of our business strategy is balance. We seek to consistently deliver strong financial results in the near-term while making meaningful investments for our future. We believe our customer first strategy can serve customers, associates, and shareholders well in a variety of economic and competitive conditions.[7]

Sales

Sales objectives are related to the volume of goods and services a retailer sells. Growth, stability, and market share are the sales goals most often sought.

Some retailers set sales growth as a top priority. They want to expand their business. There may be less emphasis on short-run profits. The assumption is that investments in the present will yield future profits. A firm that does well often becomes interested in opening new units and enlarging revenues. However, management skills and the personal touch are sometimes lost with overly fast expansion.

Stability is the goal of retailers that emphasize maintaining their sales volume, market share, price lines, and so on. Small retailers often seek stable sales that enable the owners to make a satisfactory living every year without downswings or upsurges. And certain firms develop a loyal customer following and are intent not on expanding but on continuing the approach that attracted the original consumers.

For some firms, market share—the percentage of total retail-category sales contributed by a given company—is another goal. It is often an objective only for large retailers or retail chains. The small retailer is more concerned with competition across the street than with total sales in a metropolitan area.

Sales objectives may be expressed in dollars and units. To reach dollar goals, a retailer can engage in a discount strategy (low prices and high unit sales), a moderate strategy (medium prices and medium unit sales), or a prestige strategy (high prices and low unit sales). In the long run, having unit sales as a performance target is vital. Dollar sales by year may be difficult to compare due to changing retail prices and inflation; unit sales are easier to compare. A firm with sales of $350,000 three years ago and $500,000 today might assume it is doing well, until unit sales are computed: 10,000 then and 8,000 now.

Profit

With profitability objectives, retailers seek at least a minimum profit level during a designated period, usually a year. Profit may be expressed in dollars or as a percentage of sales. For a firm with yearly sales of $5 million and total costs of $4.2 million, pre-tax dollar profit is $800,000 and profits as a percentage of sales are 16 percent. If the profit goal is equal to or less than $800,000, or 16 percent, the retailer is satisfied. If the goal is higher, the firm has not attained the minimum desired profit and is dissatisfied.

Firms with large capital expenditures in land, buildings, and equipment often set return on investment (ROI) as a goal. ROI is the relationship between profits and the investment in capital items. A satisfactory rate of return is pre-defined and compared with the actual return at the end of the year or other period. For a retailer with annual sales of $5 million and expenditures (including payments for capital items) of $4 million, the yearly profit is $1 million. If the total capital investment is $10 million, ROI is $1 million/$10 million, or 10 percent per year. The goal must be 10 percent or less for the firm to be satisfied.

Operating efficiency may be expressed as $1 -$ (operating expenses/company sales). The higher the result, the more efficient the firm. A retailer with sales of $2 million and operating costs of $1 million has a 50 percent efficiency rating ($[1 - (\$1 \text{ million}/\$2 \text{ million})]$). Of every sales dollar, 50 cents goes for nonoperating costs and profits, and 50 cents for operating expenses. The retailer might set a goal to increase efficiency to 60 percent. On sales of $2 million, operating costs would have to drop to $800,000 ($[1 - (\$800,000/\$2 \text{ million})]$).

Sixty cents of every sales dollar would then go for nonoperating costs and profits, and 40 cents for operations, which would lead to better profits. If a firm cuts expenses too much, customer service may decline; this may lead to a decline in sales and profit.

Satisfaction of Publics

Retailers typically strive to satisfy their publics: stockholders, customers, suppliers, employees, and government. Stockholder satisfaction is a goal for any publicly owned retailer. Some firms set policies leading to small annual increases in sales and profits (because these goals can be sustained over the long run and indicate good management) rather than ones based on innovative ideas that may lead to peaks and valleys in sales and profits (indicating poor management). Stable earnings lead to stable dividends.

Customer satisfaction with the total retail experience is a well-entrenched goal at most firms now. A policy of *caveat emptor* ("Let the buyer beware") will not work in today's competitive marketplace. Retailers must listen to criticism and adapt. If shoppers are pleased, other goals are more easily reached. Yet, for many retailers, other objectives rate higher in their list of priorities.

Good supplier relations is also a key goal. Retailers must understand and work with their suppliers to secure favorable purchase terms, new products, good return policies, prompt shipments, and cooperation. Relationships are very important for small retailers due to the many services that suppliers offer them.

Cordial labor relations is another goal that is often critical to retailers' performance. Good employee morale means less absenteeism, better treatment of customers, and lower staffing turnover. Relations can be improved by effective selection, training, and motivation.

Because all levels of government impose rules affecting retailing practices, another goal should be to understand and adapt to these rules. In some cases, firms can influence rules by acting as members of large groups, such as trade associations or chambers of commerce.

Image (Positioning)

An **image** represents how a given retailer is perceived by consumers and others. A firm may be seen as innovative or conservative, specialized or broad-based, discount-oriented or upscale. The key to a successful image is that consumers view the retailer in the manner the firm intends.

Through **positioning**, a retailer devises its strategy in a way that projects an image relative to its retail category and its competitors and that elicits a positive consumer response. A firm selling women's apparel could generally position itself as an upscale or mid-priced specialty retailer, a traditional department store, a discount department store, or a discount specialty retailer, and it could specifically position itself with regard to other retailers carrying women's apparel.

Two opposite positioning philosophies have gained popularity in recent years: mass merchandising and niche retailing. **Mass merchandising** is a positioning approach whereby retailers offer a discount or value-oriented image, a wide and/or deep merchandise selection, and large store facilities. Wal-Mart has a wide, deep merchandise mix whereas Dick's Sporting Goods has a narrower, deeper assortment. These firms appeal to a broad customer market, attract a lot of customer traffic, and generate high stock turnover. Because mass merchants have relatively low operating costs, achieve economies in operations, and appeal to value-conscious shoppers, their continuing popularity is forecast.

Babies "R" Us (**www. babiesrus.com**) has a very focused strategy and an online tie-in with Toys "R" Us.

In **niche retailing**, retailers identify specific customer segments and deploy unique strategies to address the desires of those segments rather than the mass market. Niching creates a high level of loyalty and shields retailers from more conventional competitors. Babies "R" Us appeals to parents with very young children, whereas Catherines Stores has fashions for plus-size women. This approach will have a strong future since it lets retailers stress factors other than price and have a better focus. See Figure 3-6.

Because both mass merchandising and niche retailing are popular, some observers call this the era of **bifurcated retailing**. They believe this may mean the decline of middle-of-the-market retailing. Firms that are neither competitively priced nor particularly individualistic may have difficulty competing.

TECHNOLOGY IN RETAILING

| Bad Boy: Improving the Delivery Experience for Customers |

Bad Boy (**www.nooobody.com**) is an eight-store, Toronto-based retail chain that sells furniture, appliances, and electronics. Bad Boy uses independent contractors to deliver products to customers' homes from its distribution center.

Until recently, Bad Boy relied on these contractors to estimate delivery times for customers, who were then called the morning of each delivery and given a four-hour delivery window. Now, Bad Boy relies on software developed by Cube Route (**www.cuberoute.com**) to handle route optimization, dispatch management, and customer notification functions. After an upfront set-up charge, Cube Route bills retailers on the basis of the number of deliveries.

Each evening, Bad Boy's drivers upload information concerning the next day's deliveries to Cube Route's Web site. Cube Route's system then generates routes for each driver and calculates an estimated arrival time with a two-hour range for each customer. The following morning, Cube Route contacts each Bad Boy customer via an automated telephone system with an estimated delivery time. Customers can also track their orders at Bad Boy's Web site that is linked to the Cube Route system. After they have entered their order numbers, customers receive a delivery window specifying the estimated delivery time.

Sources: "Cube Route Inc.," **www.directionsmag.com/companies/Cube_Route_Inc./** (March 3, 2009); and "Track Your Delivery," **www.nooobody.com/trackdelivery.php** (March 3, 2009).

Let's further examine the concept of positioning through these examples:

▶ bebe (the apparel store chain) "designs, develops, and produces a distinctive line of contemporary women's apparel and accessories, which it markets under the bebe, BEBE SPORT, bbsp, bebe O, and 2b bebe brand names." The firm was "founded as a San Francisco boutique in 1976, a time when three categories dominated the women's wear market: junior, bridge, and missy. Having discovered a demographic

FIGURE 3-6

Niche Retailing by Babies "R" Us

As the Babies "R" Us Web site (**www.babiesrus.com**) notes, the chain "features a wide selection of products for newborns and infants, including cribs and furniture, car seats, strollers, formula, diapers, bedding, clothing for preemies through size 48 months, toys, and plenty of unique gift ideas."

Source: Reprinted by permission of Susan Berry, Retail Image Consulting, Inc.

that was neither junior nor bridge, bebe aimed to break the mold by offering this under represented population of stylish women distinctive and inspirational fashion bearing an unmistakable hint of sensuality. The concept stuck and bebe reaped long-lasting success."[8]

Trader Joe's (**www. traderjoes.com**) is a shopping haven for consumers looking for distinctive, fairly priced food items.

▶ At Trader Joe's food stores, "people ask us all the time how we manage to sell our high quality products at our great value prices. We could make it sound really complicated—making us look really smart—but the answer is simple. We travel the world in search of interesting, unique, great-tasting foods and beverages. We buy direct from the producer whenever possible. We strip away all the fancy stuff and focus on the important things like natural ingredients and inspiring flavors. We run a pretty lean ship, too—you won't find any fancy offices around here. Our CEO doesn't even have a secretary! What does our fanatical frugality do for you? It guarantees you the best values you can find anywhere around on the best foods and beverages we can find from everywhere around the world."[9]

Figure 3-7 shows a retail positioning map based on two shopping criteria: (1) price and service and (2) product lines offered. Our assumption: There is a link between price and service (high price equals excellent service). Upscale department stores (Neiman Marcus) offer outstanding customer service and carry several product lines. Traditional department stores (Sears) carry more electronics and other product lines than upscale stores. They have a trained sales staff to help customers. Discount department stores (Wal-Mart) carry a lot of product lines and rely on self-service. Membership clubs (Costco) have a limited selection in a number of product categories. They have very low prices and plain surroundings. Upscale specialty stores (Tiffany) offer outstanding customer service and focus on one general product category. Traditional specialty stores (Gap) have a trained sales staff to help customers and focus on one general product category. Discount specialty stores (Old Navy) rely more on self-service and focus on one general product category. Power retailers (Home Depot) offer moderate service and prices and a huge assortment within one general product category.

FIGURE 3-7

Selected Retail Positioning Strategies

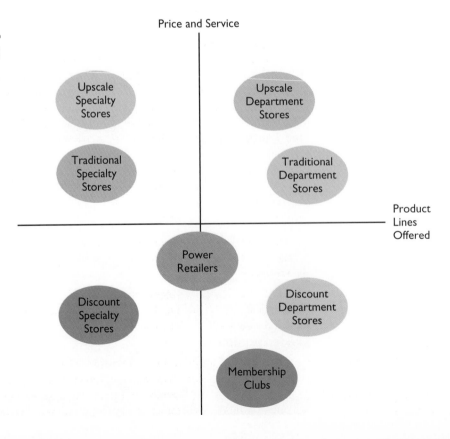

Selection of Objectives

A firm that clearly sets its goals and devises a strategy to achieve them improves its chances of success.

An example of a retailer with clear goals and a proper strategy to attain them is Papa John's, the nearly 3,000-outlet pizza chain. As reported at its Web site (**www.papajohns.com**):

> *Customers:* Papa John's will create superior brand loyalty—"raving fans"— through (a) authentic, superior-quality products, (b) legendary customer service, and (c) exceptional community service. *Team Members:* People are our most important asset. Papa John's will provide clear, consistent, strategic leadership and career opportunities for team members who (a) exhibit passion toward their work, (b) uphold our core values, (c) take pride of ownership in building the long-term value of the Papa John's brand, and (d) have ethical business practices. *Franchisees:* We will work as a team with our franchisees to create continued opportunity for outstanding financial returns to those franchisees who (a) adhere to Papa John's proven core values and systems, (b) exhibit passion in running their businesses, and (c) take pride of ownership in building the long-term value of the Papa John's brand. *Shareholders:* We will produce superior long-term value for our shareholders.

Identification of Consumer Characteristics and Needs

The customer group sought by a retailer is called the **target market**. In selecting its target market, a firm may use one of three techniques: **mass marketing**, selling goods and services to a broad spectrum of consumers; **concentrated marketing**, zeroing in on one specific group; or **differentiated marketing**, aiming at two or more distinct consumer groups, with different retailing approaches for each group.

Supermarkets and drugstores define their target markets broadly. They sell a wide assortment of medium-quality items at popular prices. In contrast, a small upscale men's shoe store appeals to a specific consumer group by offering a narrow, deep product assortment at above-average prices (or in other cases, below-average prices). A retailer aiming at one segment does not try to appeal to everyone.

Department stores are among the retailers seeking multiple market segments. They cater to several customer groups, with unique goods and services for each. Apparel may be sold in a number of distinctive boutiques in the store. Large chains frequently have divisions that appeal to different market segments. Darden Restaurants operates Red Lobster (seafood), Olive Garden (Italian), Capital Grill (American-style with "relaxed elegance"), Seasons 52 (seasonal grill and wine bar), and Bahama Breeze (Caribbean-style) restaurants for customers with different food preferences.

After choosing the target market, a firm can determine its best competitive advantages and devise a strategy mix. See Table 3-3. The significance of **competitive advantages**— the distinct competencies of a retailer relative to competitors—must not be overlooked. Some examples will demonstrate this.

> Tiffany seeks affluent, status-conscious consumers. It places stores in prestigious shopping areas, offers high-quality products, uses elegant ads, has extensive customer services, and sets rather high prices.

> Kohl's targets middle-class, value-conscious shoppers. It locates mostly in suburban shopping areas, offers national brands and Kohl's brands of medium quality, features good values in ads, has some customer services, and charges below-average to average prices.

> T.J. Maxx, an off-price store chain, aims at extremely price-conscious consumers. It locates in low-rent strip shopping centers or districts, offers national brands (sometimes overruns and seconds) of average to below-average quality, emphasizes low prices, offers few customer services, and sets very low prices.

Is the T.J. Maxx Web site (**www.tjmaxx.com**) on target for the customers it wants to reach?

TABLE 3-3 **Target Marketing Techniques and Their Strategic Implications**

	Target Market Techniques		
Strategic Implications	Mass Marketing	Concentrated Marketing	Differentiated Marketing
Retailer's location	Near a large population base	Near a small or medium population base	Near a large population base
Goods and service mix	Wide selection of medium-quality items	Selection geared to market segment—high- or low-quality items	Distinct goods/services aimed at each market segment
Promotion efforts	Mass advertising	Direct mail, E-mail, subscription	Different media and messages for each segment
Price orientation	Popular prices	High or low	High, medium, and low—depending on market segment
Strategy	One general strategy for a large homogeneous (similar) group of consumers	One specific strategy directed at a specific, limited group of customers	Multiple specific strategies, each directed at different (heterogeneous) groups of consumers

The key to the success of each of these retailers is its ability to define customers and cater to their needs in a distinctive manner. See Figure 3-8.

A retailer is better able to select a target market and satisfy customer needs if it has a good understanding of consumer behavior. This topic is discussed in Chapter 7.

FIGURE 3-8

Jean-Philippe Patisserie: A Shop of Distinction

The Bellagio Hotel & Casino (**www.bellagio.com**) in Las Vegas wants to stand out in a competitive environment. One way it does so is through this upscale food shop: "A mesmerizing fountain of cascading liquid chocolate awaits you at the Jean-Philippe Patisserie. Delight the imagination as well as the appetite, with an incredible selection of sweet and savory items including chocolates, cookies, cakes, crepes, salads, sandwiches, and much more."

Source: Reprinted by permission of Susan Berry, Retail Image Consulting, Inc.

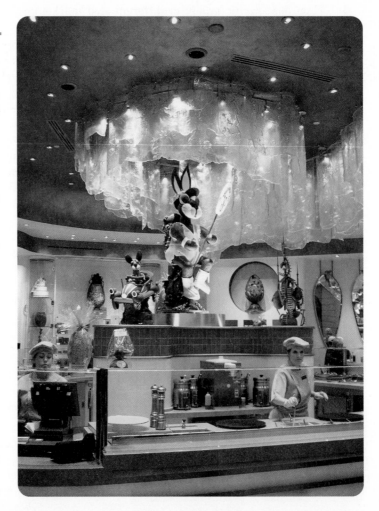

Overall Strategy

Next, the retailer develops an in-depth overall strategy. This involves two components: the aspects of business the firm can directly affect and those to which the retailer must adapt. The former are called **controllable variables**, and the latter are called **uncontrollable variables**. See Figure 3-9.

A strategy must be devised with both variables in mind. The ability of retailers to grasp and predict the effects of controllable and uncontrollable variables is greatly aided by the use of suitable data. In Chapter 8, information gathering and processing in retailing are described.

Controllable Variables

The controllable parts of a retail strategy consist of the basic categories shown in Figure 3-9: store location, managing a business, merchandise management and pricing, and communicating with the customer. A good strategy integrates these areas. These elements are covered in depth in Chapters 9 through 19.

STORE LOCATION

A retailer has several store location decisions to make. The initial one is whether to use a store or nonstore format. Then, for store-based retailers, a general location and a specific site are determined. Competitors, transportation access, population density, the type of neighborhood, nearness to suppliers, pedestrian traffic, and store composition are considered in picking a location. See Figure 3-10.

The terms of tenancy (such as rent and operating flexibility) are reviewed and a build, buy, or rent decision is made. The locations of multiple outlets are considered if expansion is a goal.

MANAGING A BUSINESS

Two major elements are involved in managing a business: the retail organization and human resource management, and operations management. Tasks, policies, resources, authority, responsibility, and rewards are outlined via a retail organization structure. Practices regarding employee hiring, training, compensation, and supervision are instituted through human resource management. Job descriptions and functions are communicated, along with the responsibility of all personnel and the chain of command.

Operations management oversees the tasks that satisfy customer, employee, and management goals. The financial aspects of operations involve asset management, budgeting, and resource allocation. Other elements include store format and size, personnel use, store maintenance, energy management, store security, insurance, credit management, computerization, and crisis management.

MERCHANDISE MANAGEMENT AND PRICING

In merchandise management, the general quality of the goods and services offering is set. Decisions are made as to the width of assortment (the number of product categories carried) and the depth of assortment (the variety of products carried in any category). Policies are set with respect to introducing new items. Criteria for buying decisions (how often, what terms, and which suppliers) are established. Forecasting, budgeting, and accounting procedures are outlined, as is the level of inventory for each type of merchandise. Finally, the retailer devises procedures to assess the success or failure of each item sold.

FIGURE 3-9

Developing an Overall
Retail Strategy

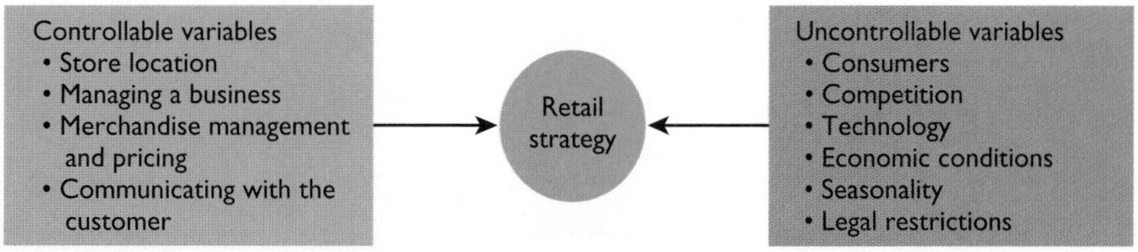

Controllable variables
• Store location
• Managing a business
• Merchandise management and pricing
• Communicating with the customer

Retail strategy

Uncontrollable variables
• Consumers
• Competition
• Technology
• Economic conditions
• Seasonality
• Legal restrictions

FIGURE 3-10

Pushcart Retailing: Stores on Wheels

Pushcart retailers are popular around the world. They have the flexibility to set up wherever the best opportunities exist and move when business slows. Although they are welcome in many areas, they are discouraged in others. This pushcart retailer operates in Coconut Grove, Florida.

Source: Reprinted by permission.

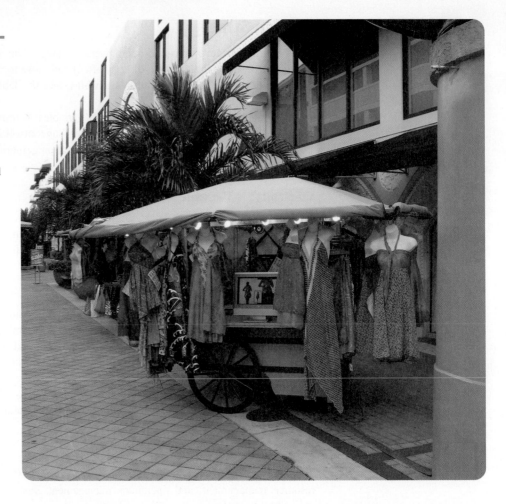

With regard to pricing, a retailer chooses from among several techniques; and it decides what range of prices to set, consistent with the firm's image and the quality of goods and services offered. The number of prices within each product category is determined, such as how many prices of luggage to carry. And the use of markdowns is planned in advance.

 **RETAILING AROUND THE WORLD** Grocery Retailing in India

Annual sales in the Indian retail grocery market are estimated to be more than $250 billion; this makes it the sixth largest grocery market in the world. Yet, even though modern retailing formats are growing quickly in India, close to 80 percent of fast-moving consumer goods (such as detergents, toiletries, shaving supplies, batteries, and paper goods) are still sold at local "kirana" stores. Much of the growth in the Indian grocery market can be attributed to the increase in India's middle class (consumers earning between $5,000 and $25,000 per year).

Large grocery retail chains are using multiple formats in India, including supermarkets, discount stores, and even hypermarkets. There has also been a large increase in the demand for Western-branded products.

Firms that wish to expand in Indian markets need to understand Indian consumers:

▶ Because rice and lentils are basic staples of the Indian diet, many private-label goods focus on these products.
▶ Indian consumers shop at grocery stores frequently and travel short distances to grocery stores.
▶ Indian consumers are extremely value conscious.
▶ India has poor roads, retail channels are long, and supply chains are not well developed. These contribute to high costs.

Source: Mala Morris, "Retailing: The Indian Challenge," *Retail Digest* (Spring 2008), pp. 46–51.

COMMUNICATING WITH THE CUSTOMER

An image can be created and sustained by applying various techniques.

The physical attributes, or atmosphere, of a store and its surrounding area greatly influence consumer perceptions. The impact of the storefront (the building's exterior or the home page for a Web retailer) should not be undervalued, as it is the first physical element seen by customers. Once inside, layouts and displays, floor colors, lighting, scents, music, and the kind of sales personnel also contribute to a retailer's image. Customer services and community relations generate a favorable image for the retailer.

The right use of promotional tools enhances sales performance. These tools range from inexpensive flyers for a take-out restaurant to an expensive national ad campaign for a franchise chain. Three forms of paid promotion are available: advertising, personal selling, and sales promotion. In addition, a retailer can obtain free publicity when stories about it are written, televised, broadcast, or blogged.

While the preceding discussion outlined the controllable parts of a retail strategy, uncontrollable variables (discussed next) must also be kept in mind.

Uncontrollable Variables

The uncontrollable parts of a strategy consist of the factors shown in Figure 3-9: consumers, competition, technology, economic conditions, seasonality, and legal restrictions. Farsighted retailers adapt the controllable parts of their strategies to take into account elements beyond their immediate control.

CONSUMERS

A skillful retailer knows it cannot alter demographic trends or lifestyle patterns, impose tastes, or "force" goods and services on people. The firm learns about its target market and forms a strategy consistent with consumer trends and desires. It cannot sell goods or services that are beyond the price range of customers, that are not wanted, or that are not displayed or advertised in the proper manner.

COMPETITION

There is often little that retailers can do to limit the entry of competitors. In fact, a retailer's success may encourage the entry of new firms or cause established competitors to modify their strategies to capitalize on the popularity of a successful retailer. A major increase in competition should lead a company to re-examine its strategy, including its target market and merchandising focus, to ensure that it sustains a competitive edge. A continued willingness to satisfy customers better than any competitor is fundamental.

TECHNOLOGY

Computer systems are available for inventory control and checkout operations. There are more high-tech ways to warehouse and transport merchandise. Toll-free 800 numbers are popular for consumer ordering. And, of course, there is the Web. Nonetheless, some advancements are expensive and may be beyond the reach of small retailers. For example, although small firms might have computerized checkouts, they will probably be unable to use fully automated inventory systems. As a result, their efficiency may be less than that of larger competitors. They must adapt by providing more personalized service.

ECONOMIC CONDITIONS

Economic conditions are beyond any retailer's control, no matter how large it is. Unemployment, interest rates, inflation, tax levels, and the annual gross domestic product (GDP) are just some economic factors with which a retailer copes. In outlining the controllable parts of its strategy, a retailer needs to consider forecasts about international, national, state, and local economies.

SEASONALITY

A constraint on certain retailers is their seasonality and the possibility that unpredictable weather will play havoc with sales forecasts. Retailers selling sports equipment, fresh food, travel services, and car rentals cannot control the seasonality of demand or bad weather. They can diversify offerings to carry a goods/service mix with items that are popular in different seasons. Thus, a sporting goods retailer can emphasize ski equipment and snowmobiles in the winter, baseball and golf equipment in the spring, scuba equipment and fishing gear in the summer, and basketball and football supplies in the fall.

LEGAL RESTRICTIONS

Table 3-4 shows how each controllable aspect of a retail strategy is affected by the legal environment.

The Federal Trade Commission has a section of its Web site (**www.ftc.gov/ ftc/business.htm**) devoted to do's and don'ts for business.

Retailers that operate in more than one state are subject to federal laws and agencies. The Sherman Act and the Clayton Act deal with monopolies and restraints of trade. The Federal Trade Commission deals with unfair trade practices and consumer complaints. The Robinson-Patman Act prohibits suppliers from giving unjust merchandise discounts to large retailers that could adversely affect small ones. The Telemarketing Sales Rule protects consumers.

At the state and local levels, retailers have to deal with many restrictions. Zoning laws prohibit firms from operating at certain sites and demand that building specifications be met. Blue laws limit the times during which retailers can conduct business. Construction,

TABLE 3-4 The Impact of the Legal Environment on Retailing[a]

Controllable Factor Affected	Selected Legal Constraints on Retailers
Store location	*Zoning laws* restrict the potential choices for a location and the type of facilities constructed.
	Blue laws restrict the days and hours during which retailers may operate.
	Environmental laws limit the retail uses of certain sites.
	Door-to-door (direct) selling laws protect consumer privacy.
	Local ordinances involve fire, smoking, outside lighting, capacity, and other rules.
	Leases and mortgages require parties to abide by stipulations in tenancy documents.
Managing the business	*Licensing provisions* mandate minimum education and/or experience for certain personnel.
	Personnel laws involve nondiscriminatory hiring, promoting, and firing of employees.
	Antitrust laws limit large firm mergers and expansion.
	Franchise agreements require parties to abide by various legal provisions.
	Business taxes include real-estate and income taxes.
	Recycling laws mandate that retailers participate in the recycling process for various materials.
Merchandise management and pricing	*Trademarks* provide retailers with exclusive rights to the brand names they develop.
	Merchandise restrictions forbid some retailers from selling specified goods or services.
	Product liability laws allow retailers to be sued if they sell defective products.
	Lemon laws specify consumer rights if products, such as autos, require continuing repairs.
	Sales taxes are required in most states, although *tax-free days* have been introduced in some locales to encourage consumer shopping.
	Unit-pricing laws require price per unit to be displayed (most often applied to supermarkets).
	Collusion laws prohibit retailers from discussing selling prices with competitors.
	Sale prices must be a reduction from the retailer's normal selling prices.
	Price discrimination laws prohibit suppliers from offering unjustified discounts to large retailers that are unavailable to smaller ones.
Communicating with the customer	*Truth-in-advertising* and *-selling laws* require retailers to be honest and not omit key facts.
	Truth-in-credit laws require that shoppers be informed of all terms when buying on credit.
	Telemarketing laws protect the privacy and rights of consumers regarding telephone sales.
	Bait-and-switch laws make it illegal to lure shoppers into a store to buy low-priced items and then to aggressively try to switch them to higher-priced ones.
	Inventory laws mandate that retailers must have sufficient stock when running sales.
	Labeling laws require merchandise to be correctly labeled and displayed.
	Cooling-off laws let customers cancel completed orders, often made by in-home sales, within three days of a contract date.

[a]This table is broad in nature and omits a law-by-law description. Many laws are state or locally oriented and apply only to certain locations; the laws in each place differ widely. The intent here is to give the reader some understanding of the current legal environment as it affects retail management.

ETHICS IN RETAILING

False Advertising and Hidden Fees: Deception with Prepaid Phone Cards

The prepaid phone-card industry brings in annual revenues of $4 billion per year in the United States. Many prepaid phone-card users are consumers who have such a poor credit history that they could not qualify for traditional cellular phone services. Often, these users purchase prepaid cards that entitle them to designated minutes for calls to friends and relatives in foreign countries.

In June 2008, Florida's Attorney General reached agreement with 10 phone-card companies that were accused of false advertising and assessing hidden charges. A dozen other states have been conducting similar investigations of these practices. In addition, the Federal Trade Commission (**www.ftc.gov**) has brought enforcement actions against seven companies.

A survey of 45 prepaid phone cards conducted in November 2007 found that the card companies delivered only 60 percent of the minutes indicated in voice prompts. Researchers used a single international phone call to compare the fees and minutes. If they had used several calls, the fees would have been even higher. Some firms charged "connection" and "hang-up" fees, while others rounded up calls in three- or four-minute increments. Many disclosures were only posted in English. The Hispanic Institute (**www.thehispanicinstitute.net**), a nonprofit research group, estimates that Hispanics are cheated out of close to $1 million per day through use of these cards.

Source: Diana Holden, "Calling Out Prepaid Phone Cards," **www.businessweek.com/technology** (July 9, 2008).

smoking, and other codes are imposed by the state and city. The licenses to operate some businesses are under state or city jurisdiction.

For more information, contact the Federal Trade Commission (**www.ftc.gov**), state and local bodies, the Better Business Bureau (**www.bbb.org**), the National Retail Federation (**www.nrf.com**), or a specialized group such as the Direct Marketing Association (**www.the-dma.org**).

Integrating Overall Strategy

*What do you think about the overall strategy of Sears (**www.sears.com**)?*

At this point, the firm has set an overall strategy. It has chosen a mission, an ownership and management style, and a goods/service category. Goals are clear. A target market has been designated and studied. Decisions have been made about store location, managing the business, merchandise management and pricing, and communications. These factors must be coordinated to have a consistent, integrated strategy and to account for uncontrollable variables (consumers, competition, technology, economy, seasonality, and legal restrictions). The firm is then ready to do the specific tasks to carry out its strategy productively.

Specific Activities

Short-run decisions are now made and enacted for each controllable part of the strategy in Figure 3-9. These actions are known as **tactics** and encompass a retailer's daily and short-term operations. They must be responsive to the uncontrollable environment. Here are some tactical moves a retailer may make:

*Stores (**www.stores.org**) tracks all kinds of tactical moves made by retailers.*

▶ *Store location.* Trading-area analysis gauges the area from which a firm draws its customers. The level of competition in a trading area is studied regularly. Relationships with nearby retailers are optimized. A chain carefully decides on the sites of new outlets. Facilities are actually built or modified.

▶ *Managing the business.* There is a clear chain of command from managers to workers. An organization structure is set into place. Personnel are hired, trained, and supervised. Asset management tracks assets and liabilities. The budget is spent properly. Operations are systemized and adjusted as required.

▶ *Merchandise management and pricing.* The assortments within departments and the space allotted to each department require constant decision making.

Innovative firms look for new merchandise and clear out slow-moving items. Purchase terms are negotiated and suppliers sought. Selling prices reflect the firm's image and target market. Price ranges offer consumers some choice. Adaptive actions are needed to respond to higher supplier prices and react to competitors' prices.

▶ *Communicating with the customer.* The storefront and display windows, store layout, and merchandise displays need regular attention. These elements help gain consumer enthusiasm, present a fresh look, introduce new products, and reflect changing seasons. Ads are placed during the proper time and in the proper media. The deployment of sales personnel varies by merchandise category and season.

The essence of retailing excellence is building a sound strategy and fine-tuning it. A firm that stands still is often moving backward. Tactical decision making is discussed in detail in Chapters 9 through 19.

Control

In the **control** phase, a review takes place (Step VI in Figure 3-1), as the strategy and tactics (Steps IV and V) are assessed against the business mission, objectives, and target market (Steps I, II, and III). This procedure is called a retail audit, which is a systematic process for analyzing the performance of a retailer. The retail audit is covered in Chapter 20.

The strengths and weaknesses of a retailer are revealed as performance is reviewed. The aspects of a strategy that have gone well are maintained; those that have gone poorly are revised, consistent with the mission, goals, and target market. The adjustments are reviewed in the firm's next retail audit.

Feedback

During each stage in a strategy, an observant management receives signals or cues, known as **feedback**, as to the success or failure of that part of the strategy. Refer to Figure 3-1. Positive feedback includes high sales revenue, no problems with the government, and low employee turnover. Negative feedback includes falling sales revenue, government sanctions (such as fines), and high employee turnover.

Retail executives look for positive and negative feedback so they can determine the causes and then capitalize on opportunities or rectify problems.

A Strategic Planning Template for Retail Management

A comprehensive, user-friendly strategic planning template, *Computer-Assisted Strategic Retail Management Planning*, appears at our Web site (**www.pearsonhighered.com/berman**). This template uses a series of drop-down menus, based on Figure 3-1, to build a strategic plan. You may apply the template to one of the retail business scenarios that are provided— or devise your own scenario. You have the option of printing each facet of the planning process individually, or printing the entire plan as an integrated whole.

TABLE 3-5   Outline of the Computerized Strategic Planning Template

1. **Situation Analysis**
   • Current organizational mission
   • Current ownership and management alternatives
   • Current goods/service category

2. **SWOT Analysis**
   • Strengths: Current and long term
   • Weaknesses: Current and long term
   • Opportunities: Current and long term
   • Threats: Current and long term

TABLE 3-5 *(Continued)*

3. **Objectives**
   - Sales
   - Profit
   - Positioning
   - Satisfaction of publics

4. **Identification of Consumers**
   - Choice of target market
     - Mass marketing
     - Concentrated marketing
     - Differentiated marketing

5. **Overall Strategy**
   - Controllable variables
     - Goods/services strategy
     - Location strategy
     - Pricing strategy
     - Promotion strategy
   - Uncontrollable variables
     - Consumer environment
     - Competitive environment
     - Legal environment
     - Economic environment
     - Technological environment

6. **Specific Activities**
   - Daily and short-term operations
   - Responses to environment

7. **Control**
   - Evaluation
   - Adjustment

Table 3-5 highlights the steps used in *Computer-Assisted Strategic Retail Management Planning* as the basis for preparing a strategic plan. Table 3-6 presents an example of how the template may be used.

TABLE 3-6   Sample Strategic Plan: A High-Fashion Ladies Clothing Shop

Sally's is a small, independently owned, high-fashion ladies clothing shop located in a suburban strip mall. It is a full-price, full-service store for fashion-forward shoppers. Sally's carries sportswear from popular designers, has a personal shopper for busy executives, and has an on-premises tailor. The store is updating its strategic plan as a means of getting additional financing for an anticipated expansion.

1. **Situation Analysis**
   - Current organizational mission: A high-fashion clothing retailer selling high-quality and designer-label clothing and accessories in an attractive full-service store environment.
   - Current ownership and management alternatives: Sole proprietor, independent store.
   - Current goods/service category: Ladies coats, jackets, blouses, and suits from major designers, as well as a full line of fashion accessories (such as scarves, belts, and hats).

2. **SWOT Analysis**
   - Strengths
     - Current
       - A loyal customer base.
       - An excellent reputation for high-fashion clothing and accessories within the community.
       - Little competition within a target market concerned with high-fashion.
       - Acceptance by a target market more concerned with fashion, quality, and customer service than with price.
       - Unlike shoppers favoring classic clothing, Sally's fashion-forward shopper spends a considerable amount of money on clothing and accessories per year.
       - Sally's has a highly regarded personal shopper (who assembles clothing based on customer preferences, visits customers, and arranges for a tailor to visit customers).

(Continued)

TABLE 3-6   Sample Strategic Plan: A High-Fashion Ladies Clothing Shop *(Continued)*

- Long term
    - A fashion-forward image with the store's target market.
    - Exclusive relationships with some well-known and some emerging designers.
    - A low-rent location in comparison to a regional shopping center.
    - Excellent supplier relationships.
    - Loyal employees.
    - Excellent relationships within the community.
- Weaknesses
    - Current
        - Difficulty in recruiting appropriate part-time personnel for peak seasonal periods.
        - The store's small space limits assortment and depth. Too often, the tailor has to perform major alterations.
        - Delivery times for certain French and Italian designers are too long.
        - The retailer does not have a computer-based information system which would better enable it to access key information concerning inventory, sales, customer preferences, and purchase histories.
    - Long term
        - Sally's small orders limit bargaining power with vendors. This affects prices paid, as well as access to "hot-selling" clothing.
        - The store's suburban strip mall location substantially reduces its trading area. The store gets little tourist trade.
        - Over-reliance on the owner-manager, and on several key employees.
        - No long-term management succession plan.
- Opportunities
    - Current
        - Sally's can hire another experienced tailor with a following to create a custom-made clothing department.
        - The store can hire an assistant to better coordinate trunk and fashion shows. This would solidify Sally's reputation among fashion-forward shoppers and in the community.
        - An adjacent store is vacant. This would enable Sally's to increase its size by 50 percent.
        - Sally's is considering developing a Web site. This would enable it to appeal to a larger trading area, offer a medium to announce events (such as a fashion show), and provide links to designers.
    - Long term
        - The larger store would allow Sally's to expand the number of designers, as well as the product lines carried. This would also improve Sally's bargaining power with suppliers.
        - A custom-made clothing department would enable Sally's to appeal to customers who dislike "ready-to-wear apparel" and to customers with highly individualized tastes.
        - The Web site should expand Sally's market.
- Threats
    - Current
        - There are rumors that Bloomingdale's, a fashion-based department store, may soon locate a new store within 10 miles of Sally's. This could affect relationships with suppliers, as well as customers. Bloomingdale's offers one-stop shopping and has a flexible return policy for unaltered merchandise with its labels intact.
        - The current local recession has reduced revenues significantly as many customers have cut back on purchases.
    - Long term
        - Many of Sally's customers are in their 50s and 60s. Some are close to retirement; others intend to spend more time in Florida and Arizona during the winter. The store needs to attract and hold on to younger shoppers.

3. **Objectives**
    - Sales: Achieve sales volume of $4 million per year.
    - Profit: (a) Achieve net profit before tax of $300,000. (b) Increase inventory turnover from 4 times a year to 6 times a year. (c) Increase gross margin return on inventory (GMROI) by 50 percent through more effective inventory management.
    - Positioning: (a) Reposition store to appeal to younger shoppers without losing current clientele. (b) Increase acceptance by younger shoppers. (c) Establish more of a Web presence.
    - Satisfaction of publics: (a) Maintain store loyalty among current customers. (b) Increase relationship with younger designers selling less costly, younger apparel. (c) Maintain excellent relationship with employees.

4. **Identification of Consumers**
    - Choice of target market
        - Mass marketing: This is not a mass-market store.
        - Concentrated marketing: This is Sally's current target market strategy.
        - Differentiated marketing: Sally's might consider attracting multiple target markets: its current fashion-forward customers seeking designer apparel and accessories in a full-service environment; younger, professional customers who desire more trendy clothing; and fashion-forward customers who desire custom-made clothing.

TABLE 3-6 *(Continued)*

5. Overall Strategy
- Controllable variables
  - Goods/service strategy: Clothing is fashion-forward from established and emerging designers. The fashion accessories sold include such items as scarves, belts, and hats. The retailer has no plans to sell ladies' shoes or pocketbooks. Most of the designer merchandise is selectively distributed. A planned custom-made clothing department would enable Sally's to attract hard-to-fit and hard-to-please shoppers. Custom-made clothing shoppers would have a wide variety of swatches and fashion books from which to choose.
  - Location strategy: Sally's currently occupies a single location in a suburban strip mall. This site has comparatively low rent, is within 10 miles of 80 percent of the store's customers, has adequate parking, and has good visibility from the road.
  - Pricing strategy: Sally's charges list price for all of its goods. Included in the price are full-tailoring service, as well as a personal shopper for important customers. Twice a year, the store has a 50 percent off sale on seasonal goods. This is followed by 70 percent off sales to clear the store of remaining off-season inventory.
  - Promotion strategy: Sally's sales personnel are well-trained and highly motivated. They know key customers by name and by their style, color, and designer preferences. Sally's plans to upgrade its regular fashion and trunk shows where new styles are exhibited to important customers. Sally's also maintains a customer data base. The best customers are called when suitable merchandise arrives and are allowed to preview it. Some other customers are contacted by mail. The new Web site will feature the latest styles, the Web address of major designers, and color availability. Sally's has a display listing in the Yellow Pages.
- Uncontrollable variables
  - Consumer environment: Business is subject to the uncertainty of the acceptance of new fashions by the target market. Although Sally's wants to attract two additional segments (custom-made clothing buyers and younger buyers), there is no assurance that it will be successful with these target markets. The store needs to be careful that in seeking these new segments, it does not alienate its current shoppers.
  - Competitive environment: The rumored opening of a fashion-oriented department store in the area would significantly affect sales.
  - Legal environment: Sally's is careful in fully complying with all laws. Unlike some competitors, it does not eliminate sales taxes for cash purchases or ship empty boxes out-of-state to avoid sales tax.
  - Economic environment: Local recessions can reduce sales substantially.
  - Technological environment: Sally's is in the process of investigating a new retail information system to track purchases, inventories, credit card transactions, and more.

6. Specific Activities
- Daily and short-term operations: Sally's policy is to match competitors' prices, correct alteration problems immediately, have longer store hours during busy periods, and offer exclusive merchandise.
- Responses to environment: Sally's acts appropriately with regard to trends in the economy, competitor actions, and so forth.

7. Control
- Evaluation: The new retail information system will better enable Sally's to ascertain fashion trends, adjust inventories to reduce markdowns, and contact customers with specific offerings. Sales by color, size, style, and designer will be more carefully monitored.
- Adjustment: The retail information system will enable Sally's store to reduce excess inventories, maximize sales opportunities, and better target individual customers.

Chapter **Summary**

1. *To show the value of strategic planning for all types of retailers.* A retail strategy is the overall plan that guides a firm. It consists of situation analysis, objectives, identification of a customer market, broad strategy, specific activities, control, and feedback. Without a well-conceived strategy, a retailer may be unable to cope with environmental factors.

2. *To explain the steps in strategic planning for retailers.* Situation analysis is the candid evaluation of opportunities and threats. It looks at the firm's current marketplace position and where it should be heading. This analysis includes defining an organizational mission, evaluating ownership and management options, and outlining the goods/service category.

An organizational mission is a commitment to a type of business and a place in the market. Ownership/management options include sole proprietorship, partnership, or corporation; starting a business, buying an existing one, or being a franchisee; owner management or professional management; and being centralized or decentralized. The goods/service category depends on personal abilities, finances, and time resources.

A firm may pursue one or more of these goals: sales (growth, stability, and market share), profit (level, return on investment, and efficiency), satisfaction of publics (stockholders, consumers, and others), and image/positioning (customer and industry perceptions).

Next, consumer characteristics and needs are determined, and a target market is selected. A firm can sell to a broad spectrum of consumers (mass marketing); zero in on one customer group (concentrated marketing); or aim at two or more distinct groups of consumers (differentiated marketing), with separate retailing approaches for each.

A broad strategy is then formed. It involves controllable variables (aspects of business a firm can directly affect) and uncontrollable variables (factors a firm cannot control and to which it must adapt).

After a general strategy is set, a firm makes and implements short-run decisions (tactics) for each controllable part of that strategy. Tactics must be forward-looking and respond to the environment.

Through a control process, strategy and tactics are evaluated and revised continuously. A retail audit systematically reviews a strategy and its execution on a regular basis. Strengths are emphasized and weaknesses minimized or eliminated.

An alert firm seeks out signals or cues, known as feedback, that indicate the level of performance at each step in the strategy.

3. *To examine the individual controllable and uncontrollable elements of a retail strategy, and to present strategic planning as a series of integrated steps.* There are four major controllable factors in retail planning: store location, managing the business, merchandise management and pricing, and communicating with the customer. The principal uncontrollable factors affecting retail planning are consumers, competition, technology, economic conditions, seasonality, and legal restrictions.

Each stage in the strategic planning process needs to be performed, undertaken sequentially, and coordinated in order to have a consistent, integrated, unified strategy.

4. *To demonstrate how a strategic plan can be prepared.* A comprehensive, user-friendly strategic planning template, *Computer-Assisted Strategic Retail Management Planning,* appears at our Web site. This template uses a series of drop-down menus to build a strategic plan.

Key Terms

retail strategy (p. 58)
situation analysis (p. 58)
opportunities (p. 58)
threats (p. 58)
organizational mission (p. 59)
sole proprietorship (p. 61)
partnership (p. 61)
corporation (p. 61)
goods/service category (p. 63)

objectives (p. 66)
image (p. 68)
positioning (p. 68)
mass merchandising (p. 68)
niche retailing (p. 68)
bifurcated retailing (p. 68)
target market (p. 71)
mass marketing (p. 71)
concentrated marketing (p. 71)

differentiated marketing (p. 71)
competitive advantages (p. 71)
controllable variables (p. 73)
uncontrollable variables (p. 73)
tactics (p. 77)
control (p. 78)
feedback (p. 78)

Questions for Discussion

1. Why is it necessary to develop a thorough, well-integrated retail strategy? What could happen if a firm does not develop such a strategy?

2. How would situation analysis differ for a major luggage store chain and an online luggage retailer?

3. What are the pros and cons of starting a new toy store versus buying an existing one?

4. Develop a checklist to help a prospective service retailer choose the proper service category in which to operate. Include personal abilities, financial resources, and time demands.

5. Why do retailers frequently underestimate the financial and time requirements of a business?

6. Draw and explain a positioning map showing the kinds of retailers selling HD TVs.

7. Discuss local examples of retailers applying mass marketing, concentrated marketing, and differentiated marketing.

8. Marsha Hill is the store manager at a popular gift shop. She has saved $100,000 and wants to open her own store. Devise an overall strategy for Marsha, including each of the controllable factors listed in Figure 3-9 in your answer.

9. A competing computer software store has a better location than yours. It is in a modern shopping center with a lot of customer traffic. Your store is in an older neighborhood and requires customers to travel farther to reach you. How could you use a merchandising, pricing, and communications strategy to overcome your disadvantageous location?

10. Describe how a retailer can use fine-tuning in strategic planning.
11. How are the control and feedback phases of retail strategy planning interrelated? Give an example.
12. Should a catalog-based shoe retailer use the strategic planning process differently from an Internet retailer? Why or why not?

Web **Exercise**

Visit the Web site of Sephora (www.sephora.com), a retail chain with a major presence in Europe, the United States, Asia, and the Middle East. Describe and evaluate the company based on the information you find there. Why do you think that Sephora has been so successful?

Note: Stop by our Web site (www.pearsonhighered.com/berman) to experience a number of highly interactive, appealing Web exercises based on actual company demonstrations, and sample materials related to retailing.

Appendix The Special Dimensions of Strategic Planning in a Global Retailing Environment

There are about 270 countries and dependent areas—with 7 billion people and a $60 trillion economy—in the world. The United States accounts for less than 5 percent of the world's population and more than one-fifth of the worldwide economy. Although the United States is a huge marketplace, there are also many other opportunities. Annual worldwide retailing sales have reached $10 trillion—and they are growing.[1] When we talk about the global environment of retailing, we mean both U.S. firms operating in foreign markets and foreign retailers operating in U.S. markets.

The strategic planning challenge is clear:

Michigan State University's CIBER (http://ciber.bus.msu.edu) is an excellent source of information on global business practices.

Economic conditions have made for a tougher operating environment, but they are also among the most compelling reasons for the move toward a more global market. Despite recent setbacks in the United States and Europe, GDP growth across India, China, and Russia has been better. This makes the retail opportunity in emerging economies more compelling. Even when faced with tough economic conditions in their home markets, global retailers can realize double-digit sales growth and profits in their emerging markets. This kind of growth creates a powerful incentive for large retailers in developed countries. Pursuing expansion into new markets appears to be the best means to further diversify their customer and operations bases, and deliver shareholder returns. This is a landmark period for visionary retailers, those that have already begun entering emerging markets. It will allow them to muscle through the economic turmoil and become truly differentiated from the competition.[2]

In embarking on an international retailing strategy, firms should consider the various factors shown in Figure A3-1.

The Strategic Planning Process and Global Retailing

Retailers looking to operate globally should follow these four steps *in conjunction with* the strategic planning process described in Chapter 3:

1. *Assess your international potential.* "You must first focus on assessing your international potential to get a picture of the trends in your industry, your domestic position

FIGURE A3-1

Factors to Consider When
Engaging in Global
Retailing

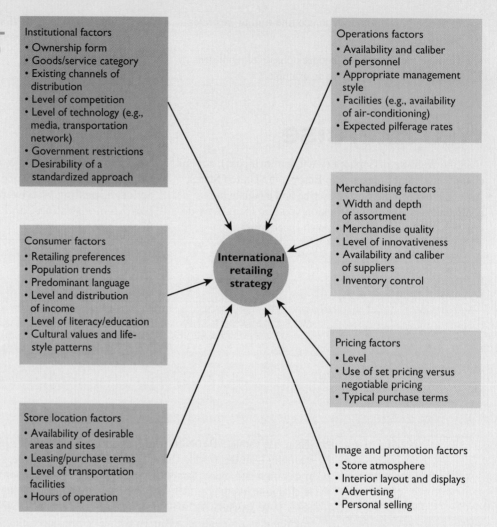

Institutional factors
• Ownership form
• Goods/service category
• Existing channels of
  distribution
• Level of competition
• Level of technology (e.g.,
  media, transportation
  network)
• Government restrictions
• Desirability of a
  standardized approach

Operations factors
• Availability and caliber
  of personnel
• Appropriate management
  style
• Facilities (e.g., availability
  of air-conditioning)
• Expected pilferage rates

Merchandising factors
• Width and depth
  of assortment
• Merchandise quality
• Level of innovativeness
• Availability and caliber
  of suppliers
• Inventory control

Consumer factors
• Retailing preferences
• Population trends
• Predominant language
• Level and distribution
  of income
• Level of literacy/education
• Cultural values and life-
  style patterns

**International
retailing
strategy**

Pricing factors
• Level
• Use of set pricing versus
  negotiable pricing
• Typical purchase terms

Store location factors
• Availability of desirable
  areas and sites
• Leasing/purchase terms
• Level of transportation
  facilities
• Hours of operation

Image and promotion factors
• Store atmosphere
• Interior layout and displays
• Advertising
• Personal selling

in that industry, the effects that international activity may have on current operations, the status of your resources, and an estimate of your sales potential. Find out about candidate countries by using research. It's easy to ruin a good plan by making fundamental cultural, partnering, or resource allocation mistakes."

2. *Get expert advice and counseling.* "Many groups in the private sector and government provide guidance to those planning to go international. Trade associations are useful, as are consulting firms and business departments of universities. Contact a district office of the Commerce Department's International Trade Administration (**www.ita.doc.gov**). State governments are another source."

Global Retail Insights
(**www.globalretail-insights.
com**) reports on the "Latest
News" at its Web site.

3. *Select your countries.* "You need to prioritize information about each country's economic strength, political stability, regulatory environment, tax policy, infrastructure development, population size, and cultural factors. For example, the economy of a country is generally considered critical to most businesses. Equally critical are political factors, particularly government regulations. Others are more dependent on which product you market. The technological stage of a country has a more influential role for computers than for cosmetics."

4. *Develop, implement, and review the international retailing strategy.* "A successful strategy identifies and manages your objectives, specifies tactics you will use, schedules activities and deadlines, and allocates resources among activities. The plan should cover a two- to five-year period, depending on what you are selling, competitors' strength, conditions in target countries, and so on. Keep the strategy flexible because often it is only after entering a country that you realize that your way of doing business needs modifying. The best strategies can be changed to exploit local conditions and circumstances. Don't underestimate the local competition, but don't overestimate it either."[3]

Opportunities and Threats in Global Retailing

For participating firms, there are wide-ranging opportunities and threats in global retailing.

Opportunities

▶ Foreign markets may be used to supplement domestic sales.
▶ Foreign markets may represent growth opportunities if domestic markets are saturated or stagnant.
▶ A retailer may be able to offer goods, services, or technology not yet available in foreign markets.
▶ Competition may be less in some foreign markets.
▶ There may be tax or investment advantages in foreign markets.
▶ Due to government and economic shifts, many countries are more open to the entry of foreign firms.
▶ Communications are easier than before. The Internet enables retailers to reach customers and suppliers well outside their domestic markets.

Threats

▶ There may be cultural differences between domestic and foreign markets.
▶ Management styles may not be easily adaptable.
▶ Foreign governments may place restrictions on some operations.
▶ Personal income may be poorly distributed among consumers in foreign markets.
▶ Distribution systems and technology may be inadequate (e.g., poor roads and lack of refrigeration). This may minimize the effectiveness of the Web as a selling tool.
▶ Institutional formats vary greatly among countries.
▶ Currencies are different. The countries in the European Union have sought to alleviate this problem by introducing the euro, a common currency, in most of their member nations.

Standardization: An Opportunity and a Threat

When devising a global strategy, a retailer must pay attention to the concept of *standardization*. Can the home market strategy be standardized and directly applied to foreign markets, or do personnel, physical facilities, operations, advertising messages, product lines, and other factors have to be adapted to local conditions and needs? Table A3-1 shows how the economies differ in 15 countries. And consider this:

> If you intend to enter a foreign market, you must be very sensitive to local cultural issues, and then be humble enough to accept that no matter how well you have prepared, some aspect of local culture will probably surprise you. Your entry plans must consist of some measure of humility and flexibility. You will inevitably be facing execution challenges that you had not adequately considered in the planning stage of your market entry.[4]

Ten Trends in Global Retailing

Several factors can affect the level of success of an international retailing strategy:

1. *Social responsibility.* "More consumers are becoming concerned about the impact that companies have on society. This includes the impact on the physical environment, on workers in countries that supply products, and the impact that products have on the consumers who purchase them."
2. *Global consumer growth shifts away from the United States.* "For the world's largest retailers, this means increased growth opportunities in Asia. It also means that the U.S. market will be a bit more challenging. Retailers in the U.S. market will increasingly face a market share battle."

TABLE A3-1 The Global Economy, Selected Countries

Country	2008 Population (millions)	2008 Population Density (per square kilometer)	2007 Per Capita GDP (U.S. $)	2007 Per Capita Retail Sales— Excluding Autos (U.S. $)	2007–2012 Projected Annual Retail Growth Rate— After Inflation (%)	2008 World Competitiveness Ranking Among the 15 Countries Listed
Brazil	197	24	9,500	1,600	4.0	11
Canada	33	3	38,600	10,500	3.5	2
China	1,330	135	5,400	655	8.1	4
France	64	114	32,600	11,100	1.8	7
Germany	82	231	34,100	10,100	0.6	3
Great Britain	61	248	35,000	12,500	4.0	5
India	1,150	346	2,600	350	6.0	8
Indonesia	238	126	3,600	850	3.9	15
Italy	58	195	30,900	10,400	1.2	12
Japan	127	336	33,500	9,000	1.7	6
Mexico	110	56	12,400	2,800	3.7	14
Philippines	96	316	3,200	750	6.0	10
Russia	141	8	14,800	3,000	8.6	13
South Korea	48	483	25,000	4,500	1.9	9
United States	304	32	45,800	11,830	4.0	1

GDP is a country's gross domestic product. Per capita GDP is expressed in terms of purchasing power parity.
World Competitiveness Ranking is based on a country's economic performance, government efficiency, business efficiency, and infrastructure.

Sources: Compiled by the authors from *World Factbook,* **https://www.cia.gov/library/publications/the-world-factbook** (updated online as of November 20, 2008); Retail Forward, *Global Retail Outlook* (March 2008); and *IMD World Competitiveness Yearbook 2008.*

3. *Commoditization run amok.* "Consumers are jaded. To demonstrate differentiation from competitors, it is no longer sufficient for retailers to simply do everything right. Those that differentiate on the basis of something other than price will be the winners of the future."

4. *The rise of "long tail" retailing.* "The long tail means focusing on niche opportunities that can be quite lucrative. Consider how consumer income in any country is distributed. The mass market is where the greatest share of income exists and where most retailers compete. The ends of the tail are smaller, representing a smaller share of income. Yet, these ends have often been ignored by retailers intent on reaping the economies of scale associated with the mass market in the middle."

5. *The fight to plant the flag in India.* "India has become the next big thing for the world's leading retailers. Even though India remains relatively closed to foreign retail investment, its business environment is riddled with obstacles, and its rapid economic growth is so new that it is not clear whether it can be sustained, it is a country with more than a billion people."

6. *Retail investment in services.* "As countries grow and achieve economic affluence, consumer spending on goods as a share of GDP tends to decline while spending on services grows disproportionately."

7. *Emerging market investment in developed retailers.* "One of the notable aspects of the global economy lately has been the huge surpluses of key emerging countries. Not only may funds in such countries seek to acquire retail companies, but in some cases they may invest in the development of startup retailers as well."

8. *Multi-channel integration.* "The best retailers will most likely focus on enriching the brand experience for distinct customer segments across multiple channels. They will use Web sites not just to sell, but to build brand identity, engage consumers in dialog, and obtain feedback from consumers."

9. *Focus on customer experience.* "One way to tackle the problem of a lack of retailer differentiation is to focus on improving the experience of consumers in the store. This encompasses far more than customer service and includes all the elements influencing consumers (such as store layout, signage, lighting, service, and the ease and speed of transactions)."

10. *Retailers as world-class marketers.* "Today, some of the world's top retailers are aggressively hiring top marketers away from manufacturing companies. Their goal is to become marketing powerhouses, to build strong brand identity in order to compete with other retailers, and, increasingly, to compete with branded suppliers through private label sales."[5]

U.S. Retailers in Foreign Markets

Here are three of the many examples of U.S. retailers with high involvement in foreign markets.

Toys "R" Us has nearly 700 stores abroad. Among the 33 nations in which it has stores are Australia, Canada, France, Germany, Great Britain, Japan, Singapore, Spain, and Sweden. In some of its markets, such as Indonesia, South Africa, Turkey, and United Arab Emirates, the firm emphasizes franchising rather than direct corporate ownership. Why? This enables Toys "R" Us to better tap the local knowledge of franchisees in certain markets while still setting corporate policies.[6]

The majority of McDonald's restaurants are outside the United States. Sales at the 18,000 outlets in nearly 120 foreign nations account for two-thirds of total revenues. Besides Europe, McDonald's has outlets in such nations as Argentina, Australia, Brazil, Canada, China, Colombia, Egypt, Greece, India, Japan, Malaysia, Mexico, New Zealand, Pakistan, Russia, South Africa, and South Korea. The restaurants in India are particularly distinctive because they do not use beef as an ingredient: "Maharaja Mac is the Indian version of the Big Mac. It is like a hamburger made with stuffing two lamb or chicken patties into a sesame seed bun, and garnishing it with iceberg lettuce, cheese, pickles, onions, and a special sauce."[7]

Amazon.com has rapidly expanded globally by introducing dedicated Web sites for specific nations. They include Canada (**www.amazon.ca**), China (**www.joyo.com**), France (**www.amazon.fr**), Germany (**www.amazon.de**), Great Britain (**www.amazon.co.uk**), and Japan (**www.amazon.co.jp**). While these sites all have the familiar Amazon Web design, they differ by language, products offered, and currency.

Foreign Retailers in the U.S. Market

A large number of foreign retailers have entered the United States to appeal to the world's most affluent mass market. Here are three examples.

Ikea is a Swedish-based home-furnishings retailer operating in more than 35 nations. In 1985, Ikea opened its first U.S. store in Pennsylvania. Since then, it has added about 35 other U.S. stores in such cities as Baltimore, Chicago, Elizabeth (New Jersey), Hicksville (Long Island, New York), Houston, Los Angeles, San Francisco, Seattle, and Washington, DC. The firm offers durable, stylish, ready-to-assemble furniture at low prices. Stores are huge, have enormous selections, and include a playroom for children and other amenities. Today, Ikea generates 94 percent of its sales from international operations, and 15 percent of total company sales (more than $4 billion per year) are from its North American stores.[8]

The Netherlands' Royal Ahold ranks among the world's top retailers with annual worldwide retail sales of $50 billion. It has food stores in about a dozen countries and serves millions of shoppers weekly. In the United States, Royal Ahold has acquired several chains, making it the leading supermarket firm on the East Coast. Its 725 U.S. stores include Stop & Shop, Giant Food, and Martin's. The firm also owns Peapod, the online food retailer.[9]

Body Shop International is a British-based chain that sells natural cosmetics and lotions that "cleanse, beautify, and soothe the human form." There are 2,500 Body Shop stores in 60 countries, including the United States. The firm has several hundred U.S. stores (60 percent company-owned and 40 percent franchised), which generate nearly one-quarter of total revenues.[10]

Although the revenues of U.S.-based retailers owned by foreign firms are hard to measure, they are several hundred billion dollars annually. Foreign ownership in U.S. retailers is highest for general merchandise stores, food stores, and apparel and accessory stores. Examples of U.S.-based retailers owned by foreign firms are shown in Table A3-2.

TABLE A3-2 Selected Ownership of U.S. Retailers by Foreign Firms

U.S. Retailer	Principal Business	Foreign Owner	Country of Owner
Circle K	Convenience stores	Couche-Tard	Canada
Crate & Barrel	Housewares stores	Otto GmbH	Germany
Food Lion	Supermarkets	Delhaize Group	Belgium
Giant Food	Supermarkets	Royal Ahold	Netherlands
Great Atlantic & Pacific (A&P)	Supermarkets	Tengelmann	Germany
Hannaford Bros.	Supermarkets	Delhaize Group	Belgium
LensCrafters	Optical stores	Luxottica	Italy
Motel 6	Economy motels	Accor	France
7-Eleven	Convenience stores	Seven & I Holdings	Japan
Stop & Shop	Supermarkets	Royal Ahold	Netherlands
Sunglass Hut	Sunglass stores	Luxottica	Italy
Talbots	Apparel	Aeon	Japan

part one
Short Cases

CASE 1: BED BATH & BEYOND'S PLAN FOR GROWTH[C-1]

Bed Bath & Beyond (BB&B, **www.bedbathandbeyond.com**), the power retailer of domestics and home furnishings, has annual sales of $7 billion and a net income of $562 million. The firm's profitability can be explained by its increasing gross profit margins at the same time it decreases selling, general, and administrative (SG&A) expenses as a percent of sales. BB&B is able to increase its gross profit margins due to its excellent atmosphere, wide assortments, and a deep variety within most merchandise lines. Its control over SG&A expenses is partly due to the outsourcing of its distribution centers to a third party.

BB&B has opened hundreds of stores over the last few years, ranging in size from 30,000 to 80,000 square feet. Because it uses a flexible real-estate strategy, BB&B is able to situate in a variety of locations. BB&B is now also being allowed into large shopping centers. In the past, department store anchor tenants blocked BB&B. In 2004, BB&B had about 630 stores with a total of 20.5 million square feet of store space. By the end of 2008, these numbers had expanded to nearly 1,000 stores with 31 million square feet of store space. Its long-term goal is to operate 1,300 stores. In addition, BB&B plans to remodel and expand many existing stores.

In 2003, BB&B purchased Christmas Tree Shops (**www.christmastreeshops.com**), a chain of stores specializing in giftware and household items. Although the Christmas Tree Shops' name suggests that it concentrates on Christmas merchandise, the chain is positioned against Pier 1 (**www.pier1.com**). In March 2007, BB&B acquired buybuyBABY (**www.buybuybaby.com**), a retailer specializing in infant and toddler merchandise. In December 2007, BB&B opened its first foreign BB&B store in Ontario, Canada. In May 2008, BB&B purchased a 50 percent equity interest in Home & More, a Mexican home goods retailer that operated two stores in Mexico City.

BB&B management (as well as many retail analysts) attributes the chain's strong sales performance to its superior customer service. BB&B is obsessive about its consumers receiving a consistently high level of customer service. For example, one recent shopper at a suburban Long Island store reported that a sales clerk was highly attentive: When the shopper asked the clerk where she could find a set of dishes listed on a bridal registry, the clerk immediately dropped what she was doing. The clerk then located the dishes and stood by the shopper as she decided whether to purchase the set and even had the dishes brought to a nearby checkout so that the shopper could continue buying at the store. The sales clerk then met the shopper at the checkout to facilitate the transaction.

In 2008, BB&B was tied for second place in an annual study of the top "20 Most Competitive Retailers" in the United States. The study, conducted by Capgemini (**www.capgemini.com**) and W Ratings Corporation (**www.wratings.com**), measured the ability of retailers to beat consumer expectations and deliver superior profitability. Each firm's rankings were based on its profits over the prior five years and the responses from a sample of 6,000 consumers.

Questions

1. Explain how Bed Bath & Beyond practices the retailing concept.
2. Evaluate Bed Bath & Beyond's growth plans.
3. How can Bed Bath & Beyond further increase the overall quality of its customer service?
4. Explain the concept of value from the perspective of a Bed Bath & Beyond customer.

CASE 2: NETFLIX: COMPETING VIA TECHNOLOGY[C-2]

In 1999, Netflix (**www.netflix.com**) introduced its online DVD rental service; this has been its major offering ever since. For a flat monthly fee, Netflix subscribers can order as many movies as they desire—up to three movies at a time—and they can keep the movie rentals for as long as they want. The movie rentals generally arrive the next day, and titles are rarely out of stock. By the end of 2008, Netflix had 8.5 million subscribers, an increase of 25 percent from a year earlier.

Netflix recently began offering its vast library of movies and TV shows, which were once only available in DVD format, in an online download as well. Since early 2008, Netflix account owners who pay the $9 minimum monthly fee for an unlimited account have had the ability to stream videos to a Windows-based PC. Those willing to purchase a $100 Roku Netflix (**www.roku.com**) player can watch these movies on their televisions (with no additional charge other than the purchase of the player). Netflix hopes that its partnership with Roku could enable the company to have as many as 10 million subscribers that would connect to Netflix via the Internet as of the end of 2009. According to Reed Hastings, Netflix's chief executive officer, "We named our company 'Netflix' and not 'DVD by Mail' for a reason."

Netflix has increased the selections available in streaming video to more than 12,000 titles, about 12 percent of its total DVD offerings. (The offerings available via streaming

[c-1]The material in this case is drawn from *Bed Bath & Beyond 2008 10-K*; Cecile B. Corral, "Bed Bath & Beyond Eager to Grow," *Home Textiles Today* (July 7, 2008), pp. 1, 21; and "Most Competitive Retailers," *Chain Store Age* (January 2008), p. 22.

[c-2]The material in this case is drawn from Danny King, "Netflix Suns Grow 25%," *Video Business* (July 28, 2008), pp. 1, 36; Danny King, "Netflix Streaming Video to Double Subs," *Video Business* (June 2, 2008), p. 5; and "Netflix No. 1 in Online Customer Service," *Video Business* (May 19, 2008), p. 2.

video are not necessarily Netflix's most popular movies, as the availability of a movie on streaming video must be approved by the movie studio.) Netflix has also partnered with Microsoft to enable owners of Microsoft's Xbox 360 videogame console to stream Netflix's service using Microsoft's Xbox Live Marketplace. In comparison to its competitors, Netflix's "all-you-can-watch" subscription pricing model offers excellent value. It is much less costly than a movie download, which can cost as much as $18, and less costly than a one-day rental over an iTunes, Movielink, or cable on-demand service.

Unlike other services that download the video to a hard drive, Netflix's video is pure streaming with quality equal to a standard-definition digital television. Netflix also requires that consumers have an Internet connection that can consistently deliver at least 2 megabits per second. Although no content is saved, users can restart a movie where they left off.

In contrast to Netflix, Blockbuster (**www.blockbuster. com**) offers in-store rentals, a mail-to-home program, and download options. Its mail-based program provides access to 85,000 titles. Blockbuster customers can exchange mailed videos for in-store videos. Blockbuster also has a streaming video option that features current titles. Download rentals generally cost between $1.99 and $3.99 for 24 hours of use. Downloads can also be purchased for between $9.99 to $20.00.

In 2008, Netflix received the top ranking in Foresee's Top 100 Online Retail Satisfaction Index (**www.foreseeresults. com**) report. Netflix's ranking was a score of 86 out of a possible 100; 2008 marked the seventh straight year that it received the top ranking.

Questions

1. Develop specific objectives for Netflix's strategic plan over the next five years.
2. What target market strategy is most appropriate for Netflix? Explain your answer.
3. Evaluate Netflix's competitive advantages and disadvantages relative to Blockbuster.
4. Explain how Netflix can better practice relationship retailing.

CASE 3: LOYALTY PROGRAMS IN THE NETHERLANDS[C-3]

In a recent research project, the authors studied the use of loyalty programs among 180 retailers doing business in 15 different retail sectors in The Netherlands. To be included in the study, a retailer had to have at least seven retail outlets or 100 employees in The Netherlands. Each responding firm was asked to indicate whether it uses a

[C-3]The material in this case is drawn from Jorna Leenheer and Tammo H.A. Bijmolt, "Which Retailers Adopt a Loyalty Program? An Empirical Study," *Journal of Retailing and Consumer Services*, Vol. 15 (2008), pp. 429–442.

loyalty program. For purposes of this project, a loyalty program was defined as consisting of these components: an explicit membership decision, registration and identification at every purchase decision, and special membership benefits (such as frequency rewards and privileges).

Here are the major findings of the research:

▶ 37 percent of the retailers studied had a loyalty program.
▶ Loyalty programs are more commonly used in retail sectors that have product assortments that are similar among competing retailers and for goods with a high purchase frequency. These include such retail formats as supermarkets, online grocery outlets, and specialty stores.
▶ Companies are more likely to adopt loyalty programs when their customers differ in profitability. Loyalty programs can be designed to both attract and retain a retailer's most profitable customers.
▶ Loyalty programs are more apt to be established when competition is intense among retailers in a given market area. These programs can be used to both increase the attractiveness of a retailer and to record information on the purchasing behavior of that retailer's customers.
▶ Loyalty program adopters have a greater customer orientation than nonadopting retailers.
▶ Surprisingly, a retailer's technological skills had little effect on its decision to adopt a loyalty program. Firms with lower degrees of technological skills were able to adopt simpler systems.

Although many retailers focus on the benefits of loyalty programs in stimulating customer loyalty (through savings features, special programs to members, and directed mailings), another major benefit is the increased information available through the study of the transactions of individual and groups of customers. The authors found that loyalty programs have a substantial effect on a retailer's knowledge of customer behavior. By applying loyalty card data, retailers can study cross-category purchases, the extent to which a special buy increases overall sales, the impact of coupons on long-term sales of a product, and so on.

Retailers can also take loyalty card data and break out customers into key segments. Through this process, a retailer can target each segment with different promotions that are most meaningful to that segment. For example, a segment that purchases organic fresh fruits and vegetables would receive a very different promotion than a group that focuses on frozen and canned vegetables.

The authors state that a major concern with loyalty programs is the false assumption among retailers that their most frequent customers are its most profitable customer group. This may not be the case if this group concentrates its purchases on a retailer's weekly specials. Retailers must study which of its customers are its most profitable to accurately determine whether profitable customers are also loyal.

Questions

1. What material from this case can be used by a U.S. supermarket chain considering a loyalty program?
2. How can a retail grocery store determine its most profitable customers?
3. Discuss the types of information a retailer can obtain through a loyalty card program.
4. Explain why a retailer's most frequent customers may not necessarily be its most profitable customer group and how to rectify this.

CASE 4: EBAY EXPANDS AROUND THE GLOBE[C-4]

As recently as 2000, eBay (**www.ebay.com**) had virtually no international operations. Then, international expansion became a major strategic initiative. By 2005, the firm had Web sites in 31 countries around the world—ranging from Brazil to Germany to China. eBay's 2005 foreign operations generated well over $1 billion in revenues, accounting for 46 percent of eBay's trading revenues. By 2008, 54 percent of sales of eBay's shopping Web sites and 43 percent of the revenues generated through eBay's PayPal (**www.paypal. com**) division (eBay's online person-to-person payment processing business) came from global markets outside the United States.

eBay has succeeded abroad because its global strategy is flexible enough to adapt to countries with different cultures, while retaining the core elements of its online business model. The global strategy is based on a playbook that is a "how-to" manual that covers such topics as online marketing, category management, and community outreach. The playbook, which is constantly updated, consists of several hundred Web pages that summarize the ongoing collective wisdom of all of eBay's worldwide managers.

eBay's playbook details how to drive customer traffic to a local eBay site through online ads at a country's most popular Web sites and search engines. The playbook also dictates that products, information, and chat groups be created by buyers and sellers in that country. Thus, eBay looks and feels like a particular foreign country's Web site brand. This strategy also avoids problems associated with a cookie-cutter approach to Web site planning on a global basis.

[C-4]The material in this case is drawn from Steve Bills, "Almost 35 Million PayPal Accounts in Europe," *American Banker* (May 22, 2007), p. 17; and Catherine Holohan, "IBM, eBay: The Boost from Overseas," *Business Week Online* (April 18, 2008), p. 5.

Meg Whitman, who became eBay's CEO in 1998, originally wanted to perfect eBay's concept in the United States before going abroad. However, she soon realized that many small competitors were springing up around the world. She became concerned that unless eBay went global, she would forfeit many opportunities to these small local firms or to major firms such as Amazon.com and Yahoo!. She also realized that growth on eBay's shopping sites would slow as small-business owners could choose to list items on sale on Amazon.com, through free classified sites, or on their own Web site.

eBay's first foreign market was Germany, chosen in part due to the country's 40 million Internet users. eBay purchased Alando (which changed its name from **www.alando.de** to **www.ebay.de** after purchase), an eBay copycat site, for $47 million in June 1999. A German business student had started Alando four months earlier. From the beginning, eBay was careful to adapt its sites to a country's culture. A lot of effort went into figuring out how to structure categories based on German customers' needs.

Shortly after buying Alando, eBay launched its own sites in Great Britain and Australia. In 2001, eBay acquired Korea's Internet Auction Co. and Europe's iBazar (**www. ibazar.es**). The latter gave eBay access to Italy, The Netherlands, and Spain. eBay then bought a minority interest in MercadoLibre (**www.mercadolibre.com**), Latin America's leading auction firm. eBay also has ownership interests in Web sites such as Kijii (**www.calgary.kijii.ca**), Canada; Gumtree.com (**www.gumtree.com**), Great Britain; LoQUo.com (**www.loquo.com**), Spain; Marktplaats.nl (**www. marktplaats.nl**), The Netherlands; mobile.de (**www. mobile.de**), Germany; and Craigslist (**www.craigslist.org**), which operates globally.

Questions

1. Evaluate the pros and cons of eBay's playbook strategy.
2. Comment on the choice of Germany as eBay's first international market.
3. Describe the pros and cons of eBay's entering an international market by purchasing a foreign firm rather than building an operation from scratch.
4. Comment on this statement: "eBay has succeeded abroad because its global strategy is flexible enough to adapt to countries with different cultures, while retaining the core elements of its online business model."

part one
Comprehensive Case

BEST BUY IN A GLOBAL GROWTH MODE*

INTRODUCTION

Best Buy (**www.bestbuy.com**) continues to weather a difficult business environment better than most consumer electronics retailers. Despite the tough environment, the retailer will continue to move forward with aggressive growth plans. New stores, new countries, a new partnership with Carphone Warehouse, and new categories and services are all part of Best Buy's strategy to expand its dominance in consumer electronics and increase its total annual sales to $80 billion within five years.

Industry Outlook and Structure

Total consumer electronics spending is forecast to grow at a slower compound annual rate through 2012. Growth was

*The material in this case is adapted by the authors from TNS Retail Forward (**www.retailforward.com**), *Industry Outlook: Consumer Electronics* (Columbus, OH: TNS Retail Forward, July 2008). Reprinted by permission.

weak in 2008, buffeted by a potent combination of negative drivers: the housing market slump, a credit crunch, record high gasoline prices, rising food costs, and job and income concerns. Yet a couple of key factors buoyed the otherwise soft near-term outlook: Government economic stimulus payments and purchases related to the 2009 all-digital TV broadcast conversion provided a boost for retailers. Strong price deflation will persist and continue to stimulate demand, although it will temper near-term growth amid a weak economy and competitive pressures.

Consumer electronics/appliance stores and big-box stores hold the lead in U.S. consumer electronics sales. Electronics-only and computer stores continue to lose share of electronics spending, key victims of the growing domination of Best Buy and Wal-Mart (**www.walmart.com**) in the category. The nonstore channel is showing signs of aging as its share gains in electronics have leveled off. See Figure 1.

Dell (**www.dell.com**) remains the leading online retailer of electronics by a wide margin, but it experienced double-digit sales declines for the second year in a row in 2007. Dell is aggressively adjusting its go-to-market strategies in order to sell more products in the United States and other countries. The major pure-play Internet retailers, Amazon.com (**www. amazon.com**) and Newegg.com (**www.newegg.com**), have continued their strong growth trends. Amazon.com has added new services, while Newegg.com continues to expand its

FIGURE 1

Share of U.S. Consumer Electronics Sales by Channel (among the top 100 consumer electronics retailers)

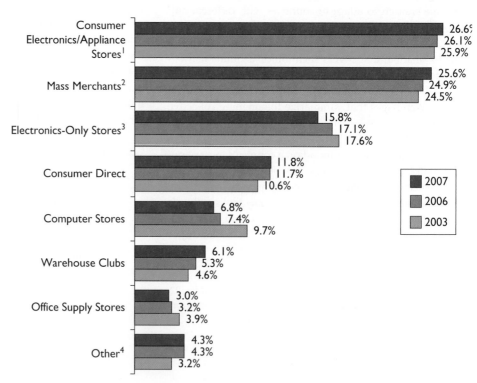

[1] Inclues Best Buy and other CE specially retailers that also sell appliances.
[2] Includes Wal-Mart, other discount department stores and supercenters, and Sears.
[3] Includes Circuit City and other CE specialty retailers that do not sell appliances.
[4] Includes home furnishings stores, drug stores, grocery stores, department stores, home improvement centers, catalog showrooms, and other retailers.
Note: Some 2006 results have been revised.

Sources: Company reports, TWICE, and TNS Retail Forward.

online presence to bolster its Web site traffic. Most of the other leading online consumer electronics retailers also posted strong growth in 2007, although they remain relatively small players.

Spending in the overall consumer electronics category increased 4.0 percent in 2007, a sharp slowdown compared with the strong gains in prior years. Growth was expected to slow to a 3.4 percent increase in 2008 (dragged lower primarily by weaker computer spending growth) then accelerate slightly

to a still-subpar 4.0 percent increase in 2009. Growth should pick up again in 2010 to 6.1 percent before tapering off slightly in the final two years of the forecast period. Category price deflation should ease a bit throughout the forecast period but remain steep. (Note: The government calculates quality enhancements as price declines in the consumer electronics and computer categories, which contributes to the downward price trends for these categories.) Table 1 shows annual U.S. consumer spending on consumer electronics.

TABLE 1 **U.S. Spending on Consumer Electronics (Audio and Video Products and Computers)**

	$ Millions	% Ch	Prices 2000=1.00	% Ch
1985	35,908	12.2%	3.513	−5.4%
1986	41,809	16.4%	3.277	−6.7%
1987	46,155	10.4%	3.171	−3.2%
1988	50,956	10.4%	3.055	−3.7%
1989	52,499	3.0%	2.973	−2.7%
1990	53,039	1.0%	2.846	−4.3%
1991	55,371	4.4%	2.724	−4.3%
1992	57,040	3.0%	2.537	−6.8%
1993	63,865	12.0%	2.359	−7.0%
1994	73,667	15.3%	2.246	−4.8%
1995	81,501	10.6%	2.063	−8.1%
1996	87,575	7.5%	1.793	−13.1%
1997	92,340	5.4%	1.530	−14.7%
1998	99,716	8.0%	1.301	−15.0%
1999	108,144	8.5%	1.117	−14.2%
2000	116,598	7.8%	1.000	−10.5%
2001	115,513	−0.9%	0.874	−12.6%
2002	120,010	3.9%	0.771	−11.7%
2003	123,095	2.6%	0.688	−10.8%
2004	133,269	8.3%	0.629	−8.5%
2005	142,258	6.7%	0.568	−9.6%
2006	151,513	6.5%	0.511	−10.1%
2007	157,567	4.0%	0.461	−9.7%
2008	162,927	3.4%	0.419	−9.2%
2009	169,515	4.0%	0.381	−9.1%
2010	179,848	6.1%	0.347	−8.7%
2011	190,716	6.0%	0.318	−8.6%
2012	201,387	5.6%	0.291	−8.5%
Compound Annual Growth Rate				
1997–2002	5.4%		−12.8%	
2002–2007	5.6%		−9.8%	
2007–2012	5.0%		−8.8%	

Note: Category includes spending on video equipment (TVs, VCRs, DVD players, video media, etc.), audio equipment (stereo components, speakers, audio media, musical instruments, etc.) and computer hardware and software.

Sources: TNS Retail Forward and U.S. Department of Commerce.

The consumer electronics channel will continue to become increasingly competitive as mass retailers step up efforts to grow their consumer electronics business and consumers become more comfortable with purchasing consumer electronics products online. As retailers such as Wal-Mart add more popular brands to the assortment, consumer electronics products including high-definition (HD) TVs are becoming commoditized at a quicker pace, and price becomes even more important as shoppers balance the price–selection equation when selecting a retailer. This has led to increased pressure on specialty consumer electronics retailers to find the niches where they can compete effectively. It also is causing them to slash prices and increase promotions, which will continue to feed consumer electronics deflation in the coming years. Additionally, the continuing shift in global sourcing to the most cost-effective countries will shape price trends.

Best Buy's Global Strategy

As shown in Table 2, Best Buy, Wal-Mart, Circuit City, Target, and Dell were the five largest U.S. sellers of consumer electronics during 2003 to 2007. Both Circuit City and Dell lost market share, while Best Buy, Wal-Mart, and Target (**www.target.com**) increased market share. Things continued to go quite badly through 2008 for Circuit City, so much so that it went out of business in 2009.

A Multi-Pronged Global Growth Strategy

Big Store-Growth Plans Home and Abroad The company planned to open about 140 stores in 2008. In the United States, plans included 85 to 100 Best Buy stores and four relocations. During 2007, Best Buy opened 101 net new Best Buy stores in the United States; 5 to 10 new Pacific Sales Kitchen and Bath stores in Western states were slated for 2008, with plans to eventually expand the format nationwide.

In China, the company planned to open up to three Best Buy stores and up to 16 Five Star Appliance stores during 2008. These plans were pared down from the start of the year given weaker-than-expected profits and the Chinese government's delay in approving new stores. For the Best Buy format, the goal was to open 10 Chinese stores in 2009 and 10 to 12 stores a year thereafter. The retailer currently operates 175 Five Star stores in China.

TABLE 2   The Leading U.S. Retailers of Consumer Electronics, 2007

Rank	Retailer	Estimated CE Sales ($ Millions)	% Change From Prior Year	4-Year CAGR	Share of Total CE Sales 2003	2006	2007
1	Best Buy[1]	$29,329	7.4%	9.7%	16.4%	18.0%	18.6%
2	Wal-Mart[2]	$24,000	6.1%	11.2%	12.7%	14.9%	15.2%
3	Circuit City[3]	$10,318	− 5.7%	2.0%	7.7%	7.2%	6.5%
4	Target	$6,384	23.8%	15.1%	3.0%	3.4%	4.1%
5	Dell[4]	$6,224	−12.0%	− 1.9%	5.5%	4.7%	4.0%
6	GameStop[5]	$5,439	27.4%	36.6%	1.3%	2.8%	3.5%
7	Costco Wholesale	$4,914	28.6%	24.8%	1.6%	2.5%	3.1%
8	Apple Stores	$3,956	19.8%	58.9%	0.5%	2.2%	2.5%
9	RadioShack[6]	$3,904	−10.8%	− 1.8%	3.4%	2.9%	2.5%
10	Sears	$2,965	1.9%	− 2.4%	2.7%	1.9%	1.9%
	Total Top 10	$97,432	6.2%	9.6%	54.8%	60.6%	61.8%
	Total CE Sales	$157,567	4.0%	6.4%	100.0%	100.0%	100.0%

[1]Best Buy domestic sales exclude appliances and services; sales include Best Buy Mobile (launched 2006), Magnolia Audio Video (acquired 2000), Pacific Sales Kitchen and Bath Centers (acquired 2006), and Speakeasy (acquired 2007).
[2]Wal-Mart's sales estimate has been revised to improve comparability with other CE retailers. For example, the estimate now includes prerecorded audio and video media. The sales estimate does not include sales at Sam's Club.
[3]Circuit City sales exclude services and warranties.
[4]Dell sales include sales through its retail partners in the United States. Dell began selling through Best Buy, Staples, and Wal-Mart in the second half of 2007.
[5]GameStop revenue includes sales of Game Informer, the retailer's monthly gaming magazine.
[6]RadioShack sales exclude services.

Note: Includes sales of video and audio hardware, video and audio media, computers and software, and related accessories. Sales are for United States only.

Sources: Company reports, TWICE, U.S. Department of Commerce, and TNS Retail Forward.

In Canada, six new Future Shop stores, along with one closure and six relocations, and six Best Buy stores were scheduled for 2008. Best Buy entered Mexico with two to five stores in the latter part of 2008 and intended to open one or two stores in Turkey in 2010. India is also being studied, as are other countries that the company won't disclose.

Making Chinese Customers Happy Best Buy says it is moving slowly in China as it continues to study the market to find out what Chinese consumers expect and want. The new Best Buy stores will all be located in and around Shanghai, where the first Chinese Best Buy opened in early 2007. That first Chinese store already ranks among the company's top 50 in revenue globally. The company will maintain its dual-brand strategy with Best Buy and Five Star as it has in Canada with Best Buy and Future Shop. The company says it wants to maintain separate cultures, but offer the same value, believing this is the best way to meet local needs. Best Buy expects to launch online sales in China within the next two years.

New Plans for Canada's Future Shop Best Buy's other banner in Canada, Future Shop, is going after appliance and game sales more aggressively. Also, Best Buy plans to test a new Future Shop prototype that focuses on home networking:

▶ Future Shop has launched a strategy to double its market share in appliances. The retailer is investing in new associate training initiatives to boost service levels by bringing in new regional appliance managers and certified product experts. Additionally, appliance departments are being enhanced to improve the shopping experience. Future Shop also has added KitchenAid to its appliance lineup both in stores and online to beef up its premium appliance offer.

▶ Following a trial at six Future Shop stores in Calgary, Best Buy said it plans to expand its used games test offering to all of its Future Shop stores in Canada.

▶ In summer 2008, Future Shop introduced a new prototype store designed to help customers connect all the gadgets in their homes. A feature of the new store will be an area that demonstrates, for example, how a computer in the bedroom can be linked to the TV in the living room along with the audio system throughout the house. To support home-network project sales, associates are being trained to provide more customized service in home networking. If tests are successful, Best Buy has said it will export the upgraded Future Shop store internationally, including the United States.

▶ Also in 2008, Future Shop announced that it was launching its own installation service for home theaters, computers, and car audio systems. The service, called ConnectPro, provides expert staff to help customers optimize electronics purchases and ensure that all components work together seamlessly.

Setting the Stage for European Entry As a first step toward launching consumer electronics stores in Europe, Best Buy in June 2008 closed on a 50 percent joint venture interest in Carphone Warehouse, the company's British-based partner in its Best Buy Mobile rollout in the United States. The two companies believe the new venture provides the best platform for Carphone Warehouse (**www.carphonewarehouse.com**) to expand its business model into new geographic areas and for Best Buy to enter the European consumer electronics market, the fastest-growing category in European retailing for the last five years according to Best Buy.

Carphone Warehouse currently operates more than 2,400 stores in nine European countries under the Carphone Warehouse and Phone House nameplates. The venture was subject to approval by Carphone Warehouse shareholders and went into effect in August 2008.

Locations of First British Stores Announced Best Buy opened the first four locations in London as the initial phase of its entry into Great Britain. The retailer chose Bath Road Retail Park in Slough, Two Rivers Retail Park in Staines, Thurrock Retail Park in Essex, and Enfield Retail Park in north London as the locations for the first phase of its British entry. Press reports in Great Britain indicated that Best Buy could open up to 20 stores in that country during 2009–2010, with a focus on out-of-town stores in retail parks, although the retailer did not rule out a flagship store in central London.

Loyalty and Service Programs Go International In 2008, Best Buy expanded its Geek Squad (**www.geeksquad.com**) service to Great Britain through its relationship with Carphone Warehouse. Additionally, the Best Buy Reward Zone loyalty program was recently extended to Canada. Points are earned that can be cashed in on future purchases. Exclusive offers, sweepstakes, and members-only sales are other perks of the program. As in the United States, where the program has operated since 2003, there is no membership fee, but one purchase per year is required to keep the account active.

Other Best Buy Growth Initiatives

Mobile Format Sees Heavy Investment Best Buy Mobile, developed in concert with Carphone Warehouse, continues to be a key strategic platform for Best Buy. There were 14 standalone Best Buy Mobile stores in operation as of mid-2008. Best Buy planned to open about 400 Mobile stores in the United States by the end of 2009. Most are in locations close to Best Buy stores. There were 599 Best Buy Mobile areas inside U.S. Best Buy stores at the end of May 2008, compared with 181 at the end of 2007. The company expanded the store-within-a-store concept to the majority of U.S. Best Buy stores as of the end of 2008. Best Buy Mobile is based on the European model, wherein multiple service providers and expanded cell phone choices are available under one roof. The company's goal is to grow its share of the mobile market from about 2 percent to double digits within the next five years, and it reported that same-store sales of mobile phones in upgraded stores grew 50 percent in the first quarter of fiscal 2009.

Apple Departments Grow in U.S. Stores and China Apple (**www.apple.com**) and Best Buy got back together in 2007 after an eight-year hiatus. As of mid-2008, Best Buy operated about 500 store-within-a-store Apple areas in the United States, up from about 200 the year before, and approached the 600-boutique goal announced at the start of 2008, or about two-thirds of Best Buy's U.S. stores. The remaining stores, at about 30,000 square feet, apparently are too small for the Apple areas. Stores that include the areas range from about 35,000 to 50,000 square feet. The Apple shops vary in design by store and are designed much like Apple's own stores, with light wood displays housing an embedded display screen. The latest layouts feature mini-theaters embedded in black walls with glowing Apple logos and stereo sound systems. In April 2008, Best Buy opened its first Apple store-within-a-store in China, inside the four-floor, 80,000-square-foot Shanghai store. Apple sent two technical consultants to the store to provide support.

Dell Completes the Computer Assortment In January 2008, Best Buy began selling a wide assortment of Dell computers in all its U.S. stores. With the addition of Dell, Best Buy's computer offer includes the five leading computer brands in the United States under one roof. In April 2008, Dell products also were added to the assortment at Best Buy Canadian stores.

Exploring New Categories and More Private Brands Best Buy plans to move further into product categories and brands that are outside its traditional consumer electronics offer:

▶ The retailer has opened store-within-a-store formats inside stores in the Twin Cities area of Minnesota and several other locations around the country that are focused on musical instruments beyond the basic electronic keyboards available in all its stores, such as guitars, drums, microphones, and amplifiers. The first opened in November 2007 and the second in February 2008. The company planned to extend the concept to about 85 stores by the end of fiscal 2008. The in-store shops occupy about 2,500 square feet of retail space and offer about 1,000 products.

▶ The company is expanding its private-brand business, providing more affordable alternative products in categories such as home theater, computers, and MP3 players. Best Buy also is increasing its range of private-label Insignia brand flat-panel TVs, including smaller, value-oriented TVs. It has said it will begin selling its private-brand products to other retailers internationally, including retailers in countries where Best Buy currently does not operate.

▶ In 2007, to attract more women to the stores, Best Buy introduced new exclusive product lines such as Liz Claiborne accessory bags and cases and home theater furniture designed by Maria Yee. This idea is being extended with the addition of upscale accessories from designer Steve Madden and the Betseyville collection by Betsey Johnson. The collections include edgy designs for cell phone, digital camera, and iPod cases.

Better Serving Hispanics During 2007, Best Buy made several changes to better serve its growing Hispanic customers. In September, the company launched a transactional, bilingual Web site. On the new site, Hispanic customers can browse, research, and order products in their preferred language. A click-to-call feature connects customers with a Spanish-speaking customer service representative if personal help is needed. The company also has added bilingual signage at more than 220 stores, developed Spanish advertising materials, and hired more sales and call center associates who are fluent in Spanish.

Free Help for Customers Best Buy has partnered with FixYa.com (**www.fixya.com**), a Web site that allows customers to seek help with technology issues. Customers can access FixYa.com from the Best Buy Web site and post questions for experts in troubleshooting forums. The site also has manuals and troubleshooting guides for more than a half-million products. The FixYa technical support community provides customers with a way to resolve many issues without having to pay for Geek Squad service.

E-Waste Recycling Tested Best Buy has been testing a free electronics recycling program in more than 100 stores. Beginning in June 2008, consumers could bring up to two products per day into the stores for recycling at no charge. TVs, microwaves, and air conditioners were among the items accepted in the program. Best Buy is evaluating the test before deciding about adding the program to other stores.

Wal-Mart's Consumer Electronics Expansion

Today, Best Buy's marketing-leading position faces an ever-stronger challenge from Wal-Mart for the sales of consumer electronics in the United States. Wal-Mart is pulling out all the stops to dominate the consumer electronics business. The retailer has completed the rollout of its new consumer electronics department configuration and continues to add new brands. The company also is exploring the addition of an installation component to its offer. The rollout is designed in part to lure more mid-to-higher-income shoppers—customers the retailer needs if it wants to overtake Best Buy as the largest U.S. electronics retailer.

The chainwide rollout of the new configuration began in May 2007; the company announced in 2008 that the redesign had been completed. The redesign efforts were focused on improving the customer CE experience in the stores and included:

▶ Wider, more navigable aisles.

▶ A large increase in the assortment of HD TVs, including more full-HD (1080p resolution) and larger models.

▶ A wider assortment of Blu-ray players and media, including brands such as Magnavox, Panasonic, and Samsung to go along with the Sony brand.

▶ A new computer display center, along with an expanded assortment of accessories and signage designed to help shoppers choose the right computer for their needs.

▶ An increased assortment of global positioning system (GPS) devices, including the addition of the Magellan brand to go along with the previous offering of Garmin and TomTom devices.

▶ A wider assortment of digital picture frames.

▶ Improved product information to provide customers with basic information about consumer electronics, necessary add-ons, and developments such as the conversion to all-digital signals.

▶ A social gaming area where game players can try out their favorite games (available in 800 stores).

▶ New gift cards for music, digital albums, and ring tones along with more exclusive CDs and DVDs with popular music artists.

▶ New lower prices in the photo services center, including 15¢ prints for orders of 100 prints or more.

▶ Increased levels of training for associates on consumer electronics and requirements to better handle customer questions and concerns, an area where Wal-Mart has fallen short in the past.

One area that has been a competitive weakness for Wal-Mart, compared with consumer electronics specialists, has been the lack of an installation or maintenance/repair offer. However, Wal-Mart recently indicated interest in expanding into consumer electronics services. Consumer electronics products such as HD TV and home theater systems are complex, and there is a clear need for installation and other services related to the sales of these products. Best Buy's Geek Squad has been a key competitive advantage for that company. If Wal-Mart follows suit, it has the potential to neutralize a major differentiator of Best Buy. This may boost sales among the well heeled, although Wal-Mart better do its homework before adding an installed offer, whose operating model is starkly different from product selling and requires different management and technical knowledge skill sets. It also requires managing a nationwide network of technicians. Best Buy had stumbled in implementing its installed services offer.

Wal-Mart has already taken the first step toward developing a service offer. It is teaming up with Dell to launch a pilot program in the Dallas area. Fifteen "Solution Centers by Dell" at stores in Dallas provide home setup services for HD TVs, home theater installations, computer repair services, and wireless technology advice. Wal-Mart is using the pilot program to learn what customers need and expect in the realm of technology services and says it has no current plans to expand the program.

Questions

1. What can *any* retailer learn from this case?
2. Analyze the data in Tables 1 and 2. What conclusions do you reach?
3. Why has Best Buy been able to weather the recent economic downturn better than many other retailers?
4. Does Best Buy do a good job with regard to the retailing concept? Explain your answer.
5. Assess Best Buy's global strategy.
6. Look at the Web site of Best Buy's Geek Squad (**www.geeksquad.com**). Why has this service business done so well?
7. From a strategic planning perspective, what must Best Buy do in the future to try to stay ahead of Wal-Mart? Will it be able to do so in the long run? Explain your answers.

PART 2 Situation Analysis

In Part Two, we talk about the organizational missions, ownership and management alternatives, goods/service categories, and objectives of a broad range of retail institutions. By understanding the unique attributes of these institutions, better retail strategies can be developed and implemented.

Chapter 4 examines the characteristics of retail institutions on the basis of ownership type: independent, chain, franchise, leased department, vertical marketing system, and consumer cooperative. We also discuss the methods used by manufacturers, wholesalers, and retailers to obtain control in a distribution channel. A chapter appendix has additional information on franchising.

Chapter 5 describes retail institutions in terms of their strategy mix. We introduce three key concepts: the wheel of retailing, scrambled merchandising, and the retail life cycle. Strategic responses to the evolving marketplace are noted. Several strategy mixes are then studied, with food and general merchandise retailers reviewed separately.

Chapter 6 focuses on nonstore retailing, electronic retailing, and nontraditional retailing approaches. We cover direct marketing, direct selling, vending machines, the World Wide Web, video kiosks, and airport retailing. The dynamics of Web-based retailing are featured. A chapter appendix covers the emerging area of multi-channel retailing in more depth.

Source: © Tom Hahn/iStockPhoto.

4

Retail Institutions by Ownership

Chapter Objectives

1. To show the ways in which retail institutions can be classified

2. To study retailers on the basis of ownership type, and to examine the characteristics of each

3. To explore the methods used by manufacturers, wholesalers, and retailers to exert influence in the distribution channel

In 1954, Ray Kroc, then a salesman of milkshake mixers, visited two of his best customers—Maurice and Richard McDonald—in San Bernadino, California. The McDonald brothers had just purchased eight Multimixers, one of Kroc's largest orders; and he wanted to observe their operations in action. What Kroc saw astounded him. Although many burger places of that era were dirty and had poor reputations, the McDonald brothers' operation was clean and modern, and there was even a burger production line.

The following day, Kroc approached the brothers and came to an agreement with them whereby he would sell franchises for $950 each and 1.4 percent of the sales while the brothers received 0.5 percent. Kroc became so obsessed with the business that he was often quoted as saying, "I believe in God, family, and McDonald's." He soon bought out the McDonald brothers.

As the chain expanded, Kroc was careful to ensure that the eating experience was identical at each restaurant. McDonald's (**www.mcdonalds.com**) controlled franchisees' menu items and décor, automated many of the operations, instituted training programs at its Hamburger University, and developed precise operating standards. Kroc passed on his obsession with quality and cleanliness to franchisees. An often quoted motto was, "if you have time to lean, you have time to clean."

Currently, McDonald's foreign sales are far larger than its domestic sales and are growing at a faster rate. In addition, it is aiming at Starbucks. As of 2009, McDonald's planned to have its 14,000 U.S. units equipped with automatic espresso machines. McDonald's projects an additional $1 billion in annual sales revenue from its new coffees.[1]

Source: Reprinted by permission of Susan Berry, Retail Image Consulting, Inc.

OVERVIEW

A **retail institution** is the basic format or structure of a business. In the United States, there are 2.3 million retail firms (including those with no payroll, whereby only the owner and/or family members work for the firm), and they operate 3.1 million establishments. An institutional discussion shows the relative sizes and diversity of different kinds of retailing, and indicates how various retailers are affected by the external environment. Institutional analysis is important in strategic planning when selecting an organizational mission, choosing an ownership alternative, defining the goods/service category, and setting objectives.

We examine retail institutions from these perspectives: ownership (Chapter 4); store-based strategy mix (Chapter 5); and nonstore-based, electronic, and non-traditional retailing (Chapter 6). Figure 4-1 shows a breakdown. An institution may be correctly placed in more than one category: A department store may be part of a chain, have a store-based strategy, accept mail-order sales, and operate a Web site.

Please interpret the data in Chapters 4, 5, and 6 carefully. Because some institutional categories are not mutually exclusive, care should be taken in combining statistics so double counting does not occur. We have drawn in the data in these chapters from a number of government and nongovernment sources. Although data are as current as possible, not all information corresponds to a common date. *Census of Retail Trade* data are only collected twice a decade. Furthermore, our numbers are based on the broad interpretation of retailing used in this book, which includes auto repair shops, hotels and motels, movie theaters, real-estate brokers, and others who sell to the final consumer.

FIGURE 4-1

A Classification Method for Retail Institutions

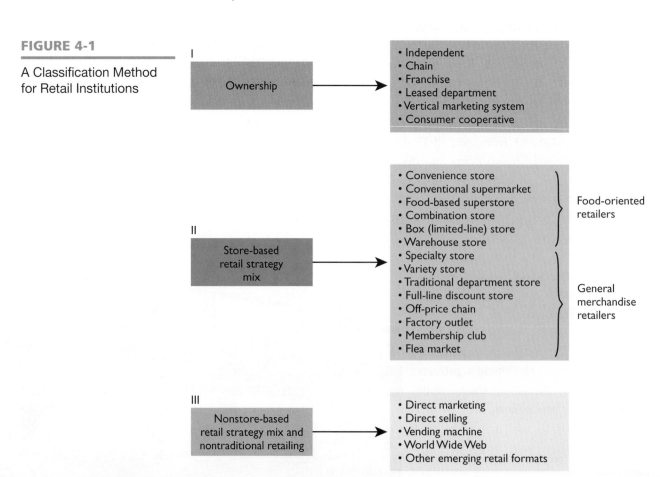

Retail Institutions Characterized by Ownership

Retail firms may be independently owned, chain-owned, franchisee-operated, leased departments, owned by manufacturers or wholesalers, or consumer-owned.

Although retailers are primarily small (three-quarters of all stores are operated by firms with one outlet and more than one-half of all firms have two or fewer paid employees), there are also very large retailers. The five leading U.S. retailers total more than $650 billion in sales and employ 3 million people. Ownership opportunities abound. According to the U.S. Census Bureau (**www.census.gov**), women own 1.1 million retail firms, African Americans (men and women) 110,000 retail firms, Hispanic Americans (men and women) 175,000 retail firms, and Asian Americans (men and women) 170,000 retail firms.

Each ownership format serves a marketplace niche, if the strategy is executed well:

▶ Independent retailers capitalize on a very targeted customer base and please shoppers in a friendly, informal way. Word-of-mouth communication is important. These retailers should not try to serve too many customers or enter into price wars.

▶ Chain retailers benefit from their widely known image and from economies of scale and mass promotion possibilities. They should maintain their image chainwide and not be inflexible in adapting to changes in the marketplace.

▶ Franchisors have strong geographic coverage—due to franchisee investments—and the motivation of franchisees as owner-operators. They should not get bogged down in policy disputes with franchisees or charge excessive royalty fees.

▶ Leased departments enable store operators and outside parties to join forces and enhance the shopping experience, while sharing expertise and expenses. They should not hurt the image of the store or place too much pressure on the lessee to bring in store traffic.

▶ A vertically integrated channel gives a firm greater control over sources of supply, but it should not provide consumers with too little choice of products or too few outlets.

▶ Cooperatives provide members with price savings. They should not expect too much involvement by members or add facilities that raise costs too much.

Independent

The Business Owner's Toolkit (**www.toolkit.com**) is an excellent resource for the independent retailer.

An **independent** retailer owns one retail unit. There are 2.2 million independent U.S. retailers—accounting for about one-third of total store sales. Seventy percent of independents are run by the owners and their families; these firms generate just 3 percent of U.S. store sales (averaging under $100,000 in annual revenues) and have no paid workers (there is no payroll).

The high number of independents is associated with the **ease of entry** into the marketplace, due to low capital requirements and no, or relatively simple, licensing provisions for many small retail firms. The investment per worker in retailing is usually much lower than for manufacturers, and licensing is pretty routine. Each year, tens of thousands of new retailers, mostly independents, open in the United States.

The ease of entry—which leads to intense competition—is a big factor in the high rate of failures among newer firms. One-third of new U.S. retailers do not survive the first year, and two-thirds do not continue beyond the third year. Most failures involve independents. Annually, thousands of U.S. retailers (of all sizes) file for bankruptcy protection—besides the thousands of small firms that simply close.[2]

The U.S. Small Business Administration (SBA) has a Small Business Development Center (SBDC) to assist current and prospective small business owners (**www.sba.gov/aboutsba/sbaprograms/sbdc**). There are 63 lead SBDCs (at least one in every state) and more than 1,100 local SBDCs, satellites, and specialty centers. The purpose "is to provide management assistance to current and prospective small business owners." Centers offer individual counseling, seminars and training sessions, conferences, and information through the Internet, as well as in person and by phone. The SBA also has many free downloadable publications at its Web site. See Figure 4-2.

CAREERS IN RETAILING

Pat: Senior Vice-President and Chief Operating Officer

A bachelor's degree in marketing helped Pat grasp the business elements of retailing, but she says that working part time in a retail store during high school was a great learning experience. She suggests that "you have to try it to know if you like it" and adds that retailing is the greatest opportunity to experience the real career world at a young age.

After graduating college, Pat entered a national department store chain's training program to become an assistant buyer, where she learned all aspects of retailing. She attributes this experience to the excellent start she got in her full-time retailing career. Pat then discovered that the aspect of the job she enjoyed the most was working with people—selling merchandise, as opposed to buying it. She made a career move to the specialty store environment because she felt it offered her more opportunity to focus on what she liked to do the most. Supervisors helped Pat evaluate and change her supervisory style; they taught her to focus on the human side of the business.

Though every day is different, Pat typically works from 8:00 A.M. to 6:00 P.M., Monday through Friday. She also works some weekends. Her typical work activities include phone and E-mail communication, planning, presentations, evaluating financial reports, managing people, and negotiating. She also does some national and international travel.

Pat currently earns $200,000-plus annually. In addition, she receives employer-provided benefits such as health, dental, and life insurance; a 401(k) and retirement plan; and stock options. Her advice to career seekers is simple: "Helping customers is what it's all about. If you like working with people, retail is a good career for you."

Source: Reprinted by permission of the National Retail Federation.

FIGURE 4-2

Useful Online Publications for Small Retailers
Go to **www.sba.gov/tools/ resourcelibrary/publications** and download any of the U.S. Small Business Administration publications at this Web site. They're free!

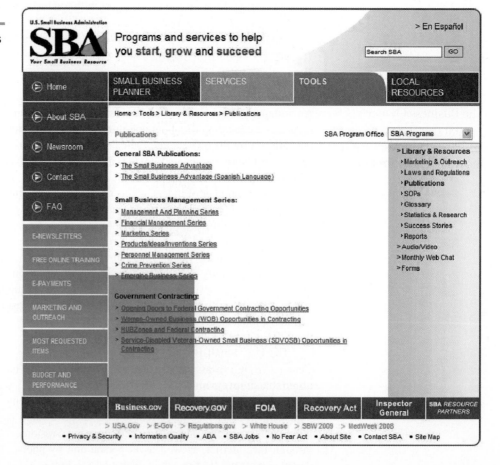

Read the Aunt Annie's story (**www.auntieannes. com/corporate_ingredients. aspx**)—from a farmer's market to a worldwide chain.

COMPETITIVE ADVANTAGES AND DISADVANTAGES OF INDEPENDENTS
Independent retailers have a variety of advantages and disadvantages. These are among their advantages:

▶ There is flexibility in choosing retail formats and locations, and in devising strategy. Because only one location is involved, detailed specifications can be set for the best site and a thorough search undertaken. Uniform location standards are not needed, as they are for chains, and independents do not have to worry about stores being too close together. Independents have great latitude in selecting target markets. Because they often have modest goals, small segments may be selected rather than the mass market. Assortments, prices, hours, and other factors are then set consistent with the segment.

▶ Investment costs for leases, fixtures, workers, and merchandise can be held down; and there is no duplication of stock or personnel functions. Responsibilities are clearly delineated within a store.

▶ Independents frequently act as specialists in a niche of a particular goods/service category. They are then more efficient and can lure shoppers interested in specialized retailers.

▶ Independents exert strong control over their strategies, and the owner-operator is typically on the premises. Decision making is centralized and layers of management personnel are minimized.

▶ There is a certain image attached to independents, particularly small ones, that chains cannot readily capture. This is the image of a personable retailer with a comfortable atmosphere in which to shop.

▶ Independents can easily sustain consistency in their efforts because only one store is operated.

▶ Independents have "independence." They do not have to fret about stockholders, board of directors meetings, and labor unrest. They are often free from unions and seniority rules.

▶ Owner-operators typically have a strong entrepreneurial drive. They have made a personal investment and there is a lot of ego involvement: "No matter what the size, to succeed in your business you will need to be good at what you do, know how to market it to get customers, be able to keep proper records of expenses and payments, and plan for weeks and even months ahead."[3]

These are some of the disadvantages of independent retailing:

▶ In bargaining with suppliers, independents may not have much power because they often buy in small quantities. Suppliers may even bypass them. Reordering may be hard if minimum order requirements are high. Some independents, such as hardware stores, belong to buying groups to increase their clout.

▶ Independents generally cannot gain economies of scale in buying and maintaining inventory. Due to financial constraints, small assortments are bought several times per year. Transportation, ordering, and handling costs per unit are high.

▶ Operations are labor intensive, sometimes with little computerization. Ordering, taking inventory, marking items, ringing up sales, and bookkeeping may be done manually. This is less efficient than computerization. In many cases, owner-operators are unwilling or unable to spend time learning how to set up and apply computerized procedures.

▶ Due to the relatively high costs of TV ads and the broad geographic coverage of magazines and some newspapers (too large for firms with one outlet), independents are limited in their access to certain media. Yet, there are various promotion tools available for creative independents (see Chapter 19).

▶ A crucial problem for independents is overdependence on the owner. All decisions may be made by that person, and there may be no management continuity when the owner-boss is ill, on vacation, or retires. Long-run success and employee morale can be affected by this. As one small business owner said: "There is no one that is going to work like me. I am always running at 65 miles per hour."[4]

▶ A limited amount of time is allotted to long-run planning, because the owner is intimately involved in daily operations of the firm.

Chain

A **chain** retailer operates multiple outlets (store units) under common ownership; it usually engages in some level of centralized (or coordinated) purchasing and decision making. In the United States, there are roughly 110,000 retail chains that operate about 900,000 establishments.

There are more than 6,000 U.S. Radio Shack (**www. radioshack.com**) stores and 700 wireless kiosks. See if there is one near you.

The relative strength of chain retailing is great, even though the number of firms is small (less than 5 percent of all U.S. retail firms). Chains today operate nearly 30 percent of retail establishments, and because stores in chains tend to be considerably larger than those run by independents, chains account for roughly two-thirds of total U.S. store sales and employment. Although the majority of chains have 5 or fewer outlets, the several hundred firms with 100 or more outlets account for more than 60 percent of U.S. retail sales. Some big U.S. chains have at least 1,000 outlets each. There are also many large foreign chains. See Figure 4-3.

The dominance of chains varies by type of retailer. Chains generate at least 75 percent of total U.S. category sales for department stores, discount department stores, and grocery stores. On the other hand, stationery, beauty salon, furniture, and liquor store chains produce far less than 50 percent of U.S. retail sales in their categories.

Sears' Kenmore brand (**www.kenmore.com**) is so powerful that many different appliances are sold under the Kenmore name.

COMPETITIVE ADVANTAGES AND DISADVANTAGES OF CHAINS

There are abundant competitive advantages for chain retailers:

▶ Many chains have bargaining power due to their purchase volume. They receive new items when introduced, have orders promptly filled, get sales support, and obtain volume discounts. Large chains may also gain exclusive rights to certain items and have goods produced under the chains' brands.
▶ Chains achieve cost efficiencies when they buy directly from manufacturers and in large volume, ship and store goods, and attend trade shows sponsored by suppliers to learn about new offerings. They can sometimes bypass wholesalers, with the result being lower supplier prices.

FIGURE 4-3

Louis Vuitton: A Powerhouse of Upscale Retailing

Louis Vuitton (**www.louisvuitton. com**) is a huge French-based chain with stores in more than 60 different markets around the world. Its Web site may be accessed in nine languages.

Source: Reprinted by permission of Susan Berry, Retail Image Consulting, Inc.

TECHNOLOGY IN RETAILING

Power Sellers on eBay

According to Alexa (**www.alexa.com**), a Web-based marketing research firm, in any given month, eBay (**www. ebay.com**) draws tens of millions of visitors to its site, exceeding Amazon.com's (**www.amazon.com**), AOL's (**www.aol.com**), Microsoft's (**www.microsoft.com**), and Flickr's (**www.flickr.com**) average number of visitors.

Today, many of eBay's "power sellers"—firms that sell at least $1,000 of goods each month—are traditional retailers that use this channel to expand their trading areas beyond their store-based locations. Other power sellers sell goods only online and use eBay to supplement their regular jobs or as a main source of income.

eBay recently changed its fee structure to further entice the power sellers that often sell high-value goods at fixed prices. eBay's revamped fee structure has reduced its upfront listing fees for goods priced at $100 or more by up to 25 percent and by up to 50 percent on store items that have fixed sale prices. eBay has also offered its power sellers discounts of up to 15 percent of eBay's final value fee. To further win over power sellers, eBay has also changed its search technology. As of March 2008, the items that buyers are most likely to see first are those from eBay's most reputable sellers.

Source: Catherine Holahan, "eBay Courts 'Power Sellers,'" **www. businessweek.com/print/technology/content/jan2008** (January 29, 2008).

▶ Efficiency is gained by sharing warehouse facilities, purchasing standardized store fixtures, and so on; by centralized buying and decision making; and by other practices. Chains typically give headquarters executives broad authority for personnel policies and for buying, pricing, and advertising decisions.
▶ Chains use computers in ordering merchandise, taking inventory, forecasting, ringing up sales, and bookkeeping. This increases efficiency and reduces overall costs.
▶ Chains, particularly national or regional ones, can take advantage of a variety of media, from TV to magazines to newspapers.
▶ Most chains have defined management philosophies, with detailed strategies and clear employee responsibilities. There is continuity when managerial personnel are absent or retire because there are qualified people to fill in and succession plans in place. See Figure 4-4.
▶ Many chains expend considerable time on long-run planning and assign specific staff to planning on a permanent basis. Opportunities and threats are carefully monitored.

FIGURE 4-4

Anthropologie: Keeping Its Eye on the Ball
As the Web site of this innovative chain (**www.anthropologie.com**) notes, "People who make up Anthropologie—our store staff, designers, merchandisers, art directors, and production teams—truly love what they do. Every day we create warm and engaging store, catalog, and Web site environments for our customers to visit. Our success comes from the Anthropologie community and the atmosphere of creative freedom and collaboration we have taken great care to nurture over the years."

Source: Reprinted by permission of Susan Berry, Retail Image Consulting, Inc.

Chain retailers do have a number of disadvantages:

▶ Once chains are established, flexibility may be limited. New nonoverlapping store locations may be hard to find. Consistent strategies must be maintained throughout all units, including prices, promotions, and product assortments. It may be difficult to adapt to local diverse markets.

▶ Investments are higher due to multiple leases and fixtures. The purchase of merchandise is more costly because a number of store branches must be stocked.

▶ Managerial control is complex, especially for chains with geographically dispersed branches. Top management cannot maintain the control over each branch that independents have over their single outlet. Lack of communication and delays in making and enacting decisions are particular problems.

▶ Personnel in large chains often have limited independence because there are several management layers and unionized employees. Some chains empower personnel to give them more authority.

Franchising[5]

The International Franchise Association (**www.franchise.org**) is a leading source of information about franchising.

Franchising involves a contractual arrangement between a *franchisor* (a manufacturer, wholesaler, or service sponsor) and a retail *franchisee,* which allows the franchisee to conduct business under an established name and according to a given pattern of business. The franchisee typically pays an initial fee and a monthly percentage of gross sales in exchange for the exclusive rights to sell goods and services in an area. Small businesses benefit by being part of a large, chain-type retail institution.

In **product/trademark franchising**, a franchisee acquires the identity of a franchisor by agreeing to sell the latter's products and/or operate under the latter's name. The franchisee operates rather autonomously. There are certain operating rules, but the franchisee sets store hours, chooses a location, and determines facilities and displays. Product/trademark franchising represents two-thirds of retail franchising sales. Examples are auto dealers and many gasoline service stations.

With **business format franchising**, there is a more interactive relationship between a franchisor and a franchisee. The franchisee receives assistance on site location, quality control, accounting systems, startup practices, management training, and responding to problems besides the right to sell goods and services. Prototype stores, standardized product lines, and cooperative advertising foster a level of coordination previously found only in chains. Business format franchising arrangements are common for restaurants and other food outlets, real-estate, and service retailing. Due to the small size of many franchisees, business formats account for about 80 percent of franchised outlets, although just one-third of total sales.

McDonald's (**www.mcdonalds.com/corp/franchise/franchisinghome.html**) is a good example of a business format franchise arrangement. The firm provides franchisee training at "Hamburger U," a detailed operating manual, regular visits by service managers, and brush-up training. In return for a 20-year franchising agreement with McDonald's, a traditional franchisee generally must put up a minimum of $300,000 of nonborrowed personal resources and pays ongoing royalty fees totaling at least 12.5 percent of gross sales to McDonald's. See Figure 4-5.

SIZE AND STRUCTURAL ARRANGEMENTS

Although auto and truck dealers provide more than one-half of all U.S. retail franchise sales, few sectors of retailing have been unaffected by franchising's growth. In the United States, there are 3,000 retail franchisors doing business with 340,000 franchisees. They operate 775,000 franchisee- and franchisor-owned outlets, employ several million people, and generate one-third of total store sales. In addition, hundreds of U.S.-based franchisors have foreign operations, with tens of thousands of outlets.

Nearly 80 percent of U.S. franchising sales and franchised outlets involve franchisee-owned units; the rest involve franchisor-owned outlets. If franchisees operate one outlet, they are independents; if they operate two or more outlets, they are chains. Today, a large number of franchisees operate as chains.

FIGURE 4-5

McDonald's Qualifications for Potential Franchisees

Source: Figure developed by the authors based on information in McDonald's "Frequently Asked Questions—Qualifications," **www. mcdonalds.com/corp/franchise/ faqs2/qualifications. html** (February 19, 2009).

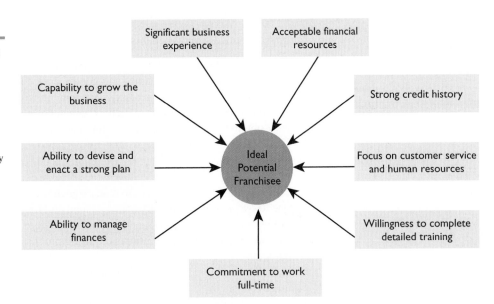

Three structural arrangements dominate retail franchising. See Figure 4-6.

1. *Manufacturer–retailer.* A manufacturer gives independent franchisees the right to sell goods and related services through a licensing agreement.
2. *Wholesaler–retailer.*
   a. *Voluntary.* A wholesaler sets up a franchise system and grants franchises to individual retailers.
   b. *Cooperative.* A group of retailers sets up a franchise system and shares the ownership and operations of a wholesaling organization.
3. *Service sponsor–retailer.* A service firm licenses individual retailers so they can offer specific service packages to consumers.

FIGURE 4-6

Structural Arrangements in Retail Franchising

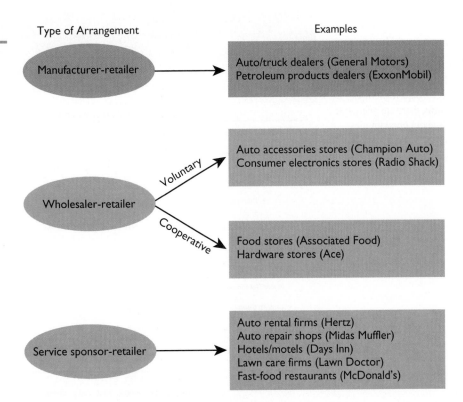

Want to learn more about what it takes to be a franchisee? Check out the Jazzercise Web site (**www. jazzercise.com/become_ franchise.htm**).

COMPETITIVE ADVANTAGES AND DISADVANTAGES OF FRANCHISING

Franchisees receive several benefits by investing in successful franchise operations:

▶ They own a retail enterprise with a relatively small capital investment.
▶ They acquire well-known names and goods/service lines.
▶ Standard operating procedures and management skills may be taught to them.
▶ Cooperative marketing efforts (such as regional or national advertising) are facilitated.
▶ They obtain exclusive selling rights for specified geographical territories.
▶ Their purchases may be less costly per unit due to the volume of the overall franchise.

Some potential problems do exist for franchisees:

▶ Oversaturation could occur if too many franchisees are in one geographic area.
▶ Due to overzealous selling by some franchisors, franchisees' income potential, required managerial ability, and investment may be incorrectly stated.
▶ They may be locked into contracts requiring purchases from franchisors or certain vendors.
▶ Cancellation clauses may give franchisors the right to void agreements if provisions are not satisfied.
▶ In some industries, franchise agreements are of short duration.
▶ Royalties are often a percentage of gross sales, regardless of franchisee profits.

The preceding factors contribute to **constrained decision making**, whereby franchisors limit franchisee involvement in the strategic planning process.

The Federal Trade Commission (FTC) has a recently revised rule regarding disclosure requirements and business opportunities (**www.ftc.gov/bcp/edu/pubs/business/franchise/ bus70.pdf**) that applies to all U.S. franchisors. It is intended to provide adequate information to potential franchisees prior to their making an investment. Although the FTC does not regularly review disclosure statements, several states do check them and may require corrections. Also, a number of states (including Arizona, California, Indiana, New Jersey, Virginia, Washington, and Wisconsin) have fair practice laws that do not permit franchisors to terminate, cancel, or fail to renew franchisees without just cause. The FTC has an excellent franchising Web site (**www.ftc.gov/bcp/franchise/netfran.shtm**), as highlighted in Figure 4-7.

FIGURE 4-7

Franchises and Business Opportunities

At the FTC's franchising site, **www. ftc.gov/ bcp/ franchise/ netfran.shtm**, there are many free downloads about opportunities— and warnings, as well.

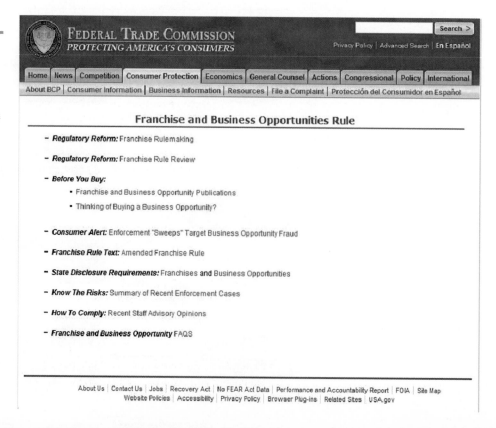

Franchisors accrue lots of benefits by having franchise arrangements:

▶ A national or global presence is developed more quickly and with less franchisor investment.
▶ Franchisee qualifications for ownership are set and enforced.
▶ Agreements require franchisees to abide by stringent operating rules set by franchisors.
▶ Money is obtained when goods are delivered rather than when they are sold.
▶ Because franchisees are owners and not employees, they have a greater incentive to work hard.
▶ Even after franchisees have paid for their outlets, franchisors receive royalties and may sell products to the individual proprietors.

Franchisors also face potential problems:

▶ Franchisees harm the overall reputation if they do not adhere to company standards.
▶ A lack of uniformity among outlets adversely affects customer loyalty.
▶ Intrafranchise competition is not desirable.
▶ The resale value of individual units is injured if franchisees perform poorly.
▶ Ineffective franchised units directly injure franchisors' profitability that results from selling services, materials, or products to the franchisees and from royalty fees.
▶ Franchisees, in greater numbers, are seeking to limit franchisors' rules and regulations.

Further information on franchising is contained in the appendix at the end of this chapter. Also, visit our Web site for a lot of links on this topic (**www.pearsonhighered. com/berman**).

Leased Department

A **leased department** is a department in a retail store—usually a department, discount, or specialty store—that is rented to an outside party. The leased department proprietor is responsible for all aspects of its business (including fixtures) and normally pays a percentage of sales as rent. The store sets operating restrictions for the leased department to ensure overall consistency and coordination.[6]

Leased departments are used by store-based retailers to broaden their offerings into product categories that often are on the fringe of the store's major product lines. They are most common for in-store beauty salons; banks; photographic studios; and shoe, jewelry, cosmetics, watch repair, and shoe repair departments. Leased departments are also popular in shopping center food courts. They account for $18 billion in annual department store sales. Data on overall leased department sales are not available.

Meldisco Corporation (**www.footstar.com**) runs leased shoe departments in 2,200 stores (especially Kmart and Rite Aid) and has annual leased department sales of $650 million. It owns the inventory and display fixtures, staffs and merchandises the departments, and pays a fee for the space occupied. The stores where Meldisco operates typically cover the costs of utilities, maintenance, advertising, and checkout services.

COMPETITIVE ADVANTAGES AND DISADVANTAGES OF LEASED DEPARTMENTS
From the *stores' perspective*, leased departments offer a number of benefits:

▶ The market is enlarged by providing one-stop customer shopping.
▶ Personnel management, merchandise displays, and reordering items are undertaken by lessees.
▶ Regular store personnel do not have to be involved.
▶ Leased department operators pay for some expenses, thus reducing store costs.
▶ A percentage of revenues is received regularly.

There are also some potential pitfalls, from the stores' perspective:

▶ Leased department operating procedures may conflict with store procedures.
▶ Lessees may adversely affect stores' images.
▶ Customers may blame problems on the stores rather than on the lessees.

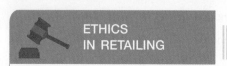

Simon Property: Resolving a Gift Card Dispute

For several years, the gift card practices of Simon Property Group (**www.simon.com**), the largest U.S. shopping center developer, have been criticized by the Attorneys General of a number of states—including Connecticut, Massachusetts, New Hampshire, New York, Illinois, and Georgia. Simon charges cardholders a $2.50 per year fee and a $5 fee for lost or stolen cards.

In October 2007, Simon won a ruling from the U.S. Court of Appeals for the Second Circuit. Simon's attorneys successfully argued that nationally chartered banks do not have to obey state gift card rules as to fees and other terms. As a result, Simon shifted its gift cards to the American Express (**www.americanexpress.com**) network. Simon also gave banks more control over pricing

when a federal regulator said that the way its credit card program was initially set up, it was not viewed as a bank product.

As of 2009, more than 35 states had enacted rules relating to gift card expiration dates or fees. In general, these state laws ban monthly service fees on gift cards after a period of nonuse. For example, the Illinois law states that expiration dates, fees, and a toll-free customer service number must be easy to see. Illinois law requires that unused funds on gift cards must revert to the state, which then tries to find the card's purchaser.

Sources: "Gift Cards and Gift Certificates Statutes and Recent Legislation," **www.ncsl.org/programs/banking/GiftCardsandCerts. htm** (July 29, 2008); and H. Michael Jalili, "A New Gift Product from Simon," *American Banker* (October 31, 2007), p. 7.

For *leased department operators*, there are these advantages:

▶ Stores are known, have steady customers, and generate immediate sales for leased departments.
▶ Some costs are reduced through shared facilities, such as security equipment and display windows.
▶ Their image is enhanced by their relationships with popular stores.

Lessees face these possible problems:

▶ There may be inflexibility as to the hours they must be open and the operating style.
▶ The goods/service lines are usually restricted.
▶ If they are successful, stores may raise rent or not renew leases when they expire.
▶ In-store locations may not generate the sales expected.

CPI (**www.cpicorp.com**) has flourished with its leased department relationship at Sears.

An example of a thriving long-term lease arrangement is one between CPI Corporation and Sears. In exchange for space in more than 1,000 U.S. and Canadian Sears stores, CPI pays 15 percent of its sales. Its annual sales per square foot are much higher than Sears' overall average. CPI's agreement with Sears has been renewed several times. Annual revenues through Sears exceed $275 million.[7]

Vertical Marketing System

A **vertical marketing system** consists of all the levels of independently owned businesses along a channel of distribution. Goods and services are normally distributed through one of these systems: independent, partially integrated, and fully integrated. See Figure 4-8.

In an *independent vertical marketing system*, there are three levels of independently owned firms: manufacturers, wholesalers, and retailers. Such a system is most often used if manufacturers or retailers are small, intensive distribution is sought, customers are widely dispersed, unit sales are high, company resources are low, channel members seek to share costs and risks, and task specialization is desirable. Independent vertical marketing systems are used by many stationery stores, gift shops, hardware stores, food stores, drugstores, and many other firms. They are the leading form of vertical marketing system.

With a *partially integrated system*, two independently owned businesses along a channel perform all production and distribution functions. It is most common when

FIGURE 4-8

Vertical Marketing
Systems: Functions and
Ownership

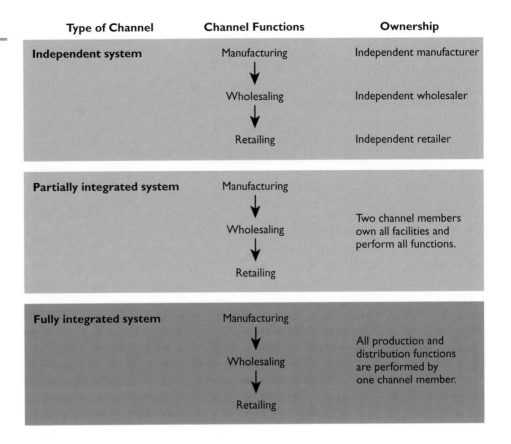

Type of Channel	Channel Functions	Ownership
Independent system	Manufacturing ↓ Wholesaling ↓ Retailing	Independent manufacturer Independent wholesaler Independent retailer
Partially integrated system	Manufacturing ↓ Wholesaling ↓ Retailing	Two channel members own all facilities and perform all functions.
Fully integrated system	Manufacturing ↓ Wholesaling ↓ Retailing	All production and distribution functions are performed by one channel member.

Kroger, the food retailer, manufactures more than 6,000 food and nonfood products in its 41 plants (**www.thekrogerco.com/ operations/operations.htm**).

a manufacturer and a retailer complete transactions and shipping, storing, and other distribution functions in the absence of a wholesaler. This system is most apt if manufacturers and retailers are large, selective or exclusive distribution is sought, unit sales are moderate, company resources are high, greater channel control is desired, and existing wholesalers are too expensive or unavailable. Partially integrated systems are often used by furniture stores, appliance stores, restaurants, computer retailers, and mail-order firms.

Through a *fully integrated system*, one firm performs all production and distribution functions. The firm has total control over its strategy, direct customer contact, and exclusivity over its offering; it also keeps all profits. This system can be costly and requires a lot of expertise. In the past, vertical marketing was employed mostly by manufacturers, such as Avon and Sherwin-Williams. At Sherwin-Williams, its own 3,350 paint stores account for nearly two-thirds of total company sales.[8] Today, more retailers (such as Kroger) use fully integrated systems for at least some products.

Some firms use **dual marketing** (a form of *multi-channel retailing*) and engage in more than one type of distribution arrangement. In this way, firms appeal to different consumers, increase sales, share some costs, and retain a good degree of strategic control. Here are two examples. (1) Sherwin-Williams sells Sherwin-Williams' paints at company stores. It sells Dutch Boy paints in home improvement stores, full-line discount stores, hardware stores, and others. See Figure 4-9. (2) In addition to its traditional standalone outlets, Dunkin' Donuts and Baskin-Robbins share facilities in a number of locations, so as to attract more customers and increase the revenue per transaction.

Besides partially or fully integrating a vertical marketing system, a firm can exert power in a distribution channel because of its economic, legal, or political strength; superior knowledge and abilities; customer loyalty; or other factors. With **channel control**, one member of a distribution channel dominates the decisions made in that channel due to the power it possesses. Manufacturers, wholesalers, and retailers each have a combination of tools to improve their positions relative to one another.

FIGURE 4-9

Sherwin-Williams' Dual
Marketing System

Manufacturers exert control by franchising, developing strong brand loyalty, pre-ticketing items (to designate suggested prices), and using exclusive distribution with retailers that agree to certain standards in exchange for sole distribution rights in an area. *Wholesalers* exert influence when they are large, introduce their own brands, sponsor franchises, and are the most efficient members in the channel for tasks such as processing reorders. *Retailers* exert clout when they represent a large percentage of a supplier's sales volume and when they foster their own brands. Private brands let retailers switch vendors with no impact on customer loyalty, as long as the same product features are included.

Strong long-term channel relationships often benefit all parties. They lead to scheduling efficiencies and cost savings. Advertising, financing, billing, and other tasks are dramatically simplified.

Consumer Cooperative

As an REI member (**www. rei.com/help/membership. html**), look at what $20 will get you!

A **consumer cooperative** is a retail firm owned by its customer members. A group of consumers invests, elects officers, manages operations, and shares the profits or savings that accrue.[9] In the United States, there are several thousand such cooperatives, from small buying clubs to Recreational Equipment Inc. (REI), with $1.4 billion in annual sales. Consumer cooperatives have been most popular in food retailing. Yet, the 500 or so U.S. food cooperatives account for less than 1 percent of total grocery sales.

Consumer cooperatives exist for these basic reasons: Some consumers feel they can operate stores as well as or better than traditional retailers. They think existing retailers inadequately fulfill customer needs for healthful, environmentally safe products. They also assume existing retailers make excessive profits and that they can sell merchandise for lower prices.

REI sells outdoor recreational equipment to 3.5 million members and other customers. It has more than 80 stores, a mail-order business, and a Web site (**www. rei.com**). Unlike other cooperatives, REI is run by a professional staff that adheres to policies set by the member-elected board. There is a $20 one-time membership fee, which allows customers to shop at REI, vote for directors, and share in profits (based on the amount spent by each member). REI's goal is to distribute a regular dividend to members.

Cooperatives are only a small part of retailing because they involve consumer initiative and drive, consumers are usually not expert in retailing functions, cost savings and low selling prices are often not as expected, and consumer boredom in running a cooperative frequently occurs.

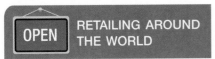

RETAILING AROUND THE WORLD | Franchising Re/Max Overseas

Re/Max (**www.remax.com**) is a real-estate brokerage franchise network with nearly 7,000 offices worldwide (4,300 in the United States, 650 in Canada, and 2,000 in the rest of the world). These franchises have a staff of 118,000 real-estate agents.

Re/Max has expanded in many foreign countries through the use of master franchise holders who purchase franchising rights for an entire foreign country. For example, franchising rights for Poland, Serbia, and Montenegro have been purchased by separate groups of investors. Those investors then sell individual franchises to foreign entrepreneurs.

The master franchisors have had to adapt the Re/Max model to the European marketplace. Real-estate salespeople in Europe commonly receive 80 percent of the total commissions and pay the balance as a desk and management fee to their brokerage firms. In contrast, Canadian salespeople commonly receive 95 percent of the total commission. There is also no multiple listing service throughout Europe, and there is little cooperation among brokers.

Although financial terms vary, the average investment in a Re/Max franchise is $113,000, which includes a $20,000 initial franchise fee. The average initial contract is for five years with an additional five-year renewal option. Passive ownership by investors is allowed, but it's discouraged.

Sources: "RE/MAX Franchising Rights Purchased for Poland," *RE/MAX Press Release* (March 16, 2007); "RE/MAX Franchising Rights Acquired for Serbia and Montenegro," *RE/MAX Press Release* (March 20, 2007); and "RE/MAX International: World Franchising," **www.worldfranchising.com/franchises.remax-international. html** (December 27, 2008).

Chapter **Summary**

1. *To show the ways in which retail institutions can be classified.* There are 2.3 million retail firms in the United States operating 3.1 million establishments. They can be grouped on the basis of ownership, store-based strategy mix, and nonstore-based and nontraditional retailing. Many retailers can be placed in more than one category. This chapter deals with retail ownership. Chapters 5 and 6 report on the other classifications.

2. *To study retailers on the basis of ownership type, and to examine the characteristics of each.* About 70 percent of U.S. retail establishments are independents, each with one store. This is mostly due to the ease of entry. Independents' competitive advantages include their flexibility, low investments, specialized offerings, direct strategy control, image, consistency, independence, and entrepreneurial spirit. Disadvantages include limited bargaining power, few economies of scale, labor intensity, reduced media access, overdependence on owner, and limited planning.

Chains are multiple stores under common ownership, with some centralized buying and decision making. They account for nearly 30 percent of U.S. retail outlets but two-thirds of retail sales. Chains' advantages are bargaining power, functional efficiencies, multiple-store operations, computerization, media access, well-defined management, and planning. They face these potential problems: inflexibility, high investments, reduced control, and limited independence of personnel.

Franchising embodies arrangements between franchisors and franchisees that let the latter do business under established names and according to detailed rules. It accounts for one-third of U.S. store sales. Franchisees benefit from small investments, popular company names, standardized operations and training, cooperative marketing, exclusive selling rights, and volume purchases. They may face constrained decision making, resulting in oversaturation, lower than promised profits, strict contract terms, cancellation clauses, short-term contracts, and royalty fees. Franchisors benefit by expanding their businesses, setting franchisee qualifications, improving cash flow, outlining procedures, gaining motivated franchisees, and receiving ongoing royalties. They may suffer if franchisees hurt the company image, do not operate uniformly, compete with one another, lower resale values and franchisor profits, and seek greater independence.

Leased departments are in-store locations rented to outside parties. They usually exist in categories on the fringe of their stores' major product lines. Stores gain from the expertise of lessees, greater traffic, reduced costs, merchandising support, and revenues. Potential store disadvantages are conflicts with lessees and adverse effects on store image. Lessee benefits are well-known store names, steady customers, immediate sales, reduced expenses, economies of scale, and an image associated with the store. Potential lessee problems are operating inflexibility, restrictions on items sold, lease nonrenewal, and poorer results than expected.

Vertical marketing systems consist of all the levels of independently owned firms along a channel of distribution. Independent systems have separately owned manufacturers, wholesalers, and retailers. In partially integrated systems, two separately owned firms, usually manufacturers and retailers, perform all production and distribution functions. With fully integrated systems, single firms do all production and distribution functions. Some firms use dual marketing, whereby they are involved in more than one type of system.

Consumer cooperatives are owned by their customers, who invest, elect officers, manage operations, and share savings or profits. They account for a tiny piece of retail sales. Cooperatives are formed because consumers think they can do retailing functions, traditional retailers are inadequate, and prices are high. They have not grown much because consumer initiative is required, expertise may be lacking, expectations have frequently not been met, and boredom occurs.

3. *To explore the methods used by manufacturers, wholesalers, and retailers to exert influence in the distribution channel.* Even without an integrated vertical marketing system, channel control can be exerted by the most powerful firm(s) in a channel. Manufacturers, wholesalers, and retailers each have ways to increase their impact. Retailers' influence is greatest when they are a large part of their vendors' sales and private brands are used.

Key Terms

retail institution (p. 102)
independent (p. 103)
ease of entry (p. 103)
chain (p. 106)
franchising (p. 108)

product/trademark franchising (p. 108)
business format franchising (p. 108)
constrained decision making (p. 110)
leased department (p. 111)

vertical marketing system (p. 112)
dual marketing (p. 113)
channel control (p. 113)
consumer cooperative (p. 114)

Questions for Discussion

1. What are the characteristics of each of the ownership forms discussed in this chapter?

2. Do you believe that independent retailers will soon disappear from the retail landscape? Explain your answer.

3. Why does the concept of ease of entry usually have less impact on chain retailers than on independent retailers?

4. How can an independent retailer overcome the problem of little computerization?

5. What difficulties might an independent encounter if it tries to expand into a chain?

6. What competitive advantages and disadvantages do regional chains have in comparison with national chains?

7. What are the similarities and differences between chains and franchising?

8. From the *franchisor's* perspective, under what circumstances would product/trademark franchising be advantageous? When would business format franchising be better?

9. Why would a supermarket want to lease space to an outside operator rather than run a business, such as dry cleaning, itself? What would be its risks in this approach?

10. What are the pros and cons of Sherwin-Williams using dual marketing?

11. How could a small independent restaurant increase its channel power?

12. Would REI be as successful if it operated as a traditional chain? Explain your answer.

Web **Exercise**

Visit the Web site of Subway (www.subway.com), one of the largest retail franchisors in the world. Based on the information you find there, would you be interested in becoming a Subway franchisee? Why or why not?

Note: Stop by our Web site (www.pearsonhighered.com/berman) to experience a number of highly interactive,

appealing Web exercises based on actual company demonstrations, and sample materials related to retailing.

Appendix The Dynamics of Franchising

This appendix is presented because of franchising's strong retailing presence and the exciting opportunities in franchising. Over the past two decades, annual U.S. franchising sales have more than tripled! We go beyond the discussion of franchising in Chapter 4 and provide information on managerial issues in franchising and on franchisor–franchisee relationships.

Consider this, for example: In 1999, Tariq and Kamran Farid opened their first Edible Arrangements store in East Haven, Connecticut. The initial franchised store opened during 2001 in Waltham, Massachusetts. Edible Arrangements was listed in a 2003 *Wall Street Journal* article as one of the "Twenty-five franchises that may surprise you." Now, due to franchising, Edible Arrangements has more than 900 stores worldwide, almost all franchised. The firm's niche is clear, as described at its Web site (**www.ediblearrangements.com**): "Edible Arrangements has a fresh fruit bouquet to make any occasion special—from birthdays, anniversaries, and congratulations to business events and client gifts. Our bouquets are made fresh with premium fruit arranged in a variety of stunning displays."

Look at Blockbuster's "Franchising" section of its Web site (**www.blockbuster. com/corporate/franchise**).

How about Blockbuster? Although it has a base of company-owned outlets, it also has nearly 1,500 franchised stores. Consider this:

> If you become a Blockbuster franchisee, you will be in very good company. Today, we have more than 8,000 corporate and franchise stores in 23 countries. The Blockbuster franchising initiative is one of the fastest and most exciting ways to grow in attractive new markets and in underserved existing markets. Our franchisees get to associate with a world leader in home entertainment. In return, we're assured high-quality, on-site management to service customers. Financial requirements are a minimum net worth of $650,000 and a minimum liquidity of $100,000 for the first store.[1]

U.S. franchisors are situated in well over 160 countries, a number that is rising due to these factors: U.S. firms see the foreign market potential. Franchising is accepted as a retailing format in more nations. Trade barriers are fewer due to such pacts as the North American Free Trade Agreement, which makes it easier for firms based in the United States, Canada, and Mexico to operate in each other's marketplaces.

Here are four Web sites for you to get more information on franchising. And remember, we have a special listing of franchising links at our Web site (**www. pearsonhighered.com/berman**):

▶ Federal Trade Commission (**www.ftc.gov/bcp/edu/pubs/consumer/invest/inv05.shtm**).
▶ International Franchise Association (**www.franchise.org**).
▶ Franchising.org (**www.franchising.org**).
▶ Small Business Administration (**www.sba.gov/smallbusinessplanner/start/ buyafranchise**).

Managerial Issues in Franchising

Franchising appeals to franchisees for several reasons. Most franchisors have easy-to-learn, standardized operating methods that they have perfected. New franchisees do not have to learn from their own trial-and-error method. Franchisors often have facilities where franchisees are trained to operate equipment, manage employees, keep records, and improve customer relations; there are usually follow-up field visits.

A new outlet of a nationally advertised franchise (such as Burger King) can attract a large customer following rather quickly and easily because of the reputation of the firm. And not only does franchising result in good initial sales and profits, it also reduces franchisees' risk of failure *if the franchisees affiliate with strong, supportive franchisors.*

What kind of individual is best suited to being a franchisee? This is what one expert says:

One of the myths that has been perpetuated is that franchise ownership is easy. This is just simply not true! While the franchisor will give the start-up training and offer ongoing support, you, the franchisee, must be prepared to manage the business. While some franchises may lend themselves to absentee ownership, most are best run by hands-on management. You must be willing to work harder than you have perhaps ever worked before. Forty-hour weeks are also a myth, particularly in the start-up phase of the business. It is more like 60- to 70-hour weeks. You must also be willing to mop floors, empty garbage, fire employees, and handle upset customers.[2]

What makes McDonald's such an admired franchise operator? Read on:

Being a McDonald's Owner/Operator offers you many advantages—from the training, and the support of a solid organization, to the opportunity to own a thriving and successful business. Essentially, here's what you receive when you become a McDonald's Owner/Operator:

▶ With McDonald's unique approach to training and support, you are in business for yourself, but not by yourself.
▶ Use of the trademarks and operating system of the number one brand in the world.
▶ The tools to help you in your business: local and national support in the areas of operations, training, advertising, marketing, human resources, real-estate, construction, purchasing, and equipment purchasing and maintenance.
▶ The enjoyment that comes from working with people, from your restaurant crew to your customers and community.
▶ The opportunity to contribute to the success of McDonald's: Big Mac, Filet-O-Fish, and Egg McMuffin sandwiches have all been developed by owner/operators.
▶ Personal and business growth and satisfaction, both as an individual owner/operator and as a member of McDonald's respected worldwide organization.[3]

Investment and startup costs for a franchised outlet can be as low as a few thousand dollars for a personal service business to as high as several million dollars for a hotel. In return for its expenditures, a franchisee gets exclusive selling rights for an area; a business format franchisee gets training, equipment and fixtures, and support in site selection, supplier negotiations, advertising, and so on. One-half of U.S. business format franchisors require franchisees to be owner-operators and work full-time. Besides receiving fees and royalties from franchisees, franchisors may sell goods and services to them. This may be required; more often, for legal reasons, such purchases are at the franchisees' discretion (subject to franchisor specifications). Each year, franchisors sell billions of dollars worth of items to franchisees.

Table A4-1 shows the franchise fees, startup costs, and royalty fees for new franchisees at 10 leading franchisors in various business categories. Financing support—either through in-house financing or third-party financing—is offered by most of the firms cited in Table A4-1. In addition, with its guaranteed loan program, the U.S. Small Business Administration is a good financing option for prospective franchisees, and some banks offer special interest rates for franchisees affiliated with established franchisors.

Franchised outlets can be bought (leased) from franchisors, master franchisees, or existing franchisees. Franchisors sell either new locations or company-owned outlets (some of which may have been taken back from unsuccessful franchisees). At times, they sell the rights in entire regions or counties to master franchisees, which then deal with individual franchisees. Existing franchisees usually have the right to sell their units if they first offer them to their franchisor, if potential buyers meet all financial and other criteria, and/or if buyers undergo training. Of interest to prospective franchisees is the emphasis a firm places on franchisee-owned outlets versus franchisor-owned ones. This indicates the commitment to franchising. As indicated in Table 4-1, leading franchisors typically own a small percentage of outlets.

TABLE A4-1   The Costs of Becoming a New Franchisee with Selected Franchisors (as of 2005)

Franchising Company	Total Startup Costs (Including Franchise Fee)	Franchise Fee	Royalty Fee as a % of Sales	Franchisee-Owned Outlets as a % of All Outlets	Offers Financing Support
Aamco Transmissions	$196,800–$252,400	$31,500	7.5	100	Third party
Carvel Ice Cream	$46,000–$388,700	$30,000	$1.93/gallon	100	Third party
Fantastic Sams	$100,500–$230,100	$25,000–$35,000	Varies	100	Third party
Jazzercise	$2,990–$33,100	$500-$1,000	up to 20	99+	None
LA Weight Loss	$84,600–$149,000	$20,000	7	99+	In-house and third party
Medicine Shoppe	$74,300–$253,400	$10,000–$18,000	2–5.5	97	In-house
Pearle Vision	$108,600–$492,400	$10,000-$30,000	7	45	In-house and third party
Petland	$550,500–$1,500,000	$30,000	4.5	97	Third party
Super 8 Motels	$278,900–$2,900,000	Varies	5.5	100	In-house and third party
UPS Store	$170,800–$279,400	$29,950	5	100	In-house and third party

Source: Computed by the authors from "2008 Franchise 500 Rankings," **www.entrepreneur.com/franchise500.**

One last point regarding managerial issues in franchising concerns the failure rate of new franchisees. For many years, it was believed that success as a franchisee was a "sure thing"—and much safer than starting a business—due to the franchisor's well-known name, its experience, and its training programs. However, some recent research has shown franchising to be as risky as opening a new business. Why? Some franchisors have over-saturated the market and not provided promised support, and unscrupulous franchisors have preyed on unsuspecting investors.

With the preceding in mind, Figure A4-1 has a checklist by which potential franchisees can assess opportunities. In using the checklist, franchisees should also obtain full prospectuses and financial reports from all franchisors under consideration, and talk to existing franchise operators and customers.

FIGURE A4-1

A Checklist of Questions for Prospective Franchisees Considering Franchise Opportunities

✓ What are the required franchise fees: initial fee, advertising appropriations, and royalties?
✓ What degree of technical knowledge is required of the franchisee?
✓ What is the required investment of time by the franchisee? Does the franchisee have to be actively involved in the day-to-day operations of the franchise?
✓ How much control does the franchisor exert in terms of materials purchased, sales quotas, space requirements, pricing, the range of goods sold, required inventory levels, and so on?
✓ Can the franchisee tolerate the regimentation and rules of the franchisor?
✓ Are the costs of required supplies and materials purchased from the franchisor at market value, above market value, or below market value?
✓ What degree of name recognition do consumers have of the franchise? Does the franchisor have a meaningful advertising program?
✓ What image does the franchise have among consumers and among current franchisees?
✓ What are the level and quality of services provided by the franchisor: site selection, training, bookkeeping, human relations, equipment maintenance, and trouble-shooting?
✓ What is the franchisor policy in terminating franchisees? What are the conditions of franchise termination? What is the rate of franchise termination and nonrenewal?
✓ What is the franchisor's legal history?
✓ What is the length of the franchise agreement?
✓ What is the failure rate of existing franchises?
✓ What is the franchisor's policy with regard to company-owned and franchisee-owned outlets?
✓ What policy does the franchisor have in allowing franchisees to sell their business?
✓ What is the franchisor's policy with regard to territorial protection for existing franchisees? With regard to new franchisees and new company-owned establishments?
✓ What is the earning potential of the franchise during the first year? The first five years?

Franchisor–Franchisee Relationships

Taco John's (www.tacojohns. com) prides itself on its collegial relationships with franchisees.

Many franchisors and franchisees have good relationships because they share goals for company image, operations, the goods and services offered, cooperative ads, and sales and profit growth. This two-way relationship is illustrated by the actions of Taco John's International (**www.tacojohns.com**), a firm with about 425 franchised pizza restaurants in more than 25 states. As the franchisor says at its Web site:

Our customers are our franchisees, their employees, and their customers. Everything we do is aimed at helping franchisees better serve customers:

> *Franchise Development.* The design of our restaurants is the result of careful, independent research and hands-on development with company prototypes. We provide conceptual floor plans and site sketches. We also provide construction consultation.
> *Marketing and Advertising.* The marketing department is responsible for planning, producing, and distributing effective and impactful programs and materials to help you grow your business and build the Taco John's brand image. Our national campaign is funded by Taco John's, suppliers, and franchisees. Each restaurant also belongs to a regional marketing co-op to participate in advertising that would otherwise not be cost-effective. Special promotions for individual restaurants are part of Taco John's local store marketing program.
> *Franchise Business Consultants.* Each restaurant is assigned a franchise business consultant.
> *Human Resources and Training.* Our human resources department will provide you with materials to help attract, motivate, and retain people. The training department teaches franchisees and their team members our operating system and how to best deliver the Taco John's promise to every customer.
> *Your New Restaurant Opening.* A grand opening team will work with you in your restaurant, just before and during your opening.
> *Menu Development.* The menu development department's primary activities include conducting consumer research, coordinating operations testing and evaluation, and documenting customer feedback during initial in-store testing.
> *Purchasing and Distribution.* Purchasing and distribution personnel negotiate with manufacturers and distribution centers to make sure our system receives the best possible quality, service, and purchase prices. A nationwide system of approved distributors warehouse all products necessary to operate a restaurant. Weekly orders are delivered to each restaurant's door.

Nonetheless, for several reasons, tensions do sometimes exist between various franchisors and their franchisees:

> The franchisor–franchisee relationship is not one of employer to employee. Franchisor controls are often viewed as rigid.
> Many agreements are considered too short by franchisees. Nearly half of U.S. agreements are 10 years or less (one-sixth are 5 years or less), usually at the franchisor's request.
> The loss of a franchise generally means eviction, and the franchisee gets nothing for "goodwill."
> Some franchisors believe their franchisees do not reinvest enough in their outlets or care enough about the consistency of operations from one outlet to another.
> Franchisors may not give adequate territorial protection and may open new outlets near existing ones.
> Franchisees may refuse to participate in cooperative advertising programs.
> Franchised outlets up for sale must usually be offered first to franchisors, which also have approval of sales to third parties.
> Some franchisees believe franchisor marketing support is low.

▶ Franchisees may be prohibited from operating competing businesses.
▶ Restrictions on suppliers may cause franchisees to pay higher prices and have limited choices.
▶ Franchisees may band together to force changes in policies and exert pressure on franchisors.
▶ Sales and profit expectations may not be realized.

Tensions can lead to conflicts—even litigation. Potential negative franchisor actions include terminating agreements; reducing marketing support; and adding red tape for orders, information requests, and warranty work. Potential negative franchisee actions include terminating agreements, adding competitors' products, refusing to promote goods and services, and not complying with data requests. Each year, business format franchisors terminate the contracts of 10 percent of the franchisee-owned stores that opened within the preceding five years.

Although franchising has been characterized by franchisors having more power than franchisees, this inequality is being reduced. First, franchisees affiliated with specific franchisors have joined together. For example, the Association of Kentucky Fried Chicken Franchisees and National Coalition of Associations of 7-Eleven Franchisees represent thousands of franchisees. Second, large umbrella groups, such as the American Franchisee Association (**www.franchisee.org**) and the American Association of Franchisees & Dealers (**www.aafd.org**), have been formed. Third, many franchisees now operate more than one outlet, so they have greater clout. Fourth, there has been a substantial rise in litigation.

Better communication and better cooperation help resolve problems. Here are two progressive tactics: First, the International Franchise Association has an ethics code for its franchisor and franchisee members, founded on these principles (**www.franchise.org/ industrysecondary.aspx?id=3554**):

> Every franchise relationship is founded on the mutual commitment of both parties to fulfill their obligations under the franchise agreement. Each party will fulfill its obligations, will act consistent with the interests of the brand, and will not act so as to harm the brand and system. This willing interdependence between franchisors and franchisees, and the trust and honesty upon which it is founded, has made franchising a worldwide success as a strategy for business growth. Honesty embodies openness, candor, and truthfulness. Franchisees and franchisors commit to sharing ideas and information and to face challenges in clear and direct terms. Our members will be sincere in word, act, and character—reputable and without deception.

Second, the National Franchise Mediation Program seeks to resolve franchisor–franchisee disagreements: "Disputes between franchisors and franchisees continue to arise. On occasion, those disputes result in mutually destructive litigation. This procedure is designed to encourage more effective and efficient management of those disputes. Since inception, a success rate of about 80 percent has been achieved in mediations in which the franchisee agreed to participate, with many more cases resolved without a mediator. Parties report that, through the Program, they are resolving many disputes through informal negotiations without either party needing to report to formal mediation.[4]

5

Retail Institutions by Store-Based Strategy Mix

Chapter Objectives

1. To describe the wheel of retailing, scrambled merchandising, and the retail life cycle, and to show how they can help explain the performance of retail strategy mixes

2. To discuss ways in which retail strategy mixes are evolving

3. To examine a wide variety of food-oriented retailers involved with store-based strategy mixes

4. To study a wide range of general merchandise retailers involved with store-based strategy mixes

Ikea (**www.ikea.com**) is the world's leading home-furnishings retailer with nearly 300 stores in about three dozen countries, including 35 U.S. stores. Since the firm's founding, Ikea has offered a wide range of home furnishings and accessories of good design at attractive price levels.

Although Ikea has had stores in the United States for just over 20 years, Ingvar Kamprad began selling furniture in Almhult, Sweden, under the Ikea name nearly 60 years ago. Kamprad got the idea for producing ready-to-assemble furniture to reduce his delivery costs when the milk wagon that was used to ship his small orders changed its route. In 1953, he purchased an empty factory and opened a showroom. Five years later, when he opened a large store, Kamprad cleverly added roof racks so customers could more easily take their purchases home.

Today, Ikea strives to facilitate the shopping process. Most stores have a spacious and open layout, a cafeteria, and even a playroom that offers baby-sitting assistance for customers. The layout encourages browsing and increases impulse purchases. The inexpensive cafeteria, which serves Swedish-style delicacies (such as potatoes with meat balls and lingonberry juice at low prices), encourages customers to spend more time on the premises. The playroom enables shoppers to go through the store without their children tagging behind them.

Ikea has consistently been named on *Working Mother* magazine's annual listing of "100 Best Companies for Working Mothers," due to its family-friendly program for workers. It has also been recognized on *Fortune*'s "100 Best Companies to Work For" and in *Fast Company*'s "Fast 50" for its environmentally responsible products.[1]

Source: Reprinted by permission of TNS Retail Forward.

OVERVIEW

In Chapter 4, retail institutions were described by type of ownership. In this chapter, we discuss three key concepts in planning retail strategy mixes: the wheel of retailing, scrambled merchandising, and the retail life cycle. We then look at how retail strategies are evolving and study the basic strategies of several store-based institutions. Chapter 6 deals with nonstore-based, electronic, and nontraditional strategies.

Considerations in Planning a Retail Strategy Mix

A retailer may be categorized by its **strategy mix**, the firm's particular combination of store location, operating procedures, goods/services offered, pricing tactics, store atmosphere and customer services, and promotional methods.

Store location refers to the use of a store or nonstore format, placement in a geographic area, and the kind of site (such as a shopping center). Operating procedures include the kinds of personnel employed, management style, store hours, and other factors. The goods/services offered may encompass several product categories or just one; quality may be low, medium, or high. Pricing refers to a retailer's use of prestige pricing (creating a quality image), competitive pricing (setting prices at the level of rivals), or penetration pricing (underpricing other retailers). Store atmosphere and customer services are reflected by the physical facilities and personal attention provided, return policies, delivery, and other factors. Promotion involves activities in such areas as advertising, displays, personal selling, and sales promotion. By combining these elements, a retailer can develop a unique strategy.

To flourish today, a retailer should strive to be dominant in some way. The firm may then reach **destination retailer** status—whereby consumers view the company as distinctive enough to become loyal to it and go out of their way to shop there. We tend to link "dominant" with "large." Yet, both small and large retailers can dominate in their own way. As follows, there are many ways to be a destination retailer, and combining two or more approaches can yield even greater appeal for a given retailer:

- ▶ Be price-oriented and cost-efficient to attract price-sensitive shoppers.
- ▶ Be upscale to attract full-service, status-conscious consumers.
- ▶ Be convenient to attract those wanting shopping ease, nearby locations, or long hours.
- ▶ Offer a dominant assortment in the product lines carried to appeal to consumers interested in variety and in-store shopping comparisons.
- ▶ Offer superior customer service to attract those frustrated by the decline in retail service.
- ▶ Be innovative or exclusive and provide a unique way of operating (such as kiosks at airports) or carry products/brands not stocked by others to reach people who are innovators or bored.

Before looking at specific strategy mixes, let's look at three concepts that help explain the use of these mixes: the wheel of retailing, scrambled merchandising, and the retail life cycle—as well as the ways in which retail strategies are evolving.

The Wheel of Retailing

According to the **wheel of retailing** theory, retail innovators often first appear as low-price operators with low costs and low profit margin requirements. Over time, the innovators upgrade the products they carry and improve their facilities and customer service (by adding better-quality items, locating in higher-rent sites, providing credit and delivery, and so on), and prices rise. As innovators mature, they become vulnerable to new discounters with lower costs, hence, the wheel of retailing.[2] See Figure 5-1.

The wheel of retailing is grounded on four principles: (1) There are many price-sensitive shoppers who will trade customer services, wide selections, and convenient locations for lower prices. (2) Price-sensitive shoppers are often not loyal and will switch to retailers with lower prices. However, prestige-sensitive customers enjoy shopping at retailers with

FIGURE 5-1

The Wheel of Retailing

As a low-end retailer upgrades its strategy to increase sales and profit margins, a new form of discounter takes its place.

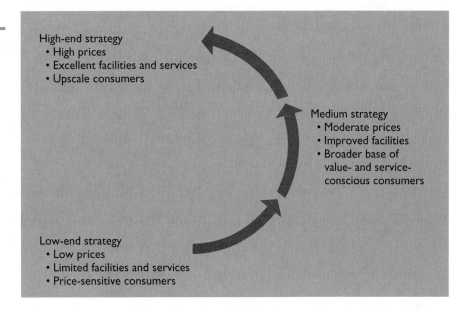

High-end strategy
• High prices
• Excellent facilities and services
• Upscale consumers

Medium strategy
• Moderate prices
• Improved facilities
• Broader base of value- and service-conscious consumers

Low-end strategy
• Low prices
• Limited facilities and services
• Price-sensitive consumers

high-end strategies. (3) New institutions are frequently able to have lower operating costs than existing institutions. (4) As retailers move up the wheel, they typically do so to increase sales, broaden the target market, and improve their image.

For example, when traditional department store prices became too high for many consumers, the growth of the full-line discount store (led by Wal-Mart) was the result. The full-line discount store stressed low prices because of such cost-cutting techniques as having a small sales force, situating in lower-rent store locations, using inexpensive fixtures, emphasizing high stock turnover, and accepting only cash or check payments for goods. Then, as full-line discount stores prospered, they typically sought to move up a little along the wheel. This meant enlarging the sales force, improving locations, upgrading fixtures, carrying a greater selection of merchandise, and accepting credit. These improvements led to higher costs, which led to somewhat higher prices. The wheel of retailing

---

CAREERS IN RETAILING

Jay: Manager of College Relations

During college, Jay was a sales associate for a regional discount store chain. At that time, he decided that he didn't want to make his career in discount retailing and thought the department-store format would be more in line with his goals.

For his first position out of training as a merchandise manager, Jay was put in a department he knew little about. But he remembered the lesson he had learned in the management training program and relied on his people. Jay involved the staff in the buying process; they knew the customer and could tell him what they always ran out of, what would beat the competition, and so on. The department earned a 25 percent gain in Jay's first year. Jay earned a promotion in just 18 months to a senior merchandise manager, where he was managing and buying a larger merchandise volume. Under his leadership, the department enjoyed four

years of strong growth. Ultimately, he became a district personnel and operations manager, which involved multiple relocations.

Jay then moved into human resources as a regional college relations manager. He worked out of his home and visited colleges, exhibiting, recruiting, and interviewing candidates for internships and full-time positions. In his current position, Jay is the manager of college relations at the corporate office. He oversees recruitment programs across the country and does some local recruiting for entry-level management and corporate positions, as well as corporate and store-based interns. In this position, Jay is exposed to all and the highest levels within the company. He earns more than $100,000 per year.

Source: Reprinted by permission of the National Retail Federation.

again came into play as newer discounters, such as off-price chains, factory outlets, and permanent flea markets, expanded to satisfy the needs of the most price-conscious consumer. More recently, we have witnessed the birth of discount Web retailers, some of which have very low costs because they do not have "bricks-and-mortar" facilities.

As indicated in Figure 5-1, the wheel of retailing reveals three basic strategic positions: low end, medium, and high end. The medium strategy may have some difficulties if retailers in this position are not perceived as distinctive: "An unfocused firm stuck in the mushy middle of its category is ripe picking for competition. As an industry matures, competitors come in and steal market share from above you as well as below you. This is what happened to Sears. While Sears stayed in the middle of the department-store market, the department-store industry was diverging into two separate industries, one at the low end and one at the high end."[3] Figure 5-2 shows the opposing alternatives in considering a strategy mix.

The wheel of retailing suggests that established firms should be wary in adding services or converting a strategy from low end to high end. Because price-conscious shoppers are not usually loyal, they are apt to switch to lower-priced firms. Furthermore, retailers may then eliminate the competitive advantages that have led to profitability. This occurred with the retail catalog showroom, which is now a defunct format.

Scrambled Merchandising

Whereas the wheel of retailing focuses on product quality, prices, and customer service, scrambled merchandising involves a retailer increasing its width of assortment (the number of different product lines carried). **Scrambled merchandising** occurs when a retailer adds goods and services that may be unrelated to each other and to the firm's original business. See Figure 5-3.

Scrambled merchandising is popular for many reasons: Retailers want to increase overall revenues; fast-selling, highly profitable goods and services are usually the ones added; consumers make more impulse purchases; people like one-stop shopping; different target markets may be reached; and the impact of seasonality and competition is reduced. In addition, the popularity of a retailer's original product line(s) may fall, causing it to scramble to maintain and grow the customer base. Blockbuster, due to the advent of pay-per-view and premium movie channels on cable and satellite TV, as well as competition from Netflix, now carries magazines, movie merchandise, candy, video games, game players, DVD players, and more—and it offers its own online rental service.

Where would you place AutoNation (www.autonation.com) along the wheel of retailing?

FIGURE 5-2

Retail Strategy Alternatives

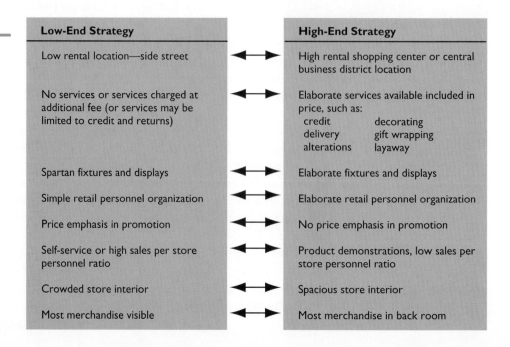

Low-End Strategy	High-End Strategy
Low rental location—side street	High rental shopping center or central business district location
No services or services charged at additional fee (or services may be limited to credit and returns)	Elaborate services available included in price, such as: credit / decorating / delivery / gift wrapping / alterations / layaway
Spartan fixtures and displays	Elaborate fixtures and displays
Simple retail personnel organization	Elaborate retail personnel organization
Price emphasis in promotion	No price emphasis in promotion
Self-service or high sales per store personnel ratio	Product demonstrations, low sales per store personnel ratio
Crowded store interior	Spacious store interior
Most merchandise visible	Most merchandise in back room

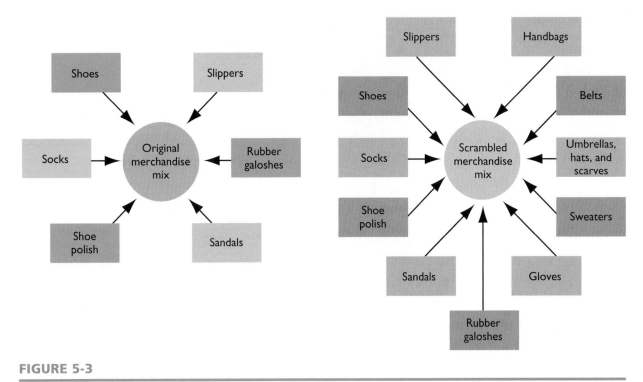

FIGURE 5-3

Scrambled Merchandising by a Show Store

How much of a practitioner of scrambled merchandising is Hammacher Schlemmer (**www. hammacherschlemmer. com**)?

Scrambled merchandising is contagious. Drugstores, bookstores, florists, video stores, and photo-developing firms are all affected by supermarkets' scrambled merchandising. A significant amount of U.S. supermarket sales are from general merchandise, health and beauty aids, and other nongrocery items, such as pharmacy items, magazines, flowers, and video rentals. In response, retailers such as drugstores are pushed into scrambled merchandising to fill the sales void caused by supermarkets. They have added toys and gift items, greeting cards, batteries, and cameras. This then creates a void for additional retailers, which are also forced to scramble.

The prevalence of scrambled merchandising means greater competition among different types of retailers and that distribution costs are affected as sales are dispersed over more retailers. There are other limitations to scrambled merchandising, including the potential lack of retailer expertise in buying, selling, and servicing unfamiliar items; the costs associated with a broader assortment (including lower inventory turnover); and the possible harm to a retailer's image if scrambled merchandising is ineffective.

The Retail Life Cycle

The **retail life cycle** concept states that retail institutions—like the goods and services they sell—pass through identifiable life stages: introduction (early growth), growth (accelerated development), maturity, and decline. The direction and speed of institutional changes can be interpreted from this concept.[4] Take a look at Figure 5-4. Figure 5-4(a) shows the business characteristics of the four stages, and Figure 5-4(b) indicates the stages in which several mall-based retail formats are now operating.

Let's examine the stages of the retail life cycle as they apply to individual institutional formats and show specific examples. During the first stage of the cycle (introduction), there is a strong departure from the strategy mixes of existing retail institutions. A firm in this stage significantly alters at least one element of the strategy mix from that of traditional competitors. Sales and then profits often rise sharply for the first firms in a category. There are risks that new institutions will not be accepted by shoppers, and there may be large initial losses due to heavy investments. At this stage, long-run success is not assured.

One institution in the innovation stage is the online grocery store. How will the format do?

FIGURE 5-4

The Retail Life Cycle

Source: TNS Retail Forward, "Mall Retailers—The Search for Growth," *Industry Outlook* (October 2001), p. 3. Reprinted by permission of TNS Retail Forward, Inc. (**www.retailforward.com**).

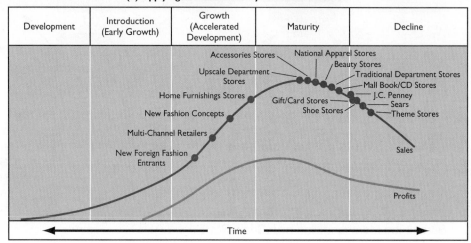

(a) Key Business Characteristics During the Stages of the Retail Life Cycle

	Life Cycle Stage			
	Introduction	Growth	Maturity	Decline
Sales	Low/growing	Rapid acceleration	High, leveling off	Dropping
Profitability	Negative to break even	High yield	High/declining	Low to break even
Positioning	Concept innovation	Special need	Broad market	Niche
Competition	None	Limited	Extensive/ saturation	Intensive/ consolidated

(b) Applying the Retail Life Cycle to Mall Retailers

Development	Introduction (Early Growth)	Growth (Accelerated Development)	Maturity	Decline

Accessories Stores
National Apparel Stores
Upscale Department Stores
Beauty Stores
Traditional Department Stores
Mall Book/CD Stores
Home Furnishings Stores
Gift/Card Stores
J.C. Penney
New Fashion Concepts
Shoe Stores
Sears
Theme Stores
Multi-Channel Retailers
New Foreign Fashion Entrants
Sales
Profits
Time

Of the big national grocery chains, only two—Royal Ahold, which owns and operates Peapod.com and Safeway—have a substantial presence online. The online merchants that rank highest are direct marketers with a long history of selling specialized food items or Web-only grocers with a national marketing base, but local and refrigerated supply chains. The leading Web-only firm is FreshDirect. To succeed in the online grocery business, retailers need to build successful supply chain and delivery models—such as FreshDirect is doing. In the high-density area of Manhattan, the difficulty of getting to the grocery store and hauling groceries home is already enough to have helped gain FreshDirect home delivery service a loyal following in the city and surrounding areas. Then, in May 2008, FreshDirect developed a program to further encourage loyalty that targets a key barrier keeping more consumers from buying groceries online—the cost of delivery. Under FreshDirect's Unlimited Delivery Pass program, customers can buy a pass for six months for $59, or for a year for $99. The pass covers delivery charges for as many online orders as the customer places during that period.[5]

See Intouch Kiosk's (**www. intouchinteractive.com**) view of the future for video kiosks.

In the second stage (growth), both sales and profits exhibit rapid growth. Existing firms expand geographically, and newer companies of the same type enter. Toward the end of accelerated development, cost pressures (to cover a larger staff, a more complex inventory system, and extensive controls) may begin to affect profits.

The interactive electronic video kiosk is an institution in the growth stage. Today, kiosks sell everything from clothing to magazines to insurance to personal computers (PCs). According to various sources, U.S. retail sales revenues generated by kiosks are expected to rise from $1.1 billion in 2001 to more than $10 billion in 2010. Worldwide, the number of installed interactive kiosks is projected to go from 246,000 kiosks in 2001 to more than 1 million kiosks in 2010.[6] This institution is examined further in Chapter 6.

The third stage (maturity) is characterized by slow sales growth for the institutional type. Although overall sales may continue to go up, that rise is at a much lower rate than during prior stages. Profit margins may have to be reduced to stimulate purchases.

Maturity is brought on by market saturation caused by the high number of firms in an institutional format, competition from newer institutions, changing societal interests, and inadequate management skills to lead mature or larger firms. Once maturity is reached, the goal is to sustain it as long as possible and not to fall into decline.

The liquor store, a form of specialty store, is an institution in the maturity stage; sales are rising, but very slowly as compared with earlier years. From 1992 to 2008, U.S. liquor store sales went up an average of 3 to 4 percent annually, which was far less than the rate for all U.S. retailers. This was due to competition from membership clubs, mail-order wine retailers, and supermarkets (in states allowing wine or liquor sales); changing lifestyles and attitudes regarding liquor; the national 21-year-old drinking age requirement; and limits on the nonalcoholic items that liquor stores are permitted to sell in some locales.

The final stage in the retail life cycle is decline, whereby industrywide sales and profits for a format fall off, many firms abandon the format, and newer formats attract consumers previously committed to that retailer type. In some cases, a decline may be hard or almost impossible to reverse. In others, it may be avoided or postponed by repositioning the institution.

After peaking in the 1980s, the retail catalog showroom declined thereafter; it vanished in 1998 as the leading firms went out of business. With this format, consumers chose items from a catalog, shopped in a warehouse setting, and wrote up orders. Why did it fade away? Many other retailers cut costs and prices, so showrooms were no longer low-price leaders. Catalogs had to be printed far in advance. Many items were slow-sellers or had low margins. Some consumers found showrooms crowded and disliked writing orders, the lack of displays reduced browsing, and the paucity of apparel goods held down revenues.[7]

On the other hand, conventional supermarkets have slowed their decline by placing new units in suburban shopping centers, redesigning interiors, lengthening store hours, having low prices, expanding the use of scrambled merchandising, closing unprofitable smaller units, and converting to larger outlets.

The life-cycle concept highlights the proper retailer response as institutions evolve. Expansion should be the focus initially, administrative skills and operations become critical in maturity, and adaptation is essential at the end of the cycle.

How Retail Institutions Are Evolving

Forward-looking firms know their individual strategies must be modified as retail institutions evolve over time. Complacency is not appropriate. Many retailers have witnessed shrinking profit margins due to intense competition and consumer interest in lower prices. This puts pressure on them to tighten internal cost controls and to promote higher-margin goods and services while eliminating unprofitable items. Let's see how firms are reacting to this formidable challenge through mergers, diversification, and downsizing, as well as cost containment and value-driven retailing.

Mergers, Diversification, and Downsizing

Some firms use mergers and diversification to sustain sales growth in a highly competitive environment (or when the institutional category in which they operate matures). For stronger firms, this trend is expected to carry over into the future.

Mergers involve the combination of separately owned retail firms. Some mergers take place between retailers of different types, such as the ones between Sears (the department store chain) and Kmart (the full-line discount store chain). Other mergers occur between similar types of retailers, such as two banks (as took place when Bank of America acquired Commerce Bank). By merging, retailers hope to jointly maximize resources, enlarge their customer base, improve productivity and bargaining power, limit weaknesses, and gain competitive advantages. It is a way for resourceful retailers to grow more rapidly and for weaker ones to enhance their long-term prospects for survival (or sell assets).

FIGURE 5-5

**west elm from
Williams-Sonoma**

Williams-Sonoma
(**www.williams-sonomainc.com**)
launched west elm as a new store
concept: By "offering a unique
combination of design, quality,
and value, west elm has grown
significantly since its 2002
launch. Customers can shop
west elm for signature products,
affordable prices, and new
decorating ideas that will update
their homes with style and ease."

Source: Reprinted by permission
of Susan Berry, Retail Image
Consulting, Inc.

Through its various
divisions, Yum! Brands
(www.yum.com) is a
restaurant retailing
dynamo.

With **diversification**, retailers become active in businesses outside their normal operations—and add stores in different goods/service categories. That is why Yum! Brands' family of restaurants now consists of KFC, Long John Silver's, Pizza Hut, and Taco Bell—franchised leaders of the quick-service chicken, seafood, pizza, and Mexican-style food categories—as well as A&W Restaurants, a more traditional quick-service franchise chain. Figure 5-5 illustrates a new Williams-Sonoma concept: west elm.

The size of many retail chains has grown due to mergers and diversification. All have not done well with that approach. Thus, even though stronger firms are expanding, we are also witnessing **downsizing**—whereby unprofitable stores are closed or divisions are sold off—by retailers unhappy with performance. Because Kmart's diversification efforts had poor results, it closed or sold its ventures outside the general merchandise store field (including Borders bookstores, Builders Square, Office Max, Payless shoe stores, and Sports Authority). It also closed a number of Kmart stores after merging with Sears.

The interest in downsizing should continue. Various retailers have overextended themselves and do not have the resources or management talent to succeed without retrenching. In their quest to open new stores, certain firms have chosen poor sites (having already saturated the best locations). Retailers such as Barnes & Noble are more interested in operating fewer, but much larger, stores and using the Web. Retailers such as supermarkets are finding they can do better if they are regional rather than national.

Cost Containment and Value-Driven Retailing

With a cost-containment approach, retailers strive to hold down both initial investments and operating costs. Many firms use this strategy because of intense competition from discounters, the need to control complicated chain or franchise operations, high land and construction costs, the volatility of the economy, and a desire to maximize productivity. Today, "retailers are examining every aspect of their businesses in order to streamline processes and costs."[8]

Save-On-Closeouts.com
has a cost-containment
approach that even
extends to its austere
Web site (www.save-
on-closeouts.com).

Cost containment can be accomplished through one or more of these approaches:

▶ Standardizing operating procedures, store layouts, store size, and product offerings.
▶ Using secondary locations, freestanding units, and locations in older strip centers and by occupying sites abandoned by others (second-use locations).

▶ Placing stores in smaller communities where building regulations are less strict, labor costs are lower, and construction and operating costs are reduced.

▶ Using inexpensive construction materials, such as bare cinder-block walls and concrete floors.

▶ Using plainer fixtures and lower-cost displays.

▶ Buying refurbished equipment.

▶ Joining cooperative buying and advertising groups.

▶ Encouraging manufacturers to finance inventories.

A driving force behind cost containment is the quest to provide good value to customers:

Value remains a retailing buzzword. Its meaning is subjective; it can mean price, quality, service, convenience, or a combination thereof. Price clearly plays a big role in what consumers buy and where they buy it. Retailers' pricing policies—particularly discounters—have encouraged consumers to shop for bargains and to distrust traditional sales. Pragmatic consumers have discovered they can get reasonable quality at everyday low prices. Price is no longer an accurate reflection of quality.[9]

Retail Institutions Categorized by Store-Based Strategy Mix

Selected aspects of the strategy mixes of 14 store-based retail institutions, divided into food-oriented and general merchandise groups, are highlighted in this section and Table 5-1. Although not all-inclusive, the strategy mixes do provide a good overview of store-based strategies. Please note that *width of assortment* is the number of different product lines carried by a retailer; *depth of assortment* is the selection within the product lines stocked. Visit our Web site (**www.pearsonhighered.com/berman**) for many links related to retail institutions' strategies.

Food-Oriented Retailers

The following food-oriented strategic retail formats are described next: convenience store, conventional supermarket, food-based superstore, combination store, box (limited-line) store, and warehouse store.

TABLE 5-1 Selected Aspects of Store-Based Retail Strategy Mixes

Type of Retailer	Location	Merchandise	Prices	Atmosphere and Services	Promotion
Food-Oriented					
Convenience store	Neighborhood	Medium width and low depth of assortment; average quality	Average to above average	Average	Moderate
Conventional supermarket	Neighborhood	Extensive width and depth of assortment; average quality; manufacturer, private, and generic brands	Competitive	Average	Heavy use of newspapers, flyers, and coupons; self-service
Food-based superstore	Community shopping center or isolated site	Full assortment of supermarket items, plus health and beauty aids and general merchandise	Competitive	Average	Heavy use of newspapers and flyers; self-service

(Continued)

TABLE 5-1   **Selected Aspects of Store-Based Retail Strategy Mixes (Continued)**

Type of Retailer	Location	Merchandise	Prices	Atmosphere and Services	Promotion
Combination store	Community shopping center or isolated site	Full selection of supermarket and drugstore items or supermarket and general merchandise; average quality	Competitive	Average	Heavy use of newspapers and flyers; self-service
Box (limited-line) store	Neighborhood	Low width and depth of assortment; few perishables; few national brands	Very low	Low	Little or none
Warehouse store	Secondary site, often in industrial area	Moderate width and low depth; emphasis on manufacturer brands bought at discounts	Very low	Low	Little or none
General Merchandise					
Specialty store	Business district or shopping center	Very narrow width and extensive depth of assortment; average to good quality	Competitive to above average	Average to excellent	Heavy use of displays; extensive sales force
Traditional department store	Business district, shopping center, or isolated store	Extensive width and depth of assortment; average to good quality	Average to above average	Good to excellent	Heavy ad and catalog use, direct mail; personal selling
Full-line discount store	Business district, shopping center, or isolated store	Extensive width and depth of assortment; average to good quality	Competitive	Slightly below average to average	Heavy use of newspapers; price-oriented; moderate sales force
Variety store	Business district, shopping center, or isolated store	Good width and some depth of assortment; below-average to average quality	Average	Below average	Use of newspapers; self-service
Off-price chain	Business district, sub-urban shopping strip, or isolated store	Moderate width but poor depth of assortment; average to good quality; lower continuity	Low	Below average	Use of newspapers; brands not advertised; limited sales force
Factory outlet	Out-of-the-way site or discount mall	Moderate width but poor depth of assortment; some irregular merchandise; lower continuity	Very low	Very low	Little; self-service
Membership club	Isolated store or secondary site (industrial park)	Moderate width but poor depth of assortment; lower continuity	Very low	Very low	Little; some direct mail; limited sales force
Flea market	Isolated site, racetrack, or arena	Extensive width but poor depth of assortment; variable quality; lower continuity	Very low	Very low	Limited; self-service

CONVENIENCE STORE

A **convenience store** is typically a well-located, food-oriented retailer that is open long hours and carries a moderate number of items. The store facility is small (only a fraction of the size of a conventional supermarket), has average to above-average prices, and average atmosphere and customer services. The ease of shopping at convenience stores and the impersonal nature of many large supermarkets make convenience stores particularly appealing to their customers, many of whom are male.

There are 145,000 U.S. convenience stores (excluding the stores where food is a small fraction of revenues), and their total annual sales are $165 billion (excluding gasoline).[10] 7-Eleven, Circle K, and Casey's General Store are major food-based U.S. convenience store chains. Speedway SuperAmerica is a leading gasoline service station-based convenience store chain with nearly 1,600 outlets.

Items such as milk, eggs, and bread once represented the major portion of sales; now sandwiches, tobacco products, snack foods, soft drinks, general merchandise, beer and wine, ATMs, and lottery tickets are also key items. And gasoline generates 30 percent or more of total sales at most of the convenience stores that carry it. See Figure 5-6.

The convenience store's advantages are its usefulness when a consumer does not want to travel to or shop at a supermarket, the availability of both fill-in items and gas, long hours, and drive-through windows. Many customers shop there multiple times a week, and the average transaction is small. Due to limited shelf space, stores receive frequent deliveries and there are high handling costs. Customers are less price-sensitive than those at other food-oriented retailers.

The industry does have problems: Some areas are saturated with stores; supermarkets have longer hours and more nonfood items; some stores are too big, making shopping less convenient; the traditional market (blue-collar workers) has shrunk; and some chains have had financial woes.

CONVENTIONAL SUPERMARKET

A **supermarket** is a self-service food store with grocery, meat, and produce departments and minimum annual sales of $2 million. Included are conventional supermarkets, food-based superstores, combination stores, box (limited-line) stores, and warehouse stores. See Figure 5-7.

A **conventional supermarket** is a departmentalized food store with a wide range of food and related products; sales of general merchandise are rather limited. This

7-Eleven (**www.7-eleven. com**) dominates the convenience store category.

The Food Marketing Institute (**www.fmi.org**) is the leading industry association for food retailers.

FIGURE 5-6

Jack in the Box Restaurants and Quick Stuff Convenience Stores: A New Combination

Jack in the Box (**www.jackinthebox.com**) has begun opening co-branded stores in a number of locations. The Quick Stuff shops are about 2,000 square feet in size, and they are open 24 hours. They include ATMs and branded gasoline pumps, complete with pay-at-the-pump credit-card readers.

Source: Reprinted by permission of Susan Berry, Retail Image Consulting, Inc.

FIGURE 5-7

Supermarkets Have Come a Long Way

Kroger (**www.kroger.com**) has been introducing a number of new Kroger Marketplace stores: "These multi-department stores offer full-service grocery, pharmacy, and expanded general merchandise—including outdoor living products, electronics, home goods, and toys." They range in size from 80,000 square feet to 125,000 square feet.

Source: Reprinted by permission of Susan Berry, Retail Image Consulting, Inc.

institution started more than 75 years ago when it was recognized that large-scale operations would let a retailer combine volume sales, self-service, and low prices. Self-service enabled supermarkets to both cut costs and increase volume. Personnel costs were reduced, and impulse buying increased. The car and the refrigerator contributed to the supermarket's success by lowering travel costs and adding to the life span of perishables.

For several decades, overall supermarket sales have been about 70 to 75 percent of U.S. grocery sales, with conventional supermarkets now yielding one-fifth of total supermarket sales. There are 17,000 conventional units, with annual sales of $110 billion.[11] Chains account for the great majority of sales. Among the leaders are Kroger, Safeway, and Ahold USA. Many independent supermarkets are affiliated with cooperative or voluntary organizations, such as IGA and Supervalu.

Conventional supermarkets generally rely on high inventory turnover (volume sales). Their profit margins are low. In general, average gross margins (selling price less merchandise cost) are 20 to 22 percent of sales, and net profits are 1 to 3 percent of sales.

These stores face intense competition from other food stores: Convenience stores offer greater customer convenience; food-based superstores and combination stores have more product lines and greater variety within them, as well as better margins; and box and warehouse stores have lower operating costs and prices. Membership clubs (discussed later), with their low prices, also provide competition—especially now that they have much expanded food lines. Variations of the supermarket are covered next.

FOOD-BASED SUPERSTORE

A **food-based superstore** is larger and more diversified than a conventional supermarket but usually smaller and less diversified than a combination store. This format originated in the 1970s as supermarkets sought to stem sales declines by expanding store size and the number of nonfood items carried. Some supermarkets merged with drugstores or general merchandise stores, but more grew into food-based superstores. There are 11,000 food-based U.S. superstores, with sales of $250 billion.[12]

The typical food-based superstore occupies at least 30,000 to 50,000 square feet of space, and 20 to 25 percent of sales are from general merchandise, including garden supplies, flowers, small appliances, and film developing. It caters to consumers' complete grocery needs, along with fill-in general merchandise.

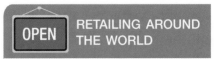

RETAILING AROUND THE WORLD

The Retail Operations of India's RPG Enterprises

RPG Enterprises (**www.rpggroup.com**), with annual sales of $3.25 billion, is one of India's largest conglomerates. The firm operates retail stores in Hong Kong, Mainland China, Macau, Taiwan, Singapore, Malaysia, Indonesia, Vietnam, and Brunei—as well as India—under a variety of store brands (including Wellcome, Giant, Marketplace, GNC, and Foodworld).

RPG operates mostly in three industry sectors in India: Spencer's Retail (**www.spencersretail.com**), a multiple-format retailer selling apparel, fashion, electronics, music and books; Music World (**www.musicworldofindia.com**), India's largest chain of music stores; and Books and Beyond, a retailer of books, toys, gifts, and stationery. RPG also owns supermarket chains, health-and-beauty stores, music stores, and a single hypermarket. RPG's expansion into retailing began when U.S.-based McKinsey & Company

(**www.mckinsey.com**), a management consulting firm, identified retailing as a growth area.

With a Hong Kong-based foreign partner, Dairy Farm International (**www.dairyfarmgroup.com**), RPG developed FoodWorld, a new supermarket chain. FoodWorld, with a wide variety of local and imported products, operates nearly 100 supermarkets in India.

In Malaysia, RPG operates more than 90 Giant (**www.giant.com.my**) hypermarkets and supermarkets. Giant's success under its founders is due to its low prices. After purchasing the chain, RPG redesigned the stores, centralized buying, and improved cleanliness standards.

Sources: "About Giant," **www.giant.com.my/about_us.html** (January 7, 2009); "Dairy Farm Brands," **www.dairyfarmgroup.com/companies/overview.htm** (January 7, 2009); and "RPG Group Overview," **www.rpggroup.com/about.html** (January 7, 2009).

Like combination stores, food-based superstores are efficient, offer a degree of one-stop shopping, stimulate impulse purchases, and feature high-profit general merchandise. But they also offer other advantages: It is easier and less costly to redesign and convert supermarkets into food-based superstores than into combination stores. Many consumers feel more comfortable shopping in true food stores than in huge combination stores. Management expertise is better focused.

Over the past two decades, U.S. supermarket chains have turned more to food-based superstores. They have expanded and remodeled existing supermarkets and built numerous new stores. Many independents have also converted to food-based superstores.

COMBINATION STORE

Meijer's (**www.meijer.com**) combination stores are quite popular with shoppers. They carry 120,000 items.

A **combination store** unites supermarket and general merchandise in one facility, with general merchandise accounting for 25 to 40 percent of sales. The format began in the late 1960s and early 1970s, as common checkout areas were set up for separately owned supermarkets and drugstores or supermarkets and general merchandise stores. The natural offshoot was integrating operations under one management. There are 4,000 U.S. combination stores (including supercenters), and annual sales are $145 billion.[13] Among those with combination stores are Meijer, Fred Meyer, and Albertson's.

Combination stores are large, from 30,000 up to 100,000 or more square feet. This leads to operating efficiencies and cost savings. Consumers like one-stop shopping and will travel to get there. Impulse sales are high. Many general merchandise items have better margins than food items. Supermarkets and drugstores have commonalities in the customers served and the low-price, high-turnover items sold. Drugstore and general merchandise customers are drawn to the store more often.

A **supercenter** is a combination store blending an economy supermarket with a discount department store. It is the U.S. version of the even larger **hypermarket** (the European institution pioneered by firms such as Carrefour that did not succeed in the United States). As a rule, the majority of supercenter sales are from nonfood items. Stores usually range from 75,000 to 150,000 square feet in size, and they stock up to 50,000 and more items—much more than the 30,000 or so items carried by other combination stores. Wal-Mart, Target, and Kmart all operate some supercenters.

BOX (LIMITED-LINE) STORE

The **box (limited-line) store** is a food-based discounter that focuses on a small selection of items, moderate hours of operation (compared with other supermarkets), few services, and limited manufacturer brands. They carry fewer than 2,000 items, few refrigerated perishables, and few sizes and brands per item. Prices are on shelves or overhead signs. Items are displayed in cut cases. Customers bag purchases. Box stores rely on low-priced private-label brands. Their prices are 20 to 30 percent below supermarkets.

The box store originated in Europe and was exported to the United States in the mid-1970s. The growth of these stores has not been as anticipated, and sales have actually fallen modestly in recent years. Some other food stores have matched box-store prices. Many people are loyal to manufacturer brands, and box stores cannot fulfill one-stop shopping needs. There are 2,500 box stores in the United States, with sales of $15 billion.[14] The leading box store operators are Save-A-Lot and Aldi.

WAREHOUSE STORE

A **warehouse store** is a food-based discounter offering a moderate number of food items in a no-frills setting. It appeals to one-stop food shoppers, concentrates on special purchases of popular brands, uses cut-case displays, offers little service, posts prices on shelves, and locates in secondary sites. Warehouse stores began in the late 1970s. There are now 1,600 U.S. stores with $50 billion in annual sales.[15]

The largest warehouse store is known as a super warehouse. There are more than 600 of them in the United States. They have annual sales exceeding $20 million each, and they contain a variety of departments, including produce. High ceilings accommodate pallet loads of groceries. Shipments are made directly to the store. Customers pack their own groceries. Super warehouses are profitable at gross margins far lower than for conventional supermarkets. The leading super warehouse chain is Cub Foods.

Many consumers do not like shopping in warehouse settings. Furthermore, because products are usually acquired when special deals are available, brands may be temporarily or permanently out of stock.

Table 5-2 shows selected operating data for the food-oriented retailers just described.

General Merchandise Retailers

We now examine these general merchandise strategic retail formats highlighted in Table 5-1: specialty store, traditional department store, full-line discount store, variety store, off-price chain, factory outlet, membership club, and flea market.

SPECIALTY STORE

A **specialty store** concentrates on selling one goods or service line, such as young women's apparel. It usually carries a narrow but deep assortment in the chosen category and tailors the strategy to a given market segment. This enables the store to maintain a better selection and sales expertise than competitors, which are often department stores. Investments are controlled, and there is a certain amount of flexibility. Among the most popular categories of specialty stores are apparel, personal care, auto supply, home furnishings, electronics, books, toys, home improvement, pet supplies, jewelry, and sporting goods.

Consumers often shop at specialty stores because of the knowledgeable sales personnel, the variety of choices within the given category, customer service policies, intimate store size and atmosphere (although this is not true of the category killer store), the lack of crowds (also not true of category killer stores), and the absence of aisles of unrelated merchandise that they must pass through. Some specialty stores have elaborate fixtures and upscale merchandise for affluent shoppers, whereas others are discount-oriented and aim at price-conscious consumers.

Total specialty store sales are difficult to determine because these retailers sell virtually all kinds of goods and services, and aggregate specialty store data are not compiled by the government. We do estimate that annual nonfood specialty store sales in the United States exceed $2 trillion (including auto dealers). The top 50 specialty store

TABLE 5-2   Selected Typical Operating Data for Food-Oriented Retailers, as of 2008

Factor	Convenience Stores	Conventional Supermarkets	Food-Based Superstores	Combination Stores	Box (Limited-Line) Stores	Warehouse Stores
Number of stores	145,000	17,000	11,000	4,000	2,500	1,600
Total annual sales	$165 billion[a]	$110 billion	$250 billion	$145 billion[b]	$15 billion	$50 billion[c]
Average store selling area (sq. ft.)	5,000 or less	15,000–20,000	30,000–50,000+	30,000–100,000+	5,000–9,000	15,000+
Number of checkouts per store	1–3	6–10	10+	10+	3–5	5+
Gross margin	25–30%	20–22%	20–25%	25%	10–12%	12–15%
Number of items stocked per store	3,000–4,000	12,000–17,000	20,000+	30,000+	Under 2,000	2,500+
Major emphasis	Daily fill-in needs; dairy, sandwiches, tobacco, gas, beverages, magazines	Food; only 5–10% of sales from general merchandise	Positioned between supermarket and combo store; 20–25% of sales from general merchandise	One-stop shopping; general merchandise is 25–40% of sales (higher at supercenters)	Low prices; few or no perishables	Low prices; variable assortments; may or may not stock perishables

[a]Excluding gasoline.

[b]Including supermarket-item sales at the supercenters of Wal-Mart, Target, and Kmart (which are more heavily oriented to general merchandise than other combination stores).

[c]Including supermarket-item sales at Costco, Sam's, and other membership clubs.

Sources: Various issues of *Progressive Grocer;* Food Marketing Institute, "Facts & Figures," **www.fmi.org/facts_figs**; *Convenience Store News,* **www.csnews.com**; and authors' estimates.

chains (excluding auto dealers) have sales of $400 billion and operate more than 115,000 outlets. Among those chains, about one-third are involved with apparel. Specialty store leaders include Home Depot (home improvement), Best Buy (consumer electronics), T.J. Maxx (apparel), Toys "R" Us (toys), GameStop (video games), and Barnes & Noble (books).[16]

As noted earlier in the chapter, one type of specialty store—the category killer—has gained particular strength. A **category killer** (also known as a **power retailer**) is an especially large specialty store. It features an enormous selection in its category and relatively low prices. Consumers are drawn from wide geographic areas. See Figure 5-8. Blockbuster, Sephora, Home Depot, Sports Authority, and Staples are among the chains almost fully based on the concept. At Sephora's 515 stores around the world, the "unique, open-sell environment features over 200 classic and emerging brands across a broad range of product categories including skincare, color, fragrance, bath & body, smilecare, and haircare, in addition to Sephora's own private label."[17]

Sometimes the focus of specialty stores is as narrow as the Joy of Socks (**www.joyofsocks.com**).

Nonetheless, smaller specialty stores (even ones with under 1,000 square feet of space) can prosper if they are focused, offer strong customer service, and avoid imitating larger firms. Many consumers do not like going to category killer stores: "Shoppers looking for just one or a few basic items and a quick checkout may not want to scour a cavernous warehouse to find what they need." Furthermore, "some categories of merchandise, such as high-tech consumer electronics products, require greater support at retail, from specially trained, knowledgeable employees, than the support typically offered at category killer stores."[18]

FIGURE 5-8

Old Navy: A Discount Power in Apparel
At many of its stores, Old Navy carries a huge selection of casual apparel and accessories, all under the Old Navy brand.

Source: Reprinted by permission of Susan Berry, Retail Image Consulting, Inc.

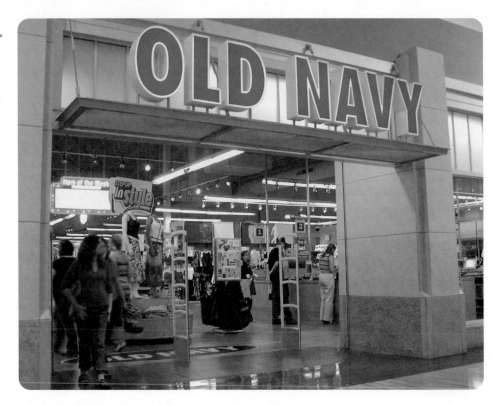

Any size specialty store can be adversely affected by seasonality or a decline in the popularity of its product category. This type of store may also fail to attract consumers who are interested in one-stop shopping for multiple product categories.

TRADITIONAL DEPARTMENT STORE

A **department store** is a large retail unit with an extensive assortment (width and depth) of goods and services that is organized into separate departments for purposes of buying, promotion, customer service, and control. It has the most selection of any general merchandise retailer, often serves as the anchor store in a shopping center or district, has strong credit card penetration, and is usually part of a chain. To be classified as a department store, a retailer must sell a wide range of products (such as apparel, furniture, appliances, and home furnishings), and selected other items (such as paint, hardware, toiletries, cosmetics, photo equipment, jewelry, toys, and sporting goods) with no one merchandise line predominating.

Two basic types of retailers meet the preceding criteria: the traditional department store and the full-line discount store. They account for more than $450 billion in annual sales (including supercenters, where general merchandise sales exceed food sales and leased departments), nearly one-tenth of all U.S. retail sales.[19] The traditional department store is discussed here; the full-line discount store is examined next.

Belk, Inc. (**www.belk.com**) is the nation's largest privately owned department store company, with more than 300 fashion department stores in 16 states.

At a **traditional department store**, merchandise quality ranges from average to quite good. Pricing is moderate to above average. Customer service ranges from medium levels of sales help, credit, delivery, and so forth to high levels of each. For example, Macy's targets middle-class shoppers interested in assortment and moderate prices, whereas Bloomingdale's aims at upscale consumers through more trendy merchandise and higher prices. Few traditional department stores sell all of the product lines that the category used to carry. Many place greater emphasis on apparel and may not carry such lines as furniture, electronics, and major appliances.

Over its history, the traditional department store has contributed many innovations, such as advertising prices, enacting a one-price policy (whereby all shoppers pay the same price for the same item), developing computerized checkouts, offering money-back guarantees, adding branch stores, decentralizing management, and moving into suburban shopping centers. However, in recent years, the performance of traditional department stores has lagged far behind that of full-line discount stores. Today, traditional department store sales ($90 billion annually) represent one-fifth of total department store sales. These are some reasons for traditional department stores' difficulties:

▶ They no longer have brand exclusivity for a lot of the popular items they sell.
▶ Instead of creating more of their own brands, they have often signed exclusive licensing agreements with fashion designers to use the designers' names. This generates loyalty to the designer, not the retailer.
▶ Price-conscious consumers are more attracted to discounters than to traditional department stores.
▶ The popularity of shopping centers has aided specialty stores because consumers can engage in one-stop shopping at several specialty stores in the same shopping center. Department stores do not dominate the smaller stores around them as they once did.
▶ Specialty stores often have better assortments in the lines they carry.
▶ Customer service has deteriorated. Often, store personnel are not as loyal, helpful, or knowledgeable as in prior years.
▶ Some stores are too big and have too much unproductive selling space and low-turnover merchandise.
▶ Many department stores have had a weak focus on market segments and a fuzzy image.
▶ Such chains as Sears have repeatedly changed strategic orientation, confusing consumers as to their image. (Is Sears a traditional department store chain or a full-line discount store chain?)
▶ Some companies are not as innovative in their merchandise decisions as they once were.

Traditional department stores need to clarify their niche in the marketplace (retail positioning); place greater emphasis on customer service and sales personnel; present more exciting, better-organized store interiors; use space better by downsizing stores and eliminating slow-selling items (such as J.C. Penney dropping consumer electronics); and open outlets in smaller, less developed towns and cities (as Sears has done). They can also centralize more buying and promotion functions, do better research, and reach customers more efficiently (by such tools as targeted mailing pieces).

Casual Male's Inventory System that Serves Its Big and Tall Customers

Casual Male (**www.casualmale.com**) is the largest specialty retailer of big and tall men's apparel, with more than 520 store locations throughout the United States, Great Britain, and Canada. Casual Male operates under Casual Male XL, Rochester Big & Tall Clothing, and Sears Canada-Casual Male names.

In most recent years, Casual Male has experienced strong same-store sales increases. These increases can be attributed to Casual Male's stores featuring assortments that are three to four times larger than what most clothing chains stock. Casual Male's stores carry such brands as Nautica (**www.nautica.com**), Izod (**www.izod.com**), and Reebok (**www.reebok.com**); private-label brands (such as Comfort Zone and Platinum); and a custom clothing line.

Although the large inventories effectively serve its customers, Casual Male is concerned about both potential overstocks and stockouts. To address the matter, Casual Male uses the QuantiSense (**www.quantisense.com**) data warehouse, which stores sales and inventory data by product. The retailer is then better able to develop and implement merchandising decisions. One component of this system even ranks each of Casual Male's stores based on the sales of particular product categories. Especially important is QuantiSense's sizing tool, which offers detailed analyses of the chain's various sizes and styles. QuantiSense also generates exception reports such as slow-selling inventory items and out-of-stock products.

Sources: "Casual Male Retail Group," *Apparel Magazine* (May 2008), p. 26; and Jack McKinney, "Casual Male Rapidly Adds BI Solution," *Chain Store Age* (April 2008), p. 62.

FULL-LINE DISCOUNT STORE

A **full-line discount store** is a type of department store with these features:

▶ It conveys the image of a high-volume, low-cost outlet selling a broad product assortment for less than conventional prices.

▶ It is more apt to carry the range of product lines once expected at department stores, including electronics, furniture, and appliances—as well as auto accessories, gardening tools, and housewares.

▶ Shopping carts and centralized checkout service are provided.

▶ Customer service is not usually provided within store departments but at a centralized area. Products are normally sold via self-service with minimal assistance in any single department.

▶ Nondurable (soft) goods feature private brands, whereas durable (hard) goods emphasize well-known manufacturer brands.

▶ Less fashion-sensitive merchandise is carried.

▶ Buildings, equipment, and fixtures are less expensive; and operating costs are lower than for traditional department stores and specialty stores.

Annual U.S. full-line discount store revenues exceed $360 billion (including general merchandise-based supercenters and leased departments), roughly 80 percent of all U.S. department store sales. Together, Wal-Mart, Target, and Kmart operate 6,300 full-line discount stores (including supercenters), with $330 billion in full-line discount store sales.[20]

The success of full-line discount stores is due to many factors. They have a clear customer focus: middle-class and lower-middle-class shoppers looking for good value. The stores feature popular brands of average- to good-quality merchandise at competitive prices. They have expanded their goods and service categories and often have their own private brands. Firms have worked hard to improve their image and provide more customer services. The average outlet (not the supercenter) tends to be smaller than a traditional department store, and sales per square foot are usually higher, which improves productivity. Some full-line discount stores are located in small towns where competition is less intense. Facilities may be newer than those of many traditional department stores.

The greatest challenges facing full-line discount stores are the competition from other retailers (especially lower-priced discounters and category killers), too rapid expansion of some firms, saturation of prime locations, and the dominance of Wal-Mart and Target (as Kmart has fallen off dramatically over the past decade). The industry has undergone a number of consolidations, bankruptcies, and liquidations.

VARIETY STORE

A **variety store** handles an assortment of inexpensive and popularly priced goods and services, such as apparel and accessories, costume jewelry, notions and small wares, candy, toys, and other items in the price range. There are open displays and few salespeople. The stores do not carry full product lines, may not be departmentalized, and do not deliver products. Although the conventional variety store format has faded away, there are two successful spin-offs from it: dollar discount stores and closeout chains.

Dollar discount stores sell similar items to those in conventional variety stores but in plainer surroundings and at much lower prices. They generate $20 billion in yearly sales. Dollar General and Family Dollar are the two leading dollar discount store chains. The two firms operate a total of 14,500 stores and have $17 billion in annual sales. *Closeout chains* sell similar items to those in conventional variety stores but feature closeouts and overruns. They account for $8 billion annually. Big Lots is the leader in that category with 1,400 stores and annual sales of $4.7 billion.[21]

The conventional variety store format (which included Woolworth and McCrory) disappeared from the U.S. marketplace in the mid-1990s after a long, successful run. What happened? There was heavy competition from specialty stores and discounters, most of the stores were older facilities, and some items had low profit margins. At one time, Woolworth had 1,200 variety stores with annual sales of $2 billion.

OFF-PRICE CHAIN

An **off-price chain** features brand-name (sometimes designer) apparel and accessories, footwear (primarily women's and family), linens, fabrics, cosmetics, and/or housewares and sells them at everyday low prices in an efficient, limited-service environment. It frequently has community dressing rooms, centralized checkout counters, no gift wrapping, and extra charges for alterations. The chains buy merchandise opportunistically, as special deals occur. Other retailers' canceled orders, manufacturers' irregulars and overruns, and end-of-season items are often purchased for a fraction of their original wholesale prices. The total sales of U.S. off-price apparel stores are $45 billion. The biggest chains are T.J. Maxx and Marshalls (both owned by TJX), Ross Stores, and Burlington Coat Factory.

TJX (www.tjx.com) operates two of the biggest off-price apparel chains: T.J. Maxx and Marshalls.

Off-price chains aim at the same shoppers as traditional department stores—but with prices reduced by 40 to 50 percent. Shoppers are also lured by the promise of new merchandise on a regular basis. At T.J. Maxx, "our off-price mission is to deliver a rapidly changing assortment of quality, brand name merchandise at prices that are 20 to 60 percent less than department and specialty store regular prices, every day. Our target customer includes the middle- to upper-middle-income shopper, who is fashion- and value-conscious."[22] Off-price shopping centers now appeal to people's interest in one-stop shopping.

The most crucial strategic element for off-price chains involves buying merchandise and establishing long-term relationships with suppliers. To succeed, the chains must secure large quantities of merchandise at reduced wholesale prices and have a regular flow of goods into the stores. Sometimes manufacturers use off-price chains to sell samples, products that are not doing well when they are introduced, and merchandise remaining near the end of a season. At other times, off-price chains employ a more active buying strategy. Instead of waiting for closeouts and canceled orders, they convince manufacturers to make merchandise during off-seasons and pay cash for items early. Off-price chains are less demanding in terms of the support requested from suppliers, they do not return products, and they pay promptly.

Off-price chains face some market pressure because of competition from other institutional formats that run frequent sales throughout the year, the discontinuity of merchandise, poor management at some firms, insufficient customer service for some shoppers, and the shakeout of underfinanced companies.

FACTORY OUTLET

A **factory outlet** is a manufacturer-owned store selling closeouts; discontinued merchandise; irregulars; canceled orders; and, sometimes, in-season, first-quality merchandise. Manufacturers' interest in outlet stores has risen for four basic reasons:

1. Manufacturers can control where their discounted merchandise is sold. By placing outlets in out-of-the-way spots with low sales penetration of the firm's brands, outlet revenues do not affect sales at key specialty and department store accounts.
2. Outlets are profitable despite prices up to 60 percent less than customary retail prices due to low operating costs—few services, low rent, limited displays, and plain store fixtures.
3. The manufacturer decides on store visibility, sets promotion policies, removes labels, and ensures that discontinued items and irregulars are disposed of properly.
4. Because many specialty and department stores are increasing private label sales, manufacturers need revenue from outlet stores to sustain their own growth.

More factory stores now operate in clusters or in outlet malls to expand customer traffic, and they use cooperative ads. Large outlet malls are in Connecticut, Florida,

FIGURE 5-9

Brooks Brothers: Realizing
the Value of Outlet Centers
Brooks Brothers has stores in
more than 80 outlet centers
around the country, 32 states
in all.

Source: Reprinted by permission.

Georgia, New York, Pennsylvania, Tennessee, and other states. There are 16,500 U.S. factory outlet stores representing hundreds of manufacturers, many in the 225 outlet malls nationwide. These stores have $18 billion in yearly sales, with three-quarters from apparel and accessories.[23] Manufacturers with a major outlet presence include Bass (footwear), Brooks Brothers (apparel), Harry & David (fruits and gift items), Levi's (apparel), Liz Claiborne (apparel), Samsonite (luggage), and Totes (rain gear). See Figure 5-9.

When deciding whether to utilize factory outlets, manufacturers must be cautious. They must evaluate their retailing expertise, the investment costs, the impact on existing retailers that buy from them, and the response of consumers. Manufacturers do not want to jeopardize their products' sales at full retail prices.

MEMBERSHIP CLUB

A **membership (warehouse) club** appeals to price-conscious consumers, who must be members to shop there. It straddles the line between wholesaling and retailing. Some members are small business owners and employees who pay a membership fee to buy merchandise at wholesale prices. They make purchases for use in operating their firms or for personal use and yield 60 percent of club sales. Most members are final consumers who buy for their own use; they represent 40 percent of club sales. They must pay an annual fee to be a member. Prices may be slightly more than for business customers. There are 1,350 U.S. membership clubs, with annual sales to final consumers of $50 billion. Costco and Sam's Club generate 90 percent of industry sales.[24]

Sam's (**www.samsclub. com**) is Wal-Mart's membership club division. It has lower prices and plainer settings than Wal-Mart's full-line discount stores.

The operating strategy of the modern membership club centers on large stores (up to 100,000 or more square feet), inexpensive isolated or industrial locations, opportunistic buying (with some merchandise discontinuity), a fraction of the items stocked by full-line discount stores, little advertising, plain fixtures, wide aisles to give forklift trucks access to shelves, concrete floors, limited delivery, fewer credit options, and very low prices. A typical club carries general merchandise, such as consumer electronics, appliances, computers, housewares, tires, and apparel (35 to 60 percent of sales); food (20 to 35 percent of sales); and sundries, such as health and beauty aids, tobacco, liquor, and candy (15 to 30 percent of sales). It may also have a pharmacy, photo developing, a car-buying service, a gasoline service station, and other items once viewed as frills for this format. Inventory turnover is several times that of a department store.

The major retailing challenges relate to the allocation of company efforts between business and final consumer accounts (without antagonizing one group or the other and without presenting a blurred store image), the lack of interest by many consumers in shopping at warehouse-type stores, the power of the two industry leaders, and the potential for saturation caused by overexpansion.

FLEA MARKET

At a **flea market**, many retail vendors sell a range of products at discount prices in plain surroundings. It is rooted in the centuries-old tradition of street selling—shoppers touch and sample items, and they haggle over prices. Vendors used to sell only antiques, bric-a-brac, and assorted used merchandise. Today, they also frequently sell new goods, such as clothing, cosmetics, watches, consumer electronics, housewares, and gift items. Many flea markets are located in nontraditional sites such as racetracks, stadiums, and arenas. Some are at sites abandoned by other retailers. Typically, vendors rent space. A flea market might rent individual spaces for $30 to $100 or more per day, depending on location. Some flea markets impose a parking fee or admission charge for shoppers.

There are a few hundred major U.S. flea markets, but overall sales data are not available. The credibility of permanent flea markets, consumer interest in bargaining, the broader product mix, the availability of brand-name goods, and the low prices all contribute to the format's appeal. One of the best-known businesses in this genre is the Rose Bowl Flea Market, which is open the second Sunday of each month. It regularly features 2,500 vendors and attracts 20,000 shoppers a day. "The only restricted items are food, animals, guns, ammunition, and pornography." The costs of vendor spaces range from $50 to $250 for one day.[25]

At a flea market, price haggling is encouraged, cash is the predominant currency, and many vendors gain their first real experience as retail entrepreneurs. One recent trend involves nonstore, Web-based flea markets such as eBay (**www.ebay.com**), eBid (**www.ebid.com**), OnlineAuction (**www.onlineauction.com**), and OZtion (**www.oztion.com**). Online auction sites account for several billion dollars in sales annually and are popular among bargain hunters.

ETHICS IN RETAILING

The Community Role of the PX

The Army and Air Force Exchange Service (AAFES, **www.aafes.com**)—also referred to as PX for post exchange—is a U.S. government-run retail chain that is unknown by many traditional consumers. Federal rules restrict entrance at AAFES shops to military personnel, retirees, and their families.

AAFES operates a number of different retail formats, including convenience stores; beer, wine, and spirit stores; and troop stores close to military installations. The 3,100 AAFES facilities account for retail sales of $10 billion a year and serve as community centers for active and retired military personnel and their families. Military personnel stationed overseas often see the PX as a place to shop that reflects contemporary American culture and values. For example, home entertainment goods and portable navigation systems are popular sellers. The motto of AAFES is

"We go where you go." AAFES has operated a number of outlets in Iraq, owns the largest bakery in Europe, and provides school lunches in Germany.

The PXs are efficiently operated by the Department of Defense (**www.defenselink.com**). A recent report found that its prices were about 20 percent less than traditional retailers. In addition, AAFES' net profit margin was 4.9 percent of sales. Profits go to support morale, welfare, and recreational programs of all branches of the military.

Sources: Deena M. Amato-McCoy, "AAFES' Miracle," *Retail Technology Quarterly* (May 2008), pp. 132–134; Mehgan Belanger, "Serving Those Who Serve the U.S.," *Convenience Store News* (October 22, 2007), pp. 183–185; and Mile Troy, "Marching Forward: AAFES Armed for Transformation," *Retailing Today* (October 8, 2007), pp. 212–224.

Many traditional retailers believe flea markets represent an unfair method of competition because the quality of merchandise may be misrepresented, consumers may buy items at flea markets and return them to other retailers for higher refunds, suppliers are often unaware their products are sold there, sales taxes can be easily avoided, and operating costs are quite low. Flea markets may also cause traffic congestion.

The high sales volume from off-price chains, factory outlets, membership clubs, and flea markets is explained by the wheel of retailing. These institutions are low-cost operators appealing to price-conscious consumers who are not totally satisfied with other retail formats that have upgraded their merchandise and customer service, raised prices, and moved along the wheel.

Chapter **Summary**

1. *To describe the wheel of retailing, scrambled merchandising, and the retail life cycle, and to show how they can help explain the performance of retail strategy mixes.* In Chapter 4, retail institutions were examined by ownership. This chapter takes a store-based strategic retailing perspective. A retail strategy mix involves a combination of factors: location, operations, goods/services offered, pricing, atmosphere and customer services, and promotion. To flourish, a firm should strive to be dominant in some way and, thus, reach destination retailer status.

Three important concepts help explain the performance of diverse retail strategies. According to the wheel of retailing, retail innovators often first appear as low-price operators with low costs and low profit margins. Over time, they upgrade their offerings and customer services and raise prices. They are then vulnerable to new discounters with lower costs that take their place along the wheel. With scrambled merchandising, a retailer adds goods and services that are unrelated to each other and its original business to increase overall sales and profits. Scrambled merchandising is contagious and often used in self-defense. The retail life cycle states that institutions pass through identifiable stages of introduction, growth, maturity, and decline. Strategies change as institutions mature.

2. *To discuss ways in which retail strategy mixes are evolving.* Many institutions are adapting to marketplace dynamics. These approaches have been popular for various firms, depending on their strengths, weaknesses, and goals: mergers, by which separately owned retailers join together; diversification, by which a retailer becomes active in businesses outside its normal operations; and downsizing, whereby unprofitable stores are closed or divisions sold. Sometimes, single companies use all three approaches. More firms also utilize cost containment and value-driven retailing. They strive to hold down both investment and operating costs. There are many ways to do this.

3. *To examine a wide variety of food-oriented retailers involved with store-based strategy mixes.* Retail institutions may be classified by store-based strategy mix and divided into food-oriented and general merchandise groups. Fourteen store-based strategy mixes are covered in this chapter.

These are the food-oriented store-based retailers: A convenience store is well located, is open long hours, and offers a moderate number of fill-in items at average to above-average prices. A conventional supermarket is departmentalized and carries a wide range of food and related items, there is little general merchandise, and prices are competitive. A food-based superstore is larger and more diversified than a conventional supermarket but smaller and less diversified than a combination store. A combination store unites supermarket and general merchandise in a large facility and sets competitive prices; the food-based supercenter (hypermarket) is a type of combination store. The box (limited-line) store is a discounter focusing on a small selection, moderate hours, few services, and few manufacturer brands. A warehouse store is a discounter offering a moderate number of food items in a no-frills setting that can be quite large.

4. *To study a wide range of general merchandise retailers involved with store-based strategy mixes.* A specialty store concentrates on one goods or service line and has a tailored strategy; the category killer is a special kind of specialty store. A department store is a large retailer with an extensive assortment of goods and services. The traditional one has a range of customer services and average to above-average prices. A full-line discount store is a department store with a low-cost, low-price strategy. A variety store has inexpensive and popularly priced items in a plain setting. An off-price chain features brand-name items and sells them at low prices in an austere environment. A factory outlet is manufacturer-owned and sells closeouts, discontinued merchandise, and irregulars at very low prices. A membership club appeals to price-conscious shoppers who must be members to shop. A flea market has many vendors offering items at discount prices in nontraditional venues.

Key Terms

strategy mix (p. 124)
destination retailer (p. 124)
wheel of retailing (p. 124
scrambled merchandising (p. 126)
retail life cycle (p. 127)
mergers (p. 129)
diversification (p. 130)
downsizing (p. 130)
convenience store (p. 133)

supermarket (p. 133)
conventional supermarket (p. 133)
food-based superstore (p. 134)
combination store (p. 135)
supercenter (p. 135)
hypermarket (p. 135)
box (limited-line) store (p. 136)
warehouse store (p. 136)
specialty store (p. 136)

category killer (power retailer) (p. 137)
department store (p. 138)
traditional department store (p. 138)
full-line discount store (p. 140)
variety store (p. 140)
off-price chain (p. 141)
factory outlet (p. 141)
membership (warehouse) club (p. 142)
flea market (p. 143)

Questions for Discussion

1. Describe how a small café could be a destination retailer.

2. Explain the wheel of retailing. Is this theory applicable today? Why or why not?

3. Develop a high-end retail strategy mix for a shoe store. Include location, operating procedures, goods/services offered, pricing tactics, and promotion methods.

4. How could these retailers best apply scrambled merchandising? Explain your answers.
   a. Radio Shack.
   b. 1-800 Flowers.
   c. A local movie theater.
   d. Ben & Jerry's.

5. What strategic emphasis should be used by institutions in the growth stage of the retail life cycle compared with the emphasis by institutions in the maturity stage?

6. Contrast the strategy mixes of convenience stores, conventional supermarkets, food-based superstores, and warehouse stores. Is there room for each? Explain your answer.

7. Do you think U.S. combination stores (supercenters) will dominate grocery retailing? Why or why not?

8. What are the pros and cons of Sephora carrying more than 200 brands of personal-care products?

9. Contrast the strategy mixes of specialty stores, traditional department stores, and full-line discount stores.

10. What must the off-price chain do to succeed in the future?

11. Do you expect factory outlet centers to keep growing? Explain your answer.

12. Comment on the decision of many membership clubs to begin selling gasoline.

Web **Exercise**

Visit the Web site of Kohl's (www.kohls.com). In your view, (a) where is Kohl's positioned along the wheel of retailing, and (b) how would you describe its use of scrambled merchandising? Explain whether you think that Kohl's is doing the right thing in terms of these two concepts.

Note: Stop by our Web site (www.pearsonhighered.com/berman) to experience a number of highly interactive, appealing Web exercises based on actual company demonstrations, and sample materials related to retailing.

6

Web, Nonstore-Based, and Other Forms of Nontraditional Retailing

Chapter **Objectives**

1. To contrast single-channel and multi-channel retailing

2. To look at the characteristics of the three major retail institutions involved with nonstore-based strategy mixes: direct marketing, direct selling, and vending machines—with an emphasis on direct marketing

3. To explore the emergence of electronic retailing through the World Wide Web

4. To discuss two other nontraditional forms of retailing: video kiosks and airport retailing

About 15 years ago, after learning that Web usage was growing at 2,300 percent per year, Jeff Bezos analyzed a list of the 20 best products to sell online. Books topped the list, largely due to the vast number of available titles. After deciding to sell books, Bezos moved to Seattle because of the number of computer professionals located there. He created an online strategy based on the concept of creating a place where people could not only find and buy any book they wanted, but also get great customer service. To Bezos, the three most important components of this strategy were—and still are—service, selection, and price.

Sales for the company that Bezos named Amazon.com (**www.amazon. com**) took off immediately, as the firm concentrated on books and sought to have the largest selection that could be found anywhere. Almost from the start, industry analysts believed that Amazon.com's Web site had several distinctive advantages: an emphasis on information over graphics; a separate page for each book, including a brief description; customer reviews; and one-click shopping to speed the checkout process. Although Amazon.com started off selling only books, it has since branched out into many other product lines, such as electronics, small appliances, a bridal registry, toys, and even diamonds. Amazon.com also operates Web sites for other retailers. It is now the world's largest online retailer.

Under a relatively new shipping plan called Amazon Prime, customers who pay an annual $79 membership fee can get unlimited two-day shipping. These members will also be eligible for overnight shipping for $3.99 per item.[1]

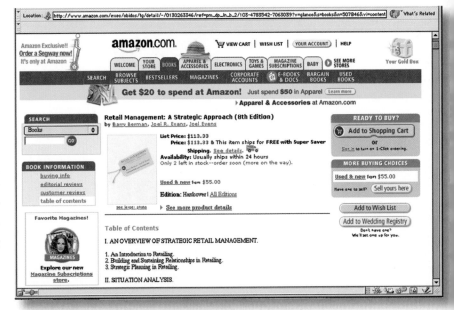

Source: Reprinted by permission of Amazon.com.

OVERVIEW

In this chapter, we contrast single-channel and multi-channel retailing and then examine nonstore-based retailing, electronic retailing, and two other types of nontraditional retailing: video kiosks and airport retailing. These formats influence the strategies of current store retailers and newly formed retailers. Visit our Web site (**www.pearsonhighered.com/berman**) for links to nonstore and nontraditional topics.

When it begins, a retailer often relies on **single-channel retailing,** whereby it sells to consumers through one retail format. That one format may be store-based (a corner shoe store) or nonstore-based (catalog retailing, direct selling, or Web retailing). As the firm grows, it may turn to **multi-channel retailing,** whereby a retailer sells to consumers through multiple retail formats.

Multi-channel retailing lets a firm reach different customer groups, share costs among various formats, and diversify its supplier base. Retail leader Wal-Mart sells at stores (including Wal-Mart, Sam's Club, and Neighborhood Market) and a Web site (**www.walmart.com**). Figure 6-1 shows examples of single- and multi-channel retailing. An end-of-chapter appendix explores multi-channel retailing in more detail.

Why have we introduced this concept here? Because even though some non-store-based firms are "pure players" (single-channel retailers), a rapidly growing number of firms are combining store and nonstore retailing to actively pursue multi-channel retailing:

According to a global retail industry executive for Sterling Commerce: "Shoppers don't care how challenging it is for retailers to organize their firms to meet their needs. Retailers without cross-channel plans in place will be left behind. But, there are opportunities to leapfrog competitors by automating cross-channel processes and achieving global order, shipment, and inventory visibility across all channels." In a survey of retailers, 98 percent agreed that the inability to meet customer cross-channel expectations threatens customer loyalty and competitive advantage. Though 81 percent of the retailers said they are fully or partially integrated across all of their sales channels (store, call center, Web

From its roots as a full-line discount store chain, Wal-Mart (www.walmart.com) has become a master of multi-channel retailing.

FIGURE 6-1

Approaches to Retailing Channels

Examples of Single-Channel Retailing

| Store-based retailer, such as a local apparel store, operating only one store format | Mail-order sporting goods retailer selling only through catalogs | Online CD/DVD retailer that only does business through the Web |

Examples of Multi-Channel Retailing

| Store-based retailer, such as a local gift store, also selling through catalogs | Store-based retailer, such as a jewelry store, also selling through the Web | Store-based retailer, such as Target, affiliating with a Web-based firm, such as CyberMonday.com |
| Store-based retailer, such as a local gift store, also selling through catalogs and the Web | Store-based retailer, such as a jewelry store, also selling through the Web and leased departments in select department stores | Store-based retailer, such as Target, affiliating with a Web-based firm, such as CyberMonday.com, and having multiple store formats (SuperTarget) |

site, kiosk, and so on), many still do not offer innovative cross-channel capabilities such as allowing consumers to buy online and pick up or return to a store. Only 43 percent of retailers said they have an automated process that allows customers to pick up orders in the store regardless of the purchasing channel. Only slightly more (48 percent) have an automated process allowing customers to return their orders to the store regardless of the channel through which it was purchased.[2]

The ever-popular eBay (www.ebay.com) is a pure Web retailer.

Retailers—single-channel or multi-channel—engage in **nonstore retailing** when they use strategy mixes that are not store-based to reach consumers and complete transactions. U.S. nonstore retailing sales exceed $410 billion annually, with 80 percent of that from direct marketing (hence, the direct marketing emphasis in this chapter). The fastest-growing form of direct marketing involves electronic (Web-based) retailing. From sales of $500 million in 1996, U.S. Web retailing revenues are expected to reach $180 billion in 2012.[3] See Figure 6-2.

Nontraditional retailing also comprises video kiosks and airport retailing, two key formats not fitting neatly into "store-based" or "nonstore-based" retailing. Sometimes they are store-based; other times they are not. What they have in common is their departure from traditional retailing strategies.

Direct Marketing

Direct magazine (www. directmag.com) is a vital source of direct marketing information.

In **direct marketing,** a customer is first exposed to a good or service through a nonpersonal medium (direct mail, TV, radio, magazine, newspaper, or computer) and then orders by mail, phone, or fax—and increasingly by computer. Annual U.S. sales are more than $325 billion (including the Web), and more than half of adults make at least one such purchase a year.[4] Japan, Germany, Great Britain, France, and Italy are among the direct marketing leaders outside the United States. Popular products are gift items, apparel, magazines, books and music, sports equipment, home accessories, food, and insurance.

In the United States, direct marketing customers are more apt to be married, middle class, and 35 to 50 years of age. Mail shoppers are more likely to live in areas away from malls. Phone shoppers are more likely to live in upscale metropolitan areas; they want to

FIGURE 6-2

Aldo: Combining Bricks-and-Mortar with Clicks-and-Mortar

Retailers of every size and type are stepping up their use of Web retailing. Aldo Shoes has a carefully constructed Web site (**www.aldoshoes.com**) to complement its 840 stores in 35 countries.

Source: Reprinted by permission of Susan Berry, Retail Image Consulting, Inc.

FIGURE 6-3

Peapod: Specializing in Food Delivery Services

Peapod (**www.peapod.com**) is an Internet grocer that serves about 270,000 customers each year. It is owned by Netherlands-based Royal Ahold. Its acquisition has enabled Peapod to use a more integrated bricks-and-clicks business strategy. It partners with other Royal Ahold stores (Peapod by Stop & Shop and Peapod by Giant).

Source: Reprinted by permission of Peapod.

avoid traffic and save time. The share of direct marketing purchases made by men has grown: The average consumer who buys direct spends several hundred dollars per year; and he or she wants convenience, unique products, and good prices.[5]

Direct marketers can be divided into two broad categories: general and specialty. General direct marketing firms offer a full line of products and sell everything from clothing to housewares. J.C. Penney (with its mail-order and Web businesses) and QVC (with its cable TV and Web businesses) are general direct marketers. Specialty direct marketers focus on more narrow product lines. L.L. Bean, Publishers Clearinghouse, and Franklin Mint are among the thousands of U.S. specialty firms. See Figure 6-3.

Direct marketing has a number of strategic business advantages:

▶ Many costs are reduced—low startup costs are possible; inventories are reduced; no displays are needed; a prime location is unnecessary; regularly staffed store hours are not important; a sales force may not be needed; and business may be run out of a garage or basement.

▶ It is possible for direct marketers to have lower prices (due to reduced costs) than store-based retailers with the same items. A huge geographic area can be covered inexpensively and efficiently.

▶ Customers shop conveniently—without crowds, parking congestion, or checkout lines. And they do not have safety concerns about shopping early in the morning or late at night.

▶ Specific consumer segments are pinpointed through targeted mailings.

▶ Consumers may sometimes legally avoid sales tax by buying from direct marketers not having retail facilities in their state (however, some states want to eliminate this loophole).

▶ A store-based firm can supplement its regular business and expand its trading area (even becoming national or global) without adding outlets.

Direct marketing also has its limits, but they are not as critical as those for direct selling:

▶ Products cannot be examined before purchase. Thus, the range of items purchased is more limited than in stores, and firms need liberal return policies to attract and keep customers.

▶ Firms may underestimate costs. Catalogs can be expensive. A computer system is required to track shipments, purchases, and returns, and to keep lists current. A 24-hour phone staff may be needed.

▶ Even successful catalogs often draw purchases from less than 10 percent of recipients.

Dan: Vice-President, Retail Trade Association

As a full-time college student (majoring in communications), Dan also worked full-time at a regional department store. He doesn't know where he found the energy, but he is glad that he did! After his graduation, Dan was hired by one national department store chain and then moved to other ones. His jobs included sales manager, assistant buyer, divisional sales manager, store manager, and vice-president.

Dan consistently exceeded financial goals for sales plans, inventory controls, and payroll costs. He was named divisional sales manager of the year twice before being promoted to store manager. Dan says that he moved between companies when there was an opportunity to advance his career to a higher position. He notes that it is important to recognize that each opportunity for advancement came about because he had proven results in his positions.

Dan's position at the retail trade association is distinctive in that it allows him to utilize his 26 years of retailing experience while learning new skills such as media relations and public speaking. If he was not working for the association, he would be working for a retailer. He was not looking to leave the department store arena when he received this offer. The uniqueness of the position grabbed his interest. He says the experience has been great and given him unparalleled exposure to the wide world of retailing, including consulting. Dan's trade association salary exceeds $100,000 annually, plus benefits.

Here's Dan's advice: "Be realistic and be willing to work hard. Dress appropriately for your job and meetings. Work in a store before making your career choice. Be sure you like working with the public and understand nonselling support work that everyone in retailing has to do. Know that it can be a lot of fun while it is a lot of hard work."

Source: Reprinted by permission of the National Retail Federation.

▶ Clutter exists. Each year, billions of catalogs are mailed in the United States alone.
▶ Printed catalogs are prepared well in advance, causing difficulties in price and style planning.
▶ Some firms have given the industry a bad name due to delivery delays and shoddy goods.

The full 30-day rule is available online (**www.ftc. gov/bcp/edu/pubs/ business/adv/bus02.pdf**).

The Federal Trade Commission's "30-day rule" is a U.S. regulation that affects direct marketers. It requires firms to ship orders within 30 days of their receipt or notify customers of delays. If an order cannot be shipped in 60 days, the customer must be given a specific delivery date and offered the option of canceling an order or waiting for it to be filled. The rule covers mail, phone, fax, and computer orders.

Despite its limitations, long-run growth for direct marketing is projected. Consumer interest in convenience and the difficulty in setting aside shopping time will continue. More direct marketers will offer 24-hour ordering and improve their efficiency. Greater product standardization and the prominence of well-known brands will reduce consumer perceptions of risk when buying from a catalog or the Web. Technological breakthroughs, such as purchases on the Web, will attract more consumer shopping.

Due to its vast presence and immense potential, our detailed discussion is intended to give you an in-depth look into direct marketing. Let's study the domain of direct marketing, emerging trends, steps in a direct marketing strategy, and key issues facing direct marketers.

The Domain of Direct Marketing

As defined earlier, *direct marketing* is a form of retailing in which a consumer is exposed to a good or service through a nonpersonal medium and then orders by mail, phone, fax, or computer. It may also be viewed as "an interactive system that uses one or more advertising media to effect a measurable response and/or transaction at any location, with this activity stored on a data base."[6]

Accordingly, we *do* include these as forms of direct marketing: any catalog; any mail, TV, radio, magazine, newspaper, phone directory, fax, or other ad; any computer-based transaction; or any other nonpersonal contact that stimulates customers to place orders by mail, phone, fax, or computer (counting interactive TV).

We *do not* include these as forms of direct marketing: (1) Direct selling—consumers are solicited by in-person sales efforts or seller-originated phone calls and the firm uses personal communication to initiate contact. (2) Conventional vending machines, whereby consumers are exposed to nonpersonal media but do not complete transactions via mail, phone, fax, or computer; they do not interact with the firm in a manner that allows a data base to be generated and kept.

Direct marketing *is* involved in many computerized kiosk transactions; when items are mailed to consumers, there is a company–customer interaction and a data base can be formed. Direct marketing is also in play when consumers originate phone calls, based on catalogs or ads they have seen.

The Customer Data Base: Key to Successful Direct Marketing

Because direct marketers often initiate contact with customers (in contrast to store shopping trips that are initiated by the consumer), it is imperative that they develop and maintain a comprehensive customer data base. They can then pinpoint their best customers, make offers aimed at specific customer needs, avoid costly mailings to nonresponsive shoppers, and track sales by customer. A good data base is the major asset of most direct marketers, and *every* thriving direct marketer has a strong data base.

Data-base retailing is a way to collect, store, and use relevant information about customers. Such information typically includes a person's name, address, background data, shopping interests, and purchase behavior. Although data bases are often compiled through large computerized information systems, they may also be used by small firms that are not overly computerized.

Here's an example of how data-base retailing can be beneficial:

> Your family clothing store is going to have a sale on children's clothing. Rather than mail a postcard to the whole customer list (both men and women), you mail the postcard only to customers who have purchased children's clothing from you in the past. The result of that targeting effort will be reduced promotion costs and increased return on your investment.[7]

Data-base retailing is discussed further in Chapter 8.

Emerging Trends

Several trends are relevant for direct marketing: the evolving activities of direct marketers, changing consumer lifestyles, increased competition, the greater use of multi-channel retailing, the newer roles for catalogs and TV, technological advances, and the interest in global direct marketing.

EVOLVING ACTIVITIES OF DIRECT MARKETERS

Over the past 35 years, these direct marketing activities have evolved:

▶ Technology has moved to the forefront in all aspects of direct marketing—from lead generation to order processing.
▶ Multiple points of customer contact are offered by many more firms today.
▶ There is an increased focus on data-base retailing.
▶ Many more firms now have well-articulated and widely communicated privacy policies.

CHANGING CONSUMER LIFESTYLES

Consumer lifestyles in America have shifted dramatically over the past several decades, mostly due to the large number of women who are now in the labor force and the longer commuting time to and from work for suburban residents. Many consumers no longer have the time or inclination to shop at stores. They are attracted by the ease of purchasing through direct marketing.

These are some of the factors consumers consider in selecting a direct marketer:

▶ Company reputation (image).
▶ Ability to shop whenever the consumer wants.
▶ Types of goods and services, as well as the assortment and brand names carried.

▶ Availability of a toll-free phone number or Web site for ordering.
▶ Credit card acceptance.
▶ Speed of promised delivery time.
▶ Competitive prices.
▶ Satisfaction with past purchases and good return policies.

INCREASED COMPETITION AMONG FIRMS

As direct marketing sales have risen, so has competition; although there are a number of big firms, such as J.C. Penney and Spiegel, there are also thousands of small ones. The Direct Marketing Association estimates that there are more than 10,000 U.S. mail-order companies.

Spiegel (www.spiegel.com) has largely been a direct marketer since the early 1900s. It faces more competition now than ever before.

Intense competition exists because entry into direct marketing is easier and less costly than entry into store retailing. A firm does not need a store; can operate with a small staff; and can use low-cost one-inch magazine ads, send brochures to targeted shoppers, and have an inexpensive Web site. It can keep a low inventory and place orders with suppliers after people buy items (as long as it meets the 30-day rule).

About one out of every two new direct marketers fails. Direct marketing lures many small firms that may poorly define their market niche, offer nondistinctive goods and services, have limited experience, misjudge the needed effort, have trouble with supplier continuity, and attract many consumer complaints.

GREATER USE OF MULTI-CHANNEL RETAILING

Today, many stores add to their revenues by using ads, brochures, catalogs, and Web sites to obtain mail-order, phone, and computer-generated sales. They see that direct marketing is efficient, targets specific segments, appeals to people who might not otherwise shop with those firms, and needs a lower investment to reach other geographic areas than opening branch outlets.

REI—the outdoor recreational equipment chain—is a good example of a store-based retailer that has flourished with its distinctive multi-channel approach, winning several accolades along the way: "For our more than 3.5 million active members and other customers, REI provides the knowledge and confidence to explore and discover new adventures. We do this through frequent educational clinics and expert advice at our retail stores and at REI.com from trusted REI staff who share our members' passion for outdoor recreation. Above all, we provide a convenient and seamless shopping experience, whether at an REI retail store, online, by phone, or by mail order."[8]

NEWER ROLES FOR CATALOGS AND TV

Direct marketers are recasting the ways in which they use their catalogs and their approach to TV retailing. Here's how.

We are witnessing three key changes in long-standing catalog tactics: (1) Many firms now print "specalogs" in addition to or instead of the annual catalogs showing all of their products. With a **specalog**, a retailer caters to a particular customer segment, emphasizes a limited number of items, and reduces production and postage costs (as a specalog is much shorter than a general catalog). Each year, such firms as Spiegel, L.L. Bean, and Travelsmith send out separate specalogs by market segment or occasion. (2) To help defray costs, some companies accept ads from noncompeting firms that are compatible with their image. (3) To stimulate sales and defray costs, some catalogs are sold in bookstores, supermarkets, and airports, and at company Web sites. The percentage of consumers buying a catalog who actually make a purchase is far higher than that for those who get catalogs in the mail.

TV retailing has two major components (not including interactive TV shopping, which is just getting off the ground): shopping networks and infomercials. On a *shopping network,* the programming focuses on merchandise presentations and their sales (usually by phone). The two biggest players are cable giants QVC and Home Shopping Network (HSN), with combined annual worldwide revenues of $10 billion. QVC has access to a global TV audience of more than 166 million households, and HSN has access to 90 million households. About 10 percent of U.S. consumers buy goods through TV shopping programs each year.

Ron Popeil became a very rich man through his Ronco (**www.ronco.com**) infomercials.

Once regarded as a medium primarily for shut-ins and the lower middle class, the typical TV-based shopper is now younger, more fashion-conscious, and as apt to be from a high-income household as the overall U.S. population. QVC and HSN feature jewelry, women's clothing, and personal-care items and do not stress nationally known brands. Most items must be bought as they are advertised to encourage shoppers to act quickly. The firms also have active Web sites (**www.qvc.com** and **www.hsn.com**).[9]

An **infomercial** is a program-length TV commercial (typically, 30 minutes) for a specific good or service that airs on cable or broadcast television, often at a fringe time. As they watch an infomercial, shoppers call in orders, which are delivered to them. Infomercials work well for products that benefit from demonstrations. Good infomercials present detailed information, include customer testimonials, are entertaining, and are divided into timed segments (since the average viewer watches only a few minutes at a time) with ordering information displayed in every segment. Infomercials account for more than $5 billion in annual U.S. revenues. Popular infomercials have included those for the Ronco Showtime Rotisserie, Magic Bullet blenders, "Fitness Made Simple" videos, and a variety of exercise equipment. The Electronic Retailing Association (**www.retailing.org**) is the trade association for infomercial firms.

TECHNOLOGICAL ADVANCES

The technology revolution is improving operating efficiency and offering enhanced sales opportunities:

- ▶ Market segments can be better targeted. Through selective binding, bigger catalogs are sent to the best customers and shorter catalogs to new prospects.
- ▶ Firms inexpensively use computers to enter mail and phone orders, arrange for shipments, and monitor inventory on hand.
- ▶ It is simple to set up and maintain computerized data bases using inexpensive software.
- ▶ Huge, automated distribution centers efficiently accumulate and ship orders.
- ▶ Customers dial toll-free phone numbers or visit Web sites to place orders and get information. The cost per call for the direct marketer is quite low.
- ▶ Consumers can conclude transactions from more sites, including kiosks at airports and train stations.
- ▶ Cable TV programming and the Web offer 24-hour shopping and ordering.
- ▶ Both in-home and at-work Web-based shopping transactions can be conducted.

ETHICS IN RETAILING

The Flood of Junk Mail: No End in Sight

Since the Can Spam Act (**www.spamlaws.com/federal/can-spam.shtml**), a major federal anti-spam law, went into effect in January 2004, the amount of unsolicited junk E-mail has increased significantly. Unsolicited E-mail accounts for as much as 90 percent of all E-mail sent. Spam activity thrives because messages can be delivered to large audiences at a very low cost.

According to data compiled by Symantec (**www.symantec.com**), a leading security software firm, much of spam now involves the use of documents that are attached to E-mail messages. These documents are often in either Microsoft Office or flash animation formats.

To many observers, the increase in junk E-mail comes as no surprise. Anti-spam groups argue that the 2004 law effectively gave spammers permission to send junk E-mails if they followed several guidelines. The most recent Can Spam Act revisions in 2008 (**www.ftc.gov/opa/2008/05/canspam.shtm**) make it easier to determine which of several parties that jointly advertise in a single E-mail message are responsible for complying with op-out requirements. A major weakness of the law is that it puts the burden on recipients to be removed from an E-mailer's mailing list through an "opt-out" feature. The "opt-out" message can be used by spammers as a means of verifying that the E-mail address used is current.

Sources: Chandra Johnson-Greene, "FTC Approves New Rule Provisions for Can-Spam," *Circulation Management* (June 2008), p. 9; and Jacob Stoller, "The War Against Spam," *CMA Management* (February 2008), pp. 48–49.

Lands' End has many different Web sites to service customers around the world, such as its German site (**www. landsend.de**). Because of Lands' End's customer commitment, this site is in German.

MOUNTING INTEREST IN GLOBAL DIRECT MARKETING

More retailers are involved with global direct marketing because of the growing consumer acceptance of nonstore retailing in other countries. Among the U.S.-based direct marketers with a significant international presence are Brookstone, Eddie Bauer, Lands' End, and Williams-Sonoma.

Outside the United States, annual direct marketing sales (by both domestic and foreign firms) are hundreds of billions of dollars. Direct marketing trade associations—each representing many member firms—exist in such diverse countries as Australia, Brazil, China, France, Germany, Japan, Russia, and Spain. In Europe alone, there are well over 10,000 direct marketing companies. Korean shoppers can view a TV shopping channel from Japan on the Internet and order through their computers.[10]

The Steps in a Direct Marketing Strategy

A direct marketing strategy has eight steps: business definition, generating customers, media selection, presenting the message, customer contact, customer response, order fulfillment, and measuring results and maintaining the data base. See Figure 6-4.

BUSINESS DEFINITION

First, a company makes two decisions regarding its business definition: (1) Is the firm going to be a pure direct marketer, or is it going to engage in multi-channel retailing? If the firm chooses the latter, it must clarify the role of direct marketing in its overall retail strategy. (2) Is the firm going to be a general direct marketer and carry a broad product assortment, or will it specialize in one goods/service category?

GENERATING CUSTOMERS

A mechanism for generating business is devised next. A firm can

▶ Buy a printed mailing list from a broker. For one mailing, a list usually costs $50 to $100 or more per 1,000 names and addresses; it is supplied in mailing-label format. Lists may be broad or broken down by gender, location, and so on. In purchasing a list, the direct marketer should check its currency.

▶ Download a mailing list from the Web that is sold by a firm such as infoUSA (**www.infousa.com**), which has data on 110 million U.S. households. With a download, a firm can use the list multiple times, but it is responsible for selecting names and printing labels.

▶ Send out a blind mailing to all the residents in a particular area. This method can be expensive (unless done through E-mail) and may receive a very low response rate.

▶ Advertise in a newspaper, magazine, Web site, or other medium, and ask customers to order by mail, phone, fax, or computer.

▶ Contact consumers who have bought from the firm or requested information. This is efficient, but it takes a while to develop a data base. To grow, a firm cannot rely solely on past customers.

FIGURE 6-4

Executing a Direct Marketing Strategy

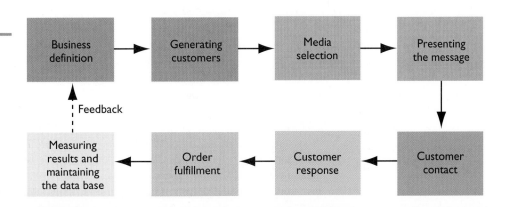

MEDIA SELECTION

Several media are available to the direct marketer:

- ▶ Printed catalogs.
- ▶ Direct mail ads and brochures.
- ▶ Inserts with monthly credit card and other bills ("statement stuffers").
- ▶ Freestanding displays with coupons, brochures, or catalogs (such as magazine subscription cards at the supermarket checkout counter).
- ▶ Ads or programs in the mass media—newspapers, magazines, radio, TV.
- ▶ Banner ads or "hot links" on the World Wide Web.
- ▶ Video kiosks.

In choosing among media, costs, distribution, lead time, and other factors should be considered.

PRESENTING THE MESSAGE

Now, the firm prepares and presents its message in a way that engenders interest, creates (or sustains) the proper image, points out compelling reasons to purchase, and provides data about goods or services (such as prices and sizes). The message must also contain ordering instructions, including the payment method; how to designate the chosen items; shipping fees; and a firm's address, phone number, and Web address.

The message, and the medium in which it is presented, should be planned in the same way that a traditional retailer plans a store. The latter uses a storefront, lighting, carpeting, the store layout, and displays to foster an image. In direct marketing, the headlines, message content, use of color, paper quality, personalization of mail, space devoted to each item, and other elements affect a firm's image.

CUSTOMER CONTACT

For each campaign, a direct marketer decides whether to contact all customers in its data base or to seek specific market segments (with different messages and/or media for each). It can classify prospective customers as *regulars* (those who buy continuously), *nonregulars* (those who buy infrequently), *new contacts* (those who have never been sought before by the firm), and *nonrespondents* (those who have been contacted but never made a purchase).

Regulars and nonregulars are the most apt to respond to a firm's future offerings, and they can be better targeted because the firm has their purchase histories. For example, customers who have bought clothing before are prime prospects for specialogs. New contacts probably know little about the firm. Messages to them must build interest, accurately portray the firm, and present meaningful reasons for consumers to buy. This group is important if growth is sought.

Nonrespondents who have been contacted repeatedly without purchasing are unlikely to ever buy. Unless a firm can present a very different message, it is inefficient to pursue this group. Firms such as Publishers Clearinghouse send mailings to millions of people who have never bought from them; this is okay because they sell inexpensive impulse items and need only a small response rate to succeed.

CUSTOMER RESPONSE

Customers respond to direct marketers in one of three ways: (1) They buy through the mail, phone, fax, or computer. (2) They request further information, such as a catalog. (3) They ignore the message. Purchases are generally made by no more than 2 to 3 percent of those contacted. The rate is higher for specialogs, mail-order clubs (e.g., for music), and firms focusing on repeat customers.

ORDER FULFILLMENT

A system is needed for order fulfillment. If orders are received by mail or fax, the firm must sort them, determine if payment is enclosed, see whether the item is in stock, mail announcements if items cannot be sent on time, coordinate shipments, and replenish inventory. If phone orders are placed, a trained sales staff must be available when people may call. Salespeople answer questions, make suggestions, enter orders, note the payment method, see whether items are in stock, coordinate shipments, and replenish inventory. If orders are placed by computer, there must be a process to promptly and efficiently handle credit transactions, issue receipts, and forward orders to a warehouse. In all cases, names, addresses, and purchase data are added to the data base for future reference.

In peak seasons, additional warehouse, shipping, order processing, and sales workers supplement regular employees. Direct marketers that are highly regarded by consumers fill orders promptly, have knowledgeable and courteous personnel, do not misrepresent quality, and provide liberal return policies.

MEASURING RESULTS AND MAINTAINING THE DATA BASE

The last step is analyzing results and maintaining the data base. Direct marketing often yields clear outcomes:

▶ *Overall response rate*—the number and percentage of people who make a purchase after receiving or viewing a particular brochure, catalog, or Web site.
▶ *Average purchase amount*—by customer location, gender, and so forth.
▶ *Sales volume by product category*—revenues correlated with the space allotted to each product in brochures, catalogs, and so forth.
▶ *Value of list brokers*—the revenues generated by various mailing lists.

After measuring results, the firm reviews its data base and makes sure that new shoppers are added, address changes are noted for existing customers, purchase and consumer information is current and available in segmentation categories, and nonrespondents are purged (when desirable).

This stage provides feedback for the direct marketer as it plans each new campaign.

Key Issues Facing Direct Marketers

In planning and applying their strategies, direct marketers must keep the following in mind.

Many people dislike one or more aspects of direct marketing. They are the most dissatisfied with late delivery or nondelivery, deceptive claims, broken or damaged items, the wrong items being sent, and the lack of information. Nonetheless, in most cases, leading direct marketers are rated well by consumers.

Most U.S. households report that they open all direct mail, but many would like to receive less of it. Because the average American household receives numerous catalogs each year, besides hundreds of other mailings, firms must be concerned about clutter. It is hard to be distinctive in this environment.

A lot of consumers are concerned that their names and other information are being sold by list brokers, as well as by some retailers. They feel this is an invasion of privacy and that their decision to purchase does not constitute permission to pass on personal data. To counteract this, members of the Direct Marketing Association remove people's names from list circulation if they make a request.

Multiple-channel retailers need a consistent image for both store-based and direct marketing efforts. They must also perceive the similarities and differences in each approach's strategy. The steady increase in postal rates makes mailing catalogs, brochures, and other promotional materials costly for some firms. Numerous direct marketers are turning more to newspapers, magazines, and cable TV—and the Web.

Direct marketers must monitor the legal environment. They must be aware that, in the future, more states will probably require residents to pay sales tax on out-of-state direct marketing purchases; the firms would have to remit the tax payments to affected states. New laws will be contested by retailers.

Direct Selling

Direct selling includes both personal contact with consumers in their homes (and other nonstore locations such as offices) and phone solicitations initiated by a retailer. Cosmetics, jewelry, vitamins, household goods and services (such as carpet cleaning),

TABLE 6-1 A Snapshot of the U.S. Direct Selling Industry

Major Product Groups (as a percent of sales dollars)	
Clothing and accessories/personal care	32.8
Home/family care products (cleaning products, cookware, cutlery, etc.)	25.6
Wellness products (weight loss products, vitamins, etc.)	21.4
Services/miscellaneous/other	16.2
Leisure/educational products (books, encyclopedias, toys/games, etc.)	4.0
Place of Sales (as a percent of sales dollars)	
In the home	70.4
Over the Internet	11.4
Over the phone	8.8
At a temporary location (such as a fair, exhibition, shopping mall, etc.)	3.7
In a workplace	2.5
Other locations	3.2
Sales Approach (method used to generate sales, as a percent of sales dollars)	
Individual/one-to-one selling	64.5
Party plan/group sales	27.7
Customer placing order directly with firm	6.6
Other	1.2
Demographics of Salespeople (as a percent of all salespeople)	
Female/male	87.9/12.1
Education (high school grad or less/at least some college)	28.0/72.0
Married/not married	77.0/23.0
Hours per week in direct selling (less than 20/20 or more)	88.0/12.0

Source: Direct Selling by the Numbers (Washington, DC: Direct Selling Association, 2008).

vacuum cleaners, and magazines and newspapers are among the items sometimes sold in this way. The industry has $31 billion in annual U.S. sales and employs 15 million people (more than 80 percent part-time). Annual foreign direct selling revenues are $85 billion, generated by 48 million salespeople.[11] Table 6-1 shows an industry overview.

A direct-selling strategy mix emphasizes convenient shopping and a personal touch, and detailed demonstrations can be made. Consumers often relax more in their homes than in stores. They are also likely to be attentive and are not exposed to competing brands (as they are in stores). For some shoppers, such as older consumers and those with young children, in-store shopping is hard due to limited mobility. For the retailer, direct selling has lower overhead costs because stores and fixtures are not necessary.

Despite its advantages, direct selling in the United States is growing slowly:

▶ More women work, and they may not be interested in or available for in-home selling.
▶ Improved job opportunities in other fields and the interest in full-time careers have reduced the pool of people interested in direct-selling jobs.
▶ A firm's market coverage is limited by the size of its sales force.
▶ Sales productivity is low because the average transaction is small and most consumers are unreceptive—many will not open their doors to salespeople or talk to telemarketers.
▶ Sales force turnover is high because employees are often poorly supervised part-timers.
▶ To stimulate sales personnel, compensation is usually 25 to 50 percent of the revenues they generate. This means average to above-average prices.
▶ There are various legal restrictions due to deceptive and high-pressure sales tactics. One such restriction is the FTC's Telemarketing Sales Rule (**www.ftc.gov/bcp/rulemaking/tsr**), which mandates that firms must disclose their identity and that the purpose of the call is selling.
▶ Because *door-to-door* has a poor image, the industry prefers the term *direct selling*.

The Direct Selling Association (**www.dsa.org**) is working hard to promote the image and professionalism of this retail format.

**TECHNOLOGY
IN RETAILING**

Direct Selling: Avon Turns to the Internet to Improve
Salesperson Performance

The use of Web-based technology has simplified the life of many direct sellers—such as Avon—by facilitating salesperson training. Avon (**www.avon.com**), the world's largest direct sales organization, has 5 million independent sales representatives worldwide—about 500,000 based in the United States.

Because Avon's sales representatives are independent workers, the firm can only recommend that all new sales reps complete Avon's Beauty of Knowledge Web site and learning management system (LMS). The LMS program is made up of 19 courses ranging from makeup management to financial management. The LMS program also includes assessment tools so that Avon's leadership members can determine what their reps have actually learned. When a rep completes one

of the 19 courses, the LMS program sends data back to a new rep's leadership mentor, who can assess which aspects of the program worked best.

In the first seven months that LMS was offered, more than 240,000 reps completed close to 850,000 courses. Part of the popularity of the program can be attributed to its flexibility. Unlike traditional classroom-based learning, reps are able to complete a course module at their convenience. Course instruction can also be stopped and started multiple times during the course of a day to accommodate a rep's multiple responsibilities to her family as well as work.

Sources: Tegan Jones, "Avon: Raising Online Education," *Clomedia* (February 2007), pp. 46–47, 56; and Ellen Byron, "Lean Times Swell Avon's Sales Force," *Wall Street Journal*, **http://online.wsj.com/article/sb122402888043134519.html** (October 15, 2008).

Firms are reacting to these issues. Avon places greater emphasis on workplace sales, offers free training to sales personnel, rewards the best workers with better territories, pursues more global sales, and places cosmetics kiosks in shopping centers. Mary Kay hires community residents as salespeople and has a party atmosphere rather than a strict door-to-door approach; this requires networks of family, friends, and neighbors. And every major direct selling firm has a Web site to supplement revenues.

Among the leading direct sellers are Avon and Mary Kay (cosmetics), Amway (household supplies), Tupperware (plastic containers), Shaklee (health products), Fuller Brush (small household products), and Kirby (vacuum cleaners). Some stores, such as J.C. Penney, also use direct selling. Penney's decorator consultants sell a complete line of furnishings, not available in its stores, to consumers in their homes. See Figure 6-5.

FIGURE 6-5

Direct Selling and Mary Kay

Throughout the world (in 35 markets), Mary Kay employs more than 1.8 million direct sales consultants, who mostly visit customers in their homes and account for several billion dollars in revenues. Through its Web site (**www.marykay.com**), the company even provides links to the home pages of its U.S. consultants.

Source: Reprinted by permission of Mary Kay.

Vending Machines

A **vending machine** is a cash- or card-operated retailing format that dispenses goods (such as beverages) and services (such as electronic arcade games). It eliminates the use of sales personnel and allows 24-hour sales. Machines can be placed wherever convenient for consumers—inside or outside stores, in motel corridors, at train stations, or on street corners.

The Canteen Corporation (www.canteen.com) has vending machines at 18,500 client locations.

Although there have been many attempts to "vend" clothing, magazines, and other general merchandise, 95 percent of the $50 billion in annual U.S. vending machine sales involve hot and cold beverages and food items. Because of health issues, over the past 30 years, cigarettes' share of sales has gone from 25 to just 1 to 2 percent. The greatest sales are achieved in factory, office, and school lunchrooms and refreshment areas; public places such as service stations are also popular sites. Newspapers on street corners and sidewalks, various machines in hotels and motels, and candy machines in restaurants and at train stations are visible aspects of vending but account for a small percentage of U.S. vending machine sales.[12] Leading vending machine operators are Canteen Corporation and Aramark Refreshment Services.

Items priced above $1.50 have not sold well; too many coins are required, and some vending machines do not have dollar bill changers. Consumers are reluctant to buy more expensive items that they cannot see displayed or have explained. However, their expanded access to and use of debit cards are expected to have a major impact on resolving the payment issue, and the video-kiosk type of vending machine lets people see product displays and get detailed information (and then place a credit or debit card order). Popular brands and standardized nonfood items are best suited to increasing sales via vending machines.

To improve productivity and customer relations, vending operators are applying several innovations. Popular products such as French fries are being made fresh in vending machines. Machine malfunctions are reduced by applying electronic mechanisms to cash-handling controls. Microprocessors track consumer preferences, trace malfunctions, and record receipts. Some machines have voice synthesizers that are programmed to say "Thank you, come again" or "Your change is 25 cents."

Operators must still deal with theft, vandalism, stockouts, above-average prices, and the perception that vending machines should be patronized only when a fill-in convenience item is needed.

Electronic Retailing: The Emergence of the World Wide Web

We are living through enormous changes from the days when retailing simply meant visiting a store, shopping from a printed catalog, greeting the Avon lady in one's home, or buying candy from a vending machine. Who would have thought that a person could "surf the Web" to research a stock, learn about a new product, search for bargains, save a trip to the store, and complain about customer service? Well, these activities are real and they're here to stay. Let's take a look at the World Wide Web from a retailing perspective, remembering that selling on the Web is a form of direct marketing.

Let's define two terms that may be confusing: The **Internet** is a global electronic superhighway of computer networks that use a common protocol and that are linked by telecommunications lines and satellite. It acts as a single, cooperative virtual network and is maintained by universities, governments, and businesses. The **World Wide Web (Web)** is one way to access information on the Internet, whereby people work with easy-to-use Web addresses (sites) and pages. Web users see words, charts, pictures, and video, and hear audio—which turn their computers into interactive multimedia centers. People can easily move from site to site by pointing at the proper spot on the monitor and clicking a mouse button. Browsing software, such as Microsoft Internet Explorer and Mozilla Firefox, facilitate Web surfing.

Both *Internet* and *World Wide Web* convey the same central theme: online interactive retailing. Because almost all online retailing is done via the World Wide Web, we use *Web* in our discussion, which is comprised of these topics: the role of the Web, the scope of Web retailing, characteristics of Web users, factors to consider in planning whether to have a Web site, and examples of Web retailers. Visit our Web site (**www.pearsonhighered. com/berman**) for several valuable links on E-retailing.

The Role of the Web

From the vantage point of the retailer, the World Wide Web can serve one or more roles:

- ▶ Project a retail presence and enhance the retailer's image.
- ▶ Generate sales as the major source of revenue for an online retailer or as a complementary source of revenue for a store-based retailer.
- ▶ Reach geographically dispersed consumers, including foreign ones.
- ▶ Provide information to consumers about products carried, store locations, usage information, answers to common questions, customer loyalty programs, and so on.
- ▶ Promote new products and fully explain and demonstrate their features.
- ▶ Furnish customer service in the form of E-mail, "hot links," and other communications.
- ▶ Be more "personal" with consumers by letting them point and click on topics they choose.
- ▶ Conduct a retail business in a cost-efficient manner.
- ▶ Obtain customer feedback.
- ▶ Promote special offers and send coupons to Web customers.
- ▶ Describe employment opportunities.
- ▶ Present information to potential investors, potential franchisees, and the media.

The role a retailer assigns to the Web depends on (1) whether its major goal is to communicate interactively with consumers or to sell goods and services, (2) whether it is predominantly a traditional retailer that wants to have a Web presence or a newer firm that wants to derive most or all of its sales from the Web, and (3) the level of resources the retailer wants to commit to site development and maintenance. There are millions of Web sites worldwide and hundreds of thousands in retailing.

The Scope of Web Retailing

Internet Retailer (**www. internetretailer.com**) tracks online retailing.

The potential of the Web is enormous: As of 2009, there were already 250 million Web users in North America, nearly 400 million in Europe, 600 million in Asia-Pacific, 140 million in Latin America, and 95 million in Africa/the Middle East. More than 90 percent of U.S. Web users have made at least one online purchase; and about three-quarters of U.S. Web users have made at least one online purchase in the last six months. A decade ago, U.S. shoppers generated 75 percent of worldwide online retail sales; the amount is now less than 40 percent and falling. U.S. retail Web sales have doubled over the past five years; and 80 percent of current purchases are made by those with broadband connections (rather than dialup). At least 5 percent or more of the U.S. sales of these goods and services are made online: apparel, banking, books, computer hardware and software, consumer electronics, gifts, greeting cards, insurance, music, newspapers/magazines, sporting goods, toys, travel, and videos. A real milestone in Web retailing was achieved just a few years ago, when—for the first time—the majority of U.S. E-retailers reported a profit.[13] Figure 6-6 indicates the percentage of projected 2012 online sales by selected product category.

Despite the foregoing data, the Web accounts for only 3 to 4 percent of U.S. retail sales! It will not be the death knell of store-based retailing but another choice for shoppers, like other forms of direct marketing. There is much higher sales growth for "clicks-and-mortar" Web retailing (multi-channel retailing) than "bricks-and-mortar" stores (single-channel retailing) and "clicks-only" Web firms (single-channel retailing). Store-based retailers account for more than three-quarters of U.S. online sales:

> Much has been written about the rapid growth of E-commerce and the predicted damage it would have on brick-and-mortar stores. But the emerging reality is that the Internet is much more effective as a marketing vehicle, while the store is—and will remain—the more effective purchasing vehicle. The "shop online, purchase in-store" phenomenon is driven by two primary consumer-shopping

FIGURE 6-6

Web-Based Retail Sales Projections for Selected Product Categories (Excluding Travel)

Source: Chart developed by the authors from data by Forester Research, 2008.

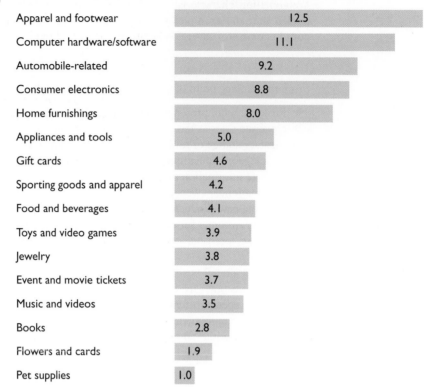

Product Category | **% of Total Web-Based Retail Sales in 2012**

Product Category	%
Apparel and footwear	12.5
Computer hardware/software	11.1
Automobile-related	9.2
Consumer electronics	8.8
Home furnishings	8.0
Appliances and tools	5.0
Gift cards	4.6
Sporting goods and apparel	4.2
Food and beverages	4.1
Toys and video games	3.9
Jewelry	3.8
Event and movie tickets	3.7
Music and videos	3.5
Books	2.8
Flowers and cards	1.9
Pet supplies	1.0

needs: efficiency and convenience. Shoppers are using the efficiency of the Internet to research products on retailer, manufacturer, and comparison shopping sites, and they are using the convenience of the local store to see, touch, and ultimately buy the product.[14]

Characteristics of Web Users

U.S. Web users have these characteristics, many of which are highlighted in Figure 6-7:

▶ *Gender and age.* There almost as many males as females on the Web; however, females shop more often. Eighteen- to 30-year-olds are most likely to use the Web; those 72 and older are least likely.

▶ *Average time online.* The typical Web user spends 14 hours per week on the Web.

▶ *Income and education.* Three-fifths of households with an annual income under $40,000 use the Web; in contrast, 91 percent of households with an annual income of at least $40,000 use the Web. Those who have attended college are more likely to use the Internet as those who have not attended college.

▶ *What shoppers have researched.* Well over one-half of Web users research holidays/destinations, consumer electronics, and portable devices (such as MP3 players) online.

▶ *Web-influenced store sales.* By 2012, it is expected the Web will stimulate more than $1.1 trillion of in-store sales annually.

According to recent research, these are some of the key factors to online shoppers with regard to their continued patronage: (1) *Website design/interaction*—"Includes all elements of the consumer's experience at the Web site (except for customer service), including navigation, information search, order processing, shipment tracking, product availability, and product and price offerings." (2) *Fulfillment/reliability*—"Customers receive what they thought they ordered based on the display and description provided at the Web site, and/or delivery of the right product at the right price (i.e., billed correctly) in good condition within the time frame promised." (3) *Customer service*—"Helpful,

FIGURE 6-7

A Snapshot of U.S. Web Users

Sources: Charts developed by the authors from data in "Where Is Generation X?" **www.emarketer. com/Article.aspx?id=1006699** (November 3, 2008); "Can You Count on Savvy Web Users?" **www. emarketer.com/Article.aspx?id=10 06790** (December 8, 2008); "What Do Shoppers Research on the Web?" **www.emarketer.com/Article.aspx? id=1006629** (October 13, 2008); and "Online Research Drives Offline Sales," **www.emarketer.com/ Article.aspx?id=1005971** (February 26, 2008).

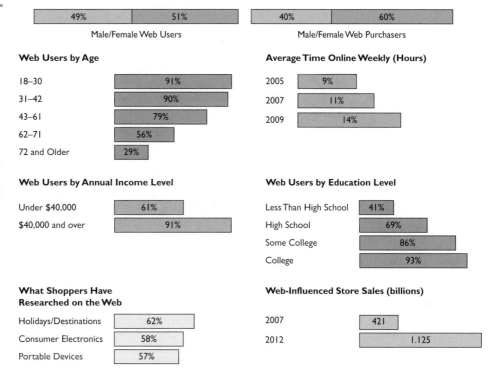

Gender Comparisons

responsive service that responds to customer inquiries and returns/complaints quickly during or after the sale." (4) *Security/privacy*—"The security of credit-card payments and the privacy of shared information during or after the sale."[15]

Web users can be enticed to shop more often if they are assured of privacy, retailers are perceived as trustworthy, sites are easy to maneuver, prices are lower than at stores, there are strong money-back guarantees, they can return a product to a store, shipping costs are not hidden until the end of the purchase process, transactions are secure, they can speak with sales representatives, and download time is faster.

Factors to Consider in Planning Whether to Have a Web Site

The Web generally offers many *advantages* for retailers. It is usually less costly to have a Web site than a store. The potential marketplace is huge and dispersed, yet relatively easy to reach. Web sites can be quite exciting, due to their multimedia capabilities. People can visit Web sites at any time, and their visits can be as short or long as they desire. Information can be targeted, so that, for example, a person visiting a toy retailer's Web site could click on the icon labeled "Educational Toys—ages three to six." A customer data base can be established and customer feedback obtained.

The Web also has *disadvantages* for retailers: If consumers do not know a firm's Web address, it may be hard to find. For various reasons, some people are not yet willing to buy online. There is tremendous clutter with regard to the number of Web sites. Because Web surfers are easily bored, a Web site must be regularly updated to ensure repeat visits. The more multimedia features a Web site has, the slower it may be for people with dialup connections to access. Some firms have been overwhelmed with customer service requests and questions from E-mail. It may be hard to coordinate store and Web transactions. There are few standards or rules as to what may be portrayed at Web sites. Consumers expect online services to be free and are reluctant to pay for them.

There is a large gulf between full-scale, integrated Web selling and a basic "telling"— rather than "selling"—Web site. To better understand this gulf, the model highlighted in Figure 6-8 was introduced at a National Retail Federation Information Technology Power Summit so that retailers can envision Web site development as a set of building blocks comprising a five-step process: "Many large, successful retailers are happy to be at Stage 2,

FIGURE 6-8

The Five Stages of
Developing a Retail Web
Presence

Source: Chart developed by the
authors from the discussion in Tracy
Mullin, "Determining Web
Presence," *Chain Store Age* (October
1999), p. 42.

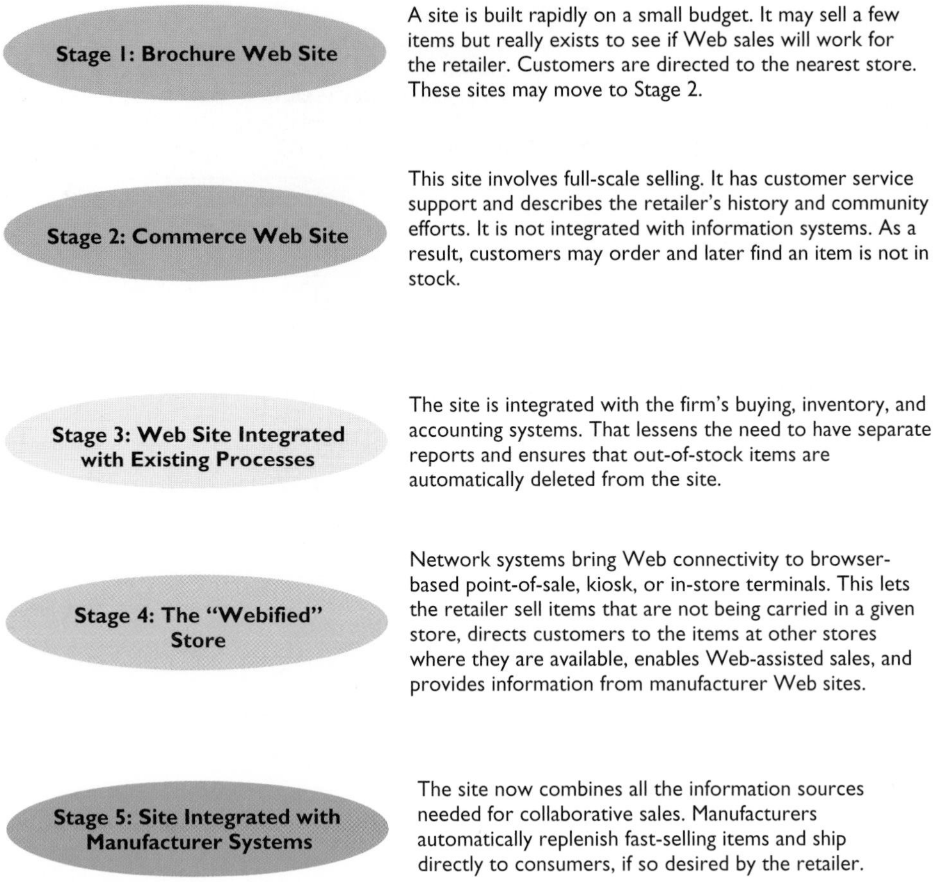

Stage 1: Brochure Web Site

A site is built rapidly on a small budget. It may sell a few items but really exists to see if Web sales will work for the retailer. Customers are directed to the nearest store. These sites may move to Stage 2.

Stage 2: Commerce Web Site

This site involves full-scale selling. It has customer service support and describes the retailer's history and community efforts. It is not integrated with information systems. As a result, customers may order and later find an item is not in stock.

Stage 3: Web Site Integrated with Existing Processes

The site is integrated with the firm's buying, inventory, and accounting systems. That lessens the need to have separate reports and ensures that out-of-stock items are automatically deleted from the site.

Stage 4: The "Webified" Store

Network systems bring Web connectivity to browser-based point-of-sale, kiosk, or in-store terminals. This lets the retailer sell items that are not being carried in a given store, directs customers to the items at other stores where they are available, enables Web-assisted sales, and provides information from manufacturer Web sites.

Stage 5: Site Integrated with Manufacturer Systems

The site now combines all the information sources needed for collaborative sales. Manufacturers automatically replenish fast-selling items and ship directly to consumers, if so desired by the retailer.

and find that it brings them new customers and increased visibility. Stage 3, where the Web becomes simply another channel, was, for a time, the ideal that retailers sought. Stages 4 and 5 represent the next steps on the road to retail nirvana—the total integration of the virtual with the physical. Yet, as history tells us, Stages 6, 7, 8, and beyond are out there, waiting for technology to mature and new applications."[16]

Web retailers should carefully consider these recommendations, compiled from several industry experts:

Keep current on E-retailing
news with TSN Retail
Forward's information-rich
Web site (http://eretail.
retailforward.com).

▶ Develop (or exploit) a well-known, trustworthy retailer name.
▶ Tailor the product assortment for Web shoppers, and keep freshening the offerings.
▶ With download speed in mind, provide pictures and ample product information.
▶ Enable the shopper to make as few clicks as possible to get product information and place orders.
▶ Provide the best possible search engine at the firm's Web site.
▶ Capitalize on customer information and relationships.
▶ Integrate online and offline businesses, and look for partnering opportunities.
▶ With permission, save customer data to make future shopping trips easier.
▶ Indicate shipping fees upfront and be clear about delivery options.
▶ Do not promote items that are out of stock; and let shoppers know immediately if items will not be shipped for a few days.
▶ Offer online order tracking.
▶ Use a secure order entry system for shoppers.
▶ Prominently state the firm's return and privacy policies.

See Figure 6-9.

Consistent with the preceding discussion, a firm has many decisions to make if it wants to utilize the Web (as enumerated in Figure 6-9). A firm cannot just put up a site and wait for consumers to visit it in droves and then expect them to happily return. In

FIGURE 6-9

A Checklist of Retailer
Decisions in Utilizing
the Web

✓ What are the company's Web goals? At what point is it expected that the site will be profitable?
✓ What budget will be allocated to developing and maintaining a Web site?
✓ Who will develop and maintain the Web site, the retailer itself or an outside specialist?
✓ Should the firm set up an independent Web site for itself or should it be part of a "cybermall?"
✓ What features will the Web site have? What level of customer service will be offered?
✓ What information will the Web site provide?
✓ How will the goods and services assortment differ at the Web site from the firm's store?
✓ Will the Web site offer benefits not available elsewhere?
✓ Will prices reflect a good value for the consumer?
✓ How fast will the user be able to download the text and images from the Web site, and point and click from screen to screen?
✓ How often will Web site content be changed?
✓ What staff will handle Web inquiries and transactions?
✓ How fast will turnaround time be for Web inquiries and transactions?
✓ How will the firm coordinate store and Web transactions and customer interactions?
✓ What will be done to avoid crashes and slow site features during peak shopping hours and seasons?
✓ How will online orders be processed?
✓ How easy will it be for shoppers to enter and complete orders?
✓ What online payment methods will be accepted?
✓ What search engines (such as Yahoo!) will list the retailer's Web site?
✓ How will the site be promoted: (a) on the Web and (b) by the company?
✓ How will Web data be stored and arranged? How will all of the firm's information systems be integrated?
✓ How will Web success be measured?
✓ How will the firm determine which Web shoppers are new customers and which are customers who would otherwise visit a company store?
✓ How will the firm ensure secure (encrypted) transactions?
✓ How will consumer privacy concerns be handled?
✓ How will returns and customer complaints be handled?

many cases: (1) It is still difficult for people to find exactly what they are looking for. (2) Once the person finds what he or she wants, it may be hard to envision the product. "Subtleties of color and texture often don't come across well on the Web. Until someone figures out how to send a cashmere scarf digitally, you won't be able to touch it." (3) Customer service is sometimes lacking. (4) Web sites and their store siblings may not be in sync. "Send someone a gift from CompanyA.com and the recipient may be surprised to find it can't be returned or exchanged at a Company A store." (5) Privacy policies may not be consumer-oriented. "Order from a site, fill out a survey, or merely browse, and you find your E-mail box swamped with unsolicited ads and other junk."[17]

Examples of Web Retailing in Action

These examples show the breadth of retailing on the World Wide Web.

Amazon.com (**www.amazon.com**) is probably the most famous pure Web retailer in the world, with revenues exceeding $8 billion and tens of millions of customers purchasing from the firm each year. This is how *Hoover's Online* sums up the Amazon.com phenomenon:

> What started as Earth's biggest bookstore has rapidly become Earth's biggest anything store. Expansion has propelled Amazon.com in innumerable directions. The firm's main Web site offers millions of books, music, DVDs, and videos (which still account for the majority, more than 60 percent, of the firm's sales), not to mention auto parts, toys, tools, electronics, home furnishings, apparel, health and beauty aids, prescription drugs, groceries, and services including film processing. Long a model for Internet companies that put market share ahead of profits, Amazon.com also made acquisitions funded by meteoric market capitalization and is now focused on profits. Founder Jeff Bezos owns about 24 percent of the firm.[18]

At the opposite end of the spectrum from Amazon.com is the specialty business of SeamlessWeb.com (**www.seamlessweb.com**):

> Ordering food is made simple. View up-to-date menus from 2,000+ restaurants in 14 cities. Find and sort through restaurants that deliver to your address. Pay and tip by credit card. Faster than ordering over the phone. Avoid waiting on hold for busy restaurants. Re-order favorite meals in just two clicks. Search through millions of dishes instantly. Make a more informed eating decision. Food photos and extra information are featured at many restaurants. Find the most popular restaurants and menu items in your area. Benefit from thousands of helpful user reviews. Save 20 percent automatically at select restaurants with Delicious Discounts! Our process works through four steps: (1) Order your meal at SeamlessWeb.com. (2) Your order prints out at the restaurant within seconds. (3) The restaurant confirms your order, which generates an E-mail. (4) The restaurant prepares and delivers your meal. In some locations, pick-up ordering is also possible.[19]

Netflix (**www.netflix.com**) is a very successful online service retailer that was started in September 1999. It rents movies in a customer-friendly way:

> Netflix, Inc. is the world's largest online movie rental service, with more than eight million subscribers. For one low monthly price, Netflix members can get DVDs delivered to their homes and can instantly watch movies and TV episodes streamed to their TVs and PCs, all in unlimited amounts. Members can choose from over 100,000 DVD titles and a growing library of more than 12,000 choices that can be watched instantly. There are never any due dates or late fees. DVDs are delivered free to members by first-class mail, with a postage-paid return envelope, from 55 distribution centers. More than 95 percent of Netflix members live in areas that generally receive shipments in one business day. Netflix is also partnering with leading consumer electronics companies to offer a range of devices that can instantly stream movies and TV episodes to members' TVs from Netflix.[20]

Finally, here are three other interesting Web retailing illustrations: First, eBay (**www.ebay.com**), Priceline.com (**www.priceline.com**), and uBid.com (**www.ubid.com**)

Online Shopping: Opportunities in Great Britain

According to the IMRG Capgemini (**www.imrg.org**) E-Retail Sales Index, British shoppers were expected to spend nearly $100 billion in 2008, a substantial increase from the online sales level in 2007. A marketing analyst for Verdict Research (**www.verdict.co.uk**) stated that much of this growth was due to consumers seeking bargains and more extensively using price-comparison Web sites. Verdict forecasts that online shopping among U.K. consumers will grow from 5.2 percent of total retail sales in 2007 to 13.8 percent during 2012.

Among the fastest-growing categories in British Web-based retailing are clothing and groceries. For example, online grocer Ocado (**www.ocado.com**) has been experiencing annual sales growth of 25 percent per year with an average transaction amount of about $150. According to

Ocado's chief financial and marketing officer, "The growth is coming from new customers. Interestingly, new customers spend less and as they become regular customers, they spend more and more."

Asda's (**www.asda.co.uk**) multi-channel director planned to distribute online grocery purchases throughout Great Britain by the end of 2008. The director believes that, in the past, online grocers received bad press due to shipping products with limited expiration dates, shipping substitute products, and selling damaged goods. These assumptions are no longer correct.

Sources: Julian Goldsmith, "Online Nearing 20 Percent of British Shopping," **www.businessweek.com/globalbiz** (July 18, 2008); and James Thompson, "What Slowdown? Brit Shoppers Hit the Web," **www.businessweek.com/globalbiz** (June 4, 2008).

FIGURE 6-10

Priceline.com: Online
Auctions for Travel

At Priceline.com
(**www.priceline.com**), "you can
now choose your exact flights
and times for incredible travel
savings or Name Your Own Price
and save even more! All it takes
is a little flexibility with your
travel plans. If you can fly any
time of day, agree to fly on any
major airline, stay in any name-
brand hotel, or rent from any of
the top 5 U.S. rental car
agencies—you can save a lot of
money with Priceline!"

Source: Reprinted by permission of
Priceline.com.

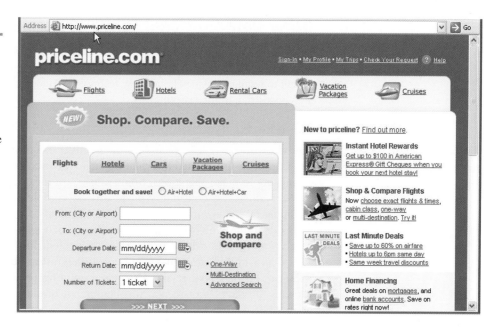

are just three of the retailers with online auctions, featuring everything from consumer
electronics and textbooks to hotel rates and air fares. See Figure 6-10. Even nonprofit
Goodwill has an auction Web site (**www.shopgoodwill.com**) to sell donated items.
Second, Starbucks offers high-speed wireless Internet service at thousands of stores:
"There are a number of complimentary and paid Wi-Fi options, whether you need to
check your E-mail, download files for your next meeting, or just surf the Web in coffee-
house comfort. When you register your Starbucks Card and use it at least once a month,
you'll receive two consecutive hours a day of complimentary Wi-Fi, courtesy of AT&T.
AT&T's more than 12 million DSL customers already qualify for free Wi-Fi at their
neighborhood Starbucks. All other customers can receive two consecutive hours of Wi-Fi
access for $3.99."[21] Third, J.C. Penney has an optimal multi-channel mix, as highlighted
in Figure 6-11.

FIGURE 6-11

J.C. Penney: A Master of
Multi-Channel Retailing

Source: Reprinted by permission of
TNS Retail Forward.

Other Nontraditional Forms of Retailing

Two other nontraditional institutions merit discussion: video kiosks and airport retailing. Although both formats have existed for years, they are now much more popular. They appeal to retailers' desires to use new technology (video kiosks) and to locate in sites with high pedestrian traffic (airports).

Video Kiosks

Kiosks.org (**www.kiosks. org**) tracks the trends with video kiosks.

The **video kiosk** is a freestanding, interactive, electronic computer terminal that displays products and related information on a video screen; it often has a touch screen for consumers to make selections. Some kiosks are located in stores to enhance customer service; others let consumers place orders, complete transactions (typically with a credit card), and arrange for shipping. Kiosks can be linked to retailers' computer networks or to the Web. There are 2.2 million video kiosks in use throughout the world, nearly 1 million of which are Internet-connected. In the United States, they generate $12 to $15 billion in annual retail sales. It is estimated that kiosks *influence* $75 to $150 billion in global retail sales—by providing product and warranty information, showing product assortments, displaying out-of-stock products, listing products by price, and so forth—and *generate* $20 billion in retail sales annually. North America accounts for the majority of kiosk sales, follow by the Pacific Rim, Europe, and the rest of the world.[22]

How exactly do video kiosks work?

Interactive kiosks are self-contained computing terminals that provide access to on-demand information and transactions. Some examples include airport self-check-in systems, retail product locators, and bill pay terminals. Other variations include kiosks that rent DVD movies, burn custom CDs and DVDs on demand, or download multimedia files to handheld media players. These systems employ modular hardware designs that can be expanded to include numerous peripherals, such as touch screens, thermal printers, and card scanners. You will typically see a touch screen and on-screen keyboard used for data entry, along with card readers and barcode scanners. A thermal printer is the most common output device. Interactive kiosks may have a customized, hardened enclosure, or may simply be a standard PC that has been repurposed for interactive kiosk duties. Virtually any kiosk application in this context will be "interactive," so this term was probably adopted to reduce confusion among the different kinds of kiosks (both high-tech and low-tech) that are in use today.[23]

Video kiosks can be placed almost anywhere (from a store aisle to the lobby of a college dormitory to a hotel lobby), require few employees, and are an entertaining and easy way to shop. See Figure 6-12. Many shopping centers and individual stores are putting their space to better, more profitable use by setting up video kiosks in previously underutilized areas. These kiosks carry everything from gift certificates to concert tickets to airline tickets. Take the case of Macy's: In 2007, it began testing out consumer electronics kiosks in 180 stores. The test was so successful that Macy's deployed them in more than 430 stores by the end of 2008: "The kiosks sell an array of small consumer electronics including iPods, accessories, and digital cameras from top manufacturers such as Sony and Apple. The touch-screen system retrieves products from the kiosk with a robotic arm and accepts debit and credit cards."[24]

The average hardware cost to a retailer per video kiosk is $5,500. This does not include content development and kiosk maintenance. Hardware prices range from under $500 per kiosk to $10,000 to $15,000 per kiosk, depending on its functions—the more "bells and whistles," the higher the price.[25]

Airport Retailing

In the past, the leading airport retailers were fast-food outlets, tiny gift stores, and newspaper/magazine stands. Today, airports are a major mecca of retailing. At virtually every large airport, as well as at many medium ones, there are full-blown shopping areas. And

FIGURE 6-12

Borders' Title Sleuth Video Kiosk

At each of Borders' more than 500 book superstores, there are 5 to 10 Title Sleuth kiosks. Each week, more than 1 million searches are conducted at these kiosks as customers track down the books they are most interested in buying. Shoppers can locate nearby stores that have their selections in stock or place an order for delivery.

Source: Reprinted by permission.

most small airports have at least a fast-food retailer and vending machines for newspapers, candy, and so forth. See Figure 6-13.

The potential retail market is huge. Worldwide, more than 1,200 commercial airports handle nearly 5 billion passengers each year—with North America accounting for one third of global passenger traffic. U.S. airports alone fly millions of passengers each day and employ nearly 2 million people (who often buy something for their personal use at the airport). There are more than 400 primary commercial U.S. airports. Overall, airport retailing generates $30 billion in global sales annually, and many airports generate annual retail revenues of at least $50 million.[26] Consider this:

New York's Kennedy Airport (**www.ifly.com/ john-f-kennedy- international-airport/ shops-stores**) typifies the retailing environment at the world's major airports.

> Not only do airports increasingly resemble malls, but they are starting to think like them, too. Airport terminals these days are designed so that passengers are channeled past and even through the stores. This happened with the first expansion of Panama's Tocumen airport, which was completed in 2007 and increased the retail area at the international terminal by 35 percent, to nearly 36,000 square feet. This attention to retail has generated sales figures that would surely be the envy of any mall. Lima Airport Partners, which has a 30-year concession to operate the Jorge Chávez International Airport, in Lima, Peru, reports revenues of $50 million per year from its retail, food, and restaurant activities. Counting the Perú Plaza and the duty-free shops in the terminals, sales at the airport were $21,000 per square meter last year—several times the sales per square meter at the average U.S. shopping mall.[27]

These are some of the distinctive features of airport retailing:

▶ There is a large group of prospective shoppers. In an average year, a big airport may have 20 million or more people passing through its concourses. In contrast, a typical regional shopping mall attracts 5 million to 6 million annual visits.

FIGURE 6-13

Airport Retailing and Starbucks

As airport retailing has grown, more nationally recognized retailers have located stores there. A leader is Starbucks, with multiple units at most major airports.

Source: Reprinted by permission.

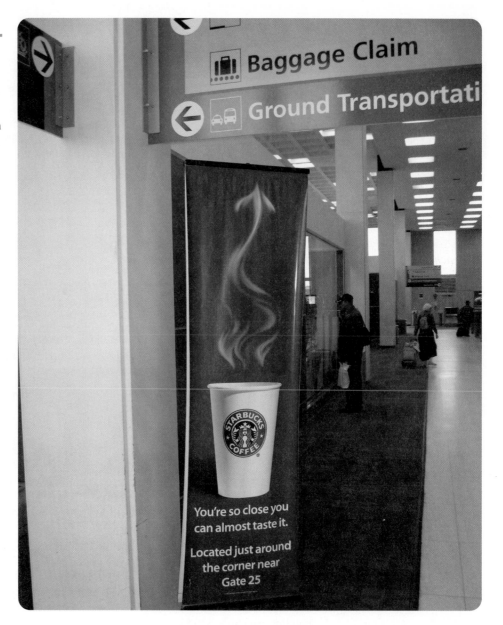

▶ Air travelers are a temporarily captive audience at the airport and looking to fill their waiting time, which could be up to several hours. They tend to have above-average incomes.

▶ Sales per square foot of retail space are much higher than at regional malls. Rent is about 20 to 30 percent higher per square foot for airport retailers.

▶ Airport stores are smaller, carry fewer items, and have higher prices than traditional stores.

▶ Replenishing merchandise and stocking shelves may be difficult at airport stores because they are physically removed from delivery areas and space is limited.

▶ The sales of gift items and forgotten travel items, from travelers not having the time to shop elsewhere, are excellent. Brookstone, which sells garment bags and travel clocks at airport shops, calls these products "I forgot" merchandise.

▶ Passengers are at airports at all times of the day. Thus, longer store hours are possible.

▶ International travelers are often interested in duty-free shopping.

▶ There is much tighter security at airports than before, which has had a dampening effect on some shopping.

Chapter **Summary**

1. *To contrast single-channel and multi-channel retailing.* A new retailer often relies on single-channel retailing, whereby it sells to consumers through one retail format. As the firm grows, it may turn to multi-channel retailing and sell to consumers through multiple retail formats. This allows the firm to reach different customers, share costs among various formats, and diversify its supplier base.

2. *To look at the characteristics of the three major retail institutions involved with nonstore-based strategy mixes: direct marketing, direct selling, and vending machines—with an emphasis on direct marketing.* Firms employ nonstore retailing to reach customers and complete transactions. Nonstore retailing encompasses direct marketing, direct selling, and vending machines.

In direct marketing, a consumer is exposed to a good or service through a nonpersonal medium and orders by mail, phone, fax, or computer. Annual U.S. retail sales from direct marketing exceed $325 billion. Direct marketers fall into two categories: general and specialty. Among the strengths of direct marketing are its reduced operating costs, large geographic coverage, customer convenience, and targeted segments. Among the weaknesses are the shopper's inability to examine items before purchase, the costs of printing and mailing, the low response rate, and marketplace clutter. Under the "30-day rule," there are legal requirements that a firm must follow as to shipping speed. The long-run prospects for direct marketing are strong due to consumer interest in reduced shopping time, 24-hour ordering, the sales of well-known brands, improvements in operating efficiency, and technology.

The key to successful direct marketing is the customer data base, with data-base retailing being a way to collect, store, and use relevant information. Several trends are vital to direct marketers: their attitudes and activities, changing consumer lifestyles, increased competition, the use of dual distribution, the roles for catalogs and TV, technological advances, and the growth in global direct marketing. Specialogs and infomercials are two tools being used more by direct marketers.

A direct marketing plan has eight stages: business definition, generating customers, media selection, presenting the message, customer contact, customer response, order fulfillment, and measuring results and maintaining the data base. Firms must consider that many people dislike shopping this way, feel overwhelmed by the amount of direct mail, and are concerned about privacy.

Direct selling includes personal contact with consumers in their homes (and other nonstore sites) and phone calls by the seller. It yields $31 billion in annual U.S. retail sales, covering many goods and services. The strategy mix stresses convenience, a personal touch, demonstrations, and relaxed consumers. U.S. sales are not going up much due to the rise in working women, the labor intensity of the business, sales force turnover, government rules, and the poor image of some firms.

A vending machine uses coin- and card-operated dispensing of goods and services. It eliminates salespeople, allows 24-hour sales, and may be put almost anywhere. Beverages and food represent 95 percent of the $50 billion in annual U.S. vending revenues. Efforts in other product categories have met with customer resistance, and items priced above $1.50 have not done well.

3. *To explore the emergence of electronic retailing through the World Wide Web.* The Internet is a global electronic superhighway that acts as a single, cooperative virtual network. The World Wide Web (Web) is a way to access information on the Internet, whereby people turn their computers into interactive multimedia centers. The Web can serve one or more retailer purposes, from projecting an image to presenting information to investors. The purpose chosen depends on the goals and focus. There is a great contrast between store retailing and Web retailing.

The growth of Web-based retailing has been enormous. U.S. revenues from retailing on the Web are expected to reach $180 billion in 2012. Nonetheless, the Web still garners only 3 to 4 percent of total U.S. retail sales.

Somewhat more females than males shop on the Web. Web usage declines by age group and increases by income and education level. Shoppers are attracted by Web site design, reliability, customer service, and security. Nonshoppers worry about the trustworthiness of online firms, want to see and handle products first, and do not like shipping cost surprises.

The Web offers these positive features for retailers: It can be inexpensive to have a Web site. The potential marketplace is huge and dispersed, yet easy to reach. Sites can be quite exciting. People can visit a site at any time. Information can be targeted. A customer data base can be established and customer feedback obtained. Yet, if consumers do not know a firm's Web address, it may be hard to find. Many people will not buy online. There is clutter with regard to the number of retail sites. Because Web surfers are easily bored, a firm must regularly update its site to ensure repeat visits. The more multimedia features a site has, the slower it may be to access. Some firms have been deluged with customer service requests. Improvements are needed to coordinate store and Web transactions. There are few standards or rules as to what may be portrayed at Web sites. Consumers expect online services to be free and are reluctant to pay for them.

A Web strategy can move through five stages: brochure site, commerce site, site integrated with existing processes, "Webified" store, and site integrated with manufacturer systems.

4. *To discuss two other nontraditional forms of retailing: video kiosks and airport retailing.* The video kiosk is a freestanding, interactive computer terminal that displays products and other information on a video screen; it often has a touchscreen for people to make selections.

Although some kiosks are in stores to upgrade customer service, others let consumers place orders, complete transactions, and arrange shipping. Kiosks can be put almost anywhere, require few personnel, and are an entertaining and easy way for people to shop. They yield $12 to $15 billion in annual U.S. revenues.

Due to the huge size of the air travel marketplace, airports are popular as retail shopping areas. Travelers (and workers) are temporarily captive at the airport, often with a lot of time to fill. Sales per square foot, as well as rent, are high. Gift items and "I forgot" merchandise sell especially well. Globally, annual retail revenues are $30 billion at airports.

Key Terms

single-channel retailing (p. 148)
multi-channel retailing (p. 148)
nonstore retailing (p. 149)
direct marketing (p. 149)

data-base retailing (p. 152)
specialog (p. 153)
infomercial (p. 154)
direct selling (p. 157)

vending machine (p. 160)
Internet (p. 160)
World Wide Web (Web) (p. 160)
video kiosk (p. 168)

Questions for Discussion

1. Contrast single-channel and multi-channel retailing. What do you think are the advantages of each?

2. Do you think nonstore retailing will continue to grow faster than store-based retailing? Explain your answer.

3. How would you increase a direct marketer's response rate from less than 1 percent of those receiving E-mail sales offers by the firm to 3 percent?

4. Explain the "30-day rule" for direct marketers.

5. What are the two main decisions to be made in the business definition stage of planning a direct marketing strategy?

6. How should Buy.com (**www.buy.com**) handle consumer concerns about their privacy?

7. Differentiate between direct selling and direct marketing. What are the strengths and weaknesses of each?

8. Select a product not heavily sold through vending machines, and present a brief plan for doing so.

9. From a consumer's perspective, what are the advantages and disadvantages of the World Wide Web?

10. From a retailer's perspective, what are the advantages and disadvantages of having a Web site?

11. What must retailers do to improve customer service on the Web?

12. What future role do you see for video kiosks? Why?

Web **Exercise**

Visit the "E-Commerce & Internet" section of Plunkett Research's Web site (www.plunkettresearch.com) by scrolling down the "Industries List." Describe four key facts that a retailer could learn from this site.

Note: Stop by our Web site (www.pearsonhighered.com/berman) to experience a number of highly

interactive, appealing Web exercises based on actual company demonstrations and sample materials related to retailing.

Appendix Multi-Channel Retailing*

As we noted at the beginning of Chapter 6, a retail firm relies on single-channel retailing if it sells to consumers through one format. A firm uses multi-channel retailing if it sells to consumers through multiple formats. We devote this appendix to multi-channel retailing because so many firms are combining store and nonstore retailing—as well as using multiple store formats.

Multi-channel retailing enables consumers to conveniently shop in a number of different ways, including stores, catalogs, a Web site, kiosks, and even PDAs (personal digital assistants) with Web access. Some firms have even developed advanced multi-channel retailing systems that enable consumers to examine products at one format, buy them at another format, and pick them up—and possibly return them—at a third format. Consider Cabela's, an outdoor lifestyle retailer:

> In addition to its 26 stores located in 19 states, Cabela's publishes 120 catalogs each year, with a circulation of 130 million households. Cabela's also maintains a Web site (**www.cabelas.com**). Cabela's typically stocks as many as 400,000 SKUs over an average yearly period. According to James Landsman, Cabela's senior applications channel manager, "Even our largest stores can carry 50 percent to 60 percent of the assortment at any one time." A major incentive for Cabela's adopting a multi-channel strategy is its increased ability to extend its product assortments.[1]

In recognition of the increasing importance of multi-channel retailing, *Catalog Age* was renamed and repositioned as *Multi-Channel Merchant* (www. multichannelmerchant.com).

Planning and maintaining a well-integrated multi-channel strategy is not easy. At a minimum, it requires setting up an infrastructure that can effectively link multiple channels. A retailer that accepts a Web purchase for exchange at a retail store needs an information system to verify the purchase, the price paid, the method of payment, and the date of the transaction. That firm also needs a mechanism for delivering goods regardless of which channel was used by a customer to purchase the goods.

These are just some of the strategic and operational issues for multi-channel retailers to address:

▶ What multi-channel cross-selling opportunities exist? A firm could list its Web site on its business cards, store invoices, and shopping bags. It could also list the nearest store locations when a consumer inputs a ZIP code at the Web site.

▶ How should the product assortment/variety strategy be adapted to each channel? How much merchandise overlap should exist across channels?

▶ How can the retailer's distribution center handle both direct-to-store and direct-to-consumer shipments?

▶ Should prices be consistent across channels (except for shipping and handling, as well as closeouts)?

▶ How can a consistent image be devised and sustained across all channels?

▶ What is the role of each channel? Some consumers prefer to search the Web to determine pricing and product information, and then they purchase in a store due to their desire to see the product, try it on, and gain the immediacy that accompanies an in-store transaction.

▶ What are the best opportunities for leveraging a firm's assets through a multi-channel strategy? Many catalog-based retailers have logistics systems that can be easily adapted to Web-based sales.

▶ Do relationships with current suppliers prevent the firm from expanding into new channels?

---

*The material in this appendix is adapted by the authors from Barry Berman and Shawn Thelen, "A Guide to Developing and Managing a Well-Integrated Multi-Channel Retail Strategy," *International Journal of Retail & Distribution Management*, Vol. 32 (No. 3, 2004), pp. 147–156. Updated January 2009. Used by permission of Barry Berman and Shawn Thelen.

Advantages of Multi-Channel Retail Strategies

There are several advantages to a retailer's enacting a multi-channel approach, including the selection of specific channels based upon their unique strengths, opportunities to leverage assets, and opportunities for increased sales and profits by appealing to multi-channel shoppers.

Selecting Among Multiple Channels Based on Their Unique Strengths

A retailer with a multi-channel strategy can use the most appropriate channels to sell particular goods or services or to reach different target markets. Because each channel has a unique combination of strengths, a multi-channel retailer has the best opportunities to fulfill its customers' shopping desires.

Store-based shopping enables customers to see an item, feel it, smell it (e.g., candles or perfumes), try it out, and then pick it up and take it home on the same shopping trip without incurring shipping and handling costs. Catalogs offer high visual impact, a high-quality image, and portability (they can be taken anywhere by the shopper). The Web offers high-quality video/audio capabilities, an interactive format, a personalized customer interface, virtually unlimited space, the ability for a customer to verify in-stock position and order status, and, in some cases, tax-free shopping. In-store kiosks are helpful for shoppers not having Web access, can lead to less inventory in the store (and reduce the need to stock low-turnover items in each store), facilitate self-service by providing information, and offer high video/audio quality.

To plan an appropriate channel mix and the role of each channel, retailers must recognize how different channels complement one another. Both Costco (**www.costco.com**) and BJ's (**www.bjs.com**) have a broader selection of items on the Web to encourage consumers to shop in multiple ways. They also send out catalogs to their customers to encourage them to either place orders on their Web sites or to visit their stores.

Opportunities to Leverage Assets

Multi-channel retailing presents opportunities for firms to leverage both tangible assets and intangible assets. A store-based retailer can leverage tangible assets by using excess capacity in its warehouse to service catalog or Web sales; that same firm can leverage its well-known brand name (an intangible asset) by selling online in geographic areas where it has no stores.

Retailers can also work with channel partners to leverage their collective assets. Checkout by Amazon is a new service by Amazon.com that enables other Web-based retailers to use Amazon.com's one-click ordering system, and it enables customers to easily determine applicable sales tax and track their orders through delivery. Amazon.com has begun an additional service, called Amazon Simple Pay, to compete with PayPal (owned by eBay). This enables customers to order merchandise without giving their credit card number over the Web.

Opportunities for Increased Sales and Profits by Appealing to Multi-Channel Shoppers

Although many people associate the American Automobile Association (AAA) with its emergency towing services, AAA is one of the nation's largest automobile, property, and casualty insurers—as well as one of the largest travel agencies. AAA uses multiple channels such as retail stores, telephone, ATMs, kiosks, direct mail, and online. Among its cross-channel features for customers are the opportunity for in-store browsing before a Web-based purchase, online registration for a store-based consultation, and loyalty programs based on multi-channel purchases.[2]

Research indicates that multi-channel consumers spend more than those who confine their shopping to a single channel. Smithsonian Business Ventures, a Washington, DC, museum complex, generates more than $200 million annually via its museum stores, catalog operations, Web sales, and off-site stores (such as those located at airports). According to the chief executive of this business, the average purchase in the museum's stores is less than $20 compared with an average catalog order of $100.[3]

Developing a Well-Integrated Multi-Channel Strategy

A well-integrated multi-channel strategy requires linkages among all of the channels. Customers should be able to easily make the transition from looking up products on the Web or in a catalog to picking up the products in a retail store. TSN Retail Forward, a retail consulting firm, analyzes multi-channel shopping behavior through a monthly survey of 4,000 nationally representative households. According to a recent survey:

- ▶ 27 percent of apparel shopping consumer respondents looked up information online about stores (location), maps, events, and phone numbers.
- ▶ 22 percent researched merchandise online prior to shopping in a store.
- ▶ 21 percent compared prices among online sites, stores, and/or catalogs.
- ▶ 21 percent downloaded coupons for use in stores.
- ▶ 18 percent shopped at a store as a result of receiving an E-mail promotion.[4]

There should be a good deal of commonality in the description and appearance of each item regardless of channel. For example, in-store personnel should be able to verify a Web or catalog purchase and arrange for returns or exchanges. At Brooks Brothers' Web site (**www.brooksbrothers.com**), shoppers can access copies of current catalogs by page number. In addition, salespeople in stores have copies of catalogs available so that customers can place orders for items not carried in a particular outlet.

These are characteristics common to superior multi-channel strategies: integrated promotions across channels; product consistency across channels; an integrated information system that shares customer, pricing, and inventory data across multiple channels; a store pickup process for items purchased on the Web or through a catalog; and the search for multi-channel opportunities with appropriate partners.

Integrating Promotions Across Channels

Cross-promotion enables consumers to use each promotional forum in its best light. Here is a list of some cross-promotion tactics:

- ▶ Include the Web site address on shopping bags, in catalogs, and in newspaper ads.
- ▶ Provide in-store kiosks so customers can order out-of-stock merchandise without a shipping fee.
- ▶ Include store addresses, phone numbers, hours, and directions on the Web site and in catalogs.
- ▶ Make it possible for customers to shop for items on the Web using the catalog order numbers.
- ▶ Distribute store coupons by direct mail and online; offer catalogs in stores and at the Web site.
- ▶ Target single-channel customers with promotions from other channels.
- ▶ Send store-based shoppers targeted E-mails (on an opt-in basis) for selected goods and services.

Ensuring Product Consistency Across Channels

Too little product overlap across channels may result in an inconsistent image. However, too much overlap may result in the loss of sales opportunities. According to research by Forrester Research, 74 percent of the sku's available in the average retailer's store can also be found in their online outlet, and 12 percent of the sku's found in an online store are available only in their online channel.[5]

Multi-channel retailers often use the Web as a way to offer highly specialized merchandise that cannot be profitably offered in stores. For example, Williams-Sonoma's (www.williams-sonoma.com) and Radio Shack's (www.radioshack.com) Web sites offer consumers highly specialized items that are not stocked in these chains' local retail stores. This strategy maximizes store space while, at the same time, it fulfills specialized needs of niche market segments.

Having an Information System That Effectively Shares Data Across Channels

To best manage a multi-channel system, a retailer needs an information system that shares customer, pricing, and inventory information across channels:

▶ Sierra Trading Post sells outdoor recreation gear, boots, and home décor items through eight specialty catalogs, four retail stores, and a Web site (www.sierratradingpost. com). It shares information across channels to increase cross-selling activities. According to the firm's online marketing manager, "Through [sharing of information], we can have a retail E-mail program and use geographic segmentation to define which customers fall within a certain radius of our stores so that stores can cater specific offers to that group. We can get a better return on the E-mails we send out and minimize the number of E-mails a specific customer receives."[6]

▶ Best Buy (www.bestbuy.com) and Sears (www.sears.com) have Web sites that enable shoppers to not only confirm whether merchandise is in stock, but also to set up in-store pickup.

Enacting a Store-Pickup Process for Items Purchased on the Web or Through a Catalog

In-store pickup requires that a retailer's inventory data base be integrated and that the firm has a logistics infrastructure that can pick and route merchandise to customers. Increasingly, shoppers are ordering big-ticket items such as digital cameras, computers, and appliances online but picking them up at nearby stores. Consumers favor this approach to avoid shipping and handling charges, to reduce their having to navigate through a big-box store, and to avoid wasting time looking for items that may be out-of-stock. Store pickup also enables shoppers to get items on the same day they are bought.

As a senior vice-president of direct commerce at Sears Holdings noted:

Some people want to go online, research something 12 times before they buy it, and then get it shipped to them. Others want it right now, and they want to be able to come in the store and pick it up. They may be doing that to save shipping, or they may want some additional interaction, or instructions on how to use the item. So providing the maximum number of choices is essential.[7]

Searching for Multi-Channel Opportunities with Appropriate Partners

The retailer needs to understand that in almost all cases a multi-channel strategy requires additional resources and competencies that are significantly greater than those demanded by a single-channel strategy. Although some retailers may conclude that they do not have these competencies or resources, others look for strategic partnerships with firms having complementary resources.

Special Challenges

A multi-channel strategy is not appropriate for every retailer. Not all retailers possess the financial and managerial resources to do so—or have the same potential synergies.

A key challenge for many retailers, particularly small to middle size firms, is the consolidation of their disparate retail management systems into one customer focused system. Many retailers started out with a single channel—typically bricks-and-mortar—and then added telephone sales, Web sales, and maybe even eBay sales. These retailers often developed separate information systems for each channel. Thus, each of these channels has a distinct information system with its own set of customer, product, sales, and inventory data. With a multi-channel-based system, a retailer's overall information center must be unified. In this way, a retailer can determine whether a large Web site or catalog user base exists within the trading area of a proposed retail location. Web buyers, for example, could then be offered an introductory 10 percent off coupon to a new store.[8]

Another potential difficulty is the management of a retailer's distribution center. Such a center requires efficient procedures for handling both large orders that are shipped directly to stores and small shipments that are made to its thousands or tens of thousands of customers. The system for handling large store-based retail purchase orders (which are often full-case loads) are quite different than shipping individual items to a customer's home.

part two
Short Cases

CASE 1: COMPETING SUCCESSFULLY AGAINST BIG BOX RETAILERS[C-1]

Most retail analysts define "big-box" retailers as discounters with stores between 50,000 and 200,000 square feet, single-story buildings, and strategies based on high volume via low markups. Big-box retailers include Wal-Mart (**www.walmart.com**), Costco (**www.costco.com**), Target (**www.target.com**), Lowe's (**www.lowes.com**), Best Buy (**www.bestbuy.com**), and Home Depot (**www.homedepot.com**).

In general, these retailers have built their strategies on the basis of four components: (1) Economies of scale—purchasing costs are reduced through ordering large quantities. (2) Low prices—it is difficult for smaller retailers to match their prices. (3) Broad merchandise offerings—one-stop shopping appeals are used. (4) A predictable shopping experience—because all the stores in a chain typically sell the same products, shoppers can easily plan their shopping trip.

The big-box stores have a considerable impact on other retailers that sell similar products. A new big-box store can even change customer shopping patterns because many customers may drive further distances to secure lower prices or to be able to shop at later times. To compete against the big-box stores, there are alternative strategies to consider. These are based on low costs, focus/differentiation, and value. The first two strategies are based on Michael Porter's competitive strategy model.

In general, it is difficult for smaller retailers to compete against big box stores on the basis of price. One way is for a small retailer to reduce its assortment and thereby generate buying power by concentrating purchases among fewer vendors. Small noncompeting retailers can also join cooperatives and jointly purchase goods. For example, on Long Island, New York, many local appliance retailers pool their purchases and then operate a joint warehouse to compete against larger appliance retailers and box stores that now sell refrigerators, ranges, and washing machines and dryers.

A second competitive strategy is to use a focus/differentiation strategy based on product quality, selection, convenience, and service. Typically, a focus/differentiation strategy is based on the concept that smaller retailers can compete against box stores as long as their pricing strategy is "within striking distance" of the box stores. A focus/differentiation strategy is predicated on a retailer's carrying specialized brands, its stocking related items, and its

capability in delivering and installing products. Smaller retailers can also cater to a market niche such as bicycle enthusiasts or safety-prone or time-pressed parents who would prefer that an experienced bicycle shop employee assemble a child's bicycle. Lastly, smaller retailers are also generally better able to tailor their merchandise and service offerings to a local market's specialized needs than big-box stores.

The third strategy is based on a value orientation. Instead of focusing attention solely on price, smaller retailers need to vigorously control those costs that do not directly enhance the attractiveness of its products or services. Value-oriented retailers should pursue cost-reduction opportunities that result in minimal reductions in value. Such retail value orientations may be based on home delivery, assembly, and after-sales service. In contrast, Wal-Mart and other big-box stores' value orientation is primarily due to low prices.

Questions

1. Differentiate between a big-box store and a category killer.
2. Discuss the competitive advantages of independents as contrasted with big-box chains.
3. What factors explain the increased popularity of big-box stores in many sectors of retailing?
4. Describe the pros and cons of a retailer's pursuit of a niche strategy to effectively compete with a big-box retailer.

CASE 2: FRANCHISING IN CHINA[C-2]

With its population of 1.3 billion people and a middle class estimated at 200 million people as of 2009, the Chinese market has been described by some retail analysts as "the mother of all franchise markets." In addition to the large target audience of consumers, China is attractive because a significant number of Chinese nationals now have the required investment to purchase a franchise there.

According to Michael Isakson, the chairman of the International Franchise Association (**www.franchise.org**): "There are currently about 500 franchise companies in China, and we expect that to grow exponentially over the next few years." A study by the China Chain Store and Franchise Association (CCFA) (**www.chinaretail.org**) found that 14 of the top 20 franchises in the United States have already entered the Chinese market. As the chief executive of iFranchise Group (**www.ifranchisegroup.com**) says, China is "in the early stages of a franchise boom of unparalleled magnitude."

c-1The material in this case is drawn from John A. Parnell and Donald L. Lester, "Competitive Strategy and the Wal-Mart Threat: Positioning for Survival and Success," *SAM Advanced Management Journal* (Spring 2008), pp. 14–24.

c-2The material in this case is drawn from "Does Franchising Fit in Asia?" *Hotels* (October 2007), pp. 44–45; Rebecca Ordish, "Testing the Franchising Waters in China," *ChinaBusinessReview.com* (November–December 2006). pp. 30–33; and Kem Pollard, "IFA and ServiceMaster Clean Discover a World of Opportunity in China," *Franchising World* (March 2008), pp. 33–34.

Prior to 2004, China lacked the laws to enable foreign companies to establish franchises in China. At that time, foreign companies had to partner with a local franchise that held import and export licenses. Until recently, Yum! Brands (**www.yum.com**)—which now operates KFC (**www.kfc.com**), Pizza Hut (**www.pizzahut.com**), and Taco Bell (**www.tacobell.com**) franchises in China— did not franchise outlets in China. Yum! Brands' initial Chinese stores were all company-owned due to concerns with intellectual property protection and China's weak legal framework. Similarly, prior to 2004, all of McDonald's (**www.mcdonalds.com**) Chinese stores were company-owned and operated with a local Chinese partner.

In 2005, as part of China's World Trade Organization commitments, franchising opportunities were opened up to foreign-invested enterprises. As of 2005, Yum! Brands began franchising stores that were company-owned for 12 months or had become profitable. Yum! Brands does not want new Chinese franchisees either losing money or struggling with the initial operation of stores. To encourage the growth of its units in second-tier cities, Yum! Brands has reduced the franchising fee to the equivalent of $250,000, and McDonald's has been franchising to Chinese nationals since new legislation was passed.

Despite the changes in franchising laws, significant challenges still exist in China. These relate to problems associated with quality control, uncertainty about the franchising regulatory environment, and weak intellectual property enforcement. For example, General Mills (**www.generalmills.com**), owner of the Häagen-Dazs (**www.haagendazs.com**) ice cream franchise, learned that it was not properly supervising a local franchise in Shanzhen. The franchisee apparently had been making ice cream cakes in an unsanitary environment. It seems that ice cream was produced in an apartment that did not have an appropriate food preparation license. Adverse publicity associated with the incident had a major negative impact on the brand's image in China.

In an incident related to intellectual property rights in China, Starbucks (**www.starbucks.com**) discovered that a Chinese firm registered its trademark prior to Starbucks' entering China. Recovering its rightful trademark became a costly and prolonged legal battle.

Questions

1. Describe the pros and cons of a multinational retailer expanding into the Chinese market via franchising.
2. What are the pros and cons of Yum! Brands developing its own stores versus using franchising as a means of selling to the China market?
3. Should Yum! Brands modify its menu to meet Chinese tastes? If yes, how? Explain your answer.
4. Comment on Yum! Brands' strategy of franchising its Chinese stores only after they have been company- owned for 12 months or have become profitable.

CASE 3: TRADER JOE'S DISTINCTIVE APPROACH[C-3]

In 1979, Joe Coulombe sold Trader Joe's (**www.traderjoes. com**)—the chain he founded in Southern California—to the German-based Albrecht family (which owns more than 1,000 Aldi, **www.aldi.com**, supermarkets located in 29 states). Trader Joe's now has 250 stores in 22 states nationwide; although the company does not disclose its sales, they have been estimated to be in excess of $6.5 billion annually.

Trader Joe's mission is to provide its customers with the best food and beverage values anywhere. It also seeks to provide nutritional and product information so its customers can make informed decisions. Unlike a typical supermarket with 25,000 or more different products and 60,000 square feet of space, the average Trader Joe's sells 3,000 products in stores that range in size from 8,000 to 15,000 square feet.

There are several cornerstones to Trader Joe's overall retail strategy. These include the importance of customer service, private labels, high sales of imported and organic foods, and use of word-of-mouth promotions.

Trader Joe's really cares about customer service. The chain was among the first to have its cashiers ask all customers if they found everything they wanted. Cashiers are even trained to leave their post and get an item a shopper cannot locate. All items in the store have an unconditional "no questions asked" money-back guarantee. Many stores also feature a sampling area where consumers can snack on freshly prepared products.

About 80 percent of the products at Trader Joe's are private label. Jokingly, it changes its name to "Trader Ming," "Trader Jacques," and "Trader Giotto," depending upon the origin associated with the product. The private-label strategy enables Trader Joe's to achieve store loyalty through product loyalty and to have more power in negotiations with vendors.

All of Trader Joe's products are purchased directly from suppliers, not intermediaries. It uses this strategy to reduce costs. Trader Joe's private-label brand was recently selected as the second most respected brand (out of 12) by 21- to 27- year-olds, behind only Apple. It was higher than Ben & Jerry's (**www.benandjerrys.com**) at number 5 and Whole Foods Markets (**www.wholefoods.com**) at number 6.

About 20 percent of Trader Joe's suppliers are located overseas. This enables the chain to have distinctive products such as pastas imported from Italy, grape leaves from Greece, eastern European jams and jellies, and French dessert items. Distinctive merchandise sourcing is a difficult strategy for competitors to copy.

Thirty percent of Trader Joe's products are organic. These include bakery items, beverages, cereals, dried fruits

---

[C-3]The material in this case is drawn from Cecily Hall, "Trendsetting Brands," *Women's Wear Daily* (April 19, 2007); and "Where Is Trader Joe's?" **www.traderjoes.com/locations/index.asp** (October 25, 2008).

and nuts, snacks, and produce. Although other supermarkets such as Whole Foods and Wild Oats (**www.wildoats.com**) also sell organic foods, Trader Joe's sells these items for 25 to 30 percent less.

Unlike traditional supermarkets that build store traffic with their freestanding advertising inserts and coupon offers, Trader Joe's promotional strategy relies on its quarterly *Fearless Flyer;* this is sent via mail and distributed in its stores. *Fearless Flyer* outlines the features of specific products by using a quirky sense of humor, including cartoons and recipes. Otherwise, most of Trader Joe's communication is based on word of mouth.

Questions

1. How would you describe Trader Joe's in terms of the wheel of retailing? Explain your answer.
2. Describe the vertical marketing system used by Trader Joe's.
3. How can a traditional supermarket effectively compete against Trader Joe's?
4. How can Trader Joe's most effectively use the Web?

CASE 4: SHUTTERFLY EXPANDS BEYOND ITS DIGITAL PHOTO PROCESSING[C-4]

By constantly monitoring customer needs and changing its retail mix, Shutterfly (**www.shutterfly.com**) has grown from a digital photo processor of standard 4-inch by 6-inch prints to a firm with annual revenues of $200 million. Shutterfly now sells a wide variety of goods and services, including do-it-yourself photo books, holiday cards featuring photos of the family, baby and wedding announcements, and stationery.

Shutterfly recently entered the social networking marketplace by allowing users to post photos. According to IDC (**www.idc.com**), an Internet-based research firm, 87 percent of U.S. Internet users indicate that they have used social networks. The research firm also found that 87 percent of the U.S. population uses the Internet as a part of their everyday routine.

Through Shutterfly Gallery, members can now post their photo books and share Gallery projects with friends and family members, as well as comment on other members' books. Photo books posted on the Shutterfly Gallery can also be embedded on a user's personal Web page or

blog. To facilitate viewing, Shutterfly Gallery is classified into 16 occasion-based categories. Viewers can select material to view by classification or by such filters as "most popular," "most commented," and "most copied."

Shutterfly recognizes that its competitive environment is a tough one. Its two major competitors are Snapfish (**www.snapfish.com**), which was acquired by Hewlett-Packard in 2005 and Kodak Gallery (**www.kodakgallery.com**), a division of Kodak. Together, these three firms control about 85 percent of the market for online photo processing and related merchandise. Each firm has some significant competitive advantages.

As the Snapfish Web site reports: "Customers can share and store their photos for free and create prints and personalized photo gifts online for the best value. Our online photo sharing, storage, and editing tools and software are free; and customers can even create private group rooms for event sharing with friends and family. We also provide mobile photo services and a subscription video sharing and storage plans. Snapfish offers more than 100 unique, customizable photo gifts, from a full line of display-quality photo books, calendars, and posters, to photo mugs, mouse pads, key chains, and jewelry."

Kodak Gallery has used its brand equity to sell related products such as digital picture frames that can be purchased with a customer's photos preloaded on its memory card. Through a partnership with Rite Aid, Kodak Gallery customers can pick up their online print orders in a local Rite Aid store. Similarly, Shutterfly consumers can pick up their photos at a local Target.

According to the Photo Marketing Association, online photo ordering has been growing at a rapid clip. Of those who order online, about 10 percent are later picked up at a retail location. As one industry analyst notes, this "net-to-store" model will likely grow faster than "net-to-mail." "People want to avoid shipping costs as they inflate the price per print, while retailers want the traffic back in their stores." Other advantages of the net-to-store model are the faster delivery of the photos and the opportunity to discuss photo quality and options with store personnel.

Questions

1. Describe the advantages and disadvantages of Shutterfly's use of a bricks-and-clicks (multi-channel) strategy.
2. What are the pros and cons of a retailer's partnering with Shutterfly?
3. What should be the contract terms in an agreement between a retailer and Shutterfly?
4. What must Shutterfly do to stay competitive with Snapfish and Kodak?

[C-4]The material in this case is drawn from Andrew Murr, "It's Picture Perfect," *Newsweek* (June 2, 2008); Greg Scoblete, "Retailers Get Online Partners to Help Drive Photo Revenue," *Twice* (May 21, 2007), pp. 12, 131; and "Shutterfly Gallery Launches to Inspire and Engage Storytellers," *Business Wire* (February 20, 2008).

part two
Comprehensive Case

TARGET'S TO-DO LIST IN A TOUGH ECONOMY*

INTRODUCTION

Target (**www.target.com**)—whose relatively affluent shopper base was once thought to be fairly insulated from economic pressures such as rising gasoline prices and food price inflation—is now feeling the pinch as a myriad of challenges come to a head. While Target's performance is suffering, Wal-Mart (**www.walmart.com**) is benefiting from the challenging economic environment.

Annual Performance Slips

U.S. households face economic challenges on a variety of fronts. In recent years, consumers have struggled with climbing gasoline prices, sliding home values, rising food prices, tightening credit conditions, and emerging job weakness. Target's performance suggests that it is feeling the effects of the difficult economic environment.

Target's sales and earnings slowed considerably during the second half of 2007, causing its year-end results to fall short of company expectations. The retailer's sales growth slowed from a double-digit gain of 13 percent in 2006 to 6 percent in 2007. Performance on a category-by-category basis was mixed:

▶ The consumables/commodities category (now representing one-third of total Target sales) was the fastest growing category at 13 percent, double the pace of the retailer's overall sales growth. Apparel/accessories

*The material in this case is adapted by the authors from TNS Retail Forward (**www.retailforward.com**), *Target's To-Do List in a Tough Economy* (Columbus, OH: TNS Retail Forward, May 2008). Reprinted by permission.

sales slowed from a 13 percent gain in 2006 to 6 percent in 2007. This was consistent with Target's overall sales growth slowdown.
▶ Gains in home furnishings/décor were slightly below the pace set during the prior year.
▶ The combined categories of electronics/entertainment/sporting goods/toys saw sales growth slow substantially from a double-digit gain of 13 percent in 2006 to 2 percent in 2007.

Target's start to 2008 was characterized by weak same-store sales growth. The retailer reported that gains in average transaction size were offset by decreases in traffic. Starting in the crucial holiday month of December 2007, Wal-Mart reported stronger comparable-store sales than Target for most months. See Figure 1.

Prior to December 2007, Wal-Mart's comparable-store monthly performance had only trumped that of Target three times since August 2003. Continued spending by Target's more affluent guests, who typically were cushioned from the effects of high fuel prices, coupled with some merchandising missteps by Wal-Mart contributed to Target's string of monthly same-store sales wins. But as shoppers got pinched more from multiple sources, in addition to high gas prices, they began looking for ways to lower their spending—which included turning to Wal-Mart.

Target's performance during the first quarter of 2008 as a whole was disappointing. Net sales grew 5.0 percent compared with a 9.0 percent gain the prior year. Net profits fell 7.5 percent, representing Target's third consecutive quarterly profit decline. The company also reported a −0.7 percent same-store sales decline. The last time Target reported a negative quarterly comp was in the fourth quarter of 2002. Other players, such as J.C. Penney (**www.jcpenney.com**), Kohl's (**www.kohls.com**), and Macy's (**www.macys.com**), also struggled with same-store sales declines, which Target management was quick to point out during the company's 2008 first quarter conference call.

FIGURE 1

Target's Monthly Same-Store Sales Growth Versus Industry Composites

Sources: Company reports and TNS Retail Forward.

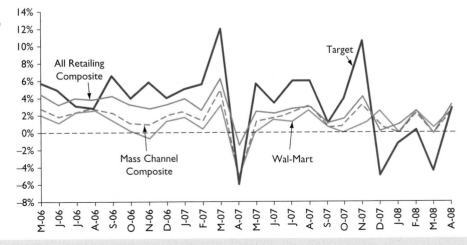

Target Loses Shoppers While Wal-Mart Wins

TNS Retail Forward's data indicate that a greater number of households shopped Target less often in 2008 than in 2007 compared with those shopping the retailer more. The reverse was true for Wal-Mart: The challenging economic environment worked in Wal-Mart's favor. See Figure 2.

Target Loses Shoppers A higher percentage of shoppers reported that they shopped Target general merchandise stores less often (18 percent) in 2008 than in 2007, compared with those that reported shopping the format more often (14 percent). Although a greater percentage of shoppers indicated that they shopped SuperTarget more often than less often, only 1 in 10 Target stores was a SuperTarget in 2008. About one out of five shoppers who reported shopping Target less said they shopped Wal-Mart more often in 2008 than in 2007.

Wal-Mart Wins Shoppers Almost a quarter of shoppers reported that they shopped at a Wal-Mart Supercenter more often in 2008 than in 2007, compared with 16 percent who shopped the format less often in 2008. More people were shopping Wal-Mart discount stores less often than more often—but this was a reflection of Wal-Mart's store conversion strategy to the supercenter format. Overall, more households were shopping Wal-Mart more often in 2008 than were shopping the retailer less often. Recent efforts to improve the store shopping experience, such as store remodels, better merchandising, brighter lighting, and wider aisles, could help Wal-Mart retain shoppers post-economic turnaround.

Target's To-Do List

Target is determined not to stray from its existing strategy—a decision that will serve Target well in the long run. But at present, it should focus on some initiatives to minimize the immediate impact of the economic downturn.

Target has earned a unique position in the retail landscape. Five years ago, TNS Retail Forward summarized Target's position in the marketplace as follows: "Rather than focusing primarily on price, Target strives to differentiate. Blending fashion, quality, and value, Target brings pizzazz to the everyday and panache to even the most mundane merchandise." This position still holds and has value today. A knee-jerk reaction to the current economic conditions is not the solution to revitalizing Target's performance and could risk deteriorating the image Target has built through the years. Instead, Target should focus on tactics that will help it weather the storm.

Here is TNS Retail Forward's suggested to-do list for Target.

Communicate Value

Target has reiterated during company quarterly conference calls that it maintains a position of being "competitively priced with Wal-Mart on like and identical items in local markets." Although it is important for Target to share its positioning with its stakeholders, it is probably even more important to be forthcoming about its competitive price position with shoppers. The challenge for Target is to make the message more about value than price, which will serve the retailer better in the long run. It isn't Target's style to shout, "We've got low prices too." Instead, it needs to put its marketing savvy to work to tell shoppers that they don't need to go anywhere else for everyday value—an approach that could appeal both to price-sensitive shoppers and those looking to reduce the run-around in an effort to save time and gas. Watch for Target to place greater emphasis on the "pay less" side of its brand promise in the company's weekly circular, in-store signing, and value pricing on endcap displays.

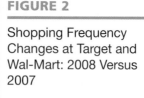

FIGURE 2

Shopping Frequency Changes at Target and Wal-Mart: 2008 Versus 2007

Source: TNS Retail Forward ShopperScape™, February 2008.

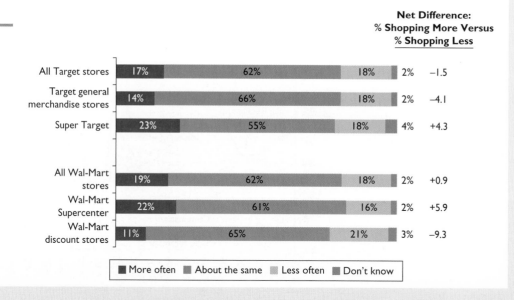

Don't Take Wal-Mart Lightly

Target's president recently commented, "We wouldn't characterize Wal-Mart's marketing campaign of lower prices as a massive price action or really any change to their normal cadence or rhythm of going to market." He further suggested that, "Perhaps [Wal-Mart is] doing a better job of marketing that message. But in all practicality, what we're observing in the marketplace is no real change in terms of the number of items [Wal-Mart is] marking down or rolling back, or the depth of those discounts." Although Wal-Mart's price rollbacks may not intimidate Target, Wal-Mart's getting its message across via better marketing should—particularly when Wal-Mart pairs it with an improved shopping experience.

Grow Share of Stomach

The timing was right when Target increased its emphasis on food in its P2004 prototype. While shoppers may be curbing their general merchandise such as apparel and home spending, they can still look to Target to fill their pantries. Food also serves as a traffic driver. But Target needs to convert more guests into grocery buyers. According to TNS Retail Forward's research, only 6 percent of Target general merchandise store shoppers purchase groceries on every trip.

Target should study how rising food prices are impacting shoppers and shopping behavior. See Figure 3. If it can give shoppers more reasons to shop its food aisles during tough economic times, it could lead to loyal grocery guests. Some opportunities in the food department include:

▶ *Promote dinner solutions.* About 43 percent of all shoppers report that they are trying to save money by forgoing restaurant dining. Although Target appears to be moving in the direction of offering meal solutions, it continues to fall short. For example, when a new store opened in fall 2007, Target sent a direct-mail piece that positioned Target as the answer to shoppers' "daily dinner dilemmas." The marketing piece also included various recipes featuring products found at the Target general merchandise store. But the buck stopped there. Target did not carry the recipe ideas from the direct-mail piece into the store—a big miss, especially considering that Target already features its "Simple Solutions" recipe cards in SuperTarget stores. Target's recipes can serve as easy solutions for guests: They appeal to time-starved shoppers and also the many shoppers curtailing their eating-out habits. The company should consider a bigger promotional push related to its recipe ideas beyond SuperTarget. In related news, Target is teaming with Travel Channel show *Bizarre Foods* host Andrew Zimmern, who will serve as the SuperTarget Meal Adventure Guide and is charged with developing easy, imaginative meals for SuperTarget guests.

▶ *Emphasize one-stop shopping.* One-third of shoppers report consolidating spending at stores they think offer the best overall value. Thus, retailers with one-stop shopping appeal could win out. Target is doing a good job of promoting its grocery offer in circulars with fun quips and quotes to encourage shoppers to skip a trip to the grocery store. More marketing efforts like this could be worthwhile.

▶ *Make gourmet affordable.* Almost one-quarter of shoppers say that they have been buying fewer gourmet and specialty products as a result of rising food prices. Target can appeal to gourmands who may be cutting back by touting its premium food brand Archer Farms as affordable gourmet.

▶ *Encourage private-brand purchases.* One out of five shoppers has reported that they are buying more private-brand products in response to rising food prices. This bodes well for Target's Archer Farms and Market Pantry private brands.

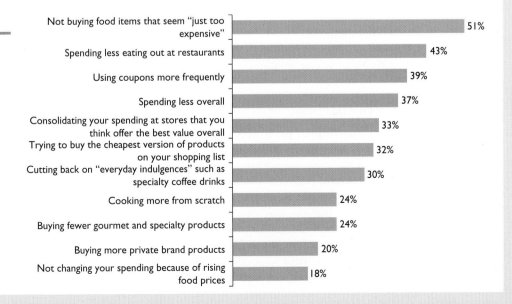

FIGURE 3

Reaction to Rising Food Prices (multiple answers allowed)

Source: TNS Retail Forward ShopperScape™, February 2008.

Not buying food items that seem "just too expensive"	51%
Spending less eating out at restaurants	43%
Using coupons more frequently	39%
Spending less overall	37%
Consolidating your spending at stores that you think offer the best value overall	33%
Trying to buy the cheapest version of products on your shopping list	32%
Cutting back on "everyday indulgences" such as specialty coffee drinks	30%
Cooking more from scratch	24%
Buying fewer gourmet and specialty products	24%
Buying more private brand products	20%
Not changing your spending because of rising food prices	18%

Sustain Traffic

This is hard to do in a struggling economy. Shoppers look to cut spending simply by shopping less. Target needs to figure out how to draw shoppers in more frequently. It could utilize its in-store register coupon program to get shoppers back in the door. Some examples: Entice shoppers with $5 off their total bill when they come back to the store in the next week and spend $50, or spend $25 in grocery and get $5 off their next bill. These types of incentives could "train" shoppers to use Target as a grocery destination. Offering a Target gift card with purchase also is a good repeat-traffic generator. Another benefit of the gift card tactic: Shoppers typically spend more than the card's value upon redemption.

Enhance the Treasure Hunt Appeal

Much of the shopping experience at Target already is about a treasure hunt because the company's go-to-market strategy is about delivering the unexpected at affordable prices. But with the economy sputtering, there are ways to up the ante. One possibility is to leverage the popular dollar section, now called "See Spot Save," because it includes 2 for $5 items in addition to $1 finds. Integrating this type of value-priced treasure hunt concept in other departments could add excitement and encourage add-on purchases. Target has taken this idea to the toy department with a selection of value-priced items promoted in bins and on an endcap. Value items in the pet department are merchandised in a similar fashion.

The dollar section has legs beyond toys and pets and even more so now because Target has stretched the idea of the value offer by incorporating 2 for $5 items: Broadening the price offer provides flexibility in terms of assortment. The "See Spot Save," concept could work in a number of other areas, such as beauty, jewelry/accessories, entertainment, school/office, stationary, and so on. To pursue this kind of initiative, it is important that Target be careful not to "cheapen" its aisles but instead focus on the treasure hunt aspect. This could mean implementing the concept in just a few departments or rotating the concept through different areas of the store. A revolving initiative through different departments would provide Target an opportunity to study shoppers' response in various categories.

Inspire New Designs for the Home

The slow-growth economy has been particularly challenging for the home category as shoppers delay discretionary purchases. Target is making some adjustments in pricing and assortment to address some near-term challenges. But it also needs to engage the customer. Shoppers are looking for smaller, less expensive projects and easy ways to improve the look of the home without a major investment.

To assist shoppers, Target could show guests how they can upgrade the look of a room with some simple decorating tips. Shoppers know they can visit Target for the latest styles and designer fashions for less, but that might not be motivation enough to spend. Project and/or room makeover guidance, tips, and tricks could deliver inspiration. A first step for Target: Work with designers not only to produce affordable designs but utilize partnerships to craft room solutions and ideas for guests. For example, the 2008 Global Bazaar allowed Target guests to shop rooms online by color themes. Why not let guests shop a certain designer's room, such as Victoria Hagan or Thomas O'Brien? This could motivate full-room (or at least multiple-item) purchases.

Keep Costs in Check

Target needs to keep a close eye on expenses, especially in light of slow sales and declining gross margins. Food is a helpful addition because of its traffic-driving potential, but the category is a drag on margins. Compared with other store categories, Target has experienced faster sales growth in the low-margin consumables and commodities category, which represented one-third of Target's total sales in 2007 versus 30 percent in 2005. At the same time, gross margins have leveled off: Gross margin remained flat at 31.9 percent in 2005 and 2006 before falling 0.1 percentage point to 31.8 percent in 2007.

Target planned to open its first company-owned food distribution center in late 2008, which would provide some benefit to food margins; self-distribution should lower costs and in turn boost margins. Continuing to promote private brands also will alleviate some margin pressure.

Target's selling, general, and administrative (SG&A) expense ratio increased from 25.0 percent in 2003 to 25.6 percent in 2007. But Target did hold its expense rate flat during the fourth quarter of 2007, in large part due to tighter control of hourly payroll expense in stores. Target has noted that it is "keenly focused on controlling the growth of our expenses particularly in light of our current slow pace of comparable-store sales. We are pleased with the progress we have made so far, but the evaluation of potential opportunities is far from complete. We remain keenly focused on making smart decisions that eliminate unnecessary expense without compromising anything that makes Target a great place to shop and a great place to work." Expect Target to continue to keep a lid on costs. Efforts have been working: 2008 first quarter growth in SG&A dollars grew at 6.2 percent—the lowest increase in more than 20 consecutive quarters, according to the company.

Maintain Inventory on Hand

According to previous TNS Retail Forward discussions with food suppliers, grocery out-of-stocks is a problem for Target in some categories, particularly for sale items. Sufficient in-stocks in the food/consumables business must be a priority for Target. Shoppers will quickly get frustrated if they seek out value items only to find empty shelves.

Looking Forward

These are challenging times for Target. The company's best bet is to reinforce its value proposition in shoppers' minds. Target can and should promote low prices, but the low-price message must also evoke value. To do both is difficult, but innovative campaigns should steer future efforts. It is crucial that Target's brand promise "Expect More. Pay Less." remain relevant regardless of economic conditions.

Expect Target to take the necessary steps to turn things around. Competitors should be mindful of potential alterations in Target's strategy and/or at least in its short-term tactics. Meanwhile, Target's recent lackluster performance has provided an entrée for other retailers to gain some ground. As Target moves forward, it must continue to innovate to ensure its differentiated position in the marketplace. More players, such as Kohl's and J.C. Penney, are taking a page from Target and exploring designer partnerships. Competitors also are becoming better brand managers, a skill that Target has been honing for a number of years.

Manufacturers must help Target deliver on its priorities. Target will look to partners to help it find ways to cut costs without forsaking value so that the guest experience remains a positive one. Manufacturer partners that can deliver helpful insights that show how shoppers are dealing with economic pressures and provide Target with ways of responding will find themselves in good stead with the retailer.

Questions

1. What lessons should Target learn based on its performance as described in this case?
2. In general, what can an independent retailer learn from this case? A chain retailer?
3. Discuss the information presented in Figures 1, 2, and 3.
4. Comment on this statement: "Target is determined not to stray from its existing strategy—a decision that will serve Target well in the long run. But at present, it should focus on some initiatives to minimize the immediate impact of the economic downturn."
5. Should Target place more emphasis on food sales and "dinner solutions"? Explain your answer.
6. How can manufacturers (suppliers) help Target in tough economic times?
7. What should be the role of the Internet for Target? Why?

PART 3 Targeting Customers and Gathering Information

In Part Three, we first present various key concepts for retailers to better identify and understand consumers and develop an appropriate target market plan. Information-gathering methods—which can be used in identifying and understanding consumers, as well as in developing and implementing a retail strategy—are then described.

Chapter 7 discusses many influences on retail shoppers: demographics, lifestyles, needs and desires, shopping attitudes and behavior, retailer actions that influence shopping, and environmental factors. We place these elements within a target marketing framework, because it is critical for retailers to recognize what makes their customers and potential customers tick—and for them to act accordingly.

Chapter 8 deals with information gathering and processing in retailing. We first consider the information flows in a retail distribution channel and review the difficulties that may arise from basing a retail strategy on inadequate information. Then we examine in depth the retail information system, its components, and recent advances in information systems—with particular emphasis on data warehousing and data mining. The last part of the chapter describes the marketing research process.

Source: Mario Ragma, Jr./istockphoto.com.

7 Identifying and Understanding Consumers

Chapter Objectives

1. To discuss why it is important for a retailer to properly identify, understand, and appeal to its customers

2. To enumerate and describe a number of consumer demographics, lifestyle factors, and needs and desires—and to explain how these concepts can be applied to retailing

3. To examine consumer attitudes toward shopping and consumer shopping behavior, including the consumer decision process and its stages

4. To look at retailer actions based on target market planning

5. To note some of the environmental factors that affect consumer shopping

Thomas Stemberg, a Harvard MBA, was working on a business plan in his home during summer 1985. While printing spreadsheets, he realized that his printer ribbon was broken. Attempts to purchase a new ribbon over the Fourth of July weekend were unsuccessful. His local stationery store and a nearby computer store were both closed, and the nearest BJ's did not carry the correct ribbon. All of a sudden, a thought occurred to Stemberg: what the world needed was a superstore selling nothing but office supplies at great prices.

On May 1, 1986, Staples (**www.staples.com**) opened its first superstore in Brighton, Massachusetts. The store was so successful that about 20 competitors launched similar store formats within the next two years. Today, Staples is the world's largest office-supply retailer with more than 1,700 superstores in the United States, Canada, and Europe. Staples also has catalog and Web-based businesses that are serviced through its Staples Business Delivery, Quill, and Contract operations.

Staples appeals to three distinct market segments: small and large businesses, home offices, and final consumers. Its stores have changed the way each of these consumers purchases supplies. Recently, Staples introduced a new private-label brand called "M by Staples." This line features fancy leather journals, business card holders, and even high-fashion file folders. According to Staples' executive vice-president for merchandising, "Instead of 100 folders for $6.20, which we lose money on, [customers] may buy $6.99-for-12 folders that we make money on."[1]

Source: Reprinted by permission of Susan Berry, Retailing Image Consulting, Inc.

OVERVIEW

The quality of a retail strategy depends on how well a firm identifies and understands its customers and how well it forms a strategy mix to appeal to them. This entails identifying consumer characteristics, needs, and attitudes; recognizing how people make decisions; and then devising the proper target market plan. It also means studying environmental factors that affect purchase decisions. Consider the following:

> The empowered consumer, faced with a multitude of choices about where, when, and how they shop, is leading to increasingly high expectations. A competitive retail sector, facing an uncertain economic future, is being challenged by consumers to compete for their business. In this environment, only the fittest and those really listening to what their customers really want are likely to survive. Customers select their shopping destination based upon their particular needs for that specific shopping occasion. Are they looking to purchase groceries, a wedding outfit, or a gift—or to design a new kitchen? On top of this, a customer's expectations for a shopping trip differ greatly depending upon very specific needs, for example, a customer visiting a supermarket for a pint of milk wants a speedy, efficient service, whereas a customer looking for menu inspiration for a dinner party desires an entirely different experience. Retailers are judged on the range, availability, quality, and ease with which customers can access and use the various services they offer.[2]

In this chapter, we explore—from a retailing perspective—the impact on shoppers of each of the elements shown in Figure 7-1: demographics, lifestyles, needs and desires, shopping attitudes and behavior, retailer actions that influence shopping, and environmental factors. By studying these elements, a retailer can devise the best possible target market plan and do so in the context of its overall strategy.

Please note: We use *consumer*, *customer*, and *shopper* interchangeably in this chapter.

FIGURE 7-1

What Makes Retail
Shoppers Tick

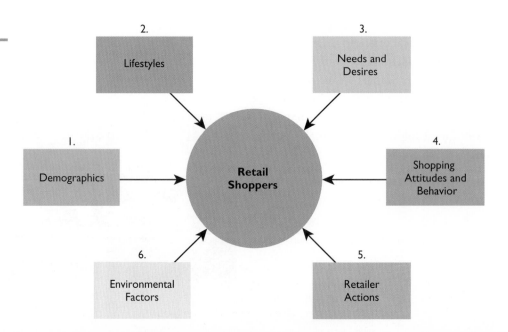

Consumer Demographics and Lifestyles

Demographics are objective, quantifiable, easily identifiable, and measurable population data. **Lifestyles** are the ways in which individual consumers and families (households) live and spend time and money. Visit our Web site (**www.pearsonhighered.com/berman**) for several useful links on these topics.

Consumer Demographics

At *The Rite Site* (**www. easidemographics.com**), retailers can access lots of useful demographic data. Take a look at the free reports.

Both groups of consumers and individual consumers can be identified by such demographics as gender, age, population growth rate, life expectancy, literacy, language spoken, household size, marital and family status, income, retail sales, mobility, place of residence, occupation, education, and ethnic/racial background. These factors affect people's retail shopping and retailer actions.

A retailer should have some knowledge of overall trends, as well as the demographics of its own target market. Table 7-1 indicates broad demographics for 10 nations around the world, and Table 7-2 shows U.S. demographics by region. Regional data are useful since most retailers are local and regional.

In understanding U.S. demographics, it is helpful to know these facts:

▶ The typical household has an annual income of $50,000. The top one-fifth of households earn $100,000 or more; the lowest one-fifth earn $21,000 or less. If income is high, people are apt to have **discretionary income**—money left after paying taxes and buying necessities.

▶ One-seventh of people move each year, yet 60 percent of all moves are in the same county.

▶ There are 5 million more females than males, and three-fifths of females aged 20 and older are in the labor force (many full-time).

▶ Most U.S. employment is in services. In addition, there are now more professionals and white-collar workers than before and fewer blue-collar and agricultural workers.

TABLE 7-1 Population Demographics: A Global Perspective—Selected Countries

Country	Male/ Female (%)	Age Distribution (%) 0–14 Years	15–64 Years	65 Years and Over	Annual Population Growth (%)	Life Expectancy in Years	Literacy Rate (%)	Principal Languages Spoken
Canada	48.8/51.2	16	69	15	0.83	81.2	99	English, French
China	51.0/49.0	20	72	8	0.63	73.2	91	More than a dozen versions of Chinese
Great Britain	48.8/51.2	17	67	16	0.28	78.9	99	English, Welsh
India	50.7/49.3	32	63	5	1.58	69.3	61	Hindi, English, 14 other official languages
Italy	48.5/51.5	14	66	20	−0.02	80.1	98	Italian, German, French, Slovene
Japan	48.5/51.5	14	65	21	−0.14	82.1	99	Japanese
Mexico	48.5/51.5	30	64	6	1.14	75.8	91	Spanish
Poland	47.5/52.5	15	72	13	−0.05	75.4	99+	Polish
South Africa	48.0/52.0	29	66	5	0.83	48.9	86	Afrikaans, English, 9 other official languages
United States	49.0/51.0	20	67	13	0.88	78.1	99	English, Spanish

The literacy rate is the percentage of people who are 15 and older who can read and write.

Source: Compiled by the authors from *World Factbook,* **https://www.cia.gov/library/publications/the-world-factbook** (December 18, 2008).

TABLE 7-2   Selected U.S. Demographics by Region

Region	Percent of Population	Percent of Household Income	Percent Ages 18–24	Percent Ages 62 and Older	Population Per Square Mile
ENC	15.2	15.8	9.7	16.0	156
ESC	5.8	5.3	9.4	16.7	98
M	7.0	7.2	9.9	15.5	25
MA	13.3	14.6	9.6	17.4	377
NE	4.8	5.3	9.6	17.3	207
P	16.3	16.8	10.7	14.7	50
SA	19.4	17.6	9.7	17.4	206
WNC	6.6	6.9	9.7	16.7	39
WSC	11.6	10.5	10.0	14.2	81

ENC (East North Central) = Illinois, Indiana, Michigan, Ohio, Wisconsin
ESC (East South Central) = Alabama, Kentucky, Mississippi, Tennessee
M (Mountain) = Arizona, Colorado, Idaho, Montana, Nevada, New Mexico, Utah, Wyoming
MA (Middle Atlantic) = New Jersey, New York, Pennsylvania
NE (New England) = Connecticut, Maine, Massachusetts, New Hampshire, Rhode Island, Vermont
P (Pacific) = Alaska, California, Hawaii, Oregon, Washington
SA (South Atlantic) = Delaware, District of Columbia, Florida, Georgia, Maryland, North Carolina, South Carolina, Virginia, West Virginia
WNC (West North Central) = Iowa, Kansas, Minnesota, Missouri, Nebraska, North Dakota, South Dakota
WSC (West South Central) = Arkansas, Louisiana, Oklahoma, Texas
Source: Computed by the authors from U.S. Bureau of the Census, 2008 data.

▶ Many adults have attended some level of college, with more than one-quarter of all U.S. adults aged 25 and older graduating from a four-year college (at the least).
▶ The population comprises many ethnic and racial groups. African Americans, Hispanic Americans, and Asian Americans account for one-third of U.S. residents—a steadily rising figure. Each of these groups represents a large potential target market; their total annual buying power is $1.7 trillion.[3]

Although the preceding gives an overview of the United States, demographics vary by area (as Table 7-2 indicates). Within a state or city, some locales have larger populations and more affluent, older, and better-educated residents. Because most retailers are local or operate in only part of a region, they must compile data about the people living in their trading areas and those most apt to shop there. *For a given business and location*, the characteristics of the target market (the customer group to be sought by the retailer) can be studied on the basis of some combination of these demographic factors—and a retail strategy planned accordingly:

▶ *Market size*—How many people are in the potential target market?
▶ *Gender*—Is the potential target market more male or female, or are they equal in proportion?
▶ *Age*—What are the prime age groups to which the retailer wants to appeal?
▶ *Household size*—What is the average household size of potential consumers?
▶ *Marital and family status*—Are potential consumers single or married? Do families have children?
▶ *Income*—Is the potential target market lower income, middle income, or upper income? Is discretionary income available for luxury purchases?
▶ *Retail sales*—What is the area's sales forecast for the retailer's goods/services category?
▶ *Birth rate*—How important is the birth rate for the retailer's goods/services category?
▶ *Mobility*—What percent of the potential target market moves into and out of the trading area yearly?

 **TECHNOLOGY IN RETAILING** Reaching Customers in New Ways

QVC (**www.qvc.com**) recently teamed up with Case Western Reserve University (**www.case.edu**) to launch the use of two-dimensional (2D) scanning codes in the United States. These scanning codes are barcodes that contain information in both horizontal and vertical directions. Through this approach, consumers can scan a code on their cell phone and it will be automatically directed to a retailer's Web site. Although this technology has been used extensively in Asia and Europe, it is new to the United States.

According to QVC's chief marketing officer, "It's [2D] the next killer app in advertising, and we're taking it to the next level." Using 2D, a consumer who scans a picture of a QVC product would be taken directly to that product's

specific Web site within QVC. This technology has obvious applications for product or service information, as well as to facilitate placing an order.

In QVC's teaming with Case Western University, students were encouraged to develop their own 2D codes and then get other students to use the new codes. In one application, a student placed a code on his business card. When scanned, the code directed the user to the student's online résumé.

Sources: Linda Haugsted, "QVC Goes '2D' with Cellphone Test," *Multichannel News* (April 7, 2008), p. 3; and "QVC Challenges Case Western Reserve Students to 'Make It' Or 'Break It,'" *QVC Press Release* (September 2, 2008).

▶ *Where people live*—How large is the trading area from which potential customers can be drawn?
▶ *Employment status*—Does the potential target market include working women?
▶ *Occupation*—In what industries and occupations are people in the area working? Are they professionals, office workers, or of some other designation?
▶ *Education*—Are potential customers college-educated?
▶ *Ethnic/racial background*—Does the potential target market cover a distinctive racial or ethnic group?

Consumer Lifestyles

Consumer Insight Magazine (**www.nielsen.com/ consumer_insight**) provides a good perspective on emerging consumer trends.

Consumer lifestyles are based on social and psychological factors and are influenced by demographics. As with demographics, a retailer should first have some knowledge of consumer lifestyle concepts and then determine the lifestyle attributes of its own target market.

These *social factors* are useful in identifying and understanding consumer lifestyles:

▶ A **culture** is a distinctive heritage shared by a group of people that passes on a series of beliefs, norms, and customs. The U.S. culture stresses individuality, success, education, and material comfort; there are also various subcultures (such as African, Asian, and Hispanic Americans) due to the many countries from which residents have come.
▶ **Social class** involves an informal ranking of people based on income, occupation, education, and other factors. People often have similar values in each social class.
▶ **Reference groups** influence people's thoughts and behavior: aspirational groups— a person does not belong but wishes to join; membership groups—a person does belong; and dissociative groups—a person does not want to belong. Face-to-face groups, such as families, have the most impact. Within reference groups, there are opinion leaders whose views are well respected and sought.
▶ The **family life cycle** describes how a traditional family moves from bachelorhood to children to solitary retirement. At each stage, attitudes, needs, purchases, and income change. Retailers must also be alert to the many adults who never marry, divorced adults, single-parent families, and childless couples. The **household life cycle** incorporates life stages for both family and nonfamily households.
▶ *Time utilization* refers to the activities in which a person is involved and the amount of time allocated to them. The broad categories are work, transportation, eating, recreation, entertainment, parenting, sleeping, and (retailers hope) shopping. Today, many consumers allocate less time to shopping.

Consumer psychology can be studied with tools such as the Keirsey Temperament Sorter. Take the online test (www.keirsey.com/cgi-bin/keirsey/newkts.cgi) to learn about yourself.

These *psychological factors* help in identifying and understanding consumer lifestyles:

▶ A **personality** is the sum total of an individual's traits, which make that individual unique. They include a person's level of self-confidence, innovativeness, autonomy, sociability, emotional stability, and assertiveness.

▶ **Class consciousness** is the extent to which a person desires and pursues social status. It helps determine the use of reference groups and the importance of prestige purchases. A class-conscious person values the status of goods, services, and retailers.

▶ **Attitudes (opinions)** are the positive, neutral, or negative feelings a person has about different topics. They are also feelings consumers have about a given retailer and its activities. Does the consumer feel a retailer is desirable, unique, and fairly priced?

▶ **Perceived risk** is the level of risk a consumer believes exists regarding the purchase of a specific good or service from a given retailer, whether or not the belief is correct. There are six types: *functional* (Will a good or service perform well?), *physical* (Can a good or service hurt me?), *financial* (Can I afford it?), *social* (What will peers think of my shopping here?), *psychological* (Am I doing the right thing?), and *time* (How much shopping effort is needed?). Perceived risk is high if a retailer or its brands are new, a person is on a budget or has little experience, there are many choices, and an item is socially visible or complex. See Figure 7-2. Firms can reduce perceived risk with information.

▶ *The importance of a purchase* to the consumer affects the amount of time he or she will spend to make a decision and the range of alternatives considered. If a purchase is important, perceived risk tends to be higher, and the retailer must adapt to this.

A retailer can develop a lifestyle profile of its target market by answering these questions and then use the answers in developing its strategy:

▶ *Culture*—What values, norms, and customs are most important to the potential target market?

▶ *Social class*—Are potential consumers lower, middle, or upper class? Are they socially mobile?

▶ *Reference groups*—To whom do people look for purchasing advice? Does this differ by good or service category? How can a firm target opinion leaders?

▶ *Family (or household) life cycle*—In what stage(s) of the cycle are the bulk of potential customers?

▶ *Time utilization*—How do people spend time? How do they view their shopping time?

▶ *Personality*—Do potential customers have identifiable personality traits?

FIGURE 7-2

The Impact of Perceived Risk on Consumers

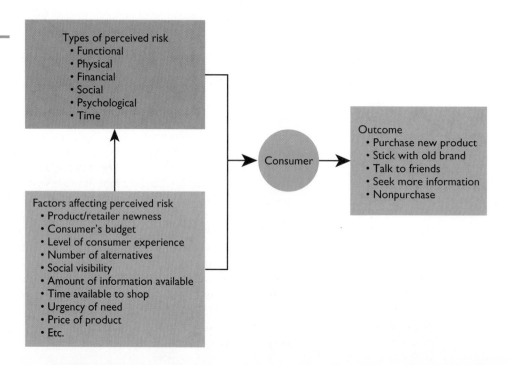

▶ *Class consciousness*—Are potential consumers status-conscious? How does this affect purchases?

▶ *Attitudes*—How does the potential target market feel about the retailer and its offerings in terms of specific strategy components?

▶ *Perceived risk*—Do potential customers feel risk in connection with the retailer? Which goods and services have the greatest perceived risk?

▶ *Importance of the purchase*—How important are the goods/services offered to potential customers?

Retailing Implications of Consumer Demographics and Lifestyles

Demographic and lifestyle factors need to be considered from several perspectives. Here are some illustrations. By no means do the examples cover the full domain of retailing.

Gender Roles: The huge number of working women, who put in 60 to 70 hours or more each week between their job and home responsibilities, is altering lifestyles significantly. Compared with women who have not worked outside the home, they tend to be more self-confident and individualistic, more concerned with convenience, more interested in sharing household and family tasks with spouses or significant others, more knowledgeable and demanding as consumers, more interested in leisure activities and travel, more involved with self-improvement and education, more appearance-conscious, and more indifferent to small price differences among retailers. They are less interested in unhurried shopping trips.

Due to the trend toward working women, male lifestyles are also changing. More men now take care of their children, shop for food, do laundry, wash dishes, cook, vacuum, and clean the bathroom. Eighteen percent of U.S. grocery shoppers are men who shop alone and 20 percent are men who shop as part of a couple.[4] See Figure 7-3. In the future, there will be still more changes in men's and women's roles. The clout and duties of husbands and wives will be shared more often. Retailers need to appreciate this trend.

FIGURE 7-3

Blurring Gender Roles
Due to changing lifestyles, more husbands and wives shop together now, as at this A&P store.

Source: Reprinted by permission.

FIGURE 7-4

King Kullen: Addressing
the Poverty of Time
To make shopping and food
preparation much more
convenient for today's
time-pressed customers,
King Kullen's Web site
(**www.kingkullen.com**) offers
weekly specials, easy-to-access
recipes, a section that describes
each in-store department, gift
cards, and a lot more.

Source: Reprinted by permission of
King Kullen.

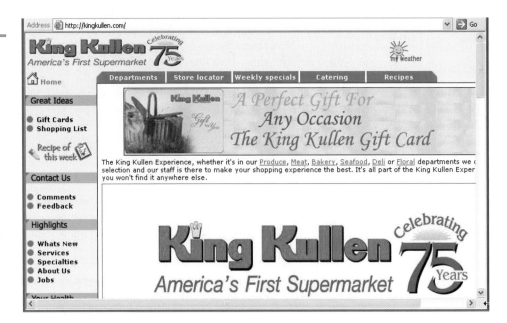

Consumer Sophistication and Confidence: Many shoppers are now more knowledge-able and cosmopolitan; more aware of trends in tastes, styles, and goods and services; and more sophisticated. Nonconforming behavior is accepted when consumers are self-assured and better appreciate the available choices. Confident shoppers experiment more. For example, some "shoppers are cutting back, trading down to less-expensive brands, shopping in less-expensive stores, putting less on the credit card. They are incorporating old and new techniques to be smarter shoppers—cutting coupons (again), reading retail circulars (again), and taking advantage of shopping online to buy more efficiently. Buying pre-owned products is another method some shoppers have adopted to stretch their dollars. This is now a legitimate way for shoppers to get everything from cars and books to home décor, clothes, even baby products."[5]

Poverty of Time: The increase in working women, the desire for personal fulfillment, the daily job commute, and the tendency of some people to have second jobs contribute to many consumers feeling time-pressured: "No matter how rich or poor consumers are, time is the great social equalizer. A new priority of making the most of the limited time we have is taking over. Consumers are looking at all the ways they spend their time, including shopping, and demanding a more time-efficient, time-conscious way to shop."[6] There are ways for retailers to respond to the poverty-of-time concept. Firms can add branch stores to limit customer travel time; be open longer hours; add on-floor sales personnel; reduce checkout time; and use mail order, Web sites, and other direct marketing practices. See Figure 7-4.

Component Lifestyles: In the past, shoppers were typecast, based on demographics and lifestyles. Now, it is recognized that shopping is less predictable and more individualistic. It is more situation-based, hence, the term *component lifestyle:* "Have you wondered what's going on with consumers? Why the contradictions when it comes to spending money? Why they will buy a $500 leather jacket at full price but wait for a $50 sweater to go on sale? Will buy a top-line sports utility vehicle then go to Costco for tires? Will pay $3.50 for a cup of coffee but think $1.29 is too much for a hamburger? Will spend $2.00 for a strawberry-smelling bath soap but wait for a coupon to buy a $0.99 twin pack of toilet soap?"[7]

VALS (**www.sric-bi.com/
VALS**) classifies lifestyles
into several profiles. Visit
the site to learn about the
profiles and take the
"VALS Survey" to see
where you fit.

Consumer Profiles

Considerable research has been aimed at describing consumer profiles in a way that is useful for retailers. Here are three examples:

In creating the ideal shopping experience for teenage shoppers, retailers need to acknowledge the desire of teens to socialize and belong—regardless of

Understanding Russian Car Shoppers

According to PricewaterhouseCoopers (**www.pwc.com**), a consulting firm, Russia recently passed Germany to become Europe's largest car market. During the first half of 2008, 1.65 million new cars were registered in Russia versus 1.63 million new cars for Germany. There are currently 26.8 million vehicles on the road in Russia, about 184 cars per 1,000 people. However, more than one-half of all vehicles are 10 years or older, 27 percent are 5 to 10 years old, and only 22 percent are less than 5 years old. One analyst predicts that as of 2010, there will be 230 cars per 1,000 people.

There are two of the major attributes of the Russian car-buying market:

▶ Daria Fomina, a spokesperson for Chrysler Russia (**www.chrysler.ru/en**), says that Russian consumers have more strict demands than many American consumers. Russians are especially concerned with safety, comfort, and interior trim.

▶ Andriy Ivchenko, a consultant with Frost & Sullivan (**www.frost.com**), notes that Russia is the number one market for SUVs (sport utility vehicles) in all of Europe due to "severe climate conditions, poor road quality, and sometimes the absence of the road itself." Ivchenko also states that Russia constitutes a major market for car accessories and enhancements such as custom paint, security systems, and audio-visual electronics.

Sources: Jason Bush, "Russian Auto Market Now Europe's Largest," **www.businessweek.com/globalbiz** (July 11, 2008); and James E. Guyette, "Russian Auto Market Open for Business," *Aftermarket Business* (January 2008), pp. 60–70.

whether they are shopping in stores or online. And although stores tend to be the venue for most transactions, the Internet often is where the teen shopper journey begins. Specialty apparel retailers tend to focus more on the store environment while department stores and mass retailers are using the Internet to compensate for the difficulty in adapting the store environment to the teen shopper.[8]

Hispanics can be found across America. For example, in Indianapolis, there are close to 40,000 Hispanics living within a two-mile radius of one of the 20 Kroger supermarkets in the market. Within that same radius, 7,500 Hispanic households are entirely dependent on Spanish. Hispanic buying power can be seen in sales of beef and pork. They spend almost $10 million annually on beef and pork inside Kroger's Indianapolis units, accounting for double-digit market shares in five of the stores. Hispanics tend to gravitate toward products they recognize. If popular brands sold well in their countries of origin, typically these goods continue to be purchased by them in the United States.[9]

According to Claritas' "geodemographic segmentation," these are the wealthiest demographic groups in America. (1) Upper crust—This is the wealthiest demographic. They live in elite suburbs and are 45- to 65-year-old empty nesters. Favorite store: Bloomingdales. (2) Blue-blood estates—The second wealthiest group, these are mostly white-collar baby boomers with kids who accumulate wealth as their family matures. They live in elite suburbs. They are well educated and often white or Asian. Favorite store: Talbot's. (3) Young digerati—Tech-savvy, young (25–44), and often childless, they tend to be highly educated, ethnically mixed, and live in fashionable urban neighborhoods. Favorite stores: Banana Republic, J. Crew. (4) Country squires—These are well-educated baby boomers with kids who've fled the city for the spacious estates in small towns or scenic rural areas. Favorite stores: Amazon.com, Target. (5) Movers & shakers—These are dual-income couples without kids who are highly educated, and typically are between the ages of 35 and 54. They achieved affluence in middle age, tend to be executives or business owners, and live in suburbs. Favorite stores: Apple, Costco.[10]

Consumer Needs and Desires

Catherines (**www.catherines.com**), a retailer of plus-size women's apparel, seeks to satisfy both consumer needs and desires, especially the latter.

When developing a target market profile, a retailer should identify key consumer needs and desires. From a retailing perspective, *needs* are a person's basic shopping requirements consistent with his or her present demographics and lifestyle. *Desires* are discretionary shopping goals that have an impact on attitudes and behavior. A person may need a new car to get to and from work, and he or she may seek a dealer with Saturday service hours. The person may desire a Porsche and a free loaner car when the vehicle is serviced but be satisfied with a Toyota that can be serviced on the weekend and fits within the budget.

Consider this: "All types of consumer expenditures vie for the same pool of limited resources—the consumer's discretionary income. Thus, consumer spending in a particular retail sector can be better understood in relation to spending in others. It is important to understand how consumers, with a given budget, make trade-offs between meeting different consumption needs. For example, how much would gas prices affect spending on food and apparel? Which retail sectors would gain most in consumer spending due to a tax rebate?"[11] And this: "Women have felt disrespected and ignored when shopping for consumer electronics products. Yet, it is all about the experience. Some stores generate fun and confidence. How you design your stores is very important. In many cases, women don't like the consumer electronics shopping experience because retailers don't know what they want. Many women want reliable, beautiful products that they are interested in using—and that match the décor of their homes."[12]

When a retail strategy aims to satisfy consumer needs and desires, it appeals to consumer **motives**, the reasons for their behavior. These are just a few of the questions to resolve:

▶ How far will customers travel to get to the retailer?
▶ How important is convenience?
▶ What hours are desired? Are evening and weekend hours required?
▶ What level of customer services is preferred?
▶ How extensive a goods/service assortment is desired?
▶ What level of goods/service quality is preferred?
▶ How important is price?
▶ What retailer actions are necessary to reduce perceived risk?
▶ Do different market segments have special needs? If so, what are they?

Let's address the last question by looking at three particular market segments that attract retailer attention: in-home shoppers, online shoppers, and outshoppers.

In-Home Shopping: The in-home shopper is not always a captive audience. Shopping is often discretionary, not necessary. Convenience in ordering an item, without traveling for it, is important. These shoppers are often active store shoppers, and they are affluent and well educated. Many in-home shoppers are self-confident, younger, and venturesome. They like in-store shopping but have low opinions of local shopping. For some catalog shoppers, time is not important. In households with young children, in-home shopping is more likely if the woman works part-time or not at all than if she works full-time. In-home shoppers may be unable to comparison shop; may not be able to touch, feel, handle, or examine products firsthand; are concerned about service (such as returns); and may not have a salesperson to ask questions.

Check out the Pew Internet & American Life Project Web site (**www.pewinternet.org**) to find out more about Web users.

Online Shopping: People who shop online are often well educated and have above-average incomes (as stated in Chapter 6). As we noted earlier, Web shopping encompasses more than just purchasing online. At REI, online shoppers can research items, check out prices, and place orders. Some shoppers have items shipped to them, while others go to the store: "REI is respected for its smart approach to multi-channel integration. Especially dazzling is the company's in-store pickup program for online orders. Customers like in-store pickup because they save shipping costs. REI likes it because it brings customers into the store, where they spend even more. About 35 percent of REI.com's sales are designated for customer pickup, and that figure climbs above 40 percent during special sales and promotional events. One in three REI.com online shoppers who opt for store pickup, rather than delivery, buy additional goods on that store visit. This adds $70 to $85 to the purchase."[13]

Outshopping: Out-of-hometown shopping, **outshopping**, is important for both local and surrounding retailers. The former want to minimize this behavior, whereas the latter want to maximize it. Outshoppers are often young, members of a large family, and new to the community. Income and education vary by situation. Outshoppers differ in their lifestyles from those who patronize hometown stores. They enjoy fine foods, like to travel, are active, like to change stores, and read out-of-town newspapers. They also downplay hometown stores and compliment out-of-town stores. This is vital data for suburban shopping centers. Outshoppers have the same basic reasons for out-of-town shopping whether they reside in small or large communities—easy access, liberal credit, store diversity, product assortments, prices, the presence of large chains, entertainment facilities, customer services, and product quality.

Shopping Attitudes and Behavior

In this section, we look at people's attitudes toward shopping, where they shop, and the way in which they make purchase decisions.

Attitudes Toward Shopping

Considerable research has been done on people's attitudes toward shopping. Such attitudes have a big impact on the ways in which people act in a retail setting. Retailers must strive to turn around some negative perceptions that now exist. Let us highlight some research findings.

Shopping Enjoyment: In general, people do not enjoy shopping as much as in the past. So, what does stimulate a pleasurable shopping experience—a challenge that retailers must address? "Customers derive enjoyment in their shopping from an assessment of accessibility, atmosphere, environment, and personnel. If a shopping center facilitates fast, efficient shopping, this would appeal to men, who would enjoy shopping in that region, and may therefore be more likely to return to the location in the future. At the same time, since women comprise a higher proportion of the shopping population, there is a need to promote aspects of the shopping center as a relaxing and fun leisure activity to increase female enjoyment of the shopping location, to retain these customers and increase the likelihood of repatronage."[14]

Attitudes Toward Shopping Time: Retail shopping is often viewed as a chore. "This observation suggests that retailers should not lose sight of the importance of time-related factors in catering to customers. No matter how much effort the retailer invests in order to improve store ambience, the effects of those efforts can be tempered by the consumer's level of chronic time pressure. Therefore, retailers should not only invest more in store atmospherics (e.g., music, color, lighting, smell, and visual merchandising) but pay equal attention to the efficiency of store location, parking, and sales personnel assistance that may deactivate shoppers' chronic time pressure."[15]

Shifting Feelings About Retailing: There has been a major change in attitudes toward spending, value, and shopping with established retailers: "The same shopper who buys commodity goods at Target may also buy expensive apparel at Nordstrom. This shift does not appear to be transitory, but rather seems to define a more enduring pattern of behavior." In addition, the "rapid expansion of specialty chains, combined with heightened competition from mass merchandisers and department stores, has led to price wars and homogenization in several subsegments. Specialty retailers must therefore constantly try to find ways to distinguish themselves from competitors in consumers' eyes."[16]

Why People Buy or Do Not Buy on a Shopping Trip: It is critical for retailers to determine why shoppers leave without making a purchase. Is it prices? A rude salesperson? Not accepting the consumer's credit card? Not having an item in stock? Or some other factor? According to one retail consulting company, here are the top 10 reasons shoppers leave an apparel store without buying:

1. Cannot find an appealing style.
2. Cannot find the right size or the item is out of stock.
3. Nothing fits.

4. No sales help is available.
5. Cannot get in and out of the store easily.
6. Prices are too high.
7. In-store experience is stressful.
8. Cannot find a good value.
9. Store is not merchandised conveniently.
10. Seasonality is off.[17]

Attitudes by Market Segment: Research has shown that shoppers may be classified into several types based on their outlook to shopping. For example, according to one classification, shoppers can be broken into four types. "Thrifties" are most interested in price and convenience. They are apt to shop at Wal-Mart. "Allures" want a "fun, social shopping experience." They gravitate toward retailers such Bloomingdale's and Limited Brands. "Speedsters" want to shop quickly. They shop disproportionately at Target and Costco. "Elites" want quality merchandise, an unhurried shopping experience, and the ability to be educated about products. They patronize retailers such as Neiman Marcus and Amazon.com. Many "retailers don't know how their customers prefer their shopping experience and compete by doing what their competitors do. But that doesn't work. Customer insight will allow a retailer not only to survive but to thrive against even the toughest competition."[18]

Attitudes Toward Private Brands: Many consumers believe private (retailer) brands are as good as or better than manufacturer brands: "For American consumers, private brands are brands like any other brands. In a new nationwide study by Ipsos-MORI, seven out of ten shoppers believe that the private-label products they buy are as good, if not better, than their national-brand counterparts. Four in ten now identify themselves as 'frequent' store-brand shoppers, and nearly one-half of all consumers say that their typical market basket contains 25 percent or more of private-brand products."[19]

Where People Shop

Consumer patronage differs sharply by type of retailer. Thus, it is vital for firms to recognize the venues where consumers are most likely to shop and plan accordingly. Table 7-3 shows where people shop.

Many consumers do **cross-shopping**, whereby they (1) shop for a product category at more than one retail format during the year or (2) visit multiple retailers on one shopping trip.

Do *you* shop at both Tiffany (**www.tiffany.com**) and BJ's (**www.bjswholesale.com**)?

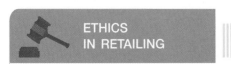
ETHICS IN RETAILING

Selling to the Poor Can Be Good—For the Consumer and for Business

Although there is a market of 4 billion people in the world who live on less than the equivalent of $3,000 per year, many businesses wrongfully assume that this market is not economically viable. David Dean, an industry consultant, has identified people with monthly household incomes of between $63 and $700 as the "next billion" potential consumers. Nonetheless, according to various marketing experts, selling to the poor requires a different perspective from selling to middle-class consumers in affluent countries.

Retailing to the poor means that firms should offer small package sizes. India, China, Africa, and the Philippines are examples of countries where the sale of single-serve packs of shampoo, detergents, tea, and ketchup are common. Henkel (**www.henkel.com**), a

German consumer products marketer, for example, sells dishwashing detergent in miniature packages for one rupee (less than 2 cents).

Another product aimed at this market segment is a simple mobile phone that contains a built-in flashlight. The flashlight is an important feature in countries with daily electrical outages. As C. K. Prahalad (author of *The Fortune at the Bottom of the Pyramid*) notes, retailers also need to consider pay-per-use options—such as Internet access at 10 cents per hour—or monthly payment options.

Sources: Julia Bonstein, "European Firms Eye Developing World," **www.businessweek.com/globalbiz** (January 16, 2008); and Kim Shiffman, "Your Next Big Thing: Selling to the Poor," **www.canadianbusiness.com/entrepreneur/managing** (December 2007).

TABLE 7-3 Retailers Where Primary Household Shoppers Purchase at Least Once Per Month (percentage of primary household shoppers)

Where America Shops:

Supermarkets	79
Discount department stores/supercenters	60
Power centers	60
Drugstores	56
Online shopping sites	42
Local neighborhood food stores	36
Home improvement centers/hardware stores	31
Regional malls	30
Membership clubs	27
Deep discount food stores	17
Apparel stores	16
Traditional department stores	15
Consumer electronics stores	14
Downtown shopping districts	8

Where the World Shops:

	Canada	China	France	Germany	Great Britain	Japan	Spain
Apparel stores	18	42	28	23	48	40	47
Consumer electronics stores	20	32	15	32	24	43	14
Deep discount food stores	34	40	45	84	63	38	28
Drugstores	77	45	55	78	38	81	50
Home improvement centers/hardware stores	31	24	31	26	21	49	25
Hypermarkets/supercenters	62	90	82	63	77	36	64
Local neighborhood food stores	60	90	56	60	66	47	59
Membership clubs/cash and carry stores	22	37	3	10	9	7	8
Supermarkets	86	82	70	81	93	91	95
Traditional department stores	22	49	16	38	51	31	39

Sources: Compiled by the authors from TNS Retail Forward, *Strategic Focus: Global Shopper Insights into Shopping Frequency* (Columbus, OH: April 2008), various pages; and TNS Retail Forward, *American Shopperscape 2008* (Columbus, OH: July 2008), p. 5.

The first scenario occurs because these consumers feel comfortable shopping at different formats during the year, their goals vary by occasion (they may want bargains on everyday clothes and fashionable items for weekend wear), they shop wherever sales are offered, and they have a favorite format for themselves and another one for other household members. Visiting multiple outlets on one trip occurs because consumers want to save travel time and shopping time. Here are cross-shopping examples:

▶ Some supermarket customers also regularly buy items carried by the supermarket at convenience stores, full-line department stores, drugstores, and specialty food stores.
▶ Some department-store customers also regularly buy items carried by the department store at factory outlets and full-line discount stores.
▶ The majority of Web shoppers also buy from catalog retailers, mass merchants, apparel chains, and department stores.
▶ Cross-shopping is high for apparel, home furnishings, shoes, sporting goods, and personal-care items.

The Consumer Decision Process

Besides identifying target market characteristics, a retailer should know how people make decisions. This requires familiarity with **consumer behavior**, which is the process by which people determine whether, what, when, where, how, from whom, and how often to purchase goods and services. Such behavior is influenced by a person's background and traits.

The consumer's decision process must be grasped from two different perspectives: (1) what good or service the consumer is thinking about buying and (2) where the consumer is going to purchase that item (if the person opts to buy). A consumer can make these decisions separately or jointly. If made jointly, he or she relies on the retailer for support (information, assortments, and knowledgeable sales personnel) over the entire decision process. If the decisions are made independently—what to buy versus where to buy—the person gathers information and advice before visiting a retailer and views the retailer merely as a place to buy (and probably more interchangeable with other firms).

In choosing whether or not to buy a given item *(what)*, the consumer considers features, durability, distinctiveness, value, ease of use, and so on. In choosing the retailer to patronize for that item *(where)*, the consumer considers location, assortment, credit availability, sales help, hours, customer service, and so on. Thus, the manufacturer and retailer have distinct challenges: The manufacturer wants people to buy its brand *(what)* at any location carrying it *(where)*. The retailer wants people to buy the product, not necessarily the manufacturer's brand *(what)*, at its store or nonstore location *(where)*.

The **consumer decision process** has two parts: the process itself and the factors affecting the process. There are six steps in the process: stimulus, problem awareness, information search, evaluation of alternatives, purchase, and post-purchase behavior. The consumer's demographics and lifestyle affect the process. The complete process is shown in Figure 7-5.

The best retailers assist consumers at each stage in the process: stimulus (newspaper ads), problem awareness (stocking new models), information search (point-of-sale displays and good salespeople), evaluation of alternatives (clearly noticeable differences among products), purchase (acceptance of credit cards), and post-purchase behavior (extended warranties and money-back returns). The greater the role a retailer assumes in the decision process, the more loyal the consumer will be.

Each time a person buys a good or service, he or she goes through a decision process. In some cases, all six steps in the process are utilized; in others, only a few steps are employed. For example, a consumer who has previously and satisfactorily bought luggage at a local store may not use the same extensive process as one who has never bought luggage.

The decision process outlined in Figure 7-5 assumes that the end result is a purchase. However, at any point, a potential customer may decide not to buy; the process then stops.

The Federal Citizen Information Center facilitates consumer decision making for such products as food by providing free online information (www.pueblo.gsa.gov/food.htm).

FIGURE 7-5

The Consumer Decision Process

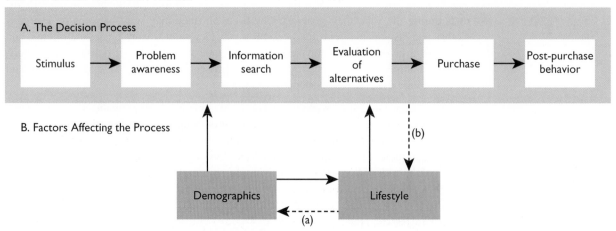

Note: Solid arrows connect all the elements in the decision process and show the impact of demographics and lifestyle upon the process. Dashed arrows show feedback. (a) shows the impact of lifestyle on certain demographics, such as family size, location, and marital status. (b) shows the impact of a purchase on elements of lifestyle, such as social class, reference groups, and social performance.

A good or service may be unneeded, unsatisfactory, or too expensive. Before discussing the ways in which retail consumers use the decision process, we explain the entire process.

Stimulus: A **stimulus** is a cue (social or commercial) or a drive (physical) meant to motivate or arouse a person to act. When a person talks with friends, fellow employees, and others, a social cue is received. The special attribute of a social cue is that it involves an interpersonal, noncommercial source. A commercial cue is a message sponsored by a retailer or some other seller. Ads, sales pitches, and store displays are commercial stimuli. Such cues may not be regarded as highly as social ones by consumers because they are seller-controlled. A third type of stimulus is a physical drive. It occurs when one or more of a person's physical senses are affected. Hunger, thirst, cold, heat, pain, or fear could cause a physical drive. A potential consumer may be exposed to any or all three types of stimuli. If aroused (motivated), he or she goes to the next step in the process. If a person is not sufficiently aroused, the stimulus is ignored—terminating the process for the given good or service.

Problem Awareness: At **problem awareness**, the consumer not only has been aroused by social, commercial, and/or physical stimuli but also recognizes that the good or service under consideration may solve a problem of shortage or unfulfilled desire. It is sometimes hard to learn why a person is motivated enough to move from a stimulus to problem awareness. Many people shop with the same retailer or buy the same good or service for different reasons; they may not know their own motivation, and they may not tell a retailer their real reasons for shopping there or buying a certain item.

Recognition of shortage occurs when a person discovers a good or service should be repurchased. A good could wear down beyond repair, or the person might run out of an item such as milk. Service may be necessary if a good such as a car requires a repair. Recognition of unfulfilled desire takes place when a person becomes aware of a good or service that has not been bought before or a retailer that has not been patronized before. An item (such as contact lenses) may improve a person's lifestyle, self-image, and so on in an untried manner, or it may offer new performance features (such as a voice-activated computer). People are more hesitant to act on unfulfilled desires. Risks and benefits may be tougher to see. When a person becomes aware of a shortage or an unfulfilled desire, he or she acts only if it is a problem worth solving. Otherwise, the process ends.

Nonprofit Consumer World is an online, noncommercial guide with more than 2,000 sources to aid the consumer's information search (www. consumerworld.org).

Information Search: If problem awareness merits further thought, information is sought. An **information search** has two parts: (1) determining the alternatives that will solve the problem at hand (and where they can be bought) and (2) ascertaining the characteristics of each alternative.

First, the person compiles a list of goods or services that address the shortage or desire being considered. This list does not have to be formal. It may be a group of alternatives the person thinks about. A person with a lot of purchase experience normally uses an internal memory search to determine the goods or services—and retailers—that are satisfactory. A person with little purchase experience often uses an external search to develop a list of alternatives and retailers. This search can involve commercial sources such as retail salespeople, noncommercial sources such as *Consumer Reports,* and social sources such as friends. Second, the person gathers information about each alternative's attributes. An experienced shopper searches his or her memory for the attributes (pros and cons) of each alternative. A consumer with little experience or a lot of uncertainty searches externally for information.

The extent of an information search depends, in part, on the consumer's perceived risk regarding a specific good or service. Risk varies among individuals and by situation. For some, it is inconsequential; for others, it is quite important. The retailer's role is to provide enough information for a shopper to feel comfortable in making decisions, thus reducing perceived risk. Point-of-purchase ads, product displays, and knowledgeable sales personnel can provide consumers with the information they need.

Once the consumer's search for information is completed, he or she must decide whether a current shortage or unfulfilled desire can be met by any of the alternatives. If one or more are satisfactory, the consumer moves to the next step in the decision process. The consumer stops the process if no satisfactory goods or services are found.

Evaluation of Alternatives: Next, a person selects one option from among the choices. This is easy if one alternative is superior on all features. An item with excellent quality and a low price is a certain pick over expensive, average-quality ones. However, a choice may not be that simple, and the person then does an **evaluation of alternatives** before making a decision. If two or more options seem attractive, the person determines the criteria to evaluate and their importance. Alternatives are ranked and a choice made.

The criteria for a decision are those good or service attributes that are considered relevant. They may include price, quality, fit, durability, and so on. The person sets standards for these characteristics and rates each alternative according to its ability to meet the standards. The importance of each criterion is also determined, and attributes are usually of differing importance to each person. One shopper may consider price to be most important while another places greater weight on quality and durability.

At this point, the person ranks alternatives from most favorite to least favorite and selects one. For some items, it is hard to rate attributes of available alternatives because they are technical, intangible, new, or poorly labeled. When this occurs, shoppers often use price, brand name, or store name as an indicator of quality and choose based on this criterion. Once a person ranks alternatives, he or she chooses the most satisfactory good or service. In situations where no alternative is adequate, a decision not to buy is made.

Purchase Act: A person is now ready for the **purchase act**—an exchange of money or a promise to pay for the ownership or use of a good or service. Important decisions are still made in this step. For a retailer, the purchase act may be the most crucial aspect of the decision process because the consumer is mainly concerned with three factors, as highlighted in Figure 7-6:

1. *Place of purchase*—this may be a store or a nonstore location. Many more items are bought at stores than through nonstore retailing, although the latter are growing more quickly. The place of purchase is evaluated in the same way as the good or the service: alternatives are listed, their traits are defined, and they are ranked. The most desirable place is then chosen. Criteria for selecting a store retailer include store location, store layout, service, sales help, store image, and prices. Criteria for selecting a nonstore retailer include image, service, prices, hours, interactivity, and convenience. A consumer will shop with the firm that has the best combination of criteria, as defined by that consumer.
2. *Purchase terms*—these include the price and method of payment. Price is the dollar amount a person must pay to achieve the ownership or use of a good or service. Method of payment is the way the price may be paid (cash, short-term credit, long-term credit).
3. *Availability*—this relates to stock on hand and delivery. Stock on hand is the amount of an item that a place of purchase has in stock. Delivery is the time span between placing an order and receiving an item and the ease with which an item is transported to its place of use.

FIGURE 7-6

Key Factors in the
Purchase Act

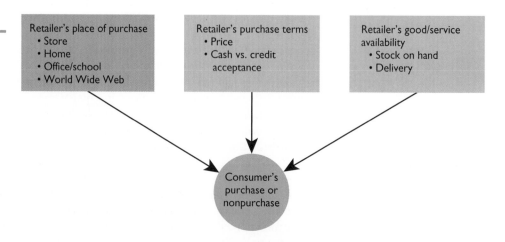

If a person is pleased with all aspects of the purchase act, the good or service is bought. If there is dissatisfaction with the place of purchase, the terms of purchase, or availability, the consumer may not buy, although there is contentment with the item itself:

> Karen wanted to buy a stereo. But, after a month of trying, she gave up: "The system I wanted was sold in only three stores and through an online firm. Two stores overpriced the stereo by $75. The third had a good price, but insisted I drive to the warehouse to get the stereo. The Web retailer had a good deal, but it ran out of the model I wanted. When I heard that, I decided to keep my old stereo."

Post-Purchase Behavior: After buying a good or service, a consumer may engage in **post-purchase behavior**, which falls into either of two categories: further purchases or re-evaluation. Sometimes, buying one item leads to further purchases and decision making continues until the last purchase is made. For instance, a car purchase leads to insurance; a retailer that uses scrambled merchandising may stimulate a shopper to make further purchases, once the primary good or service is bought.

A person may also re-evaluate a purchase. Is performance as promised? Do actual attributes match the expectations the consumer had? Has the retailer acted as expected? Satisfaction typically leads to contentment, a repurchase when a good or service wears out, and positive ratings to friends. Dissatisfaction may lead to unhappiness, brand or store switching, and unfavorable conversations with friends. The latter situation (dissatisfaction) may result from **cognitive dissonance**—doubt that the correct decision has been made. A consumer may regret that the purchase was made at all or may wish that another choice had been made. To overcome cognitive dissonance and dissatisfaction, the retailer must realize that the decision process does not end with a purchase. After-care (by phone, a service visit, or E-mail) may be as important as anything a retailer does to complete the sale. When items are expensive or important, after-care takes on greater significance because the person really wants to be right. Also, the more alternatives from which to choose, the greater the doubt after a decision is made and the more important the after-care. Department stores pioneered money-back guarantees so customers could return items if cognitive dissonance occurred.

Realistic sales presentations and ad campaigns reduce post-sale dissatisfaction because consumer expectations do not then exceed reality. If overly high expectations are created, a consumer is more apt to be unhappy because performance is not at the level promised. Combining an honest sales presentation with good customer after-care reduces or eliminates cognitive dissonance and dissatisfaction.

Types of Consumer Decision Making

Every time a person buys a good or service or visits a retailer, he or she uses a form of the decision process. The process is often undertaken subconsciously, and a person is not even aware of its use. And, as indicated in Figure 7-5, the process is affected by consumer characteristics. Older people may not spend as much time as younger ones in making some decisions due to their experience. Well-educated consumers may consult many information sources before making a decision. Upper-income consumers may spend less time making a decision because they can afford to buy again if they are dissatisfied. In a family with children, each member may have input into a decision, which lengthens the process. Class-conscious shoppers may be more interested in social sources. Consumers with low self-esteem or high perceived risk may use all the steps in detail. People under time pressure may skip steps to save time.

The use of the decision process differs by situation. The purchase of a new home usually means a thorough use of each step in the process; perceived risk is high regardless of the consumer's background. In the purchase of a magazine, the consumer often skips certain steps; perceived risk is low regardless of the person's background. There are three types of decision processes: extended decision making, limited decision making, and routine decision making.

Extended decision making occurs when a consumer makes full use of the decision process. A lot of time is spent gathering information and evaluating alternatives—both what to buy and where to buy it—before a purchase. The potential for cognitive dissonance is great.

Chris: Regional Director of Loss Prevention

While in college, Chris worked in mall security—before obtaining an internship at a bank. For the internship, he did internal auditing and operational processes work. Upon college graduation, he was promoted to assistant bank manager.

Shortly thereafter, Chris attended a career fair where he talked with a recruiter for a specialty store chain that specialized in high-end men's suits. He dropped off his résumé because he had a personal interest in the investigative side of the auditing process that had been part of his responsibilities at the bank—digging in and finding the details. He wanted to explore how he could apply this personal interest in his professional life. Chris was hired as a loss prevention (LP) analyst. In this position, he had the opportunity and the challenge to develop the LP department from the ground up. There was only one other person in the department when Chris started. He enjoyed the work.

Chris had been with the company three years when a headhunter called. An up-and-coming specialty store chain was recruiting a District LP Manager, and Chris was offered and accepted this new challenge. Later on, after switching companies again, Chris' boss recognized his responsibility and the initiative Chris took in implementing projects above and beyond his job description. Because of Chris's work ethic and performance, this next position was created for him in order to retain Chris and develop his career path. As Senior Regional LP Manager, Chris had staff reporting directly to him and took on more of an LP-policy role.

At the age of 35, five years ahead of his personal schedule, Chris became Regional Director of LP, thus achieving his goal of a having a director-level title by age 40. He currently earns more than $100,000 per year, plus generous fringe benefits.

Source: Reprinted by permission of the National Retail Federation.

In this category are expensive, complex items with which the person has had little or no experience. Perceived risk of all kinds is high. Items requiring extended decision making include a house, a first car, and life insurance. At any point in the process, a consumer can stop, and for expensive, complex items, this occurs often. Consumer traits (such as age, education, income, and class consciousness) have the most impact with extended decision making.

Because their customers tend to use extended decision making, such retailers as real-estate brokers and auto dealers emphasize personal selling, printed materials, and other communication to provide as much information as possible. A low-key informative approach may be best, so shoppers feel comfortable and not threatened. In this way, the consumer's perceived risk is minimized.

With **limited decision making**, a consumer uses each step in the purchase process but does not spend a great deal of time on each of them. It requires less time than extended decision making because the person typically has some experience with both the what and the where of the purchase. This category includes items that have been bought before but not regularly. Risk is moderate, and the consumer spends some time shopping. Priority may be placed on evaluating known alternatives according to the person's desires and standards, although information search is important for some. Items requiring limited decision making include a second car, clothing, a vacation, and gifts. Consumer attributes affect decision making, but the impact lessens as perceived risk falls and experience rises. Income, the importance of the purchase, and motives play strong roles in limited decision making.

This form of decision making is relevant to such retailers as department stores, specialty stores, and nonstore retailers that want to sway behavior and that carry goods and services that people have bought before. The shopping environment and assortment are very important. Sales personnel should be available for questions and to differentiate among brands or models.

Routine decision making takes place when the consumer buys out of habit and skips steps in the purchase process. He or she wants to spend little or no time shopping, and the same brands are usually repurchased (often from the same retailers). This category includes items that are bought regularly. They have little risk because of consumer experience. The key step is problem awareness. When the consumer realizes a good or service is needed, a repurchase is often automatic. Information search, evaluation of alternatives, and post-purchase behavior are unlikely. These steps are not undertaken as long as a person is satisfied. Items involved with routine decision making include groceries, newspapers, and haircuts. Consumer attributes have little impact. Problem awareness almost inevitably leads to a purchase.

This type of decision making is most relevant to such retailers as supermarkets, dry cleaners, and fast-food outlets. For them, these strategic elements are crucial: a good location, long hours, clear product displays, and, most important, product availability. Ads should be reminder-oriented. The major task is completing the transaction quickly and precisely.

Impulse Purchases and Customer Loyalty

Impulse purchases and customer loyalty merit our special attention.

Impulse purchases arise when consumers buy products and/or brands they had not planned on buying before entering a store, reading a mail-order catalog, seeing a TV shopping show, turning to the Web, and so forth. At least part of consumer decision making is influenced by the retailer. There are three kinds of impulse shopping:

▶ *Completely unplanned.* Before coming into contact with a retailer, a consumer has no intention of making a purchase in a goods or service category.
▶ *Partially unplanned.* Before coming into contact with a retailer, a consumer has decided to make a purchase in a goods or service category but has not chosen a brand or model.
▶ *Unplanned substitution.* A consumer intends to buy a specific brand of a good or service but changes his or her mind about the brand after coming into contact with a retailer.

With the partially unplanned and substitution kinds of impulse purchases, some decisions take place before a person interacts with a retailer. In these cases, a shopper may be involved with extended, limited, or routine decision making. Completely unplanned shopping is often related to routine decision making or limited decision making; there is little or no time spent shopping, and the key step is problem awareness.

According to recent research from OgilvyAction, (1) "A little more than 39 percent of U.S. shoppers really wait until they're in the store to decide what brand to buy." (2) "About 10 percent change their minds about brands in the store." (3) "Twenty-nine percent buy from categories they didn't intend to buy from." (4) "Almost 20 percent leave a product they'd planned to buy on the shelf."[20]

Impulse purchases are more influenced by retail displays than are pre-planned purchases. As the chief executive of Procter & Gamble, the huge consumer products manufacturer, said: "More and more of our communication is moving to store. And the reason it's moving to store is that more and more consumers are saying that they're making their purchase decisions in store. And in a period where you have a fair amount of food price inflation, we think more of that shopping list, whether it's just in [a shopper's] head or actually written down, is being decided in the store."[21] See Figure 7-7.

In studying impulse buying, these are some of the consumer attitudes and behavior patterns that retailers should take into consideration:

▶ In-store browsing is positively affected by the amount of time a person has to shop.
▶ Some individuals are more predisposed toward making impulse purchases than others.
▶ Those who enjoy shopping are more apt to make in-store purchase decisions.
▶ Impulse purchases are greater if a person has discretionary income to spend.[22]

L.L. Bean (**www.llbean. com**) has some of the most loyal customers around. See why.

When **customer loyalty** exists, a person regularly patronizes a particular retailer (store or nonstore) that he or she knows, likes, and trusts. This lets a person reduce decision making because he or she does not have to invest time in learning about and choosing the retailer from which to purchase. Loyal customers tend to be time-conscious, like shopping locally, do not often engage in outshopping, and spend more per shopping trip. In a service setting, such as an auto repair shop, customer satisfaction often leads to shopper loyalty; price has less bearing on decisions.

It can be testing to gain customer loyalty—a retailer's greatest asset. As the chairman of America's Research Group says: "What classifies as customer loyalty today only lasts until the next, better deal comes along. More people shop somewhere only because that

FIGURE 7-7

Stimulating Impulse
Purchases
Could you pass by this vending
machine without making a
purchase?

Source: Reprinted by permission.

place has the best selection and price of the moment. If someone else comes along with a
better offer, loyalty just isn't an issue."[23] Applying the retailing concept certainly enhances
the chances of gaining and keeping loyal customers: customer orientation, coordinated
effort, value-driven, and goal orientation. Relationship retailing helps also!

Consider this:

> The biggest problem with loyalty programs is that most retailers adopt a one-
> size-fits-all approach: They use monetary rewards to encourage repeat pur-
> chases. But product discounts won't change buying behavior in the long run in
> shoppers who value things like personalized service, convenience, or shopping
> pleasure more. These types of consumers may change their behavior to access
> the price promotion, but they likely will revert back to their regular brands or
> buying habits shortly thereafter, resulting in, at best, a temporary change in sales
> and market share. A more effective way to woo customers and maintain their
> patronage is to offer them individualized rewards, based on what they value. By
> offering different types of rewards to different groups of shoppers, companies
> set themselves apart and give people a reason to keep coming back. Providing
> access to a speedy checkout lane, for example, would be a more powerful way to
> win the loyalty of a person who hates grocery shopping than would a discount
> on a future purchase.[24]

Retailer Actions

As noted in Chapter 3, in *mass marketing,* a firm such as a supermarket or a drugstore sells
to a broad spectrum of consumers; it does not really focus efforts on any one kind of customer. In *concentrated marketing,* a retailer tailors its strategy to the needs of one distinct
consumer group, such as young working women; it does not attempt to satisfy people outside that segment. With *differentiated marketing,* a retailer aims at two or more distinct
consumer groups, such as men and boys, with a different strategy mix for each; it can do
this by operating more than one kind of outlet (such as separate men's and boys' clothing

stores) or by having distinct departments grouped by market segment in a single store (as a department store might do). In deciding on a target market approach, a retailer considers its goods/service category and goals, competitors' actions, the size of various segments, the efficiency of each target market alternative for the particular firm, the resources required, and other factors. See Figure 7-8.

FIGURE 7-8

Contrasting Target Market Strategies
Saks Fifth Avenue is an upscale department store chain, while 99¢ only appeals to customers looking for deep discounts and no frills.

Source: Reprinted by permission of TNS Retail Forward (top photo) and Susan Berry, Retail Image Consulting, Inc. (bottom photo).

FIGURE 7-9

Devising a Target Market Strategy

After choosing a target market method, the retailer selects the target market(s) to which it wants to appeal; identifies the characteristics, needs, and attitudes of the target market(s); seeks to understand how its targeted customers make purchase decisions; and acts appropriately. The process for devising a target market strategy is shown in Figure 7-9. Visit our Web site (**www.pearsonhighered.com/berman**) for several useful links on target marketing.

We now present several examples of retailers' target market activities.

Retailers with Mass Marketing Strategies

Walgreens drugstore chain and Kohl's Department Stores engage in mass marketing.

Walgreens is a national chain with 7,000 drugstores. The firm attracts a broad array of customers. About 5.5 million people visit a Walgreens store daily. The firm "provides the most convenient access to consumer goods and services, and pharmacy, health and wellness services, in America. We are transforming into a more efficient and customer-focused firm. We offer patients a way to stretch their dollars and maintain their prescriptions in one place without sacrificing the safety, service, or convenience of their nearby neighborhood drugstore. We have expanded our private-brand offerings, which provide greater value to customers. We continue to offer competitively priced consumables, whose sales have been very strong, particularly for fast, easy, midweek fill-in needs in our conveniently located retail stores."[25]

Find out why Kohl's is appealing (www.kohls.com).

Kohl's is a popular general merchandise retailer. And it is capitalizing on a mass marketing approach: "If you've ever shopped one of our clean, bright department stores, you've already experienced our commitment to family, value, and national brands. Our stores are stocked with everything you need for yourself and your home—apparel, shoes, and accessories for women, children and men, plus home products like small electrics, bedding, luggage, and more. Online, we've taken our commitment to convenience even further, and you'll find there's more to like at Kohls.com with every click of your mouse. We not only offer the best merchandise at the best prices, but we're always working to make your shopping experience enjoyable."[26]

Retailers with Concentrated Marketing Strategies

Family Dollar and Wet Seal engage in concentrated marketing.

Family Dollar (www.familydollar.com) has carved out a distinctive, narrow niche for itself.

Family Dollar operates 6,500 dollar stores (a type of variety store) in 44 states. It has a very focused target market strategy: The average Family Dollar customer is a female with an annual income of less than $30,000 who shops for her family. Customers depend on Family Dollar for the good prices they need to stretch their budgets. Stores are rather small and often situated in rural areas and small towns, as well as in urban areas. "Our merchandise is sold at everyday low prices in a no-frills, low overhead, self-service environment. Most merchandise is priced under $10.00."[27]

Wet Seal is a 400-store apparel chain that caters to young women. According to the company, "Wet Seal is the junior apparel brand for teenage girls that seek trend-focused and value competitive clothing with a target customer age of 13 to 19 years old. Wet Seal seeks to provide its customer base with a balance of affordably priced fashionable apparel and accessories. Wet Seal stores average approximately 3,900 square feet in size." Wet Seal brings in new apparel and accessories on a regular basis.[28]

Retailers with Differentiated Marketing Strategies

Through its KFC, Pizza Hut, Taco Bell, Long John Silver's, A&W, and Wing Street restaurants, Yum! (www.yum.com) is another retailer practicing differentiated marketing—by food preference.

Foot Locker, Inc. and Gap Inc. engage in differentiated marketing.

Besides its mainstream Foot Locker stores, the parent company (Foot Locker, Inc.) also operates chains geared specially toward women and children. Lady Foot Locker "stores offer an extensive assortment of branded athletic footwear and select branded and private-label athletic apparel dedicated to women who are fashion-minded, active, and brand-conscious." At Kids Foot Locker, "the typical customer is the parent of a child who is sports- and fashion-conscious."[29]

For many years, Gap Inc. has applied differentiated marketing through its Gap ("fashion-updated, casual clothing and accessories—including Gap, Gap Kids, Baby Gap, Gap Maternity, and Gap Body"), Old Navy ("great fashion at great prices, for everyone"), Banana Republic ("an accessible luxury brand, offering high-quality apparel and accessories collections for men and women"), and the new Piperlime ("a fresh online shop that handpicks the world's best shoes and handbags for women, men, and kids") chains.[30]

Environmental Factors Affecting Consumers

Several environmental factors influence shopping attitudes and behavior, including:

▶ State of the economy.
▶ Rate of inflation (how quickly prices are rising).
▶ Infrastructure where people shop, such as traffic congestion, the crime rate, and the ease of parking.
▶ Price wars among retailers.
▶ Emergence of new retail formats.
▶ Trend toward more people working at home.
▶ Government and community regulations regarding shopping hours, new construction, consumer protection, and so forth.
▶ Evolving societal values and norms.

Although all of these elements may not necessarily have an impact on any particular shopper, they do influence the retailer's overall target market.

When considering the strategy that they offer their customers, retailers should also know the following about the standard of living:

Factors such as discretionary income are important, but the standard of living includes not only the material articles of consumption but also the number of dependents in a family, the environment, the educational opportunities, and the amount spent for health, recreation, and social services. Unemployment, low wages, crowded living conditions, and physical calamities, such as drought, flood, or war, may bring a drop in the standard of living, and, conversely, an increase in social benefits and higher wages may bring about a rise. While the standard of living may vary greatly among various groups within a country, it also varies from nation to nation, and international comparisons are sometimes made by analyzing gross national products, per capita incomes, or any number of other indicators from life expectancy to clean water. Overall, industrialized nations tend to have a higher standard of living than developing countries. In the United States, as in most Western nations, the standard of living has shown a steady trend upward.[31]

Chapter Summary

1. *To discuss why it is important for a retailer to properly identify, understand, and appeal to its customers.* To properly develop a strategy mix, a retailer must identify the characteristics, needs, and attitudes of consumers; understand how consumers make decisions; and enact the proper target market plan. It must study environmental influences, too.

2. *To enumerate and describe a number of consumer demographics, lifestyle factors, and needs and desires—and to explain how these concepts can be applied to retailing.* Demographics are easily identifiable and measurable population statistics. Lifestyles are the ways in which consumers live and spend time and money.

Consumer demographics include gender, age, life expectancy, literacy, languages spoken, income, retail sales, education, and ethnic/racial background. These data usually have to be localized to be useful for retailers. Consumer lifestyles comprise social and psychological elements and are affected by demographics. Social factors include culture, social class, reference groups, the family life cycle, and time utilization. Psychological factors include personality, class consciousness, attitudes, perceived risk, and purchase importance. As with demographics, a firm can generate a lifestyle profile of its target market by analyzing these concepts.

There are several demographic and lifestyle trends that apply to retailing. These involve gender roles, consumer sophistication and confidence, the poverty of time, and component lifestyles. Research has enumerated consumer profiles in a useful way for retailers.

When preparing a target market profile, consumer needs and desires should be identified. Needs are basic shopping requirements, and desires are discretionary shopping goals. A retail strategy geared toward satisfying consumer needs is appealing to their motives—the reasons for behavior. The better needs and desires are addressed, the more apt people are to buy.

3. *To examine consumer attitudes toward shopping and consumer shopping behavior, including the consumer decision process and its stages.* Many people do not enjoy shopping and no longer feel high prices reflect value. Different segments have different attitudes. More people now believe private brands are of good quality. Consumer patronage differs by retailer type. People often cross-shop, whereby they shop for a product category at more than one retail format during the year or visit multiple retailers on the same shopping trip.

Retailers should have an awareness of consumer behavior—the process individuals use to decide whether, what, when, where, how, from whom, and how often to buy. The consumer's decision process must be grasped from two perspectives: (a) the good or service the consumer thinks of buying and (b) where the consumer will buy that item. These decisions can be made separately or jointly.

The consumer decision process consists of stimulus, problem awareness, information search, evaluation of alternatives, purchase, and post-purchase behavior. It is influenced by a person's background and traits. A stimulus is a cue or drive meant to motivate a person to act. At problem awareness, the consumer not only has been aroused by a stimulus but also recognizes that a good or service may solve a problem of shortage or unfulfilled desire. An information search determines the available alternatives and their characteristics. Alternatives are then evaluated and ranked. In the purchase act, a consumer considers the place of purchase, terms, and availability. After a purchase, there may be post-purchase behavior in the form of additional purchases or re-evaluation. The consumer may have cognitive dissonance if there is doubt that a correct choice has been made.

In extended decision making, a person makes full use of the decision process. In limited decision making, each step is used, but not in depth. In routine decision making, a person buys out of habit and skips steps. Impulse purchases occur when shoppers make purchases they had not planned before coming into contact with the retailer. With customer loyalty, a person regularly patronizes a retailer.

4. *To look at retailer actions based on target market planning.* Retailers can deploy mass marketing, concentrated marketing, or differentiated marketing. Several examples are presented.

5. *To note some of the environmental factors that affect consumer shopping.* Consumer attitudes and behavior are swayed by the economy, the inflation rate, the infrastructure where people shop, and other factors. Retailers also need to consider how the standard of living is changing.

Key Terms

demographics (p. 191)
lifestyles (p. 191)
discretionary income (p. 191)
culture (p. 193)
social class (p. 193)
reference groups (p. 193)
family life cycle (p. 193)
household life cycle (p. 193)
personality (p. 194)
class consciousness (p. 194)

attitudes (opinions) (p. 194)
perceived risk (p. 194)
motives (p. 198)
outshopping (p. 199)
cross-shopping (p. 200)
consumer behavior (p. 201)
consumer decision
 process (p. 202)
stimulus (p. 203)
problem awareness (p. 203)

information search (p. 203)
evaluation of alternatives (p. 204)
purchase act (p. 204)
post-purchase behavior (p. 205)
cognitive dissonance (p. 205)
extended decision making (p. 205)
limited decision making (p. 206)
routine decision making (p. 206)
impulse purchases (p. 207)
customer loyalty (p. 207)

Questions for Discussion

1. Comment on this statement: "A competitive retail sector, facing an uncertain economic future, is being challenged by consumers to compete for their business. In this environment, only the fittest and those really listening to what their customers really want are likely to survive."

2. Analyze the global population data in Table 7-1 from a retailing perspective.

3. How could a national consumer electronics chain use the U.S. population data presented in Table 7-2?

4. Explain how a retailer selling expensive art could reduce the six types of perceived risk.

5. Why is it important for retailers to know the difference between needs and desires?

6. Why do some consumers engage in outshopping? What could be done to encourage them to shop closer to home?

7. Is cross-shopping good or bad for a retailer? Explain your answer.

8. Describe how the consumer decision process would operate for these goods and services. Include "what" and "where" in your answers: an HD TV, a lawn mower, and a haircut. Which elements of the decision process are most important to retailers in each instance? Explain your answers.

9. Differentiate among the three types of impulse purchases. Give an example of each.

10. Contrast the mass-market approach used by a supermarket with the concentrated marketing approach used by a fruit-and-vegetable store. What is the key to each firm succeeding?

11. Visit a nearby Toys "R" Us (**www.toysrus.com**), and then describe its target market strategy.

12. Why is it valuable for retailers to understand the complexity of the standard-of-living concept?

Web **Exercise**

Best Buy has widely promoted its "Geek Squad" as a major customer service initiative. Visit the Geek Squad Web site (www.geeksquad.com). Evaluate the target marketing efforts that you find described there, in terms of the concepts in this chapter.

Note: Stop by our Web site (www.pearsonhighered.com/berman) to experience a number of highly interactive, appealing Web exercises based on actual company demonstrations and sample materials related to retailing.

8

Information Gathering and Processing in Retailing

Chapter Objectives

1. To discuss how information flows in a retail distribution channel

2. To show why retailers should avoid strategies based on inadequate information

3. To look at the retail information system, its components, and the recent advances in such systems

4. To describe the marketing research process

When Debbi Fields opened her first cookie store in Palo Alto, California, in 1977, she was a 20-year-old housewife with no business experience. Mrs. Fields Original Cookies (**www.mrsfields.com**) became popular very quickly, and several new stores were set up. To grow even faster, Mrs. Fields started franchising in 1990. Today, Mrs. Fields has close to 390 stores in the United States and more than 80 units in foreign countries. The firm is the largest retailer of baked-on-premises specialty cookies and brownies.

In addition to Mrs. Fields Cookies, the firm sells soft-serve frozen yogurt in the United States through its TCBY (**www.tcby.com**) division, which "serves millions of customers a variety of delicious and healthier snacks and treats through almost 900 franchise locations worldwide. And, with a renewed national interest in the health aspects of yogurt, a whole new generation of loyal consumers is discovering the delicious difference of TCBY's real dairy yogurt."

Both Mrs. Fields and TCBY share certain characteristics:

▶ Raw ingredients are purchased from outside suppliers according to proprietary recipes.
▶ The parent company oversees each supplier with vigorous quality control procedures.
▶ Goods are mixed and produced by individual store owners so that they are fresh.
▶ There is a high level of quality control to ensure consistency across all outlets.
▶ Virtually all units are owned by franchises.

Many of the operations also share similar marketing research issues relating to site-location questions, pricing issues, the need to adapt recipes to foreign tastes, and which combination of units in a single-store location maximizes overall sales and profitability.[1]

Source: Reprinted by permission of Susan Berry, Retail Image Consulting, Inc.

OVERVIEW

When a retailer sets a new strategy or modifies an existing one, gathering and analyzing information is crucial because it reduces the chances of wrong decisions. The firm can study the attributes and buying behavior of current and potential customers, alternative store and nonstore sites, store management and operations, product offerings, prices, and store image and promotion to prepare the best plan.

Research activity should, to a large degree, be determined by the risk involved. Although it may be risky for a department store to open a new branch store, there is much less risk if that retailer is deciding whether to carry a new line of sweaters. In the branch store situation, thousands of research dollars and months of study may be necessary. In the case of the new sweaters, limited research may be sufficient.

iTools (**www.itools.com**) offers very useful research tools, including multiple search engines, a dictionary, a thesaurus, a language translator, and more.

Information gathering and processing should be conducted in an ongoing manner, yielding enough data for planning and analysis. Consider these two examples:

At Sherwin-Williams paint stores, "The need for timely information is essential in making the best management decisions, especially as the speed of business continues to accelerate." The chain's new Netezza Performance Server (NPS) from Netezza, Framingham, Massachusetts, is comprised of a server, data base, and storage. It delivers data between 10 and 100 times the speed of Sherwin-Williams' traditional configuration. Since adding the solution, the chain has cut its analysis from days to seconds, giving the company the opportunity to speed up its decision-making processes.[2]

Revitalized by its transformation as a specialty retailer, Dress Barn (once an off-price discounter) overhauled its information technology systems and chose Oracle software. Using a phased approach, Dress Barn first implemented systems prioritized around performance improvements for finance and merchandising teams, then rolled out the new solutions across all parts of the firm. The retailer cites improved reporting and better, more accurate insight to customer demand, inventory, and sales. To illustrate, one report generated with Dress Barn's prior IT system, developed for weekly pricing recap, required about 200 hours to complete. Through the new system, Dress Barn can complete the same report by an end user in fewer than eight hours. Managers use the Oracle Retail systems to fine-tune merchandise and store operations and improve the overall customer shopping experience.[3]

This chapter first looks at the information flows in a retail distribution channel and notes the ramifications of inadequate research. We then describe the retail information system, data-base management and data warehousing, and the marketing research process in detail.

Information Flows in a Retail Distribution Channel

In an effective retail distribution channel, information flows freely and efficiently among the three main parties: supplier (manufacturer and/or wholesaler), retailer, and consumer. This enables the parties to better anticipate and address each other's performance expectations. We highlight the flows in Figure 8-1 and describe the information needs of the parties next.

FIGURE 8-1

How Information Flows
in a Retail Distribution
Channel

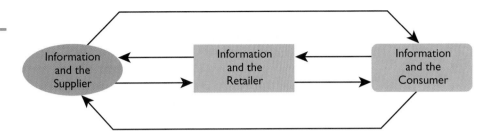

A *supplier* needs these kinds of information: (1) from the retailer—estimates of category sales, inventory turnover rates, feedback on competitors, the level of customer returns, and so on; and (2) from the consumer—attitudes toward given styles and models, the extent of brand loyalty, the willingness to pay a premium for superior quality, and so on. A *retailer* needs these kinds of information: (1) from the supplier—advance notice of new models and model changes, training materials for complex products, sales forecasts, justification for price hikes, and so on; and (2) from the consumer—why people shop with the retailer, what they like and dislike about the retailer, where else people shop, etc. A *consumer* needs these kinds of information: (1) from the supplier—assembly and operating instructions, the extent of warranty coverage, where to send a complaint, and so on; and (2) from the retailer—where specific merchandise is stocked in the store, the methods of payment accepted, the rain check policy when a sale item is out of stock, etc.

Retailers often play a crucial role in collecting data for other members of the value delivery chain because they have the most direct contact with shoppers. Retailers can assist other channel members by:

**CAREERS
IN RETAILING**

Is Retail for Me? IT and E-Commerce—Part 1

Technology careers are numerous in retailing. From technology-driven training programs delivered over satellites or the Internet to state-of-the-art cash register and credit systems, from Web design to servers and network systems management, technology careers are only growing in the retail industry:

▶ *Head of Information Systems and Data Processing.* Top position with overall responsibility for the data-processing efforts within the firm, including systems design, programming, computer operations, and information systems (IS) capital purchasing.

▶ *Head of Systems Applications Programming.* Top position responsible for coordinating systems planning and programming. This person typically reports to the head of information systems and data processing. In some chains, there may be multiple software heads, responsible separately for merchandising, finance, and operations systems, for example.

▶ *Systems Development Manager.* Coordinates systems planning and programming with user requirements. This position reports to the head of systems applications programming. Typically responsible for programming one business segment, such as merchandising, finance, or logistics.

▶ *Head of Computer Operations/Technical Services.* This is the top computer operations/technical service position and reports to the head of information systems and data processing. Establishes operating standards, and may initiate capital budgets. Responsible for coordinating computer operations with workstation networks, telecommunications, and any other data operations.

▶ *Point of Sales Administrator.* Controls the daily processing of sales and inventory information. Sets procedures for POS applications, reviews store systems, and may maintain a help desk for users.

Source: Reprinted by permission of the National Retail Federation.

▶ Permitting data to be gathered on their premises. Many research firms like to conduct surveys at shopping centers because of the large and broad base of shoppers.

▶ Gathering specific data requested by suppliers, such as how shoppers react to displays.

▶ Passing along information on the attributes of consumers buying particular brands and models. Because many credit transactions involve retailer cards, these retailers can link purchases with consumer age, income, occupation, and other factors.

For the best information flows, collaboration and cooperation are necessary—especially between suppliers and retailers. This is not always easy, as the view of one senior retail executive indicates: "Traditionally, retailers and suppliers just don't like to share supply-chain information with each other. They're more inclined to guard that valuable data than to give the data away, even when sharing would be in their own best interest. As it is, there's friction between retailer and supplier in every step of the supply chain. That's why we still have a messed-up supply chain."[4]

Fortunately, many retailers are working to improve their information-sharing efforts. And as in many aspects of retailing, Wal-Mart is leading the way. Thousands of suppliers have online access to Wal-Mart's data base through its password-protected Retail Link system (**https://retaillink.wal-mart.com**), which handles hundreds of thousands of information queries weekly. Retail Link was developed to promote more collaboration in inventory planning and product shipping, and it is a linchpin of Wal-Mart's information efforts today:

> Retail Link provides information and an array of products that allow a supplier to impact all aspects of their business. By using the information available in Retail Link, you can easily plan, execute, and analyze your business—thus providing better service to our common customers. The Retail Link Web site is accessible to any area within your company. We require all suppliers to participate in Retail Link because of the benefits it provides. Should you become one of our suppliers, you'll be provided with the requirements for accessing Retail Link.[5]

Avoiding Retail Strategies Based on Inadequate Information

Retailers are often tempted to rely on nonsystematic or incomplete ways of obtaining information due to time and costs, as well as a lack of research skills. The results can be devastating. Here are examples.

Using intuition. A movie theater charges $10 for tickets at all times. The manager feels that because all patrons are seeing the same movie, prices should be the same for a Monday matinee as a Saturday evening. Yet, by looking at data stored in the theater's information system, she would learn attendance is much lower on Mondays, indicating that because people prefer Saturday evening performances, they will pay $10 to see a movie then. Weekday customers have to be lured, and a lower price is a way to do so.

Continuing what was done before. A toy store orders conservatively for the holiday season because prior year sales were weak. The store sells out two weeks before the peak of the season, and more items cannot be received in time for the holiday. The owner assumed that last year's poor sales would occur again. Yet, a consumer survey would reveal a sense of optimism and an increased desire to give gifts.

Copying a successful competitor's strategy. A local bookstore decides to cut the prices of best-sellers to match the prices of a nearby chain bookstore. The local store then loses a lot of money and has to go out of business. Its costs are too high to match the chain's prices. The firm lost sight of its natural strengths (personal service, a more customer-friendly atmosphere, and long-time community ties).

Devising a strategy after speaking to a few individuals about their perceptions. A family-run gift store decides to have a family meeting to determine the product assortment for the next year. Each family member gives an opinion, and an overall "shopping list" is then compiled. Sometimes, the selections are right on target; other times, they result in a lot of excess inventory. The family would do better by also attending trade shows and reading industry publications.

Automatically assuming that a successful business can easily expand. A Web retailer does well with small appliances and portable TVs. It has a good reputation and wants to add other product lines to capitalize on its customer goodwill. However, the addition of custom furniture yields poor results. The firm did not first conduct research, which would have indicated that people buy standard, branded merchandise via the Web but are more reluctant to buy custom furniture that way.

Not having a good read on consumer perceptions. A florist cuts the price of two-day-old flowers from $17 to $5 a dozen because they have a shorter life expectancy, but they don't sell. The florist assumes bargain-hunting consumers will want the flowers as gifts or for floral arrangements. What the florist does not know (due to a lack of research) is that people perceive the older flowers to be of poor quality. The extremely low price actually turns off customers!

What conclusion should we draw from these examples? Inadequate information can cause a firm to enact a bad strategy. These situations can be avoided by using a well-conceived retail information system and properly executing marketing research.

The Retail Information System

A retail information system requires a lot of background information, which makes the SecondaryData.com Web site (**www.secondarydata. com/marketing/retailing. asp**) valuable.

Data gathering and analysis should not be regarded as a one-shot resolution of a single retailing issue. They should be part of an ongoing, integrated process. A **retail information system (RIS)** anticipates the information needs of retail managers; collects, organizes, and stores relevant data on a continuous basis; and directs the flow of information to the proper decision makers.

These topics are covered next: building and using a retail information system, data-base management, and gathering information through the UPC and EDI.

Building and Using a Retail Information System

Figure 8-2 presents a general RIS. The retailer begins with its business philosophy and objectives, which are influenced by environmental factors (such as competitors and the economy). The philosophy and goals provide broad guidelines that direct strategic planning. Some aspects of plans are routine and need little re-evaluation. Others are nonroutine and need evaluation each time they arise.

FIGURE 8-2

A Retail Information System

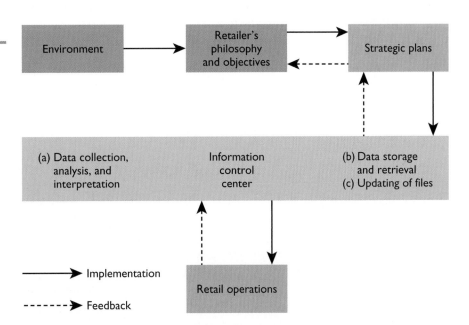

Once a strategy is outlined, the data needed to enact it are collected, analyzed, and interpreted. If data already exist, they are retrieved from files. When new data are acquired, files are updated. All of this occurs in the information control center. Based on data in the control center, decisions are enacted.

Performance results are fed back to the information control center and compared with pre-set criteria. Data are retrieved from files or further data are collected. Routine adjustments are made promptly. Regular reports and exception reports (to explain deviations from expected performance) are given to the right managers. Sometimes, managers may react in a way that affects the overall philosophy or goals (such as revising an old-fashioned image or sacrificing short-run profits to introduce a computer system).

All types of data should be stored in the control center for future and ongoing use, and the control center should be integrated with the firm's short- and long-run plans and operations. Information should not be gathered sporadically and haphazardly but systematically.

Retail Info Systems News (**www.risnews.com**) provides good insights for retailers.

A good RIS has several strengths. Information gathering is organized and company focused. Data are regularly gathered and stored so opportunities are foreseen and crises averted. Strategic elements can be coordinated. New strategies can be devised more quickly. Quantitative results are accessible, and cost-benefit analysis can be done. Information is routed to the right personnel. Yet, deploying an RIS may require high initial time and labor costs, and complex decisions may be needed to set up such a system.

In building a retail information system, a number of decisions have to be made:

▶ *How active a role should be given to the RIS?* Will it be used to proactively search for and distribute any relevant information or will it be used to reactively respond to requests from managers when problems arise? The best systems are more proactive, because they anticipate events.

▶ *Should an RIS be managed internally or be outsourced?* Although many retailers engage in RIS functions, some use outside specialists. Either style can work, as long as the RIS is guided by the retailer's information needs. Several firms have their own RIS and use outside firms for specific tasks (such as conducting surveys or managing networks).

▶ *How much should an RIS cost?* Retailers typically spend 0.5 to 2.0 percent of their sales on an RIS. This lags behind most of the suppliers from which retailers buy goods and services.[6]

 **ETHICS IN RETAILING**   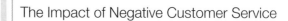   The Impact of Negative Customer Service

Since Sprint (**www.sprint.com**) acquired Nextel in 2005, the firm has become a lightning rod for stores about customer service. It has consistently received the poorest grade of the five major mobile telecommunications carriers in J.D. Powers and Associates' (**www.jdpower.com**) semi-annual customer service surveys. As a result, it lost millions of customers in a short period of time.

A major problem for Sprint was the large amount of billing errors, many of which were due to mistakes in the company's account setup process. On average, it took four to six calls to get just one customer's billing problem resolved. To compound the matter, Sprint paid its customer service agents based on the average time that was spent with a customer. Thus, too often, customer service

agents tried to get off the phone as quickly as possible to reduce the average time.

To more satisfactorily address these issues, Sprint now measures its customer service staff on the basis of first-call resolution, the ability to resolve a problem on the initial call. Sprint has simplified its billing process through a campaign called "Simply Everything," which has unlimited voice and data transmission. Lastly, Sprint representatives can now easily access a customer's service contract that contains the person's electronic signature to verify the service plan the customer selected.

Source: Michael Lev-Ram, "Sprint Tries to Clean-Up Customer Service Mess," **http://techland.blogs.fortune.cnn.com** (June 3, 2008).

▶ *How technology-driven should an RIS be?* Although retailers can gather data from trade associations, surveys, and so forth, more firms now rely on technology to drive the information process. With the advent of personal computers, inexpensive networks, and low-priced software, technology is easy to use. Even a neighborhood deli can generate sales data by product and offer specials on slow-sellers.

▶ *How much data are enough?* The purpose of an RIS is to provide enough information, on a regular basis, for a retailer to make the proper strategy choices—not to overwhelm retail managers. This means a balancing act between too little information and information overload. To avoid overload, data should be carefully edited to eliminate redundancies.

▶ *How should data be disseminated throughout the firm?* This requires decisions as to who receives various reports, the frequency of data distribution, and access to data bases. When a firm has multiple divisions or operates in several regions, information access and distribution must be coordinated.

▶ *How should data be stored for future use?* Relevant data should be stored in a manner that makes information retrieval easy and allows for adequate longitudinal (period-to-period) analysis.

Larger retailers tend to have a chief information officer (CIO) overseeing their RIS. Their information systems departments often have formal, written annual plans. Computers are used by most companies that conduct information systems analysis, and many firms use the Web for some RIS functions. Growth in the use of retail information systems is expected. There are many differences in information systems among retailers, on the basis of revenues and retail format.

Twenty-five years ago, most computerized retail systems were used only to reduce cashier errors and improve inventory control. Today, they often form the foundation for a retail information system and are used in surveys, ordering, merchandise transfers between stores, and other tasks. These activities are conducted by both small and large retailers. The vast majority of small and medium retailers—as well as large retailers—have computerized financial management systems, analyze sales electronically, and use computerized inventory management systems. Here are illustrations of the ways in which retailers are using the latest technological advances to computerize their information systems.

Retail Pro, Inc. markets Retail Pro management information software to retailers. See Figure 8-3. This software is used at stores around the world. Although popular with large retailers, Retail Pro software also has an appeal among smaller retailers due to flexible pricing based on the number of users and stores, the type of hardware, and so forth:

To see the various applications of Retail Pro, visit this Web site (**www. retailpro.com/solutions**).

Retail Pro is the leading point-of-sale and inventory management software used by specialty retailers worldwide. Over 10,000 retail companies have purchased Retail Pro since 1986. Retailers in almost every sector are experiencing the benefits of Retail Pro on a daily basis, such as a best-of-breed point-of-sales system, sophisticated business intelligence tools for stock replenishment, and an easy-to-use fully-integrated report designer module. The software is an integrated system for point-of-sales and store operations, merchandising planning and analysis, and customer management. 25,000+ installations. Running in over 75 countries. Available in 18 languages.[7]

MicroStrategy typically works with larger retailers—including two-thirds of the top 500 retailers in the world—to prepare computerized information systems. Clients include Benetton, Charming Shoppes, Dick's Sporting Goods, eBay, and Lowe's. One of its leading products is MicroStrategy Desktop:

This software provides integrated monitoring, reporting, powerful analytics, and decision support workflow on an intuitive Windows-based interface. It provides users with the means to easily access and share critical corporate information from the data base in order to make cost-cutting decisions and improve business processes. Even complex reports are easy to create; they can be viewed in various

FIGURE 8-3

Retail Pro Management
Information Software

Source: Reprinted by permission of
Retail Technologies International.

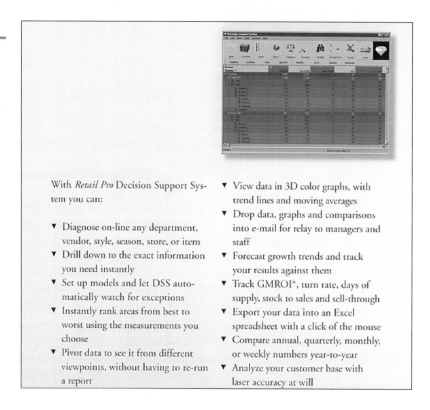

With *Retail Pro* Decision Support System you can:

▼ Diagnose on-line any department, vendor, style, season, store, or item
▼ Drill down to the exact information you need instantly
▼ Set up models and let DSS automatically watch for exceptions
▼ Instantly rank areas from best to worst using the measurements you choose
▼ Pivot data to see it from different viewpoints, without having to re-run a report

▼ View data in 3D color graphs, with trend lines and moving averages
▼ Drop data, graphs and comparisons into e-mail for relay to managers and staff
▼ Forecast growth trends and track your results against them
▼ Track GMROI*, turn rate, days of supply, stock to sales and sell-through
▼ Export your data into an Excel spreadsheet with a click of the mouse
▼ Compare annual, quarterly, monthly, or weekly numbers year-to-year
▼ Analyze your customer base with laser accuracy at will

formats, polished into production reports, distributed to other users, and extended through a host of features that include drilling, pivoting, and data slicing. Developers and power users alike employ MicroStrategy Desktop as the primary development interface for the MicroStrategy platform; however, the interface can also be customized for different users' skill levels and security profiles.[8]

Brinker International owns or franchises 1,800 casual dining places such as Chili's Grill & Bar, Romano's Macaroni Grill, On the Border Mexican Grill & Cantina, and Maggiano's Little Italy:

> Managers at all levels of Brinker depend on business intelligence technology to plan, manage, and control many aspects of the firm. Brinker selected WebFOCUS to build an operational reporting environment. Brinker has a custom point-of-sale system in each restaurant, which collects data on sales transactions, cook times, employee time cards, and other data. Each night, every restaurant is polled to gather this detailed information. Every single check (bill) issued to a customer is recorded, including what was purchased, how much it cost, and how much tip was included. Brand analysts at each restaurant chain continually review this data to fine-tune their operations.[9]

Data-Base Management

In **data-base management**, a retailer gathers, integrates, applies, and stores information related to specific subject areas. It is a major element in an RIS and may be used with customer data bases, vendor data bases, product category data bases, and so on. A firm may compile and store data on customer attributes and purchase behavior, compute sales figures by vendor, and store records by product category. Each of these would represent a separate data base. Among retailers that have data bases, most use them for frequent shopper programs, customer analysis, promotion evaluation, inventory planning, trading-area analysis, joint promotions with manufacturers, media planning, and customer communications.

Data-base management should be approached as a series of five steps:

1. Plan the particular data base and its components, and determine information needs.
2. Acquire the necessary information.

3. Retain the information in a usable and accessible format.
4. Update the data base regularly to reflect changing demographics, recent purchases, and so forth.
5. Analyze the data base to determine company strengths and weaknesses.

Information can come from internal and external sources. A retailer can develop data bases internally by keeping detailed records and arranging them. It could generate data bases *by customer*—purchase frequency, items bought, average purchase, demographics, and payment method; *by vendor*—total retailer purchases per period, total sales to customers per period, the most popular items, retailer profit margins, average delivery time, and service quality; and *by product category*—total category sales per period, item sales per period, retailer profit margins, and the percentage of items discounted.

Donnelley (**www. donnelleymarketing.com**) offers a number of useful products to help small firms build and manage their data bases.

There are firms that compile data bases and make them available for a fee. Donnelley Marketing, a subsidiary of infoUSA, provides custom reports drawn from infoUSA's U.S. data base, which has data on more than 95 percent of households. It "offers access to the most comprehensive source for demographic and lifestyle information. Available data enhancements include: geography to the street level, fine-tuned demographics (e.g., actual age, new mover), ethnicity, lifestyle dimensions/interests, property/financial characteristics (e.g., homeowner, credit-card holder), and buy behavior by channel."[10]

To effectively manage a retail data base, these are vital considerations:

▶ Is senior management knowledgeable in data-base strategies, and does it know how company data bases are currently being used?
▶ Is there a person or department responsible for overseeing the data base?
▶ Does the firm have data-base acquisition and retention goals?
▶ Is every data-base initiative analyzed to see if it is successful?
▶ Is there a mechanism to flag data that indicates potential problems or opportunities?
▶ Are customer purchases of different products or company divisions cross-linked?
▶ Is there a clear privacy policy that is communicated to those in a data base? Are there opt-out provisions for those who do not want to be included in a data base?
▶ Is the data base updated each time there is a customer interaction?
▶ Are customers, personnel, suppliers, and others invited to update their personal data?
▶ Is the data base periodically checked to eliminate redundant files?[11]

Let's now discuss two aspects of data-base management: Data warehousing is a mechanism for storing and distributing information. Data mining and micromarketing are ways in which information can be utilized. Figure 8-4 shows the interplay of data warehousing with data mining and micromarketing.

DATA WAREHOUSING

The *Teradata Online Magazine* (**www.teradata. com/tdmo**) explores data warehousing in depth.

One advance in data-base management is **data warehousing**, whereby copies of all the data bases in a firm are maintained in one location and are accessible to employees at any locale. A data warehouse is a comprehensive compilation of the data used to support management decision making: "Typically, a data warehouse is housed on an enterprise server. It is a central repository for all or significant parts of the data that a firm collects. Data warehousing describes the process of defining, populating, and using a data warehouse." The process focuses on "data capture from diverse sources for useful analysis and access."[12]

A data warehouse has the following components: (1) the data warehouse, where data are physically stored; (2) software to copy original data bases and transfer them to the warehouse; (3) interactive software to process inquiries; and (4) a directory for the categories of information kept in the warehouse.

Data warehousing has several advantages. Executives and other employees are quickly, easily, and simultaneously able to access data wherever they may be. There is more companywide entrée to new data when they are first available. Data inconsistencies are reduced by consolidating records in one location. Better data analysis and manipulation are possible because information is stored in one location.

FIGURE 8-4

Retail Data-Base Management in Action

The data warehouse is where information is collected, sorted, and stored centrally. Information is disseminated to retailer personnel, as well as to channel partners (such as alerting them to what merchandise is hot and what is not hot) and customers (such as telling them about order status). In data mining, retail executives and other employees—and sometimes channel partners—analyze information by customer type, product category, and so forth in order to determine opportunities for tailored marketing efforts. With micromarketing, the retailer applies differentiated marketing. Focused retail strategy mixes are planned for specific customer segments—or even for individual customers.

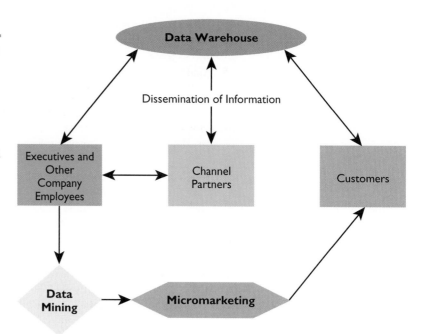

Computerized data warehouses were once costly to build (an average of $2.2 million in the 1990s) and, thus, feasible only for the largest retailers. This has changed. A simple data warehouse can now be put together for less than $25,000, making it affordable to all but very small retailers (which do not have to deal with far-flung executives, making data warehousing less necessary for them).

Macy's, Hollywood Video, 7-Eleven, and Sears are just a few of the thousands of firms that use data warehousing: "Retailers have collected vast amounts of data for years, but they have not had the means to apply it effectively to their planning and buying because, until a decade ago, no computer or software application could process all of that data. The applications available today offer retailers better results because they incorporate more than just historical sales data."[13] See Figure 8-5.

FIGURE 8-5

7-Eleven's Forward-Looking Approach to Data Warehousing

By electronically connecting all parties in the 7-Eleven supply chain, its retail information system creates a higher level of coordination and much better decision making. Store operators have actual sales information presented in logical formats and are able to order more effectively. Receiving exact orders in an organized fashion allows vendors to provide better service to the stores. Field offices are able to reduce administration costs by receiving information in electronic format. Headquarters merchandising staff are able to judge new product acceptance and communicate upcoming advertising and promotions from manufacturers that will affect sales.

Source: Reprinted by permission of 7-Eleven.

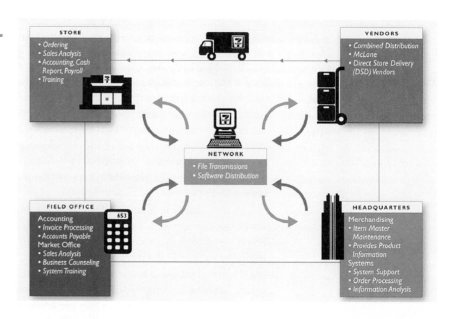

Helzberg Diamonds, which operates more than 260 U.S. jewelry stores, is one of many retailers that is positioning itself for long-term growth and focusing on cost reductions through a new data warehousing structure:

> To improve customer relationships, Helzberg Diamonds has added an enterprise-wide data-warehouse platform that supports business-intelligence applications. Until recently, its former data-warehouse system "was struggling to process and analyze data in an acceptable time frame, especially during peak seasons." Following an extensive evaluation, Helzberg switched to a new system designed specifically for high-performance analytics. It integrates a relational data base, server, and storage in a single compact unit. Helzberg utilizes the system for real-time, point-of-sale reporting that will aid in its customer-relationship-management initiatives.[14]

DATA MINING AND MICROMARKETING

Data mining is the in-depth analysis of information to gain specific insights about customers, product categories, vendors, and so forth. The goal is to learn if there are opportunities for tailored marketing efforts that would lead to better retailer performance. One application of data mining is **micromarketing**, whereby the retailer uses differentiated marketing and develops focused retail strategy mixes for specific customer segments, sometimes fine-tuned for the individual shopper.

For an in-depth discussion, go to About Retail Industry (**http://retailindustry.about.com**), and type "customer data mining" in the search engine.

Data mining relies on special software to sift through a data warehouse to uncover patterns and relationships among different factors. The software allows vast amounts of data to be quickly searched and sorted. That is why many firms, such as the Best Buy consumer electronics chain, have made the financial commitment to data mining: Best Buy "believes bottom-up insights could have an outsize impact on sales growth. In a sense, the national chain is trying to go 'hyperlocal,' asking on-the-ground employees to spot fresh customer groups."[15]

Look at how Fairmont Resort Hotels uses data mining in the firm's micromarketing efforts:

> The hotel chain wanted to learn more about its customers, but there were some questions it couldn't ask them directly. So, the Toronto-based hotel chain decided to use MapInfo's Psyte data mining tool to get a better understanding of who its customers were and what kinds of vacations they were likely to take: "We were looking for a partner that could provide us with more information about our guests in terms of their lifestyle—things that would be inappropriate to ask directly of our guests." The hotel overlays the information it gets from customers when they enroll in its loyalty program with data from MapInfo. It has used the data to help it make purchase decisions for new resorts, place ads where they will reach customers, and send better-targeted advertising brochures to its customers.[16]

Gathering Information Through the UPC and EDI

To be more efficient with their information systems, most retailers now rely on the Universal Product Code (UPC) and many utilize electronic data interchange (EDI).

With the **Universal Product Code (UPC)**, products (or tags attached to them) are marked with a series of thick and thin vertical lines, representing each item's identification code. The preferred UPC includes both numbers and lines. The lines are "read" by scanners at checkout counters. Cashiers do not enter transactions manually—although they can, if needed. Because the UPC itself is not readable by humans, the retailer or vendor must attach a ticket or sticker to a product specifying its size, color, and other information (if not on the package or the product). Given that the UPC does not include price information, this too must be added by a ticket or sticker.

By using UPC-based technology, retailers can record data instantly on an item's model number, size, color, and other factors when it is sold, as well as send the data to a computer that monitors unit sales, inventory levels, and so forth. The goals are to produce better merchandising data, improve inventory management, speed transaction time, raise productivity, reduce errors, and coordinate information. Since its inception, UPC technology has improved substantially. It is now the accepted standard in retailing:

Today, there are about five billion scans every day. The UPC has allowed retailers to control their inventory more efficiently, provided a faster and more accurate check out for customers, and made gathering information for accurate and immediate marketing studies incredibly simple.[17]

Virtually every time sales or inventory data are scanned by computer, UPC technology is involved. More than 250,000 U.S. manufacturers and retailers belong to GS1 US (formerly known as the Uniform Code Council), a group that has taken the lead in setting and promoting inter-industry product identification and communication standards. Figure 8-6 shows how far UPC technology has come. The UPC is discussed further in Chapter 16.

FIGURE 8-6

Applying UPC Technology to Gain Better Information

As this photo montage shows, Symbol Technologies has devised a host of scanning products (some of which are wireless) that make UPC data capture and processing quite simple. For example, Symbol products can be used at the point of sale to enter transaction data and transmit them to a central office, at product displays to verify shelf prices, at storage areas to aid in taking physical inventories, at receiving stations to log in the receipt of new merchandise, and at delivery points to track the movement of customer orders.

Source: Reprinted by permission of Symbol Technologies.

GXS is one of the leaders in EDI technology (**www. gxs.com**).

With **electronic data interchange (EDI)**, retailers and suppliers regularly exchange information through their computers with regard to inventory levels, delivery times, unit sales, and so on of particular items. As a result, both parties enhance their decision-making capabilities, better control inventory, and are more responsive to demand. UPC scanning is often the basis for product-related EDI data. Tens of thousands of firms around the world use some form of EDI system. Consider this scenario:

> The magic that brings the hottest, most sought-after toys, dolls, and electronic games to store shelves come holiday time doesn't spring from Santa's sleigh; rather, EDI, or Electronic Data Interchange, ensures that stockings get stuffed in a timely manner. EDI prevents a paperwork nightmare by standardizing and automating vital business processes and reducing the manual labor, red tape, and cost involved in getting goods onto shelves.[18]

Today, more retailers are expanding their EDI efforts to incorporate Internet communications with suppliers. This is known as *I-EDI (Internet electronic data interchange)*. For example: "The adoption of I-EDI by Wal-Mart signals that I-EDI is ready for heavy-duty corporate use after years of development. Wal-Mart has adopted I-EDI for most of its domestic sourcing and requires its suppliers to comply with the standard. I-EDI also helped retailer Piggly Wiggly reduce EDI costs by 20 percent when Piggly Wiggly replaced its old system with I-EDI."[19]

EDI is covered further in Chapter 15; CPFR (collaborative planning, forecasting, and replenishment) is also discussed there.

The Marketing Research Process

Marketing research in retailing entails the collection and analysis of information relating to specific issues or problems facing a retailer. At farsighted firms, marketing research is just one element in a retail information system. At others, marketing research may be the only type of data gathering and processing.

The **marketing research process** embodies a series of activities: defining the issue or problem to be studied, examining secondary data, generating primary data (if needed), analyzing data, making recommendations, and implementing findings. It is not a single act; it is a systematic process. Figure 8-7 outlines the research process. Each activity is done sequentially. Secondary data are not examined until after an issue or problem is defined. The dashed line around the primary data stage means these data are generated only if secondary data do not yield actionable information. The process is described next.

Issue (problem) definition involves a clear statement of the topic to be studied. What information does the retailer want to obtain to make a decision? Without clearly knowing the topic to be researched, irrelevant and confusing data could be collected. Here are examples of issue definitions for a shoe store. The first one seeks to compare three locations and is fairly structured; the second is more open-ended:

1. "Of three potential new store locations, which should we choose?"
2. "How can we improve the sales of our men's shoes?"

When **secondary data** are involved, a retailer looks at data that have been gathered for purposes other than addressing the issue or problem currently under study. Secondary data may be internal (such as company records) or external (such as government reports and trade publications). When **primary data** are involved, a retailer looks at data that are

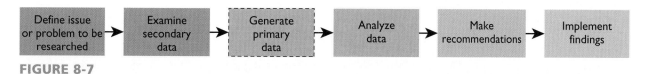

FIGURE 8-7

The Marketing Research Process in Retailing

collected to address the specific issue or problem under study. This type of data may be generated via survey, observation, experiment, and simulation.

Secondary data are sometimes relied on; other times, primary data are crucial. In some cases, both are gathered. It is important that retailers keep these points in mind: (1) There is great diversity in the possible types of data collection (and in the costs). (2) Only data relevant to the issue being studied should be collected. (3) Primary data are usually acquired only if secondary data are inadequate (thus, the dashed box in Figure 8-7). Both secondary and primary data are described further in the next sections.

These kinds of secondary and primary data can be gathered for the shoe store issues just stated:

Issue (Problem) Definition	Information Needed to Solve Issue (Problem)
1. Which store location?	1. Data on access to transportation, traffic, consumer profiles, rent, store size, and types of competition are gathered from government reports, trade publications, and observation by the owner for each of the three potential store locations.
2. How to improve sales of shoes?	2. Store sales records for the past five years by product category are gathered. A consumer survey in a nearby mall is conducted.

After data are collected, data analysis is performed to assess that information and relate it to the defined issue. Alternative solutions are also clearly outlined. For example:

Issue (Problem) Definition	Alternative Solutions
1. Which store location?	1. Each site is ranked for all of the criteria (access to transportation, traffic, consumer profiles, rent, store size, and types of competition).
2. How to improve sales of shoes?	2. Alternative strategies to boost sales are analyzed and ranked.

At this point, the pros and cons of each alternative are enumerated. See Table 8-1. Recommendations are then made as to the best strategy for the retailer. Of the available options, which is best? Table 8-1 also shows recommendations for the shoe-store issues discussed in this section.

Last, but not least, the recommended strategy is implemented. If research is to replace intuition in strategic retailing, a decision maker must follow the recommendations from research studies, even if they seem to contradict his or her own ideas.

Let's now look at secondary data and primary data in greater depth.

Secondary Data

ADVANTAGES AND DISADVANTAGES

Secondary data have several advantages:

Through Annual Report Service (www. annualreportservice.com), a retailer can learn about other firms around the globe. Get an annual report here. [free login required]

▶ Data assembly is inexpensive. Company records, trade journals, and government publications are all rather low cost. No data collection forms, interviewers, and tabulations are needed.

▶ Data can be gathered quickly. Company records, library sources, and Web sites can be accessed immediately. Many firms store reports in their retail information systems.

▶ There may be several sources of secondary data—with many perspectives.

▶ A secondary source may possess information that would otherwise be unavailable to the retailer. Government publications often have statistics no private firm could acquire.

TABLE 8-1   Research-Based Recommendations

Issue (Problem)	Alternatives	Pros and Cons of Alternatives	Recommendation
1. Which store location?	Site A	Best transportation, traffic, and consumer profiles. Highest rent. Smallest store space. Extensive competition.	Site A: the many advantages far outweigh the disadvantages.
	Site B	Poorest transportation, traffic, and consumer profiles. Lowest rent. Largest store space. No competition.	
	Site C	Intermediate on all criteria.	
2. How to improve sales of shoes?	Increased assortment	Will attract and satisfy many more customers. High costs. High level of inventory. Reduces turnover for many items.	Lower prices and increase ads: additional customers offset higher costs and lower margins; combination best expands business.
	Drop some lines and specialize	Will attract and satisfy a specific consumer market. Excludes many segments. Costs and inventory reduced.	
	Slightly reduce prices	Unit sales increase. Markup and profit per item decline.	
	Advertise	Will increase traffic and new customers. High costs.	

▶ When data are assembled by a source such as *Progressive Grocer*, A.C. Nielsen, *Stores*, or the government, results are usually quite credible.

▶ The retailer may have only a rough idea of the topics to investigate. Secondary data can then help to define issues more specifically. In addition, background information about a given issue can be gathered from secondary sources before undertaking a primary study.

TECHNOLOGY IN RETAILING

HyperActive Bob: Predictive Technology Comes to Fast Food

As a result of a robot manager known as "HyperActive Bob" (**www.hyperactivetechnologies.com**), fast-food franchises now have extra help. HyperActive Bob interprets data from video cameras that analyze the number of cars in a restaurant's parking lot to predict customer flow. The system is tied to point-of-sale registers so that HyperBob knows how many purchases are being made.

Using this information, HyperBob can accurately determine the minimum amount of specific foods that need to be on hand to satisfy short-term demand. HyperBob can also calculate the amount the chef needs to prepare of each major cooked food. HyperBob even knows how long it will take to prepare each food and calculates when the finished product will be added to the prepared food bins. According to the chief executive officer of HyperActive Technologies, "It [HyperActive Bob] actually takes over the kitchen product management in a quick service restaurant."

HyperActive Bob has been installed in numerous fast-food and quick casual restaurants in the United States. Each unit costs about $5,000 for the hardware and installation. An additional $3,000 annual fee is charged for software, upgrades, and system maintenance. Benefits of HyperActive Bob are fresher food, less food waste, and shorter customer waiting times.

Sources: Amanda C. Kooser, "Robot Invasion," *Restaurant Business* (June 2007), p. 18; and "HyperActive Technologies Reports Upward Sales Trend," **www.qsrweb.com/view_article.php?id=12445&prc=69** (November 14, 2008).

Secondary data also have several potential disadvantages:

▶ Available data may not suit the purposes of the current study because they have been collected for other reasons. Neighborhood statistics may not be found in secondary sources.

▶ Secondary data may be incomplete. A service station owner would want car data broken down by year, model, and mileage driven, so as to stock parts. A motor vehicle bureau could provide data on the models but not the mileage driven.

▶ Information may be dated. Statistics gathered every two to five years may not be valid today. The *U.S. Census of Retail Trade* is conducted every five years. Furthermore, there is often a long time delay between the completion of a census and the release of information.

▶ The accuracy of secondary data must be carefully evaluated. Thus, a retailer needs to decide whether the data have been compiled in an unbiased way. The purpose of the research, the data collection tools, and the method of analysis should each be examined—if they are available for review.

▶ Some secondary data sources are known for poor data collection techniques; they should be avoided. If there are conflicting data, the source with the best reputation for accuracy should be used.

▶ In retailing, many secondary data projects are not retested and the user of secondary data has to hope results from one narrow study are applicable to his or her firm.

Whether secondary data resolve an issue or not, their low cost and availability require that primary data not be amassed until after studying secondary data. Only if secondary data are not actionable should primary data be collected. We now present various secondary data sources for retailers.

SOURCES

There are many sources and types of secondary data. The major distinctions are between internal and external sources.

Internal secondary data are available within the company, sometimes from the data bank of a retail information system. Before searching for external secondary data or primary data, the retailer should look at information available inside the firm.

At the beginning of the year, most retailers develop budgets for the next 12 months. They are based on sales forecasts and outline planned expenditures for that year. A firm's budget and its performance in attaining budgetary goals are good sources of secondary data.

Retailers use sales and profit-and-loss reports to judge performance. Many have data from electronic registers that can be studied by store, department, and item. By comparing data with prior periods, a firm gets a sense of growth or contraction. Overdependence on sales data may be misleading. Sales should be examined along with profit-and-loss data to indicate strengths and weaknesses in operations and management and to help lead to improvements.

Through customer billing reports, a retailer learns about inventory movement, sales by different personnel, and sales volume. For credit customers, sales by location, repayment time, and types of purchases can be reviewed. Purchase invoices show the retailer's own buying history and let it evaluate itself against budgetary goals. See Figure 8-8.

Inventory records indicate the merchandise carried throughout the year and the turnover of these items. Knowing the lead time to place and receive orders from suppliers, as well as the extra merchandise kept on hand to prevent running out at different times during the year, aids planning.

If a firm does primary research, the resultant report should be kept for future use (hopefully in the retail information system). When used initially, a report involves primary data. Later reference to it is secondary in nature since the report is no longer used for its primary purpose.

Written reports on performance are another source of internal secondary data. They may be prepared by senior executives, buyers, sales personnel, or others. All phases of retail management can be improved through formal report procedures.

FIGURE 8-8

Internal Secondary Data: A Valuable Source of Information

The sales receipt (invoice) contains a lot of useful data, from the name of the person involved in each sales transaction to the items sold to the selling price. Weekly, monthly, and yearly performance can easily be tracked by carefully storing and retrieving sales receipt data.

Source: Reprinted by permission of Retail Technologies International.

External secondary data are available from sources outside the firm. They should be consulted if internal information is insufficient for a decision to be made on a defined issue. These sources are comprised of government and nongovernment categories.

To use external secondary data well, appropriate online data bases should be consulted. They contain all kinds of written materials, usually by subject or topic heading, for a specified time. Here are several data bases, chosen for their retailing relevance. They are available through the Internet (for online access, you must use your company, college, or local library Web connection—direct entry to the sites is password-protected):

▶ Academic Search Premier/EBSCOhost.
▶ Business Source Premier/EBSCOhost.
▶ Dow Jones Factiva.
▶ Emerald.
▶ Gale Business & Company Resource Center.
▶ Gale Virtual Reference Library.
▶ IngentaConnect.
▶ LexisNexis Academic Universe.
▶ Mergent Online.
▶ Plunkett Research Online.
▶ Standard & Poor's NetAdvantage.

The U.S. Census Bureau has a Web site (**www.census.gov/ econ/www/retmenu.html**) listing recent retailing reports, which can be viewed and downloaded.

The government distributes a wide range of materials. Here are several publications, chosen for their retailing value. They are available in any business library or other large library or through the Web:

▶ *Annual Retail Trade Survey.*
▶ *U.S. Census of Retail Trade.* Every five years ending in 2 and 7.
▶ *U.S. Census of Service Industries.* Every five years ending in 2 and 7.
▶ *Monthly Retail Trade and Food Services Sales.*
▶ *Statistical Abstract of the United States.*
▶ *U.S. Survey of Current Business.*
▶ *Other.* Registration data (births, deaths, automobile registrations, etc.). Available through federal, state, and local agencies.

Government agencies, such as the Federal Trade Commission, provide pamphlets on topics such as franchising, unit pricing, deceptive ads, and credit policies. The Small Business Administration provides smaller retailers with literature and advice. Pamphlets are distributed free or sold for a nominal fee.

Looking for secondary data on direct marketing (**www.colinear.com/resource.htm**) or E-commerce (**www.wilsonweb.com/research**)? Check out these sites.

Nongovernment secondary data come from many sources, often cited in reference guides. Major nongovernment sources are regular periodicals; books, monographs, and other nonregular publications; channel members; and commercial research houses.

Regular periodicals are available at most libraries or by personal subscription. A growing number are also available online; some Web sites provide free information, whereas others charge a fee. Periodicals may have a broad scope (such as *Business Week*) and discuss diverse business topics, or they may have narrower coverage (such as *Chain Store Age*) and deal mostly with retail topics.

Many firms publish books, monographs, and other nonregular retailing materials. Some, such as Pearson Higher Education (**www.pearsonhighered.com**), have textbooks and practitioner books. Others have more distinct goals. The American Marketing Association (**www.marketingpower.com**) offers information to enhance readers' business knowledge. The Better Business Bureau (**www.bbb.org**) wants to improve the public's image of business and expand industry self-regulation. The International Franchise Association (**www.franchise.org**) and the National Retail Federation (**www.nrf.com**) describe industry practices and trends, and they act as spokespersons to advocate the best interests of members. Other associations can be uncovered by consulting Gale's *Encyclopedia of Associations*.

Retailers often get information from channel members such as ad agencies, franchise operators, manufacturers, and wholesalers. When these firms do research for their own purposes and present some or all of the findings to their retailers, external secondary data are involved. Channel members pass on findings to enhance their sales and retailer relations. They usually do not charge for the information.

The last external source is the commercial research house that conducts ongoing studies and makes results available to many clients for a fee. This source is secondary if the retailer is a subscriber and does not request tailored studies. Information Resources Inc., A.C. Nielsen, and Standard Rate & Data Service provide subscriptions at lower costs than a retailer would incur if data were collected only for its use.

Our Web site (**www.pearsonhighered.com/berman**) has links to about 50 online sources of free external secondary data—both government and nongovernment.

Primary Data

ADVANTAGES AND DISADVANTAGES

After exhausting the available secondary data, a defined issue may still be unresolved. In this instance, primary data (collected to resolve a specific topic at hand) are needed. When secondary data are sufficient, primary data are not collected. There are several advantages associated with primary data:

▶ They are collected to fit the retailer's specific purpose.
▶ Information is current.
▶ The units of measure and data categories are designed for the issue being studied.
▶ The firm either collects data itself or hires an outside party. The source is known and controlled, and the methodology is constructed for the specific study.
▶ There are no conflicting data from different sources.
▶ When secondary data do not resolve an issue, primary data are the only alternative.

There are also several possible disadvantages often associated with primary data:

▶ They are normally more expensive to obtain than secondary data.
▶ Information gathering tends to be more time-consuming.
▶ Some types of information cannot be acquired by an individual firm.
▶ If only primary data are collected, the perspective may be limited.
▶ Irrelevant information may be collected if the issue is not stated clearly enough.

In sum, a retailer has many criteria to weigh in evaluating the use of primary data. In particular, specificity, currency, and reliability must be weighed against high costs, time, and limited access to materials. A variety of primary data sources for retailers are discussed next.

SOURCES

Want to learn about conducting an Internet survey? Go to this Business Research Lab Web site (**www.busreslab. com/onlinesurvey.htm**).

The first decision is to determine who collects the data. A retailer can do this itself (internal) or hire a research firm (external). Internal collection is usually quicker and cheaper. External collection is usually more objective and formal. Second, a sampling method is specified. Instead of gathering data from all stores, all products, and all customers, a retailer may obtain accurate data by studying a sample of them. This saves time and money. With a **probability (random) sample**, every store, product, or customer has an equal or known chance of being chosen for study. In a **nonprobability sample**, stores, products, or customers are chosen by the researcher—based on judgment or convenience. A probability sample is more accurate but is also more costly and complex. Third, the retailer chooses among four methods of data collection: survey, observation, experiment, and simulation. All of the methods are capable of generating data for each element of a strategy.

SURVEY. With a **survey**, information is systematically gathered from respondents by communicating with them. Surveys are used in many retail settings. Spiegel combines a computer-assisted telephone interviewing system with mail and personal surveys to monitor customer tastes and needs. Food Lion uses in-store surveys to learn how satisfied customers are and what their attitudes are on various subjects.

A survey may be conducted in person, over the phone, by mail, or online. Typically, a questionnaire is used. A *personal survey* is face-to-face, flexible, and able to elicit lengthy responses; unclear questions can be explained. It may be costly, and interviewer bias is possible. A *phone survey* is fast and rather inexpensive. Responses are often short, and nonresponse may be a problem. A *mail survey* can reach a wide range of respondents, has no interviewer bias, and is not costly. Slow returns, high nonresponse rates, and participation by incorrect respondents are potential problems. An *online survey* is interactive, can be adapted to individuals, and yields quick results. Yet, only certain customers shop online or answer online surveys. The technique chosen depends on the goals and requirements of the research project.

A survey may be nondisguised or disguised. In a nondisguised survey, the respondent is told the real purpose of the study. In a disguised survey, the respondent is not told the true purpose so that person does not answer what he or she thinks a firm wants to hear. Disguised surveys use word associations, sentence completions, and projective questions (such as, "Do your friends like shopping at this store?").

The **semantic differential**—a listing of bipolar adjective scales—is a survey technique that may be disguised or nondisguised. The respondent is asked to rate one or more retailers on several criteria, each evaluated by bipolar adjectives (such as unfriendly–friendly). By computing the average rating of all respondents for each criterion, an overall profile can be developed. A semantic differential comparing two furniture retailers appears in Figure 8-9. Store A is a prestige, high-quality store and Store B is a medium-quality, family-run store. The semantic differential graphically portrays the store images.

OBSERVATION. The form of research in which present behavior or the results of past behavior are noted and recorded is known as **observation**. Because people are not questioned, observation may not require respondents' cooperation, and survey biases are minimized. Many times, observation is used in actual situations. The key disadvantage of using observation alone is that attitudes are not elicited.

Retailers use observation to determine the quality of sales presentations (by having researchers pose as shoppers), to monitor related-item buying, to determine store activity by time and day, to make pedestrian and vehicular traffic counts (to measure the potential of new locations), and to determine the proportion of patrons using mass transit.

With **mystery shoppers**, retailers hire people to pose as customers and observe their operations, from sales presentations to how well displays are maintained to service calls.[20] One research firm, Michelson & Associates (**www.michelson.com/mystery**), has a pool of more than 80,000 mystery shoppers: "We qualify, train, and manage our shoppers to gather factual data and give objective observations. Our people range from 21 to 70 years of age with the majority being women between age 30 and 45. They are pre-selected based on client criteria such as demographics, type of car, shopping habits, etc."[21]

FIGURE 8-9

A Semantic Differential for Two Furniture Stores

Please check the blanks that best indicate your feelings about Stores A and B.

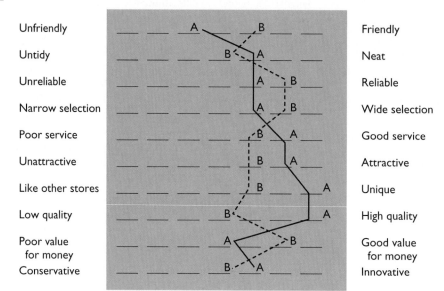

Observation may be disguised or nondisguised, structured or unstructured, direct or indirect, and human or mechanical. In disguised observation, the shopper or company employee is not aware he or she is being watched by a two-way mirror or hidden camera. In nondisguised observation, the participant knows he or she is being observed—such as a department manager watching a cashier's behavior. Structured observation calls for the observer to note specific behavior. Unstructured observation requires the observer to note all of the activities of the person being studied. With direct observation, the observer watches people's present behavior. With indirect observation, the observer examines evidence of past behavior such as food products in consumer pantries. Human observation is carried out by people. It may be disguised, but the observer may enter biased notations and miss behavior. Mechanical observation, such as a camera filming in-store shopping, eliminates viewer bias and does not miss behavior.

RETAILING AROUND THE WORLD

Mystery Shoppers: A Research Tool Comes to Puerto Rico

Puerto Rico is so competitive as a retail marketplace that shoppers often see the same products priced at identical prices at different stores throughout the island. As a result, merchants are well aware of the importance of customer service as a differential advantage.

The trend of using mystery shoppers to assess a store's customer service is now catching on in Puerto Rico. A number of mystery shopping firms, such as Shoppers' Critique International (**www.shopperscritique.com**) and BMA Mystery Shopping (**www.mystery-shopping.com**), conduct mystery shopping for fast-food chains, apparel stores, and video rental stores in Puerto Rico.

Although mystery shopping can be used to evaluate employee integrity and product quality, its major objective in Puerto Rico is to help improve customer service. Questionnaires used by mystery shoppers generally include both open- and closed-ended questions, as well as a comments section where suggestions for improvement can be noted. Among the areas covered are politeness, store cleanliness, and product quality. According to the Mystery Shopping Providers Association (**www.mysteryshop.org**), if mystery shopping uncovers poor performance, the affected employees should be retrained or told of the firm's customer service policies. It is inappropriate to fire an employee strictly based on a low score by a mystery shopper.

Sources: Jeremy Michael, "Mystery Shopping Solved," *Marketing* (July 2, 2008), p. 11; and Christopher Warzynski, "Misuse of Mystery Shopping Scores," **www.mysteryshop.org/news** (February 22, 2008).

EXPERIMENT   An **experiment** is a type of research in which one or more elements of a retail strategy mix are manipulated under controlled conditions. An element may be a price, a shelf display, or store hours. If a retailer wants to find out the effects of a price change on a brand's sales, only the price of that brand is varied. Other elements of the strategy stay the same, so the true effect of price is measured.

An experiment may use survey or observation techniques to record data. In a survey, questions are asked about the experiment: Did you buy Brand Z because of its new shelf display? Are you buying more ice cream because it's on sale? In observation, behavior is watched during the experiment: Sales of Brand Z rise by 20 percent when a new display is used. Ice cream sales go up 25 percent during a special sale.

Surveys and observations are experimental if they occur under closely controlled situations. When surveys ask broad attitude questions or unstructured behavior is observed, experiments are not involved. Experimentation can be difficult since many uncontrollable factors (such as the weather, competition, and the economy) come into play. Yet, a well-controlled experiment yields a lot of good data.

The major advantage is an experiment's ability to show cause and effect (a lower price results in higher sales). It is also systematically structured and enacted. The major potential disadvantages are high costs, contrived settings, and uncontrollable factors.

SIMULATION   A type of experiment whereby a computer program is used to manipulate the elements of a retail strategy mix rather than test them in a real setting is **simulation**. Two kinds are now being applied in retail settings: those based on mathematical models and those involving "virtual reality."

With the first kind of simulation, a model of the expected controllable and uncontrollable retail environment is constructed. Factors are manipulated by computer so their effects on the overall strategy and specific elements of it are learned. No consumer cooperation is needed, and many combinations of factors can be analyzed in a controlled, rapid, inexpensive, and risk-free manner. This format is gaining popularity because good software is available. However, it is still somewhat difficult to use.

In the second kind of simulation, a retailer devises or buys interactive software that lets participants simulate actual behavior in as realistic a format as possible. This approach creates a "virtual shopping environment." At present, there is limited software for these simulations and personnel must be trained to use it. One application of a virtual reality simulation—used by numerous clients—is from IFOP-CMR:

> Visionary Shopper is a computer-generated shopping simulation where you can create the retail environment you want, without the expense of controlling a store or creating a product prototype; vary the marketing stimuli at the touch of a button; send consumers shopping on a touch-screen monitor; and measure purchase behavior in response to changes in the marketing variables; all in a controlled and confidential setting, within a central location facility. Visionary Shopper provides a unique focus on consumer behavior—what they do, not what they say they will do. It allows you to understand buying behavior in the context of realistic store environments, not products in isolation or shelf subsets. It runs faster, and at a lower cost than current in-store research techniques.[22]

Chapter **Summary**

1. *To discuss how information flows in a retail distribution channel.* In an effective retail distribution channel, information flows freely and efficiently among the three main parties (supplier, retailer, and consumer). As a result, the parties can better anticipate and address each other's performance expectations. Retailers often have a vital role in collecting data because they have the most direct contact with shoppers.

2. *To show why retailers should avoid strategies based on inadequate information.* Whether developing a new strategy or modifying an existing one, good data are necessary to reduce a retailer's chances of making incorrect decisions. Retailers that rely on nonsystematic or incomplete research, such as intuition, increase their probabilities of failure.

3. *To look at the retail information system, its components, and the recent advances in such systems.* Useful information should be acquired through an ongoing, well-integrated process. A retail information system anticipates the data needs of retail managers; continuously collects, organizes, and stores relevant data; and directs the flow of information to decision makers. Such a system has several components: environment, retailer's philosophy, strategic plans, information control center, and retail operations. The most important component is the information control center. It directs data collection, stores and retrieves data, and updates files.

Data-base management is used to collect, integrate, apply, and store information related to specific topics (such as customers, vendors, and product categories). Data-base information can come from internal (company generated) and external (purchased from outside firms) sources. A key advance in data-base management is data warehousing, whereby copies of all the data bases in a firm are kept in one location and can be accessed by employees at any locale. It is a huge repository separate from the operational data bases that support departmental applications. Through data mining and micromarketing, retailers use data warehouses to pinpoint the specific needs of customer segments.

Retailers have increased their use of computerized retail information systems, and the Universal Product Code (UPC) is now the dominant technology for processing product-related data. With electronic data interchange (EDI) and Internet electronic data interchange (I-EDI), the computers of retailers and their suppliers regularly exchange information, sometimes through the Web.

4. *To describe the marketing research process.* Marketing research in retailing involves these sequential activities: defining the issue or problem to be researched, examining secondary data, gathering primary data (if needed), analyzing the data, making recommendations, and implementing findings. It is systematic in nature and not a single act.

Secondary data (gathered for other purposes) are inexpensive, can be collected quickly, may have several sources, and may yield otherwise unattainable information. Some sources are very credible. When an issue is ill defined, a secondary data search can clarify it. There are also potential pitfalls: These data may not suit the purposes of the study, units of measurement may not be specific enough, information may be old or inaccurate, a source may be disreputable, and data may not be reliable.

Primary data (gathered to resolve the specific topic at hand) are collected if secondary data do not adequately address the issue. They are precise and current, data are collected and categorized with the units of measures desired, the methodology is known, there are no conflicting results, and the level of reliability can be determined. When secondary data do not exist, primary data are the only option. The potential disadvantages are the cost, time, limited access, narrow perspective, and amassing of irrelevant information.

Key Terms

retail information system
(RIS) (p. 219)
data-base management (p. 222)
data warehousing (p. 223)
data mining (p. 225)
micromarketing (p. 225)
Universal Product Code
(UPC) (p. 225)
electronic data interchange
(EDI) (p. 227)

marketing research in retailing
(p. 227)
marketing research process
(p. 227)
issue (problem) definition
(p. 227)
secondary data (p. 227)
primary data (p. 227)
internal secondary data (p. 230)
external secondary data (p. 231)

probability (random)
sample (p. 233)
nonprobability sample
(p. 233)
survey (p. 233)
semantic differential (p. 233)
observation (p. 233)
mystery shoppers (p. 233)
experiment (p. 235)
simulation (p. 235)

Questions for Discussion

1. Relate the information flows in Figure 8-1 to a travel agency near your college or university.

2. What would you recommend to guard against this comment? "Traditionally, retailers and suppliers just don't like to share supply-chain information with each other."

3. Can a retailer ever have too much information? Explain your answer.

4. How could a small retailer devise a retail information system?

5. Explain the relationship among the terms *data warehouse, data mining,* and *micromarketing.* How can GameStop (**www.gamestop.com**) apply these concepts?

6. What are the opportunities and potential problems with electronic data interchange (EDI) for a drugstore chain?

7. Cite the major advantages and disadvantages of secondary data.

8. As a greeting-card store owner, what kinds of secondary data would you use to learn more about your industry and consumer trends in leisure activities?

9. Describe the major advantage of each method of gathering primary data: survey, observation, experiment, and simulation.

10. Develop a 10-item semantic differential for a local pet supplies store to judge its image. Who should be surveyed? Why?

11. Why would a retailer use mystery shoppers rather than other forms of observation? Are there any instances when you would not recommend their use? Why or why not?

12. Why do you think that "virtual shopping" has not taken off faster as a research tool for retailers?

Web **Exercise**

Visit the Web site of Global Retail Insights (http://www.idc.com/GRI/index.jsp), a firm that specializes in retailing research. Describe some of the services it offers for retailers. Which would you most recommend? Why?

Note: Stop by our Web site (www.pearsonhighered.com/berman) to experience a number of highly interactive, appealing Web exercises based on actual company demonstrations and sample materials related to retailing.

part three
Short Cases

CASE 1: ABERCROMBIE'S RUEHL NO. 925 TARGETS A DIFFERENT CUSTOMER NICHE[C-1]

Abercrombie & Fitch (**www.abercrombie.com**) hopes that when its current male and female shoppers grow up and graduate from college, they will become shoppers at Ruehl No. 925 (**www.ruehl.com**), its most recent store concept. Ruehl targets 22- to 35-year-olds. In contrast, Abercrombie & Fitch targets 18- to 22-year-olds, Hollister (**www.hollisterco.com**) aims at 14- to 18-year-olds, and Abercrombie Kids (**www.abercrombiekids.com**) is geared for 7- to 14-year-olds. In addition to the age difference, Hollister features a California/beach design.

The concept of Ruehl No. 925 is based on a lifestyle appropriate to the Ruehls, a German family that settled in New York City in the late 19th century and founded a leather goods company in a Greenwich Street townhouse. The store exterior resembles a row of three brick townhouses with iron gates. The interior is laid out like a home. Shoppers enter rooms on each side of an entranceway that leads to a "porch" with a central checkout and fitting rooms. Although the interior is attractive, some shoppers have complained that the compartment-based layout makes going from one section to another difficult. There is no indication that the chain is owned by Abercrombie & Fitch. Noticeably absent from Ruehl are the bright lights, loud music, and large graphics that are characteristic of Abercrombie & Fitch stores. Some customers have even commented that Ruehl's lighting is subdued or even dark.

Retailers such as J. Crew (**www.jcrew.com**), Banana Republic (**www.bananarepublic.com**), and Ralph Lauren (**www.polo.com**)—while also selling goods to 20-somethings—serve a much broader target market. Like Abercrombie & Fitch, Ruehl's merchandise is casual. However, its sweaters, instead of being wool, are cashmere; its jeans are a better grade of denim; and the leather purses are embossed.

The reaction of shoppers to the 30 Ruehl stores is generally positive, even though some have complained about high prices. Cashmere sweaters, for example, have been selling at more than $160, and some purses are priced at more than $900. Ruehl's management believes that the concept's New York feel will definitely work in San Francisco and other northern California markets, but may not play out in other areas.

One retail analyst has noted that Ruehl is closer to breaking even than American Eagle's new 30-store Martin + Osa (**www.martinandosa.com**) unit. According to one report, Abercrombie has delayed further expanding Ruehl until it has become profitable. In the interim,

Abercrombie is working on improving the quality of Ruehl's merchandise.

Another retail analyst has been critical of Ruehl's positioning. This analyst says that although Ruehl targets a specific age group, its lifestyle positioning is less clear. As the analyst notes: "Maybe it is easier to be a genuine lifestyle retailer if one defines its customers based on life experiences rather than on age range."

Although Ruehl's store expansion is slow, it has enhanced its Web site. Initially, the Web site limited the offerings to handbags, cologne, and perfume. Later, it added its entire men's and women's casual apparel including jeans, outerwear, and gift cards.

Questions

1. Is Abercrombie & Fitch following a mass marketing, a concentrated marketing, or a differentiated marketing strategy? Explain your answer.
2. Describe the pros and cons of Ruehl's choice of a target market.
3. How can Ruehl's help shoppers more effectively evaluate alternative products?
4. Discuss how Ruehl's can reduce shoppers' cognitive dissonance.

CASE 2: THE DIGITAL SAVVY CONSUMER[C-2]

Scarborough Research (**www.scarboroughresearch.com**), a consumer and media research firm, recently conducted a six-month national study of 111,051 U.S. adults to learn more about consumer usage and ownership of 18 high-technology products (such as DVRs, satellite radio, and VoIP), likelihood to use certain Internet features (such as blogging, downloading music, and online gaming), and use of cellular device features (such as E-mail and text messaging). Consumers who engaged in certain behaviors were classified as "digital savvy." The study did not include digital camera ownership because of its common ownership and usage. The study focused on new and emerging technologies. Based on this study, 6 percent of U.S. consumers were defined as "digital savvy." In contrast, 68.6 percent of the population had low scores on the usage and ownership of these products.

The study suggests that digital savvy consumers are early adopters of new technologies and an important market to study. Digital savvy consumers are an especially vital target audience for new innovations and a key word-of-mouth communication source for the mass market.

Let's look at some of the characteristics of the digital savvy market segment:

▶ Six of the top 10 digital savvy cities are in the West (Las Vegas, Sacramento, San Diego, Seattle, Phoenix, and San Francisco).

[c-1]The material in this case is drawn from David Moin, "Ruehl Begins E-Commerce," *Women's Wear Daily* (October 29, 2007), p. 2; and Jeanine Poggi, "Contemporary Concept Chains Face Tough Times," *Women's Wear Daily* (February 25, 2008), p. 26.

[c-2]The material in this case is drawn from "Understanding the Digital Savvy Consumer," **www.scarborough.com/press_releases** (May 2008).

▶ Digital savvy consumers are more likely to be male. Three-quarters are under the age of 44. More than one-half are under 34.

▶ 57 percent of digital savvy consumers live in a household with an income of $75,000 or more; 36 percent have a college degree (as compared with 24 percent of all consumers).

▶ Digital savvy consumers are more likely to shop at the following stores that feature audio/video goods: Costco, Sam's Club, Best Buy, and Target.

▶ Digital savvy consumers are active and athletic. They are likely to participate in basketball, yoga/Pilates, free weights/circuit training, jogging/running, bowling, photography, hiking/backpacking, golf, swimming, and bicycling.

▶ Digital savvy consumers are heavy online spenders. Fifty-four percent of the digital savvy consumers spend more than $500 online annually, versus 35 percent of the total population. These consumers are the most likely to purchase books, clothing, music, toys/games, and office supplies online during a typical year.

▶ Popular sites visited by digital savvy consumers include ESPN.com, NFL.com, CNN.com, Ask.com, and Amazon.com. Interesting, digital savvy consumers are three times more likely than the average consumer to have visited ESPN.com in the prior month, but only 38 percent as likely to have watched ESPN on cable TV within the prior week.

Questions

1. Explain the relative importance of consumer demographic and lifestyle information in targeting digital savvy consumers.

2. Discuss the relative benefits of studying digital savvy consumers over a six-month period versus a one-month period.

3. List and describe the major benefits of such a large sample.

4. How could a retailer such as Best Buy use these findings in refining its overall retail strategy to better appeal to digital savvy consumers?

CASE 3: 7-ELEVEN TURNS UP ITS RETAIL INFORMATION SYSTEM[C-3]

7-Eleven (**www.7-eleven.com**), the convenience store chain widely known for selling gasoline, cigarettes, and the Big Gulp, is now seeking to appeal to a more upscale audience with offerings that include chardonnay wine, cappuccino,

[c-3]The material in this case is drawn from Elizabeth Esfahani, "7-Eleven Gets Sophisticated," *Business 2.0* (January/February 2005), pp. 93–100; "7-Eleven, IRI Extend and Enhance IRI 7-Exchange Program," *Business Wire* (July 19, 2007); and "7-Eleven Works to Reduce OOS, Improve Turns," *Chain Store Age* (August 2008), p. 74.

artisan breads, focaccia sandwiches, and even sushi. 7-Eleven has already made strong inroads with female shoppers by being one of the first convenience stores to install credit card readers at the gas pumps (instead of in the store). The chain recognized that many mothers do not want to leave their children in the car while they pay for gasoline purchases. 7-Eleven has also begun to roll out fancier stores located in downtown business districts, at airports, and at colleges.

Central to the change in target market focus is 7-Eleven's reliance on a sophisticated retail information system that isolates trends, forecasts sales, and reorders merchandise. The system consists of its own internal corporate data, data accessed through Information Resources, Inc. (IRI, **www.infores.com**), and data from local franchise owners.

Through the internal corporatewide system, each store manager can tap into 7-Eleven's computer system to determine which products are selling best at his or her location; store managers can also determine best-selling products for the chain as a whole. In addition, the system provides other key information, such as weather reports, and notifies managers of major local sporting events and special functions at a local school. This information enables store mangers to constantly revise their selections.

In addition to its internal data base, 7-Eleven now provides access to all of its U.S. point-of-sales data to Information Resources, Inc., a major provider of single-source data. The data are on a store-specific, daily, and item level. The data are even used in conjunction with a 7-Exchange program.

The 7-Exchange program allows multiple companies to access sales information for all items. Thus, 7-Eleven can determine the overall success of a new product, better assemble an assortment, and improve its pricing strategies based on data from other convenience stores. According to Kevin Elliott, 7-Eleven's senior vice-president of merchandising, "We worked with IRI to develop the 7-Exchange data community to facilitate improved collaboration between 7-Eleven and manufacturers and suppliers. This exchange enables us to identify consumer trends and buying patterns and to gain additional insight through the 'same looking glass.'"

Many 7-Eleven franchisees have also developed their own information systems. A privately owned operator of more than 100 7-Eleven stores in Oklahoma recently added a forecasting and inventory replenishment system to avoid out-of-stock situations. The operator uses a DemandAnalytX (DAX) software system that interprets point-of-sales data to forecast demand and replenishment on a store-by-store level. As that franchisee's president says: "Orders that used to take up to an hour to write are now generated automatically by DAX, affording our managers more time to take care of customers." In addition, the system has reduced inventory by 15 percent, out-of-stocks by 50 percent, and spoilage by 45 percent.

Questions

1. Assess 7-Eleven's retail information system.

2. How can 7-Eleven effectively coordinate its use of marketing research with its retail information system?

3. Discuss how 7-Eleven can use data mining to improve its sales and profitability.
4. Describe the potential benefits of better collaboration among 7-Eleven and its suppliers.

CASE 4: THE HALLMARK OF RETAIL RESEARCH[C-4]

Even though Hallmark (**www.hallmark.com**) cards, gifts, and other related goods are sold at 43,000 retail outlets in more than 100 countries throughout the world, the greatest selection of Hallmark products can be found in Hallmark's 3,500 independently owned Hallmark Gold Crown stores and in Hallmark's close to 500 company-owned stores. A key element of Hallmark's customer data base and overall marketing efforts is its Crown Rewards loyalty program. About 14 million customers participate in this program. According to Jay T. Dittman, Hallmark's vice-president for marketing strategy, "At corporate we provide insight that turns data-base information technology into marketing programs."

Prior to shifting to its current SAS Enterprise Intelligence Platform in 2007, Hallmark had to perform several steps before its data base could be used for marketing strategy development and analysis. Data had to be downloaded from a mainframe to a server and then imported into Microsoft Access. Then Microsoft Excel was used to view and analyze the data. In the past, this process could take several days. Now, data analysis can occur without these intermediate steps. This enables Hallmark to more quickly ascertain trends, to respond faster to business opportunities, to better segment customers, and to more effectively use marketing expenditures. The new system also allows its marketing analysts to do more data mining by looking at information over multiple years of data.

One recurring problem/opportunity for Hallmark is to identify which market segment is most likely to respond to a specific promotion, such as Mother's Day. Because uniform promotions are costly and sometimes ineffective, Hallmark seeks to send different versions of

cards to different Crown Rewards segments. One version of a card might be more appropriate for older mothers who are purchasing cards for their daughters, while another version may be more fitting for young mothers with children. The new software enables Hallmark to easily track the results of different versions of each communication and then compute the return on investment with each advertisement or E-mail used.

Dittman and his fellow market researchers have also used the Enterprise Intelligence Platform to evaluate Hallmark's marketing budget expenditures throughout the year. Their research concluded that Hallmark was spending too much in January and at Easter but was underspending for Father's Day. Their analysis concluded that Hallmark could build on the momentum of Mother's Day and then reassign advertising spending from Easter to Father's Day. They also found that direct mail–based promotions were more effective than television advertising. As a result, for Father's Day, Hallmark experienced double-digit increases in sales with no adverse effect on Easter sales.

Another important research finding is that consumer card purchasing in July, August, and September is important in driving holiday sales in November and December. Because there are no traditional card or gift-purchasing events during these summer months, Hallmark is now heavily promoting birthdays and anniversaries during this time period. Direct mail- and E-mail-based promotions are used in favor of television during the summer season.

Questions

1. Explain how Hallmark's loyalty-card program can be tied into its overall retail information system.
2. Discuss important data bases that Hallmark should develop by customers as well as by product category.
3. Develop a questionnaire to study the types and size of market segments for Father's Day cards.
4. Show how the semantic differential can be used to describe Hallmark's overall image versus (a) other national brands such as Ambassador Cards and (b) half-priced cards available in many local stationery and candy stores.

[C-4]The material in this case is drawn from Karen M. Kroll, "Sending the Very Best: BI Program Helps Hallmark Target Marketing Promotions," *Stores* (October 2008), pp. 47–48.

part three ▌▌▌ ▌▌▌
Comprehensive Case

RETAILING LESSONS FROM LOYALTY PROGRAMS AROUND THE GLOBE*

INTRODUCTION

Even though retail leaders have taken diverse approaches to loyalty programs, one clear conclusion is that the programs must be a source of shopper insights that can be leveraged in multiple ways to be successful. The insights must be used to identify and execute marketing and merchandising initiatives that generate sales and profit growth from the retailer's key shoppers—and among the brands most important to those shoppers—in a way that is incremental to gains generated by existing initiatives.

The path of successful programs starts with defining the retailer's key shopper segments and using insights about the shopping behavior of shoppers in those segments to drive direct marketing, as well as in-store marketing and merchandising. Looming large in the process is the choice of the right partners in terms of manufacturers, third-party data providers, and data analytics vendors. Tailoring the choices and approach to the retailer's unique circumstances ensures that an investment in loyalty marketing yields a worthwhile return on investment. This case is based on an analysis of six retailers (CVS, Carrefour, Kroger, Seven-Eleven Japan, Tesco, and Wal-Mart) and other industry research.

CVS

U.S.-based CVS (**www.cvs.com**) introduced its Extra Care loyalty program in 2001. Today, it has more than 50 million members—making it the largest loyalty-card program in the United States and globally. Members receive 2 percent on purchases in the form of ExtraBucks and $1.00 to spend on front-end products for every two prescriptions bought.

Among retailer loyalty programs, the CVS Extra Care program is among the most innovative as the drugstore chain is willing to take risks by experimenting with new consumer touchpoints, payment systems, technologies, and third-party partnerships. Using the shopper data collected through its loyalty program, CVS has been able to segment its customers by lifestyle and life stage.

Because the firm knows that 80 percent of its shoppers are women, its segmentation includes three groups of female shoppers at different life stages: (1) Caroline is a young, single, or newly married working woman aged 18 to 34; she shops CVS for affordable beauty products. (2) Vanessa is the core CVS customer—with little free time and who juggles a family and work. As a married 35- to 54-year-old female with

*The material in this case is adapted by the authors from TNS Retail Forward (**www.retailforward.com**), *Strategic Focus: Global Loyalty Marketing Lessons* (Columbus, OH: TNS Retail Forward, July 2008). Reprinted by permission.

kids, she likes the drive-through pharmacy. (3) Sophie is an older (55+) empty nester who regularly shops for discounts; she also is a major customer of over-the-counter and prescription drugs.

Extra Care members receive targeted offers via circulars, E-mail, coupons, and direct mail. Due to rising costs, CVS is shifting some of its promotions to E-mail. CVS is also looking for other new ways to advertise and offer discounts to customers. One way is ExtraBucks—store credits earned on a quarterly basis that can be used toward front-end purchases. They are instantly available on the back of store receipts or can be downloaded from the Web. ExtraBucks are often available on promotional products.

CVS sponsors publications such as *Great Health* and *Reinventing Beauty.* Its direct marketing now includes more explicit "calls to action" in the form of discounts and coupons. For instance, in a recent issue of *Reinventing Beauty,* coupons were displayed on the cover and throughout the publication. *Great Health,* aimed at women, includes ads for products at CVS along with coupons.

CVS first piloted interactive coupon kiosks or "coupon centers" in stores in 2005. By 2007, there were coupon kiosks in 1,379 stores. By the end of 2008, half of the 6,300 CVS stores were expected to have kiosks. Through kiosks, shoppers receive targeted coupons based on past purchases tracked through the CVS Extra Care program.

CVS believes that segmentation enables merchandising, marketing, operations, and other teams to have a common language when talking about their customers. In 2003, CVS launched its Project Life format, which targets women. The new flagship store in Manhattan incorporates elements gleaned from shopper insights. CVS found that to accommodate its core female customer, whose average height is 5 feet 4 inches, it had to lower its gondola and shelf height to 60 inches. Because these core customers have little time, CVS tried to make the format easy to shop with color-coded departments and wide aisles. For convenience, the checkout is modeled after grocery stores with several lanes and self-checkout areas. The beauty department resembles an upscale specialty shop and carries European brands. A "coupon center" also is available where shoppers can scan their Extra Care loyalty card and print out discounts.

Launched in September 2007 as a pilot program, CVS Extra Care Plus is a partnership with HSBC bank to create a rewards debit card. CVS is looking at number of transactions, number of store visits, pre- and post-spending levels per cardholder, test-versus-control spending comparisons, migration of transactions to the debit card, and Extra Care Plus signups online. The loyalty debit card is not linked to a particular financial institution, so shoppers can sign up for the card and earn loyalty discounts and points without switching banks. Cardholders can pay, receive savings, and earn rewards at the checkout with one swipe of their CVS Extra Care Plus debit card and the entry of their PIN number. CVS benefits from savings on interchange fees because, among the different payment options (credit cards, signature debit cards, checks, and cash), debit-card purchases using a PIN have the lowest fee. Customers can use the loyalty debit card at CVS and other stores, so shoppers are not tied to one retailer with the program.

In 2008, CVS began to help loyalty-card holders track over-the-counter drugs, prescriptions, and other purchases that qualify for reimbursement through their health savings and flexible spending accounts. Register receipts conveniently track eligible items with a special symbol and a separate subtotal. Extra Care shoppers also receive targeted discounts and promotions on these items.

CVS says that the Extra Care loyalty program means larger transactions, more frequent shopping, and higher front-end margins. CVS credits the program for driving more profitable sales because the company can manage its promotional spending more precisely. The average cardholder visits CVS 11 times a year, while a top cardholder, in the upper 30th percentile, visits 27 times a year.

Carrefour

French-based Carrefour (**www.carrefour.com**), the second-largest global retailer after Wal-Mart, has had a loyalty program since the early 1990s but did not get serious about customer relationship management until 2004. The Club Carrefour program is available around the world in different forms and levels of development. Many of the loyalty programs involve coupons, discounts, gifts, and contests. For some markets, accumulated discounts and coupons are available online. Club Carrefour members also get exclusive promotions. Carrefour has 16.2 million French loyalty-card members.

The affinity card has become a strategic tool for Carrefour to offer consumers value in France's intense retail environment. Cardholders receive a 5 percent discount on 8,000 products, including many value-priced private brands. Carrefour is using its loyalty program to help fine-tune its customer-focused strategy and pricing and to reinforce its single-brand strategy. In addition to receiving discounts available to all cardholders, Carrefour loyalty members in France accumulate points based on the volume of their purchases. These points translate into a quarterly loyalty check.

In January 2007, French advertising laws became more lax. At that point, Carrefour began to promote its loyalty program on TV to position its stores as a place where families can save on food shopping.

Carrefour credits its loyalty program with helping it to better understand what shoppers want. For instance, member information and transaction analysis are helpful in the retailer's quest to simplify and segment its large, diverse, private-brand portfolio of 17,500 stock-keeping units (sku's) under the Carrefour brand. Recently, Carrefour has been able to reposition its brands through a three-tier system of premium, core, and entry-level private-brand products while also introducing brand extensions such as Carrefour Baby, Carrefour Kids, and Carrefour Light. As part of a localization strategy, Carrefour also is working closely with regional food suppliers to offer regional products.

By linking its transactional data to membership information, Carrefour is able to better gauge the success of its newest store prototypes. The latest hypermarket and new Carrefour Market prototypes are easier to shop with improved customer flow and simplified in-store communications. Both prototypes also build on the strength of the retailer's single-brand strategy. Carrefour's newest stores have a central walkway running along the entire length of the store. Merchandise is clustered logically, and departments are color-coded to help customers easily find the product they want. Directional signage has been improved for greater visibility while promotional signage is limited and simplified.

Because of the successful collaboration between Carrefour France and the Emnos business intelligence firm (**www.emnos.com**), in the later months of 2007, Carrefour announced it was extending the relationship to Spain so the region could become more customer-focused by segmenting customers, developing better assortments, and improving pricing and promotion policies. Emnos now has a branch office in Madrid to better serve Carrefour Spain. In 2006, Carrefour began working with Retalix (**www.retalix.com**) to implement loyalty software for the retailer's French hypermarkets. The software integrates and manages loyalty and promotion functionality. The system incorporates online tracking of customer data and real-time transmission of store transactions to a central data base. Carrefour uses Retalix in other markets, including its convenience stores in Italy. Carrefour operates loyalty programs in Asia and attributes part of its success in Taiwan to its loyalty program. In Malaysia, Carrefour is partnering with regional firms.

In France, Carrefour's loyalty program has "dramatically improved the company's knowledge of its customers." Thus, Carrefour is reconfiguring stores to improve customer flow and simplifying in-store communications. And the development of the company's private brands has benefited from improved customer insights. Leveraging shopper insights appears to be a key part of Carrefour's strategy for sustaining its leadership position in Europe and expanding its market share in foreign markets.

Kroger

About 85 percent of U.S. grocery stores have a loyalty initiative, but most are merely discount programs. Kroger (**www.kroger.com**) is at the vanguard of shopper insights in the United States, moving beyond simple discounts. Kroger is among the top retailers to leverage its loyalty program to provide its customers with relevant and targeted offers. The Kroger Plus Card (the loyalty-card programs at the company's other store banners take their store names) is held by 42 million U.S. households. These households receive 7 million targeted coupon mailings from Kroger each quarter. This puts Kroger's program among the largest retail loyalty programs in the world after CVS.

Due to U.S. concerns about privacy, Kroger asks members only for their name, address, and preference for mail in

English or Spanish. Great Britain's Tesco (**www.tesco.com**) asks card applicants for more detailed information such as age, household size, and dietary needs. Nonetheless, Kroger is able to supplement loyalty-card members' personal information with other demographic data.

Kroger gives discounts on Kroger fuel to Plus Card members based on store purchases. When gasoline prices were so high in 2008, this was viewed by members as one of the most important program benefits.

Shoppers are grouped together and classified based on price, package sizes, and types of products purchased. Through research, Kroger has segmented its customers into seven distinct groups: (1) Budget shoppers look for values and any way to stretch the food budget. (2) Convenience shoppers prefer easy-to-prepare foods and want to enter and exit the store quickly. (3) Family-focused shoppers make large purchases and take into account the needs of several members in their households. (4) Quality shoppers put a premium on quality and often shop for fresh, gourmet, and organic foods. (5) Grab-and-go shoppers have little time for cooking and want prepared and frozen meals. (6) Traditional shoppers prefer to cook, so they buy basic ingredients and fresh foods. (7) Watching-the-waist-line shoppers buy low-fat, low-carb, and other products that are indicative of their healthy lifestyles.

Kroger's best customers get useful targeted mailings more frequently. For instance, Kroger recently sent out a booklet called *My Magazine*, highlighting its Private Selection brand and offering articles, recipes, and coupons. Kroger's direct marketing can be seasonal. A recent summer *My Magazine* provided grilling tips and recipes for the discounted marinades and meats.

The loyalty program has had a major impact on Kroger's assortment, prices, package sizes, and other merchandising efforts. In concert with its loyalty data, Kroger is able to use sophisticated production planning and forecasting models to balance in-stock and overproduction in fresh foods. In terms of product development, Kroger uses individual shopper data to anticipate the needs of its customers over their lifetimes as they go through their various life stages.

Kroger takes a multi-pronged approach to providing store and manufacturer coupons on the Internet. Its Web site allows shoppers to print coupons from their computers. Kroger has partnered with Procter & Gamble (**www.pg.com**) to offer a link to P&G E-coupons. It provides another link to E-coupons from Unilever as well. Kroger has teamed up with AOL's paperless coupon program at **www.shortcuts.com** that allows online users to link coupons directly to their Kroger loyalty account. Shoppers can choose coupons by category, brand, or product. They can be redeemed at any Kroger store. Kroger is partnering with various suppliers to provide coupons on shoppers' mobile phones.

Seven-Eleven Japan

Seven-Eleven Japan (SEJ, **www.sej.co.jp/english**) is a subsidiary of Seven & I Holdings, Japan's largest retailer and the seventh-largest globally. In 2007, it began a loyalty program linked to a new contactless payment system called nanaco. Japan is mainly a cash-based economy (90 percent of retail purchases are made with cash) because the Japanese people are reluctant to use credit cards. E-wallets, which are electronic smart cards or mobile phones charged with money or linked to a bank account, are popular among Japanese consumers.

To become competitive with other Japanese convenience stores that are increasingly taking multiple brands of contactless payments, SEJ launched its own electronic money, nanaco, in April 2007. This way, SEJ (with 12,000 convenience stores in Japan) avoided paying interchange fees.

SEJ is the first retailer to offer its own electronic payment program. To differentiate nanaco from competing contactless payment systems, the program is tied to a loyalty scheme in which the user earns 1 point (1 yen) for every 100 yen in purchases. Nanaco is available in either a smart card or a mobile phone format, which is waved over a point-of-sale (POS) reader to complete a purchase. The program targets frequent shoppers, speeds up register transactions, and provides a convenient payment method.

Seven & I is trying multiple strategies to leverage nanaco to create more financial services and traffic. Because its credit card division manages the nanaco program, Seven & I can generate new revenue streams. Nanaco cards or mobile phones can be recharged with money at group stores and ATMs. Because convenience stores in Japan often operate as payment centers, where customers pay bills and payment counters are enhanced with ATMs, the new services generate more traffic and financial service fees.

SEJ expects that insights gleaned from its loyalty program will allow it to further hone a store offer that is tailored to specific demographics and day parts. Convenience stores are a major focal point of Japanese communities. Customers pay bills, pick up prepared meals, grab a refreshment, and purchase panty hose or cosmetics. School kids shop in the morning and afternoon. Teens hang out at the local SEJ after school, nights, and weekends. Housewives might shop in the afternoon for stock-up items, and husbands coming home from work might pick up bread for dinner. The elderly, like teens, also see the stores as both a place to socialize and a finance center where they can pay bills and do banking.

Convenience stores receive multiple deliveries throughout the day to accommodate different shopper groups. For instance, SEJ receives oven-fresh bread several times a day. By constantly rotating a new stream of fresh products, SEJ can keep customers coming back. Stores display a small number of sku's (2,500), so the merchandise is constantly changing.

Until 2007, without any loyalty program, SEJ was already a master of gleaning information from transaction data and tailoring its offering to customer needs. In pursuit of its objective to be "the most convenient store in the region," SEJ analyzes store data by region and by individual store to provide the correct assortment, guide product development, and develop "community-based, store-by-store services."

SEJ's major strategic advantage is its interconnected business infrastructure, which links the store network, information systems, distribution, and product development. SEJ's core strategy is to gain consumer insights to develop differentiated goods and services. With the nanaco program, SEJ can sharpen its shopper insights and deliver innovative, targeted products. Seven & I's plan is to expand nanaco beyond the convenience stores to its other formats including Denny's restaurants (**www.dennys.com**) and Ito-Yokado supermarkets. Seven & I is upping the number of locales where the nanaco can be used to 62,000 sites.

Tesco

Tesco's Clubcard program in Great Britain boasts 13.5 million members. The Clubcard is a points system in which Tesco shoppers can redeem points every quarter. For each £1, shoppers collect 1 point. Shoppers must collect 150 Clubcard points to qualify for a Clubcard voucher that can be redeemed in-store or online. The vouchers also can be used for discounts on magazines, travel, entertainment, and restaurants. Additionally, customers can accumulate points using the Tesco credit card.

Tesco has been a rarity in its ability to use a loyalty program to differentiate itself from competitors. Tesco's success starts with a strategic commitment to use its loyalty program to understand shoppers and drive targeted marketing, merchandising, and new product and format development.

In its collaboration with data analytics vendor dunnhumby (**www.dunnhumby.com**), Tesco clusters customers into six core groups based on life stage, lifestyle, and shopping basket: (1) The convenience segment includes busy urban shoppers who buy ready-made meals. (2) Fine-foods shoppers are upscale consumers who enjoy gourmet meals. They often buy fresh meat and fish, as well as organic and exotic items. (3) Healthy shoppers are concerned about their well-being and tend to buy fresh, low-calorie, and low-fat foods. (4) Mainstream shoppers like easy-to-prepare meals, including pasta. (5) Price-sensitive shoppers are on a budget and shop for the best value. They are most apt to use their rewards vouchers. (6) Traditional shoppers tend to be older and have a smaller number of items in their shopping baskets.

Customers are further segmented based on membership in various Tesco clubs, including the Wine Club, Baby & Toddler Club, Food Club, Healthy Living Club, and Christmas Savers Club. In 2007, Tesco launched the Green Clubcard program in Great Britain to include its sustainability efforts. These members receive extra points for reusing shopping bags or recycling inkjet cartridges and mobile phones.

Tesco and dunnhumby have led the industry's use of loyalty programs since the mid-1990s when they began creating targeted mailings for Clubcard holders using transaction analysis and loyalty member personal information. These mailings depended on Tesco's ability to segment customers and understand each segment's shopping needs. Using this knowledge, Tesco also has successfully ventured into new product categories, formats, and businesses.

Shoppers receive a quarterly statement in the mail tallying their accumulated points, along with vouchers and targeted promotional coupons. Because mailings are customized to each shopper, Tesco sends out more than 80,000 unique coupon combinations for each quarterly mailing. In addition to the quarterly statement, a Tesco magazine reaches 5.3 million readers.

Tesco Clubcard holders can earn extra points when using Tesco Personal Finance products such as the Tesco credit card and loan, mortgage, and insurance products. If shoppers use their Tesco credit card at Tesco stores or at Tesco.com, they receive 5 points for every £4 in purchases. Members of the Clubcard also can get points when doing business through loyalty partners such as Avis, Eon, National Tyres, and Autocare.

dunnhumby, beginning with its partnership with Tesco in 1995, is among the leaders in using data-base technology and analytics to study shopper transactions for shopper insights. dunnhumby, majority owned by Tesco, is credited with the retailer's success and rise as a major global player. Tesco and dunnhumby continue to explore partnerships using new media and in new markets beyond Great Britain.

Tesco has separate loyalty schemes in South Korea, China, and Malaysia, with offerings unique to each country. These programs have yet to exploit the transaction and customer data to the extent that Tesco has achieved at home. As a result, in April 2008, Tesco announced that it was partnering with dunnhumby to launch a global loyalty test with a goal to reach 60 million customers across the world. The test is being rolled out in nine countries, including the existing foreign loyalty programs. Tesco will be adding the Czech Republic, Hungary, Poland, Slovakia, Thailand, and Turkey to the test.

With shopper insights gleaned from the loyalty program, Tesco has moved into new growth vehicles such as convenience stores, online shopping, mobile phones, and financial services. The promotions linked to the loyalty program also allow Tesco to drive business to specific areas giving extra points for certain merchandise categories or for online sales.

Wal-Mart

Unlike other top global food retailers, Wal-Mart has not pursued a loyalty program. Wal-Mart has nevertheless sought to develop a more customer-focused, localized approach to merchandising and marketing its stores. This approach appears to be generating benefits for Wal-Mart. Wal-Mart gains shopper insights through high-level consumer segment research, transaction analysis, and category management. Rather than distributing targeted mailings and providing exclusive discounts, Wal-Mart is able to tailor its assortment to local needs without sacrificing everyday low prices.

In a three-year remerchandising effort beginning in 2006, Wal-Mart conducted consumer research to learn what mattered most to its customers. The company was embarking on its "Store of the Community" efforts, which required customer segmentation. Initially, Wal-Mart segmented its shoppers by ethnicity, income, and geography and derived six groups: African Americans, affluents, baby boomers/empty nesters, Hispanics, rural, and suburban.

More recently, the retailer's segmentation has been simplified, based on how and why people shop. These are the more streamlined segments: (1) Brand aspirationals include low-income shoppers interested in brand-name products. (2) Affluent, price-sensitive shoppers are wealthier consumers who like to shop for deals. (3) Price-value shoppers like low prices and cannot afford much due to limited budgets.

Wal-Mart still focuses on ethnic differences and continues to roll out Store of the Community initiatives that provide food and merchandise to match local tastes. With this strategy, Wal-Mart can personalize its offer to be more like a local neighborhood store than a big corporate entity. For example, in May 2008, Wal-Mart opened its first store that was designed from the start to target the Hispanic community in the Dallas suburb of Garland, Texas. With a customer base that is more than 50 percent Latino, the Garland store features Hispanic foods and many products imported from Mexico. The bakery makes corn tortilla chips from scratch. A Flor de Michoacan juice bar and ice cream shop is situated at the front of the store. Lifestyle signage is in Spanish and English and features Latino models.

Wal-Mart has changed its policy of dealing with third-party data suppliers. In 2007, it announced that it was partnering with NPD Group to gain consumer insights for its Wal-Mart and Sam's Club businesses. The partnership is part of Wal-Mart's effort to make its merchandising and marketing more customer-focused by providing integrated data to vendors so they are more informed. The Consumer Tracking Service, recently expanded by Wal-Mart and NPD, follows spending across categories and retail channels for a consumer panel representing 3.5 million consumers. Vendors doing business with Wal-Mart and Sam's Club have access to a cross-category view of what is going on across Wal-Mart's three consumer segments. NPD data are aligned with the way data are presented to vendors via Wal-Mart's Retail Link, which is the online system by which Wal-Mart provides suppliers with access to information about their own products at Wal-Mart. The NPD data, however, are separate from Wal-Mart's transaction history.

Questions

1. What overall conclusions do you reach after reading this case?
2. Comment on this statement: "CVS believes that segmentation enables merchandising, marketing, operations, and other teams to have a common language when talking about their customers."
3. Why are collaborations between retailers and such information specialists as Emnos and Retalix so valuable?
4. How should Kroger tailor its retailing strategy to take into account the seven main segmentation groups it has identified?
5. Explain Seven-Eleven Japan's nanaco program.
6. How should Tesco adapt its customer loyalties for the different countries in which it operates?
7. Why do you think that Wal-Mart has chosen *not* to have a customer loyalty program? Do you agree with this approach? Explain your answer.

PART 4 Choosing a Store Location

Once a retailer has conducted a situation analysis, set its goals, identified consumer characteristics and needs, and gathered adequate information about the marketplace, it is ready to develop and enact an overall strategy. In Parts Four through Seven, we examine the elements of such a strategy: choosing a store location, managing a business, merchandise management and pricing, and communicating with the customer. Part Four concentrates on store location.

Chapter 9 deals with the crucial nature of store location for retailers and outlines a four-step approach to location planning. In this chapter, we focus on Step 1, trading-area analysis. Among the topics we look at are the use of geographic information systems, the size and shape of trading areas, how to determine trading areas for existing and new stores, and the major factors to consider in assessing trading areas. Several data sources are described.

Chapter 10 covers the last three steps in location planning: deciding on the most desirable type of location, selecting a general location, and choosing a particular site within that location. We first contrast isolated store, unplanned business district, and planned shopping center locales. Criteria for rating each location are then outlined and detailed.

Source: Robert Simon/istockphoto.com.

9

Trading-Area Analysis

Best Buy is the nation's largest seller of consumer electronics, personal computers, entertainment software, and appliances. Best Buy operates more than 400 retail stores in 41 states, as well as a Web site (**www.bestbuy.com**), and the firm recognizes that consumer demographics and lifestyles vary significantly from store to store.

Although Best Buy has a customer data base of its credit card holders, it needed to create a more comprehensive data base for E-mail, traditional direct marketing, and trading-area analysis purposes. Best Buy's data base was developed in partnership with Experian, a firm that compiles data from more than 3,500 public and proprietary sources to provide a comprehensive analysis of U.S. households in a community. Best Buy then added more than 50 million customer records with INSOURCE data that include such demographic information as age, income, occupation, lifestyles, and purchase history.

As a result of its data-base analysis, Best Buy has been able to classify customers into three key market segments:

- ▶ Affluent suburban families.
- ▶ Trend-setting urban dwellers.
- ▶ Closely knit families of Middle America.

Every Best Buy store location has a different combination of these segments. For example, affluent downtown locations may have large concentrations of trend-setting urban dwellers, while working-class areas have more close-knit families.

Each of the three segments desires different types of merchandise and has special customer service needs. Trend-setting urban dwellers may desire the latest technology and desire top-of-the-line products, while Middle America families may value more middle-of-the-line, family-oriented goods such as high-definition LCD televisions. And the trend-setting urban dwellers may desire custom installation of surround systems, while Middle American families may install these units as a family project.[1]

Source: Reprinted by permission of Susan Berry, Retail Image Consulting, Inc.

OVERVIEW

More than 90 percent of retail sales are made at stores. Thus, the selection of a store location is one of the most significant strategic decisions in retailing. Consider the detailed planning of TaMolly's, a Mexican food restaurant chain with about a dozen locations in Texas, Arkansas, and Louisiana—and soon in Oklahoma. TaMolly's

> puts a premium on freshness—for both its food and its restaurant locations. When seeking out new locations in the secondary markets in which it competes, the Texarkana, Texas-based firm seeks a similar level of freshness as it builds its stores from scratch. But developing a restaurant from the ground up in new markets can be a problematic venture if all the pieces of the puzzle—site selection, direct real-estate investment, attracting new customers—don't fit. "We build to own, " says TaMolly's general counsel. "We actually are making an investment in real-estate, not just a restaurant. When we go to a place, obviously, we want to be successful with our restaurant and we try to find the best locations for us. It may not be the most expensive place or the most desirable site for some chains, but we want to go to where our customers are most concentrated. Everything is prepared on site. We need a lot of prep space. Most restaurant kitchens are not designed for that. It works better for us to build and have control over the design and size of our kitchens."[2]

This chapter and the next explain why the proper store location is so crucial, as well as the steps a retailer should take in choosing a store location and deciding whether to build, lease, or buy facilities. Visit our Web site (**www.pearsonhighered.com/berman**) for many links on store location.

At the Entrepreneur Web site (**www.entrepreneur.com**), type in "Finding a Location" to access a wealth of helpful articles on location planning.

The Importance of Location to a Retailer

Location decisions are complex, costs can be quite high, there is little flexibility once a site is chosen, and locational attributes have a big impact on a strategy. One of the oldest adages in retailing is that "location, location, location" is the major factor leading to a firm's success or failure. See Figure 9-1.

FIGURE 9-1

The Importance of Location to Nine West
Nine West (**www.ninewest.com**), part of the Jones Apparel Group, operates about 220 stores that are located in upscale and regional malls and urban retail centers. These locales are critical for Nine West, which sells merchandise categorized as "better." The typical store is about 1,600 square feet.

Source: Reprinted by permission of Nine West.

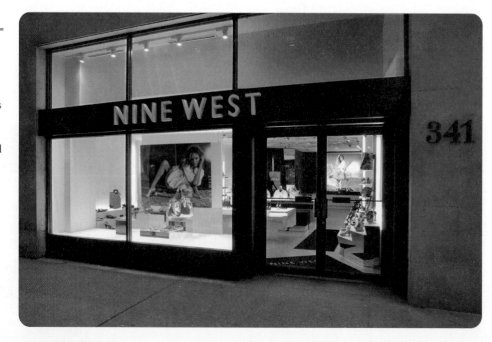

A good location may let a retailer succeed even if its strategy mix is mediocre. A hospital gift shop may do well, although its assortment is limited, prices are high, and it does not advertise. On the other hand, a poor location may be such a liability that even superior retailers cannot overcome it. A mom-and-pop store may do poorly if it is across the street from a category killer store; although the small firm features personal service, it cannot match the selection and prices. At a different site, it might prosper.

The choice of a location requires extensive decision making due to the number of criteria considered, including population size and traits, the competition, transportation access, parking availability, the nature of nearby stores, property costs, the length of the agreement, legal restrictions, and other factors.

A store location typically necessitates a sizable investment and a long-term commitment. Even a retailer that minimizes its investment by leasing (rather than owning a building and land) can incur large costs. Besides lease payments, the firm must spend money on lighting, fixtures, a storefront, and so on.

Although leases of less than 5 years are common in less desirable retailing locations, leases in good shopping centers or shopping districts are often 5 to 10 years or more. It is not uncommon for a supermarket lease to be 15 or 20 years. Department stores and large specialty stores on major downtown thoroughfares occasionally sign leases longer than 20 years.

Due to its fixed nature, the investment, and the length of the lease, store location is the least flexible element of a retail strategy. A firm cannot easily move to another site or convert to another format. It may also be barred from subleasing to another party during the lease period; if a retailer breaks a lease, it may be responsible to the property owner for financial losses. In contrast, ads, prices, customer services, and assortment can be modified as the environment (consumers, competition, the economy) changes.

Even a retailer that owns its store's building and land may also find it hard to change locations. It has to find an acceptable buyer, which might take several months or longer, and it may have to assist the buyer with financing. It may incur a loss, should it sell during an economic downturn.

Any retailer moving from one location to another faces three potential problems. (1) Some loyal customers and employees may be lost; the greater the distance between the old and new locations, the bigger the loss. (2) A new site may not have the same traits as the original one. (3) Store fixtures and renovations at an old site usually cannot be transferred to a new site; their remaining value is lost if they have not been fully depreciated.

Store location affects long- and short-run planning. In the *long run,* the choice of location influences the overall strategy. A retailer must be at a site that is consistent with its mission, goals, and target market for an extended time. It also must regularly study and monitor the status of the location as to population trends, the distances people travel to the store, and competitors' entry and exit—and adapt accordingly.

In the *short run,* the location has an impact on the specific elements of a strategy mix. A retailer in a downtown area with many office buildings may have little pedestrian traffic on weekends. It would probably be improper to sell items such as major appliances there (these items are often bought jointly by husbands and wives). The retailer could either close on weekends and not stock certain products or remain open and try to attract customers to the area by aggressive promotion or pricing. If the retailer closes on weekends, it adapts its strategy mix to the attributes of the location. If it stays open, it invests additional resources in an attempt to alter shopping habits. A retailer that strives to overcome its location, by and large, faces greater risks than one that adapts.

Retailers should follow these four steps in choosing a store location:

1. Evaluate alternate geographic (trading) areas in terms of the characteristics of residents and existing retailers.
2. Determine whether to locate as an isolated store, in an unplanned business district, or in a planned shopping center within the geographic area.
3. Select the general isolated store, unplanned business district, or planned shopping center location.
4. Analyze alternate sites contained in the specified retail location type.

RETAILING AROUND THE WORLD

Chain Stores Grow in Russia

A number of foreign retailers have been expanding their efforts in Russia. They are doing so because many segments of the marketplace remain understored. Until a couple of years ago, fast-food restaurants such as McDonald's (**www.mcdonalds.com**) had been the most aggressive foreign retailers there.

Wal-Mart (**www.walmartstores.com**) recently appointed Stephen Fanderl as president of Wal-Mart Emerging Markets Europe to explore retail opportunities in Russia. Coach (**www.coach.com**), the American clothing accessories marketer, has also announced plans to open at least 15 retail stores in Moscow and St. Petersburg with a Jamilco, a Russian partner. These stores will sell the full assortment of Coach products, including handbags, small leather goods, outerwear, and eyeglasses.

Local retailers such as X5 Retail Group (**www.x5ru/en**), a major Russian food retailer, are also expanding. X5 announced plans to purchase Karusel, a Russian operator of hypermarkets.

Increasingly, developers have begun to build shopping centers in smaller Russian cities. A major concern is that many residents there feel uncomfortable shopping in modern shopping centers, especially those with food courts and entertainment facilities.

Sources: Sophia Chabbott, "Coach to Open First Russian Unit in April," *Women's Wear Daily* (January 31, 2008), p. 3; Antonio Guerrero, "Russia's Retail Therapy," *Global Finance* (June 2008), pp. 42–44; and Denis Sokolov, "Russia's Retail Revolution," *Estates Gazette; 2007 Centre Retailing*, pp. 75–78.

This chapter concentrates on Step 1. Chapter 10 details Steps 2, 3, and 4. The selection of a store location is a process involving each of these steps.

Trading-Area Analysis

The first step in the choice of a retail store location is to describe and evaluate alternate trading areas and then decide on the most desirable one. A **trading area** is "a geographic area containing the customers of a particular firm or group of firms for specific goods or services."[3] After a trading area is picked, it should be reviewed regularly.

A thorough analysis of trading areas provides several benefits:

▶ Consumers' demographic and socioeconomic characteristics are examined. For a new store, the study of proposed trading areas reveals opportunities and the retail strategy necessary to succeed. For an existing store, it can be determined if the current strategy still matches consumer needs.

▶ The focus of promotional activities is ascertained, and the retailer can look at media coverage patterns of proposed or existing locations. If 95 percent of customers live within three miles of a store, it would be inefficient to advertise in a paper with a citywide audience.

▶ A retailer learns whether the location of a proposed branch store will service new customers or take business from its existing stores. Suppose a supermarket chain has a store in Jackson, Mississippi, with a trading area of two miles, and it considers adding a new store, three miles from the Jackson branch. Figure 9-2 shows the distinct trading areas and expected overlap of the stores. The shaded portion represents the **trading-area overlap**, where the same customers are served by both branches. The chain must find out the overall net increase in sales if it adds the proposed store (total revised sales of existing store + total sales of new store - total previous sales of existing store).

▶ Chains anticipate whether competitors want to open nearby stores if the firm does not do so itself. That is why TJX has two of its chains, T.J. Maxx and Marshalls, situate within 1.5 miles of each other in more than 100 U.S. markets, even though they are both off-price apparel firms.

▶ The best number of stores for a chain to operate in a given area is calculated. How many outlets should a retailer have in a region to provide good service for customers

FIGURE 9-2

The Trading Areas of
Current and Proposed
Supermarket Outlets

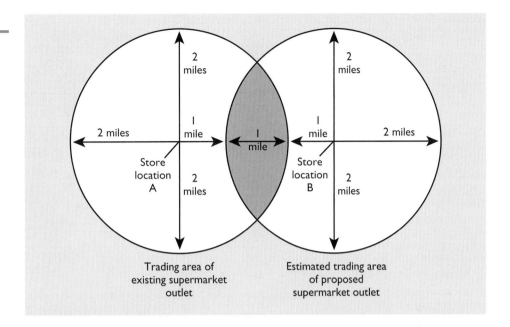

Trading area of
existing supermarket
outlet

Estimated trading area
of proposed
supermarket outlet

(without raising costs too much or having too much overlap)? When CVS entered Atlanta, it opened nine new drugstores in one day. This gave it enough coverage of the city to service residents, without placing stores too close together. A major competitive advantage for Canadian Tire Corporation is that four-fifths of the Canadian population live within a 15-minute drive of a Canadian Tire store.

▶ Geographic weaknesses are highlighted. Suppose a suburban shopping center does an analysis and discovers that most of those residing south of town do not shop there, and a more comprehensive study reveals that people are afraid to drive past a dangerous railroad crossing. Due to its research, the shopping center exerts political pressure to make the crossing safer.

▶ The impact of the Internet is taken into account. Store-based retailers must examine trading areas more carefully than ever to see how their customers' shopping behavior is changing due to the Web.

▶ Other factors are reviewed. The competition, financial institutions, transportation, labor availability, supplier location, legal restrictions, and so on can each be learned for the trading area(s) examined.

The Use of Geographic Information Systems in Trading-Area Delineation and Analysis

Increasingly, retailers are using **geographic information system (GIS)** software, which combines digitized mapping with key locational data to graphically depict trading-area characteristics such as population demographics; data on customer purchases; and listings of current, proposed, and competitor locations. Commercial GIS software lets firms quickly research the attractiveness of different locations and access computer-generated maps. Before, retailers often placed different color pins on paper maps to show current and proposed locales—and competitors' sites—and had to collect and analyze data.[4]

Learn more about TIGER
mapping at its Web site
(**www.census.gov/geo/
www/tiger/index.html**).

Most GIS software programs are extrapolated from the decennial *Census of Population* and the U.S. Census Bureau's national digital map (known as TIGER—topologically integrated geographic encoding and referencing). TIGER incorporates all streets and highways in the United States. TIGER files may be ordered free of charge by calling 301-763-4636. Commercial GIS software can be bought and accessed through Web site downloads or by DVDs or CDs.

TIGER maps may be adapted to reflect census tracts, railroads, highways, waterways, and other physical attributes of any U.S. area. They do not show retailers, other commercial entities, or population traits, and the Web site is hard to use. The federal government recently invested several hundred million dollars to upgrade the TIGER program.

FIGURE 9-3

GIS Software in Action

(A) This map shows the relative location of customers who patronize a particular store. Desire lines (spider lines) indicate the relationship between the location of each customer and the store location. The analysis examines the relationship between total purchase behavior and the distance each customer travels to patronize the store.

(B) This map illustrates the impact, on existing customers, if the location of a store/site (in this case, a bank) is changed. The "x" represents the proposed location and the "check" represents the existing location. The red and yellow polygons represent a 9-minute drive around each location. This 9-minute value represents 80 percent of the customer base.

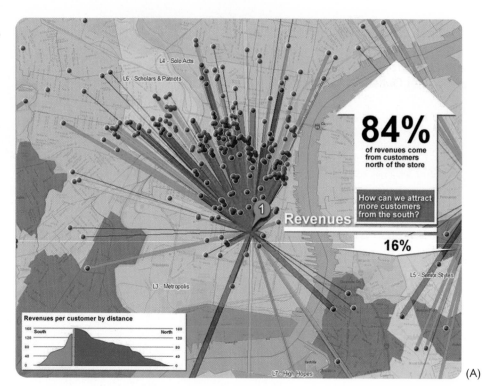

(A)

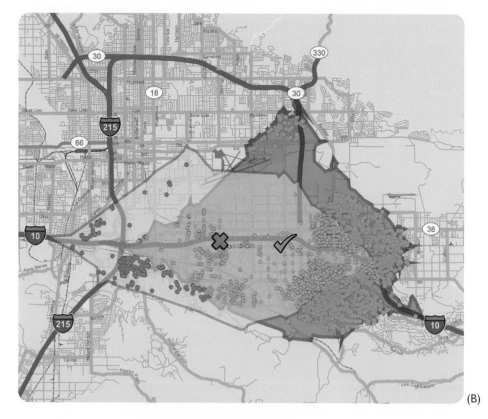

(B)

Mapping software from private firms has many more enhancements than TIGER. These firms often offer free demonstrations, but they expect to be paid for their software packages. Although GIS software differs by vendor, it generally can be accessed or bought for as little as $100 (or less) or for as much as several thousand dollars, is designed to work with personal computers, and allows for some manipulation of trading-area data. Illustrations appear in Figure 9-3. Private firms that offer mapping software include:

(Continued)

(C) In this map, a retail location is interested in understanding the correlation between the purchase behavior of customers and the lifestyle segment of the neighborhood in which they live. The company markets a customized message to each lifestyle segment in the primary trade area. The message is tailored to reflect the historic product purchases in each segment and is the basis of the customer behavior profile.

(D) This 3-D map is a synthesis of customer spending for one retail site. The customer data base (with customer spending) is "geocoded." The number of customers who live in each grid cell is calculated and their total dollar purchases aggregated or summed. The result is a polygonal grid with a count of customers and the total dollars spent at the store/site/location.

Source: © ESRI, Tele Atlas, HandsOn-BI. Used by permission. All rights reserved.

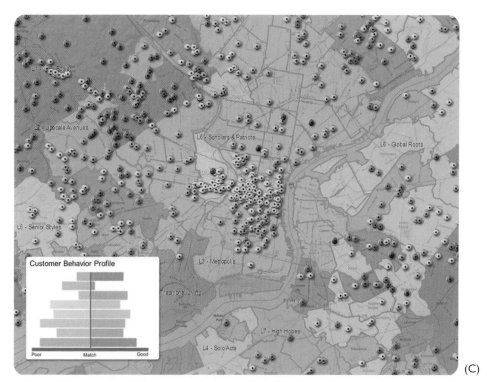

(C)

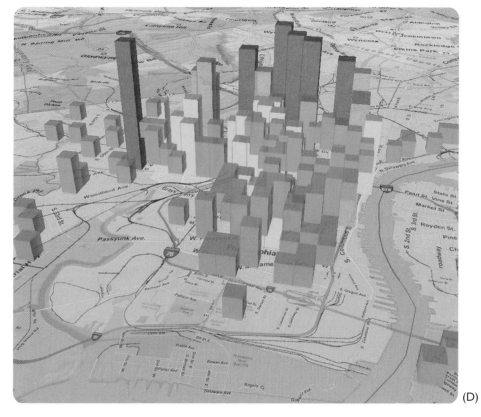

(D)

In the "Cases " section of the MapInfo Web site (www.mapinfo.com), take a look at the retail case studies.

▶ Autodesk (**http://usa.autodesk.com**).
▶ Caliper Corporation (**www.caliper.com**).
▶ Claritas (**www.claritas.com**).
▶ ESRI (Environmental Systems Research Institute) (**www.esri.com**).
▶ geoVue (**www.geovue.com**).

> ▶ MPSI Systems (**www.mpsisys.com**).
> ▶ Pitney Bowes MapInfo (**www.mapinfo.com**).
> ▶ SRC (**www.demographicsnow.com**).
> ▶ TeleAtlas (**www.teleatlas.com**).
> ▶ Tetrad Computer Applications (**www.tetrad.com**).

At our Web site (**www.pearsonhighered.com/berman**), we provide links to the descriptions of the GIS software for all of these firms. Many of the companies have free demonstrations at their sites.

Do you like *colorful* trading-area maps? Enter SRC's site (**www. demographicsnow.com**) and click "View Sample Reports & Maps" on the left toolbar.

GIS software can be applied in various ways. A chain retailer could learn which of its stores have trading areas containing households with a median annual income of more than $50,000. That firm could derive the sales potential of proposed new store locations and those stores' potential effect on sales at existing branches. It could use GIS software to determine the demographics of customers at its best locations and set up a computer model to find the potential locations with the most desirable attributes. A retailer could even use the software to pinpoint its geographic areas of strength and weakness.

These two examples show how retailers benefit from GIS software:

▶ Walgreens uses its GIS software to "marry map information, such as locations of streets, bridges, parks, and public transportation, with proprietary business data, such as market share, demographics, and household income." At Walgreens, "GIS data analysis guides decision making in a number of operational areas, from real-estate (choosing optimum sites for new stores) to human resources (gauging the sales impact of relocating a pharmacist with a loyal customer following)." Walgreens relies on software from ESRI, which enables the chain to "analyze data in a highly local fashion."[5]

▶ Ace Hardware has relied on GIS software for several years. Recently, it enhanced its Web site by introducing an interactive store-locator application from GSI Commerce Interactive and integrating geolocation technology to the store-locator tool. This technology, from Digital Element, "analyzes the numerical Internet Protocol address on the user's computer. After identifying the person's city location, it targets them with local information, including the number of retail stores within a certain radius, store news, promotions featured in weekly circulars, and events. It even provides the user with a Google map that highlights the closest Ace store."[6]

TECHNOLOGY IN RETAILING | Using GIS to Enhance Retail Decisions

At one time, retailers had to rely on ZIP code-based geographic mapping. Although ZIP codes could be easily obtained from consumers, retailers were unable to determine whether two customers lived one block or three miles from one another. And ZIP code-based data could not be used to calculate the number of households with certain annual income levels that lived within two miles of a planned store location. Through geographic information system (GIS) software, retailers can draw or create a territory in digital format.

Although most detailed GIS maps are generated by government agencies, private service bureaus reorganize maps from multiple agencies in a more user-friendly manner. GIS mapping assigns latitude–longitude coordinates to each customer based upon his or her address.

The software is then able to develop demographic profiles of residents in a particular area (block, ZIP code, census tract, and county).

By understanding the demographics of a retailer's best customers, that retailer can undertake more intelligent store location decisions, more effectively target direct mail, better understand changes in a location's demographics, and revise its merchandise and service offerings based on customer preferences. Franchises and chains can also use this information to determine the optimal number of store units in a given market area and identify potentially profitable new sites.

Sources: Jane Moore, "Strengthening Growth Through Technology Applications," *Franchising World* (April 2007), pp. 37–39; and "Web Sites for Digital GIS Data," **http://www-sul.stanford.edu/depts/gis/web.html**.

The Size and Shape of Trading Areas

Each trading area has three parts: The **primary trading area** encompasses 50 to 80 percent of a store's customers. It is the area closest to the store and possesses the highest density of customers to population and the highest per capita sales. There is little overlap with other trading areas. The **secondary trading area** contains an additional 15 to 25 percent of a store's customers. It is located outside the primary area, and customers are more widely dispersed. The **fringe trading area** includes all the remaining customers, and they are the most widely dispersed. A store could have a primary trading area of 4 miles, a secondary trading area of 5 miles, and a fringe trading area of 10 miles. The fringe trading area typically includes some outshoppers who travel greater distances to patronize certain stores.

Figures 9-4, 9-5, and 9-6 show the makeup of trading areas and their segments. In reality, trading areas do not usually follow such circular patterns. They adjust to the physical environment. The size and shape of a trading area are influenced by store type, store size, the location of competitors, housing patterns, travel time and traffic barriers (such as toll bridges), and media availability. These factors are discussed next.

Two stores can have different trading areas even if they are in the same shopping district or shopping center. Situated in one shopping center could be a branch of an apparel chain with a distinctive image and people willing to travel up to 20 miles and a shoe store seen as average and people willing to travel up to 5 miles. When one store has a better assortment, promotes more, and/or creates a stronger image, it may then become a **destination store** and generate a trading area much larger than that of a competitor with a "me-too" appeal. That is why Dunkin' Donuts uses the slogan "America Runs on Dunkin'."

Visit this site to see the complexity of factors in site selection (**www.conway.com/cheklist**).

FIGURE 9-4

The Segments of a Trading Area

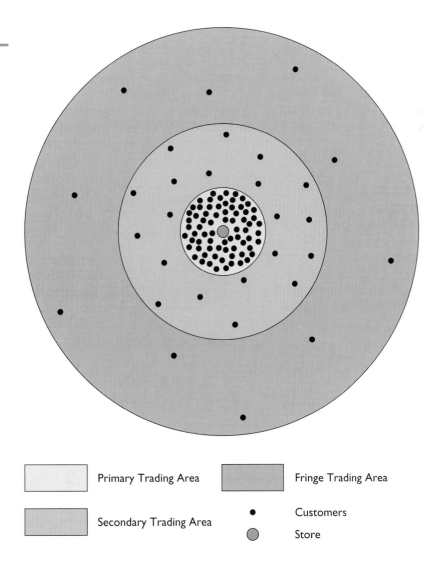

	Primary Trading Area		Fringe Trading Area
	Secondary Trading Area	•	Customers
			Store

FIGURE 9-5

Delineating Trading-Area Segments

This GIS map clearly depicts primary, secondary, and fringe trading areas for a store. However, the shapes are rarely so concentric.

Source: Reprinted by permission of ESRI and GDT.

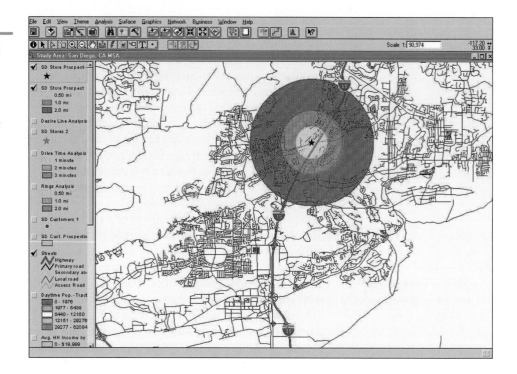

A **parasite store** does not create its own traffic and has no real trading area of its own. This store depends on people who are drawn to the location for other reasons. A magazine stand in a hotel lobby and a snack bar in a shopping center are parasites. While they are there, customers patronize these shops.

The extent of a store's or center's trading area is affected by its own size. As a store or center gets larger, its trading area usually increases, because store or center size generally reflects the assortment of goods and services. Yet, trading areas do not grow proportionately with store or center size. As a rule, supermarket trading areas are bigger than those of convenience stores. Supermarkets have a better product selection, and convenience stores

FIGURE 9-6

Prime Outlets, Grand Prairie, Texas: Outlining Its Trading Areas

In doing research for its new outlet shopping center in Grand Prairie, Texas (opening in 2010), Prime Outlets did a thorough job of identifying the population characteristics for households within a 60-mile radius of the outlet center.

Source: Reprinted by permission of Prime Retail.

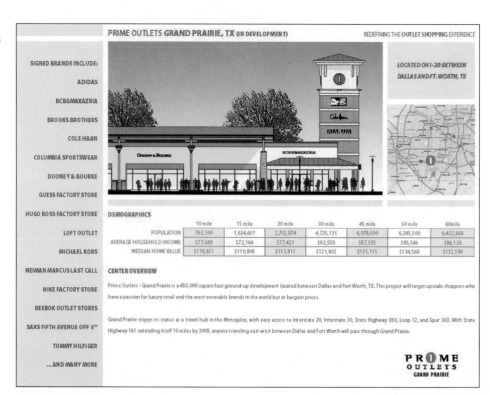

FIGURE 9-7

Le P'tit Paris: A Neighborhood Draw

Many retailers, such as Florida's Le P'tit Paris—a French restaurant/café, are dependent on the visibility of their locations, the pedestrian traffic, and the attractiveness of their decors. For Le P'tit, outdoor dining is quite appealing during good weather.

Source: Reprinted by permission.

appeal to the need for fill-in merchandise. In a regional shopping center, department stores typically have the largest trading areas, followed by apparel stores; gift stores have comparatively small trading areas. See Figure 9-7.

Whenever potential shoppers are situated between two competing stores, the trading area is often reduced for each store. The size of each store's trading area normally increases as the distance between stores grows (target markets do not then overlap as much). On the other hand, when stores are situated very near one another, the size of each store's trading area does not necessarily shrink. This store grouping may actually increase the trading area for each store if more consumers are attracted to the location due to the variety of goods and services. Yet, each store's market penetration (its percentage of sales in the trading area) may be low with such competition. Also, the entry of a new store may change the shape or create gaps in the trading areas of existing stores.

In many urban communities, people are clustered in multi-unit housing near the center of commerce. With such population density, it is worthwhile for a retailer to be quite close to consumers; trading areas tend to be small because there are several shopping districts in close proximity to one another, particularly for the most densely populated cities. In many suburbs, people live in single-unit housing—which is more geographically spread out. To produce satisfactory sales volume there, a retailer needs to attract shoppers from a greater distance.

The influence of travel or driving time on a trading area may not be clear from the population's geographic distribution. Physical barriers (toll bridges, poor roads, railroad tracks, one-way streets) usually reduce trading areas' size and contribute to their odd shapes. Economic barriers, such as different sales taxes in two towns, also affect the size and shape of trading areas.

In a community where a newspaper or other local media are available, a retailer could afford to advertise and enlarge its trading area. If local media are not available, the retailer would have to weigh the costs of advertising in countywide or regional media against the possibilities of a bigger trading area.

Delineating the Trading Area of an Existing Store

The size, shape, and characteristics of the trading area for an existing store—or shopping district or shopping center—can usually be delineated quite accurately. Store records (secondary data) or a special research study (primary data) can measure the trading area. And many firms offer computer-generated maps that can be tailored to individual retailers' needs.

Store records can reveal customer addresses. For credit customers, the data can be obtained from a retailer's billing department; for cash customers, addresses can be acquired by analyzing deliveries, cash sales slips, store contests (sweepstakes), and checks. In both instances, the task is relatively inexpensive and quick because the data were originally collected for other purposes and are readily available.

Because many big retailers have computerized credit card systems, they can delineate primary, secondary, and fringe trading areas in terms of the:

▶ Frequency with which people from various geographic locales shop at a particular store.
▶ Average dollar purchases at a store by people from given geographic locales.
▶ Concentration of a store's credit card holders from given geographic locales.

Although it is easy to get data on credit card customers, the analysis may be invalid if cash customers are not also studied. Credit use may vary among shoppers from different locales, especially if consumer characteristics in the locales are dissimilar. A firm reduces this problem if both cash and credit customers are studied.

MetroCount (**www. metrocount.com**) offers software to provide vehicular traffic counts. Click on "Products."

A retailer can also collect primary data to determine trading-area size. It can record the license plate numbers of cars parked near a store, find the general addresses of those vehicle owners by contacting the state motor vehicle office, and then note them on a map. Typically, only the ZIP code and street of residence are provided to protect people's privacy. When using license plate analysis, nondrivers and passengers—customers who walk to a store, use mass transit, or are driven by others—should not be omitted. To collect data on these customers, questions must often be asked (survey).

Visit this site (**www.claritas. com/MyBestSegments/ Default.jsp**) to study your area's lifestyles and purchasing preferences. Click on "You Are Where You Live."

If a retailer desires more demographic and lifestyle information about consumers in particular areas, it can buy the data. PRIZM NE is Claritas's system for identifying communities by lifestyle clusters. It identifies 66 neighborhood types, including "Gray Power," "Urban Achievers," and "Suburban Sprawl." This system was originally based on ZIP codes; it now also incorporates census tracts, block groups and enumeration districts, phone exchanges, and postal routes. Online PRIZM NE reports can be downloaded for as little as a few hundred dollars; costs are higher if reports are tailored to the individual retailer.

No matter how a trading area is delineated, a time bias may exist. A downtown business district is patronized by different customers during the week (those who work there) than on weekends (those who travel there to shop). Special events may attract people from great distances for only a brief time. Thus, an accurate estimate of a store's trading area requires complete and continuous investigation.

After delineating a trading area, the retailer should map people's locations and densities—either manually or with GIS software. In the manual method, a paper map of the area around a store is used. Different color dots or pins are placed on this map to represent *population* locations and densities, incomes, and other factors. *Customer* locations and densities are then indicated; primary, secondary, and fringe trading areas are denoted by ZIP code. Customers can be lured by promotions aimed at particular ZIP codes. With GIS software, vital customer data (such as purchase frequencies and amounts) are combined with other information sources (such as census data) to yield computer-generated digitized maps depicting primary, secondary, and fringe trading areas.

Delineating the Trading Area of a New Store

A new store opening in an established trading area can use the methods just cited. The discussion in this section refers to a trading area with less-defined shopping and traffic patterns. Such an area must normally be evaluated in terms of opportunities rather than current patronage and traffic (pedestrian and vehicular) patterns. Accordingly, additional tools must be utilized.

Trend analysis—projecting the future based on the past—can be employed by examining government and other data for predictions about population location, auto registrations, new housing starts, mass transportation, highways, zoning, and so on. Through consumer surveys, information can be gathered about the time and distance people would be willing to travel to various possible retail locations, the factors attracting people to a new store, the addresses of those most apt to visit a new store, and other topics. Either technique may be a basis for delineating alternate new store trading areas.

Three computerized trading-area analysis models are available for assessing new store locations:

▶ An **analog model** is the simplest and most popular trading-area analysis model. Potential sales for a new store are estimated on the basis of revenues for similar stores in existing areas, the competition at a prospective location, the new store's expected market share at that location, and the size and density of the location's primary trading area.

▶ A **regression model** uses a series of mathematical equations showing the association between potential store sales and several independent variables at each location, such as population size, average income, the number of households, nearby competitors, transportation barriers, and traffic patterns.

▶ A **gravity model** is based on the premise that people are drawn to stores that are closer and more attractive than competitors' stores. The distance between consumers and competitors, the distance between consumers and a given site, and store image are included in this model.

Computerized trading-area models offer several benefits to retailers: They operate in an objective and systematic way. They offer insights as to how each locational attribute should be weighted. They are useful in screening a large number of locations. They can assess management performance by comparing forecasts with results.

More specific methods for delineating new trading areas are described next.[7]

REILLY'S LAW

The traditional means of trading-area delineation is **Reilly's law of retail gravitation**.[8] It establishes a point of indifference between two cities or communities, so the trading area of each can be determined. The **point of indifference** is the geographic breaking point between two cities (communities) at which consumers are indifferent to shopping at either. According to Reilly's law, more consumers go to the larger city or community because there are more stores; the assortment makes travel time worthwhile. Reilly's law rests on these assumptions: Two competing areas are equally accessible from a major road, and retailers in the two areas are equally effective. Other factors (such as population dispersion) are held constant or ignored.

The law may be expressed algebraically as:[9]

$$D_{ab} = \frac{d}{1 + \sqrt{P_b/P_a}}$$

where

D_{ab} = Limit of city (community) A's trading area, measured in miles along the road to city (community) B

d = Distance in miles along a major roadway between cities (communities) A and B

P_a = Population of city (community) A

P_b = Population of city (community) B

A city with a population of 90,000 (A) would draw people from three times the distance as a city with 10,000 (B). If the cities are 20 miles apart, the point of indifference for the larger city is 15 miles, and for the smaller city, it is 5 miles:

$$D_{ab} = \frac{20}{1 + \sqrt{10,000/90,000}} = 15 \text{ miles}$$

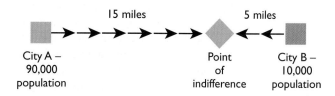

Reilly's law is an important contribution to trading-area analysis because of its ease of calculation. It is most useful when other data are not available or when compiling other data is costly. Nonetheless, Reilly's law has three limitations: (1) Distance is only measured by major thoroughfares; some people will travel shorter distances along cross streets. (2) Travel time does not necessarily reflect the distance traveled. Many people are more concerned about time than distance. (3) Actual distance may not correspond with the perceptions of distance. A store with few services and crowded aisles is apt to be a greater perceived distance from the person than a similarly located store with a more pleasant atmosphere.

HUFF'S LAW

Huff's law of shopper attraction delineates trading areas on the basis of the product assortment (of the items desired by the consumer) carried at various shopping locations, travel times from the shopper's home to alternative locations, and the sensitivity of the kind of shopping to travel time. Assortment is rated by the total square feet of selling space a retailer expects all firms in a shopping area to allot to a product category. Sensitivity to the kind of shopping entails the trip's purpose (restocking versus shopping) and the type of good/service sought (such as clothing versus groceries).[10]

Huff's law is expressed as:

$$P_{ij} = \frac{\dfrac{S_j}{(T_{ij})^\lambda}}{\displaystyle\sum_{j}^{n} \dfrac{S_j}{(T_{ij})^\lambda}}$$

where

P_{ij} = Probability of a consumer's traveling from home i to shopping location j
S_j = Square footage of selling space in shopping location j expected to be devoted to a particular product category
T_{ij} = Travel time from consumer's home i to shopping location j
λ = Parameter used to estimate the effect of travel time on different kinds of shopping trips
n = Number of different shopping locations

λ must be determined through research or by a computer program.

Assume a leased department operator studies three possible locations with 200, 300, and 500 total square feet of store space allocated to men's cologne (by all retailers in the areas). A group of potential customers lives 7 minutes from the first location, 10 minutes from the second, and 15 minutes from the third. The operator estimates the effect of travel time to be 2. Therefore, the probability of consumers' shopping is 43.9 percent for Location 1, 32.2 percent for Location 2, and 23.9 percent for Location 3:

$$P_{i1} = \frac{(200)/(7)^2}{(200)/(7)^2 + (300)/(10)^2 + (500)/(15)^2} = 43.9\%$$

$$P_{i2} = \frac{(300)/(10)^2}{(200)/(7)^2 + (300)/(10)^2 + (500)/(15)^2} = 32.2\%$$

$$P_{i3} = \frac{(500)/(15)^2}{(200)/(7)^2 + (300)/(10)^2 + (500)/(15)^2} = 23.9\%$$

If 200 men live 7 minutes from Location 1, about 88 of them will shop there.

These points should be considered in using Huff's law:

▶ To determine Location 1's trading area, similar computations would be made for people living at a driving time of 10, 15, 20 minutes, and so on. The number of people at each distance who would shop there are then summed. Thus, stores in Location 1 could estimate their total market, the trading-area size, and the primary, secondary, and fringe areas for a product category.

▶ If new retail facilities in a product category are added to a locale, the percentage of people living at every travel time from that location who would shop there goes up.

▶ The probability of people shopping at a location depends on the effect of travel time. If a product is important, such as dress watches, consumers are less travel sensitive. A λ of 1 leads to these figures: Location 1, 31.1 percent; Location 2, 32.6 percent; and Location 3, 36.3 percent (based on the space in the cologne example). Location 3 would be popular for the watches due to its assortment.

▶ All the variables are rather hard to calculate; for mapping purposes, travel time must be converted to miles. Travel time also depends on the transportation form used.

▶ Since people buy different items on different shopping trips, the trading area varies by trip.

Today, the Huff model is incorporated in such GIS software as ESRI's ArcGIS Business Analyst.

Learn more about the current use of the Huff model (**www.esri.com/library/whitepapers/pdfs/calibrating-huff-model.pdf**).

OTHER TRADING-AREA RESEARCH

Over the years, many researchers have examined trading-area size in a variety of settings. They have introduced additional factors and advanced statistical techniques to explain the consumer's choice of shopping location.

In his model, Gautschi added to Huff's analysis by including shopping-center descriptors and transportation conditions. Weisbrod, Parcells, and Kern studied shopping center appeal on the basis of expected population changes, store characteristics, and the transportation network. LeBlang demonstrated that consumer lifestyles could be used to predict sales at new department store locations. Albaladejo-Pina and Aranda-Gallego looked at the effects of competition among stores in different sections of a trading area. Bell, Ho, and Tang devised a model with fixed and variable store choice factors. Rogers examined the role of human decision making versus computer-based models in site choice. Smith and Hay reviewed the role of competition in trading areas. ReVelle, Murray, and Serra examined the impact of a firm's reducing the number of facilities in an area. Wood and Browne focused on the specifics of convenience store location planning. Diep and Sweeney studied shopping trip value.[11]

Characteristics of Trading Areas

PCensus with MapInfo (**www.tetrad.com/industry/franchising.html**) is a useful tool for scrutinizing potential franchise locations.

After the size and shape of alternative trading areas are determined, the characteristics of those areas are studied. Of special interest are the attributes of residents and how well they match the firm's definition of its target market. An auto repair franchisee may compare opportunities in several locales by reviewing the number of car registrations; a hearing aid retailer may evaluate the percentage of the population 60 years of age or older; and a bookstore retailer may be concerned with residents' education level.

Among the trading-area factors that should be studied by most retailers are the population size and characteristics, availability of labor, closeness to sources of supply, promotion facilities, economic base, competition, availability of locations, and regulations. The **economic base** is an area's industrial and commercial structure—the companies and industries that residents depend on to earn a living. The dominant industry (company) in an area is important because its drastic decline may have adverse effects on a large segment of residents. An area with a diverse economic base, where residents work for a variety of nonrelated industries, is more secure than an area with one major industry. Table 9-1 summarizes a number of factors to consider in evaluating retail trading areas.

Much of the data needed to describe an area can be obtained from the U.S. Bureau of the Census, the *American Community Survey, Editor & Publisher Market Guide, Survey of Buying Power, Rand McNally Commercial Atlas & Marketing Guide, Standard Rate & Data Service,* regional planning boards, public utilities, chambers of commerce, local government offices, shopping-center owners, and renting agents. In addition, GIS software provides data on potential buying power in an area, the location of competitors, and highway access. Both demographic and lifestyle information may also be included in this software.

CAREERS IN RETAILING

Is Retail for Me? IT and E-Commerce—Part 2

There are many opportunities specifically related to E-commerce:

▶ *E-Commerce Director.* This person may come from a merchandising, marketing, or information technology (IT) background, but holds the top position over all Internet initiatives. The individual is responsible for the Internet retailing strategies, Web site content and appearance, Internet partnerships, effectiveness, and financial results of the E-tailing effort.

▶ *Web Site Designer/Art Director.* This is the top designer position responsible for the creative look and feel of the Web site environment. This individual will determine the use and layout of graphics, pictures, placement, and content of copywriting text, etc. She or he may have a graphic arts or advertising background, for example, rather than a technical background installing gifs, jpegs, etc.

▶ *Web Site Project Manager.* This is a technical position assigning work to programming staff (internal and/or contract staff), ensuring that deadlines, hardware, and programming specifications are met.

Has typical IT project manager responsibilities, but all are related to E-commerce. Duties may include project budgeting and hiring staff or directing an outsourced programming service.

▶ *Top E-Merchant (Merchandise Manager).* This position is responsible for selecting the merchandise displayed on the Web and determining the inventory quantities needed for Internet sales. Decides prices, markdowns, and when to remove end-of-stock items from the Web site. May negotiate bulk sales of returns and closeouts with other retailers. May supervise a staff of merchants and/or inventory planners. This person is not responsible for the technical IT part of the Web site.

▶ *Fulfillment Manager.* This position is responsible for the pick, pack, and send operations for all customer Web orders. May also be responsible for the call center. May manage an internal processing staff or may direct an outsourced distribution center service provider.

Source: Reprinted by permission of the National Retail Federation.

Although the yardsticks in Table 9-1 are not equally important in all location decisions, each should be considered. The most important yardsticks should be "knockout" factors: If a location does not meet minimum standards on key measures, it should be immediately dropped from further consideration.

These are examples of desirable trading-area attributes, according to several retailers:

▶ When selecting new markets, AutoZone studies the number and age of the vehicles that residents are driving—in addition to demographics, the level of competition, and the cost of real-estate: "In reviewing the vehicle profile, we consider the number of vehicles that are seven years old and older, 'our kind of vehicles,' as these are generally no longer under the original manufacturers' warranties and require more maintenance and repair than younger vehicles."

▶ Abercrombie & Fitch, which places an emphasis on upscale teenage shoppers, looks for store space in already successful shopping centers. It usually seeks out "upscale malls with a minimum of four anchors or street locations because it would not get enough foot traffic in a lower-grade property."

▶ About 4,500 Dollar General stores serve communities with populations of less than 20,000. This lets it take advantage of its brand awareness, maximize operating efficiencies, and serve untapped markets: "We believe that our target customers prefer the convenience of a small, neighborhood store with a focused merchandise assortment at value prices."

▶ The Syms off-price apparel chain seeks locations near highways or thoroughfares in suburban areas populated by a least 1 million persons and readily accessible by car. In certain areas, with over 2 million people, Syms has more than one store.[12]

TABLE 9-1 Chief Factors to Consider in Evaluating Retail Trading Areas

Population Size and Characteristics

Total size and density	Total disposable income
Age distribution	Per-capita disposable income
Average educational level	Occupation distribution
Percentage of residents owning homes	Trends

Availability of Labor

Management

Management trainee

Clerical

Closeness to Sources of Supply

Delivery costs	Number of manufacturers and wholesalers
Timeliness	Availability and reliability of product lines

Promotion Facilities

Availability and frequency of media

Costs

Waste

Economic Base

Dominant industry	Freedom from economic and seasonal fluctuations
Extent of diversification	Availability of credit and financial facilities
Growth projections	

Competitive Situation

Number and size of existing competitors	Short-run and long-run outlook
Evaluation of competitor strengths/ weaknesses	Level of saturation

Availability of Store Locations

Number and type of locations	Zoning restrictions
Access to transportation	Costs
Owning versus leasing opportunities	

Regulations

Taxes	Minimum wages
Licensing	Zoning
Operations	

Several stages of the process for gathering data to analyze trading areas are shown in Figure 9-8, which includes not only the attributes of residents but also those of the competition. By studying these factors, a retailer sees how desirable an area is for its business.

We next discuss three elements in trading-area selection: population characteristics, economic base characteristics, and the nature of competition and the level of saturation.

Characteristics of the Population

Extensive knowledge about an area's population characteristics can be gained from secondary sources. They offer data about the population size, number of households, income distribution, education level, age distribution, and more. Because the *Census of Population* and other public sources are so valuable, we briefly describe them next.

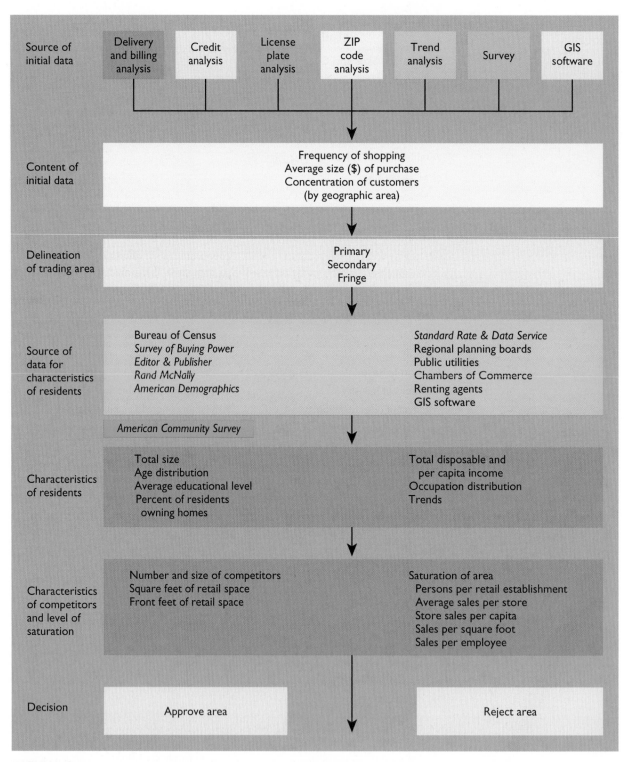

FIGURE 9-8

Analyzing Retail Trade Areas

Find out about the 2010 U.S. Census (www.census. gov/2010census).

CENSUS OF POPULATION

The **Census of Population** supplies a wide range of demographic data for all U.S. cities and surrounding vicinities. Data are organized on a geographic basis, starting with blocks and continuing to census tracts, cities, counties, states, and regions. There are less data for blocks and census tracts than for larger units due to privacy issues. The major advantage of census data is the information on small geographic units. Once trading-area boundaries are outlined, a firm can look at data for each of the geographic units in that area and study aggregate demographics. There are also data categories that are especially helpful for retailers interested in segmenting the market—including racial and ethnic data, small-area income data, and commuting patterns. Census data are available on DVDs and CDs, on computer tapes, and online.

The U.S. Census Bureau's TIGER computerized data base contains extremely detailed physical breakdowns of areas in the United States. The data base has digital descriptions of geographic areas (area boundaries and codes, latitude and longitude coordinates, and address ranges). Because TIGER data must be used in conjunction with population and other data, GIS software is necessary. As noted earlier in this chapter, many private firms have devised location analysis programs, based in large part on TIGER. These firms also usually project data to the present year and into the future.

The major drawbacks of the *Census of Population* are that it is undertaken only once every 10 years and that all data are not immediately available when collected. The last set of published U.S. census data is still the 2000 *Census of Population*. Data from the 2010 *Census of Population* will be released in phases from 2011 through 2013. Thus, census material can be out-of-date and inaccurate—particularly several years after collection. Other sources, such as municipal building departments or utilities, state government offices, other Census reports (such as the *Current Population Survey*), and computerized projections by private firms such as Dun & Bradstreet must be used to update *Census of Population* data.

The value of the *Census of Population's* actual 2000 census tract data can be shown by an illustration of Long Beach, New York, which is 30 miles east of New York City on Long Island's south shore. Long Beach encompasses six census tracts: 4164, 4165, 4166, 4167.01, 4167.02, and 4168. See Figure 9-9. Although tract 4163 is contiguous with Long Beach, it represents another community. Table 9-2 shows various population statistics for each Long Beach census tract. Resident characteristics in each tract differ; thus, a retailer might choose to locate in one or more tracts but not in others.

Suppose a bookstore chain wants to evaluate two potential trading areas. Because of the demographic differences of tract 4165 from the other tracts, the chain decides not to include this tract in its analysis. Trading area A corresponds with tracts 4164 and 4166. Area B is similar to tracts 4167.01, 4167.02, and 4168. Population data for these areas (extracted from Table 9-2) are presented in Table 9-3. Area A differs from Area B, despite their proximity and similar physical size:

▶ The population in Area B is 13 percent larger.

▶ Although the population in both areas rose from 1990 to 2000, Area B grew very little.

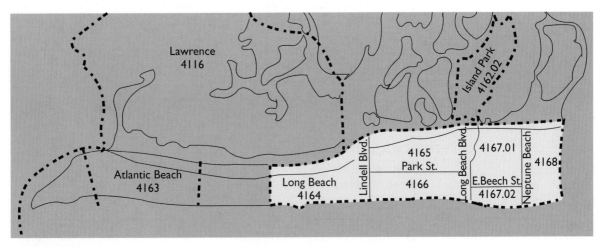

FIGURE 9-9

The Census Tracts of Long Beach, New York

TABLE 9-2   Selected Characteristics of Long Beach, New York, Residents by Census Tract, 1990 and 2000[a]

| | Tract Number | | | | | |
	4164	4165	4166	4167.01	4167.02	4168
Total Population						
1990	7,082	5,694	5,613	4,162	4,479	6,480
1990 population 25 and older	5,315	3,331	4,306	3,003	3,620	5,074
2000	7,406	6,231	6,326	4,471	4,443	6,585
2000 population 25 and older	5,772	4,073	4,904	3,163	3,739	5,173
Number of Households						
1990	2,735	1,812	2,219	1,465	2,295	3,066
2000	3,138	2,002	2,592	1,601	2,440	3,165
Education						
College graduates (% of population 25 and older), 2000	38.4	18.6	44.9	35.8	35.9	43.7
Income						
Median household income, 2000 (estimate)	$59,188	$46,261	$63,716	$68,680	$52,334	$64,348
Selected Occupations						
Managerial, professional, and related occupations (% of employed persons 16 and older), 2000	42.6	25.2	49.1	45.4	40.9	47.6

[a]According to the New York State Data Center, **www.nylovesbiz.com/nysdc/popandhous/ESTIMATE.asp** (December 24, 2008) from 2000 to mid-2007, the total population in Long Beach declined by 2.5 percent.

Sources: Census of Population (Washington, DC: U.S. Bureau of the Census, 2000); and authors' computations.

▶ In Area A, a slightly greater percentage of residents aged 25 and older have college degrees.
▶ The annual median income and the proportion of workers who are managers or professionals are roughly equal in Areas A and B.

TABLE 9-3   Selected Population Statistics for Long Beach Trading Areas A and B

	Area A (Tracts 4164 and 4166)	Area B (Tracts 4167.01, 4167.02, and 4168)
Total population, 2000	13,732	15,499
Population change, 1990–2000 (%)	+8.2	+2.5
College graduates, 25 and older, 2000 (%)	41.4	39.2
Median household income, 2000	$61,236	$61,242
Managerial and professional specialty occupations (% of employed persons 16 and older), 2000	45.3	45.0

The bookstore chain would have a tough time selecting between the areas because they are so similar. Thus, the chain might also consider the location of the sites available in Area A and Area B, relative to the locations of its existing stores, before making a final decision.

OTHER PUBLIC SOURCES

There are many other useful, easily accessible public sources for current population information, in addition to the *Census of Population*—especially on a city or county basis. These sources typically update their data annually. They also provide some data not available from the *Census of Population:* total annual retail sales by area, annual retail sales for specific product categories, and population projections. The biggest disadvantage of these sources is their use of geographic territories that are often much larger than a store's trading area and that cannot be broken down easily.

One rather new national source of annual population data is the *American Community Survey,* which provides "demographic, social, economic, and housing data for over 800 geographical areas." The Survey has an excellent, user-friendly Web site (**www.census.gov/acs/www**). On the state and local level, public data sources include planning commissions, research centers at public universities, county offices, and many other institutions.

Let us demonstrate the usefulness of public sources through the following example. Note: We obtained all of the information for our example on the Internet—free!

Suppose a prospective new car dealer investigates three counties near Chicago: DuPage, Kane, and Lake. The dealer decides to focus on one source of information that is available in print and online versions: *Northern Illinois Market Facts* (prepared annually by the Regional Development Institute, Northern Illinois University, in cooperation with the Illinois Department of Commerce & Economic Opportunity). Table 9-4 lists selected population and retail sales data for these counties.

What can the car dealer learn? DuPage is by far the largest county; Kane is the smallest. However, the population growth rate from 2000 to 2007 was much higher for Kane. Lake has the highest median household income; and Lake has the most adult college graduates. On a per capita basis, DuPage residents account for 57 percent more

---

ETHICS IN RETAILING

Is Wal-Mart Really a Bad Neighbor for Cities?

There have been many anecdotal reports indicating that Wal-Mart (**www.walmart.com**) has been largely responsible for turning "main street" into "ghost towns" and for the destruction of small local businesses. One such report noted that Wal-Mart's expansion into Iowa was solely responsible for the closings of 555 grocery stores, 298 hardware stores, 293 building suppliers, 161 variety shops, 158 women's stores, and 116 pharmacies.

However, after recently completing a major independent research study, two West Virginia University professors found that Wal-Mart had no statistically significant impact on small-business activity in the United States. These authors concluded that the negative reports are misleading for the following reasons:

▶ Many of the studies just examined the number of small stores in counties with Wal-Mart stores versus those counties without a Wal-Mart presence.

▶ Many reports count such large-store formats as Kmart (**www.kmart.com**), Target (**www.target.com**), and Home Depot (**www.homedepot.com**) as small businesses.

▶ Even though a new Wal-Mart might lead to the failure of a hardware store or an antique store, another new retailer might then open in the hardware store's location.

The authors found that, since 1985, the number of small U.S. retail establishments has been practically unchanged. States with a larger number of Wal-Mart stores also have more small establishments per capita than states with relatively fewer Wal-Mart stores.

Source: Andrea M. Dean and Russell S. Sobel, "Has Wal-Mart Buried Mom and Pop?" *Regulation* (Spring 2008), pp. 38–45.

TABLE 9-4   Selected Data Relating to Three Illinois Counties (2007, unless otherwise specified)

	County		
	DuPage	Kane	Lake
Total population	932,670	493,735	713,362
Annual population growth, 2000–2007	0.44%	2.90%	1.46%
Number of households	351,469	170,268	251,891
Number of people 20 and over	672,455	337,221	493,647
Median household income	$67,066	$65,752	$70,368
Households with $50,000 or more in annual income	65.6%	63.9%	66.3%
College graduates, 25 and older (%)	43.6%	30.5%	40.3%
Total retail sales	$18,150,690,087	$6,108,489,420	$11,305,360,098
Annual per-capita retail sales	$19,461	$12,372	$15,848
Employment in retail trade	124,250	39,050	75,100
Total Retail Sales by Category			
Apparel	$ 744,178,294	$ 335,966,918	$ 395,687,603
Automotive and gas stations	4,319,864,241	1,093,419,606	2,509,789,942
Eating, drinking, and hotel	1,579,110,038	568,089,516	972,260,968
Food (grocery)	1,742,466,248	775,778,156	1,187,062,810
General merchandise	1,869,521,079	678,042,326	1,220,978,891
Home improvement and hardware	925,685,194	476,462,175	734,848,406
Household goods	1,270,548,306	317,641,450	938,344,888
Pharmaceutical	2,541,096,612	806,320,603	1,763,636,175
Other	3,158,220,075	1,056,768,670	1,582,750,414
Percentage of Total Retail Sales by Category			
Apparel	4.1%	5.5%	3.5%
Automotive and gas stations	23.8	17.9	22.2
Eating, drinking, and hotel	8.7	9.3	8.6
Food (grocery)	9.6	12.7	10.5
General merchandise	10.3	11.1	10.8
Home improvement and hardware	5.1	7.8	6.5
Household goods	7.0	5.2	8.3
Pharmaceutical	14.0	13.2	15.6
Other	17.4	17.3	14.0

Source: Computed by the authors from *Northern Illinois Market Facts 2008* (DeKalb, IL: Regional Development Institute, Northern Illinois University).

retail sales than Kane residents and 23 percent more than Lake residents. Lake and DuPage residents both allocate more than one-fifth of their retail spending to autos and recreational vehicles, while Kane residents account for the highest percentage of their retail spending on groceries and home improvement stores.

A Cadillac dealer using these data might select DuPage or Lake, and a Ford dealer might select Kane. But because the data are broad in nature, several subsections of Kane may actually be superior choices to subsections in DuPage or Lake for the Cadillac dealer. The competition in each area also must be noted.

The location decision for a fast-food franchise usually requires less data than for a bookstore or an auto dealer. Fast-food franchisors often seek communities with many people living or working within a three- or four-mile radius of their stores. However, bookstore owners and auto dealers cannot locate merely on the basis of population density. They must consider a more complex set of population factors.

Economic Base Characteristics

The economic base reflects a community's commercial and industrial infrastructure and residents' sources of income. A firm seeking stability normally prefers an area with a diversified economic base (a large number of nonrelated industries) to one with an economic base keyed to a single major industry. The latter area is more affected by a strike, declining demand for an industry, and cyclical fluctuations.

In assessing a trading area's economic base, a retailer should investigate the percentage of the labor force in each industry, transportation, banking facilities, the impact of economic fluctuations, and the future of individual industries (firms). Data can be obtained from such sources as Easy Analytic Software, *Editor & Publisher Market Guide,* regional planning commissions, industrial development organizations, and chambers of commerce.

Easy Analytic Software (**www.easidemographics.com**) provides a wide range of inexpensive economic reports. It also produces several "Census 2000 Reports" that can be downloaded free (after a simple sign-in procedure), including Quick Reports, Quick Tables, Quick Maps, Site Analysis, Rank Analysis, and Profile Analysis.

Editor & Publisher Market Guide offers annual economic base data for cities, including employment sources, transportation networks, financial institutions, auto registrations, newspaper circulation, and shopping centers. It also has data on population size and total households. *Editor & Publisher Market Guide* data cover broad geographic areas. The bookstore chain noted earlier would find the information on shopping centers to be helpful. The auto dealer would find the information on the transportation network, the availability of financial institutions, and the number of passenger cars to be useful. *Editor & Publisher Market Guide* is best used to supplement other sources.

The Nature of Competition and the Level of Saturation

A trading area may have residents who match the characteristics of the desired market and a strong economic base, yet still be a poor location for a new store if competition is too intense. A locale with a small population and a narrow economic base may be a good location if competition is minimal.

When examining competition, these factors should be analyzed: the number of existing stores, the size distribution of existing stores, the rate of new store openings, the strengths and weaknesses of all stores, short-run and long-run trends, and the level of saturation.

Over the past two decades, many U.S. retailers have expanded into foreign markets due to the lower level of competition there. That is why Wal-Mart has entered into Mexico, El Salvador, Argentina, Brazil, and China; Lowe's is now in Mexico, Vietnam, and China; and Baskin-Robbins has stores in Russia, Malaysia, Greece, and Thailand. Yet, in the future, even these locales may become oversaturated due to all the new stores. Furthermore, although the Northeast population in the United States has been declining relative to the Southeast and the Southwest—and is often considered to be too saturated with stores—its high population density (the number of persons per square mile) is crucial for retailers. In New Jersey, there are 1,170 people per square mile; in Massachusetts, 825; in Florida, 340; in Louisiana, 100; in Arizona, 57; and in Utah, 32.

An **understored trading area** has too few stores selling a specific good or service to satisfy the needs of its population. An **overstored trading area** has so many stores selling a specific good or service that some retailers cannot earn an adequate profit. A **saturated trading area** has the proper amount of stores to satisfy the needs of its population for a specific good or service, and to enable retailers to prosper.

Despite the large number of areas in the United States that are overstored, there still remain plentiful opportunities in understored communities. For example, CVS, the large drugstore chain (with 7,000 stores, after acquiring California-based Longs Drugs in late 2008):

> looks for highly-visible locations in a high-traffic areas that are easily accessible
> and in trading areas of at least 18,000 people. We prefer sites that can support a
> freestanding store with drive-thru capability, between 1.5 to 2 acres, with park-
> ing for at least 80 vehicles. The U.S. retail pharmacy industry is expected to

more than double in the next few years. An aging population and the increased utilization of prescription drugs is fueling the demand for more pharmacy services. Several markets in the United States with high-growth population rates are relatively understored and need more pharmacies. We will meet this demand by opening new stores in these high-growth markets.[13]

MEASURING TRADING-AREA SATURATION

Because any trading area can support only a given number of stores or square feet of selling space per goods/service category, these ratios can help to quantify retail store saturation:

▶ Number of persons per retail establishment.
▶ Average sales per retail store.
▶ Average sales per retail store category.
▶ Average store sales per capita or household.
▶ Average sales per square foot of selling area.
▶ Average sales per employee.

The saturation level in a trading area can be measured against a goal or compared with other trading areas. An auto accessory chain might find that its current trading area is saturated by computing the ratio of residents to auto accessory stores. On the basis of this calculation, the owner could then decide to expand into a nearby locale with a lower ratio rather than to add another store in its present trading area.

Data for saturation ratios can be obtained from a retailer's records on its performance, city and state records, phone directories, consumer surveys, economic census data, *Editor & Publisher Market Guide, County Business Patterns,* trade publications, and other sources. Sales by product category, population size, and number of households per market area can be found with other national and state sources.

When investigating an area's saturation for a specific good or service, ratios must be interpreted carefully. Differences among areas are not always reliable indicators of saturation. For instance, car sales per capita are different for a suburban area than an urban area because suburbanites have a much greater need for cars. Each area's level of saturation should be evaluated against distinct standards—based on optimum per capita sales figures in that area.

In calculating saturation based on sales per square foot, a new or growing retailer must take its proposed store into account. If that store is not part of the calculation, the relative value of each trading area is distorted. Sales per square foot decline most if new outlets are added in small communities. The retailer should also consider if a new store will expand the total consumer market for a good or service category in a trading area or just increase its market share in that area without expanding the total market.

These are three examples of how retailers factor trading-area saturation into their decisions:

▶ Kroger knows "the supermarket industry is highly competitive, and generally characterized by high inventory turnover and narrow profit margins. The most significant competitive trend in the industry is the growth of low-priced retailers. In many locations, the company regularly engages with competitors in price competition, which sometimes adversely affects operating margins. Also, the chain competes with national, regional, and local supermarket chains, in addition to independent supermarkets, as well as with supercenters and other nontraditional grocers." Kroger deals with the situation by situating at locations that "are large enough to offer the high-margin specialty departments that customers desire and trading on the one-stop appeal of its stores with new departments and offerings.[14]

▶ Ralph Lauren's new Atlanta store in the Lenox Square shopping center is positioned as the chain's flagship store in the South. "This is by far our biggest store in the South; and in glamour, the level of sophistication, and product range, it rivals our stores in Milan or Tokyo," said Charles Fagan, executive vice-president. "Our New York store is the Northeast flagship, Chicago is the flagship of the middle of the country, and Beverly Hills is it for the West Coast. The new store reflects our commitment to Atlanta and this region—which is now a mix of everything from the most conservative banker to the trendiest people in the music industry. We no longer count on just the more traditional, classic items to be best-sellers." The store is also intended to attract customers from a wide trading area of surrounding Southern states.[15]

Look at the *Marketing Guidebook* sample (**www. tradedimensions.com/ tours/mg_samples.asp**) to see the saturation levels of supermarkets. Click "County Level Data."

▶ Supermarket chains buy annual data from Trade Dimensions (**www.tradedimensions. com**) that measure the level of saturation by U.S. city, including the number of supermarkets, overall supermarket sales, supermarket sales per capita, weekly sales per square foot, chain supermarkets versus independents, total supermarket space, the number of supermarket employees, and more.

Chapter **Summary**

1. *To demonstrate the importance of store location for a retailer and outline the process for choosing a store location.* The location choice is critical because of the complex decision making, the high costs, the lack of flexibility once a site is chosen, and the impact of a site on the strategy. A good location may let a retailer succeed even if its strategy mix is relatively mediocre.

    The selection of a store location includes (1) evaluating alternative trading areas, (2) determining the best type of location, (3) picking a general site, and (4) settling on a specific site. This chapter looks at Step 1. Chapter 10 details Steps 2, 3, and 4.

2. *To discuss the concept of a trading area and its related components.* A trading area is the geographical area from which customers are drawn. When shopping locales are nearby, they may have trading-area overlap.

    Many retailers utilize geographic information system (GIS) software to delineate and analyze trading areas. The software combines digitized mapping with key data to graphically depict trading areas. This lets retailers research alternative locations and display findings on computerized maps. Several vendors market GIS software, based on TIGER mapping by the U.S. government.

    Each trading area has primary, secondary, and fringe components. The farther people live from a shopping area, the less apt they are to travel there. The size and shape of a trading area depend on store type, store size, competitor locations, housing patterns, travel time and traffic barriers, and media availability. Destination stores have larger trading areas than parasites.

3. *To show how trading areas may be delineated for existing and new stores.* The size, shape, and characteristics of the trading area for an existing store or group of stores can be learned accurately—based on store records, contests, license plate numbers, surveys, and so on. Time biases must be considered in amassing data. Results should be mapped and customer densities noted.

    Potential trading areas for a new store must often be described in terms of opportunities, rather than current patronage and traffic. Trend analysis and consumer surveys may be used. Three computerized models are available for planning a new store location: analog, regression, and gravity. They offer several benefits.

    Two techniques for delineating new trading areas are Reilly's law, which relates the population size of different cities to the size of their trading areas; and Huff's law, which is based on each area's shopping assortment, the distance of people from various retail locales, and sensitivity to travel time.

4. *To examine three major factors in trading-area analysis: population characteristics, economic base characteristics, and competition and the level of saturation.* The best sources for population data are the *Census of Population* and other publicly available sources. Census data are detailed and specific, but become dated. Information from public sources such as the *American Community Survey* may be more current, but they report on broader geographic areas.

    An area's economic base reflects the community's commercial and industrial infrastructure, as well as residents' income sources. A retailer should look at the percentage of the labor force in each industry, the transportation network, banking facilities, the potential impact of economic fluctuations on the area, and the future of individual industries. Easy Analytic and *Editor & Publisher Market Guide* are good sources of data on the economic base.

    A trading area cannot be properly analyzed without studying the nature of competition and the level of saturation. An area may be understored (too few retailers), overstored (too many retailers), or saturated (the proper number of retailers). Saturation may be measured in terms of the number of persons per store, average sales per store, average store sales per capita or household, average sales per square foot of selling space, and average sales per employee.

Key Terms

trading area (p. 252)
trading-area overlap (p. 252)
geographic information system (GIS) (p. 253)
primary trading area (p. 257)
secondary trading area (p. 257)
fringe trading area (p. 257)
destination store (p. 257)

parasite store (p. 258)
analog model (p. 261)
regression model (p. 261)
gravity model (p. 261)
Reilly's law of retail gravitation (p. 261)
point of indifference (p. 261)

Huff's law of shopper attraction (p. 262)
economic base (p. 263)
Census of Population (p. 266)
understored trading area (p. 271)
overstored trading area (p. 271)
saturated trading area (p. 271)

Questions for Discussion

1. Comment on this statement: "A poor location may be such a liability that even superior retailers cannot overcome it." Is it always true? Give examples.

2. If a retailer has a new 10-year store lease, does this mean the next time it studies the characteristics of its trading area should be 5 years from now? Explain your answer.

3. What is trading-area overlap? Are there any advantages to a chain retailer's having some overlap among its various stores? Why or why not?

4. Describe three ways in which a camera store chain could use geographic information system (GIS) software in its trading-area analysis.

5. How could an off-campus store selling dormitory-style furniture near a college campus determine its primary, secondary, and fringe trading areas? Why should the store obtain this information?

6. How could a parasite store increase the size of its trading area?

7. Explain Reilly's law. What are its advantages and disadvantages?

8. Use Huff's law to compute the probability of consumers' traveling from their homes to each of three

shopping areas: Square footage of selling space—Location 1, 12,000; Location 2, 15,000; Location 3, 25,000. Travel time—to Location 1, 15 minutes; to Location 2, 21 minutes; to Location 3, 25 minutes. Effect of travel time on shopping trip—2. Explain your answer.

9. What are the major advantages and disadvantages of *Census of Population* data in delineating trading areas?

10. Look at the most recent online data from the American Community Survey (**www.census.gov/acs/www**) for the area in which your college is located. What retailing-related conclusions do you draw?

11. If a retail area is acknowledged to be "saturated," what does this signify for existing retailers? For prospective retailers considering this area?

12. How could a Web-based retailer determine the level of saturation for its product category? What should this retailer do to lessen the impact of the level of saturation it faces?

Note: At our Web site (**www.pearsonhighered.com/berman**), there are several math questions related to the material in this chapter so that you may review these concepts.

Web **Exercise**

Visit the Web site of Site Selection Online (**www.siteselection.com**). What could a retailer learn from *Site Selection Magazine*? What Web site feature do you like best? Why?

Note: Stop by our Web site (**www.pearsonhighered.com/berman**) to experience a number of highly interactive,

appealing Web exercises based on actual company demonstrations and sample materials related to retailing.

10 Site Selection

Shortly after World War II, William Rosenberg started Industrial Luncheon Services to sell donuts, sandwiches, and coffee to factory workers. He purchased 10 unused cab-and-chassis platforms from the New England Telephone Company and had each outfitted with stainless steel bodies and side flaps that could be lifted. Despite the popularity of the sandwiches, coffee and donuts were the real bestsellers. In 1948, Rosenberg opened his first store, Open Kettle, as an additional outlet for the sale of donuts.

In 1950, Rosenberg changed the Open Kettle name to Dunkin' Donuts (**www.dunkindonuts.com**) and began franchising. Allied Domecq PLC acquired the chain in 1990. The chain was recently sold to a group of private equity firms. Today, Dunkin' Donuts has more than 5,800 locations in the United States alone. It is the world's largest seller of donuts, bagels, and muffins. The company signed more than 1,000 new franchise agreements, which will result in several new store openings, during one recent five-year period.

Dunkin' Donuts has very specific location standards. Its standalone stores generally require a population of 15,000 or more within a three-minute drive and 25,000 within a five-minute drive, a median household income of more than $30,000, and a minimum average traffic count of 20,000 for 24 hours (based on 12 months of data). Dunkin' Donuts also has specific site requirements. These include a minimum of one parking spot for every three seats, easy access from all traffic directions (no more than two turns in or out of the store), high visibility from major vehicular roadways, and a 10-year lease with two 5-year renewal options.[1]

Source: Reprinted by permission of Susan Berry, Retail Image Consulting, Inc.

OVERVIEW

After a retailer investigates alternative trading areas (Step 1), it determines what type of location is desirable (Step 2), selects the general location (Step 3), and evaluates alternative specific store sites (Step 4). Steps 2, 3, and 4 are discussed in this chapter.

As an example, at Bed Bath & Beyond (BB&B), which has more than 800 stores,

Is there now a Bed Bath & Beyond near you (**www. bedbathandbeyond.com**)? Click on "Stores."

continued growth depends, in part, on our ability to open new stores and operate profitably. Our ability to open additional stores successfully will depend on a number of factors, including our identification and availability of suitable store locations; our success in negotiating leases on acceptable terms; our hiring and training of skilled store operating personnel, especially management; and our timely development of new stores, including the availability of construction materials and labor and the absence of significant construction and other delays in store openings based on weather or other events. Most of our stores are located in suburban areas of medium- and large-sized cities. These stores are situated in strip and power strip shopping centers, as well as in major off-price and conventional malls, and in freestanding buildings.[2]

Types of Locations

There are three different location types: isolated store, unplanned business district, and planned shopping center. Each has its own attributes as to the composition of competitors, parking, nearness to nonretail institutions (such as office buildings), and other factors. Step 2 in the location process is to determine which type of location to use.

The Isolated Store

An **isolated store** is a freestanding retail outlet located on either a highway or a street. There are no adjacent retailers with which this type of store shares traffic.

The advantages of this type of retail location are many:

▶ There is no competition in close proximity.
▶ Rental costs are relatively low.
▶ There is flexibility; no group rules must be followed in operations, and larger space may be obtained.
▶ Isolation is good for stores involved in one-stop or convenience shopping.
▶ Better road and traffic visibility is possible.
▶ Facilities can be adapted to individual specifications.
▶ Easy parking can be arranged.
▶ Cost reductions are possible, leading to lower prices.

There are also various disadvantages to this retail location type:

▶ Initial customers may be difficult to attract.
▶ Many people will not travel very far to get to one store on a continuous basis.
▶ Most people like variety in shopping.
▶ Advertising expenses may be high.
▶ Costs such as outside lighting, security, grounds maintenance, and trash collection are not shared.
▶ Other retailers and community zoning laws may restrict access to desirable locations.
▶ A store must often be built rather than rented.
▶ As a rule, unplanned business districts and planned shopping centers are much more popular among consumers; they generate most of retail sales.

Large-store formats (such as Wal-Mart supercenters and Costco membership clubs) and convenience-oriented retailers (such as 7-Eleven) are usually the retailers best suited to isolated locations because of the challenge of attracting a target market. A small specialty

FIGURE 10-1

At Starbucks, Isolated Locations Are a Key Part of the Mix

These days, Starbucks (**www.starbucks.com**) has stores at all types of locations—including standalone sites, shopping centers, downtown business districts, and other sites. In this way, it efficiently reaches different geographic markets—and consumers who are working, shopping, traveling, and so forth.

Source: Reprinted by permission of Susan Berry, Retail Image Consulting, Inc.

store would probably be unable to develop a customer following; people would be unwilling to travel to a store that does not have a large assortment of products or a strong image for merchandise and/or prices.

Years ago, numerous shopping centers forbade the entry of discounters because discount operations were frowned on by traditional retailers. This forced the discounters to become isolated stores or to build their own centers, and they have been successful. Today, diverse retailers are in isolated locations, as well as at business district and shopping center sites. Retailers using a mixed-location strategy include McDonald's, Target, Sears, Starbucks, Toys "R" Us, Wal-Mart, and 7-Eleven. Some retailers, including many gas stations and convenience stores, still emphasize isolated locations. See Figure 10-1.

The Unplanned Business District

An **unplanned business district** is a type of retail location where two or more stores situate together (or in close proximity) in such a way that the total arrangement or mix of stores is not due to prior long-range planning. Stores locate based on what is best for them, not the district. Four shoe stores may exist in an area with no pharmacy. There are four kinds of unplanned business district: central business district, secondary business district, neighborhood business district, and string. A description of each follows.

CENTRAL BUSINESS DISTRICT

A **central business district (CBD)** is the hub of retailing in a city. It is synonymous with the term *downtown*. The CBD exists where there is the greatest density of office buildings and stores. Both vehicular and pedestrian traffic are very high. The core of a CBD is often no more than a square mile, with cultural and entertainment facilities surrounding it. Shoppers are drawn from the whole urban area and include all ethnic groups and all classes of people. The CBD has at least one major department store and a number of specialty and convenience stores. The arrangement of stores follows no pre-set format; it depends on history (first come, first located), retail trends, and luck.

Here are some strengths that allow CBDs to draw a large number of shoppers:

▶ Excellent goods/service assortment.
▶ Access to public transportation.
▶ Variety of store types and positioning strategies within one area.
▶ Wide range of prices.
▶ Variety of customer services.
▶ High level of pedestrian traffic.
▶ Nearness to commercial and social facilities.

RETAILING AROUND THE WORLD

| Times Square in Hong Kong |

Five years ago, Hong Kong's Times Square mall opened. Today, it is one of Hong Kong's largest shopping malls with 900,000 square feet of retail space and more than 230 shops, including Armani Exchange (**www.armaniexchange.com**), Bally (**www.bally.com**), Bose (**www.bose.com**), Brooks Brothers (**www.brooksbrothers.com**), Coach (**www.coach.com**), Kate Spade (**www.katespace.com**), MaxMara (**www.maxmarafashion.com**), Patagonia (**www.patagonia.com**), and Tumi (**www.tumi.com**). The mall is one of the 10 most popular tourist destinations in Hong Kong. In addition to retail space, the mall has more than 1 million square feet of office space, a multicinema complex, and a variety of restaurants.

One of the difficulties with vertical malls, such as Times Square, has been getting shoppers to the higher floors. Many consumers get tired of going up and down escalators. To encourage shoppers to visit a given floor, Times Square groups the retailers with similar offerings on the same floor. For example, there is a high concentration of electronics retailers on the top floor of Times Square.

Until recently, most of Times Square's promotions focused on its dining options and its annual New Year's Eve countdown party. The Hong Kong center has started using a series of promotions such as a contest that coincided with the Beijing Olympics, a charity sale, a design road show, and Times Square Live (featuring amateur performances).

Source: **www.timessquare.com.hk/en/module/about/index.php** (February 20, 2009).

In addition, chain headquarters stores are often situated in CBDs.

These are some of the inherent weaknesses of the CBD:

▶ Inadequate parking as well as traffic and delivery congestion.
▶ Travel time for those living in the suburbs.
▶ Frail condition of some cities—such as aging stores—compared with their suburbs.
▶ Relatively poor image of central cities to some potential consumers.
▶ High rents and taxes for the most popular sites.
▶ Movement of some popular downtown stores to suburban shopping centers.
▶ Discontinuity of offerings (such as four shoe stores and no pharmacy).

The CBD remains a major retailing force, although its share of overall sales has fallen over the years, as compared with the planned shopping center. Besides the weaknesses cited, much of the drop-off is due to suburbanization. In the first half of the 20th century, most urban workers lived near their jobs. Gradually, many people moved to the suburbs—where they are served by planned shopping centers.

A number of CBDs are doing quite well, and many others are striving to return to their former stature. They use such tactics as modernizing storefronts and equipment, forming cooperative merchants' associations, modernizing sidewalks and adding brighter lighting, building vertical malls (with several floors of stores), improving transportation networks, closing streets to vehicular traffic (sometimes with disappointing results), bringing in "razzmatazz" retailers such as Nike Town, and integrating a commercial and residential environment known as mixed-use facilities.

As one retail location expert has noted, a superior CBD "embodies a character, look, flavor, and heritage that are not found in other locations, especially within the surrounding region. To best enhance its distinct qualities, a downtown should build upon its intrinsic historic, economic, natural, and cultural amenities. Why would a person choose a downtown as a destination with so many other alternatives available? The answer is a strong sense of place, a characteristic rarely associated with regional malls, big box retailers, or suburban commercial corridors."[3]

A good example of the value of a revitalized CBD is Dallas, where there is a strong effort under way to make the central city more competitive with suburban shopping centers:

A 12-year-old effort to breathe life into the Dallas city center appears to be paying off. There are new restaurants, hotels, nightlife, and a thriving arts community.

More than $1.8 billion has been invested in the CBD. The revitalization's cornerstone is the $348 million Dallas Center for the Performing Arts, which will be open 340 nights a year with performances by the Dallas Opera, dance, theater, and touring Broadway productions. It is expected to draw 800,000 people and pump $200 million into the economy each year, not including ticket sales. "You will see Dallas come alive," predicted one business leader. "We've never had a beautiful heart-of-the-city, and once we have it, people will want to take part and take ownership." New stores include Jos. A. Bank men's clothier, Crimson in the City contemporary boutique, and Benji's Collezioni designer store. All are within a block of Neiman Marcus' flagship store, which stood as downtown's sole fashion merchant for years.[4]

Boston's Faneuil Hall is another key CBD renovation. When developer James Rouse took over the site containing three 150-year-old, block-long former food warehouses, it had been abandoned for almost 10 years. Rouse used landscaping, fountains, banners, open-air courts, street performers, and colorful graphics to enable Faneuil Hall to capture a festive spirit. Faneuil Hall combines shopping, eating, and watching activities and makes them fun. Today, it has more than 100 shops and pushcarts, 17 restaurants and pubs, more than 40 food stalls, and entertainment. It attracts millions of shoppers and visitors yearly.

Grand Central Terminal (**www.grandcentralterminal.com**) is all dressed up and open for business.

Other major CBD revitalization projects include Annapolis Town Centre (Maryland), Branson Landing (Missouri), Circle Centre (Indianapolis), Grand Central Terminal (New York City), Harborplace (Baltimore), Horton Plaza (San Diego), Peabody Place (Memphis), Pioneer Place (Portland, Oregon), Riverchase Galleria (Birmingham, Alabama), Tower City Center (Cleveland), and Union Station (Washington, DC). See Figure 10-2.

Visit our Web site (**www.pearsonhighered.com/berman**) for links to all of the CBD projects mentioned in this section.

SECONDARY BUSINESS DISTRICT

A **secondary business district (SBD)** is an unplanned shopping area in a city or town that is usually bounded by the intersection of two major streets. Cities—particularly larger ones—often have multiple SBDs, each with at least a junior department store (a branch of a traditional department store or a full-line discount store) and/or some larger specialty stores, besides many smaller stores. This format is now more important because cities have "sprawled" over larger geographic areas.

FIGURE 10-2

Harborplace: A Revitalized Central Business District

Large Business districts rely on the customer traffic drawn by office buildings, as well as cultural and entertainment facilities. One popular, revitalized business district is depicted here: The Gallery at Harborplace in Baltimore.

Source: Reprinted by permission of The Rouse Company.

The kinds of goods and services sold in an SBD mirror those in the CBD. However, an SBD has smaller stores, less width and depth of merchandise assortment, and a smaller trading area (consumers will not travel as far), and it sells a higher proportion of convenience-oriented items.

The SBD's major strengths include a solid product selection, access to thoroughfares and public transportation, less crowding and more personal service than a CBD, and placement nearer to residential areas than a CBD. The SBD's major weaknesses include the discontinuity of offerings, the sometimes high rent and taxes (but not as high as in a CBD), traffic and delivery congestion, aging facilities, parking difficulties, and fewer chain outlets than in the CBD. These weaknesses have generally not affected the SBD as much as the CBD—and parking problems, travel time, and congestion are less for the SBD.

NEIGHBORHOOD BUSINESS DISTRICT

A **neighborhood business district (NBD)** is an unplanned shopping area that appeals to the convenience shopping and service needs of a single residential area. An NBD contains several small stores, such as a dry cleaner, a stationery store, a barber shop and/or a beauty salon, a liquor store, and a restaurant. The leading retailer is typically a supermarket or a large drugstore. This type of business district is situated on the major street(s) of its residential area.

An NBD offers a good location, long store hours, good parking, and a less hectic atmosphere than a CBD or SBD. On the other hand, there is a limited selection of goods and services, and prices tend to be higher because competition is less than in a CBD or SBD.

STRING

A **string** is an unplanned shopping area comprising a group of retail stores, often with similar or compatible product lines, located along a street or highway. There is little extension of shopping onto perpendicular streets. A string may start with an isolated store, success then breeding competitors. Car dealers, antique stores, and apparel retailers often situate in strings.

A string location has many of the advantages of an isolated store site (lower rent, more flexibility, better road visibility and parking, and lower operating costs), along with some disadvantages (less product variety, increased travel for many consumers, higher advertising costs, zoning restrictions, and the need to build premises). Unlike an isolated store, a string store has competition at its location. This draws more people to the area and allows for some sharing of common costs. It also means less control over prices and less loyalty toward each outlet. An individual store's increased traffic flow, due to being in a string rather than an isolated site, may be greater than the customers lost to competitors. This explains why four gas stations locate on opposing corners.

Figure 10-3 shows a map with various forms of unplanned business districts and isolated locations.

The Planned Shopping Center

A **planned shopping center** consists of a group of architecturally unified commercial establishments on a site that is centrally owned or managed, designed and operated as a unit, based on balanced tenancy, and accompanied by parking facilities. Its location, size, and mix of stores are related to the trading area served. Through **balanced tenancy**, the stores in a planned shopping center complement each other as to the quality and variety of their product offerings, and the kind and number of stores are linked to overall population needs. To ensure balanced tenancy, the management of a planned center usually specifies the proportion of total space for each kind of retailer, limits the product lines that can be sold by every store, and stipulates what kinds of firms can acquire unexpired leases. At a well-run center, a coordinated and cooperative long-run retailing strategy is followed by all stores.

The planned shopping center has several positive attributes:

▶ Well-rounded assortments of goods and services based on long-range planning.
▶ Strong suburban population.

Shopping centers in some form have existed for more than 1,000 years. Learn more about this phenomenon (**www.icsc. org/srch/about/ impactofshoppingcenters**).

FIGURE 10-3

Unplanned Business
Districts and Isolated
Locations

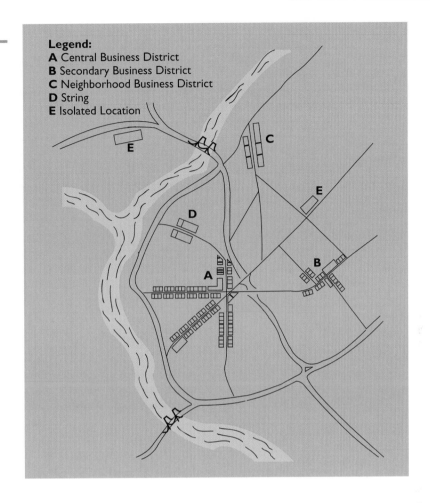

Legend:
A Central Business District
B Secondary Business District
C Neighborhood Business District
D String
E Isolated Location

- Interest in one-stop, family shopping.
- Cooperative planning and sharing of common costs.
- Creation of distinctive, but unified, shopping center images.
- Maximization of pedestrian traffic for individual stores.
- Access to highways and availability of parking for consumers.
- More appealing than city shopping for some people.
- Generally lower rent and taxes than CBDs (except for enclosed regional malls).
- Generally lower theft rates than CBDs.
- Popularity of malls—both *open* (shopping area off-limits to vehicles) and *closed* (shopping area off-limits to vehicles and all stores in a temperature-controlled facility).
- Growth of discount malls and other newer types of shopping centers.

There are also some limitations associated with the planned shopping center:

- Landlord regulations that reduce each retailer's flexibility, such as required hours.
- Generally higher rent than an isolated store.
- Restrictions on the goods/services that can be sold by each store.
- A competitive environment within the center.
- Required payments for items that may be of little or no value to an individual retailer, such as membership in a merchants' association.
- Too many malls in a number of areas ("the malling of America").
- Rising consumer boredom with and disinterest in shopping as an activity.
- Aging facilities of some older centers.
- Domination by large anchor stores.

Shopping Centers Today, in print and online (www.icsc.org/sct/index.php), is the bible of the industry.

How important are planned shopping centers? According to recent research, there are almost 91,000 U.S. shopping centers, about 1,100 of which are fully enclosed shopping

FIGURE 10-4

Macy's: A Dominant Shopping Center Retailer

Macy's has department stores in planned shopping centers around the United States. It is usually one of the lead anchors in these shopping centers, with multiple entrances/exits and easy access from parking lots.

Source: Reprinted by permission of Susan Berry, Retail Image Consulting, Inc.

malls. Shopping center revenues are about $2.35 trillion annually and account for nearly one-half of total U.S. retail-store sales (including autos and gasoline). About 12.5 million people work in shopping centers. Eighty-five percent of Americans over age 18 visit some type of center in an average month. Gap, Nordstrom, and Macy's are among the vast number of chains with a substantial presence at shopping centers. Some big retailers have also been involved in shopping center development. Sears has participated in the construction of dozens of shopping centers, and Publix Super Markets operates centers with hundreds of small tenants. Each year, numerous new centers of all kinds and sizes are built, and retail space is added to existing centers.[5] See Figure 10-4.

To sustain their long-term growth, shopping centers are engaging in these practices:

▶ Several older centers have been renovated, expanded, or repositioned. The Alderwood Mall in Lynnwood, Washington; Clifton Park Center in New Jersey; East Towne Mall in Madison, Wisconsin; Eaton Centre in Toronto, Canada; Park Place in Tucson, Arizona; Queens Center in New York; Westfield Shoppingtown in Santa Anita, California; and Yorktown Center Mall in Lombard, Illinois, have all been revitalized. Visit our Web site (**www.pearsonhighered.com/berman**) for links to these shopping centers.

▶ Certain derivative types of centers are fostering consumer interest and enthusiasm. Three of these, megamalls, lifestyle centers, and power centers, are discussed a little later in this chapter.

▶ Shopping centers are responding to shifting consumer lifestyles. They have made parking easier; added ramps for baby strollers and wheelchairs; and included more distinctive retailers such as the Apple Store, Apricot Lane, BCBG Max Azira, Juicy Couture, MaxMara, and Michael Kors. They have also introduced more information booths and center directories.

▶ The retailer mix has broadened at many centers to attract people interested in one-stop shopping. More centers now include banks, stockbrokers, dentists, doctors, beauty salons, TV repair outlets, and/or car rental offices. Many centers also include "temporary tenants," retailers that lease space (often in mall aisles or walkways) and sell from booths or moving carts. The tenants benefit from the lower rent and short-term commitment; the centers benefit by creating more excitement and diversity in shopping. Consumers often happen on new vendors in unexpected places.

▶ Open-air malls are gaining in popularity: They "are affordable—for developers to build and for tenants to lease." They "have lower common area maintenance fees." Customers like them, "as warm-weather shoppers appreciate the opportunity to be outdoors—and cold-weather stalwarts prove their hardiness out in the elements."

And "amenities are important, because wide-open spaces offer a plethora of land-scaping and gathering opportunities."[6]

▶ More shopping center developers are striving to build their own brand loyalty. Simon and Westfield are among the developers who have spent millions of dollars to boost their images by advertising their own names—with slogans such as "Simon Malls—More Choices." Simon (**www.simon.com**) owns and manages about 390 properties in 41 states, Europe, Japan, and elsewhere.

▶ Some shopping centers use frequent-shopper programs to retain customers and track spending. Prizes range from pre-paid calling cards to Caribbean vacations.

There are three types of planned shopping centers: regional, community, and neighborhood. Their characteristics are noted in Table 10-1, and they are described next.

REGIONAL SHOPPING CENTER

A **regional shopping center** is a large, planned shopping facility appealing to a geographically dispersed market. It has at least one or two department stores (each with a minimum of 100,000 square feet) and 50 to 150 or more smaller retailers. A regional center offers a very broad and deep assortment of shopping-oriented goods and services

TABLE 10-1 **Characteristics of Typical Neighborhood, Community, and Regional Types of U.S. Planned Shopping Centers**

Features of a Typical Center	Type of Center		
	Regional	Community	Neighborhood
Total site area (acres)	30–100+	10–40	3–15
Total sq. ft. leased to retailers	400,001–2,000,000+	100,001–400,000	30,000–100,000
Principal tenant	One, two, or more full-sized department stores	Branch department store (traditional or discount), variety store, and/or category killer store	Supermarket or drugstore
Number of stores	50–150 or more	15–25	5–15
Goods and services offered	Largest assortment for customers, focusing on goods that encourage careful shopping and services that enhance the shopping experience (such as a food court)	Moderate assortment for customers, focusing on a mix of shopping-and convenience-oriented goods and services	Lowest assortment for customers, emphasizing convenience-oriented goods and services
Minimum number of people living/working in trading area needed to support center	100,000+	20,000–100,000	3,000–50,000
Trading area in driving time	Up to 30 minutes	Up to 20 minutes	Fewer than 15 minutes
Location	Outside central city, on arterial highway or expressway	Close to one or more populated residential area(s)	Along a major thoroughfare in a single residential area
Layout	Mall, often enclosed with anchor stores at major entrances/exits	Strip or L-shaped	Strip
Percentage of all centers	3	17	80
Percentage of all centers' selling space	28	40	32

Sources: Adapted by the authors from the International Council of Shopping Centers definitions data base; and Michael P. Niemira and Jay Spivey, "The U.S. Shopping Center Industry—Size, Shape and Impact," *Research Review*, Vol. 14 (No. 2, 2007), pp. 33–37.

intended to enhance the consumer's visit. The market is 100,000+ people who live or work up to a 30-minute drive away. On average, people travel less than 20 minutes.

The regional center is the result of a planned effort to re-create the shopping variety of a central city in suburbia. Some regional centers have even become the social, cultural, and vocational focal point of an entire suburban area. Frequently, it is used as a town plaza, a meeting place, a concert hall, and a place for a brisk indoor walk. Despite the declining overall interest in shopping, on a typical visit to a regional shopping center, many people spend an average of an hour or more there.

The first outdoor regional shopping center opened in 1950 in Seattle, anchored by a branch of Bon Marche, a leading downtown department store. Southdale Center (outside Minneapolis), built in 1956 for the Target Corporation (then Dayton Hudson), was the first fully enclosed, climate-controlled mall. Today, there are about 2,515 U.S. regional centers, and this format is popping up around the world (where small stores still remain the dominant force) from Australia to Brazil to India to Malaysia.

One type of regional center is the **megamall**, an enormous planned shopping center with 1 million+ square feet of retail space, multiple anchor stores, up to several hundred specialty stores, food courts, and entertainment facilities. It seeks to heighten interest in shopping and expand the trading area. There are 520 U.S. megamalls, including Mall of America (**www.mallofamerica.com**) in Minnesota. It has four anchors (Bloomingdale's, Macy's, Nordstrom, and Sears), 520 other stores, a 14-screen movie theater, a health club, 50 restaurants, a Nickelodeon Universe indoor amusement park, and 12,550 parking spaces—on 4.2 million square feet. The mall has stores for every budget, attracts 40 percent of visitors from outside a 150-mile radius, and draws 600,000 to 900,000 visitors weekly. Beijing, China's Jin Yuan shopping center is the largest megamall in the world. See Figure 10-5 for another leading regional center.

Mall of America's attractions (**www. mallofamerica.com**) are as impressive as the mall itself.

COMMUNITY SHOPPING CENTER

A **community shopping center** is a moderate-sized, planned shopping facility with a branch department store (traditional or discount) and/or a category killer store, as well as several smaller stores (similar to those in a neighborhood center). It offers a moderate assortment of shopping- and convenience-oriented goods and services to consumers from

TECHNOLOGY IN RETAILING

Site-Selection Software Hits the Spot

geoVue (**www.geovue.com**), Customer Analytics Report (**www.buxtonco.com**), and MapInfo (**www.mapinfo.com**) are examples of site-selection technological applications that are used by a wide variety of retailers. According to the chief executive of geoVue, "Retailers that are sophisticated realize that a market is dynamic, not static." Thus, the value of a location can rapidly change due to such factors as new competition, housing developments, and even long-term road construction. For example, using geoVue's input data and iPlan market planning software, Walgreens determined that it needed to move one of its drugstores two times in a three-year period to keep up with changed market conditions. As a result of these relocations, store sales increased by 30 percent.

Buxton's Customer Analytics Report provides retailers with insights into its customers' purchasing behavior based on such factors as customer hobbies, media preferences, and brand preferences. Retailers can determine what products customers are purchasing at specific stores; for example, very high Internet-based sales levels within a particular ZIP code may indicate the need for additional retail locations. This report can also be used to predict the impact of potential competitors.

Pitney Bowes' MapInfo has an application called AnySite Online RM. This software generates a trading-area profile for a proposed shopping center that is matched against a data base of preferred trading-area profiles. MapInfo then generates a list of tenants that can optimize the developer's retail tenant mix.

Sources: Beth Mattson-Teig, "Site Seeing," *Retail Traffic* (October 2007), p. 110; and Kerry Pipes, "Site Selection Grows Up: Improved Tech Tools Make the Process Faster, Better," **www.franchise-update.com/article/667** (December 5, 2008).

FIGURE 10-5

Festival Walk: Hong Kong Megamall

"Festival Walk is an energized environment of innovation, originality, and pleasure. Boasting a world-class design of natural light and open space, Festival Walk offers an unparalleled environment for business and pleasure: over 200 shops and 25 restaurants; an 11-screen cinema multiplex; Hong Kong's largest ice rink; over 220,000 square feet of office space; an 850-space car park; and direct access to buses, taxis, and a train station. Its dramatic setting and accessibility have made it the location of choice for some of the world's best-known retail names and reputable companies." [**www.festivalwalk.com**]

Source: Reprinted by permission of TNS Retail Forward.

one or more nearby, well-populated, residential areas. About 20,000 to 100,000 people, who live or work within a 10- to 20-minute drive, are served by this location.

There is better long-range planning for a community shopping center than a neighborhood shopping center. Balanced tenancy is usually enforced, and cooperative promotion is more apt. Store composition and the center's image are kept pretty consistent with pre-set goals.

Two noteworthy types of community center are the power center and the lifestyle center. A **power center** is a shopping site with (1) up to a half-dozen or so category killer stores and a mix of smaller stores or (2) several complementary stores specializing in one product category. A power center usually occupies 200,000 to 400,000 square feet on a major highway or road intersection. It seeks to be quite distinctive to draw shoppers and better compete with regional centers. There are more than 2,500 U.S. power centers, such as Pennsylvania's Whitehall Square. That 315,000-square-foot center is a category killer center with a 55,000-square-foot Raymour & Flanigan Furniture Store, a 52,000-square-foot Redner's Warehouse Market, a 49,000-square-foot Sports Authority, a 30,000-square-foot Ross Dress for Less, a 23,000-square-foot PetSmart, and a 21,000-square-foot Staples, as well as several smaller stores.

Centro Properties (www.centroprop.com) is a leading retail-estate developer with several power centers. Visit its properties online.

A **lifestyle center** is an open-air shopping site that typically includes 150,000 to 500,000 square feet of space dedicated to upscale, well-known specialty stores. The focus is often on apparel, home products, books, music, and restaurants. Popular stores at lifestyle centers include Ann Taylor, Banana Republic, Barnes & Noble, Bath & Body Works, Gap, GapKids, Pottery Barn, Talbots, Victoria's Secret, and Williams-Sonoma. Aspen Grove in Littleton, Denver; Deer Park Town Center in Illinois; Rookwood Commons in Norwood, Ohio; and CocoWalk in Coconut Grove, Florida, are examples of lifestyle shopping centers. See Figure 10-6. At present, there are about 160 such centers in the United States.

NEIGHBORHOOD SHOPPING CENTER

A **neighborhood shopping center** is a planned shopping facility, with the largest store being a supermarket or a drugstore. Other retailers often include a bakery, a laundry, a dry cleaner, a stationery store, a barbershop or beauty parlor, a hardware store, a restaurant, a liquor store, and a gas station. This center focuses on convenience-oriented goods and services for people living or working nearby. It serves 3,000 to 50,000 people who are within a 15-minute drive (usually less than 10 minutes).

A neighborhood center is usually arranged in a strip. Initially, it is carefully planned and tenants are balanced. Over time, the planned aspects may lessen and newcomers may face fewer restrictions. Thus, a liquor store may replace a barbershop—leaving a void. A center's ability to maintain balance depends on its attractiveness to potential tenants (expressed

FIGURE 10-6

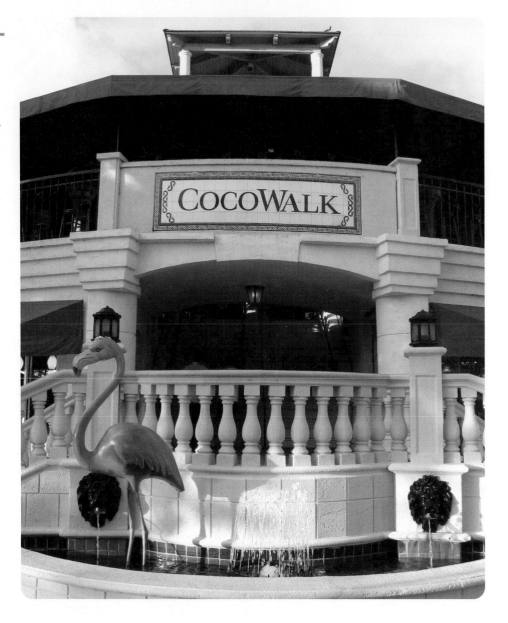

CocoWalk: A Lifestyle Center

CocoWalk is an open-air, lifestyle shopping center in Coconut Grove, Florida. It has 38 retailers, including a state-of-the-art movie theater, several restaurants, and more. Its shops include Azul Boutique, Goldiamor Fine Jewelry, and White House Black Market.

Source: Reprinted by permission.

by the extent of store vacancies). In number, but not in selling space or sales, neighborhood centers account for 80 percent of all U.S. shopping centers.

The Choice of a General Location

The last part of Step 2 in location planning requires a retailer to select a locational format: isolated, unplanned district, or planned center. The decision depends on the firm's strategy and a careful evaluation of the advantages and disadvantages of each alternative.

Next, in Step 3, the retailer chooses a broadly defined site. Two decisions are needed here. First, the specific kind of isolated store, unplanned business district, or planned shopping center location is picked. If a firm wants an isolated store, it must decide on a highway or side street. Should it desire an unplanned business area, it must decide on a CBD, an SBD, an NBD, or a string. A retailer seeking a planned area must choose a regional, community, or neighborhood shopping center—and whether to use a derivative form such as a megamall or power center. Here are the preferences of three retailers:

> Radio Shack operates about 4,400 company-owned stores, 1,500 franchise stores, and 700 kiosks in the United States. It has the advantage of convenience, owing to its smaller stores and greater scale. Radio Shack stores measure about

2,500 square feet and are located in malls and open-air centers, as well as store-fronts. Roughly 9 out of 10 Americans live or work within five minutes of a Radio Shack store, the company says. And its "small-box format enables customers to generally get in and out of a store quickly without having to deal with the hassles associated with big-box shopping—including parking issues, navigating a large store to find the exact items you need, and the occasional lengthy checkout lines," according to an analyst at RBC Capital Markets.[7]

Guitar Center (**www. guitarcenter.com**) has a well-conceived location plan.

The Guitar Center chain has developed unique and, what historically have been, highly effective selection criteria to identify prospective store sites for our Guitar Center units. In evaluating the suitability of a particular location, we concentrate on the demographics of our target customer, as well as traffic patterns and specific site characteristics such as visibility, accessibility, traffic volume, shopping patterns, and availability of adequate parking. Stores are typically located in freestanding locations to maximize their outside exposure and signage.[8]

Apple Stores are typically placed at high-traffic locations in quality shopping malls and urban shopping districts. By operating its own stores and locating them in desirable locations, the firm is better positioned to control the customer buying experience and attract new customers. The stores are designed to simplify and enhance the presentation and marketing of Apple products and related solutions. To that end, retail-store configurations have evolved into various sizes in order to accommodate market-specific demands. The Company has certain retail stores that have been designed and built to serve as high-profile venues to promote brand awareness and serve as vehicles for corporate sales and marketing activities. Because of their unique design elements, locations, and size, these stores require substantially more investment than Apple's more typical retail stores.[9]

Second, a firm must select its general store placement. For an isolated store, this means picking a specific highway or side street. For an unplanned district or planned center, this means picking a specific district (e.g., downtown Los Angeles) or center (e.g., Seminary South in Fort Worth, Texas).

In Step 3, the retailer narrows down the decisions made in the first two steps and then chooses a general location. Step 4 requires the firm to evaluate specific alternative sites, including their position on a block (or in a center), the side of the street, and the terms of tenancy. The factors to be considered in assessing and choosing a general location and a specific site within that location are described together in the next section because many strategic decisions are similar for these two steps.

Location and Site Evaluation

The assessment of general locations and the specific sites contained within them requires extensive analysis. In any area, the optimum site for a particular store is called the **one-hundred percent location**. Because different retailers need different kinds of locations, a location labeled as 100 percent for one firm may be less than optimal for another. An upscale ladies' apparel shop would seek a location unlike that sought by a convenience store. The apparel shop would benefit from heavy pedestrian traffic, closeness to major department stores, and proximity to other specialty stores. The convenience store would rather be in an area with ample parking and heavy vehicular traffic. It does not need to be close to other stores.

Figure 10-7 contains a location and site evaluation checklist. A retailer should rate every alternative location (and specific site) on all the criteria and develop overall ratings for them. Two firms may rate the same site differently. This figure should be used in conjunction with the trading-area data noted in Chapter 9, not instead of them.

Pedestrian Traffic

The most crucial measures of a location's and site's value are the number and type of people passing by. Other things being equal, a site with the most pedestrian traffic is often best.

FIGURE 10-7

A Location/Site Evaluation Checklist
Rate each of these criteria on a scale of 1 to 10, with 1 being excellent and 10 being poor.

Pedestrian Traffic	Number of people	_____
	Type of people	_____
Vehicular Traffic	Number of vehicles	_____
	Type of vehicles	_____
	Traffic congestion	_____
Parking Facilities	Number and quality of parking spots	_____
	Distance to store	_____
	Availability of employee parking	_____
Transportation	Availability of mass transit	_____
	Access from major highways	_____
	Ease of deliveries	_____
Store Composition	Number and size of stores	_____
	Affinity	_____
	Retail balance	_____
Specific Site	Visibility	_____
	Placement in the location	_____
	Size and shape of the lot	_____
	Size and shape of the building	_____
	Condition and age of the lot and building	_____
Terms of Occupancy	Ownership or leasing terms	_____
	Operations and maintenance costs	_____
	Taxes	_____
	Zoning restrictions	_____
	Voluntary regulations	_____
Overall Rating	General location	_____
	Specific site	_____

Not everyone passing a location or site is a good prospect for all types of stores, so many firms use selective counting procedures, such as counting only those carrying shopping bags. Otherwise, pedestrian traffic totals may include too many nonshoppers. It would be improper for an appliance retailer to count as prospective shoppers all the people who pass a downtown site on the way to work. In fact, much of the downtown pedestrian traffic may be from people who are there for nonretailing activities.

A proper pedestrian traffic count should encompass these four elements:

▶ Separation of the count by age and gender (with very young children not counted).
▶ Division of the count by time (this allows the study of peaks, low points, and changes in the gender of the people passing by the hour).
▶ Pedestrian interviews (to find out the proportion of potential shoppers).
▶ Spot analysis of shopping trips (to verify the stores actually visited).

Vehicular Traffic

The quantity and characteristics of vehicular traffic are very important for retailers that appeal to customers who drive there. Convenience stores, outlets in regional shopping centers, and car washes are retailers that rely on heavy vehicular traffic. Automotive traffic studies are essential in suburban areas, where pedestrian traffic is often limited. See Figure 10-8.

As with pedestrian traffic, adjustments to the raw count of vehicular traffic must be made. Some retailers count only homeward-bound traffic, some exclude vehicles on the other side of a divided highway, and some omit out-of-state cars. Data may be available from the state highway department, the county engineer, or the regional planning commission.

Besides traffic counts, the retailer should study the extent and timing of congestion (from traffic, detours, and poor roads). People normally avoid congested areas and shop where driving time and driving difficulties are minimized.

CAREERS IN RETAILING

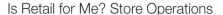

Is Retail for Me? Store Operations

Retailers offer a large variety of career opportunities—complete with competitive wages, fringe benefits, positive working conditions, and opportunities for career and educational advancement. In this chapter and the next several chapters, we provide information from the NRF about specific career tracks. This information is general in nature; individual firms will vary in the details based on size, retail format, etc.

Are you a big picture person? Retail professionals in the store operations career area oversee overall store operations and profits. Responsibilities may include managing staff functions like loss prevention and/or human resources. Here are several positions at the top of the store operations career ladder:

▶ *Head of Store Operations.* Top executive in charge of overall store operation and profits. May supervise some staff functions like loss prevention, distribution, and/or a field human resources group. Does not have buying or accounting responsibility. Typically reports to the head of a chain.

▶ *Zone Manager.* This position exists only in very large chains to supervise a geographic group of regional managers. This position is the third level above the store managers (store manager to district manager to regional manager to zone manager).

▶ *Regional Manager.* This manager supervises a geographic group of district managers and is two levels above store managers.

▶ *District Manager.* This position is the first level above a group of store and/or area managers and does not personally manage a specific store.

▶ *Area Manager.* This position is a "super store manager" role, running one store as the store manager while supervising one or more other store managers. This arrangement may also be called a district manager trainee or senior store manager, among other titles.

Source: Reprinted by permission of the National Retail Federation.

FIGURE 10-8

Vehicular Traffic Analysis
In determining the location for its new outlet center in Grand Prairie, Texas, Prime Outlets did a vehicular traffic study. It learned that 176,000 vehicles pass by the site each day.

Source: Reprinted by permission of Prime Retail.

PRIME OUTLETS **GRAND PRAIRIE, TX** (IN DEVELOPMENT)   REDEFINING THE OUTLET SHOPPING EXPERIENCE

DALLAS
15 miles

176,000 vehicles pass daily

FT. WORTH
17 miles

AERIAL / GLA: 450,000 sq. ft.

Parking Facilities

Most U.S. retail stores include some provision for nearby off-street parking. In many business districts, parking is provided by individual stores, arrangements among stores, and local government. In planned shopping centers, parking is shared by all stores there. The number and quality of parking spots, their distances from stores, and the availability of employee parking should all be evaluated.

The need for retailer parking facilities depends on the store's trading area, the type of store, the proportion of shoppers using a car, the existence of other parking, the turnover of spaces (which depend on the length of a shopping trip), the flow of shoppers, and parking by nonshoppers. A shopping center normally needs 4 to 5 parking spaces per 1,000 square feet of gross floor area, a supermarket 10 to 15 spaces, and a furniture store 3 or 4 spaces.

Free parking sometimes creates problems. Commuters and employees of nearby businesses may park in spaces intended for shoppers. This problem can be lessened by validating shoppers' parking stubs and requiring payment from nonshoppers. Another problem may occur if the selling space at a location increases due to new stores or the expansion of current ones. Existing parking may then be inadequate. Double-deck parking or parking tiers save land and shorten the distance from a parked car to a store—a key factor because customers at a regional shopping center may be unwilling to walk more than a few hundred feet from their cars to the center.

Transportation

Mass transit, access from major highways, and ease of deliveries must be examined.

In a downtown area, closeness to mass transit is important for people who do not own cars, who commute to work, or who would not otherwise shop in an area with traffic congestion. The availability of buses, taxis, subways, trains, and other kinds of public transit is a must for any area not readily accessible by vehicular traffic.

Locations dependent on vehicular traffic should be rated on their nearness to major thoroughfares. Driving time is a consideration for many people. In addition, drivers heading eastbound on a highway often do not like to make a U-turn to get to a store on the westbound side of that highway.

The transportation network should be studied for delivery truck access. Many thoroughfares are excellent for cars but ban large trucks or cannot bear their weight.

Store Composition

The number and size of stores should be consistent with the type of location. A retailer in an isolated site wants no stores nearby; a retailer in a neighborhood business district wants an area with 10 or 15 small stores; and a retailer in a regional shopping center wants a location with many stores, including large department stores (to generate customer traffic).

If the stores at a given location (be it an unplanned district or a planned center) complement, blend, and cooperate with one another, and each benefits from the others' presence, **affinity** exists. When affinity is strong, the sales of each store are greater, due to the high customer traffic, than if the stores are apart. The practice of similar or complementary stores locating near each other is based on two factors: (1) Customers like to compare the prices, styles, selections, and services of similar stores. (2) Customers like one-stop shopping and purchase at different stores on the same trip. Affinities can exist among competing stores, as well as among complementary stores. More people travel to shopping areas with large selections than to convenience-oriented areas, so the sales of all stores are enhanced.

One measure of compatibility is the degree to which stores exchange customers. Stores in these categories are very compatible with each other and have high customer interchange:

▶ Supermarket, drugstore, bakery, fruit-and-vegetable store, meat store.
▶ Department store, apparel store, hosiery store, lingerie shop, shoe store, jewelry store.

Retail balance, the mix of stores within a district or shopping center, should also be considered. Proper balance occurs when the number of store facilities for each merchandise or service classification is equal to the location's market potential, a range of goods and services is provided to foster one-stop shopping, there is an adequate assortment within any category, and there is a proper mix of store types (balanced tenancy).

Specific Site

Visibility, placement in the location, size and shape of the lot, size and shape of the building, and condition and age of the lot and building should be reviewed for the specific site.

Visibility is a site's ability to be seen by pedestrian or vehicular traffic. A site on a side street or at the end of a shopping center is not as visible as one on a major road or at the center's entrance. High visibility aids store awareness; and some people hesitate to go down a side street or to the end of a center.

Placement in the location is a site's relative position in the district or center. A corner location may be desirable because it is situated at the intersection of two streets and has "corner influence." It is usually more expensive because of the greater pedestrian and vehicular passersby due to traffic flows from two streets, increased window display area, and less traffic congestion through multiple entrances. Corner influence is greatest in high-volume locations. That is why some Pier 1 stores, Starbucks restaurants, and other retailers occupy corner sites. See Figure 10-9.

A convenience-oriented firm, such as a stationery store, is very concerned about the side of the street, the location relative to other convenience-oriented stores, nearness to parking, access to a bus stop, and the distance from residences. A shopping-oriented retailer, such as a furniture store, is more interested in a corner site to increase window display space, proximity to wallpaper and other related retailers, the accessibility of its pickup platform to consumers, and the ease of deliveries to the store.

When a retailer buys or rents an existing building, its size and shape should be noted. The condition and age of the lot and the building should also be studied. A department store requires significantly more space than a boutique; and it may desire a square site, while the boutique seeks a rectangular one. Any site should be viewed in terms of total space needs: parking, walkways, selling, nonselling, and so on.

Due to the saturation of many desirable locations and the lack of available spots in others, some firms have turned to nontraditional sites—often to complement their existing stores. T.G.I. Friday's, Staples, and Bally have airport stores. McDonald's has outlets in many Wal-Marts and at several gas stations. Some fast-food retailers share facilities to provide more variety and to share costs. See Figure 10-10.

FIGURE 10-9

Corner Influence and Hershey's
Consider the pedestrian and vehicular traffic—and the eye-catching appeal—generated by this Hershey's store in Ohio.

Source: Reprinted by permission of Susan Berry, Retail Image Consulting, Inc.

FIGURE 10-10

Multi-Store Locations

To draw more customers and split overhead costs, various retailers are sharing store locations. The location shown here includes Starbucks, Popeye's, Pizza Hut, and Taco Bell.

Source: Reprinted by permission of Susan Berry, Retail Image Consulting, Inc.

The National Trust for Historic Preservation (**www.preservationnation. org**) has revitalized communities across the United States.

Terms of Occupancy

Terms of occupancy—ownership versus leasing, the type of lease, operations and maintenance costs, taxes, zoning restrictions, and voluntary regulations—must be evaluated for each prospective site.

OWNERSHIP VERSUS LEASING

A retailer with adequate funding can either own or lease premises. Ownership is more common in small stores, in small communities, or at inexpensive locations. It has several advantages. There is no chance that a property owner will not renew a lease or double the rent when a lease expires. Monthly mortgage payments are stable. Operations are flexible; a retailer can engage in scrambled merchandising and break down walls. It is also likely that property value will appreciate over time, resulting in a financial gain if the business is sold. Ownership disadvantages are the high initial costs, the long-term commitment, and the inability to readily change sites. Home Depot owns about 87 percent of its store properties.[10]

If a retailer chooses ownership, it must decide whether to construct a new facility or buy an existing building. The retailer should consider the purchase price and maintenance costs, zoning restrictions, the age and condition of existing facilities, the adaptability of existing facilities, and the time to erect a new building. To encourage building rehabilitation in towns with 5,000 to 50,000 people, Congress enacted the Main Street program (**www.mainstreet.org**) of the National Trust for Historic Preservation. There is currently a network of 40 statewide, citywide, and countywide Main Street programs actively serving more than 1,200 towns. These towns benefit from planning support, tax credits, and low-interest loans.

The great majority of stores in central business districts and regional shopping centers are leased, mostly due to the high investment for ownership. Department stores tend to have renewable 20- to 30-year leases, supermarkets usually have renewable 15- to 20-year leases, and specialty stores often have 5- to 10-year leases with options to extend. Some leases give the retailer the right to end an agreement before the expiration date—under given circumstances and for a specified retailer payment.

Leasing minimizes the initial investment, reduces risk, allows access to prime sites that cannot hold more stores, leads to immediate occupancy and traffic, and reduces the long-term commitment. Many retailers also feel they can open more stores or spend more on other aspects of their strategies by leasing. Firms that lease accept limits on operating flexibility, restrictions on subletting and selling the business, possible nonrenewal problems, rent increases, and not gaining from rising real-estate values.

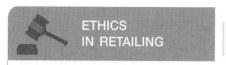

ETHICS IN RETAILING

Tesco Ireland: Strong Corporate Social Responsibility

Tesco Ireland (**www.tesco.ie**) serves more than 1.2 million customers a week from its more than 95 stores located throughout Ireland. It has enacted a strong corporate social responsibility statement concerning the firm's strategy and values, customers, employees, the surrounding community, suppliers, property, and the environment.

Here is a summary of some of the more important aspects of Tesco's social responsibility statement as related to store construction:

▶ Tesco addresses environmental impact concerns when planning and building retail stores, including environmental impact assessment regulations.

▶ When proposing new store development, Tesco's policy is to meet with local community representatives,

elected officials, and members of the public. Tesco is committed to addressing all of the issues raised.

▶ Tesco seeks to build environmentally responsible buildings. Its newer buildings use composite sandwich panel construction instead of steel, concrete, and bricks. These newer materials are more fuel efficient.

▶ Parking spaces for disabled persons are provided close to each store. Nearby spaces are also designated for parent and child use; these parking bays are the same size as disabled parking bays and are always located next to a walkway to the store.

Source: "Corporate Social Responsibility," **www.tesco.ie/csr/index.html** (August 14, 2008).

Through a *sale-leaseback*, some large retailers build stores and then sell them to real-estate investors who lease the property back to the retailers on a long-term basis. Retailers using sale-leasebacks build stores to their specifications and have bargaining power in leasing—while lowering capital expenditures.

TYPES OF LEASES

Property owners do not rely solely on constant rent leases, partly due to their concern about interest rates and the related rise in operating costs. Terms can be quite complicated.[11]

Tiffany (**www.tiffany.com**), a name synonymous with glamour, is one of the cornerstone retailers on New York's high-rent Fifth Avenue.

The simplest, most direct arrangement is the **straight lease**—a retailer pays a fixed dollar amount per month over the life of the lease. Rent usually ranges from $1 to $75 annually per square foot, depending on the site's desirability and store traffic. At some sites, rents can be much higher. At the intersection of New York's Fifth Avenue and 57th Street, the yearly rent is up to $1,500 per square foot![12]

A **percentage lease** stipulates that rent is related to sales or profits. This differs from a straight lease, which provides for constant payments. A percentage lease protects a property owner against inflation and lets it benefit if a store is successful; it also allows a tenant to view the lease as a variable cost—rent is lower when its performance is weak and higher when performance is good. The percentage rate varies by type of shopping district or center and by type of store.

Percentage leases have variations. With a specified minimum, low sales are assumed to be partly the retailer's responsibility; the property owner receives minimum payments (as in a straight lease) no matter what the sales or profits. With a specified maximum, it is assumed that a very successful retailer should not pay more than a maximum rent. Superior merchandising, promotion, and pricing should reward the retailer. Another variation is the sliding scale: the ratio of rent to sales changes as sales rise. A sliding-down scale has a retailer pay a lower percentage as sales go up and is an incentive to the retailer.

A **graduated lease** calls for precise rent increases over a stated period of time. Monthly rent may be $4,800 for the first five years and $5,600 for the last five years of a lease. Rent is known in advance by the retailer and the property owner, and it is based on expected increases in sales and costs. There is no problem auditing sales or profits, as there is for percentage leases. This lease is often used with small retailers.

A **maintenance-increase-recoupment lease** has a provision allowing rent to increase if a property owner's taxes, heating bills, insurance, or other expenses rise beyond a certain point. This provision most often supplements a straight rental lease agreement.

A **net lease** calls for all maintenance costs (such as heating, electricity, insurance, and interior repair) to be paid by the retailer. It frees the property owner from managing the facility and gives the retailer control over store maintenance. It is used to supplement a straight lease or a percentage lease.

OTHER CONSIDERATIONS

After assessing ownership and leasing opportunities, a retailer must look at the costs of operations and maintenance. The age and condition of a facility may cause a retailer to have high monthly costs, even though the mortgage or rent is low. Furthermore, the costs of extensive renovations should be calculated.

Differences in sales taxes (those customers pay) and business taxes (those retailers pay) among alternative sites must be weighed. Business taxes should be broken down into real-estate and income categories. The highest statewide sales tax is in Indiana, Mississippi, New Jersey, Rhode Island, and Tennessee (7 percent); Alaska, Delaware, Montana, New Hampshire, and Oregon have no state sales tax.

There may be zoning restrictions as to the kind of stores allowed, store size, building height, the type of merchandise carried, and other factors that have to be hurdled (or another site chosen). For example,

> Dozens of communities have enacted zoning rules that prohibit stores over a certain size. Store size caps help to sustain the vitality of small-scale, pedestrian-oriented business districts, which in turn nurture local business development. Store size caps keep out some national retailers that refuse to build outlets smaller than their standard formats. Others will opt to comply with a community's size limit by designing smaller stores. What constitutes an appropriate upper limit for the size of retail stores depends on many factors, including the size of the town, the scale of its existing buildings, and its long-term goals with regard to retail development. Some communities have banned only the biggest of the big boxes. Belfast, Maine, caps stores at 75,000 square feet. Others, such as Hailey, Idaho, and Ashland, Oregon, have chosen much smaller limits (36,000 and 45,000 square feet).[13]

Voluntary restrictions—not mandated by the government—are most prevalent in planned shopping centers and may include required membership in merchant groups, uniform hours, and cooperative security forces. Leases for many stores in regional shopping centers have included clauses protecting anchor tenants from too much competition—especially from discounters. These clauses involve limits on product lines, bans against discounting, fees for common services, and so forth. Anchors are protected by developers because the developers need their long-term commitments to finance the centers. The Federal Trade Commission discourages "exclusives"—whereby only a particular retailer in a center can carry specified merchandise—and "radius clauses"—whereby a tenant agrees not to operate another store within a certain distance.

Because of overbuilding, some retailers are in a good position to bargain over the terms of occupancy. This differs from city to city and from shopping location to shopping location.

Overall Rating

The last task in choosing a store location is to compute overall ratings: (1) Each location under consideration is given an overall rating based on the criteria in Figure 10-7. (2) The overall ratings of alternative locations are compared, and the best location is chosen. (3) The same procedure is used to evaluate the alternative sites within the location.

It is often difficult to compile and compare composite evaluations because some attributes may be positive while others are negative. The general location may be a good shopping center, but the site in the center may be poor, or an area may have excellent

What is the sales tax in Utah? California? Go to this site (**www. salestaxinstitute.com/ sales_tax_rates.php**) to find out the sales tax in all 50 states.

Lease agreements used to be so simple that they could be written on a napkin—not today (**www. icsc.org/srch/sct/sct9905/ 16.php**).

potential but take two years to build a store. The attributes in Figure 10-7 should be weighted according to their importance. An overall rating should also include *knockout factors*—those that preclude consideration of a site. Possible knockout factors are a short lease, little or no evening or weekend pedestrian traffic, and poor tenant relations with the landlord.

Chapter **Summary**

1. *To thoroughly examine the types of locations available to a retailer: isolated store, unplanned business district, and planned shopping center.* After a retailer rates alternative trading areas, it decides on the type of location, selects the general location, and chooses a particular site. There are three basic locational types.

An isolated store is freestanding, not adjacent to other stores. It has no competition, low rent, flexibility, road visibility, easy parking, and lower property costs. It also has a lack of traffic, no variety for shoppers, no shared costs, and zoning restrictions.

An unplanned business district is a shopping area with two or more stores located together or nearby. Store composition is not based on planning. There are four categories: central business district, secondary business district, neighborhood business district, and string. An unplanned district generally has these favorable points: variety of goods, services, and prices; access to public transit; nearness to commercial and social facilities; and pedestrian traffic. Yet, its shortcomings have led to the growth of the planned shopping center: inadequate parking, older facilities, high rents and taxes in popular CBDs, discontinuity of offerings, traffic and delivery congestion, high theft rates, and some declining central cities.

A planned shopping center is centrally owned or managed and well balanced. It usually has one or more anchor stores and many smaller stores. The planned center is popular, due to extensive goods and service offerings, expanding suburbs, shared strategic planning and costs, attractive locations, parking facilities, lower rent and taxes (except for regional centers), lower theft rates, the popularity of malls (although some people are now bored with them), and the lesser appeal of inner-city shopping. Negative aspects include operations inflexibility, restrictions on merchandise carried, and anchor store domination. There are three forms: regional, community, and neighborhood centers.

2. *To note the decisions necessary in choosing a general retail location.* First, the specific form of isolated store, unplanned business district, or planned shopping center location is determined, such as whether to be on a highway or side street; in a CBD, an SBD, an NBD, or a string; or in a regional, community, or neighborhood shopping center. Then the general store location is specified—singling out a particular highway, business district, or shopping center.

3. *To describe the concept of the one-hundred percent location.* Extensive analysis is required when evaluating each general location and specific sites within it. Most importantly, the optimum site for a given store must be determined. This is the one-hundred percent location, and it differs by retailer.

4. *To discuss several criteria for evaluating general retail locations and the specific sites within them.* Pedestrian traffic, vehicular traffic, parking facilities, transportation, store composition, the attributes of each specific site, and terms of occupancy should be studied. An overall rating is then computed for each location and site, and the best one selected.

Affinity occurs when the stores at the same location complement, blend, and cooperate with one another; each benefits from the others' presence.

5. *To contrast alternative terms of occupancy.* A retailer can opt to own or lease. If it leases, terms are specified in a straight lease, percentage lease, graduated lease, maintenance-increase-recoupment lease, and/or net lease. Operating and maintenance costs, taxes, zoning restrictions, and voluntary restrictions also need to be reviewed.

Key Terms

isolated store (p. 276)
unplanned business district (p. 277)
central business district (CBD) (p. 277)
secondary business district (SBD) (p. 279)
neighborhood business district (NBD) (p. 280)
string (p. 280)
planned shopping center (p. 280)
balanced tenancy (p. 280)
regional shopping center (p. 283)
megamall (p. 284)
community shopping center (p. 284)
power center (p. 285)
lifestyle center (p. 285)
neighborhood shopping center (p. 285)
one-hundred percent location (p. 287)

affinity (p. 290)
retail balance (p. 291)
terms of occupancy (p. 292)

straight lease (p. 293)
percentage lease (p. 293)
graduated lease (p. 293)

maintenance-increase-recoupment
   lease (p. 294)
net lease (p. 294)

Questions for Discussion

1. A drugstore chain has decided to open outlets in a combination of isolated locations, unplanned business districts, and planned shopping centers. Comment on this strategy.

2. From the retailer's perspective, compare the advantages of locating in unplanned business districts versus planned shopping centers.

3. Differentiate among the central business district, the secondary business district, the neighborhood business district, and the string.

4. Develop a brief plan to revitalize a neighborhood business district near your campus.

5. What is a megamall? What is a lifestyle center? Describe the strengths and weaknesses of each.

6. Evaluate a regional shopping center near your campus.

7. Explain why a one-hundred percent location for Macy's may not be a one-hundred percent location for a local apparel store.

8. What criteria should a small retailer use in selecting a general store location and a specific site within it? A large retailer?

9. What difficulties are there in using a rating scale such as that shown in Figure 10-7? What are the benefits?

10. How do the parking needs for a gift shop, a shoe repair store, and a luggage store differ?

11. Under what circumstances would it be more desirable for a retailer to buy or lease an existing facility rather than to build a new store?

12. What are the pros and cons of a straight lease versus a percentage lease for a prospective retail tenant? For the landlord?

Web **Exercise**

Visit the Web site of the National Trust Main Street Center (www.mainstreet.org). What could the retailers in a small community learn from this site?

Note: Stop by our Web site (www.pearsonhighered.com/ berman) to experience a number of highly interactive,

appealing Web exercises based on actual company demonstrations and sample materials related to retailing.

part four
Short Cases

CASE 1: THE PAVILION AT PORT ORANGE, FLORIDA[C-1]

The Pavilion at Port Orange, Florida (located less than five miles south of Daytona Beach), is a 550,000-square-foot, open-air shopping center. The shopping center is anchored by a Belk (**www.belk.com**) fashion-oriented department store and a state-of-the-art, 14-screen Hollywood theater. Belk's 75,000-square-foot store specializes in fashion apparel for the entire family, cosmetics, and home furnishings. The store features such brands as Estée Lauder, Clinique, Ralph Lauren, Izod, and Nautica, as well as the retailer's private labels. The theater offers plush, high-backed seating and digital-surround capabilities.

In addition to the anchor tenants, The Pavilion at Port Orange includes 190,000 square feet of upscale specialty retailers and restaurants. As with many other lifestyle centers, The Pavilion has a Main Street format in its building design, a community performance area, a beach-themed children's play area, extensive landscaping, and miles of walking trails. The focal point of the center is a seven-acre lake surrounded by upscale water-view restaurants.

The center is targeted to the area's 500,000 permanent residents, as well as the more than 8 million annual visitors. Let's look at some of the important population facts about this shopping center:

▶ It has excellent visibility from I-95, a major highway, and is located directly off one of three major thoroughfares to the beach.
▶ The center's primary trade area is estimated to be 166,000 people. Its secondary trade area comprises 304,000 people. These numbers are projected to be 182,000 people for the primary trade area and 328,000 people for the secondary trade area as of 2011.
▶ The full-time residents of Port Orange are relatively affluent. Although the average single-family home sells for $250,000, waterfront homes sell in the millions of dollars. One estimate is that the median household income for the primary trade area is $44,000; the corresponding figure for the secondary trade area is $40,000.
▶ In addition to the primary and secondary trade-area population, the area attracts millions of tourists each year. These tourists are attracted to the area due to the close by Daytona International Speedway (**www.daytonainternationalspeedway.com**), NASCAR Headquarters (**www.nascar.com**), the beaches, and

visits to friends and family members. The center is also located less than 10 miles from Ocean Center, Volusia County's convention, entertainment, and sports complex. According to one estimate, tourism generates $4 billion in revenues for the area annually.
▶ The area has a well-diversified economic base. More than one-third of the manufacturing work force is employed in the engineering and production of medical and surgical supplies, robotic pharmaceutical dosing systems, and biohazard containment systems for public and military applications.

Questions

1. How could shopping center developers in Daytona Beach use geographic information systems in their planning?
2. Analyze the economic base of Daytona Beach, Florida, using online research data bases, as well as *Editor & Publisher* (if available at your college library).
3. Explain how the trading area of Port Orange can be delineated for an existing mall. For a new mall.
4. Describe the dangers in Port Orange's becoming over-stored. How can the level of saturation for Port Orange be controlled?

CASE 2: EXPERIAN'S MICROMARKETER G3 GIS[C-2]

Micromarketer Generation 3 (**www.micromarketerg3.com**), also known as Micromarketer G3, is a geographic information system tool that enables retailers to develop consumer profiles by area, provides data useful in analyzing the suitability of locations, and assists retailers in responding to changes in neighborhood composition. Micromarketer G3 is available in desktop, network, and Internet-based versions. The software is already used by more than 500 organizations throughout the world.

Micromarketer G3 allows retailers to identify their best-performing locations and the potential of current and new store sites. Because Micromarketer G3 uses the most current data, it is often much more relevant than census data that can be as much as 10 years old. For example, a retailer evaluating the Dallas/Fort Worth area using the most current census data might infer that an area north of Fort Worth is relatively unpopulated. MicromarketerG3, in contrast, would show that the very same area is now very densely populated due to new construction.

Let's look at different potential applications for Micromarketer G3. The software can

▶ Identify suitable locations for new stores.
▶ Determine trading-area overlap for chain and franchise-based retailers.

[C-1]The material in this case is drawn from "Springing Up in the Southeast," *Chain Store Age* (August 2008), pp. 134–140; and "The Pavilion at Port Orange: Creating a Shopper's Paradise," **www.cblproperties.com** (January 10, 2009).

[C-2]The material in this case is drawn from Rick Erwin, "Site Selection's New Look," *Chain Store Age* (July 2008), p. 32; "Experian Releases Micromarketer Generation3," **www.business-strategies.com.hk** (September 7, 2008); and "Micromarketer Generation 3: Geographical Information Solutions," **www.micromarketerg3.com** (January 14, 2009).

▶ Evaluate changes in buyer behavior due to new competitors, the impact of the Web on selected store-based retailers, and shifts in demographic factors.

▶ Compute market share for large retailers on a local, regional, and/or national basis.

▶ Determine threats and opportunities due to changes in consumer behavior (such as the increased use of super-stores or less driving due to high gasoline prices).

▶ Use customer profiles to better target and attract new customers.

▶ Better understand the demographic, lifestyle, and purchasing habits of customers who are concentrated around each current and proposed location.

▶ Study optimal drive times for each location and for different groups of customers.

On a monthly basis, Experian's INSOURCE data base enters new information into the Micromarketer G3 system. Micromarketer G3 then integrates geographic data, census data, household demographic data, and behavioral segmentation data. This information is derived from publicly available sources (such as directories and data on real-estate construction and sales), as well as proprietary sources such as product registration and mail-order data. Incorporated within Micromarketer G3 is Experian's consumer segmentation system that classifies more than one-third of the world's population.

These are some of the major characteristics of the Micromarketer G3 GIS system: Micromarketer G3 is easy to maintain. It enables users to add information from additional sources, and to switch between old and newer data sets. Reporting and data visualization are flexible. Maps and charts can be customized, and multiple data sets can be contained in the same report. Among the formats supported are Microsoft Excel, html, and Adobe Reader. Micromarketer G3 is compatible with such industry-standard applications as Oracle, MS Access, and SPSS.

Questions

1. What are the advantages of using GIS software versus using manual systems?
2. How can GIS software be useful in delineating trading area segments?
3. Explain how Target can use GIS software in determining the placement of its discount supercenters.
4. Develop 10 criteria to rank alternative GIS software solutions for retail applications.

CASE 3: HOME DEPOT IN NEW YORK CITY[C-3]

Home Depot's (**www.homedepot.com**) first store in Manhattan was the chain's first three-story unit, as well as its first with a doorman and concierge. This store caters to multiple markets: decorators, building contractors and superintendents, brownstone owners, householders who own or rent individual apartments, and suburban commuters.

Before its Manhattan expansion, Home Depot successfully opened and managed stores in downtown Detroit, downtown Seattle, and the Lincoln Park neighborhood of Chicago. These stores are a clear indication that Home Depot is seeking growth opportunities outside suburban markets and that it is able to tailor its merchandise selections to meet the needs of urban customers.

Because the Manhattan store is in a landmark preservation area, the store exterior cannot be modified. So, instead of large permanent signs, the store's signage consists of orange-color banners. The store stocks 20,000 different products; special ordering capability increases this number to 100,000 items. The selection in many product categories is unparalleled for both Home Depot and for Manhattan shoppers. The store offers 1,000 different varieties of lighting fixtures; 500 of these are in stock. Its customers can choose among 2,000 different types of flooring, including area rugs priced from $200 to $8,000. The store even offers 3,200 different paint colors that can be mixed from its nine paint-mixing stations. Despite the large selection of these items, the store does not have a lumber department and does not stock plasterboard, insulation, or plywood. These items require special orders.

The store's Chelsea neighborhood location, which used to be full of independent retailers, now has such retail category killers as Old Navy (**www.oldnavy.com**), Staples (**www.staples.com**), Bed Bath & Beyond (**www. bedbathandbeyond.com**), and Best Buy (**www.bestbuy.com**). The trend of large retailers coming to this area has some independents concerned. Others, however, feel that stores such as Home Depot will increase sales for all merchants in the neighborhood due to the cumulative attraction of chain and independent retailers.

The idea of the doorman for Home Depot stemmed from the need to help get customers a taxi or to help load their cars. The concierge offers directions to a product's location and sends customers to the proper aisles. All signs in the store are in English, Spanish, and Mandarin to appeal to the area's diverse clientele.

Home Depot has been careful in selecting sites for additional stores due to high rent costs and the low availability of parking. It recently decided not to open an additional store in lower Manhattan near SoHo and Tribeca. Real-estate executives at Home Depot were concerned about whether that area's population density warranted the $40 per square foot rent for the 125,000-square-foot building. Home Depot has also been re-evaluating whether it will sublet its 110,000 square foot space at an East Harlem shopping plaza.

[C-3]The material in this case is drawn from Mike Duff, "Home Depot Hangs New Shingle in Manhattan," *DSN Retailing Today* (January 10, 2005), pp. 4–5, 38; Elizabeth Lazarowitz, "Costco

Eyeing Harlem Site: Struggling Home Depot Looks to Back Out; Warehouse Club May Take Its Place," *Daily News* (June 23, 2008), p. 4; and Peter Slatin, "Home Depot Dumps Downtown; Apple Peels 34th," *Statin Report* (January 24, 2007).

Questions

1. Discuss the differences in trading-area size and characteristics for a downtown versus a suburban location for Home Depot.
2. Describe how location and site selection would vary between downtown versus a suburban location for Home Depot.
3. Beyond the factors mentioned in this case, how should Home Depot adapt its Manhattan stores to the community?
4. Do you think Home Depot's presence in Manhattan help or hurt existing hardware and lighting stores? Explain your answer.

CASE 4: LEASE NEGOTIATION: POWER SHIFTS TO RETAILERS[C-4]

In 2007, demand for quality retail space was so strong that many were content to get any reasonable deal they could find. However, since 2008, the leasing market has changed dramatically. According to the chief investment officer of Regency Centers (**www.regencycenters.com**), a shopping-center investor that manages several million square feet of retail space, "The leasing environment is tougher. The anchor tenants have cut back on store openings; and as a result, secondary markets have been completely out of favor. And those retailers that do go to smaller markets will try to get very tough deals."

The increased leasing power that has flowed to retailers is largely due to the great number of retailers that have slowed down their expansion pace and/or closed their underperforming retail stores due to economic uncertainty. For example, Charming Shoppes (**www.charmingshoppes.com**), which operates women's apparel stores including Lane Bryant (**www.lanebryant.com**) and Fashion Bug (**www.fashionbug. com**), closed 150 underperforming stores. It also opened fewer than 60 new stores in 2008, a 50 percent decrease from 2007. Similarly, Home Depot (**www.homedepot.com**) opened 50 new stores in 2008, versus 87 stores in 2007.

To add to the uncertain retail environment, Borders (**www.borders.com**)—among others—put itself up for sale; and Circuit City closed approximately 20 percent of its stores

[C-4]The material in this case is drawn from Elaine Misonzhnik, "Gravitational Pull," *Retail Traffic* (May 2008), pp. 171–174.

in late 2008 and then went out of business in 2009 due to weak performance. In addition, many national chains have begun to insist on high-traffic locations in major markets.

Concessions desired by retail tenants range from lower rents, free rents for the beginning of a lease period, allowances for renovation expenses, and the use of percentage leases (which have lower rental costs when sales volume expectations are not met). Let's look at two such requests for concessions:

▶ Gene Speigelman, an executive director of Cushman & Wakefield (**www.cushwake.com**)—a leading real-estate brokerage firm—represented a specialty clothing chain looking for new locations in the Southeast. In its negotiations for retail space at a "Class A" regional mall, the chain wanted a 15 percent reduction from the asking rent for 2008 and a switch to a percentage lease arrangement in 2009. As Speigelman said, "They want the landlord to partner with them on the risk in 2009; they are taking less of a gamble."
▶ A Florida-based real-estate developer with a 5.5-million-square-foot portfolio, reported that an apparel chain wanted a $60-per-square-foot tenant improvement allowance in 2008. In 2007, the chain had been willing to accept $47 per square foot. In addition, the chain wanted a rent reduction to $24 per square foot from the $27 it agreed to in 2007.

The increased power of the tenants in negotiating with owners of retail space has significantly lengthened the time that all parties (landlords, tenants, real-estate attorneys, and real-estate brokers) need to negotiate a deal. According to one expert, a lease that would have taken two to three months to negotiate in 2007 now typically requires from four months to up to a full year.

Questions

1. Explain the significance of the increased power of retail tenants beyond securing lower rents in lease agreements.
2. Explain the pros and cons of a percentage lease versus a straight lease for a retail tenant.
3. Explain the pros and cons of a percentage lease versus a straight lease for a shopping center developer.
4. What can a shopping center developer do with unoccupied retail space to generate retail mall traffic and to reduce potential blight?

part four ▮▮▮ ▮▮▮
Comprehensive Case

TOUGH TIMES FOR SHOPPING CENTERS*

INTRODUCTION

According to TNS Retail Forward survey data, shoppers continue to pare retailers from their consideration, with the average number of firms visited in the past four weeks close to all-time lows. Additionally, the shares of survey respondents shopping most shopping center types monthly again declined in 2008. Monthly shopping incidence remains strongest among the two youngest shopper segments—those age 18 to 24 and 25 to 34—and tends to increase along with household income.

Survey participants were asked how often they shop and whether or not they purchase anything, at each of the following locations:

▶ *Regional mall:* large enclosed mall or shopping center that includes one or more department stores.
▶ *Lifestyle center:* large, mostly nonenclosed (outdoor), shopping center that includes fashion-oriented specialty stores and may also include department stores, restaurants, and entertainment.
▶ *Big-city downtown shopping district* (that is not a mall).
▶ *Power center:* large, strip shopping center that includes at least one discount department store (e.g., Target, Wal-Mart) or category superstore (e.g., Best Buy, Lowe's, Borders, Office Depot).
▶ *Small to mid-sized strip mall with supermarket anchor.*

*The material in this case is adapted by the authors from TNS Retail Forward (**www.retailforward.com**), *Shopping Centers Battle Declining Traffic; Shoppers Shrink Consideration Set* (July 2008); and TNS Retail Forward, *Industry Outlook: Department Stores* (July 2008). Reprinted by permission.

▶ *Small strip mall where the largest stores are small specialty stores.*
▶ *Factory outlet/off-price shopping center.*
▶ *Online shopping site.*

Consumers Visit Fewer Stores

Shoppers are visiting fewer retailers each month. The average number of different retailers that primary household shoppers say they shopped during the previous four weeks declined from 14.4 in July 2004 to 12.3 in June 2008, or roughly two fewer retailers. See Figure 1. The decline in the average number of soft goods retailers (i.e., department stores, apparel specialty stores, and shoe and accessories stores) shopped has been smaller (in absolute terms), dipping from 3.3 in July 2004 to 2.6 in June 2008.

Fewer Monthly Shoppers Across Most Shopping Center Types

The shares of monthly shoppers and monthly clothing shoppers declined both year-to-year and from 2006 to 2008 across most shopping center types that typically feature retailers whose offer includes soft goods categories. See Table 1. The only locations to capture larger shares of monthly shoppers, as well as monthly clothing shoppers in 2008 were power centers, strip malls with a supermarket anchor, and online sites. During the past three years, however, only power centers and outlet malls recorded an increase in their monthly all-shopper bases. The share of monthly clothing shoppers was down across all shopping locations except strip malls with a supermarket anchor, outlet malls, and online sites during that same time period.

One-Stop Shopping Appeal Keeping Power Centers Popular

With three out of five primary household shoppers shopping power centers monthly, the format boasts the largest monthly shopper base. And although the share of shoppers visiting power centers on a monthly basis declined in 2007, surging

FIGURE 1

Average Number of Retailers Shopped During the Prior Four Weeks

Source: TNS Retail Forward Shopper Scape™, July 2004–June 2008.

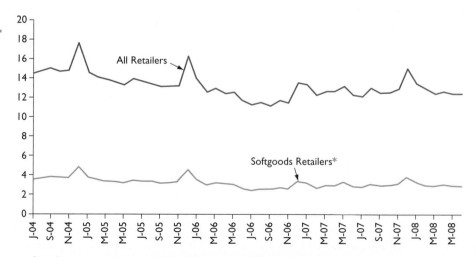

*i.e., department stores, apparel specialty stores, and shoe and accessory stores.

TABLE 1 Monthly Shoppers by Shopping Location

	2006		2007		2008	
	Monthly Shoppers	Monthly *Clothing* Shoppers	Monthly Shoppers	Monthly *Clothing* Shoppers	Monthly Shoppers	Monthly *Clothing* Shoppers
Power Center[1]	59%	38%	56%	36%	60%	37%
Strip mall with supermarket anchor	55%	23%	49%	22%	49%	23%
Online shopping sites	43%	27%	42%	27%	42%	29%
Regional mall[2]	34%	26%	32%	25%	30%	23%
Small strip mall with specialty stores	25%	16%	22%	15%	20%	13%
Lifestyle center[3]	24%	18%	21%	16%	20%	16%
Factory outlet/off-price shopping center	10%	11%	13%	13%	13%	11%
Downtown shopping district	10%	9%	9%	9%	8%	8%

[1]Large, strip shopping center that includes at least one discount department store or category superstore.
[2]Large enclosed mall or shopping center that includes one or more department stores.
[3]Large mostly nonenclosed (outdoor) shopping center that includes fashion-oriented specialty stores and may also include department stores, restaurants, and entertainment.
Source: TNS Retail Forward ShopperScape July 2006, June 2007, and June 2008.

gasoline prices likely contributed to the increased popularity of power centers in 2008 both for general shopping and clothes shopping.

Appeal of Regional Malls Continuing to Dwindle

The share of primary household shoppers visiting regional malls monthly has decreased nearly 4 percentage points during the past few years. Although the decline was slightly less pronounced (−2.9 percentage points) among those respondents shopping specifically for clothes during that time frame, the format now ties with strip malls anchored by a supermarket for the third-largest monthly clothing shopper base (23 percent of respondents).

Lifestyle Centers Not Gaining Traction

Despite the acceleration of lifestyle center development in 2006 and 2007, only a fifth of primary household shoppers shop the format monthly. And although specialty apparel retailers are a cornerstone of the format, even fewer shoppers frequent lifestyle centers monthly for clothing.

Economy Not Luring More Shoppers to Outlets

The monthly all-shopper base at factory outlet/off-price shopping centers was virtually static from 2007 to 2008, and the share of respondents shopping the format for clothing declined 1.3 percentage points year-to-year. Although the economy has spurred more shoppers into bargain-hunting mode, the high transportation costs associated with visiting outlet centers—often miles from population centers and their full-price regional mall counterparts—likely offset some of the savings to be found from clearance buys. Still, with several new outlet centers expected to be built through 2010, according to the International Council of Shopping Centers, more shoppers will likely find the format more accessible in the near future.

Shopping Frequency About the Same or Down Across All Venues

A majority of shoppers say they are shopping all types of shopping venues—except downtown shopping districts—with the same frequency as before. See Figure 2.

However, among those consumers whose shopping behavior has changed, a larger share are shopping each format less often than those who are shopping the respective format more often. In fact, the share of shoppers who are shopping each format less often exceeds the share of more-frequent shoppers by a margin of 20-plus percentage points for all shopping center types except for online shopping sites and power centers.

The difference is smallest among shoppers of online sites: 17 percent of shoppers say they shop Web sites more often than a year ago, compared with 21 percent of shoppers who now shop the channel less often. And although power centers are attracting the largest share of shoppers with the same frequency as a year ago (63 percent), the share of shoppers visiting the format less often still tops the share shopping more often.

Shopping Incidence Favors Youth and Wealth

Shoppers age 25 to 34 tend to shop a variety of shopping center types monthly, both in general and specifically for clothing, compared with other shopper segments. See Table 2.

The swell of youth-oriented retailers at regional malls, however, makes for one of the exceptions. Although about a third of all primary household shoppers visit regional malls monthly, that share surges to more than half for respondents age 18 to 24. Among those shopping specifically for clothing, slightly more than a quarter of all shoppers are in a regional mall at least once a month, compared with nearly 40 percent of 18- to 24-year-olds. This age group also has the

FIGURE 2

Shopping Frequency
Compared with
Previous Year

Source: TNS Retail Forward
Shopper Scape™, July 2008.

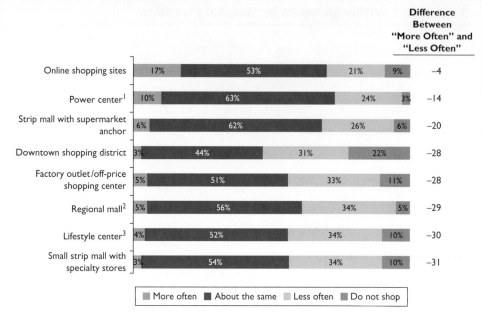

Difference
Between
"More Often" and
"Less Often"

Location	More often	About the same	Less often	Do not shop	Difference
Online shopping sites	17%	53%	21%	9%	−4
Power center[1]	10%	63%	24%	3%	−14
Strip mall with supermarket anchor	6%	62%	26%	6%	−20
Downtown shopping district	3%	44%	31%	22%	−28
Factory outlet/off-price shopping center	5%	51%	33%	11%	−28
Regional mall[2]	5%	56%	34%	5%	−29
Lifestyle center[3]	4%	52%	34%	10%	−30
Small strip mall with specialty stores	3%	54%	34%	10%	−31

■ More often ■ About the same ■ Less often ■ Do not shop

[1]Large strip shopping center that includes at least one discount department store or category superstore.
[2]Large enclosed mall or shopping center that includes one or more department stores.
[3]Large mostly nonenclosed (outdoor) shopping center that includes fashion-oriented specialty stores and may also
include department stores, restaurants, and entertainment.

TABLE 2   Monthly Shopping Incidence by Demographics, 2008

	Regional Mall[1]		Lifestyle Center[2]		Downtown Shopping District		Power Center[3]	
	Monthly Shopper	Monthly *Clothing* Shoppers	Monthly Shopper	Monthly *Clothing* Shoppers	Monthly Shoppers	Monthly *Clothing* Shoppers	Monthly Shoppers	Monthly *Clothing* Shoppers
18–24	51%*	39%	26%	27%	24%	21%	59%	42%
25–34	39%	32%	27%	24%	16%	16%	66%	43%
35–44	30%	23%	18%	15%	7%	8%	63%	39%
45–54	27%	22%	20%	15%	5%	5%	61%	39%
55–64	26%	18%	18%	11%	3%	4%	54%	30%
65+	22%	16%	15%	9%	3%	3%	53%	32%
Less than $25,000	22%	16%	14%	13%	10%	8%	51%	33%
$25,000–$49,000	26%	21%	18%	15%	7%	8%	58%	36%
$50,000–$74,999	31%	23%	19%	12%	6%	6%	61%	35%
$75,000–$99,999	36%	28%	24%	20%	7%	9%	67%	44%
$100,000+	41%	33%	28%	21%	8%	8%	67%	42%
Young singles	39%	33%	26%	22%	21%	14%	63%	38%
Middle singles	20%	14%	13%	9%	6%	6%	49%	28%
Older singles	22%	15%	14%	9%	2%	3%	49%	27%
Young couple	36%	29%	25%	23%	13%	13%	62%	37%
Working older couple	28%	22%	23%	15%	5%	5%	62%	38%
Retired older couple	25%	18%	17%	9%	3%	3%	56%	34%
Young parent	39%	29%	21%	20%	10%	10%	67%	45%
Middle parent	35%	28%	23%	21%	12%	13%	64%	44%
Older parent	30%	24%	20%	16%	4%	5%	63%	40%
Roommates	30%	29%	23%	13%	16%	17%	50%	25%

TABLE 2 Continued

	Strip Mall with Supermarket Anchor		Small Strip Mall with Specialty Stores		Factory Outlet/Off-Price Shopping Center		Online Sites	
	Monthly Shoppers	Monthly *Clothing* Shoppers	Monthly Shoppers	Monthly *Clothing* Shoppers	Monthly Shoppers	Monthly *Clothing* Shoppers	Monthly Shoppers	Monthly *Clothing* Shoppers
18–24	40%	25%	25%	22%	21%	24%	46%	34%
25–34	50%	25%	27%	19%	22%	18%	51%	36%
35–44	46%	20%	24%	14%	13%	12%	43%	29%
45–54	53%	27%	19%	13%	10%	9%	44%	31%
55–64	50%	20%	18%	10%	8%	7%	42%	27%
65+	50%	23%	12%	7%	6%	7%	29%	21%
Less than $25,000	40%	19%	17%	10%	13%	10%	33%	21%
$25,000–$49,999	47%	23%	18%	13%	13%	11%	37%	27%
$50,000–$74,999	53%	23%	19%	12%	13%	10%	43%	30%
$75,000–$99,999	53%	28%	24%	16%	13%	14%	51%	39%
$100,000+	57%	27%	26%	18%	12%	12%	54%	37%
Young singles	45%	23%	27%	18%	22%	20%	48%	34%
Middle singles	47%	19%	16%	9%	10%	8%	42%	24%
Older singles	48%	20%	13%	9%	5%	5%	26%	22%
Young couple	43%	24%	24%	17%	16%	17%	51%	35%
Working older couple	56%	25%	18%	12%	11%	10%	41%	30%
Retired older couple	48%	22%	13%	8%	7%	7%	32%	22%
Young parent	50%	24%	24%	16%	16%	12%	47%	32%
Middle parent	44%	24%	28%	18%	20%	18%	44%	32%
Older parent	54%	28%	22%	15%	10%	9%	41%	31%
Roommates	54%	22%	30%	18%	20%	14%	54%	28%

*Read as: 51% of 18-to-24-year-olds shop regional malls monthly.
[1]Large enclosed mall or shopping center that includes one or more department stores.
[2]Large mostly nonenclosed (outdoor) shopping center that includes fashion-oriented specialty stores and may also include department stores, restaurants, and entertainment.
[3]Large, strip shopping center that includes at least one discount department store or category superstore.

Source: TNS Retail Forward ShopperScape™, June 2008.

highest incidence of monthly clothing shoppers at lifestyle centers, downtown shopping districts, factory outlets, and strip malls with a supermarket anchor (tied with the 25- to 34-year-old cohort).

Monthly shopping incidence tends to increase along with income across most formats. Downtown shopping districts, however, have the highest incidence of monthly shoppers among the less affluent. One out of 10 shoppers with a household income of less than $25,000 shops downtown shopping districts once a month, compared with 8 percent of all shoppers.

The Evolving Store Base of Department Stores

Department store retailers are adjusting their store planning and diversifying their store portfolio amid the difficult economic environment in the United States. Value department stores J.C. Penney (**www.jcpenney.com**) and Kohl's (**www.kohls.com**) are pulling back from aggressive store-opening plans, while traditional department stores are tweaking their formats and looking to new venues (such as lifestyle centers) for store growth. Upscale department stores, meanwhile, increasingly are looking to outlets as a new distribution channel and to faster-growing markets abroad.

Value Department Stores Pare Expansion Plans

Kohl's and newly expansion-oriented J.C. Penney have driven store growth in the department store channel during the past couple of years. The current slowdown in consumer spending, however, has prompted the two to revise their initial growth plans.

Kohl's won't reach 1,400 stores by 2012. After having opened an average of 90-plus stores a year from 2003 through 2007, Kohl's announced in 2008 that it would slow its store growth, opening 70 to 75 stores compared with an initially planned 90 stores. Consequently, Kohl's backed off its target of 1,400 stores by 2012, with chief executive Larry Montgomery saying after the company's annual meeting that it would likely take a couple more years to reach that number. The year 2008, however, did bring about the retailer's entrance into one major new market: Miami–Ft. Lauderdale–West Palm Beach, where it opened eight stores in the fall.

J.C. Penney developed a bridge plan. In 2005, J.C. Penney ended a nearly decade-long program of store closings that left the retailer with nearly 220 fewer stores. After opening a couple of net new stores in 2005 and more than a dozen a year later, J.C. Penney announced a sweeping store expansion and renovation program calling for 50 new or relocated stores a year and 65 remodeled stores a year through 2011. But after just one year, J.C. Penney trimmed its store opening and remodeling plans because of the weak consumer spending environment. In 2008, the retailer expected to open 36 new or relocated stores and renovate 20 others. In June 2008, J.C. Penney further slashed its planned capital expenditures for 2009, saying it would open only 20 new or relocated stores (including its first in Manhattan) and renovate 10 to 15 locations.

Traditional Department Stores Try New Locations and Prototypes

In part because of slow to nonexistent growth in regional malls, traditional department stores, including Macy's (**www.macys.com**), are increasingly looking to lifestyle centers and other nontraditional formats for new store growth. Others tweaked not only the format but also the merchandise mix in an attempt to deliver the best shopping experience for the target customer.

Although more than 50 percent of Macy's capital spending through 2010 is expected to pay for store remodels, maintenance, and expansions, the retailer does intend to spend more than $670 million on new stores from 2008 through 2010. According to Macy's, "most" of the approximately 20 planned new stores will open in lifestyle centers being developed in markets where Macy's already operates.

In May 2008, Macy's announced it would discontinue the Bloomingdale's By Mail catalog by early 2009 and instead shift its resources to further growing the brand's E-commerce business. (Note: Bloomingdale's will continue to mail advertising pieces.) Macy's previously said that it expected its nonstore business to generate $1 billion in sales in 2008. In the past two years, Macy's has invested more than $200 million to improve the infrastructure for its nonstore business. These investments included two new fulfillment centers and investments in warehouse management and order management systems.

In November 2007, Gottschalks opened its first store featuring a new smaller format with a dramatically pared-back assortment of housewares and home textiles. Instead, the 58,000-plus square-foot store emphasized cosmetics, women's apparel, shoes, and accessories. In terms of design, Gottschalks transformed the former grocery store site in a Wal-Mart-anchored shopping center with plenty of natural lighting, updated décor, and an open floor plan. However, due to the fallout from the collapse of the California housing market in its trading areas, Gottschalks called off plans to open additional smaller-format stores. Then in late March 2009, Gottschalks announced that it was going out of business. Even its ambitious plans to retool with small formats were unable to protect it from the negative effects of the worst economy in decades.

Upscale Department Stores Emphasize Outlets

During the past several years, Neiman Marcus (**www.neimanmarcus.com**) has aggressively grown its outlet channel, adding nine net new Last Call/Horchow stores in the past five years and a Last Call micro Web site to NeimanMarcus.com. In fiscal 2009, the upscale department store chain opened an additional three outlet branches, which took total Last Call doors to 27.

Nordstrom (**www.nordstrom.com**) and Saks (**www.saks.com**), meanwhile, had been less focused on the outlet channel. Since disposing of its mid-tier department store businesses, Saks was making its operations more efficient and renovating its existing store base. Nordstrom was more focused on growing its network of full-line stores. That, however, is changing.

Saks is rebranding and repositioning its outlet channel in an effort to establish it as a destination rather than a clearinghouse for end-of-season or marked-down merchandise. First, the retailer changed the name of the outlets from Off Fifth to Saks Fifth Avenue Off 5th to more closely align the stores with its luxury department store parent. In April 2008, Saks replaced its existing outlet in a Prime Outlets International center in Orlando, Florida, with the prototype Saks Fifth Avenue Off 5th. Three additional stores also opened by the end of 2008; some of Saks' existing outlets are being completely remodeled, and others will incorporate only some of the features from the prototype. According to media reports, the retailer's outlet stores generate about $400 million in annual sales.

Nordstrom is accelerating the pace of its Rack store openings. After having opened a total of two net new Rack outlets and one net new Last Chance outlet from 2003 through 2007, Nordstrom decided to open six new Rack stores in 2008–2009: Danvers, Massachusetts (fall 2008); Cleveland (fall 2008); Orange County, California (fall 2008); San Antonio (fall 2008); White Plains, New York (fall 2008); and Orlando (spring 2009).

International Opportunities

As the U.S. economy slowed, department stores joined the growing list of U.S.-based apparel specialists seeking expansion in faster-growing international markets, where American brands and high-end designers are in demand. Although Barneys New York (**www.barneys.com**) has licensed its name in Japan for more than a decade and is widely believed to be preparing for more widespread international expansion under its new owners, Dubai-based Istithmar World Capital, other department store retailers have only recently begun investigating opportunities abroad.

Questions

1. What are the major lessons for retailers to learn from this case?
2. Comment on the monthly shopping behavior trends by shopping location as shown in Table 1, Table 2, and Figure 2.
3. Are the negative shopping center trends cited in this case reversible? Why or why not?
4. Visit a nearby regional shopping mall, and analyze the store mix that you find there.
5. What must shopping centers do to attract young shoppers? Older shoppers?
6. Discuss the decision of some upscale retailers to place more emphasis on store locations in outlet centers.
7. What special factors must be considered by a U.S. retailer when opening a new store in a foreign country rather than in the United States?

PART 5 Managing a Retail Business

In Part Five, the elements of managing a retail enterprise are discussed. We first look at the steps in setting up a retail organization and the special human resource management environment of retailing. Operations management is then examined—from both financial and operational perspectives.

Chapter 11 reports how a retailer can use its organizational structure to assign tasks, policies, resources, authority, responsibilities, and rewards to satisfy the needs of the target market, employees, and management. We also show how human resource management can be applied so that the structure works properly. Human resource management consists of recruiting, selecting, training, compensating, and supervising personnel.

Chapter 12 focuses on the financial dimensions of operations management in enacting a retail strategy. We discuss these topics: profit planning, asset management (including the strategic profit model, other key ratios, and financial trends in retailing), budgeting, and resource allocation.

Chapter 13 presents the operational aspects of operations management. We cover these specific concepts: operations blueprint; store format, size, and space allocation; personnel utilization; store maintenance, energy management, and renovations; inventory management; store security; insurance; credit management; computerization; and crisis management.

Source: Michael DeLeon/istockphoto.com.

11

Retail Organization and Human Resource Management

Chapter Objectives

1. To study the procedures involved in setting up a retail organization

2. To examine the various organizational arrangements utilized in retailing

3. To consider the special human resource environment of retailing

4. To describe the principles and practices involved with the human resource management process in retailing

James Nordstrom and Carl Wallin opened their first Wallin & Nordstrom shoe store in downtown Seattle in 1901. Today, Nordstrom (**www.nordstrom.com**) has evolved into a retailing powerhouse with annual sales approaching $9 billion. The company operates about 100 department stores, 50 discount Nordstrom Rack stores, two Jeffrey Boutiques, and two Last Chance clearance stores. In addition, Nordstrom has a strong online presence and serves customers through its direct mail catalogs. It recently sold off its four U.S. Faconnable boutiques and its 37 international Faconnable boutiques.

Although each of its store divisions has its own internal organizational structure, Nordstrom is constantly seeking synergies among these units. To increase its fashion-forward image, Jeffrey Kalinsky, the founder of Jeffrey New York and Jeffrey Atlanta, has taken on a greater role. While he continues to work with the head merchants of women's and men's designer apparel, shoes, and accessories, Kalinsky now also guides the overall vision at Nordstrom.

And though Nordstrom.com is a separate organizational entity, customers can now pick up merchandise purchased through Nordstrom's Web site in the customer service department at a Nordstrom location of their choice. This enables customers to do related-item purchasing at the store and saves Nordstrom some shipping expenses.

Nordstrom also has an excellent human resources strategy. It has a "promote-from-within" philosophy, and many of its executives started as sales personnel. Today, at a time when many retailers have curtailed employee benefits, Nordstrom includes medical, dental, and vision benefits. In addition, it offers employee discounts and profit sharing.[1]

Source: Reprinted by permission of TNS Retail Forward.

OVERVIEW

Managing a retail business comprises three steps: setting up an organization structure, hiring and managing personnel, and managing operations—financially and nonfinancially. In this chapter, the first two steps are covered. Chapters 12 and 13 deal with operations management.

Setting Up a Retail Organization

Through a **retail organization**, a firm structures and assigns tasks (functions), policies, resources, authority, responsibilities, and rewards to efficiently and effectively satisfy the needs of its target market, employees, and management. Figure 11-1 shows various needs that should be taken into account when planning and assessing an organization structure.

As a rule, a firm cannot survive unless its organization structure satisfies the target market, regardless of how well employee and management needs are met. A structure that reduces costs through centralized buying but that results in the firm's being insensitive to geographic differences in customer preferences would be improper. Although many retailers perform similar tasks or functions (buying, pricing, displaying, and wrapping merchandise), there are many ways of organizing to carry out these functions. The process of setting

FIGURE 11-1

Selected Factors That Must Be Considered in Planning and Assessing a Retail Organization

TARGET MARKET NEEDS

Are there sufficient personnel to provide appropriate customer service?

Are personnel knowledgeable and courteous?

Are store facilities well maintained?

Are the specific needs of branch store customers met?

Are changing needs promptly addressed?

EMPLOYEE NEEDS

Are positions challenging and satisfying enough?

Is there an orderly promotion program from within?

Is the employee able to participate in the decision making?

Are the channels of communication clear and open?

Is the authority-responsibility relationship clear?

Is each employee treated fairly?

Is good performance rewarded?

MANAGEMENT NEEDS

Is it relatively easy to obtain and retain competent personnel?

Are personnel procedures clearly defined?

Does each worker report to only one supervisor?

Can each manager properly supervise all of the workers reporting to him or her?

Do operating departments have adequate staff support (e.g., marketing research)?

Are the levels of organization properly developed?

Are the organization's plans well integrated?

Are employees motivated?

Is absenteeism low?

Is there a system to replace personnel in an orderly manner?

Is there enough flexibility to adapt to changes in customers or the environment?

FIGURE 11-2

The Process of Organizing a Retail Firm

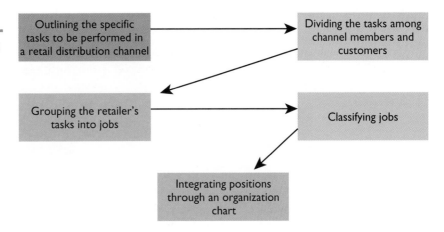

up a retail organization is outlined in Figure 11-2 and described next. Visit our Web site (**www.pearsonhighered.com/berman**) for a variety of links on running a retail business.

Specifying Tasks to Be Performed

The tasks in a distribution channel must be enumerated, and then keyed to the chosen strategy mix, for effective retailing to occur:

- ▶ Buying merchandise for the retailer.
- ▶ Shipping merchandise to the retailer.
- ▶ Receiving merchandise and checking incoming shipments.
- ▶ Setting prices.
- ▶ Marking merchandise.
- ▶ Inventory storage and control.
- ▶ Preparing merchandise and window displays.
- ▶ Facilities maintenance (e.g., keeping the store clean).
- ▶ Customer research and exchanging information.
- ▶ Customer contact (e.g., advertising, personal selling).
- ▶ Facilitating shopping (e.g., convenient site, short checkout lines).
- ▶ Customer follow-up and complaint handling.
- ▶ Personnel management.
- ▶ Repairs and alteration of merchandise.
- ▶ Billing customers.
- ▶ Handling receipts and financial records.
- ▶ Credit operations.
- ▶ Gift wrapping.
- ▶ Delivery to customers.
- ▶ Returning unsold or damaged merchandise to vendors.
- ▶ Sales forecasting and budgeting.
- ▶ Coordination.

Dividing Tasks Among Channel Members and Customers

Sysco is a wholesaler serving 400,000 restaurants, hotels, schools, and other locales. It offers them a wide range of support services (**www.sysco.com/services/services.html**).

Although the preceding tasks are typically performed in a distribution channel, they do not have to be done by a retailer. Some can be completed by the manufacturer, wholesaler, specialist, or consumer. Figure 11-3 shows the types of activities that could be carried out by each party. Following are some criteria to consider in allocating the functions related to consumer credit.

A task should be carried out only if desired by the target market. For some retailers, liberal credit policies may provide significant advantages over competitors. For others, a cash-only policy may reduce their overhead and lead to lower prices.

A task should be done by the party with the best competence. Credit collection may require a legal staff and computerized records—most affordable by medium or large retailers.

FIGURE 11-3

The Division of Tasks
in a Distribution Channel

Performer	Tasks
Retailer	Can perform all or some of the tasks in the distribution channel, from buying merchandise to coordination.
Manufacturer or Wholesaler	Can take care of few or many functions, such as shipping, marking merchandise, inventory storage, displays, research, etc.
Specialist(s)	Can undertake a particular task: buying office, delivery firm, warehouse, marketing research firm, ad agency, accountant, credit bureau, computer service firm.
Consumer	Can be responsible for delivery, credit (cash purchases), sales effort (self-service), product alterations (do-it-yourselfers), etc.

Smaller retailers are likely to rely on bank credit cards. There is a loss of control when an activity is delegated to another party. A credit collection agency, pressing for past-due payments, may antagonize customers.

The retailer's institutional framework can have an impact on task allocation. Franchisees are readily able to get together to have their own private-label brands. Independents cannot do this as easily.

Task allocation depends on the savings gained by sharing or shifting tasks. The credit function is better performed by an outside credit bureau if it has expert personnel and ongoing access to financial data, uses tailored computer software, pays lower rent (due to an out-of-the-way site), and so on. Many retailers cannot attain these savings themselves.

This site (http://retailindustry.about.com/od/retailjobscareers) highlights the range of jobs available in retailing.

Grouping Tasks into Jobs

After the retailer decides which tasks to perform, they are grouped into jobs. The jobs must be clearly structured. Here are examples of grouping tasks into jobs:

Tasks	Jobs
Displaying merchandise, customer contact, gift wrapping, customer follow-up	Sales personnel
Entering transaction data, handling cash and credit purchases, gift wrapping	Cashier(s)
Receiving merchandise, checking incoming shipments, marking merchandise, inventory storage and control, returning merchandise to vendors	Inventory personnel
Window dressing, interior display setups, use of mobile displays	Display personnel
Billing customers, credit operations, customer research	Credit personnel
Merchandise repairs and alterations, resolution of complaints, customer research	Customer service personnel
Cleaning store, replacing old fixtures	Janitorial personnel
Employee management, sales forecasting, budgeting, pricing, coordinating tasks	Management personnel

CAREERS IN RETAILING

Is Retail for Me? Human Resources

Human resources is the people side, the legal side, and the detail side of retail. Recruiting and hiring employees are the most obvious parts. But retail careers in human resources also include a wealth of other responsibilities such as training, designing training programs, overseeing compensation and benefits, and planning for and ensuring legal compliance in hiring and employment practices.

▶ *Head of Human Resources (HR).* Top HR job, responsible for policies in employment, employee relations, wages and benefits, orientation and training, safety and health, and employee services.

▶ *Compensation and Benefits Manager.* Responsible for plan design recommendations, legal compliance, and administration of both the compensation and employee benefits programs.

▶ *Benefits Manager.* Responsible for plan design recommendations, legal compliance, and administration of the employee benefits programs.

▶ *Compensation Manager.* Responsible for plan design recommendations, legal compliance, and administration of the compensation programs.

▶ *Head of Training and Development.* Responsible for training and development of associates through the creation and management of training programs and the effective communication of information.

▶ *HR Generalist: Home Office Staff.* Typically responsible for employee relations, recruiting/outplacement, and answering routine employee questions on benefits and HR policies in general, perhaps for specified job levels or operating groups.

▶ *HR Generalist: Regional or In-Store.* Typically responsible for employee relations, training, recruiting/outplacement, and answering routine questions on benefits and HR policies for a geographic group of stores. Typically reports to store operations management.

Source: Reprinted by permission of the National Retail Federation.

While grouping tasks into jobs, specialization should be considered so that each employee is responsible for a limited range of functions (as opposed to performing many diverse tasks). Specialization has the advantages of clearly defined tasks, greater expertise, reduced training, and hiring people with narrow education and experience. Problems can result due to extreme specialization: poor morale (boredom), people not being aware of their jobs' importance, and the need for more employees. Specialization means assigning explicit duties to individuals so a job position encompasses a homogeneous cluster of tasks.

Once tasks are grouped, job descriptions are constructed. These outline the job titles, objectives, duties, and responsibilities for every position. They are used as a hiring, supervision, and evaluation tool. Figure 11-4 contains a job description for a store manager.

Classifying Jobs

Jobs are then broadly grouped into functional, product, geographic, or combination classifications. *Functional classification* divides jobs by task—such as sales promotion, buying, and store operations. Expert knowledge is utilized. *Product classification* divides jobs on a goods or service basis. A department store hires different personnel for clothing, furniture, appliances, and so forth. This classification recognizes the differences in personnel requirements for different products.

Geographic classification is useful for chains operating in different areas. Employees are adapted to local conditions, and they are supervised by branch managers. Some firms, especially larger ones, use a *combination classification*. If a branch unit of a chain hires its selling staff, but buying personnel for each product line are hired by headquarters, the functional, product, and geographic formats are combined.

FIGURE 11-4

A Job Description
for a Store Manager

JOB TITLE: Store Manager for 34th Street Branch of Pombo's Department Stores

POSITION REPORTS TO: Senior Vice-President

POSITIONS REPORTING TO STORE MANAGER: All personnel in the 34th Street store

OBJECTIVES: To properly staff and operate the 34th Street store

DUTIES AND RESPONSIBILITIES:
- Sales forecasting and budgeting
- Personnel recruitment, selection, training, motivation, and evaluation
- Merchandise display, inventory management, and merchandise reorders
- Transferring merchandise among stores
- Handling store receipts, preparing bank transactions, opening and closing store
- Reviewing customer complaints
- Reviewing computer data forms
- Semi-annual review of overall operations and reports for top management

COMMITTEES AND MEETINGS:
- Attendance at monthly meetings with Senior Vice-President
- Supervision of weekly meetings with department managers

Developing an Organization Chart

The format of a retail organization must be designed in an integrated, coordinated way. Jobs must be defined and distinct; yet, interrelationships among positions must be clear. As one human resources consultant recently noted:

> The first step in unlocking your company's true potential is ensuring your employees understand how their specific job/role contributes to achieving your business objectives. Without a consistent process of setting goals for each individual employee that map directly to the firm's objectives, they may be spending too much time on the wrong activities. In fact, leading industry analysts estimate nearly 95 percent of workers are unaware of their firm's top objectives. And that's often because an effective process to communicate and track progress against these objectives does not exist. So how can your company expect people to work toward a shared vision—and deliver bottom-line results—if they're unclear what's expected of them? Establishing a formal process for creating relevant goals for each employee, and monitoring/measuring performance against company objectives, unquestionably results in both individual and company success.[2]

The **hierarchy of authority** outlines the job interactions within a company by describing the reporting relationships among employees (from the lowest level to the highest level). Coordination and control are provided by this hierarchy. A firm with many workers reporting to one manager has a *flat organization*. Its benefits are good communication, quicker handling of problems, and better employee identification with a job. The major problem tends to be the number of people reporting to one manager. A *tall organization* has several management levels, resulting in close supervision and fewer workers reporting to each manager. Problems include a long channel of communication, the impersonal impression given to workers regarding access to upper-level personnel, and inflexible rules.

With these factors in mind, a retailer devises an **organization chart,** which graphically displays its hierarchical relationships. Table 11-1 lists the principles to consider in establishing an organization chart. Figure 11-5 shows examples of basic organization charts.

Organizational Patterns in Retailing

An independent retailer has a simple organization. It operates only one store, the owner-manager usually supervises all employees, and workers have access to the owner-manager if there are problems. In contrast, a chain must specify how tasks are delegated, coordinate

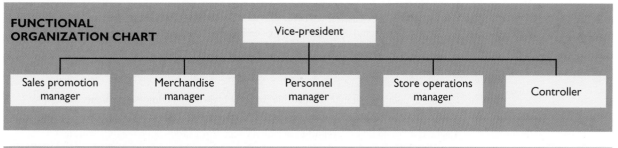

FUNCTIONAL ORGANIZATION CHART

Vice-president

- Sales promotion manager
- Merchandise manager
- Personnel manager
- Store operations manager
- Controller

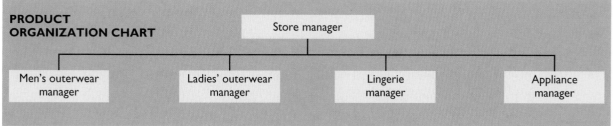

PRODUCT ORGANIZATION CHART

Store manager

- Men's outerwear manager
- Ladies' outerwear manager
- Lingerie manager
- Appliance manager

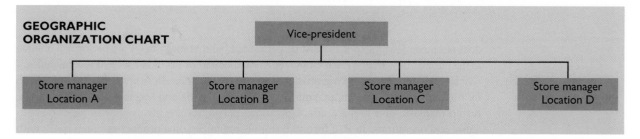

GEOGRAPHIC ORGANIZATION CHART

Vice-president

- Store manager Location A
- Store manager Location B
- Store manager Location C
- Store manager Location D

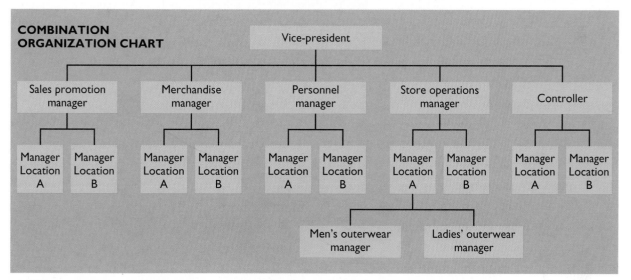

COMBINATION ORGANIZATION CHART

Vice-president

- Sales promotion manager
  - Manager Location A
  - Manager Location B
- Merchandise manager
  - Manager Location A
  - Manager Location B
- Personnel manager
  - Manager Location A
  - Manager Location B
- Store operations manager
  - Manager Location A
    - Men's outerwear manager
    - Ladies' outerwear manager
  - Manager Location B
- Controller
  - Manager Location A
  - Manager Location B

FIGURE 11-5

Different Forms of Retail Organization

multiple stores, and set common policies for employees. The organizational arrangements used by independent retailers, department stores, chain retailers, and diversified retailers are discussed next.

Organizational Arrangements Used by Small Independent Retailers

Small independents use uncomplicated arrangements with only two or three levels of personnel (owner-manager and employees), and the owner-manager personally runs the firm and oversees workers. There are few employees, little specialization, and no branch units. This

TABLE 11-1 Principles for Organizing a Retail Firm

An organization should show interest in its employees. Job rotation, promotion from within, participatory management, recognition, job enrichment, and so forth improve worker morale.

Employee turnover, lateness, and absenteeism should be monitored, because they may indicate personnel problems.

The line of authority should be traceable from the highest to the lowest positions. In this way, employees know to whom they report and who reports to them *(chain of command)*.

A subordinate should only report to one direct supervisor *(unity of command)*. This avoids the problem of workers receiving conflicting orders.

There is a limit to the number of employees a manager can directly supervise *(span of control)*.

A person responsible for a given objective needs the power to achieve it.

Although a supervisor can delegate authority, he or she is still responsible for subordinates.

The greater the number of organizational levels, the longer the time for communication to travel and the greater the coordination problems.

An organization has an informal structure aside from the formal organization chart. Informal relationships exercise power in the organization and may bypass formal relationships and procedures.

does not mean fewer activities must be performed but that many tasks are performed relative to the number of workers. Each employee must allot part of his or her time to several duties.

Figure 11-6 shows the organizations of two small firms. In A, a boutique is organized by function. Merchandising personnel buy and sell goods and services, plan assortments, set up displays, and prepare ads. Operations personnel are involved with store maintenance and operations. In B, a furniture store is organized on a product-oriented basis, with personnel in each category responsible for selected activities. All products get proper attention, and some expertise is developed. This is important because different skills are necessary to buy and sell each type of furniture.

Organizational Arrangements Used by Department Stores

Many department stores continue to use organizational arrangements that are a modification of the **Mazur plan,** which divides all retail activities into four functional areas—merchandising, publicity, store management, and accounting and control:

1. *Merchandising*—buying, selling, stock planning and control, promotion planning.
2. *Publicity*—window and interior displays, advertising, planning and executing promotional events (along with merchandise managers), advertising research, public relations.

FIGURE 11-6

Organization Structures
Used by Small
Independents

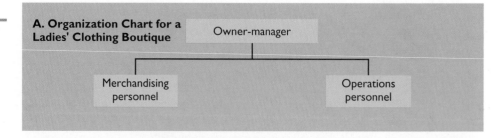

A. Organization Chart for a Ladies' Clothing Boutique

Owner-manager

Merchandising personnel

Operations personnel

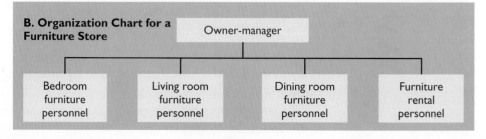

B. Organization Chart for a Furniture Store

Owner-manager

Bedroom furniture personnel

Living room furniture personnel

Dining room furniture personnel

Furniture rental personnel

3. *Store management*—merchandise care, customer services, buying store supplies and equipment, maintenance, operating activities (such as receiving and delivering products), store and merchandise protection (insurance and security), employee training and compensation, workroom operations.
4. *Accounting and control*—credit and collections, expense budgeting and control, inventory planning and control, recordkeeping.[3]

These areas are organized into *line* (direct authority and responsibility) and *staff* (advisory and support) components. Thus, a controller and a publicity manager provide staff services to merchandisers, but within their disciplines, personnel are organized on a line basis. Figure 11-7 illustrates the Mazur plan.

The merchandising division is responsible for buying and selling. It is headed by a merchandising manager, who is often viewed as the most important area executive. He or she supervises buyers, devises financial controls for each department, coordinates merchandise plans (so there is a consistent image among departments), and interprets the effects of economic data. In some cases, divisional merchandise managers are utilized, so the number of buyers reporting to a single manager does not become unwieldy.

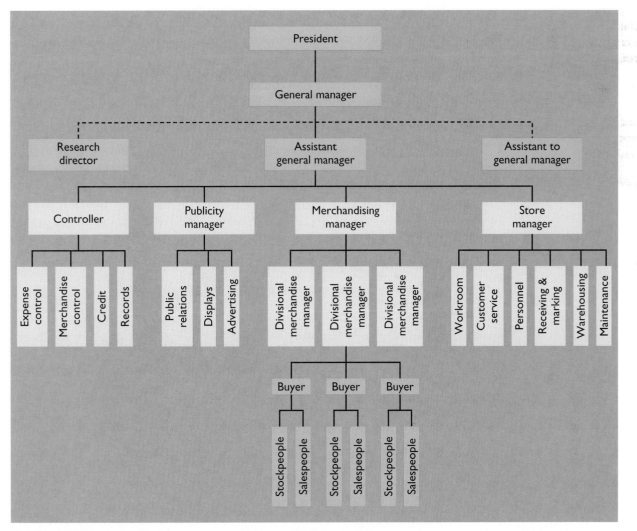

FIGURE 11-7

The Basic Mazur Organization Plan for Department Stores

Source: Adapted from Paul Mazur, *Principles of Organization Applied to Modern Retailing* (New York: Harper & Brothers, 1927), frontispiece. Reprinted by permission.

In the basic Mazur plan, the buyer has complete accountability for expenses and profit goals within a department. Duties include preparing preliminary budgets, studying trends, negotiating with vendors over price, planning the number of salespeople, and informing sales personnel about the merchandise purchased. Grouping buying and selling activities into one job (buyer) may present a problem. Because buyers are not constantly on the selling floor, training, scheduling, and supervising personnel may suffer.

The growth of branch stores led to three Mazur plan derivatives: *main store control,* by which headquarters executives oversee and operate branches; *separate store organization,* by which each branch has its own buying responsibilities; and **equal store organization,** by which buying is centralized and branches become sales units with equal operational status. The latter is the most popular format.

In the main store control format, most authority remains at headquarters. Merchandise planning and buying, advertising, financial controls, store hours, and other tasks are centrally managed to standardize the performance. Branch store managers hire and supervise employees, but daily operations conform to company policies. This works well if there are few branches and the preferences of their customers are similar to those at the main store. As branch stores increase, buyers, the advertising director, and others may be overworked and give little attention to branches. Because headquarters personnel are not at the branches, differences in customer preferences may be overlooked.

The separate store format places merchandise managers in branch stores, which have autonomy for merchandising and operations. Customer needs are quickly noted, but duplication of tasks is possible. Coordination can also be a problem. Transferring goods between branches is more complex and costly. This format is best if stores are large, branches are dispersed, or local customer tastes vary widely.

In the equal store format, the benefits of both centralization and decentralization are sought. Buying—forecasting, planning, purchasing, pricing, distribution to branches, and promotion—is centralized. Selling—presenting merchandise, selling, customer services, and operations—is managed locally. All stores, including headquarters, are treated alike. Buyers are freed from managing so many workers. Data gathering is critical since buyers have less customer contact.

Organizational Arrangements Used by Chain Retailers

Various chain retailers use a version of the equal store organization, as depicted in Figure 11-8. Although chains' organizations may differ, they generally have these attributes:

▶ There are many functional divisions, such as sales promotion, merchandise management, distribution, operations, real-estate, personnel, and information systems.
▶ Overall authority is centralized. Store managers have selling responsibility.
▶ Many operations are standardized (fixtures, store layout, building design, merchandise lines, credit policy, and store service).
▶ An elaborate control system keeps management informed.
▶ Some decentralization lets branches adapt to localities and increases store manager responsibilities. Although large chains standardize most of the items their outlets carry, store managers often fine-tune the rest of the strategy mix for the local market. This is empowerment at the store manager level.

Organizational Arrangements Used by Diversified Retailers

A **diversified retailer** is a multi-line firm operating under central ownership. Like other chains, a diversified retailer operates multiple stores; unlike typical chains, a diversified firm is involved with different types of retail operations. Here are two examples:

▶ Kroger Co. (**www.kroger.com**) operates supermarkets, warehouse stores, supercenters, convenience stores, and jewelry stores; and it also has a manufacturing group. The firm owns multiple store chains in each of its retail categories. See Figure 11-9.

To discover how Kroger operates, go to this section of its Web site (**www. thekrogerco.com/operations/ operations.htm**).

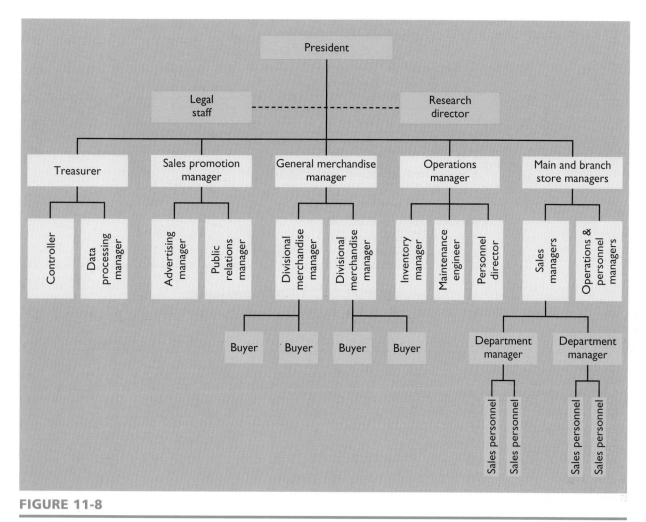

FIGURE 11-8

The Equal Store Organizational Format Used by Many Chain Stores

▶ Japan's Aeon Co. (**www.aeon.info/en**) comprises superstores, supermarkets, discount stores, home centers, specialty stores, convenience stores, financial services stores, restaurants, and more. Besides Japan, Aeon has facilities in numerous other countries. It is also a shopping center developer.

Due to their multiple strategy mixes, diversified retailers face complex organizational considerations. Interdivision control is needed, with operating procedures and goals clearly communicated. Interdivision competition must be coordinated. Resources must be divided among different divisions. Potential image and advertising conflicts must be avoided. Management skills must adapt to different operations.

Human Resource Management in Retailing

Human resource management involves recruiting, selecting, training, compensating, and supervising personnel in a manner consistent with the retailer's organization structure and strategy mix. Personnel practices are dependent on the line of business, the number of employees, the location of outlets, and other factors. Because good personnel are needed to develop and carry out retail strategies, and labor costs can amount to 50 percent or more of expenses, the value of human resource management is clear.

U.S. retailing employs 25 million people. Thus, there is a constant need to attract new employees—and retain existing ones. For example, 2 million fast-food workers are aged 16 to 20, and they stay in their jobs for only short periods. In general, retailers

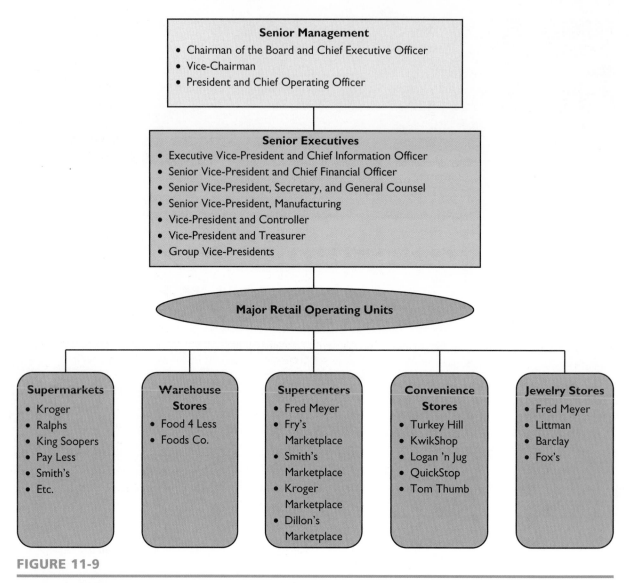

FIGURE 11-9

The Organizational Structure of Kroger Co. (Selected Store Chains and Positions)

Source: Compiled by the authors from the *Kroger Co. 2008 Annual Report.*

need to reduce the turnover rate; when workers quickly exit a firm, the results can be disastrous. See Table 11-2.

Consider the approaches of Target, Uno Chicago Grill, Nordstrom, and Whole Foods:

▶ Target is committed to employee development and retention: "Goals are clear, challenging, and met through teamwork. In our stores, guests find a clean, organized, welcoming atmosphere, and smart, stylish merchandise. Creating this shopping experience for guests begins with creating a great workplace for team members: 'The Strength of Many. The Power of One.' We know that an inclusive environment, where all contributions are valued, is critical to ensuring future success. The power of individuality and the strength created when teams leverage those unique capabilities and experiences are essential to our shared vision of remaining an industry leader."[4]

Uno Chicago Grill (**www. unos.com/employ.html**) has a clear employee development plan.

▶ Uno Chicago Grill regularly recruits college graduates for its management training program: "If you're ready to move ahead with a dynamic national chain, team up with Uno today. Each restaurant has a team made up of a general manager, assistant general manager, and 1 to 3 managers. In building this team, Uno works hard to offer the right mix to meet career aspirations, training opportunities, work/family considerations, and pay and benefits expectations."[5]

TABLE 11-2 The True Cost of Employee Turnover

Costs of using fill-in employees until permanent replacements are found.

Severance pay for exiting employees.

Costs of hiring new employees: advertising, interviewing time, travel expenses, testing, screening.

Training costs: trainers, training materials and technology, trainee compensation, supervisor time (on-the-job training).

Costs of mistakes and lower productivity while new employees gain experience.

Customer dissatisfaction due to the departure of previous employees and the use of inexperienced workers.

Loss of continuity among co-workers.

Poor employee morale when turnover is high.

Lower employee loyalty to retailer when turnover is high.

▶ At Nordstrom, buying is decentralized and salespeople have considerable input. They can place special orders and are empowered to resolve customer problems: "Our goal is to provide outstanding service every day, one customer at a time. The 'Inverted Pyramid' represents our philosophy and our structure, placing our customers at the top. Next are those who directly serve our customers—our salespeople and those supporting them. Department managers, buyers, merchandise managers, store managers, regional managers, our executive team, and our board of directors then support this group. We work hard to make decisions in the best interest of our customers and those serving them."[6]

▶ Whole Foods Market has been widely honored for its employee-nurturing environment: "We mentor our team members through education and on-the-job experience. We encourage participation and involvement at all levels of our business. Team expertise is developed by fostering creativity, self-responsibility, and self-directed teamwork, and by rewarding productivity and performance. We encourage all qualified team members to apply for any available opportunity in their store or facility, their region, or the company as they expand their product knowledge, develop their skills, and enhance their value to their teams. To support advancement from within, all openings for positions at team leader level and higher are listed on our internal job site."[7]

ETHICS IN RETAILING | How Retailers Can Succeed by Doing the Right Thing

Costco (**www.costco.com**), Wegmans (**www.wegmans.com**), and Ikea (**www.ikea.com**) are just a few of the retailers that believe treating their employees well is good business. These are among the common advantages of providing employees with fair wages and healthcare benefits: lower employee turnover, lower costs associated with hiring and firing (such as reduced advertising, lower training costs for new employees, and lower severance costs), and a positive corporate culture that is related to employee satisfaction.

Wegmans Food Markets was ranked number three in *Fortune*'s "100 Best Companies to Work For" for 2008. The 71-unit, family-owned chain consistently ranks close to the top of this *Fortune*'s annual study. Salaries are higher at Wegmans than at many other supermarkets

(the average department manager earns $50,000), and during the past 20 years, Wegmans has paid out more than $50 million in college scholarships to its employees.

Wegmans' labor costs are between 15 and 17 percent of its sales (versus 12 percent for the typical supermarket chain), while its employee turnover rate among full-time employees is 6 percent (versus 19 percent for similar-sized supermarket chains). And Wegmans' sales per square foot are 50 percent higher than the industry average.

Sources: "100 Best Companies to Work For," **http://money.cnn.com/magazines/fortune/bestcompanies/2008/snapshots/3.html** (August 19, 2008); and "Wegmans: I Have Never Given Away More Than I Got Back," **http://givingypcontrol.wordpress.com/category/wegmans** (August 19, 2008).

The Special Human Resource Environment of Retailing

The Bureau of Labor Statistics compiles current employment data on such jobs as retail sales worker supervisors and managers (www.bls.gov/oco).

Retailers face a human resource environment characterized by a large number of inexperienced workers, long hours, highly visible employees, a diverse workforce, many part-time workers, and variable customer demand. These factors complicate employee hiring, staffing, and supervision.

The need for a large retail labor force often means hiring those with little or no prior experience. Sometimes, a position in retailing represents a person's first "real job." People are attracted to retailing because they find jobs near to home; and retail positions (such as cashiers, stock clerks, and some types of sales personnel) may require limited education, training, and skill. Also, the low wages paid for some positions result in the hiring of inexperienced people. Thus, high employee turnover and cases of poor performance, lateness, and absenteeism may result.

The long working hours in retailing, which may include weekends, turn off certain prospective employees; many retailers now have longer hours since more shoppers want to shop during evenings and weekends. Accordingly, some retailers require at least two shifts of full-time employees.

Retailing employees are highly visible to the customer. Therefore, when personnel are selected and trained, special care must be taken with regard to their manners and appearance. Some small retailers do not place enough emphasis on employee appearance (neat grooming and appropriate attire).

It is common for retailers to have a diverse labor force, with regard to age, work experience, gender, race, and other factors. This means that firms must train and supervise their workers so that they interact well with one another—and are sensitive to the perspectives and needs of one another. Consider the employee strategy of Home Depot: "We have partnered with national nonprofit and government agencies and educational organizations to reach out to the communities in which we operate and to provide us with a broad range of qualified candidates with diverse backgrounds." Home Depot has partnerships with the U.S. military, AARP (American Association of Retired Persons), and several Hispanic groups.[8]

Due to their long hours, retailers regularly hire part-time workers. In many supermarkets, more than one-half of the workers are part-time, and problems may arise. Some part-time employees are more lackadaisical, late, absent, or likely to quit than full-time employees. They must be closely monitored.

Variations in customer demand by day, time period, or season may cause difficulties. Nearly 40 percent of U.S. shoppers make their major supermarket trips on Saturday or Sunday. So, how many employees should there be on Monday through Friday and how many on Saturday and Sunday? Demand differences by day part (morning, afternoon, evening) and by season (fall, holidays) also affect planning. When stores are very busy, even administrative and clerical employees may be needed on the sales floor.

As a rule, retailers should consider these points:

▶ Recruitment and selection procedures must efficiently generate sufficient applicants.
▶ Some training must be short because workers are inexperienced and temporary.
▶ Compensation must be perceived as "fair" by employees.
▶ Advancement opportunities must be available to employees who view retailing as a career.
▶ Employee appearance and work habits must be explained and reviewed.
▶ Diverse workers must be taught to work together well and amicably.
▶ Morale problems may result from high turnover and the many part-time workers.
▶ Full- and part-time workers may conflict, especially if some full-timers are replaced.

Various retail career opportunities are available to women and minorities. There is still some room for improvement.

WOMEN IN RETAILING

Retailing has made a lot of progress in career advancement for women. According to the "2008 Catalyst Census of Women Board Directors of the *Fortune* 500," these retailers are among the U.S. public companies with at least 25 percent of corporate officers who are women: Avon, Macy's, Circuit City, Nordstrom, Office Depot, Target, Barnes & Noble, Publix Super Markets, Amazon.com, Avis, CVS, J.C. Penney, Sears, TJX, and Walt Disney. In the lodging and food service sectors, the female-to-male mix for managerial jobs is nearly 50 percent. More than two-thirds of supervisors at eating and drinking establishments are women. Ikea, Marriott, Patagonia, Sears, Target, and other retailers are regularly rated as excellent companies for working mothers.

Women have more career options in retailing than ever before, as the following examples show. Mary Kay Ash (Mary Kay cosmetics), Debbi Fields (Mrs. Fields' Cookies), and Lillian Vernon (the direct marketer) founded retailing empires. As of 2009, women were chief executive officers of such U.S.-based retailers as Ann Taylor Stores, Avon, Charming Shoppes, Jack in the Box, PC Connection, Rite Aid, TJX, and Wendy's.

At Avon, Andrea Jung, the chairman and chief executive officer, is an Asian American woman, and 40 percent of its board of directors are women:

> Andrea Jung has been Chairman of the Board of Avon Products since September 6, 2001 and also its Chief Executive Officer since November 4, 1999. She is responsible for developing and executing all of Avon's long-term growth strategies, launching new brand initiatives, developing earnings opportunities for women worldwide, and defining Avon as the premier direct seller of beauty products.[9]

Rite Aid's chairman and chief executive officer is Mary Sammons. She became chairman in 2007, after being appointed as chief executive officer in 2003. She joined Rite Aid in late 1999 as president and chief operating officer:

> Before joining Rite Aid, Sammons was President and Chief Executive Officer of Fred Meyer Stores, a food, drug, and general merchandise retailer in the Pacific Northwest and a unit of Fred Meyer, Inc., which was bought by The Kroger Company in 1999. In 26 years at Fred Meyer, she held positions of increasing responsibility in all areas of operations and merchandising before becoming chief executive officer. Sammons is a member of the executive committee of the National Association of Chain Drug Stores—the chain drugstore trade association—and president of the Rite Aid Foundation.[10]

Despite recent progress, women still account for only 15 percent of corporate officers at publicly owned retail firms. These are some of the issues for retailers to address with regard to female workers:

▶ Meaningful training programs.
▶ Advancement opportunities.
▶ Flex time—the ability of employees to adapt their hours.
▶ Job sharing among two or more employees who each work less than full-time.
▶ Child care.

MINORITIES IN RETAILING

As with women, retailers have done many good things in the area of minority employment, with more still to be accomplished. Consider these examples of retailers cited in *Fortune*'s "100 Best Companies to Work for 2008: Minorities:"[11]

> At eBay, our business model is a little unusual. We've created a place where people come together to exchange ideas and experiences. They're why we're committed to keeping the eBay culture fun and unique and why we give back through the eBay Foundation, eBay Giving Works, volunteer programs, and our charity program outreach. We believe in diversity in both thought and experience because it helps us lead with our head, our hands, and our heart. We are committed to hiring, promoting, and compensating employees based on their qualifications and demonstrated ability to perform job responsibilities. eBay promotes equal employment opportunity to all employees and applicants, without regard to age, race, color, national origin, physical or mental disability, gender, religion, sexual orientation, gender identity, marital or veteran status, condition of pregnancy, or any other legally protected characteristic.

As part of her legacy, Mary Kay Ash left behind a charitable foundation (www.mkacf.org).

See why Avon calls itself "The Company for Women" (www.avoncompany.com/women).

Fortune annually lists the best employers among public companies (http://money.cnn.com/magazines/fortune/bestcompanies).

Stew Leonard's fast-paced, energetic environment is designed to bring out the very best in our team members. We are dedicated to making sure that our team members are safe, healthy, and happy. Being an equal opportunity employer is a source of great pride for us, and we actively promote this in all of our recruiting efforts. We celebrate the diversity of all of our team members. We believe that diversity is about more than just physical traits, but is a celebration of cultures, experiences, opinions, and life itself.

One of the best ways that Nordstrom has found to provide excellent customer service is by ensuring that we reflect the communities we serve. Having a workplace that attracts and supports diversity, benefits both our customers and employees. We believe each of our employees has the opportunity to realize their potential and contribute to the success of our company. Nordstrom is committed to recruiting, hiring, and promoting qualified people of all backgrounds, regardless of sex; race; color; creed; national origin; religion; age; marital status; pregnancy; physical, mental, or sensory disability; sexual orientation; gender identity; or any other basis protected by federal, state, or local law.

At Wal-Mart, the labor force includes more than 251,000 African American associates, more than 39,000 Asian and 5,000 Pacific Islander associates, more than 165,000 Hispanic associates, and more than 16,000 American Indian and Alaskan Native associates. Enterprise Rent-A-Car not only has a diverse work force itself, but it also requires the same for its suppliers: "Enterprise wants the supplier base to bear a reasonable relationship to the communities in which we do business. Our supplier diversity program identifies and encourages equal opportunities for minority-owned, women-owned, and other types of disadvantaged businesses. National partnerships with organizations such as the National Minority Supplier Development Council, Women Business Enterprise Council, and Airport Minority Advisory Council assist us in reaching our goals." Walgreens even has a special Web site devoted to employee diversity (**http://diversity.walgreens.com/default.html**).[12]

As the president of the National Retail Federation—the leading trade association in the industry—has observed: "African Americans, Hispanics, and other minorities will find prime opportunities for career development and advancement in this dynamic industry as retailers recognize the need for diversity to be reflected on the selling floor and in upper management."[13]

These are some of the ways for retailers to better address the needs of minority workers:

McDonald's (**http://www. mcdonalds.com/usa/work/ diversity.html**) actively encourages diversity and understanding.

▶ Clear policy statements from top management as to the value of employee diversity.
▶ Active recruitment programs to stimulate minority applications.
▶ Meaningful training programs.
▶ Advancement opportunities.
▶ Zero tolerance for insensitive workplace behavior.

The Human Resource Management Process in Retailing

The **human resource management process** consists of these interrelated personnel activities: recruitment, selection, training, compensation, and supervision. The goals are to obtain, develop, and retain employees. When applying the process, diversity, labor laws, and privacy should be considered.

Diversity involves two premises: (1) that employees be hired and promoted in a fair and open way, without regard to gender, ethnic background, and other related factors; and (2) that in a diverse society, the workplace should be representative of such diversity.

There are several aspects of labor laws for retailers to satisfy. They must not

▶ Hire underage workers.
▶ Pay workers "off the books."
▶ Require workers to engage in illegal acts (such as bait-and-switch selling).
▶ Discriminate in hiring or promoting workers.
▶ Violate worker safety regulations.
▶ Disobey the Americans with Disabilities Act.
▶ Deal with suppliers that disobey labor laws.

Retailers must also be careful not to violate employees' privacy rights. Only necessary data about workers should be gathered and stored, and such information should not be freely disseminated.

We now discuss each activity in human resource management for sales and middle-management jobs. For more insights on the process, go to our Web site (**www. pearsonhighered.com/berman**).

RECRUITING RETAIL PERSONNEL

Recruitment is the activity whereby a retailer generates a list of job applicants. Table 11-3 indicates the features of several key recruitment sources. In addition to these sources, the Web now plays a bigger role in recruitment. Many retailers have a career or job section at their Web site, and some sections are as elaborate as the overall sites. Visit Target Stores' site (**www. target.com**), for example. Scroll down to the bottom of the home page and click on "Careers."

For entry-level sales jobs, retailers rely on educational institutions, ads, walk-ins (or write-ins), Web sites, and employee recommendations. For middle-management positions, retailers rely on employment agencies, competitors, ads, and current employee referrals. The retailer's typical goal is to generate a list of potential employees, which is reduced during selection. However, retailers that only accept applications from those who meet minimum background standards can save a lot of time and money.

SELECTING RETAIL PERSONNEL

The firm next selects new employees by matching the traits of potential employees with specific job requirements. Job analysis and description, the application blank, interviewing, testing (optional), references, and a physical exam (optional) are tools in the process; they should be integrated.

In **job analysis,** information is amassed on each job's functions and requirements: duties, responsibilities, aptitude, interest, education, experience, and physical tasks. It is used to select personnel, set performance standards, and assign salaries. For example,

TABLE 11-3   Recruitment Sources and Their Characteristics

Sources	Characteristics
Outside the Company	
Educational institutions	a. High schools, business schools, community colleges, universities, graduate schools b. Good for training positions; ensure minimum educational requirements are met; especially useful when long-term contacts with instructors are developed
Other channel members, competitors	a. Employees of wholesalers, manufacturers, ad agencies, competitors; leads from each of these b. Reduce extent of training; can evaluate performance with prior firm(s); must instruct in company policy; some negative morale if current employees feel bypassed for promotions
Advertisements	a. Newspapers, trade publications, professional journals, Web sites b. Large quantity of applicants; average applicant quality may not be high; cost/applicant is low; additional responsibility placed on screening; can reduce unacceptable applications by noting job qualifications in ads
Employment agencies	a. Private organizations, professional organizations, government, executive search firms b. Must be carefully selected; must be determined who pays fee; good for applicant screening; specialists in personnel
Unsolicited applicants	a. Walk-ins, write-ins b. Wide variance in quality; must be carefully screened; file should be kept for future positions
Within the Company	
Current and former employees	a. Promotion or transfer of existing full-time employees, part-time employees; rehiring of laid-off employees b. Knowledge of company policies and personnel; good for morale; honest appraisal from in-house supervisor
Employee recommendations	a. Friends, acquaintances, relatives b. Value of recommendations depend on honesty and judgment of current employees

department managers often act as the main sales associates for their areas, oversee other sales associates, have some administrative duties, report to the store manager, are eligible for bonuses, and are paid $25,000 to $40,000+ annually.

Job analysis should lead to written job descriptions. A **traditional job description** contains a position's title, relationships (superior and subordinate), and specific roles and tasks. Figure 11-4 showed a store manager job description. Yet, using a traditional description alone has been criticized. This may limit a job's scope, as well as its authority and responsibility; not let a person grow; limit activities to those listed; and not describe how positions are coordinated. To complement a traditional description, a **goal-oriented job description** can enumerate basic functions, the relationship of each job to overall goals, the interdependence of positions, and information flows. See Figure 11-10.

FIGURE 11-10

A Goal-Oriented Job Description for a Management Trainee

Attributes Required	Ability	Desire	In the Retailing Environment
ANALYTICAL SKILLS: ability to solve problems; strong numerical ability for analysis of facts and data for planning, managing, and controlling.			Retail executives are problem solvers. Knowledge and understanding of past performance and present circumstances form the basis for action and planning.
CREATIVITY: ability to generate and recognize imaginative ideas and solutions; ability to recognize the need for and be responsive to change.			Retail executives are idea people. Successful buying results from sensitive, aware decisions, while merchandising requires imaginative, innovative techniques.
DECISIVENESS: ability to make quick decisions and render judgments, take action, and commit oneself to completion.			Retail executives are action people. Whether it's new fashion trends or customer desires, decisions must be made quickly and confidently in this ever-changing environment.
FLEXIBILITY: ability to adjust to the ever-changing needs of the situation; ability to adapt to different people, places, and things; willingness to do whatever is necessary to get the task done.			Retail executives are flexible. Surprises in retailing never cease. Plans must be altered quickly to accommodate changes in trends, styles, and attitudes, while numerous ongoing activities cannot be ignored.
INITIATIVE: ability to originate action rather than wait to be told what to do and ability to act based on conviction.			Retail executives are doers. Sales volumes, trends, and buying opportunities mean continual action. Opportunities for action must be seized.
LEADERSHIP: ability to inspire others to trust and respect your judgment; ability to delegate and to guide and persuade others.			Retail executives are managers. Running a business means depending on others to get the work done. One person cannot do it all.
ORGANIZATION: ability to establish priorities and courses of action for self and/or others; skill in planning and following up to achieve results.			Retail executives are jugglers. A variety of issues, functions, and projects are constantly in motion. To reach your goals, priorities must be set and work must be delegated to others.
RISK-TAKING: willingness to take calculated risks based on thorough analysis and sound judgment and to accept responsibility for the results.			Retail executives are courageous. Success in retailing often comes from taking calculated risks and having the confidence to try something new before someone else does.
STRESS TOLERANCE: ability to perform consistently under pressure, to thrive on constant change and challenge.			Retail executives are resilient. As the above description should suggest, retailing is fast-paced and demanding.

An **application blank** is usually the first tool used to screen applicants; providing data on education, experience, health, reasons for leaving prior jobs, outside activities, hobbies, and references. It is usually short, requires little interpretation, and can be used as the basis for probing in an interview. With a **weighted application blank,** factors having a high relationship with job success are given more weight than others. Retailers that use such a form analyze the performance of current and past employees and determine the criteria (education, experience, and so on) best correlated with job success (as measured by longer tenure, better performance, and so on). After weighted scores are awarded to all job applicants (based on data they provide), a minimum total score becomes a cutoff point for hiring. An effective application blank aids retailers in lessening turnover and selecting high achievers.

An application blank should be used along with a job description. Those meeting minimum job requirements are processed further; others are immediately rejected. In this way, the application blank provides a quick and inexpensive method of screening.

The interview seeks information that can be amassed only by personal questioning and observation. It lets an employer determine a candidate's verbal ability, note his or her appearance, ask questions keyed to the application, and probe career goals. Interviewing decisions must be made about the level of formality, the number and length of interviews, the location, the person(s) to do the interviewing, and the interview structure. These decisions often depend on the interviewer's ability and the job's requirements.

Small firms tend to hire an applicant who has a good interview. Large firms may add testing. In this case, a candidate who does well in an interview then takes a psychological test (to measure personality, intelligence, interest, and leadership) and/or achievement tests (to measure learned knowledge).[14]

Tests must be administered by qualified people. Standardized exams should not be used unless proven effective in predicting job performance. Because achievement tests deal with specific skills or information (like the ability to make a sales presentation), they are easier to interpret than psychological tests, and direct relationships between knowledge and ability can be shown. In administering tests, retailers must not violate any federal, state, or local law. The federal Employee Polygraph Protection Act bars retailers from using lie detector tests in most hiring situations (drugstores are exempt).

CVS (**www.cvscaremark. com/careers**) encourages potential employees to apply online.

To save time and operate more efficiently, some retailers—large and small—use computerized application blanks and testing. Advance Auto Parts, Babies "R" Us, Best Buy, Blockbuster, CVS, Family Dollar, Lowe's, PetSmart, and Sports Authority are among those with in-store kiosks that allow people to apply for jobs, complete application blanks, and answer several questions. This speeds up the hiring process and attracts a lot of applicants.

Many retailers get references from applicants that can be checked either before or after an interview. References are contacted to see how enthusiastically they recommend an applicant, check the applicant's honesty, and ask why an applicant left a prior job. Mail and phone checks are inexpensive, fast, and easy.

Some firms require a physical exam because of the physical activity, long hours, and tensions involved in many retailing positions. A clean bill of health means the candidate is offered a job. Again, federal, state, and local laws must be followed.

Each step in the selection process complements the others; together they give the retailer a good information package for choosing personnel. As a rule, retailers should use job descriptions, application blanks, interviews, and reference checks. Follow-up interviews, psychological and achievement tests, and physical exams depend on the retailer and the position. Inexpensive tools (such as application blanks) are used in the early screening stages; more costly, in-depth tools (such as interviews) are used after reducing the applicant pool. Equal opportunity, nondiscriminatory practices must be followed.

TRAINING RETAIL PERSONNEL

Every new employee should receive **pre-training,** an indoctrination on the firm's history and policies, as well as a job orientation on hours, compensation, the chain of command, and job duties. New employees should also be introduced to co-workers: "It is important that employees learn as soon as possible what is expected of them, and what to expect from others, in addition to learning about the values and attitudes of the organization. While people can learn from experience, they will make many mistakes that are unnecessary and potentially damaging. The main reasons orientation programs fail: The program was not planned; the employee was unaware of the job requirements; the employee does not feel welcome."[15]

Training programs teach new (and existing) personnel how best to perform their jobs or how to improve themselves. Training can range from one-day sessions on operating a computerized cash register, personal selling techniques, or compliance with affirmative action programs to two-year programs for executive trainees on all aspects of the retailer and its operations:

▶ For each new employee, The Container Store provides extensive formal training, which includes learning about how to perform multiple jobs: "We place so much importance on service that every first-year, full-time salesperson receives about 241 hours of training—in a retail industry where the average is about seven hours. And training continues throughout an employee's career. Our trainers are in the stores every day ensuring that store employees are knowledgeable and empowered to offer the unparalleled customer service that we are known for in the industry."[16]

▶ Best Buy now uses an online "Learning Lounge" to help facilitate employee training for new and continuing workers and to let employees easily communicate with one another: The portal "provides course materials from Best Buy and its suppliers to learn about product details and how to help customers. There are incentives for workers to choose from a variety of audio, video, and document resources. Employees are encouraged to share ideas with others through message boards, blogs, and social networks." The portal is also "designed for employees to take online tests to get certified as having completed assigned learning tasks and to let managers monitor participation."[17]

▶ At the Panda Express restaurant chain: "The Panda Leadership Forum is designed for high-potential area coaches (Panda's designation for multi-unit supervisors). After receiving a nomination by a supervisor, the selected employee will travel to the company's headquarters four times a year to participate in various personal self-awareness and skill-development activities and events. To date, no senior executive has come from outside the Panda ranks."[18]

Training should be an ongoing activity. New equipment, legal changes, new product lines, job promotions, low employee morale, and employee turnover necessitate not only training but also retraining. Macy's has a program called "clienteling," which tutors sales associates on how to have better long-term relations with specific repeat customers. Core vendors of Macy's teach sales associates about the features and benefits of new merchandise when it is introduced.

There are several training decisions, as shown in Figure 11-11. They can be divided into three categories: identifying needs, devising appropriate training methods, and evaluation.

Short-term training needs can be identified by measuring the gap between the skills that workers already have and the skills desired by the firm (for each job). This training should

FIGURE 11-11

A Checklist of Selected Training Decisions

✓ When should training occur? (At the time of hiring and/or after being at the workplace?)

✓ How long should training be?

✓ What training programs should there be for new employees? For existing employees?

✓ Who should conduct each training program? (Supervisor, co-worker, training department, or outside specialist?)

✓ Where should training take place? (At the workplace or in a training room?)

✓ What material (content) should be learned? How should it be taught?

✓ Should audiovisuals be used? If yes, how?

✓ Should elements of the training program be computerized? If yes, how?

✓ How should the effectiveness of training be measured?

TECHNOLOGY IN RETAILING

Employee Scheduling Software at Ann Taylor Stores

Retailers increasingly are seeking to increase the productivity of their employees. Firms such as Limited Brands (**www.limitedbrands.com**), Gap (**www.gap.com**), Williams-Sonoma (**www.williams-sonoma.com**), and Ann Taylor Stores (**www.anntaylor.com**) have installed employee special software that schedules their employees into specific time shifts. Software suppliers say that their products can increase worker productivity by 15 percent.

At Ann Taylor Stores, which uses software developed by Red Prairie (**www.redprairie.com**), store managers can determine each retail salesperson's key performance metrics: average sales per hour, units sold, and average transaction amount. Based on these measures, the most productive employees can be scheduled to work at a store's peak selling times. Because the system rewards productive salespeople with favorable hours, it gives employees an incentive to suggest additional fashion accessories and to trade up customers to more costly apparel items. Before the system was operational, Ann Taylor did not properly align staff availability with store traffic. In many instances, stores had too many employees at 9:00 A.M. and too few at peak hours such as 2:00 P.M. or later in the afternoon.

One major concern is that this software system may encourage retail salespeople to fight over customers. Retail salespeople who are assigned the poorest hours will also find it very difficult to have high sales productivity.

Source: Vanessa O'Connell, "Retailers Reprogram Workers in a Push for More Efficiency," *Wall Street Journal* (September 11, 2008), pp. A1, A11.

prepare employees for possible job rotation, promotions, and changes in the company. A longer training plan lets a firm identify future needs and train workers appropriately.

There are many training methods for retailers: lectures, demonstrations, videos, programmed instruction, conferences, sensitivity training, case studies, role playing, behavior modeling, and competency-based instruction. Some techniques may be computerized—as more firms are doing. The methods' attributes are noted in Table 11-4. Retailers often use more than one technique to reduce employee boredom and cover the material better.

Take a look at Centurion Systems' "Résumé" of retail training solutions (**www.centurionsys.com**).

Computer-based training software is available from a variety of vendors. For example, Centurion Systems has devised more than 100 training modules that have been used to train more than 1 million retail employees in such areas as point-of-sales systems, labor scheduling, customer service, manager training, store operations, merchandise management, and more. Among its many clients are BJ's, Domino's, Godiva, Gymboree, Kohl's, Macy's, and Tiffany.

TABLE 11-4   The Characteristics of Retail Training Methods

Method	Characteristics
Lectures	Factual, uninterrupted presentations of material; can use professional educator or expert in the field; no active participation by trainees
Demonstrations	Good for showing how to use equipment or do a sales presentation; applies relevance of training; active participation by trainees
Videos	Highly visual, good for demonstration; can be used many times; no active participation by trainees
Programmed instruction	Presents information in a structured manner; requires response from trainees; provides performance feedback; adjustable to trainees' pace; high initial investment
Conferences	Useful for supervisory training; conference leaders must encourage participation; reinforce training
Sensitivity training	Extensive interaction; good for supervisors as a tool for understanding employees
Case studies	Actual or hypothetical problems presented, including circumstances, pertinent information, and questions; learning by doing; exposure to a wide variety of problems
Role playing	Trainees placed into real-life situations and act out roles
Behavior modeling	Trainees taught to imitate models shown in videos or in role-playing sessions
Competency-based instruction	Trainees given a list of tasks or exercises that are presented in a self-paced format

For training to succeed, a conducive environment is needed, based on several principles:

▶ All people can learn if taught well; there should be a sense of achievement.
▶ A person learns better when motivated; intelligence alone is not sufficient.
▶ Learning should be goal-oriented.
▶ A trainee learns more when he or she participates and is not a passive listener.
▶ The teacher must provide guidance, as well as adapt to the learner and to the situation.
▶ Learning should be approached as a series of steps rather than a one-time occurrence.
▶ Learning should be spread out over a reasonable period of time rather than be compressed.
▶ The learner should be encouraged to do homework or otherwise practice.
▶ Different methods of learning should be combined.
▶ Performance standards should be set and good performance recognized.

A training program must be regularly evaluated. Comparisons can be made between the performance of those who receive training and those who do not, as well as among employees receiving different types of training for the same job. Evaluations should always be made in relation to stated training goals. In addition, training effects should be measured over different time intervals (such as immediately, 30 days later, and six months later), and proper records maintained.

COMPENSATING RETAIL PERSONNEL

Total **compensation**—direct monetary payments (salaries, commissions, and bonuses) and indirect payments (paid vacations, health and life insurance, and retirement plans)—should be fair to both the retailer and its employees. To better motivate employees, some firms also have profit-sharing. Smaller retailers often pay salaries, commissions, and/or bonuses and have fewer fringe benefits. Bigger ones generally pay salaries, commissions, and/or bonuses and offer more fringe benefits.

This site (**www.dol.gov/ esa/minwage/america.htm**) shows the minimum wage in every state.

Since July 2009, the hourly federal minimum wage has been $7.25 (up from $6.55 as of July 2008 and $5.85 as of July 2007). In addition, 45 states have their own laws—about a dozen higher than the federal minimum and six lower. The minimum wage has the most impact on retailers hiring entry-level, part-time workers. Full-time, career-track retailing jobs are paid an attractive market rate; to attract part-time workers during good economic times, retailers must often pay salaries above the minimum.

At some large firms, compensation for certain positions is set through collective bargaining. According to the U.S. Bureau of Labor Statistics, about 850,000 retail employees are represented by labor unions. However, union membership varies greatly. Unionized grocery stores account for more than one-half of total U.S. supermarket sales, while independent supermarkets are not usually unionized.

With a *straight salary,* a worker is paid a fixed amount per hour, week, month, or year. Advantages are retailer control, employee security, and known expenses. Disadvantages are retailer inflexibility, the limited productivity incentive, and fixed costs. Clerks and cashiers are usually paid salaries. With a *straight commission,* earnings are directly tied to productivity (such as sales volume). Advantages are retailer flexibility, the link to worker productivity, no fixed costs, and employee incentive. Disadvantages are the retailer's potential lack of control over the tasks performed, the risk of low earnings to employees, cost variability, and the lack of limits on worker earnings. Sales personnel for autos, real estate, furniture, jewelry, and other expensive items are often paid a straight commission—as are direct-selling personnel.

To combine the attributes of salary and commission plans, some retailers pay their employees a *salary plus commission.* Shoe salespeople, major appliance salespeople, and some management personnel are among those paid in this manner. Sometimes, bonuses supplement salary and/or commission, normally for outstanding performance. At Finish Line footwear and apparel stores, regional, district, and store managers receive fixed salaries and earn bonuses based on sales, the size of the payroll, and theft rate goals. In certain cases, retail executives are paid via a "compensation cafeteria" and choose their own combination of salary, bonus, deferred bonus, fringe benefits, life insurance, stock options, and retirement benefits.

Sears (**www.searsholdings. com/careers/whyus/ benefits.htm**) has a generous employee benefits package.

A thorny issue facing retailers today involves the benefits portion of employee compensation, especially as related to pensions and healthcare. It is a challenging time due to intense price competition, the use of part-time workers, and escalating medical costs as retailers try to balance their employees' needs with company financial needs.

SUPERVISING RETAIL PERSONNEL

Supervision is the manner of providing a job environment that encourages employee accomplishment. The goals are to oversee personnel, attain good performance, maintain morale, motivate people, control costs, communicate, and resolve problems. Supervision is provided by personal contact, meetings, and reports.

Every firm wants to continually motivate employees so as to harness their energy on behalf of the retailer and achieve its goals. **Job motivation** is the drive within people to attain work-related goals. It may be positive or negative. These 10 attitude questions can be used to help predict employee behavior, based on their motivation:

1. Do you like the kind of work you do?
2. Does your work give you a sense of accomplishment?
3. Are you proud to say you work with us?
4. How does the amount of work expected from you influence your overall job attitude?
5. How do physical working conditions influence your overall job attitude?
6. How does the way you are treated by supervisors influence your overall job attitude?
7. Do you feel good about the future of the company?
8. Do you think the company is making the changes necessary to compete effectively?
9. Do you understand the company's business strategy?
10. Do you see a connection between your work and the company's strategic objectives?[19]

Employee motivation should be approached from two perspectives: What job-related factors cause employees to be satisfied or dissatisfied with their positions? What supervision style is best for both the retailer and its employees? See Figure 11-12.

Each employee looks at job satisfaction in terms of minimum expectations ("dissatisfiers") and desired goals ("satisfiers"). A motivated employee requires fulfillment of both factors. *Minimum expectations* relate mostly to the job environment, including a safe workplace, equitable treatment for those with the same jobs, some flexibility in company policies (such as not docking pay if a person is 10 minutes late), an even-tempered boss,

---

OPEN | RETAILING AROUND THE WORLD   How ASDA Motivates Employees

ASDA (**www.asda.co.uk**) is the largest value-oriented retailer in Great Britain, with about 330 stores and 170,000 employees. Several times, ASDA has been voted one of the leading employee-friendly British employers based on the *Sunday Times'* "Top 100 Best Companies to Work For" survey. ASDA has also received a prize for having employed more than 30,000 people aged over 50. Since ASDA became part of the Wal-Mart (**www.walmart.com**) family in June 1999, its sales have increased dramatically.

An important part of ASDA's human resource management philosophy is based on listening to employees and reacting to their suggestions. There are three central components to this orientation:

▶ A corporate culture based on managers walking around and providing feedback to employees.

Listening groups are also formed; these groups are encouraged to develop action plans. A "no jacket" rule makes the workplace environment less formal.

▶ A corporate mission based on respect for the individual, service to the customer, and constant striving for excellence.

▶ A family-friendly environment. ASDA allows employees with children under 6 or with disabled children under 18 to have flexible hours. Maternity/adoption leave can extend to 52 weeks; and paternity leave is up to two weeks paid leave or up to three months unpaid leave.

Source: "ASDA Careers," **www.asda.jobs** (March 9, 2009).

Tom Holmes

SEARS

TYPE OF STORE:
Department Store

HEADQUARTERS:
Hoffman Estates, Ill.

Upcoming grads anxious to climb to the top might take a look at Tom Holmes. At 29, he has already been general store manager at two Sears stores.

This political science major from the University of Illinois worked retail as an undergrad, but planned a career in investment banking. At graduation, he realized retail offered the chance to develop professionally.

"If you're confused about your direction, find an organization that lets you develop a base foundation of skill sets you can use throughout your career," notes Holmes. "Management and leadership skills are important virtually anywhere."

He contacted Sears, and was brought on board in 1993. He started in an executive development program and became a sales manager. Promotions have been quick to come ever since. He presently manages a Sears in West Dundee, Ill.

Holmes values the adventure of dealing with different personalities. "I really like working with people, both having an impact on customers and being able to coach and

mentor teams to success," he says.

He is currently earning his MBA from Northwestern University's Kellogg Graduate School of Management, with a focus on strategy and marketing. Sears has tuition reimbursement for graduate and undergraduate students, which helps its employees contribute more to the company and their mutual futures.

With a college degree, employees start higher up on the food chain, get management responsibilities from square one and a sense of accomplishment as a result.

"The first time you're in charge when you realize your boss is two hours away, it makes you feel really responsible," he adds. "I like it that there are lots of plans, direction from Sears as a company, yet there's autonomy as well."

Holmes also enjoys the variety his position offers. "Yes, it's a cliché, but it really is different every day. Sometimes I do human resources things, sometimes presentations, and on other days customer service is the focus. There's a lot of flexibility day-to-day, and in how you shape your career." ∎

FIGURE 11-12

Sears: Providing a Motivating Career Path for Employees

Source: Reprinted by permission of *DSN Retailing Today.*

some freedom in attire, a fair compensation package, basic fringe benefits (such as vacation time and medical coverage), clear communications, and job security. These elements can generally influence motivation in only one way—negatively. If minimum expectations are not met, a person will be unhappy. If these expectations are met, they are taken for granted and do little to motivate the person to go "above and beyond."

Desired goals relate more to the job than to the work environment. They are based on whether an employee likes the job, is recognized for good performance, feels a sense of achievement, is empowered to make decisions, is trusted, has a defined career path, receives extra compensation when performance is exceptional, and is given the chance to learn and grow. These elements can have a huge impact on job satisfaction and motivate a person to go "above and beyond." Nonetheless, if minimum expectations are not met, an employee might still be dissatisfied enough to leave, even if the job is quite rewarding.

There are three basic styles of supervising retail employees:

▶ Management assumes that employees must be closely supervised and controlled and that only economic inducements really motivate. Management further believes that the average worker lacks ambition, dislikes responsibility, and prefers to be led. This is the traditional view of motivation and has been applied to lower-level retail positions.

▶ Management assumes employees can be self-managers and assigned authority, motivation is social and psychological, and supervision can be decentralized and participatory. Management also thinks that motivation, the capacity for assuming responsibility, and a readiness to achieve company goals exist in people. The critical supervisory task is to create an environment so people achieve their goals by attaining company objectives. This is a more modern view and applies to all levels of personnel.

▶ Management applies a self-management approach and also advocates more employee involvement in defining jobs and sharing overall decision making. There is mutual loyalty between the firm and its workers, and both parties enthusiastically cooperate for the long-term benefit of each. This is also a modern view and applies to all levels of personnel.

It is imperative to motivate employees in a manner that yields job satisfaction, low turnover, low absenteeism, and high productivity. Consider these suggestions from one leading consultant:

(1) Motivate Employees to Find Solutions—Encourage employees to be solution creators instead of problem creators. When employees communicate a problem, look at it as an opportunity to empower the employees. **(2) Motivate Employees by Soliciting Opinions**—Just asking for opinions tells employees that you value their input. **(3) Motivate Employees by Managing to Their Level**—Learn employees' skills, experience, and motivation levels for performing workplace tasks. Follow-up based on your findings. **(4) Motivate Employees by Delegating Tasks**—Delegating a task shows employees you have confidence that they can do the job. **(5) Motivate Employees by Encouraging Ideas**—Create a safe environment for employees to share their ideas. Always give them credit for the ideas they express. **(6) Motivate Employees by Embracing Mistakes**—Allowing employees to make mistakes allows them to grow, be creative, and be empowered. **(7) Motivate Employees by Assigning Leadership Roles**—Leadership comes at all levels and doesn't require a title. Take the time to align employees' skills with leadership opportunities. **(8) Motivate Employees by Rewarding Initiative**—Publicly recognize employees during meetings, with reward bonuses, etc., so other employees are motivated to take initiative. (9) **Motivate Employees by Getting Goal Setting Buy-In**—Employees will be more motivated to achieve your goals if they help develop those goals.[20]

Chapter **Summary**

1. *To study the procedures involved in setting up a retail organization.* A retail organization structures and assigns tasks, policies, resources, authority, responsibilities, and rewards to satisfy the needs of its target market, employees, and management. There are five steps in setting up an organization: outlining specific tasks to be performed in a distribution channel, dividing tasks, grouping tasks into jobs, classifying jobs, and integrating positions with an organization chart.

Specific tasks include buying, shipping, receiving and checking, pricing, and marking merchandise; inventory control; display preparation; facilities maintenance; research; customer contact and follow-up; and a lot more. These tasks may be divided among retailers, manufacturers, wholesalers, specialists, and customers.

Tasks are next grouped into jobs, such as sales personnel, cashiers, inventory personnel, display personnel, customer service personnel, and management. Then jobs are arranged by functional, product, geographic, or combination classification. An organization chart displays the hierarchy of authority and the relationship among jobs, and it helps coordinate personnel.

2. *To examine the various organizational arrangements utilized in retailing.* Retail organization structures differ by institution. Small independents use simple formats, with little specialization. Many department stores use a version of the Mazur plan and place functions into four

categories: merchandising, publicity, store management, and accounting and control. The equal store format is used by numerous chain stores. Diversified firms have very complex organizations.

3. *To consider the special human resource environment of retailing.* Retailers are unique due to the large number of inexperienced workers, long hours, highly visible employees, a diverse work force, many part-time workers, and variations in customer demand. There is a broad range of career opportunities available to women and minorities, although improvement is still needed.

4. *To describe the principles and practices involved with the human resource management process in retailing.* This process comprises several interrelated activities: recruitment, selection, training, compensation, and supervision. In applying the process, diversity, labor laws, and employee privacy should be kept in mind.

Recruitment generates job applicants. Sources include educational institutions, channel members, competitors, ads, employment agencies, unsolicited applicants, employees, and Web sites.

Personnel selection requires thorough job analysis, creating job descriptions, using application blanks, interviews, testing (optional), reference checking, and physical exams. After personnel are selected, they go through pretraining and job training. Good training identifies needs, uses proper methods, and assesses results. Training is usually vital for continuing, as well as new, personnel.

Employees are compensated by direct monetary payments and/or indirect payments. The direct compensation plans are straight salary, straight commission, and salary plus commission and/or bonus. Indirect payments involve such items as paid vacations, health benefits, and retirement plans.

Proper supervision is needed to sustain superior employee performance. A main task is employee motivation. The causes of job satisfaction/dissatisfaction and the supervisory style must be reviewed.

Key Terms

retail organization (p. 310)
hierarchy of authority (p. 314)
organization chart (p. 314)
Mazur plan (p. 316)
equal store organization (p. 318)
diversified retailer (p. 318)
human resource management (p. 319)

human resource management process (p. 324)
recruitment (p. 325)
job analysis (p. 325)
traditional job description (p. 326)
goal-oriented job description (p. 326)
application blank (p. 327)

weighted application blank (p. 327)
pre-training (p. 327)
training programs (p. 328)
compensation (p. 330)
supervision (p. 331)
job motivation (p. 331)

Questions for Discussion

1. Cite at least five objectives a small hardware store chain should set when setting up its organization structure.

2. Why are employee needs important in developing a retail organization?

3. Are the steps involved in setting up a retail organization the same for small and large retailers? Explain your answer.

4. Describe the greatest similarities and differences in the organization structures of small independents, chain retailers, and diversified retailers.

5. How can retailers attract and retain more women and minority workers?

6. How would small and large retailers act differently for each of the following?
   a. Diversity.
   b. Recruitment.
   c. Selection.
   d. Training.
   e. Compensation.
   f. Supervision.

7. Why are the job description and the application blank so important in employee selection?

8. What problems can occur while interviewing and testing prospective employees?

9. Present a plan for the ongoing training of both existing lower-level and middle-management employees without making it seem punitive.

10. Describe the goals of a compensation plan (both direct and indirect components) in a retail setting.

11. Are the minimum job expectations of entry-level workers and middle-level managers similar or dissimilar? What about the desired goals? Explain your answers.

12. How would you supervise and motivate a 19-year-old Gap employee? A 45-year-old Gap employee?

Web **Exercise**

Visit the Web site that Macy's, Inc. has dedicated to college recruiting (www.macysjobs.com/college/index.asp) for its Macy's and Bloomingdale's department chains. What do you think of this site as a mechanism for attracting new college graduates to Macy's and Bloomingdale's? Why?

Note: Stop by our Web site (www.pearsonhighered. com/berman) to experience a number of highly interactive, appealing Web exercises based on actual company demonstrations and sample materials related to retailing.

12

Operations Management: Financial Dimensions

Chapter **Objectives**

1. To define operations management
2. To discuss profit planning
3. To describe asset management, including the strategic profit model, other key business ratios, and financial trends in retailing
4. To look at retail budgeting
5. To examine resource allocation

About 75 years ago, the top management of Lazarus and the John Shillito Company met with senior executives of Abraham & Straus, Filene's, and Bloomingdale's. They agreed to merge and form Federated Department Stores to reduce their vulnerability to economic downturns. Over the years, Federated acquired such chains as Bon Marche, Burdines, Goldsmith's, Macy's, and Rich's, and it closed or divested itself of Shillito, Abraham & Straus, and Filene's.

In 2005, Federated Department Stores reached an agreement to purchase May Department Stores. Among May's chains were May Department Stores, Filene's, and Marshall Field's. After the purchase, some May stores were closed and others were converted into Macy's stores. As of June 1, 2007, Federated Department Stores was renamed Macy's, Inc. (**www.macysinc. com**) and given "M" as a new stock market ticker symbol.

As part of its overall retail strategy, the firm converted its regional chains such as Rich's, Burdine's, and Goldsmith's into Macy's stores. Some analysts believe the purchase of May Department Stores and the conversion of stores into Macy's will better enable the retailer to achieve long-run economies of scale, as well as increased bargaining power with suppliers. There is concern among other analysts, however, that some of the regional differences in merchandising may become lost due to increased centralization.

Until recently, the department store sector of retailing was able to attract a large number of customers through one-stop shopping appeals, fashion-forward apparel, and attentive service. Although traditional department store chains were once considered the darlings of retailing, they have been losing market share to discount stores for years.[1]

Source: Reprinted by permission of Susan Berry, Retail Image Consulting, Inc.

OVERVIEW

After devising an organization structure and a human resource plan, a retailer concentrates on **operations management**—the efficient and effective implementation of the policies and tasks necessary to satisfy the firm's customers, employees, and management (and stockholders, if a public company). This has a major impact on sales and profits. High inventory levels, long hours, expensive fixtures, extensive customer services, and widespread advertising may lead to higher revenues. But at what cost? If a store pays night-shift workers a 25 percent premium, is being open 24 hours per day worthwhile (do the higher sales justify the costs and add to overall profit)?

This chapter covers the financial aspects of operations management, with emphasis on profit planning, asset management, budgeting, and resource allocation. The operational dimensions of operations management are explored in detail in Chapter 13. A number of useful financial operations links may be found at our Web site (**www.pearsonhighered.com/berman**).

Profit Planning

Learn more about the profit-and-loss statement (**www.toolkit.cch.com/text/ P06_1578.asp**).

A **profit-and-loss (income) statement** is a summary of a retailer's revenues and expenses over a given period of time, usually a month, quarter, or year. It lets the firm review its overall and specific revenues and costs for similar periods (such as January 1, 2009, to December 31, 2009, versus January 1, 2008, to December 31, 2008), and analyze profitability. By having frequent statements, a firm can monitor progress toward goals, update performance estimates, and revise strategies and tactics.

In comparing profit-and-loss performance over time, it is crucial that the same time periods be used (such as the third quarter of 2009 with the third quarter of 2008) due to seasonality. Some fiscal years may have an unequal number of weeks (53 weeks one year versus 51 weeks another). Retailers that open new stores or expand existing stores between accounting periods should also take into account the larger facilities. Yearly results should reflect total revenue growth and the rise in same-store sales.

A profit-and-loss statement consists of these major components:

▶ **Net sales**—the revenues received by a retailer during a given period after deducting customer returns, markdowns, and employee discounts.
▶ **Cost of goods sold**—the amount a retailer pays to acquire the merchandise sold during a given time period. It is based on purchase prices and freight charges, less all discounts (such as quantity, cash, and promotion).
▶ **Gross profit (margin)**—the difference between net sales and the cost of goods sold; it consists of operating expenses plus net profit.
▶ **Operating expenses**—the cost of running a retail business.
▶ **Taxes**—the portion of revenues turned over to the federal, state, and/or local government.
▶ **Net profit after taxes**—the profit earned after all costs and taxes have been deducted.

Table 12-1 shows the most recent annual profit-and-loss statement for Donna's Gift Shop, an independent retailer. The firm uses a fiscal year (September 1 to August 31) rather than a calendar year in preparing its accounting reports. These observations can be drawn from the table:

▶ Annual net sales were $330,000—after deducting returns, markdowns on the items sold, and employee discounts from total sales.
▶ The cost of goods sold was $180,000, computed by taking the total purchases for merchandise sold, adding freight, and subtracting quantity, cash, and promotion discounts.

TABLE 12-1 **Donna's Gift Shop, Fiscal 2009 Profit-and-Loss Statement**

Net sales	$330,000
Cost of goods sold	$180,000
Gross profit	$150,000
Operating expenses	
Salaries	$ 75,000
Advertising	4,950
Supplies	1,650
Shipping	1,500
Insurance	4,500
Maintenance	5,100
Other	2,550
Total	$ 95,250
Other costs	$ 20,000
Total costs	$115,250
Net profit before taxes	$ 34,750
Taxes	$ 15,500
Net profit after taxes	$ 19,250

▶ Gross profit was $150,000, calculated by subtracting the cost of goods sold from net sales. This went for operating and other expenses, taxes, and profit.

▶ Operating expenses totaled $95,250, including salaries, advertising, supplies, shipping, insurance, maintenance, and other expenses.

▶ Unassigned costs were $20,000.

▶ Net profit before taxes was $34,750, computed by deducting total costs from gross profit. The tax bill was $15,500, leaving a net profit after taxes of $19,250.

Overall, fiscal 2009 was pretty good for Donna; her personal salary was $43,000 and the store's after-tax profit was $19,250. A further analysis of Donna's Gift Shop's profit-and-loss statement appears in the budgeting section of this chapter.

Asset Management

Try out the Business Owner's Toolkit's downloadable Excel-based balance sheet template (www.toolkit.cch.com/ tools/balshe_m.asp).

Each retailer has assets to manage and liabilities to control. This section covers the balance sheet, the strategic profit model, and other ratios. A **balance sheet** itemizes a retailer's assets, liabilities, and net worth at a specific time—based on the principle that Assets = Liabilities + Net worth. Table 12-2 has a balance sheet for Donna's Gift Shop.

Assets are any items a retailer owns with a monetary value. Current assets are cash on hand (or in the bank) and items readily converted to cash, such as inventory on hand and accounts receivable (amounts owed to the firm). Fixed assets are property, buildings (a store, warehouse, and so on), fixtures, and equipment such as cash registers and trucks; these are used for a long period. The major fixed asset for many retailers is real-estate. Unlike current assets, which are recorded at cost, fixed assets are recorded at cost less accumulated depreciation. Thus, records may not reflect the true value of these assets. Many retailing analysts use the term **hidden assets** to describe depreciated assets, such as buildings and warehouses, that are noted on a retail balance sheet at low values relative to their actual worth.

Liabilities are financial obligations a retailer incurs in operating a business. Current liabilities are payroll expenses payable, taxes payable, accounts payable (amounts owed to

TABLE 12-2 A Retail Balance Sheet for Donna's Gift Shop (as of August 31, 2009)

Assets		Liabilities	
Current		Current	
Cash on hand	$ 19,950	Payroll expenses payable	$ 6,000
Inventory	36,150	Taxes payable	13,500
Accounts receivable	1,650	Accounts payable	32,100
Total	$ 57,750	Short-term loan	1,050
		Total	$ 52,650
Fixed (present value)			
Property	$187,500	Fixed	
Building	63,000	Mortgage	$ 97,500
Store fixtures	14,550	Long-term loan	6,750
Equipment	2,550	Total	$104,250
Total	$267,600	Total liabilities	$156,900
Total assets	$325,350		
		Net Worth	$168,450
		Liabilities + net worth	$325,350

suppliers), and short-term loans; these must be paid in the coming year. Fixed liabilities comprise mortgages and long-term loans; these are generally repaid over several years.

A retailer's **net worth** is computed as assets minus liabilities. It is also called owner's equity and represents the value of a business after deducting all financial obligations.

In operations management, the retailer's goal is to use its assets in the manner providing the best results possible. There are three basic ways to measure those results: net profit margin, asset turnover, and financial leverage. Each component is discussed next.

Net profit margin is a performance measure based on a retailer's net profit and net sales:

$$\text{Net profit margin} = \frac{\text{Net profit after taxes}}{\text{Net sales}}$$

At Donna's Gift Shop, fiscal year 2009 net profit margin was 5.83 percent—a very good percentage for a gift shop. To enhance its net profit margin, a retailer must either raise gross profit as a percentage of sales or reduce expenses as a percentage of sales.[2] It could lift gross profit by purchasing opportunistically, selling exclusive products, avoiding price competition through excellent service, and adding items with higher margins. It could reduce operating costs by stressing self-service, lowering labor costs, refinancing the mortgage, cutting energy costs, and so on. The firm must be careful not to lessen customer service to the extent that sales and profit would decline.

Asset turnover is a performance measure based on a retailer's net sales and total assets:

$$\text{Asset turnover} = \frac{\text{Net sales}}{\text{Total assets}}$$

Donna's Gift Shop had a very low asset turnover, 1.0143, and it averaged $1.01 in sales per dollar of total assets. To improve the asset turnover ratio, a firm must generate increased sales from the same level of assets or keep the same sales with fewer assets. A firm might increase sales by having longer hours, accepting Web orders, training employees to sell additional products, or stocking better-known brands. None of these tactics requires expanding the asset base. Or a firm might maintain its sales on a lower asset base by moving to a smaller store, simplifying fixtures (or having suppliers install fixtures), keeping a smaller inventory, and negotiating for the property owner to pay part of the costs of a renovation.

Is Retail for Me? Finance

Are numbers your game? Financial and accounting skills are more than a game in retail; they can be your career! The finance retail career area includes all accounting and treasury functions such as accounting for income, paying expenses, compiling and maintaining financial records, money management and cash flow control, banking, investment, and credit lines. Auditory responsibilities may also fall into this retail career area.

Here are some senior-level positions in finance:

▶ *Chief Financial Officer (CFO).* The head of all accounting and treasury functions for the firm. May also supervise the information systems department.

▶ *Controller.* This position is responsible for compiling and maintaining the integrity of the firm's fiscal records and reports. May have accounting department managers as subordinates but is not the CFO; this position reports to the CFO.

▶ *Treasurer.* Responsible for money management and cash flow control, which includes banking, investment, and credit lines.

▶ *Top Internal Auditor.* Department head responsible for verifying the accuracy of fiscal records and/or policy compliance. May also do operations audits.

Source: Reprinted by permission of the National Retail Federation.

By looking at the relationship between net profit margin and asset turnover, **return on assets (ROA)** can be computed:

$$\text{Return on assets} = \text{Net profit margin} \times \text{Asset turnover}$$

$$\text{Return on assets} = \frac{\text{Net profit after taxes}}{\text{Net sales}} \times \frac{\text{Net sales}}{\text{Total assets}}$$

$$= \frac{\text{Net profit after taxes}}{\text{Total assets}}$$

Donna's Gift Shop had an ROA of 5.9 percent ($0.0583 \times 1.0143 = 0.059$). This return is below average for gift stores; the firm's good net profit margin does not adequately offset its low asset turnover.

Financial leverage is a performance measure based on the relationship between a retailer's total assets and net worth:

$$\text{Financial leverage} = \frac{\text{Total assets}}{\text{Net worth}}$$

Donna's Gift Shop's financial leverage ratio was 1.9314. Assets were just under twice the net worth, and total liabilities and net worth were almost equal. This ratio was slightly lower than the average for gift stores (a conservative group). The store is in no danger.

A retailer with a high financial leverage ratio has substantial debt, while a ratio of 1 means it has no debt—assets equal net worth. If the ratio is too high, there may be an excessive focus on cost-cutting and short-run sales so as to make interest payments, net profit margins may suffer, and a firm may be forced into bankruptcy if debts cannot be paid. When financial leverage is low, a retailer may be overly conservative—limiting its ability to renovate and expand existing stores and to enter new markets. Leverage is too low if owner's equity is relatively high; equity could be partly replaced by increasing short- and long-term loans and/or accounts payable. Some equity funds could be taken out of a business by the owner (stockholders, if a public firm).

FIGURE 12-1

The Strategic Profit Model

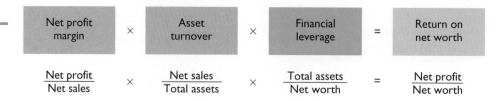

The Strategic Profit Model

The relationship among net profit margin, asset turnover, and financial leverage is expressed by the **strategic profit model,** which reflects a performance measure known as **return on net worth (RONW).** See Figure 12-1. The strategic profit model can be used in planning or controlling assets. Thus, a retailer could learn that the major cause of its poor return on net worth is weak asset turnover or financial leverage that is too low. A firm can raise its return on net worth by lifting the net profit margin, asset turnover, or financial leverage. Because these measures are multiplied to determine return on net worth, doubling *any* of them would double the return on net worth.

This is how the strategic profit model can be applied to Donna's Gift Shop:

$$\text{Return on net worth} = \frac{\text{Net profit after taxes}}{\text{Net sales}} \times \frac{\text{Net sales}}{\text{Total assets}} \times \frac{\text{Total assets}}{\text{Net worth}}$$

$$= \frac{\$19,250}{\$330,000} \times \frac{\$330,000}{\$325,350} \times \frac{\$325,350}{\$168,450}$$

$$= .0583 \quad \times 1.0143 \quad \times 1.9314$$

$$= .1142 \quad = 11.4\%$$

Overall, Donna's return on net worth was above average for gift stores.

Table 12-3 applies the strategic profit model to various retailers. It is best to make comparisons among firms within given retail categories. For example, the net profit margins of general merchandise retailers have historically been higher than those of food retailers. Because financial performance differs from year to year, caution is advised in studying these data. Furthermore, the individual components of the strategic profit model must be analyzed, not just the return on net worth. For example,

Visit this site (www. pnwassoc.com/issues/ codbanalysis.htm) to see how the strategic profit model can be applied to a hardware store.

▶ TJX had the highest return on net worth among all 18 retailers shown in Table 12-3. Its net profit margin was lower than The Gap, Inc., but its asset turnover was quite strong. TJX was also more financially leveraged than The Gap, Inc.

▶ Best Buy's profit margin was solid, while Circuit City incurred losses in 2007 and was the only retailer in Table 12-3 to have a negative net worth. Circuit City went out of business in 2009.

▶ Sears Holdings (which includes Sears and Kmart) had a return on net worth that lagged well behind other general merchandise retailers. Its profit margins were especially low.

Other Key Business Ratios

Additional ratios can also measure retailer success or failure in reaching performance goals. Here are several key business ratios—besides those covered in the preceding discussion:

▶ *Quick ratio*—cash plus accounts receivable divided by total current liabilities, those due within one year. A ratio above 1-to-1 means the firm is liquid and can cover short-term debt.

▶ *Current ratio*—total current assets (cash, accounts receivable, inventories, and marketable securities) divided by total current liabilities. A ratio of 2-to-1 or more is good.

▶ *Collection period*—accounts receivable divided by net sales and then multiplied by 365. If most sales are on credit, a collection period one-third or more over normal terms (such as 40.0 for a store with 30-day credit terms) means slow-turning receivables.

TABLE 12-3 Application of Strategic Profit Model to Selected Retailers (2007 Data)

Retailer	Net Profit Margin	× Asset Turnover	× Financial Leverage	= Return on Net Worth
Apparel Retailers				
TJX	4.24%	2.86	2.66	32.23%
The Gap, Inc.	5.28%	2.01	1.83	19.49%
Consumer Electronics Retailers				
Best Buy	3.52%	3.14	2.85	31.38%
Circuit City	−2.72%	3.14	2.49	−21.29%
Drugstore Retailers				
Walgreen	3.80%	2.78	1.74	18.38%
CVS	3.45%	5.39	0.45	8.42%
Food Retailers				
Publix	5.10%	2.88	1.43	20.99%
Safeway	2.10%	2.40	2.63	13.25%
General Merchandise Retailers				
Wal-Mart	3.36%	2.32	2.53	19.70%
Target	4.50%	1.42	2.91	18.61%
Sears Holdings	1.63%	3.96	1.20	7.74%
Costco	1.68%	3.28	2.27	12.56%
Macy's, Inc.	3.39%	0.95	2.80	9.01%
J.C. Penney	5.59%	1.39	2.69	20.91%
Home Improvement Retailers				
Home Depot	5.68%	1.75	2.50	24.81%
Lowe's	5.82%	1.56	1.92	17.45%
Office Supplies Retailers				
Staples	5.14%	2.14	1.58	17.42%
Office Depot	2.55%	2.14	2.35	12.84%

Note: Because the data in this table are from 2007, they do NOT take into account the weakened performance of many retailers during the 2008–2009 economic downturn.

Source: Computed by the authors from data in company annual reports.

▶ *Accounts payable to net sales*—accounts payable divided by annual net sales. This compares how a retailer pays suppliers relative to volume transacted. A figure above the industry average indicates that a firm relies on suppliers to finance operations.

▶ *Overall gross profit*—net sales minus the cost of goods sold and then divided by net sales. This companywide average includes markdowns, discounts, and shortages.[3]

The Census Bureau, online, provides more than a decade of gross profit (gross margin) percentage data by line of business (**www.census.gov/svsd/ retlann/view/table7.txt**).

For any retailer, large or small, the goal is to do as well as possible on these key business ratios. Areas of weakness must be identified and corrected for the firm to enhance its long-term results—and to avoid negative financial results. Table 12-4 describes ways to improve performance for each of the preceding ratios, as well as asset turnover and return on net worth.

At our Web site (**www.pearsonhighered.com/berman**), we have links to each of the Yahoo! Finance sites related to retailers' financial performance.

TABLE 12-4   **Selected Ways for a Retailer to Improve Its Key Business Ratios**

Ratios	Causes of Poor Performance	Suggestions to Improve Performance
Quick ratio	Too low a quick ratio indicates too much current liabilities relative to cash and accounts receivable.	Reduce current liabilities by outsourcing delivery and installation, leasing equipment (instead of purchasing), and turning over inventory more quickly.
Current ratio	Too low a current ratio indicates too much current liabilities relative to cash, accounts receivable, inventories, and marketable securities.	Reduce current liabilities. Consider outsourcing delivery and installation, as well as leasing equipment (instead of purchasing).
Collection period	Too long a collection period indicates too many slow-paying accounts.	Increase payment requirements for store-credit accounts and encourage marginal shoppers to use debit cards, layaway programs, and bank cards.
Accounts payable to net sales purchase	Too high an accounts-payable-to-net-sales ratio indicates that a firm heavily relies on suppliers to finance inventories.	Increase inventory turnover of key items by reducing slow-turnover items, paying accounts payable on time, and purchasing more goods on consignment.
Overall gross profit margin	Too low an overall gross profit margin indicates a combination of low net sales and a high cost of goods sold.	Increase profit margins through better negotiation with vendors to reduce the cost of goods sold, lessen the use of discounting, avoid "meeting the price" of competition tactics, and better focus on merchandise with higher profit margins (such as private-label items).
Asset turnover	Too low an asset turnover indicates insufficient sales per dollar of assets.	Improve asset turnover by extending store hours, using central warehousing, outsourcing delivery and other services, and leasing instead of purchasing.
Return on net worth	Too low a return on new worth indicates insufficient profit as a percent of net worth.	Increase gross profit (through better negotiation and by selling a mix of more profitable goods) and lower operating expenses (by eliminating costly services that are not valued by consumers).

Financial Trends in Retailing

Entrepreneur's "Money" section (**www.entrepreneur. com/money**) has a lot of valuable advice for small businesses.

Several trends relating to asset management merit discussion: the state of the economy; funding sources (including initial public offerings); mergers, consolidations, and spin-offs; bankruptcies and liquidations; and questionable accounting and financial reporting practices.

Many retailers are affected by the strength or weakness of the economy. During a strong economy, high consumer demand may mask retailer weaknesses. But when the economy is weak, sales stagnate, cash flow problems may occur, heavy markdowns may be needed (which cut profit margins), and consumers are more reluctant to buy big-ticket items. Furthermore, public firms may see their stock prices plummet, as happened in the past few years: "The recent retailing slide—when stores were forced to cut prices to convince wary consumers to spend—promises to have a lasting impact on the way the retail industry operates. Many retailers are rethinking how they do business. Some are saying they will trim inventory and reduce the number of suppliers. That, in turn, will cause a ripple effect, prompting a number of weaker manufacturers, small brands, and underfunded fashion labels to fail. New retail formats and concept stores are likely to be curtailed. And luxury-goods makers already are working to cut the long lead times between orders and store delivery as a way to reduce risk."[4]

Three sources of funding are important to retailers. First, because interest rates have remained quite low, many companies have sought to refinance their mortgages and leases—which can dramatically decrease their monthly payments. Even though funding was tight in 2008 and 2009 due to the decline of the financial markets, retailers retained some leverage: "Many stores pushed to negotiate lower rents, warning that they mightn't be able to make it unless their costs were cut. Those in stronger positions were finding that the market's turmoil provided them clout to haggle for lower lease rates."[5]

Second, shopping center developers often use a retail real-estate investment trust (REIT) to fund construction. With this strategy, investors buy shares in a REIT as they would a stock. Until recently, investors liked participating in REITs because real-estate had historically been a good investment. However, during the 2008–2009 economic decline, many REITS struggled and their value fell. Nonetheless, the long-term forecast for REITs is good: "Even looking at all the negatives, most retail REITs remain well capitalized, have decent debt-to-capitalization ratios, have manageable refinancing loads coming through, and have portfolios that can weather vacancies. Many retail REITs represent phenomenal bargains and should be great investments when the stock market does mount its recovery."[6]

Third, a funding source that has gained retailing acceptance over the past two decades is the initial public offering (IPO), whereby a firm raises money by selling stock. An IPO is typically used to fund expansion. What do investors look for in an IPO? "They want a company to have a history of profitability. They want to see revenue growth and strong backing. And they want a company to match up well against companies already trading." In 2008–2009, IPOs were scarce due to the economic downturn. But, in 2007, firms such as Lumber Liquidators, Cinemark Holdings, and U.S. Auto Parts became public companies. Once the economy stabilizes and then turns around, retailers such as Dave & Buster's will probably be involved with IPOs.[7]

Mergers and consolidations represent a way for retailers to add to their asset base without building new facilities or waiting for new business units to turn a profit. They also present a way for weak retailers to receive financial transfusions. For example, in the last several years, Kmart acquired Sears and became Sears Holdings, Dick's Sporting Goods acquired Gaylan's, Federated Department Stores (now Macy's, Inc.) acquired May Department Stores, TD Bank acquired Commerce Bancorp, and Foot Locker acquired Foot Action. All of these deals were driven by the weakness of the acquired firms. Typically, mergers and consolidations lead to some stores being shut, particularly those with trading-area overlap, and cutbacks among management personnel.

The leveraged buyout (LBO) is a type of acquisition in which a retail ownership change is mostly financed by loans from banks, investors, and others. The LBO phenomenon has had a big effect on retail budgeting and cash flow. At times, because debts incurred with LBOs can be high, some well-known retailers have had to focus more on paying interest on their debts than on investing in their businesses, run sales to generate enough cash to cover operating costs and buy new goods, and sell store units to pay off debt. Two major retailers involved with LBOs were weakened: Toys "R" Us and Barneys New York.

Retailers sometimes consolidate their businesses to streamline operations and improve profits. Winn-Dixie, Eddie Bauer, Circuit City, Kmart, Macy's, Pier 1, Michaels, and many other firms have closed underperforming stores. Other times, retailers use spin-offs to generate more money or to sell a division that no longer meets expectations. Target sold off its Mervyns and Marshall Field's divisions, Saks Inc. sold off Proffitt's and McRae's department store chains, and Viacom spun off its Blockbuster store division. As the Saks chief executive stated at the time of the spin-off: "We believe it is appropriate to divide our department store businesses into distinct enterprises and permit each to have its own focused future. The decision to sell Proffitt's and McRae's was made very deliberately. We believe this strategy is in the long-term best interests of our shareholders, our customers, and our associates."[8]

When they want to continue in business, weak retailers file Chapter 11. If they want to liquidate, they file Chapter 7 (**www.uscourts. gov/bankruptcycourts/ bankbasics0908.pdf**).

To safeguard themselves against mounting debts, as well as to continue in business, faltering retailers may seek bankruptcy protection under Chapter 11 of the Federal Bankruptcy Code (which was toughened in 2005). In November 2006, when the economy was quite strong, only 3.8 percent of the large retailers tracked by a turnaround consulting firm were facing a high possibility of bankruptcy or financial distress. By November 2008, the figure had risen to 25.8 percent.[9]

With bankruptcy protection, retailers can renegotiate bills, get out of leases, and work with creditors to plan for the future. Declaring bankruptcy has major ramifications: "While some believe that filing for bankruptcy results in the loss of key executives, disruptions in supply, and demoralization on those who stay, others say it fends off creditors and lets firms pay off debt and survive what may be a temporary upheaval. Executives who are not in favor of filing also cite the cost of legal and financial advisory fees of bankruptcy protection."[10]

TECHNOLOGY IN RETAILING

Analyzing Data: The Wal-Mart Way

Wal-Mart (**www.walmart.com**) operates one of the world's largest commercial data warehouses. The warehouse contains sales data on every item sold in all of its stores. This encompasses 800 million transactions from its 30 million customers on a daily basis, as well as data relating to sales and inventory from Wal-Mart's 20,000 suppliers. Since Wal-Mart has pushed for the adoption of RFID technology by its major suppliers, the magnitude of its data has grown substantially.

In the past, Wal-Mart used its data warehouse to analyze in-store sales, its in-stock rate (Wal-Mart seeks to maintain a 98.5 percent in-stock rate), markdowns, and related-item purchasing by consumers. It now also seeks to better analyze the ideal mix of products in each store and to improve store layouts.

Wal-Mart became one of Hewlett-Packard's (**www.hp. com**) earliest customers for Hewlett-Packard's new Neoview data warehousing system. Neoview will be used in conjunction with Wal-Mart's Retail Link system that supplies Wal-Mart with data on its suppliers' sales and inventory turnover. After several months of testing, Wal-Mart shifted over to Neoview in June 2007. Prior to Wal-Mart, Bon-Ton Stores (**www.bonton.com**), a department store chain, was one of Neoview's first major users. Bon-Ton uses Neoview to measure supplier profitability.

Sources: Mary Hayes Weier, "Hewlett-Packard Data Warehouse Lands In Wal-Mart's Shopping Cart," **www.informationweek.com** (August 4, 2007); and "HP Delivers Real-Time Business Information with Enhanced Neoview Capabilities" **www.hp.com/hpinfo/ newsroom/press/2008/080602a.html** (June 2, 2008).

Here's a recent retail bankruptcy example involving Hancock Fabrics. It entered bankruptcy in March 2007 and successfully emerged from it in August 2008:

> During the first quarter of 2007, we closed 30 retail stores and began going-out-of-business sales in 104 other stores that were completed by the end of June. Our bankruptcy plan provides for payment in full in cash plus interest, as applicable, or reinstatement of allowed administrative, secured, priority, and general unsecured claims in addition to the retention of ownership by holders of equity interest in the firm. As of November 1, 2008, we operated 265 stores in 37 states and an Internet store called hancockfabrics.com. We conduct our business in one operating business segment. Hancock is committed to serving creative enthusiasts with a complete selection of fashion and home decorating textiles, sewing accessories, needlecraft supplies, and sewing machines.[11]

Not all bankruptcies end up with rejuvenated retailers. Many end up in liquidations, where the firms ultimately go out of business. This recently happened with Mervyns, Linens 'n Things, Sharper Image, Steve & Barry's, Goody's Family Clothing, and other firms. When a retailer goes out of business, it is painful for all parties: the owner/stockholders, employees, creditors, landlords (who then have vacant store sites), and customers. See Figure 12-2.

As with several other sectors of business, over the last few years, some retailers have been heavily criticized for questionable accounting and financial practices. Here are two examples:

▶ Sometimes, illegalities are at the root of the problem. In 2008, a federal jury "convicted Bradley Stinn, former chief executive at Friedman's, Inc. and its affiliate, Crescent Jewelers, of securities fraud, mail fraud, and conspiracy, for participating in what prosecutors called a 'massive accounting fraud scheme designed to inflate Friedman's financial performance.' The government investigation also led to guilty pleas by Friedman's and Crescent's former chief financial officer and Friedman's former controller. During the time of the conspiracy, Friedman's was the third-largest U.S. specialty retailer of fine jewelry with 686 stores in 20 states."[12]

▶ Other times, ineffective practices are involved: In 2008, "an independent investigation into a $152 million accounting shortfall at Ace Hardware concluded that the retailer's problems with its books stemmed from a lack of controls and human error over a period

FIGURE 12-2

The Demise of Linens 'n Things

After a long, successful run as a leading retailer of household goods, Linens 'n Things went out of business in late 2008. The firm was adversely affected by the weak economy, heavy competition, and its unsuccessful conversion from a publicly owned to a privately owned company in 2006. At the end, it was unable to get support from its creditors or to find a buyer.

Source: Reprinted by permission of TNS Retail Forward.

of years." Ace's chief executive said that the auditors "found no missing inventory, no missing money, and no fraud. Obviously, it's an embarrassing situation for Ace and one we would rather not have had to deal with." Ace then restated three years of financial reports and replaced its chief financial officer who had resigned when the shortfall was uncovered (which was before the independent report was produced).[13]

To bolster public confidence and stockholder equity, retailers need to be as "transparent" as possible in their accounting and financial reporting practices:

> In the aftermath of the Enron scandal, more retailers are being proactive in sharing their views on disclosure and accurate financial reporting with investors. Wal-Mart, in its annual report noted that, "The financial results reported here will provide you, the stakeholders, with a review of our company, and will provide a detailed discussion about those financial matters that are significant to your company. Although it is not the most exciting reading, our team has worked hard to make these reports comprehensive, yet simple, and I would encourage you to review them." The increased disclosure now practiced by retailers and the relatively straightforward accounting involved in a retail business have made the industry attractive to investors looking for stability in turbulent times. Yet, retailers will almost certainly be forced to live with new and unknown finance-related requirements from elected officials and government regulators who don't want another Enron.[14]

Budgeting

Why does a new business need a formal budget? Type "Budgeting" at this site (**www.entrepreneur. com**).

Budgeting outlines a retailer's planned expenditures for a given time based on expected performance. Costs are linked to satisfying target market, employee, and management goals. What should personnel costs be to attain a certain level of customer service? What compensation amount will motivate salespeople? What operating expenses will generate intended revenues and reach profit goals?

There are several benefits from a retailer's meticulously preparing a budget:

▶ Expenditures are clearly related to expected performance, and costs can be adjusted as goals are revised. This enhances productivity.
▶ Resources are allocated to the right departments, product categories, and so on.

▶ Spending for various departments, product categories, and so on is coordinated.
▶ Because planning is structured and integrated, the goal of efficiency is prominent.
▶ Cost standards are set, such as advertising equals 5 percent of sales.
▶ A firm prepares for the future rather than reacts to it.
▶ Expenditures are monitored during a budget cycle. If a firm allots $50,000 to buy new merchandise, and it has spent $33,000 halfway through a cycle, it has $17,000 remaining.
▶ A firm can analyze planned budgets versus actual budgets.
▶ Costs and performance can be compared with industry averages.

A retailer should be aware of the effort in the budgeting process, recognize that forecasts may not be fully accurate (due to unexpected demand, competitors' tactics, and so forth), and modify plans as needed. It should not be too conservative (or inflexible) to simply add a percentage to each expense category to arrive at the next budget, such as increasing spending by 3 percent across the board based on anticipated sales growth of 3 percent. The budgeting process is shown in Figure 12-3 and described next.

Preliminary Budgeting Decisions

There are six preliminary decisions.

First, budgeting authority is specified. In top-down budgeting, senior executives make centralized financial decisions and communicate them down the line to succeeding levels of managers. In bottom-up budgeting, lower-level executives develop departmental budget requests; these requests are assembled, and a company budget is designed. Bottom-up budgeting includes varied perspectives, holds managers more accountable, and enhances employee morale. Many firms combine aspects of the two approaches.

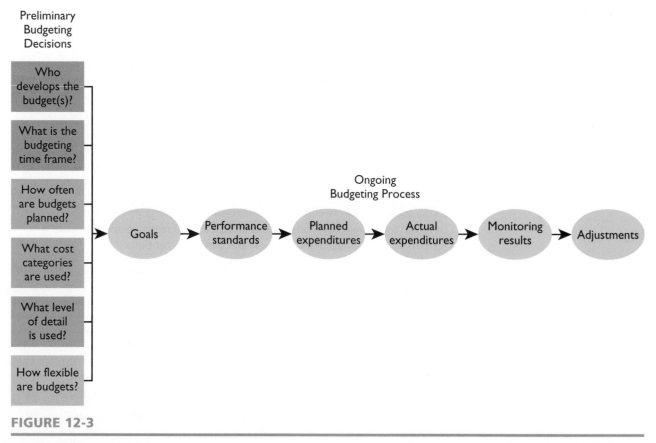

FIGURE 12-3

The Retail Budgeting Process

Second, the time frame is defined. Most firms have budgets with yearly, quarterly, and monthly components. Annual spending is planned, while costs and performance are regularly reviewed. This responds to seasonal or other fluctuations. Sometimes, the time frame is longer than a year or shorter than a month. When a firm opens new stores over a five-year period, it sets construction costs for the entire period. When a supermarket orders perishables, it has weekly budgets for each item.

Third, budgeting frequency is determined. Many firms review budgets on an ongoing basis, but most plan them yearly. In some firms, several months may be set aside each year for the budgeting process; this lets all participants have time to gather data and facilitates taking the budgets through several drafts.

Fourth, cost categories are established:

▶ *Capital expenditures* are long-term investments in land, buildings, fixtures, and equipment. *Operating expenditures* are the short-term expenses of running a business.

▶ *Fixed costs,* such as store security, remain constant for the budget period regardless of the retailer's performance. *Variable costs,* such as sales commissions, are based on performance. If performance is good, these expenses often rise.

▶ *Direct costs* are incurred by specific departments, product categories, and so on, such as the earnings of department-based salespeople. *Indirect costs,* such as centralized cashiers, are shared by multiple departments, product categories, and so on.

▶ *Natural account expenses* are reported by the names of the costs, such as salaries, and not assigned by purpose. *Functional account expenses* are classified on the basis of the purpose or activity for which expenditures are made, such as cashier salaries.

Fifth, the level of detail is set. Should spending be assigned by department (produce), product category (fresh fruit), product subcategory (apples), or product item (McIntosh apples)? With a very detailed budget, every expense subcategory must be adequately covered.

Sixth, budget flexibility is prescribed. A budget should be strict enough to guide planned spending and link costs to goals. Yet, a budget that is too inflexible may not let a retailer adapt to changing market conditions, capitalize on new opportunities, or modify a poor strategy (if further spending is needed to improve matters). Budget flexibility is often expressed in quantitative terms, such as allowing a buyer to increase a quarterly budget by a certain maximum percentage if demand is higher than anticipated.

OPEN · RETAILING AROUND THE WORLD | Zara's Unique Supply Chain Management Strategy

To be successful, retailers must pay particular attention to the impact of off-shore manufacturing on sales levels and inventory due to longer lead times than for domestic production. A retailer that is often mentioned for its successful sourcing operations is Zara (**www.zara.com**), which is headquartered in Spain. Zara, with more than 750 stores in 55 countries, has been growing at 10 percent per year for the past decade.

Although many of Zara's competitors produce at least 90 percent of their goods in Asia in order to achieve lower manufacturing costs, their goods may arrive late or miss the fashion trend and then have to be sold at significant markdowns. In contrast, Zara produces 40 percent of its most fashionable clothing and accessories in fully owned factories in Europe after the season has begun. Zara says that its higher production costs are offset by savings in markdown reductions and higher profits due to increased sales revenues.

To gain additional control over product quality, a subsidiary of Zara—Comditel—manages the purchase and treatment of all fabrics. All goods, including those whose production is outsourced, are sent to Zara's distribution center. Goods are then distributed to Zara's retail stores twice each week based on communication from store managers. This system eliminates markdowns and wasted warehouse space.

Source: "Zara SM," **http://articles.directorym.com/Zara-a869. html** (February 9, 2009).

Ongoing Budgeting Process

After making preliminary budgeting decisions, the retailer engages in the ongoing budgeting process shown in Figure 12-3:

▶ Goals are set based on customer, employee, and management needs.

▶ Performance standards are specified, including customer service levels, the compensation needed to motivate employees, and the sales and profits needed to satisfy management. Typically, the budget is related to a sales forecast, which projects revenues for the next period. Forecasts are usually broken down by department or product category.

▶ Expenditures are planned in terms of performance goals. In **zero-based budgeting,** a firm starts each new budget from scratch and outlines the expenditures needed to reach that period's goals. All costs are justified each time a budget is done. With **incremental budgeting**, a firm uses current and past budgets as guides and adds to or subtracts from them to arrive at the coming period's expenditures. Most retailers use incremental budgeting because it is easier, less time-consuming, and not as risky.

▶ Actual expenditures are made. The retailer pays rent and employee salaries, buys merchandise, places ads, and so on.

▶ Results are monitored: (1) Actual expenditures are compared with planned spending for each expense category, and reasons for any deviations are reviewed. (2) The firm learns if performance standards have been met and tries to explain deviations.

▶ The budget is adjusted. Revisions are major or minor, depending on how closely a firm has come to reaching its goals. The funds allotted to some expense categories may be reduced, while greater funds may be provided to other categories.

Table 12-5 compares budgeted and actual revenues, expenses, and profits for Donna's Gift Shop during fiscal 2009. The actual data come from Table 12-1. The variance figures

TABLE 12-5 **Donna's Gift Shop, Fiscal 2006 Budgeted Versus Actual Profit-and-Loss Statement (in Dollars and Percent)**

	Budgeted		Actual		Variance[a]	
	Dollars	*Percent*	*Dollars*	*Percent*	*Dollars*	*Percent*
Net sales	$300,000	100.00	$330,000	100.00	+$30,000	—
Cost of goods sold	$165,000	55.00	$180,000	54.55	−$15,000	+0.45
Gross profit	$135,000	45.00	$150,000	45.45	+$15,000	+0.45
Operating expenses:						
Salaries	$ 75,000	25.00	$ 75,000	22.73	—	+2.27
Advertising	5,250	1.75	4,950	1.50	+$ 300	+0.25
Supplies	1,800	0.60	1,650	0.50	+$ 150	+0.10
Shipping	1,350	0.45	1,500	0.45	−$ 150	—
Insurance	4,500	1.50	4,500	1.36	—	+0.14
Maintenance	5,100	1.70	5,100	1.55	—	+0.15
Other	3,000	1.00	2,550	0.77	+$ 450	+0.23
Total	$ 96,000	32.00	$ 95,250	28.86	+$ 750	+3.14
Other costs	$ 18,000	6.00	$ 20,000	6.06	−$ 2,000	−0.06
Total costs	$114,000	38.00	$115,250	34.92	−$ 1,250	+3.08
Net profit before taxes	$ 21,000	7.00	$ 34,750	10.53	+$13,750	+3.53
Taxes	$ 9,000	3.00	$ 15,500	4.70	−$ 6,500	−1.70
Net profit after taxes	$ 12,000	4.00	$ 19,250	5.83	+$ 7,250	+1.83

There are small rounding errors.

[a] Variance is a positive number if actual sales or profits are higher than expected or actual expenses are lower than expected. Variance is a negative number if actual sales or profits are lower than expected or actual expenses are higher than expected.

compare expected and actual results for each profit-and-loss item. Variances are positive if performance is better than expected and negative if it is worse.

As Table 12-5 indicates, in *dollar terms,* net profit after taxes was $7,250 higher than budgeted. Sales were $30,000 higher than expected; thus, the cost of goods sold was $15,000 higher. Actual operating expenses were $750 lower than expected, while other costs were $2,000 higher. Table 12-5 also shows results in *percentage terms.* This lets a firm evaluate budgeted versus actual performance on a percent-of-sales basis. In Donna's case, actual net profit after taxes was 5.83 percent of sales—better than planned. The higher net profit was mostly due to the actual operating costs percentage being lower than planned.

A firm must closely monitor its **cash flow**, which relates the amount and timing of revenues received to the amount and timing of expenditures for a specific time. In cash flow management, the usual intention is to make sure revenues are received before expenditures are made.[15] Otherwise, short-term loans may be needed or profits may be tied up in inventory and other expenses. For seasonal retailers, this may be unavoidable. Underestimating costs and overestimating revenues, both of which affect cash flow, are leading causes of new business failures. Table 12-6 has cash flow examples.

Learn more about cash flow management by typing "Cash Flow" at this site (www.entrepreneur.com).

TABLE 12-6   The Effects of Cash Flow

A.

A retailer has rather consistent sales throughout the year. Therefore, the cash flow in any given month is positive. This means no short-term loans are needed, and the owner can withdraw funds from the firm if she so desires:

Linda's Luncheonette, Cash Flow for January

Cash inflow:		
Net sales		$21,000
Cash outflow:		
Cost of goods sold	$8,000	
Operating expenses	5,500	
Other costs	2,000	
Total		$15,500
Positive cash flow		$ 5,500

B.

A retailer has highly seasonal sales that peak in December. Yet, to have a good assortment of merchandise on hand during December, it must order merchandise in September and October and pay for it in November. As a result, it has a negative cash flow in November that must be financed by a short-term loan. All debts are paid off in January, after the peak selling season is completed:

Dave's Party Favors, Cash Flow for November

Cash inflow:		
Net sales		$14,000
Cash outflow:		
Cost of goods sold	$12,500	
Operating expenses	3,000	
Other costs	2,100	
Total		$17,600
Net cash flow		−$ 3,600
Short-term loan (to be paid off in January)		$ 3,600

Resource Allocation

In allotting financial resources, both the magnitude of various costs and productivity should be examined. Each has significance for asset management and budgeting.

The Magnitude of Various Costs

To easily study the financial operating performance of publicly owned retailers, go to AnnualReports.com (**www. annualreports.com**), enter a company name, and download its 10K report.

As noted before, spending can be divided into two categories. **Capital expenditures** are long-term investments in fixed assets. **Operating expenditures** are short-term selling and administrative costs in running a business. It is vital to have a sense of the magnitude of various capital and operating costs.

In 2008, these were the average capital expenditures (for the basic building shell; heating, ventilation, and air-conditioning; lighting; flooring; fixtures; ceilings; interior and exterior signage; and roofing) for erecting a single store for a range of retailers: department store—$6.1 million; supermarket—$3.3 million; big-box store—$2.7 million; home center—$2.6 million; drugstore—$1.2 million; and apparel specialty store—$1.0 million.[16] Thus, a typical home center chain must be prepared to invest $2.6 million to build each new store (which averaged 60,000 square feet industrywide in 2008), not including land and merchandise costs; the total could be higher if a bigger store is built.

Remodeling can also be expensive. It is prompted by competitive pressures, mergers and acquisitions, consumer trends, the requirement of complying with the Americans with Disabilities Act, environmental concerns, and other factors.

To reduce their investments, some retailers insist that real-estate developers help pay for building, renovating, and fixturing costs. These demands by retail tenants reflect some areas' oversaturation, the amount of retail space available due to the liquidation of some retailers (as well as mergers), and the interest of developers in gaining retailers that generate consumer traffic (such as category killers).

Operating expenses, usually expressed as a percentage of sales, range from 20 percent or so in supermarkets to more than 40 percent in some specialty stores. To succeed, these costs must be in line with competitors'. Costco has an edge over many rivals due to lower SGA (selling, general, and administrative expenses as a percentage of sales): Costco, 10 percent; Wal-Mart, 19 percent; Kohl's, 22 percent; Target, 22 percent; and Dillard's, 29 percent. However, BJ's SGA is 8 percent.[17]

Resource allocation must also take into account **opportunity costs**—the possible benefits a retailer forgoes if it invests in one opportunity rather than another. If a supermarket chain

---

ETHICS IN RETAILING

Are Visa and MasterCard Imposing Unfair Transaction Fees?

In mid-2008, a House Judiciary Committee held a hearing on proposed laws that would prevent credit card companies such as Visa (**www.visa.com**) and MasterCard (**www.mastercard.com**) from imposing unfair transaction fees. Intercharge fees, the amounts charged to merchants on every credit or debit card transaction, have been increasing at a rate of 17 percent per year.

During 2007 alone, Visa and MasterCard received $42 billion in these fees (slightly less than 2 percent per transaction). The average U.S. family was expected to pay $427 in hidden credit and debit card fees in 2008, up from $159 in 2001. One proposed law would allow merchants to individually negotiate their own fees.

To combat high fees, some merchants have begun to charge different prices for transactions paid in cash versus those paid with credit or debit cards. For example, to combat the interchange fees of 9 cents to 12 cents per gallon, Flash Foods (**www.flashfoods.com**), the operator of 180 gas service stations in Georgia and Florida, now charges motorists several cents less per gallon for cash. Flash Foods reports that its credit card fees now total $14 million per year versus $4 million in 2004. About 60 percent of total U.S. gasoline purchases are made with credit or debit cards each year.

Sources: Brian Burnsed, "To Save Money at the Gas Pump, Pay Cash," **www.businessweek.com/bwdaily** (June 20, 2008); and Michael Sanson, "Fighting the Credit Card Companies," *Restaurant Hospitality* (June 2008), p. 6.

renovates 15 existing stores at a total cost of $3.3 million, it cannot open a new outlet requiring a $3.3 million investment (excluding land and merchandise). Financial resources are finite, so firms often face either/or decisions.

Productivity

Look at the various ways in which retailers can improve their financial performance (www.toolkit. cch.com/text/P06_0100. asp).

Due to erratic sales, mixed economic growth, high labor costs, intense competition, and other factors, many retailers place great priority on their **productivity,** the efficiency with which a retail strategy is carried out. Productivity can be described in terms of costs as a percentage of sales, the time it takes a cashier to complete a transaction, profit margins, sales per square foot, inventory turnover, and so forth. The key question is: How can sales and profit goals be reached while keeping control over costs?

Because different retail strategy mixes have distinct resource needs as to store location, fixtures, personnel, and other elements, productivity must be based on norms for each type of strategy mix (such as department stores versus full-line discount stores). Sales growth should also be measured on the basis of comparable seasons, using the same stores. Otherwise, the data will be affected by seasonality and/or the increased square footage of stores.

There are two ways to enhance productivity: (1) A firm can improve employee performance, sales per foot of space, and other factors by upgrading training programs, increasing advertising, and so forth. (2) It can reduce costs by automating, having suppliers do certain tasks, and so forth. A retailer could use a small core of full-time workers during nonpeak times, supplemented with part-timers in peak periods.

Productivity must not be measured from a cost-cutting perspective alone. This may undermine customer loyalty. One of the more complex dilemmas for store retailers that are also online is how to handle customer returns. To control costs, some of them have decided not to allow online purchases to be returned at their stores. This policy has gotten a lot of customers upset.

These are two examples of strategies that diverse retailers have used to raise productivity:

▶ Department stores such as Sears are paying more attention to space productivity. Sears has cleared hundreds of thousands of square feet of space by removing some furniture departments, converting space that was previously used by its affiliated home improvement contractors to retail use, and better managing and displaying its merchandise categories.

Tuesday Morning uses a variety of E-mail formats (http://etreasures. tuesdaymorning.com) to offer bargains to consumers and to reduce its costs by minimizing the need for printed circulars and newspaper ads.

▶ Tuesday Morning, a chain selling quality closeouts, opens its stores for about 300 days per year. Operating costs are low because the stores save on labor expenses (part-time workers are used extensively), utilities, and insurance. The firm further reduces its costs by locating in low-rent sites and offering a no-frills shopping environment: "Our successful concept was founded on a unique philosophy: sell first-quality, famous designer and name-brand merchandise at extraordinarily discounted prices on an event basis. Our 10 major events usually kick off on the first Tuesday of the month. We receive new merchandise shipments daily, and customers can return often to find the shelves replenished with new items." It does not sell merchandise online.[18]

It is vital that retailers, in their quest to become more productive, do not alienate their customers and diminish the shopping experience: "Increasing retail sales productivity is important, but the true challenge—and the true benchmark of retail management performance—is to build productivity profitably."[19]

Chapter Summary

1. *To define operations management.* Operations management involves efficiently and effectively implementing the tasks and policies to satisfy the retailer's customers, employees, and management. This chapter covered the financial aspects of operations management. Operational dimensions are studied in Chapter 13.

2. *To discuss profit planning.* The profit-and-loss (income) statement summarizes a retailer's revenues and expenses over a specific time, typically on a monthly, quarterly, and/or yearly basis. It consists of these major components: net sales, cost of goods sold, gross profit (margin), operating expenses, and net profit after taxes.

3. *To describe asset management, including the strategic profit model, other key business ratios, and financial trends in retailing.* Each retailer has assets and liabilities to manage. A balance sheet shows assets, liabilities, and net worth at a given time. Assets are items with a monetary value owned by a retailer; some appreciate and may have a hidden value. Liabilities are financial obligations. The retailer's net worth, also called owner's equity, is computed as assets minus liabilities.

Asset management may be measured by reviewing the net profit margin, asset turnover, and financial leverage. Net profit margin equals net profit divided by net sales. Asset turnover equals net sales divided by total assets. By multiplying the net profit margin by asset turnover, a retailer can find its return on assets—which is based on net sales, net profit, and total assets. Financial leverage equals total assets divided by net worth. The strategic profit model incorporates asset turnover, profit margin, and financial leverage to yield the return on net worth. It allows a retailer to better plan and control its asset management.

Other key ratios for retailers are the quick ratio, current ratio, collection period, accounts payable to net sales, and overall gross profit (in percent).

Important financial trends involve the state of the economy; funding sources; mergers, consolidations, and spin-offs; bankruptcies and liquidations; and questionable accounting and financial reporting practices.

4. *To look at retail budgeting.* Budgeting outlines a retailer's planned expenditures for a given time based on expected performance; costs are linked to goals.

There are six preliminary decisions: (a) Responsibility is defined by top-down and/or bottom-up methods. (b) The time frame is specified. (c) Budgeting frequency is set. (d) Cost categories are established. (e) The level of detail is ascertained. (f) Budgeting flexibility is determined.

The ongoing budgeting process then proceeds: goals, performance standards, planned spending, actual expenditures, monitoring results, and adjustments. With zero-based budgeting, each budget starts from scratch; with incremental budgeting, current and past budgets are guides. The budgeted versus actual profit-and-loss statement and the percentage profit-and-loss statement are vital tools. In all budgeting decisions, cash flow, which relates the amount and timing of revenues received with the amount and timing of expenditures made, must be considered.

5. *To examine resource allocation.* Both the magnitude of costs and productivity need to be examined. Costs can be divided into capital and operating categories; both must be regularly reviewed. Opportunity costs mean forgoing possible benefits if a retailer invests in one opportunity rather than another. Productivity is the efficiency with which a retail strategy is carried out; the goal is to maximize sales and profits while keeping costs in check.

Key Terms

operations management (p. 336)
profit-and-loss (income) statement (p. 336)
net sales (p. 336)
cost of goods sold (p. 336)
gross profit (margin) (p. 336)
operating expenses (p. 336)
taxes (p. 336)
net profit after taxes (p. 336)
balance sheet (p. 337)

assets (p. 337)
hidden assets (p. 337)
liabilities (p. 337)
net worth (p. 338)
net profit margin (p. 338)
asset turnover (p. 338)
return on assets (ROA) (p. 339)
financial leverage (p. 339)
strategic profit model (p. 340)
return on net worth (RONW) (p. 340)

budgeting (p. 345)
zero-based budgeting (p. 348)
incremental budgeting (p. 348)
cash flow (p. 349)
capital expenditures (p. 350)
operating expenditures (p. 350)
opportunity costs (p. 350)
productivity (p. 351)

Questions for Discussion

1. Describe the relationship of assets, liabilities, and net worth for a retailer. How is a balance sheet useful in examining these items?

2. A retailer has net sales of $975,000, net profit of $165,000, total assets of $600,000, and a net worth of $225,000.
   a. Calculate net profit margin, asset turnover, and return on assets.
   b. Compute financial leverage and return on net worth.

   c. Evaluate the financial performance of this retailer.

3. How can a small apparel store increase its asset turnover?

4. Is too low a financial leverage ratio good or bad? Why?

5. Differentiate between an IPO and an LBO.

6. Present five recommendations for retailers to improve their accounting and financial reporting practices with regard to disclosure ("transparency") of all relevant information to stockholders and others.

7. What is zero-based budgeting? Why do most retailers utilize incremental budgeting, despite its limitations?

8. What is the value of a percentage profit-and-loss statement?

9. How could a seasonal retailer improve its cash flow during periods when it must buy goods for future selling periods?

10. Distinguish between capital spending and operating expenditures. Why is this distinction important to retailers?

11. What factors should retailers consider when assessing opportunity costs?

12. How can these retailers improve their productivity?
    a. House-painting service.
    b. Optical store.
    c. College bookstore.
    d. Upscale luggage store.

Note: At our Web site (**www.pearsonhighered.com/berman**), there are several math problems related to the material in this chapter so that you may review these concepts.

Web **Exercise**

Visit the Web site of QuickBooks (**http://oe.quickbooks. com/interactive_tour_movie.cfm**) to take the online interactive tour. What are benefits of a product such as this for a small retailer?

Note: Stop by our Web site (**www.pearsonhighered.com/ berman**) to experience a number of highly interactive,

appealing Web exercises based on actual company demonstrations and sample materials related to retailing.

13 Operations Management: Operational Dimensions

Chapter Objectives

1. To describe the operational scope of operations management

2. To examine several specific aspects of operating a retail business: operations blueprint; store format, size, and space allocation; personnel utilization; store maintenance, energy management, and renovations; inventory management; store security; insurance; credit management; computerization; outsourcing; and crisis management

The term "black gold" is typically used to describe oil. However, this term is also appropriate for the coffee shops created by Howard Schultz, the founder of Starbucks (**www.starbucks.com**). While traveling in Italy in 1983, Schultz became excited over the coffee-bar culture there. He was very enthusiastic about the growth prospects in the United States because Milan, a city about the size of Philadelphia, supported 1,500 espresso bars.

Schultz was able to convince his Starbucks bosses to sell espresso at a new store in Seattle in 1984. However, they were reluctant to move into the prepared coffee business. As a result, Schultz began his own coffee-bar operation in 1985. Currently, Starbucks has about 8,800 company-owned stores and 7,000 licensed stores worldwide.

After opening more than 1,000 new stores during each of the prior two years, Starbucks announced that it was slowing down its U.S. growth strategy to less than 400 new stores beginning in 2009. And in 2008 and 2009, Starbucks embarked on a plan to close down a number of underperforming outlets. These actions were in response to poor store saturation in some areas. Market analysts also attributed Starbucks' recent stagnant performance to the economic downturn, and the recent push by both McDonald's and Dunkin' Donuts to sell espresso and other more exotic coffees.

In response to the poor performance, Starbucks has implemented a number of initiatives. It developed a new "everyday" coffee blend called Pike Place Roast that was introduced with free samples on a nationwide basis. To enhance the in-store experience, qualifying AT&T high speed Internet and Wi-Fi customers now enjoy free Wi-Fi access at Starbucks. And to further restore confidence, Howard Schulz resumed his position as Starbucks' chief executive officer (which he had left some time before).[1]

Source: Reprinted by permission of Susan Berry, Retail Image Consulting, Inc.

OVERVIEW

For a good operations overview, go to the About.com: Retailing Web site (http://retail.about.com/od/storeoperations).

As defined in Chapter 12, *operations management* is the efficient and effective implementation of the policies and tasks that satisfy a retailer's customers, employees, and management (and stockholders, if it is publicly owned). While Chapter 12 examined the financial dimensions of operations management, this chapter covers the operational aspects.

For firms to succeed in the long term, operational areas need to be managed well. A decision to change a store format or to introduce new anti-theft equipment must be carefully reviewed because these acts greatly affect performance. In running their businesses, retail executives must make a wide range of operational decisions, such as these:

▶ What operating guidelines are used?
▶ What is the optimal format and size of a store? What is the relationship among shelf space, shelf location, and sales for each item in the store?
▶ How can personnel best be matched to customer traffic flows? Would increased staffing improve or reduce productivity? What impact does self-service have on sales?
▶ What effect does the use of various building materials have on store maintenance? How can energy costs be better controlled? How often should facilities be renovated?
▶ How can inventory best be managed?
▶ How can the personal safety of shoppers and employees be ensured?
▶ What levels of insurance are required?
▶ How can credit transactions be managed most effectively?
▶ How can computer systems improve operating efficiency?
▶ Should any aspects of operations be outsourced?
▶ What kinds of crisis management plans should be in place?

Operating a Retail Business

To address these questions, we now look at the operations blueprint; store format, size, and space allocation; personnel utilization; store maintenance, energy management, and renovations; inventory management; store security; insurance; credit management; computerization; outsourcing; and crisis management.

Operations Blueprint

To encourage more compatibility among different retail hardware and software systems, the National Retail Federation has established its ARTS program (www.nrf-arts.org).

An **operations blueprint** systematically lists all operating functions to be performed, their characteristics, and their timing. When developing a blueprint, the retailer specifies, in detail, every operating function from the store's opening to closing—and those responsible for them.[2] For example, who opens the store? When? What are the steps (turning off the alarm, turning on the power, setting up the computer, and so forth)? The performance of these tasks must not be left to chance.

A large or diversified retailer may use multiple blueprints and have separate blueprints for such areas as store maintenance, inventory management, credit management, and store displays. Whenever a retailer modifies its store format or operating procedures (such as relying more on self-service), it must also adjust the operations blueprint(s).

Figure 13-1 has an operations blueprint for a quick-oil-change firm. It identifies employee and customer tasks (in order) and expected performance times for each activity. Among the advantages of this blueprint—and others—are that it standardizes activities (within a location and between locations), isolates points at which operations may be weak or prone to failure (Do employees actually check transmission, brake, and power-steering fluids in one minute?), outlines a plan that can be evaluated for completeness (Should customers be offered different grades of oil?), shows personnel needs (Should

Expected Average

Time per Activity

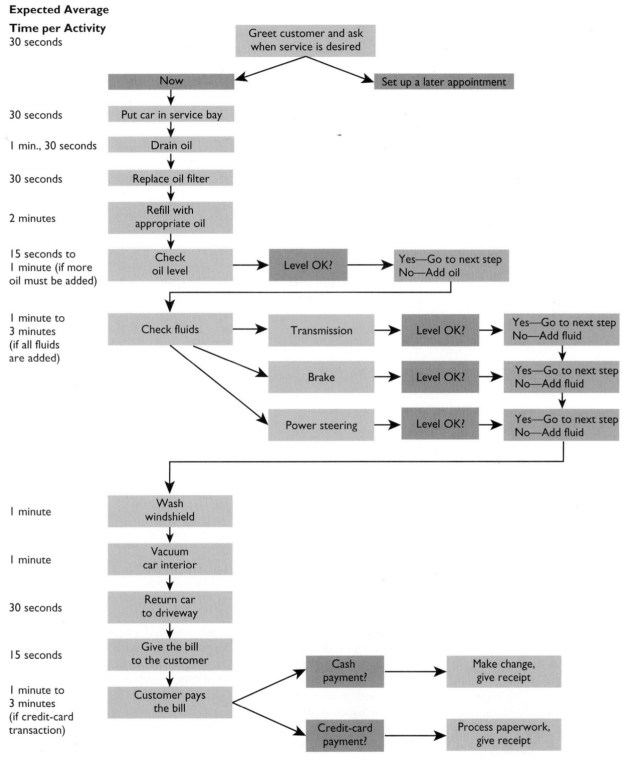

Total expected time = 10 minutes to 14 minutes, 45 seconds.

FIGURE 13-1

An Operations Blueprint for a Quick-Oil-Change Firm's Employees

CAREERS IN RETAILING

Is Retail for Me? Store Management

Store management is where people skills and running a business meet. The store manager or management team has responsibility ranging from departmental to overall establishment. Managers at all levels supervise and assist sales and other employees. Additional responsibilities, depending on store/company size and management level, include opening and closing the store, staffing, administration, and financial functions. Promotions to management positions can be earned through experience, or a college degree may afford direct entry to management trainee programs:

▶ *Store Manager.* Responsible for the overall sales, administration, and staffing of one store.
▶ *Assistant Store Manager.* This position is the "Number 2" person or level in the store, in charge of the whole store when the Store Manager is absent.

Specific duties and title vary by the merchandise type and volume size of store.

▶ *Department Sales Manager.* This position supervises merchandising and staff in a department or zone in a large-square-footage store. May be a keyholder.
▶ *"Third Key"—Hourly Keyholder.* This position is a job level and not a title. A retail store typically has 12 to 14 shifts per week that require a keyholder to open or close. Because the manager and assistant are typically scheduled for 5 shifts each, for a total of 10, there has to be another Associate holding the "third key." In smaller-volume stores, this may be a part-time associate. In a big-box store, the third key may be held by a senior department sales manager.

Source: Reprinted by permission of the National Retail Federation.

one person change the oil and another wash the windshield?), and helps identify productivity improvements (Should the customer or an employee drive a car into and out of the service bay?).

Store Format, Size, and Space Allocation

The Benchmark Group (www.bgark.com) has collaborated with a number of retailers to develop their stores. Click on "Project Experience."

With regard to store format, it should be determined whether productivity can be raised by such tactics as locating in a planned shopping center rather than in an unplanned business district, using prefabricated materials in construction, and applying certain kinds of store design and layouts.

A key store format decision for chain retailers is whether to use **prototype stores,** whereby multiple outlets conform to relatively uniform construction, layout, and operations standards. Such stores make centralized management control easier, reduce construction costs, standardize operations, facilitate the interchange of employees among outlets, allow fixtures and other materials to be bought in quantity, and display a consistent chain image. Yet, a strict reliance on prototypes may lead to inflexibility, failure to adapt to or capitalize on local customer needs, and too little creativity. Pep Boys, Office Depot, Starbucks, McDonald's, and most supermarket chains are among those with prototype stores.

Together with prototype stores, some chains use **rationalized retailing** programs to combine a high degree of centralized management control with strict operating procedures for every phase of business. Most of these chains' operations are performed in a virtually identical manner in all outlets. Rigid control and standardization make this technique easy to enact and manage, and a firm can add a significant number of stores in a short time. Radio Shack, Toys "R" Us, and Starbucks use rationalized retailing. They operate many stores that are similar in size, layout, and merchandising. See Figure 13-2.

Many retailers use one or both of two contrasting store-size approaches to be distinctive and to deal with high rents in some metropolitan markets. Home Depot, Barnes & Noble, and Sports Authority have category killer stores with huge assortments that try to dominate smaller stores. Food-based warehouse stores and large discount-oriented stores often situate in secondary sites, where rents are low—confident that they can draw customers. Cub Foods (a warehouse chain) and Wal-Mart engage in this approach. At the same time, some retailers believe large stores are not efficient in serving saturated

FIGURE 13-2

Rationalized Retailing and
Toys "R" Us
To present a uniform look for its
stores and to be more efficient,
Toys "R" Us frequently utilizes
rationalized retailing as part of
its prototype store formats.

Source: Reprinted by permission
of Susan Berry, Retail Image
Consulting, Inc.

(or small) markets; they have been opening smaller stores or downsizing existing ones
because of high rents:

> Tiffany is putting its contemporary foot forward with a new smaller retail
> format at the lifestyle center Americana at Brand in Glendale, California. The
> 2,600-square-foot store spotlights Tiffany pieces in a comfortable, airy environ-
> ment meant to exemplify the opposite of buttoned-down selling. Customers are
> encouraged to try on the jewelry, with entry and middle price points ranging
> from $80 to $42,000 and averaging $200 to $5,000. Engagement rings and
> statement pieces, the steepest-priced category, aren't available. "Our whole
> intent is to zero in on the contemporary fashion collections and showcase them
> in a more artful and accessible way. Take the blinders off. Forget about the
> rules for how we merchandise today. Let's think about how women shop." The
> standard Tiffany jewelry groupings by metal are abandoned in favor of group-
> ings by style and category. There are displays featuring Tiffany's array of ban-
> gles and stackable rings, and a charm bar. The design imbues the store with a
> "hushed elegance." Tiffany's signature blue is present on digital screens with
> soothing imagery, in glass in select displays on which jewelry is set with the
> signature blue boxes. Robert DuGrenier designed two crystal chandeliers, and
> local artist Suzanne Erickson contributed two works of the abstracted human
> form that can be draped with Tiffany pieces. Jewelry is openly exhibited on
> mountings, under glass that's not fully enclosed and in drawers that customers
> are invited to open.[3]

Retailers often focus on allocating store space. They use facilities productively by determining the amount of space, and its placement, for each product category. Sometimes, retailers
drop merchandise lines because they occupy too much space. That is why J.C. Penney eliminated home electronics, large sporting goods, and photo equipment from its department stores.
With a **top-down space management approach,** a retailer starts with its total available
store space (by outlet and for the overall firm, if a chain), divides the space into categories, and

then works on product layouts. In contrast, a **bottom-up space management approach** begins planning at the individual product level and then proceeds to the category, total store, and overall company levels.

These are among the tactics that some retailers use to improve store space productivity: Vertical displays, which occupy less room, hang on store walls or from ceilings. Formerly free space now has small point-of-sale displays and vending machines; sometimes, product displays are in front of stores. Open doorways, mirrored walls, and vaulted ceilings give small stores a larger appearance. Up to 75 percent or more of total floor space may be used for selling; the rest is for storage, rest rooms, and so on. Scrambled merchandising (with high-profit, high-turnover items) occupies more space in stores, in catalogs, and at Web sites than before. By staying open longer, retailers use space better.

Our Web site (**www.pearsonhighered.com/berman**) has many links on these topics.

Personnel Utilization

From an operations perspective, efficiently utilizing retail personnel is vital: (1) Labor costs are high. For various retailers, wages and benefits may account for up to one-half of operating costs. (2) High employee turnover means increased recruitment, training, and supervision costs. (3) Poor personnel may have weak sales skills, mistreat shoppers, mis-ring transactions, and make other errors. (4) Productivity gains in technology have exceeded those in labor; yet, some retailers are labor intensive. (5) Labor scheduling is often subject to unanticipated demand. Although retailers know they must increase staff in peak periods and reduce it in slow ones, they may still be over- or understaffed if weather changes, competitors run specials, or suppliers increase promotions. (6) There is less flexibility for firms with unionized employees. Working conditions, compensation, tasks, overtime pay, performance measures, termination procedures, seniority rights, and promotion criteria are generally specified in union contracts.

These are among the tactics that can maximize personnel productivity:

Kronos' Workforce Scheduler (**www.kronos. com/Products/wf_ Scheduler.htm**) allows retailers to better manage employee scheduling.

▶ *Hiring process.* By very carefully screening potential employees before they are offered jobs, turnover is reduced and better performance secured.

▶ *Workload forecasts.* For each time period, the number and type of employees are predetermined. A drugstore may have one pharmacist, one cashier, and one stockperson from 2 P.M. to 5 P.M. on weekdays and add a pharmacist and a cashier from 5 P.M. to 7:30 P.M. (to accommodate people shopping after work). In doing workload forecasts, costs must be balanced against the possibilities of lost sales if customer waiting time is excessive. The key is to be both efficient (cost-oriented) and effective (service-oriented). Many retailers use computer software as an aid in scheduling personnel.

▶ *Job standardization and cross-training.* Through **job standardization,** the tasks of personnel with similar positions in different departments, such as cashiers in clothing and candy departments, are rather uniform. With **cross-training,** personnel learn tasks associated with more than one job, such as cashier, stockperson, and gift wrapper. A firm increases personnel flexibility and reduces the number of employees needed at any time by job standardization and cross-training. If one department is slow, a cashier could be assigned to a busy one; and a salesperson could process transactions, set up displays, and handle complaints. Cross-training even reduces employee boredom. See Figure 13-3.

▶ *Employee performance standards.* Each worker is given clear goals and is accountable for them. Cashiers are judged on transaction speed and mis-rings, buyers on department revenues and markdowns, and senior executives on the firm's reaching sales and profit targets. Personnel are more productive when working toward specific goals.

▶ *Compensation.* Financial remuneration, promotions, and recognition that reward good performance help to motivate employees. A cashier is motivated to reduce mis-rings if there is a bonus for keeping mistakes under a certain percentage of all transactions.

FIGURE 13-3

Productive Customer-
Oriented Employees at
Home Depot
Home Depot employees are
trained to be knowledgeable and
flexible when helping customers.

Source: Reprinted by permission
of Home Depot.

▶ *Self-service.* Costs are reduced with self-service. However: (1) Self-service
requires better displays, popular brands, ample assortments, and products with
clear features. (2) By reducing sales personnel, some shoppers may feel service is
inadequate. (3) There is no cross-selling (whereby customers are encouraged to
buy complementary goods they may not have been thinking about).

▶ *Length of employment.* Generally, full-time workers who have been with a firm for
an extended time are more productive than those who are part-time or who have
worked there for a short time. They are often more knowledgeable, are more anxious
to see the firm succeed, need less supervision, are popular with customers, can be
promoted, and are adaptable to the work environment. The superior productivity of
these workers normally far outweighs their higher compensation.

Store Maintenance, Energy Management, and Renovations

Store maintenance encompasses all the activities in managing physical facilities. These
are just some of the facilities to be managed: exterior—parking lot, points of entry and exit,
outside signs and display windows, and common areas adjacent to a store (e.g., sidewalks);
interior—windows, walls, flooring, climate control and energy use, lighting, displays and
signs, fixtures, and ceilings. See Figure 13-4.

The quality of store maintenance affects consumer perceptions, the life span of facilities, and operating costs. Consumers do not like stores that are decaying or otherwise poorly
maintained. This means promptly replacing burned-out lamps and periodically repainting
room surfaces.

Thorough, ongoing maintenance may extend current facilities for a longer period before
having to invest in new ones. At home centers, the heating, ventilation, and air-conditioning

Visit this Web site
(**www.bltllc.com/
commercial_industrial_
floor.htm**) to learn more
about commercial flooring.

FIGURE 13-4

A Checklist of Selected
Store Maintenance
Decisions

✓ What responsibility should the retailer have for maintaining outside facilities? For instance, does a lease agreement make the retailer or the property owner accountable for snow removal in the parking lot?

✓ Should store maintenance activities be done by the retailer's personnel or by outside specialists? Will that decision differ by type of facility (e.g., air-conditioning versus flooring) and by type of service (e.g., maintenance versus repairs)?

✓ What repairs should be classified as emergencies? How promptly should nonemergency repairs be made?

✓ What should be the required frequency of store maintenance for each type of facility (e.g., daily vacuuming of floors versus weekly washing of exterior windows)? How often should special maintenance activities be done (e.g., restriping spaces in a parking lot)?

✓ How should store maintenance vary by season and by time of day (e.g., when a store is open versus when it is closed)?

✓ How long should existing facilities be utilized before acquiring new ones? What schedule should be followed?

✓ What performance standards should be set for each element of store maintenance? Do these standards adequately balance costs against a desired level of maintenance?

equipment lasts an average of 15 years; display fixtures an average of 12 years; and interior signs an average of 7 years. But maintenance is costly.[4] In a typical year, a home center spends $15,000 on floor maintenance alone.

Due to rising costs over the last 35-plus years, energy management is a major factor in retail operations. For firms with special needs, such as food stores, it is especially critical. To manage their energy resources more effectively, many retailers now:

► Use better insulation in constructing and renovating stores.
► Carefully adjust interior temperature levels during nonselling hours. In summer, air-conditioning is reduced at off-hours; in winter, heating is lowered at off-hours.
► Use computerized systems to monitor temperature levels. Some chains' systems even allow operators to adjust the temperature, lighting, heat, and air-conditioning in multiple stores from one office.
► Substitute high-efficiency bulbs and fluorescent ballasts for traditional lighting.
► Install special air-conditioning systems that control humidity levels in specific store areas, such as freezer locations—to minimize moisture condensation.

Here is an example of how seriously some retailers take energy management:

Office Depot opened its first "green" store in Austin, Texas. It includes energy-efficient lighting; more than 50 active skylights that adjust with the path of the sun; solar panels on the roof, which generate about 10 percent of the store's energy and power exterior signage; reflective roofing, which prevents absorption of the heat from the sun and keeps the interior of the store much cooler; steel decking and joists made of recycled steel and recycled concrete partitions; water conservation fixtures, including dual flush toilets, low-flow urinals, and automatic shutoff sensors in restrooms; an exterior landscaping system with "xeriscaping," a water-efficient technique; an energy-management system that allows tracking of energy usage and trends from one central location; and more.[5]

Besides everyday maintenance and energy management, retailers need decision rules regarding renovations: How often are renovations necessary? What areas require renovations more frequently than others? How extensive will renovations be at any one time? Will the retailer be open for business as usual during renovations? How much money must be set aside in anticipation of future renovations? Will renovations result in higher revenues, lower operating costs, or both?

ETHICS IN RETAILING

Hannaford Supermarkets: Leadership in Energy and Environmental Design

Leadership in Energy and Environmental Design (LEED) is a certification program that provides nationally accepted standards for high-performance "green" buildings. LEED provides specific benchmarks in five key areas: sustainable site development, water savings, energy efficiency, material selection, and indoor environmental quality.

Hannaford Supermarkets (**www.hannaford.com**), which operates 160 stores in New York and New England areas, has been building the first supermarket in the United States to meet the stringent LEED Platinum specifications. The platinum rating is the highest designation provided by the U.S. Green Building Council (**www. usgbc.org**), which awards ratings at the silver, gold, and platinum levels. To achieve a platinum rating, a building needs such features as solar photovoltaic panels, geothermal heating and cooling,

high-efficiency refrigeration systems, energy-efficient lighting, and advanced recycling programs.

Hannaford's new Augusta, Maine, store, scheduled to open in mid-2009, will be 40 percent more efficient than a traditional supermarket: "It plans to reduce greenhouse gas emissions, water consumption, and waste and to provide an improved indoor environment for both store associates and shoppers." So among other things, the store will have "a 'green' roof with plants and natural lighting. The site will also be used to test new technology tied to energy efficiency and sustainability."

Source: Warren Thayer, "Got Sustainability?" **www. rffretailer.com/Articles/Cover_Story/BNP_GUID_9-5-2006_A_ 1000000000000450006** (October 21, 2008).

Sometimes, the complexities of store renovations are addressed quite cleverly:

Three years after the devastation of Hurricane Katrina, Dillard's heralded the top-to-bottom renovation of its 270,000-square-foot store at Lakeside Shopping Center: "We have spared no expense in this renovation. It is now our crown jewel." The one-year project was completed while the store remained open, but at least one-third of the space had been closed for three years due to storm damage. The store now emphasizes ready-to-wear, which has almost doubled to 70,000 square feet. The assortment has shifted to a 60–40 ratio of better and contemporary merchandise to traditional. Before, the ratio was 40–60. Ready-to-wear departments are islands offset with marble, bamboo, tile, and carpet flooring. Spacious aisles have replaced narrow paths previously obstructed by racks jammed with indecipherable merchandise. Lighting is brighter to highlight merchandise; and modern colorful platforms and tables have replaced stainless steel and glass rounders. The shoe department has increased to 20,000 square feet, with stockroom space available for 90,000 pairs of shoes.[6]

Inventory Management

A retailer uses inventory management to maintain a proper merchandise assortment while ensuring that operations are efficient and effective. Although the role of inventory management in merchandising is covered in Chapter 15, these are some operational issues to consider:

▶ How can the handling of merchandise from different suppliers be coordinated?
▶ How much inventory should be on the sales floor versus in a warehouse or storeroom? See Figure 13-5.
▶ How often should inventory be moved from nonselling to selling areas of a store?
▶ What inventory functions can be done during nonstore hours?
▶ What are the trade-offs between faster supplier delivery and higher shipping costs?
▶ What supplier support is expected in storing merchandise or setting up displays?
▶ What level of in-store merchandise breakage is acceptable?
▶ Which items require customer delivery? When? By whom?

FIGURE 13-5

Inventory Management
at Wal-Mart
As with every aspect of
operations, Wal-Mart has a very
efficient approach to inventory
management. Its stores are well
stocked, have most merchandise
in the selling area (and not in
a storeroom), and have display
counters that facilitate a lot
of stock on shelves.

Source: Reprinted by permission
of TNS Retail Forward.

Store Security

Store security relates to two basic issues: personal security and merchandise security. Personal security is examined here. Merchandise security is covered in Chapter 15.

Many shoppers and employees feel less safe at retail shopping locations than before, with these results: Some people are unwilling to shop at night. Some shoppers believe malls are not as safe as they once were. Parking is a source of anxiety for people who worry about walking through a dimly lit parking lot. In response, retailers need to be proactive. For example, the Arden Fair Mall, near Sacramento, California, has a sophisticated camera-surveillance network. Because the mall spans 75 acres of land, "management knew it was crucial that security be beefed up from the previous use of just a few fixed cameras and a VHS tape deck." According to Arden's security manager: "The difference between our old system and the new one is like night and day. We only had 19 cameras compared to the 128 cameras now, and the quality of the images is excellent! We wanted something that would be able to monitor mall property while helping shoppers feel safe, and we are very pleased with how the system has turned out."[7]

These are among the practices retailers are utilizing to address this issue:

▶ Uniformed security guards provide a visible presence that reassures customers and employees, and it is a warning to potential thieves and muggers. Some shopping areas even have horse-mounted guards or guards who patrol on motorized Segway Personal Transporters. As one security expert noted: "The standard practice is for guards to walk the floor to provide a visual reminder that they are there, and report unusual behavior to superiors or directly to police."[8]

▶ Undercover personnel are used to complement uniformed guards.

▶ Brighter lighting is used in parking lots, which are also patrolled more frequently by guards. These guards more often work in teams.

▶ TV cameras and other devices scan the areas frequented by shoppers and employees. 7-Eleven has an in-store cable TV and alarm monitoring system, complete with audio.

▶ Some shopping areas have curfews for teenagers. This is a controversial tactic.

▶ Access to store backroom facilities (such as storage rooms) has been tightened.

▶ Bank deposits are made more frequently—often by armed security guards.

Insurance

Among the types of insurance that retailers buy are workers' compensation, product liability, fire, accident, property, and officers' liability. Many firms also offer health insurance to full-time employees; sometimes, they pay the entire premiums, other times, employees pay part or all of the premiums.

Insurance decisions can have a big impact on a retailer: (1) In recent years, premiums have risen dramatically. (2) Several insurers have reduced the scope of their coverage; they now require higher deductibles or do not provide coverage on all aspects of operations (such as the professional liability of pharmacists). (3) There are fewer insurers servicing retailers today than a decade ago; this limits the choice of carrier. (4) Insurance against environmental risks (such as leaking oil tanks) is more important due to government rules.

To protect themselves financially, a number of retailers have enacted costly programs aimed at lessening their vulnerability to employee and customer insurance claims due to unsafe conditions, as well as to hold down premiums. These programs include no-slip carpeting, flooring, and rubber entrance mats; more frequently mopping and inspecting wet floors; doing more elevator and escalator checks; having regular fire drills; building more fire-resistant facilities; setting up separate storage areas for dangerous items; discussing safety in employee training; and keeping records showing proper maintenance activity.

Credit Management

Visa presents a lot of advice (**http://usa.visa. com/merchants/merchant_ resources**) for retailers. Scroll down to "Tips & Tools" and click on "Downloads."

These are the operational decisions to be made in the area of credit management:

▶ What form of payment is acceptable? A retailer may accept cash only, cash and personal checks, cash and credit card(s), cash and debit cards, or all of these.
▶ Who administers the credit plan? The firm can have its own credit system and/or accept major credit cards (such as Visa, MasterCard, American Express, and Discover). It may also work with PayPal and Google Checkout for online payments.
▶ What are customer eligibility requirements for a check or credit purchase? With a check purchase, a photo ID might be sufficient. To open a new credit account, a customer must meet age, employment, income, and other conditions; an existing customer would be evaluated in terms of the outstanding balance and credit limit. A minimum purchase amount may be specified for a credit transaction.
▶ What credit terms will be used? A retailer with its own plan must determine when interest charges begin to accrue, the rate of interest, and minimum monthly payments.
▶ How are late payments or nonpayments to be handled? Some retailers with their own credit plans rely on outside collection agencies to follow up on past-due accounts.

The retailer must weigh the ability of credit to increase revenues against the costs of processing payments—screening, transaction, and collection costs, as well as bad debts. If a retailer completes credit functions itself, it incurs these costs; if outside parties (such as Visa) are used, the retailer covers the costs by its fees to the credit organization.

The *Nilson Report* presents information on retail payment methods. At its site (**www.nilsonreport.com**), you can access highlights.

In the United States, there are more than 1.5 billion credit and debit cards in use. During the Christmas holiday season alone, there are more than 2 billion retail credit and debit card transactions—involving $165 billion—yearly. The average transaction involving a credit/debit card or a check is far higher than a cash one. Overall, one-third of U.S. retail transactions are in cash, one-sixth are by check, and one-half are by credit and debit card. Among retailers accepting credit and debit cards, one-third have their own card, virtually all accept MasterCard and/or Visa, 80 percent accept Discover, and more than one-half accept American Express. Most firms that accept credit cards handle two or more cards.[9]

Credit card fees paid by retailers typically range from 1.5 percent to 5.0 percent of sales for Visa, MasterCard, Discover, and American Express—depending on volume and the card provider. There may also be transaction and monthly fees. The total costs of retailers' own credit operations as a percent of credit sales are usually lower, at 2.0 percent. Costco offers a merchant credit-processing program in partnership with Elavon so that small firms may carry Visa or MasterCard. It charges a 1.64 percent of sales fee and a transaction charge of 20 cents for store retailers; the amounts are 1.99 percent and 27 cents per transaction for nonstore retailers.[10]

Many retailers—of all types—now place greater emphasis on a **debit card system,** whereby the purchase price is immediately deducted from a consumer's bank account and entered into a retailer's account through a computer terminal. The retailer's risk of nonpayment is eliminated, and its costs are reduced with debit rather than credit transactions. For traditional credit cards, monthly billing is employed; with debit cards, monetary account transfers are made at the time of the purchase. There is some resistance to debit transactions by consumers who like the delayed-payment benefit of conventional credit cards. On the other hand, the prepaid gift card, a form of debit card, is popular.

As the payment landscape evolves, new operational issues must be addressed:

Click on "About Deluxe" (**www.deluxe.com**) to learn about one of the premier payment systems support companies for retailers.

▶ Retailers have more payment options. For example, online retailers offer an average of 3.5 payment choices.[11] At store-based retailers, training cashiers is more complex due to all the payment formats, such as cash, third-party and retailer credit and debit cards, personal checks, gift cards, and more.

▶ Hardware and software are available to process paper checks electronically. This means cost savings for the retailer and faster payments from the bank.

▶ Visa and MasterCard have been sued for requiring retailers to accept both credit and debit cards.

▶ Nonstore retailers have less legal protection against credit card fraud than store retailers that secure written authorization.

▶ Credit card transactions on the Web must instantly take into account different sales tax rates and currencies (for global sales).

CAM Commerce Solutions (**www.camcommerce.com**) offers very inexpensive operations software to small retailers in the hope that as these retailers grow, they will upgrade to advanced software.

▶ In Europe, retailers are still grappling with the intricacies of using the euro as currency because the euro is not the standard currency for countries such as Great Britain.

Computerization

Many retailers have substantially improved their operations productivity through computerization; with the continuing decline in the prices of computer systems and related software, even more small firms will do so in the near future. At the same time, retailers must consider this: "The supply chain is no longer characterized by the old plan-buy-build-move-sell principle, but

---

TECHNOLOGY IN RETAILING

mConfirm: Fighting Credit-Card Fraud

Credit-card fraud is getting more sophisticated. Several types of fraud involve mail/Internet orders (where the thief does not have to have the actual credit card present during a transaction), account takeover (where criminals use stolen or fake documents to open a business or credit card account in someone else's name), skimming (where criminals retain a consumer's account number during an actual transaction), and carding (where credit card numbers are generated via computer programs). In one massive credit card fraud case, the Department of Justice charged 11 people with stealing more than 40 million payment card numbers from such retailers as TJX Companies, DSW, and Forever 21.

To reduce credit card fraud, mConfirm (**www.mconfirm.com**) has developed a system to reduce credit

card theft by determining whether the cardholder's mobile phone is located close to the point of sale. Data on the location of the mobile phone location and other information are used to determine a risk score for each transaction. mConfirm's chief executive officer says that such information should not cause privacy concerns because the consumer's location would be known based on their purchasing activity. mConfirm is also working on a means of expanding this service to Web-based sales.

Sources: Matthew Lynch, Cate T. Corcoran, and Justin Sullivan, "11 Charged in Retail Credit Card Fraud Scam," *Women's Wear Daily* (August 6, 2008), p. 2; Daniel Wolf, "System Verifies Transactions by Phone's Location," *American Banker* (March 5, 2008), p. 5; and Bill Zalus, "Credit Card and Transaction Fraud Schemes," *Security* (June 2008), p. 94.

rather by a highly integrated and collaborative, sense-and-respond network. In this network, retailers and their supply partners sense changes in consumer demand in real time and react accordingly, so the right product is in the right place for the right customer."[12] Let's look at various examples of the operational benefits of computerization.

Retailers such as Home Depot, Wal-Mart, and J.C. Penney use videoconferencing. This lets them link store employees with central headquarters, as well as interact with vendors. Videoconferencing can be done through satellite technology and by computer (with special hardware and software). In both cases, audio/video communications train workers, spread news, stimulate employee morale, and so on.

Polycom (**www.polycom. com/usa/en/products/ voice/wireless_solutions**) has a variety of wireless communications products.

In-store telecommunications aid operations via low-cost, secure in-store transmissions. See Figure 13-6. Polycom, with its SpectraLink product line, is one of the firms that markets lightweight phones so workers can talk to one another anywhere in a store. There are no time charges or monthly fees. Polycom clients have included Barnes & Noble, Ikea, Kmart, Neiman Marcus, Rite Aid, and Toys "R" Us.

Software provides computerized inventory control and order tracking. For example, "One challenge grocers face is matching perishable inventory supply to demand. Underestimate demand and shelves go bare. Overestimate demand and you have a lot of spoiled goods. To strike a balance between the two, Price Chopper turned to technology. The role of the software the grocer chose—Fresh Market Manager from Park City Group—was to measure day-to-day demand of fresh items based on sales history and to manage production of those items accordingly."[13] LXE hardware and software (**www.lxe.com**) also enable retailers to be more efficient in performing a wide variety of functions. See Figure 13-7.

Nowhere is computerization more critical than in the checkout process. Let's examine the computerized checkout, the electronic point-of-sale system, and scanning formats.

The **computerized checkout** is used by both large and small retailers so they can efficiently process transactions and monitor inventory. Firms rely on UPC-based systems; cashiers manually ring up sales or pass items over or past scanners. Computerized

FIGURE 13-6

Effective In-Store Communications

Foot Locker employees are equipped with battery-powered headsets that enable them to communicate easily within individual stores.

Source: Reprinted by permission of Foot Locker.

FIGURE 13-7

How Computerization
Improves Productivity
"Do you and your employees
have enough time to manage
staff, help customers, check
inventory, stock shelves, set the
store, process returns and
product transfers, make sales,
conduct cycle counts, and handle
all of the other small tasks that
come up in any given day? If
not, the use of LXE's rugged
mobile computers can improve
your store's efficiency and
accuracy in many areas. Get rid
of those manual, paper processes
and increase the speed and
precision of your tasks that take
away from helping customers
and making sales."

Source: Reprinted by permission
of LXE.

registers instantly record and display sales, provide detailed receipts, and store inventory data. See Figure 13-8. This type of checkout lowers costs by reducing transaction time, employee training, mis-rings, and the need for item pricing. Retailers also have better inventory control, reduced spoilage, and improved ordering. They even get item-by-item data—which aid in determining store layout and merchandise plans, shelf space, and inventory replenishment. Recent technological developments related to computerized checkouts include wireless scanners that let workers scan heavy items without lifting them, radio frequency identification tags (RFID) that emit a radio frequency code when placed near a receiver (which is faster than UPC codes and better for harsh climates), and speech recognition (that can tally an order on the basis of a clerk's verbal command).

Retailers do face two potential problems with computerized checkouts. First, UPC-based systems do not reach peak efficiency unless all suppliers attach UPC labels to merchandise; otherwise, retailers incur labeling costs. Second, because UPC symbols are unreadable by humans, some states have laws that require price labeling on individual items. This lessens the labor savings of posting only shelf prices.

Many retailers have upgraded to an **electronic point-of-sale system,** which performs all the tasks of a computerized checkout and verifies check and charge transactions, provides instantaneous sales reports, monitors and changes prices, sends intra- and inter-store messages, evaluates personnel and profitability, and stores data. A point-of-sale system is often used along with a retail information system. Point-of-sale terminals can stand alone or be integrated with an in-store or a headquarters computer.

Retail scanning equipment
comes in a wide variety
of models and price ranges
(**www.barcodediscount.com**).

Retailers have specific goals for scanning equipment: "The first barcode scanner was used in business 30 years ago. Since then, they have proven their value in automating workflow applications. Today, the system enables data management for multiple inventory items in an efficient and simplified manner. In retail stores, the barcode scanner can be used to receive stock to the outlet, track the location on the sales floor (when used with inventory management software), count inventory, and ring up sales while lessening the human error and fatigue of these steps."[14] Among the recent advances in scanning technology are hand-held scanners; wearable, hands-free scanners; and miniaturized data transceivers.

FIGURE 13-8

An Innovative Use of Checkout Technology

At Giant Eagle, customers can use a portable scanning device to assist them as they shop in the store. This device allows them to keep a running total of the items they select and obtain other product information as well. When they complete their shopping, customers can quickly checkout by using the scanner at a self-checkout station.

Source: Reprinted by permission of TNS Retail Forward.

As noted in Chapter 2, one scanning option with growing retailer interest is **self-scanning,** whereby the consumer himself or herself scans items being purchased at a checkout counter, pays by credit or debit card, and bags items. According to the *Market Study: 2008 North American Self-Checkout Systems:*

> Seventy-nine percent of respondents used a self-checkout in the prior 12 months. In 2007, consumers spent over $161 billion on self-checkout transactions at retailers. Thirty-seven percent of respondents say they really like self-checkout. Only 13 percent say they will not use the technology. Recent installations at Kroger, Home Depot, Lowe's, Albertson's, and others suggest that a large volume of transactions in these stores is being handled by self-checkout. This allows employees to focus on other aspects of the retail operation and on the highest-margin customers in the store.[15]

Outsourcing

More retailers have turned to outsourcing for some of the operating tasks they previously performed themselves. With **outsourcing,** a retailer pays an outside party to undertake one or more of its operating functions. The goals are to reduce the costs and employee time devoted to particular tasks. For example, Limited Brands uses outside firms to oversee its energy use and facilities maintenance. Crate & Barrel outsources the management of its E-mail programs. Kmart uses logistics firms to consolidate small shipments and to process returned merchandise; it also outsources electronic data interchange tasks. Home Depot outsources most trucking operations. J.C. Penney, which for decades managed its credit operations, now has a long-term contract with GE Money (formerly GE Capital).

GE Money (www.gemoney.com/en/business) handles credit operations for a number of retailers.

RETAILING AROUND THE WORLD | Fujitsu's GlobalSTORE Software Application

A major benefit to Fujitsu's GlobalSTORE software application is that it is a true international retail solution. GlobalSTORE enables a retailer to use a single point-of-sale system worldwide. Through the use of GlobalSTORE, a retailer's staff can ship goods directly to a customer from any number of retail locations worldwide. GlobalSTORE also reflects different currencies and different languages. A customer seeking a special size and color shirt in Boston may receive the shirt from a retailer's store in Quebec, Canada. This system increases a retailer's customer service capability, while lowering inventory holding costs. GlobalSTORE's capability also makes it easier for a retailer to globally expand while keeping the same point of sales system.

Another important feature of GlobalSTORE is that this software supports different store formats and different departments within a store. Global operations are likely to involve different store formats than deployed in the United States. Lastly, many global retailers use different data input devices in different countries or in different store formats. GlobalSTORE supports multiple data input devices.

GlobalSTORE is currently being used by more than 150 retailers located in 36 countries. These include Nordstrom (**www.nordstrom.com**), Payless ShoeSource (**www.payless.com**), OfficeMax (**www.officemax.com**), and Daniel's Leather (**www.danielsleather.com**).

Sources: "Fujitsu's GlobalSTORE Software Named Best-in-Class for Current Offering by Independent Research Firm," **www.fujitsu.com/us/news/pr/ftxs_20061002.html** (October 2, 2006); and "GlobalSTORE POS Application," **www.fujitsu.com/us/services/retailing/software/globalstore** (March 3, 2009).

This comment sums up the benefits of outsourcing:

> In the past, retailers were guilty of outsourcing for negative reasons. Some simply moved a problem from in-house to outsourcer, handing over functions they didn't understand. Now, retailers appear to be outsourcing positively—to concentrate on what they are good at and what makes them different in a market where everyone is in competition. "Every retailer believes there are things that make them distinctive," says the business development director at outsourcing company Retail Assist. "If the retailer is all about having the right product at the right time, then it wouldn't want to outsource its supply chain, but could outsource store systems, for example. Every retailer can't be good at everything, but if you're best at one thing, keep that close to the business."[16]

Crisis Management

Despite the best intentions, retailers may sometimes be faced with crisis situations that need to be managed as smoothly as feasible. Crises may be brought on by an in-store fire or broken water pipe, access to a store being partially blocked due to picketing by striking workers, a car accident in the parking lot, a burglary, a sudden illness by the owner or a key employee, a storm that knocks out a retailer's power, unexpectedly high or low consumer demand for a good or service, a sudden increase in a supplier's prices, a natural disaster such as a flood or an earthquake, or other factors.

Although many crises may be anticipated, and some adverse effects may occur regardless of retailer efforts, these principles are important:

1. There should be contingency plans for as many different types of crisis situations as possible. That is why retailers buy insurance, install backup generators, and prepare management succession plans. A firm can have a checklist to follow if there is an incident such as a store fire or a parking-lot accident.
2. Essential information should be communicated to all affected parties, such as the fire or police department, employees, customers, and the media, as soon as a crisis occurs.
3. Cooperation—not conflict—among the involved parties is essential.
4. Responses should be as swift as feasible; indecisiveness may worsen the situation.
5. The chain of command should be clear and decision makers given adequate authority.

Crisis management is a key task for both small and large retailers: "If you haven't thought about how to deal with customers before a crisis happens, you're actually too late if one occurs. You have to plan how messages and actions are taken to key constituents, and the customer is often overlooked as the key constituent."[17] And consider this: "Many companies avoid planning for disaster. It's human nature. But when you think about what it would cost you if you are not prepared, it's just good business sense to plan for the worst. You'll need to avoid the following common mistakes: Put it off until tomorrow. Only big companies can afford continuity planning. Plan only for natural disasters. You have to do it yourself."[18]

Visit our Web site (**www.pearsonhighered.com/berman**) for several links on crisis management.

Chapter **Summary**

1. *To describe the operational scope of operations management.* Operations management efficiently and effectively seeks to enact the policies needed to satisfy customers, employees, and management. In contrast to Chapter 12, which dealt with financial aspects, Chapter 13 covered operational facets.

2. *To examine several specific aspects of operating a retail business.* An operations blueprint systematically lists all operating functions, their characteristics, and their timing, as well as the responsibility for performing the functions.

Store format and size considerations include the use of prototype stores and store dimensions. Firms often use prototype stores in conjunction with rationalized retailing. Some retailers emphasize category killer stores; others open smaller stores. In space allocation, retailers deploy a top-down or a bottom-up approach. They want to optimize the productivity of store space.

Personnel utilization activities that improve productivity range from better screening applicants to workload forecasts to job standardization and cross-training. Job standardization routinizes the tasks of people with similar positions in different departments. With cross-training, people learn tasks associated with more than one job. A firm can advance its personnel flexibility and minimize the total number of workers needed at any given time by these techniques.

Store maintenance includes all activities in managing physical facilities. It influences people's perceptions of the retailer, the life span of facilities, and operating costs. To better control energy resources, retailers are doing everything from using better-quality insulation materials when building and renovating stores to substituting high-efficiency bulbs. Besides everyday facilities management, retailers need decision rules as to the frequency and manner of store renovations.

Good inventory management requires that retailers acquire and maintain the proper merchandise while ensuring efficient and effective operations. This encompasses everything from coordinating different supplier shipments to planning customer deliveries (if needed).

Store security measures protect both personal and merchandise safety. Because of safety concerns, fewer people now shop at night and some avoid shopping in areas they view as unsafe. In response, retailers are employing security guards, using better lighting in parking lots, tightening access to facilities, and deploying other tactics.

Among the insurance that retailers buy are workers' compensation, product liability, fire, accident, property, and officers' liability. Many firms also have employee health insurance.

Most U.S. adults use credit cards. Check and credit payments generally mean larger transactions than cash payments. One-third of retail transactions are in cash, one-sixth by check, and one-half by credit or debit card. Retailers pay various fees to be able to offer noncash payment options to customers, and there is a wide range of payment systems available for retailers.

A growing number of retailers have computerized elements of operations. Videoconferencing and wireless in-store telephone communications are gaining in popularity. Computerized checkouts and electronic point-of-sale systems are quite useful. Electronic point-of-sale systems perform all the tasks of computerized checkouts and verify check and charge transactions, provide instant sales reports, monitor and change prices, send intra- and inter-store messages, evaluate personnel and profitability, and store data. Self-scanning is gaining in popularity.

With outsourcing, the retailer pays another party to handle one or more operating functions. The goals are to reduce costs and better utilize employees' time.

Crisis management must handle unexpected situations as smoothly as possible. There should be contingency plans, information should be communicated to those affected, all parties should cooperate, responses should be swift, and the chain of command for decisions should be clear.

Key Terms

operations blueprint (p. 356)
prototype stores (p. 358)
rationalized retailing (p. 358)
top-down space management
approach (p. 359)

bottom-up space management
approach (p. 360)
job standardization (p. 360)
cross-training (p. 360)
store maintenance (p. 361)

debit card system (p. 366)
computerized checkout (p. 367)
electronic point-of-sale system (p. 368)
self-scanning (p. 369)
outsourcing (p. 369)

Questions for Discussion

1. Present a brief operations blueprint for a dry cleaning store.

2. What are the pros and cons of prototype stores? For which kind of firms is this type of store *most* desirable?

3. Why would a retailer be interested in job standardization and cross-training for its employees?

4. Comment on this statement: "The quality of store maintenance efforts affects consumer perceptions of the retailer, the life span of facilities, and operating expenses."

5. Talk to two local retailers and ask them what they have done to maximize their energy efficiency. Present your findings.

6. As a grocery store owner, you are planning a complete renovation of the fresh fruit section. What decisions must you make?

7. Present a five-step plan for a retailer to reassure customers that it is safe to shop there.

8. An appliance store does not accept checks because of the risks involved. However, it does accept Visa and MasterCard. Evaluate this strategy.

9. What potential problems may result if a retailer relies on its computer system to implement too many actions (such as employee scheduling or inventory reordering) automatically?

10. What operations criteria would you use to evaluate the success of self-scanning at Home Depot?

11. Are there any operating functions that should *never* be outsourced? Explain your answer.

12. Outline the contingency plan a retailer could have in the event of each of these occurrences:
    a. A shopper's accidentally setting off the fire alarm.
    b. A broken store display window.
    c. A firm's Web site inadvertently making personal customer information available to a mailing list company.
    d. The bankruptcy of a key supplier.

Web **Exercise**

Visit the Web site of the Outsourcing Center (www. outsourcing-center.com), and type "Retail" in the search bar. What useful information do you find there?

Note: Stop by our Web site (www.pearsonhighered. com/berman) to experience a number of highly

interactive, appealing Web exercises based on actual company demonstrations and sample materials related to retailing.

part five
Short Cases

CASE 1: THE EMPLOYEE CULTURE AT UMPQUA BANK[C-1]

Umpqua Bank (**www.umpquabank.com**), with nearly 150 branches (from Napa Valley, California, to Seattle, Washington) and $8.3 billion in assets, is committed to creating and maintaining a corporate culture that provides excellent customer service. A key component of the bank's overall retail strategy is its "universal associate" program (that is what Umpqua calls its employees).

At Umpqua, each universal associate is trained to perform every banking task. A teller can take a loan application, and a mortgage officer is able to assist a customer in opening a safe-deposit box. A significant side benefit of this culture is that Umpqua's employee turnover is one-half the industry average. Another benefit is that employee boredom is reduced by performing multiple tasks daily. An employee's workday varies based on which departments are slow and/or busy. In contrast, at a typical bank, employees specialize in certain tasks; thus, employees often have an "it's not my job" mentality.

Umpqua's employees are empowered to satisfy customers. Many branches place dog bowls full of water at the bank entrance for clients with dogs. At a bank location in Portland, Oregon, Umpqua partners with such technology-based companies as Cisco (**www.cisco.com**), Intel (**www.intel.com**), and Microsoft (**www.microsoft.com**) to enhance the customer experience via an Innovation Lab.

This location features a 25-foot plasma product wall featuring touch-screen technology, a computer café for customer use, and an interactive wall providing information on volunteer opportunities and community events. A social networking site—LocalSpace—invites local firms to seek advice from one another. Based on their use, these features may be rolled-out to Umpqua's network of branch locations.

Some Umpqua bank locations even play music produced by local talent. According to a former project manager for Umpqua Bank, the firm proves its story in its branches because "visually, every square inch is dedicated to aligning the bank branch with the neighborhood it resides in."

Umpqua believes that it needs to continually measure and reward customer service on a team level. The bank gives out a total of $175,000 in bonuses each month. The team award is based on (1) new-account surveys, (2) in-lobby "your opinion counts cards," (3) the results of three mystery telephone shopping experiences per month, (4) the retention of existing customers, (5) lost accounts per month, and (6) cross-selling scores. Due to the bank's incentive program, it averages 4.9 cross-selling products per sales session versus an industry average of 3.5 products.

Umpqua understands the difficulties in sustaining its customer service strategy as the firm acquires banks with different cultures and personnel who do not share Umpqua's customer philosophy. Thus, when it acquires a local bank, Umpqua conveys its culture to employees and customers. After acquiring one local bank, it announced its opening with ice-cream trucks filled with ice-cream sandwiches.

Questions

1. Discuss the pros and cons of Umpqua's universal associate program from the perspective of the bank's management.
2. Discuss the pros and cons of Umpqua's universal associate program from the perspective of the bank's employees.
3. Is a tall or flat organization most appropriate for Umpqua? Explain your answer.
4. Develop a goal-oriented job description for an Umpqua teller.

CASE 2: SONY LOOKS TO A SMALL-STORE FORMAT [C-2]

Sony (**www.sony.com**) is now gearing up to sell its TVs, DVD players, and other electronics through a number of small company-owned Sony Style (**www.sonystyle.com**) stores. Since it began this strategy, Sony has opened more than 60 U.S. stores. Although apparel manufacturers such as Coach (**www.coach.com**), Burberry (**www.burberry.com**), and Ralph Lauren (**www.polo.com**) often have hundreds of company-owned stores that compete with department and specialty stores, this strategy is uncommon for electronics manufacturers.

Due to its belief that many conventional electronics stores do a poor job in demonstrating merchandise to women, Sony is planning to place more Sony Style stores in upscale shopping centers and central business districts. It is opening stores near such female-oriented firms as Sephora (**www.sephora.com**), Tiffany (**www.tiffany.com**), and Louis Vuitton (**www.vuitton.com**). Sony has also sought out U.S. mall locations in the nation's largest 50 major metropolitan markets and bids for the best locations in these malls. Sony is currently close to reaching that goal. This location strategy is in sharp contrast with that of large electronics stores such as Best Buy (**www.bestbuy.com**) that are situated in smaller malls.

[C-1] The material in this case is drawn from Linda Daily, "Umpqua Bank Debuts Innovation Lab," *Community Banker* (January 2008), p. 11; Anthony Malakin, "Incentives: Serving Rewards," *US Banker* (August 2008), p. 12; and Bryan Ochalla, "Not Cookie Cutter Branches," *Credit Union Management* (June 2008), pp. 51–54.

[C-2] The material in this case is drawn from Colleen Bohen, "Sony Style Named Best Vendor Retailer," *Twice* (October 8, 2007), p. 24; Alan Wolf, "Sony Style Enhances In-Store Services," *Twice* (August 4, 2008), p. 12; and Alan Wolf, "Toys 'R' Us Opens Sony In-Store Shop," *Twice* (August 6, 2007), p. 22.

Sony's newest strategy focuses on using small store formats. It recently opened an in-store Sony shop in Toys "R" Us' Manhattan Times Square flagship store. The 550-square-foot store features Sony Cyber-shot digital cameras, Walkman portable MP3 players and CD players, Vaio notebooks, and Sony Readers. Employees are especially trained to allow shoppers to try out Sony products in the store so that they can get hands-on experience prior to purchasing goods.

According to Sony Style's retail senior vice-president, Sony opened its first Sony Style store in response to consumer confusion about "the shift in technology from an analog to a digital world." The chain is targeted to women because Sony correctly anticipated that women would become an increasingly "major force of consumer electronics purchasing."

Sony Style stores feature a concierge desk where each shopper is greeted. Aisles are designed to easily accommodate strollers. And unlike conventional electronics store where competing brands are lined up in rows, every Sony model is placed on a different stand. This gives consumers a better idea of what the TVs or home theaters will look like in their living room or den. And all TVs are tuned to the Discovery Channel or to movie clips from Sony Corporation movies, not to sports channels.

Sales at Sony Style locations reached $740 million as of 2006, making this division the 22nd largest consumer electronics chain in the United States. In 2007, Sony Style received *Twice* magazine's "Excellence in Retailing Award in the Best Vendor Category." Today, annual revenues are in the $1 billion range.

Many electronics retailers fear that Sony will become a direct competitor, as well as their supplier. To reduce their concerns, Sony invites retailers that have nearby stores to their newest locations prior to their opening. Sony has also undertaken marketing research studies showing that the new stores, by better educating customers about the features of a Sony model, increase the sales of all stores in the area.

Questions

1. Identify the pros and cons of Sony's small-store format.
2. Should Sony use prototype stores? Should it use rationalized retailing? Explain your answers.
3. Describe the pros and cons of a top-down space management approach for Sony, as well a bottom-up space management system.
4. Discuss the inventory management issues Sony needs to understand in managing its stores.

CASE 3: MANAGING HIGH PRODUCTIVITY: PUBLIX SUPER MARKETS[C-3]

With Wal-Mart's (**www.walmart.com**) increased emphasis on food products, many small and medium-sized supermarkets have had difficulty competing against Wal-Mart's low prices, long store hours, and one-stop shopping

appeals. One notable exception is Publix Super Markets (**www.publix.com**), which recently opened its 900th store. Publix has a market share of more than 40 percent in its home state of Florida and is reportedly taking business away from Wal-Mart and other supermarkets as Publix continues to expand into Alabama, Georgia, Tennessee, and South Carolina.

Let's look at Publix's performance as judged by the strategic profit model. For 2007, Publix had a net profit margin of 5.14 percent, asset turnover of 2.86 times, and financial leverage of 1.42. Publix's return on net worth was 20.98 percent. During the same period, Wal-Mart had a return on net worth of 19.7 percent—with a net profit margin of 3.40 percent, asset turnover of 2.29 times, and financial leverage of 2.53 times. And Whole Foods' (**www.wholefoods.com**) return on net worth was 12.50 percent—with a net profit margin of 2.77 percent, asset turnover of 2.05 times, and financial leverage of 2.20 times.

Retail analysts generally credit Publix's employee ownership, high customer service ratings, and ability to tailor products to specific customer groups as the three major factors that account for Publix's strong productivity. Ever since the American Consumer Satisfaction Index (**www.theacsi.org**) began rating firms in 1997, Publix has ranked number one in customer satisfaction. Publix has a long-standing reputation for customer service: Its employees place customers' goods into shopping bags, take the bags to the customer's car, and even load them in the trunk. Employees are trained to refuse tips and accept them only if the customer offers the tip more than once. The same philosophy extends to Publix's pharmacy, where prescriptions are filled within 15 minutes of being dropped off.

Publix's employees own 31 percent of the equity in the firm through a stock ownership plan. This makes Publix the largest employee-owned company in the United States. According to the founder of wRatings (**www.wratings.com**), a research firm that ranks the most competitive retail and consumer goods companies annually, the fact that Publix is employee managed has a large impact on the retailer's success: "If you're an employee and you own stock, you're going to do a better job."

Many other retail analysts also believe that stock ownership plans increase worker productivity because higher profits directly contribute to an employee's wealth. Employee-owners may also be more prone to skip or reduce lunch hours on an especially busy day, cover for other workers who are sick, and seek to increase the low productivity of a fellow worker.

As part of its strategy of appealing to key market segments with special offerings, Publix has opened Publix

---

[C-3]The material in this case is drawn from Sharon Edelson, "Rating the Most Competitive Retailers," *Women's Wear Daily* (July 28, 2008), p. 30; "The Opposite of Wal-Mart," *Economist* (May 5, 2007), p. 79; and Mike Troy, "Publix Achieves Record Expansion, Stays No. 1 in Service," *Drug Store News* (April 21, 2008), pp. 136, 170.

Sabor (**www.publix.com/sabor**) stores in south Florida markets with large Hispanic and Caribbean populations. These Publix Sabor markets offer packaged goods that appeal to Hispanic shoppers, as well as specially prepared dishes such as red beans with pigs' feet and stewed chicken and perishables such as yucca root. It has also opened up a number of stores especially devoted to organic foods.

Questions

1. Discuss the significance of Publix's versus Wal-Mart's performance on the strategic profit model.
2. Explain how employee ownership can contribute to increased productivity.
3. How can a publicly owned supermarket chain better motivate its employees?
4. Develop a plan for Publix to further reduce employee turnover.

CASE 4: IMAX AND AMC JOIN TOGETHER[C-4]

IMAX (**www.imax.com**) recently entered into a joint venture with AMC Entertainment (**www.amctheaters.com**) to bring IMAX's state-of-the-art projection systems to 33 U.S. market areas by 2011. This joint venture will more than double the number of Imax theaters in the United States.

Under this agreement, IMAX pays for the cost of new projection systems (valued at about $500,000 each) and AMC agrees to retrofit its existing theaters to accommodate screens that are 25 percent larger than existing screens and provide IMAX-friendly seating. In the past, many of the IMAX-equipped theaters were limited to such sites as museums and space domes (e.g., the San Diego Hall of Science or the Smithsonian Institute). By using digital technology that reduces the high cost of screens and costly film, IMAX technology can now be used in traditionally sized movie theaters.

AMC either owns or has partial financial interest in 360 movie theaters with more than 5,000 screens. According to AMC's chairman and chief executive officer: "Deployment of the IMAX digital projection system is consistent with AMC's commitment to install digital cinema technology throughout its circuit theaters." As an indication of the effectiveness of the new format, IMAX posted same-store sales growth of 65 percent from the prior year. Although three-dimensional (3-D) versions of Dreamworks' (**www.**

c-4The material in this case is drawn from Jesse Serwer, "IMAX Enters New Dimension," *Retailing Today* (March 2008).

dreamworks.com) *Beowulf* feature were available in less than one-third of the screens (mostly in larger markets), these screens accounted for two-thirds of the gross revenues on *Beowulf*'s opening weekend.

Another favorable development is the increased number of 3-D movies produced by movie studios. Dreamworks' chief executive has announced that all of his studio's animated features will now be made in a 3-D format. In the past, many 3-D films featured special-effects movies and enhanced animated films. Recently, a U2 concert was filmed in 3-D. As the president of Media by Numbers (**www.paintbynumbers.com**) noted: "With these 3-D movies, they are trying to bring the level of the visual plane up to the level of the sonic experience, and that's what's going to make the difference."

Industry observers have remarked that the IMAX/AMC joint venture will be very closely watched by competitors. According to Media by Numbers' president: "Everyone in the film industry will be watching that deal very closely. If it's successful, and I think they will be very successful, other chains will be interested in working out similar deals with IMAX."

The IMAX-AMC deal is not exclusive. This opens up the opportunity for other partnerships with additional movie chains. The new 3-D format also faces competition on a number of fronts. One, a competing technology, Real D, has equipped 1,100 screens worldwide to show its format. Another technology, developed by Digital3.com, enables consumers to view 3-D movies without the use of special glasses. A third competitive threat is the greater number of homes that have sophisticated projection systems, high-definition televisions, and high-definition DVD players. There are also more films that can be downloaded on demand from the Internet via firms such as Netflix and from cable stations.

Questions

1. Comment on the budgeting process for an IMAX-AMC theater.
2. Develop a financial plan to increase the profitability for an IMAX-AMC theater.
3. Differentiate between capital expenditures and operating expenditures for an IMAX-AMC theater. Why is the distinction important?
4. List and discuss five retail productivity measures to assess the IMAX-AMC joint venture in terms of sales and profitability.

part five

Comprehensive Case

REACHING GEN Y AS RETAIL EMPLOYEES*

INTRODUCTION

Four key current American generations include Generation Y (or Gen Y, born 1978 to 2000), who are hopeful, have a determined work ethic, and are polite to authority figures. Next is Generation X (or Gen X, born 1965 to 1977), who are skeptical, have a balanced work ethic, and are unimpressed by authority. Baby boomers (born 1946 to 1964) follow. They are optimistic, strongly driven at work, and have a love/hate view of authority. Finally, there are the Veterans or Silent/GI Generation (born 1900 to 1945), who are practical, have a dedicated work ethic, and are respectful of authority.

At last count, there were 70 million Gen Yers in the United States, or nearly one-quarter of the overall population. Viewed collectively, this group shares a number of characteristics important to retailers. Members of Gen Y, also known as "Millennials," make many of their own purchasing decisions and also heavily influence purchase decisions within their households. However, because the Gen Y consumer is so tech savvy, marketing to them is different from any other generation in history. Likewise, retailers are presented with new opportunities and challenges with recruiting and retaining Gen Y employees. Examining how technological advances have shaped Gen Y provides a better understanding of how to reach them on both sides of the cash register, as both customers and retail employees.

What sets Gen Y apart? Rapid advancements in technology and connectivity (E-mail, the Internet, instant messaging, cell phones, DVDs, MP3 players, digital cameras, camera phones, etc.) have greatly shaped Gen Y shopping preferences

*The material in this case is adapted by the authors from Maritz Research (**www.maritzresearch.com**), "Reaching Gen Y on Both Sides of the Cash Register," *Retailing Issues Letter* (College Station, TX: Center for Retail Studies at Texas A&M University, Maritz Research, and FKM, Number 2, 2007). Reprinted by permission.

compared with prior generations. Demographers and others have been tracking trends associated with Gen Y since they first became visible as consumers more than 20 years ago and began entering the work force in the late 1990s. Retailers that understand the aspects that differentiate Gen Y from other generations can be better prepared to satisfy Gen Y customers and employees.

Engaging the Gen Y Retail Employee

Popularity of Retail Employment for Gen Y

A Job Opportunity Study conducted by Maritz Poll found that retail is extremely popular with Gen Y. Eighty-three percent of the 16- to 24-year-old respondents who were looking for a job want a retail position. In addition, potential retail employees (44 percent) are significantly more likely to be 16- to 24-years-old than those seeking nonretail employment (9 percent). Because a substantial portion of the retail industry is comprised of Gen Y, retailers need to be equipped to recruit and retain younger employees who come to the work force with a different set of expectations than previous generations.

Longevity on the Job

A frequently asked question is: "Once our employees have been hired and trained, how long will they stay with the company?" Gen Y is all about change and has virtually no loyalty to their employers. As a result, Gen Y employees are less likely to stay in their current jobs. Our Employee Engagement research shows that 94 percent of 16- to 24-year-olds currently employed in retail say they foresee themselves changing careers in the future. See Figure 1.

Retail Employee Engagement

Given that so many Gen Y retail employees expect to change jobs, it becomes even more important to retain current employees. However, because Gen Y has different expectations for employment than did its predecessors, retailers may find "the rules have changed."

Gen Yers want meaningful work that fulfills them or helps others. The Employee Engagement research focused on how well the retail industry is meeting the needs of its employees. The good news is that the retail industry is hitting

FIGURE 1

Retail Employees Foreseeing a Change in Careers

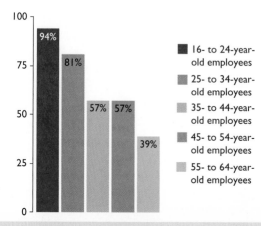

Legend:
- 16- to 24-year-old employees
- 25- to 34-year-old employees
- 35- to 44-year-old employees
- 45- to 54-year-old employees
- 55- to 64-year-old employees

(Bar values: 94%, 81%, 57%, 57%, 39%)

the mark on many work-related aspects that are important to Gen Y. Although there is still room for improvement in the retail industry on the key attributes related to employee engagement, Gen Y retail employees are significantly more likely than other generations of retail employees to have higher levels of satisfaction with the attributes that lead to engagement with their job.

Provide Work–Life Balance

Gen Yers want to find a balance between work and life. "They separate career and home lives, and want flexibility." Our research shows that Gen Yers are more likely to find that balance with their retail employment than are older retail employees. Significantly more of the 16- to 24-year-olds than 25- to 34-year-olds or 55- to 64-year-olds agree or strongly agree with the statement: "My organization actively works to help its employees achieve an appropriate balance between work and personal life."

Similarly, significantly more of the 16- to 24- year-olds than of the 35- to 64-year-olds agree or strongly agree with the statement: "Work expectations at my company are realistic and fair." Apparently, Gen Yers are able to achieve the work–life balance that "workaholic" baby boomers were unable to find.

Give a Sense of Personal Accomplishment

Feeling personal accomplishment with their employment is one major area in which the retail industry has failed to reach its goal with Gen Y. The 16- to 24-year-olds are significantly more likely than the 45- to 64-year-olds to disagree or strongly disagree with the statement: "My work gives me a strong sense of personal accomplishment." A broader Maritz Poll study on Employee Incentives with all types of employees (not just retail employees) also found Gen Y significantly less likely to feel their work gives them a sense of strong personal accomplishment. Employers can overcome this obstacle with coaching and by allowing retail workers to use and develop their skills, which leads to deeper feelings of personal accomplishment.

Provide Meaningful Feedback

Gen Y has grown up with constant feedback, recognition, and praise from their parents and at school. As a result, they expect immediate feedback at work. A *Wall Street Journal* article dubbed them, "The Most Praised Generation" and drives home the point that Gen Yers require more praise in the workplace and in their personal relationships than did previous generations. Although there is still some improvement to be made in providing employee recognition in the retail industry, evidently Gen Yers are more likely to receive meaningful feedback than are some older generations.

Our Retail Employee Engagement research shows Gen Y employees are much more likely to receive the praise they desire than those aged 55 to 64. The Employee Incentives study also found younger employees (in this case, Gen X versus those over 35) were much more likely to be recognized in meaningful ways, to be satisfied with

the firm's efforts to recognize employees, and to feel the firm uses recognition to reinforce actions that positively affect customers and uses recognition to reinforce corporate values.

Casey Priest, Vice-President of Marketing at the Container Store (**www.containerstore.com**), says: "We adopt a coaching mentality, among other managerial practices, so that when managers observe good work they give specific praise immediately." The Container Store's many strategies must work because the chain has ranked near the top of *Fortune*'s best firms to work for eight years straight. It is not clear whether Gen Yers actively seek this praise or if employers are more focused on providing praise to Gen Yers than to other generations. Regardless of generation, employers should ascertain from each employee what type of feedback (public, private, merchandise, time off, etc.) is most valued by the employee.

Possibly, Gen Y's politeness to authority figures leads to more open dialog than with other generations. Significantly more of the 16- to 24-year-olds than 25- to 34-year-olds and the 55- to 64-year-olds either agree or strongly agree with the statement: "Open and honest dialog is encouraged here."

Promote Teamwork

Gen Yers like working with a team and, compared with other generations, are finding the support they need in the retail environment. The majority of 16- to 24-year-olds (65 percent) either agree or strongly agree with the statement: "At my company, it seems like we're all on the same team, working for the same goals." This level of agreement is significantly higher than that of any other age group. Retailers should keep in mind that a degree of finesse may be necessary if teams are composed of members from multiple generations who may approach situations with different styles.

Encourage Creative Thinking

Gen Yers are well-educated, creative thinkers, and they crave creative thinking in their work life. Overall, differences in creative thinking did not vary as greatly between generations as did other factors in the employee engagement battery. However, significantly more 16- to 24-year-olds than 25- to 34-year-olds agree/strongly agree with the statement "My company actively encourages creativity and innovative thinking." Both the employee and employer have a great deal to gain from encouraging creative thinking.

Offer Perks

Many companies are promoting flexible work schedules for Gen Yers. Our Job Opportunity study found flexible work hours are important to Gen Yers seeking any type of employment (not necessarily retail employment). Employers benefit from flexible work hours as a perk because it does not require additional cash expenditures.

The vast majority of those aged 16 to 24 seeking a retail job agree or strongly agree with the statement: "I want flexible work hours." Their desire for flexible hours is significantly greater for these younger employees than it is for the

35- to 44-year-olds. However, overall, this did not vary as greatly between generations as did other factors.

Interactions with Customers

Given the large percentage of Gen Y in retail positions, it is inevitable that younger retail employees will interact with customers. The customer's experience during the transaction can greatly influence their opinion of the retailer and impact sales. Our Retail Employee Engagement research assessed the extent to which employees enjoy their interactions with customers. Specifically, the study evaluated employees' opinions regarding their enjoyment with their customer interactions and the extent to which employees feel customers are "rude and impatient," "rushed and indifferent," or "friendly and understanding." The findings reveal that employees' interactions with customers vary significantly by the employees' ages.

Perhaps because of their frequent use of technology to communicate, rather than direct contact, younger retail employees (aged 16 to 24) are significantly less likely to enjoy their interactions with customers than older employees (aged 35 to 64). Only 55 percent of the 16- to 24-year-olds enjoy their interactions with customers, compared to 74 percent of the 35- to 44-year-olds and 83 percent of the 45- to 64-year-olds. It is not just the retail employees who possess this attitude. Employee Engagement research with employees from multiple industries also found Gen Yers were significantly less likely than other generations to enjoy their interactions with customers. See Figure 2.

One in four of the 16- to 24-year-olds find their customers "rude and impatient." These employees are significantly more likely to feel the customers are "rude and impatient" than are employees in the 35- to 64-year-old age range. See Figure 3. Younger employees are also more likely to believe their customers are "rushed and indifferent." Almost one in three of the 25- to 34-year-old employees feel this way. Employees in the 25- to 34-year-old age range are significantly more likely to agree with this description of their customers

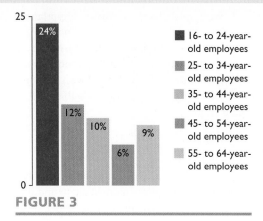

FIGURE 3

Retail Employees Who Feel Their Customers Are "Rude and Impatient"

than are employees in the 35- to 64-year-old age range. See Figure 4.

Approximately 8 in 10 of the older employees find the customers "friendly and understanding." Employees aged 35 to 64 are significantly more likely to find the customers "friendly and understanding" than are employees aged 16 to 34. See Figure 5.

Importance of Employee Interactions on Customer Satisfaction

Virtually every retailer intuitively knows employee interactions play a key role in customer satisfaction. Our Retail Customer Loyalty study confirmed that "helpful and friendly employees" is the most important factor related to overall store satisfaction. By comparison, "helpful/ friendly employees" is almost twice as important as "reasonable prices" as related to overall store satisfaction. See Figure 6.

Given the importance rating of "helpful and friendly employees," the significantly higher percent of younger employees who don't enjoy their interactions with customers can have huge implications for retailers. At the

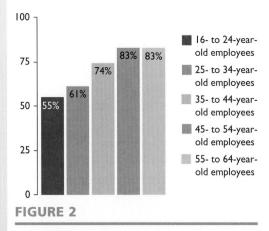

FIGURE 2

Retail Employees Who "Enjoy Their Interactions with Customers"

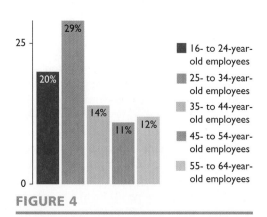

FIGURE 4

Percent of Retail Employees Who Feel Their Customers Are "Rushed and Indifferent"

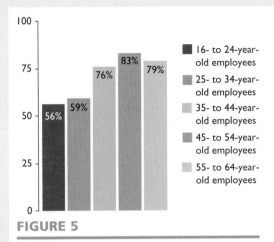

FIGURE 5

Retail Employees Who Feel Their Customers Are "Friendly and Understanding"

very least, this finding should affect the methods for hiring and training younger employees who interact with customers.

The Driver Importance Ratings can be compared as follows: "product variety and availability" with a score of 25 is five times more important than "easy to return products," which has a score of 5 as it relates to overall satisfaction with the store.

Learning Styles and Training

Gen Y has specific learning styles that differentiate them from other age groups. Having grown up with technology and MTV, they tend to have shorter attention spans and respond to rapid visuals that might appear as stimulation overload to their older counterparts. They are visually oriented, like graphics, and thrive on change and variety. This technologically savvy generation is receptive to online training.

For Gen Yers, it is important to provide a thorough orientation to the company (including what's good, not so

good, expectations, and long-term goals). Because Gen Y values creative thinking and education, developing a strong training department and establishing mentor programs are also vital.

Defining the Gen Y Employee

Gen Y employees bring many positive skills and traits to the work force. However, they are motivated and engaged in different ways than older employees. Reaching them will be both a rewarding and necessary component in the retail world.

Gen Yers recognize they are getting support from their employer, but are still dissatisfied, bored at work, and are the most likely to move on. They are particularly demanding of their workplace, which is bad news for a low-margin, high-turnover industry such as retail. What can you do? This is where providing meaningful incentives are probably going to be even more necessary than in the past to keep turnover down and productivity high.

Employers should ask themselves:

▶ Are we effectively using technology to recruit employees?
▶ Does our hiring and training process focus on creating positive interactions with customers?
▶ Is our training in a format that best reaches this generation?
▶ Does the job include the components which engage Gen Y, such as:
   ✓ Balance between work life and personal life.
   ✓ A chance to feel a sense of personal accomplishment.
   ✓ Feedback that is immediate and meaningful.
   ✓ An opportunity to work with a team.
   ✓ An environment that promotes creative thinking.
   ✓ Perks that include flexible work hours.

For organizations with a large proportion of their employees falling in the Gen Y group, employers should ask themselves, "What is the impact of my employees on my customer base?"

FIGURE 6

Importance of Factors in Retail Shopper Satisfaction

Factor	Importance Ratings for Overall Satisfaction with Store
Helpful and friendly employees	27
Product variety and availability	25
Store layout/ neat and clean	23
Reasonable prices	15
Easy-to-return products	5
Not crowded/ adequate parking	3
Convenient location	2
Loyalty program membership	1

Appealing to the Generation Y Customer

Gen Y's purchasing behavior is based on different criteria than previous generations. Overall, Gen Y is more concerned with how the product makes them appear and keeping up with trends than are older shoppers who more greatly value the shopping experience.

A study conducted by Maritz Poll (a consumer opinion poll that reflects the opinions and attitudes of Americans and Europeans on a variety of topics) evaluated how decision factors for making a purchase vary by generation. The study found that "status of the product," "keeping up with what my friends/colleagues have," and "being the newest product of its kind" were significantly more important to younger shoppers (Gen Y and Gen X) than either baby boomers or the Silent/GI Generation.

This finding highlights the "viral" element of marketing to Gen Y, which relies heavily on "word of mouth" (or, actually, text messaging/E-mails, blogs, etc.) and peer groups to influence their purchase decisions. *Chain Store Age*'s feature on Gen Y supports this finding. The article noted that "because they are in constant communication, the influence of peers is more important than that of traditional cultural authorities such as brand advertising."

A second, recently conducted Maritz Poll study focusing specifically on Gen Y shoppers aged 18–30, found this constant communication dynamic takes on many forms and often has a retail bent to it. Sixty-nine percent of the poll's Gen Y shoppers said they send between 1 and 10 text messages per day; individuals in this generational group, on average, text approximately 17 messages per day. More specific to retail, 48 percent of Gen Y respondents said they belong to an online group hosted by a retailer. Also, approximately one-fourth have posted an online review for a product or specific retailer, and about two-thirds use online reviews as a source when making purchasing decisions. The emergence of online retail boards and retail-themed blogs, and frequent word-of-mouth communications through online and texting, have encouraged retailers to rethink their marketing strategies for Gen Y.

Interestingly, while Gen Y shoppers are communicating through online and wireless media with one another, they are not as receptive to retailers sending messages and offers via text messages. Although texting seems like a perfect channel for retailers to reach Gen Y shoppers, because it's used so much and is so accessible, it isn't actually the best. The poll revealed that approximately two-thirds of respondents said they were "unlikely to or would definitely not subscribe" to offers solicited via cell phone. Only 5 percent of those polled were signed up with retailers to receive text offers and information.

Older shoppers (Gen Xers and baby boomers) rate the "quality of the shopping experience when making a purchase" as significantly more important than Gen Y shoppers. It is not surprising the youngest group of shoppers is less appreciative of the shopping experience. Given that Gen Y is adept at using technology for virtually every facet of their lives, a personalized shopping experience is far less important to them. Even though a quality shopping experience appeals to older shoppers, the retailer's Gen Y strategy should be to help them make purchases quickly and easily.

Gen Y rates "need for the product" as significantly less important than Gen X, baby boomers, or the Silent/GI Generation. Consumers in life stages after Gen Y (those with mortgages, children in college, or nearing retirement/in retirement) are more concerned with spending their money wisely. However, it is somewhat surprising that Gen Y rated the "price of the product" and "quality of the product" as significantly less important than Gen X or baby boomers. For Gen Y, keeping up with their peer group overrides factors that older generations find important. This finding also provides insight that Gen Yers are more prone to impulse spending than older shoppers.

Questions

1. What are the major lessons to be learned from this case?
2. What would you recommend that a retailer do to (a) attract, (b) train, and (c) retain good Gen Y employees?
3. How would you improve productivity of Gen Y employees?
4. What would you do to ensure that Gen Y and baby boomer employees in a retail firm feel that they are on the same team?
5. How could a retailer satisfy its needs with regard to proper staffing during all store hours—including mornings, evenings, and weekends—and the desire by Gen Y employees for a work–life balance?
6. According to Figures 2 and 5, a substantial number of Gen Y retail employees do not enjoy their interactions with customers and do not find customers to be friendly and understanding. What would you recommend to turn around these attitudes?
7. From a human resource management perspective, comment on this statement: "Older shoppers rate the 'quality of the shopping experience when making a purchase' as significantly more important than Gen Y shoppers."

PART 6 Merchandise Management and Pricing

In Part Six, we present the merchandise management and pricing aspects of the retail strategy mix. Merchandise management consists of the buying, handling, and financial aspects of merchandising. Pricing decisions deal with the financial aspects of merchandise management and affect their interaction with other retailing elements.

Chapter 14 covers the development of merchandise plans. We begin by discussing the concept of a merchandising philosophy. We then look at buying organizations and their processes, as well as the major considerations in formulating merchandise plans. The chapter concludes by describing category management and merchandising software.

Chapter 15 focuses on implementing merchandise plans. We study each stage in the buying and handling process: gathering information, selecting and interacting with merchandise sources, evaluation, negotiation, concluding purchases, receiving and stocking merchandise, reordering, and re-evaluation. We also examine logistics and inventory management, as well as their effects on merchandising.

Chapter 16 concentrates on financial merchandise management. We introduce the cost and retail methods of accounting. The merchandise forecasting and budgeting process is presented. Unit control systems are discussed. Dollar and unit financial inventory controls are integrated.

Chapter 17 deals with pricing. We review the outside factors affecting price decisions: consumers, government, suppliers, and competitors. A framework for developing a price strategy is then shown: objectives, broad policy, basic strategy, implementation, and adjustments.

14 Developing Merchandise Plans

Chapter Objectives

1. To demonstrate the importance of a sound merchandising philosophy

2. To study various buying organization formats and the processes they use

3. To outline the considerations in devising merchandise plans: forecasts, innovativeness, assortment, brands, timing, and allocation

4. To discuss category management and merchandising software

In 1993, the chief executive of The Gap, Inc. (**www.gap.com**) realized that his Gap and Banana Republic stores were ineffective in reaching consumers who did not want to spend much money on clothes. So, he converted 48 underperforming Gap stores into Gap Warehouse stores. Soon thereafter, these stores were renamed Old Navy (**www.oldnavy. com**). Old Navy now generates about $7 billion in annual sales.

Today, Old Navy is the most often purchased brand by two of the three generations that together account for about 80 percent of apparel spending by women and girls: the Millennials (aged 10 to 27) and Generation Xers (aged 28 to 38), according to research studies on the chain.

A recent report by Scarborough Research found that 26 percent of female respondents indicated that they shopped at Old Navy in the prior three months. That's a higher percentage than Victoria's Secret (16 percent), Macy's (14 percent), and Gap (13 percent).

Old Navy has achieved its success through a strategy that combines value pricing, timely styling, an updated image, and sizing to fit American's growing waistlines. Old Navy is able to hold prices at discount levels by using lower-cost materials. For example, although a Gap sweater is typically made from merino wool, an Old Navy sweater is more likely to be made with lower-cost acrylic fabric. Since fall 2007, Old Navy's design team has been headed by successful designer Todd Oldham, who created home accessories for Target and furniture for La-Z-Boy. Despite its low prices, Old Navy apparel is stylish and well displayed, and the sales staff is well trained.[1]

Source: Reprinted by permission of Susan Berry, Retail Image Consulting, Inc.

OVERVIEW

Retail Detail Merchandising (**www. rdmerchandising.com**) is a third-party vendor of several merchandising services.

Retailers must have the proper product assortments and sell them in a manner consistent with their overall strategy. **Merchandising** consists of the activities involved in acquiring particular goods and/or services and making them available at the places, times, and prices and in the quantity that enable a retailer to reach its goals. Merchandising decisions can dramatically affect performance. Consider these observations of the late Stanley Marcus, former chief executive of Neiman Marcus:

> I believe that retail merchandising is actually very simple: it consists of two factors, customers and products. If you take good care in the buying of the product, it doesn't come back. If you take good care of your customers, they do come back. It's just that simple and just that difficult. This is obviously an oversimplification of the problems of retailing. It's not quite that easy—but almost.
>
> Yet, no wonder customer loyalty has dropped. There is little reason for a shopper to go across town to a store when it's a forgone conclusion that she'll find the same merchandise in store C that she has already seen in stores A and B. I fully expect to come upon a newspaper headline that proclaims, "Customers Found Bored to Death in the Sportswear Department of the XYZ Department Store."
>
> Merchandise sameness emanates from the training of buyers who have been taught to play it safe by avoiding risky fashions, to play it cautiously by buying from a limited number of standard vendors who sell the same "packages" to all major accounts, to play it for profit by advertising only the goods supported by manufacturers' advertising allowances. Many retailers erroneously believe the goal is to make a profit and fail to realize that a profit is due to having goods or services that are so satisfactory that the customer is willing to pay a bonus, or a profit, over and above the distributor's cost.[2]

In this chapter, the *planning* aspects of merchandising are discussed. The *implementation* aspects of merchandising are examined in Chapter 15. The *financial* aspects of merchandising are described in Chapter 16. Retail *pricing* is covered in Chapter 17.

Visit our Web site (**www.pearsonhighered.com/berman**) for a broad selection of links related to merchandising strategies and tactics.

Merchandising Philosophy

At Cost Plus World Market, you never know what you'll find (**www. worldmarket.com**).

A **merchandising philosophy** sets the guiding principles for all the merchandise decisions that a retailer makes. It must reflect target market desires, the retailer's institutional type, the marketplace positioning, the defined value chain, supplier capabilities, costs, competitors, product trends, and other factors. The retail merchandising philosophy drives every product decision, from what product lines to carry to the shelf space allotted to different products to inventory turnover to pricing—and more: "Retailers have to decide on the breadth of assortment across the store (narrow or wide) and the depth of the assortment within each category (deep or shallow). In addition, they must select the quality of the items within the assortment—high or low, national brands or store brands. They need to decide on their pricing policies, across categories and within. Finally, retailers must decide if assortments should generally be stable over time or whether there should be surprise, specials, or customization in assortments."[3] See Figure 14-1.

FIGURE 14-1

Dick's Merchandising Philosophy

As Dick's Sporting Goods notes at its Web site (**www.dickssportinggoods.com**): "Our mission is to be the number one sporting and fitness specialty retailer for all athletes and outdoor enthusiasts through the relentless improvement of everything we do. With over 300 stores, Dick's offers the finest quality products at competitive prices, backed by the best service anywhere. From fairway woods to the backwoods, there's plenty here to be excited about. Our Sportsman's Lodge offers everything for hunting, fishing, hiking, water sports, and camping, while golfers enjoy a Pro Shop that boasts a premium selection. Sportswear lovers will find a separate department designed specifically for them, offering a huge selection of both footwear and apparel. We've even got an indoor track where runners can test gear before purchase."

Source: Reprinted by permission of Dick's Sporting Goods.

Costco, the membership club giant, flourishes with its individualistic merchandising philosophy:

> We provide our members with a broad range of high-quality merchandise at prices consistently lower than they can obtain elsewhere. It is important to carry only products on which we can provide our members significant savings. We limit specific items in each product line to fast-selling models, sizes, and colors. Therefore, we carry about 4,000 active stock-keeping units (sku's) per store in our core business, as opposed to 40,000 to 140,000 sku's or more at discount retailers, supermarkets, and supercenters. Many consumable products are offered for sale in case, carton, or multiple-pack quantities only. We have direct buying relationships with many producers of nationally branded merchandise. No significant portion of merchandise is from any one of these or any other single supplier. We also purchase selected private-label merchandise, as long as quality and customer demand are comparable and the value to our members is greater as compared to name brand items.[4]

In forming a merchandising philosophy, the scope of responsibility for merchandise personnel must be stated. Are these personnel to be involved with the full array of *merchandising functions,* both buying and selling goods and services (including selection, pricing, display, and customer transactions)? Or are they to focus on the *buying function,* with others responsible for displays, personal selling, and so on? Many firms consider merchandising to be the foundation for their success, and buyers (or merchandise managers) engage in both buying and selling tasks. Other retailers consider their buyers to be skilled specialists who should not be active in the selling function, which is done by other skilled specialists. For example, store managers at full-line discount stores often have great influence on product displays but have little impact on whether to stock or promote particular brands.

With a merchandising-oriented philosophy, the buyer's expertise is used in selling, responsibility and authority are clear, the buyer ensures that items are properly displayed, costs are reduced (fewer specialists), and the buyer is close to consumers due to selling involvement. When buying and selling are separate, specialized skills are applied to each task, the morale of store personnel goes up as they get more authority, selling is not viewed as a secondary task, salesperson–customer interaction is better, and buying and selling personnel are distinctly supervised. Each firm must see which format is best for it.

To capitalize on opportunities, more retailers now use micromerchandising and cross-merchandising. With **micromerchandising,** a retailer adjusts shelf-space allocations to respond to customer and other differences among local markets. Dominick's supermarkets assign shelf space to children's and adult's cereals to reflect demand patterns at different stores. Wal-Mart allots the space to product lines at various stores to reflect differences in demographics, weather, and shopping. Micromerchandising is easier today due to the date generated. Consider this observation: Micromerchandisers "plan differently. They respond differently. Their approach to localization is no exception. Retail winners combine science and process improvements to achieve better performance, use customer segmentation and market basket data to drive merchandising and other decisions, localize assortments armed with customer insights and advanced tools, and collaborate with vendors to make better localized assortment decisions."[5]

 **CAREERS IN RETAILING**

 Is Retail for Me? Merchandise Buying and Planning—Part 1

Merchandise buying and planning involve the intersection of retail art and statistics. These retail professionals select the merchandise to be sold. They facilitate order follow-up, inventory flow, and the allocation of merchandise to stores. Statistical development and analysis are woven into this retail career area, where team members also coordinate gross margin planning/analysis responsibilities, develop distribution plans for merchandise categories and subclasses, and balance stock unit ratios by store:

▶ *Head of Merchandise Buying/General Merchandise Manager (GMM).* Top executive in charge of all merchandise buying for a chain. This position will typically be a GMM position or, in very large volume chains, may be executive vice-president level with multiple GMMs reporting to him or her.

▶ *Divisional Merchandise Manager (DMM).* This position is one level above and directly supervises a group of buyers, typically in related merchandise categories.

▶ *Senior Merchandise Buyer.* These buyers are senior to merchandise buyers due to unusually high dollar volume or product complexity of the goods being

bought. Senior buyers may train other buyers and may supervise a small staff but are ranked between buyer and DMM.

▶ *Merchandise Buyer.* This position selects the merchandise to be sold by sourcing vendors in the United States or overseas markets and/or by working with vendors to produce private labels.

▶ *Associate Merchandise Buyer.* This position assists the buyer but typically has an open-to-buy authority over a portion of the buyer's category or for reorders and test quantities. The buyer typically retains responsibility over the merchandise category.

▶ *Assistant Merchandise Buyer.* Supports the buyer in merchandise selection, order follow-up, and inventory flow-through. May not have an open-to-buy, although some may have authority to make replenishment orders. This is a buyer trainee professional position, not clerical support.

Source: Reprinted by permission of the National Retail Federation.

In **cross-merchandising,** a retailer carries complementary goods and services to encourage shoppers to buy more. That is why apparel stores stock accessories and auto dealers offer extended warranties. Cross-merchandising, like scrambled merchandising, can be ineffective if taken too far. Yet, it has tremendous potential. Consider this creative approach:

> Specialty food retailers constantly search for the next method to expand their business. For many, opening a café or restaurant seems like the perfect extension, adding sales while increasing interest in the foods within their retail mix. A successful restaurant allows retailers to take advantage of myriad cross-merchandising opportunities. A restaurant is, in effect, a built-in tasting station where merchants have a captive audience. Making the foray into the café business was a no-brainer for West Point Market, a specialty food store in Akron, Ohio. From croutons made in the bakery to a sauce on a sandwich that can be bought off the shelf, West Point Market is diligent about promoting ingredients used in the café that are also sold in the store, highlighting its private-label products.[6]

Buying Organization Formats and Processes

A merchandising plan cannot be properly devised unless the buying organization and its processes are well defined: Who is responsible for decisions? What are their tasks? Do they have sufficient authority? How does merchandising fit with overall operations? Figure 14-2 highlights the range of organizational attributes from which to choose.

Level of Formality

With a *formal buying organization,* merchandising (buying) is a distinct retail task and a separate department is set up. The functions involved in acquiring merchandise and making it available for sale are under the control of this department. A formal organization is most often used by larger firms and involves distinct personnel. In an *informal buying organization,* merchandising (buying) is not a distinct task. The same personnel handle both merchandising (buying) and other retail tasks; responsibility and authority are not always clear-cut. Informal organizations generally occur in smaller retailers.

FIGURE 14-2

The Attributes and Functions of Buying Organizations

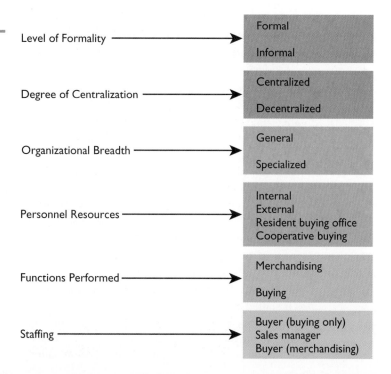

Level of Formality → Formal / Informal

Degree of Centralization → Centralized / Decentralized

Organizational Breadth → General / Specialized

Personnel Resources → Internal / External / Resident buying office / Cooperative buying

Functions Performed → Merchandising / Buying

Staffing → Buyer (buying only) / Sales manager / Buyer (merchandising)

The advantages of a formal organization are the clarity of responsibilities and the use of full-time, specialized merchandisers. The disadvantage is the cost of a separate department. The advantages of an informal format are the low costs and flexibility. The disadvantages are less-defined responsibilities and the lesser emphasis on merchandise planning. Both structures exist in great numbers. It is not critical for a firm to use a formal department. It is crucial that the firm recognizes the role of merchandising (buying) and ensures that responsibility, activities, and operational relationships are aptly defined and enacted.

Degree of Centralization

Multi-unit retailers must choose whether to have a centralized buying organization or a decentralized one. In a *centralized buying organization,* all purchase decisions emanate from one office. A chain may have eight stores, with all merchandise decisions made at the headquarters store. In a *decentralized buying organization,* purchase decisions are made locally or regionally. A 40-store chain may allow each outlet to select its own merchandise or divide the branches into geographic territories (such as four branches per region) with regional decisions made by the headquarters store in each territory.

The advantages of centralized buying are the integration of effort, strict controls, consistent image, proximity to top management, staff support, and volume discounts. Possible disadvantages are the inflexibility, time delays, poor morale at local stores, and excessive uniformity. Decentralized buying has these advantages: adaptability to local conditions, quick order processing, and improved morale because of branch autonomy. Potential disadvantages are disjointed planning, an inconsistent image, limited controls, little staff support, and a loss of volume discounts.

See what Zara's merchandisers think is "hot" (**www.zara.com**).

Many chains combine the formats by deploying a centralized buying organization while also giving store managers some input. This is how Zara, the Madrid-based global apparel chain, operates:

> Zara is present in 72 countries, with a network of 1,530 stores in prime locations of major cities. Its international presence is a testament to the idea that national borders are no impediment to sharing a single fashion culture. Design is conceived as a process closely linked to the public. Information from our stores is constantly transmitted to a design team of over 200 professionals, informing them of customer needs and concerns. Zara has stores specialized in junior fashion called Kiddy's Class. The stores are in Spain, Portugal, France, Italy, and Greece. Zara is in step with society, dressing the ideas, trends, and tastes that society itself has developed. That is the key to its success among people, cultures, and generations that, despite their differences, all share a special feeling for fashion.[7]

Organizational Breadth

In a general buying organization, one or several people buy all of a firm's merchandise. The owner of a small hardware store may buy the merchandise for his or her store. With a specialized organization, each buyer is responsible for a product category. A department store usually has separate buyers for girls', juniors', and women's clothes.

A general approach is better if the retailer is small or there are few products involved. A specialized approach is better if the retailer is large or many products are carried. By specializing, there is greater expertise and responsibility is well defined; however, costs are higher and extra personnel are required.

Personnel Resources

A retailer can choose an inside or outside buying organization. An *inside buying organization* is staffed by a retailer's personnel, and merchandise decisions are made by permanent employees. See Figure 14-3. With an *outside buying organization,* a company or personnel external to the retailer are hired, usually on a fee basis. Most retailers use either an inside or an outside organization; some employ a combination.

Melissa Davies

WAL★MART

TYPE OF STORE:
Mass Market

HEADQUARTERS:
Bentonville, Ark.

Networking helped Melissa Davies score a job as a buyer for the nation's largest retailer, Wal-Mart.

While a student and basketball player at Eastern Washington University in Cheney, Wash., Davies was part of a group called Students in Free Enterprise. "The program allows you to network with businesses locally," explains Davies, a business administration marketing and management major. While giving a presentation, a Wal-Mart executive heard her speak and invited her to pursue a career with the chain's training program.

After starting as a buyer trainee, Davies rose through the ranks with four promotions. Now she is a buyer of outdoor decorative merchandise in the lawn and garden department.

"I love the challenge. I find it amazing that I'm 24 years old and have the responsibility for a category that is somewhere in the $300 million range," says Davies. What she finds refreshing at Wal-Mart is that the company is willing to let even young associates follow their gut instincts. "At Wal-Mart, it isn't about experience or tenure, it is about performance," adds Davies, who once vowed she'd never work in retail and wanted to pursue a career in sports marketing because of her college basketball experience. She is now a great supporter of a retail career path. "I've entrusted my career to Wal-Mart," she adds.

During a typical day, Davies finds herself meeting with suppliers, talking to store associates and answering at least 170 e-mails. "It is fast paced, and I find it exciting to work with suppliers on long-term ideas and strategies." Although she's young, she says she's earned the respect of top-level executives from major manufacturers who supply Wal-Mart.

What's her gameplan? "I'd like to stay in merchandising and ultimately have a leadership role in the company." She's still involved in Students in Free Enterprise, and she helps show others the opportunity presented by not only retailing, but Wal-Mart in particular. ■

FIGURE 14-3

At Wal-Mart: Developing an Inside Buying Organization

Source: Reprinted by permission of *DSN Retailing Today.*

An inside buying organization is most often used by large retailers and very small retailers. Large retailers do this to have greater control over merchandising decisions and to be more distinctive. They have the financial clout to employ their own specialists. At very small retailers, the owner or manager does all merchandising functions to save money and keep close to the market.

Ross Stores has merchandising career opportunities in New York and Los Angeles. Scroll down to "corporate/ buying office/distribution opportunities" (**www. rossstores.com/job_search. aspx**).

Ross Stores (**www.rossstores.com**), the off-price apparel chain with stores in 27 states, is an example of a retailer with an inside buying organization. Ross operates buying offices in New York City and Los Angeles, the two largest U.S. apparel markets: "We have about 250 merchants—including merchandise managers, buyers, and assistant buyers." Ross relies on "a network of 6,400 merchandise vendors and manufacturers and has adequate sources of first-quality merchandise to meet our requirements. We purchase the vast majority of our merchandise directly from manufacturers, and we have not experienced any difficulty in obtaining sufficient merchandise inventory."[8]

An outside organization is most frequently used by small or medium-sized retailers or those far from supply sources. It is more efficient for them to hire outside buyers than to use company personnel. An outside organization has purchase volume clout in dealing with suppliers, usually services noncompeting retailers, offers research, and may sponsor private brands. Outside buying organizations may be paid by retailers that subscribe to their services or by vendors that give commissions. An individual retailer may set up its own internal organization if it feels its outside group is dealing with direct competitors or the firm finds it can buy items more efficiently on its own.

The Doneger Group (**www.doneger.com**) is the leading independent resident buying office, with hundreds of retailer clients. As its Web site notes, the firm "was founded in 1946 by Henry Doneger and originally served as a resident buying office for women's specialty retailers throughout the United States. Having experienced significant growth through the years, our clients, both U.S.-based and international, now also include department stores, family apparel stores, mass merchandisers, and discount stores. Today, we are proud to be the largest, most dynamic independent resident buying office and fashion merchandising consulting firm in the world."

Learn more about AMC (www.theamc.com), Target's buying organization.

The Federation of Pharmacy Networks (www.fpn.org) provides many services for its members.

Macy's, Inc. (www. macyscollege.com/college) has exciting career paths in both merchandising and operations.

Associated Merchandising Corporation (AMC) is a hybrid buying organization. For decades, it was a nonprofit organization co-owned by numerous retailers. Target acquired AMC in 1998, mostly to serve its own stores. Currently, AMC still provides merchandising functions for several other retailers as well. It is involved with global trend identification; product design and development; global product sourcing; quality assurance; and production, delivery, and order tracking for apparel, accessories, and home goods.

A **resident buying office,** which can be an inside or outside organization, is used when a retailer wants to keep in close touch with key market trends and cannot do so through just headquarters buying staff. Such offices are situated in important merchandise centers and provide valuable data and contacts. A few large specialized U.S. firms operate resident buying offices that serve several thousand retailers. Each organization just cited (Ross, Doneger, and AMC) has multiple resident buying offices to get a better sense of local markets and merchandise sources. Besides the major players, there are many smaller outside resident buying offices that assist retailers.

Today, independent retailers and small chains are involved with cooperative buying to a greater degree than before to compete with large chains. In **cooperative buying,** a group of retailers gets together to make quantity purchases from suppliers and obtain volume discounts. It is most popular among food, hardware, and drugstore retailers. As an illustration, the Federation of Pharmacy Networks (FPN) comprises 22 buying groups across the United States. It represents 13,000 independent drugstore owners: "FPN negotiates with selected vendors to establish favorable contracts based on the volume purchasing power achieved through our pharmacies. Many of our programs provide the independent pharmacist with significant net savings. Additionally, each member group office benefits from FPN's programs."[9]

Functions Performed

At this juncture, the responsibilities and functions of merchandise and in-store personnel are assigned. With a "merchandising" view, merchandise personnel oversee all buying and selling functions, including assortments, advertising, pricing, point-of-sale displays, employee utilization, and personal selling approaches. With a "buying" view, merchandise personnel oversee the buying of products, advertising, and pricing, while in-store personnel oversee assortments, displays, employee utilization, and sales presentations. The functions undertaken must reflect the retailer's level of formality, the degree of centralization, and personnel resources.

Staffing

The last organizational decision involves staffing. What positions must be filled and with what qualifications? Firms with a merchandising viewpoint are most concerned with hiring good buyers. Firms with a buying perspective are concerned about hiring sales managers, as well. Many large firms hire college graduates, train them, and promote them to buyers and sales managers.

A **buyer** is responsible for selecting the merchandise to be carried by a retailer and setting a strategy to market that merchandise. He or she devises and controls sales and profit projections for a product category (generally for all stores in a chain); plans proper merchandise assortments, styling, sizes, and quantities; negotiates with and evaluates vendors; and often oversees in-store displays. He or she must be attuned to the marketplace, be able to bargain with suppliers, and be capable of preparing detailed plans; and he or she may travel to the marketplace. A **sales manager** typically supervises the on-floor selling and operational activities for a specific retail department. He or she must be a good organizer, administrator, and motivator. A *merchandising buyer* must possess the attributes of each. Most retailers feel the critical qualification for good merchandisers is their ability to relate to customers and methodically anticipate future needs. In addition, to some extent, buyers are involved with many of the remaining tasks described in this and the next chapter.

Macy's, Inc., which operates the Macy's and Bloomingdale's department store chains, has career tracks that recognize the value of both merchandising and in-store personnel. Figure 14-4 shows two distinct career tracks.

FIGURE 14-4

Merchandising Versus Store Management Career Tracks at Macy's, Inc.

Source: Figure developed by the authors based on information at "Career Paths," **www.macysjobs. com/college/careers/careerpaths** (March 11, 2009).

Merchandising Track	*Store Management Track*
Divisional Merchandise Manager — Oversees merchandise selection and procurement for a particular business segment. Sets the merchandise direction to ensure continuity on the selling floor. Develops strategy to ensure customer satisfaction and maximize performance and profits.	**Store Manager** — Responsible for all aspects of running a profitable store. Sets the tone to ensure success in customer service, profits, operations, people development, merchandise presentation, and merchandise assortment.
Buyer — Expected to maximize sales and profitability of a given business area by developing and implementing a strategy, analyzing it, and reacting to trends. Overall support of company sales, gross margin, and turnover objectives.	**Assistant Store Manager** — Directs merchandise flow, store maintenance, expense management, shortage prevention, and store sales support activities for a large portion of store volume. Acts as Store Manager in his or her absence.
Associate Buyer — Responsible for merchandise development, marketing, and financial management of a particular business area. This is a developmental step to buyer.	**Sales Manager** — In charge of store activities in a specific merchandise area. Includes merchandise presentation, employee development, customer service, operations, and inventory control.
Assistant Buyer — Aids buyer in selecting and procuring merchandise, which supports overall sales, gross margin, and turnover goals. Provides operational support to buyers. Assumes some buying responsibility, once buyer determines proficiency.	**Assistant Sales Manager** — Responsible for supervising daily store activities in a specific merchandise area. Includes selling and service management, selecting and developing associates, merchandising, and business management.

Here's what it's like at the top of the merchandising world:

> Lynne Ronon joined HSN (Home Shopping Network) as Executive Vice-President of Merchandising in October 2007. In this role, she is responsible for planning and directing all merchandising strategies, programs, and policies in the key categories of apparel and accessories, beauty, jewelry, health/personal care, home lifestyle, and electronics and housewares. Among her responsibilities is the continued evolution of HSN's merchandising strategy, including the cultivation of brand name partners and the development of exclusive HSN brands, the expansion of product assortments, and product development. Prior to HSN, Ronon was with Burberry as Senior Vice-President, North Asia. In that capacity, Ronon's responsibilities included merchandise buying and product development, uniting franchises and core operations, and implementing a cohesive global strategy.[10]

Devising Merchandise Plans

There are several factors to consider in devising merchandise plans, as discussed next. See Figure 14-5.

Forecasts

Forecasts are projections of expected retail sales for given periods. They are the foundation of merchandise plans and include these components: overall company projections, product category projections, item-by-item projections, and store-by-store projections (if a chain). Consider the process used by Ikea, the global furniture chain:

Ikea (**www.ikea.com/ms/ en_US/about_ikea_new/ about**) scours the globe for interesting new items that will be popular in its stores.

> Ikea manages production from raw materials to finished product. To do so, Ikea must coordinate with more than 2,000 suppliers in 55 nations. At any time, Ikea

FIGURE 14-5

Considerations in Devising
Merchandise Plans

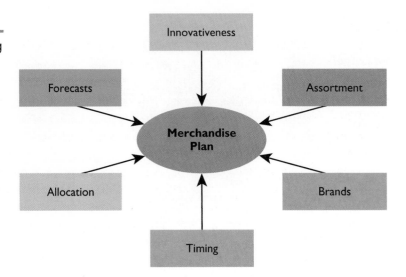

has about 11,000 items to manage, 30 percent of which are less than 12 months old. Thus, forecasting is quite important: "We decided we needed a unified planning solution with a top-down approach. The idea was to have a system that would first forecast demand at the highest level, across continents. Then, to drill down to forecasts for individual countries, and then automatically break down those forecasts to the store level."[11]

In this section, forecasting is examined from a general planning perspective. In Chapter 16, the financial dimensions of forecasting are reviewed.

When preparing forecasts, it is essential to distinguish among different types of merchandise. **Staple merchandise** consists of the regular products carried by a retailer. For a supermarket, staples include milk, bread, canned soup, and facial tissues. For a department store, staples include everyday watches, jeans, glassware, and housewares. Because these items have relatively stable sales (sometimes seasonal) and their nature may not change much over time, a retailer can clearly outline the quantities for these items. A **basic stock list** specifies the inventory level, color, brand, style category, size, package, and so on for every staple item carried by the retailer.

Assortment merchandise consists of apparel, furniture, autos, and other products for which the retailer must carry a variety of products in order to give customers a proper selection. This merchandise is harder to forecast than staples due to demand variations, style changes, and the number of sizes and colors to be carried. Decisions are two-pronged: (1) Product lines, styles, designs, and colors are projected. (2) A **model stock plan** is used to project specific items, such as the number of green, red, and blue pullover sweaters of a certain design by size. With a model stock plan, many items are ordered for popular sizes and colors, and small amounts of less popular sizes and colors fill out the assortment.

Fashion merchandise consists of products that may have cyclical sales due to changing tastes and lifestyles. For these items, forecasting can be hard because styles may change from year to year. "Hot" colors often change back and forth. **Seasonal merchandise** consists of products that sell well over nonconsecutive time periods. Items such as ski equipment and air conditioner servicing have excellent sales during one season per year. Because the strongest sales of seasonal items usually occur at the same time each year, forecasting is straightforward.

With **fad merchandise,** high sales are generated for a short time. Often, toys and games are fads, such as Harry Potter toys that flew off store shelves each time a related movie was released. It is hard to forecast whether such products will reach specific sales targets and how long they will be popular. Sometimes, fads turn into extended fads—and sales continue for a long period at a fraction of earlier sales. Trivial Pursuit board games are in the extended fad category.

ETHICS IN RETAILING

Tom's of Maine: Bringing All-Natural Idealism to Retailers

Tom's of Maine (**www.tomsofmaine.com**) makes and markets more than 90 all-natural products that are sold at 40,000 locations throughout North America (including small health-food stores, mass merchants, and drugstores). Tom's positions itself as a company with a conscience. Examples of its social responsibility include sponsorships of important environmental, human need, and educational activities; giving 10 percent of pre-tax profits to charities; and encouraging volunteer work among its employees. Colgate-Palmolive, the world's largest marketer of toothpaste, purchased an 84 percent interest in Tom's in 2006.

Tom's of Maine has a Common Good Partnerships program (**www.tomsofmaine.com/cgp**) that encourages retailers to work on community projects. One of its major activities involves the National Rivers Awareness program, which stimulates people to volunteer to clean up local rivers. Through this program, participating retailers receive in-store displays, posters, and brochures describing the program.

Tom's has also developed a special toothpaste that highlights the National Rivers Awareness program. Consumers who purchase any two Tom's of Maine products are eligible to receive a free Rivers Awareness Kit. The kit includes a video, a book produced by the River Network, postcards, and information about joining the River Network. These programs help retailers to project a socially conscious image while increasing sales of Tom's high-profit margin items.

Sources: "Community Involvement," **www.tomsofmaine.com/toms/community** (December 19, 2008); and "Tom's of Maine National Rivers Awareness Program," **http://www2.rivernetwork.org/hottopics/index.cfm?doc_id=76** (December 19, 2008).

In forecasting for best-sellers, many retailers use a **never-out list** to determine the amount of merchandise to purchase for resale. The goal is to purchase enough of these products so they are always in stock. Products are added to and deleted from the list as their popularity changes. Before a new James Patterson novel is released, stores order large quantities to be sure they meet anticipated demand. After it disappears from best-seller lists, smaller quantities are kept. It is a good strategy to use a combination of a basic stock list, a model stock plan, and a never-out list. These lists may overlap.

Innovativeness

The innovativeness of a merchandise plan depends on a number of factors. See Table 14-1.

An innovative retailer has a great opportunity—distinctiveness (by being first in the market)—and a great risk—possibly misreading customers and being stuck with large inventories. By assessing each factor in Table 14-1 and preparing a detailed plan for merchandising new goods and services, a firm can better capitalize on opportunities and reduce risks. As shown in Figure 14-6, Saks Fifth Avenue takes innovativeness quite seriously. So do companies such as Hammacher Schlemmer and 7-Eleven:

Check out Hammacher Schlemmer's (www. hammacher.com) unique product offerings.

▶ Hammacher Schlemmer offers an eclectic mix of housewares, personal care products, home and office products, apparel, sports and leisure goods, gift items, and more. It has stores in major cities, catalogs, and a Web site. Its slogan is "Offering the Best, the Only, and the Unexpected." The firm carries such items as a $7,000 acoustic resonance massage chair, a $499.95 ultrasonic vegetable cleaner, and $29.95 support walking socks.

▶ The convenience store format is quite innovative, as exemplified by 7-Eleven, which "introduces 25 new products to stores weekly. Some new items are introduced nationwide, some regionally. For instance, you'll find new sushi-type products in California, new Cuban sandwiches in Florida, new cheesecake doughnuts in the Northeast, and new carnitas pitas in Colorado." As a 7-Eleven executive says: "Our goal is to have first-mover advantage in our channel or exclusivity for a period of time. Customers want something new, fresh, and fun to satisfy their daily needs, and we try to meet this."[12]

Retailers should assess the growth potential for each new good or service they carry: How fast will a new good or service generate sales? What are the most sales (dollars and units) to be reached in a season or year? Over what period will a good or service continue

TABLE 14-1 **Factors to Bear in Mind When Planning Merchandise Innovativeness**

Factor	Relevance for Planning
Target market(s)	Evaluate whether the target market is conservative or innovative.
Goods/service growth potential	Consider each new offering on the basis of rapidity of initial sales, maximum sales potential per time period, and length of sales life.
Fashion trends	Understand vertical and horizontal fashion trends, if appropriate.
Retailer image	Carry goods/services that reinforce the firm's image. The level of innovativeness should be consistent with this image.
Competition	Lead or follow competition in the selection of new goods/services.
Customer segments	Segment customers by dividing merchandise into established-product displays and new-product displays.
Responsiveness to consumers	Carry new offerings when requested by the target market.
Amount of investment	Consider all of the possible investment for each new good/service: product costs, new fixtures, and additional personnel (or further training for existing personnel).
Profitability	Assess each new offering for potential profits.
Risk	Be aware of the possible tarnishing of the retailer's image, investment costs, and opportunity costs.
Constrained decision making	Restrict franchisees and chain branches from buying certain items.
Declining goods/services	Delete older goods/services if sales and/or profits are too low.

selling? One tool to assess potential is the **product life cycle,** which shows the expected behavior of a good or service over its life. The basic cycle comprises introduction, growth, maturity, and decline stages—shown in Figure 14-7 and described next.

During introduction, the retailer should anticipate a limited target market. The good or service will probably be supplied in one basic version. The manufacturer (supplier) may

FIGURE 14-7

The Traditional Product
Life Cycle

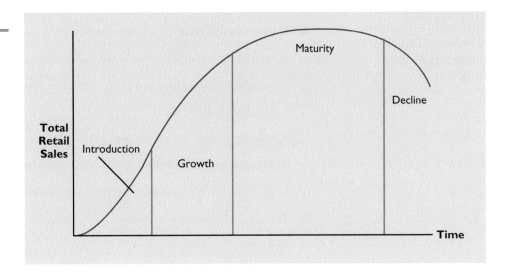

limit distribution to "finer" stores. Yet, new convenience items such as food and house-wares products are normally mass distributed. Items initially distributed selectively tend to have high prices. Mass distributed products typically involve low prices to foster faster consumer acceptance. Early promotion must be explanatory, geared to informing shoppers. At this stage, there are very few possible suppliers.

As innovators buy a new product and recommend it to friends, sales increase rapidly and the growth stage is entered. The target market includes middle-income consumers who are more innovative than average. The assortment expands, as do the number of retailers carrying the product. Price discounting is not widely used, but competing retailers offer a range of prices and customer service. Promotion is more persuasive and aimed at acquainting shoppers with availability and services. There are more suppliers.

In maturity, sales reach their maximum, the largest portion of the target market is attracted, and shoppers select from very broad product offerings. All types of retailers (discount to upscale) carry the good or service in some form. Prestige retailers stress brand names and customer service, while others use active price competition. Price is more often cited in ads. Competition is intense.

The decline stage is brought on by a shrinking market (due to product obsolescence, newer substitutes, and boredom) and lower profit margins. The target market may become the lowest-income consumers and laggards. Some retailers cut back on the assortment; others drop the good or service. At retailers still carrying the items, promotion is reduced and geared to price. There are fewer suppliers.

Many retailers pay a lot of attention to new-product additions but not enough to deciding whether to drop existing items. Yet, because of limited resources and shelf space, some items have to be dropped when others are added. Instead of intuitively pruning products, a retailer should use structured guidelines:

▶ Select items for possible elimination on the basis of declining sales, prices, and profits, as well as the appearance of substitutes.
▶ Gather and analyze detailed financial and other data about these items.
▶ Consider nondeletion strategies such as cutting costs, revising promotion efforts, adjusting prices, and cooperating with other retailers.
▶ After making a deletion decision, do not overlook timing, parts and servicing, inventory, and holdover demand.

Sometimes, a seemingly obsolete good or service can be revived. An innovative retailer recognizes the potential in this area and merchandises accordingly. Direct marketers heavily promote "greatest hits" recordings featuring individual music artists and compilations of multiple artists.

FIGURE 14-8

A Selected Checklist for
Predicting Fashion
Adoption

√ Does the fashion satisfy a consumer need?

√ Is the fashion compatible with emerging consumer lifestyles?

√ Is the fashion oriented toward the mass market or a market segment?

√ Is the fashion radically new?

√ Are the reputations of the designer(s) and the retailers carrying the fashion good?

√ Are several designers marketing some version of the fashion?

√ Is the price range for the fashion appropriate for the target market?

√ Will appropriate advertising be used?

√ Will the fashion change over time?

√ Will consumers view the fashion as a long-term trend?

Apparel retailers must be familiar with fashion trends. A *vertical trend* occurs when a fashion is first accepted by upscale consumers and undergoes changes in its basic form before it is sold to the general public. A fashion goes through three stages: distinctive—original designs, designer stores, custom-made, worn by upscale shoppers; emulation—modification of original designs, finer stores, alterations, worn by middle class; and economic emulation—simple copies, discount stores, mass produced, mass marketed.

With a *horizontal trend,* a new fashion is accepted by a broad spectrum of people upon its introduction while retaining its basic form. Within any social class, there are innovative customers who act as opinion leaders. New fashions must be accepted by these leaders, who then convince other members of the same social class (who are more conservative) to buy the items. Fashion is sold across the class and not from one class to another. Figure 14-8 has a checklist for predicting fashion adoption.

Assortment

An **assortment** is the selection of merchandise a retailer carries. It includes both the breadth of product categories and the variety within each category.

A firm first chooses the quality of merchandise. Should it carry top-line, expensive items and sell to upper-income customers? Or should it carry middle-of-the-line, moderately priced items and cater to middle-income customers? Or should it carry lesser-quality, inexpensive items and attract lower-income customers? Or should it try to draw more than one market segment by offering a variety, such as middle- and top-line items for middle- and upper-income shoppers? The firm must also decide whether to carry promotional products (low-priced closeout items or special buys used to generate store traffic). Several factors must be reviewed in choosing merchandise quality. See Table 14-2.

Family Dollar has an overall strategy that is very consistent with its approach to merchandise quality:

Look at Family Dollar's
(**www.familydollar.com**)
targeted merchandising
approach. Click on
"About Us."

With more than 6,500 U.S. units, Family Dollar has carved a niche as the go-to store for shoppers in need of a few quick essentials that won't break the budget. "We are focused on delivering good-value, low-cost items in a convenient shopping environment to a growing value-conscious customer base. The single mom shopping at Family Dollar might not have as much cash in her wallet as someone else, but she's every bit as savvy. Our customers truly know the value of a dollar."[13]

After deciding on product quality, a retailer determines its width and depth of assortment. **Width of assortment** refers to the number of distinct goods/service categories (product lines) a retailer carries. **Depth of assortment** refers to the variety in any one goods/service category (product line) a retailer carries. As noted in Chapter 5, an

TABLE 14-2   Factors to Take into Account When Planning Merchandise Quality

Factor	Relevance for Planning
Target market(s)	Match merchandise quality to the wishes of the desired target market(s).
Competition	Sell similar quality (follow the competition) or different quality (to appeal to a different target market).
Retailer's image	Relate merchandise quality directly to the perception that customers have of retailer.
Store location	Consider the impact of location on the retailer's image and the number of competitors, which, in turn, relate to quality.
Stock turnover	Be aware that high quality and high prices usually yield a lower turnover than low quality and low prices.
Profitability	Recognize that high-quality goods generally bring greater profit per unit than lesser-quality goods; turnover may cause total profits to be greater for the latter.
Manufacturer versus private brands	Understand that, for many consumers, manufacturer brands connote higher quality than private brands.
Customer services offered	Know that high-quality goods require personal selling, alterations, delivery, and so on. Lesser-quality merchandise may not.
Personnel	Employ skilled, knowledgeable personnel for high-quality merchandise. Self-service may be used with lesser-quality merchandise.
Perceived goods/ service benefits	Analyze consumers. Lesser-quality goods attract customers who desire functional product benefits. High-quality goods attract customers who desire extended product benefits (e.g., status, services).
Constrained decision making	Face reality. a. Franchisees or chain store managers have limited or no control over products. b. Independent retailers that buy from a few large wholesalers are limited to the range of quality offered by those wholesalers.

assortment can range from wide and deep (department store) to narrow and shallow (box store). Figure 14-9 shows advantages and disadvantages for each basic strategy.

Assortment strategies vary widely. Web retailer Discount Art (**www.discountart.com**) says it is geared toward "the artist who demands good-quality art materials, but also appreciates good prices." KFC's thousands of worldwide outlets emphasize chicken and related quick-service products. They do not sell hamburgers, pizza, or many other popular fast-food items. Macy's department stores feature thousands of general merchandise items, and Amazon.com is a Web-based department store with millions of items for sale. Figure 14-10 features Ikea, the home furnishings giant. This is the dilemma that retailers may face in determining how big an assortment to carry:

> The importance of merchandising as a differentiator among retailers is increasing. More than 47 percent of consumers surveyed said that offering a "Wide Variety" or "Popular Styles and Brands" were the most important things retailers could do from a merchandising perspective. Yet, a wide variety of inventory left at the end of the season to mark down is not an attractive condition. So, although difficult to achieve, it is critical for retailers to have the right product assortment at the right time. Even advanced supply chains can suffer due to over-assorted conditions. Coordination with a variety of worldwide suppliers is essential to getting the product assortment desired in a timely manner. Customer choice also means product life-cycle management is an everyday consideration.[14]

Advantages	Disadvantages
Wide and Deep (many goods/service categories and a large assortment in each category)	
Broad market	High inventory investment
Full selection of items	General image
High level of customer traffic	Many items with low turnover
Customer loyalty	Some obsolete merchandise
One-stop shopping	
No disappointed customers	
Wide and Shallow (many goods/service categories and a limited assortment in each category)	
Broad market	Low variety within product lines
High level of customer traffic	Some disappointed customers
Emphasis on convenience customers	Weak image
Less costly than wide and deep	Many items with low turnover
One-stop shopping	Reduced customer loyalty
Narrow and Deep (few goods/service categories and a large assortment in each category)	
Specialist image	Too much emphasis on one category
Good customer choice in category(ies)	No one-stop shopping
Specialized personnel	More susceptible to trends/cycles
Customer loyalty	Greater effort needed to enlarge the size of the trading area
No disappointed customers	Little (no) scrambled merchandising
Less costly than wide and deep	
Narrow and Shallow (few goods/service categories and a limited assortment in each category)	
Aimed at convenience customers	Little width and depth
Least costly	No one-stop shopping
High turnover of items	Some disappointed customers
	Weak image
	Limited customer loyalty
	Small trading area
	Little (no) scrambled merchandising

FIGURE 14-9

Retail Assortment Strategies

Retailers should take several factors into account in planning their assortment: If variety is increased, will overall sales go up? Will overall profits? How much space is required for each product category? How much space is available? Carrying 10 varieties of cat food will not necessarily yield greater sales or profits than stocking 4 varieties. The retailer must look at the investment costs that occur with a large variety. Because selling space is limited, it should be allocated to those goods and services generating the most customer traffic and sales. The inventory turnover rate should also be studied.

A distinction should be made among scrambled merchandising, complementary goods and services, and substitute goods and services. With *scrambled merchandising,* a retailer adds unrelated items to generate more revenues and lift profit margins (such as a florist carrying umbrellas). Handling *complementary goods and services* lets the retailer sell both basic items and related offerings (such as stereos and CDs) via cross-merchandising. Although scrambled merchandising and cross-merchandising both increase overall sales, carrying too many *substitute goods and services* (such as competing brands of toothpaste) may shift sales from one brand to another and have little impact on overall retail sales.

FIGURE 14-10

Ikea's Wide and Deep Assortment

Not only does Ikea carry a wide range of product lines—from bedroom and living room furniture to kitchen gears and appliances to lighting and a whole lot more—it also stocks a large array of colors, designs, and styles within its product categories.

Source: Reprinted by permission of TNS Retail Forward.

These factors are also key as a retailer considers a wider, deeper assortment: (1) Risks, merchandise investments, damages, and obsolescence may rise dramatically. (2) Personnel may be spread too thinly over dissimilar products. (3) Both the positive and negative ramifications of scrambled merchandising may occur. (4) Inventory control may be difficult; overall turnover probably will slow down.

A retailer may not have a choice about stocking a full assortment within a product line if a powerful supplier insists that the retailer carry its entire line or it will not sell at all to that retailer. But large retailers—and smaller ones belonging to cooperative buying groups—are now standing up to suppliers, and many retailers stock their own brands next to manufacturers'.

OPEN RETAILING AROUND THE WORLD

At Left Foot, Mass Customization Comes to the Fore with a Global Supply Chain

Jarno Fonsen runs Pomarfin, a Finland-based firm that sells customized footwear via the Internet. Its retail name is Leftfoot Company. Through Pomarfin, shoe shops located around the world can purchase or rent scanners that measure customer's feet in their store. The specifications are then sent to Pomarfin's headquarters in Finland and then passed onto its factory in Estonia. Because Pomarfin keeps the customer's precise foot dimensions on file, reorders can be made without an additional measurement. Setting up the technology cost Pomarfin the equivalent of $13.1 million. Jarno Fonsen now plans to offer his shoe fittings services at between 20 to 30 of his own stores—mostly in Finland, Germany, Great Britain, and Sweden.

The shoes typically cost between $265 and $400 at retail. To save production costs, each shoe is put together

from a number of different building blocks as opposed to being made from individual custom components. This is a true example of mass customization. Costs are also reduced because labor costs in Estonia are about one-third those in Finland.

To encourage retailers to purchase or lease the foot-scanning equipment, retailers receive the same profit from continuing as initial orders, even though the consumer does not need to remeasure his or her feet.

Sources: Peter Marsh, "The Shoe That Is Sure to Fit," *Financial Times* (March 7, 2007), **www.ft.com/cms/s/1b78833c-cd1b-11db-a938-000b5df10621.html;** and "Left: The Right One," **https://shop.leftfootcompany.com** (February 25, 2009).

Brands

As part of its assortment planning, a retailer chooses the proper mix of manufacturer, private, and generic brands—a challenge made more complex with the proliferation of brands. **Manufacturer (national) brands** are produced and controlled by manufacturers. They are usually well known, supported by manufacturer ads, somewhat pre-sold to consumers, require limited retailer investment in marketing, and often represent maximum quality to consumers. Such brands dominate sales in many product categories. Popular manufacturer brands include Apple, Liz Claiborne, Coke, Gillette, Microsoft, Nike, Nintendo, Revlon, and Sony. The retailers likely to rely most heavily on manufacturer brands are small firms, Web firms, discounters, and others that want the credibility associated with well-known brands or that have low-price strategies (so consumers can compare the prices of different retailers on name-brand items).

Although they face extensive competition from private bands, manufacturer brands remain the dominant type of brand, accounting for more than 80 percent of all retail sales worldwide: "What would a supermarket without national brands look like? I can describe it in one lonely word—empty. It's hard to imagine a store with no Pepsi, Cheerios, Fritos, or Tide. No Colgate, Oreos, Tylenol, or Hellmann's. No Hershey bars, Campbell's soup, Heinz ketchup, Quaker oatmeal, or Tropicana orange juice. Where are this imaginary store's shoppers? At a supermarket where the aisles are lined with national brands."[15]

Private (dealer) brands, also known as **store brands,** contain names designated by wholesalers or retailers, are more profitable to retailers, are better controlled by retailers, are not sold by competing retailers, are less expensive for consumers, and lead to customer loyalty to retailers. With most private brands, retailers must line up suppliers, arrange for distribution and warehousing, sponsor ads, create displays, and absorb losses from unsold items. This is why retailer interest in private brands is growing:

▶ In *dollar sales,* private brands account for about 17 percent of U.S. retail revenues; they account for 22 percent of *unit sales.* Private brands represent 19 percent of dollar sales at food stores, 15 percent at drugstores (excluding prescription drugs), and 12 percent at mass merchandisers in the United States. In Northern Europe, the dollar sales figure for private brands ranges from 13 percent of retail store revenues in Italy to 32 percent in Spain.[16]

▶ Private brands are typically priced 20 to 30 percent below manufacturer brands. This benefits consumers, as well as retailers (costs are lower and revenues are shared by fewer parties). Retailer profits are higher from private brands, despite the lower prices.

▶ Most U.S. shoppers are aware of private brands—80 percent buy them regularly.

▶ At The Gap, Old Navy, The Limited, McDonald's, and many other retailers, private brands represent most or all of company revenues.

▶ At virtually all large retailers, both private brands and manufacturer brands are strong. Sears' Kenmore appliance line is the market-leading brand—ahead of GE, Maytag, and others. J.C. Penney private brands include American Living (created by Polo Ralph Lauren), St. John's Bay, and Worthington. Amazon.com sells private brands along with millions of manufacturer-branded items. Great Britain's Tesco supermarkets has four different private brands that encompass at least 500 product items *each.* Take our private brand challenge in Table 14-3.

The best-selling U.S. appliance brand (**www. kenmore.com**) is not GE or Whirlpool.

In the past, private brands were only discount versions of mid-tier products. They are now seen in a different light: "Retailers are helping to fuel private-label growth with new strategies including more distinctive labels, innovative packaging, in-store merchandising, and even feature ad support. Efforts such as these are successfully changing consumer perceptions of private label. No longer is private label seen as a low-cost alternative to brand-name products. Consumers increasingly believe that private label offerings are as good, sometimes even better, in quality as their brand name counterpart."[17] See Figure 14-11.

A new form of private branding has also emerged—the *premium private brand.* For example, H.T. Traders is a popular brand by Harris Teeter (the supermarket chain). The brand is exclusive to the chain: "Our H.T. Traders brand represents so many aspects of fine cooking and dining it's hard to put it into words. We studied classical Mediterranean cooking

TABLE 14-3   The Berman/Evans Private Brand Test

Think you know a lot about private brands? Then take our test. Match the retailers and the brand names. The answers are at the bottom of the table. No peeking. First, take the test.

Please note: Retailers may have more than one brand on the list.

Retailer	Brand
1. A&P	a. Alfani men's apparel
2. Bloomingdale's	b. America's Choice cookies
3. Costco	c. Craftsman tools
4. Kmart	d. Jaclyn Smith bed and bath accessories
5. Macy's	e. Joseph & Lyman men's apparel
6. Kohl's	f. Kirkland Signature coffee
7. J.C. Penney	g. Master Choice jams and preserves
8. Sears	h. Mossimo women's apparel
9. Target	i. Ol' Roy dog food
10. Wal-Mart	j. Roadhandler tires
	k. Simply Vera sleepwear
	l. Stafford men's apparel

Answers: 1—b, g; 2—e; 3—f; 4—d; 5—a; 6—k; 7—l; 8—i; 9—c, j; 10—i

and developed our own recipes based on time-honored traditional flavors and methods, but we made them simple for you to bring home and blend into your menu planning. Intensely flavored vinegars, excellent-quality extra virgin olive oils, bronze die-cut pastas, slow-cooked pasta sauces, classical bruschettas, and tapenades—we could go on and on. The best way to really appreciate these restaurant-quality favorites of ours is to experience them yourself, and your satisfaction is guaranteed!"[18]

FIGURE 14-11

Wal-Mart's New Approach to Private Brands
Wal-Mart is well known for its discount prices and value-oriented private brands. Through its George line, Wal-Mart is now aggressively trying to create more of a "designer" look for its apparel to better compete with Target's designer brands.

Source: Reprinted by permission of Susan Berry, Retail Image Consulting, Inc.

FIGURE 14-12

Sears' Distinctive Branding Strategy
Even though Sears is a powerhouse in private brands with Craftsman, Kenmore, and other brands of its own, the retailer realizes that many of its customers also like to be able to select from well-known manufacturer brands.

Source: Reprinted by permission of TNS Retail Forward.

Care must be taken in deciding how much to emphasize private brands. As previously noted, many consumers are loyal to manufacturer brands and would shop elsewhere if those brands are not stocked or their variety is pruned. See Figure 14-12.

Generic brands feature products' generic names as brands (such as canned peas); they are no-frills goods stocked by some retailers. They are a form of private brand. These items usually receive secondary shelf locations, have little or no promotion support, may be of lesser quality, are stocked in limited assortments, and have plain packages. Retailers control generics and price them well below other brands. In supermarkets, generics account for less than 1 percent of sales. In the prescription drug industry, where the quality of manufacturer brands and generics is similar, generics provide 60 percent of sales.

The competition between manufacturers and retailers for shelf space and profits has led to a **battle of the brands,** whereby manufacturer, private, and generic brands fight each other for more space and control. Nowhere is this battle clearer than at large retail chains: "Walk down the aisle of a Staples store, and you'll see a lot of big-name brands—Avery, Duracell, Hewlett-Packard, 3M, and more. But you'll also find more than a thousand products sold under the retailer's own brand: Staples' yellow self-stick notes, Staples' stainless-steel shears, even Staples' ink cartridges for laser printers."[19] In 2008, Staples' brand sales exceeded 22 percent of total sales.

Timing

For new products, the retailer must decide when they are first purchased, displayed, and sold. For established products, the firm must plan the merchandise flow during the year. The retailer should take into account its forecasts and other factors: peak seasons, order and delivery time, routine versus special orders, stock turnover, discounts, and the efficiency of inventory procedures.

Some goods and services have peak seasons. These items (such as winter coats) require large inventories in peak times and less stock during off seasons. Because some people like to shop during off seasons, the retailer should not eliminate the items.

With regard to order and delivery time, how long does it take the retailer to process an order request? After the order is sent to the supplier, how long does it take to receive merchandise? By adding these two periods together, the retailer can get a good idea of the lead time to restock shelves. If it takes a retailer 7 days to process an order and the supplier another 14 days to deliver goods, the retailer should begin a new order at least 21 days before the old inventory runs out.

Routine orders involve restocking staples and other regularly sold items. Deliveries are received weekly, monthly, and so on. Planning and problems are minimized. Special orders involve merchandise not sold regularly, such as custom furniture. They need more planning and cooperation between retailer and supplier. Specific delivery dates are usually arranged.

Stock turnover (how quickly merchandise sells) greatly influences how often items must be ordered. Convenience items such as milk and bread (which are also highly perishable) have a high turnover rate and are restocked quite often. Shopping items such as refrigerators and color TVs have a lower turnover rate and are restocked less often.

In deciding when and how often to buy merchandise, the availability of quantity discounts should be considered. Large purchases may result in lower per-unit costs. Efficient inventory procedures, such as electronic data interchange and quick response planning procedures, also decrease costs and order times while raising merchandise productivity.

Allocation

The last part of merchandise planning is the allocation of products. A single-unit retailer chooses how much merchandise to place on the sales floor, how much to place in a stockroom, and whether to use a warehouse. A chain also apportions products among stores. Allocation is covered further in Chapter 15.

Some retailers rely on warehouses as distribution centers. Products are shipped from suppliers to these warehouses, and then they are assigned and shipped to individual stores. Other retailers, including many supermarket chains, do not rely as much on warehouses. They have at least some goods shipped directly from suppliers to individual stores.

It is vital for chains, whether engaged in centralized or decentralized merchandising, to have a clear store-by-store allocation plan. Even if merchandise lines are standardized across the chain, store-by-store assortments must reflect the variations in the size and diversity of the customer base, in store size and location, in the climate, and in other factors.

Category Management

As noted in Chapter 2, **category management** is a merchandising technique that some firms—including several supermarkets, drugstores, hardware stores, and general merchandise retailers—use to improve productivity. It is a way to manage a retail business that focuses on the performance of product category results rather than individual brands. It arranges product groupings into strategic business units to better meet consumer needs and to achieve sales and profit goals. Retail managers make merchandising decisions that maximize the total return on the assets assigned to them.

This is how category management typically works:

> Category management is a retailing process in which first of all, all likeminded products in a retailer's total portfolio are lumped together into product groups called "categories." Some examples of categories would be toothpaste, washing-up liquids, baked beans, dog foods, cosmetics, and walking shoes. Each category is then run like a "mini-business" in its own right, managed by both the retailer and suppliers, with its own category turnover and/or profitability targets. The relationship between retailer and supplier moves to a more collaborative nature with more openness and sharing of information. Importantly, suppliers are expected to propose actions (such as new products or promotions) only if they add to the total category sales and the satisfaction of the shopper.[20]

According to the A.C. Nielsen research company, good category management involves these steps:

1. Define the category based on the needs of the target market.
2. Assign a role to the category based on several questions: How important is the category to the consumer? How important is the category to the retailer? How important is the category to the retailer's competitors? What is the category's outlook in the marketplace?

3. Assess the category to find opportunities for improvement.
4. Set performance targets and measure progress with a category scorecard.
5. Create a marketing strategy that draws the overarching picture of how to achieve the category role and scorecard targets.
6. Choose tactics for category assortment, pricing, promotion, merchandising, and supply chain strategies.
7. Roll out the plan.
8. Review performance regularly and adjust as needed.[21]

A fundamental premise is that a retailer must empower specific personnel to be responsible for the financial performance of each product category. As with micromerchandising, category management means adapting merchandise for each store or region to best satisfy customers. In deciding on the space per product category, there are several crucial measures of performance. Comparisons can be made by studying company data from period to period and by looking at categorical statistics in trade magazines:

▶ *Sales per linear foot of shelf space*—annual sales divided by the total linear footage devoted to the product category.
▶ *Gross profit per linear foot of shelf space*—annual gross profit divided by the total linear footage devoted to the product category.
▶ *Return on inventory investment*—annual gross profit divided by average inventory at cost.
▶ *Inventory turnover*—the number of times during a given period, usually one year, that the average inventory on hand is sold.
▶ *Days' supply*—the number of days of supply of an item on the shelf.
▶ *Direct product profitability (DPP)*—an item's gross profit less its direct retailing costs (warehouse and store support, occupancy, inventory, and direct labor costs, but not general overhead).

Some collaborative aspects of category management are working well, while other aspects are not—due to the differing roles of manufacturers and retailers in the channel of distribution:[22]

What Manufacturers Feel About Retailers
SUCCESSFUL APPLICATIONS OF CATEGORY MANAGEMENT

▶ Retailers act as equal partners.
▶ Retailers get input from manufacturers so they put the best possible plan together.
▶ Retailers are open minded and willing to change.
▶ Retailers that give manufacturers proper lead time—and timely goals and suggestions—receive the highest-quality work.

UNSUCCESSFUL APPLICATIONS OF CATEGORY MANAGEMENT

▶ Different goals among the retailers' senior managers, category managers, and operations managers impede the process.
▶ Retailers have a "template fixation." Yet, a template alone cannot explain why shoppers choose a given product or category.
▶ Retailers expect manufacturers to do more than their share or to pay more than their share for gathering and analyzing data.

What Retailers Feel About Manufacturers
SUCCESSFUL APPLICATIONS OF CATEGORY MANAGEMENT

▶ Manufacturers gather data on consumer purchases and make recommendations to retailers.
▶ Manufacturers with clearly defined and supported plans are viewed favorably.
▶ Manufacturers help the retailers understand how to get more out of shopper traffic and build shopper loyalty, incremental volume, and return on merchandising assets.

FIGURE 14-13

Applying Category
Management to Heavy-
Duty Liquid Detergent

Note: The criteria are based on the
average profit and movement of the
items in the product category of
heavy-duty liquid detergent. The
averages change for each product
category.

Source: Walter H. Heller,
"Profitability; Where It's Really At,"
(December 1992), p. 27. Copyright
Progressive Grocer. Reprinted by
permission.

More than $0.69 per item	**High Potential ("sleepers")** Action: Promote more, better position, more facings, display more, sample, back with store coupons	**Winners** Action: Promote more, better position, more facings, display more
Less than $0.69 per item	**Underachievers ("dogs")** Action: Raise prices, lower position, cut promotions, consider delisting	**Traffic Builders** Action: Review prices, lower position, expand space, mix with sleepers, display
	Fewer than 12.3 items per week	More than 12.3 items per week

Direct Product Profitability (vertical axis)

Unit Sales (horizontal axis)

UNSUCCESSFUL APPLICATIONS OF CATEGORY MANAGEMENT

▶ Manufacturers make recommendations that consistently favor their brands.
▶ Manufacturers just drop a completed template off with their retailers.
▶ Manufacturers do not maintain confidentiality for shared data or recommendations.

Figure 14-13 indicates how a retailer could use category management to better merchandise liquid detergent. One axis relates to direct product profitability. For the supermarket in this example, $0.69 per item is the average DPP for all liquid detergents. Those with higher amounts are placed in the top half of the grid and those with lower amounts in the bottom half. The other axis classifies detergents in terms of unit sales (an indicator of inventory turnover), with 12.3 items weekly being the dividing line between slow- and fast-moving detergents. All detergents can be placed into one of four categories: high potential ("sleepers"), products with high profitability but low sales; winners, products with high profitability and high sales; underachievers ("dogs"), products with low profitability and low sales; and traffic builders, products with low profitability and high sales. Specific strategies are recommended in the figure.

Merchandising Software

This site (www.business. com/directory/retail_and_ consumer_services/ software) provides a directory of retail software providers.

One of the most significant advances in merchandise planning is the widespread availability of computer software, which gives retailers an excellent support mechanism to systematically prepare forecasts, try out various assortment scenarios, coordinate the data for category management, and so forth. In an era when many retailers carry thousands of items, merchandising software is a part of everyday business life.

Some merchandising software is provided by suppliers and trade associations at no charge—as part of the value delivery chain and relationship retailing. Other software is sold by marketing firms, often for $1,500 or less (although some software sells for $25,000 or more). Let's now discuss the far-reaching nature of merchandising software. The links to several retail merchandising software products, including category management, may be found at our Web site (**www.pearsonhighered.com/berman**).

General Merchandise Planning Software

Some retailers prefer functionally driven software, while others use integrated software packages. Pacific Sunwear, a 950-store national chain, is an example of the latter. It utilizes MicroStrategy's (**www.microstrategy.com**) Business Intelligence Platform software "to analyze key merchandise sales and inventory metrics to glean insight on the sales trends and inventory investments of its products by specific regions, demographics, and stores." The software "converts detailed transactional data into personalized reports through dashboards and exception reporting for Pacific Sunwear's executives, merchants, merchandise planners, and allocators." The retailer chose MicroStrategy software "for its ease-of-use, superior reporting, and analytical capabilities, and its Web-based platform."[23]

Forecasting Software

Many retailers use their data warehouses to make merchandise forecasts. JDA Software (**www.jda.com**) is one of the firms that produces software that lets them do so. Fred Meyer is a major retail client. JDA's Allocation & Replenishment software enables Fred Meyer to "ensure forecasts are up-to-date and are at the right level. Other benefits include reduced safety-stock levels and increased customer satisfaction, as well as the ability to recover lost sales and reduce lead-time with improved forecasts." As a Fred Meyer executive notes: "We have been able to provide our vendors with more accurate and timely forecasts. The right forecast, paired with delivering the right product to the right location at the right time, have all played a role in increasing our average in-stock percentage from 92 percent to 96 percent."[24]

Firms such as SAS (**www.sas.com**) offer sophisticated software for retail forecasting purposes: "You can analyze and forecast processes that take place over time. You can identify previously unseen trends and anticipate fluctuations so you can more effectively plan for the future. Whether you want to understand past trends, forecast the future, or better understand how your business functions, we provide a wide range of analytical tools that ensure your success."[25]

 **TECHNOLOGY IN RETAILING**   Enhanced Merchandise Planning at Abercrombie & Fitch

Abercrombie & Fitch (A&F, **www.abercrombie.com**) is in its first stages of international expansion. The retailer's Canadian stores currently generate three times the sales and profit levels of similarly sized U.S. stores. And its first London store, which opened in 2007, has sales comparable to Abercrombie & Fitch's New York City store.

To better ensure success, A&F has begun to use Oracle's Retail Merchandising System (**www.oracle.com**) to replace its current system that is between 10 and 20 years old. In Phase One, A&F will focus on merchandise planning and purchase order processes. Phase Two will help manage A&F's perpetual inventory, sales auditing, and pricing management activities.

Part of the attraction of the new IT system is its tighter inventory management. Until recently, A&F would place new products in the front of each store on a seasonal or monthly basis. This has now been upgraded to a weekly activity. Although the weekly timing encourages customers to visit A&F more frequently, it requires a much more effective inventory management system to be sure that the right mix of goods is available in all sizes and colors. Better stocking of stores gives A&F's sales associates more time to sell goods rather than attempt to locate a customer's preferred product at a nearby A&F store.

Source: "Top Innovators: Abercrombie & Fitch," *Apparel Magazine* (May 2008), p. 30.

Innovativeness Software

Because today's software provides detailed data rapidly, it allows retailers to monitor and more quickly react to trends. Processes that once took months now are done in weeks or days. Instead of missing a selling season, retailers are prepared for the latest craze.

Wal-Mart, among others, uses Web-based color control software from Datacolor: "Wal-Mart is encouraging its suppliers to implement Datacolor's color-matching technology to streamline the color approval process that precedes production runs for new products, thus resulting in time and cost savings." Datacolor software enables retailers and their suppliers to reduce the process from weeks to days: "By eliminating physical samples, our technology streamlines the process so you can deliver uncompromised color on time and on target."[26]

Assortment Software

Learn more about SAS retail software (**www.sas. com/industry/retail**).

A number of retailers employ merchandising software to better plan assortments. One such retailer is AutoZone, which relies on a variety of SAS (**www.sas.com**) software programs. AutoZone sells nearly one-half million products at its 3,300 stores and retains information in a comprehensive data warehouse. As AutoZone's director of product and price optimization notes: "With SAS, AutoZone ensures efficient, profitable retail operations, not to mention more satisfied customers—by knowing store-by-store which products sell and how to price them effectively to keep them moving off the shelves. SAS helps us sift the important signals from all the noise coming at us, so to speak, so we can make decisions that leverage our inventory and assets optimally and give us good profitability in the market."[27]

Allocation Software

Chains of all sizes and types want to improve how they allocate merchandise to stores. There are several software programs to let them do so. Consider the Allocation software from JustEnough. Most retail planners would like to better tailor their merchandise to local needs: "JustEnough forecasts customer demand and then, taking into account the current stock at each location and what has been sold, calculates both the optimal inventory to send to each location and how much to reorder across the supply chain." In situations where inventory needs to be cleared at the end of a season, the software "will allocate the inventory to the stores where JustEnough thinks it will have the best chance to be sold. JustEnough protects you from sending the inventory to the wrong place, and then having to transport the inventory again to the stores that need it."[28]

Category Management Software

A wide range of software programs is available to help manufacturers and retailers deal with category management's complexities. A few retailers have even developed their own software. Programs typically base space allocation on sales, inventory turnover, and profits at individual stores. Because data are store specific, space allocations reflect actual sales. These are examples of category management software:

Spaceman Merchandiser (**http://us.nielsen.com/ products/ms_spaceman_ merchandiser.shtml**) is Nielsen's entry-level software.

▶ Nielsen offers Category Business Planner (**www.us.nielsen.com/products/rs_ cbp.shtml**) and Spaceman (**http://us.nielsen.com/products/ms_spaceman.shtml**) software.
▶ MEMRB IRI markets the popular Apollo Pro merchandising software (**www.memrb.com**).
▶ Shelf Logic (**www.shelflogic.com**) markets Shelf Logic Pro category management software for only $750 and Shelf Logic Quik plan for $479. See Figure 14-14.

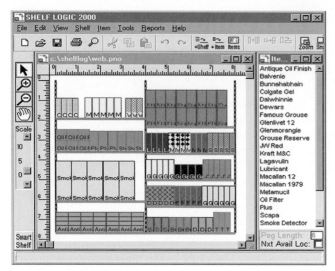
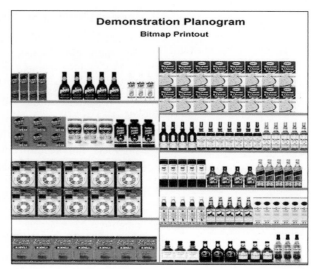

FIGURE 14-14

Shelf Logic: Software for Category Management Planning

Source: Reprinted by permission of Logical Planning Systems.

Chapter Summary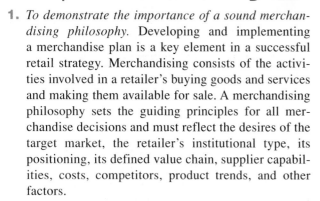

1. *To demonstrate the importance of a sound merchandising philosophy.* Developing and implementing a merchandise plan is a key element in a successful retail strategy. Merchandising consists of the activities involved in a retailer's buying goods and services and making them available for sale. A merchandising philosophy sets the guiding principles for all merchandise decisions and must reflect the desires of the target market, the retailer's institutional type, its positioning, its defined value chain, supplier capabilities, costs, competitors, product trends, and other factors.

2. *To study various buying organization formats and the processes they use.* The buying organization and its processes must be defined in terms of its formality, degree of centralization, organizational breadth, personnel resources, functions performed, and staffing.

   With a formal buying organization, merchandising is a distinct task in a separate department. In an informal buying organization, the same personnel handle both merchandising and other retail tasks. Multi-unit retailers must choose whether to have a centralized or a decentralized buying organization. In a centralized organization, all purchases emanate from one office. In a decentralized organization, decisions are made locally or regionally. For a general organization, one person or a few people buy all merchandise. For a specialized organization, each buyer is responsible for a product category.

   An inside buying organization is staffed by a retailer's personnel and decisions are made by its permanent employees. An outside buying organization involves a company or personnel external to the retailer. Most retailers use either an inside or an outside buying organization; some employ a combination. A resident buying office, which can be an inside or outside organization, is used when a retailer wants to keep in close touch with key markets and cannot do so through headquarters buying staff. Independents and small chains often use cooperative buying to compete with large chains.

   If a retailer has a "merchandising" view, merchandise personnel oversee all buying and selling functions. If it has a "buying" view, merchandise personnel oversee buying, advertising, and pricing, while store personnel oversee assortments, displays, personnel deployment, and sales presentations.

   A buyer is responsible for selecting merchandise and setting a strategy to market that merchandise. He or she devises and controls sales and profit projections for a product category; plans assortments, styling, sizes, and quantities; negotiates with and evaluates vendors; and oversees store displays. A sales manager supervises the on-floor selling and operational activities for a specific retail department. He or she must be a good organizer, administrator, and motivator.

3. *To outline the considerations in devising merchandise plans: forecasts, innovativeness, assortment, brands, timing, and allocation.* Forecasts are projections of expected retail sales and form the foundation of merchandise plans. Staple merchandise consists of the

regular products a retailer carries. A basic stock list specifies the inventory level, color, brand, and so on for every staple item carried. Assortment merchandise consists of products for which there must be a variety so customers have a proper selection. A model stock plan projects levels of specific assortment merchandise. Fashion merchandise has cyclical sales due to changing tastes and lifestyles. Seasonal merchandise sells well over nonconsecutive periods. With fad merchandise, sales are high for a short time. When forecasting for best-sellers, many retailers use a never-out list.

A retailer's innovativeness is related to the target market(s), product growth potential, fashion trends, the retailer's image, competition, customer segments, responsiveness to consumers, investment costs, profitability, risk, constrained decision making, and declining goods and services. Three issues are of particular interest: How fast will a new good or service generate sales? What are the most sales to be achieved in a season or a year? Over what period will a good or service continue to sell? A useful tool is the product life cycle.

An assortment is the merchandise selection carried. The retailer first chooses the quality of merchandise. The assortment is then determined. Width of assortment refers to the number of distinct product categories carried. Depth of assortment refers to the variety in any category. As part of assortment planning, a retailer chooses its mix of brands. Manufacturer brands are produced and controlled by manufacturers. Private brands contain names designated by wholesalers or retailers. Generic brands feature generic names as brands and are a form of private brand. The competition between manufacturers and retailers is called the battle of the brands.

For new goods and services, it must be decided when they are first to be displayed and sold. For established goods and services, the firm must plan the merchandise flow during the year. In deciding when and how often to buy merchandise, quantity discounts should be considered. A single-unit retailer chooses how much merchandise to allocate to the sales floor and how much to the stockroom, and whether to use a warehouse. A chain also allocates items among stores.

4. *To discuss category management and merchandising software.* Category management is a technique for managing a retail business that focuses on product category results rather than the performance of individual brands. It arranges product groups into strategic business units to better address consumer needs and meet financial goals. Category management helps retail personnel make the merchandising decisions that maximize the total return on the assets. There is now plentiful PC- and Web-based merchandising software available for retailers, in just about every aspect of merchandise planning.

Key Terms

merchandising (p. 384)	staple merchandise (p. 392)	assortment (p. 396)
merchandising philosophy (p. 384)	basic stock list (p. 392)	width of assortment (p. 396)
micromerchandising (p. 386)	assortment merchandise (p. 392)	depth of assortment (p. 396)
cross-merchandising (p. 387)	model stock plan (p. 392)	manufacturer (national) brands
resident buying office (p. 390)	fashion merchandise (p. 392)	(p. 400)
cooperative buying (p. 390)	seasonal merchandise (p. 392)	private (dealer, store) brands (p. 400)
buyer (p. 390)	fad merchandise (p. 392)	generic brands (p. 402)
sales manager (p. 390)	never-out list (p. 393)	battle of the brands (p. 402)
forecasts (p. 391)	product life cycle (p. 394)	category management (p. 403)

Questions for Discussion

1. Describe and evaluate the merchandising philosophy of your favorite restaurant.

2. What is the distinction between *merchandising functions* and the *buying function?*

3. Is micromerchandising a good approach? Why or why not?

4. What are the advantages and disadvantages of a centralized buying organization?

5. Interview a local store owner and determine how he or she makes merchandise decisions. Evaluate that approach.

6. How could a drugstore use a basic stock list, a model stock plan, and a never-out list?

7. Under what circumstances could a retailer carry a wide range of merchandise quality without hurting its image? When should the quality of merchandise carried be quite narrow?

8. How should a major appliance retailer use the product life-cycle concept?

9. What are the trade-offs in a retailer's deciding how much to emphasize private brands rather than manufacturer brands?

10. Present a checklist of five factors for a chain retailer to review in determining how to allocate merchandise among its stores.

11. What is the basic premise of category management? Why do you think that supermarkets have been at the forefront of the movement to use category management?

12. What do you think are the risks of placing too much reliance on merchandising software? Do the risks outweigh the benefits? Explain your answer.

Web **Exercise**

Visit this section of the Planning Factory's Web site (www. planfact.co.uk/mp.htm). Look at several of the merchandising resources listed there. Discuss what you learn from these resources.

Note: Stop by our Web site (www.pearsonhighered.com/ berman) to experience a number of highly interactive,

appealing Web exercises based on actual company demonstrations and sample materials related to retailing.

15 Implementing Merchandise Plans

Chapter **Objectives**

1. To describe the steps in the implementation of merchandise plans: gathering information, selecting and interacting with merchandise sources, evaluation, negotiation, concluding purchases, receiving and stocking merchandise, reordering, and re-evaluation

2. To examine the prominent roles of logistics and inventory management in the implementation of merchandise plans

In 1961, Dr. Stanley Pearle had the idea to create a store that combined a complete eye exam, an extensive selection of frames and corrective lenses, and convenient store hours. Pearle could not possibly have foreseen that his first one-stop, total-eye-care center located in Savannah, Georgia, would grow into Pearle Vision Center (**www.pearlevision.com**).

Cole National Corporation acquired Pearle Vision Center in 1996 from Grand Metropolitan. In 2004, Milan-based Luxottica Group SpA (the owner of the LensCrafters and Sunglass Hut International chains, as well as Ray-Ban, Revo, and other premium brands) purchased Cole National in a $441 million transaction. At the time of the merger, Cole National with its Pearle Vision franchises had close to 3,000 locations in the United States, Canada, Puerto Rico, and the Virgin Islands. This deal joined the two largest eyeglass retailing companies in America.

In addition to Pearle Vision, Luxottica Group SpA (the parent company) sells eyewear through its Sears Optical, Target Optical, and Cole Managed Vision (which serves more than 23 million subscribers in medium and large organizations) units. Its more than 6,700 optical and sunglass retail stores give Luxottica the ability to market its products to different segments, as well as clout in negotiating with its key vendors. Luxottica also has licensing agreements with Prada, Versace, Donna Karan, Burberry, Chanel, and Dolce & Gabbana.

Despite the large size of Luxottica and the power of mass retailers that sell optical products, the U.S. eyeglass/sunglass market is still highly fragmented.[1]

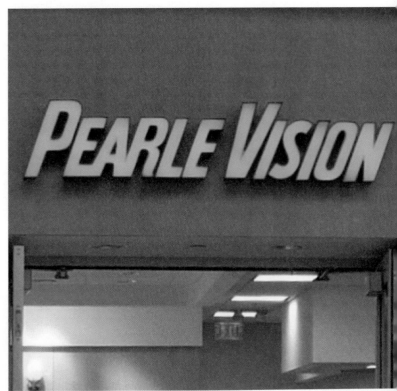

Source: Reprinted by permission of Susan Berry, Retail Image Consulting, Inc.

OVERVIEW

Enter the 7-Eleven Web site (www.7-eleven.com) and click on "News Room" to find out what this creative retailer is doing.

This chapter builds on Chapter 14 and covers the implementation of merchandise plans, including logistics and inventory management. Sometimes, it is simple to enact merchandise plans. Other times, it requires a lot of hard work. Home Depot's supply chain management illustrates the latter situation:

> When CEO Frank Blake first took the helm of Home Depot, he visited a store in Prescott, Arizona. There, he saw a pyramid of John Deere tractors. He asked the store manager whether he sold a lot of tractors. "I sold one last year," the manager told Blake. "Well, you've got 35 years of supply then," the CEO replied. Blake recounted this anecdote at a Cobb County Chamber of Commerce meeting to describe just how broken Atlanta-based Home Depot's supply chain had become. After 30 years in business—and taking pride in towering shelves of in-stock items—Home Depot is going to a more traditional supply chain. It's one of the company's largest initiatives. Home Depot spent $118 million on it in 2008 alone and will spend $260 million through 2010. When it's done in several years, it could free up $1.5 billion in working capital. That hinges on getting better inventory onto shelves when customers want it. The firm says that every one-tenth improvement in turning over inventory equals about $150 million in cash. The company is hoping for one full turn of improvement.[2]

Implementing Merchandise Plans

The implementation of merchandise plans comprises the eight sequential steps shown in Figure 15-1 and discussed next.

Gathering Information

After overall merchandising plans are set, more information about target market needs and prospective suppliers is required before buying or rebuying merchandise. In gathering data *about the marketplace,* a retailer has several possible sources. The most valuable is the consumer. By regularly researching target market demographics, lifestyles, product preferences, and potential shopping plans, a retailer can learn about consumer demand directly. Loyalty programs are especially useful in tracking consumer purchases and interests.

Other information sources can be used when direct consumer data are insufficient. Suppliers (manufacturers and wholesalers) usually do their own sales forecasts and marketing research (such as test marketing). They also know how much outside promotional

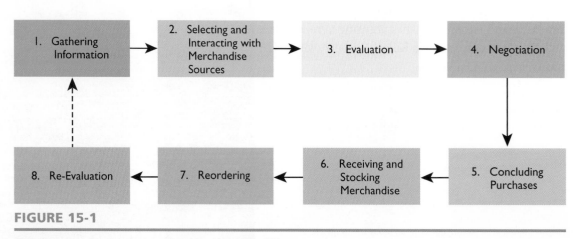

FIGURE 15-1

The Process for Implementing Merchandise Plans

support a retailer will get. In closing a deal with the retailer, a supplier may present charts and graphs, showing forecasts and promotional support. Yet, the retailer should remember that it is the party with direct access to the target market and its needs.

Retail sales and display personnel interact with consumers and can pass their observations along to management. A **want book (want slip)** system is a formal way to record consumer requests for unstocked or out-of-stock merchandise. It is very helpful to a retailer's buyers. Outside of customers, salespeople may provide the most useful information for merchandising decisions.

Competitors represent another information source. A conservative retailer may not stock an item until competitors do and may employ comparison shoppers to study the offerings and prices of competitors. The most sophisticated comparison shopping involves the use of Web-based shopping bots such as mySimon.com, whereby competitors' offerings and prices are tracked electronically. Buy.com, for one, constantly checks its prices to make sure that it is not undersold. In addition, trade publications report on trends in each aspect of retailing and provide another way of gathering data from competitors. See Figure 15-2 for an example of a competition shopping report.

In addition, government sources indicate unemployment, inflation, and product safety data; independent news sources conduct their own consumer polls and do investigative reporting; and commercial data can be purchased.

To learn about the attributes of *specific suppliers* and their merchandise, retailers can

▶ Talk to suppliers, get specification sheets, read trade publications, and seek references.
▶ Attend trade shows with numerous exhibitors (suppliers). There are hundreds of trade shows yearly in New York. In Paris, the semi-annual Prêt À Porter show attracts 1,100 exhibitors and about 43,000 attendees. The National Hardware

See how mySimon (**www. mysimon.com**) can help retailers track competitors.

Learn why High Point (**www.highpointmarket.org**) is a world-class market.

FIGURE 15-2

A Competition Shopping Report

COMPETITION SHOPPING REPORT

Store #_____   Date_____

Dept. #_____   Qualified Competition Shopped:

1._____
2._____

Our Style No.	Mfr. Model or Style	Description	Our Price	1st Compet. Price	2nd Compet. Price	Store's Recom. Price	Buyer's Recom. Price

Item Seen at Our Competitor's Store Which We Should Carry:					
Manufacturer	Mfr. Model or Style	Description	Reg. or List Price	Sale Price	Buyer's Comments

_____   _____
Signature of Shopper   *Store Manager*

Show in Las Vegas has more than 2,000 exhibitors and 30,000 attendees each year. The High Point Furniture Market in North Carolina has semi-annual shows that attract more than 2,000 manufacturers and 85,000 attendees—from all 50 states and 110 countries.

California Market Center (**www.californiamarketcenter. com**) offers a lot of online information for retailers. Click on "exhibitor/tenant."

▶ Visit year-round merchandise marts such as AmericasMart Atlanta (**www.americasmart. com**), Merchandise Mart in Chicago (**www.merchandisemart.com/mmart**), California Market Center in Los Angeles (**www.californiamarketcenter.com**), and Dallas Market Center (**www.dallasmarketcenter.com**). These marts have daily hours for permanent vendor showrooms and large areas for trade shows.

▶ Search the Web. One newer application is GoExhibit (**www.goexhibit.com**). A trade show coordinator "puts all the sights and sounds of a physical show right on its Web site." The GoExhibit virtual trade show lets the coordinator "customize every element of the virtual exhibit hall, including the graphics and clickable elements of each booth." Trade show attendees "visit the virtual exhibit hall right on the trade show's Web site, moving from booth to booth and visiting exhibitors that have paid the trade show for their virtual booth space."

Whatever the information acquired, a retailer should feel comfortable that it is sufficient for making good decisions. For routine decisions (staple products), limited information may be adequate. On the other hand, new fashions' sales fluctuate widely and require extensive data for forecasts.

At our Web site (**www.pearsonhighered.com/berman**), we have more than a dozen links to leading trade shows and merchandise marts.

Selecting and Interacting with Merchandise Sources

The next step is to select sources of merchandise and to interact with them. Three major options exist:

▶ *Company-owned.* A large retailer owns a manufacturing and/or wholesaling facility. A company-owned supplier handles all or part of the merchandise the retailer requests.

▶ *Outside, regularly used supplier.* This supplier is not owned by the retailer but used regularly. A retailer knows the quality of merchandise and the reliability of the supplier from its experience.

▶ *Outside, new supplier.* This supplier is not owned by the retailer, which has not bought from it before. The retailer may be unfamiliar with merchandise quality and supplier reliability.

A retailer can rely on one kind of supplier or utilize a combination (the biggest retailers often use all three formats). The types of outside suppliers (regularly used and new) are described in Figure 15-3. In choosing vendors, the criteria listed in the Figure 15-4 checklist should be considered.

Big Lots places emphasis on supplier relations (**www.biglotscorporate. com/vendor/index.asp**).

Big Lots, which buys merchandise to stock its national chain of closeout stores, is a good example of how complicated choosing suppliers can be:

An integral part of our business is the sourcing and purchasing of quality brand-name merchandise directly from manufacturers and other vendors typically at prices substantially below those paid by traditional retailers. We have the ability to purchase significant quantities of a vendor's closeout merchandise in specific product categories and to control distribution in accordance with vendor instructions. Our sourcing channels also include bankruptcies, liquidations, and insurance claims. We supplement our traditional brand-name closeout purchases with direct import and domestically sourced merchandise in departments such as furniture, home decorative, and lawn and garden. Our top ten vendors account for only 14 percent of total purchases. We buy about 25 percent of our merchandise directly from overseas vendors, including 21 percent from vendors in China.[3]

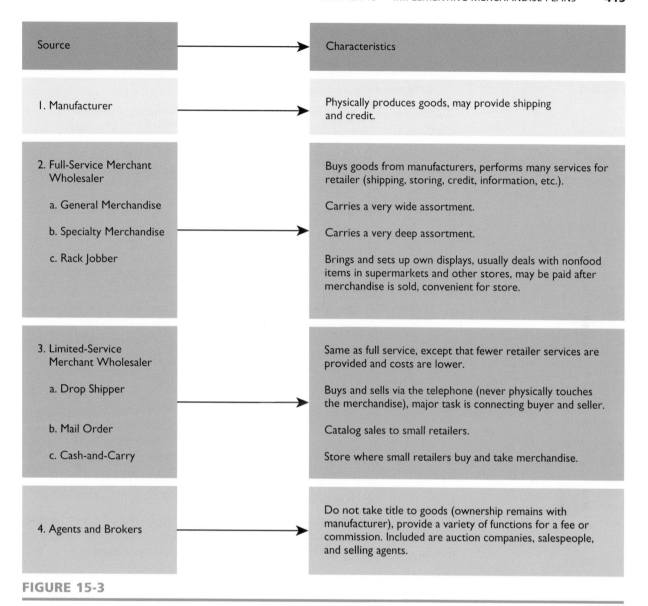

FIGURE 15-3

Outside Sources of Supply

Retailers and suppliers often interact well together, as highlighted in Figure 15-5. Other times, there are conflicts. As noted earlier, relationship building can be invaluable. Yet, there remain sore points between retailers and suppliers. On the one hand, many retailers have beefed up their use of private brands because they are upset when suppliers such as Gucci open their own stores in the same shopping centers. Most Gucci sales now come from company-owned and franchised shops. On the other hand, many suppliers are distressed by what they believe is retailers' excessive use of **chargebacks,** whereby retailers, at their sole discretion, make deductions in their bills for infractions ranging from late shipments to damaged and expired goods. Some suppliers have even taken their retailers to court: "The last thing a company wants to do is sue one of its biggest customers. But disputes over stores' payments to their suppliers are growing increasingly bitter, spawning numerous lawsuits over the last several years, involving almost every large American department store chain."[4]

Selecting merchandise sources must be viewed as a two-way street. For example, in 2005, Nike announced that it would no longer distribute its products through Sears' stores, out of concern that Nike items would end up being sold at Sears' sister chain Kmart. And Nike products are not available at Wal-Mart. As one observer noted: "Nike

FIGURE 15-4

A Checklist of Points to Review in Choosing Vendors

✓ Reliability—Will a supplier consistently fulfill all written promises?

✓ Price–quality—Who provides the best merchandise at the lowest price?

✓ Order-processing time—How fast will deliveries be made?

✓ Exclusive rights—Will a supplier give exclusive selling rights or customize products?

✓ Functions provided—Will a supplier undertake shipping, storing, and other functions, if needed?

✓ Information—Will a supplier pass along important data?

✓ Ethics—Will a supplier fulfill all verbal promises and not engage in unfair business or labor practices?

✓ Guarantee—Does a supplier stand behind its offerings?

✓ Credit—Can credit purchases be made from a supplier? On what terms?

✓ Long-term relationships—Will a supplier be available over an extended period?

✓ Reorders—Can a supplier promptly fill reorders?

✓ Markup—Will markup (price margins) be adequate?

✓ Innovativeness—Is a supplier's line innovative or conservative?

✓ Local advertising—Does a supplier advertise in local media?

✓ Investment—How large are total investment costs with a supplier?

✓ Risk—How much risk is involved in dealing with a supplier?

does not sell its products in Wal-Mart and has long argued that its brand would be devalued if sold in discount chains."[5]

Evaluating Merchandise

Whatever source is chosen, there must be a procedure to evaluate the merchandise under consideration. Three procedures are possible: inspection, sampling, and description. The technique depends on the item's cost, its attributes, and purchase regularity.

FIGURE 15–5

Zara: A Collaborative Supplier–Retailer Program

For its fast-paced merchandise planning and development processes to work properly, Zara personnel need to foster close relationships with suppliers around the world. As the retailer's Web site notes, "Zara offers the latest trends in international fashion in an environment of thought-out design."

Source: Reprinted by permission of Susan Berry, Retail Image Consulting, Inc.

Inspection occurs when every single unit is examined before purchase and after delivery. Jewelry and art are examples of expensive, rather unique purchases for which the retailer carefully inspects all items.

Sampling is used with regular purchases of large quantities of breakable, perishable, or expensive items. Because inspection is inefficient, items are sampled for quality and condition. A retailer ready to buy several hundred light fixtures, bunches of bananas, or inexpensive watches does not inspect each item. A number of units are sampled, and the entire selection is bought if the sample is okay. An unsatisfactory sample might cause a whole shipment to be rejected (or a discount negotiated). Sampling may also occur upon receipt of merchandise.

Description buying is used with standardized, nonbreakable, and nonperishable merchandise. Items are not inspected or sampled; they are ordered in quantity based on a verbal, written, or pictorial description. A stationery store can order paper clips, pads, and printer paper from a catalog or Web site. After it receives an order, only a count of those items is conducted.

Negotiating the Purchase

Next, a retailer negotiates the purchase and its terms. A new or special order usually results in a negotiated contract, and a retailer and a supplier carefully discuss all aspects of the purchase. A regular order or reorder often involves a uniform contract, because terms are standard or have already been set and the order is handled routinely.

Off-price retailers and other deep discounters may require negotiated contracts for most purchases. These firms employ **opportunistic buying,** by which especially low prices are negotiated for merchandise whose sales have not lived up to expectations, end-of-season goods, items consumers have returned to the manufacturer or another retailer, and closeouts. At TJX, "buyers are in the marketplace virtually every week, buying mostly for the current selling season. By having a liquid inventory position, our buyers can buy close to need, enabling them to buy into current market trends and take advantage of the opportunities in the marketplace."[6]

Several purchase terms must be specified, whether a negotiated or a uniform contract is involved. These include the delivery date, quantity purchased, price and payment arrangements, discounts, form of delivery, and point of transfer of title, as well as special clauses.

The delivery date and the quantity purchased must be clear. A retailer should be able to cancel an order if either provision is not carried out. The purchase price, payment arrangements, and permissible discounts must also be addressed. What is the retailer's cost per item (including handling)? What forms of payment are permitted (cash and credit)? What discounts are given? Retailers' purchase prices are often discounted for early payments ("2/10/net 30" means there is a 2 percent discount if the full bill is paid in 10 days; the full bill is due in 30 days), support activities (setting up displays), and quantity purchases. Stipulations are needed for the form of delivery (truck, rail, and so on) and the party responsible for shipping fees (FOB factory—free on board—means a supplier places merchandise with the shipper, but the retailer pays the freight). Last, the point of transfer of title—when ownership changes from supplier to buyer—must be stated in a contract.

To learn more about the slotting allowance controversy, visit this Web site (**www.ftc.gov/opa/ 2003/11/slottingallowance. htm**).

Special clauses may be inserted by either party. Sometimes, they are beneficial to both parties (such as an agreement about the advertising support each party provides). Other times, the clauses are inserted by the more powerful party. As noted in Chapter 1, a major disagreement between vendors and large retailers is the latter's increasing use of **slotting allowances**—payments that retailers require of vendors for providing shelf space:

> For small suppliers, the need to fund slotting allowances can severely limit distribution or cause the diversion of resources that could be better spent on other parts of the business. For consumers, the practice leads to artificially restricted product assortments. Category managers who decide which items to put on store shelves are often forced to choose between conflicting goals—maximizing profits by accepting slotting allowances or doing what is in the best interests of their customers.[7]

Unlike many other retailers, industry leader Wal-Mart does not charge any slotting allowances and often gets new products first from suppliers as a result of this policy.

Concluding Purchases

Many medium-sized and large retailers use computers to complete and process orders (based on electronic data interchange [EDI] and quick response [QR] inventory planning), and each purchase is fed into a computer data bank. Smaller retailers often write up and process orders manually, and purchase amounts are added to their inventory in the same way. Yet, with the advances in computerized ordering software, even small retailers may have the capability of placing orders electronically—especially if they buy from large wholesalers that use EDI and QR systems.

Multi-unit retailers must determine whether the final purchase decision is made by central or regional management or by local managers. Advantages and disadvantages accrue to each approach.

Several alternatives are possible regarding the transfer of title between parties. The retailer's responsibilities and rights differ in each of these situations:

There is EDI/QR software (**www.gxs.com/solution/smb**) to fit almost any budget.

▶ The retailer takes title immediately on purchase.
▶ The retailer assumes ownership after items are loaded onto the mode of transportation.
▶ The retailer takes title when a shipment is received.
▶ The retailer does not take title until the end of a billing cycle, when the supplier is paid.
▶ The retailer accepts merchandise on consignment and does not own the items. The supplier is paid after merchandise is sold.

A consignment or memorandum deal may be possible if a vendor is in a weak position and wants to persuade retailers to carry its items. In a **consignment purchase,** a retailer has no risk because title is not taken; the supplier owns the goods until sold. An electronic version (scan-based trading) is being tried at some supermarkets. It saves time and money for all parties due to the paperless steps in a purchase. In a **memorandum purchase,** risk is still low, but a retailer takes title on delivery and is responsible for damages. In both options, retailers do not pay for items until they are sold and can return items.

CAREERS IN RETAILING

|||||| **Is Retail for Me? Merchandise Buying and Planning— Part 2**

Besides the typical merchandising positions noted in Chapter 14, there are many other opportunities:

▶ *Head of Merchandise Planning and Allocation.* Top executive responsible for allocation of merchandise to stores. This position may advise the GMM (general merchandise manager) and buying staff on flow quantities and timing, as well as assist in planning quantities for merchandise events. Does not buy goods but may have gross margin planning/analysis responsibilities.
▶ *Senior Merchandise Planner/Controller.* In very large chains, this position is between the head of planning and planners. This position supervises planners responsible for selected product categories, often corresponding to the DMM (divisional merchandise manager) merchandise groupings.
▶ *Merchandise Planner/Controller.* This position advises on flow quantities and timing and develops distribution plans for specific merchandise categories and subclasses. Responsible for balancing stock unit ratios by store. May directly supervise a crew of merchandise distributors/allocators.

▶ *Merchandise Distributor/Allocator/Analyst.* Responsible for allocating new merchandise into stores by replenishment needs or stock ratios. May also coordinate inter-store transfers of goods. Will generally do analysis only upon instruction from a planner. Primary duty is allocation, not planning.
▶ *Head of Import Coordination and Production.* Top executive over imports and/or offshore merchandise production, which includes licensing and monitoring production at offshore factories. May be responsible for quota management. May assist traffic department or third-party contractor with shipping arrangements through Customs.
▶ *Production Manager.* Monitors factory production of private label goods, ensuring conformity to specifications and quality. May coordinate shipping from factory to distribution centers. May work with overseas factories. May have responsibility for import shipping arrangements through Customs.

Source: Reprinted by permission of the National Retail Federation.

Receiving and Stocking Merchandise

The retailer is now ready to receive and handle items. This involves receiving and storing, checking and paying invoices, price and inventory marking, setting up displays, figuring on-floor assortments, completing transactions, arranging delivery or pickup, processing returns and damaged goods, monitoring pilferage, and controlling merchandise. See Figure 15-6. Good distribution management is key.

Items may be shipped from suppliers to warehouses (for storage and disbursement) or directly to retailers' store(s). The Walgreens drugstore chain has fully automated warehouses that stock thousands of products and speed their delivery to stores. Amazon.com uses U.S. and international fulfillment centers and warehouses that it operates itself, as well as fulfillment centers that are operated under co-sourcing arrangements. J.C. Penney has separate distribution centers for its store and catalog operations.

One important emerging technology that may greatly advance the merchandise tracking and handling process for retailers involves **RFID (radio frequency identification)** systems. RFID is a method of "storing and remotely retrieving data using devices called RFID tags or transponders. The technology requires some extent of cooperation of an RFID reader and an RFID tag. An RFID tag is an object, such as an adhesive sticker, that can be applied to or incorporated into a product or its package to identify and track it using radio waves. Some tags can be read from several feet away and beyond the line of sight of the reader. There are generally two types of RFID tags: active RFID tags, which contain a battery, and passive RFID tags, which have no battery. Most RFID tags contain two parts: an integrated circuit for storing and processing information and an antenna for receiving and transmitting the signal."[8]

At present, RFID use is limited. It is too early to predict how widespread RFID use will be or how long it will take to be accepted by most retailers and their suppliers. Suppliers are responsible for most of the work and costs. The current costs for an RFID system range from $100,000 to $300,000 for a small supplier to several million dollars for a large supplier. But the benefits are clear:

> Several years into the RFID revolution, it's clear that implementation is occurring more slowly than Wal-Mart originally envisioned: "Our goal is to track all pallets and cases." Yet, as of 2008, only 600 of Wal-Mart's 60,000 suppliers plus

FIGURE 15-6

Receiving and Stocking Merchandise at REI's Category Killer Stores
With its wide and deep product assortment, along with some very tall vertical displays, in-store merchandising at REI can be quite challenging.

Source: Reprinted by permission of Susan Berry, Retail Image Consulting, Inc.

750 Sam's Club suppliers had deployed RFID to some degree. On Wal-Mart's end, RFID is deployed at about 1,000 of the roughly 4,000 Wal-Mart and Sam's Club stores in the United States. Wal-Mart's original goal was to have 12 of its approximately 120 distribution centers outfitted for RFID by 2006. By 2008, only five were set up for RFID, because the company shifted its RFID focus to in-store implementations.

Wal-Mart is unshakable in its belief that RFID delivers benefits: "We've reduced out-of-stocks by 8 percent worldwide, and we can resupply three times faster. Suppliers have seen a significant increase in sales. We've also done recent tests that showed perpetual inventory improving by 20 percent." As Wal-Mart and its suppliers become more familiar with RFID, new benefits are emerging. The initial focus was on simple inventory tracking: Did the pallet arrive in Dallas? Then firms realized that RFID can play a big role in asset management: Did that HDTV just walk out the door? There also are the benefits of robust, two-way supply-chain-based communication.[9]

When orders are received, they must be checked for completeness and product condition. Invoices must be reviewed for accuracy and payments made as specified. This step cannot be taken for granted.

At this point, prices and inventory information are marked on merchandise. Supermarkets estimate that price marking on individual items costs them an amount equal to their annual profits. Marking can be done in various ways. Small firms may hand-post prices and manually keep inventory records. Some retailers use their own computer-generated price tags and rely on pre-printed UPC data on packages to keep records. Others buy tags, with computer- and human-readable price and inventory data, from outside suppliers. Still others expect vendors to provide source tagging. An inventory system works best when there is more data on labels or tags. With Monarch portable printers, hand-held devices print UPC-based labels and can be connected to store computers. See Figure 15-7.

Seagull Scientific (www.seagullscientific.com) markets popular labeling software.

FIGURE 15-7

The Monarch 1130 Series Labeler
The 1130 Series labelers represent a complete family of identification and pricing solutions. The labelers are simple and easy to use. They have ergonomic handle grips, lift-up covers for quick maintenance, label-viewing windows, and other features.

Source: Reprinted by permission of Monarch Marking Systems.

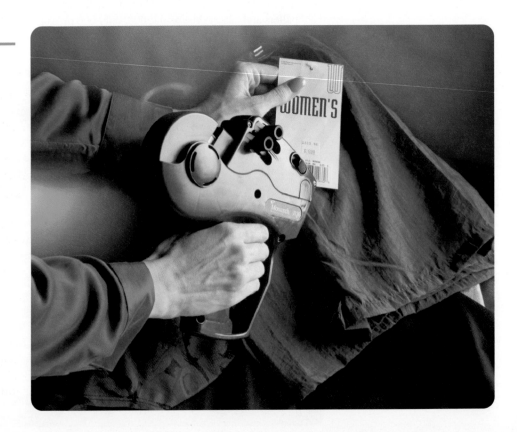

Store displays and on-floor quantities and assortments depend on the retailer and products involved. Supermarkets usually have bin-and-rack displays and place most inventory on the sales floor. Traditional department stores have all kinds of interior displays and place a lot of inventory in the back room, off the sales floor. Displays and on-floor merchandising are discussed in Chapter 18.

Merchandise handling is not complete until the customer buys and receives it from a retailer. This means order taking, credit or cash transactions, packaging, and delivery or pickup. Automation has improved retailer performance in each of these areas.

A procedure for processing returns and damaged goods is also needed. The retailer must determine the party responsible for customer returns (supplier or retailer) and the situations in which damaged goods would be accepted for refund or exchange (such as the length of time a warranty is honored).

As discussed later in the chapter, more retailers are taking aggressive actions to monitor and reduce inventory losses. This is a major problem due to the high costs of merchandise theft.

Merchandise control involves assessing sales, profits, turnover, inventory shortages, seasonality, and costs for each product category and item carried. Control is usually achieved by preparing computerized inventory data and doing physical inventories. A physical inventory must be adjusted to reflect damaged goods, pilferage, customer returns, and other factors. See Figure 15-8. A discussion of this topic appears in Chapter 16.

Merchandise receiving and handling is covered further later in this chapter.

Reordering Merchandise

Four factors are critical in reordering merchandise that the retailer purchases more than once: order and delivery time, inventory turnover, financial outlays, and inventory versus ordering costs.

How long does it take for a retailer to process an order and a supplier to fulfill and deliver it? It is possible for delivery time to be so lengthy that a retailer must reorder while having a full inventory. On the other hand, overnight delivery may be available for some items.

How long does it take for a retailer to sell out its inventory? A fast-selling product gives a retailer two choices: (1) order a surplus of items and spread out reorder periods or (2) keep a low inventory and order frequently. A slow-selling item may let a retailer reduce its initial inventory and spread out reorders.

What are the financial outlays under various purchase options? A large order, with a quantity discount, may require a big cash outlay. A small order, while more expensive per item, results in lower total costs at any one time since less inventory is held.

There are trade-offs between inventory holding and ordering costs. A large inventory fosters customer satisfaction, volume discounts, low per-item shipping costs, and easier handling. It also means high investments; greater obsolescence and damages; and storage, insurance, and opportunity costs. Placing many orders and keeping a small inventory mean a low investment, low opportunity costs, low storage costs, and little obsolescence. Yet, there may be disappointed customers if items are out of stock, higher unit costs, adverse effects from order delays, a need for partial shipments, service charges, and complex handling. Retailers try to hold enough stock to satisfy customers while not having a high surplus. Quick response inventory planning lowers inventory and ordering costs via close retailer-supplier relationships.

Re-evaluating on a Regular Basis

A merchandising plan should be re-evaluated regularly, with management reviewing the buying organization and that organization assessing the implementation. The overall procedure, as well as the handling of individual goods and services, should be monitored. Conclusions during this stage become part of the information-gathering stage for future efforts.

LXE'S HANDS-FREE PLATFORM ALLOWS:

- Real-time inventory updates

- Real-time selection and let-downs

- Easy management of product shortages as they occur

- Automatic priority updates for replenishments to short picked locations

- Support for multi-language environments

- Automatic or manual assignment by selection zone

- Ability to send the order-picker back to short picked locations that have been replenished

- Picking activity information to be captured, such as assignment times, end times and status

- Reactions to changing distribution needs through the availability of real-time data.

- Much more...

FIGURE 15-8

State-of-the-Art Inventory Control

Source: Reprinted by permission of LXE.

Logistics

Logistics is the total process of planning, implementing, and coordinating the physical movement of merchandise from manufacturer (wholesaler) to retailer to customer in the most timely, effective, and cost-efficient manner possible. Logistics regards order processing and fulfillment, transportation, warehousing, customer service, and inventory management as interdependent functions in the value delivery chain. If a logistics system works well,

FIGURE 15-9

The Multi-Faceted Logistics Approach of Home Depot

Home Depot pays a lot of attention to both its supply chain and its customers. The thousands of items that are carried by Home Depot must be efficiently delivered to individual stores (top photo), with the final step typically involving large commercial vehicles. In addition, many customers rent small Home Depot trucks to easily and immediately bring large purchases to their homes (bottom photo).

Source: Reprinted by permission of Home Depot.

firms reduce stockouts, hold down inventories, and improve customer service—all at the same time. See Figure 15-9. Logistics can also be quite challenging:

> St. Louis-based Save-A-Lot, a subsidiary of Supervalu, operates 15 distribution centers from Florida to New York. It buys and sells grocery commodities in full-pallet quantities and limits the number of sku's to generate operating efficiencies: "Our business model drives efficiency in both warehousing and transportation, which is critical with the cost structures that we're faced with today." Save-A-Lot uses Ryder System to provide all the dedicated transportation for four distribution centers. Whenever a Ryder truck carries a Save-A-Lot load, Ryder looks for additional hauling opportunities to offset costs. So a Ryder truck may be carrying five pallets of tomatoes for Save-A-Lot as well as crates of lettuce for a regional burger chain; both companies get their products on time and split the fees.[10]

In this section, we discuss these logistics concepts: performance goals, the supply chain, order processing and fulfillment, transportation and warehousing, and customer transactions and customer service. Inventory management is covered in the final section of this chapter.

Performance Goals

Among retailers' major logistics goals are to:

▶ Match the costs incurred to specific logistics activities, thereby fulfilling all activities as economically as possible, given the firms' other performance objectives.
▶ Place and receive orders as easily, accurately, and satisfactorily as possible.

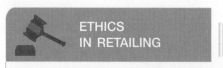

ETHICS IN RETAILING

Rolling Out Green Products at Home Depot

In mid-2007, Home Depot (**www.homedepot.com**) began to roll-out its "Eco Options" (**www.homedepot.com/ecooptions**) line of products in its nearly 1,900 U.S. stores. Products that meet appropriate standards are given a distinctive label made up of an orange-colored halo on top of a house and tree design. This label was placed on such Home Depot's products as compact fluorescent light bulbs, organic plants housed in biodegradable pots, front-loading washing machines, all-natural cleaning products, low-flow toilets, and energy efficient appliances.

Home Depot projected that this line would include 6,000 products and about 12 percent of its total sales in 2009. Suppliers who earn the Eco Option label will receive superior shelf placement; they will also be heavily featured in Home Depot's freestanding newspaper inserts.

To qualify for this label, suppliers must respond to a detailed questionnaire that examines energy efficiency, clean air, sustainable forestry, and water efficiency issues. Many products have had their claims verified by an independent standards and certification firm.

As an additional part of Home Depot's commitment to ecology, the chain refuses to purchase wood products from endangered forests, and it was the first retailer to have a new store certified as "green" by the U.S. Green Building Council (**www.usgbc.com**).

Sources: Doug Desjardins, "Hardware's New Shade of Green," *Retailing Today* (May 7, 2007), pp. 23–24; Rebecca Harris, "Turning Green," *Marketing Magazine* (June 11, 2007), pp. 18–24; and Lori Tripoli, "Corporate Profile: Home Depot: A Big-Box Store Makes Strides in Sustainability," *Sustainability: The Journal of Record* (February 2008), pp. 18–21.

▶ Minimize the time between ordering and receiving merchandise.
▶ Coordinate shipments from various suppliers.
▶ Have enough merchandise on hand to satisfy customer demand, without having so much inventory that heavy markdowns will be necessary.
▶ Place merchandise on the sales floor efficiently.
▶ Process customer orders efficiently and in a manner satisfactory to customers.
▶ Work collaboratively and communicate regularly with other supply chain members.
▶ Handle returns effectively and minimize damaged products.
▶ Monitor logistics performance.
▶ Have backup plans in case of breakdowns in the system.

At Sears, there is an entire division devoted to logistics. Sears Logistics Services (SLS) is the sole point of contact for all of the logistical activity at Sears: It "arranges the home delivery of appliances, electronics, furniture, and home improvement products from more than 2,000 Sears locations. In addition, SLS handles the transportation of apparel and other products from manufacturers' facilities to store shelves and manages other transportation and warehousing services for the Sears retail network."[11]

Bon-Ton (http://logistics.bonton.com) is very serious about maximizing its logistics performance.

The Bon-Ton department store chain has a detailed *Merchandise Logistical Standards* guide, as stated at its Web site (**http://logistics.bonton.com/pdfs/2008MerchandiseLogisticalStandards.pdf**):

> Every vendor relationship is important. As you find in any working relationship, it is critical to clearly define expectations. Product quality, shipping windows, production, and product availability are just some of the expectations that we define. Additionally, critical consideration must be given to the environmental impact (including the impact of fuel costs) of processes upon the supply chain. The management of the supply chain has become a critical role in producing higher levels of productivity, improving product flow to the selling floor, reducing inventories and overall cost reduction for both the retailer and supplier. As an organization, we have developed specific vendor and transportation requirements. These are definitive and clear expectations consistent with the standard practices prevalent throughout retailing. While critical to our mutual success, these provisions allow us to minimize costs and receive and process merchandise

in a timely cost-effective manner, thus assuring a continuous flow of merchandise to the selling floor. All suppliers (including all domestic private-brand vendors) are required to comply with the instructions, purchase order terms, and logistical and transportation standards contained here and elsewhere on our Web site.

Supply Chain Management

The **supply chain** is the logistics aspect of a value delivery chain. It comprises all of the parties that participate in the retail logistics process: manufacturers, wholesalers, third-party specialists (shippers, order-fulfillment houses, and so forth), and the retailer. For numerous links related to supply chain management, visit our Web site (**www.pearsonhighered.com/berman**).

The CPFR Committee (**www.vics.org/committees/cpfr/**) is actively working to expand the use of integrated supply chain planning.

Many retailers and suppliers are seeking closer logistical relationships. One technique for larger retailers is **collaborative planning, forecasting, and replenishment (CPFR)—** a holistic approach to supply chain management among a network of trading partners. According to the Voluntary Interindustry Commerce Standards Association, hundreds of leading manufacturers, service providers, and retailers (including Ace Hardware, Best Buy, Macy's, J.C. Penney, Safeway, Staples, Target, Walgreens, and Wal-Mart) have participated in CPFR programs. Nonetheless, CPFR has not been an unqualified success:

> CPFR is an evolving business practice that seeks to reduce supply chain costs by promoting greater integration, visibility, and cooperation between trading partners' supply chains. It represents the most encompassing, well-defined framework for enabling supply chain integration across organizational boundaries. Aligning business goals can be challenging, since this often means that business practices or processes that benefit one party must be discontinued or modified if they're not equally rewarding to a potential collaborative partner. Examples include the practice of so-called "channel stuffing," wherein a retailer is persuaded to periodically absorb larger-than-needed replenishment orders to help a supplier achieve key objectives, such as a quarterly revenue goal. In collaborative alliances, mutually agreeable metrics and shared inventory goals/targets would make such practices impractical. There are many case studies detailing the effectiveness of CPFR relationships and many examples of positive financial and intangible benefits to be gained by both trading partners. On the surface, such benefits may seem tempting, but it's also important to fully weigh the costs, implications, and requirements of engaging in CPFR relationships.[12]

Third-party logistics (outsourcing) is becoming more popular. For example, many retailers (including Internet-based firms) rely on UPS Supply Chain Solutions, a division of United Parcel Service, as their logistics specialist: "In a retail environment where it is increasingly more difficult to show a competitive advantage while maintaining profit margins, you need to focus on your retail strategy rather than deal with supply chain issues." At UPS Supply Chain Solutions, "experienced professionals work closely with retail businesses to improve service, optimize distribution and transportation networks, and streamline their global supply chains."[13] Logistics specialists work with retailers of all sizes to ship and warehouse merchandise.

Target's Partners Online program (**www.partnersonline.com**) is a proactive relationship retailing activity.

The Web is a growing force in supplier–retailer communications. A number of manufacturers and retailers have set up dedicated sites exclusively to interact with their channel partners. For confidential information exchanges, passwords and secure encryption technology are utilized. Target Corporation has a very advanced Web site called Partners Online, which took several years to develop and test. At the Web site, vendors can access sales data and inventory reports, accounts payable figures, invoices, and report cards on their performance. There are also manuals and newsletters.

Order Processing and Fulfillment

To optimize order processing and fulfillment, many firms now engage in **quick response (QR) inventory planning,** by which a retailer reduces the amount of inventory it holds by ordering more frequently and in lower quantity. A QR system requires a retailer to have good relationships with suppliers, coordinate shipments, monitor inventory levels closely to avoid stockouts, and regularly communicate with suppliers by electronic data interchange (via the Web or direct PC connections) and other means.

For the retailer, a QR system reduces inventory costs, minimizes the space required for storage, and lets the firm better match orders with market conditions—by replenishing stock more quickly. For the manufacturer, a QR system can also improve inventory turnover and better match supply and demand by giving the vendor the data to track actual sales. These data were less available in the past. In addition, an effective QR system makes it more unlikely that a retailer would switch suppliers. The most active users of QR are department stores, full-line discount stores, apparel stores, home centers, supermarkets, and drugstores. Among the firms using QR are Dillard's, Giant Food, Home Depot, Limited Brands, Macy's, J.C. Penney, Sears, Target Corporation, and Wal-Mart.

A QR system works best in conjunction with floor-ready merchandise, lower minimum order sizes, properly formatted store fixtures, and electronic data interchange (EDI). **Floor-ready merchandise** refers to items that are received at the store in condition to be put directly on display without any preparation by retail workers. For example, in this approach, apparel manufacturers are responsible for pre-ticketing garments (with information specified by the retailer) and placing them on hangers. At Bon-Ton Stores, "distribution facilities are electronically monitored by our merchandising staff to facilitate distribution of goods to our stores. We use electronic technology with most vendors, so as to move merchandise onto the selling floor quickly and cost effectively by allowing vendors to deliver floor-ready merchandise pre-labeled for individual stores. In addition, we use high-speed automated conveyor systems to scan barcoded labels on incoming cartons of merchandise and direct cartons to the proper processing areas."[14]

Quick response also means suppliers need to rethink the minimum order sizes they will accept. Although a minimum order size of 12 for a given size or color was once required by sheet and towel makers, minimum order size is now as low as 2 units. Minimum order sizes for men's shirts have been reduced from six to as few as two units. The lower order sizes have led some retailers to refixture in-store departments. Previously, fixtures were often configured on the basis of a retailer's stocking full inventories. Today, the retailer must make a visual impact with smaller inventories.

Electronic data interchange (EDI, described in Chapter 8), lets retailers do QR inventory planning efficiently—via a paperless, computer-to-computer relationship between retailers and vendors. Research suggests that retail prices could be reduced by an average of 10 percent with the industrywide usage of QR and EDI. This illustration shows the value of QR and EDI:

> What lean management does, above all else, is provide quick, flexible response to customer demand. Wal-Mart is the world's grand champion of lean supply chains. While advanced information technology gets most of the credit, collaboration is the foundation. Wal-Mart's 2,000-odd suppliers near the retailer's Bentonville, Arkansas, headquarters maintain multi-functional teams on site. Daily, along with their Wal-Mart counterparts, they work out pricing, packaging, logistics, promotions, product options, product coding, weights, and measures by sharing actual and forecast demand data, and so forth. The on-site team from each supplier must get itself together at home before it can present itself collaboratively with Wal-Mart.[15]

ECR Europe (**www.ecrnet. org**) has taken a lead role in trying to popularize this business tool.

A number of firms in the food sector of retailing are striving to use **efficient consumer response (ECR)** planning, which permits supermarkets to incorporate aspects of quick response inventory planning, electronic data interchange, and logistics planning. The goal is "to develop a responsive, consumer-driven system in which manufacturers, brokers, and distributors work together to maximize consumer value and minimize supply chain cost. To meet this goal, we need a smooth, continual product flow matched to consumer consumption. And to support the flow of products, we need timely, accurate data flowing through a paperless system between the retail checkout and the manufacturing line."[16] Although ECR has enabled supermarkets to cut tens of billions of dollars in distribution costs, applying it has not been easy. Many supermarkets are still unwilling to trade their ability to negotiate short-term purchase terms with vendors in return for routine order fulfillment without special deals.

Retailers are also addressing two other aspects of order processing and fulfillment. (1) With *advanced ship notices,* retailers that utilize QR and EDI receive an alert when bills of lading are sent electronically as soon as a shipment leaves the vendor. This gives the retailers more time to efficiently receive and allocate merchandise. (2) Because more retailers are buying from multiple suppliers, from multi-location sources, and from overseas, they must better coordinate order placement and fulfillment. Home Depot, among others, has added an import logistics group to coordinate overseas forecasting, ordering, sourcing, and logistics. Supervalu is dealing with its practice of buying products from so many different countries around the globe.

Sometimes, the order-processing-and-fulfillment process can be quite challenging:

> Tony Stallone works for Peapod, an online grocery-delivery service, near Chicago. His title is vice-president of perishables, so for him a delicate strawberry has value beyond measure. "This is the most important item we sell. If customers receive mushy strawberries, they may never shop with us again." Online grocers have to work so hard to win new customers that any slipup— one bad strawberry, one late delivery—could send the recipient back to the store down the street.[17]

Transportation and Warehousing

Several transportation decisions are necessary:

- ▶ How often will merchandise be shipped to the retailer?
- ▶ How will small order quantities be handled?
- ▶ What shipper will be used (the manufacturer, the retailer, or a third-party specialist)?
- ▶ What transportation form will be used? Are multiple forms required (such as manufacturer trucks to retailer warehouses and retailer trucks to individual stores)?
- ▶ What are the special considerations for perishables and expensive merchandise?
- ▶ How often will special shipping arrangements be necessary (such as rush orders)?
- ▶ How are shipping terms negotiated with suppliers?
- ▶ What delivery options will be available for the retailer's customers? This is a critical decision for nonstore retailers, especially those selling through the Web.

 **TECHNOLOGY IN RETAILING** | 99 Cents Only Stores: Optimizing Logistics

99 Cents Only Stores (**www.99only.com**) is the nation's oldest existing one-price retailer. This retailer operates about 250 stores in California, Nevada, Arizona, and Texas. Unlike other retailers that sell a consistent product mix over time, 99 Cents Only Stores purchases many of its goods on an opportunistic basis. Often, goods are one-time purchases due to bankruptcies, cancelled orders, oversupplies at vendors, and even products that have been discontinued during test markets. The high amount of opportunistic purchases complicates the inventory management process.

99 Cents Only Stores uses HighJump's Warehouse Advantage WMS system (**www.highjumpsoftware.com**) to control inventory movement from the time the products enter its warehouse until they leave. Voice-picking software, which is an important part of the system, provides specific voice-picking directions to the retailer's warehouse personnel as to which goods need to be chosen and where these goods can be found. Once picked, goods are separated into one of 20 lanes that are set up for specific stores. After going through this sorting operation, an item's inventory status is changed to "picked."

After sorting, HighJump's Yard Advantage yard management software keeps track of inventory on each delivery truck. This system component gives 99 Cents Only Stores' store managers information about late shipments via exception reports.

Source: "99 Cents Only Stores: Discount Retailer Drives Expansion with Solutions from HighJunp Software," **www.highjumpsoftware.com/ FinalDocsLibrary** (September 15, 2008).

Transportation effectiveness is influenced by the caliber of the logistics infrastructure (including access to refrigerated trucks, airports, waterway docking, and superhighways), traffic congestion, parking, and other factors. Retailers operating outside the United States must come to grips with the logistical problems in many foreign countries, where the transportation network and the existence of modern technology may be severely lacking.

With regard to warehousing, some retailers focus on warehouses as central or regional distribution centers. Products are sent from suppliers to these warehouses, and then they are allotted and shipped to individual stores. Claire's Stores has its central buying and store operations offices, as well as its North American distribution center, in Hoffman Estates, Illinois. The distribution facility occupies 373,000 square feet of space. See Figure 15-10. Toys "R" Us has separate regional distribution centers for U.S. Toys "R" Us stores and its international Toys "R" Us stores. Most centers are owned; some are leased.

HighJump (www.highjump.com) offers integrated "Direct Store Delivery" software.

Other retailers, including many supermarket chains, do not rely as much on central or regional warehouses. Instead, they have at least some goods shipped right from suppliers to individual stores through **direct store distribution (DSD)**. This approach works best with retailers that also utilize EDI. It is a way to move high turnover, high bulk, perishable products from the manufacturer directly to the store. The items most apt to involve DSD (such as beverages, bread, and snack foods) have an average shelf life of 60 days or less, while warehoused items have an average shelf life of one year or more. About one-quarter of the typical supermarket's sales are from items with DSD.[18]

The advantages of central warehousing are the efficiency in transportation and storage, mechanized processing of goods, improved security, efficient merchandise marking, ease of returns, and coordinated merchandise flow. Key disadvantages are the excessive centralized control, extra handling of perishables, high costs for small retailers, and potential ordering delays. Centralized warehousing may also reduce the capability of QR systems by adding another step. These are the pros and cons of DSD:

Logistics managers constantly find themselves between a rock and a hard place, trying to balance customer service with the demands of chief financial officers for lower inventories and operating costs. Those demands are multiplied many times over when the products involved are perishable or have a limited shelf life due to other concerns. To get those products to market in a timely manner to avoid spoilage, the most practical answer is the implementation of direct store-delivery. However, DSD does not come without a price. One expert says: "There's no doubt that DSD, in terms of perishables, is the most efficient way to maximize the residual shelf life of a product. Without maximizing residual shelf life, you end up either throwing away product or losing sales. It's also adding to your total costs." Another expert notes that "It's a high-cost system, but you're managing your brand and adding value to that brand. There's a trade-off between cost and control."[19]

FIGURE 15-10

Claire's Aggressive Use of Central Warehousing
Claire's Stores has a central warehouse in Hoffman Estates, Illinois. The mammoth warehouse has been designed to accommodate a second level and can support up to 6,000 stores. At present, the firm operates 3,000 shops, mostly in shopping malls. They sell inexpensive jewelry and accessories for girls. Its stores include Claire's and Icing by Claire's.

Source: Reprinted by permission of Claire's Stores, Inc.

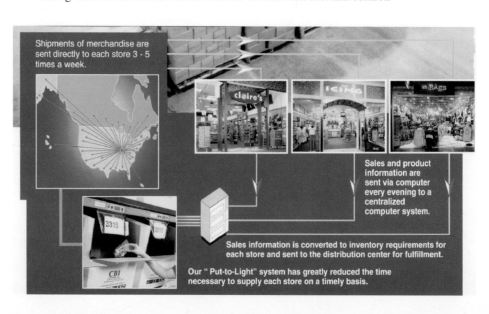

Customer Transactions and Customer Service

Retailers must plan for outbound logistics (as well as inbound logistics): completing transactions by turning over merchandise to customers. This can be as simple as having a shopper take an item from a display area to the checkout counter or driving his or her car to a loading area. It can also be as complex as concluding a Web transaction that entails shipments from multiple vendors to the customer. A shopper's purchase of a computer, a fax machine, and an answering machine from Buy.com may result in three separate shipments. That is why UPS, Federal Express, and others are doing more home deliveries. They can readily handle the diversity of shipping requests that retailers often cannot.

Even basic deliveries can have a breakdown. Think of the local pharmacy whose high school delivery person fails to come to work one day—or the pizzeria that gets no customer orders between 2:00 P.M. and 5:00 P.M. and 25 delivery orders between 5:00 P.M. and 7:00 P.M.

There are considerable differences between store-based and nonstore retailers. Most retail stores know that the customer wants to take the purchase or to pick it up when it is ready (such as a new car). All direct marketers, including Web retailers, are responsible for ensuring that products are delivered to the shopper's door or another convenient nearby location.

Customer service expectations are affected by logistical effectiveness. That is why Amazon.com emphasizes excellent logistics: "Our supply chain is designed to be as efficient as possible so we can have the widest variety of products available for immediate shipment to customers all over the world. And technology plays a pivotal role in ensuring a great customer experience, especially during the holiday season when having products arrive on time is critical."[20]

Inventory Management

As part of its logistics efforts, a retailer utilizes **inventory management** to acquire and maintain a proper merchandise assortment while ordering, shipping, handling, storing, displaying, and selling costs are kept in check. First, a retailer places an order based on a sales forecast or actual customer behavior. Both the number of items and their variety are requested when ordering. Order size and frequency depend on quantity discounts and inventory costs. Second, a supplier fills the order and sends merchandise to a warehouse or directly to the store(s). Third, the retailer receives products, makes items available for sale (by removing them from packing, marking prices, and placing them on the sales floor), and completes customer transactions. Some transactions are not concluded until items are delivered to the customer. The cycle starts anew as a retailer places another order. Let's look at these aspects of inventory management: retailer tasks, inventory levels, merchandise security, reverse logistics, and inventory analysis.

Retailer Tasks

Due to the comprehensive nature of inventory management, and to be more cost-effective, some retailers now expect suppliers to perform more tasks, or they outsource at least part of their inventory management activities: "In 1990, producers shipped products to retailers in a *warehouse-ready* mode. Retailers then reprocessed merchandise to package and price it for sale in the store where consumers make purchases. Today, in the era of *floor-ready,* producers ship products that have already been packaged and prepared for immediate movement to the sales floor. In the future, there will be a shift to *consumer-ready* manufacturing where the links between producer and consumer are even more direct than traditionally."[21] Here are some examples:

▶ Wal-Mart and other retailers count on key suppliers to participate in their inventory management programs. Industrywide, this practice is known as **vendor-managed inventory (VMI)**.[22] Procter & Gamble even has its own employees stationed at Wal-Mart headquarters to manage the inventory replenishment of that manufacturer's products.

The National Association for Retailing Merchandising Services offers a national online "JobBank" (www.narms.com/jobbank.html) by category and job location.

▶ Target Corporation is at the forefront of another trend—store retailers outsourcing customer order fulfillment for their online businesses. Through its arrangement with Amazon.com, Target.com offers shoppers a patented one-click online shopping experience: "Powered by Amazon.com, 1-Click Ordering is the fastest, easiest way to place most orders. This convenient tool is turned on immediately after you place your first credit card order. You can place an order to any address you've shipped to before by clicking just one button. We will automatically reference your account for shipping and billing information."[23]

▶ According to the National Association for Retail Merchandising Services (**www.narms.com**), more than $3 billion in retail merchandising services—ranging from reordering to display design—are annually provided by specialized firms. One specialist is New Concepts in Marketing, which provides ordering and inventory control, promotional selling, display placement, and other such services for such clients as Babies "R" Us, Kmart, Publix, and Sam's Clubs.

One contentious inventory management activity involves who is responsible for source tagging, the manufacturer or the retailer. In *source tagging,* anti-theft tags are put on items when they are produced, rather than at the store. Although both sides agree on the benefits of this, in terms of the reduced costs and the floor-readiness of merchandise, there are disagreements about who should pay for the tags.

Inventory Levels

Having the proper inventory on hand is a difficult balancing act:

1. The retailer wants to be appealing and never lose a sale by being out of stock. Yet, it does not want to be "stuck" with excess merchandise that must be marked down drastically.
2. The situation is more complicated for retailers that carry fad merchandise, that handle new items for which there is no track record, and that operate in new business formats where demand estimates are often inaccurate. Thus, inventory levels must be planned in relation to the products involved: staples, assortment merchandise, fashion merchandise, fads, and best-sellers.
3. Customer demand is *never* completely predictable—even for staple items. Weather, special sales, and other factors can have an impact on even the most stable items.
4. Shelf space allocations should be linked to current revenues, which means that allocations must be regularly reviewed and adjusted.

RETAILING AROUND THE WORLD — Dealing with Overloaded U.S. Ports of Entry

The Los Angeles–Long Beach ports are favored by importers because they are equipped to handle large freighters that can hold more than 4,000 containers. These two ports handle about 40 percent of all U.S. container trade. Many of these freighters are too big to pass through the Panama Canal to Eastern seaports.

Two key factors have the potential to dramatically reduce trucking capacity from shippers using Los Angeles–Long Beach ports: a worker identification program and the clean truck program. The Coast Guard (**www.uscg.mil**) intended to make the federal government's Transportation Worker Identification Credential program (TWIC) mandatory in 2008. This program, which affects all U.S. ports, could result in a loss of thousands of drivers who will not be able to establish legal residency, which is a requirement for obtaining the TWIC card. In addition, southern California's clean truck program will ban all trucks made in 1989 or earlier from the harbor. An estimate is that about 2,700 of the 16,800 trucks used in Los Angeles–Long Beach ports will be banned.

One forecast is that the combined effect of these two factors will be to reduce harbor capacity by about 25 percent. As a result, many shippers will have to choose longer routes to the United States. This would substantially increase the transportation and inventory requirements for many retailers.

Source: Bill Mongelluzzo, "SoCal Tricking Squeeze," *Traffic World* (April 28, 2008), p. 32.

One of the advantages of QR and EDI is that retailers hold "leaner" inventories because they receive new merchandise more often. Yet, when merchandise is especially popular or the supply chain breaks down, stockouts may still occur. A Food Marketing Institute study found that even supermarkets, which carry more staples than most other retailers, lose 3 percent of sales due to out-of-stock goods.

This illustration shows just how tough inventory management can be:

Longo Brothers Fruit Markets (**www.longos.com**) is a family-owned, full-service chain of 16 grocery stores in the Toronto area, complete with fresh produce, large butcher areas, and other offerings. Managing inventory is a key to profitability for Longo's, as it is with other grocery store chains. Longo's tried to control inventory through its enterprise resource planning system, but encountered numerous problems: "The solution we had had a lot of issues with data integrity. We have a lot of different systems within the company, and it's important to maintain the integrity of the data between the different applications." For example, shelf pricing and register pricing are contained in two different applications, but changes on the shelf (such as short-term sales) weren't always reflected accurately at the cash register, leading to price checks, longer waits in line, and dissatisfied customers. The inventory system wasn't integrated either, causing the stores to run out of stock. That problem was aggravated by the chain's online ordering system, which allows customers to order over the Internet and receive goods shipped directly from a store, not from a central warehouse. Company officials decided to purchase Tomax software, designed to integrate different systems to provide a comprehensive management system. Now all Longo's has to do is enter price changes one time and the system automatically coordinates shelf and register (and online) pricing. Similarly, when a customer buys an item, the inventory adjusts, helping to minimize the chances of running out.[24]

Inventory level planning is discussed further in the next chapter.

Merchandise Security

Each year, $40 billion in U.S. retail sales—and about $105 billion worldwide—are lost due to **inventory shrinkage** caused by employee theft, customer shoplifting, vendor fraud, and administrative errors. Of the U.S. amount, employees account for 46 percent, customers 34 percent, vendors 5 percent, and administrative errors (faulty paperwork and computer entries) 15 percent. As the figures show, employee theft is much higher than shopper theft.[25] Shrinkage typically ranges from under 1 percent of sales to more than 3 percent of sales at retail stores. This means a small store with $500,000 in annual sales might lose up to $15,000 or more due to shrinkage, and a large store with $3 million in sales might lose up to $90,000 or more due to shrinkage. Thus, some form of merchandise security is needed by all retailers.

To reduce merchandise theft, there are three key points to consider: (1) Loss prevention measures should be incorporated as stores are designed and built. The placement of entrances, dressing rooms, and delivery areas is critical. (2) A combination of security measures should be enacted, such as employee background checks, in-store guards, electronic security equipment, and merchandise tags. (3) Retailers must communicate the importance of loss prevention to employees, customers, and vendors—and the actions they are prepared to take to reduce losses (such as firing workers and prosecuting shoplifters).

Here are some activities that are reducing losses from merchandise theft:

▶ Product tags, guards, video cameras, point-of-sale computers, employee surveillance, and burglar alarms are being used by more firms. Storefront protection is also popular.

Sensormatic (**www. sensormatic.com**) is a leader in electronic security.

▶ Many general merchandise retailers and some supermarkets use **electronic article surveillance**—whereby special tags are attached to products so that the tags can be sensed by electronic security devices at store exits. If the tags are not removed by store personnel or desensitized by scanning equipment, an alarm goes off. Retailers also have access to nonelectronic tags. These are snugly attached to products and

FIGURE 15-11

Sensormatic: The Leader in Store Security Systems
These aesthetically pleasing, acrylic pedestals (part of Sensormatic's Euro Pro Max system) provide an unobstructed vision of exits, as well as the ultimate electronic article surveillance system. An alarm goes off if a person tries to leave a store without a product's security tag being properly removed.

Source: Reprinted by permission of Sensormatic Electronics Corporation.

must be removed by special detachers; otherwise products are unusable. Dye tags permanently stain products, if not removed properly. See Figure 15-11.

▶ A number of retailers do detailed background checks for each prospective new employee. Some use loss prevention software that detects suspicious employee behavior.

▶ Various retailers have employee training programs and offer incentives for reducing merchandise losses. Others use written policies on ethical behavior that are signed by all personnel, including senior management. Target has enrolled managers at problem stores in a Stock Shortage Institute. Neiman Marcus has shown workers a film with interviews of convicted shoplifters in prison to highlight the problem's seriousness.

▶ More retailers are apt to fire employees and prosecute shoplifters involved with theft. Courts are imposing stiffer penalties; in some areas, store detectives are empowered by police to make arrests. In more than 40 states, there are civil restitution laws; shoplifters must pay for stolen goods or face arrests and criminal trials. In most states, fines are higher if goods are not returned or are damaged. Shoplifters must also contribute to court costs.

▶ Some mystery shoppers are hired to watch for shoplifting, not just to research behavior.

Figure 15-12 presents a list of tactics retailers can use to combat employee and shopper theft, by far the leading causes of losses.

When devising a merchandise security plan, a retailer must assess the plan's impact on its image, employee morale, shopper comfort, and vendor relations. By setting strict rules for fitting rooms (by limiting the number of garments) or placing chains on very expensive coats, a retailer may cause some shoppers to avoid this merchandise—or visit another store.

Reverse Logistics

The term **reverse logistics** encompasses all merchandise flows from the customer and/or the retailer back through the supply channel. It typically involves items returned because of shopper second thoughts, damaged or defective products, or retailer over-stocking. In the United States, customer returns alone are estimated by the National Retail Federation at about 9 percent of total retail sales. Sometimes, retailers may use closeout firms that buy back unpopular merchandise (at a fraction of the original cost) that suppliers will not take back; these firms then resell the goods at a deep discount. To avoid channel conflicts, the conditions for reverse logistics should be specified in

FIGURE 15-12

Ways Retailers Can Deter Employee and Shopper Theft

A. Employee Theft

- Use honesty tests as employee screening devices.
- Lock up trash to prevent merchandise from being thrown out and then retrieved.
- Verify through cameras and undercover personnel whether all sales are rung up.
- Centrally control all exterior doors to monitor opening and closing.
- Divide responsibilities—have one employee record sales and another make deposits.
- Give rewards for spotting thefts.
- Have training programs.
- Vigorously investigate all known losses and fire offenders immediately.

B. Shopper Theft While Store Is Open

- Use uniformed guards.
- Set up cameras and mirrors to increase visibility—especially in low-traffic areas.
- Use electronic article surveillance for high-value and theft-prone goods.
- Develop comprehensive employee training programs.
- Offer employee bonuses based on an overall reduction in shortages.
- Inspect all packages brought into store.
- Use self-locking showcases for high-value items such as jewelry.
- Attach expensive clothing together.
- Alternate the direction of hangers on clothing near doors.
- Limit the number of entrances and exits to the store, and the dollar value and quantity of merchandise displayed near exits.
- Prosecute all individuals charged with theft.

C. Employee/Shopper Theft While Store Is Closed

- Conduct a thorough building check at night to make sure no one is left in store.
- Lock all exits, even fire exits.
- Utilize ultrasonic/infrared detectors, burglar alarm traps, or guards with dogs.
- Place valuables in a safe.
- Install shatterproof glass and/or iron gates on windows and doors to prevent break-ins.
- Make sure exterior lighting is adequate.
- Periodically test burglar alarms.

advance. U.S. firms spend $50 billion per year for the handling, transportation, and processing costs associated with returns.[26]

These are among the decisions that must be made for reverse logistics:

▶ Under what conditions (the permissible time, the condition of the product, and so forth) are customer returns accepted by the retailer and by the manufacturer?

▶ What is the customer refund policy? Is there a fee for returning an opened package?

▶ What party is responsible for shipping a returned product to the manufacturer?

▶ What customer documentation is needed to prove the date of purchase and the price paid?

▶ How are customer repairs handled (an immediate exchange, a third-party repair, or a refurbished product sent by the manufacturer)?

▶ To what extent are employees empowered to process customer returns?

The Reverse Logistics Association (www.reverselogisticstrends.com) presents a lot of good information on this topic at its Web site.

Inventory Analysis

Inventory status and performance must be analyzed regularly to gauge the success of inventory management. Recent advances in computer software have made such analysis much more accurate and timely. See Figure 15-13. According to surveys of retailers, these

FIGURE 15-13

Inventory Management with Everest Software

As Everest Software, Inc. (**www.everestsoftwareinc.com**) says at its Web site: "Keeping inventory management costs down is crucial to any business. Everest provides your business with real-time inventory management that allows you to operate your business efficiently. Inventory details are kept up to date for all your sales channels including Web, retail, and distribution so your sales team can promise orders confidently and provide excellent service to your customers."

Source: Reprinted by permission of Everest Software, Inc.

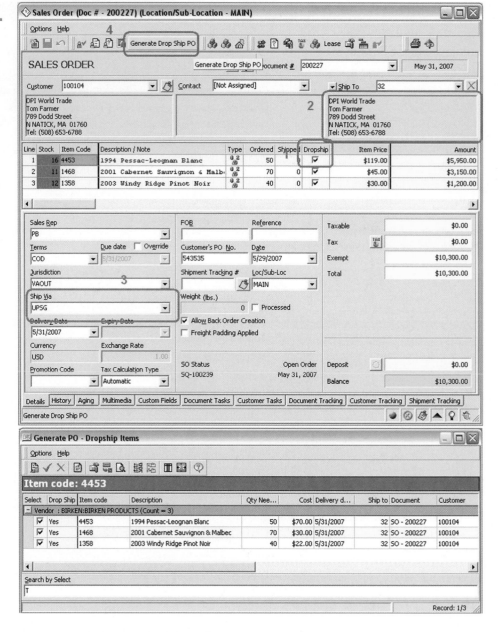

are the elements of inventory performance that are deemed most important: gross margin dollars, inventory turnover, gross profit percentage, gross margin return on inventory, the weeks of supply available, and the average in-stock position.

Inventory analysis is discussed further in the next chapter.

Chapter **Summary**

1. *To describe the steps in the implementation of merchandise plans.* (a) Information is gathered about target market needs and prospective suppliers. Data about shopper needs can come from customers, suppliers, personnel, competitors, and others. A want book (want slip) is helpful. To acquire information about suppliers, the retailer can talk to prospects, attend trade shows, visit merchandise marts, and search the Web.

(b) The retailer chooses firm-owned; outside, regularly used; and/or outside, new supply sources. Relationships may become strained with suppliers because their goals differ from those of retailers.

(c) The merchandise under consideration is evaluated by inspection, sampling, and/or description. The method depends on the product and situation.

(d) Purchase terms may be negotiated (as with opportunistic buying) or uniform contracts may be used. Terms must be clear, including the delivery date, quantity purchased, price and payment arrangements, discounts, form of delivery, and point of transfer. There may also be special provisions.

(e) The purchase is concluded automatically or manually. Sometimes, management approval is needed. The transfer of title may take place as soon as the order is shipped or not until after merchandise is sold by the retailer.

(f) Handling involves receiving and storing, price and inventory marking, displays, floor stocking, customer transactions, delivery or pickup, returns and damaged goods, monitoring pilferage, and control. RFID (radio frequency identification) is an emerging technology in this area.

(g) Reorder procedures depend on order and delivery time, inventory turnover, financial outlays, and inventory versus ordering costs.

(h) Both the overall merchandising procedure and specific goods and services must be reviewed.

2. *To examine the prominent roles of logistics and inventory management in the implementation of merchandise plans.* Logistics includes planning, implementing, and coordinating the movement of merchandise from supplier to retailer to customer. Logistics goals are to relate costs to activities, accurately place and receive orders, minimize ordering/receiving time, coordinate shipments, have proper merchandise levels, place merchandise on the sales floor, process customer orders, work well in the supply chain, handle returns effectively and minimize damaged goods, monitor performance, and have backup plans.

A supply chain covers all parties in the logistics process. Collaborative planning, forecasting, and replenishment (CPFR) uses a holistic approach. Third-party logistics is more popular than before. Many manufacturers and retailers have Web sites to interact with channel partners.

Some retailers engage in QR inventory planning. Floor-ready merchandise is received at the store ready to be displayed. EDI lets retailers use QR planning through computerized supply chain relationships. Numerous supermarkets use efficient consumer response. Several transportation decisions are needed, as are warehousing choices. Certain retailers have goods shipped by direct store distribution. Retailers must also plan outbound logistics: completing transactions by turning over merchandise to the customer.

As part of logistics, a retailer uses inventory management. Due to its complexity, and to reduce costs, retailers may expect suppliers to perform more tasks or they may outsource some inventory activities. Vendor-managed inventory (VMI) is growing in popularity.

Having the proper inventory is a balancing act: The retailer does not want to lose sales due to being out of stock. It also does not want to be stuck with excess merchandise. Each year, $40 billion in U.S. retail sales are lost due to employee theft, customer shoplifting, vendor fraud, and administrative errors. Many retailers use electronic article surveillance, with special tags attached to products.

Reverse logistics involves all merchandise flows from the customer and/or the retailer back through a supply channel. It includes returns due to damages, defects, or poor retail sales.

Inventory performance must be analyzed regularly.

Key Terms

want book (want slip) (p. 413)
chargebacks (p. 415)
opportunistic buying (p. 417)
slotting allowances (p. 417)
consignment purchase (p. 418)
memorandum purchase (p. 418)
RFID (radio frequency identification) (p. 419)
logistics (p. 422)
supply chain (p. 425)
collaborative planning, forecasting, and replenishment (CPFR) (p. 425)
quick response (QR) inventory planning (p. 425)
floor-ready merchandise (p. 426)
efficient consumer response (ECR) (p. 426)
direct store distribution (DSD) (p. 428)
inventory management (p. 429)
vendor-managed inventory (VMI) (p. 429)
inventory shrinkage (p. 431)
electronic article surveillance (p. 431)
reverse logistics (p. 432)

Questions for Discussion

1. What information should a department store gather before adding a new women's apparel brand to its product mix?

2. What are the pros and cons of a retailer's relying too much on a want book?

3. Cite the advantages and disadvantages associated with these merchandise sources for your regular gift store. How would your answers differ for a local watch store?
   a. Company-owned.
   b. Outside, regularly used.
   c. Outside, new.

4. Devise a checklist a retailer could use to negotiate opportunistic buying terms with suppliers.

5. Under what circumstances should a retailer try to charge slotting allowances? How may this strategy backfire?

6. Which is more difficult, implementing a merchandise plan for a small deli or Wal-Mart? Explain your answer.

7. Distinguish between these two terms: *logistics* and *inventory management*. Give an example of each.

8. What are the benefits of quick response inventory planning? What do you think are the risks?

9. Why are some retailers convinced that distribution centers must be used as the shipping points for merchandise from manufacturers while other retailers favor direct store distribution?

10. How could a neighborhood drugstore be prepared for the variations in customer demand for home delivery during the day?

11. What is vendor-managed inventory? How do both manufacturers and retailers benefit from its use?

12. Present a seven-item checklist for a retailer to use with its reverse logistics.

Web **Exercise**

Visit the "Retail Industry Solutions" section of the Federal Express Web site (www.fedex.com/us/supplychain/industrysolutions/retail.html). Describe the services that it offers for retailers. What are the benefits of a retailer's using FedEx Supply Chain Services?

Note: Stop by our Web site (www.pearsonhighered.com/berman) to experience a number of highly interactive, appealing Web exercises based on actual company demonstrations and sample materials related to retailing.

16

Financial Merchandise Management

eBay (**www.ebay.com**) was founded in 1995 by Pierre Omidyar as a place for his girlfriend to trade Pez dispensers with fellow collectors. In its first years under Omidyar, eBay quickly grew by popularizing the online auction environment for a host of goods.

In 1998, Meg Whitman took over as eBay's chief executive. Under Whitman, more goods were sold at fixed prices, new categories of merchandise were added, and large retailers began selling goods at their own online eBay stores. John Donahue assumed the role of chief executive March 31, 2008. Using data from the most recent 12-month period, eBay has approximately 85 million active users who bid on, buy, or list an item.

Even though eBay sells only a small fraction as much as Wal-Mart, the difference in the two firms' operations is dramatic. Wal-Mart relies on 143 distribution centers, numerous trucks, thousands of stores, and 2.1 million worldwide employees (1.4 million in the United States). In comparison, eBay has about 15,500 employees worldwide (including temporary employees), about 9,500 of whom are based in the United States. And unlike Wal-Mart, eBay does not take title to or possession of a single item. eBay earns its profits by charging sellers a placement fee to list items for sale, an extra fee to highlight "Featured Auction" items, and a success fee if a transaction is made. Some retailing analysts cite Wal-Mart as the model of the modern, centralized mass marketer, while eBay is the model of the decentralized, virtual marketing company.[1]

Source: Reprinted by permission of Susan Berry, Retail Image Consulting, Inc.

OVERVIEW

Sage Accpac (www.
sageaccpac.com/products/
accounting) is one of many
firms that offer integrated
accounting software that is
widely used by retailers.

Through **financial merchandise management,** a retailer specifies which products
(goods and services) are purchased, when products are purchased, and how
many products are purchased. **Dollar control** involves planning and monitoring
a retailer's financial investment in merchandise over a stated period. **Unit control**
relates to the quantities of merchandise a retailer handles during a stated period.
The dollar investment is determined before assortment decisions are made.

Well-structured financial merchandise plans offer these benefits:

▶ The value and amount of inventory in each department and/or store unit
during a given period are delineated. Stock is balanced, and fewer markdowns may be necessary.

▶ The amount of merchandise (in terms of investment) a buyer can purchase
during a given period is stipulated. This gives a buyer direction.

▶ The inventory investment in relation to planned and actual revenues is
studied. This improves the return on investment.

▶ The retailer's space requirements are partly determined by estimating
beginning-of-month and end-of-month inventory levels.

▶ A buyer's performance is rated. Various measures may be used to set standards.

▶ Stock shortages are determined, and bookkeeping errors and pilferage are
uncovered.

▶ Slow-moving items are classified—leading to increased sales efforts or markdowns.

▶ A proper balance between inventory and out-of-stock conditions is maintained.

Yet, "many companies suffer from poor inventory control which leads to inefficiency and wasted expenditures on goods that sit on the shelf." With the right
software and techniques, a firm "can optimize inventory levels, eliminate stockouts, increase sales, and squeeze the most out of a supply chain."[2]

This chapter divides financial merchandise management into four areas:
methods of accounting, merchandise forecasting and budgeting, unit control systems, and financial inventory control. The hypothetical Handy Hardware Store
illustrates the concepts.

Inventory Valuation: The Cost and Retail Methods of Accounting

This site (www.ssinet.com/
accounting/docs/imcd.pdf)
has an excellent guide on
inventory management.

Retail inventory accounting systems can be complex because they entail a great deal of data
(due to the number of items sold). A typical retailer's dollar control system must provide
such data as the sales and purchases made by that firm during a budget period, the value of
beginning and ending inventory, markups and markdowns, and merchandise shortages.

Table 16-1 shows a profit-and-loss statement for Handy Hardware Store for the period
from January 1, 2009, through June 30, 2009. The sales amount represents total receipts
over this time. Beginning inventory was computed by counting the merchandise in stock
on January 1, 2009—recorded at cost. Purchases (at cost) and transportation charges (costs
incurred in shipping items from suppliers to the retailer) were derived by adding the
invoice slips for all merchandise bought by Handy in the period.

Together, beginning inventory, purchases, and transportation charges equal the cost of
merchandise available for sale. The **cost of goods sold** equals the cost of merchandise
available for sale minus the cost value of ending inventory. Sales less cost of goods sold
yields **gross profit,** while **net profit** is gross profit minus retail operating expenses.
Because Handy does a physical inventory twice yearly, ending inventory was figured by
counting the items in stock on June 30, 2009—recorded at cost (Handy codes each item).

Retailers have different data needs than manufacturers. Assortments are larger. Costs
cannot be printed on cartons unless coded (due to customer inspection). Stock shortages
are higher. Sales are more frequent. Retailers require monthly, not quarterly, profit data.

TABLE 16-1 **Handy Hardware Store Profit-and-Loss Statement, January 1, 2009–June 30, 2009**

Sales		$417,460
Less cost of goods sold:		
Beginning inventory (at cost)	$ 44,620	
Purchases (at cost)	289,400	
Transportation charges	2,600	
Merchandise available for sale	$336,620	
Ending inventory (at cost)	90,500	
Cost of goods sold		246,120
Gross profit		$171,340
Less operating expenses:		
Salaries	$ 70,000	
Advertising	25,000	
Rental	16,000	
Other	26,000	
Total operating expenses		137,000
Net profit before taxes		$ 34,340

Two inventory accounting systems are available: (1) The cost accounting system values merchandise at cost plus inbound transportation charges. (2) The retail accounting system values merchandise at current retail prices. Let's study both methods in terms of the frequency with which data are obtained, the difficulties of a physical inventory and record keeping, the ease of settling insurance claims (if there is inventory damage), the extent to which shortages can be computed, and system complexities.

CAREERS IN RETAILING

Is Retail for Me? Distribution, Logistics, and Supply Chain Management

The logistics retail career area oversees the movement and storage of consumer products. Responsibilities include the management and facilitation of distribution centers, logistics traffic management, trucking, and other transportation operations. It may also include import/export shipping and related duties.

Here are three management-level jobs in logistics:

▶ *Head of (Physical) Distribution and Logistics.* Top executive position over all domestic distribution centers and logistics traffic management. May have some trucking operations for merchandise movement to and among stores. May handle import/export shipping.

▶ *Distribution Center Manager.* This position manages one distribution center in a firm with two or more centers. Typically will not supervise a full traffic

department function, because distribution is centrally run.

▶ *Traffic Manager (Head of Transport Logistics).* This position is responsible for selecting trucking firms, negotiating carrier rates, and managing inbound/outbound shipments in the United States. May be responsible for overseas merchandise only after it clears Customs. Does not run a distribution center. Variations to job description: (a) Position is generally as described; or (b) Doesn't negotiate the trucking contracts, just administers the shipping, damage claims, and carrier billings; or (c) Also handles overseas shipping and clearing goods through U.S. Customs.

Source: Reprinted by permission of the National Retail Federation.

At our Web site (**www.pearsonhighered.com/berman**), there are a number of links related to retail accounting and inventory valuation, including several from the Internal Revenue Service.

The Cost Method

With the **cost method of accounting,** the cost to the retailer of each item is recorded on an accounting sheet and/or is coded on a price tag or merchandise container. As a physical inventory is done, item costs must be learned, the quantity of every item in stock counted, and total inventory value at cost calculated. One way to code merchandise cost is to use a 10-letter equivalency system, such as M = 0, N = 1, O = 2, P = 3, Q = 4, R = 5, S = 6, T = 7, U = 8, and V = 9. An item coded with STOP has a cost value of $67.23. This technique is useful as an accounting tool and for retailers that allow price bargaining by customers (profit per item is easy to compute).

A retailer can use the cost method as it does physical or book inventories. A physical inventory means an actual merchandise count; a book inventory relies on record keeping.

A PHYSICAL INVENTORY SYSTEM USING THE COST METHOD

In a **physical inventory system**, ending inventory—recorded at cost—is measured by counting the merchandise in stock at the close of a selling period. Gross profit is not computed until ending inventory is valued. A retailer using the cost method along with a physical inventory system derives gross profit only as often as it performs a full merchandise count. Because most firms do so just once or twice yearly, a physical inventory system alone imposes limits on planning. In addition, a firm might be unable to compute inventory shortages (due to pilferage and unrecorded breakage) because ending inventory value is set by adding the costs of all items in stock. It does not compute what the ending inventory *should be.*

A BOOK INVENTORY SYSTEM USING THE COST METHOD

Retail ICE software facilitates perpetual inventory calculations (**www.retailice.com/demo/ purchasing.htm**).

A **book (perpetual) inventory system** avoids the problem of infrequent financial analysis by keeping a running total of the value of all inventory on hand at cost at a given time. End-of-month inventory values can be computed without a physical inventory, and frequent financial statements can be prepared. In addition, a book inventory lets a retailer uncover stock shortages by comparing projected inventory values with actual inventory values through a physical inventory.[3]

A book inventory is kept by regularly recording purchases and adding them to existing inventory value; sales are subtracted to arrive at the new current inventory value (all at cost). Table 16-2 shows Handy Hardware's book inventory system for July 1, 2009, through December 31, 2009; the beginning inventory in Table 16-2 is the ending inventory from Table 16-1. Table 16-2 assumes that merchandise costs are rather constant and monthly sales at cost are easy to compute. Yet, suppose merchandise costs rise. How would inventory value then be computed?

TABLE 16-2 **Handy Hardware Store Perpetual Inventory System, July 1, 2009–December 31, 2009[a]**

Date	Beginning-of-Month Inventory (at Cost)	+	Net Monthly Purchases (at Cost)	−	Monthly Sales (at Cost)	=	End-of-Month Inventory (at Cost)
7/1/09	$90,500		$ 40,000		$ 62,400		$ 68,100
8/1/09	68,100		28,000		38,400		57,700
9/1/09	57,700		27,600		28,800		56,500
10/1/09	56,500		44,000		28,800		71,700
11/1/09	71,700		50,400		40,800		81,300
12/1/09	81,300		15,900		61,200		36,000
		Total	$205,900		$260,400		(as of 12/31/09)

[a]Transportation charges are not included in computing inventory value in this table.

At its Web site, SourceCorp provides good background information on LIFO (www.lifochannel. com).

FIFO and LIFO are two ways to value inventory. The **FIFO (first-in-first-out) method** logically assumes old merchandise is sold first, while newer items remain in inventory. The **LIFO (last-in-first-out) method** assumes new merchandise is sold first, while older stock remains in inventory. FIFO matches inventory value with the current cost structure—the goods in inventory are the ones bought most recently, while LIFO matches current sales with the current cost structure—the goods sold first are the ones bought most recently. When inventory values rise, LIFO offers retailers a tax advantage because lower profits are shown.

In Figure 16-1, the FIFO and LIFO methods are illustrated for Handy Hardware's snow blowers for 2009; the store carries only one model of snow blower. Handy knows that it sold 220 snow blowers in 2009 at an average price of $320. It began 2009 with an inventory of 30 snow blowers, purchased for $150 each. During January 2009, it bought 100 snow blowers at $175 each; from October to December 2009, Handy bought another 150 snow blowers for $225 apiece. Because Handy sold 220 snow blowers in 2009, as of the close of business on December 31, it had 60 units remaining.

With the FIFO method, Handy assumes its beginning inventory and initial purchases were sold first. The 60 snow blowers remaining in inventory would have a cost value of $225 each, a total cost of goods sold of $42,250, and a gross profit of $28,150. With the LIFO method, Handy assumes the most recently purchased items were sold first and the remaining inventory would consist of beginning goods and early purchases. Of the snow blowers remaining in inventory, 30 would have a cost value of $150 each and 30 a cost value of $175 apiece, resulting in a total cost of goods sold of $46,000 and a gross profit of $24,400. The FIFO method presents a more accurate picture of the cost of goods sold and the true cost value of ending inventory. The LIFO method indicates a lower profit, leading to the payment of lower taxes but an understated ending inventory value at cost.

The retail method of inventory, which combines FIFO and LIFO concepts, is explained shortly.

FIGURE 16-1

Applying FIFO and LIFO Inventory Methods to Handy Hardware, January 1, 2009– December 31, 2009

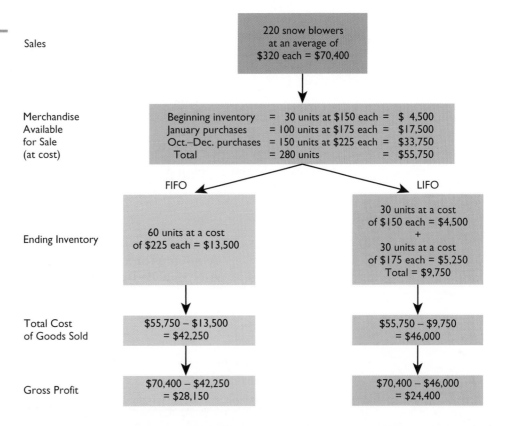

DISADVANTAGES OF COST-BASED INVENTORY SYSTEMS

Cost-based physical and book systems have significant disadvantages. First, both require that a cost be assigned to each item in stock (and to each item sold). When merchandise costs change, cost-based valuation systems work best for firms with low inventory turnover, limited assortments, and high average prices—such as car dealers.

Second, neither cost-based method adjusts inventory values to reflect style changes, end-of-season markdowns, or sudden surges of demand (which may raise prices). Thus, ending inventory value based on merchandise cost may not reflect its actual worth. This discrepancy could be troublesome if inventory value is used in filing insurance claims for losses.

Despite these factors, retailers that make the products they sell—such as bakeries, restaurants, and furniture showrooms—often keep records on a cost basis. A department store with these operations can use the cost method for them and the retail method for other areas.

The Retail Method

With the **retail method of accounting,** closing inventory value is determined by calculating the average relationship between the cost and retail values of merchandise available for sale during a period. Although the retail method overcomes the disadvantages of the cost method, it requires detailed records and is more complex because ending inventory is first valued in retail dollars and then converted to compute gross margin (gross profit).

There are three basic steps to determine ending inventory value by the retail method:

1. Calculating the cost complement.
2. Calculating deductions from retail value.
3. Converting retail inventory value to cost.

CALCULATING THE COST COMPLEMENT

The value of beginning inventory, net purchases, additional markups, and transportation charges are all included in the retail method. Beginning inventory and net purchase amounts (purchases less returns) are recorded at both cost and retail levels. Additional markups represent the extra revenues received when a retailer increases selling prices, due to inflation or unexpectedly high demand. Transportation charges are the retailer's costs for shipping the goods it buys from suppliers to the retailer. Table 16-3 shows the total merchandise available for sale at cost and at retail for Handy Hardware from July 1, 2009, through December 31, 2009, using the costs in Table 16-2.

By using Table 16-3 data, the average relationship of cost to retail value for all merchandise available for sale by Handy Hardware—the **cost complement**—can be computed:

$$\text{Cost complement} = \frac{\text{Total cost valuation}}{\text{Total retail valuation}}$$

$$= \frac{\$299{,}892}{\$496{,}126} = 0.6045$$

Because the cost complement is 0.6045 (60.45 percent), on average, 60.45 cents of every retail sales dollar went to cover Handy Hardware's merchandise cost.

TABLE 16-3   Handy Hardware Store, Calculating Merchandise Available for Sale at Cost and at Retail, July 1, 2009–December 31, 2009

	At Cost	At Retail
Beginning inventory	$ 90,500	$139,200
Net purchases	205,900	340,526
Additional markups	—	16,400
Transportation charges	3,492	—
Total merchandise available for sale	$299,892	$496,126

TABLE 16-4   Handy Hardware Store, Computing Ending Retail Book Value, as of December 31, 2009

Merchandise available for sale (at retail)		$496,126
Less deductions:		
Sales	$422,540	
Markdowns	11,634	
Employee discounts	2,400	
Total deductions		436,574
Ending retail book value of inventory		$ 59,552

CALCULATING DEDUCTIONS FROM RETAIL VALUE

The ending retail value of inventory must reflect all deductions from the total merchandise available for sale at retail. Besides sales, deductions include markdowns (for special sales and end-of-season goods), employee discounts, and stock shortages (due to pilferage and unrecorded breakage). Although sales, markdowns, and employee discounts can be recorded throughout an accounting period, a physical inventory is needed to learn about stock shortages.

From Table 16-3, it is known that Handy Hardware had a retail value of merchandise available for sale of $496,126 for the period from July 1, 2009, through December 31, 2009. As shown in Table 16-4, this was reduced by sales of $422,540 and recorded markdowns and employee discounts of $14,034. The ending book value of inventory at retail as of December 31, 2009, was $59,552.

To compute stock shortages, the retail book value of ending inventory is compared with the actual physical ending inventory at retail. If book inventory exceeds physical inventory, a shortage exists. Table 16-5 shows the results of Handy's physical inventory. Shortages were $3,082 (at retail), and book value was adjusted accordingly. Although Handy knows the shortages were from pilferage, bookkeeping errors, and overshipments not billed to customers, it cannot learn the proportion of shortages from each factor.

Occasionally, a physical inventory may reveal a stock overage—an excess of physical inventory value over book value. This may be due to errors in a physical inventory or in keeping a book inventory. If overages occur, ending retail book value is adjusted upward. Inasmuch as a retailer has to conduct a physical inventory to compute shortages (overages), and a physical inventory is usually taken only once or twice a year, shortages (overages) are often estimated for monthly merchandise budgets.

CONVERTING RETAIL INVENTORY VALUE TO COST

The retailer must next convert the adjusted ending retail book value of inventory to cost so as to compute dollar gross profit (gross margin). The ending inventory at cost equals the adjusted ending retail book value multiplied by the cost complement. For Handy Hardware, this was:

Ending inventory = Adjusted ending retail book value $\times$ Cost complement
(at cost)

$$= \$56,470 \times .6045 = \$34,136$$

This computation does not yield the exact inventory cost. It shows the average relationship between cost and the retail selling price for all merchandise available for sale.

TABLE 16-5   Handy Hardware Store, Computing Stock Shortages and Adjusting Retail Book Value, as of December 31, 2009

Ending retail book value of inventory	$59,552
Physical inventory (at retail)	56,470
Stock shortages (at retail)	3,082
Adjusted ending retail book value of inventory	$56,470

TABLE 16-6   Handy Hardware Store Profit-and-Loss Statement, July 1, 2009–December 31, 2009

Sales		$422,540
Less cost of goods sold:		
Total merchandise available for sale (at cost)	$299,892	
Adjusted ending inventory (at cost)[a]	34,136	
Cost of goods sold		265,756
Gross profit		$156,784
Less operating expenses:		
Salaries	$ 70,000	
Advertising	25,000	
Rental	16,000	
Other	28,000	
Total operating expenses		139,000
Net profit before taxes		$ 17,784

[a]Adjusted ending inventory (at cost) = Adjusted retail book value × Cost complement = $56,470 × 0.6045 = $34,136

The adjusted ending inventory at cost can be used to find gross profit. As Table 16-6 shows, Handy's six-month cost of goods sold was $265,756, resulting in gross profit of $156,784. By deducting operating expenses of $139,000, Handy learns that the net profit before taxes for this period was $17,784.

ADVANTAGES OF THE RETAIL METHOD

Compared with other techniques, there are several advantages to the retail method of accounting:

▶ Valuation errors are reduced when conducting a physical inventory because merchandise value is recorded at retail and costs do not have to be decoded.
▶ Because the process is simpler, a physical inventory can be completed more often. This lets a firm be more aware of slow-moving items and stock shortages.
▶ The physical inventory method at cost requires a physical inventory to prepare a profit-and-loss statement. The retail method lets a firm set up a profit-and-loss statement based on book inventory. The retailer can then estimate the stock shortages between physical inventories and study departmental profit trends.
▶ A complete record of ending book values helps determine insurance coverage and settle insurance claims. The retail book method gives an estimate of inventory value throughout the year. Because physical inventories are usually taken when merchandise levels are low, the book value at retail lets retailers plan insurance coverage for peak periods and shows the values of goods on hand. The retail method is accepted in insurance claims.

LIMITATIONS OF THE RETAIL METHOD

The greatest weakness is the bookkeeping burden of recording data. Ending book inventory figures can be correctly computed only if the following are accurately noted: the value of beginning inventory (at cost and at retail), purchases (at cost and at retail), shipping charges, markups, markdowns, employee discounts, transfers from other departments or stores, returns, and sales. Although personnel are freed from taking many physical inventories, ending book value at retail may be inaccurate unless all required data are precisely recorded. With computerization, this potential problem is lessened.

Another limitation is that the cost complement is an average based on the total cost of merchandise available for sale and total retail value. The ending cost value only approximates the true inventory value. This may cause misinformation if fast-selling items have different markups from slow-selling items or if there are wide variations among the markups of different goods.

Familiarity with the retail and cost methods of inventory is essential for understanding the financial merchandise management material described in the balance of this chapter.

Go here (**www.microsoft.com/dynamics/rms/product/numberswhitepaper.mspx**) to download a good discussion on "Numbers That Matter in Retailing."

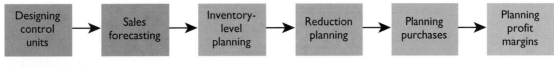

FIGURE 16-2

The Merchandise Forecasting and Budgeting Process: Dollar Control

Merchandise Forecasting and Budgeting: Dollar Control

As we noted earlier, dollar control entails planning and monitoring a firm's inventory investment over time. Figure 16-2 shows the six-step dollar control process for merchandise forecasting and budgeting. This process should be followed sequentially since a change in one stage affects all the stages after it. If a sales forecast is too low, a firm may run out of items because it does not plan to have enough merchandise during a selling season and planned purchases will also be too low.

Visit our Web site (**www.pearsonhighered.com/berman**) for a detailed listing of links related to both dollar control and unit control in merchandise management.

Designating Control Units

Merchandise forecasting and budgeting requires the selection of **control units,** the merchandise categories for which data are gathered. Such classifications must be narrow enough to isolate opportunities and problems with specific merchandise lines. A retailer wishing to control goods within departments must record data on dollar allotments separately for each category.

Knowing that total markdowns in a department are 20 percent above last year's level is less valuable than knowing the specific merchandise lines in which large markdowns are being taken. A retailer can broaden its control system by combining categories that comprise a department. However, a broad category cannot be broken down into components.

It is helpful to select control units consistent with other company and trade association data. Internal comparisons are meaningful only when categories are stable. Classifications that shift over time do not permit comparisons. External comparisons are

---

ETHICS IN RETAILING

 Auto Dealers and Ethics: Not an Oxymoron

Ethical behavior by auto dealers has become increasingly important because consumers are now more knowledgeable (due to information on the Web) and because auto retailing is a popular target of regulators and attorneys. Two ways for car dealers to instill ethical behavior among their sales personnel involve rethinking sales force compensation and re-examining how car dealers operate as business leaders.

Traditionally, many salespeople have been paid on the basis of the gross profit of each sale. This practice encourages salespeople to inflate the sales price to an unsuspecting consumer or to push high-profit, dealer-installed options or unnecessary high-profit services. Alternative methods are to place fixed prices on cars, provide bonuses to sales staff based on customer satisfaction scores, and link bonuses to referral and repeat business.

As the lead manager, the owner of a dealership should set an example for the practices of his or her employees. The firm's code of ethics needs to reflect what behavior is unacceptable, including restrictions on high-pressure tactics and misrepresentation of prices or credit costs. Salespeople who continually violate the ethical code should be terminated regardless of profitability. The Washington State Independent Auto Dealers (WSIADA) is one of several dealer groups that has a comprehensive code of ethics for its members: "If at any time a dealer violates WSIADA's Code of Ethics, WSIADA has the ability to revoke their membership."

Sources: Lee Harkins, "Scare Tactics Hurt Business," *Ward's Dealer Business* (November 2007), p. 44; and "Code of Ethics," **www.wsiada.com/ethics.html** (January 10, 2009).

not meaningful if control units are dissimilar for a retailer and its trade associations. Control units may be based on departments, classifications within departments, price line classifications, and standard merchandise classifications. A discussion of each follows.

The broadest practical classification for financial record keeping is the department, which lets a retailer assess each general merchandise grouping or buyer. Even the small Handy Hardware needs to acquire data on a departmental basis (tools and equipment, supplies, housewares, and so on) for buying, inventory control, and markdown decisions.

To obtain more financial data, **classification merchandising** can be used, whereby each department is subdivided into further categories for related types of merchandise. In planning its tools and equipment department, Handy Hardware can keep financial records on both overall departmental performance and the results of such categories as lawn mowers/ snow blowers, power tools, hand tools, and ladders.

A special form of classification merchandising uses *price line classifications*—sales, inventories, and purchases are analyzed by price category. This helps if different models of a product are sold at different prices to different target markets (such as Handy's having $20 power tools for do-it-yourselfers and $135 models for contractors). Retailers with deep assortments most often use price line control.

To best contrast its data with industry averages, a firm's merchandise categories should conform to those cited in trade publications. The National Retail Federation devised a *standard merchandise classification* with common reporting categories for a range of retailers and products. It annually produces *Retail Horizons,* using its classifications. Specific classifications are also popular for some retailers. *Progressive Grocer* regularly publishes data based on standard classifications for supermarkets.

Once appropriate dollar control units are set, all transactions—including sales, purchases, transfers, markdowns, and employee discounts—must be recorded under the proper classification number. Thus, if house paint is Department 25 and brushes are 25-1, all transactions must carry these designations.

Sales Forecasting

Sport Chalet succeeds with SAS software (**www.sas. com/success/sportchalet. html**).

A retailer estimates its expected future revenues for a given period by *sales forecasting.* Forecasts may be companywide, departmental, and for individual merchandise classifications. Perhaps the most important step in financial merchandise planning is accurate sales forecasting, because an incorrect projection of sales throws off the entire process. That is why many retailers use state-of-the art forecasting software. Sport Chalet has dramatically improved its inventory productivity by using such software from SAS.[4]

Larger retailers often forecast total and department sales by techniques such as trend analysis, time series analysis, and multiple regression analysis. A discussion of these techniques is beyond the scope of this book. Small retailers rely more on "guesstimates," projections based on experience. Even for larger firms, sales forecasting for merchandise classifications within departments (or price lines) relies on more qualitative methods. One way to forecast sales for narrow categories is first to project sales on a company basis and by department and then to break down figures judgmentally into merchandise classifications.

External factors, internal company factors, and seasonal trends must be anticipated and taken into account. Among the external factors that can affect projected sales are consumer trends, competitors' actions, the state of the economy, the weather, and new supplier offerings. For example, Planalytics offers a patented methodology to analyze and forecast the relationship among consumer demand, store traffic, and the weather.[5] Internal company factors that can affect future sales include additions and deletions of merchandise lines, revised promotion and credit policies, changes in hours, new outlets, and store remodeling. With many retailers, seasonality must be considered in setting monthly or quarterly sales forecasts. Handy's yearly snow blower sales should not be estimated from December sales alone.

A sales forecast can be developed by examining past trends and projecting future growth (based on external and internal factors). Table 16-7 shows a sales forecast for Handy Hardware. It is an estimate, subject to revisions. Various factors may be hard to incorporate when devising a forecast, such as merchandise shortages, consumer reactions to new products, the rate of inflation, and new government legislation. That is why a financial merchandise plan needs some flexibility.

TABLE 16-7 Handy Hardware Store, A Simple Sales Forecast Using Product Control Units

Product Control Units	Actual Sales 2009	Projected Growth/ Decline (%)	Sales Forecast 2010
Lawn mowers/snow blowers	$200,000	+10.0	$220,000
Paint and supplies	128,000	+3.0	131,840
Hardware supplies	108,000	+8.0	116,640
Plumbing supplies	88,000	−4.0	84,480
Power tools	88,000	+6.0	93,280
Garden supplies/chemicals	68,000	+4.0	70,720
Housewares	48,000	−6.0	45,120
Electrical supplies	40,000	+4.0	41,600
Ladders	36,000	+6.0	38,160
Hand tools	36,000	+9.0	39,240
Total year	$840,000	+4.9[a]	$881,080

[a]There is a small rounding error.

After a yearly forecast is derived, it should be broken into quarters or months. In retailing, monthly forecasts are usually required. Jewelry stores know December accounts for nearly one-quarter of annual sales, while drugstores know December sales are slightly better than average. Stationery stores and card stores realize that Christmas cards generate more than 60 percent of seasonal greeting card sales, while Valentine's Day cards are second with about 25 percent.[6]

To acquire more specific estimates, a retailer could use a **monthly sales index,** which divides each month's actual sales by average monthly sales and multiplies the results by 100. Table 16-8 shows Handy Hardware's 2009 actual monthly sales and monthly sales indexes. The store is seasonal, with peaks in late spring and early summer (for lawn mowers, garden supplies, and so on), as well as December (for lighting fixtures, snow blowers, and gifts). Average monthly 2009 sales were $70,000 ($840,000/12). Thus, the monthly sales index for January is 67 [($46,800/$70,000) × 100]; other monthly indexes are computed similarly.

TABLE 16-8 Handy Hardware Store, 2009 Sales by Month

Month	Monthly Actual Sales	Sales Index[a]
January	$ 46,800	67
February	40,864	58
March	48,000	69
April	65,600	94
May	112,196	160
June	103,800	148
July	104,560	149
August	62,800	90
September	46,904	67
October	46,800	67
November	66,884	96
December	94,792	135
Total yearly sales	$840,000	
Average monthly sales	$ 70,000	
Average monthly index		100

[a]Monthly sales index = (Monthly sales/Average monthly sales) × 100

TABLE 16-9   Handy Hardware Store, 2010 Sales Forecast by Month

Month	Actual Sales 2009	Monthly Sales Index	Monthly Sales Forecast for 2010[a]
January	$ 46,800	67	$73,423 × 0.67 = $ 49,193
February	40,864	58	73,423 × 0.58 = 42,585
March	48,000	69	73,423 × 0.69 = 50,662
April	65,600	94	73,423 × 0.94 = 69,018
May	112,196	160	73,423 × 1.60 = 117,477
June	103,800	148	73,423 × 1.48 = 108,666
July	104,560	149	73,423 × 1.49 = 109,400
August	62,800	90	73,423 × 0.90 = 66,081
September	46,904	67	73,423 × 0.67 = 49,193
October	46,800	67	73,423 × 0.67 = 49,193
November	66,884	96	73,423 × 0.96 = 70,486
December	94,792	135	73,423 × 1.35 = 99,121
Total sales	$840,000		Total sales forecast $881,080[b]
Average monthly sales	$ 70,000		Average monthly forecast $ 73,423

[a]Monthly sales forecast = Average monthly forecast × (Monthly index/100). In this equation, the monthly index is computed as a fraction of 1.00 rather than 100.
[b]There is a small rounding error.

Each monthly index shows the percentage deviation of that month's sales from the average month's. A May index of 160 means May sales are 60 percent higher than average. An October index of 67 means sales in October are 33 percent below average.

Once monthly sales indexes are determined, a retailer can forecast monthly sales, based on the yearly sales forecast. Table 16-9 shows how Handy's 2010 monthly sales can be forecast if average monthly sales are expected to be $73,423.

Inventory-Level Planning

ILOG offers software such as Inventory Analyst (**www.ilog.com/products/ inventory_analyst**) to enhance inventory planning.

At this point, a retailer plans its inventory. The level must be sufficient to meet sales expectations, allowing a margin for error. Techniques to plan inventory levels are the basic stock, percentage variation, weeks' supply, and stock-to-sales methods.

With the **basic stock method,** a retailer carries more items than it expects to sell over a specified period. There is a cushion if sales are more than anticipated, shipments are delayed, or customers want to select from a variety of items. It is best when inventory turnover is low or sales are erratic over the year. Beginning-of-month planned inventory equals planned sales plus a basic stock amount:

Basic stock (at retail)   = Average monthly stock at retail − Average monthly sales

Beginning-of-month planned inventory level = Planned monthly sales + Basic stock (at retail)

If Handy Hardware, with an average monthly 2010 forecast of $73,423, wants extra stock equal to 10 percent of its average monthly forecast and expects January 2010 sales to be $49,193:

Basic stock (at retail)   = ($73,423 × 1.10) − $73,423 = $7,342

Beginning-of-January planned inventory level = $49,193 + $7,342 = $56,535 (at retail)

In the **percentage variation method,** beginning-of-month planned inventory during any month differs from planned average monthly stock by only one-half of that month's variation from estimated average monthly sales. This method is recommended if stock turnover is more than six times a year or relatively stable, since it results in planned inventories closer to the monthly average than other techniques:

$$\text{Beginning-of-month planned inventory level (at retail)} = \text{Planned average monthly stock at retail} \times 1/2 \, [1 + (\text{Estimated monthly sales}/\text{Estimated average monthly sales})]$$

If Handy Hardware plans average monthly stock of $80,765 and November 2010 sales are expected to be 4 percent less than average monthly sales of $73,423, the store's planned inventory level at the beginning of November 2010 would be:

$$\text{Beginning-of-November planned inventory level (at retail)} = \$80,765 \times 1/2 \, [1 + (\$70,486/\$73,423)] = \$79,150$$

Handy Hardware should not use this method due to its variable sales. If it did, Handy would plan a beginning-of-December 2010 inventory of $94,899, less than expected sales ($99,121).

The **weeks' supply method** forecasts average sales weekly, so beginning inventory equals several weeks' expected sales. It assumes inventory is in proportion to sales. Too much merchandise may be stocked in peak periods and too little during slow periods:

$$\text{Beginning-of-month planned inventory level (at retail)} = \text{Average estimated weekly sales} \times \text{Number of weeks to be stocked}$$

If Handy Hardware forecasts average weekly sales of $10,956.92 from January 1, 2010, through March 31, 2010, and it wants to stock 13 weeks of merchandise (based on expected turnover), beginning inventory would be $142,440:

$$\text{Beginning-of-January planned inventory level (at retail)} = \$10,956.92 \times 13 = \$142,440$$

With the **stock-to-sales method,** a retailer wants to maintain a specified ratio of goods on hand to sales. A ratio of 1.3 means that if Handy Hardware plans sales of $69,018 in April 2010, it should have $89,723 worth of merchandise (at retail) available

TECHNOLOGY IN RETAILING

Tesco: Applying Weather-Related Demand Forecasting

Tesco (**www.tesco.com**), Great Britain's largest retailer and the fourth largest retailer in the world, applies sophisticated weather-related demand forecasting for its grocery products. According to Tesco's supply chain systems development director, "sales of individual products can fluctuate by up to 300 percent day-to-day. Getting it wrong could mean you lose £1 to £2 million straight away [$1.5 to $3.0 million U.S. dollars]."

Research by Tesco showed that sales of its washed salads in its Extra stores located in southeast England increase by as much as 19 percent as temperatures climb from 20 to 25°C (68 to 75°F). A high degree of sunshine (eight hours or more) also increases sales of these products. Products such as broccoli work in the opposite direction, with declining sales as temperatures "heat up."

Tesco is now expanding its demand forecasting model so that it will take into account different regions. It is also seeking to more accurately forecast the effect of promotions on sales of specific products. Tesco's research found that customers in different regions respond differently to temperature and sunshine hours. In Scotland, increases in demand for some products occur at lower temperatures than in southern England.

Source: Rod Addy, "Tesco Keeps a Keen Eye on Its Fair-Weather Customers," *Food Manufacture* (April 2008), p. 6.

during the month. Like the weeks' supply method, this approach tends to adjust inventory more drastically than changes in sales require.

Yearly stock-to-sales ratios by retail type are provided by sources such as *Industry Norms & Key Business Ratios* (New York: Dun & Bradstreet) and *Annual Statement Studies* (Philadelphia: Risk Management Association). A retailer can, thus, compare its ratios with other firms'.

Reduction Planning

Besides forecasting sales, a firm should estimate its expected **retail reductions,** which represent the difference between beginning inventory plus purchases during the period and sales plus ending inventory. Planned reductions incorporate anticipated markdowns (discounts to stimulate sales), employee and other discounts (price cuts to employees, senior citizens, and others), and stock shortages (pilferage, breakage, and bookkeeping errors):

$$\text{Planned reductions} = \begin{aligned}&\text{(Beginning inventory + Planned purchases)}\\&- \text{(Planned sales + Ending inventory)}\end{aligned}$$

Reduction planning revolves around two key factors: estimating expected total reductions by budget period and assigning the estimates monthly. The following should be considered in planning reductions: past experience, markdown data for similar retailers, changes in company policies, merchandise carryover from one budget period to another, price trends, and stock-shortage trends.

Past experience is a good starting point. This information can then be compared with the performance of similar firms—by reviewing data on markdowns, discounts, and stock shortages in trade publications. A retailer with higher markdowns than competitors could investigate and correct the situation by adjusting its buying practices and price levels or training sales personnel better.

A retailer must consider its own procedures in reviewing reductions. Policy changes often affect the quantity and timing of markdowns. If a firm expands its assortment of seasonal and fashion merchandise, this would probably lead to a rise in markdowns.

Merchandise carryover, price trends, and stock-shortage trends also affect planning. If such items as gloves and antifreeze are stocked in off seasons, markdowns are often not used to clear out inventory. Yet, the carryover of fad items merely postpones reductions. Price trends of product categories have a strong impact on reductions. Many full computer systems now sell for less than $1,000, down considerably from prior years. This means higher-priced computers must be marked down. Recent stock shortage trends (determined by comparing prior book and physical inventory values) can be used to project future reductions due to employee, customer, and vendor theft; breakage; and bookkeeping mistakes. If a firm has total stock shortages of less than 2 percent of annual sales, it is usually deemed to be doing well. Figure 16-3 shows a checklist to reduce shortages from clerical and handling errors. Suggestions for reducing shortages from theft were covered in Chapter 15.

After determining total reductions, they must be planned by month because reductions as a percentage of sales are not the same during each month. Stock shortages may be much higher during busy periods, when stores are more crowded and transactions happen more quickly.

Planning Purchases

The formula for calculating planned purchases for a period is:

$$\begin{aligned}\text{Planned}\\\text{purchase} =\\\text{(at retail)}\end{aligned}\quad\begin{aligned}&\text{Planned sales for the month + Planned reductions for the month}\\&+ \text{Planned end-of-month stock} - \text{Beginning-of-month stock}\end{aligned}$$

If Handy Hardware projects June 2010 sales to be $108,666 and total planned reductions to be 5 percent of sales, plans end-of-month inventory at retail to be $72,000, and has a beginning-of-month inventory at retail of $80,000, planned purchases for June are:

$$\begin{aligned}\text{Planned purchases}\\\text{(at retail)}\end{aligned} = \$108,666 + \$5,433 + \$72,000 - \$80,000 = \$106,099$$

FIGURE 16-3

A Checklist to Reduce Inventory Shortages Due to Clerical and Handling Errors

Answer yes or no to each of the following questions. A no means corrective action must be taken.

Buying
1. Is the exact quantity of merchandise purchased always specified in the contract?
2. Are special purchase terms clearly noted?
3. Are returns to the vendor recorded properly?

Marking
4. Are retail prices clearly and correctly marked on merchandise?
5. Are markdowns and additional markups recorded by item number and quantity?
6. Does a cashier check with a manager if a price is not marked on an item?
7. Are old price tags removed when an item's price changes?

Handling
8. After receipt, are purchase quantities checked against the order?
9. Is merchandise handled in a systematic manner?
10. Are items sold in bulk (such as produce, sugar, candy) measured accurately?
11. Are damaged, soiled, returned, or other special goods handled separately?

Selling
12. Do sales personnel know correct prices or have easy access to them?
13. Are misrings by cashiers made on a very small percentage of sales?
14. Are special terms noted on sales receipts (such as employee discounts)?
15. Are sales receipts numbered and later checked for missing invoices?

Inventory Planning
16. Is a physical inventory conducted at least annually and is a book inventory kept throughout the year?
17. Are the differences between physical inventory and book inventory always explained?

Accounting
18. Are permanent records on all transactions kept and monitored for accuracy?
19. Are both retail and cost data maintained?
20. Are inventory shortages compared with industry averages?

Because Handy Hardware expects 2010 merchandise costs to be about 60 percent of retail selling price, its plan is to purchase $63,659 of goods at cost in June 2010:

$$\text{Planned purchases (at cost)} = \text{Planned purchases at retail} \times \text{Merchandise costs as a percentage of selling price}$$
$$= \$106,099 \times 0.60 = \$63,659$$

Take an online tour of *The OTB Book* (www.otb-retail.com/tour1.htm).

Open-to-buy is the difference between planned purchases and the purchase commitments already made by a buyer for a given period, often a month. It represents the amount the buyer has left to spend for that month and is reduced each time a purchase is made. At the beginning of a month, a firm's planned purchases and open-to-buy are equal if no purchase commitments have been made before that month starts. Open-to-buy is recorded at cost.

At Handy Hardware, the buyer has made purchase commitments for June 2010 in the amount of $55,000 at retail. Accordingly, Handy's open-to-buy at retail for June is $51,099:

$$\text{Open-to-buy (at retail)} = \text{Planned purchases for the month} - \text{Purchase commitments for that month}$$
$$= \$106,099 - \$55,000 = \$51,099$$

To calculate the June 2010 open-to-buy at cost, $51,099 is multiplied by Handy Hardware's merchandise costs as a percentage of selling price:

$$\text{Open-to-buy (at cost)} = \text{Open-to-buy at retail} \times \text{Merchandise costs as a percentage of selling price}$$

$$= \$51,099 \times 0.60 = \$30,659$$

The open-to-buy concept has two major strengths: (1) It maintains a specified relationship between inventory and planned sales; this avoids overbuying and underbuying. (2) It lets a firm adjust purchases to reflect changes in sales, markdowns, and so on. If Handy revises its June 2010 sales forecast to $120,000 (from $108,666), it automatically increases planned purchases and open-to-buy by $11,334 at retail and $6,800 at cost.

It is advisable for a retailer to keep at least a small open-to-buy figure for as long as possible—to take advantage of special deals, purchase new models when introduced, and fill in items that sell out. An open-to-buy limit sometimes must be exceeded due to underestimated demand (low sales forecasts). A retailer should not be so rigid that merchandising personnel are unable to have the discretion (employee empowerment) to purchase below-average-priced items when the open-to-buy is not really open.

Planning Profit Margins

In preparing a profitable merchandise budget, a retailer must consider planned net sales, retail operating expenses, profit, and retail reductions in pricing merchandise:

$$\text{Required initial markup percentage} = \frac{\text{Planned retail expenses} + \text{Planned profit} + \text{Planned reductions}}{\text{Planned net sales} + \text{Planned reductions}}$$

The required markup is a companywide average. Individual items may be priced according to demand and other factors, as long as the average is met. A fuller markup discussion is in Chapter 17. The concept of initial markup is introduced here for continuity in the description of merchandise budgeting.

Handy has an overall 2010 sales forecast of $881,080 and expects annual expenses to be $290,000. Reductions are projected at $44,000. The total net dollar profit margin goal is $60,000 (6.8 percent of sales). Its required initial markup is 42.6 percent:

$$\text{Required initial markup percentage} = \frac{\$290,000 + \$60,000 + \$44,000}{\$881,080 + \$44,000} = 42.6\%$$

$$\text{Required initial markup percentage (all factors expressed as a percentage of net sales)} = \frac{32.9\% + 6.8\% + 5.0\%}{100.0\% + 5.0\%} = 42.6\%$$

Unit Control Systems

RWS Information Systems offers unit control software capabilities in its POS-IM program (www.rwsinfo.com/invcon2.html).

Unit control systems deal with quantities of merchandise in units rather than in dollars. Information typically reveals

▶ Items selling well and those selling poorly.
▶ Opportunities and problems in terms of price, color, style, size, and so on.
▶ The quantity of goods on hand (if book inventory is used). This minimizes overstocking and understocking.
▶ An indication of inventory age, highlighting candidates for markdowns or promotions.
▶ The optimal time to reorder merchandise.
▶ Experiences with alternative sources (vendors) when problems arise.
▶ The level of inventory and sales for each item in every store branch. This improves the transfer of goods between branches and alerts salespeople as to which branches have desired products. Also, less stock can be held in individual stores, reducing costs.

FIGURE 16-4

Physical Inventory Systems Made Simpler

Taking a physical inventory using a Retail Pro portable terminal takes only a fraction of the time required for a traditional manual count. It also yields a more accurate result. After each scan with the laser gun, the physical count is recorded in the portable terminal. Once a section of inventory is complete, an employee connects the portable terminal to a computer and Retail Pro compares the recorded inventory with the physical counts. Any discrepancies are immediately isolated and reported. When the firm is ready, it can automatically adjust the recorded inventory to reflect the physical counts and record this adjustment. The portable terminal can also perform quantity and price verifications by pre-loading inventory quantity and price information. When merchandise is scanned, the unit displays the correct retail price and the expected quantity on hand. This makes it easy to detect pricing errors and missing merchandise.

Source: Photo reprinted by permission of Retail Technologies International.

Physical Inventory Systems

A *physical inventory unit control system* is similar to a physical inventory dollar control system. However, the latter is concerned with the financial value of inventory, while a unit control system looks at the number of units by item classification. With unit control, inventory levels are monitored either by visual inspection or actual count. See Figure 16-4.

In a visual inspection system, merchandise is placed on pegboard (or similar) displays, with each item numbered on the back or on a stock card. Minimum inventory quantities are noted, and sales personnel reorder when inventory reaches the minimum level. This is accurate only if items are placed in numerical order on displays (and sold accordingly). The system is used in the housewares and hardware displays of various discount and hardware stores. Although easy to maintain and inexpensive, it does not provide data on the rate of sales of individual items. And minimum stock quantities may be arbitrarily defined and not drawn from in-depth analysis.

The other physical inventory system, actual counting, means regularly compiling the number of units on hand. This approach records—in units—inventory on hand, purchases, sales volume, and shortages during specified periods. A stock-counting system requires more clerical work but lets a firm obtain sales data for given periods and stock-to-sales relationships as of the time of each count. A physical system is not as sophisticated as a book system. It is more useful with low-value items having predictable sales. Handy Hardware could use the system for its insulation tape:

	Number of Rolls of Tape for the Period 12/1/09–12/31/09
Beginning inventory, December 1, 2009	100
Total purchases for period	70
Total units available for sale	170
Closing inventory, December 31, 2009	60
Sales and shortages for period	110

Perpetual Inventory Systems

A *perpetual inventory unit control system* keeps a running total of the number of units handled by a retailer through record keeping entries that adjust for sales, returns, transfers to other departments or stores, receipt of shipments, and other transactions. All additions to and subtractions from beginning inventory are recorded. Such a system can be applied manually, use merchandise tags processed by computers, or rely on point-of-sale devices such as optical scanners.

A manual system requires employees to gather data by examining sales checks, merchandise receipts, transfer requests, and other documents. Data are then coded and tabulated. A merchandise tagging system relies on pre-printed tags with data by department, classification, vendor, style, date of receipt, color, and/or material. When an item is sold, a copy of the tag is removed and sent to a tabulating facility for computer analysis. Since pre-printed tags are processed in batches, they can be used by smaller retailers that subscribe to service bureaus and by branches of chains (with data processed at a central location). Point-of-sale (POS) systems feed data from merchandise tags or product labels directly to in-store computers for immediate data processing. Computer-based systems are quicker, more accurate, and of higher quality than manual ones.

Want to look up a UPC code? Go here (www. upcdatabase.com/ itemform.asp).

Newer POS systems are easy to network, have battery backup capabilities, and run on standard components. Many of these systems use optical scanners to transfer data from products to computers by wands or other devices that pass over sensitized strips on the items. Figure 16-5 shows how barcoding works. As noted earlier, the UPC is the dominant format for coding data onto merchandise. This is how to interpret a barcode:

(1) The *number system* uses two digits (sometimes three digits) to identify the country (or economic region) numbering authority which assigns the manufacturer code. In the traditional UPC code, the first digit is 0, and it is not displayed on the label. (2) The *manufacturer code* is a unique code assigned to each manufacturer by

OPEN RETAILING AROUND THE WORLD

Using Tracking Software to Pinpoint Unsafe Products

In 2008 and 2009, the mass media focused attention on a number of safety issues associated with Chinese goods, including Mattel's (**www.mattel.com**) recall of almost a million toys that contained lead-based paint, Foreign Tire Sales' (**www.foreigntire.com**) recall of about 450,000 Chinese-made tires that fell apart at high speeds, and RC2's (**www.rc2.com**) recall of Thomas & Friends Wooden Railway toys that had excessive levels of lead and rechargeable lithium-ion batteries that could overheat and catch fire.

As a result, technology firms such as SmartOnline (**www.smartonline.com**) and FoodLogiQ (**www. foodlogiq.com**) have been designing chips that can better track the source of unsafe products and better manage the recall process. Some experts feel that retailers will

have to nudge suppliers to participate in such a tracking program. Wal-Mart is currently pushing its suppliers to add auditing features to their scanning activities. These auditing activities will let retailers know which supplier, farm, and acreage was the cause of a specific outbreak. As a result, only specific products would be recalled.

Retailers can also use loyalty card data to determine which customers purchase the affected lots. Harris Teeter (**www.harristeeter.com**) recently used its enhanced scanning system to notify shoppers of specific shipments of a cereal product that may have been mislabeled.

Source: Sue Stock, "Making Food Easier to Track: Local Companies Ramp Up Scanning Technology That Could Prevent Millions in Lost Products and Revenue," *McClatchy-Tribune Business News* (June 18, 2008).

FIGURE 16-5

How Does a UPC-Based Scanner System Work?

When a scanner is passed over an item with a UPC symbol, that symbol is read by a low-energy laser. The UPC symbol consists of a series of vertical lines. with numbers below them. Each product has its own unique identification code, and the price is not in the symbol. Scanned information is transmitted to an in-store computer that identifies the item and searches its memory for the current price. This information is then sent back to the checkout terminal.

Source: Reprinted by permission of TNS Retail Forward.

the numbering authority indicated by the number system code. All products from a given firm use the same manufacturer code, which is typically 5 digits. (3) The *product code* is a unique code assigned by the manufacturer. Unlike its assigned manufacturer code, the manufacturer is free to assign 5-digit product codes to each of its products without consulting any other organization. (4) The *check digit* is an additional digit used to verify that a barcode has been scanned correctly. It is calculated based on the rest of the digits of the barcode.[7]

Many retailers combine perpetual and physical systems, whereby items accounting for a large proportion of sales are controlled by a perpetual system and other items are controlled by a physical inventory system. Thus, attention is properly placed on the retailer's most important products.

Unit Control Systems in Practice

Conducting a physical inventory is extremely time-consuming and labor-intensive. It is also crucial: "Having too much stock, or too little, is costly." The National Retail Federation has found that each year retailers in the United States lose about $225 billion due to excessive inventory and $45 billion from not having sufficient inventory on hand.[8]

Consider this:

The cost of inventory to a smaller retailer is far greater than simply the invoice cost and freight. There are inventory carrying costs, shrink, damage and obsolescence costs, and even the cost of lost sales due to too much inventory. These costs can add up quickly, almost imperceptibly. But these costs are real, and they do end up on the income statement eroding profits. While many smaller retailers think that they need more inventory to be sure they don't miss making any sales, the reality is that too much inventory almost always leads to lost sales. This is where having too much inventory can actually impact a retailer on the very top line of the income statement.

If there's too much inventory, stores are simply harder to shop, and when stores are harder to shop, customers buy less. This can play out in several ways: When stores are overstocked, it's harder for customers to find what they came in for and more likely they'll leave without it. When there's too much stuff, aisles can become narrower, discouraging customers from exploring deeper into the store. When displays are overstuffed, customers become afraid to touch, afraid of breaking something on a shelf simply packed too tightly or starting an avalanche on a display piled too high. When there's too much assortment, too many things to choose from, customers can become paralyzed. If the retailer hasn't been able to focus the assortment for the customer, how can the customer know with confidence that they'll be happy with what they purchase?[9]

Financial Inventory Control: Integrating Dollar and Unit Concepts

Oracle (**www.oracle.com/ applications/retail/iso**) markets sophisticated inventory analysis software.

Until now, we have discussed dollar and unit control separately. In practice, they are linked. A decision on how many units to buy is affected by dollar investments, inventory turnover, quantity discounts, warehousing and insurance costs, and so on. Three aspects of financial inventory control are covered next: stock turnover and gross margin return on investment, when to reorder, and how much to reorder.

Stock Turnover and Gross Margin Return on Investment

Stock turnover represents the number of times during a specific period, usually one year, that the average inventory on hand is sold. It can be measured by store, product line, department, and vendor. With high turnover, inventory investments are productive on a per-dollar basis, items are fresh, there are fewer losses due to changes in styles, and interest, insurance, breakage, and warehousing costs are reduced. A retailer can raise stock turnover by reducing its assortment, eliminating or having little inventory for slow-selling items, buying in a timely way, applying quick response (QR) inventory planning, and using reliable suppliers.

Stock turnover can be computed in units or dollars (at retail or cost). The choice of a formula depends on the retailer's accounting system:

$$\text{Annual rate of stock turnover (in units)} = \frac{\text{Number of units sold during year}}{\text{Average inventory on hand (in units)}}$$

$$\text{Annual rate of stock turnover (in retail dollars)} = \frac{\text{Net yearly sales}}{\text{Average inventory on hand (at retail)}}$$

$$\text{Annual rate of stock turnover (at cost)} = \frac{\text{Cost of goods sold during the year}}{\text{Average inventory on hand (at cost)}}$$

In computing turnover, the average inventory for the entire period needs to be reflected. Turnover rates are invalid if the true average is not used, as occurs if a firm mistakenly views the inventory level of a peak or slow month as the yearly average. Table 16-10 shows annual turnover rates for various retailers. Eating places, gasoline service stations, and grocery stores have high rates. They rely on sales volume for their success. Jewelry stores, shoe stores, department stores, and some clothing stores have low rates. They require larger profit margins on each item sold and maintain a sizable assortment.

Despite the advantages of high turnover, buying items in small amounts may also result in the loss of quantity discounts and in higher transportation charges. Because high turnover might be due to a limited assortment, some sales may be lost, and profits may be lower if prices are reduced to move inventory quickly. The return on investment depends on both turnover and profit per unit.

TABLE 16-10   Annual Median Stock Turnover Rates for Selected Types of Retailers

Type of Retailer	Annual Median Stock Turnover Rate (Times)
Auto and home supply stores	7.6
Car dealers (new and used)	5.8
Department stores	4.7
Drug and proprietary stores	13.0
Eating places	95.8
Family clothing stores	3.8
Furniture stores	5.1
Gasoline service stations	46.7
Grocery stores	18.9
Hardware stores	5.1
Household appliance stores	6.2
Jewelry stores	2.3
Lumber and other materials dealers	7.3
Men's and boys' clothing stores	4.3
Shoe stores	4.2
Women's clothing stores	7.4

Source: Industry Norms & Key Business Ratios (New York: Dun & Bradstreet, 2007–2008), pp. 98–108.

Learn more about GMROI (**http://rtfurniture.net/worksheet.html**).

Gross margin return on investment (GMROI) shows the relationship between the gross margin in dollars (total dollar operating profits) and the average inventory investment (at cost) by combining profitability and sales-to-stock measures:

$$\text{GMROI} = \frac{\text{Gross margin in dollars}}{\text{Net sales}} \times \frac{\text{Net sales}}{\text{Average inventory at cost}}$$

$$= \frac{\text{Gross margin in dollars}}{\text{Average inventory at cost}}$$

The gross margin in dollars equals net sales minus the cost of goods sold. The gross margin percentage is derived by dividing dollar gross margin by net sales. A sales-to-stock ratio is derived by dividing net sales by average inventory at cost. That ratio may be converted to stock turnover by multiplying it by [(100 − Gross margin percentage)/100].

GMROI is a useful concept for several reasons:

▶ It shows how diverse retailers can prosper. A supermarket may have a gross margin of 20 percent and a sales-to-stock ratio of 25—a GMROI of 500 percent. A women's clothing store may have a gross margin of 50 percent and a sales-to-stock ratio of 10—a GMROI of 500 percent. Both firms have the same GMROI due to the trade-off between item profitability and turnover.
▶ It is a good indicator of a manager's performance because it focuses on factors controlled by that person. Interdepartmental comparisons can also be made.
▶ It is simple to plan and understand, and data collection is easy.
▶ It can be determined if GMROI performance is consistent with other company goals.

The gross margin percentage and the sales-to-stock ratio must be studied individually. If only overall GMROI is reviewed, performance may be assessed improperly.

When to Reorder

One way to control inventory investment is to systematically set stock levels at which new orders must be placed. Such a stock level is called a **reorder point,** and it is based on three factors. **Order lead time** is the period from the date an order is placed by a retailer to the date merchandise is ready for sale (received, price-marked, and put on the selling floor). **Usage rate** refers to average sales per day, in units, of merchandise. **Safety stock** is the extra inventory that protects against out-of-stock conditions due to unexpected demand and delays in delivery. It depends on the firm's policy toward running out of items.

This is the formula for a retailer that does not plan to carry safety stock. It believes customer demand is stable and that its orders are promptly filled by suppliers:

$$\text{Reorder point} = \text{Usage rate} \times \text{Lead time}$$

If Handy Hardware sells 10 paintbrushes a day and needs 8 days to order, receive, and display them, it has a reorder point of 80 brushes. It would reorder brushes once inventory on hand reaches 80. By the time brushes from that order are placed on shelves (8 days later), stock on hand will be zero, and the new stock will replenish the inventory.

This strategy is proper only when Handy has a steady customer demand of 10 paintbrushes daily and it takes exactly 8 days to complete all stages in the ordering process. This does not normally occur. If customers buy 15 brushes per day during the month, Handy would run out of stock in 5-1/3 days and be without brushes for 2-2/3 days. If an order takes 10 days to process, Handy would have no brushes for 2 days, despite correctly estimating demand. Figure 16-6 shows how stockouts may occur.

For a retailer interested in keeping a safety stock, the reorder formula becomes:

$$\text{Reorder point} = (\text{Usage rate} \times \text{Lead time}) + \text{Safety stock}$$

Suppose Handy Hardware decides on safety stock of 30 percent for paintbrushes; its reorder point is $(10 \times 8) + (0.30 \times 80) = 80 + 24 = 104$. Handy still expects to sell an average of 10 brushes per day and receive orders in an average of 8 days. The safety stock of 24 extra brushes is kept on hand to protect against unexpected demand or a late shipment.

By combining a perpetual inventory system and reorder point calculations, ordering can be computerized and an **automatic reordering system** can be mechanically activated

FIGURE 16-6

How Stockouts May Occur

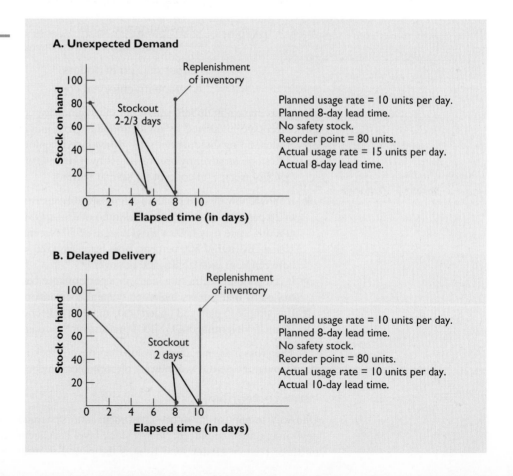

when stock-on-hand reaches the reorder point. However, intervention by a buyer or manager must be possible, especially if monthly sales fluctuate greatly.

How Much to Reorder

A firm placing large orders generally reduces ordering costs but increases inventory-holding costs. A firm placing small orders often minimizes inventory-holding costs while ordering costs may rise (unless EDI and a QR inventory system are used).

Economic order quantity (EOQ) is the quantity per order (in units) that minimizes the total costs of processing orders and holding inventory. Order-processing costs include computer time, order forms, labor, and handling new goods. Holding costs include warehousing, inventory investment, insurance, taxes, depreciation, deterioration, and pilferage. EOQ calculations can be done by large and small firms.

As Figure 16-7 shows, order-processing costs drop as the order quantity (in units) goes up because fewer orders are needed for the same total annual quantity, and inventory-holding costs rise as the order quantity goes up because more units must be held in inventory and they are kept for longer periods. The two costs are summed into a total cost curve. Mathematically, the economic order quantity is:

$$EOQ = \sqrt{\frac{2DS}{IC}}$$

where

EOQ = quantity per order (in units)
D = annual demand (in units)
S = costs to place an order (in dollars)
I = percentage of annual carrying cost to unit cost
C = unit cost of an item (in dollars)

Handy estimates it can sell 150 power tool sets per year. They cost $90 each. Breakage, insurance, tied-up capital, and pilferage equal 10 percent of the costs of the sets (or $9 each). Order costs are $25 per order. The economic order quantity is 29:

$$EOQ = \sqrt{\frac{2(150)(\$25)}{(0.10)(\$90)}} = \sqrt{\frac{\$7,500}{\$9}} = 29$$

The EOQ formula must often be modified to take into account changes in demand, quantity discounts, and variable ordering and holding costs.

FIGURE 16-7

Economic Order Quantity

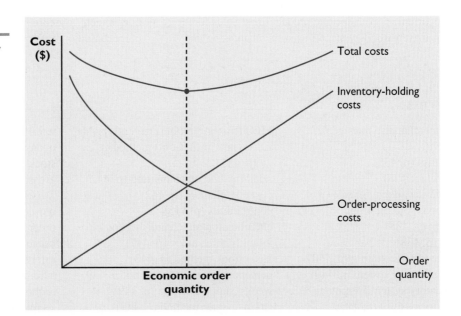

Chapter **Summary**

1. *To describe the major aspects of financial merchandise planning and management.* The purpose of financial merchandise management is to stipulate which products are bought by the retailer, when, and in what quantity. Dollar control monitors inventory investment, while unit control relates to the amount of merchandise handled. Financial merchandise management encompasses accounting methods, merchandise forecasts and budgets, unit control, and integrated dollar and unit controls.

2. *To explain the cost and retail methods of accounting.* The two accounting techniques for retailers are the cost and retail methods of inventory valuation. Physical and book (perpetual) procedures are possible with each. Physical inventory valuation requires counting merchandise at prescribed times. Book inventory valuation relies on accurate bookkeeping and a smooth data flow.

   The cost method obligates a retailer to have careful records or to code costs on packages. This must be done to find the exact value of ending inventory at cost. Many firms use LIFO accounting to project that value, which lets them reduce taxes by having a low ending inventory value. In the retail method, closing inventory value is tied to the average relationship between the cost and retail value of merchandise. That more accurately reflects market conditions but can be complex.

3. *To study the merchandise forecasting and budgeting process.* This is a form of dollar control with six stages: designating control units, sales forecasting, inventory-level planning, reduction planning, planning purchases, and planning profit margins. Adjustments require all later stages to be modified.

   Control units—merchandise categories for which data are gathered—must be narrow to isolate problems and opportunities with specific product lines. Sales forecasting may be the key stage in the merchandising and budgeting process. Through inventory-level planning, a firm sets merchandise quantities for specified periods through the basic stock, percentage variation, weeks' supply, and/or stock-to-sales methods. Reduction planning estimates expected markdowns, discounts, and stock shortages. Planned purchases are linked to planned sales, reductions, and ending and beginning inventory. Profit margins depend on planned net sales, operating expenses, profit, and reductions.

4. *To examine alternative methods of inventory unit control.* A unit control system involves physical units of merchandise. It monitors best-sellers and poor-sellers, the quantity of goods on hand, inventory age, reorder time, and so on. A physical inventory unit control system may use visual inspection or stock counting. A perpetual inventory unit control system keeps a running total of the units handled through record keeping entries that adjust for sales, returns, transfers, and so on. A perpetual system can be applied manually, by merchandise tags processed by computers, or by point-of-sale devices. Virtually all larger retailers conduct regular complete physical inventories; two-thirds use a perpetual inventory system.

5. *To integrate dollar and unit merchandising control concepts.* Three aspects of financial inventory management integrate dollar and unit control concepts: stock turnover and gross margin return on investment, when to reorder, and how much to reorder. Stock turnover is the number of times during a period that average inventory on hand is sold. Gross margin return on investment shows the relationship between gross margin in dollars (total dollar operating profits) and average inventory investment (at cost). A reorder point calculation—when to reorder—includes the retailer's usage rate, order lead time, and safety stock. The economic order quantity—how much to reorder—shows how big an order to place, based on both ordering and inventory costs.

Key Terms

financial merchandise management (p. 438)
dollar control (p. 438)
unit control (p. 438)
merchandise available for sale (p. 438)
cost of goods sold (p. 438)
gross profit (p. 438)
net profit (p. 438)
cost method of accounting (p. 440)
physical inventory system (p. 440)
book inventory system (perpetual inventory system) (p. 440)

FIFO (first-in-first-out) method (p. 441)
LIFO (last-in-first-out) method (p. 441)
retail method of accounting (p. 442)
cost complement (p. 442)
control units (p. 445)
classification merchandising (p. 446)
monthly sales index (p. 447)
basic stock method (p. 448)
percentage variation method (p. 449)
weeks' supply method (p. 449)
stock-to-sales method (p. 449)

retail reductions (p. 450)
open-to-buy (p. 451)
stock turnover (p. 456)
gross margin return on investment (GMROI) (p. 457)
reorder point (p. 457)
order lead time (p. 457)
usage rate (p. 458)
safety stock (p. 458)
automatic reordering system (p. 458)
economic order quantity (EOQ) (p. 459)

Questions for Discussion

1. Which retailers can best use a perpetual inventory system based on the cost method? Explain your answer.

2. The FIFO method seems more logical than the LIFO method, because it assumes the first merchandise purchased is the first merchandise sold. So, why do more retailers use LIFO?

3. Explain the basic premise of the retail method of accounting. Present an example.

4. Why should a local appliance store designate control units, even though this may be time-consuming?

5. Why use sophisticated weather forecasting services if daily weather predictions tend to be inaccurate?

6. Contrast the weeks' supply method and the percentage variation method of merchandise planning.

7. Present two situations in which it would be advisable for a retailer to take a markdown instead of carry over merchandise from one budget period to another.

8. A retailer has yearly sales of $800,000. Inventory on January 1 is $300,000 (at cost). During the year, $600,000 of merchandise (at cost) is purchased. The ending inventory is $305,000 (at cost). Operating costs are $90,000. Calculate the cost of goods sold and net profit, and set up a profit-and-loss statement. There are no retail reductions in this problem.

9. A retailer has a beginning monthly inventory valued at $80,000 at retail and $52,500 at cost. Net purchases during the month are $190,000 at retail and $115,000 at cost. Transportation charges are $10,500. Sales are $225,000. Markdowns and discounts equal $30,000. A physical inventory at the end of the month shows merchandise valued at $15,000 (at retail) on hand. Compute the following:
   a. Total merchandise available for sale—at cost and at retail.
   b. Cost complement.
   c. Ending retail book value of inventory.
   d. Stock shortages.
   e. Adjusted ending retail book value.
   f. Gross profit.

10. The sales of a full-line discount store are listed. Calculate the monthly sales indexes. What do they mean?

January	$400,000	May	$460,000	September	$460,000
February	415,000	June	430,000	October	400,000
March	415,000	July	370,000	November	490,000
April	460,000	August	430,000	December	610,000

11. If the planned average monthly stock for the discount store in Question 10 is $520,000 (at retail), how much inventory should be planned for August if the retailer uses the percentage variation method? Comment on this retailer's choice of the percentage variation method.

12. The store in Questions 10 and 11 knows its cost complement for all merchandise purchased last year was 0.61; it projects this to remain constant. It expects to begin and end December with inventory valued at $240,000 at retail and estimates December reductions to be $18,000. The firm already has purchase commitments for December worth $180,000 (at retail). What is the open-to-buy at cost for December?

Note: At our Web site (**www.pearsonhighered.com/berman**), there are several math problems related to the material in this chapter so that you may review these concepts.

Web **Exercise**

Visit the Retail Owners Institute Web site (www. retailowner.com). Describe how a small retailer could use the information found at the site in its financial merchandise management efforts. Describe how a large retailer could use the information found at the site.

Note: Stop by our Web site (www.pearsonhighered. com/berman) to experience a number of highly interactive, appealing Web exercises based on actual company demonstrations and sample materials related to retailing.

17

Pricing in Retailing

During the 1950s, Sol Price founded FedMart, the nation's first membership club. Initially, FedMart was open only to government employees due to strict laws regarding discounting. In 1975, Price sold his interest in FedMart and a year later opened Price Club in an aircraft hanger in an industrial section of San Diego. In 1983, some former Price Club executives opened their own membership club and named it Costco. Price Club and Costco merged as Price Costco in 1993, and the name of the company was changed to Costco (**www.costco.com**) in 1995.

There are now 1,250 membership clubs in the United States, operated mostly by Costco, Sam's Club (**www.samsclub.com**), and BJ's (**www. bjswholesale.com**). Costco operates more than 480 membership clubs serving nearly 50 million cardholders in 36 states and Puerto Rico, Canada, Great Britain, Japan, South Korea, and Taiwan. Costco averages $918 a square foot in sales versus $552 for Sam's Club.

To attract upscale customers, Costco carries fine wines and charges a retail markup of no more than 14 percent. In contrast, local merchants typically mark up wine by 40 percent. As a result, Costco is probably the largest retailer of premium wines in the United States. According to Costco's chief financial officer, "If we were a country, we would be the third largest seller of Dom Perignon champagne in the world." Costco also lures affluent shoppers with Ralph Lauren clothing and Waterford crystal at deep discounts. It is even known for stocking treasure-hunt items, such as Prada handbags, that are offered briefly to encourage bargain hunters to visit the store more frequently.[1]

Source: Reprinted by permission of Susan Berry, Retail Image Consulting, Inc.

OVERVIEW

Learn about the complexities of setting prices (**www.pricepointreport.com**).

Goods and services must be priced in a way that both achieves profitability for the retailer and satisfies customers. A pricing strategy must be consistent with the retailer's overall image (positioning), sales, profit, and return on investment goals.

There are three basic pricing options for a retailer: (1) A *discount orientation* uses low prices as the major competitive advantage. A low-price image, fewer shopping frills, and low per-unit profit margins mean a target market of price-oriented customers, low operating costs, and high inventory turnover. Off-price retailers and full-line discount stores are in this category. (2) With an *at-the-market orientation,* the retailer has average prices. It offers solid service and a nice atmosphere to middle-class shoppers. Margins are moderate to good, and average to above-average quality products are stocked. This firm may find it hard to expand its price range, and it may be squeezed by retailers positioned as discounters or prestige stores. Traditional department stores and many drugstores are in this category. (3) Through an *upscale orientation,* a prestigious image is the retailer's major competitive advantage. A smaller target market, higher expenses, and lower turnover mean customer loyalty, distinctive services and products, and high per-unit profit margins. Upscale department stores and specialty stores are in this category.

Nordstrom is the world's largest online shoe retailer (**http://store.nordstrom.com/category/default_shoes.asp**), with its usual upscale prices and service.

One important key to successful retailing is offering a good *value* in the consumer's mind—for the price orientation chosen. That is why Sports Authority shifted from its long-time good, better, and best strategy to one that emphasizes better and best products in order to improve gross margins and achieve greater customer loyalty: "We are dedicated to providing our customers with the best shopping experience possible by consistently providing great brands at great values. We are dedicated to increasing that value by providing industry-leading customer service and product knowledge. We are dedicated to you, and helping you take your game to the next level. If this is what you have been looking for in a sporting goods retailer, then you've come to the right store!"[2]

Every customer, whether buying an inexpensive $4 ream of paper or a $40 ream of embossed, personalized stationery, wants to feel his or her purchase represents a good value. The consumer is not necessarily looking only for the best price. He or she is often interested in the best value—which may be reflected in a superior shopping experience. See Figure 17-1.

Consider this observation by a *Business Week* reporter:

> I inherited a ring that was somewhat dated, but with a beautiful aquamarine, my wife's birthstone. I knew she would love the stone, so I set out to find a jeweler who could redesign the ring into a pendant for her birthday. I visited three or four different jewelry stores, trying to find one that would offer design talent, a personal touch, and a willingness to work within my budget. As I evaluated my decision process, I observed something interesting and somewhat surprising—I gravitated to the most expensive option. I can't say that the jeweler I chose was definitively better, but for some reason I felt more comfortable with it, not in spite of its higher prices, but because of them. I felt that by paying a little extra I would be more assured of ending up with a piece my wife would love.[3]

Another factor shaping today's pricing environment for retailers of all types is the ease by which a shopper can compare prices on the Web. When a consumer could only do price comparisons by visiting individual stores, the process was time-consuming—which limited many people's willingness to shop

FIGURE 17-1

At Barnes & Noble:
A Huge Selection
AND Special Discounts
for Members

Source: Reprinted by permission
of Susan Berry, Retail Image
Consulting, Inc.

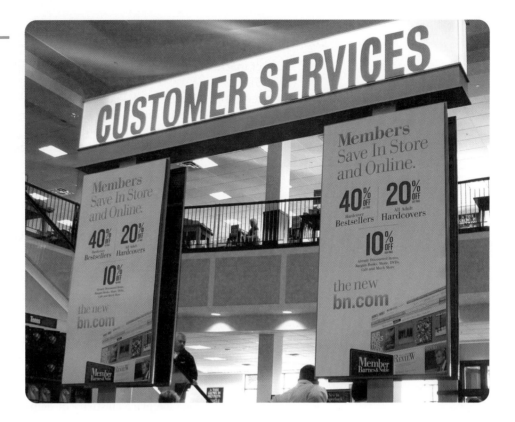

around. Now, with a few clicks of a computer mouse, a shopper can quickly gain online price information from several retailers in just minutes—without leaving home. Web sites such as PriceGrabber.com, NexTag, Shopping.com, and MySimon.com make comparison shopping very simple: As the Smarter.com Web site notes: "Our goal is to help consumers make smarter buying decisions by enabling them to research and compare products, as well as to compare prices on millions of products available at thousands of reputable online stores. We gather product and merchant data from across the Internet, organize, and structure it into a comprehensive catalog."[4] See Figure 17-2.

FIGURE 17-2

Shopping.com: A
Comparison-Shopping
Web Site

Source: Reprinted by permission.

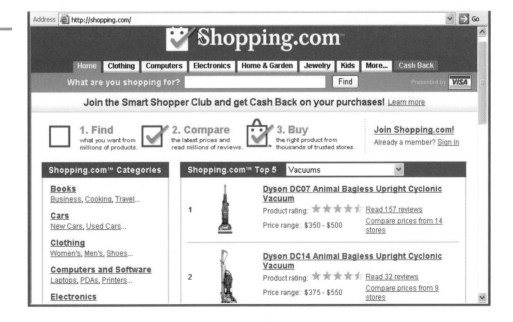

The interaction of price with other retailing mix elements can be illustrated by BE's Toy City, a hypothetical discounter. It has a broad strategy consisting of:

▶ A target market of price-conscious families that shop for inexpensive toys ($9 to $12).
▶ A limited range of merchandise quality ("better" merchandise consists of end-of-season closeouts and manufacturer overruns).
▶ Self-service in an outlet mall location.
▶ A good assortment supported by quantity purchases at deep discounts from suppliers.
▶ An image of efficiency and variety.

In this chapter, we divide retail pricing into two major sections: the external factors affecting a price strategy and the steps in a price strategy. At our site (**www.pearsonhighered.com/berman**), there are several links to information on setting a price strategy.

External Factors Affecting a Retail Price Strategy

Several factors (discussed next) have an impact on a retail pricing strategy, as shown in Figure 17-3. Sometimes, the factors have a minor effect. In other cases, they severely restrict a firm's pricing options.

The Consumer and Retail Pricing[5]

Retailers should understand the **price elasticity of demand**—the sensitivity of customers to price changes in terms of the quantities they will buy—because there is often a relationship between price and consumer purchases and perceptions. If small percentage changes in price lead to substantial percentage changes in the number of units bought, demand is *price elastic*. This occurs when the urgency to purchase is low or there are acceptable substitutes. If large percentage changes in price lead to small percentage changes in the number of units bought, demand is *price inelastic*. Then purchase urgency is high or there are no acceptable substitutes (as takes place with brand or retailer loyalty). *Unitary elasticity* occurs when percentage changes in price are directly offset by percentage changes in quantity.

Price elasticity is computed by dividing the percentage change in the quantity demanded by the percentage change in the price charged. Because purchases generally decline as prices go up, elasticity tends to be a negative number:

One look at Godiva's Web site (www.godiva.com) and you'll know why demand for its products is inelastic.

$$\text{Elasticity} = \frac{\dfrac{\text{Quantity 1} - \text{Quantity 2}}{\text{Quantity 1} + \text{Quantity 2}}}{\dfrac{\text{Price 1} - \text{Price 2}}{\text{Price 1} + \text{Price 2}}}$$

Table 17-1 shows the price elasticity for a 1,000-seat movie theater (with elasticities converted to positive numbers) that offers second-run movies. The quantity demanded (tickets

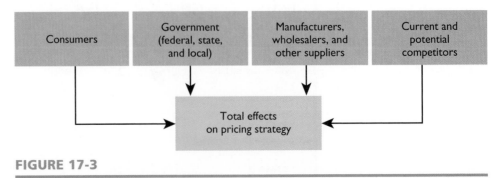

FIGURE 17-3

Factors Affecting a Retail Price Strategy

Value Retailing: Not Just a U.S. Phenomenon

Value retailing has become the fastest growing segment of the British clothing market. Among the retailers positioned in this segment are T.K. Maxx (**www.tkmaxx.com**), Matalan (**www.matalan.co.uk**), Primark (**www.primark. co.uk**), Peacocks (**www.peacocks.co.uk**), and George at ASDA (**www.george.com**). According to the managing director of Live and Breathe, a British advertising agency: "It's a great time for value retailing. If they've done well in the last five years when consumers had money to spend and credit available, then now when the economy is pinching they should do well."

Primark, a value retailer, appeals to adults under 35 years old, as well as children. It promotes itself using the slogan, "Look good, Pay less" and has used a marketing strategy based on having low prices and quickly reacting to the latest fashion trends. Industry observers believe that Primark is now the number-one value-based British clothing retailer. To keep its costs down, Primark has a very low promotional budget that stresses store openings.

To increase sales, ASDA (**www.asda.co.uk**), the British division of Wal-Mart, started selling the value-based George clothing brand (which has global sales of $3 billion) on the Web in 2008. The Web site, which serves Great Britain, features next-day delivery. Returns can be made by mail or in the store.

Sources: Rosie Baker, "Following Fast Fashion," *In-Store* (June 2008), pp. 37, 39; and Samatha Conti, "George Coming to Web, $200 Million in Sales Seen," *Women's Wear Daily* (July 24, 2007), p. 3.

sold) declines at every price from $6.00 to $10.00. Demand is inelastic from $6.00 to $7.00 and $7.00 to $8.00; ticket receipts increase because the percentage change in price is greater than the percentage change in tickets sold. Demand is unitary from $8.00 to $9.00; ticket receipts are constant because the percentage change in tickets sold exactly offsets the percentage change in price. Demand is elastic from $9.00 to $10.00; ticket receipts decline because the percentage change in tickets sold is greater than the percentage change in price.

For our movie theater example, total ticket receipts are highest at $8.00 or at $9.00. But what about total revenues? If patrons spend an average of $4.00 each at the concession stand, the best price is $6.00 (total overall revenues of $10,000). This theater is most interested in total revenues because its operating costs are the same whether there are 1,000 or 550 patrons. But typically, retailers should evaluate the costs, as well as the revenues, from serving additional customers.

TABLE 17-1   A Movie Theater's Elasticity of Demand

Price	Tickets Sold (Saturday Night)	Total Ticket Receipts	Elasticity of Demand[a]
$ 6.00	1,000	$6,000	
			E = 0.68
7.00	900	6,300	
			E = 0.79
8.00	810	6,480	
			E = 1.00
9.00	720	6,480	
			E = 2.54
10.00	550	5,500	

$$\text{Computation example (\$6.00 to \$7.00 price range)} \quad = \quad \frac{\dfrac{1,000-900}{1,000+900}}{\dfrac{\$6.00-\$7.00}{\$6.00+\$7.00}} \quad = \quad 0.68$$

[a]Expressed as a positive number.

In retailing, computing price elasticity is difficult. First, as with the movie theater, demand for individual events or items may be hard to predict. One week, the theater may attract 1,000 patrons to a movie, and the next week it may attract 400 patrons to a different movie. Second, many retailers carry thousands of items and cannot possibly compute elasticities for every one. As a result, they usually rely on average markup pricing, competition, tradition, and industrywide data to indicate price elasticity.

Price sensitivity varies by market segment, based on shopping orientation. After identifying potential segments, retailers determine which of them form their target market:

Dell (**www.dell.com/home**) appeals to multiple consumer segments—from novice to advanced computer user, with prices set accordingly.

▶ *Economic consumers.* They perceive competing retailers as similar and shop around for the lowest possible prices. This segment has grown dramatically in recent years.
▶ *Status-oriented consumers.* They perceive competing retailers as quite different. They are more interested in prestige brands and strong customer service than in price.
▶ *Assortment-oriented consumers.* They seek retailers with a strong selection in the product categories being considered. They want fair prices.
▶ *Personalizing consumers.* They shop where they are known and feel a bond with employees and the firm itself. These shoppers will pay slightly above-average prices.
▶ *Convenience-oriented consumers.* They shop because they must, want nearby stores with long hours, and may use catalogs or the Web. These people will pay higher prices for convenience.

The Government and Retail Pricing

Three levels of government may affect retail pricing decisions: federal, state, and local. When laws are federal, they apply to interstate commerce. A retailer operating only within the boundaries of one state may not be restricted by some federal legislation. Major government rules relate to horizontal price fixing, vertical price fixing, price discrimination, minimum price levels, unit pricing, item price removal, and price advertising. For retailers operating outside their home countries, a fourth level of government comes into play: international jurisdictions.

HORIZONTAL PRICE FIXING

An agreement among manufacturers, among wholesalers, or among retailers to set prices is known as **horizontal price fixing**. Such agreements are illegal under the Sherman Antitrust Act and the Federal Trade Commission Act, regardless of how "reasonable" prices may be. It is also illegal for retailers to get together regarding the use of coupons, rebates, or other price-oriented tactics.

Although few large-scale legal actions have been taken in recent years, the penalties for horizontal price fixing can be severe:

> In 2003, venerable auction houses Sotheby's and Christie's pled guilty to colluding to fix commission fees in the 1990s. The two firms paid more than $600 million in fines and to settle civil lawsuit damages. After a high-profile trial, Sotheby's chairman, A. Alfred Taubman, cooled his heels in prison for ten months and CEO Diana Brooks languished under house arrest in Manhattan.[6]

VERTICAL PRICE FIXING

When manufacturers or wholesalers seek to control the retail prices of their goods and services, **vertical price fixing** occurs. Until recently, retailers in the United States could not be forced to adhere to *minimum retail prices* set by manufacturers and wholesalers. Federal laws banning this practice were intended to encourage price competition among retailers. However, as a result of a 2007 Supreme Court ruling, the situation has changed significantly:

> Manufacturers now have more legal power to set minimum prices, thanks to a ruling overturning a century-old ban on the practice. This could lead to higher prices for consumers and make it harder for smaller retailers to compete. The case reached the Supreme Court because of a dispute between Leegin Creative Leather Products, a manufacturer of women's fashion accessories; and Kay's

Kloset, a Dallas-area boutique. Leegin stopped shipping its products to Kay's Kloset because the store was selling them below a company-mandated price. PSKS, the parent company of Kay's Kloset, filed an antitrust suit against Leegin in 2002. In June 2007, the Supreme Court ruled in Leegin's favor.

This latest ruling does not legalize minimum pricing across the board. Horizontal price fixing—when competitors group together to set prices—is still illegal. The court decision asserts that minimum pricing is not an automatic antitrust violation and that the courts should judge according to the "rule of reason," or on a case-by-case basis, to determine what is anti-competitive.

Patricia Huddleston, a professor at Michigan State University, says minimum pricing will not be pervasive because there are too many disincentives for manufacturers. Retailers can quit carrying the products in question and switch to competitors that do not require minimum prices. Consumers can quit buying higher-priced products in favor of cheaper ones. Thus, manufacturers may unwittingly create new competition in the form of more private-label goods. "I think more retailers will develop their own private-label merchandise because the manufacturer then has no power over the prices," Huddleston said. In addition, private-label goods are often cheaper to consumers and generate higher margins for retailers. Off-price retailers will be largely unaffected by minimum price restrictions, since they buy excess inventory, not current goods, from manufacturers and full-price retailers.[7]

Manufacturers and wholesalers can also legally control retail prices by one of these methods: They can screen retailers. They can set realistic list prices. They can pre-print prices on products (which retailers do not have to use). They can set regular prices that are accepted by consumers (such as 50 cents for a newspaper). They can use consignment selling, whereby the supplier owns items until they are sold and assumes costs normally associated with the retailer. They can own retail facilities. They can refuse to sell to retailers that advertise discount prices in violation of written policies. A supplier has a right to announce a policy for dealer pricing and can refuse to sell to those that do not comply. It cannot use coercion to prohibit a retailer from advertising low prices.

PRICE DISCRIMINATION

The **Robinson-Patman Act** bars manufacturers and wholesalers from discriminating in price or purchase terms in selling to individual retailers if these retailers are purchasing products of "like quality" and the effect of such discrimination is to injure competition. The intent of this Act is to stop large retailers from using their power to gain discounts not justified by the cost savings achieved by suppliers due to big orders. There are exceptions that allow justifiable price discrimination when:

▶ Products are physically different.
▶ The retailers paying different prices are not competitors.
▶ Competition is not injured.
▶ Price differences are due to differences in supplier costs.
▶ Market conditions change—costs rise or fall or competing suppliers shift their prices.

Discounts are not illegal, as long as suppliers follow the preceding rules, make discounts available to competing retailers on an equitable basis, and offer discounts sufficiently graduated so small retailers can also qualify. Discounts for cumulative purchases (total yearly orders) and for multistore purchases by chains may be hard to justify.

Although the Robinson-Patman Act restricts sellers more than buyers, retailers are covered under Section 2(F): "It shall be unlawful for any person engaged in commerce, in the course of such commerce, knowingly to induce or receive a discrimination in price which is prohibited in this section." Thus, a retail buyer must try to get the lowest prices charged to any competitor, yet not bargain so hard that discounts cannot be justified by acceptable exceptions.

MINIMUM-PRICE LAWS

About half the states have **minimum-price laws** that prevent retailers from selling certain items for less than their cost plus a fixed percentage to cover overhead. Besides general laws, some state rules set minimum prices for specific products. For instance, in New Jersey and Connecticut, the retail price of liquor cannot be less than the wholesale cost (including taxes and delivery charges).

Minimum-price laws protect small retailers from **predatory pricing**, in which large retailers seek to reduce competition by selling goods and services at very low prices, thus causing small retailers to go out of business. In one widely watched case, three pharmacies in Arkansas filed a suit claiming Wal-Mart had sold selected items below cost in an attempt to reduce competition. Wal-Mart agreed it had priced some items below cost to meet or beat rivals' prices but not to harm competitors. The Arkansas Supreme Court ruled that Wal-Mart did not use predatory pricing since the three pharmacies were still profitable.

With **loss leaders**, retailers price selected items below cost to lure more customer traffic for those retailers. Supermarkets and other retailers use loss leaders to increase overall sales and profits because people buy more than one item once in a store: "The loss leader strategy is used primarily to attract customers to your business through the introduction of a bargain. Such bargains may result in no profit being made but will be made up through the sale of other goods/services that may or may not be related to the product. The main aim of the strategy is to eliminate competition in order to gain an advantage in the market consequently building your own image. Implementing the loss leader strategy can be risky and therefore needs to be considered that it is the right approach to penetrating the market."[8]

UNIT PRICING

In some states, the proliferation of package sizes has led to **unit pricing** laws—whereby some retailers must express both the total price of an item and its price per unit of measure. Food stores are most affected by unit price rules because grocery items are more regulated than nongrocery items.[9] There are exemptions for firms with low sales. The aim of unit pricing is to enable consumers to compare prices of products available in many sizes. Thus, a 5-ounce can of tuna fish priced at $1.35 would also have a shelf label showing this as 27 cents per ounce. And a person learns that a 20-ounce bottle of soda selling for $1.00 (5 cents per ounce) costs more than a 67.6-ounce—2-liter—bottle for $1.49 (2.2 cents per ounce).

Retailer costs include computing per-unit prices, printing product and shelf labels, and keeping computer records. These costs are influenced by the way prices are attached to goods (by the supplier or the retailer), the number of items subject to unit pricing, the frequency of price changes, sales volume, and the number of stores in a chain.

Unit pricing can be a good strategy for retailers to follow, even when not required. At many supermarkets, the unit pricing system more than pays for itself because of decreased price-marking errors, better inventory control, and improved space management.

ITEM PRICE REMOVAL

The boom in computerized checkout systems has led many firms, especially supermarkets, to advocate **item price removal**—whereby prices are marked only on shelves or signs and not on individual items. Scanning equipment reads pre-marked product codes and enters price data at the checkout counter. This practice is banned in several states and local communities.

Many retailers oppose item pricing laws: "In the eyes of the typical retailer, item-pricing laws are relics of a bygone era, inappropriate for the world of scanners and shelf labeling, electronic or manual. And instead of serving customers and cutting costs, employees are forced to work the aisles with a sticker gun." Yet, consumer advocates support them: "Price tags help people shop and help reduce checkout errors. Consumers have the right to compare a price tag to the amount charged at the checkout."[10]

PRICE ADVERTISING

The FTC has guidelines pertaining to advertising price reductions, advertising prices in relation to competitors' prices, and bait-and-switch advertising. To access several FTC publications on acceptable pricing practices, visit our Web site (**www.pearsonhighered.com/berman**).

A retailer cannot claim or imply that a price has been reduced from some former level (a suggested list price) unless the former price was one that the retailer had actually offered for a good or service on a regular basis during a reasonably substantial, recent period of time.

When a retailer says its prices are lower than competitors', it must make certain that its comparisons pertain to firms selling large quantities in the same trading area. A somewhat controversial, but legal, practice is price matching. For the most part, a retailer makes three assumptions when it "guarantees to match the lowest price" of any competing retailer: (1) This guarantee gives shoppers the impression that the firm always offers low prices or else it would not make such a commitment. (2) Most shoppers will not return to a store after a purchase even if they see a lower price advertised elsewhere. (3) The guarantee may exclude most deep discounters and online firms by stating they are not really competitors.

Bait-and-switch advertising is an illegal practice in which a retailer lures a customer by advertising goods and services at exceptionally low prices; once the customer contacts the retailer (by entering a store, calling a toll-free number, or going to a Web site), he or she is told the good/service of interest is out of stock or of inferior quality. A salesperson (or Web script) tries to convince the person to buy a more costly substitute. The retailer does not intend to sell the advertised item. In deciding if a promotion uses bait-and-switch advertising, the FTC considers how many transactions are made at the advertised price, whether sales commissions are excluded on sale items, and total sales relative to advertising costs.

Manufacturers, Wholesalers, and Other Suppliers—and Retail Pricing

There may be conflicts between manufacturers (and other suppliers) and retailers in setting final prices since each would like some control. Manufacturers usually want a certain image and to enable all retailers, even inefficient ones, to earn profits. In contrast, most retailers want to set prices based on their own image, goals, and so forth. A supplier can control prices by using exclusive distribution, not selling to price-cutting retailers, or being its own retailer. A retailer can gain control by being a vital customer, threatening to stop carrying suppliers' lines, stocking private brands, or selling gray market goods.

Many manufacturers set their prices to retailers by estimating final retail prices and then subtracting required retailer and wholesaler profit margins. In the men's apparel industry, the common retail markup is 50 percent of the final price. Thus, a man's shirt retailing at $50 can be sold to the retailer for no more than $25. If a wholesaler is involved, the manufacturer's wholesale price must be far less than $25.

Retailers sometimes carry manufacturers' brands and place high prices on them so rival brands (such as private labels) can be sold more easily. This is called "selling against the brand" and is disliked by manufacturers because sales of their brands are apt to decline. Some retailers also sell **gray market goods**, brand-name products bought in foreign markets or goods transshipped from other retailers. Manufacturers dislike gray market goods because they are often sold at low prices by unauthorized dealers. They may sue gray market goods resellers on the basis of copyright and trademark infringement.

When suppliers are unknown or products are new, retailers may seek price guarantees. For example, to get its radios stocked, a new supplier might have to guarantee the $30 suggested retail price. If the retailers cannot sell the radios for $30, the manufacturer pays a refund. Should the retailers have to sell the radios at $25, the manufacturer gives back $5. Another guarantee is one in which a supplier tells the retailer that no competitor will buy an item for a lower price. If anyone does, the retailer gets a rebate. The relative power of the retailer and its suppliers determines whether such guarantees are provided.

A retailer also has other suppliers: employees, fixtures manufacturers, landlords, and outside parties (such as ad agencies). Each has an effect on price because of their costs to the retailer.

See how Auto-by-Tel (www.autobytel.com) and CarsDirect.com (www.carsdirect.com) approach the selling of cars.

Competition and Retail Pricing

Market pricing occurs when shoppers have a large choice of retailers. In this instance, retailers often price similarly to each other and have less control over price because consumers can easily shop around. Supermarkets, fast-food restaurants, and gas stations may

ETHICS
IN RETAILING

Is "Free" Really Free?

Many Web users get pop-up messages, such as: "Congratulations. You have won a $500 gift certificate to a major electronics store or a free Dell notebook computer. Just complete a simple survey and get ready to redeem your gift." In these instances, the consumer really must be wary.

An editor of *Promo* magazine received such a message and spent an hour or so completing the survey and signing up for mandatory memberships to Netflix (**www.netflix. com**) and the BMG Music Club (**www.bmgmusicservice. com**), and for credit cards that he neither needed nor wanted. [*Please note:* Neither Netflix, BMG, nor the credit card companies were participants in these offers.] The Web site never let the editor know how many questions or offers he needed to address. As anticipated, the certificates for the free goods never arrived. The Web site for the offer did

not provide a phone number or address for inquiries or complaints. A check of the offering firm's Web site (**www. consumergain.com**) with the Complaints Board (**www. complaintsboard.com**) found many other complaints from consumers who did not receive the promised free goods.

The firm's behavior meets the classic test for the Federal Trade Commission's (**www.ftc.gov**) definition of bait-and-switch-advertising as "an alluring, but insincere offer to sell a good or service. The primary aim of a bait advertisement is to obtain leads as to persons interested in buying merchandise of the type so advertised."

Sources: Larry Jaffe, "Bait & Switch Chronicles," *Promo* (May 2007), p. 6; and "Inside Bait-and-Switch Advertising," **www. brandingstrategyinsider.com/2008/05/inside-bait-and.html** (May 3, 2008).

use market pricing due to their competitive industries. Demand for specific retailers may be weak enough so that some customers would switch to a competitor if prices are raised much.

With *administered pricing,* firms seek to attract consumers on the basis of distinctive retailing mixes. This occurs when people consider image, assortment, service, and so forth to be important and they are willing to pay above-average prices to unique retailers. Upscale department stores, fashion apparel stores, and expensive restaurants are among those with unique offerings and solid control over their prices.

Most price-oriented strategies can be quickly copied. Thus, the reaction of competitors is predictable if the leading firm is successful. This means a price strategy should be viewed from both short-run and long-run perspectives. If competition becomes too intense, a price war may erupt—whereby various firms continually lower prices below regular amounts and sometimes below their cost to lure consumers from competitors. Price wars are sometimes difficult to end and can lead to low profits, losses, or even bankruptcy for some competitors. This is especially so for Web retailers.

Developing a Retail Price Strategy

As Figure 17-4 shows, a retail price strategy has five steps: objectives, policy, strategy, implementation, and adjustments. Pricing policies must be integrated with the total retail mix, which occurs in the second step. The process can be complex due to the

FIGURE 17-4

A Framework for Developing a Retail Price Strategy

often erratic nature of demand, the number of items carried, and the impact of the external factors already noted.

Retail Objectives and Pricing

A retailer's pricing strategy has to reflect its overall goals and be related to sales and profits. There must also be specific pricing goals to avoid such potential problems as confusing people by having too many prices, spending too much time bargaining with customers, offering frequent discounts to stimulate customer traffic, having inadequate profit margins, and placing too much emphasis on price.

OVERALL OBJECTIVES AND PRICING

Sales goals may be stated in terms of revenues and/or unit volume. An aggressive strategy, known as **market penetration pricing**, is used when a retailer seeks large revenues by setting low prices and selling many units. Profit per unit is low, but total profit is high if sales projections are reached. This approach is proper if customers are price sensitive, low prices discourage actual and potential competition, and retail costs do not rise much with volume.

With a **market skimming pricing** strategy, a firm sets premium prices and attracts customers less concerned with price than service, assortment, and prestige. It usually does not maximize sales but does achieve high profit per unit. It is proper if the targeted segment is price insensitive, new competitors are unlikely to enter the market, and added sales will greatly increase retail costs. See Figure 17-5.

Return on investment and early recovery of cash are other possible profit-based goals for retailers using a market skimming strategy. *Return on investment* is sought if a retailer wants profit to be a certain percentage of its investment, such as 20 percent of inventory investment. *Early recovery of cash* is used by retailers that may be short on funds, wish to expand, or be uncertain about the future.

BE's Toy City, the discounter we introduced earlier in this chapter, may be used to illustrate how a retailer sets sales, profit, and return-on-investment goals. The firm sells inexpensive toys and overruns to avoid competing with mainstream toy stores, has one price for all toys (to be set within the $9 to $12 range), minimizes operating costs, encourages self-service, and carries a good selection. Table 17-2 has data on BE's Toy City

Nielsen's Priceman (www.us.nielsen.com/products/ms_priceman.shtml) is a powerful software tool for strategic pricing.

SecondSpin.com (www.secondspin.com) sells used CDs and DVDs at a discount. Tiffany (www.tiffany.com) has great jewelry—although it can be a little pricey.

FIGURE 17-5

Bulgari's Market Skimming Approach

As Hoovers.com (**www.hoovers.com**) notes, "If you have to ask, 'How much?' you probably can't afford Bulgari. The world's number three jewelry company (behind Cartier and Tiffany & Co.) has been crafting prized baubles for the rich and famous for more than a hundred years. Today Bulgari reaches a larger—but no less exclusive— market through more than 150 Bulgari stores, as well as select retailers worldwide."

Source: Reprinted by permission of Susan Berry, Retail Image Consulting, Inc.

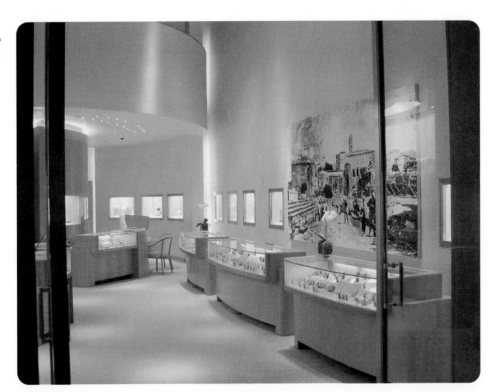

TABLE 17-2 BE's Toy City: Demand, Costs, Profit, and Return on Inventory Investment[a]

Selling Price ($)	Demand (units)	Total Sales Revenue ($)	Average Cost of Goods ($)	Total Cost of Goods ($)	Total Operating Costs ($)	Total Costs ($)	Average Total Costs ($)	Total Profit ($)
9.00	114,000	1,026,000	7.60	866,400	104,000	970,400	8.51	55,600
10.00	104,000	1,040,000	7.85	816,400	94,000	910,400	8.75	129,600
11.00	80,000	880,000	8.25	660,000	88,000	748,000	9.35	132,000
12.00	60,000	720,000	8.75	525,000	80,000	605,000	10.08	115,000

Selling Price ($)	Profit/ Unit ($)	Markup at Retail (%)	Profit/ Sales (%)	Average Inventory on Hand (units)	Inventory Turnover (units)	Average Inventory Investment at Cost ($)	Inventory Turnover ($)	Return-on-Inventory Investment (%)
9.00	0.49	16	5.4	12,000	9.5	91,200	9.5	61
10.00	1.25	22	12.5	13,000	8.0	102,050	8.0	127
11.00	1.65	25	15.0	14,000	5.7	115,500	5.7	114
12.00	1.92	27	16.0	16,000	3.8	140,000	3.8	82

Note: The average cost of goods reflects quantity discounts. Total operating costs include all retail operating expenses.
[a]Numbers have been rounded.

pertaining to demand, costs, profit, and return-on-inventory investment at prices from $9 to $12. The firm must select the best price within that range. Table 17-3 shows how the figures in Table 17-2 were derived. Several conclusions can be drawn from Table 17-2:

▶ A sales goal would lead to a price of $10. Total sales are highest ($1,040,000).
▶ A dollar profit goal would lead to a price of $11. Total profit is highest ($132,000).
▶ A return-on-inventory investment goal would lead to a price of $10. Return on inventory investment is 127 percent.

TABLE 17-3 Derivation of BE's Toy City Data

Column in Table 17-2	Source of Information or Method of Computation
Selling price	Trade data, comparison shopping, experience
Demand (in units) at each price	Consumer surveys, trade data, experience
Total sales revenue	Selling price × Quantity demanded
Average cost of goods	Supplier contacts, quantity discount structure, estimates of order sizes
Total cost of goods	Average cost of goods × Quantity demanded
Total operating costs	Experience, trade data, estimation of individual retail expenses
Total costs	Total cost of goods + Total operating costs
Average total costs	Total costs/Quantity demanded
Total profit	Total sales revenue − Total costs
Profit per unit	Total profit/Quantity demanded
Markup (at retail)	(Selling price − Average cost of goods)/Selling price
Profit as a percentage of sales	Total profit/Total sales revenue
Average inventory on hand	Trade data, inventory turnover data (in units), experience
Inventory turnover (in units)	Quantity demanded/Average inventory on hand (in units)
Average inventory investment (at cost)	Average cost of goods × Average inventory on hand (in units)
Inventory turnover (in $)	Total cost of goods/Average inventory investment (at cost)
Return-on-inventory investment	Total profit/Average inventory investment (at cost)

▶ Although the most items can be sold at $9, that price would lead to the least profit ($55,600).

▶ A price of $12 would yield the highest profit per unit ($1.92) and as a percentage of sales, but total dollar profit is not maximized at this price.

▶ The highest inventory turnover (16,000 units at $12.00) would not lead to the highest total profits.

As a result, BE's Toy City decides on a price of $11 because it would earn the highest dollar profits, while generating good profit per unit and good profit as a percentage of sales.

SPECIFIC PRICING OBJECTIVES

Figure 17-6 lists specific pricing goals other than sales and profits. Each retailer must determine their relative importance given its situation—and plan accordingly. Some goals may be incompatible, such as "to not encourage shoppers to be overly price-conscious" and a "we-will-not-be-undersold" philosophy.

Broad Price Policy

KSS (www.kssg.com) offers a lot of software solutions that enable retailers to better integrate their price strategies.

Through a broad price policy, a retailer generates an integrated price plan with short- and long-run perspectives (balancing immediate and future goals) and a consistent image (vital for chains and franchises). The retailer interrelates its price policy with the target market, the retail image, and the other elements of the retail mix. These are some of the price policies from which a firm could choose:

▶ No competitors will have lower prices, no competitors will have higher prices (for prestige purposes), or prices will be consistent with competitors'.

▶ All items will be priced independently, depending on the demand for each, or the prices for all items will be interrelated to maintain an image and ensure proper markups.

▶ Price leadership will be exerted, competitors will be price leaders and set prices first, or prices will be set independently of competitors.

▶ Prices will be constant over a year or season, or prices will change if costs change.

FIGURE 17-6

Specific Pricing Objectives from Which Retailers May Choose

✓ To maintain a proper image.

✓ To encourage shoppers not to be overly price-conscious.

✓ To be perceived as fair by all parties (including suppliers, employees, and customers).

✓ To be consistent in setting prices.

✓ To increase customer traffic during slow periods.

✓ To clear out seasonal merchandise.

✓ To match competitors' prices without starting a price war.

✓ To promote a "we-will-not-be-undersold" philosophy.

✓ To be regarded as the price leader in the market area by consumers.

✓ To provide ample customer service.

✓ To minimize the chance of government actions relating to price advertising and antitrust matters.

✓ To discourage potential competitors from entering the marketplace.

✓ To create and maintain customer interest.

✓ To encourage repeat business.

See how retailers can improve pricing decisions (www.gofso.com/Premium/ BS/fg/fg-Pricing.html).

Price Strategy

In **demand-oriented pricing**, a retailer sets prices based on consumer desires. It determines the range of prices acceptable to the target market. The top of this range is the demand ceiling, the most that people will pay for a good or service. With **cost-oriented pricing**, a retailer sets a price floor, the minimum price acceptable to the firm so it can reach a specified profit goal. A retailer usually computes merchandise and operating costs and adds a profit margin to these figures. For **competition-oriented pricing**, a retailer sets its prices in accordance with competitors'. The price levels of key competitors are studied and applied.

As a rule, retailers should combine these approaches in enacting a price strategy. The approaches should not be viewed as operating independently.

DEMAND-ORIENTED PRICING

Retailers use demand-oriented pricing to estimate the quantities that customers would buy at various prices. This approach studies customer interests and the psychological implications of pricing. Two aspects of psychological pricing are the price–quality association and prestige pricing.

According to the **price–quality association** concept, many consumers feel high prices connote high quality and low prices connote low quality. This association is especially important if competing firms or products are hard to judge on bases other than price, consumers have little experience or confidence in judging quality (as with a new retailer), shoppers perceive large differences in quality among retailers or products, and brand names are insignificant in product choice. Although various studies have documented a price–quality relationship, research also indicates that if other quality cues, such as retailer atmospherics, customer service, and popular brands, are involved, these cues may be more important than price in a person's judgment of overall retailer or product quality.

Prestige pricing—which assumes that consumers will not buy goods and services at prices deemed too low—is based on the price–quality association. Its premise is that consumers may feel too low a price means poor quality and status. Some people look for prestige pricing when selecting retailers and do not patronize those with prices viewed as too low. Saks Fifth Avenue and Neiman Marcus do not generally carry low-end items because their customers may feel they are inferior. Prestige pricing does not apply to all shoppers. Some people may be economizers and always shop for bargains; and neither the price–quality association nor prestige pricing may be applicable for them.

COST-ORIENTED PRICING

One form of cost-oriented pricing, markup pricing, is the most widely used pricing technique. In **markup pricing**, a retailer sets prices by adding per-unit merchandise costs, retail operating expenses, and desired profit. The difference between merchandise costs and selling price is the **markup**. If a retailer buys a desk for $200 and sells it for $300, the extra $100 covers operating costs and profit. The markup is $33\frac{1}{3}$ percent at retail or 50 percent at cost. The level of the markup depends on a product's traditional markup, the supplier's suggested list price, inventory turnover, competition, rent and other overhead costs, the extent to which the product must be serviced, and the selling effort.

Markups can be computed on the basis of retail selling price or cost but are typically calculated using the retail price. Why? (1) Retail expenses, markdowns, and profit are always stated as a percentage of sales. Thus, markups expressed as a percentage of sales are more meaningful. (2) Manufacturers quote selling prices and discounts to retailers as percentage reductions from retail list prices. (3) Retail price data are more readily available than cost data. (4) Profitability seems smaller if expressed on the basis of price. This can be useful in communicating with the government, employees, and consumers.

This is how a **markup percentage** is calculated. The difference is in the denominator:

$$\frac{\text{Markup percentage}}{\text{(at retail)}} = \frac{\text{Retail selling price} - \text{Merchandise cost}}{\text{Retail selling price}}$$

$$\frac{\text{Markup percentage}}{\text{(at cost)}} = \frac{\text{Retail selling price} - \text{Merchandise cost}}{\text{Merchandise cost}}$$

TABLE 17-4 Markup Equivalents

Percentage at Retail	Percentage at Cost
10.0	11.1
20.0	25.0
30.0	42.9
40.0	66.7
50.0	100.0
60.0	150.0
70.0	233.3
80.0	400.0
90.0	900.0

Table 17-4 shows several markup percentages at retail and at cost. As markups go up, the disparity between the percentages grows. Suppose a retailer buys a watch for $20 and considers whether to sell it for $25, $40, or $100. The $25 price yields a markup of 20 percent at retail and 25 percent at cost, the $40 price a markup of 50 percent at retail and 100 percent at cost, and the $80 price a markup of 80 percent at retail and 400 percent at cost.

These three examples indicate the usefulness of the markup concept in planning:

1. A discount clothing store can buy a shipment of men's long-sleeve shirts at $12 each and wants a 30 percent markup at retail.[11] What retail price should the store charge to achieve this markup?

$$\text{Markup percentage (at retail)} = \frac{\text{Retail selling price} - \text{Merchandise cost}}{\text{Retail selling price}}$$

$$0.30 = \frac{\text{Retail selling price} - \$12.00}{\text{Retail selling price}}$$

$$\text{Retail selling price} = \$17.14$$

2. A stationery store desires a minimum 40 percent markup at retail.[12] If standard envelopes retail at $7.99 per box, what is the maximum price the store should pay for each box?

$$\text{Markup percentage (at retail)} = \frac{\text{Retail selling price} - \text{Merchandise cost}}{\text{Retail selling price}}$$

$$0.40 = \frac{\$7.99 - \text{Merchandise cost}}{\$7.99}$$

$$\text{Merchandise cost} = \$4.794$$

3. A sporting goods store has been offered a closeout purchase for bicycles. The cost of each bike is $105, and it should retail for $160. What markup at retail would the store obtain?

$$\text{Markup percentage (at retail)} = \frac{\text{Retail selling price} - \text{Merchandise cost}}{\text{Retail selling price}}$$

$$= \frac{\$160.00 - \$105.00}{\$160.00} = 34.4$$

A retailer's markup percentage may also be determined by examining planned retail operating expenses, profit, and net sales. Suppose a florist estimates yearly operating expenses to be $55,000. The desired profit is $50,000 per year, including the owner's salary. Net sales are forecast to be $250,000. The planned markup would be:

$$\text{Markup percentage (at retail)} = \frac{\text{Planned retail operating expenses} + \text{Planned profit}}{\text{Planned net sales}}$$

$$= \frac{\$55,000 + \$50,000}{\$250,000} = 42$$

If potted plants cost the florist $8.00 each, the retailer's selling price would be:

$$\text{Retail selling price} = \frac{\text{Merchandise cost}}{1 - \text{Markup}}$$

$$= \frac{\$8.00}{1 - 0.42} = \$13.79$$

The florist must sell about 18,129 plants (assuming that this is the only item it carries) at $13.79 apiece to achieve sales and profit goals. To reach these goals, all plants must be sold at the $13.79 price.

Because it is rare to sell all items in stock at their original prices, initial markup, maintained markup, and gross margin should each be computed. **Initial markup** is based on the original retail value assigned to merchandise less the costs of the merchandise. **Maintained markup** is based on the actual prices received for merchandise sold during a time period less merchandise cost. Maintained markups relate to actual prices received, so they can be hard to predict. The difference between the initial and maintained markups is that the latter reflect adjustments for markdowns, added markups, shortages, and discounts.

The initial markup percentage depends on planned retail operating expenses, profit, reductions, and net sales:

$$\begin{array}{l}\text{Initial markup} \\ \text{percentage} \\ \text{(at retail)}\end{array} = \frac{\begin{array}{c}\text{Planned retail operating expenses} + \text{Planned profit} \\ + \text{Planned retail reductions}\end{array}}{\text{Planned net sales} + \text{Planned retail reductions}}$$

If planned retail reductions are 0, the initial markup percentage equals planned retail operating expenses plus profit, both divided by planned net sales. To resume the florist example, suppose the firm projects that retail reductions will be 20 percent of estimated sales, or $50,000. To reach its goals, the initial markup and the original selling price would be:

$$\begin{array}{l}\text{Initial markup} \\ \text{percentage} \\ \text{(at retail)}\end{array} = \frac{\$55,000 + \$50,000 + \$50,000}{\$250,000 + \$50,000} = 51.7$$

$$\text{Retail selling price} = \frac{\text{Merchandise cost}}{1 - \text{Markup}} = \frac{\$8.00}{1 - 0.517} = \$16.56$$

The original retail value of 18,129 plants is about $300,000. Retail reductions of $50,000 lead to net sales of $250,000. Thus, the retailer must begin by selling plants at $16.56 apiece if it wants an average selling price of $13.79 and a maintained markup of 42 percent.

The maintained markup percentage is:

$$\begin{array}{l}\text{Maintained markup} \\ \text{percentage} \\ \text{(at retail)}\end{array} = \frac{\text{Actual retail operating expenses} + \text{Actual profit}}{\text{Actual net sales}}$$

or

$$\begin{array}{l}\text{Maintained markup} \\ \text{percentage} \\ \text{(at retail)}\end{array} = \frac{\text{Average selling price} - \text{Merchandise cost}}{\text{Average selling price}}$$

Gross margin is the difference between net sales and the total cost of goods sold (which adjusts for cash discounts and additional expenses):

$$\text{Gross margin (in \$)} = \text{Net sales} - \text{Total cost of goods}$$

The florist's gross margin (the dollar equivalent of maintained markup) is roughly $105,000.

Although a retailer must set a companywide markup goal, markups for categories of merchandise or individual products may differ—sometimes dramatically. At many full-line discount stores, maintained markup as a percentage of sales ranges from under 20 percent for consumer electronics to more than 40 percent for jewelry and watches.

Price Optimization Software: The Price Is Right

Although large supermarket chains have been using price optimization software for many years, this software is increasingly being used by smaller grocery chains. Several software firms have recently developed scaled-down Web versions of their software. In addition, some major wholesalers have struck deals with software providers to offer their services to the wholesalers' clients. Nash Finch has signed a contract with Revionics (**www.revionics. com**), for the software provider to offer its price and promotional modeling software to the independent retailers and military commissaries it serves in 31 states. Supervalu, another leading wholesaler, has a similar arrangement with Revionics.

Unlike larger chains, small to medium-sized firms do not have in-house information technology experts, cannot afford the resources to troubleshoot computer systems issues, and do not have specialized staffs to analyze complex reports.

Let's look at how well this software has been applied at two small to medium-sized chains:

▶ The owner of Delano's IGA Markets (**www. delanomarkets.com**), an eight-store chain based in San Francisco, reports that "The service [Revionics Web-based pricing system] helps us balance sales growth with achieving maximum profitability."
▶ The director of purchasing for Earth Fare (**www.earthfare.com**), an 11-store chain in Asheville, North Carolina, states that "We can focus more on servicing the customer, because Revionics automates and improves many of the tasks related to pricing."

Sources: Joseph Tarnowski, "The Price Is Just Right," *Progressive Grocer* (April 1, 2008), p. 66; and Joseph Tarnowski, "The Price Software Is Right," *Progressive Grocer* (September 15, 2007), p. 100.

With a **variable markup policy**, a retailer purposely adjusts markups by merchandise category. Such a policy:

▶ Recognizes that the costs of different goods/service categories may fluctuate widely. Some items require alterations or installation. Even within a product line, expensive items may require greater end-of-year markdowns than inexpensive ones. The high-priced line needs a larger initial markup.
▶ Allows for differences in product investments. For major appliances, where the retailer orders regularly from a wholesaler, lower markups are needed than with fine jewelry, where the retailer must have a complete stock of unique merchandise.
▶ Accounts for differences in sales efforts and merchandising skills. A feature-laden food processor may require a substantial effort, whereas a standard toaster involves much less effort.
▶ May help a retailer to generate more customer traffic by advertising certain products at deep discounts. This entails leader pricing (discussed later in the chapter).

One way to plan variable markups is **direct product profitability (DPP)**, a technique that enables a retailer to find the profitability of each category of merchandise by computing adjusted per-unit gross margin and assigning direct product costs for such expense categories as warehousing, transportation, handling, and selling. The proper markup for each category or item is then set. DPP is used by some supermarkets, discounters, and other retailers. However, there is complexity in assigning costs.

Figure 17-7 illustrates DPP for two items with a selling price of $20. The retailer pays $12 for Item A, whose per-unit gross margin is $8. Since the retailer gets a $1 per unit allowance to set up a special display, the adjusted gross margin is $9. Total direct retail costs are estimated at $5. Direct product profit is $4—20 percent of sales. The retailer pays $10 for Item B, whose per-unit gross margin is $10. There are no special discounts or allowances. Because Item B needs more selling effort, total direct retail costs are $6. The direct profit is $4—20 percent of sales. To attain the same direct profit per unit, Item A needs a 40 percent markup (per-unit gross margin/selling price), and Item B needs 50 percent.

Cost-oriented (markup) pricing is popular among retailers. It is simple, because a retailer can apply a standard markup for a product category more easily than it can estimate demand at various prices. The firm can also adjust prices according to demand or segment its customers.

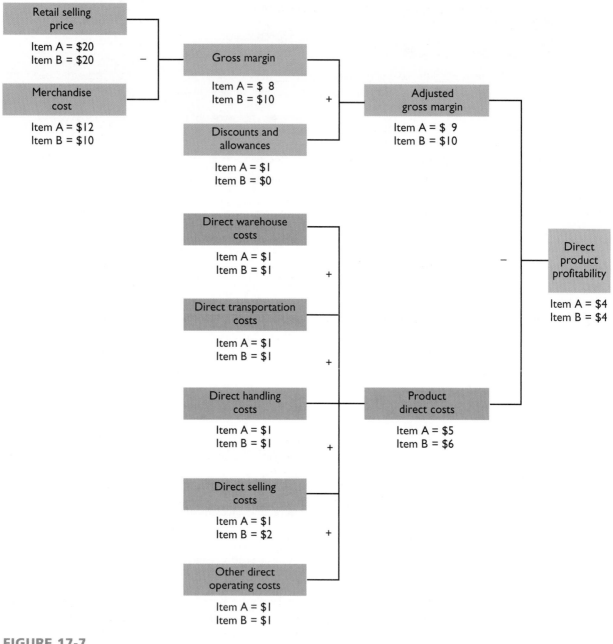

FIGURE 17-7

How to Determine Direct Product Profitability

Markup pricing has a sense of equity given that the retailer earns a fair profit. When retailers have similar markups, price competition is reduced. Markup pricing is efficient if it takes into account competition, seasonal factors, and the intricacies in selling some products.

COMPETITION-ORIENTED PRICING

A retailer can use competitors' prices as a guide. That firm might not alter prices in reaction to changes in demand or costs unless competitors alter theirs. Similarly, it might change prices when competitors do, even if demand or costs remain the same.

As shown in Table 17-5, a competition-oriented retailer can price below, at, or above the market. A firm with a strong location, superior service, good assortments, a favorable image, and exclusive brands can set prices above competitors. However, above-market pricing is not suitable for a retailer that has an inconvenient location, relies on self-service, is not innovative, and offers no real product distinctiveness.

TABLE 17-5   Competition-Oriented Pricing Alternatives

Retail Mix Variable	Alternative Price Strategies		
	Pricing Below the Market	Pricing At the Market	Pricing Above the Market
Location	Poor, inconvenient site; low rent	Close to competitors, no location advantage	Few strong competitors, convenient to consumers
Customer service	Self-service, little salesperson support, limited displays	Moderate assistance by sales personnel	High levels of personal selling, delivery, etc.
Product assortment	More emphasis on best-sellers	Medium or large assortment	Small or large assortment
Atmosphere	Inexpensive fixtures, racks for merchandise	Moderate atmosphere	Attractive and pleasant décor
Innovativeness in assortment	Follower, conservative	Concentration on best-sellers	Quite innovative
Special services	Not available	Not available or extra fee	Included in price
Product lines carried	Some name brands, private labels, closeouts	Selection of name brands, private labels	Exclusive name brands and private labels

Competition-oriented pricing does not require calculations of demand curves or price elasticity. The average market price is assumed to be fair for both the consumer and the retailer. Pricing at the market level does not disrupt competition and therefore does not usually lead to retaliation.

INTEGRATION OF APPROACHES TO PRICE STRATEGY

To properly integrate the three approaches, questions such as these should be addressed:

▶ If prices are reduced, will revenues increase greatly? (Demand orientation)
▶ Should different prices be charged for a product based on negotiations with customers, seasonality, and so on? (Demand orientation)
▶ Will a given price level allow a traditional markup to be attained? (Cost orientation)
▶ What price level is needed for an item with special buying, selling, or delivery costs? (Cost orientation)
▶ What price levels are competitors setting? (Competitive orientation)
▶ Can above-market prices be set due to a superior image? (Competitive orientation)

Implementation of Price Strategy

Implementing a price strategy involves a variety of separate but interrelated specific decisions, in addition to those broad concepts already discussed. A checklist of selected decisions is shown in Figure 17-8. In this section, the specifics of a pricing strategy are detailed.

CUSTOMARY AND VARIABLE PRICING

With **customary pricing**, a retailer sets prices for goods and services and seeks to maintain them for an extended period. Examples of items with customary prices are newspapers, candy, arcade games, vending machine items, and foods on restaurant menus. In each case, the retailer wants to establish set prices and have consumers take them for granted.

Bi-Lo (www.bi-lo.com), the southeastern supermarket chain, offers both everyday low prices and regular promotions.

A version of customary pricing is **everyday low pricing (EDLP)**, in which a retailer strives to sell its goods and services at consistently low prices throughout the selling season. Low prices are set initially; and there are few or no advertised specials, except on discontinued items or end-of-season closeouts. The retailer reduces its advertising and product re-pricing costs, and this approach increases the credibility of its prices in the consumer's mind. On the other hand, with EDLP, manufacturers may eliminate the special trade allowances designed to encourage retailers to offer price promotions during the year. Wal-Mart and Ikea are among the retailers successfully utilizing EDLP. See Figure 17-9.

FIGURE 17-8

A Checklist of Selected Specific Pricing Decisions

✓ How important is price stability? How long should prices be maintained?

✓ Is everyday low pricing desirable?

✓ Should prices change if costs and/or customer demand vary?

✓ Should the same prices be charged to all customers buying under the same conditions?

✓ Should customer bargaining be permitted?

✓ Should odd pricing be used?

✓ Should leader pricing be utilized to draw customer traffic? If yes, should leader prices be above, at, or below costs?

✓ Should consumers be offered discounts for purchasing in quantity?

✓ Should price lining be used to provide a price range and price points within that range?

✓ Should pricing practices vary by department or product line?

In many instances, a retailer cannot or should not use customary pricing. A firm *cannot* maintain constant prices if its costs are rising. A firm *should not* hold prices constant if customer demand varies. Under **variable pricing**, a retailer alters its prices to coincide with fluctuations in costs or consumer demand. Variable pricing may also provide excitement due to special sales opportunities for customers.

Cost fluctuations can be seasonal or trend-related. Supermarket and florist prices vary over the year due to the seasonal nature of many food and floral products. When seasonal items are scarce, the cost to the retailer goes up. If costs continually rise (as with luxury cars) or fall (as with computers), the retailer must change prices permanently (unlike temporary seasonal changes).

Demand fluctuations can be place- or time-based. Place-based fluctuations exist for retailers selling seat locations (such as concert halls) or room locations (such as hotels). Different prices can be charged for different locations, such as tickets close to the stage commanding higher prices. Time-based fluctuations occur if consumer demand differs by hour,

FIGURE 17-9

Wal-Mart and Everyday Low Prices

Source: Reprinted by permission of TNS Retail Forward.

day, or season. Demand for a movie theater is greater on Saturday than on Wednesday. Prices should be lower during periods of less demand.

Yield management pricing is a computerized, demand-based, variable pricing technique, whereby a retailer (typically a service firm) determines the combination of prices that yield the greatest total revenues for a given period. It is widely used by airlines and hotels. A crucial airline decision is how many first-class, full-coach, and discount tickets to sell on each flight. With this approach, an airline offers fewer discount tickets for flights in peak periods than flights in off-peak times. The airline has two goals: fill as many seats as possible on every flight and sell as many full-fare tickets as it can ("You don't want to sell a seat for $99 if someone will pay $599"). Yield management pricing may be too complex for small firms and requires complex software. Our Web site (**www.pearsonhighered.com/berman**) has many links that illustrate the uses of yield management and other pricing software.

It is possible to combine customary and variable pricing. A movie theater can charge $5 every Wednesday night and $9 every Saturday. A bookstore can lower prices by 20 percent for best-sellers that have been out for three months.

ONE-PRICE POLICY AND FLEXIBLE PRICING

Under a **one-price policy**, a retailer charges the same price to all customers buying an item under similar conditions. This policy may be used together with customary pricing or variable pricing. With variable pricing, all customers interested in a particular section of concert seats would pay the same price. This approach is easy to manage, does not require skilled salespeople, makes shopping quicker, permits self-service, puts consumers under less pressure, and is tied to price goals. One-price policies are the rule for most U.S. retailers, and bargaining is often not permitted.

Looking to bargain? Go to eBay (**www.ebay.com**) or Overstock.com Auctions (**www.auctions.overstock. com**).

Flexible pricing lets consumers bargain over prices; those who are good at it obtain lower prices. Many jewelry stores, auto dealers, and others use flexible pricing. They do not clearly post bottom-line prices; shoppers need prior knowledge to bargain successfully. Flexible pricing encourages consumers to spend more time, gives an impression the firm is discount-oriented, and generates high margins from shoppers who do not like haggling. It requires high initial prices and good salespeople.

A special form of flexible pricing is **contingency pricing**, whereby a service retailer does not get paid until after the service is performed and payment is contingent on the service's

---

CAREERS IN RETAILING — Is Retail for Me? Loss Prevention

Do you have an eye for detail, an appetite for solving puzzles, or a knack for proactivity? The loss prevention career area is responsible for safeguarding company assets and may include risk management issues, such as customer and employee safety. Loss prevention team members work together to prevent and handle merchandise loss due to shoplifting, employee theft, paperwork errors, and vendor fraud. Physical security of store and company buildings may also be included, as well as financial auditing responsibilities:

Here are three jobs in the area of loss prevention.

▶ *Head of Loss Prevention.* Top position responsible for safeguarding company assets. Primary emphasis is preventing merchandise shrinkage through theft or poor paperwork. May also be responsible for physical security of home office building(s) and warehouse(s).

May do executive investigations. May have an auditing department monitoring cash flow documents.

▶ *Regional Loss Prevention Manager.* Responsible for safeguarding company assets within a geographic area. May emphasize preventing merchandise loss through employee training and audits but will also investigate known losses and coordinate with police/courts on theft prosecutions.

▶ *Store Detective.* Primarily responsible for prevention of merchandise theft, apprehension, and prosecution of shoplifters. May do investigations of suspected employee theft. This is a "plain clothes" position, not a uniformed security guard or watchperson.

Source: Reprinted by permission of the National Retail Federation.

being satisfactory. In some cases, such as real-estate, consumers like contingency payments so they know the service is done properly. This represents some risk to the retailer since a lot of time and effort may be spent without payment. A real-estate broker may show a house 25 times, not sell it, and, therefore, not be paid.

ODD PRICING

In **odd pricing**, retail prices are set at levels below even dollar values, such as $0.49, $4.98, and $199. The assumption is that people feel these prices represent discounts or that the amounts are beneath consumer price ceilings. Odd pricing is a form of psychological pricing. Realtors hope consumers with a price ceiling of less than $350,000 are attracted to houses selling for $349,500. See Figure 17-10.

Odd prices that are 1 cent or 2 cents below the next highest even price ($0.29, $0.99, $2.98) are common up to $10.00. Beyond that point and up to $50.00, 5-cent reductions from the highest even price ($19.95, $49.95) are more usual. For more expensive items, prices are in dollars ($399, $4,995).

LEADER PRICING

In **leader pricing**, a retailer advertises and sells selected items in its goods/service assortment at less than the usual profit margins. The goal is to increase customer traffic for the retailer so that it can sell regularly priced goods and services in addition to the specially priced items. This is different from bait-and-switch, in which sale items are not sold.

Leader pricing typically involves frequently purchased, nationally branded, high turnover goods and services because it is easy for customers to detect low prices. Supermarkets, home centers, discount stores, drugstores, and fast-food restaurants are just some of the retailers that utilize leader pricing to draw shoppers. There are two kinds of leader pricing: loss leaders and sales at lower than regular prices (but higher than cost). Loss leaders are regulated on a statewide basis under minimum-price laws.

MULTIPLE-UNIT PRICING

With **multiple-unit pricing**, a retailer offers discounts to customers who buy in quantity or who buy a product bundle. By selling items at two for $0.75, a retailer attempts to sell more products than at $0.39 each. There are three reasons to use multiple-unit pricing: (1) A firm could seek to have shoppers increase their total purchases of an item. (If people buy multiple units to stockpile them, instead of consuming more, the firm's overall sales do not increase.) (2) This approach can help sell slow-moving and end-of-season merchandise. (3) Price bundling may increase sales of related items.

FIGURE 17-10

Odd Pricing: A Popular Retailing Tactic

At Aeropostale, odd pricing is widely employed so that the chain projects a value-driven image to shoppers.

Source: Reprinted by permission of Susan Berry, Retail Image Consulting, Inc.

In **bundled pricing**, a retailer combines several elements in one basic price. A digital camera bundle could include a camera, batteries, a telephoto lens, a case, and a tripod for $229. This approach increases overall sales and offers people a discount over unbundled prices. However, it is unresponsive to the needs of different customers. As an alternative, many retailers use **unbundled pricing**—they charge separate prices for each item sold. A TV rental firm could charge separately for TV set rental, home delivery, and a monthly service contract. This closely links prices with costs and gives people more choice. Unbundled pricing may be harder to manage and may result in people buying fewer related items.

PRICE LINING

Marriott International (**www.marriott.com/ corporateinfo/glance.mi**) really knows how to use price lining.

Rather than stock merchandise at all different price levels, retailers often employ **price lining** and sell merchandise at a limited range of price points, with each point representing a distinct level of quality. Retailers first determine their price floors and ceilings in each product category. They then set a limited number of price points within the range.[13] Department stores generally carry good, better, and best versions of merchandise consistent with their overall price policy—and set individual prices accordingly.

Price lining benefits both consumers and retailers. If the price range for a box of handkerchiefs is $6 to $15 and the price points are $6, $9, and $15, consumers know that distinct product qualities exist. However, should a retailer have prices of $6, $7, $8, $9, $10, $11, $12, $13, $14, and $15, the consumer may be confused about product differences. For retailers, price lining aids merchandise planning. Retail buyers can seek those suppliers carrying products at appropriate prices, and they can better negotiate with suppliers. They can automatically disregard products not fitting within price lines and thereby reduce inventory investment. Also, stock turnover goes up when the number of models carried is limited.

Difficulties do exist: (1) Depending on the price points selected, price lining may leave excessive gaps. A parent shopping for a graduation gift might find a $30 briefcase to be too cheap and a $200 one to be too expensive. (2) Inflation can make it tough to keep price points and price ranges. (3) Markdowns may disrupt the balance in a price line, unless all items in a line are reduced proportionally. (4) Price lines must be coordinated for complementary product categories, such as blazers, skirts, and shoes.

Price Adjustments

Retailers needs to be focused in making price adjustments (**www. bizmove.com/general/ m6h4.htm**).

Price adjustments enable retailers to use price as an adaptive mechanism. Markdowns and additional markups may be needed due to competition, seasonality, demand patterns, merchandise costs, and pilferage. Figure 17-11 shows a price change authorization form.

A **markdown** from an item's original price is used to meet the lower price of another retailer, adapt to inventory overstocking, clear out shopworn merchandise, reduce assortments of odds and ends, and increase customer traffic. An **additional markup** increases an item's original price because demand is unexpectedly high or costs are rising. In today's competitive marketplace, markdowns are applied much more frequently than additional markups.

A third price adjustment, the employee discount, is noted here because it may affect the computation of markdowns and additional markups. Although an employee discount is not an adaptive mechanism, it influences morale. Some firms give employee discounts on all items and also let workers buy sale items before they are made available to the general public.

COMPUTING MARKDOWNS AND ADDITIONAL MARKUPS

Markdowns and additional markups can be expressed in dollars or percentages.

The **markdown percentage** is the total dollar markdown as a percentage of net sales (in dollars):

$$\text{Markdown percentage} = \frac{\text{Total dollar markdown}}{\text{Net sales (in \$)}}$$

Although it is simple to compute, this formula does not enable a retailer to learn the percentage of items that are marked down relative to those sold at the original price.

FIGURE 17-11

A Price Change Authorization Form

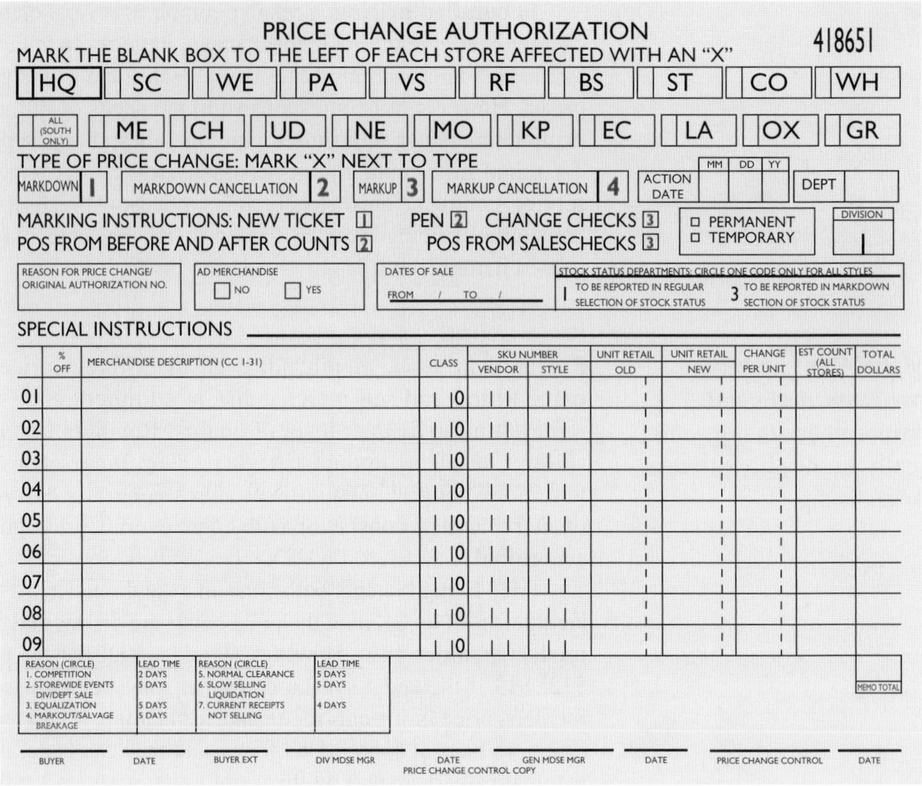
PRICE CHANGE AUTHORIZATION 418651

MARK THE BLANK BOX TO THE LEFT OF EACH STORE AFFECTED WITH AN "X"

HQ SC WE PA VS RF BS ST CO WH

ALL (SOUTH ONLY) ME CH UD NE MO KP EC LA OX GR

TYPE OF PRICE CHANGE: MARK "X" NEXT TO TYPE

MARKDOWN 1 MARKDOWN CANCELLATION 2 MARKUP 3 MARKUP CANCELLATION 4 ACTION DATE MM DD YY DEPT

MARKING INSTRUCTIONS: NEW TICKET 1 PEN 2 CHANGE CHECKS 3 ☐ PERMANENT ☐ TEMPORARY DIVISION 1

POS FROM BEFORE AND AFTER COUNTS 2 POS FROM SALESCHECKS 3

REASON FOR PRICE CHANGE/ ORIGINAL AUTHORIZATION NO. | AD MERCHANDISE ☐ NO ☐ YES | DATES OF SALE FROM / TO / | STOCK STATUS DEPARTMENTS: CIRCLE ONE CODE ONLY FOR ALL STYLES 1 TO BE REPORTED IN REGULAR SELECTION OF STOCK STATUS 3 TO BE REPORTED IN MARKDOWN SECTION OF STOCK STATUS

SPECIAL INSTRUCTIONS

	% OFF	MERCHANDISE DESCRIPTION (CC 1-31)	CLASS	SKU NUMBER VENDOR	SKU NUMBER STYLE	UNIT RETAIL OLD	UNIT RETAIL NEW	CHANGE PER UNIT	EST COUNT (ALL STORES)	TOTAL DOLLARS
01			10							
02			10							
03			10							
04			10							
05			10							
06			10							
07			10							
08			10							
09			10							

REASON (CIRCLE)	LEAD TIME	REASON (CIRCLE)	LEAD TIME
1. COMPETITION	2 DAYS	5. NORMAL CLEARANCE	5 DAYS
2. STOREWIDE EVENTS DIV/DEPT SALE	5 DAYS	6. SLOW SELLING LIQUIDATION	5 DAYS
3. EQUALIZATION	5 DAYS	7. CURRENT RECEIPTS NOT SELLING	4 DAYS
4. MARKOUT/SALVAGE BREAKAGE	5 DAYS		

MEMO TOTAL

BUYER DATE BUYER EXT DIV MDSE MGR DATE GEN MDSE MGR DATE PRICE CHANGE CONTROL DATE

PRICE CHANGE CONTROL COPY

A complementary measure is the **off-retail markdown percentage**, which looks at the markdown for each item or category of items as a percentage of original retail price. The markdown percentage for every item can be computed, as well as the percentage of items marked down:

$$\text{Off-retail markdown percentage} = \frac{\text{Original price} - \text{New price}}{\text{Original price}}$$

Suppose a gas barbecue grill sells for \$400 at the beginning of the summer and is reduced to \$280 at the end of the summer. The off-retail markdown is 30 percent [(\$400 − \$280)/\$400]. If 100 grills are sold at the original price and 20 are sold at the sale price, the percentage of items marked down is 17 percent, and the total dollar markdown is \$2,400.

The **additional markup percentage** looks at total dollar additional markups as a percentage of net sales, while the **addition to retail percentage** measures a price rise as a percentage of the original price:

$$\text{Additional markup percentage} = \frac{\text{Total dollar additional markups}}{\text{Net sales (in \$)}}$$

$$\text{Addition to retail percentage} = \frac{\text{New price} - \text{Original price}}{\text{Original price}}$$

Retailers must realize that many more customers would have to buy at reduced prices for those retailers to have a total gross profit equal to that at higher prices. A retailer's judgment regarding price adjustments is affected by its operating expenses at various sales volumes and customer price elasticities. The true impact of a markdown or an additional markup can be learned from this formula:

$$\text{Unit sales required to earn the same total gross profit with a price adjustment} = \frac{\text{Original markup (\%)}}{\text{Original markup (\%)} \pm \text{Price change (\%)}} \times \text{Expected unit sales at original price}$$

Suppose a Hewlett-Packard printer with a cost of $50 has an original retail price of $100 (a markup of 50 percent). A retailer expects to sell 500 units over the next year, generating a total gross profit of $25,000 ($50 × 500). How many units does the retailer have to sell if it reduces the price to $85 or raises it to $110—and still earn a $25,000 gross profit? Here are the answers:

$$\text{Unit sales required (at \$85)} = \frac{50\%}{50\% - 15\%} \times 500 = 1.43 \times 500 = 714$$

$$\text{Unit sales required (at \$110)} = \frac{50\%}{50\% + 10\%} \times 500 = 0.83 \times 500 = 417$$

MARKDOWN CONTROL

Through markdown control, a retailer evaluates the number of markdowns, the proportion of sales involving markdowns, and the causes. The control must be such that buying plans can be altered in later periods to reflect markdowns. A good way to evaluate the cause of markdowns is to have retail buyers record the reasons for each markdown and then examine them periodically. Possible buyer notations are "end of season," "to match the price of a competitor," and "obsolete style."

Through markdown control, a retailer can monitor its policies, such as the way items are displayed. Careful planning may also enable a retailer to avoid some markdowns by running more ads, training workers better, shipping goods more efficiently among branch units, and returning items to vendors.

The need for markdown control should not be interpreted as meaning that all markdowns can or should be minimized or eliminated. In fact, too low a markdown percentage may indicate that a retailer's buyers have not assumed enough risk in purchasing goods.

TIMING MARKDOWNS

There are different perspectives among retailers about the best markdown timing sequence, but much can be said about the benefits of an *early markdown policy:* It requires lower markdowns to sell products than markdowns late in the season. Merchandise is offered at reduced prices while demand is still fairly active. Early markdowns free selling space for new merchandise. The retailer's cash flow position can be improved. The main advantage of a *late markdown policy* is that a retailer gives itself every opportunity to sell merchandise at original prices. Yet, the advantages associated with an early markdown policy cannot be achieved under a late markdown policy.

Retailers can also use a *staggered markdown policy* and discount prices throughout a selling period. One pre-planned staggered markdown policy is an *automatic markdown plan,* in which the amount and timing of markdowns are controlled by the length of time merchandise remains in stock. Syms, the off-price chain, uses this approach to ensure fresh stock and early markdowns:

> All garments are sold with the brand-name as affixed by the manufacturer. Because women's dresses are susceptible to considerable style fluctuation, Syms has long utilized a 10-day automatic markdown pricing policy to promote movement of merchandise. The date of placement on the selling floor of each women's dress is stamped on the back of the price ticket. The front of each ticket contains what the Company believes to be the nationally advertised price, the initial Syms price, and three reduced prices. Each reduced price becomes effective after the passage of 10 selling days. Syms also offers "dividend" prices consisting of additional price reductions on various types of merchandise at various times.[14]

A *storewide clearance,* conducted once or twice a year, is another way to time markdowns. It often takes place after peak selling periods such as Christmas and Mother's Day. The goal is to clean out merchandise before taking a physical inventory and beginning the next season. The advantages of a storewide clearance are that a longer period is

FIGURE 17-12

Giant Eagle: Going Even
Further Than Everyday
Low Pricing
To constantly promote its low-
price philosophy, Giant Eagle
stores have an entire section
devoted to weekly specials.

Source: Reprinted by permission of
TNS Retail Forward.

provided for selling merchandise at original prices and that frequent markdowns can destroy a consumer's confidence in regular prices: "Why buy now, when it will be on sale next week?" Clearance sales limit bargain hunting to once or twice a year.

In the past, many retailers would introduce merchandise at high prices and then mark down many items by as much as 60 percent to increase store traffic and improve inventory turnover. This caused customers to wait for price reductions and treat initial prices skeptically. Today, more retailers start out with lower prices and try to run fewer sales and apply fewer markdowns than before. See Figure 17-12. Nonetheless, a big problem facing some retailers is that they have gotten consumers too used to buying when items are discounted.

Chapter **Summary**

1. *To describe the role of pricing in a retail strategy and to show that pricing decisions must be made in an integrated and adaptive manner.* Pricing is crucial to a retailer because of its interrelationship with overall objectives and the other components of the retail strategy. A price plan must be integrated and responsive—and provide a good value to customers.

2. *To examine the impact of consumers; government; manufacturers, wholesalers, and other suppliers; and current and potential competitors on pricing decisions.* Before designing a price plan, a retailer must study the factors affecting its decisions. Sometimes, the factors have a minor effect on pricing discretion; other times, they severely limit pricing options.

Retailers should be familiar with the price elasticity of demand and the different market segments that are possible. Government restrictions deal with price fixing, price discrimination, minimum prices, unit pricing, item

price removal, and price advertising. There may be conflicts about which party controls retail prices; and manufacturers, wholesalers, and other suppliers may be asked to provide price guarantees (if they are in a weak position). The competitive environment may foster market pricing, lead to price wars, or allow administered pricing.

3. *To present a framework for developing a retail price strategy.* This framework consists of five stages: objectives, broad price policy, price strategy, implementation of price strategy, and price adjustments.

Retail pricing goals can be chosen from among sales, dollar profits, return on investment, and early recovery of cash. Next, a broad policy outlines a coordinated series of actions, consistent with the retailer's image and oriented to the short and long run.

A good price strategy incorporates demand, cost, and competitive concepts. Each of these orientations must be understood separately and jointly. Psychological pricing;

markup pricing; alternative ways of computing markups; gross margin; direct product profitability; and pricing below, at, or above the market are among the key aspects of strategy planning.

When enacting a price strategy, specific tools can be used to supplement the broad base of the strategy. Retailers should know when to use customary and variable pricing, one-price policies and flexible pricing, odd pricing, leader pricing, multiple-unit pricing, and price lining.

Price adjustments may be required to adapt to internal and external conditions. Adjustments include markdowns, additional markups, and employee discounts. It is important that adjustments are controlled by a budget, the causes of markdowns are noted, future company buying reflects prior performance, adjustments are properly timed, and excessive discounting is avoided.

Key Terms

price elasticity of demand (p. 466)
horizontal price fixing (p. 468)
vertical price fixing (p. 468)
Robinson-Patman Act (p. 469)
minimum-price laws (p. 470)
predatory pricing (p. 470)
loss leaders (p. 470)
unit pricing (p. 470)
item price removal (p. 470)
bait-and-switch advertising (p. 471)
gray market goods (p. 471)
market penetration pricing (p. 473)
market skimming pricing (p. 473)
demand-oriented pricing (p. 476)
cost-oriented pricing (p. 476)
competition-oriented pricing (p. 476)

price–quality association (p. 476)
prestige pricing (p. 476)
markup pricing (p. 476)
markup (p. 476)
markup percentage (p. 476)
initial markup (p. 478)
maintained markup (p. 478)
gross margin (p. 478)
variable markup policy (p. 479)
direct product profitability (DPP) (p. 479)
customary pricing (p. 481)
everyday low pricing (EDLP) (p. 481)
variable pricing (p. 482)
yield management pricing (p. 483)
one-price policy (p. 483)

flexible pricing (p. 483)
contingency pricing (p. 483)
odd pricing (p. 484)
leader pricing (p. 484)
multiple-unit pricing (p. 484)
bundled pricing (p. 485)
unbundled pricing (p. 485)
price lining (p. 485)
markdown (p. 485)
additional markup (p. 485)
markdown percentage (p. 485)
off-retail markdown percentage (p. 486)
additional markup percentage (p. 486)
addition to retail percentage (p. 486)

Questions for Discussion

1. Why is it important for retailers to understand the concept of price elasticity even if they are unable to compute it?

2. Comment on each of the following from the perspective of a large retailer:
   a. Horizontal price fixing.
   b. Vertical price fixing.
   c. Price discrimination.
   d. Minimum-price laws.
   e. Unit pricing.

3. Give an example of a price strategy that integrates demand, cost, and competitive criteria.

4. Explain why markups are usually computed as a percentage of selling price rather than of cost.

5. A floor tile retailer wants to receive a 40 percent markup (at retail) for all merchandise. If one style of tile retails for $11 per tile, what is the maximum that the retailer would be willing to pay for a tile?

6. A car dealer purchases multiple-disk CD players for $120 each and desires a 35 percent markup (at retail). What retail price should be charged?

7. A gift store charges $25.00 for a ceramic figurine; its cost is $11.25. What is the markup percentage (at cost and at retail)?

8. A firm has planned operating expenses of $170,000, a profit goal of $110,000, and planned reductions of $35,000, and it expects sales of $650,000. Compute the initial markup percentage.

9. At the end of the year, the retailer in Question 8 determines that actual operating expenses are $160,000, actual profit is $105,000, and actual sales are $630,000. What is the maintained markup percentage? Explain the difference in your answers to Questions 8 and 9.

10. What are the pros and cons of everyday low pricing to a retailer? To a manufacturer?

11. Under what circumstances do you think bundled pricing is a good idea? A poor idea? Why?

12. A retailer buys items for $55. At an original retail price of $85, it expects to sell 1,000 units.
    a. If the price is marked down to $75, how many units must the retailer sell to earn the same total gross profit it would attain with an $85 price?
    b. If the price is marked up to $90, how many units must the retailer sell to earn the same total gross profit it would attain with an $85 price?

Note: At our Web site (**www.pearsonhighered.com/berman**), there are several math problems related to the material in this chapter so that you may review these concepts.

Web **Exercise**

Visit the Web site of BJ's Wholesale Club (www.bjs.com). What are the least expensive consumer products sold through this site? The most expensive? Do you feel that this price range is consistent with BJ's image as a discount-oriented membership club chain? Explain your answer.

Note: Stop by our Web site (www.pearsonhighered. com/berman) to experience a number of highly interactive, appealing Web exercises based on actual company demonstrations and sample materials related to retailing.

part six
Short Cases

CASE 1: DESIGNER BRANDS: A GLOBAL PHENOMENON[C-1]

Nielsen (**www.nielsen.com**), a marketing research firm, conducts periodic research reports on global trends relating to designer brands. One recent study found that 16 percent of the global respondents say that they buy designer brands, and 31 percent say that they know someone who buys designer brands. Here are some of the major findings of this research report.

The five designer brands most frequently bought on a global basis (in order of purchase) are Calvin Klein (**www.calvinklein.com**), Ralph Lauren (**www.ralphlauren.com**), Diesel (**www.diesel.com**), Chanel (**www.chanel.com**), and Christian Dior (**www.dior.com**). The five most coveted global brands (in order of preference) are Gucci (**www.gucci.com**), Chanel, Calvin Klein, Louis Vuitton (**www.vuitton.com**), and Giorgio Armani (**www.armani.com**).

On a proportionate basis, Greek consumers are the most designer label-prone consumers. Nearly one-half of Greek consumers state that they are purchasers of designer brands; 73 percent report that they know a designer label buyer. The global market with the second-highest percentage of designer label shoppers is Hong Kong, mostly due to the high discretionary income of many Hong Kong shoppers. This income is partially fueled by the high proportion of Hong Kong shoppers who live at home through their late 20s or 30s or until they get married. India is the third-ranked country in terms of the importance of designer brands. According to the managing director of Nielsen South Asia, "Indian designer shoppers prefer well-known brands such as Louis Vuitton and Gucci which have an international, high-profile image—and also because these brands have opened up large stores, making their products more visible and accessible to buyers."

The vast majority of consumer respondents (71 percent) feel that designer brands are overpriced, and only 25 percent of respondents believe that designer brands are of significantly higher quality than standard brands. One theory that explains the popularity of designer brands, despite the perception that they are too costly and not of higher quality, is the "bling factor." This explanation states that designer brands are worn as a "badge of affluence."

The Nielsen study found that 52 percent of online consumers believe that shoppers purchase designer brands as a means of projecting their social status. This is particularly important in Asia, the Middle East, and Latin America, where a large middle-income market has been created and where historic class boundaries have begun to fall.

Consumer attitudes to "knockoffs" and counterfeit designer goods vary by country. Overall, only 15 percent of consumer respondents think that "knockoff" and counterfeit designer brands are just as good as authentic designer goods. The greatest aversion to these imitators is in Asia, where these products are very common. For example, only 1 percent of Japanese and 3 percent of Chinese consumers feel that imitation designer goods are equal in quality to authentic goods. On the opposite end of the spectrum, 27 percent of Canadians and 26 percent of U.S. respondents feel that copies are just as good as the real thing. Similarly, 22 percent of British and Australian consumers claim that there is no significant difference between authentic and bogus designer goods.

Questions

1. What should be the role of designer brands as part of the fashion merchandise selection process for an upscale women's clothing specialty store chain?
2. Are designer brands a form of manufacturer (national brand)? Explain your answer.
3. Explain the role of designer brands in category management.
4. Why do designer brand owners so aggressively fight knockoffs, even though many consumers know they are less costly copies?

CASE 2: MACY'S GOES LOCAL[C-2]

With the acquisition of May Department Stores in 2005 for $11.5 billion, Federated Department Stores became the world's largest department store chain. In 2007, Federated Department Stores dropped 11 of the store names (such as Marshall Field's, Robinsons-May, and Kaufmann's) that were used to brand its stores in local markets and renamed those stores as Macy's and the parent chain Macy's, Inc. (**www.macys.com**). The Bloomingdale's (**www.bloomingdales.com**) name and concept remained intact.

Macy's, Inc. hoped that using a standard merchandising strategy throughout the United States would lower merchandise costs because of greater bargaining power, enable the chain to utilize national advertising more effectively, and forge a national identity. The unified image and national clout enabled Macy's to attract Martha Stewart and other designers to create a line of products especially for the chain. The Macy's name was used on all of its stores with the exception of Bloomingdale's, which strives to differentiate itself from Macy's stores through a greater emphasis on fashion and the sale of merchandise at higher price points.

In its 2007 fiscal year, same-store sales at Macy's, Inc. dropped 1.3 percent from the 2006 level. This sales decline caused Macy's, Inc. chief executive officer, Terry Lundgren, to scrap the chain's standardized cookie-cutter merchandising

[C-1]The material in this case is drawn from "Consumer and Designer Brands: A Global Report," **http://www.nielsen.com/solutions/fashionBrands.pdf**, (April 2008).

[C-2]The material in this case is drawn from Vanessa O'Connell, "Reversing Field, Macy's Goes Local," *Wall Street Journal* (April 21, 2008).

strategy in favor of specifically tailoring merchandise selection. According to Lundgren, "What the consumer wants in the Galleria of St. Louis is different from what the consumer wants in State Street Chicago or what the consumer wants in Portland, Oregon." As part of the chain's revamped tailoring strategy, Lundgren wants 15 percent of the merchandise in each store to reflect local tastes and preferences.

As part of its initial 2008 localization strategy, inventory was customized at about one-third of Macy's stores, including all of the former Marshall Field's and many other former May Company stores. Locations in Seattle, Minneapolis, Chicago, Portland, and Salt Lake City were the first stores to be localized. Macy's strategy in going local is similar to that employed by Best Buy (**www.bestbuy.com**), the electronics retail chain.

Best Buy began to use local strategies in 2004 after identifying four specific types of customers: such as upscale suburban mom or urban trendsetter. Then Best Buy computed, on a store-by-store basis, which customer groups were the most important. Ross Stores (**www.rossstores.com**), a national discount-apparel chain, decided to tailor 15 percent of the merchandise in each of its 900 stores as of fall 2008.

Planning and implementing its localized strategy will be especially difficult for Macy's, Inc. Although Lundgren acknowledges that Bloomingdale's executives at Macy's, Inc. headquarters "have a clear understanding of what is going on in each store," the Macy's store division is so large that central management needs "to make sure we are in tune to what it is that the consumer is expecting of us—the product category, the size, or color."

A single Macy's store typically stocks between 1.5 and 4 million stock-keeping units. This means that hundreds of thousands of items can be affected by localization. To accomplish localization, 13 executives are now in charge of overseeing the merchandise assortment at a group of 10 department stores. In the past, under the standardized strategy, seven executives were in charge of merchandise assortments in as many as 23 stores.

Questions

1. List and explain the pros and cons of centralized buying for Macy's.
2. Explain the role of centralized buying with staple merchandise versus the role of decentralized buying for Macy's with fashion and seasonal merchandise.
3. List three factors you think Macy's, Inc. should consider in localizing merchandise by store location.
4. How should Macy's and Bloomingdale's merchandising decisions be coordinated?

CASE 3: BJ'S: PROFITING IN RECESSIONARY TIMES[C-3]

As of 2009, BJ's (**www.bjs.com**) operated about 175 membership (warehouse) clubs in 16 eastern states. Ninety percent of these clubs average 113,000 square feet in size; 10 percent are smaller-format clubs averaging 71,000 square feet. The smaller units serve market areas that are unable to support traditional units. BJ's has more than $9.0 billion in annual revenues, operating income of 2.1 percent of sales, and net income of 1.4 percent of sales. Membership fees comprise 2.1 percent of BJ's total revenues.

BJ's current strategy is based on three dimensions: providing everyday value, creating excitement, and having an efficient supply chain. Let's look at each of these in detail.

According to Laura Sen, BJ's chief operating officer: "It [providing everyday value] starts with the promise to our members when we sell a membership. You pay to shop with us; we should be giving you great values every day." To achieve lower prices, BJ's recently dropped its Member Insight team that data mined BJ's comprehensive customer data base and then segmented BJ's customers into such groups as pet owners, moms with babies, and golden oldies. BJ's found that the increased costs of merchandising to each segment added unnecessary costs without significantly increasing sales. As a result of this inefficiency, BJ's was forced to increase prices on such basics as milk, eggs, butter, and chicken.

The second part of BJ's strategy is to generate excitement in shopping. Sen says: "People typically don't like to go grocery shopping. It's our job to create merchandise excitement in all areas of the club to help make shopping an enjoyable experience." BJ's has begun offering more top-quality brands, as well as organics at attractive prices. For instance, BJ's recently offered a six-pack of Stonyfield 10-ounce Organic Smoothies for $6; this item often sells for more than $10 at supermarkets. BJ's also opportunistically buys closeouts, bankrupt lots, and canceled orders such as $330 kayaks. These special buys encourage customers to revisit the store frequently and to promote impulse purchasing.

The third part of the strategy is based on increasing supply chain efficiency. Two standard ways of measuring BJ's financial inventory control are the annual rate of stock turnover (10.2 times in 2008) and gross margin return on investment (GMROI; 81.4 percent in 2008). BJ's GMROI is actually more than 81.4 percent since it includes buying and occupancy costs in its cost-of-sales calculation).

As with other warehouse clubs, BJ's seeks to reduce handling costs by purchasing full truckloads of merchandise directly from manufacturers and then storing this merchandise directly on the sales floor instead of at a separate warehouse. Membership (warehouse) clubs also have low fixturing and operating costs. Instead of limiting its focus to internal efficiency, BJ's has reached out to its suppliers as well. BJ's recently had a two-day, off-site meeting with one supplier to increase overall supply chain efficiency.

[C-3]The material in this case is drawn from *BJ'S Wholesale Club 2008 10-K*; "Movers: GM, Boeing, BJ's Wholesale, Phillips-Van Heusen," *Business Week Online* (November 20, 2008), p. 21; and Mike Sharkey, "Club Comeback," *Retail Merchandiser* (July–August 2008), pp. 42–48.

For the third quarter 2008, BJ's posted earnings per share of 48 cents (versus 35 cents the year before) and had comparable store increases of 12 percent. These were remarkable numbers in a recessionary period.

Questions

1. Distinguish between the merchandise planning process for a traditional electronics store such as Best Buy and BJ's.
2. Develop a plan for minimizing inventory shrinkage at BJ's.
3. Describe five major logistics performance goals at BJ's.
4. In weak economic times, should BJ's dramatically cut back on its in-store inventory? Explain the pros and cons of doing so.

CASE 4: FAST-FOOD PRICING REVISITED[C-4]

Squeezed between the rising costs for their food products and consumer reluctance to pay higher prices, fast-food chains are experimenting with more types of value-priced meals, changing portion sizes, and presenting new promotional messages to attract more consumers. According to Domino's Pizza (**www.dominos.com**) chairman and chief executive, "First of all, everybody has to take pricing up and frankly [that] will continue to happen if we continue to see the kind of cost pressures, both in terms of minimum-wage increases and their impact, gasoline prices at the pump, and then all the commodities that drive our stores."

Domino's, which operates 5,100 stores in the United States and 8,700 units worldwide, has an intense focus on pricing. Nonetheless, external events—such as a tough economy and rising costs—can intervene. In 2008, systemwide U.S. same-store sales fell after some operators raised prices to the detriment of store traffic. So, in addition to re-analyzing its pricing structure, Domino's is attempting to increase lunch sales and to promote its $4.00 10-inch pizza. It has also begun to test a premium line of pizza and oven-baked sandwiches.

Yum! Brands (**www.yum.com**)—the franchisor of Taco Bell (**www.tacobell.com**), Pizza Hut (**www.pizzahut.com**), and KFC (**www.kfc.com**)—has faced similar pricing and cost pressures. As Yum's chief financial officer discovered, the chain incorrectly assumed that commodity cost increases for 2008 would be $55 million over the level of 2007. "It

C-4The material in this case is drawn from Sarah E. A. Lockyer, "Chains Retool Their Pricing Strategies," *Nation's Restaurant News* (August 4, 2008), pp. 1, 9.

ended up being $100 million in the United States, and we got a little bit behind on pricing." In response, Yum Brands! has featured a dual-pricing strategy based on value items—such as Taco Bell's 79 cent, 89 cent, and 99 cent "Why Pay More" menu items—and a new premium line of Tuscani Pastas in its Pizza Hut locations.

McDonald's Dollar Menu (**www.mcdonalds.com**), which represents about 14 percent of the chain's sales revenue, is also being changed to provide franchisees increased profits. Many franchisees have complained that while the Dollar Menu increased store traffic, it did not increase unit profitability because the lower-priced items did not cover increased operating costs. McDonald's is currently using a three-tiered price structure consisting of its Dollar Menu value-priced selections, its regularly priced menu items, and higher-priced premium menu selections such as Angus burgers.

Panera Bread (**www.panerabread.com**), which operates or franchises 1,250 bakery cafés, has shifted its focus from a sales per transaction to a gross profit per transaction-based pricing model. Panera has seen no meaningful drop-off in store traffic as a result of raising its price levels. Recently, Panera increased prices on its signature bagels to $1.25 each, while its traditional bagels remained at 99 cents each. In addition, Panera has focused on selling higher-price and higher-profitability items.

Many fast-causal restaurants such as P.F. Chang's China Bistro Inc. (**www.pfchangs.com**), Darden Restaurants (**www.dardenrestaurants.com**)—which operates Red Lobster, Olive Garden, and LongHorn Steakhouse)—decided not to raise prices to keep their recession-weary customers. The Cheesecake Factory (**www.cheesecakefactory.com**) recently completed a major pricing study and concluded that it should raise prices by just 1 percent. Many of these restaurants are now attracting customers who have traded-down from higher-priced more traditional restaurants.

Questions

1. Describe the pros and cons of using value-priced meals as a strategy to build retail sales for a franchisee.
2. Describe the pros and cons of changing portion sizes as a strategy to build retail sales for a franchisee.
3. Discuss the pros and cons to a restaurant's changing prices by day of week or time of day versus discounting all meals by the same percentage.
4. How can a restaurant determine the price elasticity of demand for its dinner menu? How should it use that information?

part six

Comprehensive Case

LOWE'S: CATEGORY POTENTIAL AMONG FEMALE SHOPPERS[*]

INTRODUCTION

Women who shop frequently at Lowe's (**www.lowes.com**) tend to have a higher income than the average shopper and are more likely to have shopped the various product categories at a home improvement center, according to TNS Retail Forward's ShopperScape. Still, many categories offer Lowe's room for improvement in terms of converting frequent female shoppers into purchasers. Lowe's weakest category in this

[*]The material in this case is adapted by the authors from TNS Retail Forward (**www.retailforward.com**), *Lowe's—Category Potential Among Female Frequent Shoppers* (Columbus, OH: TNS Retail Forward, July 2008); and TNS Retail Forward, *The Home Depot and Lowe's—Parsing the Gender Gap* (May 2008). Reprinted by permission.

regard is cleaning supplies. For categories such as hand and power tools, outdoor power equipment, paint, and carpet, Lowe's is losing significant numbers of female monthly shoppers to competitors. Lowe's needs to find ways to maximize the return on this key shopper segment.

Lowe's Merchandising by the Numbers

About 12 percent of all female primary household shoppers shop Lowe's on a monthly basis. These shoppers are more active home improvement shoppers when compared with all women who have ever shopped at a home improvement center, based on shopping activity in key home improvement categories. Women who shop Lowe's monthly also are much more likely than all shoppers to have incomes of $50,000 or greater, be married with children, and have college degrees.

As shown in Table 1, females who shop monthly at Lowe's may be defined in demographic terms, based upon their age, income, marital status, presence of children, household size, life stage, education, and size of the market in which they live.

TABLE 1 Profile of Female Lowe's Monthly Shoppers

	All Shoppers	Female Monthly Lowe's Shoppers	Index
Age			
18–24	6%	2%	30[*]
25–34	18	16	88
35–44	20	24	118
45–54	21	23	110
55–64	16	17	103
65+	19	19	101
Average Age (years)	47.7	48.9	103
Income			
Under $25,000	25%	17%	68
$25,000–$34,999	11	11	95
$35,000–$49,999	15	14	96
$50,000–$74,999	18	22	122
$75,000–$99,999	11	13	111
$100,000+	19	23	120
Average Income	$60,880	$67,670	111
Marital Status			
Married	54%	67%	124
Not married	46	33	72
Presence of Children			
Yes	29%	33%	116
No	71	67	93
Household Size			
1 member	27%	20%	75
2 members	33	36	108

(Continued)

TABLE 1 **Profile of Female Lowe's Monthly Shoppers** (Continued)

	All Shoppers	Female Monthly Lowe's Shoppers	Index
3 members	16	17	104
4 members	14	16	117
5 or more members	10	11	109
Life Stage			
Young singles	6%	3%	47
Middle singles	15	12	80
Older singles	6	5	87
Young couple	9	7	77
Working older couple	13	16	119
Retired older couple	12	13	113
Young parent	14	16	117
Middle parent	10	11	116
Older parent	14	16	108
Roommates	2	1	80
Female Education[1]			
Did not finish high school	2%	3%	113
High school graduate	22	20	90
Some college	40	38	96
College graduate	22	24	110
Post-graduate degree	13	14	113
Male Education[2]			
Did not finish high school	5%	6%	104
High school graduate	21	21	103
Some college	35	37	105
College graduate	22	20	92
Post-graduate degree	15	15	95
Market Size			
Large market/MSA, pop > 2 million	50%	43%	96
Mid-size MSA, pop of 500,000 to 2 million	22	25	110
Non-MSA/small market < 500,000 pop	28	33	117

Index of 100 = Average
Shading indicates segments with indices 105+, in which shoppers in the defined segment are at least 5% more likely than average to be the defined type of shopper.
*Read as: Female monthly Lowe's shoppers are 70% (100-30) less likely than all shoppers to be in the 18–24 age segment.
[1]Based on households where a female head of household is present.
[2]Based on households where a male head of household is present.
Source: TNS Retail Forward ShopperScape™, July 2008. There are rounding errors in this table.

Female primary household shoppers buy a lot of different merchandise at home improvement centers. Figure 1 compares the behavior of all women shoppers versus those who shop at Lowe's monthly.

Among women who are in a Lowe's store each month, more than 90 percent say they would likely make their next cleaning supplies purchase at another retailer, with more than one-half citing Wal-Mart (**www.walmart.com**). Forty-three percent of frequent Lowe's female shoppers would likely make their next major appliance purchase at Lowe's, while 30

percent say Sears (**www.sears.com**) would be their choice. Among the other kitchen, bath, and laundry categories, faucets are a strong point for Lowe's. More than three out of four say they would likely make their next purchase at Lowe's. Cabinets and countertops also are strong for the retailer.

About 6 out of 10 women who shop at Lowe's monthly say they would likely make their next carpet purchase at another retailer. The most-often mentioned choice is "other retailer," which likely includes specialty flooring stores. Carpeting is a category Lowe's has promoted heavily to

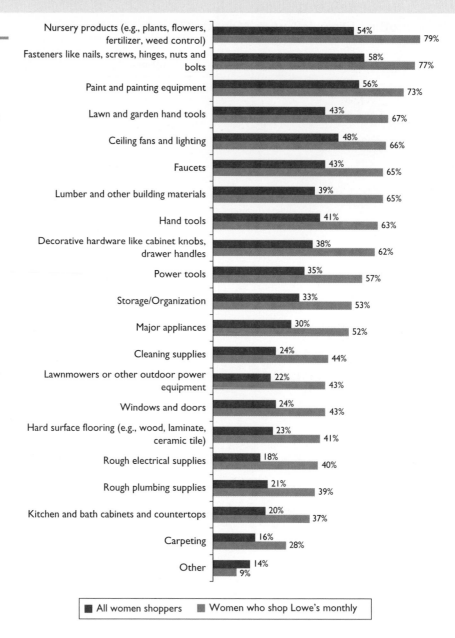

FIGURE 1

Products Ever Shopped for at a Home Improvement Center (among female primary household shoppers who have ever shopped a home improvement center)

Source: TNS Retail Forward ShopperScape™, April 2008.

convert shoppers into buyers. Similarly, nearly two-thirds say they would likely make their next storage/organization purchase elsewhere, with Wal-Mart most often mentioned. And more than one-half of women who shop at Lowe's monthly say they would likely buy their next lawn mower or other outdoor power tool at another retailer, with Sears the strongest competitor, likely reflecting the continued strength of Sears' Craftsman brand.

Among women who shop Lowe's monthly, more than 4 out of 10 say they would likely make their next hand tool purchase at another retailer and nearly half will likely go elsewhere for their next power tool purchase, with Sears edging out Home Depot (**www.homedepot. com**) as the strongest competitor for both categories. Roughly two-thirds indicate they would likely make their next purchase at Lowe's in the other core do-it-yourself categories except lumber, where the percentage jumps to nearly 75 percent.

Lowe's Versus Home Depot

Lowe's is the second-leading home-improvement retailer in the world with 1,600 stores and annual revenues of $50 billion. Home Depot is the leader with 2,200 stores and annual sales of $80 billion.

According to TNS Retail Forward's ShopperScape, there are some key differences that shape gender preference for Lowe's and Home Depot. Although both women and men prefer Lowe's to Home Depot by wide margins, women tend to be somewhat stronger advocates for their preferred retailer. Women who prefer Lowe's are much more likely than men to cite service-related factors as reasons. Additionally, women prefer Lowe's for more product categories compared with men. Yet, when it comes to reaching for their wallets, men who prefer Lowe's spend significantly more than women and outspend men who prefer Home Depot by a two-to-one margin. See Figure 2.

FIGURE 2

Store Preference Intensity (among respondents who shopped at both Home Depot and Lowe's in the past year)

Note: This data is among shoppers who have a preference for either Lowe's or Home Depot.

Source: TNS Retail Forward ShopperScape™, July 2007.

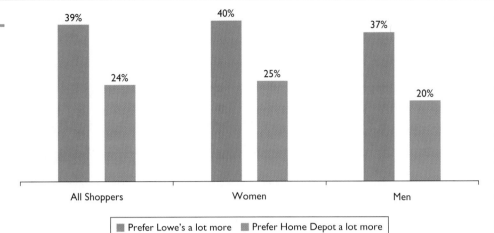

Among shoppers who prefer Lowe's, women are much more likely than men to prefer the retailer due to better-perceived customer service, brand selection, and pricing. Among shoppers who prefer Home Depot, the preference differences between the sexes are narrower, although men are more likely than women to say Home Depot has a broad selection of brands and that it is more likely to have what they need in stock. See Table 2.

TABLE 2 Perceptions That Shape Retailer Preference by Gender (among respondents who shopped at both Home Depot and Lowe's in the past year)

	Home Depot Is Better		Lowe's Is Better		Don't know/Not sure	
	Men	Women	Men	Women	Men	Women
Convenient location	42%	45%	40%	41%	19%	15%
Service (average)	25	24	26	29	49	46
Knowledgeable associates	33	31	33	42	34	28
Easy to find associates when I need help	29	29	37	43	34	29
Consistently good customer service	29	26	39	45	32	29
Good delivery service	14	12	17	18	69	70
Good options to finance my purchase	17	17	14	16	70	67
Good how-to clinics for projects I'm interested in	30	32	14	14	56	54
Production selection (average)	23	21	30	34	47	46
Broad selection of brands	29	25	36	43	35	33
Offer brands sold exclusively by one retailer	15	11	15	15	70	73
Easy to special-order products not in the store	15	15	21	21	64	64
Store is appealing/easy to shop	22	24	54	56	23	20
Good return policy	26	26	28	32	46	43
Likely to have what I need in stock	36	30	41	46	24	24
Helpful Web site	16	16	19	22	66	62
Pricing (average)	31	30	32	37	38	33
Low everyday prices for items I need	32	30	32	37	36	33
Good sale prices	29	29	28	37	43	34
Good value for the prices	30	30	36	38	34	32
Installation services (average)	17	16	16	16	67	68
Broad range of installation services	19	18	18	17	62	65
Installation services provide high-quality results	15	14	13	15	72	71

Source: TNS Retail Forward ShopperScape™, July 2007.

FIGURE 3

Product Category Ratings by Women (among respondents who shopped at both Home Depot and Lowe's in the past year)

Source: TNS Retail Forward ShopperScape™, July 2007.

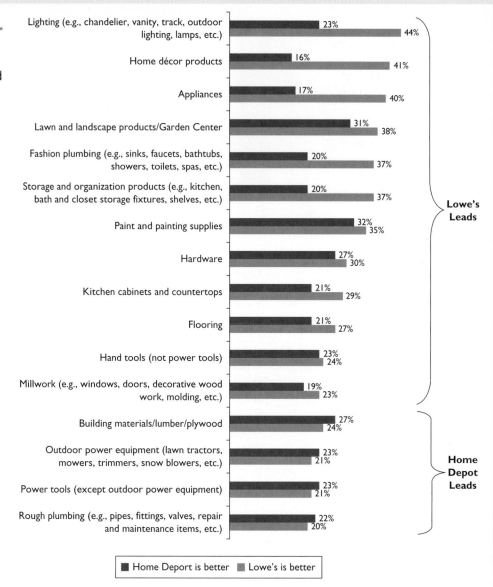

Legend: ■ Home Deport is better ■ Lowe's is better

Data (Home Depot % / Lowe's %):
- Lighting (e.g., chandelier, vanity, track, outdoor lighting, lamps, etc.): 23% / 44%
- Home décor products: 16% / 41%
- Appliances: 17% / 40%
- Lawn and landscape products/Garden Center: 31% / 38%
- Fashion plumbing (e.g., sinks, faucets, bathtubs, showers, toilets, spas, etc.): 20% / 37%
- Storage and organization products (e.g., kitchen, bath and closet storage fixtures, shelves, etc.): 20% / 37%
- Paint and painting supplies: 32% / 35%
- Hardware: 27% / 30%
- Kitchen cabinets and countertops: 21% / 29%
- Flooring: 21% / 27%
- Hand tools (not power tools): 23% / 24%
- Millwork (e.g., windows, doors, decorative wood work, molding, etc.): 19% / 23%

(Lowe's Leads)

- Building materials/lumber/plywood: 27% / 24%
- Outdoor power equipment (lawn tractors, mowers, trimmers, snow blowers, etc.): 23% / 21%
- Power tools (except outdoor power equipment): 23% / 21%
- Rough plumbing (e.g., pipes, fittings, valves, repair and maintenance items, etc.): 22% / 20%

(Home Depot Leads)

Women prefer Lowe's in more categories. Among women, Lowe's is preferred to Home Depot in 12 of the 16 categories tracked, compared with 9 of the 16 categories for men. Men tend to prefer Home Depot for most of the core tool, hardware, and building materials products. Lowe's enjoys wide preference margins for both sexes in appliances, home décor, lighting, and other soft home improvement categories. Categories for which men prefer Home Depot, but women prefer Lowe's, are hardware, paint and painting supplies, hand tools, and flooring. See Figures 3 and 4.

Thanks to men, shoppers who prefer Lowe's spend more. Overall, shoppers who prefer Lowe's spent $64 more on home improvement products (at any retailer) during the all-important spring selling season than those who prefer Home Depot. Lowe's edge is due to male shoppers, who spent on average a whopping $574 more than men who prefer Home Depot. The difference is the result of a larger proportion of big-ticket spending by men who prefer Lowe's. Among women, shoppers who prefer Lowe's spent $83 less than those who prefer Home Depot. Still, women who prefer either Home Depot or Lowe's spent significantly more than men who prefer Home Depot. See Figure 5 and Table 3.

Questions

1. Apply the concept of category management to the themes of this case, especially Table 1 and Figures 3 and 4.
2. Why do you think that both men and women prefer Lowe's over Home Depot?
3. Comment on the differences in men's and women's attitudes about product selection and pricing in Home Depot and Lowe's as reported in Table 2.

FIGURE 4

Product Category Ratings by Men (among respondents who shopped at both Home Depot and Lowe's in the past year)

Source: TNS Retail Forward ShopperScape™, July 2007.

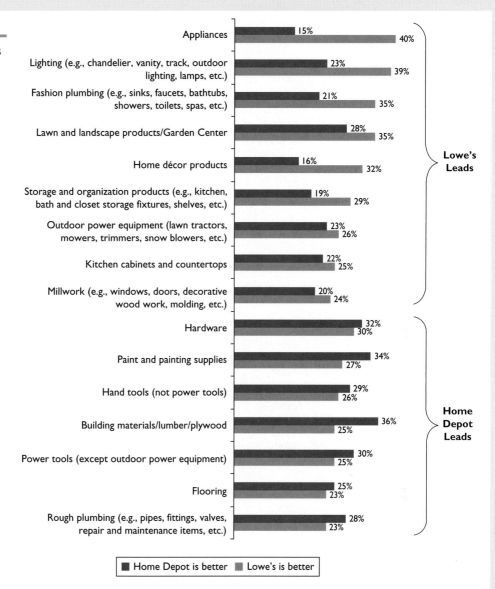

4. Should Lowe's have distinct merchandising strategies for men and women shoppers? Explain your answer.
5. Are there any risks associated with Lowe's placing greater emphasis on women shoppers in the future? Explain your answer.

6. Analyze the information regarding the level of customer spending in Home Depot and Lowe's shown in Table 3.
7. What criteria should Lowe's use in selecting new suppliers? Explain your answer.

FIGURE 5

Average Amount Spent on Home Improvement Products in the Past Three Months

Source: TNS Retail Forward ShopperScape™, July 2007.

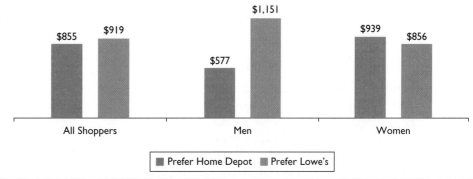

TABLE 3   **Amount Spent on Home Improvement Products in the Prior Three Months**

Men	Shopped Both Retailers	Prefer Home Depot	Index	Prefer Lowe's	Index
None	24%	21%	87*	21%	89
$1–$29	10	9	92	7	73
$30–$59	11	11	101	12	108
$60–$99	4	4	100	5	129
$100–$299	23	28	122	23	100
$300 or more	28	27	96	31	112
Average spent[1]	$841	$577	69	$1,151	137

Note: Shaded cells have an index value of 105 or more.
*Read as: Male shoppers who prefer Home Depot are 13% less likely than all shoppers (100-87) to have spent no money on home improvement products in the last three months.
[1]Average amount spent includes home improvement spending at any other retailer.

Women	Shopped Both Retailers	Prefer Home Depot	Index	Prefer Lowe's	Index
None	25%	23%	93*	24%	96
$1–$29	6	7	111	6	89
$30–$59	12	11	93	12	98
$60–$99	4	5	126	3	74
$100–$299	24	25	106	24	103
$300 or more	29	29	99	32	108
Average spent[1]	$849	$939	111	$856	101

Note: Shaded cells have an index value of 105 or more.
*Read as: Female shoppers who prefer Home Depot are 7% less likely (100-93) than all shoppers to have spent no money on home improvement products in the last three months.
[1]Average amount spent includes home improvement spending at any other retailer.

Source: TNS Retail Forward ShopperScape[TM] July 2007.

Communicating
with the Customer

In Part Seven, the elements involved in how a retailer communicates with its customers are discussed. First, we look at the role of a retail image and how it is developed and sustained. Various aspects of a promotional strategy are then detailed.

Chapter 18 discusses the importance of communications for a retailer. We review the significance of image in the communications effort and the components of a retailer's image. The creation of an image depends heavily on a retailer's atmosphere—which is comprised of all of its physical characteristics, such as the store exterior, the general interior, layouts, and displays. This applies to both store and nonstore retailers. Ways of encouraging customers to spend more time shopping and the value of community relations are also described.

Chapter 19 focuses on the promotional strategy, specifically how a retailer can inform, persuade, and remind the target market about its strategic mix. In the first part of the chapter, we deal with the four basic types of retail promotion: advertising, public relations, personal selling, and sales promotion. The second part describes the steps in a promotional strategy: objectives, budget, mix of forms, implementation of mix, and review and revision of the plan.

Source: UpperCut Images/Superstock Royalty Free.

18

Establishing and Maintaining a Retail Image

Chapter Objectives

1. To show the importance of communicating with customers and examine the concept of retail image

2. To describe how a retail store image is related to the atmosphere it creates via its exterior, general interior, layout, and displays, and to look at the special case of nonstore atmospherics

3. To discuss ways of encouraging customers to spend more time shopping

4. To consider the impact of community relations on a retailer's image

Target Corporation (**www.target.com**) has been busy building its image as a fashion-forward full-line discount store chain. And it has succeeded. The firm has come a very long way since its 1962 founding. Although many upper-middle-class customers feel uncomfortable shopping for clothing or housewares at Wal-Mart (**www.walmart.com**) or Kmart (**www.kmart.com**), their general view of Target can be summarized by the positioning statement: "Expect more. Pay less."

Target's strategy was born from its realization that it could not compete against Wal-Mart on price alone. Instead, Target decided to use its department store roots to develop partnerships with leading designers and brands in order to attract upscale shoppers. These include housewares designed by architect Michael Graves (**www.michaelgraves.com**), pots made by Calphalon (**www.calphalon.com**), maternity apparel by Liz Lange (**www.lizlange.com**), and an exclusive line of apparel by Mossimo (**www.mossimo.com**). To increase store traffic, Target has begun to offer prepared foods, wine, and USDA Choice Angus beef in many stores. Yet, despite its upscale merchandising, Target is still clearly a discounter as seen by its optical, pharmacy, and photo departments—as well as its self-service merchandising philosophy.

Its promotional campaign using a dog ("Spot") with red and white circles is another example of a successful tactic. A recent survey showed that 97 percent of Americans recognize Target's bull's eye symbol. Target's success in refining its image can be seen by examining the demographics of its current target customer: typically a suburban, professional, well-educated female with a family and an average household annual income of $45,000 per year. This is significantly higher than the demographics of the average shopper at either Wal-Mart or Kmart.[1]

Source: Reprinted by permission of Susan Berry, Retail Image Consulting, Inc.

OVERVIEW

There are many trade associations in the retail image arena. Visit a few online (http://vmsd.com/associations).

A retailer needs a superior communications strategy to properly position itself in customers' minds, as well as to nurture their shopping behavior. Once customers are attracted, the retailer must strive to create a proper shopping mood for them. Various physical and symbolic cues can be used to do this. See Figure 18-1. It is imperative to maximize the total retail experience for shoppers:

> The brand on the outside of your store may mean more to customers than the brands on the inside. It is not enough to carry fine merchandise and well-advertised brands; how you present merchandise sets you apart from the retailer to either side of you and the retailer down the street that may be carrying the same brands—or brands equally well-known. The presentation of merchandise and the displays that bring shoppers into the store are very important in creating a retail

FIGURE 18-1

Positioning and Retail Image

Polaris Fashion Place is the premier shopping center in Central Ohio—and its "look" reinforces this retail image. The shopping center has six anchor stores (Saks Fifth Avenue, Von Maur, Macy's, Sears, J.C. Penney, and Great Indoors), as well as more than 150 specialty stores. Dining options include Brio Tuscan Grille, Molly Woo's, California Pizza Kitchen, and Cheesecake Factory.

Source: Reprinted by permission of Susan Berry, Retail Image Consulting, Inc.

image. If one uses mannequins, are they distinctive? Do they represent the retailer's customer base? What do the display of stock on the wall and floor fixtures or fittings—on the display tables and racks—say about the retailer? How does a shopper quickly and conveniently find merchandise or a particular designer or brand he or she seeks inside the store? That is where the retailer's distinctive visual merchandising not only becomes part of the retail image but adds greatly to what shoppers the world over look for in a shopping experience. They look for and want selection, quality, comfort, and ease of shopping.[2]

This chapter describes how to establish and maintain an image. Retail atmosphere, storefronts, store layouts, and displays are examined. We also explore the challenge of how to encourage people to spend more time shopping and the role of community relations. Chapter 19 focuses on the common promotional tools available to retailers: advertising, public relations, personal selling, and sales promotion.

While our discussion looks more at store retailers, the basic principles do apply to nonstore retailers. For a mail-order firm, the catalog cover is its storefront, and the interior layouts and displays are the pages devoted to product categories and the individual items within them. For a Web retailer, the home page is its storefront, and the interior layouts and displays are represented by the links within the site.

The Significance of Retail Image

Display & Design Ideas (**www.ddimagazine.com**) is a leading trade magazine that often deals with retail image topics.

As defined in Chapter 3, *image* refers to how a retailer is perceived by customers and others, and *positioning* refers to how a firm devises its strategy so as to project an image relative to its retail category and its competitors—and to elicit a positive consumer response. To succeed, a retailer must communicate a distinctive, clear, and consistent image. Once its image is established in consumers' minds, a retailer is placed in a niche

CAREERS IN RETAILING

Is Retail for Me? Marketing and Advertising—Part 1

Unleash your creativity (or your strategic side) in retail. Depending on firm size, marketing functions may be centralized in one department, divided into different departments (like advertising, sales promotion, art and visual merchandising, and public/press relations), or grouped in various combinations:

▶ *Head of Marketing/Advertising/Sales Promotion.* Depending on the firm's size, marketing, advertising, sales promotion, art, and visual merchandising tasks may all be in one department or divided into any combination. Marketing conducts focus groups and statistical analysis of customer buying patterns for a strategic overview of the company's market share and positioning. Advertising creates and places media to sell either the company image or specific goods. Sales promotion commonly puts emphasis on mailings, coupons, events, and point of purchase material. Visual merchandising focuses on in-store presentation of the merchandise. The art department

creates the imagery to be used for advertising and sales promotion.

▶ *Head of Marketing (only).* Marketing conducts focus groups and statistical analysis of customer buying patterns for a strategic overview of the company's market share and positioning.

▶ *Head of Advertising.* Advertising creates and places media to sell either the company image or specific goods. Media placement and copywriting separate this position from the art department head below. The position of head of advertising and sales promotion adds extensive sales promotion activity to the advertising duties listed here.

▶ *Head of Advertising and Sales Promotion.* Advertising selects and places media to sell either the company image or specific goods. Sales promotion commonly puts emphasis on mailings, coupons, events, and point of purchase material.

Source: Reprinted by permission of the National Retail Federation.

relative to competitors. For global retailers, it can be challenging to convey a consistent image worldwide, given the different backgrounds of consumers.

Components of a Retail Image

Numerous factors contribute to a retailer's image, and it is the totality of them that forms an overall image. See Figure 18-2. We examined these factors in earlier chapters: target market, retail positioning, customer service, store location, merchandise attributes, and pricing. Our focal points for Chapters 18 and 19 are the attributes of physical facilities, shopping experiences, community service, advertising, public relations, personal selling, and sales promotion.

The Dynamics of Creating and Maintaining a Retail Image

Creating and maintaining a retail image is a complex, multi-step, ongoing process. It encompasses far more than store "atmosphere," which is discussed shortly. As J'Amy Owens, a well-known retailing consultant, noted: "A shopper should be able to determine the following about a store *in three seconds:* its name, its line of trade, its claim to fame, its price position, and its personality." Those shoppers "who need what you are selling will find you. Everyone else must be enticed to enter your store. Without a distinct image, you don't have a chance of being seen or heard through all the clutter that is retailing."[3]

Furthermore, with so many people having little time for shopping and others having less interest in it, more retailers understand that they may have to *entertain* shoppers to draw their business:

See how Jungle Jim's Web site (www.junglejims.com) reinforces its retail image.

Little did owner and store namesake Jim Bonaminio know when he started his market in Fairfield, Ohio, that he would take grocery shopping to a new level. Jungle Jim's has grown over the years from a simple roadside stand to a 300,000-square-foot food extravaganza and tourist destination, offering over 150,000 different items from more than 75 countries around the globe and employing an average of 350 employees throughout each year. Jungle Jim's resembles a theme park beginning in the parking lot and continuing to the unusual displays throughout the store. The entry is a jungle itself, with gorillas,

FIGURE 18-2

The Elements of a Retail Image

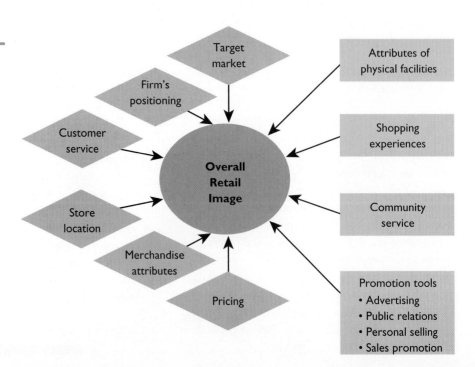

giraffes, elephants, and monkeys greeting you with the occasional roar and the splashing of a miniature waterfall in the background. Inside are several animatronic displays, such as a lion that sings Elvis Presley songs at regular intervals and a "rock band" composed of General Mills cereal mascots. The miniature storefronts in Jungle Jim's European section represent the architectural styles of various countries, and the Mexican section is covered by what appears to be the adobe façade and wooden frame of a cantina. Subtle humor is injected into many parts of the store, such as trashcans once labeled "Jungle Junk" and restroom entrances disguised as portable toilets—which, by the way, earned Jungle Jim's the "Best Restroom in America" award for 2007.[4]

Let's highlight two other examples. At Prada, the upscale 250-store apparel and accessories chain, the goal is to turn shopping into a rewarding experience. Prada stores provide sales associates with high-tech, hand-held devices tied into the Prada data base, enabling the associates to have some expertise on every item sold. The devices even serve as remote controls that associates can use to display runway videos of fashion items upon request. There are video panels on clothing racks and elsewhere. For more excitement: "Dressing rooms are equipped with RFID-enabled touch-screen panels that scan items, then provide shoppers with product information, runway videos, sizes and colors, and suggestions on which accessories are 'must haves.' Dressing room glass doors change from clear (so the shopper may show the garment to others) to opaque (for privacy) by the wave of a hand. Dressing rooms also have 'Magic Mirrors' which shoot digital video of customers wearing apparel so they may see how it looks from the back and other angles before purchasing." In addition, stores have Wi-Fi technology.[5] See Figure 18-3.

Are big-box stores becoming too impersonal? A strategist at consultancy Iconoculture thinks so: "As consumers expect more personalization, it's the big-box stores that sell rows of products created on faraway assembly lines that will suffer." Many of these stores "are still in the warehouse mentality, and the business model has shifted. If you have to spend an hour wandering around looking for what you want, forget it." Wal-Mart—which aggressively studies the marketplace—understands this trend. It "has started customizing each store to fit regional demands, such as focusing on clothes that reflect local styles. Analysts say that has helped the mammoth chain stay relevant."[6]

FIGURE 18-3

Shopping at Prada: Not a Routine Experience

Source: Reprinted by permission of Susan Berry, Retail Image Consulting, Inc.

A key goal for chain retailers, franchisors, and global retailers is to maintain a consistent image among all branches. Yet, despite the best planning, a number of factors may vary widely among branch stores and affect the image. They include management and employee performance, consumer profiles, competitors, the convenience in reaching stores, parking, safety, the ease of finding merchandise, language and cultural diversity among customers in different countries, and the qualities of the surrounding area. Sometimes, retailers with good images receive negative publicity. This must be countered in order for them to maintain their desired standing with the public.

Atmosphere

VMSD (http://vmsd.com/projects) provides many examples of excellence in retail atmospherics.

A retailer's image depends heavily on its "atmosphere," the psychological feeling a customer gets when visiting that retailer. It is the personality of a store, catalog, vending machine, or Web site. "Retail image" is a much broader and all-encompassing term relative to the communication tools a retailer uses to position itself. For a store-based retailer, **atmosphere (atmospherics)** refers to the store's physical characteristics that project an image and draw customers. For a nonstore-based firm, atmosphere refers to the physical characteristics of catalogs, vending machines, Web sites, and so forth. A retailer's sights, sounds, smells, and other physical attributes all contribute to customer perceptions.

A retailer's atmosphere may influence people's shopping enjoyment, as well as their time spent browsing, willingness to converse with personnel, tendency to spend more than originally planned, and likelihood of future patronage. Many people even form impressions of a retailer before entering its facilities (due to the store location, storefront, and other factors) or just after entering (due to displays, width of aisles, and other things). They often judge the firm prior to examining merchandise and prices.

Check out the advantages of "Visual Simulation" (www.facit.co.uk/retail.htm) in planning atmospherics.

When a retailer takes a proactive, integrated atmospherics approach to create a certain "look," properly display products, stimulate shopping behavior, and enhance the physical environment, it engages in **visual merchandising.** It includes everything from store display windows to the width of aisles to the materials used for fixtures to merchandise presentation. Through visual merchandising, the Eddie Bauer chain, highlighted in Figure 18-4, wants to

FIGURE 18-4

Visual Merchandising and Eddie Bauer
The Eddie Bauer chain is placing greater reliance on its visual merchandising efforts.

Source: Reprinted by permission of Susan Berry, Retail Image Consulting, Inc.

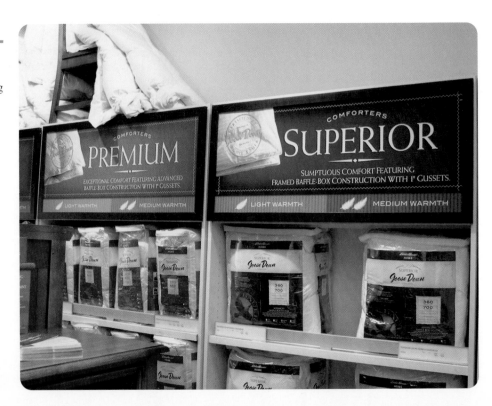

ensure that its stores "are a compelling shopping destination via powerful graphics, props, and product displays." As it says in its annual report:

> Our retail stores are designed and fixtured to create a distinctive and inviting atmosphere, with clear displays and information about product quality and fabrication. We believe that about 5,500 square feet is the appropriate size for most of our stores, as we believe this size allows us to achieve the correct balance between product assortment, inventory, and sales. We train our retail sales associates to provide a high standard of customer service and to create appealing head-to-toe outfit displays to show our customers how to wear our apparel to encourage multiple purchases by customers.[7]

Visit our Web site (**www.pearsonhighered.com/berman**) for links related to visual merchandising.

A Store-Based Retailing Perspective

Store atmosphere (atmospherics) can be divided into these key elements: exterior, general interior, store layout, and displays. Figure 18-5 contains a detailed breakdown of them.

EXTERIOR

A store's exterior has a powerful impact on its image and should be planned accordingly.

A **storefront** is the total physical exterior of the store itself. It includes the marquee, entrances, windows, lighting, and construction materials. With its storefront, a retailer can present a conservative, trendy, upscale, discount, or other image. Consumers who pass through an unfamiliar business district or shopping center often judge a store by its exterior. Besides the storefront itself, atmosphere can be enhanced by trees, fountains, and benches in front of the store. These intensify consumer feelings about shopping and about the store by establishing a relaxed environment. There are various alternatives in planning a basic storefront. Here are a few of them:

▶ Modular structure—a one-piece rectangle or square that may attach several stores.
▶ Prefabricated (prefab) structure—a frame built in a factory and assembled at the site.
▶ Prototype store—used by franchisors and chains to foster a consistent atmosphere.
▶ Recessed storefront—lures people by being recessed from the level of other stores. Customers must walk in a number of feet to examine the storefront.
▶ Unique building design—a round structure, for example.

A **marquee** is a sign that displays the store's name. It can be painted or a neon light, printed or script, and set alone or mixed with a slogan (trademark) and other information.

FIGURE 18-5

The Elements of Atmosphere

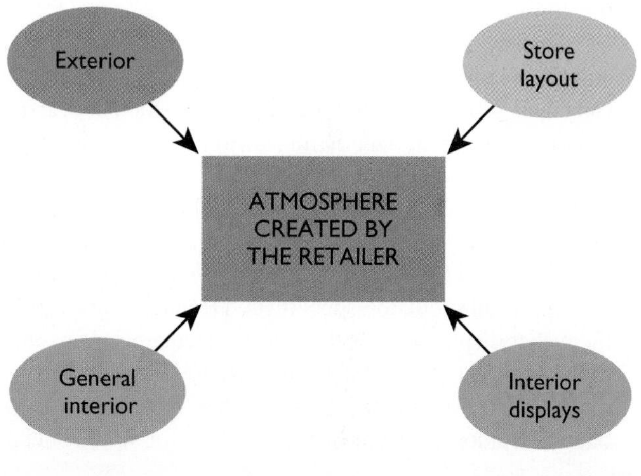

FIGURE 18-6

Using a Marquee to
Generate a Powerful
Retail Image

Source: Reprinted by permission
of Goran Petkovic.

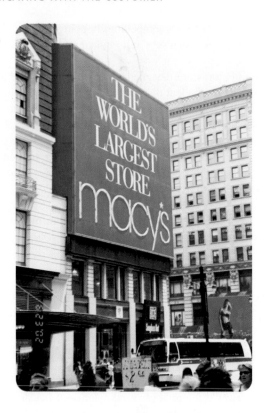

The marquee should attract attention, as Macy's Herald Square does. See Figure 18-6. Image is influenced because a marquee can be gaudy and flashy or subdued and subtle. The world's best-known marquee is McDonald's golden arch.

Store entrances require three major decisions. First, the number of entrances is determined. Many small stores have only one entrance. Department stores may have four to eight or more entrances. A store hoping to draw both vehicular and pedestrian traffic may need at least two entrances (one for pedestrians, another near the parking lot). Because front and back entrances serve different purposes, they should be designed separately. A factor that may limit the number of entrances is potential pilferage.

Second, the type of entrance(s) is chosen. The doorway can be revolving; electric, self-opening; regular, push-pull; or climate-controlled. The latter is an open entrance with a curtain of warm or cold air, set at the same temperature as inside the store. Entrance flooring can be cement, tile, or carpeting. Lighting can be traditional or fluorescent, white or colors, and/or flashing or constant. Look at how the Neiman Marcus outlet store entrance reinforces its discount image, as depicted in Figure 18-7.

Third, walkways are considered. A wide, lavish walkway creates a different atmosphere and mood than a narrow one. Large window displays may be attractive, but customers would not be pleased if there is insufficient space for a comfortable entry into the store.

Display windows have two main purposes: (1) to identify the store and its offerings and (2) to induce people to enter. By showing a representative merchandise offering, a store can create an overall mood. By showing fashion or seasonal goods, it can show it is contemporary. By showing sale items, a store can lure price-conscious consumers. By showing eye-catching displays that have little to do with its merchandise offering, a store can attract pedestrians' attention. By showing public service messages (such as a sign for the Special Olympics), the store can indicate its community involvement.

A lot of planning is needed to develop good display windows, which leads many retailers to hire outside specialists. Decisions include the number, size, shape, color, and themes of display windows—and the frequency of changes per year. Retailers in shopping malls may not use display windows for the side of the building facing the parking lot; there are solid building exteriors. They feel vehicular patrons are not lured by expensive outside windows; they invest in displays for storefronts inside the malls.

FIGURE 18-7

Last Call Clearance Center:
The Name Says It All

Source: Reprinted by permission
of TNS Retail Forward.

Exterior building height can be disguised or nondisguised. With disguised building height, part of a store or shopping center is beneath ground level. Such a building is not as intimidating to people who dislike a large structure. With nondisguised building height, the entire store or center can be seen by pedestrians. An intimate image cannot be fostered with a block-long building, nor can a department store image be linked to a small site.

Few firms succeed with poor visibility. This means pedestrian and/or vehicular traffic must clearly see storefronts or marquees. A store located behind a bus stop has poor visibility

---

**ETHICS
IN RETAILING**

Enhancing the Ethical Image of Electronics Retailing

In 1996, the Electronic Retailing Association's (ERA, **www.retailing.org**) board of directors unanimously approved a strengthened Code of Ethics for its electronics retailer members. Even though the code does not have an enforcement mechanism, ERA hopes that members will voluntarily comply. The board will seek to take action in cases involving clear and serious violations of this code.

Here is a summary of the ERA's ethical guidelines for members:

▶ To comply with ERA's marketing guidelines and all laws pertaining to the marketing of electronics.
▶ To honor all warranties and money-back guarantees, and to fairly handle all consumer complaints.

▶ To accurately reflect the nature and scope of business operations and all ownership interests.
▶ To avoid false statements concerning competitors and their products, businesses, and business practices.
▶ To fulfill all contracts and legal obligations and to avoid interfering with the legal rights of others.
▶ To refrain from improper business conduct, including discrimination based on race, color, religion, national origin, age, or sex.
▶ To support legislation that promotes fair and honest competition and the protection of consumer rights, and to oppose legislation that weakens the free market economic system.

Source: "ERA Member Code of Ethics," **www.retailing.org/node/74** (February 5, 2009).

for vehicular traffic and pedestrians across the street. Many retailers near highways use billboards since drivers go by quickly.

In every case, the goal is to have the store or center appear unique and catch the shopper's eye. A distinctive storefront, an elaborate marquee, recessed open-air entrances, decorative windows, and unusual building height and size are one set of features that could attract consumers by their uniqueness. Nonetheless, uniqueness may not be without its shortcomings. An example is the multi-level "shopping-center-in-the-round." Because this center (which often occupies a square city block) is round, parking on each floor level makes the walking distances very short. Yet, a rectangular center may have greater floor space on a lot of the same size, on-floor parking may reduce shopping on other floors, added entrances increase chances for pilferage, many people dislike circular driving, and architectural costs are higher.

As a retailer plans its exterior, the surrounding stores and the surrounding area should be studied. Surrounding stores present image cues due to their price range, level of service, and so on. The surrounding area reflects the demographics and lifestyles of those who live nearby. An overall area image rubs off on individual retailers because people tend to have a general perception of a shopping center or a business district. An unfavorable atmosphere would exist if vandalism and crime are high, people living near the store are not in the target market, and the area is rundown.

Parking facilities can add to or detract from store atmosphere. Plentiful, free, nearby parking creates a more positive image than scarce, costly, distant parking. Some potential shoppers may never enter a store if they must drive around for parking. Other customers may rush in and out of a store to finish shopping before parking meters expire. A related potential problem is that of congestion. Atmospherics are diminished if the parking lot, sidewalks, and/or entrances are jammed. Consumers who feel crushed in the crowd spend less time shopping and are in poorer moods than those who feel comfortable.

GENERAL INTERIOR

Once customers are inside a store, numerous elements affect their perceptions; and retailers need to plan accordingly:

▶ At Gander Mountain, the outdoor lifestyle chain, its merchandising philosophy guides store interior decisions: "Our large-format stores are generally located with convenient access to a major highway and have an open-style shopping environment characterized by wide aisles, open bar-joist ceilings, and high-density racking. To further build upon our reputation for high quality and exceptional value, we are outfitting certain stores and our new stores with additional features such as brick-and-stone accents, log-wrapped columns, and improved branding, fixture, flooring, and signage elements.[8]

▶ According to the designer of the popular Apple Stores, the interior reflects "three values: transparency, community, and service. The open, spacious interior with computers, iPods, and iPhones neatly on tables conveys transparency. The store encourages community via its theater and lounging areas. The commitment to service is branded into customers' minds as they visit the Genius Bar." Each store is "a place where people feel comfortable and are not intimidated by technology."[9]

▶ At the Toys "R" Times Square store in New York City, visitors are invited to "circle the center of the toy universe" on the only indoor Ferris wheel in Times Square: "There is no grander store entrance anywhere! The amazing 60-foot-tall Ferris wheel signals the start of a truly magical visit."[10]

Maxey Hayse Design Studios (**www.maxeyhayse. com/design_portfolio.html**) has designed interiors for a variety of retailers. Several are profiled here.

The general interior elements of store atmosphere were cited in Figure 18-5. They are described next.

Flooring can be cement, wood, linoleum, carpet, and so on. A plush, thick carpet creates one kind of atmosphere and a concrete floor another. Thus, 80 percent of department stores have carpeted floors, 70 percent of home centers have concrete floors, and two-thirds of big-box stores have vinyl floors.[11]

FIGURE 18-8

Eye-Catching Displays from M&M World
"Four floors of retail space devoted to our favorite chocolate-covered candies? It just doesn't get much better than that! Located in the Showcase Mall in Las Vegas, the mouth-watering exhibit features Red, Yellow, and the rest of the brightly colored gang on everything from T-shirts and golf-club covers to calculators and martini glasses." (from **www.vegas.com**)

Source: Reprinted by permission of Susan Berry, Retail Image Consulting, Inc.

Bright, vibrant colors contribute to a different atmosphere than light pastels or plain white walls. See Figure 18-8. Lighting can be direct or indirect, white or colors, constant or flashing. A teen-oriented apparel boutique might use bright colors and vibrant, flashing lights to foster one atmosphere, and a maternity dress shop could use pastel colors and indirect lighting to form a different atmosphere. Sometimes, when colors are changed, customers may be initially uncomfortable until they get used to the new scheme: "At first, shoppers were mystified by their new Sweetbay Supermarket. Was it the same company as the former Kash n' Karry store? Or was it a new company altogether? Vibrant colors such as purple and apricot were splashed about the new Sweetbay store—unlike the teal coloring of Kash n' Karry. Years ago, Kash n' Karry stores even had yucky brown-and-orange colors." In fact, Sweetbay is "working to transform Tampa-based Kash n' Karry into the more elegant Sweetbay Supermarkets."[12]

Scents and sounds influence the customer's mood. A restaurant can use food aromas to increase people's appetites. A cosmetics store can use an array of perfume scents to attract shoppers. A pet store can let its animals' natural scents and sounds woo customers. A beauty salon can play soft music or rock, depending on its customers. Slow-tempo music in super-markets encourages people to move more slowly.

Store fixtures can be planned on the basis of both their utility and aesthetics. Pipes, plumbing, beams, doors, storage rooms, and display racks and tables should be considered part of interior decorating. An upscale store usually dresses up its fixtures and disguises them. A discount store might leave fixtures exposed because this portrays the desired image.

Wall textures enhance or diminish atmospherics. Prestigious stores often use raised wallpaper. Department stores are more apt to use flat wallpaper, while discount stores may have barren walls. Chic stores might have chandeliers, while discounters have fluorescent lighting.

The customer's mood is affected by the store's temperature and how it is achieved. Insufficient heat in winter and no air-conditioning in summer can shorten a shopping trip. And image is influenced by the use of central air-conditioning, unit air-conditioning, fans, or open windows.

Wide, uncrowded aisles create a better atmosphere than narrow, crowded ones. People shop longer and spend more if they are not pushed while walking or looking at merchandise. In Boston and elsewhere, although Filene's Basement stores offer bargains, overcrowding keeps some customers away.

Dressing facilities can be elaborate, plain, or nonexistent. An upscale store has carpeted, private dressing rooms. An average-quality store has linoleum-floored, semiprivate rooms. A discount store has small stalls or no facilities. For some apparel shoppers, dressing facilities are a factor in store selection.

Multi-level stores must have vertical transportation: elevator, escalator, and/or stairs. Larger stores may have a combination of all three. Traditionally, finer stores relied on operator-run elevators and discount stores on stairs. Today, escalators are quite popular. They provide shoppers with a quiet ride and a panoramic view of the store. Finer stores decorate their escalators with fountains, shrubs, and trees. Stairs remain important for some discount and smaller stores.

Light fixtures, wood or metal beams, doors, rest rooms, dressing rooms, and vertical transportation can cause **dead areas** for the retailer. These are awkward spaces where normal displays cannot be set up. Sometimes, it is not possible for such areas to be deployed profitably or attractively. However, retailers have learned to use dead areas better. Mirrors are attached to exit doors. Vending machines are located near rest rooms. Ads appear in dressing rooms. One creative use of a dead area involves the escalator. It lets shoppers view each floor, and sales of impulse items go up when placed at the escalator entrance or exit. Many firms plan escalators so customers must get off at each floor and pass by appealing displays.

Polite, well-groomed, knowledgeable personnel generate a positive atmosphere. Ill-mannered, poorly groomed, uninformed personnel engender a negative one. A store using self-service minimizes its personnel and creates a discount, impersonal image. A store cannot develop an upscale image if it is set up for self-service. As one expert puts it, "15 feet, 15 seconds. That's how quickly your customers should be greeted, welcomed, and treated like a guest in your store."[13]

The merchandise a retailer sells can influence its image. Top-line items yield one kind of image, and lower-quality items yield another. The mood of the customer is affected accordingly.

Price levels foster a perception of retail image in consumers' minds; and the way prices are displayed is a vital part of atmosphere. Upscale stores have few or no price displays, rely on discrete price tags, and place cash registers in inconspicuous areas behind posts or in employee rooms. Discounters accentuate price displays, show prices in large print, and locate cash registers centrally, with signs pointing to them.

A store with state-of-the-art technology impresses people with its operations efficiency and speed. One with slower, older technology may have impatient shoppers. A store with a modern building (new storefront and marquee) and new fixtures (lights, floors, and walls) fosters a more favorable atmosphere than one with older facilities. Remodeling can improve store appearance, update facilities, and reallocate space. It typically results in strong sales and profit increases after completion.

Last, but certainly not least, there must be a plan for keeping the store clean. No matter how impressive the exterior and interior, an unkempt store will be perceived poorly: "A restroom with broken or malfunctioning equipment appears sloppy. It's really important that restrooms look clean."[14]

STORE LAYOUT

At this point, the specifics of store layout are *sequentially* planned and enacted.

ALLOCATION OF FLOOR SPACE.   Each store has a total amount of floor space to allot to selling, merchandise, personnel, and customers. Without this allocation, the retailer would have no idea of the space available for displays, signs, rest rooms, and so on:

▶ *Selling space* is used for displays of merchandise, interactions between salespeople and customers, demonstrations, and so on. Self-service retailers apportion most space to selling.

▶ *Merchandise space* is used to stock nondisplayed items. At a traditional shoe store, this area takes up a large percentage of total space.

The Boom in Digital Signs

Digital signs are typically used by retailers to maximize the impact of their projected images. Digital signs are also useful in automating the complex task of changing prices on outside store signs (such as in gasoline stations).

At JD Sports' flagship store in Oxford Circus, (**www.jdsports.co.uk**) digital displays constantly portray sports images to the firm's shoppers. To increase the realism of the displays and to provide maximum dramatic impact, JD Sports, a British-based retailer, uses six seamless plasma screens that can be seen as customers ride the escalator to the store's first floor. Likewise, eight plasma screens are visible in another key store location.

In a totally different digital sign application, gas stations have increasingly converted to digital signage to post the price of gasoline. The major advantages of digital signs to gas stations include the ability to more quickly respond to demand and competitive pressures, the ability to centrally control prices, and increased worker safety (as workers do not have to climb ladders to change prices). In Wisconsin, where gas stations can only legally change prices once a day, the digital signs free the stations from concern over posting incorrect prices.

Sources: "Digital Signs are Good for JD Sports," *In-Store* (March 2008), p. 7; and Tammy Mastroberte, "An Electric Price," *Convenience Store News* (May 7, 2007), pp. 35–36.

▶ *Personnel space* is set aside for employees to change clothes, to take lunch and coffee breaks, and for rest rooms. Because retail space is valuable, personnel space is strictly controlled. Yet, a retailer should consider the effect on employee morale.

▶ *Customer space* contributes to the shopping mood. It can include a lounge, benches and/or chairs, dressing rooms, rest rooms, a restaurant, a nursery, parking, and wide aisles. Discounters are more apt to skimp on these areas.

Visit Shelf Logic (**www. shelflogic.com/movies.htm**) and click on "Creating a Planogram" to learn more about this tool.

More firms now use planograms to assign space. A **planogram** is a visual (graphical) representation of the space for selling, merchandise, personnel, and customers—as well as for product categories. It also lays out their in-store placement. A planogram may be hand-drawn or computer-generated. Visit our Web site (**www.pearsonhighered.com/berman**) for several planogram links.

CLASSIFICATION OF STORE OFFERINGS. A store's offerings are next classified into product groupings. Many retailers use a combination of groupings and plan store layouts accordingly. Special provisions must be made to minimize shoplifting and pilferage. This means placing vulnerable products away from corners and doors. Four types of groupings (and combinations of them) are most commonly used:

▶ **Functional product groupings** display merchandise by common end use. A men's clothing store might group shirts, ties, cuff links, and tie pins; shoes, shoe trees, and shoe polish; T-shirts, undershorts, and socks; suits; and sports jackets and slacks.

▶ **Purchase motivation product groupings** appeal to the consumer's urge to buy products and the amount of time he or she is willing to spend on shopping. A committed customer with time to shop will visit a store's upper floors; a disinterested person with less time will look at displays on the first floor. Look at the first level of a department store. It includes impulse products and other rather quick purchases. The third floor has items encouraging and requiring more thoughtful shopping.

▶ **Market segment product groupings** place together various items that appeal to a given target market. A women's apparel store divides products into juniors', misses', and ladies' apparel. A music store separates CDs into rock, jazz, classical, R&B, country, and other sections. An art gallery places paintings into different price groups.

▶ **Storability product groupings** may be used for products needing special handling. A supermarket has freezer, refrigerator, and room-temperature sections. A florist keeps some flowers refrigerated and others at room temperature, as do a bakery and a fruit store.

FIGURE 18-9

How a Supermarket Uses a Straight (Gridiron) Traffic Pattern

Source: Illustration by Steve Cowden for *Progressive Grocer.* Reprinted by permission.

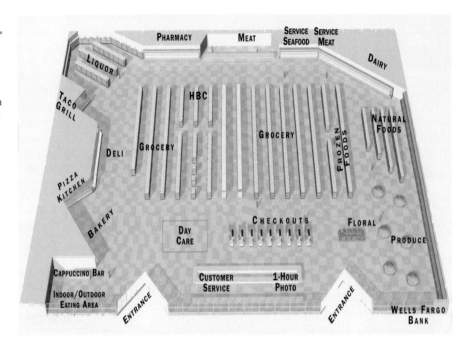

DETERMINATION OF A TRAFFIC-FLOW PATTERN.   The traffic-flow pattern of the store is then set. A **straight (gridiron) traffic flow** places displays and aisles in a rectangular or gridiron pattern, as shown in Figure 18-9. A **curving (free-flowing) traffic flow** places displays and aisles in a free-flowing pattern, as shown in Figure 18-10. Sears' innovative layout, which combines both approaches, is highlighted in Figure 18-11.

A straight traffic pattern is often used by food retailers, discount stores, drugstores, hardware stores, and stationery stores. It has several advantages:

▶ An efficient atmosphere is created.
▶ More floor space is devoted to product displays.
▶ People can shop quickly.
▶ Inventory control and security are simplified.
▶ Self-service is easy, thereby reducing labor costs.

The disadvantages are the impersonal atmosphere, more limited browsing by customers, and rushed shopping behavior.

A curving traffic pattern is used by department stores, apparel stores, and other shopping-oriented stores. This approach has several benefits:

▶ A friendly atmosphere is presented.
▶ Shoppers do not feel rushed and will browse around.
▶ People are encouraged to walk through the store in any direction or pattern.
▶ Impulse or unplanned purchases are enhanced.

The disadvantages are the possible customer confusion, wasted floor space, difficulties in inventory control, higher labor intensity, and potential loitering. Also, the displays often cost more.

DETERMINATION OF SPACE NEEDS.   The space for each product category is now calculated, with both selling and nonselling space considered. There are two different approaches: the model stock method and the space-productivity ratio.

The **model stock approach** determines the floor space necessary to carry and display a proper merchandise assortment. Apparel stores and shoe stores are among those using this method. The **sales–productivity ratio** assigns floor space on the basis of sales or profit per foot. Highly profitable product categories get large chunks of space; marginally profitable categories get less. Food stores and bookstores are among those that use this technique.

FIGURE 18-10

How a Department Store Uses a Curving (Free-Flowing) Traffic Pattern

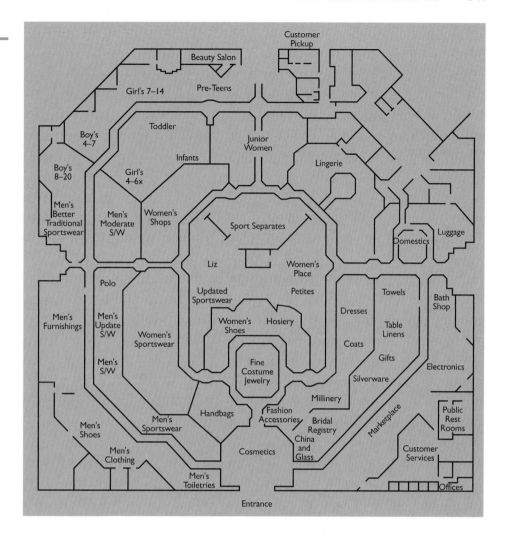

FIGURE 18-11

Sears' Open-Store Design: Combining Elements of Gridiron and Free-Flowing Traffic Patterns

Source: Reprinted by permission of TNS Retail Forward.

MAPPING OUT IN-STORE LOCATIONS. At this juncture, department locations are mapped out. For multi-level stores, that means assigning departments to floors and laying out individual floors. What products should be on each floor? What should be the layout of each floor? A single-level store addresses only the second question. These are some questions to consider:

▶ What items should be placed on the first floor, on the second floor, and so on?
▶ How should groupings be placed relative to doors, vertical transportation, and so on?
▶ Where should impulse products and convenience products be situated?
▶ How should associated product categories be aligned?
▶ Where should seasonal and off-season products be placed?
▶ Where should space-consuming categories such as furniture be located?
▶ How close should product displays and stored inventory be to each other?
▶ What shopping patterns do consumers follow once they enter the store?
▶ How can the overall appearance of store crowding be averted?

In two studies of supermarket shoppers, these interesting findings were uncovered:

1. "Grocery shoppers don't weave up and down all aisles—a pattern commonly thought to dominate store travel. Most shoppers tend only to travel select aisles, and rarely in the systematic up and down patterns most tend to consider the dominant travel pattern."
2. "Once they enter an aisle, shoppers rarely make it to the other end. They travel into and out of the aisle rather than traversing its entire length."
3. "Shoppers prefer a counter-clockwise shopping experience. They tend to shop more quickly as they approach the checkout counters. Behavior is driven more by their location in the store than the merchandise in front of them."
4. While 44 percent of shoppers "only go in select center store aisles to get specific things I need," 53 percent of shoppers "go up and down every/almost every center store aisle."
5. "The perimeter of the store—often called the 'racetrack'—is the shopper's home base, not just the space covered between aisles. Previous folklore perpetuated the myth that the perimeter was visited incidental to successive aisle traverses. We now know that it often serves as the main thoroughfare, effectively a home base from which shoppers take quick trips into the aisles."[15]

ARRANGEMENT OF INDIVIDUAL PRODUCTS. The last step in store layout planning is arranging individual products. The most profitable items and brands could be placed in the best locations, and products could be arranged by package size, price, color, brand, level of personal service required, and/or customer interest. End-aisle display positions, eye-level positions, and checkout counter positions are the most likely to increase sales for individual items. Continuity of locations is also important; shifts in store layout may decrease sales by confusing shoppers. The least desirable display position is often knee or ankle level, because consumers do not like to bend down.

Retailer goals often differ from their manufacturers. While the latter want to maximize their brands' sales and push for eye-level, full-shelf, end-aisle locations, retailers seek to maximize total store sales and profit, regardless of brand. Self-service retailers have special considerations. Besides using a gridiron layout to minimize shopper confusion, they must clearly mark aisles, displays, and merchandise.

Consider some of the tactics that supermarkets have employed:

▶ Many have produce near the entrance; some others have flowers. "The idea is to tantalize the customer, to draw you in with eye-catching displays."
▶ "Cereal theory" means placing boxes on lower shelves, which are at eye level for children.
▶ People buy more soup if the varieties are not shelved in alphabetical order.
▶ Store brands do better when located to the left of manufacturer brands. "After seeing the name brand, the eye automatically moves left (as if on a new page) to compare prices."

▶ Because "the best viewing angle is 15 degrees below the horizontal, the choicest display level has been measured at 51 to 53 inches off the floor."

▶ Virtually all stores place smaller impulse-type purchases near cash registers, "as customers often make last-minute purchases while they're waiting on line to pay."[16]

INTERIOR (POINT-OF-PURCHASE) DISPLAYS

Cahill specializes in creative retail displays (**www.cahilldisplay.com**).

Once the store layout is fully detailed, a retailer devises its interior displays. Each **point-of-purchase (POP) display** provides shoppers with information, adds to store atmosphere, and serves a substantial promotional role. Here's what the Global Association for Marketing at-Retail says:

Marketing at-retail is persuasive. Serving as the last three feet of the marketing plan, it is the only mass medium executed at the critical point where products, consumers, and the money to purchase all meet at the same time. It is no coincidence that with 74 percent of all purchase decisions in mass merchandisers made in store, an increasing number of brand marketers and retailers invest in this medium. *Retail marketing serves as the silent salesperson.* Displays and in-store media educate and draw attention to consumers about a product's availability and attributes. Coming at a time when most consumers want more information, and retailers have reduced staffing levels, retail marketing performs a vital service and augments cost-reduction efforts. *Marketing at-retail is flexible.* It is the only mass advertising medium that can convey the same overall strategic message in differing languages to varying audiences in the same village, city, or region. *Marketing at-retail is increasingly sophisticated in its construction and utilization.* Today's displays are easily assembled, maintained, and more powerful in entertaining and informing in the retail environment. *Marketing at-retail is used increasingly by retailers to enhance the shopping experience.* It is used to help overhaul a store's image, re-direct store traffic, and bolster merchandising plans.[17]

At this site (**http://dir.yahoo. com/Business_and_ Economy**), retailers can choose from many display firms. Click on "Business to Business," "Retail Management," and then "Point of Purchase Displays."

Several types of displays are described here. Most retailers use a combination of them.

An **assortment display** exhibits a wide range of merchandise. With an *open assortment,* the customer is encouraged to feel, look at, and/or try on products. Greeting cards, books, magazines, and apparel are the kinds of products for which retailers use open assortments. In addition, food stores have expanded their open displays for fruit, vegetables, and candy; some department stores have open displays for cosmetics and perfume. With a *closed assortment,* the customer is encouraged to look at merchandise but not touch it or try it on. Computer software, CDs, and DVDs are pre-packaged items that cannot be opened before buying. Jewelry is usually kept in closed glass cases that employees must unlock.

A **theme-setting display** depicts a product offering in a thematic manner and sets a specific mood. Retailers often vary their displays to reflect seasons or special events; some even have employees dress for the occasion. All or part of a store may be adapted to a theme, such as Presidents' Day, Valentine's Day, or another concept. Each special theme seeks to attract attention and make shopping more fun.

With an **ensemble display**, a complete product bundle (ensemble) is presented—rather than showing merchandise in separate categories (such as a shoe department, sock department, pants department, shirt department, and sports jacket department). Thus, a mannequin may be dressed in a matching combination of shoes, socks, pants, shirt, and sports jacket, and these items would be available in one department or adjacent departments. Customers like the ease of a purchase and envisioning an entire product bundle.

A **rack display** has a primarily functional use: to neatly hang or present products. It is often used by apparel retailers, housewares retailers, and others. This display must be carefully maintained because it may lead to product clutter and shoppers' returning items to the wrong place. Current technology enables retailers to use sliding, disconnecting, contracting/expanding, lightweight, attractive rack displays. A **case display** exhibits heavier, bulkier items than racks hold. DVD sets, books, pre-packaged goods, and sweaters typically appear in case displays.

A **cut case** is an inexpensive display that leaves merchandise in the original carton. Supermarkets and discount stores frequently use cut cases, which do not create a warm atmosphere. Neither does a **dump bin**—a case that holds piles of sale clothing, marked-down books, or other products. Dump bins have open assortments of roughly handled items. Both cut cases and dump bins reduce display costs and project a low-price image.

Posters, signs, and cards can dress up all types of displays, including cut cases and dump bins. They provide information about product locations and stimulate customers to shop. A mobile, a hanging display with parts that move in response to air currents, serves the same purpose—but stands out more. Electronic displays are also widely used today. They can be interactive, be tailored to individual stores, provide product demonstrations, answer customer questions, and incorporate the latest in multi-media capabilities. These displays are much easier to reprogram than traditional displays are to remodel.

A Nonstore-Based Retailing Perspective

Try out this demo E-store (http://sm.kemford.com/webstore/store) to experience many of the components of online retailing.

Many atmospherics principles apply to both store and nonstore retailers. However, there are also some distinctions.[18] Let's look at the storefront, general interior, store layout, displays, and checkout counter from the vantage point of one type of direct marketer, the Web retailer.

STOREFRONT

The storefront for a Web retailer is the home page. Thus, it is important that the home page:

▶ Prominently show the company name and indicate the positioning of the firm.
▶ Be inviting. A "virtual storefront" must encourage customers to enter.
▶ Make it easy to go into the store.
▶ Show the product lines carried.
▶ Use graphics as display windows and icons as access points.
▶ Have a distinctive look and feel.
▶ Include the retailer's E-mail address, mailing address, and phone number.
▶ Be highlighted at various search engines.

See Figure 18-12.

GENERAL INTERIOR

As with store retailers, a Web retailer's general interior sets a shopping mood. Colors run the gamut from plain white backgrounds to stylish black backgrounds. Some firms use audio to generate shopper interest. "Fixtures" relate to how simple or elaborate the Web site

FIGURE 18-12

The RE/MAX Online Storefront
The RE/MAX home page (its storefront) is colorful, yet easy to use. It clearly depicts the firm as a leading real-estate broker that does business across the United States—and around the globe.

Source: Reprinted by permission of RE/MAX International.

looks. "Width of aisles" means how cluttered the site appears and the size of the text and images. The general interior also involves these elements:

- ▶ Instructions about how to use the site.
- ▶ Information about the company.
- ▶ Product icons.
- ▶ News items.
- ▶ The shopping cart (how orders are placed).
- ▶ A product search engine.
- ▶ Locations of physical stores (for multi-channel retailers).
- ▶ A shopper login for firms that use loyalty programs and track their customers.

STORE LAYOUT

A Web retailer's store layout has two components: the layout of each individual Web page and the links to move from page to page. Web retailers spend a lot of time planning the traffic flow for their stores. Online consumers want to shop efficiently, and they get impatient if the "store" is not laid out properly.

Some online firms use a gridiron approach, while others have more free-flowing Web pages and links. Web companies often have a directory on the home page that indicates product categories. Shoppers click on an icon to enter the area of the site housing the category (department) of interest. Many retailers encourage customers to shop for any product from any section of the Web site by providing an interactive search engine. In that case, a person types in the product name or category and is automatically sent to the relevant Web page. As with physical stores, online retailers allocate more display space to popular product categories and brands—and give them a better position. On pages that require scrolling down, best-sellers usually appear at the top of the page and slower-sellers at the bottom.

DISPLAYS

Web retailers can display full product assortments or let shoppers choose from tailored assortments. This decision affects the open or cluttered appearance of a site, the level of choice, and possible shopper confusion. Online firms often use special themes, such as Valentine's Day. It is easy for them to show ensembles—and for shoppers to interactively mix and match to create their own ensembles. Through graphics and photos, a site can give the appearance of cut cases and dump bins for items on sale.

CHECKOUT COUNTER

A Web checkout counter can be complex: (1) Online shoppers worry more about the security and privacy of purchase transactions than those buying in a store. (2) Online shoppers often work harder to complete transactions. They must carefully enter the model number and quantity, as well as their shipping address, E-mail address, shipping preference, and credit card number. They may also be asked for their phone number, job title, and so on, because some retailers want to build their data bases. (3) Online shoppers may feel surprised by shipping and handling fees, if these fees are not revealed until they go to checkout.

At the bottom of its home page, learn how Amazon.com (**www.amazon.com**) enables shoppers to use "1-Click Settings" for easy ordering.

To simplify matters, Amazon.com has a patented checkout process—a major competitive advantage. Amazon.com's "1-Click" program lets shoppers securely store their shipping address, preferred shipping method, and credit card information. Each purchase requires just one click to set up an order form.

SPECIAL CONSIDERATIONS

Let's examine two other issues: how to set up a proper Web site and the advantages and disadvantages of Web atmospherics versus those of traditional stores.

New online retailers often have little experience with Web design or the fundamentals of store design and layout. These firms typically hire specialists to design their sites. When business grows, they may take Web design in-house. These are a few firms that design online stores for small retailers: Easy Store Creator (**www.easystorecreator.com**), Volusion (**www.volusion.com/web_design.asp**), Webfodder (**www.webfodder.com**), and Yahoo! Small Business (**http://smallbusiness.yahoo.com/ecommerce**). In this grouping, design and hosting costs are as low as $25.97 monthly (for the first three months).

Compared with physical stores, online stores have several advantages. A Web site:

▶ Has almost unlimited space to present product assortments, displays, and information.
▶ Can be tailored to the individual customer.
▶ Can be modified daily (or even hourly) to reflect changes in demand, new offerings from suppliers, and competitors' actions.
▶ Can promote cross-merchandising and impulse purchases with little shopper effort.
▶ Enables a shopper to enter and exit an online store in a matter of minutes.

Online stores also have potential disadvantages. A Web site:

▶ Can be slow for dialup shoppers. The situation worsens as more graphics and video clips are added.
▶ Can be confusing. How many clicks must a shopper make from the time he or she enters a site until a purchase is made?
▶ Cannot display the three-dimensional aspects of products as well as physical stores.
▶ Requires constant updating to reflect stockouts, new merchandise, and price changes.
▶ Is more likely to be exited without a purchase. It is easy to visit another Web site.

Encouraging Customers to Spend More Time Shopping

Underhill's Envirosell Inc. (www.envirosell.com) is a leader in shopping behavior research.

Paco Underhill, the guru of retail anthropology, has a simple explanation for why consumers should be encouraged to spend more time shopping: "The amount of minutes a shopper spends in a store (shopping, not waiting in a line) is important in determining how much she or he will buy. Over and over again, our studies have shown a direct relationship between these numbers. In an electronics store we studied, nonbuyers spent 5 minutes and 6 seconds in the store, compared to 9 minutes and 29 seconds for buyers. In a toy store, buyers spent over 17 minutes, compared to 10 for nonbuyers. In some stores, buyers spend three or four times as much time as nonbuyers.[19] Our Web site (**www.pearsonhighered.com/berman**) has links to research projects and video clips from Underhill's company Envirosell.

Among the tactics to persuade people to spend more time shopping are experiential merchandising, solutions selling, an enhanced shopping experience, retailer co-branding, and wish list programs.

RETAILING AROUND THE WORLD — Balenciaga Opens a London Flagship Store

Balenciaga (**www.balenciaga.com/us/en/eShopLanding.aspx**) is a fashion house owned by the Gucci Group. Balenciaga is most known for its line of handbags. It also produces small leather goods, shoes, sunglasses, jewelry, and gowns. Balenciaga has four U.S. boutiques, located in New York City; Costa Mesa, California; Los Angeles; and Las Vegas. In addition, Balenciaga has stores in Milan, Italy, and Paris, France. Its newest boutique is located in London's Mayfair section, near fashion designers Marc Jacobs and Luella, and Aesop (a luxury skincare retailer).

These are some characteristics of Balenciaga's flagship London store:

▶ The store resembles a spacecraft with metal lighting fixtures coming down from the ceiling and a giant "B" logo dominating the store's interior.

▶ Stands are located throughout the store that are outfitted with motion detectors. These stands, dubbed "musical forests," project video images and sounds. According to Balenciaga's creative director, "When you move in the store, it's quite an experience. One [forest] might be silent, while another is playing."
▶ Multiple materials are used for flooring: lacquer, wood covered with silver leaf, and volcanic rock. Each floor section has different colors, textures, and patterns.
▶ Balenciaga's signage is very subdued; there are no window displays and the storefront, which used to house a bank, was not changed.

Source: Miles Socha, "Balenciaga Flagship Brings Space to London," *Women's Wear Daily* (February 1, 2008), p. 4.

FIGURE 18-13

Making the Shopping
Experience More Pleasant
At Best Buy, shoppers can "test
drive" its consumer
electronics—especially the
large-screen TV sets.

Source: Reprinted by permission
of Susan Berry, Retail Image
Consulting, Inc.

The aim of **experiential merchandising** is to convert shopping from a passive activity into a more interactive one, by better engaging customers. See Figure 18-13. A number of retailers are doing so:

> Filled with all the things girls love, American Girl Place is a special destination where girls can make lasting memories. Locations in Chicago, New York, and Los Angeles offer girls a chance to share a variety of unforgettable experiences with their families and friends. Each retail and entertainment site has a Historical Boutique that features the company's flagship line of books, dolls, and accessories that celebrate girls of yesterday. Peek into the Past historical exhibits bring the worlds of all the characters to life with authentically re-created corners of each character's home. The Just Like You Boutique celebrates the interests of contemporary girls with more than 20 different dolls and a full range of accessories, plus a line of Dress Like Your Doll clothing. For younger girls, there are the Bitty Baby and Bitty Twins Nurseries. Girls can also browse the Bookstore, stocked with American Girl's best-selling historical, contemporary, and advice and activity books. They can also treat their dolls to new hairdos in the Doll Hair Salon and visit the Photo Studio for a souvenir portrait.[20]

> Our goal at Urban Outfitters is to be the brand of choice for well-educated, urban-minded young adults. We accomplish our objective by creating a differential shopping experience, which creates an emotional bond with the 18- to 30-year-old target customer we serve. Currently, we operate more than 130 stores in the U.S., Canada, and Europe. Our stores offer a unique and eclectic mix of fashion merchandise in a lifestyle sensitive store environment. Products range from women's and men's apparel, accessories, and footwear to items for the apartment, as well as gifts and novelties.[21]

> I came across a cooking demonstration at a Sam's Club the other day. Actually, I smelled it from 30 yards, I saw it from 25 yards, and I heard it from 15 yards. They were showing how to make cheese and ham crepes. The cooks wore white chef hats and were tossing around a French accent as if it were a poorly dubbed foreign film. I was first in line to get a sample. Did I buy any crepe making material? No. But it did stick in my mind for the next store visit and it took my mood from robotically going down the aisles to having a pleasurable time. The more pleasant the customer finds the environment, the longer he/she will stay in the store, the more sections they will shop, the more items they will shop, and the more items they will purchase.[22]

Solutions selling takes a customer-centered approach and presents "solutions" rather than "products." It goes a step beyond cross-merchandising. At holiday times, some retailers group gift items by price ("under $25, under $50, under $100, $100 and above") rather than by product category. This provides a solution for the shopper who has a budget to spend but a fuzzy idea of what to buy. Many supermarkets sell fully prepared, complete meals that just have to be heated and served. This solves the problem of "What's for dinner?" without requiring the consumer to shop for meal components.

An *enhanced shopping experience* means the retailer does everything possible to minimize annoyances and to make the shopping trip pleasant. Given all of the retail choices facing consumers, retailers must do all they can so that shoppers do not have unpleasant experiences. For example, shoppers often dislike waiting in line to check out. As one retailing expert says: "Think about the most frustrating experience you've had while waiting in a retail line. Remember how you felt standing with products in hand and some unseen impediment ahead costing valuable time and draining your patience? Now, picture that same experience, but imagine that a manager greets you in a friendly tone and offers you a drink or a warm chocolate-chip cookie for your trouble. The latter may seem rosy or downright silly, but smart retailers will use queue times as opportunities to connect with shoppers in a highly memorable fashion—whether that means with warm cookies or simply good, attentive customer service."[23]

Retailers can also provide an enhanced shopping experience by setting up wider aisles so people do not feel cramped, adding benches and chairs so those accompanying the main shopper can relax, using kiosks to stimulate impulse purchases and answer questions, having activities for children (such as Ikea's playroom), and opening more checkout counters. What decades-old shopping accessory is turning out to be one of the greatest enhancements of all? It is the humble shopping cart, as highlighted in Figure 18-14:

> As old-fashioned as they seem, carts are perfectly suited for the way people shop today. They're pressed for time and buy more in fewer trips. Mothers struggling to corral children love them. The growing ranks of senior citizens lean on carts for support and appreciate not having to carry their purchases. Carts empower an impulse. From category killers such as Home Depot to mass merchandisers such as Target Stores and Kmart, stores are bigger, carrying a wider array of goods, and pushing prices lower. They need customers to stay longer, cruise through the whole store, and load up. Why would any sane

See how retailers can create an enhanced shopping experience (www.merchandiseconcepts.com).

FIGURE 18-14

The Shopping Cart's Role in an Enhanced Shopping Experience

At Home Depot, shopping carts now make it easier to locate items in the store by including a convenient map of department locations on the handle—in addition to carrying customer purchases.

Source: Reprinted by permission of Home Depot.

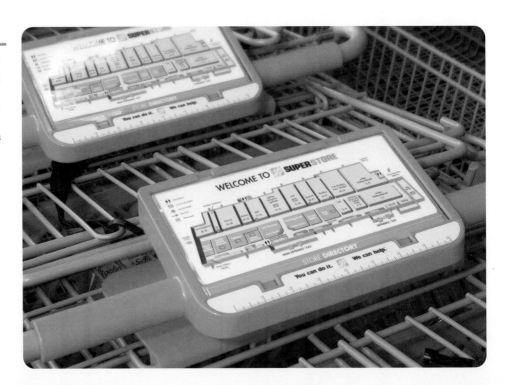

retailer deny its customers a cart? Some, it seems, are just too classy to have stainless steel contraptions junking up their stores. "I'm not sure I could see someone buying a $2,000 suit and hanging it over a cart," says the director of stores for Saks Fifth Avenue.[24]

More firms participate in *co-branding*, whereby two or more well-known retailers situate under the same roof (or at one Web site) to share costs, stimulate consumers to visit more often, and attract people shopping together who have different preferences. Here are several examples: Subway in Wal-Mart stores, Starbucks in Barnes & Noble stores, joint Dunkin' Donuts and Baskin-Robbins outlets, and numerous small retailers that sell their merchandise through Amazon.com. This illustrates why co-branding is growing in popularity: "Sean and Tina Berry often disagree on where to have lunch. But there was no dispute the other day, when they went to a combined Taco Bell and Long John Silver's restaurant not far from where they work. Mr. Berry had the Taco Bell grilled stuffed burrito while his wife opted for a fried fish platter from Long John Silver's. The combined restaurant is part of a trend in the fast-food industry. Restaurants say such combinations are preferred by customers, generate higher sales, and give the companies a chance to build lesser-known brands."[25]

Another tactic being implemented by a growing number of retailers is the *wish list program*. It is a technique that expands upon the long-standing concept of a wedding registry, and it can be used with virtually any products or life events. Wish lists are being used to great effect by Web retailers (and multi-channel retailers) to enable customers to prepare shopping lists for gift items they'd like to receive from a particular store or shopping center:

> Birthdays. Holidays. Graduations. The joy surrounding these occasions can be trumped by the stress of finding a great gift. And for those about to receive a bevy of gifts, it would be nice to actually get what you want, right? Online gift registries are the answer for both sides of the gift-giving process. The set-up is simple. You create an online wish list, which friends and relatives can easily access. And if your loved ones aren't the most computer-savvy, you can often E-mail your list to them. By viewing someone's wish list, you'll know exactly what they want. To find someone's "wish box," you simply enter some general information, such as their name, address, or home state.[26]

Community Relations

The way that retailers interact with the communities around them can have a significant impact on both their image and performance. Their stature can be enhanced by engaging in such community-oriented actions as these:

▶ Making sure that stores are barrier-free for disabled shoppers and strictly enforcing handicapped parking rules.
▶ Showing a concern for the environment by recycling trash and cleaning streets.
▶ Supporting charities and noting that support at the company Web site.
▶ Participating in antidrug programs.
▶ Employing area residents.
▶ Running special sales for senior citizens and other groups.
▶ Sponsoring Little League and other youth activities.
▶ Cooperating with neighborhood planning groups.
▶ Donating money and/or equipment to schools.
▶ Carefully checking IDs for purchases with age minimums.

Each year, 7-Eleven makes substantial charitable contributions of cash and goods to support programs addressing issues such as literacy, reading, crime, and multi-cultural understanding. It also donates hundreds of thousands of pounds of food to local food banks throughout the United States. Wal-Mart, Kmart, and Big Lots are among the numerous retailers participating in some type of antidrug program. Borders, Barnes &

Noble, Target, and others participate in national literacy programs. Safeway and Giant Food are just two of the supermarket chains that give money or equipment to schools in their neighborhoods.

As with any aspect of retail strategy planning, community relations efforts can be undertaken by retailers of any size and format:

> To help foster children sleep better, retailer Sleep Country USA sponsored its first-ever Pajama Drive. The company, which conducts six drives a year to help fill the material needs of foster kids and their foster parents, took in 7,039 pairs of pajamas in the recent effort. Contributions came from individuals, families, companies, and even children who asked for pajama donations in lieu of gifts at their birthday parties. As David Swendseid of Trillium Family Services, a provider of services to Northwest children and families, said: "Children can enter foster care with just the clothing on their backs, and given that our foster families usually provide care for more than one child, having resources to purchase new clothing is a challenge. New items, even those as simple as pajamas, provide an incredible relief to the parents and invite a sense of belonging for the child."[27]

Chapter **Summary**

1. *To show the importance of communicating with customers and examine the concept of retail image.* Customer communications are crucial for a store or nonstore retailer to position itself in customers' minds. Various physical and symbolic cues can be used.

   Presenting the proper image—the way a firm is perceived by its customers and others—is an essential aspect of the retail strategy mix. The components of a firm's image are its target market characteristics, retail positioning and reputation, store location, merchandise assortment, price levels, physical facilities, shopping experiences, community service, advertising, public relations, personal selling, and sales promotion. A retail image requires a multi-step, ongoing approach. For chains, there must be a consistent image among branches.

2. *To describe how a retail store image is related to the atmosphere it creates via its exterior, general interior, layout, and displays, and to look at the special case of nonstore atmospherics.* For a store retailer, atmosphere (atmospherics) is based on the physical attributes of the store utilized to develop an image; it is composed of the exterior, general interior, store layout, and displays. For a nonstore firm, the physical attributes of such elements as catalogs, vending machines, and Web sites affect the image.

   The store exterior is comprised of the storefront, marquee, entrances, display windows, building height and size, visibility, uniqueness, surrounding stores and area, parking, and congestion. It sets a mood before a prospective customer even enters a store.

   The general interior of a store encompasses its flooring, colors, lighting, scents and sounds, fixtures,

wall textures, temperature, width of aisles, dressing facilities, vertical transportation, dead areas, personnel, self-service, merchandise, price displays, cash register placement, technology/modernization, and cleanliness. An upscale retailer's interior is far different from a discounter's—reflecting the image desired and the costs of doing business.

In laying out a store interior, six steps are necessary: (a) Floor space is allocated among selling, merchandise, personnel, and customers based on a firm's overall strategy. More firms now use planograms. (b) Product groupings are set, based on function, purchase motivation, market segment, and/or storability. (c) Traffic flows are planned, using a straight or curving pattern. (d) Space per product category is computed by a model stock approach or sales–productivity ratio. (e) Departments are located. (f) Individual products are arranged within departments.

Interior (point-of-purchase) displays provide information for consumers, add to the atmosphere, and have a promotional role. Interior display possibilities include assortment displays, theme displays, ensemble displays, rack and case displays, cut case and dump bin displays, posters, mobiles, and electronic displays.

For Web retailers, many principles of atmospherics are similar to those for store retailers. There are also key differences. The home page is the storefront. The general interior consists of site instructions, company information, product icons, the shopping cart, the product search engine, and other factors. The store layout includes individual Web pages, as well as the links that connect them. Displays can feature full or more selective assortments. Sales are lost if the checkout counter does not function well. There are specialists that help in Web site design. Compared with traditional stores, Web stores have various pros and cons.

3. *To discuss ways of encouraging customers to spend more time shopping.* To persuade consumers to devote more time with the retailer, these tactics are often employed: experiential merchandising, solutions selling, enhancing the shopping experience, retailer co-branding, and wish list programs.

4. *To consider the impact of community relations on a retailer's image.* Consumers react favorably to retailers involved in such activities as establishing stores that are barrier-free for persons with disabilities, supporting charities, and running special sales for senior citizens.

Key Terms

atmosphere (atmospherics) (p. 508)
visual merchandising (p. 508)
storefront (p. 509)
marquee (p. 509)
dead areas (p. 514)
planogram (p. 515)
functional product groupings (p. 515)
purchase motivation product
    groupings (p. 515)

market segment product
    groupings (p. 515)
storability product groupings (p. 515)
straight (gridiron) traffic flow (p. 516)
curving (free-flowing) traffic
    flow (p. 516)
model stock approach (p. 516)
sales–productivity ratio (p. 516)
point-of-purchase (POP) display (p. 519)

assortment display (p. 519)
theme-setting display (p. 519)
ensemble display (p. 519)
rack display (p. 519)
case display (p. 519)
cut case (p. 520)
dump bin (p. 520)
experiential merchandising (p. 523)
solutions selling (p. 524)

Questions for Discussion

1. Why is it sometimes difficult for a retailer to convey its image to consumers? Give an example of a specialty store retailer with a fuzzy image.

2. How could a store selling new furniture project a value-based retail image? How could a store selling used furniture project such an image?

3. Define the concept of *atmosphere.* How does this differ from that of *visual merchandising?*

4. Which aspects of a store's exterior are controllable by a retailer? Which are uncontrollable?

5. What are meant by *selling, merchandise, personnel,* and *customer space?*

6. Present a planogram for a nearby grocery store.

7. Develop a purchase motivation product grouping for an online bookstore.

8. Which stores should *not* use a curving (free-flowing) layout? Explain your answer.

9. Visit the Web site of Petco (**www.petco.com**), and then comment on its storefront, general interior, store layout, displays, and checkout counter.

10. How could a neighborhood hardware store engage in solutions selling?

11. Do you agree with upscale retailers' decision not to provide in-store shopping carts? What realistic alternatives would you suggest? Explain your answers.

12. Present a community relations program for a dentist.

Web **Exercise**

Visit the Web site of T.G.I. Friday's (**www.tgifridays.com**). How would you rate the atmospherics and ambience of this site? What do you like most and least about the site? Explain your answers.

Note: Stop by our Web site (**www.pearsonhighered. com/berman**) to experience a number of highly

interactive, appealing Web exercises based on actual company demonstrations and sample materials related to retailing.

19 Promotional Strategy

In her second year selling Stanley Home Products, Mary Kay Ash was named "queen of sales." In 1963, when a younger male associate was promoted instead of her, Mary Kay Ash quit Stanley in frustration. One month later, with a $5,000 investment, Ash started her own skin-care business with just five items for sale. Today, Mary Kay Inc. (**www.marykay.com**) has annual sales of more than $2 billion (at the wholesale price level) and is the second-largest direct seller of skin products in the United States, with an independent sales force of 1.7 million consultants based in more than 30 countries. Mary Kay has 700,000 of its independent beauty consultants in the United States. About 500 women worldwide have become National Sales Directors, the highest rank within Mary Kay's independent sales force.

Associates characterized Mary Kay Ash as a tough businesswoman who stressed the empowerment of women, as well as positive thinking. Ash believed that "given the opportunity, encouragement, and awards, they will soar." Many of her employees feel that Mary Kay offered women with families career opportunities that were not otherwise available to them. A popular quote attributed to Mary Kay Ash is "if your mind can conceive it, and if you can believe it, you can achieve it."

Ash is also remembered for her reward dinners where top sales consultants were (and still are) given jewelry and cars. The reward for the top independent sales consultants who purchase a specified amount of Mary Kay products is a two-year lease on a new pink Cadillac. Currently, these consultants drive an estimated 2,000 "Mary Kay Pink Pearl Cadillacs."[1]

Source: Reprinted by permission of Mary Kay.

OVERVIEW

Sephora, the European and U.S. beauty chain, has a well-integrated promotion plan—from its colorful Web site (**www.sephora. com**) to its stores.

Retail promotion includes any communication by a retailer that informs, persuades, and/or reminds the target market about any aspect of that firm. In the first part of this chapter, the elements of retail promotion are detailed. The second part centers on the strategic aspects of promotion.

Consider the effort that Best Buy puts into its promotion strategy:

> We want our employees to engage with our customers and bring to bear a wide menu of capabilities to serve our customers' individual wants and needs. Our enterprise's unique, core capabilities lie in the ability of our line-level staff to recognize customers' desires and our support teams' ability to tailor new offers and to provide skill sets based on those customer needs. District managers monitor store operations and meet regularly with store managers to discuss merchandising, new product introductions, sales promotions, customer loyalty programs, employee satisfaction surveys, and store operating performance. Advertising, merchandise purchasing, and pricing, as well as inventory policies, are generally controlled centrally. Our stores compete by aggressively advertising and emphasizing a complete product and service solution, value pricing, and financing alternatives. Advertising costs consist primarily of print and television ads, as well as promotional events. Net advertising expenses were $684 million in fiscal 2008. Allowances received from vendors for advertising were $156 million in fiscal 2008.[2]

In assessing the substantial impact of the recent economic downturn, Brian Dunn, Best Buy's president and chief operating officer, said:

> In 42 years of retailing, we've never seen such difficult times for the consumer. People are making dramatic changes in how much they spend, and we're not immune from those forces. That's why it's critical that we manage spending, while preserving key growth initiatives. We believe our strategic indicators are strong. We continue to see improvements in employee turnover, customer satisfaction, and market share—and our commitment to our strategy of customer centricity is unwavering.[3]

Elements of the Retail Promotional Mix

This site (**www.promotion-strategies.net**) provides an overview on promotion planning. Click on a topic in the menu.

Advertising, public relations, personal selling, and sales promotion are the elements of promotion. In this section, we discuss each in terms of goals, advantages and disadvantages, and basic forms. A good plan integrates these elements—based on the overall strategy. A movie theater concentrates on ads and sales promotion (food displays), while an upscale specialty store stresses personal selling. See Figure 19-1.

Retailers devote significant sums to promotion. For example, a typical department store spends up to 4 to 5 percent of sales on ads and 8 to 10 percent on personal selling and support services. And most department store chains also invest heavily in sales promotions and use public relations to generate favorable publicity and reply to media information requests. We have more than a dozen links related to the retail promotion mix at our Web site (**www.pearsonhighered.com/berman**).

Advertising

Advertising is paid, nonpersonal communication transmitted through out-of-store mass media by an identified sponsor. Four aspects of this definition merit clarification:

1. *Paid form.* This distinguishes advertising from publicity (an element of public relations), for which no payment is made by the retailer for the time or space used to convey a message.

FIGURE 19-1

Best Buy: A Retailing Ace at Promotion
Best Buy recognizes the value of every aspect of promotion—from advertising and personal selling to saturation signage outside its downtown stores.

Source: Reprinted by permission of TNS Retail Forward.

2. *Nonpersonal presentation.* A standard message is delivered to the entire audience, and it cannot be adapted to individual customers (except with the Web).
3. *Out-of-store mass media.* These include newspapers, radio, TV, the Web, and other mass channels, rather than personal contacts. In-store communications (such as displays) are considered sales promotion.
4. *Identified sponsor.* The sponsor's name is clearly divulged, unlike publicity. See Figure 19-2.

Sears Holdings (which includes Sears and Kmart) has the highest annual dollar advertising expenditures among U.S. retailers—$1.6 billion, about 3.6 percent of its U.S. sales. On the other hand, Wal-Mart spends just 0.4 percent of sales on ads, relying more on word of mouth, in-store events, and everyday low prices.[4] Table 19-1 shows advertising ratios for several retailing categories.

DIFFERENCES BETWEEN RETAILER AND MANUFACTURER ADVERTISING STRATEGIES
Retailers—other than national chains—usually have more geographically concentrated target markets than manufacturers. This means they can adapt better to local needs, habits, and preferences. However, those retailers cannot utilize national media as readily as manufacturers. Only the largest retail chains and franchises can advertise on national TV programs. An exception is direct marketing (including the World Wide Web) because trading areas for even small firms can then be geographically dispersed.

Retail ads stress immediacy. Individual items are placed for sale and advertised over short time periods. Manufacturers are more often concerned with developing favorable attitudes.

Many retailers stress prices in ads, whereas manufacturers usually emphasize key product attributes. In addition, retailers often display several different products in one ad, whereas manufacturers tend to minimize the number of products mentioned in a single ad.

Media rates tend to be lower for retailers. Because of this, and the desire of many manufacturers and wholesalers for wide distribution, the costs of retail advertising are sometimes shared by manufacturers or wholesalers and their retailers. Two or more retailers may also share costs. Both of these approaches entail **cooperative advertising**.

Find out how to devise good ads (**www.inc.com/ articles_by_topic/ marketing-pr-advertising**).

OBJECTIVES
A retailer would select one or more of these goals and base advertising efforts on it (them).

▶ To grow short-term sales.
▶ To increase customer traffic.

FIGURE 19-2

Advertising and Wal-Mart
Wal-Mart not only advertises on
TV and radio, in newspapers and
magazines, and on billboards, it
also has a very sophisticated
video system that shows ads in
its stores.

Source: Reprinted by permission of
TNS Retail Forward.

▶ To develop and/or reinforce a retail image.
▶ To inform customers about goods and services and/or company attributes.
▶ To ease the job for sales personnel.
▶ To stimulate demand for private brands.

ADVANTAGES AND DISADVANTAGES
The major advantages of advertising are that:

▶ A large audience is attracted. For print media, circulation is supplemented by the
passing of a copy from one reader to another.
▶ The costs per viewer, reader, or listener are low.
▶ A number of alternative media are available, so a retailer can match a medium to the
target market.
▶ The retailer has control over message content, graphics, timing, and size (or length),
so a standardized message in a chosen format can be delivered to the entire audience.
▶ In print media, a message can be studied and restudied by the target market.

TABLE 19-1   Selected U.S. Advertising-to-Sales Ratios by Type of Retailer

Type of Retailer	Advertising Dollars as Percentage of Sales Dollars[a]	Advertising Dollars as Percentage of Margin[b]
Apparel and accessories stores	5.2	11.9
Auto and home supply stores	1.9	3.8
Department stores	5.1	13.3
Drug and proprietary stores	0.7	3.2
Eating places	2.9	10.8
Family clothing stores	1.9	5.3
Furniture stores	8.7	23.6
Grocery stores	0.8	2.9
Hobby, toy, and game shops	2.9	8.1
Hotels and motels	1.4	6.2
Lumber and building materials	1.7	4.9
Mail-order firms	3.5	12.4
Movie theaters	1.0	4.6
Radio, TV, and consumer electronics stores	2.4	9.3
Shoe stores	2.3	7.0

[a]Advertising dollars as percentage of sales = Advertising expenditures/Net company sales
[b]Advertising dollars as percentage of margin = Advertising expenditures/(Net company sales − Cost of goods sold)

Source: Schonfeld & Associates, "2008 Advertising-to-Sales Ratios for 200 Largest Ad Spending Industries," **www.adage.com**. Reprinted by permission. Copyright Crain Communications Inc.

▶ Editorial content (a TV show, a news story, and so on) often surrounds an ad. This may increase its credibility or the probability it will be read.

▶ Self-service or reduced-service operations are possible since a customer becomes aware of a retailer and its offerings before shopping.

The major disadvantages of advertising are that:

▶ Standardized messages lack flexibility (except for the Web and its interactive nature). They do not focus on the needs of individual customers.

▶ Some media require large investments. This may reduce the access of small firms.

▶ Media may reach large geographic areas, and for retailers, this may be wasteful. A small supermarket chain might find that only 40 percent of an audience resides in its trading area.

▶ Some media require a long lead time for placing ads. This reduces the ability to advertise fad items or to react to some current events themes.

▶ Some media have a high throwaway rate. Circulars may be discarded without being read.

▶ A 30-second TV commercial or small newspaper ad does not have many details.

The preceding are broad generalities. The pros and cons of specific media are covered next.

MEDIA

Retailers can choose from the media highlighted in Table 19-2 and described here.

Papers (dailies, weeklies, and shoppers) represent the most preferred medium for retailers, having the advantages of market coverage, short lead time, reasonable costs, flexibility, longevity, graphics, and editorial association (ads near columns or articles).

CAREERS IN RETAILING

Is Retail for Me? Marketing and Advertising—Part 2

In addition to the typical marketing and advertising positions noted in Chapter 18, there are many other opportunities:

▶ *Art Department Head.* Manager of the department of graphics artists and/or computer-aided designers (CAD), who create signage and imagery for the advertising, sales promotion, and store operating groups, among others.

▶ *Graphics Designer.* Graphics artists and/or computer-aided designers (CAD) who create signage and imagery for the advertising, sales promotion, and store operating groups, among others.

▶ *Print Production Coordinator.* This position is responsible for negotiating printer prices and for coordinating the production and distribution of printed media such as sales promotion materials, published reports, benefits booklets, etc. Works closely with graphic artist and printer shops.

▶ *Head of Visual Merchandising.* Top position responsible for the overall "look" of the stores, including windows, sales floor signage, and displays. May publish "planograms," indicating where and how to place merchandise on the sales floor for best visual advantage.

▶ *Visual Merchandiser (VM).* This position is typically one of three types, with similar skills and responsibilities, but different scope: (a) Regional VMs are typically found in boutique chains, responsible for visual presentation in a geographic area. This position may report to the head of visual or to a local district/regional manager of stores. (b) In-store VMs are found in big-box stores that need one or more associates per store, typically reporting to the store manager. This position is more doing and less training than the regional VM. (c) Home office-based VMs focus on training and monitoring but may be responsible for a brand or category nationwide.

Source: Reprinted by permission of the National Retail Federation.

TABLE 19-2 Advertising Media Comparison Chart

Medium	Market Coverage	Particular Suitability
Daily papers	Single community or entire metro area; local editions may be available.	All larger retailers.
Weekly papers	Single community usually; may be a metro area.	Retailers with a strictly local market.
Shopper papers	Most households in one community; chain shoppers can cover a metro area.	Neighborhood retailers and service businesses.
Phone directories	Geographic area or occupational field served by a directory.	All types of goods and service-oriented retailers.
Direct mail	Controlled by the retailer.	New and expanding firms, those using coupons or special offers, mail order.
Radio	Definable market area surrounding the station.	Retailers focusing on identifiable segments.
TV	Definable market area surrounding the station.	Retailers of goods and services with wide appeal.
World Wide Web	Global.	All types of goods and service-oriented retailers.
Transit	Urban or metro community served by transit system.	Retailers near transit routes, especially those appealing to commuters.
Outdoor	Entire metro area or single neighborhood.	Amusement and tourist-oriented retailers, well-known firms.
Local magazines	Entire metro area or region; zoned editions sometimes available.	Restaurants, entertainment-oriented firms, specialty shops, mail-order firms.
Flyers/circulars	Single neighborhood.	Restaurants, dry cleaners, service stations, and other neighborhood firms.

Disadvantages include the possible waste (circulation to a wider area than necessary), the competition among retailers, the black-and-white format, and the appeal to fewer senses than TV. To maintain a dominant position, many papers have revamped their graphics, and some run color ads. Free-distribution shopper papers ("penny savers"), with little news content and delivery to all households in a geographic area, are popular today.

The Yellow Pages (**www. yellowpages.com**) remains a key medium for retailers.

In a White Pages phone directory, retailers get free alphabetical listings along with all other phone subscribers, commercial and noncommercial. The major advantage of the White over the Yellow Pages is that those who know a firm's name are not exposed to competitors. The major disadvantage, in contrast with the Yellow Pages, is the alphabetical rather than type-of-business listing. A person unfamiliar with repair services will usually look in the Yellow Pages under "Repair." In the Yellow Pages, firms pay for listings (and display ads, if desired) in their category. Most retailers advertise in the Yellow Pages. The advantages include widespread usage by people ready to shop and their long life (one year or more). The disadvantages are that retailer awareness may not be gained and there is a lengthy lead time for new ads.

With direct mail, retailers send catalogs or ads to customers by the mail or private delivery firms. Advantages are the targeted audience, tailored format, controlled costs, quick feedback, and tie-ins (including ads with bills). Among the disadvantages are the high throwaway rate ("junk mail"), poor image to some people, low response rate, and outdated mailing lists (addressees may have moved).

Radio is used by a variety of retailers. Advantages are the relatively low costs, its value as a medium for car drivers and passengers, its ability to use segmentation, its rather short lead time, and its wide reach. Disadvantages include no visual impact, the need for repetition, the need for brevity, and waste. The use of radio by retailers has gone up in recent years.

TV ads, although increasing due to the rise of national and regional retailers, are far behind papers in retail promotion expenditures. Among the advantages are the dramatic effects of messages, the large market coverage, creativity, and program affiliation (for sponsors). Disadvantages include high minimum costs, audience waste, the need for brevity and repetition, and the limited availability of popular times for nonsponsors. Because cable TV is more focused than conventional stations, it appeals to local retailers.

From an advertising perspective, retailers use the Web to provide information to customers about store locations, to describe the products carried, to let people order catalogs, and so forth. Retailers have two opportunities to reach customers: advertising on search engines and other firms' Web sites; and communicating with customers at their own sites. See Figure 19-3.

Transit advertising is used in areas with mass transit systems. Ads are displayed on buses and in trains and taxis. Advantages are the captive audience, mass market, high level of repetitiveness, and geographically defined market. Disadvantages are the ad clutter, distracted audience, lack of availability in small areas, restricted travel paths, and graffiti. Many retailers also advertise on their delivery vehicles.

At the Outdoor Advertising Association Web site (**www.oaaa.org**), type in "Retail."

Outdoor (billboard) advertising is sometimes used by retailers. Posters and signs may be displayed in public places, on buildings, and alongside highways. Advantages are the large size of the ads, the frequency of exposure, the relatively low costs, and the assistance in directing new customers. Disadvantages include the clutter of ads, a distracted audience, the limited information, and some legislation banning outdoor ads.

Magazine usage is value for three reasons: the rise in larger retail chains, the creation of regional and local editions, and the use by nonstore and multi-channel retailers. Advantages are the tailoring to specific markets, creative options, editorial associations, longevity of messages, and color. Disadvantages include the long lead time, less sense of consumer urgency, waste, and declining readership.

Single-page (flyers) or multiple-page (circulars) ads are distributed in parking lots or to consumer homes. Advantages include the targeted audience, low costs, flexibility, and speed. Among the disadvantages are the level of throwaways, the poor image to some, and clutter. Flyers are good for smaller firms, while circulars are used by larger ones.

FIGURE 19-3

Using the Internet to Provide a New Product Line

Home Depot has a new line of environmentally friendly products. At a special section of its Web site (**www.homedepot.com/ecooptions**), the retailer provides a huge amount of information about this initiative.

Source: Reprinted by permission of Home Depot.

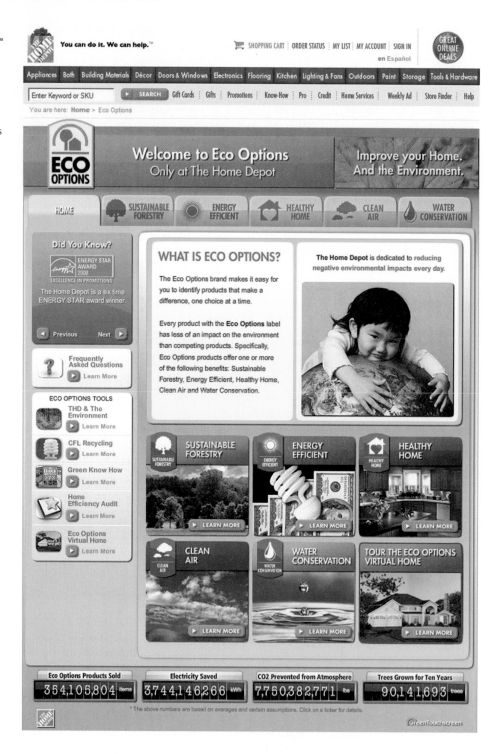

TYPES

Advertisements can be classified by content and payment method. See Figure 19-4.

Pioneer ads have awareness as a goal and offer information (usually on new firms or locations). *Competitive ads* have persuasion as a goal. *Reminder ads* are geared to loyal customers and stress the attributes that have made the retailers successful. *Institutional ads* strive to keep retailer names before the public without emphasizing the sale of goods or services. Public service messages are institutional.

Retailers may pay their own way or seek cooperative ventures in placing ads. Firms paying their own way have total control and incur all costs. With cooperative ventures, two or more parties share the costs and the decision making.[5] Billions of dollars are spent

FIGURE 19-4

Types of Advertising

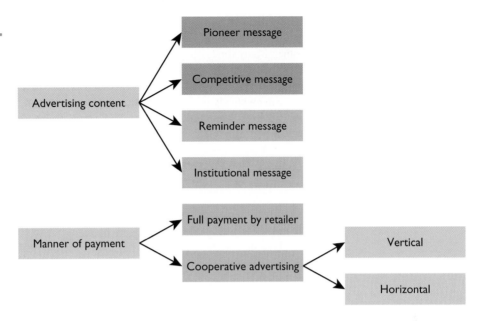

Carol Wright (**www. carolwright.com**) is a leader in horizontal cooperative promotions.

yearly on U.S. cooperative advertising, most in vertical agreements. Newspapers are preferred over other media for cooperative ads related to retailing.

In a **vertical cooperative advertising agreement**, a manufacturer and a retailer or a wholesaler and a retailer share an ad. Responsibilities are specified contractually, and retailers are typically not reimbursed until after ads run. Vertical cooperative advertising is subject to the Robinson-Patman Act; similar arrangements must be offered to all retailers on a proportional basis. Advantages to a retailer are the reduced ad costs, assistance in preparing ads, greater market coverage, and less planning time. Disadvantages to a retailer include less control, flexibility, and distinctiveness. Some retailers are concerned about the eligibility requirements to participate and the emphasis on the supplier's name in ads. In response, manufacturers and other suppliers are now more flexible and understanding.

With a **horizontal cooperative advertising agreement**, two or more retailers share an ad. A horizontal agreement is most often used by small noncompeting retailers (such as independent hardware stores), retailers in the same shopping center, and franchisees of a given firm. Advantages and disadvantages are similar to those in a vertical agreement. Two further benefits are the bargaining power of retailers in dealing with the media and the synergies of multiple retailers working together.

When planning a cooperative strategy, these questions should be considered:

▶ What ads qualify, in terms of merchandise and special requirements?
▶ What percentage of advertising is paid by each party?
▶ When can ads be run? In what media?
▶ Are there special provisions regarding message content?
▶ What documentation is required for reimbursement?
▶ How does each party benefit?
▶ Do cooperative ads obscure the image of individual retailers?

Public Relations

At Wendy's (**www.wendys. com**), public relations means community relations. After entering the site, select "Community."

Public relations entails any communication that fosters a favorable image for the retailer among its publics (consumers, investors, government, channel members, employees, and the general public). It may be nonpersonal or personal, paid or nonpaid, and sponsor controlled or not controlled. **Publicity** is any nonpersonal form of public relations whereby messages are transmitted through mass media, the time or space provided by the media is not paid for, and there is no identified commercial sponsor.

The basic distinction between advertising and publicity is that publicity is nonpaid. Thus, it is not as readily controllable. A story on a store opening may not appear, appear after the fact, or not appear in the form desired. Yet, to shoppers, publicity is often more credible and valuable. Advertising and publicity (public relations) should complement one another. Many times, the aim is for publicity to precede ads.

Public relations can benefit both large and small retailers. Although the former often spend a lot of money to publicize events such as the Macy's Thanksgiving Day Parade, small firms can creatively generate attention for themselves on a limited budget. They can feature book signings by authors, sponsor school sports teams, donate goods and services to charities, and so forth.

OBJECTIVES

Public relations seeks to accomplish one or more of these goals:

▶ Increase awareness of the retailer and its strategy mix.
▶ Maintain or improve the company image.
▶ Show the retailer as a contributor to the community's quality of life.
▶ Demonstrate innovativeness.
▶ Present a favorable message in a highly believable manner.
▶ Minimize total promotion costs.

ADVANTAGES AND DISADVANTAGES

The major advantages of public relations are that:

▶ An image can be presented or enhanced.
▶ A more credible source presents the message (such as a good restaurant review).
▶ There are no costs for message time or space.
▶ A mass audience is addressed.
▶ Carryover effects are possible (if a store is perceived as community-oriented, its value positioning is more apt to be perceived favorably).
▶ People pay more attention to news stories than to clearly identified ads.

The major disadvantages of public relations are that:

▶ Some retailers do not believe in spending any funds on image-related communication.
▶ There is little retailer control over a publicity message and its timing, placement, and coverage by a given medium.
▶ It may be more suitable for short-run, rather than long-run, planning.
▶ Although there are no media costs for publicity, there are costs for a public relations staff, planning activities, and the activities themselves (such as store openings).

TYPES

Public relations can be planned or unexpected and image enhancing or image detracting.

With planned public relations, a retailer outlines its activities in advance, strives to have media report on them, and anticipates certain coverage. Community services, such as donations and special sales; parades on holidays (such as the Macy's Thanksgiving Day Parade); the introduction of "hot" new goods and services; and a new store opening are activities a retailer hopes will gain media coverage. The release of quarterly sales figures and publication of the annual report are events a retailer knows will be covered.

When unexpected publicity occurs, the media report on a company without its having advance notice. TV and newspaper reporters may anonymously visit restaurants and other retailers to rate their performance and quality. A fire, an employee strike, or other newsworthy event may be mentioned in a story. Investigative reports on company practices may appear.

There is positive publicity when media reports are complimentary, with regard to the excellence of a retailer's practices, its community efforts, and so on. However, the media may also provide negative publicity. A story could describe a store opening in less than glowing terms, rap a firm's environmental record, or otherwise be critical.

That is why public relations must be viewed as a component of the promotion mix, not as the whole mix.

Personal Selling

The communication tips at this Web site (www.inc. com/guides/sales/23032. html) are quite helpful.

Personal selling involves oral communication with one or more prospective customers for the purpose of making a sale. The level of personal selling used by a retailer depends on the image it wants to convey, the products sold, the amount of self-service, and the interest in long-term customer relationships—as well as customer expectations. Retail salespeople may work in a store, visit consumer homes or places of work, or engage in telemarketing.

J.C. Penney believes in training superior sales associates. Why? First, higher levels of selling are needed to reinforce its image as a fashion-oriented department store. Unlike self-service discounters, Penney wants its sales staff to give advice to customers. Second, Penney wants to stimulate cross-selling, whereby associates recommend related items to customers. Third, Penney wants sales associates to "save the sale," by suggesting that customers who return merchandise try different colors, styles, or quality. Four, Penney believes it can foster customer loyalty. Figure 19-5 highlights J.C. Penney's sales associate tips.

OBJECTIVES

The goals of personal selling are to:

▶ Persuade customers to buy (since they often enter a store after seeing an ad).
▶ Stimulate sales of impulse items or products related to customers' basic purchases.
▶ Complete customer transactions.
▶ Feed back information to company decision makers.
▶ Provide proper levels of customer service.
▶ Improve and maintain customer satisfaction.
▶ Create awareness of items also marketed through the Web, mail, and telemarketing.

ADVANTAGES AND DISADVANTAGES

The advantages of selling relate to its personal nature:

▶ A salesperson can adapt a message to the needs of the individual customer.
▶ A salesperson can be flexible in offering ways to address customer needs.
▶ The attention span of the customer is higher than with advertising.
▶ There is less waste; most people who walk into a store are potential customers.
▶ Customers respond more often to personal selling than to ads.
▶ Immediate feedback is provided.

The major disadvantages of personal selling are that:

▶ Only a limited number of customers can be handled at a given time.
▶ The costs of interacting with each customer can be high.
▶ Customers are not initially lured into a store through personal selling.
▶ Self-service may be discouraged.
▶ Some customers may view salespeople as unhelpful and as too aggressive.

FIGURE 19-5

J.C. Penney's Tips for Sales Associates

Source: J.C. Penney.

✓ Greet the customer. This sets the tone for the customer's visit to your department.
✓ Listen to customers to determine their needs.
✓ Know your merchandise. For example, describe the quality features of Penney's private brands.
✓ Know merchandise in related departments. This can increase sales and lessen a customer's shopping time.
✓ Learn to juggle several shoppers at once.
✓ Pack merchandise carefully. Ask if customer wants an item on a hanger to prevent creasing.
✓ Constantly work at keeping the department looking its best.
✓ Refer to the customer by his or her name; this can be gotten from the person's credit card.
✓ Stress Penney's "hassle-free" return policy.

FIGURE 19-6

Personal Selling: Even at Costco

Although Costco operates in an austere, mostly self-service format, high-touch kiosks are often situated inside stores. Cell phone kiosks are quite popular, and they are staffed by salespeople representing the service companies being promoted. The marketing of cellular phone services requires knowledgeable salespeople.

Source: Reprinted by permission of TNS Retail Forward.

TYPES

Most sales positions involve either order taking or order getting. An **order-taking salesperson** performs routine clerical and sales functions—setting up displays, stocking shelves, answering simple questions, and ringing up sales. This type of selling is most likely in stores that are strong in self-service but also have some personnel on the floor. An **order-getting salesperson** is actively involved with informing and persuading customers and in closing sales. This is a true "sales" employee. Order getters usually sell higher-priced or complex items, such as real-estate, autos, and consumer electronics. They are more skilled and better paid than order takers. See Figure 19-6.

A manufacturer may sometimes help fund personal selling by providing **PMs (promotional or push monies)** for retail salespeople selling its brand. PMs are in addition to regular salesperson compensation. Many retailers dislike this practice because their salespeople may be less responsive to actual customer desires (if customers desire brands not yielding PMs).

FUNCTIONS

Store sales personnel may be responsible for all or many of the tasks shown in Figure 19-7 and described next. Nonstore sales personnel may also have to generate customer leads (by knocking on doors in residential areas or calling people who are listed in a local phone directory).

On entering a store or a department in it (or being contacted at home), a salesperson greets the customer. Typical in-store greetings are: "Hello, may I help you?" "Hi, is there anything in particular you are looking for?" With any greeting, the salesperson seeks to put the customer at ease and build rapport.

The salesperson next finds out what the person wants: Is the person just looking, or is there a specific good or service in mind? For what purpose is the item to be used? Is there a price range in mind? What other information can the shopper provide to help the salesperson?

At this point, the salesperson may show merchandise. He or she selects the product most apt to satisfy the customer. The salesperson may try to trade up (discuss a more expensive version) or offer a substitute (if the retailer does not carry or is out of the requested item).

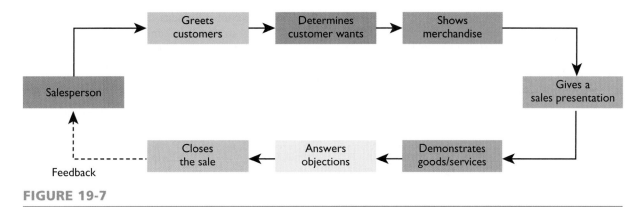

FIGURE 19-7

Typical Personal Selling Functions

The salesperson now makes a sales presentation to motivate the customer to purchase. The **canned sales presentation** is a memorized, repetitive speech given to all customers interested in a particular item. It works best if shoppers require little assistance and sales force turnover is high. The **need-satisfaction approach** is based on the principle that each customer has different wants; thus, a sales presentation should be geared to the demands of the individual customer. It is being utilized more in retailing.

A demonstration can show the utility of an item and allow customer participation. Demonstrations are often used with stereos, autos, health clubs, and watches.

A customer may have questions, and the salesperson must address them. Once all questions are answered, the salesperson tries to close the sale and get the shopper to buy. Typical closing lines are: "Will you take it with you or have it delivered?" "Cash or charge?" "Would you like this gift wrapped?"

For personal selling to work well, salespeople must be enthusiastic, knowledgeable, interested in customers, and good communicators. Figure 19-8 cites several ways that retail sales can be lost through poor personal selling and how to avoid these problems.[6]

Sales Promotion

Promo magazine (www.promomagazine.com) is a leading source of information about sales promotion.

Sales promotion encompasses the paid communication activities other than advertising, public relations, and personal selling that stimulate consumer purchases and dealer effectiveness. It includes displays, contests, sweepstakes, coupons, frequent shopper programs, prizes, samples, demonstrations, referral gifts, and other limited-time selling efforts outside of the ordinary promotion routine. The value and complexity of sales promotion are clear from this commentary:

In-store marketing—including POP, merchandising, and in-store services—is growing mostly via more (and more sophisticated) POP displays and in-store

FIGURE 19-8

Selected Reasons Retail Sales Are Lost—and How to Avoid Them

✗ *Poor qualification of the customer.* ✓ Obtain information from the customer so the sales presentation is properly tailored.
✗ *Salespersons not demonstrating the good or service.* ✓ Show the good or service in use so that benefits are visualized.
✗ *Failure to put feeling into the presentation.* ✓ Encourage salespeople to be sincere and consumer-oriented.
✗ *Poor knowledge.* ✓ Train salespeople to know the major advantages and disadvantages of the goods and services, as well as competitors', and be able to answer questions.
✗ *Arguing with a customer.* ✓ Avoid arguments in handling customer objections, even if the customer is wrong.
✗ *No suggestion selling.* ✓ Attempt to sell related items (such as service contracts, product supplies, and installation).
✗ *Giving up too early.* ✓ Try again if an attempt to close a sale is unsuccessful.
✗ *Inflexibility.* ✓ Be creative in offering alternative solutions to a customer's needs.
✗ *Poor follow-up.* ✓ Be sure that orders are correctly written, that deliveries arrive on time, and that customers are satisfied.

media such as TV and radio. InStore Broadcasting Network distributes integrated audio and video ads to retailers through a process called PerfectMedia. Its clients include Kroger, Safeway, Walgreens, and Duane Reade. Apparel and durables retailers (such as consumer electronics stores) are using more interactive displays that let shoppers interact with a brand before buying. Niketown displays let shoppers order custom shoes, delivered two weeks later by mail. Packaged-goods brands will adopt interactive displays as a bridge between static POP and speedy in-store demos. Sampling and demos are still strong.[7]

OBJECTIVES

Sales promotion goals include:

- ▶ Increasing short-term sales volume.
- ▶ Maintaining customer loyalty.
- ▶ Emphasizing novelty.
- ▶ Complementing other promotion tools.

ADVANTAGES AND DISADVANTAGES

The major advantages of sales promotion are that:

- ▶ It often has eye-catching appeal.
- ▶ Themes and tools can be distinctive.
- ▶ The consumer may receive something of value, such as coupons or free merchandise.
- ▶ It helps draw customer traffic and maintain loyalty to the retailer.
- ▶ Impulse purchases are increased.
- ▶ Customers can have fun, particularly with promotion tools such as contests and demonstrations.

The major disadvantages of sales promotion are that:

- ▶ It may be hard to terminate certain promotions without adverse customer reactions.
- ▶ The retailer's image may be hurt if trite promotions are used.
- ▶ Frivolous selling points may be stressed rather than the retailer's product assortment, prices, customer services, and other factors.
- ▶ Many sales promotions have only short-term effects.
- ▶ It should be used mostly as a supplement to other promotional forms.

RETAILING AROUND THE WORLD | Europe's Changing Laws Regarding Price Promotions and Store Hours

Although Germany's laws were finally changed in late 2007 to allow retailers to discount prices when they prefer, most German retailers did not discount prices for the Christmas 2007 season. In the past, many European retailers could cut prices only during January, too late for the Christmas season.

The concept of a Christmas sale has been so alien to Europeans that many store signs use the English word "sale" instead of the corresponding word in their language. Some European governments have also dropped regulations concerning store hours and now allow Sunday store openings. Germany, for example, leaves the decision as to store opening times to individual state governments.

The German retail federation BAG found that since the pricing regulations were lifted, retailers have more than tripled the number of large sales they hold throughout the year. Many stores also offer promotions on an almost continuous basis.

There are still reminders of the past. France sets minimum prices that retailers must pay suppliers to restrict the power of large chain retailers. Germany's "price labeling decree" requires retailers to have a price tag on all items displayed in shop windows so that consumers can determine their affordability. And Great Britain does not allow stores to open for more than six hours on Sundays.

Source: Cecilie Rohwedder, "Achtung Christmas Shoppers! Holiday Sales, Long Banned, Are Hitting Europe's Stores; Germans Give in to the Discounts," *Wall Street Journal* (December 24, 2007), p. B1.

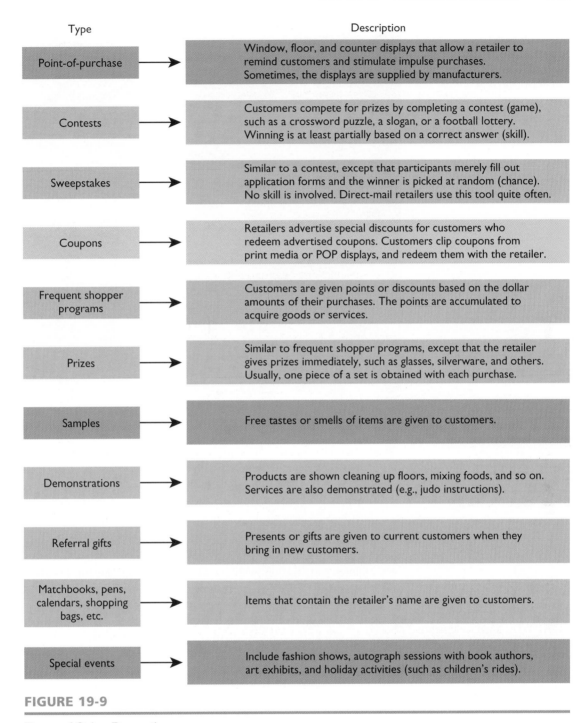

Type	Description
Point-of-purchase	Window, floor, and counter displays that allow a retailer to remind customers and stimulate impulse purchases. Sometimes, the displays are supplied by manufacturers.
Contests	Customers compete for prizes by completing a contest (game), such as a crossword puzzle, a slogan, or a football lottery. Winning is at least partially based on a correct answer (skill).
Sweepstakes	Similar to a contest, except that participants merely fill out application forms and the winner is picked at random (chance). No skill is involved. Direct-mail retailers use this tool quite often.
Coupons	Retailers advertise special discounts for customers who redeem advertised coupons. Customers clip coupons from print media or POP displays, and redeem them with the retailer.
Frequent shopper programs	Customers are given points or discounts based on the dollar amounts of their purchases. The points are accumulated to acquire goods or services.
Prizes	Similar to frequent shopper programs, except that the retailer gives prizes immediately, such as glasses, silverware, and others. Usually, one piece of a set is obtained with each purchase.
Samples	Free tastes or smells of items are given to customers.
Demonstrations	Products are shown cleaning up floors, mixing foods, and so on. Services are also demonstrated (e.g., judo instructions).
Referral gifts	Presents or gifts are given to current customers when they bring in new customers.
Matchbooks, pens, calendars, shopping bags, etc.	Items that contain the retailer's name are given to customers.
Special events	Include fashion shows, autograph sessions with book authors, art exhibits, and holiday activities (such as children's rides).

FIGURE 19-9

Types of Sales Promotion

TYPES

Figure 19-9 describes the major types of sales promotions. Each is explained here.

Visit the site of the leading point-of-purchase trade association (**www.popai. org**).

Point-of-purchase promotion consists of in-store displays designed to lift sales. Displays may remind customers, stimulate impulse behavior, facilitate self-service, and reduce retailer costs if manufacturers provide the displays. See Figure 19-10. These data show the extent of displays:

▶ U.S. manufacturers and retailers together annually spend $20 billion on in-store displays,[8] with retailers using about two-thirds of all displays provided by manufacturers.
▶ Virtually all retailers have some type of POP display.

FIGURE 19-10

An Appealing, Socially Responsible POP Display at Giant Eagle

Source: Reprinted by permission of TNS Retail Forward.

► Restaurants, apparel stores, music/video stores, toy stores, and sporting goods stores are among the retail categories with above-average use of in-store displays.
► Retailers spend one-sixth of their sales promotion budgets on displays.
► Display ads appear on shopping carts in most U.S. supermarkets. And thousands of supermarkets have electronic signs above their aisles promoting well-known brands.

Contests and sweepstakes are similar; they seek to attract customers who participate in events with large prizes. A contest requires a customer to show some skill. A sweepstakes only requires participation, with the winner chosen at random. Disadvantages of contests and sweepstakes are their costs, customer reliance on these tools for continued patronage, the customer effort, and entries by nonshoppers. Together, U.S. manufacturers and retailers spend $2 billion yearly on contests and sweepstakes.[9]

Each year, $375 billion worth of coupons—discounts from regular selling prices—are distributed in the United States, with grocery products accounting for two-thirds of them. Consumers actually redeem $3 billion in coupons annually; retailers receive several hundred million dollars for processing coupon redemptions. Coupons are offered through freestanding inserts in Sunday papers and placements in daily papers, direct mail, Web sites, regular magazines, and Sunday newspaper magazines. They are also placed in or on packages and dispensed from in-store machines.[10]

Coupons have four key advantages: (1) In many cases, manufacturers pay to advertise and redeem them. (2) According to surveys, more than 80 percent of consumers redeem coupons at least once during the year. (3) They contribute to the consumer's perception that a retailer offers good value. (4) Ad effectiveness can be measured by counting redeemed coupons. Disadvantages include the possible negative effect on the retailer's image, consumers shopping only if coupons are available, the low redemption rates, the clutter of coupons, retailer and consumer fraud, and handling costs. Less than 3 percent of coupons are redeemed by consumers due to the large number of them that are received.

Frequent shopper programs foster customer relationships by awarding discounts or prizes to people for continued patronage. In most programs, customers accumulate points (or their equivalent)—which are redeemed for cash, discounts, or prizes. Programs that follow these principles are most apt to succeed:

(1) By compiling customer data throughout the life of your program, you can tailor your offers based on past preferences and purchase histories. If your data base has a large number of lapsed customers, offering an instant reward is a great way to bring them back. (2) The best programs build excitement by letting customers know what rewards they can expect and how to earn them. (3) To stimulate participation, make rewards obtainable and graduate them so you transform a higher percentage of your data base to high-value customers. This will avoid pitfalls of programs that reward primarily on enrollment, which tend to attract price switchers. (4) Provide in-kind rewards. Suppose you own a neighborhood music store. A 20 percent bonus on the next CD purchase would bring shoppers back and make the program itself more memorable because the reward would be associated with your product. (5) Create an ongoing dialog. Since customers are actively interested in news about their rewards, they're receptive to an ongoing interaction—which ultimately leads to more sales.[11]

All sorts of retailers participate in online loyalty programs, such as e-Rewards (www.e-rewards.com).

The advantages of frequent shopper programs for retailers are the loyalty (customers amass points only by shopping at a specific firm or firms), the increased shopping, and the competitive edge for a retailer similar to others. However, some consumers feel these programs are not really free and would rather shop at lower-priced stores without loyalty programs, it may take a while for shoppers to gather enough points to earn meaningful gifts, and retail profit margins may be smaller if firms with these programs try to price competitively with those without the programs.

Prizes are similar to frequent shopper programs, but they are given with each purchase. They are most effective when sets of glasses, silverware, dishes, place mats, and so on are distributed one at a time to shoppers. These encourage loyalty. Problems are the cost of prizes, the difficulty of termination, and the possible impact on image.

Free samples (food tastings) and demonstrations (cooking lessons) can complement personal selling. About $2.3 billion is spent annually on sampling and demonstrations in U.S. stores[12]—mostly at supermarkets, membership clubs, specialty stores, and department stores. They are effective because customers become involved and impulse purchases increase. Loitering and costs may be problems.

Referral gifts may encourage existing customers to bring in new ones. Direct marketers, such as book and music clubs, often use this tool. It is a technique that has no important shortcomings and recognizes the value of friends in influencing purchases.

Matchbooks, pens, calendars, and shopping bags may be given to customers. They differ from prizes because they promote retailers' names. These items should be used as supplements. The advantage is longevity. There is no real disadvantage.

Retailers may use special events to generate consumer enthusiasm. Events can range from store grand openings to fashion shows. When new McDonald's stores open, there are typically giveaways and children's activities, and there is a guest appearance by Ronald McDonald (a human in a costume). Generally, in choosing a special event, the potential increase in consumer awareness and store traffic needs to be weighed against that event's costs. See Figure 19-11.

Planning a Retail Promotional Strategy

A systematic approach to promotional planning is shown in Figure 19-12 and explained next. Our Web site (**www.pearsonhighered.com/berman**) has links related to several aspects of promotional strategy, including word of mouth.

Determining Promotional Objectives

A retailer's broad promotional goals are typically drawn from this list:

- ▶ Increase sales.
- ▶ Stimulate impulse and reminder buying.
- ▶ Raise customer traffic.
- ▶ Get leads for sales personnel.
- ▶ Present and reinforce the retailer image.
- ▶ Inform customers about goods and services.
- ▶ Popularize new stores and Web sites.

FIGURE 19-11

Driving Business Through
Special Events

Source: Reprinted by permission
of Susan Berry, Retail Image
Consulting, Inc.

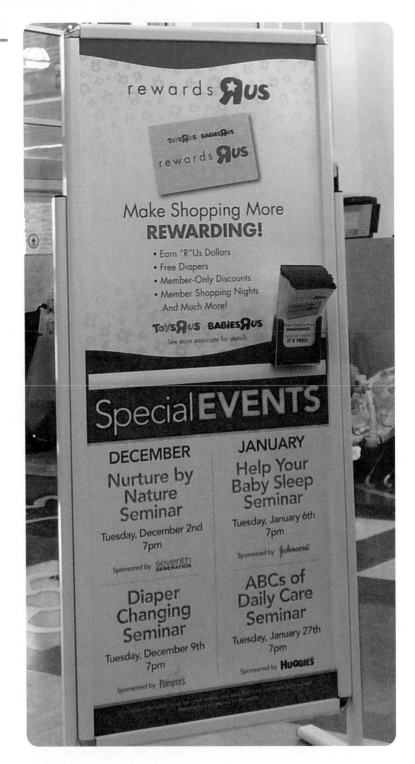

▶ Capitalize on manufacturer support.

▶ Enhance customer relations.

▶ Maintain customer loyalty.

▶ Have consumers pass along positive information to friends and others.

In developing a promotional strategy, the firm must determine which of these are most important.

It is vital to state goals as precisely as possible to give direction to the choice of promotional types, media, and messages. Increasing sales is not a specific goal. However, increasing sales by 10 percent is directional, quantitative, and measurable. With that goal, a firm would be able to prepare a thorough promotional plan and evaluate its success.

FIGURE 19-12

Planning a Retail
Promotional Strategy

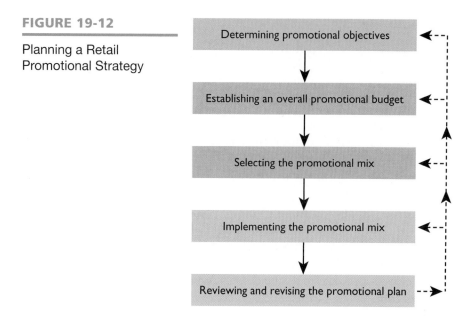

McDonald's, which has won numerous awards for creative advertising, wants its ads and promotions to drive sales, introduce new products, push special offers, create an emotional bond with customers, and deflect criticism about the firm's fast-food menu:

> Over the years, McDonald's has developed TV advertising campaigns that have become, like McDonald's, a part of our lives and culture. These commercials have focused not only on products, but on the overall McDonald's experience, portraying warmth and a real slice of everyday life. This "image" advertising has become a trademark of the firm and created memorable TV moments and themes. We are committed to communicating responsibly; and we want to use our brand to make a difference. For years, our global guidelines have helped to ensure that our advertising and marketing are clear, appropriate, and truthful and address age-appropriate communications to children:
>
> ▶ Communicate to children balanced food choices that fit within a child's nutritional needs.
> ▶ Use our licensed characters and properties to encourage activity and balanced food choices for children to make food, such as fruit and vegetables, fun to eat.
> ▶ Promote to children positive messages that support their well-being, body, mind, and spirit.
> ▶ Provide nutrition information for our food to help parents and families make informed choices.
> ▶ Engage the support of subject matter experts and informed third parties to help guide our efforts for children and families worldwide.[13]

See what tactics facilitate good WOM (www.geocities.com/wallstreet/6246/tactics1.html).

Perhaps the most vital long-term promotion goal for any retailer is to gain positive **word of mouth (WOM),** which occurs when one consumer talks to others. If a satisfied customer refers friends to a retailer, this can build into a chain of customers. No retailer can succeed if it receives extensive negative WOM (such as "The hotel advertised that everything was included in the price. Yet it cost me another $50 to play golf"). Negative WOM will cause a firm to lose substantial business.

Both goods- and services-oriented retailers must have positive word of mouth to attract and retain customers. They need WOM referrals to generate new customers. As one expert says: "Pay attention to what customers are saying, solve problems quickly, encourage feedback, and most importantly, give them something exciting to talk about. Advertising can be expensive. As firms try to figure out how they'll spend their budget to best effect, they often fail to consider the most effective and often least expensive way of getting people to know what great products and service they offer: word-of-mouth marketing."[14]

TECHNOLOGY IN RETAILING

Software Support for In-Store Demonstrations

In-store demonstrations are sometimes a vital part of retailer and supplier promotional strategies. The retailer benefits from the excitement added to the in-store experience, increased sales as a result of the promotion, and the ability to use the promotion as a test of a product's sales performance. The supplier sees an in-store promotion as an opportunity to get customers to try a product and as a means of gaining the cooperation of retailers to stock the good. If the product sells especially well, the demonstration can result in the retailer's stocking a new product without pressing the supplier to pay slotting fees.

A new software package from PromoWorks (**www.promoworks.com**) promises to help suppliers better plan and evaluate their in-store promotional activities. The firm's PromoIntelligence Reports enables suppliers to select the optimal base of stores to run in-store demonstrations based on variables such as store traffic count by hour and day of week. A supplier can query PromoWorks' data base to determine the best store location and time period by product category, retail channel, geographic market area, and individual retailer. PromoWorks also enables suppliers to determine what demonstrator is best by measuring sales performance associated with specific in-store personnel.

Sources: "Latest Software Supports In-Store Demonstrations," *Promo* (October/November 2007), pp. 17, 21; and "In-Store Demonstration Service," **www.entrepreneur.com/businessideas/116.html** (January 30, 2009).

Establishing an Overall Promotional Budget

There are five main procedures for setting the size of a retail promotional budget. Retailers should weigh the strengths and weaknesses of each technique in relation to their own requirements and constraints. To assist firms in their efforts, there is now computer software available.

With the **all-you-can-afford method,** a retailer first allots funds for each element of the retail strategy mix except promotion. The remaining funds go to promotion. This is the weakest technique. Its shortcomings are that little emphasis is placed on promotion as a strategic variable; expenditures are not linked to goals; and if little or no funds are left over, the promotion budget is too small or nonexistent. The method is used predominantly by small, conservative retailers.

The **incremental method** relies on prior promotion budgets to allocate funds. A percentage is either added to or subtracted from one year's budget to determine the next year's. If this year's promotion budget is $100,000, next year's would be calculated by adjusting that amount. A 10 percent rise means that next year's budget would be $110,000. This technique is useful for a small retailer. It provides a reference point. The budget is adjusted based on the firm's feelings about past successes and future trends. It is easy to apply. Yet, the budget is rarely tied to specific goals. "Gut feelings" are used.

With the **competitive parity method,** a retailer's promotion budget is raised or lowered based on competitors' actions. If the leading competitor raises its budget, other retailers in the area may follow. This method is useful for small and large firms, uses a comparison point, and is market-oriented and conservative. It is also imitative, takes for granted that tough-to-get competitive data are available, and assumes competitors are similar (as to years in business, size, customers, location, merchandise, prices, and so on). That last point is critical because competitors often need very different promotional budgets.

In the **percentage-of-sales method,** a retailer ties its promotion budget to revenue. A promotion-to-sales ratio is developed. Then, during succeeding years, this ratio remains constant. A firm could set promotion costs at 10 percent of sales. If this year's sales are $600,000, there is a $60,000 promotion budget. If next year's sales are estimated at $720,000, a $72,000 budget is planned. This process uses sales as a base, is adaptable, and correlates promotion and sales. Nonetheless, there is no relation to goals (for an established firm, sales growth may not require increased promotion); promotion is not used to lead sales; and promotion drops during poor periods, when increases might be helpful. This technique provides excess financing in times of high sales and too few funds in periods of low sales.

Under the **objective-and-task method,** a retailer clearly defines its promotion goals and prepares a budget to satisfy them. A goal might be to have 70 percent of the people in its trading area know a retailer's name by the end of a one-month promotion campaign, up from 50 percent. To do so, it would determine the tasks and costs required to achieve that goal:

Objective	Task	Cost
1. Gain awareness of working women.	Use eight 1/4-page ads in four successive Sunday editions of two area papers.	$20,000
2. Gain awareness of motorists.	Use twenty 30-second radio ads during prime time on local radio stations.	12,000
3. Gain awareness of pedestrians.	Give away 5,000 shopping bags.	15,000
	Total budget	$47,000

The objective-and-task method is the best budgeting technique. Goals are clear, spending relates to goal-oriented tasks, and performance can be assessed. It can be time-consuming and complex to set goals and specific tasks, especially for small retailers.

Selecting the Promotional Mix

After a budget is set, the promotional mix is determined: the retailer's combination of advertising, public relations, personal selling, and sales promotion. A firm with a limited budget may rely on store displays, flyers, targeted direct mail, and publicity to generate customer traffic. One with a large budget may rely more on newspaper and TV ads. Retailers often use an assortment of forms to reinforce each other. A melding of media ads and POP displays may be more effective than either form alone. See Figure 19-13.

FIGURE 19-13

An Integrated Promotional Mix

Macy's actively promotes its Star Rewards customer loyalty program—in the store, through direct mailings, and at the retailer's Web site. The success of this program is important for Macy's long-term growth.

Source: Reprinted by permission of Macy's.

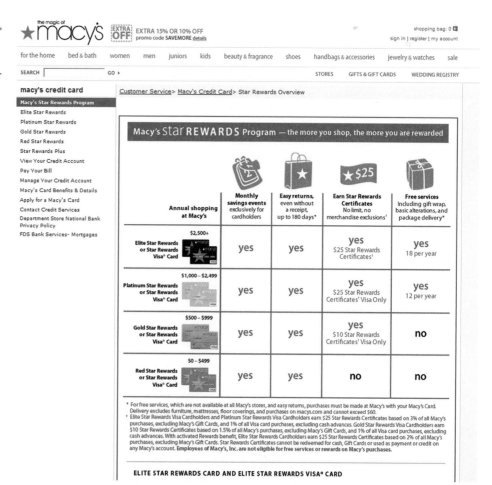

TABLE 19-3   The Promotional Mixes of Selected Small Retailers

Type of Retailer	Favorite Media	Personal Selling Emphasis	Special Considerations	Promotional Opportunities
Apparel store	Weekly papers; direct mail; radio; Internet; exterior signs.	High.	Cooperative ads available from manufacturers.	Fashion shows for community groups and charities.
Auto supply store	Local papers; Yellow Pages; POP displays; Internet; exterior signs.	Moderate.	Cooperative ads available from manufacturers.	Direct mail.
Bookstore	Local papers; Yellow Pages; radio; Internet; exterior signs.	Moderate.	Cooperative ads available from publishers.	Author-signing events.
Coin-operated laundry	Yellow Pages; flyers in area; local direct mail; exterior signs.	None.	None.	Coupons in newspaper ads.
Gift store	Weekly papers; Yellow Pages; direct mail; Internet; exterior signs.	Moderate.	None.	Special events; Web ads.
Hair grooming/ beauty salon	Yellow Pages; mentions in feature articles; exterior signs.	Moderate.	Word-of-mouth communication key.	Participation in fashion shows; free beauty clinics.
Health food store	Local papers; shoppers; POP displays; Internet; exterior signs.	Moderate.	None.	Display windows.
Restaurant	Newspapers; radio; Yellow Pages; entertainment guides; Internet; exterior signs.	Moderate.	Word-of-mouth communication key.	Write-ups in critics' columns; special events.

Freestanding inserts offer retailers many possibilities. Visit Valassis (**www.valassis. com**), click on "Products," and choose "Freestanding Inserts."

The promotional mix is affected by the type of retailer involved. In supermarkets, sampling, frequent shopper promotions, theme sales, and bonus coupons are among the techniques used most. At upscale stores, there is more attention to personal selling and less to advertising and sales promotion as compared with discounters. Table 19-3 shows a number of small-retailer promotional mixes.

In reacting to a retailer's communication efforts, consumers often go through a sequence of steps known as the **hierarchy of effects,** which takes them from awareness to knowledge to liking to preference to conviction to purchase. Different promotional mixes are needed in each step. Ads and public relations are best to develop awareness; personal selling and sales promotion are best in changing attitudes and stimulating desires. This is especially true for expensive, complex goods and services. See Figure 19-14.

Implementing the Promotional Mix

The implementation of a promotional mix involves choosing which specific media to use (such as Newspaper A and Newspaper B), timing, message content, the makeup of the sales force, specific sales promotion tools, and the responsibility for coordination. Consider this example:

> If you own an upscale jewelry store, you know from your sales history or marketing research that your target market is consumers earning more than $75,000 per year. Any print advertising should thus appear in publications in which readership income exceeds $75,000. To introduce new customers to your product, a direct-marketing technique, such as a direct-mail letter with a money-saving offer to first-time customers, might work. Or you can try a sales promotion, such as a free gift with a minimum purchase of $250. If your target

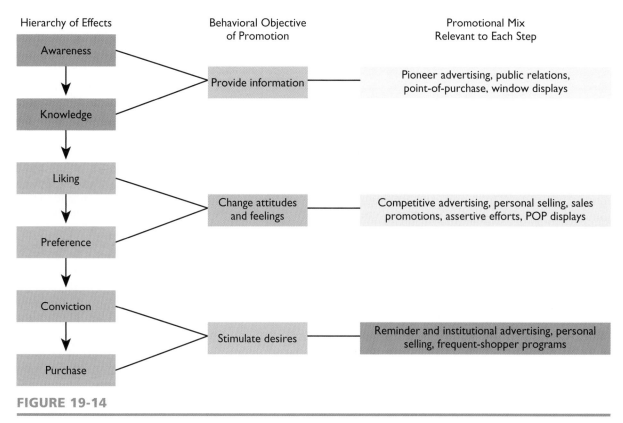

FIGURE 19-14

Promotion and the Hierarchy of Effects

market has a misconception about your store (say, that it's more expensive or less effective than rival stores), you can correct the perception by providing comparisons or testimonials.[15]

MEDIA DECISIONS

Is 3D shopping on the Web ahead of its time or on target (www.3dshopper. net)?

The choice of specific media is based on their overall costs, efficiency (the cost to reach the target market), lead time, and editorial content. Overall costs are important since heavy use of one expensive medium may preclude a balanced promotional mix, and a firm may not be able to repeat a message in a costly medium.

A medium's efficiency relates to the cost of reaching a given number of target customers. Media rates are often expressed in terms of cost per 1,000 readers, watchers, or listeners:

$$\text{Cost per thousand} = \frac{\text{Cost per message} \times 1,000}{\text{Circulation}}$$

A newspaper with a circulation of 400,000 and a one-page advertising rate of $10,000 has a per-page cost per thousand of $25.

In this computation, total circulation is used to measure efficiency. Yet, because a retailer usually appeals to a limited target market, only the relevant portion of circulation should be considered. If 70 percent of readers are target customers for a particular firm (and the other 30 percent live outside the trading area), the real cost per thousand is:

$$\begin{aligned}
\text{Cost per thousand} \atop \text{(target market)} &= \frac{\text{Cost per page} \times 1,000}{\text{Circulation} \times \dfrac{\text{Target market}}{\text{Circulation}}} \\
&= \frac{\$10,000 \times 1,000}{400,000 \times 0.70} = \$35.71
\end{aligned}$$

Different media require different lead times. A newspaper ad can be placed shortly before publication, whereas a magazine ad sometimes must be placed months in advance. In addition, the retailer must decide what kind of editorial content it wants near ads (such as a sports story or a personal care column).

Media decisions are not simple. Despite spending billions of dollars on TV and radio commercials, banner ads at search engines, and other media, many Web retailers have found that the most valuable medium for them is E-mail. It is fast, inexpensive, and targeted. Consider the following.

To generate greater *awareness* of Web retailers, costly advertising may be necessary in today's competitive and cluttered landscape. At Netflix, "We promote our service to consumers through various marketing programs, including online promotions, television and radio advertising, package inserts, direct mail, and other promotions with third parties. These programs encourage consumers to subscribe to our service and may include a free trial period."[16] Once customers have visited a Web site, E-mail can help *sustain relationships:*

> Opt-in marketing involves the customer giving permission for the retailer to send marketing materials and giving private information on where to send them. The customer is more likely to "read," "hear," or "see" a marketing message if he/she has already given prior permission to do so. In the highest form, opt-in E-mail marketing involves an ongoing, evolving relationship between the retailer and the customer. The relationship is one that becomes increasingly focused, with the relevant exchange of information and value. In order to retain customers, the retailer must continually offer value. Customer loyalty cannot be taken for granted, it has to be earned.[17]

TIMING OF THE PROMOTIONAL MIX

Reach refers to the number of distinct people exposed to a retailer's promotion efforts in a specific period. **Frequency** is the average number of times each person reached is exposed to a retailer's promotion efforts in a specific period. A retailer can advertise extensively or intensively. Extensive media coverage often means ads reach many people but with relatively low frequency. Intensive media coverage generally means ads are placed in selected media and repeated frequently. Repetition is important, particularly for a retailer seeking to develop an image or sell new goods or services.

Decisions are needed about how to address peak selling seasons and whether to mass or distribute efforts. When peak seasons occur, all elements of the promotional mix are

---

 **ETHICS IN RETAILING**   How the Jewelers Vigilance Committee Cracks Down on Deceptive Advertising

The Jewelers Vigilance Committee (JVC) is a one-hundred-year-old, not-for-profit trade association dedicated to maintaining the jewelry industry's highest ethical standards. Both jewelry dealers and government agencies that regulate the jewelry industry regularly rely on the JVC for guidance and assistance. Here's how the JVC operates.

Recently, the JVC responded to a phone call stating that a new Little Rock, Arkansas, jewelry store was promoting "wholesale prices to the public." After getting evidence of the ads, JVC's staff investigated Arkansas laws, as well as the FTC's guidelines concerning deceptive advertising. Arkansas law states that by promoting a store's prices as wholesale, the firm must be a wholesaler that does not sell to final consumers. Arkansas law also says that when a retailer promotes that it sells jewelry at wholesale prices, this means it is selling these goods at cost.

After determining that the complaint was valid, JVC sent a letter to the retailer stating that its print and radio ads were against state and federal laws. As a result of this letter, the mall retailer decided to correct its future advertising. JVC assisted the retailer in complying with the law by helping the jeweler correct its ads so they would meet all legal requirements.

Sources: "Cecilia Gardner, "False Claims of 'Wholesale Prices' in Ads Can Give Retailers Unfair Advantage," *National Jeweler* (April 2007), p. 20; and "About JVC," **www.jvclegal.org/index.php?categoryid=10** (February 28, 2009).

usually utilized; in slow periods, promotional efforts are typically reduced. A **massed promotion effort** is used by retailers, such as toy retailers, that promote seasonally. A **distributed promotion effort** is used by retailers, such as fast-food restaurants, that promote throughout the year. Although they are not affected by seasonality in the same way as other retailers, massed advertising is practiced by supermarkets, many of which use Wednesday or Thursday for weekly newspaper ads. This takes advantage of the fact that a high proportion of their consumers make their major shopping trip on Friday, Saturday, or Sunday.

Sales force size can vary by time (morning versus evening), day (weekdays versus weekends), and month (December versus January). Sales promotions also vary in their timing. Store openings and holidays are especially good times for sales promotions (and public relations).

CONTENT OF MESSAGES

The CarMax (**www.carmax.com**) message: "The Way Car Buying U.S. *Should* Be" is clear and information packed. Click on "Why CarMax."

Whether written or spoken, personally or impersonally delivered, message content is important. Advertising themes, wording, headlines, use of color, size, layout, and placement must be selected. Publicity releases must be written. In personal selling, the greeting, sales presentation, demonstration, and closing need to be applied. With sales promotion, the firm's message must be composed and placed on the promotional device.

To a large extent, the characteristics of the promotional form influence the message. A shopping bag often contains no more than a retailer's name, and a billboard (seen at 55 miles per hour) is good for visual effect but can hold only limited information. Yet, a salesperson may be able to hold a customer's attention for a while. A number of shopping centers use a glossy magazine to communicate a community-oriented image, introduce new stores to consumers, and promote the goods and services carried at stores in the center. Cluttered ads displaying many products suggest a discounter's orientation, while fine pencil drawings and selective product displays suggest a specialty store focus.

Some retailers use comparative advertising to contrast their offerings with competitors'. These ads help position a retailer relative to competitors, increase awareness of the firm, maximize the efficiency of a limited budget, and offer credibility. Yet, they provide visibility for competitors, may confuse people, and may lead to legal action. Fast-food and off-price retailers are among those using comparative ads.

MAKEUP OF SALES FORCE

Sales personnel qualifications must be detailed; and these personnel must be recruited, selected, trained, compensated, supervised, and monitored. Personnel should also be classified as order takers or order getters and assigned to the appropriate departments.

SALES PROMOTION TOOLS

Specific sales promotion tools must be chosen from among those cited in Figure 19-9. The combination of tools depends on short-term goals and the other aspects of the promotion mix. If possible, cooperative ventures should be sought. Tools inconsistent with the firm's image should never be used; and retailers should recognize the types of promotions that customers really want. For example: "In an effort to clear out the clutter of the in-store environment, supermarkets for some time now have been implementing clean-store policies. They are limiting the number and size of displays to what the stores feel complement the space, don't interfere with customer traffic flow, won't overwhelm shoppers, and generally simplify the entire experience."[18]

RESPONSIBILITY FOR COORDINATION

Regardless of the retailer's size or format, someone must be responsible for the promotion function. Larger retailers often assign this job to a vice-president, who oversees display personnel, works with the firm's ad agency, supervises the firm's advertising department (if there is one), and supplies branch outlets with POP materials. In a large retail setting, personal selling is usually under the jurisdiction of the store manager. For a promotional strategy to succeed, its components have to be coordinated with other retail mix elements.

Sales personnel must be informed of special sales and know product attributes; featured items must be received, marked, and displayed; and accounting entries must be made. Often, a shopping center or a shopping district runs theme promotions, such as "Back to School." In those instances, someone must coordinate the activities of all participating retailers.

Reviewing and Revising the Promotional Plan

An analysis of the success of a promotional plan depends on its objectives. Revisions should be made if pre-set goals are not achieved. Here are some ways to test the effectiveness of a promotional effort:

Examples of Retail Promotion Goals	Approaches for Evaluating Promotion Effectiveness
Inform current customers about new credit plans; acquaint potential customers with new offerings.	Study company and product awareness before and after promotion; evaluate size of audience.
Develop and reinforce a particular image; maintain customer loyalty.	Study image through surveys before and after public relations and other promotion efforts.
Increase customer traffic; get leads for salespeople; increase revenues above last year's; reduce customer returns from prior year's.	Evaluate sales performance and the number of inquiries; study customer intentions to buy before and after promotion; study customer trading areas and average purchases; review coupon redemption.

NET-ADS (**www.net-ads. com/articles/advertising**) presents insights on the current status of Web advertising.

Although it may at times be tough to assess promotion efforts (e.g., increased revenues might be due to several factors, not just promotion), it is crucial for retailers to systematically study and adapt their promotional mixes. Wal-Mart provides suppliers with store-by-store data and sets up-front goals for cooperative promotion programs. Actual sales are then compared against the goals. Lowe's, the home center chain, applies computerized testing to review thousands of different ideas affecting the design of circulars and media mix options. And consider this:

> The marketing executives of leading closeout retailer Big Lots sought to improve their marketing strategy by determining how specific advertising methods (involving television, newspaper, and radio) affected the firm's sales. Big Lots initially compared sales over a three-year period at 36 randomly selected stores and embarked on a 16-week MVT (multi-variable testing) process with QualPro. A selected project team began by formulating a series of improvement ideas to help determine the most effective radio stations, times of day, and so forth for Big Lots to advertise. After three improvement ideas were selected to be tested, QualPro used MVT to test 250 stores in 32 different markets and determine which of the ideas would be effective for Big Lots. Two of the initial ideas were selected for "refinement" testing and eventually implemented to result in significantly boosted sales. When combined, the two ideas increased Big Lots' weekly sales by $4.1 million.[19]

Chapter Summary

1. *To explore the scope of retail promotion.* Any communication by a retailer that informs, persuades, and/or reminds the target market about any aspect of the retailer through ads, public relations, personal selling, and sales promotion is retail promotion.

2. *To study the elements of retail promotion: advertising, public relations, personal selling, and sales promotion.* Advertising involves paid, nonpersonal communication. It has a large audience, low costs per person, many alternative media, and other factors. It also involves

message inflexibility, high absolute costs, and a wasted portion of the audience. Key advertising media are papers, phone directories, direct mail, radio, TV, the Web, transit, outdoor, magazines, and flyers/circulars. Especially useful are cooperative ads, in which a retailer shares costs and messages with manufacturers, wholesalers, or other retailers.

Public relations includes all communications fostering a favorable image. It may be nonpersonal or personal, paid or nonpaid, and sponsor controlled or not controlled. Publicity is the nonpersonal, nonpaid form of public relations. Public relations creates awareness, enhances the image, involves credible sources, and has no message costs. It also has little control over messages, is short term, and can entail nonmedia costs. Publicity can be expected or unexpected and positive or negative.

Personal selling uses oral communication with one or more potential customers and is critical for persuasion and in closing sales. It is adaptable, flexible, and provides immediate feedback. The audience is small, per-customer costs are high, and shoppers are not lured into the store. Order-taking and/or order-getting salespeople can be employed. Functions include greeting the customer, determining wants, showing merchandise, making a sales presentation, demonstrating products, answering objections, and closing the sale.

Sales promotion comprises the paid communication activities other than advertising, public relations, and personal selling. It may be eye-catching, unique, and valuable to the customer. It also may be hard to end, have a negative effect on image, and rely on frivolous selling points. Tools include POP displays, contests and sweepstakes, coupons, frequent shopper programs, prizes, samples, demonstrations, referral gifts, matchbooks, pens, calendars, shopping bags, and special events.

3. *To discuss the strategic aspects of retail promotion.* There are five steps in a promotion strategy: (a) Goals are stated in specific and measurable terms. Positive word of mouth (WOM) is an important long-term goal. (b) An overall promotion budget is set on the basis of one of these techniques: all you can afford, incremental, competitive parity, percentage of sales, and objective and task. (c) The promotional mix is outlined, based on the budget, the type of retailing, the coverage of the media, and the hierarchy of effects. (d) The promotional mix is enacted. Included are decisions involving specific media, promotional timing, message content, sales force composition, sales promotion tools, and the responsibility for coordination. (e) The retailer systematically reviews and adjusts the promotional plan, consistent with pre-set goals.

Key Terms

retail promotion (p. 530)
advertising (p. 530)
cooperative advertising (p. 531)
vertical cooperative advertising agreement (p. 537)
horizontal cooperative advertising agreement (p. 537)
public relations (p. 537)
publicity (p. 537)
personal selling (p. 539)

order-taking salesperson (p. 540)
order-getting salesperson (p. 540)
PMs (promotional or push monies) (p. 540)
canned sales presentation (p. 541)
need-satisfaction approach (p. 541)
sales promotion (p. 541)
word of mouth (WOM) (p. 547)
all-you-can-afford method (p. 548)
incremental method (p. 548)

competitive parity method (p. 548)
percentage-of-sales method (p. 548)
objective-and-task method (p. 549)
hierarchy of effects (p. 550)
reach (p. 552)
frequency (p. 552)
massed promotion effort (p. 553)
distributed promotion effort (p. 553)

Questions for Discussion

1. How would an advertising plan for a Web bike retailer differ from that for a bricks-and-mortar bike store chain?

2. How do manufacturer and retailer cooperative advertising goals overlap? How do they differ?

3. How may a local office supplies store try to generate positive publicity?

4. Are there any retailers that should *not* use personal selling? Explain your answer.

5. Are there any retailers that should *not* use sales promotion? Explain your answer.

6. How can advertising, public relations, personal selling, and sales promotion complement each other for a retailer?

7. What are the pros and cons of coupons?

8. Develop sales promotions for each of the following:
   a. A nearby regional shopping center.
   b. A new restaurant.
   c. An off-price apparel retailer.

9. Which method of promotional budgeting should a small retailer use? A large retailer? Why?

10. Explain the hierarchy of effects from a retail perspective. Apply your answer to a new health food store.

11. Develop a checklist for an upscale sporting goods chain to coordinate its promotional plan.

12. For each of these promotional goals, explain how to evaluate promotional effectiveness:
    a. To increase impulse purchases of candy.
    b. To project an innovative image.
    c. To maintain customer loyalty rates.

Web **Exercise**

Visit the Web site of Office.com (www.office.com) and click "Promote Your Business" on the toolbar. What could a retailer learn by surfing this site?

Note: Stop by our Web site (www.pearsonhighered. com/berman) to experience a number of highly interactive, appealing Web exercises based on actual company demonstrations and sample materials related to retailing.

part seven
Short Cases

CASE 1: BORDERS' NEW STORE CONCEPT[C-1]

Borders (**www.borders.com**) recently opened its ninth new concept store in Wareham Crossing, Massachusetts. The concept store format is part of Borders' overall retail strategy that seeks to modernize its 1,100 stores. According to Borders Group's chief executive officer: "We're competing with other entertainment retailers. People are spending money. Why are they going to spend it in a bookstore?" These stores also meet Borders' revised mission statement that positions its stores as a headquarters for knowledge and entertainment.

Although the music section has been reduced by one-third in concept stores, the remaining space has been replaced with a download center where customers can acquire MP3s from a huge online catalog of music selections and then burn seven songs onto a CD for $9.95. These stores also have computer kiosks in three departments: wellness, cooking, and travel. These kiosks allow shoppers to view specific recommended book titles, watch travel and cooking show segments in the store, and even purchase airplane tickets and print out recipes. The Wareham Crossing store even sells additional electronics goods such as digital cameras, iPod accessories, and a Slingbox cable box adapter that enables consumers to view television programming on their home or office computers.

One retail analyst says that this new store format should increase both sales per square foot and gross profits through the use of several creative strategies. And the kiosks should increase the sales of new and older cookbook titles due to their prominent position in the store. In addition, Borders can better cross-merchandise products, such as moving travel magazines closer to the travel books department.

Besides the high-tech features, the Wareham Crossing store features a striking two-story tower-style entrance exterior. The store also has more windows than a traditional Borders store; this provides natural lighting. At 25,000 square feet, the overall store size is similar to that of a more traditional Borders store.

Another new Borders concept store has opened in Tukwila, Washington. This store features five destination areas: cooking, travel, wellness, graphic novels, and children's—each with a "shop within a shop" look and feel. Although most Borders stores have cooking, travel, wellness, and children's departments, this store features a graphic novels section (that sell traditional as well as Japanese comics) to better attract teenage consumers.

The Tukwila store also has a digital center with a three-dimensional, 12-foot fixture with multiple computer kiosks and workstations. Consumers can use the digital center to download music, generate personalized photo books with Shutterfly.com, and even publish their own books using Borders Publishing Powered by Lulu.com.

To generate store traffic in the Tukwila store, Borders organized a weekend-long grand opening celebration. Shoppers could enter to win Borders digital services certificates; Borders $250 gift cards; cookbooks; wellness books; and gift bags filled with stationery, cards, and gifts. These prizes were chosen to emphasize the store's positioning relative to traditional Borders' stores.

Questions

1. How would you describe the retail image of Borders as a chain of bookstore superstores? How does the new concept store fit in with this image?
2. Present a one-sentence positioning slogan for the new Borders concept stores, and explain it.
3. How does the positioning of the new Borders concept stores compare with Amazon.com?
4. Describe a one-year promotion plan for opening a new Borders concept store.

CASE 2: UPPING THE ANTE IN SUPERMARKET MARKETING[C-2]

Supermarkets are increasingly competing with a variety of store formats, including Wal-Mart (**www.walmart.com**) and Target (**www.target.com**) supercenters, Costco (**www.costco.com**) and BJ's (**www.bjs.com**) membership clubs, and even small specialty food retailers that specialize in natural and organic foods. According to Publix Super Markets' (**www.publix.com**) director of media and community relations, "We are all competing for the same share of stomach." To differentiate its stores from competitors, Publix offers customers a complete shopping experience that includes deli cafés; mezzanine areas for lounging, eating, or accessing free Wi-Fi services; and DVD kiosk rental facilities.

Schnuck Markets' (**www.schnucks.com**) communications director says: "For most patrons, grocery shopping is considered a chore. It doesn't compare to shopping for fun and exciting merchandise that you enjoy day after day. So, we strive to create a wonderful shopping experience—sampling, special events, information, and prize giveaways—for our customers so they will want to come back again and again."

Let's look at how traditional supermarkets are competing via retail promotional strategies based on clean stores,

---

[c-1]The material in this case is drawn from Steve Adams, "New Borders Concept Store in Wareham Plays Up Digital Media," **www.enterprisenews.com/business** (July 11, 2008); and "Borders Celebrates the Grand Opening of its New Concept Store in Tukwila, Washington," **www.marketwatch.com/news/story** (October 23, 2008).

[c-2]The material in this case is drawn from "Channel Report: Supermarkets," **www.shoppermarketingmag.com/article.php?nid=40873** (October 23, 2008).

sampling, better supplier collaboration, cross-merchandising, technology, and private labels:

▶ As part of a "clean store" strategy, many supermarkets have reduced the number and size of displays so that these displays do not interfere with normal customer traffic, block access to goods, or limit access to handicapped individuals. This often means that manufacturers must be more sensitive to designing displays with smaller footprints.

▶ In-store sampling is increasingly used by traditional retailers to add excitement to the shopping experience. Stores such as Trader Joe's (**www.traderjoes.com**) use sampling as a means of attracting consumers to their stores, to keep customers in the store for longer time periods, and to get customers to try new products.

▶ Improved supplier collaboration can result in better-designed displays, such as permanent displays that blend with the retailer's store interior and temporary displays that are tied into specific promotions.

▶ Cross-merchandising enables supermarkets to better sell combinations of products such as wine and cheese, stuffing and turkeys, and even Coke products with cooked rotisserie chickens. Cross-merchandising is an important strategy for stimulating impulse purchases, increasing sales productivity, and suggesting the purchase of higher gross margin merchandise.

▶ Among the recent innovative technological applications are in-store television networks, recipe kiosks, and kiosks that enable customers to swipe their recipe cards and receive coupon selections based on their past purchase behavior. Publix is testing shopping cart screens that feature programming with popular children's TV characters such as Dora the Explorer, Bob the Builder, and Barney. This programming does not contain any advertising.

▶ Proactive supermarkets are promoting new lines of private-label products. Some chains, such as Schnucks, have added lines of all natural and organic foods. And Schnucks recently expanded its Full Circle line to include laundry and household cleaning items that are eco-friendly and biodegradable. It plans to add a new "green cleaning" section to its stores.

Questions

1. Explain the significance of this statement: "For most patrons, grocery shopping is considered a chore. It doesn't compare to shopping for fun and exciting merchandise that you enjoy day after day."

2. Discuss the role of customer space in contributing to or detracting from a retailer's overall image. Cite specific examples.

3. Explain the pros and cons of determining space needs via the model stock approach and the sales–productivity ratio method.

4. Develop an experiential merchandising program for a local supermarket.

CASE 3: VIRTUAL REALITY IN RETAILING: WHAT'S AHEAD?[C-3]

Although virtual Web sites such as Barbie Girls (**www.barbiegirls.com**), Habbo (**www.habbo.com**), and the World of Warcraft (**www.worldofwarcraft.com**) will ultimately affect retailers and shopping centers in many ways, one prominent analyst says: "I am convinced they will, though not in the next year or two years." This analyst believes that "Ultimately, it may end up being as important as the World Wide Web."

As evidence of the tremendous potential, Mattel announced that its Barbie Girl site, which allows girls to create Barbie-like avatars (representations of the computer user that can talk, pay, and shop with their online friends) has 14 million registered users. An increasing number of firms, such as Burger King (**www.burgerking.com**) and Wells Fargo (**www.wellfargo.com**), have also created their own online worlds as opposed to using sites developed with proprietary platforms.

Some estimates suggest that millions of consumers now spend about 20 hours per week—about 30 percent of their free time—at virtual Web sites. According to the creative director of a consulting firm: "Can you imagine consumers spending almost three hours a day, every single day in the week, in your shopping mall? Sounds like a fairy tale." Although these sites are not currently a serious competitive threat to traditional shopping centers, they may be if the number of virtual worlds continues rapidly expanding.

One technology consultant predicts that today's virtual worlds will become more photorealistic and stable as a result of the two-dimensional Internet becoming more three-dimensional. 3-D protocols that are being tested will also enable consumers to move their personal avatars from one virtual site to another. Thus, Web shoppers will be able to shop at multiple online malls. Themall.tv (**www.themalltv.com**) has signed on more than 500 brands—including Bose (**www.bose.com**), HMV (**www.hmv.com**), and the Royal Bank of Scotland (**www.rbs.co.uk**)—as tenants. Shoppers at this site can float around a realistic mall, ride elevators, and even pass by fountains as they visit virtual replicas of real-world stores.

Kinset (**www.kinset.com**), a Boston-based firm, has created a 3-D virtual mall that resembles an outdoor lifestyle center. Kinset enables shoppers to enter stores that are stocked with as many as 10,000 three-dimensional copies of actual products. If shoppers desire, they can purchase specific products through Amazon.com, a partner in Kinset. Shoppers can also browse selections by sight, as well as through keyword-based searches.

[C-3]The material in this case is drawn from Joel Groover, "Turning Virtual Reality Into Reality," **www.icsc.org/sct_article** (October 2008).

Another interesting application is to develop an avatar of yourself, with your exact profile, and then "try on specific clothing items to see how they complement your overall appearance." In Barcelona, Spain, Gran Via 2 (**www.granvia2.com**), a 54,600-square-foot shopping center, has used images of avatars as part of its Shopping 2.0 marketing campaign. The campaign is directed to shoppers under the age of 35.

One other futuristic application is a mall with 3-D replicas displaying available items for sale. An avatar going through the three-dimensional mall has the option of picking up the item at the actual store or ordering the good for in-home delivery. When a store is sold out of a particular item, the item disappears from the three-dimensional store shelf model.

Questions

1. Describe the role of selling space, merchandise space, personnel space, and customer space in a virtual retailing site.
2. Explain the relationship between visual merchandising and virtual retailing.
3. An eyeglass retailer is seeking to develop a virtual Web site where a customer can developing an avatar of him- or herself and then "try on specific eyeglasses items to see how each eyeglass frame complements a prospective customer's overall appearance." Discuss the pros and cons of this.
4. A men's clothing retailer is seeking to develop a virtual Web site where a customer can develop an avatar of himself and then "try on specific clothing items to see how each item complements a prospective customer's overall appearance." Discuss the pros and cons of this.

CASE 4: RESTAURANTS STEP UP THEIR PROMOTIONS[C-4]

Recognizing that some people are less likely to eat out in a recessionary economy, a number of upscale restaurants have been increasingly reliant on promotions to maintain their traditional sales levels. Recently, the Union Square Hospitality Group (**www.ushgnyc.com**)—which operates some of New York City's best continental and Indian-style restaurants—instituted mix-and-match price-fixed menus (where consumers can vary the selection), lower-cost wine selections, and larger dessert selections that could be shared. The chain also extended a special $30 dinner promotion beyond the customary one-week limit.

In revising its marketing strategy, Union Square Hospitality Group was very careful not to lower the quality of the ingredients or to reduce preparation time at the expense of freshness or taste. According to the president of this chain: "People who care about quality and having a great dining experience don't stop doing that when they economize. They're still going to go to restaurants that provide that for them."

Recognizing that a large number of its guests at one of its New York restaurants were European, an employee at one of the Union Square Hospitality Group's restaurants came up with the idea of pricing the wine selection in euros instead of U.S. dollars. Through this strategy, European customers were more easily able to determine the actual cost of the wine. They also were more readily able to see what great value the wine was relative to the cost of a comparable wine in their home country.

In Boston, Prezza (**www.prezza.com**), a fine Italian restaurant, entered into a joint promotion with three nearby restaurants. The promotion, called the North End Progressive Dinner, provided guests with the opportunity to eat one of four courses at each restaurant for a total charge of $50. This promotion let customers try out all four restaurants, experience different types of cuisines and atmospheres, and/or eat an entrée at their favorite restaurant and a dessert at a restaurant especially known for its pastry chef. Obviously, such a promotion can only work when restaurant owners can act collectively and do not see each other as direct competitors.

In another Boston-based promotion, Kingfish Hall, a seafood restaurant, developed "31 Days of Lobster," in which lobster was prepared differently each night for a price of $25. The promotion was offered at a time when the cost of lobster declined and when demand for lobster was not especially strong. As the restaurant's director of operations says: "Originally, it was supposed to run for the month of July, but it proved so popular, we extended it through August. It was an opportunity for us to provide a high-end food item to our guests that was price-conscious and affordable, especially given the way the economy is."

The owner of Parlor Steakhouse (**www.parlorsteakhouse.com**) in New York City developed a promotion with a varied price structure and a mix-and-match menu. The restaurant allowed customers to build a meal based on their food and budget preferences. Menu prices ranged from $24 for hanger steak to $79 for a Porterhouse steak for two as part of a three-course lunch. The restaurant attracted a steady traffic based on this offering.

Questions

1. Develop specific promotional goals and plans for a downtown restaurant having poor sales on weekends versus weekdays.
2. Describe how vertical cooperative advertising can be implemented for a restaurant.
3. Develop a promotional campaign that would feature the ability of customers to try multiple restaurants, to experience different types of cuisines, and/or to eat an entrée at their favorite restaurant and a dessert at a restaurant especially known for its pastry chef.
4. What types of advertising media are most appropriate for a restaurant that has a large population of foreign guests?

[C-4]The material in this case is drawn from Elissa Elan, "Upscale Operators Turn to Newfangled Promotions to Maintain Guest Traffic," *Nation's Restaurant News* (September 8, 2008), pp. 1, 40.

part seven

Comprehensive Case

CROSSING THE GREAT MEDIA CHANNEL DIVIDE*

INTRODUCTION

Today's consumers have many ways to research products and make retail purchases. Armed with more information than ever, they are changing the way they interact with retailers. Consumers are embracing everything from retail to E-tail, from bricks-and-mortar to clicks-and-calls. A recent study shows that in the 90 days before making a purchase, 87 percent of adults research the product online. Not surprisingly, the job of retaining customer loyalty is becoming correspondingly tough. One day, a person is among your most steadfast in-store customers. The next, he or she is buying online. A key catalog customer may suddenly change from using the catalog to purchase to merely using it to confirm product pricing.

As consumers change their retail purchasing behavior, retailers try to keep up. This is nothing new—consumers lead and business follows. For consumers, this means taking advantage of the growing number of options that give them more control over when, where, and how they shop.

Multi-Channel Versus Silo

In earlier, simpler times, each retail channel was a distinct business type. You were either a cataloger, a place-based retailer, or, more recently, an E-commerce merchant. However, the days of the single-channel retail brand are quickly coming to a close. Many retailers today have become power brands that cater to a variety of consumer touchpoints through multiple channels.

While retailers scurry to respond to consumers' shopping habits, they may struggle to make the dramatic operational changes required. Traditionally, each channel operates as a silo under the purview of one person who is responsible for thoroughly understanding that channel. There is little interaction with the other channels. But for consumers, this "one-channel, one-approach" retail management style is hopelessly out of sync—they want it all. In a nutshell, as consumers embrace a variety of channels, retailers are caught in archaic structures created for single channels.

---

*The material in this case is adapted by the authors from Larry Kelley and Kyle Allen, "Crossing the Great Channel Divide," *Retailing Issues Letter* (College Station, TX: Center for Retail Studies at Texas A&M University, Maritz Research, and FKM, No. 1, 2007); and Venky Shankar, "What Should a Retailer's Multi-Channel Retailing Strategy Be?" *Retailing Issues Letter* (College Station, TX: Center for Retail Studies at Texas A&M University, Maritz Research, and FKM, No. 1, 2007). Reprinted by permission.

Media Channel Planning

Media channel planning (sometimes called "communications planning") is a powerful way of gaining insight into consumer behavior. Originally a media tool, channel planning can now be applied to retail messaging and merchandising as well. By considering all forms of communication that can potentially reach a customer, it enables retailers to overcome the "silo effect" and promotes the exchange of ideas and tactics among the relevant channels.

Ultimately, channel planning enables retailers to align the message, merchandising, and media—and helps unify competing forces and departments within the organization. Above all, it reveals what's relevant and important to consumers and answers the question, "How can we get the right message to the right consumer in the right way?"

Today, there are more potential contact points with the consumer than ever before. So how can we identify the right channel?

Step 1

Conduct research to unlock the points important to potential customers. These may include the amount of detailed information they need, how much trust they must have in the product, how important price is to the selection process, their experience with the product, and to what extent quality is important to them.

The point to remember is that consumers can tell us what matters to them when they're making product decisions, and these factors can vary by category and product. For example, you may want to ask consumers how good each media channel is at helping them decide if they can trust a brand. Channels range from traditional media such as television, to in-store opportunities to examine the product, to recommendations from friends and family, to online or E-mail marketing—even to celebrity endorsements. Keep in mind that in today's highly fragmented media landscape, consumers are typically exposed to many points of contact beyond the traditional TV and print channels that retailers have long used.

Step 2

Once this research is complete, retailers can perform an analysis to identify the elements most important to the product purchase and the best media sources for communicating them. At that point, each medium is weighted according to its ability to deliver the targeted consumers, as well as its cost effectiveness. The resulting output enables marketers to have a thorough understanding of which factors are important to consumers and how well the various communication channels address them.

Figure 1 outlines the fundamental elements of the channel planning model. Keep in mind that each element is centered on what is important to the customers, not what is important to the advertiser.

FIGURE 1

Advertising Media Planning Model

Media Metrics
- Cost efficiency
- Reach
- Frequency

Advertising Tactics
- Time of day/week exposure
- Ad copy requires detailed messaging
- Opportunity to capture data from consumers

Consumer Channel/Preference
How consumers want to shop and buy:
- At store only
- Online only
- Comfortable with either method

Advertising Media Optimization

Media Effectiveness
How effective is media in communicating the following:
- Conveying trust
- Providing detailed information
- Conveying price information
- Communicating quality
- Generating awareness

Consumer Category Drivers
Factors important to consumers when making a decision:
- Having detailed information about brands
- Having a lot of trust in a brand
- Price
- High quality
- Previous experience with brand

The completed research and analysis phases will yield a list of the various communication channels and their order of importance for achieving optimal marketing results.

Using Channel Planning

Now that we've established what channel planning is, let's discuss how we can take this consumer-centric approach and extend it to media planning, messaging, and merchandising.

Media Planning

The beauty of channel planning is that retailers can model their advertising responses by category and by sku (stock-keeping unit). Let's take a look at a mass merchant that offers a wide range of categories and price points. One category may be high-end electronics, while another may be lottery tickets.

Different criteria are used for making these purchases. Buying a lottery ticket is more of an impulse purchase, while buying high-end electronics is usually a well-planned decision. High-end electronics are available from multiple retail channels such as online and in-store, while lottery tickets are available only at retail locations. From a consumer's perspective, each type of purchase carries very different requirements.

When making a costly consumer electronics purchase, consumers indicate that product quality and trust are very important. However, buying a lottery ticket is a relatively low-risk purchase, and the essential marketing factors that are important to consumers are price (relatively low) and previous experience (they may have won in the past).

Channel planning helps unlock the best media options for conveying essential elements important to making a purchase. This is a prime example of consumer-centric communications planning. Let's take a look at a lottery ticket, as highlighted in Figure 2.

Notice that in-store media are at the top of the list. This makes sense, because impulse purchases are operationally defined as those that are made spur of the moment. So, in this case, the category merchant and the chief marketing officer (CMO) should increase their in-store support. The second media element that affects impulse purchasing is broadcast—radio and TV. This suggests that media exposure close to the time of purchase can help trigger a sale. Knowing that in-store media and broadcast are both important drivers of purchasing behavior among lottery ticket buyers is an important insight and should be used to shape media plans to leverage communication dollars for maximum effect.

FIGURE 2

Lottery Media Channels— Strength of Fit

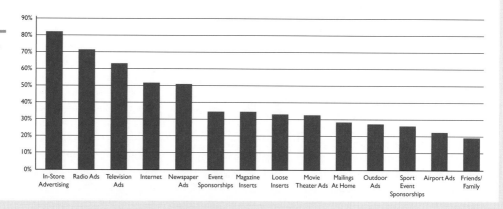

Now, let's take a look at a very different purchase situation: high-end electronics. In most cases, spending hundreds or thousands of dollars is a carefully researched and planned purchase. Consumers require a lot of trust when making such a purchase because of the significant financial and psychological risk involved. But if trust were the only variable, we would see TV and newspaper advertising rise to the top of the list. As it is, there is also a need for considerable category/product information. The list of media channels that consumers indicate can convey this successfully is shown in Figure 3.

In this case, the leading channel options include online—with a heavy emphasis on search-engine marketing—and, to a lesser degree, offline print. So the category merchant and the CMO should develop an online strategy that can deliver detailed information about the products offered. This might also include a presence in key consumer electronics magazines, as well as a URL link in the ad directing consumers to the merchant's Web site to find even more product information.

Messaging

Media channel planning also provides a consumer-centric point of view that can provide key insights for shaping the sales message.

All communication has two fundamental elements: *content* and *tone*. Content is the information conveyed. Tone is the way it is conveyed. Knowing which information is important to a customer who is in a buying state of mind can be a powerful tool. Retailers can use what they discover during channel-planning research to help determine what the advertising should say and how it should be said.

For example, in some product categories, such as computers, consumers require detailed information about brands. Thus, in this category, brands typically communicate details that help consumers make comparisons—such things as available memory, processing speed, monitor size, and so on. Computer manufacturers have responded to this consumer need by placing specifications for their systems in print ads, catalogs, and online advertising.

Because consumers spend large sums of money on computers, trust is also important. For this reason, the tone of much of the advertising in this category is typically straightforward, positive, and imparts confidence that the new computer will deliver the promised benefits.

There are exceptions, of course. A brand's context is always an important consideration. Apple's (**www.apple.com**) recent TV ad campaign takes a humorous stance as it compares Macs with Windows-based PCs. It is certainly possible that Apple's research indicated that potential Mac buyers would be more receptive to a "softer," more humorous, ad message—one that communicated the differences between Macs and PCs.

Five Consumer Needs

Following are the needs customers say are most important when making purchase decisions. Suggested responses follow:

▶ *Detailed information*. Action—show detailed product specifications; provide technical data that can be referenced online or in-store.
▶ *Trust*. Action—provide endorsement by celebrities, generational peers, or third-party groups that are trusted to provide objective opinions (such as the *Good Housekeeping* Seal of Approval).
▶ *Price*. Action—communicate the price point relative to competitive products.
▶ *Quality*. Action—utilize rankings and awards to demonstrate product superiority relative to others in the category.
▶ *Previous brand experience*. Action—leverage testimonials of brand users to reinforce core product attributes.

In many cases, consumer needs are interrelated. A trusted brand may have a reputation for good quality that is reinforced by previous positive brand experience.

By understanding what is important to consumers, retailers can shape the message to communicate detailed information about products, trust in the brand, price (high or low), and brand quality; or to leverage the consumer's previous experience with a brand.

Merchandising

Consumer insights are not limited to just making better advertising media or messaging decisions. After all, advertising is an important ingredient to retail sales but certainly not the only means of increasing sales. The consumer insight information from the channel planning process can help shape a category's merchandising and/or marketing program.

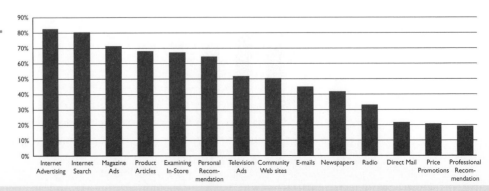

FIGURE 3

High-End Electronics
Media Channels—
Strength of Fit

Because channel planning can be honed to the sku level, a category manager can use this process as a filter to understand the consumer sales dynamics for that category. The key questions to ask are:

▶ How do consumers prefer to buy the sku?

▶ What is important to consumers in making this purchase?

▶ How is this sku best sold to the consumer?

By assessing how consumers prefer to buy each sku, the category manager will determine if he or she is in retailing, E-tailing, or a combination of the two. Let's take the home furnishings category as an example. It may become readily clear that consumers would prefer to come in to the store to buy sofas and chairs but may be much more likely to purchase lamps, tables, and desks online. This category, then, would require a combination of in-store and online selling.

Traditional retailing is undergoing a tectonic shift. Media channel planning enables retailers to adapt to the changing landscape by more tightly aligning media, messaging, and merchandising strategies, thus unlocking new potential for sales and profit. Channel planning helps break down walls that have separated these areas, by focusing on the most important aspect of the business—the consumer.

What Should a Retailer's Multi-Channel Retailing Strategy Be?

Multi-channel retailing is a buzzword. What exactly is it? What do we know about multi-channel shopping behavior? How can retailers formulate a sound multi-channel strategy? What are some of the best practices of multi-channel strategy?

Multi-channel retailing simultaneously offers information, goods, services, and support to customers through two or more synchronized channels—such as the catalog, store, and the Web. The role of each channel varies not only with shopper characteristics, but also with those of the product categories and the tasks involved. Retailers face a challenge to formulate a unifying multi-channel strategy that maximizes profits and enables them to make critical decisions on resource allocation across channels.

Several studies suggest that multi-channel shoppers might be more attractive to retailers than single-channel customers. A study by DoubleClick found that 65 percent of consumers were multi-channel shoppers and their size was increasing rapidly. Forrester Research found that more than two-thirds of the consumers search products online, but make a purchase offline. A few firms are noticing the dramatic impact of multi-channel shopping behavior on their revenues. A study by J.C. Penney (**www.jcpenney.com**) found that its customers who use all three channels (store, catalog, and the Web) spent $887 per year compared with $150, $195, and $201 spent by customers who only use the Web, store, or catalog, respectively. A study by McKinsey & Company found that, on average, retail customers using multiple channels spent about 20 to 30 percent more than customers using a single channel.

A retailer's first step in formulating a sound multi-channel retailing strategy is to understand the shopping behavior of customers for its and its rivals' products. To analyze the shopping behavior, the retailer can use different types of data such as its own point-of-sales data, loyalty program data, store-level and panel data from third-party vendors, and Internet click-stream data. Managers can use statistical models to identify segments of customers by channel, and determine the drivers of the recency, frequency, and monetary value of their purchases. They can supplement their analysis of behavioral data with analysis of shopper attitude survey data. The retailer can then determine the profitability of its customer segments and individual customers and prioritize them for targeting. Managers can use the geo-demographic information of the shoppers to come up with alternative marketing campaigns and programs. By testing some alternative campaigns on a sample of customers, the retailer can ascertain the effects of marketing actions and choose the most effective campaign. Finally, by monitoring the responses to the campaigns, the retailer can revise its multi-channel retailing strategy on an ongoing basis.

Using a large syndicated data base of the shopping behavior of about 96 million households and that from an apparel firm, we conducted a large-scale research study to develop a framework to help managers identify and target profitable customers and make appropriate channel-specific resource allocation decisions based on the current and expected future profitability of customers. We examined questions such as: Who are multi-channel shoppers? What drives multi-channel shopping behavior? How valuable are multi-channel shoppers to the firm? How responsive are multi-channel customers to a firm's marketing efforts? How should resources be allocated to different customer-channel segments?

The results from our study show that multi-channel shoppers buy more often, buy more items, and spend considerably more than single-channel shoppers. The equity (financial value) of multi-channel customers is nearly twice that of the closest single-channel customers (online or offline). The demographic characteristics and shopping traits of these multi-channel customers differ significantly from single-channel customers. The results also show that customers' responses to marketing efforts vary significantly across the customer-channel segments. We find that marketing efforts influence purchase frequency, purchase quantity, and monetary value in different ways. The findings suggest that catalog-only and multi-channel customer segments are most responsive to marketing communications, while the Web-only and store-only segments respond more to price and discounts, respectively. The findings also show that a firm can substantially improve profits by as much as about 30 percent by reallocating marketing efforts across the different customer-channel segments.

Multi-channel retailing offers retailers an important opportunity to consolidate and grow their businesses. In addition to offering customers more channels to shop from, multi-channel retailing provides organizations with greater opportunities to interact with customers, promote other channels, use price differentiation tools, segment customers specific to a channel, and target product categories to specific customer segments. By honing their multi-channel marketing capabilities, retailers can build stronger relationships with their customers and begin developing the core competency that promises to become a hallmark of world-class retailers.

Questions

1. What are the key lessons to be learned from this case?
2. How do these lessons differ for single-channel retailers versus multi-channel retailers?
3. What role does store atmosphere play in a retailer's sending a positioning message to its customers? What role does a retailer's Web site play?
4. Discuss the differences in the media channels best used by lottery retailers versus high-end consumer electronics retailers—as highlighted in Figures 2 and 3.
5. Present a promotion campaign for a new high-end consumer electronics store.
6. Describe the five needs that customers say are most important when making purchase decisions.
7. Comment on this statement: "Catalog-only and multi-channel customer segments are most responsive to marketing communications, while the Web-only and store-only segments respond more to price and discounts, respectively."

PART 8 Putting It All Together

In Part Eight, we "put it all together."

Chapter 20 connects the elements of a retail strategy that have been described throughout this book. We examine planning and opportunity analysis, productivity, performance measures, and scenario analysis. The value of data comparisons (benchmarking and gap analysis) is highlighted. Strategic control via the retail audit is covered.

20

Integrating and Controlling the Retail Strategy

Chapter Objectives

1. To demonstrate the importance of integrating a retail strategy

2. To examine four key factors in the development and enactment of an integrated retail strategy: planning procedures and opportunity analysis, defining productivity, performance measures, and scenario analysis

3. To show how industry and company data can be used in strategy planning and analysis (benchmarking and gap analysis)

4. To show the value of a retail audit

Bernard Marcus and Arthur Blank, the co-founders of Home Depot (**www.homedepot.com**), met while they worked for Handy Dan, a regional hardware store chain based in Los Angeles. After a personality clash with their boss, Marcus and Blank were both fired. The two executives were convinced that a store offering home improvement products (some of which were previously available only to contractors) could provide excellent customer service and change the way these products were sold. In 1979, the partners opened their first Home Depot store in Atlanta. Today, Home Depot dominates the do-it-yourself home improvement market with annual sales exceeding $77 billion, nearly 2,000 U.S. stores (including Expo Design Centers), 245 foreign stores, and 331,000 associates.

Home Depot is not complacent with its success as the firm plans for the future. It has rolled out a larger appliance showroom format in many of its locations in an attempt to move up from its number four position (with a 10 percent market share) in the appliance business (versus Sears with a 37 percent share and Lowe's with a 24 percent share). In 2001, Home Depot did not sell a single large appliance; Lowe's has been selling appliances nationally since 1994.

Home Depot is also developing neighborhood store prototypes intended for high-density market areas where full-size units are impractical. One of its Manhattan stores, for example, customizes services to meet the needs of interior designers, contractors, and architects. The paint department there has 11 mixers capable of producing 3,260 different colors.[1]

Source: Reprinted by permission of Susan Berry, Retail Image Consulting, Inc.

OVERVIEW

This site (**www.bizmove. com/marketing/m2c.htm**) raises a lot of good questions for retailers to think about in integrating their strategies.

This chapter focuses on integrating and controlling a retail strategy. We tie together the material detailed previously, show why retailers need coordinated strategies, and describe how to assess performance.

By integrating and regularly monitoring their strategies, firms of any size or format can take a proper view of the retailing concept and create a superior total retail experience. Consider how Dollar Tree competes with Wal-Mart—which is more than 80 times larger:

> The most significant competitive strength of Dollar Tree is its ability to price all products at a single price of $1. The firm maintains its discount pricing structure through a combination of strategic initiatives that include buying goods in huge quantities, having strong relationships with vendors and suppliers, and acquiring manufacturers' overruns. Dollar Tree buys 60 percent of its merchandise domestically and imports the remaining 40 percent from low-cost countries such as China. Owing to its value pricing, Dollar Tree attracts many price-conscious budget customers, who engage in 550 million sales transactions each year. The retailer deals with periodic market turbulence via volume buying, increasing efficiencies in its supply chain, and cutting costs by simplifying packaging or adjusting the quantity of items to keep the price of $1. Its efficient pricing structure has enabled the firm to carve out a niche position in the cluttered retail marketplace. Dollar Tree is also trying to differentiate itself by enhancing the "shopping experience" for customers. Ambience is designed in a bright fashion with ample lighting, and parking space is provided close to the storefront.[2]

See Figure 20-1.

As today's retailers look to the future, they must deal with new strategic choices due to the globalization of world markets, economic uncertainty, evolving

FIGURE 20-1

Dollar Tree Knows What Its Customers Want

Source: Reprinted by permission of TNS Retail Forward.

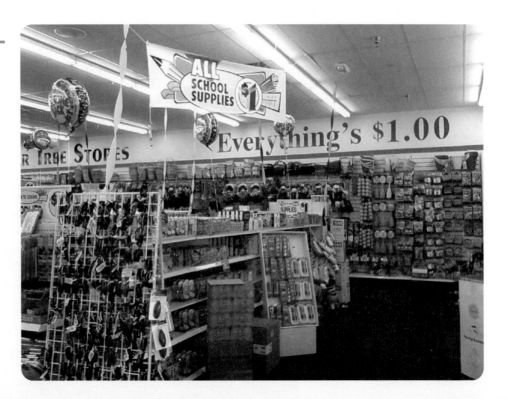

consumer lifestyles, competition among formats, and rapid technology changes. They would also be wise to study the strategies of both successful firms and those encountering significant challenges. Consider the demise of Circuit City, once the largest consumer electronics chain in the United States:

> The brutal economy swallowed another household retail name. Sixty-year-old Circuit City started liquidating in January 2009, leaving 34,000 employees without jobs and adding 567 vacant buildings to a growing list of empty retail storefronts. It expected all stores to close by the end of March 2009. A bankruptcy court approved Circuit City's liquidation after it couldn't find a buyer. A year earlier, Circuit City would have been able to reorganize, but consumer electronics firms faced a double-whammy: the recession and a market category too price-driven. In addition, growing competition online from Amazon.com and others and bigger consumer electronics departments at Wal-Mart, Target, Sam's, and Costco made the environment even tougher. As one analyst said: "Circuit City was just chasing Best Buy for a long time; and if Best Buy could make money and Circuit City couldn't, the difference was management." Circuit City's sales peaked in 2006 at $12.4 billion.[3]

Integrating the Retail Strategy

A major goal of *Retail Management* has been to describe the relationships among the elements of a retail strategy and show the need to act in an integrated way. Figures 20-2 and 20-3 highlight the integrated strategy of Coach, the accessories and gifts retailer. In 2008, Coach was cited by TNS Retail Forward and *Chain Store Age* as the leading U.S. "high performance retailer."[4] At our Web site (**www.pearsonhighered. com/berman**), there are links to several integrated retail strategies using Bplans.com software templates.

Four fundamental factors especially need to be taken into account in devising and enacting an integrated retail strategy: planning procedures and opportunity analysis, properly defining productivity, performance measures, and scenario analysis. These factors are discussed next.

Planning Procedures and Opportunity Analysis

Planning procedures are enhanced by undertaking three coordinated activities. The process is then more systematic and reflects input from multiple parties:

1. Senior executives outline the firm's overall direction and goals. This provides written guidelines for middle- and lower-level managers, who get input from various internal and external sources. These managers are encouraged to generate ideas at an early stage.
2. Top-down plans and bottom-up or horizontal plans are combined.
3. Specific plans are enacted, including checkpoints and dates.

Opportunities need to be studied with regard to their impact on overall strategy and not in an isolated manner. See Figure 20-4. As noted by TNS Retail Forward, "Retailers that apply innovative thinking to a growth market opportunity created by demographic, societal, economic, and technological trends can generate significant growth and financial performance. The needs of an aging population, ethnic consumers, and the pursuit of a healthy lifestyle provide fertile ground for innovative solutions."[5]

A useful retailer tool for evaluating opportunities is the **sales opportunity grid**, which rates the promise of new and established goods, services, procedures, and/or store outlets across a variety of criteria. It enables opportunities to be evaluated on the basis of the integrated strategies the firms would follow if the opportunities are pursued. Computerization makes it possible to apply such a grid.

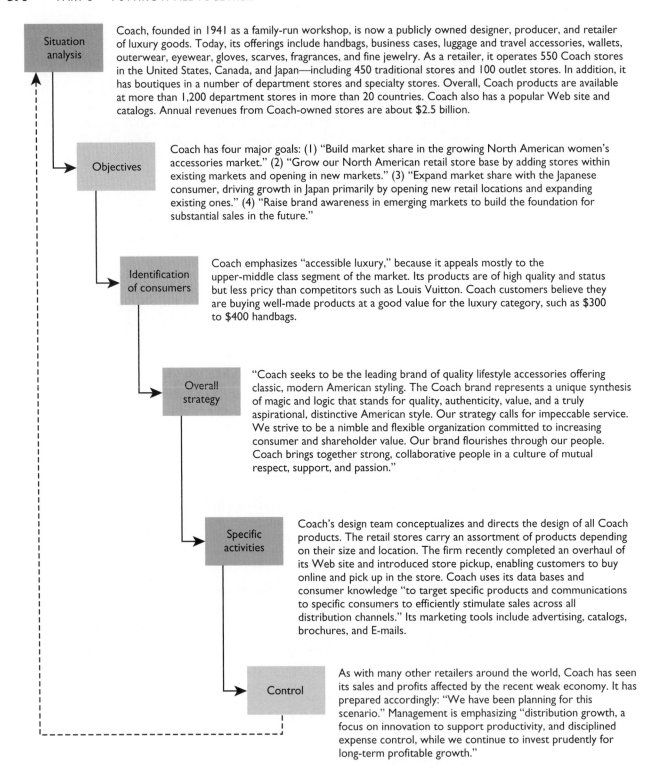

Situation analysis

Coach, founded in 1941 as a family-run workshop, is now a publicly owned designer, producer, and retailer of luxury goods. Today, its offerings include handbags, business cases, luggage and travel accessories, wallets, outerwear, eyewear, gloves, scarves, fragrances, and fine jewelry. As a retailer, it operates 550 Coach stores in the United States, Canada, and Japan—including 450 traditional stores and 100 outlet stores. In addition, it has boutiques in a number of department stores and specialty stores. Overall, Coach products are available at more than 1,200 department stores in more than 20 countries. Coach also has a popular Web site and catalogs. Annual revenues from Coach-owned stores are about $2.5 billion.

Objectives

Coach has four major goals: (1) "Build market share in the growing North American women's accessories market." (2) "Grow our North American retail store base by adding stores within existing markets and opening in new markets." (3) "Expand market share with the Japanese consumer, driving growth in Japan primarily by opening new retail locations and expanding existing ones." (4) "Raise brand awareness in emerging markets to build the foundation for substantial sales in the future."

Identification of consumers

Coach emphasizes "accessible luxury," because it appeals mostly to the upper-middle class segment of the market. Its products are of high quality and status but less pricy than competitors such as Louis Vuitton. Coach customers believe they are buying well-made products at a good value for the luxury category, such as $300 to $400 handbags.

Overall strategy

"Coach seeks to be the leading brand of quality lifestyle accessories offering classic, modern American styling. The Coach brand represents a unique synthesis of magic and logic that stands for quality, authenticity, value, and a truly aspirational, distinctive American style. Our strategy calls for impeccable service. We strive to be a nimble and flexible organization committed to increasing consumer and shareholder value. Our brand flourishes through our people. Coach brings together strong, collaborative people in a culture of mutual respect, support, and passion."

Specific activities

Coach's design team conceptualizes and directs the design of all Coach products. The retail stores carry an assortment of products depending on their size and location. The firm recently completed an overhaul of its Web site and introduced store pickup, enabling customers to buy online and pick up in the store. Coach uses its data bases and consumer knowledge "to target specific products and communications to specific consumers to efficiently stimulate sales across all distribution channels." Its marketing tools include advertising, catalogs, brochures, and E-mails.

Control

As with many other retailers around the world, Coach has seen its sales and profits affected by the recent weak economy. It has prepared accordingly: "We have been planning for this scenario." Management is emphasizing "distribution growth, a focus on innovation to support productivity, and disciplined expense control, while we continue to invest prudently for long-term profitable growth."

FIGURE 20-2

The Integrated Strategy of Coach

Sources: Figure developed by the authors based on data from the *Coach 2008 Annual Report* and Web site, **www.coach.com** (January 27, 2009).

FIGURE 20-3

Coach: Providing Value in
Every One of Its Retail
Formats

Source: Reprinted by permission of
TNS Retail Forward.

Table 20-1 shows a sales opportunity grid for a supermarket that wants to decide which of two salad dressing brands to carry. The store manager has outlined the integrated strategy for each brand; A is established; B is new. Due to its newness, the manager believes initial Brand B sales would be lower, but first year sales would be similar. The brands would be priced the same and occupy identical space. Brand B requires higher display costs but offers a larger markup. Brand B would return a greater gross profit and net profit than Brand A by the end of the first year. Based on the overall grid, the manager picks Brand B. Yet, if the store is more concerned about immediate profit, Brand A might be chosen.

Defining Productivity in a Manner Consistent with the Strategy

Intellilink (www.
intellilinksi.com) can
improve a retailer's
productivity. See how.

As we noted in Chapters 12 and 13, *productivity* refers to the efficiency with which a retail strategy is carried out; it is in any retailer's interest to reach sales and profit goals while keeping control over costs. On the one hand, a retailer looks to avoid unnecessary costs. It does not want eight salespeople working at one time if four can satisfactorily handle all customers. And it does not want to pay high rent for a site in a regional shopping center if

CAREERS IN RETAILING

Take Another Look!

Think there are few career opportunities in the retail industry? Take another look:

▶ *Marketing, Sales Promotion, and Advertising.* Develop creative and competitive ways to effectively present retail products to potential customers. Average salary $105,000.

▶ *Human Resources.* Use careful judgment to recruit, train, and develop employees, as well as manage payroll, benefits, and pensions. Average salary $95,000.

▶ *Store Manager.* Ensure that goals are met for financial success, merchandising and promotions, employees, customer relations, legal relations, and community involvement. Average salary $60,000.

▶ *Finance and Internal Auditing.* Oversee financial needs of a company, including accounting, budgeting, investments, and long- and short-term financial planning. Average salary $185,000.

▶ *Department Manager.* Supervise merchandise orders and displays, control inventories, schedule personnel, manage staff, and achieve financial goals. Average salary $45,000.

▶ *Vice-President/Director of Store Operations.* Supervise all stores, directing financial goals, strategic planning, marketing strategies, personnel development, and operations. Average salary $240,000.

▶ *Loss Prevention.* Save millions of dollars yearly for retailers using surveillance technology to ensure merchandise and facilities are not stolen or destroyed by misuse or abuse. Average salary $90,000.

▶ *E-Commerce, Information Technology, and Telecommunications.* Develop and maintain computer systems to increase efficiency, automate functions, and sell over the Web. Average salary $115,000.

▶ *Distribution, Logistics, and Supply Chain Management.* Use technology to manage the process of moving goods and information from raw material to supplier to customer. Average salary $110,000.

▶ *Merchandising and Buying.* Use expert understanding of consumer and market trends to predict what customers will want to buy. Average salary $105,000.

Source: Reprinted by permission of the National Retail Federation.

customers would willingly travel a few miles farther to a less costly site. On the other hand, a firm is not looking to lose customers because there are insufficient sales personnel to handle the rush of shoppers during peak hours. It also does not want a low rent site if this means a significant drop in customer traffic.

Potential trade-offs often mean neither the least expensive strategy nor the most expensive one is the most productive strategy; the former approach might not adequately service customers and the latter might be wasteful. An upscale retailer could not succeed with self-service, and it would be unnecessary for a discounter to have a large sales staff. The most productive approach applies a specific integrated retail strategy (such as a full-service jewelry store) as efficiently as possible.

Food Lion is a leading retailer due to its well-integrated, productive strategy:

Success is based on the principle of offering customers quality products at great prices and neighborly service in clean, conveniently located stores. Food Lion is one of the largest supermarket chains in the United States, with 1,300 supermarkets, either directly or through affiliated entities, under the names of Food Lion, Bloom, Bottom Dollar, Harveys, and Reid's. These stores meet local customer needs and preferences for the freshest and best-quality products in 11 Southeastern and Mid-Atlantic states. Stores offer nationally and regionally advertised brands, as well as a growing number of high-quality private label products made and packaged for Food Lion. The company maintains its great prices and quality assurance through technological advances and operating efficiencies such as standard store formats, innovative warehouse design and management, energy-efficient facilities, and data synchronization and integration with suppliers. Food Lion's commitment to quality is evident in its 73,000 associates. The company actively supports its associates through ongoing training programs and continuing advancement opportunities.[6]

FIGURE 20-4

Opportunity Analysis with the Small Business Administration

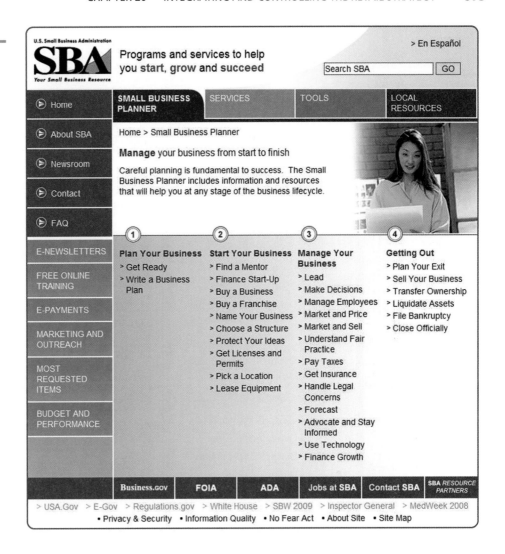

Performance Measures

By outlining relevant **performance measures**—the criteria used to assess effectiveness—and setting standards (goals) for each of them, a retailer can better develop and integrate its strategy. Among the measures frequently used by retailers are total sales, average sales per store, sales by goods/service category, sales per square foot, gross margins, gross margin return on investment, operating income, inventory turnover, markdown percentages, employee turnover, financial ratios, and profitability.

A retailer can gain insights from a visit to the Benchmarking Report Center (www.reportcenter. com).

To properly gauge a strategy's effectiveness, a firm should use **benchmarking**, whereby the retailer sets standards and measures its performance based on the achievements of its sector of retailing, specific competitors, high-performance firms, and/or the prior actions of the firm itself: "What company sets the standards in your industry, and what can you learn from them? Many executives sit around the table, beginning the budgeting process for the fiscal year and comparing performance from year to year. That is a good start but not enough. It is necessary to look at internal, as well as external, standards. The goal of benchmarking is to use peer operating results to improve the performance of all business processes."[7]

A good free source is the "Historical Retail Trade and Food Services" section of the U.S. Census Bureau's Web site (**www.census.gov/mrts/www/nmrtshist.html**). It shows more than 10 years of data involving a monthly comparison of sales, purchases, gross margins, inventories, and inventory-to-sales ratios by retail category through its "Historical Annual Benchmark Reports" link.

Learn about best practices, both retail and nonretail (http://www3.best-in-class. com).

Retailers of varying sizes—and in different goods or service lines—can also obtain comparative data from such sources as the Small Business Administration, Internal Revenue

TABLE 20-1 **Supermarket's Sales Opportunity Grid for Two Brands of Salad Dressing**

Criteria	Brand A (established)	Brand B (new)
Retail price	$2.58/8-ounce bottle	$2.58/8-ounce bottle
Floor space needed	8 square feet	8 square feet
Display costs	$10.00/month	$20.00/month for 6 months $10.00/month thereafter
Operating costs	$0.12/unit	$0.12/unit
Markup	19%	22%
Sales estimate		
During first month		
Units	250	50
Dollars	$645	$129
During first six months		
Units	1,400	500
Dollars	$3,612	$1,290
During first year		
Units	2,500	2,750
Dollars	$6,450	$7,095
Gross profit estimate		
During first month	$123	$28
During first six months	$686	$284
During first year	$1,226	$1,561
Net profit estimate		
During first month	$83	$2
During first six months	$458	$104
During first year	$806	$1,051

Example 1:
Gross profit estimate = Sales estimate − [(1.00 − Markup percentage) × (Sales estimate)]

Brand A gross profit estimate during first six months = $3,612 − [(1.00 − 0.19) × ($3,612)] = $686

Example 2:
Net profit estimate = Gross profit estimate − (Display costs + Operating costs)

Brand A net profit estimate during first six months = $686 − ($60 + $168) = $458

Service, *Progressive Grocer, Stores, Chain Store Age, DSN Retailing Today,* BizMiner, Dun & Bradstreet, the National Retail Federation, Risk Management Association, and annual reports. Those retailers can then compare their performance with others.

Table 20-2 contains revenue, expense, and income benchmarking data for small retailers in 14 different business categories. The cost of goods sold as a percentage of revenues is highest for gas stations and food and beverage stores, gross profit is greatest for hotels and motels, operating expenses are also the most for hotels and motels, and net income is highest for personal and laundry services.

One popular, independent, ongoing benchmarking survey is the American Customer Satisfaction Index (ACSI). It addresses two questions:

1. Are customer satisfaction and evaluations of quality improving or declining in the United States?
2. Are they improving or declining for particular sectors of industry and for specific companies?

TABLE 20-2 Benchmarking Through Annual Operating Statements of Typical Sole Proprietors, 2005 (Expressed in Terms of Revenues = 100%)

Type of Retailer	Total Revenues	Cost of Goods Sold	Gross Profit	Total Operating Expenses	Net Income
Apparel and accessory stores	100	51.7	48.3	33.0	15.3
Auto repair shops	100	38.6	61.4	42.8	18.6
Building materials/garden equipment	100	64.9	35.1	24.7	10.4
Eating and drinking places	100	42.1	57.9	47.0	10.9
Electronics and appliance stores	100	53.2	46.8	33.1	13.7
Food and beverage stores	100	72.7	27.3	21.0	6.3
Furniture and home furnishings stores	100	54.3	45.7	34.3	11.4
Gas stations	100	86.3	13.7	11.5	2.2
General merchandise stores	100	67.8	32.2	23.7	8.5
Health and personal care stores	100	60.0	40.0	24.6	15.4
Hotel and motels	100	5.7	94.3	76.4	17.9
Nonstore	100	46.8	53.2	30.3	22.9
Personal and laundry services	100	11.0	89.0	50.0	39.0
Sporting goods/ hobby/book/music stores	100	53.5	46.5	31.8	14.7

Source: U.S. Internal Revenue Service, as compiled by **www.bizstats.com** (February 20, 2009).

The index is based on a scale of 0 to 100, with 100 the highest possible score. A national sample of more than 65,000 people takes part in phone interviews, with 250 interviews of current customers for each of the firms studied (**www.theacsi.org**). Table 20-3 shows that the highest score by any listed retailer was 88 for Amazon.com, while the lowest was 64 for McDonald's.

TABLE 20-3 Benchmarking Through the American Customer Satisfaction Index

Retailer	1995 Index Score	1999 Index Score	2003 Index Score	2007 Index Score
Department/Discount Stores	**75**	**72**	**76**	**73**
Nordstrom	83	76	—	80
Kohl's	—	—	79	79
Dollar General	—	—	—	78
J.C. Penney	77	75	77	77
Target	76	74	75	77
Macy's	71	68	71	75
Sears	71	74	75	73
Wal-Mart	81	72	75	68
Supermarkets	**75**	**74**	**74**	**76**
Publix	82	82	82	83
Kroger	76	74	71	75
Supervalu	77	75	77	74
Whole Foods	—	—	—	73
Safeway	73	72	71	72
Winn-Dixie	75	71	73	71

(*Continued*)

TABLE 20-3 **Benchmarking Through the American Customer Satisfaction Index (Continued)**

Retailer	1995 Index Score	1999 Index Score	2003 Index Score	2007 Index Score
Specialty Retail Stores	—	**79**	**74**	**75**
Barnes & Noble	—	—	—	83
Borders	—	—	—	81
Costco	—	79	80	81
Sam's Club	—	78	77	77
Staples	—	—	—	77
The Gap, Inc.	—	—	—	75
Lowe's	—	—	77	75
Best Buy	—	—	72	74
TJX	—	—	—	74
Home Depot	—	—	73	67
Limited-Service Restaurants	**70**	**69**	**74**	**77**
Starbucks	—	—	—	78
Wendy's	73	71	74	78
Papa John's	—	76	76	77
Pizza Hut	66	68	75	72
KFC	68	64	71	71
Burger King	65	66	68	69
Taco Bell	66	64	68	69
McDonald's	63	61	64	64
E-Commerce	—	—	**84**	**83**
Amazon.com	—	—	88	88
Netflix	—	—	—	84
eBay	—	—	82	81
Overstock.com	—	—	—	80

— = insufficient data.

Source: University of Michigan Ross School of Business, American Society for Quality Control, and CFI Group, "ACSI Scores & Commentary," **www.theacsi.org** (February 20, 2009). Reprinted by permission.

There is now greater interest in the benchmarking of service retailing. One well-known measurement tool is SERVQUAL, which lets service retailers assess their quality by asking customers to react to a series of statements in five areas of performance:

▶ *Reliability.* Providing services as promised. Dependability in handling service problems. Performing services right the first time. Providing services at the promised time. Maintaining error-free records.

▶ *Responsiveness.* Keeping customers informed about when services will be done. Prompt service. Willingness to help customers. Readiness to act on customer requests.

▶ *Assurance.* Employees who instill customer confidence and make customers feel safe in transactions. Employees who are consistently courteous and have the knowledge to answer questions.

▶ *Empathy.* Giving customers individual attention in a caring way. Having the customer's best interest at heart. Employees who understand the needs of their customers. Convenient business hours.

▶ *Tangibles.* Modern equipment. Visually appealing facilities. Employees who have a neat, professional appearance. Visually appealing materials associated with the service.[8]

In reviewing the performance of others, firms should look at the *best practices* in retailing—whether involving companies in its own business sector or other sectors. For example, the Supply Chain Consortium (**www.supplychainconsortium.com**) includes a number of retailers. By joining the consortium, member companies get information that help them address issues such as these:

> **Economic Impact**—How do I stack up to my peers? Where can I improve? **Costs**—Are my supply chain costs competitive? **Operations**—How do my operating characteristics compare to my peers? **Performance Measurement**—How do my peers measure supply chain performance? Where do they stand in achieving their goals? **Collaboration**—How much collaboration is there with supply chain firms? **Outsourcing**—Where and why do my peers use outsourcing? **Technology**—What technologies are my peers using in their supply chain operations? What is working and what is not?[9]

TNS Retail Forward (**www.retailforward.com**) regularly produces a list of "high performance U.S. retailers, derived from its own proprietary ranking system. It includes firms performing well above average on a **retail performance index**, encompassing five-year trends in revenue growth and profit growth, and a six-year average return on assets. Due to its importance, return on assets is weighted twice as much as revenue growth or profit growth. An overall performance index of 100 is average. Table 20-4 cites 20 high-performance retailers and reveals that there are various ways to be one. The leader, Coach, was strong on all measures. On the other hand, although Hibbett Sporting Goods was 10th in return on assets, it was last in revenue growth and next-to-last in profit growth—among the 20 firms in Table 20-4. By

TABLE 20-4 Benchmarking High-Performance U.S. Retailers

Company	Compound Annual Revenue Growth, 2002–2007 (%)	Compound 5-Year Revenue Growth Index	Annual Profit Growth, 2002–2007 (%)	5-Year Profit Growth Index	Average Annual Return on Assets 2002–2007 (%)	5-Year Return on Assets Index	Retail Performance Index[a]
Coach	27.3	295	39.8	362	28.9	511	419
Blue Nile	34.7	375	60.7	552	16.4	291	377
Aeropostale	23.6	255	32.8	298	19.7	349	313
Urban Outfitters	29.0	313	42.4	385	14.7	261	305
Lumber Liquidators	44.0	476	18.8	171	15.5	274	299
EZCORP	13.6	147	76.6	697	8.9	158	290
Best Buy	13.8	149	70.0	637	9.7	172	282
American Eagle Outfitters	15.9	172	35.1	320	16.5	292	269
Zumiez	30.3	328	34.7	316	11.9	210	266
Fastenal Company	17.9	193	25.2	229	17.6	311	261
Abercrombie & Fitch	18.6	201	19.5	178	17.8	315	252
GameStop	39.3	425	40.6	370	5.9	104	251
Jos. A. Bank Clothiers	19.9	215	35.6	324	10.8	192	231
bebe	16.3	176	26.8	243	13.1	232	221
DSW	16.9	182	46.2	420	8.0	141	221
Citi Trends	28.5	308	23.1	210	9.9	175	217
Dick's Sporting Goods	25.0	271	32.3	294	7.6	135	208
Bed Bath & Beyond	14.0	151	13.2	120	15.3	270	203
Hibbett Sporting Goods	13.3	144	15.5	141	14.7	260	201
Cash America	19.1	206	32.7	297	8.1	143	198
U.S. Retailing Medians	*9.3*	*100*	*11.0*	*100*	*5.7*	*100*	*100*

[a]Retail performance index = [Revenue growth index + Profit growth index + 2 (Return on assets index)]/4

Source: "2008 High Performance Retailers," **www.retailforward.com** (October 20, 2008). Reprinted by permission of TNS Retail Forward.

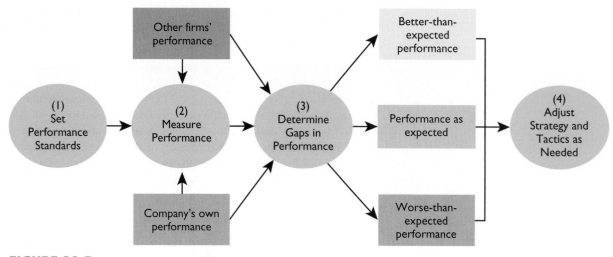

FIGURE 20-5

Utilizing Gap Analysis

learning about high performance firms in different retail categories, a prospective or existing company can study the strategies of those retailers and try to emulate their best practices.

A retailer can also benchmark its own internal performance, conduct gap analysis, and plan for the future. Through **gap analysis**, a company compares its actual performance against its potential performance and then determines the areas in which it must improve. As Figure 20-5 indicates, gap analysis has four main steps.

Let us apply gap analysis to Home Depot. Table 20-5 indicates its financial results for fiscal years 2004 through 2008. The data in the table may be used to benchmark Home Depot in terms of its own performance. Between 2004 and 2008, Home Depot saw sales growth slow, and profitability leveled off and then declined. The gross margin as a percent of sales remained strong, while operating expenses as a percent of sales rose. Although total assets were strong, working capital dropped significantly. The current ratio, inventory turnover, and return on invested capital all fell. Home Depot continued to open new stores; but comparable store sales and sales per square foot declined. Overall, Home Depot's 2004–2008 performance was not up to its

What makes a good retail Web site? Companies can close the gap by checking here ().

---

eBay: A Founder's Philanthropy

Pierre Omidyar, the founder of eBay (**www.ebay.com**) who turned 40 in 2007, was one of the richest 30-something-year-olds in history. From the time be began acquiring his wealth, it was apparent to friends that he was uncomfortable, perhaps even embarrassed, by it. While Pierre and his wife Pam Omidyar have vowed to give away all their wealth, they want their philanthropy to have a great impact.

In 2004, the Omidyars launched Omidyar Network (**www.omidyar.net**), an organization that combines a traditional foundation (which gives grants) with a for-profit venture fund (that makes investments). Unlike many other foundations, the Omidyar Network believes that market-based solutions can generate significant social returns. The network is run by Matt Bannick, the former president of eBay International. According to the organi-

zation's Web site, from 2004 through 2008, the Omidyar Network donated more than $260 million.

The Omidyar Network has helped to fund Donorschoose.org (**www.donorschoose.org**), which gives school supplies to needy children, and Prosper.com (**www.prosper.com**), a low-interest consumer lending site. It is also a major investor in Unitus Equity Fund (**www.unitusequityfund.com**), an $8.5 million microfinance investor that finances projects in Asia and Latin America. This fund provides low-interest microloans of $50 or more to small business owners.

Sources: Catherine Holahan, "eBay: The Place for Microfinance," **www.businessweek.com/technology** (October 24, 2007); and "The Face of Philanthropy," **http://money.cnn/galleries/2008/fortune/0801** (January 11, 2008).

TABLE 20-5   Home Depot: Internal Benchmarking and Gap Analysis

	Fiscal Year Ending January 30, 2004	Fiscal Year Ending January 29, 2006	Fiscal Year Ending February 3, 2008
Statement of Earnings Data			
Net sales (in millions)	$63,660	$77,019	$77,349
Earnings before taxes (in millions)	$ 6,762	$ 8,967	$ 6,620
Net earnings (in millions)	$ 4,253	$ 5,641	$ 4,210
Gross margin (% of sales)	31.7	33.7	33.6
Total operating expenses (% of sales)	21.1	21.9	24.3
Net earnings (% of sales)	6.7	7.3	5.4
Balance Sheet Data and Financial Ratios			
Total assets (in millions)	$34,437	$44,405	$44,323
Working capital (in millions)	$ 3,774	$ 2,563	$ 1,968
Merchandise inventories (in millions)	$ 9,076	$11,401	$11,731
Current ratio (times)	1.40	1.20	1.15
Inventory turnover (times)	5.0	4.7	4.2
Return on invested capital (%)	19.2	20.4	13.9
Customer and Store Data			
Number of stores	1,707	2,042	2,234
Total square footage (in millions)	183	215	235
Number of customer transactions (in millions)	1,246	1,330	1,336
Average sale per transaction	$ 51.15	$ 57.98	$ 57.48
Comparable-store sales increase (%)	3.7	3.1	–6.7
Weighted-average sales per square foot	$ 371	$ 377	$ 332

Source: Compiled by the authors from *Home Depot Annual Reports.*

prior results. This signaled that Home Depot had "gaps" to fix and that competition and the economy had an effect. Home Depot must resolve these issues to regain momentum.

To ensure that gaps are minimized in relationship retailing, firms should undertake the following:

1. *Customer insight.* Analyze known consumer information, such as sales, cost, and profits by segment.
2. *Customer profiling.* Regularly gather and merge transaction and lifestyle data to get a fuller picture of individual shoppers. Identify noncustomers who fit the profile of the firm's best segment.
3. *Customer life-cycle model.* Study shopper behavior at various life stages. Look at demographics by segment. Find the cost of serving each life cycle within each segment and the resultant profitability.
4. *Extended business model.* Based on steps 3 and 4, draw conclusions about which customers to focus on, the best ways to interact with them, and the best strategy to foster relationships. Survey individual customers to find out how to tailor the retail strategy to best satisfy their needs.

5. *Relationship program planning and design.* Identify all points of contact (in person, pickup, delivery, kiosk, phone, fax, computer) between the firm and its customers, and the communications that should flow back and forth during each contact. Select processes that please existing customers and attract new ones, promote retention, increase spending, and lift profitability per customer.

6. *Implementation.* Integrate marketing, customer service, and selling efforts.[10]

At our Web site (**www.pearsonhighered.com/berman**), we have a number of links related to benchmarking and gap analysis.

Scenario Analysis

TNS Retail Forward (http://rfkb.retailforward.com/freereports.aspx) makes various forward-looking retail research reports available online.

In **scenario analysis**, a retailer projects the future by studying factors that affect long-run performance and then forms contingency ("what if") plans based on alternate scenarios (such as low, moderate, and high levels of competition). Planning for the future is not easy:

Retailing is a zero-sum game with low profit margins. Because the U.S. market is quite competitive, a gain in sales for one store equals a loss for another. In this environment, retailers—especially department stores—have come to rely on frequent price promotions to attract customers, who now expect low prices. This dynamic keeps a lid on profits. Reinforcing this trend is Wal-Mart Stores, Inc., with its "everyday low prices" policy that offers discount prices all the time. Because of its size, Wal-Mart has gained power in its relationships with manufacturers, which it does not hesitate to wield. The world's largest retailer squeezes vendors for the greatest possible discount, which allows Wal-Mart to maintain and even lower its prices. The combination of a mature, highly saturated market, a slow sales growth environment, and merchants' inability to raise prices makes it imperative to drive down costs and/or improve economies of scale. Retailers' survival tactics include everything from closing weak units and cutting jobs to instituting inventory controls and expanding stores.[11]

Though it seems counterintuitive, promoting and discounting do not address the consumer-confidence issue. What are retailers doing to reconfigure their offerings? Making the case for why particular goods are necessary and relevant. One of the most notable efforts comes from J.C. Penney. The humble store for middle-class moms is flexing its brand attitude, getting into sync with the different identities found within the American family—offering family essentials with a light push on style. It has been steadily building its portfolio of exclusive new apparel brands, most recently targeting young men and juniors with trendy, traditional, premium, and urban looks. Women of all ages have made Sephora, Penney's "little beauty playground," into a bright financial success, and the company plans to expand its aspirational American Living collection by Polo Ralph Lauren. More innovative merchandising and enhanced store environments are being created for "encouragement and inspiration, offering style and quality at a smart price."[12]

Brazilian retailer CBD feels the global financial crisis and economic downturn creates opportunities to negotiate prices with suppliers and acquire weakened competitors. The retail group, better known by its flagship supermarket chain Pao de Acucar, created an internal division devoted to mergers and acquisitions. "The crisis generates lots of opportunities. As the rope tightens around the neck (of potential acquisitions), talks become easier." The company plans to leverage its 1.4 billion real ($620 million) cash flow to open new stores and make acquisitions. It maintained its intention to open a number of new stores, depending on the impact of the global crisis on the local economy.[13]

Predicting the future is not simple (www.futurist.com/articles).

In planning for its future, Kohl's (**www.kohls.com**) has a well-conceived—and widely praised—strategic plan. Here are selected elements of that plan:

▶ *Organizational mission and positioning.* Kohl's is positioning itself "to be the leading family-focused, value-oriented, specialty department store—offering quality exclusive and national brand merchandise to the customer in an environment that is convenient, friendly, and exciting." The slogan is "expect great things."

▶ *Goals.* There are four strategic goals that Kohl's management believes are "keys to achieving future success." These strategic goals involve enhancing merchandise content, increasing market share through targeted marketing efforts, improving inventory management, and making the in-store shopping experience more dynamic and exciting.

▶ *Basic strategy.* "If you've ever shopped one of our clean, bright department stores, you've already experienced our commitment to family, value, and national brands. Our stores are stocked with everything you need for yourself and your home—apparel, shoes, and accessories for women, children, and men, plus home products like small electrics, bedding, luggage, and more. Online, we've taken our commitment to convenience even further, and you'll find there's more to like at Kohls.com with every click of your mouse. We not only offer the best merchandise at the best prices, but we're always working to make your shopping experience enjoyable."

▶ *Merchandising.* "Expanding our merchandise offering is critical to increasing market share and engaging a broader range of customers. In the updated and contemporary categories, we introduced Simply Vera by Vera Wang, along with the ELLE Contemporary Collection. These brands were eagerly embraced by our customers. Brands such as Chaps continue to attract our core classic customer, while the introduction of Dana Buchman in spring 2009 enhanced our classic offerings."

▶ *Marketing.* "Our marketing program is designed to differentiate Kohl's in the marketplace. It uses a strategically selected variety of media to build awareness and desire for our national, private, and exclusive brands and increase traffic and sales. We're focusing efforts on encouraging our customer to explore the store to increase the number of store areas she shops for her family and herself."[14]

At our Web site (**www.pearsonhighered.com/berman**), there are several links related to scenario analysis and future planning.

Control: Using the Retail Audit

After a retail strategy is devised and enacted, it must be continuously assessed and necessary adjustments made. A vital evaluation tool is the **retail audit**, which systematically examines and evaluates a firm's total retailing effort or a specific aspect of it. The purpose of an audit is to study what a retailer is presently doing, appraise performance, and make recommendations for the future. An audit investigates a retailer's objectives, strategy, implementation, and organization. Goals are reviewed and evaluated for their clarity, consistency, and appropriateness. The strategy and the methods for deriving it are analyzed. The application of the strategy and how it is received by customers are reviewed. The organizational structure is analyzed with regard to lines of command and other factors.

Good auditing includes these elements: Audits are conducted regularly. In-depth analysis is involved. Data are amassed and analyzed systematically. An open-minded, unbiased perspective is maintained. There is a willingness to uncover weaknesses to be corrected, as well as strengths to be exploited. After an audit is completed, decision makers are responsive to the recommendations made in the audit report.

Undertaking an Audit

There are six steps in retail auditing. See Figure 20-6 for an overview of the six-step retail auditing process, which is described next: (1) Determine who does an audit. (2) Decide

RETAILING AROUND THE WORLD

Wal-Mart: The Master of Global Best Practices

Wal-Mart's (**www.walmart.com**) international division is enormous, with annual revenues that are higher than all but a handful of retailers. The firm operates thousands of store units in more than a dozen foreign countries and serves more than 48 million international customers each week.

Wal-Mart's international retail strategy involves adapting store formats to each market. For example:

▶ In Mexico, Wal-Mart operates supercenters, food and clothing stores, and restaurants. Its Banco Wal-Mart operates 16 Wal-Mart bank branches that offer installment plans on electronics and household appliances.
▶ Wal-Mart has experimented with a number of formats at its British-based ASDA (**www.asda.co.uk**) division. To complement ASDA's food-based stores, Wal-Mart recently added ASDA Living stores featuring general merchandise and George apparel stores.

▶ The Chinese market is expected to have very high levels of growth for Wal-Mart over the next several years. Wal-Mart plans to again double its number of stores over the next five years. To accomplish this objective, Wal-Mart has purchased a controlling interest in the Trust-Mart chain (**www.trust-mart. com**) for $1 billion U.S. and also plans to open 24 new Wal-Mart stores. One problem in accomplishing its goals is the shortage of prime retail locations—as well as competition from Carrefour (**www.carrefour. com**), Auchan (**www.auchan.com**), and Tesco (**www.tesco.com**).

Sources: Raphael Moreau, "Carrefour and Wal-Mart's Differing Expansion Strategies in China," *Retail Digest* (Spring 2008), pp. 42–45; Geri Smith and Keith Epstein, "Wal-Mart Banks on the 'Unbanked,'" **www.businessweek.com** (December 13, 2007); and "Wal-Mart International Operations Data Sheet—August 2008," **http://walmartstores.com/FactsNews/Newsroom/8522.aspx** (August 24, 2008).

when and how often an audit is done. (3) Establish the areas to be audited. (4) Develop audit form(s). (5) Conduct the audit. (6) Report to management.

DETERMINING WHO DOES THE AUDIT

One or a combination of three parties can be involved: a company audit specialist, a company department manager, and/or an outside auditor.

A company audit specialist is an internal employee whose prime responsibility is the retail audit. The advantages of this person include the auditing expertise, thoroughness, level of knowledge about the firm, and ongoing nature (no time lags). Disadvantages include the costs (especially for retailers that do not need full-time auditors) and the auditor's limited independence.

A company department manager is an internal employee whose prime job is operations management; that manager may also be asked to participate in the retail audit. The advantages are that there are no added personnel expenses and that the manager is knowledgeable about the firm and its operations. Disadvantages include the manager's time away from the primary job, the potential lack of objectivity, time pressure, and the complexity of companywide audits.

An outside auditor is not a retailer's employee but a paid consultant. Advantages are the auditor's broad experience, objectivity, and thoroughness. Disadvantages are the high costs per day or hour (for some retailers, it may be cheaper to hire per-diem consultants than full-time auditors; the opposite is true for larger firms), the time lag while a consultant gains familiarity with the firm, the failure of some firms to use outside specialists continuously, and the reluctance of some employees to cooperate.

DETERMINING WHEN AND HOW OFTEN THE AUDIT IS CONDUCTED

Logical times for auditing are the end of the calendar year, the end of the retailer's annual reporting year (fiscal year), or when a complete physical inventory is conducted. Each of these is appropriate for evaluating a retailer's operations during the previous period. An audit must be enacted at least annually, although some retailers desire more frequent analysis. It is important that the same period(s), such as January-December, be studied to make meaningful comparisons, projections, and adjustments.

FIGURE 20-6

The Retail Audit Process

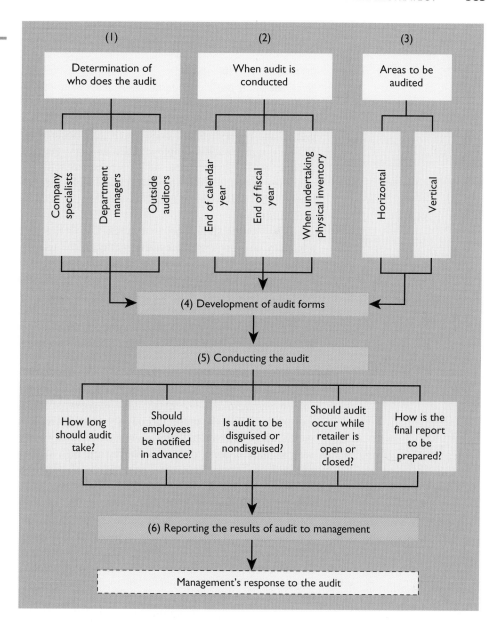

DETERMINING AREAS TO BE AUDITED

A retail audit typically includes more than financial analysis; it reviews various aspects of a firm's strategy and operations to identify strengths and weaknesses. There are two basic types of audits. They should be used in conjunction with one another because a horizontal audit often reveals areas that merit further investigation by a vertical audit.

A **horizontal retail audit** analyzes a firm's overall performance, from the organizational mission to goals to customer satisfaction to the basic retail strategy mix and its implementation in an integrated, consistent way. It is also known as a "retail strategy audit." A **vertical retail audit** analyzes—in depth—a firm's performance in one area of the strategy mix or operations, such as the credit function, customer service, merchandise assortment, or interior displays. A vertical audit is focused and specialized.

This site has a detailed online vertical pricing audit (**www.bizmove.com/marketing/m2y3.htm**) for retailers.

DEVELOPING AUDIT FORMS

To be systematic, a retailer should use detailed audit forms. An audit form lists the area(s) to be studied and guides data collection. It usually resembles a questionnaire and is completed by the auditor. Without audit forms, analysis is more haphazard and subjective. Key questions may be omitted or poorly worded. Auditor biases may appear. Most significantly, questions may differ from one audit period to another, which limits comparisons. Examples of retail audit forms are presented shortly.

CONDUCTING THE AUDIT

Next, the audit itself is undertaken. Management specifies how long the audit will take. Prior notification of employees depends on management's perception of two factors: the need to compile some data in advance to save time versus the desire to get an objective picture and not a distorted one (which may occur if employees have too much notice). With a disguised audit, employees are unaware that it is taking place. It is useful if the auditor investigates an area such as personal selling and acts as a customer to elicit employee responses. With a nondisguised audit, employees know an audit is being conducted. This is desirable if employees are asked specific operational questions and help in gathering data.

Some audits should be done while the retailer is open, such as assessing parking adequacy, in-store customer traffic patterns, the use of vertical transportation, and customer relations. Others should be done when the firm is closed, such as analyses of the condition of fixtures, inventory levels and turnover, financial statements, and employee records.

An audit report can be formal or informal, brief or long, oral or written, and a statement of findings or a statement of findings plus recommendations. It has a better chance of acceptance if presented in the format desired by management.

REPORTING AUDIT FINDINGS AND RECOMMENDATIONS TO MANAGEMENT

The last auditing step is to present findings and recommendations to management. It is the role of management—not the auditor—to see what adjustments (if any) to make. Decision makers must read the report thoroughly, consider each point, and enact the needed strategic changes. They should treat each audit seriously and react accordingly. No matter how well an audit is done, it is not a worthwhile activity if management fails to enact recommendations.

Responding to an Audit

TJX (**www.tjx.com/about. asp**) is very open about its performance. Enter "Businesses" and see how much information is available about the firm's plans and results.

After management studies audit findings, appropriate actions are taken. Areas of strength are continued and areas of weakness are revised. These actions must be consistent with the retail strategy and noted in the firm's retail information system (for further reference).

One retailer that places great reliance on its retail audits is Target. It is truly a "learning company:"

> Target has used the lessons of successful merchandising to design its stores around the purchasing needs of customers in each local market. Taking a cue from retail Web sites that track the purchases of each individual shopper, Target undertook rigorous research to determine specific consumer-shopping patterns within the store—where they went and how they bought in different markets. It used the results to organize stores based on highly specific consumer segmentation. For example, hand-sanitizing lotion may be at the front of an urban Target location, while bug spray and garden equipment may draw visitors to a more suburban store. By carefully assessing the shopping patterns of customers in all of its stores, Target has been able to create almost personalized shopping experiences for greater appeal to local audiences. The company used research to develop a merchandising strategy that led to a substantial increase in sales volume. Target has told its consumers that, no matter what market they're in, it understands precisely what they need.[15]

AuditNet (**www.auditnet. org**) has a number of good examples of auditing applications. Click on "Audit Programs."

Possible Difficulties in Conducting a Retail Audit

Several obstacles may occur in doing a retail audit. A retailer should be aware of them:

▶ An audit may be costly.
▶ It may be quite time-consuming.

TECHNOLOGY IN RETAILING

Online Checkout Systems at Sierra Trading Post

A significant proportion of online consumers have been found to abandon their purchase process at the shopping cart stage. There are several possible explanations. One is that delivery costs, which are only visible at this stage, are too high relative to the cost of the merchandise purchased. A second explanation focuses on consumer concern over credit card security. And a third issue involves the large number of steps that need to be taken by the consumer to finalize the sale.

Sierra Trading Post (**www.sierratradingpost.com**)—a multi-channel retailer that operates three stores, nine mail-order catalogs, and a Web site—is among the firms actively striving to reduce the unnecessary loss of consumers. By integrating its site with Google Checkout (**https://checkout.**

google.com), Sierra Trading Post now stores all purchasing information within Google's data base. This process eliminates the customer's having to re-enter billing and credit card information for each purchase. According to Google's group product marketing manager, "the average customer fills out at least 15 fields during an online checkout." In addition, the consumer does not have to repeatedly give out sensitive credit card information over the Web. The new system has increased sales at Sierra Trading Post, as well as reduced transaction processing costs by 20 percent.

Sources: Samantha Murphy, "Checking Out," *Chain Store Age* (January 2007), p. 66; and "Google Checkout," **http://checkout. google.com/sell** (February 7, 2009).

▶ Performance measures may be inaccurate.
▶ Employees may feel threatened and not cooperate as much as desired.
▶ Incorrect data may be collected.
▶ Management may not be responsive to the findings.

At present, many retailers—particularly small ones—do not understand or perform systematic retail audits. But this must change if they are to assess themselves properly and plan correctly for the future.

Illustrations of Retail Audit Forms

Here, we present a management audit form and a retailing effectiveness checklist to show how small and large retailers can inexpensively, yet efficiently, conduct retail audits. An internal or external auditor (or department manager) could periodically complete one of these forms and then discuss the findings with management. The examples noted are both horizontal audits. A vertical audit would involve an in-depth analysis of any one area in the forms.

A MANAGEMENT AUDIT FORM FOR SMALL RETAILERS

Under the auspices of the U.S. Small Business Administration, a *Marketing Checklist for Small Retailers* was developed. Although written for small firms, it is a comprehensive horizontal audit applicable to all retailers. Figure 20-7 shows selected questions from this audit form. "Yes" is the desired answer to each question. For questions answered negatively, the firm must learn the causes and adjust its strategy.

A RETAILING EFFECTIVENESS CHECKLIST

Figure 20-8 has another type of audit form to assess performance and prepare for the future: a retailing effectiveness checklist. It can be used by small and large firms alike. The checklist is more strategic than the *Management Audit for Small Retailers*—which is more tactical. Unlike the yes–no answers in Figure 20-7, the checklist lets a retailer rate its performance from 1 to 5 in each area; this provides more in-depth information. However, a total score should not be computed (unless items are weighted), because all items are not equally important. A simple summation would not be a meaningful score.

Planning
1. Have you thought about the long-term direction of your business?   ____
2. Have you developed a realistic set of plans for the year's operations?   ____
3. Do your plans provide methods to deal with competition?   ____
4. Is there a system for auditing your objectives?   ____

Customer Analysis (Who are your target customers and what are they seeking from you?)
1. Have you profiled your customers by age, income, education, occupation, etc.?   ____
2. Are you aware of the reasons why customers shop with you?   ____
3. Do you ask your customers for suggestions on ways to improve your operation?   ____
4. Do you know what goods and services your customers most prefer?   ____

Organization and Human Resources
1. Are job descriptions and authority for responsibilities clearly stated?   ____
2. Have you an effective system for communication with employees?   ____
3. Do you have a formal program for motivating employees?   ____
4. Have you taken steps to minimize shoplifting and internal theft?   ____

Operations and Special Services
1. Do you monitor every facet of your operations in terms of specific goals?   ____
2. Do you provide time-saving services for greater customer convenience?   ____
3. Do you have a policy for handling merchandise returned by customers?   ____
4. Do you get feedback through customer surveys?   ____

Financial Analysis and Control
1. Do your financial records give you the information to make sound decisions?   ____
2. Can sales be broken down by department?   ____
3. Do you understand the pros and cons of the retail method of accounting?   ____
4. Have you taken steps to minimize shoplifting and internal theft?   ____

Buying
1. Do you have a merchandise budget (planned purchases) for each season that is broken down by department and merchandise classification?   ____
2. Does it take into consideration planned sales, planned gross margin, planned inventory turnover, and planned markdowns?   ____
3. Do you plan exclusive or private brand programs?   ____
4. Do you take advantage of cash discounts and allowances offered by your vendor/supplier?   ____

Pricing
1. Have you determined whether to price below, at, or above the market?   ____
2. Do you set specific markups for each product category?   ____
3. Do you know which products are slow-movers and which are fast?   ____
4. Have you developed a markdown policy?   ____

Atmospherics
1. Are the unique appeals of your business reflected in your image?   ____
2. Have you figured out the best locations for displays?   ____
3. Do you know which items are bought on "impulse?"   ____
4. Do you use signs to aid your customers in shopping?   ____

Promotion
1. Are you familiar with the strengths and weaknesses of various promotional methods?   ____
2. Do you participate in cooperative advertising?   ____
3. Do you ask customers to refer your business to friends and relatives?   ____
4. Do you make use of community projects or publicity?   ____

FIGURE 20-7

A Management Audit Form for Small Retailers—Selected Questions

These questions cover areas that are the basis for retailing. You can use this form to evaluate your current status and, perhaps, to rethink certain decisions. Answer YES or NO to each question.

Source: Adapted by the authors from Michael W. Little, *Marketing Checklist for Small Retailers* (Washington, DC: U.S. Small Business Administration, Management Aids Number 4.012).

✓ A long-term organizational mission is clearly articulated.   ____

✓ The current status of the firm is taken into consideration when setting future plans.   ____

✓ Sustainable competitive advantages are actively pursued.   ____

✓ Company weaknesses have been identified and minimized.   ____

✓ The management style is compatible with the firm's way of doing business.   ____

✓ There is a logical short-run and long-run approach to the firm's chosen line of business.   ____

✓ There are specific, realistic, and measurable short- and long-term goals.   ____

✓ These goals guide strategy development and resource allocation.   ____

✓ The characteristics and needs of the target market are known.   ____

✓ The strategy is tailored to the chosen target market.   ____

✓ Customers are extremely loyal.   ____

✓ There are systematic plans prepared for each element of the strategy mix.   ____

✓ All important uncontrollable factors are monitored.   ____

✓ The overall strategy is integrated.   ____

✓ Short-, moderate-, and long-term plans are compatible.   ____

✓ The firm knows how each merchandise line, for-sale service, and business format stands in the marketplace.   ____

✓ Tactics are carried out in a manner consistent with the strategic plan.   ____

✓ The strategic plan and its elements are adequately communicated.   ____

✓ Unbiased feedback is regularly sought for each aspect of the strategic plan.   ____

✓ Information about new opportunities and threats is sought out.   ____

✓ After enacting a strategic plan, company strengths and weaknesses, as well as successes and failures, are studied on an ongoing basis.   ____

✓ Results are studied in a manner that reduces the firm's chances of overreacting to a situation.   ____

✓ Strategic modifications are made when needed and before crises occur.   ____

✓ The firm avoids strategy flip-flops (that confuse customers, employees, suppliers, and others).   ____

✓ The company has a well-executed Web site or plans to have one shortly.   ____

FIGURE 20-8

A Retailing Effectiveness Checklist

Rate your company's effectiveness in each of the following areas on a scale of 1 to 5, with 1 being strongly agree (excellent effort) and 5 being strongly disagree (poor effort). An answer of 3 or higher signifies that improvements are necessary.

Chapter **Summary**

1. *To demonstrate the importance of integrating a retail strategy.* This chapter shows why retailers need to plan and apply coordinated strategies, and it describes how to assess success or failure. The stages of a retail strategy must be viewed as an ongoing, integrated system of interrelated steps.

2. *To examine four key factors in the development and enactment of an integrated retail strategy: planning procedures and opportunity analysis, defining productivity, performance measures, and scenario analysis.* Planning procedures can be optimized by adhering to a series of specified actions, from situation analysis to control. Opportunities need to be studied in terms of their impact on overall strategy. The sales opportunity grid is good for comparing various strategic options.

   To maximize productivity, retailers need to define exactly what productivity represents to them when they enact their strategies. Although firms should be efficient, this does not necessarily mean having the lowest possible

operating costs (which may lead to customer dissatisfaction) but rather keying spending to the performance standards required by a retailer's chosen niche (such as upscale versus discount).

By applying the right performance measures and setting standards for them, a retailer can better integrate its strategy. Measures include total sales, average sales per store, sales by goods/service category, sales per square foot, gross margins, gross margin return on investment, operating income, inventory turnover, markdown percentages, employee turnover, financial ratios, and profitability. TNS Retail Forward's performance index combines sales growth, profit growth, and return on assets.

With scenario analysis, a retailer projects the future by examining the major factors that will have an impact on its long-term performance. Contingency plans are then keyed to alternative scenarios. This is not easy.

3. *To show how industry and company data can be used in strategy planning and analysis (benchmarking and gap*

analysis). With benchmarking, a retailer sets its own standards and measures performance based on the achievements of its sector of retailing, specific competitors, the best companies, and/or its own prior actions. Through gap analysis, a retailer can compare its actual performance against its potential performance and see the areas in which it must improve.

4. *To show the value of a retail audit.* A retail strategy must be regularly monitored, evaluated, and fine-tuned or revised. The retail audit is one way to do this. It is a systematic, thorough, and unbiased review and appraisal.

The audit process has six sequential steps: (a) determining who does the audit, (b) deciding when and how often it is conducted, (c) setting the areas to be audited, (d) preparing forms, (e) conducting the audit, and (f) reporting results and recommendations to management. After the right executives read the audit report, necessary revisions in strategy should be made.

In a horizontal audit, a retailer's overall strategy and performance are assessed. In a vertical audit, one element of a strategy is reviewed in detail. Among the potential difficulties of auditing are the costs, the time commitment, the inaccuracy of performance standards, the poor cooperation from some employees, the collection of incorrect data, and unresponsive management. Some firms do not conduct audits; thus, they may find it difficult to evaluate their positions and plan for the future.

Two audit forms are presented in the chapter: a management audit for retailers and a retailing effectiveness checklist.

Key Terms

sales opportunity grid (p. 569)
performance measures (p. 573)
benchmarking (p. 573)

retail performance index (p. 577)
gap analysis (p. 578)
scenario analysis (p. 580)

retail audit (p. 581)
horizontal retail audit (p. 583)
vertical retail audit (p. 583)

Questions for Discussion

1. Why is it imperative for a firm to view its strategy as an integrated and ongoing process?

2. Develop a sales opportunity grid for a drugstore planning to add DVD rentals to its services mix.

3. Cite five performance measures commonly used by retailers, and explain what can be learned by studying each.

4. What is benchmarking? Present a five-step procedure to do retail benchmarking.

5. What are the pros and cons of the retail performance index highlighted in Table 20-4?

6. How are the terms *gap analysis* and *scenario analysis* interrelated?

7. Distinguish between horizontal and vertical retail audits. Develop a vertical audit form for a watch repair store.

8. What are the attributes of good retail auditing?

9. Distinguish among these auditors. Under what circumstances would each be preferred?
   a. Outside auditor.
   b. Company audit specialist.
   c. Company department manager.

10. Under what circumstances should a nondisguised audit be used?

11. How should management respond to the findings of an audit? What can happen if the findings are ignored?

12. Why do many retailers not conduct any form of retail audit? Are these reasons valid? Explain your answer.

Web **Exercise**

Visit the Web site of the American Customer Satisfaction Index (www.theacsi.org), click on "ACSI Scores & Commentary" and then "Scores by Industry." Go into each of the current retailing industry links. What do you conclude from reviewing these scores?

Note: Stop by our Web site (www.pearsonhighered. com/berman) to experience a number of highly interactive, appealing Web exercises based on actual company demonstrations and sample materials related to retailing.

part eight
Short Cases

CASE 1: VON MAUR: LOOKING TO THE FUTURE[C-1]

Von Maur (**www.vonmaur.com**) is a 22-unit, Iowa-based department store chain with annual sales revenues of $230 million and 3,000 employees. Founded in 1872, the chain features upscale clothing, shoes, cosmetics, and fashion accessories. From 2003 through 2008, Von Maur opened two new stores annually. Although the chain's growth has focused on the geographic middle of the United States, it has begun to open new store units further south, such as in Tennessee and Oklahoma.

The chain's strategy, based on unique brands and high levels of customer service, seems to be working well. Unlike larger chains, Von Maur stocks merchandise from smaller firms that are out of favor at larger chains because they do not have the ability to cross-dock the goods. This gives Von Maur exclusive merchandise. Its buyers and salespeople are also given a large degree of latitude. Buyers can track customer requests through want books, and salespeople can even call customers to let them know that their favorite products have recently been marked down.

According to Jim von Maur, the chain's president: "Our buyers are doing a wonderful job of bringing in exciting products our customers want, and we're benefiting from a reputation for excellent service. Whether times are up or down, people are always looking for quality service."

Unlike many major chains that use frequent markdowns to build store traffic, Von Maur takes markdowns only when necessary to clear slow-selling merchandise. This gives store personnel ample opportunity to sell goods at full price and reinforces the notion among consumers that Von Maur's markdowns are meaningful.

Recently, Von Maur began to promote its goods and services via E-mail. Unlike other retailers that send out as many as three E-mails a day to some consumers, Von Maur uses E-mail selectively. Its offers are more carefully tailored to a customer's past purchase history. In 2006, the chain launched its E-commerce site, which has experienced significant growth. Although the department store managers and top executives anticipated that the Web site would mostly sell fashion accessories and basic items, they were surprised to see how well fashion products sold through this channel.

In terms of location strategy, Von Maur has opened several new stores in lifestyle and mixed-use centers. These smaller centers give the chain additional flexibility in choosing locations. As Jim von Maur notes: "Before, if we couldn't get into the traditional mall as an anchor, we were locked out of a whole market. Smaller, mixed-use centers give us easier access to new markets."

Much of Von Maur's flexibility is due to its being privately owned. Private ownership enables the firm to grow at its own pace, lets it focus on long-term profit potential as opposed to meeting analysts' expectations for each quarter, and provides the freedom to develop and implement strategies with little or no involvement from bankers or major owners of the firm's stock. Jim von Maur says: "Public companies need to focus on the bottom line to satisfy shareholders. As a private company, we can focus on what makes shopping with us special and what our shoppers want. We'll grow carefully so we don't lose what makes us special."

Questions

1. Does Von Maur have a well-integrated retail strategy? Explain your answer.
2. List 10 critical performance measures that Von Maur can use to benchmark its performance.
3. How can Von Maur utilize scenario analysis as it plans for the future?
4. In looking ahead, describe the strategic implications of Von Maur's being privately owned.

CASE 2: THE INNOVATIVE APPROACH OF UNCLE GIUSEPPE'S[C-2]

Uncle Giuseppe's (**www.uncleg.com**) is a three-unit Long Island, New York supermarket chain. Its Smithtown, Long Island, store has been described as a "culinary mecca of Italian food." It was originally designed to combine a deli, pasta shop, meat market, and fruit and vegetable stand, but it ended up being all of that and even more. As Thomas Barresi, a partner of the 33,000-square-foot store, explains, the shopping experience at Uncle Giuseppe's has the "magic of a hit record" with the ability to evoke emotion among consumers. "Our idea was to take that tradition, that food heritage, but put those stores under one roof for a completely new experience, with theater, atmosphere—and make it fun shopping."

An important part of the shopping experience is the store's atmosphere. This includes 67 strategically spaced speakers, a constant soundtrack of music (by Frank Sinatra, Tony Bennett, and other leading Italian American singers), huge murals of Rome on the walls, and a ceiling that is hand-painted with a blue sky and white clouds. No detail was spared. The store's rest room—with marble walls and floors—better resembles a prestigious restaurant's design than a supermarket's facility.

Another critical part of Uncle Giuseppe's strategy is its prepared foods section. All bakery items, except for the breads (which are baked at specialty bakeries), are prepared

[C-1]The material in this case is drawn from Meghan Flynn, "A Century of Strategy," *Retail Merchandiser* (July–August 2008), pp. 50–56.

[C-2]The material in this case is drawn from Stephen Dowdell, "All the Way," *Progressive Grocer* (June 2008), pp. 26–34.

on the premises to give Uncle Giuseppe's control over preparation and ingredient quality. The store's deli features 130 different dishes (each of which is made with a recipe approved by Thomas Barresi). Best-sellers among the prepared foods include grilled chicken, broccoli rabe, and a dietetic dish called Shrimp Delight (shrimp and spaghetti squash with a spicy fra diavolo sauce). Other favorites are fried chicken for children, Italian-style meatballs, Sicilian eggplant, and lasagna. Alongside the prepared food case is a hot grilling station that becomes a sampling station on weekends.

The store's service counter is staffed by 15 butchers and clerks. According to Barresi: "A lot of other stores have gotten away from butchers, but not us. We know that it's a cost-cutting measure, but we never look at cost first, we consider quality first, and then price." The store also purchases only American Spring lamb, not frozen imported lamb. Similarly, everything at the store's seafood counter is brought in daily from Brooklyn, New York's Fulton Fish Market. The service counter offers about 30 prepared seafood items supervised by a seafood department manager who is a skilled Italian-trained chef.

Interestingly, the chain's four owners are also partners in a wholesale produce business. So, it should come as no surprise that the store has 500 produce items. Like the meat and seafood departments, the produce department features such value-added conveniences as corn that is sold with the husks removed, peeled and pre-cut garlic, and vegetable kabobs ready for grilling with no additional preparation by the consumer.

Despite all of these culinary flourishes, Uncle Giuseppe's regularly monitors its pricing levels with those at neighboring supermarket chains. The firm's policy is to be at or below the pricing levels with local supermarket chains.

Questions

1. List 10 performance measures that are suitable for Uncle Giuseppe's.
2. Describe the pros and cons of Uncle Giuseppe's partners also having ownership of a wholesale produce business.
3. Prepare a horizontal retail audit form for Uncle Giuseppe's.
4. Prepare a vertical retail audit form for Uncle Giuseppe's to evaluate the effectiveness of its customer service.

part eight
Comprehensive Case

WHAT'S AHEAD FOR COSTCO?*

INTRODUCTION

This case is divided into two major sections. "What Is Costco?" provides an overview of the company. TNS Retail Forward's Market Positioning Model is used as a framework to analyze Costco's market strategy and execution. "What Should We Expect?" examines key management initiatives and the resulting impact on future sales and unit growth. A high-level SWOT analysis summarizes the company's competitive strengths, weaknesses, opportunities, and threats.

What Is Costco?

Costco (**www.costco.com**) is the largest U.S. membership warehouse club player with nearly one-half of total U.S. warehouse club sales. It is expected to reach more than $90 billion in annual global sales as of 2012. The company ranks among the top 10 largest retailers both in the United States and worldwide.

The firm's no-frills, self-service, members-only clubs are positioned well to attract both businesses seeking to buy in bulk and individual consumers hoping to discover a great deal while stocking up for home. It targets upscale shoppers with a treasure-hunt environment A multi-channel retailer,

---

*The material in this case is adapted by the authors from TNS Retail Forward (**www.retailforward.com**), *Costco Profile* (Columbus, OH: TNS Retail Forward, January 2008). Reprinted by permission.

Costco operates warehouse clubs; Costco Business Centers, which carry only merchandise catering to small businesses; and Costco Home, which is a furnishings-and-furniture outlet. Costco gains additional sales through its E-commerce Web sites and catalogs.

Key Markets

Costco locations are concentrated in the western United States, but are rapidly expanding to the rest of the country. At the end of 2008, Costco operated 550 clubs with 150 (27 percent of units) located outside the United States and Puerto Rico. Domestically, Costco and Sam's Club (**www.samsclub.com**) markets are beginning to blur as the two players go head-to-head throughout the nation.

Costco is pushing eastward into Sam's Club's middle-America and southern strongholds. Although market saturation constrains U.S. expansion, Costco is growing by filling in existing markets. For instance, it continues to add clubs in such saturated cities as Seattle and Los Angeles. In addition, it is beginning to experiment with a smaller format for urban areas and moving into malls as an anchor. Costco continues to increase its global presence, adding six to eight new units per year outside the United States in recent years.

Market Positioning Model

TNS Retail Forward's market positioning model provides a good framework for understanding Costco's strategy. The positioning variables on the left side of the model identify the company's market strategy objectives: target customers, core goods and services, core competition, and key appeals. Successful market positioning depends on the execution of the six key variables on the right side of the model: merchandising; pricing; promotion; customer service; location and physical facilities; and organization, systems, and processes. See Figure 1.

FIGURE 1

Market Positioning Model Applied to Costco

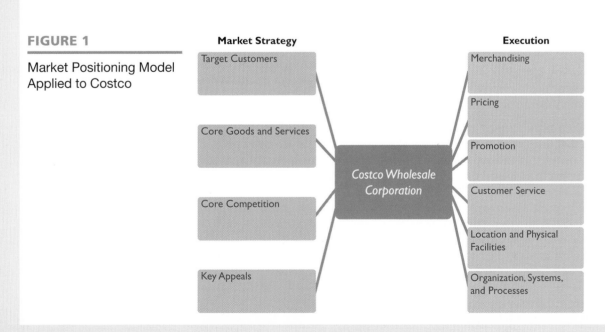

Market Strategy
- Target Customers
- Core Goods and Services
- Core Competition
- Key Appeals

Costco Wholesale Corporation

Execution
- Merchandising
- Pricing
- Promotion
- Customer Service
- Location and Physical Facilities
- Organization, Systems, and Processes

Market Strategy

Target Customers   Costco targets affluent individual consumers and small businesses by opening clubs in upscale communities. Costco has about 20 million individual members. This excludes add-on cards. Because each membership can have multiple card holders, Costco reports that there are 54 million Costco cardholders. Roughly 5.6 million Costco memberships are business customers.

Core Goods and Services   Costco's merchandise mix features a wide range, but narrow selection of some 4,000 carefully edited sku's. In comparison, Sam's Club carries around 5,000 sku's, and BJ's (www.bjs.com) typically offers 7,500 sku's. Merchandise is comprised of both national and private brands that are sold in case, carton, or multiple-pack quantities. Food accounts for 30 percent of total sales; sundries, 25 percent; hard goods, 20 percent; soft goods, 12 percent; and other, including pharmacy, optical, photo centers, and gas stations, 13 percent. More than 400 sku's are private brands or co-branded products. Through third-party providers, Costco offers loans and auto, health, and home insurance to Executive members. A quarter of the product mix is constantly changing. Unique and limited-time products create excitement. Because Costco offers a limited number of sku's, inventory turn is so rapid (12 times per year), that the company often sells a product before having to pay for it. Therefore, inventory is bought through payment terms rather than through working capital.

Core Competition   The U.S. members-only warehouse club business is highly competitive. With only three players, it is also highly concentrated. Sam's Club and BJ's are Costco's direct competitors. Yet, in any given market, Costco competes against traditional wholesalers and other food and general merchandise retailers such as supercenters, general merchandise stores, specialty chains, and gas stations. Costco, the largest player in terms of sales, is known for its on-trend merchandise. Sam's Club has the largest store network and greatest geographic coverage. It is focused on providing low-cost basics and consumables for small business owners. BJ's is a distant third on a national level, but dominates its northeastern market. BJ's offers consumables to affluent households who are looking for bulk savings. It competes more directly with supermarkets.

Key Appeals   Costco has amassed a loyal following based on a combination of three primary factors: (1) quality merchandise at low prices, (2) a treasure hunt atmosphere, and (3) one-stop shopping convenience. Costco offers a selection of quality name brands at lower prices than traditional competitors. An important element of the company's merchandising strategy is to carry only those products on which it can provide its members with significant cost savings. The company's Kirkland Signature brand has reached national-brand-name status. Cut-rate deals on upscale goods for a limited time create a treasure-hunt environment. Convenience is another draw as individuals can take care of several health-related errands through the pharmacy, hearing-aid center, and optical department while stocking up on groceries. Costco fulfills most business merchandise needs that otherwise would have to be ordered from several different wholesalers. Although traditional wholesalers sometimes charge premiums for smaller quantities, Costco's bulk sizing may be just the right amount.

Execution

Merchandising   Costco is quite innovative when it comes to selling luxury goods to drive traffic. The retailer has shown a willingness to take risks with products. High-end items have included Picasso artwork, coffins, boats, automobiles, teak lounge chairs, and platinum jewelry. Customers may come in specifically to find the latest bottle of Central Coast wines. Because of its affluent customer base, Costco has established relationships with many upscale vendors that typically would not sell their products in a discount store or a membership warehouse club atmosphere.

As a result of its emphasis on high-ticket items, Costco is able to generate average annual sales of $127 million per club at a 10.5 percent gross margin. Also, by offering a product for a limited time, Costco creates a sense of urgency or scarcity. Customers are willing to grab up the latest offer because they may not have the opportunity in the future.

Costco's food quality stands out among its peers as the company targets a more discerning customer than its competitors. For instance, a typical Costco's meat department has on-site butchers who can give advice on how to cook well-marbled cuts of beef or Australian rack of lamb. Bakers make four-layer chocolate cakes. Costco continues to expand its organic offering, including Kirkland Signature organic peanut butter and organic yogurt. Most notably, Costco has teamed up with Stoneyfield Farm (www.stoneyfieldfarm.com) to co-brand Kirkland Signature organic smoothies.

Costco also is growing its prepared food offering to include ready-to-eat chicken burritos, ribs, and hot chicken wings. The company has been recognized for its commitment to wine. In 2003, *Wine Enthusiast* named Costco the "Wine Retailer of the Year" for its willingness to carry unique and unusual wines. The Kirkland Signature line of wines is also well respected. Unlike other retailers, Costco's private-label wines target the super premium to luxury varieties.

Costco's exclusive and private brands offered at value prices represent a major point of differentiation with its peers. Kirkland Signature items currently account for one-sixth of sales, which Costco intends to increase to one-quarter over the next couple of years. Kirkland Signature brand products typically provide 20 percent savings over leading national brands. Manufacturers that refuse to accommodate Costco's demands for lower prices may find themselves displaced by a similar Costco private-brand product, which may sell just as well or better than the manufacturer's brand.

Costco's strategy also is to build co-branding partnerships with major suppliers to gain access to exclusive products. When Costco partners with upscale and/or specialty suppliers and manufacturers, such as Borghese Cosmetics, Carnegie Deli, and Martha Stewart, Costco shoppers are assured that co-branded merchandise, though offered at lower prices than the original products, has comparable quality.

Home goods is another big-ticket growth opportunity for Costco. *Furniture Today* estimates that Costco generates more than $1 billion annually in furniture and bedding sales. Costco also has grown its annual consumer electronics sales to $4 billion according to *TWICE's* "Top 100 Retailers" report, which makes the firm the ninth-largest electronics retailer in the United States.

Yet, the consumer electronics category has had its challenges. In early 2007, Costco tightened its return policy after experiencing high returns. In addition, Costco extended manufacturers' warranties and launched a technical-support program dubbed Costco Concierge. Costco tries to keep its offerings fresh with new products. In May 2007, Costco began selling Apple TVs (**www.apple.com/appletv**) in selected stores. Costco also offers home goods through its two standalone Costco Home units. Its Web sites and catalogs continue to offer more high-ticket items, such as appliances and consumer electronics.

In fiscal 2007, Costco's online sales exceeded $1 billion. Costco's goal is to grow E-commerce's annual revenues to $5 billion in the next few years. Its strategy is to complement its warehouse clubs rather than to duplicate the in-store experience. And Costco.com is a vehicle to test new product categories and create category extensions. Many of the items available online tend to be higher end with an emphasis on hard goods. Merchandise includes an extended offering of big-ticket items such as coffins, furniture, consumer electronics, jewelry, band instruments, and tires. Costco.com is even competing with home improvement retailers with its "hardware" offerings that include items such as flooring, generators, solar kits, and garage doors. Recently, Costco overhauled its Web site's overall look and improved the navigation capabilities by revamping categories and subcategories.

Pricing Costco has a competitive pricing strategy with markups limited to 14 percent over cost on manufacturer brands. Low prices are achieved through volume purchasing, efficient distribution, minimal merchandise handling, and no-frills/self-service stores. Despite a 15 percent markup cap, private brands are priced considerably below national brands.

Membership fees provide a continuing source of revenue, enabling clubs to lower prices. Business and Gold Star (individual) memberships are available for $50 a year. The Executive level ($100 per year) provides a 2 percent annual rebate capped at $500.

Store-generated coupons are limited. In 2006, Costco experimented with providing Passport coupon books in store for the first time. Management has indicated they are likely to go back to direct mailing. Additionally, Costco gas prices typically run 10 to 20 cents less than typical gas stations.

Promotion Costco does very little advertising or promoting. Instead, it relies on creating "buzz" or word-of-mouth recommendations. Costco generally limits marketing and promotions to new openings. Also, each store receives marketing dollars for canvassing businesses and for in-store promotions such as product sampling and demonstrations.

Costco's monthly magazine, *Costco Connection,* is mailed to members and distributed in stores. The magazine generates its own revenue through cooperative dollars from suppliers' coupons. It also features articles and products of interest to both small businesses and individuals. It often is used to showcase new products and co-branding partnerships. For example, one 2008 issue featured an interview with legendary exercise pioneer Jack La Lanne to highlight the Jack La Lanne Power Juicer sold exclusively at Costco.

Customer Service One of the characteristics of the warehouse club model is limited customer service. Yet, despite the no-frills warehouse atmosphere, Costco manages to build customer loyalty by providing customers with an extremely liberal return policy. Costco has a history of taking back virtually anything, regardless of purchase date and without a receipt. Recently, Costco has had to limit electronics returns to a 90-day limit due to heavy losses from excessive returns.

In-store product sampling and demonstrations provide customers with instant gratification and an opportunity to try a product before making a purchase. Costco also provides convenient shopping alternatives through its catalog and E-commerce. Many Costco warehouses have even installed in-store special-order kiosks for items such as laminate flooring, countertops, and cabinets. Those products can be ordered for delivery or store pickup. In addition, customer service is enhanced by the one-stop shopping convenience provided by the company's gas stations, pharmacies, food courts, and optical centers.

In comparison to shopping in a no-frills warehouse, Costco.com provides an added element of customer service that cannot be found in the store. The "What's New" section features the latest and limited-time offers or previews promotional savings. Perhaps, the jewelry category offers the highest level of online customer service by providing a "Diamond Education and FAQs" section. After learning about certification and diamond colors and clarity, online shoppers then can customize a diamond ring with the "Build-to-Order" feature. Higher-end jewelry can be special ordered online, as well. Costco.com provides one-stop shopping convenience because customers can arrange travel plans, purchase tickets for events, or order flowers for a loved one. The site offers gift ideas, gift baskets, and gift cards, which include restaurant and travel gift certificates. Small businesses can buy corporate gifts at Costco.com. If a customer has a shower or wedding, customized invitations and announcements can be ordered online.

Location and Physical Facilities With regard to its physical facilities, Costco has been quite flexible at adapting its club size and product offerings. For instance, it continues to open larger-than-average formats to accommodate recent merchandise initiatives. In November 2005, Costco opened a 205,000-square-foot unit in suburban Portland, Oregon (the average Costco store is 140,000 square feet), with extra space dedicated to fresh foods (including home-meal replacement) and to an expanded assortment of furniture and home furnishings. At the same time, the company has learned to edit its assortment for smaller or urban markets, particularly given its experience with smaller clubs in Japan and Taiwan. In November 2006, Costco opened a 128,000-square-foot club in downtown Vancouver. The urban club provides parking for members with a below-ground, multi-level garage. The product mix is edited with a heavier emphasis on food. Back in 2001, Costco began to anchor some regional malls as shopping malls often provide excellent real-estate opportunities.

Costco has operated in international markets for years and has patiently built market share in six countries (Canada, Great Britain, Japan, Mexico, South Korea, and Taiwan). During fiscal 2008, about a dozen new units outside the United States and Puerto Rico were opened. Costco has operated in Canada since 1986, opening an average of three new units per year, which brought the total club count to 76 Canadian locations by the end of 2008. Costco is cautious about finding the right locations and then learning to adapt its retail concept to the local market—as in the case of Japan, where it quickly had to reduce bulk package sizes to accommodate Japanese homes, which are small by U.S. standards.

Organization, Systems, and Processes Costco's distribution strategy is to deliver product to warehouse clubs either directly or through a regional network of cross-docking facilities or depots. Costco operates 11 depots in the United States and 5 abroad (including 3 depots in Canada). For fiscal 2008, Costco planned to spend $150 million upgrading and expanding its cross-docking facilities. Today, 75 percent of products are cross-docked, where container-load shipments are broken down and repackaged for shipment to individual warehouses. The other 25 percent of the merchandise is shipped directly to the club by vendors. Costco prefers to operate its own company fleet with leased trucks rather than use third-party logistics providers. Fleets serve clubs within a 100-mile radius.

Costco leverages its scale, as well as its heavy reliance on private brands, to negotiate with vendors. Vendors are expected to quote the lowest possible price. They must provide packaging and displays that meet Costco's specifications. New suppliers try to gain entry to Costco by participating in demonstration road shows, where their products can be given a trial run. All purchase orders and invoices are transmitted through electronic data interchange (EDI). Costco also prefers

to cut out the middleman and is known to challenge laws and regulations that impede its ability to work with suppliers directly. Beginning in 2004, Costco challenged Washington State's wine and liquor distribution laws prohibiting wine producers from delivering products directly to retailers, thus requiring the retailers to work through distributors. In 2006, a U.S. District Court judge ruled in Costco's favor finding that Washington's beer and wine distribution laws violated antitrust laws.

Costco continues to test new technologies such as self-checkout counters and special-order kiosks. As part of its integrated multi-channel strategy, special-order kiosks complement Costco's catalogs and E-commerce site by allowing customers to order items such as diamonds, window coverings, countertops, and caskets in the store. Costco also offers in-store photo kiosks where customers can print digital pictures. The system is tied into Costco.com's photo center powered by Snapfish (**www.snapfish.com**), whereby customers can upload images and order prints on the Internet for pickup at the nearest club's One Hour Photo Lab. Other online photo center capabilities include online image sharing with family and friends and ordering personalized gifts such as calendars, mugs, and T-shirts.

Costco is acknowledged for its good labor relations. For instance, in 2007–2008, Costco workers earned an average hourly rate of $17.25 in contrast to $10.11 for Wal-Mart. Hourly workers receive bonuses, and nearly 90 percent are eligible for health insurance. A 401(k) retirement plan with company matching is available to employees after 90 days of employment. Some 12 percent of its workers are unionized, and employee turnover is among the lowest in retail at 17 percent a year. Because of low employee theft, Costco also has an inventory shrinkage rate of just 0.2 percent of sales.

Costco's buyers are integral to the company's success because they are given full authority to make decisions and the freedom to make mistakes. Their major objective is to seek out quality products at value prices. Buyers are able to gain entry to high-end suppliers who typically would not deal with discount merchandisers.

What Should We Expect?

Costco's market positioning success has come from offering upscale products at value prices and by its ability to select the next hot-selling item or identify a new service. By being flexible and innovative, yet still conservative in exploring new merchandise categories, store formats, store concepts, and services, Costco has been able to keep up with the latest consumer trends.

TNS Retail Forward believes that the company is poised for further growth at home and abroad. With Costco's strong store productivity, Business Centers, Costco Home concept, and E-commerce, the company should continue to enjoy its leading market position.

Most of Costco's key initiatives involve continued expansion. In early 2007, Costco announced plans to grow its store base to 1,025 units by 2017. Of the 1,025 clubs, the majority (712) will be in the United States. In addition, Costco is exploring global markets such as Australia and India. Meanwhile, Costco continues to add more products online in the United States and Canada. Costco takes a cautious stance with new businesses. For instance, Costco opened its first car wash in Seattle in 2006, and its second location was slated for San Diego in 2008.

To accommodate growth, Costco continues to expand its infrastructure and hone its merchandising by partnering with vendors, tracking product trends, and developing private brands. Meanwhile, big-ticket items continue to be a growth opportunity for the company as it adds more home goods at clubs, online, and at Costco Home.

Costco leads by catering to upscale shoppers with cut-rate, limited-time, high-end products. Its treasure-hunt environment drives traffic, and its E-commerce and in-store kiosks offer a broader assortment than what ordinarily can be found in clubs. Its private brands are well respected and often outsell national brands. Costco successfully relies on vendor-paid inventory by selling products before paying for them. With a stable management team, Costco has nurtured good employee and customer relations, which translates into public goodwill. Yet, Costco relocates a number of stores each year—suggesting that its older locations are a weakness. Also, Costco operates with razor-thin profit margins (less than 2 percent) and has a relatively low household penetration (12 percent of monthly shoppers compared with 14 percent for Sam's). Yet, the warehouse club channel's outlook is healthy, and Costco continues to grow ancillary services, new concepts, and global markets. However, finding affordable real-estate will be tricky as it in-fills existing markets and encounters more cannibalization and cross-channel competition. Figure 2 shows a detailed SWOT analysis.

TNS Retail Forward expects Costco's sales growth to slow, but still remain strong at a compound annual growth rate of 7.3 percent over the 2008–2012 period, compared with 10.7 percent over the prior five years. Unit growth also will slow to a compound annual rate of 4.1 percent through 2012, which is slower than the 5.5 percent rate during 2002–2007. Costco will most certainly introduce both large and small formats, depending on the market. Also, unit growth will slow as E-commerce sales continue to take off.

Questions

1. What is Costco? Why is it so successful with upscale shoppers?
2. What could other retailers—both discounters and full-service retailers—learn from Costco?
3. Assess Costco's strategy in terms of its product mix of 4,000 sku's and its key appeals.
4. What are the basic principles underlying Costco's merchandising strategy?
5. Costco spends very little on promotion efforts. How is it able to attract shoppers without greater expenditures?
6. Describe the ideal location and store format for new Costco stores.
7. In looking to the future, discuss the SWOT analysis of Costco shown in Figure 2—from the perspectives of both Costco and Sam's Club.

FIGURE 2

SWOT Analysis of Costco

- **Strengths**
  - Channel leader
  - Affluent core customer
  - Treasure-hunt atmosphere
  - Multi-channel offer
  - Popular private labels
  - Supplier-financed inventory
  - Nimble
  - Strong corporate culture
  - Goodwill with public

- **Weaknesses**
  - Older locations
  - Razor-thin profit margins (<2%)
  - Relatively low household penetration

- **Opportunities**
  - Ancillary services
  - New concepts
  - North American and global store growth

- **Threats**
  - Real-estate issues
  - Cannibalization
  - Competition from single-category killers

Appendix   Careers in Retailing

OVERVIEW

A person looking for a career in retailing has two broad possibilities: owning a business or working for a retailer. One alternative does not preclude the other. Many people open their own retail businesses after getting experience as employees. A person can also choose franchising, which has elements of both entrepreneurship and managerial assistance (as discussed in Chapter 4).

Regardless of the specific retail career path chosen, recent college graduates often gain personnel and profit-and-loss responsibilities faster in retailing than in any other major sector of business. After an initial training program, an entry-level manager supervises personnel, works on in-store displays, interacts with customers, and reviews sales and other data on a regular basis. An assistant buyer helps in planning merchandise assortments, interacting with suppliers, and outlining the promotion effort. Our Web site (**www.pearsonhighered.com/berman**) has loads of career-related materials: We

- ► Have a table describing dozens of positions in retailing.
- ► Present career paths for several leading retailers across a variety of formats.
- ► Offer advice on résumé writing (complete with a sample résumé), interviewing, and internships.
- ► Highlight retailing-related information from the *Occupational Outlook Handbook.*
- ► Present links to a number of popular career sites, including 200 retailers' sites.

The Bright Future of a Career in Retailing

Consider these observations from Careers-in-Marketing.com, Macy's, and the National Retail Federation. According to Careers-in-Marketing.com:

> Retail is one of the fastest growing, most dynamic parts of the world economy. Careers in retail are people-oriented, fast-paced, and exciting. Retailing is worth taking a good look at, particularly if you are looking for a service-oriented, entrepreneurial profession. The options are many, including store management, buying, merchandising, and central management. There's also the booming area of online retail. If you are interested in technology, marketing, and retail, this may be the area for you.[1]

Macy's, Inc. is one of the world's leading retailers, and has a very flexible approach in choosing its high-level executives from many possible retail career paths:

> We are not only the kind of company that will help you discover and grow your interests and talents. It is our philosophy and practice to develop and promote talent from within the company—a fact that attests to the potential of career movement within Macy's, Inc. At a company like ours, your career can be a mosaic of positions in retail stores (sales, management), merchandising (buying, planning), and support operations (systems, credit, logistics, etc.).
>
> Sue joined our team as an executive trainee in the early years of her career. After spending some time in our training program learning the ropes, she moved through a series of diverse positions as an assistant buyer, sales manager, buyer, assistant store manager, store manager, divisional merchandise manager, general merchandise manager, EVP/director of stores, president-retail division,

chairman and CEO-retail division, and group president before reaching her rank as vice chair. She is also one of only seven executive officers in Macy's, Inc.'s corporate management structure. Sue's leadership today is helping Macy's, Inc. to better define its future strategy for providing superior merchandise assortments, value, and excitement on the sales floor. She is especially attuned to satisfying the customer who relies on our department stores for fashion, convenience, and service.

Diana worked her way up to the regional merchandise manager level—a path that included stops along the way as a buyer, department sales manager, group sales manager, and merchandising team manager. She's recently been promoted again. So in the progression of her career, why has Diana chosen to stay with us? In her own words, she assures us its because we offer something that's very important to both her career and lifestyle—opportunity. "I like the fact that Macy's, Inc. is, in many ways, a global business. There is not only the opportunity to move and advance within my current position, but there is an option to relocate." There are thousands of Sues and Dianas in Macy's, Inc.[2]

At its "Retail Careers Center" Web site (**www.nrffoundation.com/CareersCenter/ default.asp**), the National Retail Federation offers a lot of valuable advice and resources:

> Experience retail. With so many diverse career paths, the retail industry gives everyone the opportunity to explore their passion and interests. Our resources will excite and inspire you for a career in retail! Watch our "Go Retail!" video (**www. nrffoundation.com/CareersCenter/GoRetail.asp**), designed to promote retail as a high-energy and fast-growing industry. The video features interviews from retail CEOs and corporate employees and covers the wide array of career choices within the industry. Explore career areas and job opportunities in: marketing/advertising, store operations, loss prevention, store management, finance, human resources, IT and E-commerce, sales and sales-related, distribution, logistics, supply chain management, merchandise buying/planning, and entrepreneurship.[3]

Owning a Business

Owning a retail business is popular, and many opportunities exist. Most retail outlets are sole proprietorships; and many of today's giants began as independents, including Wal-Mart, Home Depot, J.C. Penney, McDonald's, Sears, The Cheesecake Factory, and Mrs. Fields. Consider the saga of Wendy's (**www.wendys.com/about_us/story.jsp**):

> When Dave Thomas opened the first Wendy's Old Fashioned Hamburgers restaurant, he had created something new and different—high-quality food made with the freshest ingredients, served the way the customer wanted. Quality was so important to Dave that he put the phrase "Quality is our Recipe" on the logo. Today, that passion for quality remains our number one priority at every Wendy's around the world. And it all began in 1969 with a single restaurant in Columbus, Ohio.

Wendy's is now part of the Wendy's/Arby's Group, the third largest U.S. quick-service restaurant chain, with more than 10,000 corporate-owned or franchised restaurants and systemwide sales of $12 billion.

Too often, people overlook the possibility of owning a retail business. Initial investments can be quite modest (several thousand dollars). Direct marketing (both mail order and Web retailing), direct selling, and service retailing often require relatively low initial investments—as do various franchises. Financing may also be available from banks, suppliers, store-fixture firms, and equipment companies.

Opportunities as a Retail Employee

As we've noted before, in the United States, 25 million people are employed by traditional retailers. This does not include millions of others employed by firms such as banks, insurance companies, and airlines. More people work in retailing than in any other industry.

Career opportunities are plentiful because of the number of new retail businesses that open and the labor intensity of retailing. Thousands of new outlets open each year in the United States, and certain segments of retailing are growing at particularly rapid rates. Retailers such as Wal-Mart and Costco also plan to open many new stores in foreign markets. The increased employment from new store openings and the sales growth of retail formats (such as supercenters) also mean there are significant opportunities for personal advancement for talented retail personnel. Every time a chain opens a new outlet, there is a need for a store manager and other management-level people.

Selected retailing positions, career paths, and compensation ranges are described next.

Types of Positions in Retailing

Employment is not confined to buying and merchandising. Retail career opportunities also encompass advertising, public relations, credit analysis, marketing research, warehouse management, data processing, personnel management, accounting, and real-estate. Look at the table ("Selected Positions in Retailing") in the career section of our Web site for a list and description of a wide range of retailing positions. Some highly specialized jobs may be available only in large retail firms.

The type of position a person seeks should be matched with the type of retailer likely to have such a position. Chain stores and franchises typically have real-estate divisions. Department stores and chain stores usually have large human resource departments. Mail-order firms often have advertising production departments. If one is interested in travel, a buying position or a job with a retailer having geographically dispersed operations should be sought.

Figures 1 and 2 show the retailing experiences of two diverse college graduates.

Glorie Delamin

TYPE OF STORE:
Office Superstore

HEADQUARTERS:
Framingham, Mass.

Glorie Delamin knew what she wanted before graduating last May, and she got it. She went from a career fair to a career at Staples. Originally an accounting major, she realized she wanted to pursue the retail route after a good experience as an assistant manager at a Conroy's store. She switched to a major in business administration with an emphasis in retail and earned a certificate in marketing at California State University in Los Angeles.

She started last June, and is presently operations manager at a Staples store in Glendale, Calif. "Staples is currently a great opportunity. I'm fortunate that I got in at such a good time. We're expanding and growing at a rapid rate. There's new Web site opportunities now as well."

Like many in retail, she loves that she's not anchored down to a desk from 9 to 5. Her workday is flexible. One day she works on plan-o-grams and store layouts; another, she is hiring people and always making sure everyone's duties are completed. About 60 percent of the time, she's roaming the sales floor, and she enjoys this one-on-one contact with customers.

"The most challenging part of my job is being able to satisfy customers' needs, but it's one of the best parts as well," she adds. "Our store is in an area where we get a lot of regular customers, and we're constantly talking to them. We feel really close to them because of the personal contact we get on a daily basis."

Recruits learn about satisfying customer's needs in the in-store manager trainee program that also covers merchandising and taking inventory—basically the ropes of the operation. Staples' program features workshops where trainees role-play in-store scenarios. Stores usually have three managers—general, sales and operations—and trainees see firsthand what the different positions entail.

Delamin's advice to upcoming graduates? "Take advantage of your school's career fairs, career center, and contacts. They're really useful and could lead you right into a job after school."

It worked for her. ∎

FIGURE 1

Staples

Source: Reprinted by permission of *DSN Retailing Today.*

Michael Hines

TYPE OF STORE:
Consumer Electronics Chain

HEADQUARTERS:
Eden Prairie, Minn.

After teaching abroad, working in real estate and getting his MBA, retail was the last place Michael Hines thought he would end up. But, he's found it to be the perfect career for him.

He earned his bachelor's degree in psychology from the University of Notre Dame and his MBA from Vanderbilt University before working for Best Buy, where he is presently project manager for small business development. He's proof that there's a lot of room to move up in retail, even with an advanced degree. In fact, Best Buy offers scholarships to help workers pay for MBAs. And getting your MBA pays: according to Hines, starting salaries, not including the stock options, are around $70,000 to $80,000 annually with this additional degree.

As school ended, he took advantage of an alumni contact at Best Buy, adding that many college Web sites and career centers make similar information available.

"The best part of my job is that I get to work with bright, dynamic people from very diverse backgrounds," says Hines. "It's very intellectually stimulating and very rewarding."

Hines works on cross-functional teams, addressing issues like logistics, advertising, development and brand management. There's a lot to retail that's behind-the-scenes. He's only been with the company a few months, but he's already well into the swing of things.

"It's very challenging. The company puts a lot of trust in me and really respects my opinion. What we're doing is very entrepreneurial, and I get a lot of hands-on assignments on different sides of the company."

What kind of people fit in at Best Buy? "You have to be a fun-loving person, not take yourself too seriously, enjoy life outside of the workplace," adds Hines. "Best Buy wants its employees to have time to play. They feel it makes employees well rounded and more productive overall."

Respect, fun, challenges, growth opportunity all at one job? Hines should know, that's why he's sticking with retail. ■

FIGURE 2

Best Buy

Source: Reprinted by permission of *DSN Retailing Today.*

Career Paths and Compensation in Retailing

For college graduates, executive training programs at larger retailers offer good learning experiences and advancement potential. These firms often offer careers in merchandising and nonmerchandising areas.

Here is how a new college graduate could progress in a career path at a typical department store or specialty store chain: He or she usually begins with a training program (lasting from three months to a year or more) on how to run a merchandise department. That program often involves on-the-job and classroom experiences. On-the-job training includes working with records, reordering stock, planning displays, and supervising salespeople. Classroom activities include learning how to evaluate vendors, analyze computer reports, forecast fashion trends, and administer store policy.

After initial training, the person becomes an entry-level operations manager (often called a sales manager, assistant department manager, or department manager—depending on the firm) or an assistant buyer. An entry-level manager or assistant buyer works under the direction of a seasoned department (group) manager or buyer and analyzes sales, assists in purchasing goods, handles reorders, and helps with displays. The new manager supervises personnel and learns store operations; the assistant buyer is more involved in purchases than operations. Depending on the retailer, either person may follow the same type of career path, or the entry-level operations manager may progress up the store management ladder and the assistant buyer up the buying ladder.

During this time, the responsibilities and duties depend on the department (group) manager's or buyer's willingness to delegate and teach. In a situation where a manager or buyer has authority to make decisions, the entry-level manager or assistant buyer will usually be given more responsibility. If a firm has centralized management, a manager (buyer) is more limited in his or her responsibilities, as is the entry-level manager or assistant buyer. Further, an assistant buyer will gain more experience if he or she is in a firm near a wholesale market center and can make trips to the market to buy merchandise.

The next step in a department store or specialty store chain's career path is promotion to department (group) manager or buyer. This position is entrepreneurial—running a business. The manager or buyer selects merchandise, develops a promotional campaign, decides which items to reorder, and oversees personnel and record keeping. For some retailers, *manager* and *buyer* are synonymous. For others, the distinction is as just explained for entry-level positions. Generally, a person is considered for promotion to manager or buyer after two years.

Large department store and specialty store chains have additional levels of personnel to plan, supervise, and assess merchandise departments. On the store management side, there can be group managers, store managers, branch vice-presidents, and others. On the buying side, there can be divisional managers, merchandising vice-presidents, and others.

At many firms, advancement is indicated by specific career paths. This lets employees monitor their performance, know the next career step, and progress in a clear manner. Several retail career paths are shown in the careers section of our Web site.

Table 1 lists compensation ranges for personnel in a number of retailing positions.

TABLE 1 **Typical Compensation Ranges for Personnel in Selected Retailing Positions**

Position	Compensation Range
Operations	
Customer service representative	$25,000 − $50,000+
Department manager—soft-line retailer	$30,000 − $35,000+
Store management trainee	$30,000 − $35,000+
Department manager—department store	$30,000 − $35,000+
Department manager—mass merchandiser	$30,000 − $35,000+
Department manager—hard-line retailer	$30,000 − $35,000+
Warehouse director	$30,000 − $90,000+
Store manager—specialty store, home center, drugstore	$32,000 − $70,000+
Store manager—soft-line retailer	$35,000 − $75,000+
Customer service supervisor	$40,000 − $60,000+
Security director	$42,000 − $70,000+
Store manager—department store	$45,000 − $85,000+
Operations director	$60,000 − $100,000+
Merchandising	
Assistant buyer	$25,000 − $40,000+
Buyer—specialty store, home center, drugstore, department store	$35,000 − $80,000+
Buyer—discount store	$35,000 − $85,000+
Buyer—national chain	$45,000 − $85,000+
Divisional merchandise manager	$60,000 − $100,000+
General merchandise manager—drugstore, home center	$65,000 − $100,000+
General merchandise manager—specialty store, department store	$70,000 − $125,000+
General merchandise manager—discount store, national chain	$70,000 − $125,000+
Senior merchandising executive	$80,000 − $250,000+
Marketing Research	
Market research junior analyst	$30,000 − $35,000+
Market research analyst	$30,000 − $45,000+
Market research senior analyst	$40,000 − $55,000+
Market research assistant director	$45,000 − $65,000+
Market research director	$55,000 − $75,000+

(Continued)

TABLE 1 Typical Compensation Ranges for Personnel in Selected Retailing Positions *(Continued)*

Position	Compensation Range
Top Management	
Senior human resources executive	$60,000 − $140,000+
Senior advertising executive	$65,000 − $110,000+
Senior real-estate executive	$65,000 − $120,000+
Senior financial executive	$85,000 − $200,000+
President	$250,000 − $3,000,000+
Chairman of the board	$350,000 − $10,000,000+
Other	
Public relations specialist	$35,000 − $85,000+
Retail sales analyst	$38,000 − $90,000+
Supply chain specialist	$40,000 − $60,000+

Source: Estimated by the authors from various sources.

Getting Your First Position as a Retail Professional

The key steps in getting your first professional position in retailing are the search for opportunities, interview preparation, and the evaluation of options. You must devote sufficient time to these steps so your job hunt progresses as well as possible.

Searching for Career Opportunities in Retailing

Various sources should be consulted. These include your school placement office, company directories and Web sites, classified ads in your local newspapers, Web job sites, and networking (with professors, friends, neighbors, and family members). Here are some hints to consider:

▶ *Do not "place all your eggs in one basket."* Do not rely too much on friends and relatives. They may be able to get you an interview but not a guaranteed job offer.
▶ *Be serious and systematic in your career search.* Plan in advance, and do not wait until the recruiting season starts at your school to generate a list of retail employers.
▶ *Use directories with lists of retailers and current job openings.* Online listings include CareerBuilder.com Retail Jobs (**http://retail.careerbuilder.com**), AllRetailJobs.com (**www.allretailjobs.com**), Work in Retail.com (**www.workinretail.com**), and I Hire Retail (**www.ihireretail.com**). Also visit our Web site (**www.pearsonhighered.com/berman**).
▶ *Rely on the "law of large numbers."* In sending out résumés, you may have to contact at least 10 to 20 retailers to get just two to four interviews.
▶ *Make sure your résumé and cover letter highlight your best qualities.* These may include school honors, officer status in an organization, work experience, computer skills, and the proportion of college tuition you paid. Our Web site shows a sample résumé for an entry-level position in retailing.
▶ *Show your résumé to at least one professor.* Be receptive to constructive comments. Remember, your professor's goal is to help you get the best possible first job.

Preparing for the Interview

The initial and subsequent interviews for a position, which may last for 20 to 30 minutes or longer, play a large part in determining if you get a job offer. For that reason, you should be prepared for all interviews:

▶ *Adequately research each firm.* Be aware of its goods/service category, current size, overall retail strategy, competitive developments, and so on.

▶ *Anticipate questions and plan general responses.* "Tell me about yourself." "Why are you interested in a retailing career?" "Why do you want a job with us?" "What are your major strengths?" "Your major weaknesses?" "What do you want to be doing five years from now?" "What would your prior boss say about you?" In preparation, role-play your answers to these questions with someone.

▶ *Treat every interview as if it is the most important one.* Otherwise, you may not be properly prepared if the position turns out to be more desirable than you originally thought. And remember that you represent both your college and yourself at all interviews.

▶ *Be prepared to raise your own questions when asked to do so in the interview.* They should relate to career paths, training, and opportunities for advancement.

▶ *Dress appropriately and be well groomed.*

▶ *Verify the date and place of the interview.* Be prompt.

▶ *Have a pen and pad (or PDA) available to record information after the interview is over.*

▶ *Write a note to the interviewer within a week to thank him or her for spending time with you and to express a continuing interest in the company.*

Evaluating Retail Career Opportunities

Job seekers often place too much emphasis on initial salary or the firm's image in assessing career opportunities. Many other factors should be considered, as well:

▶ What activities do you like?

▶ What are your personal strengths and weaknesses?

▶ What are your current and long-term goals?

▶ Do you want to work for an independent, a chain, or a franchise operation?

▶ Does the opportunity offer an acceptable and clear career path?

▶ Does the opportunity include a formal training program?

▶ Will the opportunity enable you to be rewarded for good performance?

▶ Will you have to relocate?

▶ Will each promotion in the company result in greater authority and responsibility?

▶ Is the compensation level fair relative to other offers?

▶ Can a good employee move up the career path much faster than an average one?

▶ If owning a retail firm is a long-term goal, which opportunity is the best preparation?

Glossary

Additional Markup Increase in a retail price above the original markup when demand is unexpectedly high or costs are rising. (p. 485)

Additional Markup Percentage Looks at total dollar additional markups as a percentage of net sales: (p. 486)

$$\text{Additional markup percentage} = \frac{\text{Total dollar additional markups}}{\text{Net sales (in \$)}}$$

Addition to Retail Percentage Measures a price rise as a percentage of the original price: (p. 486)

$$\text{Addition to retail percentage} = \frac{\text{New price} - \text{Original price}}{\text{Original price}}$$

Advertising Paid, nonpersonal communication transmitted through out-of-store mass media by an identified sponsor. (p. 530)

Affinity Exists when the stores at a given location complement, blend, and cooperate with one another, and each benefits from the others' presence. (p. 290)

All-You-Can-Afford Method Promotional budgeting procedure in which a retailer first allots funds for each element of the strategy mix except promotion. The funds that are left go to the promotional budget. (p. 548)

Americans with Disabilities Act (ADA) Mandates that persons with disabilities be given appropriate access to retailing facilities. (p. 49)

Analog Model Computerized site selection tool in which potential sales for a new store are estimated based on sales of similar stores in existing areas, competition at a prospective location, the new store's expected market share at that location, and the size and density of a location's primary trading area. (p. 261)

Application Blank Usually the first tool used to screen applicants. It provides data on education, experience, health, reasons for leaving prior jobs, outside activities, hobbies, and references. (p. 327)

Assets Any items a retailer owns with a monetary value. (p. 337)

Asset Turnover Performance measure based on a retailer's net sales and total assets. It is equal to net sales divided by total assets. (p. 338)

Assortment Selection of merchandise carried by a retailer. It includes both the breadth of product categories and the variety within each category. (p. 396)

Assortment Display An open or closed display in which a retailer exhibits a wide range of merchandise. (p. 519)

Assortment Merchandise Apparel, furniture, autos, and other products for which the retailer must carry a variety of products in order to give customers a proper selection. (p. 392)

Atmosphere (Atmospherics) Reflection of a store's physical characteristics that are used to develop an image and draw customers. The concept is also applicable to nonstore retailers. (p. 508)

Attitudes (Opinions) Positive, neutral, or negative feelings a person has about different topics. (p. 194)

Augmented Customer Service Encompasses the actions that enhance the shopping experience and give retailers a competitive advantage. (p. 33)

Automatic Reordering System Computerized approach that combines a perpetual inventory and reorder point calculations. (p. 458)

Bait-and-Switch Advertising Illegal practice in which a retailer lures a customer by advertising goods and services at exceptionally low prices and then tries to convince the person to buy a better, more expensive substitute that is available. The retailer has no intention of selling the advertised item. (p. 471)

Balanced Tenancy Occurs when stores in a planned shopping center complement each other as to the quality and variety of their product offerings. (p. 280)

Balance Sheet Itemizes a retailer's assets, liabilities, and net worth at a specific time—based on the principle that assets equal liabilities plus net worth. (p. 337)

Basic Stock List Specifies the inventory level, color, brand, style category, size, package, and so on for every staple item carried by a retailer. (p. 392)

Basic Stock Method Inventory level planning tool wherein a retailer carries more items than it expects to sell over a specified period: (p. 448)

$$\text{Basic stock} = \frac{\text{Average monthly stock at retail}}{} - \text{Average monthly sales}$$

Battle of the Brands The competition between manufacturers and retailers for shelf space and profits, whereby manufacturer, private, and generic brands fight each other for more space and control. (p. 402)

Benchmarking Occurs when the retailer sets its own standards and measures performance based on the achievements in its sector, specific competitors, high-performance firms, and/or its own prior actions. (p. 573)

Bifurcated Retailing Denotes the decline of middle-of-the-market retailing due to the popularity of both mass merchandising and niche retailing. (p. 68)

Book Inventory System Keeps a running total of the value of all inventory at cost as of a given time. This is done by recording purchases and adding them to existing inventory value; sales are subtracted to arrive at the new current inventory value (all at cost). It is also known as a perpetual inventory system. (p. 440)

Bottom-Up Space Management Approach Exists when planning starts at the individual product level and then proceeds to the category, total store, and overall company levels. (p. 360)

Box (Limited-Line) Store Food-based discounter that focuses on a small selection of items, moderate hours of operation (compared with supermarkets), few services, and limited manufacturer brands. (p. 136)

Budgeting Outlines a retailer's planned expenditures for a given time based on expected performance. (p. 345)

Bundled Pricing Involves a retailer combining several elements in one basic price. (p. 485)

Business Format Franchising Arrangement in which the franchisee receives assistance in site location, quality control, accounting, startup practices, management training, and responding to problems—besides the right to sell goods and services. (p. 108)

Buyer Person responsible for selecting the merchandise to be carried by a retailer and setting a strategy to market that merchandise. (p. 390)

Canned Sales Presentation Memorized, repetitive speech given to all customers interested in a particular item. (p. 541)

Capital Expenditures Retail expenditures that are long-term investments in fixed assets. (p. 350)

Case Display Interior display that exhibits heavier, bulkier items than racks hold. (p. 519)

Cash Flow Relates the amount and timing of revenues received to the amount and timing of expenditures made during a specific time. (p. 349)

Category Killer (Power Retailer) Very large specialty store featuring an enormous selection in its product category and relatively low prices. It draws consumers from wide geographic areas. (p. 137)

Category Management Merchandising technique that improves productivity. It focuses on product category results rather than the performance of individual brands or models. (p. 403)

Census of Population Supplies a wide range of demographic data for all U.S. cities and surrounding vicinities. These data are organized on a geographic basis. (p. 266)

Central Business District (CBD) Hub of retailing in a city. It is synonymous with "downtown." The CBD has the greatest density of office buildings and stores. (p. 277)

Chain Retailer that operates multiple outlets (store units) under common ownership. It usually engages in some level of centralized (or coordinated) purchasing and decision making. (p. 106)

Channel Control Occurs when one member of a distribution channel can dominate the decisions made in that channel by the power it possesses. (p. 113)

Channel of Distribution All of the businesses and people involved in the physical movement and transfer of ownership of goods and services from producer to consumer. (p. 7)

Chargebacks Practice of retailers, at their discretion, making deductions in the manufacturers' bills for infractions ranging from late shipments to damaged and expired merchandise. (p. 415)

Class Consciousness Extent to which a person desires and pursues social status. (p. 194)

Classification Merchandising Allows firms to obtain more financial data by subdividing each specified department into further categories for related types of merchandise. (p. 446)

Cognitive Dissonance Doubt that occurs after a purchase is made, which can be alleviated by customer after-care, money-back guarantees, and realistic sales presentations and advertising campaigns. (p. 205)

Collaborative Planning, Forecasting, and Replenishment (CPFR) Emerging technique for larger firms whereby there is a holistic approach to supply chain management among a network of trading partners. (p. 425)

Combination Store Unites supermarket and general merchandise sales in one facility, with general merchandise typically accounting for 25 to 40 percent of total sales. (p. 135)

Community Shopping Center Moderate-sized, planned shopping facility with a branch department store and/or a category killer store, in addition to several smaller stores. About 20,000 to 100,000 people, who live or work within 10 to 20 minutes of the center, are served by this location. (p. 284)

Compensation Includes direct monetary payments to employees (such as salaries, commissions, and bonuses) and indirect payments (such as paid vacations, health and life insurance benefits, and retirement plans). (p. 330)

Competition-Oriented Pricing Approach in which a firm sets prices in accordance with competitors'. (p. 476)

Competitive Advantages Distinct competencies of a retailer relative to competitors. (p. 71)

Competitive Parity Method Promotional budgeting procedure by which a retailer's budget is raised or lowered based on competitors' actions. (p. 548)

Computerized Checkout Used by large and small retailers to efficiently process transactions and monitor inventory. Cashiers ring up sales or pass items by scanners. Computerized registers instantly record and display sales, customers get detailed receipts, and inventory data are stored in a memory bank. (p. 367)

Concentrated Marketing Selling goods and services to one specific group. (p. 71)

Consignment Purchase Items not paid for by a retailer until they are sold. The retailer can return unsold merchandise. Title is not taken by the retailer; the supplier owns the goods until sold. (p. 418)

Constrained Decision Making Limits franchisee involvement in the strategic planning process. (p. 110)

Consumer Behavior The process by which people determine whether, what, when, where, how, from whom, and how often to purchase goods and services. (p. 201)

Consumer Cooperative Retail firm owned by its customer members. A group of consumers invests in the company, elects officers, manages operations, and shares the profits or savings that accrue. (p. 114)

Consumer Decision Process Stages a consumer goes through in buying a good or service: stimulus, problem awareness, information search, evaluation of alternatives, purchase, and post-purchase behavior. Demographics and lifestyle factors affect this decision process. (p. 202)

Consumerism Involves the activities of government, business, and other organizations that protect people from practices infringing on their rights as consumers. (p. 49)

Consumer Loyalty (Frequent Shopper) Programs Reward a retailer's best customers, those with whom it wants long-lasting relationships. (p. 38)

Contingency Pricing Arrangement by which a service retailer does not get paid until after the service is satisfactorily performed. This is a special form of flexible pricing. (p. 483)

Control Phase in the evaluation of a firm's strategy and tactics in which a semiannual or annual review of the retailer takes place. (p. 78)

Controllable Variables Aspects of business that the retailer can directly affect (such as hours of operation and sales personnel). (p. 73)

Control Units Merchandise categories for which data are gathered. (p. 445)

Convenience Store Well-located food-oriented retailer that is open long hours and carries a moderate number of items. It is small, with average to above-average prices and average atmosphere and services. (p. 133)

Conventional Supermarket Departmentalized food store with a wide range of food and related products; sales of general merchandise are rather limited. (p. 133)

Cooperative Advertising Occurs when manufacturers or wholesalers and their retailers, or two or more retailers, share the costs of retail advertising. (p. 531)

Cooperative Buying Procedure used when a group of retailers make quantity purchases from suppliers. (p. 390)

Core Customers Consumers with whom retailers seek to nurture long relationships. They should be singled out in a firm's data base. (p. 33)

Corporation Retail firm that is formally incorporated under state law. It is a legal entity apart from individual officers (or stockholders). (p. 61)

Cost Complement Average relationship of cost to retail value for all merchandise available for sale during a given time period. (p. 442)

Cost Method of Accounting Requires the retailer's cost of each item to be recorded on an accounting sheet and/or coded on a price tag or merchandise container. When a physical inventory is done, item costs must be learned, the quantity of every item in stock counted, and total inventory value at cost calculated. (p. 440)

Cost of Goods Sold Amount a retailer has paid to acquire the merchandise sold during a given time period. It equals the cost of merchandise available for sale minus the cost value of ending inventory. (pp. 336, 438)

Cost-Oriented Pricing Approach in which a retailer sets a price floor, the minimum price acceptable to the firm

so it can reach a specified profit goal. A retailer usually computes merchandise and retail operating costs and adds a profit margin to these figures. (p. 476)

Cross-Merchandising Exists when a retailer carries complementary goods and services so that shoppers are encouraged to buy more. (p. 387)

Cross-Shopping Occurs when consumers shop for a product category through more than one retail format during the year or visit multiple retailers on one shopping trip. (p. 200)

Cross-Training Enables personnel to learn tasks associated with more than one job. (p. 360)

Culture Distinctive heritage shared by a group of people. It passes on beliefs, norms, and customs. (p. 193)

Curving (Free-Flowing) Traffic Flow Presents displays and aisles in a free-flowing pattern. (p. 516)

Customary Pricing Used when a retailer sets prices for goods and services and seeks to maintain them for an extended period. (p. 481)

Customer Loyalty Exists when a person regularly patronizes a particular retailer (store or nonstore) that he or she knows, likes, and trusts. (p. 207)

Customer Satisfaction Occurs when the value and customer service provided through a retailing experience meet or exceed consumer expectations. (p. 38)

Customer Service Identifiable, but sometimes intangible, activities undertaken by a retailer in conjunction with the basic goods and services it sells. (p. 16)

Cut Case Inexpensive display, in which merchandise is left in the original carton. (p. 520)

Data-Base Management Procedure a retailer uses to gather, integrate, apply, and store information related to specific subject areas. It is a key element in a retail information system. (p. 222)

Data-Base Retailing Way to collect, store, and use relevant information on customers. (p. 152)

Data Mining Involves the in-depth analysis of information so as to gain specific insights about customers, product categories, vendors, and so forth. (p. 225)

Data Warehousing Advance in data-base management whereby copies of all the data bases in a company are maintained in one location and accessible to employees at any locale. (p. 223)

Dead Areas Awkward spaces where normal displays cannot be set up. (p. 514)

Debit Card System Computerized process whereby the purchase price of a good or service is immediately deducted from a consumer's bank account and entered into a retailer's account. (p. 366)

Demand-Oriented Pricing Approach by which a retailer sets prices based on consumer desires. It determines the range of prices acceptable to the target market. (p. 476)

Demographics Objective, quantifiable, easily identifiable, and measurable population data. (p. 191)

Department Store Large store with an extensive assortment (width and depth) of goods and services that has separate departments for purposes of buying, promotion, customer service, and control. (p. 138)

Depth of Assortment The variety in any one goods/service category (product line) with which a retailer is involved. (p. 396)

Destination Retailer Firm that consumers view as distinctive enough to become loyal to it. Consumers go out of their way to shop there. (p. 124)

Destination Store Retail outlet with a trading area much larger than that of a competitor with a less unique appeal. It offers a better merchandise assortment in its product category(ies), promotes more extensively, and/or creates a stronger image. (p. 257)

Differentiated Marketing Aims at two or more distinct consumer groups, with different retailing approaches for each group. (p. 71)

Direct Marketing Form of retailing in which a customer is first exposed to a good or service through a nonpersonal medium and then orders by mail, phone, or fax—and increasingly by computer. (p. 149)

Direct Product Profitability (DPP) Method for planning variable markups whereby a retailer finds the profitability of each category or unit of merchandise by computing adjusted per-unit gross margin and assigning direct product costs for such expenses as warehousing, transportation, handling, and selling. (p. 479)

Direct Selling Includes both personal contact with consumers in their homes (and other nonstore locations such as offices) and phone solicitations initiated by a retailer. (p. 157)

Direct Store Distribution (DSD) Exists when retailers have at least some goods shipped directly from suppliers to individual stores. It works best with retailers that also utilize electronic data interchange. (p. 428)

Discretionary Income Money left after paying taxes and buying necessities. (p. 191)

Distributed Promotion Effort Used by retailers that promote throughout the year. (p. 553)

Diversification Way in which retailers become active in business outside their normal operations—and add stores in different goods/service categories. (p. 130)

Diversified Retailer Multi-line firm with central ownership. It is also known as a retail conglomerate. (p. 318)

Dollar Control Planning and monitoring the financial merchandise investment over a stated period. (p. 438)

Downsizing Unprofitable stores closed or divisions sold off by retailers unhappy with performance. (p. 130)

Dual Marketing Involves firms engaged in more than one type of distribution arrangement. This enables those firms to appeal to different consumers, increase sales, share some costs, and maintain a good degree of strategic control. (p. 113)

Dump Bin Case display that houses piles of sale clothing, marked-down books, or other products. (p. 520)

Ease of Entry Occurs due to low capital requirements and no, or relatively simple, licensing provisions. (p. 103)

Economic Base Area's industrial and commercial structure—the companies and industries that residents depend on to earn a living. (p. 263)

Economic Order Quantity (EOQ) Quantity per order (in units) that minimizes the total costs of processing orders and holding inventory: (p. 459)

$$EOQ = \sqrt{\frac{2DS}{IC}}$$

Efficient Consumer Response (ECR) Form of order processing and fulfillment by which supermarkets are incorporating aspects of quick response inventory planning, electronic data interchange, and logistics planning. (p. 426)

Electronic Article Surveillance Involves special tags that are attached to products so that the tags can be sensed by electronic security devices at store exits. (p. 431)

Electronic Banking Includes both automatic teller machines (ATMs) and the instant processing of retail purchases. (p. 44)

Electronic Data Interchange (EDI) Lets retailers and suppliers regularly exchange information through their computers with regard to inventory levels, delivery times, unit sales, and so on, of particular items. (p. 227)

Electronic Point-of-Sale System Performs all the tasks of a computerized checkout and also verifies check and charge transactions, provides instantaneous sales reports, monitors and changes prices, sends intra- and inter-store messages, evaluates personnel and profitability, and stores data. (p. 368)

Employee Empowerment Way of improving customer service in which workers have discretion to do what they feel is needed—within reason—to satisfy the customer, even if this means bending some rules. (p. 34)

Ensemble Display Interior display whereby a complete product bundle (ensemble) is presented rather than showing merchandise in separate categories. (p. 519)

Equal Store Organization Centralizes the buying function. Branch stores become sales units with equal operational status. (p. 318)

Ethics Involves activities that are trustworthy, fair, honest, and respectful for each retailer constituency. (p. 46)

Evaluation of Alternatives Stage in the decision process where a consumer selects one good or service to buy from a list of alternatives. (p. 204)

Everyday Low Pricing (EDLP) Version of customary pricing whereby a retailer strives to sell its goods and services at consistently low prices throughout the selling season. (p. 481)

Exclusive Distribution Takes place when suppliers enter agreements with one or a few retailers to designate the latter as the only firms in specified geographic areas to carry certain brands or product lines. (p. 10)

Expected Customer Service Level of service that customers want to receive from any retailer, such as basic employee courtesy. (p. 33)

Experiential Merchandising Tactic whose intent is to convert shopping from a passive activity into a more interactive one, by better engaging the customer. (p. 523)

Experiment Type of research in which one or more elements of a retail strategy mix are manipulated under controlled conditions. (p. 235)

Extended Decision Making Occurs when a consumer makes full use of the decision process, usually for expensive, complex items with which the person has had little or no experience. (p. 205)

External Secondary Data Available from sources outside a firm. (p. 231)

Factory Outlet Manufacturer-owned store selling its closeouts, discontinued merchandise, irregulars, canceled orders, and, sometimes, in-season, first-quality merchandise. (p. 141)

Fad Merchandise Items that generate a high level of sales for a short time. (p. 392)

Family Life Cycle How a traditional family moves from bachelorhood to children to solitary retirement. (p. 193)

Fashion Merchandise Products that may have cyclical sales due to changing tastes and lifestyles. (p. 392)

Feedback Signals or cues as to the success or failure of part of a retail strategy. (p. 78)

FIFO (First-In-First-Out) Method Logically assumes old merchandise is sold first, while newer items remain in inventory. It matches inventory value with the current cost structure. (p. 441)

Financial Leverage Performance measure based on the relationship between a retailer's total assets and net worth. It is equal to total assets divided by net worth. (p. 339)

Financial Merchandise Management Occurs when a retailer specifies exactly which products (goods and services) are purchased, when products are purchased, and how many products are purchased. (p. 438)

Flea Market Location where many vendors offer a range of products at discount prices in plain surroundings. Many flea markets are located in nontraditional sites not normally associated with retailing. (p. 143)

Flexible Pricing Strategy that lets consumers bargain over selling prices; those consumers who are good at bargaining obtain lower prices than those who are not. (p. 483)

Floor-Ready Merchandise Items that are received at the store in condition to be put directly on display without any preparation by retail workers. (p. 426)

Food-Based Superstore Retailer that is larger and more diversified than a conventional supermarket but usually smaller and less diversified than a combination store. It caters to consumers' complete grocery needs and offers them the ability to buy fill-in general merchandise. (p. 134)

Forecasts Projections of expected retail sales for given time periods. (p. 391)

Franchising Contractual arrangement between a franchisor (a manufacturer, a wholesaler, or a service sponsor) and a retail franchisee, which allows the franchisee to conduct a given form of business under an established name and according to a given pattern of business. (p. 108)

Frequency Average number of times each person who is reached by a message is exposed to a retailer's promotion efforts in a specific period. (p. 552)

Fringe Trading Area Includes customers not found in primary and secondary trading areas. These are the most widely dispersed customers. (p. 257)

Full-Line Discount Store Type of department store with a broad, low-priced product assortment; all of the range of products expected at department stores; centralized checkout service; self-service; private-brand nondurables and well-known manufacturer-brand durables; less fashion-sensitive merchandise; relatively inexpensive building, equipment, and fixtures; and less emphasis on credit. (p. 140)

Functional Product Groupings Categorize and display a store's merchandise by common end use. (p. 515)

Gap Analysis Enables a company to compare its actual performance against its potential performance and then determine the areas in which it must improve. (p. 578)

Generic Brands No-frills goods stocked by some retailers. These items usually receive secondary shelf locations, have little or no promotion support, are sometimes of less quality than other brands, are stocked in limited assortments, and have plain packages. They are a form of private brand. (p. 402)

Geographic Information System (GIS) Combines digitized mapping with key locational data to graphically depict such trading-area characteristics as the demographic attributes of the population; data on customer purchases; and listings of current, proposed, and competitor locations. (p. 253)

Goal-Oriented Job Description Enumerates a position's basic functions, the relationship of each job to overall goals, the interdependence of positions, and information flows. (p. 326)

Goods Retailing Focuses on the sale of tangible (physical) products. (p. 41)

Goods/Service Category Retail firm's line of business. (p. 63)

Graduated Lease Calls for precise rent increases over a stated period of time. (p. 293)

Gravity Model Computerized site selection tool based on the premise that people are drawn to stores that are closer and more attractive than competitors'. (p. 261)

Gray Market Goods Brand-name products bought in foreign markets or goods transshipped from other retailers. They are often sold at low prices by unauthorized dealers. (p. 471)

Gross Margin Difference between net sales and the total cost of goods sold. It is also called gross profit. (p. 478)

Gross Margin Return on Investment (GMROI) Shows relationship between total dollar operating profits and the average inventory investment (at cost) by combining profitability and sales-to-stock measures: (p. 457)

$$\text{GMROI} = \frac{\text{Gross margin in dollars}}{\text{Net sales}}$$
$$\times \frac{\text{Net sales}}{\text{Average inventory at cost}}$$
$$= \frac{\text{Gross margin in dollars}}{\text{Average inventory at cost}}$$

Gross Profit Difference between net sales and the total cost of goods sold. It is also known as *gross margin*. (pp. 336, 438)

Hidden Assets Depreciated assets, such as store buildings and warehouses, that are reflected on a retailer's balance sheet at low values relative to their actual worth. (p. 337)

Hierarchy of Authority Outlines the job interactions within a company by describing the reporting relationships among employees. Coordination and control are provided. (p. 314)

Hierarchy of Effects Sequence of steps a consumer goes through in reacting to retail communications, which leads him or her from awareness to knowledge to liking to preference to conviction to purchase. (p. 550)

Horizontal Cooperative Advertising Agreement Enables two or more retailers (most often small, situated together, or franchisees of the same company) to share an ad. (p. 537)

Horizontal Price Fixing Agreement among manufacturers, among wholesalers, or among retailers to set certain prices. This is illegal, regardless of how "reasonable" prices may be. (p. 468)

Horizontal Retail Audit Analyzes a retail firm's overall performance, from mission to goals to customer satisfaction to basic retail strategy mix and its implementation in an integrated, consistent way. (p. 583)

Household Life Cycle Incorporates the life stages of both family and nonfamily households. (p. 193)

Huff's Law of Shopper Attraction Delineates trading areas on the basis of the product assortment carried at various shopping locations, travel times from the shopper's home to alternative locations, and the sensitivity of the kind of shopping to travel time. (p. 262)

Human Resource Management Recruiting, selecting, training, compensating, and supervising personnel in a manner consistent with the retailer's organization structure and strategy mix. (p. 319)

Human Resource Management Process Consists of these interrelated activities: recruitment, selection, training, compensation, and supervision. The goals are to obtain, develop, and retain employees. (p. 324)

Hypermarket Combination store pioneered in Europe that blends an economy supermarket with a discount department store. It is even larger than a supercenter. (p. 135)

Image Represents how a given retailer is perceived by consumers and others. (p. 68)

Impulse Purchases Occur when consumers buy products and/or brands they had not planned to before entering a store, reading a catalog, seeing a TV shopping show, turning to the Web, and so forth. (p. 207)

Incremental Budgeting Process whereby a firm uses current and past budgets as guides and adds to or subtracts from them to arrive at the coming period's expenditures. (p. 348)

Incremental Method Promotional budgeting procedure by which a percentage is either added to or subtracted from one year's budget to determine the next year's. (p. 548)

Independent Retailer that owns one retail unit. (p. 103)

Infomercial Program-length TV commercial (most often, 30 minutes in length) for a specific good or service that airs on cable television or on broadcast television, often at a fringe time. It is particularly worthwhile for products that benefit from visual demonstrations. (p. 154)

Information Search Consists of two parts: determining alternatives to solve the problem at hand (and where they can be bought) and learning the characteristics of alternatives. It may be internal or external. (p. 203)

Initial Markup (at Retail) Based on the original retail value assigned to merchandise less the merchandise costs, expressed as a percentage of the original retail price: (p. 478)

$$\text{Initial markup percentage (at retail)} =$$
$$\frac{\begin{array}{c}\text{Planned retail operating expenses}\\+\text{ Planned profit}+\text{Planned retail reductions}\end{array}}{\begin{array}{c}\text{Planned net sales}\\+\text{ Planned retail reductions}\end{array}}$$

Intensive Distribution Takes place when suppliers sell through as many retailers as possible. This often maximizes suppliers' sales and lets retailers offer many brands and product versions. (p. 10)

Internal Secondary Data Available within a company, sometimes from the data bank of a retail information system. (p. 230)

Internet Global electronic superhighway of computer networks that use a common protocol and that are linked by telecommunications lines and satellite. (p. 160)

Inventory Management Process whereby a firm seeks to acquire and maintain a proper merchandise assortment while ordering, shipping, handling, storing, displaying, and selling costs are kept in check. (p. 429)

Inventory Shrinkage Encompasses employee theft, customer shoplifting, vendor fraud, and administrative errors. (p. 431)

Isolated Store Freestanding retail outlet located on either a highway or a street. There are no adjacent retailers with which this type of store shares traffic. (p. 276)

Issue (Problem) Definition Step in the marketing research process that involves a clear statement of the topic to be studied. (p. 227)

Item Price Removal Practice whereby prices are marked only on shelves or signs and not on individual items. It is banned in several states and local communities. (p. 470)

Job Analysis Consists of gathering information about each job's functions and requirements: duties, responsibilities, aptitude, interest, education, experience, and physical tasks. (p. 325)

Job Motivation Drive within people to attain work-related goals. (p. 331)

Job Standardization Keeps tasks of employees with similar positions in different departments rather uniform. (p. 360)

Leader Pricing Occurs when a retailer advertises and sells selected items in its goods/service assortment at less than the usual profit margins. The goal is to increase customer traffic so as to sell regularly priced goods and services in addition to the specially priced items. (p. 484)

Leased Department Site in a retail store—usually a department, discount, or specialty store—that is rented to an outside party. (p. 111)

Liabilities Financial obligations a retailer incurs in operating a business. (p. 337)

Lifestyle Center An open-air shopping site that typically includes 150,000 to 500,000 square feet of space dedicated to upscale, well-known specialty stores. (p. 285)

Lifestyles Ways that individual consumers and families (households) live and spend time and money. (p. 191)

LIFO (Last-In-First-Out) Method Assumes new merchandise is sold first, while older stock remains in inventory. It matches current sales with the current cost structure. (p. 441)

Limited Decision Making Occurs when a consumer uses every step in the purchase process but does not spend a great deal of time on each of them. (p. 206)

Logistics Total process of planning, enacting, and coordinating the physical movement of merchandise from supplier to retailer to customer in the most timely, effective, and cost-efficient manner possible. (p. 422)

Loss Leaders Items priced below cost to lure more customer traffic. Loss leaders are restricted by some state minimum price laws. (p. 470)

Maintained Markup (at Retail) Based on the actual prices received for merchandise sold during a time period less merchandise cost, expressed as a percentage: (p. 478)

$$\text{Maintained markup percentage (at retail)} = \frac{\text{Actual retail operating expenses} + \text{Actual profit}}{\text{Actual net sales}}$$

or

$$\frac{\text{Average selling price} - \text{Merchandise cost}}{\text{Average selling price}}$$

Maintenance-Increase-Recoupment Lease Has a provision allowing rent to increase if a property owner's taxes, heating bills, insurance, or other expenses rise beyond a certain point. (p. 294)

Manufacturer (National) Brands Produced and controlled by manufacturers. They are usually well known, supported by manufacturer ads, somewhat pre-sold to consumers, require limited retailer investment in marketing, and often represent maximum product quality to consumers. (p. 400)

Markdown Reduction from the original retail price of an item to meet the lower price of another retailer, adapt to inventory overstocking, clear out shopworn merchandise, reduce assortments of odds and ends, and increase customer traffic. (p. 485)

Markdown Percentage Total dollar markdown as a percentage of net sales (in dollars): (p. 485)

$$\text{Markdown percentage} = \frac{\text{Total dollar markdown}}{\text{Net sales (in \$)}}$$

Marketing Research in Retailing Collection and analysis of information relating to specific issues or problems facing a retailer. (p. 227)

Marketing Research Process Embodies a series of activities: defining the issue or problem, examining secondary data, generating primary data (if needed), analyzing data, making recommendations, and implementing findings. (p. 227)

Market Penetration Pricing Strategy in which a retailer seeks to achieve large revenues by setting low prices and selling a high unit volume. (p. 473)

Market Segment Product Groupings Place together various items that appeal to a given target market. (p. 515)

Market Skimming Pricing Strategy wherein a firm charges premium prices and attracts customers less concerned with price than service, assortment, and status. (p. 473)

Markup Difference between merchandise costs and retail selling price. (p. 476)

Markup Percentage (at Cost) Difference between retail price and merchandise cost expressed as a percentage of merchandise cost: (p. 476)

$$\text{Markup percentage (at cost)} = \frac{\text{Retail selling price} - \text{Merchandise cost}}{\text{Merchandise cost}}$$

Markup Percentage (at Retail) Difference between retail price and merchandise cost expressed as a percentage of retail price: (p. 476)

$$\text{Markup percentage (at retail)} = \frac{\text{Retail selling price} - \text{Merchandise cost}}{\text{Retail selling price}}$$

Markup Pricing Form of cost-oriented pricing in which a retailer sets prices by adding per-unit merchandise costs, retail operating expenses, and desired profit. (p. 476)

Marquee Sign used to display a store's name and/or logo. (p. 509)

Massed Promotion Effort Used by retailers that promote mostly in one or two seasons. (p. 553)

Mass Marketing Selling goods and services to a broad spectrum of consumers. (p. 71)

Mass Merchandising Positioning approach whereby retailers offer a discount or value-oriented image, a wide and/or deep merchandise selection, and large store facilities. (p. 68)

Mazur Plan Divides all retail activities into four functional areas: merchandising, publicity, store management, and accounting and control. (p. 316)

Megamall Enormous planned shopping center with at least 1 million square feet of retail space, multiple anchor stores, up to several hundred specialty stores, food courts, and entertainment facilities. (p. 284)

Membership (Warehouse) Club Appeals to price-conscious consumers, who must be members to shop. (p. 142)

Memorandum Purchase Occurs when items are not paid for by the retailer until they are sold. The retailer can return unsold merchandise. However, it takes title on delivery and is responsible for damages. (p. 418)

Merchandise Available for Sale Equals beginning inventory, purchases, and transportation charges. (p. 438)

Merchandising Activities involved in acquiring particular goods and/or services and making them available at the places, times, and prices and in the quantity to enable a retailer to reach its goals. (p. 384)

Merchandising Philosophy Sets the guiding principles for all the merchandise decisions a retailer makes. (p. 384)

Mergers The combinations of separately owned retail firms. (p. 129)

Micromarketing Application of data mining whereby the retailer uses differentiated marketing and focused strategy mixes for specific segments, sometimes fine-tuned for the individual shopper. (p. 225)

Micromerchandising Strategy whereby a retailer adjusts its shelf-space allocations to respond to customer and other differences among local markets. (p. 386)

Minimum Price Laws State regulations preventing retailers from selling certain items for less than their cost plus a fixed percentage to cover overhead. These laws restrict loss leaders and predatory pricing. (p. 470)

Model Stock Approach Method of determining the amount of floor space necessary to carry and display a proper merchandise assortment. (p. 516)

Model Stock Plan Planned composition of fashion goods, which reflects the mix of merchandise available based on expected sales. It indicates product lines, colors, and size distributions. (p. 392)

Monthly Sales Index Measure of sales seasonality that is calculated by dividing each month's actual sales by average monthly sales and then multiplying the results by 100. (p. 447)

Motives Reasons for consumer behavior. (p. 198)

Multi-Channel Retailing A distribution approach whereby a retailer sells to consumers through multiple retail formats (points of contact). (pp. 8, 148)

Multiple-Unit Pricing Discounts offered to customers who buy in quantity or who buy a product bundle. (p. 484)

Mystery Shoppers People hired by retailers to pose as customers and observe their operations, from sales presentations to how well displays are maintained to service calls. (p. 233)

Need-Satisfaction Approach Sales technique based on the principle that each customer has a different set of wants; thus, a sales presentation should be geared to the demands of the individual customer. (p. 541)

Neighborhood Business District (NBD) Unplanned shopping area that appeals to the convenience shopping and service needs of a single residential area. The leading retailer is typically a supermarket or a large drugstore, and it is situated on the major street(s) of its residential area. (p. 280)

Neighborhood Shopping Center Planned shopping facility with the largest store being a supermarket or a drugstore. It serves 3,000 to 50,000 people within a 15-minute drive (usually less than 10 minutes). (p. 285)

Net Lease Calls for all maintenance costs, such as heating, electricity, insurance, and interior repair, to be paid by the retailer. (p. 294)

Net Profit Equals gross profit minus retail operating expenses. (p. 438)

Net Profit After Taxes The profit earned after all costs and taxes have been deducted. (p. 336)

Net Profit Margin Performance measure based on a retailer's net profit and net sales. It is equal to net profit divided by net sales. (p. 338)

Net Sales Revenues received by a retailer during a given time period after deducting customer returns, markdowns, and employee discounts. (p. 336)

Net Worth Retailer's assets minus its liabilities. (p. 338)

Never-Out List Used when a retailer plans stock levels for best-sellers. The goal is to purchase enough of these products so they are always in stock. (p. 393)

Niche Retailing Enables retailers to identify customer segments and deploy unique strategies to address the desires of those segments. (p. 68)

Nongoods Services Area of service retailing in which intangible personal services are offered to consumers—who experience the services rather than possess them. (p. 42)

Nonprobability Sample Approach in which stores, products, or customers are chosen by the researcher—based on judgment or convenience. (p. 233)

Nonstore Retailing Utilizes strategy mixes that are not store-based to reach consumers and complete transactions. It occurs via direct marketing, direct selling, and vending machines. (p. 149)

Objective-and-Task Method Promotional budgeting procedure by which a retailer clearly defines its promotional goals and prepares a budget to satisfy them. (p. 549)

Objectives Long-term and short-term performance targets that a retailer hopes to attain. Goals can involve sales, profit, satisfaction of publics, and image. (p. 66)

Observation Form of research in which present behavior or the results of past behavior are observed and recorded. It can be human or mechanical. (p. 233)

Odd Pricing Retail prices set at levels below even dollar values, such as $0.49, $4.98, and $199. (p. 484)

Off-Price Chain Features brand-name apparel and accessories, footwear, linens, fabrics, cosmetics, and/or housewares and sells them at everyday low prices in an efficient, limited-service environment. (p. 141)

Off-Retail Markdown Percentage Markdown for each item or category of items computed as a percentage of original retail price: (p. 486)

$$\text{Off-retail markdown percentage} = \frac{\text{Original price} - \text{New price}}{\text{Original price}}$$

One-Hundred Percent Location Optimum site for a particular store. A location labeled as 100 percent for one firm may be less than optimal for another. (p. 287)

One-Price Policy Strategy wherein a retailer charges the same price to all customers buying an item under similar conditions. (p. 483)

Open Credit Account Requires a consumer to pay his or her bill in full when it is due. (p. 36)

Open-to-Buy Difference between planned purchases and the purchase commitments already made by a buyer for a given time period, often a month. It represents the amount the buyer has left to spend for that month and is reduced each time a purchase is made. (p. 451)

Operating Expenditures (Expenses) Short-term selling and administrative costs of running a business. (pp. 336, 350)

Operations Blueprint Systematically lists all the operating functions to be performed, their characteristics, and their timing. (p. 356)

Operations Management Process used to efficiently and effectively enact the policies and tasks to satisfy a firm's customers, employees, and management (and stockholders, if a publicly owned company). (p. 336)

Opportunistic Buying Negotiates low prices for merchandise whose sales have not met expectations, end-of-season goods, items returned to the manufacturer or another retailer, and closeouts. (p. 417)

Opportunities Marketplace openings that exist because other retailers have not yet capitalized on them. (p. 58)

Opportunity Costs Possible benefits a retailer forgoes if it invests in one opportunity rather than another. (p. 350)

Option Credit Account Form of revolving account that allows partial payments. No interest is assessed if a person pays a bill in full when it is due. (p. 36)

Order-Getting Salesperson Actively involved with informing and persuading customers, and in closing sales. This is a true "sales" employee. (p. 540)

Order Lead Time Period from when an order is placed by a retailer to the date merchandise is ready for sale (received, price marked, and put on the selling floor). (p. 457)

Order-Taking Salesperson Engages in routine clerical and sales functions, such as setting up displays, placing inventory on shelves, answering simple questions, filling orders, and ringing up sales. (p. 540)

Organizational Mission Retailer's commitment to a type of business and a distinctive marketplace role. It is reflected in the attitude to consumers, employees, suppliers, competitors, government, and others. (p. 59)

Organization Chart Graphically displays the hierarchical relationships within a firm. (p. 314)

Outshopping When a person goes out of his or her hometown to shop. (p. 199)

Outsourcing Situation whereby a retailer pays an outside party to undertake one or more operating tasks. (p. 369)

Overstored Trading Area Geographic area with so many stores selling a specific good or service that some retailers will be unable to earn an adequate profit. (p. 271)

Owned-Goods Services Area of service retailing in which goods owned by consumers are repaired, improved, or maintained. (p. 41)

Parasite Store Outlet that does not create its own traffic and has no real trading area of its own. (p. 258)

Partnership Unincorporated retail firm owned by two or more persons, each with a financial interest. (p. 61)

Perceived Risk Level of risk a consumer believes exists regarding the purchase of a specific good or service from a given retailer, whether or not the belief is actually correct. (p. 194)

Percentage Lease Stipulates that rent is related to a retailer's sales or profits. (p. 293)

Percentage-of-Sales Method Promotional budgeting method in which a retailer ties its budget to revenue. (p. 548)

Percentage Variation Method Inventory level planning method where beginning-of-month planned inventory during any month differs from planned average monthly stock by only one-half of that month's variation from estimated average monthly sales. Under this method: (p. 449)

$$\text{Beginning-of-month planned inventory level (at retail)} = \text{Planned average monthly stock at retail} \times 1/2 [1 + (\text{Estimated monthly sales}/\text{Estimated average monthly sales})]$$

Performance Measures Criteria used to assess effectiveness, including total sales, sales per store, sales by product category, sales per square foot, gross margins, gross margin return on investment, operating income, inventory turnover, markdown percentages, employee turnover, financial ratios, and profitability. (p. 573)

Personality Sum total of an individual's traits, which make that individual unique. (p. 194)

Personal Selling Oral communication with one or more prospective customers to make sales. (p. 539)

Physical Inventory System Actual counting of merchandise. A firm using the cost method of inventory valuation and relying on a physical inventory can derive gross profit only when it does a full inventory. (p. 440)

Planned Shopping Center Group of architecturally unified commercial facilities on a site that is centrally owned or managed, designed and operated as a unit, based on balanced tenancy, and accompanied by parking. (p. 280)

Planogram Visual (graphical) representation of the space for selling, merchandise, personnel, and customers—as well as for product categories. (p. 515)

PMs Promotional money, push money, or prize money that a manufacturer provides for retail salespeople selling that manufacturer's brand. (p. 540)

Point of Indifference Geographic breaking point between two cities (communities), so that the trading area of each can be determined. At this point, consumers would be indifferent to shopping at either area. (p. 261)

Point-of-Purchase (POP) Display Interior display that provides shoppers with information, adds to store atmosphere, and serves a substantial promotional role. (p. 519)

Positioning Enables a retailer to devise its strategy in a way that projects an image relative to its retail category and its competitors, and elicits consumer responses to that image. (p. 68)

Post-Purchase Behavior Further purchases or re-evaluation based on a purchase. (p. 205)

Power Center Shopping site with (1) up to a half dozen or so category killer stores and a mix of smaller stores or (2) several complementary stores specializing in one product category. (p. 285)

Predatory Pricing Involves large retailers that seek to reduce competition by selling goods and services at very low prices, thus causing small retailers to go out of business. (p. 470)

Prestige Pricing Assumes consumers will not buy goods and services at prices deemed too low. It is based on the price-quality association. (p. 476)

Pre-Training Indoctrination on the history and policies of the retailer and a job orientation on hours, compensation, the chain of command, and job duties. (p. 327)

Price Elasticity of Demand Sensitivity of customers to price changes in terms of the quantities bought: (p. 466)

$$\text{Elasticity} = \frac{\dfrac{\text{Quantity 1} - \text{Quantity 2}}{\text{Quantity 1} + \text{Quantity 2}}}{\dfrac{\text{Price 1} - \text{Price 2}}{\text{Price 1} + \text{Price 2}}}$$

Price Lining Practice whereby retailers sell merchandise at a limited range of price points, with each point representing a distinct level of quality. (p. 485)

Price–Quality Association Concept stating that many consumers feel high prices connote high quality and low prices connote low quality. (p. 476)

Primary Data Those collected to address the specific issue or problem under study. This type of data may be gathered via surveys, observations, experiments, and simulation. (p. 227)

Primary Trading Area Encompasses 50 to 80 percent of a store's customers. It is the area closest to the store and possesses the highest density of customers to population and the highest per capita sales. (p. 257)

Private (Dealer, Store) Brands Contain names designated by wholesalers or retailers, are more profitable to retailers, are better controlled by retailers, are not sold by competing retailers, are less expensive for consumers, and lead to customer loyalty to retailers (rather than to manufacturers). (p. 400)

Probability (Random) Sample Approach whereby every store, product, or customer has an equal or known chance of being chosen for study. (p. 233)

Problem Awareness Stage in the decision process at which the consumer not only has been aroused by social, commercial, and/or physical stimuli, but also recognizes that the good or service under consideration may solve a problem of shortage or unfulfilled desire. (p. 203)

Productivity Efficiency with which a retail strategy is carried out. (p. 351)

Product Life Cycle Shows the expected behavior of a good or service over its life. The traditional cycle has four stages: introduction, growth, maturity, and decline. (p. 394)

Product/Trademark Franchising Arrangement in which the franchisee acquires the identity of the franchisor by agreeing to sell the latter's products and/or operate under the latter's name. (p. 108)

Profit-and-Loss (Income) Statement Summary of a retailer's revenues and expenses over a particular period of time, usually a month, quarter, or year. (p. 336)

Prototype Stores Used with an operations strategy that requires multiple outlets in a chain to conform to relatively uniform construction, layout, and operations standards. (p. 358)

Publicity Any nonpersonal form of public relations whereby messages are transmitted by mass media, the time or space provided by the media is not paid for, and there is no identified commercial sponsor. (p. 537)

Public Relations Any communication that fosters a favorable image for the retailer among its publics (consumers, investors, government, channel members, employees, and the general public). (p. 537)

Purchase Act Exchange of money or a promise to pay for the ownership or use of a good or service. Purchase variables include the place of purchase, terms, and availability of merchandise. (p. 204)

Purchase Motivation Product Groupings Appeal to the consumer's urge to buy products and the amount of time he or she is willing to spend in shopping. (p. 515)

Quick Response (QR) Inventory Planning Enables a retailer to reduce the amount of inventory it keeps on hand by ordering more frequently and in lower quantity. (p. 425)

Rack Display Interior display that neatly hangs or presents products. (p. 519)

Rationalized Retailing Combines a high degree of centralized management control with strict operating procedures for every phase of business. (p. 358)

Reach Number of distinct people exposed to a retailer's promotional efforts during a specified period. (p. 552)

Recruitment Activity whereby a retailer generates a list of job applicants. (p. 325)

Reference Groups Influence people's thoughts and behavior. They may be classified as aspirational, membership, and dissociative. (p. 193)

Regional Shopping Center Large, planned shopping facility appealing to a geographically dispersed market. It has at least one or two full-sized department stores and 50 to 150 or more smaller retailers. The market for this center is 100,000+ people who live or work up to a 30-minute drive time from the center. (p. 283)

Regression Model Computerized site selection tool that uses equations showing the association between potential store sales and several independent variables at each location under consideration. (p. 261)

Reilly's Law of Retail Gravitation Traditional means of trading-area delineation that establishes a point of indifference between two cities or communities, so the trading area of each can be determined. (p. 261)

Relationship Retailing Exists when retailers seek to establish and maintain long-term bonds with customers, rather than act as if each sales transaction is a completely new encounter with them. (p. 18)

Rented-Goods Services Area of service retailing in which consumers lease and use goods for specified periods of time. (p. 41)

Reorder Point Stock level at which new orders must be placed: (p. 457)

$$\text{Reorder point} = \frac{(\text{Usage rate} \times \text{Lead time})}{+ \text{Safety stock}}$$

Resident Buying Office Inside or outside buying organization used when a retailer wants to keep in close touch with market trends and cannot do so with just its headquarters buying staff. Such offices are usually situated in important merchandise centers (sources of supply) and provide valuable data and contacts. (p. 390)

Retail Audit Systematically examines the total retailing effort or a specific aspect of it to study what a retailer is presently doing, appraise how well it is performing, and make recommendations. (p. 581)

Retail Balance The mix of stores within a district or shopping center. (p. 291)

Retail Information System (RIS) Anticipates the information needs of managers; collects, organizes, and stores relevant data on a continuous basis; and directs the flow of information to proper decision makers. (p. 219)

Retailing Business activities involved in selling goods and services to consumers for their personal, family, or household use. (p. 4)

Retailing Concept An approach to business that is customer-oriented, coordinated, value-driven, and goal-oriented. (p.14)

Retail Institution Basic format or structure of a business. Institutions can be classified by ownership, store-based retail strategy mix, and nonstore-based, electronic, and nontraditional retailing. (p. 102)

Retail Life Cycle Theory asserting that institutions—like the goods and services they sell—pass through identifiable life stages: introduction (early growth), growth (accelerated development), maturity, and decline. (p. 127)

Retail Method of Accounting Determines closing inventory value by calculating the average relationship between the cost and retail values of merchandise available for sale during a period. (p. 442)

Retail Organization How a firm structures and assigns tasks, policies, resources, authority, responsibilities, and rewards so as to efficiently and effectively satisfy the needs of its target market, employees, and management. (p. 310)

Retail Performance Index Encompasses five-year trends in revenue growth and profit growth, and a six-year average return on assets. (p. 577)

Retail Promotion Any communication by a retailer that informs, persuades, and/or reminds the target market about any aspect of that firm. (p. 530)

Retail Reductions Difference between beginning inventory plus purchases during the period and sales plus ending inventory. They encompass anticipated markdowns, employee and other discounts, and stock shortages. (p. 450)

Retail Strategy Overall plan guiding a retail firm. It influences the firm's business activities and its response to market forces, such as competition and the economy. (pp.12, 58)

Return on Assets (ROA) Performance ratio based on net sales, net profit, and total assets: (p. 339)

$$\frac{\text{Return}}{\text{on assets}} = \frac{\text{Net profit}}{\text{Net sales}} \times \frac{\text{Net sales}}{\text{Total assets}} = \frac{\text{Net profit}}{\text{Total assets}}$$

Return on Net Worth (RONW) Performance measure based on net profit, net sales, total assets, and net worth: (p. 340)

$$\frac{\text{Return on}}{\text{net worth}} = \frac{\text{Net profit}}{\text{Net sales}} \times \frac{\text{Net sales}}{\text{Total assets}} \times \frac{\text{Total assets}}{\text{Net worth}}$$

Reverse Logistics Encompasses all merchandise flows from the customer and/or the retailer back through the supply channel. (p. 432)

Revolving Credit Account Allows a customer to charge items and be billed monthly on the basis of the outstanding cumulative balance. (p. 36)

RFID (Radio Frequency Identification) A method of storing and remotely retrieving data using devices called RFID tags or transponders. (p. 419)

Robinson-Patman Act Bars manufacturers and wholesalers from discriminating in price or purchase terms in selling to individual retailers if these retailers are purchasing products of "like quality" and the effect of such discrimination is to injure competition. (p. 469)

Routine Decision Making Takes place when a consumer buys out of habit and skips steps in the purchase process. (p. 206)

Safety Stock Extra inventory to protect against out-of-stock conditions due to unexpected demand and delays in delivery. (p. 458)

Sales Manager Person who typically supervises the on-floor selling and operational activities for a specific retail department. (p. 390)

Sales Opportunity Grid Rates the promise of new and established goods, services, procedures, and/or store outlets across a variety of criteria. (p. 569)

Sales–Productivity Ratio Method for assigning floor space on the basis of sales or profit per foot. (p. 516)

Sales Promotion Encompasses the paid communication activities other than advertising, public relations, and personal selling that stimulate consumer purchases and dealer effectiveness. (p. 541)

Saturated Trading Area Geographic area with the proper amount of retail facilities to satisfy the needs of its population for a specific good or service, as well as to enable retailers to prosper. (p. 271)

Scenario Analysis Lets a retailer project the future by studying factors that affect long-term performance and then forming contingency plans based on alternate scenarios. (p. 580)

Scrambled Merchandising Occurs when a retailer adds goods and services that may be unrelated to each other and to the firm's original business. (p. 126)

Seasonal Merchandise Products that sell well over non-consecutive time periods. (p. 392)

Secondary Business District (SBD) Unplanned shopping area in a city or town that is usually bounded by the intersection of two major streets. It has at least a junior department store and/or some larger specialty stores—in addition to many smaller stores. (p. 279)

Secondary Data Those gathered for purposes other than addressing the issue or problem currently under study. (p. 227)

Secondary Trading Area Geographic area that contains an additional 15 to 25 percent of a store's customers. It is located outside the primary area, and customers are more widely dispersed. (p. 257)

Selective Distribution Takes place when suppliers sell through a moderate number of retailers. This lets suppliers have higher sales than in exclusive distribution and lets retailers carry some competing brands. (p. 10)

Self-Scanning Enables the consumer himself or herself to scan the items being purchased at a checkout counter, pay electronically by credit or debit card, and bag the items. (p. 369)

Semantic Differential Disguised or nondisguised survey technique, whereby a respondent is asked to rate one or more retailers on several criteria; each criterion is evaluated along a bipolar adjective scale. (p. 233)

Service Retailing Involves transactions in which consumers do not purchase or acquire ownership of tangible products. It encompasses rented goods, owned goods, and nongoods. (p. 41)

Simulation Type of experiment whereby a computer program is used to manipulate the elements of a retail strategy mix rather than test them in a real setting. (p. 235)

Single-Channel Retailing A distribution approach whereby a retailer sells to consumers through one retail format. (p. 148)

Situation Analysis Candid evaluation of the opportunities and threats facing a prospective or existing retailer. (p. 58)

Slotting Allowances Payments that retailers require of vendors for providing shelf space in stores. (p. 417)

Social Class Informal ranking of people based on income, occupation, education, and other factors. (p. 193)

Social Responsibility Occurs when a retailer acts in society's best interests—as well as its own. The challenge is to balance corporate citizenship with fair profits. (p. 48)

Sole Proprietorship Unincorporated retail firm owned by one person. (p. 61)

Solutions Selling Takes a customer-centered approach and presents "solutions" rather than "products." It goes a step beyond cross-merchandising. (p. 524)

Sorting Process Involves the retailer's collecting an assortment of goods and services from various sources, buying them in large quantity, and offering to sell them in small quantities to consumers. (p. 8)

Specialog Enables a retailer to cater to the specific needs of customer segments, emphasize a limited number of items, and reduce catalog production and postage costs. (p. 153)

Specialty Store Retailer that concentrates on selling one goods or service line. (p. 136)

Staple Merchandise Consists of the regular products carried by a retailer. (p. 392)

Stimulus Cue (social or commercial) or a drive (physical) meant to motivate or arouse a person to act. (p. 203)

Stock-to-Sales Method Inventory level planning technique wherein a retailer wants to maintain a specified ratio of goods on hand to sales. (p. 449)

Stock Turnover Number of times during a specific period, usually one year, that the average inventory on hand is sold. It can be computed in units or dollars (at retail or cost): (p. 456)

$$\text{Annual rate of stock turnover (in units)} = \frac{\text{Number of units sold during year}}{\text{Average inventory on hand (in units)}}$$

$$\text{Annual rate of stock turnover (in retail dollars)} = \frac{\text{Net yearly sales}}{\text{Average inventory on hand (at retail)}}$$

$$\text{Annual rate of stock turnover (at cost)} = \frac{\text{Cost of goods sold during the year}}{\text{Average inventory on hand (at cost)}}$$

Storability Product Groupings Used for products that need special handling. (p. 515)

Storefront Total physical exterior of a store, including the marquee, entrances, windows, lighting, and construction materials. (p. 509)

Store Maintenance Encompasses all the activities in managing a retailer's physical facilities. (p. 361)

Straight (Gridiron) Traffic Flow Presents displays and aisles in a rectangular or gridiron pattern. (p. 516)

Straight Lease Requires the retailer to pay a fixed dollar amount per month over the life of a lease. It is the simplest, most direct leasing arrangement. (p. 293)

Strategic Profit Model Expresses the numerical relationship among net profit margin, asset turnover, and financial leverage. It can be used in planning or controlling a retailer's assets. (p. 340)

Strategy Mix Firm's particular combination of store location, operating procedures, goods/services offered, pricing tactics, store atmosphere and customer services, and promotional methods. (p. 124)

String Unplanned shopping area comprising a group of retail stores, often with similar or compatible product lines, located along a street or highway. (p. 280)

Supercenter Combination store blending an economy supermarket with a discount department store. (p. 135)

Supermarket Self-service food store with grocery, meat, and produce departments and minimum annual sales of $2 million. The category includes conventional supermarkets, food-based superstores, combination stores, box (limited-line) stores, and warehouse stores. (p. 133)

Supervision Manner of providing a job environment that encourages employee accomplishment. (p. 331)

Supply Chain Logistics aspect of a value delivery chain. It comprises all of the parties that participate in the retail logistics process: manufacturers, wholesalers, third-party specialists, and the retailer. (p. 425)

Survey Research technique that systematically gathers information from respondents by communicating with them. (p. 233)

Tactics Actions that encompass a retailer's daily and short-term operations. (p. 77)

Target Market Customer group that a retailer seeks to attract and satisfy. (p. 71)

Taxes The portion of revenues turned over to the federal, state, and/or local government. (p. 336)

Terms of Occupancy Consist of ownership versus leasing, the type of lease, operations and maintenance costs, taxes, zoning restrictions, and voluntary regulations. (p. 292)

Theme-Setting Display Interior display that depicts a product offering in a thematic manner and portrays a specific atmosphere or mood. (p. 519)

Threats Environmental and marketplace factors that can adversely affect retailers if they do not react to them (and sometimes, even if they do). (p. 58)

Top-Down Space Management Approach Exists when a retailer starts with its total available store space, divides the space into categories, and then works on in-store product layouts. (p. 359)

Total Retail Experience All the elements in a retail offering that encourage or inhibit consumers during their contact with a retailer. (p. 15)

Trading Area Geographic area containing the customers of a particular firm or group of firms for specific goods or services. (p. 252)

Trading-Area Overlap Occurs when the trading areas of stores in different locations encroach on one another. In the overlap area, the same customers are served by both stores. (p. 252)

Traditional Department Store Type of department store in which merchandise quality ranges from average to quite good, pricing is moderate to above average, and customer service ranges from medium levels of sales help, credit, delivery, and so forth to high levels of each. (p. 138)

Traditional Job Description Contains each position's title, supervisory relationships (superior and subordinate), committee assignments, and the specific ongoing roles and tasks. (p. 326)

Training Programs Used to teach new (and existing) personnel how best to perform their jobs or how to improve themselves. (p. 328)

Unbundled Pricing Involves a retailer's charging separate prices for each item sold. (p. 485)

Uncontrollable Variables Aspects of business to which the retailer must adapt (such as competition, the economy, and laws). (p. 73)

Understored Trading Area Geographic area that has too few stores selling a specific good or service to satisfy the needs of its population. (p. 271)

Unit Control Looks at the quantities of merchandise a retailer handles during a stated period. (p. 438)

Unit Pricing Practice required by many states, whereby retailers (mostly food stores) must express both the total price of an item and its price per unit of measure. (p. 470)

Universal Product Code (UPC) Classification for coding data onto products via a series of thick and thin vertical lines. It lets retailers record information instantaneously on a product's model number, size, color, and other factors when it is sold, as well as send the information to a computer that monitors unit sales, inventory levels, and other factors. The UPC is not readable by humans. (p. 225)

Unplanned Business District Type of retail location where two or more stores situate together (or nearby) in such a way that the total arrangement or mix of stores is not due to prior long-range planning. (p. 277)

Usage Rate Average sales per day, in units, of merchandise. (p. 458)

Value Embodied by the activities and processes (a value chain) that provide a given level of value for the consumer—from manufacturer, wholesaler, and retailer perspectives. From the customer's perspective, it is the perception the shopper has of a value chain. (p. 28)

Value Chain Total bundle of benefits offered to consumers through a channel of distribution. (p. 29)

Value Delivery System All the parties that develop, produce, deliver, and sell and service particular goods and services. (p. 39)

Variable Markup Policy Strategy whereby a firm purposely adjusts markups by merchandise category. (p. 479)

Variable Pricing Strategy wherein a retailer alters prices to coincide with fluctuations in costs or consumer demand. (p. 482)

Variety Store Outlet that handles a wide assortment of inexpensive and popularly priced goods and services, such as apparel and accessories, costume jewelry, notions and small wares, candy, toys, and other items in the price range. (p. 140)

Vending Machine Format involving the cash- or card-operated dispensing of goods and services. It eliminates the use of sales personnel and allows around-the-clock sales. (p. 160)

Vendor-Managed Inventory (VMI) Practice of retailers counting on key suppliers to actively participate in their inventory management programs. Suppliers have their own employees stationed at retailers' headquarters to manage the inventory replenishment of the suppliers' products. (p. 429)

Vertical Cooperative Advertising Agreement Enables a manufacturer and a retailer or a wholesaler and a retailer to share an ad. (p. 537)

Vertical Marketing System All the levels of independently owned businesses along a channel of distribution. Goods and services are normally distributed through one of three types of systems: independent, partially integrated, and fully integrated. (p. 112)

Vertical Price Fixing Occurs when manufacturers or wholesalers seek to control the retail prices of their goods and services. (p. 468)

Vertical Retail Audit Analyzes—in depth—performance in one area of the strategy mix or operations. (p. 583)

Video Kiosk Freestanding, interactive, electronic computer terminal that displays products and related information on a video screen; it often uses a touch-screen for consumers to make selections. (p. 168)

Visual Merchandising Proactive, integrated approach to atmospherics taken by a retailer to create a certain "look," properly display products, stimulate shopping, and enhance the physical environment. (p. 508)

Want Book Notebook in which retail store employees record requests for unstocked or out-of-stock merchandise. (p. 413)

Want Slip Slip on which retail store employees enter requests for unstocked or out-of-stock merchandise. (p. 413)

Warehouse Store Food-based discounter offering a moderate number of food items in a no-frills setting. (p. 136)

Weeks' Supply Method An inventory level planning method wherein beginning inventory equals several weeks' expected sales. It assumes inventory is in direct proportion to sales. Under this method: (p. 449)

Beginning-of-month planned inventory level (at retail) = Average estimated weekly sales × Number of weeks to be stocked

Weighted Application Blank Form whereby criteria best correlating with job success get more weight than others. A minimum total score becomes a cutoff point for hiring. (p. 327)

Wheel of Retailing Theory stating that retail innovators often first appear as low-price operators with low costs and low profit margins. Over time, they upgrade the products carried and improve facilities and customer services. They then become vulnerable to new discounters with lower cost structures. (p. 124)

Width of Assortment Number of distinct goods/service categories (product lines) a retailer carries. (p. 396)

Word-of-Mouth (WOM) Occurs when one consumer talks to others. (p. 547)

World Wide Web (Web) Way of accessing the Internet, whereby people work with easy-to-use Web addresses and pages. Users see words, colorful charts, pictures, and video, and hear audio. (p. 160)

Yield Management Pricing Computerized, demand-based, variable pricing technique whereby a retailer (typically a service firm) determines the combination of prices that yield the greatest total revenues for a given period. (p. 483)

Zero-Based Budgeting Practice followed when a firm starts each new budget from scratch and outlines the expenditures needed to reach that period's goals. All costs are justified each time a budget is done. (p. 348)

Endnotes

Chapter 1

1. Various company sources.

2. Estimated by the authors from data in "2008 Global Powers of Retailing," *Stores* (January 2008), special section.

3. *Annual Retail Trade Survey* (Washington, DC: U.S. Census Bureau, March 7, 2008); and retailer annual reports.

4. The material in this section is drawn from **http://sites.target. com/site/en/company/page.jsp**; **www.target.com**; *Target Corporation 2007 and 2008 Annual Reports*; *Target Fact Book 2008;* Sharon Edelson, "Target Reveals Plans to Address Downturn," *Women's Wear Daily* (October 24, 2008), p. 10; Andria Cheng, "Target to Intensify Value Message, May Offer Perishables," *Dow Jones News Service* (October 23, 2008); Rachel Cericola, "Target Gift Card Doubles As Digital Camera," **www.electronichouse.com/article/target_gift_car d_doubles_as_digital_camera** (November 11, 2008); Nicole Maestra, "Target Slows Store Plans, Toughens Credit Terms," *Reuters News* (October 23, 2008); Reena Jana, "Ducking the Price War, Target Highlights Fashion," *Business Week Online* (October 2, 2008); and Natalie Zmuda and Emily Bryson, "Marketers Shift Focus to Value," *Advertising Age* (August 25, 2008), pp. 4, 22.

5. "What Retailers Need Now," *Chain Store Age* (August 2008), p. 16A.

6. John Di Francis, "Treating the Customer Dissatisfaction Epidemic: How to Go Beyond Simply Masking the Symptoms," **http://moneymoz.com/treating-the-customer-dissatisfaction-epidemic-how-to-go-beyond-simply-masking-the-symptoms** (October 11, 2008).

7. "Build-A-Bear Workshop Corporate Profile," **http://phx. corporate-ir.net/phoenix.zhtml?c=182478&p=irol-home Profile** (February 5, 6212009).

8. Susan Reda, "Saving Customer Service: Are Retailers Up to the Challenge?" *Stores* (January 2001), p. 50.

9. Leonard L. Berry and Kathleen Seiders, "Serving Unfair Customers," *Retailing Issues Letter* (Number 1, 2008), p. 6.

Chapter 1 Appendix

1. "Subprime Overdues Hit 33 Percent," *National Mortgage News* (December 8, 2008), p. 1; and Elizabeth O'Brien, "Subprime Truth and Consequences," *Financial Planning* (December 2008), pp. 74–78.

2. Ibid.

3. Mark Gongloff, "Ahead of the Tape," *Wall Street Journal* (December 12, 2008), p. C1; and Peter Coy, "598,000 Jobs Lost in January," *Business Week* (February 9, 2009), p. 12.

4. Mark Potter and James Davey, "Analysis—Worst Still to Come for Europe's Retailers," *Reuters News* (December 12, 2008).

5. Ibid.

6. "Chapter 7," *BMI Global Assumptions* (London: Business Monitor International, 2008).

7. Evan Clark, "The Meltdown; The Economy Is Ailing for Most of the Year, But Dramatically Plunged in the Fall, Affecting U.S. as Well as World Markets, Employment and Overall Consumerism," *Women's Wear Daily* (December 15, 2008), p. 2B.

8. Ann Zimmerman, Jennifer Saranow, and Miguel Bustillo, "Retail Sales Plummet," *Wall Street Journal* (December 26, 2008), p. 1.

9. Vicki M. Young, "Bankrupt Steve & Barry's to Liquidate," *Women's Wear Daily* (November 21, 2008), p. 2.

10. Emily Thornton and John Cady, "What Have You Done to My Company?" *Business Week* (December 8, 2008), pp. 40–45.

11. Michael Barbaro, "The Sharper Image Files Bankruptcy Protection," *New York Times* (February 21, 2008).

12. Alan Wolf, "Tweeter Demise Ends Era in CE Retailing," *Twice News* (November 17, 2008), p. 12.

13. "You'd Better Watch Out: Gift Cards Can Be Lumps of Coal," *USA Today* (November 17, 2008).

14. Stephanie Rosenbloom, "For Wal-Mart, a Christmas That's Made to Order," *New York Times* (November 6, 2008). See also Ann Zimmerman, "Retail Sales Show Signs of Life," *Wall Street Journal* (March 6, 2009), pp. A1-A12.

15. Debra Chanil and Jenny McTaggart, "Glass Half Full," *Progressive Grocer* (April 15, 2008), pp. 24–42.

16. Kelly Nolam, "Rent-to-Own Retail Store Holds Steady," *Wall Street Journal* (December 10, 2008).

17. David Moin and Evan Clark, "Counting Every Penny: Stores Build Up Cash to Weather the Storm," *Women's Wear Daily*, (December 10, 2008), p. 1.

Chapter 2

1. Various company sources.

2. "About Us," **www.gamestop.com/gs/help/About_Us.aspx** (February 9, 2009).

3. Retail Forward, *Retailing 2005*, p. 9.

4. Barbara Hughes, "Why Loyalty and Value Really Matter Today," *H&MM* (November 3, 2008), p. 40.

5. *Shopping Centers Battle Declining Traffic; Shoppers Shrink Consideration Set* (Columbus, OH: TNS Retail Forward, July 2008); *Global Shopper Insights into Shopping Frequency* (Columbus, OH: TNS Retail Forward, April 2008); Linda Tucci, "Men Conquer a New Frontier: The Mall," *Boston.com* (April 10, 2005); *Strategic Focus: Global Food, Drug, Mass Shopper Update* (Columbus, OH: Retail Forward, April 2005); *Industry Outlook: Value Department Stores* (Columbus, OH: Retail Forward, March 2005); and *Industry Outlook: Mass Channel* (Columbus, OH: Retail Forward, May 2005).

6. "Should You Use a Shotgun or a Sniper Approach to Internet Marketing?" **www.hemsida.tv/should-you-use-a-shotgun-or-a-sniper-approach-to-internet-marketing** (September 18, 2007).

7. "Our Company, Our Culture," **www.autozoneinc.com/about_us/our_company** (March 9, 2009).

8. "America's Best Drugstores," *Consumer Reports* (June 2008), pp. 13–14.

9. "Our Culture," **http://careers.nordstrom.com/company/our-culture.asp** (March 11, 2009).

10. Rose Otieno, Chris Harrow, and Gaynor Lea-Greenwood, "The Unhappy Shopper, A Retail Experience: Exploring Fashion, Fit, and Affordability," *International Journal of Retail & Distribution Management*, Vol. 33 (Number 4, 2005), pp. 298–309.

11. "Customer Satisfaction Survey," **www.statpac.com/online-surveys/Customer_Satisfaction.htm** (March 5, 2009).

12. "Why You Need a Loyalty Program," *Profit* (November 2005), p. 1.

13. Lars Meyer Waarden and Christophe Benavent, "Rewards That Reward," **http://online.wsj.com/article/SB122160028857244783.html** (September 17, 2008).

14. *Becoming a Wal-Mart or Sam's Club Supplier* (Bentonville, AR: Wal-Mart: 2008).

15. "Strength in Numbers," **www.myace.com/index.cfm?fa=strength** (March 9, 2008).

16. Leonard L. Berry, "Relationship Marketing of Services—Growing Interest, Emerging Prospects," *Journal of the Academy of Marketing Science*, Vol. 23 (Fall 1995), pp. 237–238. See also Charlene Pleger Bebko, "Service Intangibility and Its Impact on Consumer Expectations of Service Quality," *Journal of Services Marketing*, Vol. 14 (Number 1, 2000), pp. 9–26.

17. *ATM & Debit News' 2009 EFT Data Book*.

18. Richard Sullivan, "Can Smart Cards Reduce Payments Fraud and Identity Theft?" *Economic Review* (Third Quarter, 2008), p. 35.

19. "Self-Checkout Definition," **www.pcmag.com/encyclopedia_term/0,2542,t=self-scanning+checkout&i=51072,00.asp** (December 3, 2008).

20. Jennifer Hopfinger, "Wild Cards," *Shopping Centers Today* (May 2008), pp. 45–46.

21. "EmbassyDirect Registration Kiosk," **http://embassysuites.hilton.com/en/es/promotions/es_kiosks/index.jhtml** (December 6, 2008).

22. "About Us," **https://www.chaindrugstore.net/CDSInfoV2/pages/aboutUs.htm** (December 6, 2008).

23. *Direct Marketing Association's Guidelines for Ethical Business Practices* (New York: Direct Marketing Association, revised May 2008).

24. "Sustainability," **http://walmartstores.com/Sustainability** (December 9, 2008).

25. "Community Involvement," **www.hannaford.com/Contents/Our_Company/Community** (December 11, 2008).

26. See Joel Groover, "Unhandicapped Access," *Shopping Centers Today* (September 2008), pp. 97–100.

27. Susan Haller, "Privacy: What Every Manager Should Know," *Information Management Journal*, Vol. 36 (May–June 2002), pp. 38–39.

28. J.C. Penney, public relations.

29. Giant Food, public relations.

Chapter 2 Appendix

1. Estimated by the authors based on data in *2008 Statistical Abstract* (Washington, DC: U.S. Census Bureau); and *Service Annual Survey 2007* (Washington, DC: U.S. Census Bureau).

2. Leonard L. Berry and Manjit S. Yadav, "Capture and Communicate Value in the Pricing of Services," *Sloan Management Review*, Vol. 37 (Summer 1996), pp. 41–51.

3. The material in this section is excerpted from "Baldrige Award Recipient Profile: Pal's Sudden Service," **www.nist.gov/public_affairs/pals.htm** (March 13, 2002); "Criteria for Excellence," **www.quality.nist.gov/Business_Criteria.htm** (February 7, 2009); "Pal's," **www.palsweb.com** (February 7, 2009); Leo Jacobson, "Fast and Happy," *Incentive* (November 2004), p. 22; and Margaret Littman, "Blind Faith," *Chain Leader* (August 2007), pp. 24–25.

Chapter 3

1. Various company sources.

2. "Write a Business Plan," **www.sba.gov/smallbusinessplanner/plan/writeabusinessplan** (March 30, 2009).

3. "McDonald's Values," **www.crmcdonalds.com/publish/csr/home/about/values.html** (April 2, 2009); "PetSmart Company Profile," **http://phx.corporate-ir.net/phoenix.zhtml?c=93506&p=irol-homeprofile** (April 2, 2009); and "Zumiez 411," **www.zumiez.com/411_zumiez.aspx** (April 2, 2009).

4. For additional information about business ownership formats, go to *Inc.*'s "Legal Issues-Buying/Selling a Business" site (**www.inc.com/articles_by_topic/legal-biz_finance-legal_buy_sell**).

5. "Choosing an Entity for Your Business," **www.forefieldkt.com/kt/trns.aspx?xd=BS-CORE-03&il=a2&xsl=content** (April 2, 2009).

6. Estimated by the authors from data in *Statistical Abstract of the United States 2008* (Washington, DC: U.S. Department of Commerce, 2008).

7. *2007 Kroger Factbook*, p. 42.

8. "The bebe Background," **www.bebe.com** (April 6, 2009).

9. "How We Do Business," **www.traderjoes.com/how_we_do_biz.html** (April 6, 2009).

Chapter 3 Appendix

1. *World Factbook*, **www.cia.gov/library/publications/the-world-factbook** (updated online as of November 20, 2008).

2. *Emerging Opportunities for Global Retailers* (Chicago: A.T. Kearney, Inc., 2008), p. 1.

3. William J. McDonald, "Five Steps to International Success," *Direct Marketing* (November 1998), pp. 32–36.

4. John C. Koopman, "Successful Global Retailers a Rare Breed," *Canadian Manager* (Spring 2000), p. 25.

5. "Global Powers of Retailing," *Chain Store Age* (January 2008), pp. G44–G46.

6. "About Toys "R" Us," **http://www9.toysrus.com/about** (December 22, 2008).

7. "About McDonald's," **www.mcdonalds.com/corp/about. html** (December 22, 2008); and "Maharaja Mac Sandwich," **www.encyclocentral.com/20995-Maharaja_Mac_Sandwich_ Of_International_Food_Chain_McDonalds.html** (December 22, 2008).

8. *Facts & Figures: The Ikea Group 2008.*

9. "About Us," **www.ahold.com/en/about** (December 22, 2008).

10. "Nature's Way to Beautiful," **www.thebodyshop-usa.com/ bodyshop/beauty/about-us** (December 22, 2008).

Chapter 4

1. Various company sources.

2. *Statistical Abstract of the United States 2008* (Washington, DC: U.S. Department of Commerce).

3. "Knowledge and Skills: Where the Path Begins," **www.bos.frb. org/consumer/pathways/knowledge.htm** (January 24, 2009).

4. Erin Edgemon, "Long Hours Required to Keep Family Business Running," **www.murfreesboropost.com/news. php?viewStory=13992** (November 16, 2008).

5. For a good overview of franchising and franchising opportunities, see *Entrepreneur's* "Annual Franchise 500" issue, which appears each January.

6. For more information on leased departments, see Connie Robbins Gentry, "Retailers as Landlords," *Chain Store Age* (May 2002), pp. 55–58.

7. *CPI Corp 2008 Annual Report.*

8. *Sherwin-Williams 2008 Annual Report.*

9. For more information on cooperatives, visit these Web sites: National Cooperative Business Association (**www. ncba.coop**); National Cooperative Grocers Association (**http://ncga.coop**); and Go.coop (**www.go.coop**).

Chapter 4 Appendix

1. "About Blockbuster," **www.blockbuster.com/corporate/ franchise** (March 30, 2009).

2. Robert McIntosh, "Self-Evaluation: Is Franchising for You?" **www.franchise.org/FranchiseeSecondary.aspx?id=10010** (March 30, 2009).

3. "System Support," **www.aboutmcdonalds.com/mcd/ franchising/us_franchising/why_mcdonalds/system_support. html** (March 30, 2009).

4. "Franchise Mediation Program," **www.cpradr.org/ ClausesRules/FranchiseRules/FranchiseMediationProgram/ tabid/304/Default.aspx** (March 30, 2009).

Chapter 5

1. Various company sources.

2. The pioneering works on the wheel of retailing are Malcolm P. McNair, "Significant Trends and Developments in the Postwar Period," in A. B. Smith (Editor), *Competitive Distribution in a Free High Level Economy and Its Implications for the University* (Pittsburgh: University of Pittsburgh Press, 1958), pp. 17–18; and Stanley Hollander, "The Wheel of Retailing," *Journal of Marketing*, Vol. 25 (July 1960), pp. 37–42. For further analysis of the concept, see Stephen Brown, "The Wheel of Retailing: Past and Future," *Journal of Retailing*, Vol. 66 (Summer 1990), pp. 143–149; Stephen Brown, "Postmodernism, the Wheel of Retailing, and Will to Power," *International Review of Retail, Distribution, and Consumer Research*, Vol. 5 (July 1995), pp. 387–414; Don E. Schultz, "Another Turn of the Wheel," *Marketing Management* (March–April 2002), pp. 8–9; and Susan D. Sampson, "Category Killers and Big-Box Retailing: Their Historical Impact on Retailing in the USA," *International Journal of Retail & Distribution Management*, Vol. 36 (No. 1, 2008), pp. 17–31.

3. "Ries' Pieces: The Sad Saga of Sears," **http://ries.typepad. com/ries_blog/2008/01/with-the-kmart.html** (January 29, 2008).

4. See Jonathan Reynolds, Elizabeth Howard, Christine Cuthbertson, and Latchezar Hristov, "Perspectives on Retail Format Innovation: Relating Theory and Practice," *International Journal of Retail & Distribution Management*, Vol. 35 (No. 8, 2007), pp. 647–660.

5. E-Commerce Remains Food for Thought for Big Chain Grocers," **www.internetretailer.com/dailyNews.asp?id=27735** (September 10, 2008).

6. See **www.kis-kiosk.com/interactive-kiosks.html** for an overview of kiosks.

7. "Last Catalog Showroom Retailer Now in Liquidation," *Knight Ridder/Tribune Business News* (February 3, 2002).

8. "Retailing: General," *Standard & Poor's Industry Surveys* (November 20, 2008), p. 12.

9. Ibid., p. 19.

10. "Fact Sheets," **www.nacsonline.com/NACS/News/FactSheets/ Pages/default.aspx** (March 2, 2009).

11. Various issues of *Progressive Grocer*; and Food Marketing Institute, "Facts & Figures," **www.fmi.org/facts_figs**.

12. Ibid.

13. Ibid.

14. Ibid.

15. Ibid.

16. Computed by the authors from "Retailing: Specialty," *Standard & Poor's Industry Surveys* (September 11, 2008).

17. "Sephora," **www.sephora.com/help/about_sephora.jhtml? location=sephora** (March 8, 2009).

18. "Retailing: Specialty," p. 15.

19. Computed by the authors from "Retailing: General," *Standard & Poor's Industry Surveys*; and "2008 Annual Industry Report," *Retailing Today* (2008).

20. "2008 Annual Industry Report."

21. Ibid.

22. "About Us," **www.tjx.com/about.asp** (March 9, 2009).

23. "Outlet Outlook," *Shopping Centers Today* (August 2008), pp. 47, 49.

24. "Annual Industry Report."

25. Adapted by the authors from "Rose Bowl Flea Market Selling Information," **www.rgcshows.com/ShowsMainMenu/ RoseBowlFleaMarket/RoseBowlSellingInformation/tabid/ 157/Default.aspx** (March 9, 2009).

Chapter 6

1. Various company sources.

2. "Survey Demonstrates That Gaps Are Closing Between Consumer Expectations and Retailer Readiness for Cross-Channel Execution," *Sterling Commerce Press Release* (August 26, 2008).

3. "Online Sales Are Still Growing but Far More Slowly," **www.emarketer.com/Article.aspx?id=1006765** (November 24, 2008).

4. Authors' estimates, based on "DMA's Quarterly Business Review," **www.the-dma.org/cgi/disppressrelease?article= 1229** (October 13, 2008).

5. Sherry Chiger, "Consumer Catalog Shopping Survey: Parts I to III," *Catalog Age* (August, October, and November 2001); and Amy Johannes, "Who Likes Grocery Mail? Guys Do," **http://promomagazine.com/mag/marketing_likes_grocery_ mail/index.html** (May 1, 2007).

6. "What Is the Direct Marketing Association?" **www.the-dma.org/aboutdma/whatisthedma.shtml** (March 9, 2009).

7. "Data-Base Marketing Defined," **www.itsallgoodwebdesign. com/html/database_marketing.html** (March 11, 2006).

8. "The REI Story," **www.rei.com/jobs/story.html** (March 6, 2009).

9. "About QVC," **www.qvc.com** (March 6, 2009); and "HSN Company Info," **www.hsn.com/corp/info/default.aspx** (March 6, 2009).

10. "Direct Marketing Associations of the World," **http://www. the-dma.org/subsidiaries/intdmas.pdf** (April 25, 2008); "Federation of European Direct and Interactive Marketing Press Pack," **www.fedma.org/press.74284.en.html** (January 2009); and "Japanese Shopping Channel to Debut in Korea," **www. atimes.com** (June 10, 2005).

11. *Direct Selling by the Numbers* (Washington, DC: Direct Selling Association, 2008); and "International Statistics," **www.wfdsa.org** (October 29, 2008).

12. *Vending Times Census of the Industry*, 2008 Edition.

13. "Internet World Stats," **www.internetworldstats.com/stats. htm** (March 10, 2009); "Trends in Online Global Shopping," **http://www.nielsen.com/solutions/GlobalOnlineShopping ReportFeb08.pdf** (February 2008); "Online Buyers Active But Practical," **www.emarketer.com/Articles.aspx?id= 100647** (November 18, 2008); and authors' estimates.

14. Bob Armour, "From Clicks to Bricks," *Multichannel Merchant* (May 2008), pp. 37–38.

15. Betsy Bugg Holloway and Sharon E. Beatty, "Satisfiers and Dissatisfiers in the Online Environment: A Critical Incident Assessment," *Journal of Service Research*, Vol. 10 (May 2008), p. 356.

16. Tracy Mullin, "Determining Web Presence," *Chain Store Age* (October 1999), p. 42.

17. Jodi Mardesich, "The Web Is No Shopper's Paradise," *Fortune* (November 8, 1999), pp. 188–198.

18. "Amazon.com, Inc," **www.hoovers.com/amazon.com/— ID__51493—/free-co-profile.xhtml** (March 7, 2009).

19. "How Does a Seamless Order Work?" **http://www2. seamlessweb.com/AtHome/Howitworks.htm** (March 9, 2009).

20. "About Netflix," **www.netflix.com/PressRoom?id=1005** (March 9, 2009).

21. "High-Speed Internet Access at Starbucks," **www. starbucks.com/retail/wireless.asp** (March 9, 2009).

22. Authors' projections, based on "Stats N' Facts Research Area," **www.kiomag.com/statfactoptions** (January 18, 2006); *Kiosk Industry Sector Report—Retail* (Rockville, MD: Summit Research Associates, 2008); and Lee Holman and Greg Buzek, *Market Study: 2008 North American Self-Service Kiosks* (Franklin, TN: IHL Group, June 5, 2008).

23. "Interactive Kiosks," **www.wirespring.com/Solutions/ interactive_kiosks.html** (February 28, 2009).

24. "A Small-Box Renaissance at the Big Boxes," *Retailing Today* (August 11, 2008), p. 15.

25. Authors' projections, based on a variety of sources.

26. "Statistics: World Airport Traffic," *ACI Information Brief* (July 2008); *Airport Revenue News 2008 Fact Book*; and "Airport Retail Sales Flying High Despite Credit Crunch as Tourism Booms," *In-Store* (September 2008), p. 5.

27. María Bird Picó, "Emerging Markets on the Fly," **www.icsc.org/sct/sct_article.php?i=sct1108&s=1&d=4** (November, 2008).

Chapter 6 Appendix

1. Connie Robbins Gentry, "Multi-Channel Experience," *Chain Store Age* (March 2008), pp. 74, 76.

2. Barton Goldenberg, "Multiplicity Means More: Customers Want It. Technology Allows It," *CRM Magazine* (February 2008), p. 8.

3. "Leveraging the Internet," *Chain Store Age* (April 2008), p. 17A.

4. Kelly Tackett, *Softgoods Shopper Update: Multi-Channel Shopping* (Columbus, OH: TNS Retail Forward (March 2008), p. 5.

5. Scot Meyer, "Mastering Multi-Channel Retailing," *MMR* (January 29, 2007), p. 22.

6. Pamela Oldham, "Multi-Channel Retail: On the Frontier," *DM News* (February 28, 2008), p. S4.

7. Scot Meyer, "Mastering Multi-Channel Retailing," *MMR* (January 29, 2007), p. 22.

8. Kevin Hillstrom, "Take a 360-Degree Customer View," *DM News* (August 18, 2008), p. 17.

Chapter 7

1. Various company sources.

2. Sarah Kellett, "Why Are My Customers So Disloyal?" **http://uk.fujitsu.com/POV/localData/pdf/customer-loyalty. pdf** (Spring 2008).

3. Authors' estimates, based on data from the U.S. Census Bureau (**www.census.gov**) and the U.S. Bureau of Labor (**www.bls.gov**) Web sites (February 11, 2009).

4. TNS Retail Forward, *Shopper Perspectives: Men in Grocery Stores* (Columbus, OH: July 2007).

5. WSL Strategic Retail, *How America Shops in Crisis White Paper* (New York, NY: 2008), p. 2.

6. Pamela N. Danziger, "The Lure of Shopping," *American Demographics* (July–August 2002), p. 46.

7. WSL Strategic Retail, *How America Shops 1998* (New York, NY: 1998).

8. TNS Retail Forward, *Industry Outlook: Targeting Teen Shoppers* (Columbus, OH: August 2008), p. 18.

9. Dana Joffe, "Targeting the Emerging Hispanic Market, *Chain Store Age* (September 2008), p. 64.

10. "The Color (and Age) of Money," *Retail Customer Experience* (October 2008), p. 20.

11. Rex Y. Du and Wagner A. Kamakura, "Where Did All That Money Go? Understanding How Consumers Allocate Their Consumption Budget," *Journal of Marketing,* Vol. 72 (November 2008), p. 109.

12. Steve Smith, "What Women Want When Shopping for CE," *Twice* (June 6, 2005), p. 20.

13. Anthony D. Cox, Dena Cox, and Ronald D. Anderson, "Reassessing the Pleasures of Store Shopping," *Journal of Business Research*, Vol. 58 (Number 3, 2005), pp. 250–259.

14. Cathy Hart, Andrew M. Farrell, Grazyna Stachow, Gary Reed, and John W. Cadogan, "Enjoyment of the Shopping Experience: Impact on Customers' Repatronage Intentions and Gender Influence," *Service Industries Journal*, Vol. 27 (July 2007), p. 599.

15. Hye-Young Kim and Youn-Kyung Kim, "Shopping Enjoyment and Store Shopping: The Moderating Influence of Chronic Time Pressure Modes," *Journal of Retailing and Consumer Services*, Vol. 15 (September 2008), p. 417.

16. "Retailing: General," *Standard & Poor's Industry Surveys* (November 20, 2008), p. 19; and "Retailing: Specialty," *Standard & Poor's Industry Surveys* (September 11, 2008), p. 8.

17. Kurt Salmon Associates, "Which Way to the Emerald City?" *Perspective* (February 2000), p. 3.

18. Don Peppers, "Retailers Emphasize Customer Knowledge," **www.1to1.com/View.aspx?DocID=28792** (April 4, 2005).

19. Private Label Manufacturers Association, "Store Brands Achieving New Heights of Consumer Popularity and Growth," **http://plma.com/storeBrands/sbt08.html** (November 10, 2008).

20. Jack Neff, "Pick a Product: 40% of Public Decide in Store," *Advertising Age* (July 28, 2008), pp. 1, 31.

21. Ibid., p. 31.

22. Sharon E. Beatty and M. Elizabeth Ferrell, "Impulse Buying: Modeling Its Precursors," *Journal of Retailing*, Vol. 74 (Summer 1998), pp. 169–191.

23. Richard Burnett, "Customer Loyalty Is Up for Grabs," *Knight-Ridder/Tribune Business News* (January 27, 2002).

24. Lars Meyer-Waarden and Christophe Benavent, "Rewards That," *Wall Street Journal* (September 22, 2008), p. R5.

25. "Company Overview," **http://news.walgreens.com/article_display.cfm?article_id=1046** (March 19, 2009).

26. "Corporate Profile," **www.kohlscorporation.com/InvestorRelations/Investor01.htm** (March 19, 2009).

27. "Family Dollar Stores, Inc.," **www.hoovers.com** (March 22, 2009); and "Investors," **http://familydollar.com/Investors.aspx?p=irhome** (March 22, 2009).

28. "Wet Seal," **www.wetsealinc.com/corpinfo/corpinfo.asp?id=3** (March 22, 2009).

29. "Foot Locker, Inc." **www.footlocker-inc.com** (March 22, 2009).

30. "Our Brands," **www.gapinc.com/public/OurBrands/brands.shtml** (March 22, 2009).

31. "Standard of Living," **www.encyclopedia.com/doc/1E1-stndliv.html** (December 27, 2008).

Chapter 8

1. Various company sources.

2. "Sherwin-Williams Adds Analysis Tool," *Chain Store Age* (July 2008), p. 34.

3. "Dress Barn, Inc." *Apparel Magazine* (May 2008), pp. 21–22.

4. Dan Scheraga, "Disappointment Reigns," *Chain Store Age* (August 2002), p. 83.

5. "Becoming a Wal-Mart or Sam's Club Supplier," **www.walmartstores.com/download/2048.pdf** (February 21, 2009).

6. Janet Suleski and Fenella Sirkisoon, "Retail IT and Budgeting Study: 2006–2007," **www.stores.org/Current_Issue/2008/10/WebEdit1/index.asp** (October 2008).

7. "Retail Pro," **www.expressiontech.com/retailpro.html** (February 25, 2009).

8. "MicroStrategy Desktop," **www.microstrategy.com/Software/Products/User_Interfaces/Desktop** (February 25, 2009).

9. Kenny Sullivan, "Analyzing Operational Data to Improve the Guest Experience," *What Works in Enterprise Business Intelligence* (2008), p. 12.

10. "Data Enhancement," **www.donnelleymarketing.com/products_data_enhancement.html** (February 27, 2009).

11. Adapted by the authors from Jeff St. Onge, "Direct Marketing Credos for Today's Banking," *Direct Marketing* (March 1999), p. 56.

12. "Data Warehousing: Putting Your Data to Work," **www.techdivas.com/data.htm** (June 29, 2005).

13. Meridith Levinson, "They Know What You'll Buy Next Summer (They Hope)," *CIO* (May 2002), p. 116.

14. "Helzberg Builds Data Warehouse," *Chain Store Age* (May 2008), p. 122.

15. Jenna McGregor, "At Best Buy, Marketing Goes Micro," **www.businessweek.com/magazine** (May 15, 2008).

16. Poonam Khanna, "Hotel Chain Gets Personal with Customers," *Computing Canada* (April 8, 2005), p. 18.

17. "The UPC Code," **www.gs1us.org/upc_background.html** (February 25, 2009).

18. "How Electronic Data Interchange (EDI), Santa's Little Secret, Gets Toys To Shelves," **www.businesswire.com** (November 6, 2008).

19. Zhenyu Huang, Brian D. Janz, Mark N. Frolick, and Scott Bury, "A Comprehensive Examination of Internet-EDI Adoption," *Information Systems Management*, Vol. 73 (2008), pp. 273–286.

20. For more information, see Molly Knight, "Private Eyes," *Shopping Centers Today* (April 2008), pp. 19–20.

21. "Who Are Michelson & Associates' Mystery Shoppers?" **www.michelson.com/mystery/ourshoppers.html** (February 23, 2009).

22. "Virtual Shopper: The Next Generation of Market Research," **www.ifop.com/america/to/shopper_eng.htm** (February 23, 2009).

Chapter 9

1. Various company sources.

2. M. V. Greene, "Built to Order," **www.stores.org/Current_Issue/2008/09/edit10.asp** (September 2008).

3. "Dictionary," **www.marketingpower.com/_layouts/Dictionary.aspx?dLetter=T** (March 11, 2009).

4. See "GIS Lounge," **http://gislounge.com/web-based-gis**, for more information about the technical aspects of geographic information systems.

5. Samantha Murphy, "Making It Personal," *Chain Store Age* (November 2008), p. 66.

6. Denise Power, "Walgreens Maps Out Its Plan for Apparel," *Women's Wear Daily* (May 5, 2008), p. 24.

7. For a good overview of trading-area models, see Jean-Paul Rodrigue, "Market Area Analysis," **http://people.hofstra.edu/geotrans/eng/ch7en/meth7en/ch7m2en.html** (July 19, 2008). Click on the images on the left side of this Web site.

8. William J. Reilly, *Method for the Study of Retail Relationships*, Research Monograph No. 4 (Austin: University of Texas Press, 1929), University of Texas Bulletin No. 2944. See also MacKenzie S. Bottum, "Reilly's Law," *Appraisal Journal*, Vol. 57 (April 1989), pp. 166–172; Michael D. D'Amico, Jon M. Hawes, and Dale M. Lewison, "Determining a Hospital's Trading Area: An Application of Reilly's Law," *Journal of Hospital Marketing*, Vol. 8 (Number 2, 1994), pp. 121–129; and Matt T. Rosenberg, "Gravity Models," **http://geography.about.com/library/weekly/aa031601a.htm** (March 4, 2009).

9. Matt T. Rosenberg, "Reilly's Law of Retail Gravitation," **http://geography.about.com/cs/citiesurbangeo/a/aa041403a.htm** (March 4, 2009).

10. David L. Huff, "Defining and Estimating a Trading Area," *Journal of Marketing*, Vol. 28 (July 1964), pp. 34–38; and David L. Huff and Larry Blue, *A Programmed Solution for Estimating Retail Sales Potential* (Lawrence: University of Kansas, 1966). See also Ela Dramowicz, "Retail Trade Area Analysis Using the Huff Model," **www.directionsmag.com/**printer.php?article_id=896 (July 2, 2005); and David Huff and Bradley M. McCallum, "Calibrating the Huff Model Using ArcGIS Business Analyst," **www.esri.com/library/whitepapers/pdfs/calibrating-huff-model.pdf** (September 25, 2008).

11. David A. Gautschi, "Specification of Patronage Models for Retail Center Choice," *Journal of Marketing Research*, Vol. 18 (May 1981), pp. 162–174; Glen E. Weisbrod, Robert J. Parcells, and Clifford Kern, "A Disaggregate Model for Predicting Shopping Area Market Attraction," *Journal of Retailing*, Vol. 60 (Spring 1984), pp. 65–83; Paul LeBlang, "A Theoretical Approach for Predicting Sales at a New Department-Store Location Via Lifestyles," *Direct Marketing*, Vol. 7 (Autumn 1993), pp. 70–74; Isabel P. Albaladejo-Pina and Joaquin Aranda-Gallego, "A Measure of Trade Centre Position," *European Journal of Marketing*, Vol. 32 (No. 5–6, 1998), pp. 464–479; David R. Bell, Teck-Hua Ho, and Christopher S. Tang, "Determining Where to Shop: Fixed and Variable Costs of Shopping," *Journal of Marketing Research*, Vol. 35 (August 1998), pp. 352–369; David S. Rogers, "Developing a Location Research Methodology," *Journal of Targeting, Measurement & Analysis for Marketing*, Vol. 13 (March 2005), pp. 201–208; Howard Smith and Donald Hay, "Streets, Malls, and Supermarkets," *Journal of Economics & Management Strategy*, Vol. 14. (March 2005), pp. 29–59; Charles ReVelle, Alan T. Murray, and Daniel Serra, "Location Models for Ceding Market Share and Shrinking Services," *Omega*, Vol. 35 (2007), pp. 533–540; Steve Wood and Sue Browne, "Convenience Store Location Planning and Forecasting: A Practical Research Agenda," *International Journal of Retail & Distribution Management*, Vol. 35 (No. 4, 2007), pp. 233–255; and Vien Chau, Stephanie Diep, and Jillian C. Sweeney, "Shopping Trip Value: Do Stores and Products Matter?" *Journal of Retailing and Consumer Services*, Vol. 15 (2008), pp. 399–409.

12. *AutoZone 2008 Annual Report*; Elaine Misonzhnik, "All the Right Moves," **www.retailtrafficmag.com** (October 2008); *Dollar General 2008 Annual Report*; and *Syms 2008 Annual Report*.

13. "CVS Caremark FAQs," **http://phx.corporate-ir.net/phoenix.zhtml?c=183405&p=irol-faq** (March 9, 2009).

14. "One-Stop Shop Appeal Builds Sales," *Drug Store News Annual Yearbook* (April 2008), p. 47.

15. Georgia Lee, "Lauren's Latest at Lenox: Bigger and More Glamorous," *Women's Wear Daily* (October 30, 2007). p. 16.

Chapter 10

1. Various company sources.

2. *Bed Bath & Beyond 2008 Annual Report*.

3. Kent Robertson, "Enhancing Downtown's Sense of Place," *Main Street News* (September 1999).

4. Holly Haber, "Downtown Revival," *Women's Wear Daily* (October 16, 2008), p. 10.

5. Author projections, based on International Council of Shopping Centers' data; Michael P. Niemira and Jay Spivey, "The U.S. Shopping Center Industry—Size, Shape and

Impact," *Research Review*, Vol. 14 (No. 2, 2007), pp. 33–37; and John Connolly and Brandon Rogoff, "Keeping Track of U.S. Mall Visits," *Research Review*, Vol. 15 (No. 2, 2008), pp. 5–9.

6. Katherine Field, "Raising the Roof," *Chain Store Age* (July 2008), p. 109.

7. Jennifer Hopfinger, "Radio Shack's Revamp Starts to Pay Dividends," *Shopping Centers Today* (December 2008).

8. *Guitar Center 2005 Annual Report.*

9. *Apple Inc. 2008 Annual Report.*

10. *Home Depot 2008 Annual Report.*

11. See Curt Hazlett, "The Wide World of Rent Structure," *Shopping Centers Today* (December 2008), pp. 104–108.

12. Beth Kowitt, "The Right Address," *Fortune* (September 1, 2008), p. 65.

13. "Smaller-Size Caps," **www.newrules.org/retail/size.html** (December 30, 2008).

Chapter 11

1. Various company sources.

2. "Changing the Game: 4 Ways to Unlock Your Employees' Performance Potential," **www.successfactors.com/docs/unlocking-employee-potential** (2008).

3. Paul M. Mazur, *Principles of Organization Applied to Modern Retailing* (New York: Harper & Brothers, 1927).

4. "Target Careers: Culture," **http://sites.target.com/site/en/company/page.jsp?contentId=WCMP04-031452** (April 2, 2009).

5. "Management Opportunities," **www.unos.com/mgmtJobs.html** (April 2, 2009).

6. "Our Structure," **http://careers.nordstrom.com/company/our-structure.asp** (April 2, 2009).

7. "Career Paths," **www.wholefoodsmarket.com/careers/paths.php** (April 2, 2009).

8. "National Hiring Partnerships," **https://careers.homedepot.com/cg/content.do?p=nhp** (April 4, 2009).

9. "Andrea Jung: Executive Profile & Biography," **http://investing.businessweek.com** (January 11, 2009).

10. "Rite Aid Management Team: Mary F. Sammons," **www.riteaid.com/company/about/sammons.jsf** (January 11, 2009).

11. "eBay Careers—Culture," **www.ebaycareers.com/culture.html** (April 6, 2009); "Job Culture at Stew Leonard's," **www.stewleonards.com/careers/culture.cfm** (April 6, 2009); and "Nordstrom Careers: Diversity," **http://careers.nordstrom.com/company/diversity.asp** (April 6, 2009).

12. "Wal-Mart Employment and Diversity Fact Sheet," **http://walmartstores.com/download/2305.pdf** (December 16, 2008); "Enterprise Rent-A-Car Careers," **www.erac.com/our-culture/diversity.aspx** (April 9, 2009); and "Our Commitment: Diversity at Walgreens," **http://diversity.walgreens.com/ourcommitment/default.html** (April 9, 2009).

13. Richard Feinberg, "The Retail Industry: A Giant, Hidden Career Opportunity," **www.black-collegian.com/career/industry-reports/retail.shtml** (July 1, 2005).

14. For a good illustration of the testing resources available for retailers, visit the Web site of Employee Selection & Development Inc. (**www.employeeselect.com/selectTests.htm**).

15. Judith Brown, "Employee Orientation: Keeping New Employees on Board," **http://humanresources.about.com/od/retention/a/keepnewemployee.htm** (April 10, 2009).

16. "The Container Store," **http://company.monster.com/container** (April 10, 2009).

17. "Best Buy Employees Study Up on Products in New Online Learning Lounge," **www.internetretailer.com/dailyNews.asp?id=28339** (November 3, 2008).

18. Katherine Field, "Putting Employees First," *Chain Store Age* (June 2008), p. 61.

19. Adapted by the authors from Anthony J. Rucci, Steven P. Kirn, and Richard T. Quinn, "The Employee-Customer-Profit Chain at Sears," *Harvard Business Review*, Vol. 76 (January–February 1998), pp. 82–97.

20. Adapted by the authors from Dan Sykes, "Jump Start Your Employee Motivation," **www.thesykesgrp.com/MotivateTeamJumpstart01.htm** (January 4, 2009).

Chapter 12

1. Various company sources.

2. See Suzanne P. Nimocks, "Managing Overhead Costs," *McKinsey Quarterly* (Number 2, 2005), pp. 106–117.

3. *Industry Norms & Key Business Ratios* (New York: Dun & Bradstreet, 2007–08).

4. Rachel Dodes, Ann Zimmerman, and Jeffrey McCracken, "Retailers Brace for Major Change—Chain Stores See a Future with Fewer Outlets, Brands—and Thinner Profits," *Wall Street Journal* (December 27, 2008), p. B1.

5. Kris Hudson, "Struggling Retailers Press Struggling Landlords on Rent," *Wall Street Journal* (January 7, 2009), p. C1.

6. David Bodamer, "Retail REITs Deserve Another Look," *Retail Traffic* (November 2008), p. 4.

7. Ken Clark, "Going Public: Down But Not Out," *Chain Store Age* (January 2002), pp. 55–56; and "IPO Central," **www.hoovers.com** (April 14, 2009).

8. "Saks Incorporated Agrees to Sell Proffitt's/McRae's to Belk, Inc. for $622 Million," *Business Wire* (April 29, 2005).

9. Dodes, Zimmerman, and McCracken, "Retailers Brace for Major Change—Chain Stores See a Future with Fewer Outlets, Brands—and Thinner Profits," p. B1.

10. Michael Hartnett, "Value of Chapter 11 Protections for Retailers Sparks Sharp Debate," *Stores* (April 1999), p. 92.

11. *Hancock Fabrics 10Q, for the Quarterly Period Ended November 1, 2008.*

12. "Bradley Stinn Convicted of Fraud," **http://www.jckonline.com/article/CA6545283.html** (March 26, 2008).

13. Sandra M. Jones, "No Fraud in $152M Accounting Shortfall, Ace Reports," **http://accounting.smartpros.com/x60387.xml** (January 14, 2008).

14. Mike Troy, "12 Hot Issues Facing Mass Retailing—2: Financial Reform," *DSN Retailing Today* (May 20, 2002), p. 21.

15. See Cash Miller, "Manage Your Cash Flow Or Perish," **http://ezinearticles.com/?Manage-Your-Cash-Flow-Or-Perish&id=1814745** (December 22, 2008); and Michael Lemm, "Small Business Tip: How to Manage Cash Flow," **http://small-business-management.bestmanagementarticles. com/a-30689-small-business-tip—how-to-managecash-flow. aspx** (December 31, 2008)

16. Computed by the authors from Marianne Wilson, "Cutting Back on Costs, *Chain Store Age* (July 2008), pp. 72–76.

17. Company annual reports.

18. "Corporate Information," **www.tuesdaymorning.com/ci/ci.asp** (April 12, 2009).

19. Craig R. Johnson, "Profitable Productivity," *Chain Store Age* (July 2007), p. 154.

Chapter 13

1. Various company sources.

2. See Mary Jo Bitner, Amy L. Ostrom, and Felicia N. Morgan, "Service Blueprinting: A Practical Technique for Service Innovation," *California Management Review*, Vol. 50 (Spring 2008), pp. 66–94.

3. Rachel Brown, "Tiffany's Unveils New Store Concept at Americana at Brand," **http://www.wwd.com/wwd-publications/wwd/2008-10-27** (October 27, 2008).

4. "Average Life Span of Store-Outfitting Systems," *Chain Store Age* (July 2008), p. 74.

5. Alan Wolf, "Office Depot Opens First 'Green'," *Twice* (September 3, 2008), p. 28.

6. Sharon Donovan, "Dillard's Unveils Revamped New Orleans Unit," *Women's Wear Daily* (October 13, 2008), p. 17.

7. "Success Stories," *SDM: Security Distributing & Marketing* (April 2008 Supplement), p. 13.

8. David Bodamer, "Talking Points," *Retail Traffic* (January 2008), p. 23.

9. Compiled from various sources by the authors.

10. "Merchant Credit-Card Processing," **www.elavon.com/ acquiring/costco** (February 2, 2009).

11. Marianne Crowe, "Emerging Payments—The Changing Landscape," **www.bos.frb.org/economic/eprg/presentations/ 2008/crowe04151708.pdf** (2008).

12. "Re-Inventing the Supply Chain," **www.xr23.com/page.cfm/ 141** (May 15, 2005).

13. Dan Scheraga, "Keeping It Fresh," *Chain Store Age* (May 2005), p. 111; and "Fresh Market Manager," **www.parkcitygroup.com/ products/fresh-market-manager** (February 4, 2009).

14. "Barcode Scanners," **www.posguys.com/barcode-scanner_3** (February 7, 2009).

15. *Market Study: 2008 North American Self-Checkout Systems*, **www.ihlservices.com/ihl/public_downloads/pdf4. pdf** (September 27, 2008).

16. Natalie Stevenson, "Sourcing Out the Best Deal," *Retail Week Online* (April 29, 2005).

17. Don Peppers and Martha Rogers, "Crisis Management Seeks a Customer Center," *Inside 1to1 Strategy Online* (February 24, 2005).

18. "Planning for Disaster," *Retail Merchandiser* (September–October 2008), p. 5.

Chapter 14

1. Various company sources.

2. Stanley Marcus, "Reflections on Retailing," *Retailing Issues Letter* (July 2000), p. 2.

3. Barbara E. Kahn, "Introduction to the Special Issue: Assortment Planning," *Journal of Retailing*, Vol. 75 (Fall 1999), p. 289. See also Cathy Hart and Mohammed Rafiq, "The Dimensions of Assortment: A Proposed Hierarchy of Assortment Decision Making," *International Review of Retail, Distribution & Consumer Research*, Vol. 16 (July 2006), pp. 333–351.

4. *Costco 2008 Annual Report*.

5. "Best Practices to Localize, Differentiate, and Win," **www. precima.com/webinar_sept17.html** (September 17, 2008).

6. Laura Everage, "Going Foodservice: The Restaurant Adventure," **www.specialtyfood.com/do/news/ViewNewsArticle?id=2394** (March 21, 2009).

7. "The Future of Fast Fashion," *Economist* (June 18, 2005), p. 57.

8. *Ross Stores 2008 Annual Report*.

9. "FPN History—Who We Are," **www.fpn.org/who.htm** (March 23, 2009).

10. "HSN Executives," **www.hsni.com/management.cfm?bioID= 21271&CategoryID=1811** (March 23, 2009).

11. Dan Scheraga, "Balancing Act at Ikea," *Chain Store Age* (June 2005), p. 46; and "Corporate Ikea," **www.ikea.com/us/ en/customerservices/faq** (March 25, 2009).

12. Lina Wright, "The Big Bite on QSRs," **www.qsrmagazine.com/ articles/features/121/7-eleven-2.phtml** (November 2008).

13. Susan Reda, "Family Dollar Grows by Helping Shoppers Stretch Food Budgets," **www.stores.org/Current_Issue/ 2008/07/Edit1/index.asp** (July 2008).

14. "Four Critical Elements of Retail Supply Chain Success," **www.highjumpsoftware.com/promos/download.asp?item=29** (2008).

15. Gary Rodkin, "A Balancing Act," *Progressive Grocer* (June 1999), p. 29.

16. "U.S. & Europe Private Label 2008," *Times & Trends* (October 2008).

17. "Private Label 2008," *Times & Trends* (October 2008), p. 6.

18. "H.T. Traders," **www.harristeeter.com/in_our_stores/our_ brands/ht_traders.aspx** (March 23, 2009).

19. Laurie Sullivan, "Retailers Ply Their Own Brands," *Information Week* (April 18, 2005), pp. 61–65.

20. "What Is Category Management?" **www.catmanplus.com/ whatis.html** (March 24, 2009).

21. Al Heller, "Consumer-Centric Category Management: A Fresh Spin on Maximizing Performance," **http://us.acnielsen.com/ pubs/2005_q4_ci_consumercentric.shtml** (Fourth Quarter 2005).

22. Information Resources, Inc., "Manufacturer and Retailer Report Cards," *NeoBrief* (Issue 1, 1999), pp. 3–6.

23. "Customer Success Story: Pacific Sunwear of California, Inc.," **www.islandpacific.com/images/PacSun.pdf** (January 13, 2009).

24. "Fred Meyer: Super-Sizing the Shopping Experience," **www.jda.com/company/display-collateral.html?did=595** (March 25,2009).

25. "Forecasting Software," **www.sas.com/technologies/analytics/forecasting** (March 25, 2009).

26. "Textiles and Apparel: Retailers and Brands," **www.datacolor.com/textile-apparel/retailers-brands** (March 26, 2009).

27. "Rev Up Retail Performance," **www.sas.com/success/autozone.html** (March 26, 2009).

28. "Allocation," **www.justenough.com/Solutions_Allocation.aspx** (March 26, 2009).

Chapter 15

1. Various company sources.

2. Rachel Tobin Ramos, "Home Depot's Supply Chain Overhaul to Free Up Cash, Improve Inventory," **www.ajc.com/business/content/business/stories/2008/09/28/home_depot_supply.html** (September 28, 2008).

3. *Big Lots 2007 Annual Report.*

4. Tracie Rozhon, "Stores and Vendors Take Their Haggling Over Payment to Court," *New York Times Online* (May 17, 2005).

5. "Nike Sues Wal-Mart," **www.huffingtonpost.com/2008/10/16/nike-sues-wal-mart_n_135240.html** (October 16, 2008).

6. *TJX Companies 2008 Annual Report.*

7. "Getting the Real Story on Slotting Allowances," *MMR Online* (May 9, 2005).

8. Adapted by the authors from "RFID," **http://en.wikipedia.org/wiki/RFID#The_RFID_system** (January 14, 2009).

9. John S. Webster, "Wal-Mart's RFID Revolution a Tough Sell," **www.networkworld.com/news/2008/091508-wal-mart-rfid.html?hpg1=bn** (September 15, 2008).

10. Fred Minnick, "3PLs Help Retailers, Vendors Reduce Hauling Costs," **www.stores.org/Current_Issue/2008/10/edit10.asp** (October 2008).

11. "Sears Logistics Services," **www.hoovers.com/sears-logistics-services/—ID__108358—/free-co-profile.xhtml** (March 19, 2009).

12. Jerry Andrews, "CPFR: Considering the Options, Advantages, and Pitfalls," **www.sdcexec.com/publication/index.jsp?issueId=86** (April-May 2008).

13. "Retail," **http://ups-scs.com/solutions/retail.html** (March 27, 2009).

14. *Bon-Ton Stores 2008 Annual Report.*

15. Richard Schonberger, "The Skinny on Lean Management," **www.superfactory.com/articles/featured/2009/0109-schonberger-skinny-lean-management.html** (January 2009).

16. "What Is Efficient Consumer Response?" **www.ecr.ca/en/ecrinfo.html** (March 27, 2009).

17. Ted C. Fishman, "Click Here for Tomatoes," *Money* (April 2005), p. 143.

18. Grocery Manufacturers Association, "Powering Growth Through Direct Store Delivery," **www.gmabrands.com/publications/DSD_Final_111108.pdf** (September 2008).

19. "Delivering Just in Time: Trade Partner Collaboration Could Relieve Some of DSD's Headaches," *Food Logistics Online* (October 15, 2004).

20. Dan McCue, "All I Really Need to Know (about Logistics) I Learned From Rudolph: A Holiday Demand Story," **www.inboundlogistics.com/articles/features/1108_feature02.shtml** (November 2008).

21. Kurt Salmon Associates, "Vision for the New Millennium," *KSA Brochure* (n.d.).

22. See Peter Duchessi and Indushobha Chengalur-Smith, "Enhancing Business Performance Via Vendor Managed Inventory Applications," *Communications of the ACM*, Vol. 51 (December 2008), pp. 121–127.

23. "Help: 1-Click Shopping," **www.target.com** (March 24, 2009).

24. Phil Britt, "Retailers Look to KM to Drive Business," *KM World* (January 2009), pp. 114–115.

25. Joshua Bamfield, *The Global Retail Theft Barometer 2008* (Thorofare, NJ: Checkpoint Systems).

26. Alexandria Sage, "Retailers See More Returns, Some Loosen Policy," **www.washingtonpost.com** (November 13, 2008); and C. J. Charlton, "Reverse Logistics: Customer Satisfaction, Environment Key to Success in 21st Century," *Inbound Logistics* (January 2005), p. 28.

Chapter 16

1. Various company sources.

2. "Inventory Management Software," **www.logisense.com/billing_cpe.html** (March 30, 2009).

3. For more information on inventory valuation, visit the Investopedia.com Web site, **www.investopedia.com/terms/p/perpetualinventory.asp**.

4. Marc Millstein, "Sport Chalet Improves Inventory Management," *Chain Store Age* (December 2007), p. 28A.

5. "A Solution for Every Season," **www.planalytics.com/index.php?p=retail_products** (March 30, 2009).

6. "The Facts About Greeting Cards," **www.greetingcard.org/pdf/FactsAboutGreetingCardsFactSheet.pdf** (March 30, 2009).

7. "EAN-13: Background Information," **www.barcodeisland.com/ean13.phtml** (March 30, 2009).

8. "Ready, Aim, Scan," *Business Wire* (May 2, 2005).

9. Ted Hurlbut, "The True Cost of Retail Inventory," **www.inc.com/resources/retail/articles/200707/hurlbut.html** (July 2007).

Chapter 17

1. Various company sources.

2. "Sports Authority: About Us," **www.sportsauthority.com/corp/index.jsp** (April 2, 2009).

3. Steve McKee, "Low Prices Are Not Always Your Friend Mike Troy," **www.businessweek.com/smallbiz** (April 2008).

4. "Company Info—Smarter.com," **www.smarter.com/press** (April 3, 2009).

5. See Marguerite Moore and Jason M. Carpenter, "An Examination of Consumer Price Cue Usage in U.S. Discount Formats," *International Journal of Retail & Distribution Management*, Vol. 36 (No. 4–5, 2008), pp. 345–359; and Stephan Zielke, "Exploring Asymmetric Effects in the Formation of Retail Price Satisfaction," *Journal of Retailing & Consumer Services*, Vol. 15 (September 2008), pp. 335–347.

6. Julie Creswell, "Sotheby's Is Back in Auction," *Fortune* (September 20, 2004), p. 18.

7. Jennifer Hopfinger, "Bare Minimum," *Shopping Centers Today* (November 2008), pp. 17–18.

8. "The Loss Leader," **www.bizhelp24.com/marketing/the-loss-leader-3.html** (April 3, 2009).

9. See "Item and Unit Pricing," **www.fmi.org/gr/issues/gr_issues_display.cfm?id=133** (October 2007).

10. Ken Clark, "Sticker Shock," *Chain Store Age* (September 2000), p. 88. See also David C. Wyld, "Back to the Future?: Why 'Old School' Item Pricing Laws May Hold Back the Use of RFID in Retail Settings," **www.coastal.edu/business/cbj/pdfs/articles/spring2008/wyld.pdf** (Spring 2008).

11. Selling price may also be computed by transposing the markup formula into

$$\text{Retail selling price} = \frac{\text{Merchandise cost}}{1 - \text{Markup}} = \$17.14$$

12. Merchandise cost may also be computed by transposing the markup formula into

$$\text{Merchandise cost} =$$
$$(\text{Retail selling price}) (1 - \text{Markup}) = \$4.794$$

13. See Sangkil Moon and Glenn Voss, "How Do Price Range Shoppers Differ from Reference Price Point Shoppers?" *Journal of Business Research*, Vol. 62 (January 2009), pp. 31–38.

14. *Syms 2008 Annual Report.*

Chapter 18

1. Various company sources.

2. Martin Pegler, "Creating a Brand," *Drug Store News* (June 2002), p. 27.

3. Edward O. Welles, "The Diva of Retail," *Inc.* (October 1999), p. 48.

4. "Welcome to Jungle Jim's International Market," **www.junglejims.com/about/about_jungle_jims_store_info.asp** (April 28, 2009).

5. "Prada—The Cutting Edge of Retail Technology," **www.xr23.com/Page.cfm/140** (May 15, 2005).

6. Kimberly Palmer, "The Store of YOU," *U.S. News & World Report* (November 3, 2008), pp. 54–56.

7. *Eddie Bauer 2008 Annual Report.*

8. *Gander Mountain 2008 Annual Report.*

9. Travis K. Kircher, "A Career by Design," **www.retailcustomerexperience.com/article.php?id=851** (January-February 2009).

10. "Toys 'R' Us Times Square," **http://www5.toysrus.com/TimesSquare/dsp_home.cfm** (April 29, 2009).

11. "Types of Flooring Used," *Chain Store Age* (July 2008), p. 82.

12. Michael Sasso, "Sweetbay's Bright Outlook," *Tampa Tribune Online* (June 26, 2005).

13. Steven Zarwell, "What's on Your Front Door?" *Dealernews* (March 2005), p. 38.

14. "Surface Beauty," *Chain Store Age* (July 2005), p. 94.

15. Peter S. Fader, Eric T. Bradlow, and Jeffrey S. Larson, "Tag Team: Tracking the Patterns of Supermarket Shoppers," **http://knowledge.wharton.upenn.edu/index.cfm?fa=viewArticle&id=1208** (June 1, 2005); and "Food Drug Mass—Influencing Shoppers at Store Level," *Shopper Update* (Columbus, OH: TNS Retail Forward, August 2008).

16. Jack Hitt, "The Theory of Supermarkets," *New York Times Magazine* (March 10, 1996), pp. 56–61, 94, 98; and Jennifer Lonoff Schiff, "The Layout of the Land," *Multichannel Merchant* (December 2007), p. 41.

17. "The Marketing-at-Retail Industry," **www.popai.com/AM/Template.cfm?Section=Industry** (April 30, 2009).

18. See Pookie Sautter, Michael R. Hyman, and Vaidotas Lukošius, "E-Tail Atmospherics: A Critique of the Literature and Model Extension," *Journal of Electronic Commerce Research*, Vol. 5 (No. 1, 2004), pp. 14–24; Louis K. Falk, Hy Sockel, Homer Warren, and Kuanchin Chen, "Atmospherics in the Cyber World," **www.businesscommunication.org/conventions/Proceedings/2006/12ABC06.pdf** (2006); and Chin-Shan Wu, Fei-Fei Cheng, and David C. Yen, "The Atmospheric Factors of Online Storefront Environment Design: An Empirical Experiment in Taiwan," *Information Management*, Vol. 45 (November 2008), pp. 493–498.

19. Paco Underhill, *Why We Buy: Updated and Revised* (New York: Simon & Schuster, 2009).

20. "American Girl Place," **www.americangirl.com/corp/corporate.php?section=about&id=14** (May 1, 2009).

21. "Company Profile," **www.urbn.com/profile/urban.jsp** (May 1, 2009).

22. Craig Childress, "Supermarkets Coming to Their Senses, All Five of Them," *Progressive Grocer: Equipment & Design Online* (June 4, 2004).

23. James Bickers, "A Wait They Won't Hate," **www.retailcustomerexperience.com/article.php?id=440** (June 20, 2008).

24. Joseph B. Cahill, "The Secret Weapon of Big Discounters: Lowly Shopping Cart," *Wall Street Journal* (November 24, 1999), pp. A1, A10. See also Renee DeGross, "Department Stores Try on New Ideas," *Atlanta Journal-Constitution* (August 18, 2002), p. F1.

25. Melanie Warner, "Diners Walk Through One Door and Visit Two Restaurants," *New York Times Online* (July 11, 2005).

26. Karalee Miller, "Online 'Wishes' Can Ease Gift Giving," *Fort Worth Star-Telegram Online* (June 7, 2005).

27. "Sleep Country USA Sponsors Pajama Drive," *Furniture Today* (June 23, 2008), p. 43.

Chapter 19

1. Various company sources.

2. *Best Buy 2008 Annual Report.*

3. "Best Buy Sees Softer Consumer Spending, Lowers Fiscal 2009 EPS Guidance," **http://bestbuymedia.tekgroup.com/article_display.cfm?article_id=4613** (November 12, 2008).

4. Computed by the authors from data in "Annual 2009," *Advertising Age* (December 29, 2008).

5. See Chris Prasifka, "Getting the Word Out: Building a Co-op Program," *Franchising World* (September 2008), pp. 56–59.

6. See also Mark Smock, "Don't Make These Top 10 Selling Mistakes!" **www.salesopedia.com/content/view/348/10633** (May 2, 2009).

7. Adapted by the authors from Betsy Spethmann, "Tuning In at the Shelf," *Promo* (April 2005), pp. AR29, AR32; and "PerfectMedia Overview," **www.ibnads.com/in/re_overview.php** (May 3, 2009).

8. Amy Johannes, "Watching the Carts," *Promo* (October 2008), p. 36.

9. Amy Johannes, "Playing the Game," *Promo* (October 2008), p. 26.

10. "All About Coupons," **www.couponmonth.com/pages/allabout.htm** (May 3, 2009).

11. Kim T. Gordon, "Reward Your Customers," **http://www.smallbusinessnow.com/library/Reward-Your-Customers-p-131.html** (May 4, 2009).

12. Brian Quinton, "The Hands-On Experience," *Promo* (October 2008), p. 37.

13. "Marketing," **www.mcdonalds.ca/en/aboutus/marketing_themes.aspx** (May 4, 2009); and "Food Communications—How and What We Are Telling Our Customers," **www.crmcdonalds.com** (May 4, 2009).

14. Barrie Young, "Word of Mouth: Marketing That Works," *Franchising World* (December 2008), pp. 64–65. See also Arnaud De Bruyn and Gary L. Lilien, "A Multi-Stage Model of Word-of-Mouth Influence Through Viral Marketing," *International Journal of Research in Marketing*, Vol. 25 (September 2008), pp. 151–163; and Sara Kim and Do-Hyung Park, "The Effects of Consumer Knowledge on Message Processing of Electronic Word of Mouth Via Online Consumer Reviews," *Electronic Commerce Research & Applications*, Vol. 7 (December 2008), pp. 399–410.

15. "How to Establish a Promotion Mix," **http://edwardlowe.org/index.elf?page=sserc&storyid=8816&function=story** (2000).

16. *Netflix 2008 Annual Report.*

17. Evelyn Lim, "How Opt-in Email Marketing Helps You in Your Online Business," **www.e-bizmap.com/articles/opt-in.htm** (May 4, 2009).

18. "Channel Report: Supermarkets," **www.shoppermarketingmag.com/article.php?nid=40873** (January 17, 2009).

19. "Retail Industry Successes Using MVT," **http://qualproinc.com/success/retail/retail_capabilities/biglots.html** (May 5, 2009).

Chapter 20

1. Various company sources.

2. "Dollar Tree Stores: Company Profile," *Datamonitor* (November 2008).

3. Maria Halkias, "Circuit City to Close All Its Stores," **www.dallasnews.com** (January 16, 2009).

4. To learn more about outstanding retail performers, look at the "High Performance Retailers" report in *Chain Store Age*, which appears every November.

5. "Ten Opportunities for Retail Innovation Revealed in New Retail Forward Report," **http://www.retailforward.com/pressroom/PressReleases/061305.asp** (June 13, 2005).

6. "About Food Lion: Company Information," **www.foodlion.com/AboutFoodLion/CompanyInformation.asp** (May 6, 2009).

7. Thomas Angell, "Benchmarking Strategy Vital to Business Performance," *Financial Executive* (June 2005), p. 16.

8. A. Parasuraman, Valarie A. Zeithaml, and Leonard L. Berry, "Alternative Scales for Measuring Service Quality: A Comparative Assessment Based on Psychometric and Diagnostic Criteria," *Journal of Retailing*, Vol. 70 (Fall 1994), pp. 201–230. See also Lisa J. Morrison Coulthard, "Measuring Service Quality," *International Journal of Market Research*, Vol. 46 (Quarter 4, 2004), pp. 479–497; David H. Wong, Nexhmi Rexha, and Ian Phau, "Re-Examining Traditional Service Quality in an E-Banking Era," *International Journal of Bank Marketing*, Vol. 26 (November 2008), pp. 526–545; François A. Carrillat, Fernando Jaramillo, and Jay P. Mulki, "The Validity of the SERVQUAL and SERVPERF Scales," *International Journal of Service Industry Management*, Vol. 18 (December 2007), pp. 472–490; and Wan Yusoff, Wan Zahari, Maziah Ismail, and Graeme Newell, "FM-SERVQUAL: A New Approach of Service Quality Measurement Framework in Local Authorities," *Journal of Corporate Real Estate*, Vol. 10 (July 2008), pp. 130–144.

9. "Supply Chain Consortium Overview," **www.supplychainconsortium.com/resource_center_process_overview.asp** (May 6, 2009).

10. Austen Mulinder, "Hear Today…Or Gone Tomorrow? Winners Listen to Customers," *Retailing Issues Letter* (September 1999), p. 5.

11. "Retailing General," *Standard & Poor's Industry Surveys* (November 20, 2008), p. 11.

12. "Trouble in the Second Act," *Chain Store Age* (August 2008), p. 4A.

13. "Brazil Retailer CBD Sees Opportunity in Crisis," **www.reuters.com** (January 5, 2009).

14. *Kohl's 2008 Annual Report*; and various sections of **www.kohls.com** (May 8, 2009).

15. Jane Stevenson, "Use Merchandising to Build Brand and Attract Consumers," *Advertising Age* (February 25, 2008), p. 17.

Appendix

1. "Retailing Careers," **www.careers-in-marketing.com/rt.htm** (January 29, 2009).

2. "Macy's Career Profiles," **www.macysjobs.com/common/profiles/profiles.asp** (January 29, 2009).

3. "Experience Retail," **www.nrffoundation.com/CareersCenter/Experience_Retail.asp** (January 29, 2009).

Name Index

Subject Index

Here are the Web site addresses for more than 200 of the largest retailers around the globe. Take a look at the dynamics of retailing from a worldwide perspective. See how different retailers in different nations really are. [Remember, Web sites often change. These addresses are current as of the publication of this book.]

UNITED STATES

7-Eleven (Southland)	www.7-eleven.com
Albertson's	www.albertsons.com
Amazon.com	www.amazon.com
Amway	www.amway.com
Army & Air Force Exchange Services	www.aafes.com
Auto Nation	www.autonation.com
Auto Zone	www.autozone.com
Avon	www.avon.com
Barnes & Noble	www.barnesandnoble.com
Bed Bath & Beyond	www.bedbathandbeyond.com
Belk	www.belk.com
Best Buy	www.bestbuy.com
Big Lots	www.biglots.com
BJ's Wholesale Club	www.bjs.com
Blue Nile	www.bluenile.com
Bloomingdale's	www.bloomingdales.com
Borders	www.borders.com
Burlington Coat Factory	www.burlingtoncoatfactory.com
H.E. Butt	www.heb.com
CarMax	www.carmax.com
Casey's General Stores	www.caseys.com
Charming Shoppes	www.charmingshoppes.com
Costco	www.costco.com
CVS	www.cvs.com
Darden Restaurants	www.dardenrestaurants.com
Dillard's	www.dillards.com
Dollar General	www.dollargeneral.com
Dollar Tree	www.dollartree.com
Family Dollar	www.familydollar.com
Foot Locker	www.footlocker.com
Gap	www.gap.com
Giant Eagle	www.gianteagle.com
Harris Teeter	www.harristeeter.com
Home Depot	www.homedepot.com
Home Shopping Network	www.hsn.com
Kmart	www.kmart.com
Kohl's	www.kohls.com
Kroger	www.kroger.com
LensCrafters	www.lenscrafters.com
Limited Brands	www.limitedbrands.com
Lowe's	www.lowes.com
Macy's	www.macys.com
McDonald's	www.mcdonalds.com
Meijer	www.meijer.com
Menards	www.menards.com
Michaels	www.michaels.com
Neiman Marcus	www.neimanmarcus.com
Nordstrom	www.nordstrom.com
Office Depot	www.officedepot.com
OfficeMax	www.officemax.com
Pathmark	www.pathmark.com
Payless ShoeSource	www.payless.com
J.C. Penney	www.jcpenney.com
Pep Boys	www.pepboys.com
PetsMart	www.petsmart.com
Publix	www.publix.com
QVC	www.qvc.com
Radio Shack	www.radioshack.com
Rite Aid	www.riteaid.com
Ross Stores	www.rossstores.com
Safeway	www.safeway.com
Saks, Inc.	www.saksincorporated.com
Sears	www.sears.com
Sherwin-Williams	www.sherwin-williams.com
Spiegel	www.spiegel.com
Staples	www.staples.com
Starbucks	www.starbucks.com
Super Valu	www.supervalu.com
Target	www.target.com
Tiffany	www.tiffany.com
TJX Companies	www.tjx.com
Toys "R" Us	www.toysrus.com
Victoria's Secret	www.victoriassecret.com
Walgreens	www.walgreens.com
Wal-Mart	www.walmart.com
Wendy's	www.wendys.com
Whole Foods Market	www.wholefoodsmarket.com
Williams-Sonoma	www.williams-sonoma.com
Winn-Dixie	www.winndixiegrocerystores.com
Yum! Brands	www.yum.com
Zales	www.zale.com

AUSTRALIA

Coles Myer	www.colesmyer.com
Foodland	www.foodlandsa.com.au
Wesfarmers	www.wesfarmers.com.au
Woolworths	www.woolworths.com.au

AUSTRIA

SPAR Austria	http://unternehmen.spar.at/spar/presse/english.htm

BELGIUM

Colruyt Group	www.colruytgroup.com
Delhaize Group	www.delhaizegroup.com/default.aspx?language=en-US

BRAZIL

Pao de Acucar	www.paodeacucar.com.br (in Portuguese)

CANADA

Canadian Tire	www.canadiantire.ca
Couche-Tard	www.couchetard.com/index.php?module=CMS&id=1&newlang=eng
Empire	www.empireco.ca
Hudson's Bay	www.hbc.com/hbc
Jean Coutu	www.jeancoutu.com
Loblaw	www.loblaw.com
Metro	www.metro.ca
Sears Canada	www.sears.ca
Shoppers Drug Mart	www.shoppersdrugmart.ca/english/index.html

DENMARK

Dansk Supermarked Gruppen	www.dsg.dk/da/Pages/Forside.aspx [D]
FDB	www.samvirke.dk/samvirke/Sider/InEnglish.aspx

FINLAND

Kesko	www.kesko.fi (select flag at bottom of screen for English)
S Group	www.s-kanava.fi/valtakunnallinen/etusivu?lang=2

FRANCE

Auchan	www.groupe-auchan.com/index.jsp?lang=EN
Carrefour	www.carrefour.com/cdc/home
Cora	www.cora.fr [F]
E. Leclerc	www.e-leclerc.com [F]
Galeries Lafayette	www.galerieslafayette.com (select from Languages at bottom of screen)
Group Casino	www.groupe-casino.fr/accueil/index.php?&lang=en
Intermarche	www.intermarche.com/englishpage.aspx
LeRoy Merlin	www.leroymerlin.com/html/en/home.htm
LVMH	www.lvmh.com
Magasins U	http://www.magasins-u.com [F]
Pinault-Printemps-Redoute	www.ppr.com/front__Changelang-en.html

GERMANY

Aldi International	www.aldi.de

[D] means site is in Danish
[F] means site is in French
[G] means site is in German